HOW TO INCREASE READING ABILITY

HOW TO INCREASE READING ABILITY

A Guide to Developmental and Remedial Methods

EIGHTH EDITION

Albert J. Harris

Edward R. Sipay

Longman
New York & London

LIBRARY

HOW TO INCREASE READING ABILITY, Eighth Edition

Longman Inc., 95 Church Street, White Plains, N.Y. 10601
Associated companies, branches, and representatives
throughout the world.

Developmental Editor: Lane Akers
Editorial and Design Supervisor: Irene Glynn
Production Supervisor: Diane Kleiner
Composition: Maryland Composition Co., Inc.
Printing and Binding: The Alpine Press, Inc.

Library of Congress Cataloging in Publication Data

Harris, Albert Josiah.
  How to increase reading ability.
  Bibliography: p.
  Includes index.
  1. Developmental reading. 2. Reading—Remedial
teaching. I. Sipay, Edward R. II. Title.
LB1050.53.H37   1985   372.4'1   84-28870
ISBN 0-582-28546-1

Manufactured in the United States of America
9 8 7 6 5 4 3 2 1   93 92 91 90 89 88 87 86 85

To Edith

Contents

1

Reading, Language, and Reading Disability   1

2

Readiness for Reading   32

3

Beginning Reading Instruction   58

4

An Overview of Reading Instruction   82

5

Adapting Reading Instruction
to Individual Differences   103

6

Identifying Reading Disabilities   133

7

Assessing Reading Performance   160

8

Correlates of Reading Disability, I: Cognitive Factors   229

9

Correlates of Reading Disability, II: Neurological, Physiological, and Physical Factors   266

_____ **13** _____

Improving Reading Comprehension   444

_____ **14** _____

Learning through Reading
and Learning to Read Rapidly
and Flexibly   509

_____ **15** _____

Fostering Reading Interests,
Attitudes, and Tastes   562

APPENDIX **A**
A Descriptive Listing of
Tests by Types   604

List of Figures

List of Tables

Preface

There has been a great outpouring of new research and theorizing about reading during the 5 years since the Seventh Edition was completed. Over 5000 books, articles, and monographs about reading and reading instruction have been published. New ideas have created a need for new terms, such as *schema theory* and *story grammar*. This has made it necessary for us to do another thorough revision, with comprehensive updating in every chapter.

Despite the many changes, the basic character of *How to Increase Reading Ability* has remained the same. Because of the book's continuing widespread use, we have been encouraged to maintain the guiding principles of the earlier editions: scope, balance, practicality, and clarity.

Our first principle, breadth of scope, requires that the book be useful to anyone concerned with reading improvement, including reading specialists, classroom teachers, specialists in learning disabilities, and researchers. Since many people who become interested in reading disabilities come from fields such as educational and clinical psychology, linguistics and psycholinguistics, neurology and neuropsychology, the book describes the nature of the developmental reading program, a foundation needed for understanding diagnosis and remedial teaching.

This book has been used primarily as a text in graduate courses in reading diagnosis and remedial teaching and as a desk reference for reading specialists.

It has also been used successfully in undergraduate courses on the teaching of reading and the language arts and as a reference in courses on learning disabilities.

Our second guiding principle, balance, involves a commitment to present both sides of controversial issues. We try to cite the most important research on the topic, indicate what we consider to be the strengths and weaknesses of each side, and state our own position (when we have one) on the issue. We provide references to the best recent references on the topic, making it possible for serious students to locate and study the issue from original sources.

Our third objective is to make the book practical and helpful. As in previous editions, we have included succinct descriptions of diagnostic procedures, tests, teaching methods, and materials of many kinds. We have addressed the questions considered important by teachers. We have used vignettes to illustrate many points.

Our fourth objective has been to write clearly and understandably. We have tried to keep technical terminology to a minimum. When the use of a technical term has been unavoidable, we have provided definitions, explanations, illustrations, or examples. We have revised every sentence that seemed to us to be difficult to comprehend.

Before we began to write, we solicited criticisms and suggestions from several people who had used the Seventh Edition. These included two professors of reading (James R. Layton and Dixie Lee Spiegel) and three graduate students (L. Fryer, T. King, and G. Zalud). We are very grateful for their thoughtful and helpful ideas, many of which we have used.

The organization of the book has been changed somewhat. We have done some combining of chapters, so there are now 15 chapters instead of the 19 chapters in the previous edition. This has helped to cut out many instances of redundancy. As before, the first third of the book describes the reading program from kindergarten to college, with an introductory chapter followed by chapters on readiness, beginning reading instruction, continuing reading instruction, and ways to provide for individual differences. The middle third covers evaluation and diagnosis. Chapter 6 identifies reading disabilities; Chapter 7 deals with evaluating reading performance; and Chapters 8, 9, and 10 discuss in detail the correlates of reading disability. The final third describes the developmental and remedial improvement of reading: Chapter 11 on basic principles of remedial teaching, Chapter 12 on word recognition, Chapter 13 on comprehension, Chapter 14 on study skills and rate, and Chapter 15 on developing reading interests and attitudes. Chapter sequence has been changed only slightly, with the chapter on interests now placed last instead of next to last.

We have endeavored to avoid any appearance of sexism. We have used plural pronouns (*they, them, their*) instead of the singular *he, she, his, her* whenever possible. When *children* would not fit the context, we have used masculine pronouns, since most disabled readers are boys or men. Because most elementary school teachers and reading specialists are women, we have used *she* and *her* in referring to a teacher.

As in the Seventh Edition, we have gathered all the references in one alphabetized Bibliography that contains approximately 2700 items, almost half of which were published in the 1980s.

The Appendixes have been thoroughly revised. In Appendix A the tests are listed by category and alphabetically within each category. Thus, for example, all reading readiness tests are arranged alphabetically under that heading. Descriptive information about the tests has been expanded, making it unnecessary to include such information in the body of the text.

In Appendix B the list of series books for use in remedial reading has been brought up to date. Appendix C provides an alphabetical list of the book and test publishers mentioned in the text. It also contains some distributors of audiovisual materials, materials for special education, and so on. The rapidity of changes in the publishing industry makes it inevitable that some of the names and addresses in this Appendix will change.

Appendix D contains all the information necessary for using the *Harris–Jacobson Wide Range Readability Formula*, a new, easy-to-use formula that provides readability scores from 1.1 to 11.3. Also included are the Readability List needed for using the formula and information on the reliability and validity of the formula. We are deeply indebted to the Macmillan Publishing Co. and to Mrs. Milton D. Jacobson for their permission to reproduce this material, which was first published in A. J. Harris and M. D. Jacobson, *Basic Reading Vocabularies* (New York: Macmillan, 1982), pp. 19–37.

We wish to express our appreciation to Mrs. Edith Harris; as with all of the seven previous editions, she has been helpful in many ways. We are indebted to Mrs. Charlotte Harris Wiener for her description of speed-reading instruction in Chapter 14. Our thanks go to Donna Parent for expert typing of the manuscript and to Arlene Adams for her library research.

ALBERT J. HARRIS
EDWARD R. SIPAY

1

Reading, Language, and Reading Disability

I. THE IMPORTANCE AND STATUS OF READING IN MODERN SOCIETY

The Importance of Reading

Reading ability has economic, societal, political, and personal values, and it increases in importance as a society becomes more complex and industrialized. As technology advances, more occupations require high levels of education or specialized training for which reading ability is vital. Automation and foreign competition have eliminated many unskilled and semiskilled jobs. Many displaced workers become chronically unemployable because they do not possess the minimum reading skills required for success in new positions or job-training programs.

A few illiterates have become millionaires, and there are ways of substituting for reading and for circumventing situations that require reading. Nevertheless, the number of illiterates who prosper financially in a modern, high-technology society is decreasing rapidly. The more usual fate of those who cannot read or write is deep poverty (Corbett 1982).

Children who fail to read adequately, particularly those who are severely disabled readers, are increasingly handicapped as they progress through school. They are almost sure to repeat grades, and if they get into high school, they are practically certain to drop out before graduation. Thus many desirable occupations are closed to them, and the pattern of failure and its consequences is repeated. Reading proficiency is essential if loss of self-esteem and permanent welfare status are to be avoided.

In most industrial societies there is a social stigma attached to illiteracy, so many adults attempt to become literate partly in order to gain or preserve their esteem among family and peers (Levine 1982). Illiterates are in constant fear of having their lack of reading ability discovered (Jennings 1975).

Reading ability is also important to everyday functioning. Those who cannot read street signs or notices of sales, for example, are at a disadvantage. Understanding newspaper want ads requires a sixth- to seventh-grade level of reading ability (Hirshoren, Hunt, & Davis 1974), and the readability of newspapers ranges from the eighth grade (Johns & Wheat 1984) to the tenth grade (Monteith 1980) to the college level (Fusaro & Conover 1983), with the readability levels of articles varying considerably. Directions for preparing a TV dinner are written at the eight-grade level, and instructions for taking aspirin are at the tenth-grade level (Kilty 1976). The readability of health safety pamphlets ranged from sixth-grade level to level seventeen (with a mean of twelfth grade); insurance policies ranged from the eleventh to the sixteenth grade level; and the federal income tax from 1040A was at the ninth, tenth-, or thirteenth-grade level, depending on which formula was applied (Negin & Krugler 1980).

As for the world of work, over half the training materials for seven military jobs exceeds eleventh-grade level of difficulty (Sticht 1975). Similarly, the average difficulty of materials used in various occupations is the eleventh-grade level (Harste & Mikulecky 1984).

Literacy is especially valuable in a society that has a free press. Being able to read adequately and critically allows one to obtain and reflect on varying political points of view, which are presented in print in much more detail than in other forms of media. Such knowledge may result in increased political participation and efficacy.

To a large extent those who cannot read, or who choose not to read, are cut off not only from possible intellectual enrichment but also from cultural activities, and find it difficult to mingle with educated people. Through reading we create the environment that shapes our minds and ourselves (Guthrie & Seifort 1983). Literacy enables individuals to conceptualize, to generalize, to draw inferences, and to work out logical relationships among ideas in ways that would otherwise be impossible; it alters the way people think (F. D'Angelo 1982). Reading also fulfills emotional and spiritual needs.

In the face of expanding electronic communication, there is justifiable concern for the future of the book and other printed matter as we know it (Larrick 1983). We are at present in a state of transition. It may well be that knowledge will increasingly be stored and transmitted in electronic form rather than in books, and voice and video cassettes are competing with the written word (Lupica 1982). Indeed, Wagschal (1978) predicted that the demise of the written word will be complete by the year 2001, and some believe that electronic media will make the printed word obsolete. If and when such a situation occurs, we will have to prepare our students for it by improving their listening skills. But even with our rapid technological advances in such fields as home computers, the printed word is, and will likely be for some time to come, the medium of choice (Suhor 1984). Moreover, it is unlikely that all available printed material will be available in recorded voice form in the near future at a price affordable for the masses.

Predictions of the "demise of reading ability" seem premature. Compared to most forms of communication media, reading has unique advantages (Neuman 1984). Instead of having to select from limited choices, as a reader you can select from the whole range of past and present writings. You can read in a place and at a time chosen for your convenience. You can set your own pace—slow down or speed up, take a break, reread, or pause to think and reflect. You can read what, when, where, and how you please. This flexibility ensures the continuing value of reading for both education and entertainment for some time to come.

The Status of Reading

Reading Ability

Periodically, charges have been made that American education in general, and reading achievement in particular, has declined. These reported declines have been attributed to a variety of causes, such as attempts "to remedy the political follies and social irregularities of our time by obliterating academic standards" (Cahn 1981), a permissive society that produces teachers who fail to teach reading effectively (Copperman 1978), and failure to emphasize phonics in the initial stages of reading instruction (Flesch 1955, 1981). Most often, the critics cite comments of employers, as well as college and high school teachers; or compare test results with those of previous years in the United States or with those from other industrial nations; or compare private and public schools.

The most frequently cited complaint of employers concerns the reading and writing abilities of white-collar workers. But what has been overlooked is that the percentage of the work force who are white-collar workers is increasing (e.g., it rose from 36% in 1946 to 48% in 1974). In order to fill many of these positions, people with lower intellectual abilities than was formerly the case have had to be hired (Bormuth 1982).

There is evidence that reading achievement was not as "good" in the "old days" as some would have us believe (Wolfthal 1981), but it is impossible to prove whether reading performance has declined, risen, or remained stable over the years. Many more students attend school at all levels today, and the school population is much more diverse than it was only 20 years ago. Schooling was not compulsory in the early part of this century. In the 1960s the national effort that cut the dropout rate to about a quarter of its former level had two indirect results: (1) It began to lower the average intelligence score because the former school dropouts generally had lower IQ scores than those who remained in school; and (2) since there is a substantial correlation between IQ and reading ability, average reading scores declined. Because most of the dropouts were high school students, rather than those at the elementary school level, it is not surprising to find that reading achievement declined more at the higher academic level (Bormuth 1982).

Although direct comparisons are questionable, it is possible for comparative data to indicate trends. Based on a comprehensive review of the literature, Tuinman, Rowls, and Farr (1976) concluded that a gradual improvement in reading competency took place between 1925 and 1965, and that from 1966 on there was a leveling off and perhaps a slight decline in average reading achievement in the United States.

The apparent decline in American reading achievement in the 1970s was substantiated by Flanagan (1976) and seems to have been a part of a nationwide trend above the primary grades in various academic areas (Harneschfeger & Wiley 1976b). Although there is insufficient evidence to determine the exact cause(s), the decline may have reflected fewer dropouts among low-scoring students, marked changes in school curriculum (e.g., fewer academic courses), a decrease in average daily attendance and thereby fewer days of schooling, teenage addiction to alcohol and drugs, and changing social attitudes and trends (Harneschfeger & Wiley 1976a). More recently, similar causes were reported, as well as a decline in the number of high school students taking traditional academic courses (National Commission on Excellence in Education 1983, Fiske 1983).

Other comparative data suggest some improvement, some stability, and some need for concern. In the 1970s the National Assessment of Educational Progress test results indicated that the overall reading skills of 9-year-olds improved steadily, and those of 13- and 17-year olds remained stable. The 9-year-olds improved in all three areas sampled by the NAEP tests: literal comprehension, inferential comprehension, and reference skills. Only literal comprehension improved at the 13-year-old level, and 17-year-olds showed a significant decline in inferential comprehension (Ward 1981, NAEP 1982). Reading achievement in a number of major American cities has risen consistently during the early 1980s (Micklos 1982a). Chall (1983b) hypothesized that such gains and losses reflected the changes in reading instruction that began in the late 1960s (e.g., more and earlier phonics, harder basals, and more help for those who needed it). Above the fourth grade, the reading matter goes beyond what students already know. Material to be read becomes more complicated, literary, abstract, and technical. More prior knowledge and more sophisticated language and cognitive abilities are required to comprehend such materials.

Although they still read below national levels, minority children showed improved reading skills. Whereas 9-year-old blacks were reading 14 percentage points below the national average in 1971, the gap narrowed to 8 percentage points by 1980 (Micklos 1982b). From 1970 to 1980, black 9- and 13-year-olds showed significant improvement, particularly the younger children, whose average reading score on the NAEP test improved by almost 10 percentage points (NAEP 1982). Between 1975 and 1980, Hispanic 9-year-olds improved twice as much in reading as their age counterparts across the nation; 13-year-old Hispanics' performance did not change significantly (Ward 1982).

It should be noted, however, that factors other than race and ethnicity contribute to reading performance. For example, blacks in advantaged urban areas performed much closer to national levels than black students in rural and disadvantaged urban areas (NAEP 1983a). A similar situation pertained for Hispanics (Ward 1982).

Some NAEP data are disturbing in that part of the gains made by low achievers may have come at the expense of the more able students. For example, from 1977 to 1980, the lowest quartile of the 9- and 13-year-olds improved their reading skills; the 17-year-olds did not. However, the highest quartile in the two oldest age groups lost ground (NAEP 1983b). The decline in higher-level reading skills among older students on the NAEP tests is disquieting (Micklos 1982b).

Overall, the status of reading achievement in the United States is not as bad as some would have us believe, and some conclude that it is much better (Cassidy 1978a, Farr & Blomenberg 1979, Fay 1980). Reading achievement in the United States compares somewhat favorably to that in other countries. For example, in 1973 American 14-year-olds ranked third in reading comprehension among the 15 countries studied (Thorndike 1973) and third in the interpretation of literature and fifth in the comprehension of literature among 10 countries (Purves 1973). Our 18-year-olds ranked twelfth in reading comprehension, fifth in interpreting literature, and seventh in comprehending literature. More recently, Purves *et al.* (1981) concluded that not only do our best students read as well as, or better than, those in other developed nations but the United States brings a higher percentage (75%) of its age group further along in reading than any of the other 14 countries studied.

Reading Habits

Compared to other industrialized nations, Americans read less. For example, whereas Americans spend an average of 5 minutes daily reading books that are not part of their work or schooling, Russians read 29 minutes a day and Bulgarians 20 minutes (Guthrie 1982). Reading volume, which is based on the number of books, magazines, and newspapers read monthly, and is highly correlated with reading achievement, was 20% higher in New Zealand than in the United States (Guthrie 1981c).

Only 56% of the Americans surveyed in one study claimed to have read a book in the past 6 months (*Albany Times Union* 1978), a figure that has remained fairly stable since 1978. Book readership declined from 75% in 1978 to 63% for 16- to 21-year-olds; only 39% of those over the age of 60 read books. Of those over 16, 96% reported reading books, magazines, or newspapers (Diehl 1984).

Literacy and Illiteracy

There are numerous conceptual and methodological problems in studying literacy, not the least of which is its definition. No one definition of literacy or illiteracy is generally accepted. Illiteracy does not mean a complete lack of reading ability, and there are many levels of literacy ranging from reading one's own name to enjoying a novel or understanding a highly technical journal article. The point at which literacy begins and illiteracy ends is hard to determine; a broad gray area seems to exist.

When literacy is defined in absolute terms, as it typically is, the criteria employed include school attendance for a particular number of years, a level of performance on a norm-referenced test, or successful demonstration of a defined set of competencies (Park 1981). Often those who use such definitions are referring to a minimal level of competency (see below). But staying in school for a given number of years does not ensure that a person can read at the highest grade attended. Nor does a score on a standardized test reveal what a person can comprehend.

Literacy can also be defined in relative terms. Relative definitions state that because materials vary in difficulty and are read for various purposes, a person can be literate in one situation but illiterate in another. Writers such as Bormuth (1982) and Levine (1982) suggest that a person who can read what he or she wants to, or has to, read is literate.

There has been a growing concern about literacy at national and international levels (Carroll & Chall 1975; Downing 1973a, 1978). Illiteracy in the world is massive and complex. Between 1945 and 1974, world adult illiteracy dropped from 44.3% to 34.2%; but as a result of the population explosion during the same period, the number of illiterates rose from 700 million to 800 million (Corbett 1982). Internationally, illiteracy is concentrated geographically and socially. Although it appears much more frequently in emerging countries, it still occurs in highly developed industrial nations. Illiteracy is complexly related to cultural, social, political, and economic issues (Ryan 1980, Levine 1982).

Historically, reading instruction has attempted to produce either a low level of literacy for the masses or a high level for the elite. The commitment to develop a high level of literacy for an entire population, such as the Right to Read effort in the United States (Allen 1970), is a recent innovation.

Differences in the definition of literacy and the inclusion of varying age groups have resulted in confusion about what should be measured and in estimates of illiteracy in America ranging from 1% to 20% (Kirsch & Guthrie 1977–1978). Depending on which statistic one reads, one could be led to believe that illiteracy in the United States is either practically nonexistent or rampant (IRA 1983).

Although distinctions are not always drawn between literacy and functional literacy, the current trend is to define and measure the latter. Almost all definitions of functional literacy stress reading tasks that are directly related to functioning adequately as an adult in society. These survival or real-life aptitudes usually deal with the application of reading skills to everyday needs like reading labels, forms, or schedules. They attempt to measure reading behaviors without which it would be very difficult to function in American society today.

Minimal Competency

The minimal competency movement is closely related to the concern over literacy and is part of a broad national reemphasis on basic skills. Minimal competency has had a long history in the United States, but unlike earlier responses, which involved curriculum reform, the current movement has focused on testing as the remedy (Haney & Madaus 1978). The individual's test performance usually determines whether he or she receives a high school diploma or a certificate of attendance. By 1983, 39 states had mandated minimal competency tests for students above the eighth grade, and 26 states required such tests for children below the fifth-grade level (National Center for Education Statistics 1983). Although the demands that such tests place on students differ (Chall 1983b), current minimal competency tests generally attempt to determine whether specific reading, writing, and computation skills have been mastered or whether a specified level of general achievement has been attained. The arguments for and against competency testing have been enumerated by Bunda and Sanders (1979) and Perkins (1982).

States have dealt with competency testing and programs in various ways (see Jaeger & Tittle 1980, Gorth & Perkins 1982, Fisher 1983). Based on recent court rulings, five legal principles have emerged (Citron 1982):

1. The appropriate use of competency tests is constitutional as long as the implementation procedure and the test are fair; a state may require a "functional literacy" test as a diploma requirement.
2. There must be adequate notice of the testing, and opportunity must be made available (e.g., remedial programs) for students to prepare for the test. Adequate notice of test requirements is particularly important in the case of handicapped students whose curriculum may not cover test requirements (Citron 1983).
3. Competency tests may not carry forward the effects of past discrimination. That is, the schools must demonstrate that any disproportionate failure rate on the part of minorities results from some factor other than "educational deprivation" stemming from past wrongful policies.
4. A graduation test must reflect material taught; in order to establish this requisite of validity, the state must demonstrate that what the test measures was actually taught.
5. Federal law does not prohibit requiring handicapped students to meet valid state requirements in order to receive a regular diploma; schools are not required to lower their academic standards in order to accommodate properly classified handicapped students who cannot meet these requirements. Test administration, however, may be modified for handicapped students (McKinney 1983).

II. THE NATURE OF READING

Reading Models

No one fully understands the extremely complex process we call reading. This is not surprising for, as McConkie (1982) pointed out, reading is a cognitive activity that takes place rapidly and privately in our minds, making it difficult to study. Not only is the process unobservable to others, but readers themselves are hardly aware of what they are doing.

Many of the earlier models of the nature of reading have been summarized (Geyer 1972, Harker 1972–1973, Williams 1973, Singer 1976, Samuels 1977b), and a number may be found in their original form in Singer and Ruddell (1976). Some recent models have also been summarized and critiqued (Lovett 1981, Mitchell 1982). Gibson and Levin (1975) were of the opinion that since there is no single reading process, a single model of reading is not viable. Rather than offer a number of models, Gibson and Levin stated general principles about the skilled reading process that apply to many reading situations and at various levels of proficiency.

Much of the problem with some earlier models is that their attempts were too ambitious. As Samuels and Eisenberg (1981) stated, it is dangerous to attempt a description of the reading process as a whole. Comprehensive descriptions tried to explain so much that they were untestable. Therefore it is not surprising that most models are partial in that they are concerned with specific aspects (e.g., perceptual or cognitive), stages (beginning or skilled reading), or modes (oral or silent reading) and do not attempt to account for all phases of the reading process.

Most models may be placed in one of three classes: *bottom–up, top–down,* or *interactive.*

Bottom–Up Models

According to bottom–up models, reading is essentially a process of trans-lating graphic symbols into speech during oral reading or into inner speech during silent reading. The reader then applies previously acquired listening comprehension skills. Most bottom–up theorists believe that written language is subservient to, or parasitic on, oral language; the only activity unique to read-ing is "breaking the written code."

Sensory and perceptual processes (commonly referred to as lower-level processes) are believed to occur prior to, and perhaps independent of, cognitive processes (commonly referred to as higher-level processes). The reader first picks up graphic information from the printed material (e.g., letters, groups of letters, words); after that, syntactic and semantic processing occur. As a result of this information flow, the printed material is understood. Reading compre-hension is believed to be heavily dependent on rapid, accurate word recognition. Reading is controlled by textual input; the reader plays a relatively passive role in the process (Weaver & Resnick 1979). The printed material is believed to provide more information than the reader does (Strange 1980, 1984).

Some theorists and writers attribute bottom–up models to all levels of read-ing competence. Others suggest that bottom–up processing best describes learn-ing to read (the acquisition stage), but that a top–down or interactive model more accurately describes skilled reading.

Two of the most widely cited bottom–up models are those of Gough (Gough 1972, Gough & Cosky 1977) and LaBerge and Samuels (1976). Gough appears to have remained committed to his original model, but Samuels has denied that the original LaBerge and Samuels theory was a bottom–up model and has modified the model so that it is more in line with the interactive viewpoint (Samuels & Eisenberg 1981).

Top–Down Models

In top–down models the reader's prior knowledge and cognitive and linguistic competence play key roles in the construction of meaning. Before, or very shortly after, any graphic input, the reader generates hypotheses regarding the meaning of the printed material. These predictions are based on the reader's prior knowledge of the topic, the specific content of the material, and syntactic parsing (interpreting the words in their particular grammatical functions). Graphic cues are sampled only as needed. As the information is processed, the reader's predictions about meaning are rejected, confirmed, or refined. The reader, who plays an active role in the process, is believed to supply more information than the printed material.

Many top–down theorists suggest that their models are more descriptive of skilled than of unskilled readers. Some, like the Goodmans (Goodman & Goodman 1979, 1982), believe that novice readers differ from skilled readers only in the lesser command they have over the strategies needed for extracting meaning from print.

In contrast to bottom–up models, many top–down theorists believe that skilled readers go directly from print to meaning without first recoding print to speech.

The two models most frequently cited as representative of the top–down position are those of K. Goodman (1967, 1984) and F. Smith (1971, 1975, 1976, 1977, 1979), both of which are based on psycholinguistic theories (the interaction between thought and language). K. Goodman (1981, 1982), however, has claimed that his model is, and always has been, an interactive model. More recently, he has referred to reading as a "transactive process" (K. Goodman 1984).

Few purely bottom–up or top–down models of reading have been proposed. It seems logical to conclude that there must be some bottom–up processing and some top–down processing in reading. The models differ in the importance ascribed to each kind of processing. Whatever model one holds, it is important to remember that there is a danger in overemphasizing either kind of processing. A proper balance must be struck between the information provided by the text and that which the reader brings to the text (Adams 1980).

Interactive Models

Interactive models are not merely a compromise between bottom–up and top–down theories. In interactive models different processes are believed to be responsible for providing information that is shared with other processes. Thus a hypothesis generated by top–down processing is guided by the results of bottom–up processing, and the bottom–up processing is guided in part by the expectations imposed by top–down processing. Information derived from each kind of processing is combined to determine the most likely interpretation of the printed message. The influence of each kind of processing is not equal in all interactive models. Nor is there complete agreement among interactive theorists as to which kind of processing initiates the reading process, or if they occur almost simultaneously.

In interactive models the reader assumes either an active or passive role depending on the strength and accuracy of the hypotheses generated by top–down processing (Pearson & Kamil 1978). The most widely cited interactive model is that of Rumelhart (1977). His early model postulated that, at least for skilled readers, top–down and bottom–up processing occur simultaneously. When the accumulated evidence most strongly supports a particular hypothesis, comprehension takes place. Because comprehension depends on both graphic information and the information in the reader's mind, it may be obstructed when a critical skill or a piece of information is missing. When comprehension is hampered, the skilled reader compensates by decoding key words, relying on context, or both. More recently, Rumelhart and McClelland (1981, 1982) have proposed a more limited interactive model.

Other interactive models have been developed by Perfetti and Lesgold (1979), Stanovich (1980), and J. Fredericksen (1981, 1982a, b). An interactive analysis of oral reading has been presented by Danks and Hill (1981).

Other Models

There are many other models, only a few of which are mentioned here. One of the earliest models of reading was the substrata-factor theory of Holmes (1953, 1970), which was defended by Downing (1981). Calfee (Calfee & Spector 1981, Calfee 1982) proposed a two-stage independent process model that he claimed to be task specific. A basic assumption of Calfee's model is that cognitive processes can be divided into relatively independent subprocesses, an assumption that has been challenged by Rispens (1982). Brown (1981) presented a model that stressed the aspects of comprehending language that are unique to reading. Yet other models are based on eye-movement research (Carpenter & Just 1981, 1983) or artificial intelligence (Mewhort & Campbell 1981, Schank 1982).

Instructional Implications of Models of Reading

There is a difference of opinion regarding the implications of reading models for instruction. On the one hand, authors like Pearson and Kamil (1978) were of the opinion that reading models play a vital role in the instructional process even when teachers are not consciously aware of them. They believed that most teachers operate with at least an implicit model of reading. On the other hand, writers like Venezky (1979a) warned against premature leaps from theory to practice. The importance of the "art of teaching" was stressed by Otto and White (1982), who cautioned that the conventional wisdom of teachers might be passed over too lightly as the implications of theory and research are sought and elaborated. They further commented that, for years, reading teachers have known some of the things that certain cognitive psychologists seem to have just discovered.

Those who adhere to a bottom–up model would place early and great emphasis on the mastery of decoding and word-recognition skills and on accurate word recognition, with the instruction being strongly teacher directed.

Top–down advocates would stress obtaining meaning from the printed material and would play down word-recognition skills. For example, in accord with Goodman's model of reading as a "psycholinguistic guessing game," Goodman and Goodman (1979, 1982) believed that the acquisition of reading is an extension of natural language learning and that instruction consistent with this process facilitates learning to read. They believed that children are in no more need of being taught to read than they are of being taught to understand spoken language. The role of the teacher is to guide and facilitate the children's learning, not to provide direct instruction. Rather than tell the child a word he had mispronounced, the teacher would provide feedback by giving the child a more accurate set for the meaning of the sentence or passage. Thus if the child said "house" for *horse*, the teacher would tell the child that the story is about animals (Pearson & Kamil 1978).

Although Strange (1980, 1984) has discussed the instructional implications of an interactive model, the degree to which decoding or meaning would be emphasized in an interactive model is not clear.

Despite these general instructional suggestions, it is premature to base specific instruction on a particular model of reading. At present, no model can specify exactly how decoding should be taught or how reading comprehension can be facilitated.

Diagnostic and Remedial Implications of Models of Reading

Different beliefs about the nature of the reading process should influence decisions regarding the diagnosis and treatment of reading disabilities. It is therefore not surprising to find articles relating reading disability to models of reading (e.g., Bauer 1982, Rispens 1982). What diagnosticians look for is likely to be based on what they believe the reading process to be, and what they find should influence what and how they remediate the reading problem.

Advocates of bottom–up models tend to place great emphasis on diagnosing and treating decoding and word-recognition problems, in the belief that weaknesses in these areas are the primary contributors to inadequate reading comprehension. Diagnosis probably would involve testing separate skills and strategies, and remediation would attempt to overcome specific weaknesses (Pearson & Kamil 1978). If the initial tests did not indicate that bottom–up processes were weak or if comprehension was still inadequate after remediation, the diagnostician would seek other causal or contributing factors.

The emphasis placed on diagnosing and treating decoding and word-recognition skills may reflect the fact that we know much more about bottom–up processing differences than about top–down processing differences (Garner 1983) and the availability of decoding and word-recognition tests compared to the lack of tests for determining weaknesses in top–down processing.

Most people who favor a top–down model do not see word-recognition accuracy as a primary concern. Rather, they tend to view miscues as indications of the processing strategies being employed by the reader. Attention would be focused on determining the breakdown within top–down processing. Diagnosis would stress determining to what extent the reader was using and coordinating cues from various sources of information, playing down the role of graphic information. Rather than treat specific decoding or word-recognition weaknesses, the remediation would play to the child's strengths and encompass teaching the appropriate use of strategies for employing the various cue systems that provide the information necessary for reading comprehension. Remediation would also encompass teaching the child how to generate and monitor hypotheses about the meaning of the material.

Followers of interactive models and some top–down advocates believe that the reading process is made up of highly interrelated subprocesses. The inability to coordinate the subprocesses or a weakness in any subprocess may have a negative impact on reading comprehension. Therefore, those who abide by an interactive model probably would attempt to determine possible deficiences in any of the information sources. Doing so, however, may not be an easy procedure. For example, there appear to be processes that mediate both word decoding and text comprehension (Stanovich 1982a, b).

A Definition of Reading

Reading is the meaningful interpretation of printed or written verbal symbols. Reading (comprehending) is a result of the interaction between the perception of graphic symbols that represent language and the reader's language skills, cognitive skills, and knowledge of the world. In this process the reader tries to re-create the meanings intended by the writer.

It cannot be overemphasized that meaningful response is at the heart of the reading process. "It can and should embrace all types of thinking, evaluating, judging, imagining, reasoning, and problem solving" (Gates 1949, p. 3). More than intellectual meaning may be involved; feelings of considerable intensity may be aroused, and emotional attitudes may be profoundly altered through reading.

The beginning reader must learn not only that the odd-looking marks represent the written form of language but also that written language is meaningful and differs from spoken language. In order to obtain the intended meaning, the child must be able to recognize most of the words. As the reader brings prior knowledge to bear, the response to the first words sets up an anticipation for meaning that, if correct, aids in identifying the words that follow. If too many words are mispronounced (or omitted because they are not recognized), if word recognition is so slow and halting that the words are not perceived as coming in meaningful sequences, or if sentences are run together and frequently misphrased, the approximation to oral language will not be close enough to convey the intended meaning.

For many children who are learning to read, speech serves as a mediator between visual perception and meaning; that is, they must pronounce words orally in order to retrieve meaning from them. As children become more skilled in reading, the need for using speech as a mediator lessens; reading becomes inaudible, noticeable lip and tongue movements cease, and to many an expert reader the meaning seems to leap from the printed page with scarcely any awareness of inner speech. Without word recognition, meaning cannot take place; conversely, comprehension facilitates word identification.

Skill in word recognition continues to develop as the child's reading ability matures. The recognition of common words becomes faster and more accurate, and new words are continually added to the child's store of words recognized at sight. Skill in decoding new words is acquired concurrently so that the child does not have to be told each new word.

As the child gets beyond the beginning stages in reading and recognizing words becomes nearly automatic, reading material becomes more complicated. Ideas that are outside the range of the youngster's experience are introduced, and words are employed that the child has never heard spoken. Sentences become longer and complex. Finding out what the book means gets harder because the language is more involved than the conversation to which the child is accustomed. To keep up with reading, children must increase their vocabularies, enlarge and refine their concepts and ideas, and develop mastery of complex forms of language.

Children meet a variety of reading materials and read to satisfy many needs and purposes. Story reading becomes differentiated from work reading. In pleasure reading, exclusive concern with the plot is gradually enriched by the development of appreciation for humor, characterization, accuracy and vividness of description, and the sheer beauty of artistic expression. In work-type reading, study skills and habits must be formed that differ from subject to subject, and different methods of study must be learned to cope with different phases of each subject. The efficient student learns how to locate needed information, distinguish major from minor points, follow directions, interpret, summarize, outline, and utilize facts.

Finally, reading becomes reflective and evaluative. To grasp the meaning and organization of a writer's ideas is important, but not sufficient. Mature readers bring their previous knowledge and experience to their present reading, compare the facts and arguments presented by one author with those of another, and are on the alert for errors in logic. Mature readers can distinguish factual reporting from biased propaganda and objective reasoning from wishful thinking.

To summarize, *reading may be defined as the meaningful interpretation of printed or written verbal symbols.* For the beginner, reading is concerned mainly with learning to recognize the printed symbols that represent language and to respond intellectually and emotionally as if the material were spoken rather than printed. The reasoning side of reading becomes increasingly important as word recognition is mastered. As proficiency in reading increases, individuals learn to adapt their reading strategies in accordance with the purpose for reading and the restrictions imposed by the material. The nature of the reading task, therefore, changes as learners progress to more mature levels. Reading is not one skill but a large number of highly interrelated skills that develop gradually over the years.

Reading is a complex process in which the recognition and comprehension of written symbols are influenced by readers' perceptual skills, decoding skills, experiential backgrounds, mind sets, and reasoning abilities as they anticipate meaning on the basis of what they have read. The total process is a gestalt, or whole; a serious flaw in any major function or part may prevent adequate performance.

III. READING AS LANGUAGE

Language provides us with the ability to communicate and entails much more than speech. Language consists of all the words in a person's lexicon (mental dictionary) and knowing how both to combine words into an infinite number of comprehensible sentences and to interpret sentences heard or read. By contrast, speech consists of the actual utterances spoken to particular persons in particular situations (Cazden 1972). Inner speech, which includes most thinking, is an important aspect of language.

Spoken and Written Language

There are two forms of language—spoken and written—and each has an expressive and a receptive aspect. Spoken language includes speaking and listening. Written or printed language encompasses writing (authorship, not penmanship) and reading.

Differences of opinion exist as to whether similar processes are involved in listening and reading or whether there are important processing differences. Those who believe that listening and reading are processed in the same or a similar manner propose that written language is parasitic on spoken language. Thus, to them reading is decoding, a position compatible with bottom–up models of reading. Once learners translate the printed text into its spoken form (phonological recoding[1]), they can apply the comprehension skills already developed in learning to understand spoken language.

In addition to the assumption that the comprehension processes are the same, or sufficiently similar, for reading and listening, those who argue the "reading as decoding" viewpoint assume that novice readers are linguistically mature. The latter assumption is often based on the finding that many 4- and 5-year-olds produce spoken sentences that contain all the basic syntactic transformations that underlie adult sentence structures. The claim that this means that children entering school are linguistically mature is an overstatement (Adams 1980). Oral language syntax is only moderately correlated with reading achievement in the first grade (Fletcher 1981), and there is a big difference between saying that young children can produce sentences as syntactically complex as an adult and claiming that they can understand such sentences as well as an adult.

---

[1] To *decode* means to get the intended meaning from analysis of spoken or *graphic symbols*; it is used primarily to refer to word identification. To *encode* means to change a message into symbols, for example, to encode an idea into words. To *recode* means to change information from one code into another, for example, to recode writing into speech.

Children continue to make substantial gains in their ability to understand syntactic structures until at least age 13. Moreover, young children need relatively little syntactic sophistication to understand most spoken language because of the cues provided by the speaker and the situation.

Reading demands more syntactic sophistication than listening does. Whereas syntactic and semantic information may be provided for the listeners by the speakers (e.g., phrases and clauses are "chunked" together), readers must discover the cues for themselves. Unless readers can construct the syntactic structure from the printed text, it does not matter if they have the syntactic competence to understand it (Adams 1980).

Differences between the more formal syntactic structure of written language and the less formal and often incomplete syntax of spoken language, with which children are more familiar, may cause problems for some of them (Rubin 1980b). This is especially true of children who have not been read to and thus have not been exposed to the language structures of written text.

Most 6-year-olds have mastered the most common morphological rules[2] of language, but they continue to gain mastery of the remaining features throughout their school years. For a discussion of language development during the elementary school years, refer to Hodges (1970, 1984) and Holdzkom *et al.* (1984).

Differences between the expressive forms of spoken and written language make reading more difficult than listening comprehension. Whereas speech tends to be repetitious, informal, and often incomplete in its syntax, written language tends to be concise, formal, and grammatically correct, with sentence structures that differ from those delivering the same message in spoken language. Some discourse structures used by writers are not employed often by speakers. Because authors are separated from their readers, they must use discourse structures such as subordinate and relative clauses, appositive phrases, and passive verbs that explicitly connect ideas (Bingham 1983).

The comprehension of oral language takes place in a "real world context" so that such potentially ambiguous words as *this, here,* and *now* are readily understandable because the use of such terms is usually accompanied by gestures indicating their referents.

In normal conversation each participant makes his (or her) own statements. In reading the learner must attribute comments, feelings, and the like to each character on the basis of clues such as punctuation marks. Also, the speaker is attempting to communicate with a given audience. He can see his audience's reactions, and if necessary, can adjust the way in which he is communicating. In addition, in the speaking–listening exchange, there may be opportunities for the listener to request clarification or additional information; the reader does not have these options. The face-to-face interchange also provides extralinguistic cues to meaning, such as gestures and facial expressions, which are especially helpful when the words do not really convey the intended meaning (e.g., raised

---

[2] A *morpheme* is a unit of language that conveys meaning. A *free morpheme* is a whole word that cannot be further divided into meaning-bearing units (e.g., *girl*). A *bound morpheme* (inflectional endings and affixes) must be combined with a free morpheme whose meaning it changes (e.g., *girls*).

eyebrows can mean that the speaker questions what the words seem to say). The reader must learn to rely less on situational cues and more on linguistic cues to obtain meaning.

Prosody

Speakers can provide three kinds of prosodic cues—pitch, stress, and juncture—that help to indicate the intended meaning of their utterances. *Pitch*, raising or lowering the voice, may provide cues as to the kind of sentence (e.g., most interrogative sentences end with a rising pitch). *Stress* involves accenting a syllable or word. Stressing a syllable can indicate the word's part of speech and sometimes its meaning (e.g., con'vict versus con-vict'). Accenting a word can modify meaning (e.g., **He** broke the glass. He **broke** the glass. He broke the **glass**). Stressing a pronoun helps to indicate its referent (e.g., in "Rob hit Mike and then **Susie** hit him," *him* refers to Mike. But in "Rob hit Mike and then Susie hit **him**," *him* refers to Rob). *Juncture* involves slight pauses between words, longer pauses between phrases and clauses, and even longer pauses between sentences. Pauses and changes in speed often provide clues for chunking words into clauses and phrases. Generally, pauses occur at syntactic boundaries.

The ability to comprehend written language requires the acquisition of alternative strategies to compensate for the lack of prosodic features (Schreiber 1980). In written language the only available clues to pitch are punctuation marks. Occasionally, stress is cued by italics, boldface type, or the use of all capital letters in the word. Spaces between printed words substitute for the brief pauses in speech, and wider spaces, as well as periods, question marks, and exclamation points, mark the ends of sentences. Although commas or semicolons may set off some phrases or clauses, readers often have to segment sentences into syntactic units on their own. Punctuation marks also help identify units such as possessives, which are marked by apostrophes. Quotation marks help separate and identify direct speech (Cordeiro, Giacobbe, & Cazden 1983). In conversation, who is doing the speaking is clearly indicated. In reading the conversational dialogues that appear frequently in pre-primers and primers, the characters' utterances are set off by quotation marks and phrases such as "Marcia said." The ability to interpret such cues is important for comprehension. Consider the difference in meaning between the following: Susie said, "Rob, I am here," and "Susie," said Rob, "I am here." In some reading materials, the words spoken by each character are not always indicated by quotation marks, and phrases such as "asked Jim" are dropped after the first few times. As a result, it is easy for the novice reader to lose track of who said what (Collins & Haviland 1979).

Although typographical cues and punctuation marks do not reflect all of the prosody of spoken language, they can be helpful to readers who understand their use. But children tend to rely more than adults on prosodic cues and are less able to employ lexical, syntactic, and semantic cues. Therefore they may have difficulty compensating for the lack of prosody in written text (Kleiman 1982).

Processing Oral and Silent Reading

Some writers (e.g., Juel & Holmes 1981) believe that oral and silent reading involve the same processes. Others (e.g., Mosenthal 1976–1977) argue that important differences exist between processing oral and silent reading. Yet others (e.g., Danks & Hill 1981) are of the opinion that we understand very little of the processing requirements of oral reading or how they relate to silent reading. Each group offers some evidence to support their viewpoint, but no definitive evidence has yet been presented.

Direct Versus Mediated Access to Meaning

The issue here is whether there needs to be phonological recoding during reading in order to acquire meaning. At one end of the continuum are theorists, often followers of top–down models, who believe that skilled, and perhaps even unskilled, readers can go directly from print to meaning without first recoding to speech (e.g., F. Smith 1979).

At the other end of the continuum are those, usually advocates of bottom–up models, who believe that graphic information must be recoded into phonological information. Words must be pronounced before their meanings are apparent. If the lexical entry for a word is jointly constituted by its four defining properties (a phonological form, a visual form, a grammatical class, and a meaning), as some believe it to be (see Barron 1980, 1981b), then the phonological form of a word (its sound) must be pronounced because it is a necessary part of the word (Fowler 1981). Some argue that even in skilled reading there is a form of phonological recoding, however abbreviated, that precedes comprehension (Weaver & Resnick 1979). They believe that phonological memory serves an important function in reading because it provides a link between visual memory and semantic memory. When a unit is selected from visual memory for processing, it must be recoded and a counterpart found in phonological memory. This phonological information is passed on to semantic memory where it is processed into meaning (Samuels & Eisenberg 1981). Phonological coding facilitates reading by providing a stable code for information that must be held in short-term memory until the meaning of segments (e.g., clauses, sentences) can be extracted (Stanovich 1980, Liberman et al. 1980). Studies of short-term memory suggest that skilled readers of English prefer a phonological recoding strategy (Shwedel 1983).

A third point of view holds that while speech processes seem to be unnecessary for skilled readers, they may be important for beginning reading because novice readers must learn to associate print to speech sounds. In order to become a skilled reader, however, one must learn to bypass the print-to-speech-to-meaning connection by acquiring a direct print-to-meaning connection. Extensive practice at *lexical access* (extracting meaning from words) allows attention to phonemic correspondences of letters to drop out and perception of letter patterns to activate word meanings automatically. There are, however, a few unresolved questions concerning the idea of a transition from novice to skilled reading with its accompanying change in processing. The major question is whether phonological recoding continues to serve some role subsequent to lexical access, such as aiding later memory and comprehension (Lesgold & Perfetti 1981). Within this viewpoint are those who believe that skilled readers revert to phonological recoding when the material is difficult for them.

Yet others (e.g., Baron & Treiman 1980, Glushko 1981, Barron 1981b) propose that there is evidence for both a print-to-sound-to-meaning path and a direct print-to-meaning path. They contend that in reading, all the paths that can be used are used. Juel (1983) hypothesized that usually both pathways to the lexicon operate simultaneously. Novice readers, however, seem to rely heavily on the print-to-sound-to-meaning pathway. Skilled readers seem to be adept at using both pathways.

English Orthography[3]

English uses an alphabetic writing system. Our 26 letters can be used to represent approximately 44 sounds that can be combined to construct all the words in our language. Alphabetic orthographies may be characterized by the extent to which they are phonetic representations of speech. Languages having a shallow orthography are ones in which spelling-to-sound correspondences are simple and consistent. In languages having a deep orthography, such as English, the spelling-to-sound relationships are complex. English spellings reflect not only grapheme–phoneme and phoneme–grapheme relationships but also semantic relationships at the morphophonemic level.[4] Morphophonemes follow rules that are more complex than grapheme–phoneme correspondences, and many so-called exceptions in English orthography are actually rule governed (Venezky 1970b). The underlying regularity of spellings at the morphophonemic level aids the skilled reader in understanding similarities in meaning among words, despite changes in vowel sounds and accent shifts (e.g., *courage, courageous*). Because our writing system represents meaning-bearing items directly, it functions well for a variety of dialects (C. Chomsky 1979b). Although English orthography may be "near optimal" for a formal system of rules, the speaker's internalized rules are not nearly as well defined or consistently applied as some authors suggest. However, preserving certain spellings (e.g., *s* as a plural marker), despite the variations in the sounds they represent, provides convenient clues to the reader (Taylor 1981).

Feitelson (1976) concluded that learning to read an alphabetic language that has consistent symbol–sound associations is easier than learning to read one with many irregularities because there is much less to learn and what has to be learned is less complex. Henderson (1982), however, felt that the linguists' intuition that a phonetic (shallow) orthography might be easier for children to

---

[3] Refer to Henderson (1982) for a comprehensive treatment of English orthography and a brief history of writing systems. See Taylor (1981) for a discussion of various writing systems and Weigl (1980) for a brief history of written language leading to our use of an alphabetic writing system.

[4] A *morphophoneme* is a unit of language that is intermediate between a *morpheme* and a *phoneme*. A *morpheme* is a unit of language that conveys meaning. A *phoneme* is the minimal sound unit that distinguishes one meaningful word from another (e.g., /b/at or /s/at). A *grapheme* is a written or printed letter or letters that represents a phoneme.

acquire, and a morphophonemic orthography might be more suitable for skilled readers, remains untested.

Frequently, the opinion is voiced that English is a nonphonemic language and the irregularities of its grapheme–phoneme correspondences are roadblocks in learning to read. The classic example provided is G. B. Shaw's contention that *fish* can be spelled *ghoti* (*gh* as in tou*gh*, *o* as in w*o*men, and *ti* as in na*ti*on). But such a spelling is impossible given the constraints of English orthography (L. Henderson 1982). At the beginning of words, *gh* never represents /f/, nor does *ti* represent /sh/ in the final position. Those who consider English orthography to be irregular often cite the findings of Hanna and Hanna (1966) that only half of the approximately 17,000 words they studied could be spelled correctly by applying a series of phoneme–grapheme correspondence rules. But, as Hodges (1982) pointed out, about 37% of the misspelled words had only one incorrect phoneme–grapheme match. If Hanna and Hanna had accounted for morphological relationships, approximately 87% of the words would have been spelled correctly. In English spellings there are constraints on position (e.g., *ck* never occurs in the initial position) and sequence (e.g., *q* is always followed by *u*).

English has very specific rules that restrict the combinations of letters that can occur in a word. For example, of the possible 441 combinations of two consonants, only 30 occur in English words (L. Haber & Haber 1981).

In Anglo-Saxon, Old English, and Middle English, there was a much closer relationship between the way words were spelled and pronounced. In the early days of English orthography there were no commonly agreed upon spellings for large numbers of words. Various factors throughout the years have contributed to the straying of English spelling from its alphabetic base (Barnitz 1980, Baron *et al.* 1980, Hodges 1981, L. Henderson 1982, Balmuth 1982):

1. Sound changes. Although, over time, the pronunciations of many words changed, their spellings did not. Thus the spellings no longer reflect their pronunciations.

2. Borrowed words. Words borrowed from other languages are usually pronounced as in the original language and retain their original spelling (e.g., *cello* from Italian, *bouquet* from French).

3. Adoptions of new spellings by scribes before spelling became standardized. For example, in 1066 Anglo-Saxon scribes began using the French distinction of hard and soft *c*.

4. Analogy or inverse spelling. In attempting to standardize spellings, words that were thought to be related were respelled to match existing strong spelling patterns. Thus the French *delite* became *delight*. However, the assumptions about relationships were not always correct. For example, the Old English word *caude* was spelled *could* when the spelling of *wolde* became *would*. During these changes, words like *come* and *love* came to be spelled with an *o* rather than with a *u* as in the original *cumen* and *luve*.

5. Etymology. In attempting to standardize spellings, the origins of the words were employed, particularly Classic Latin. At times, these efforts were misdirected. For example, the Middle English word *sisoures* acquired a silent *c* (*scissors*) in the belief that it was derived from the Latin *scindere* (to cut) rather than from its actual etymological source *cisorium* (a cutting tool).

6. *Homophones.* Spellings were changed to distinguish between homophones (words with the same pronunciation but which represent unrelated meanings). For example, we have *sum–some* and *whole–hole*. Interestingly, however, we have retained the spelling *holistic* rather than *wholistic*, which would more clearly designate its meaning.

Evidence from cross-linguistic and bilingual studies shows that writing systems that consistently fit the phonological structure of the language facilitate learning to read (Barnitz 1978). But this applies only to the decoding aspect of learning to read. Even in learning to read Finnish, which has a nearly optimal grapheme–phoneme relationship, Finnish children have as much difficulty as those learning to read other languages when it comes to comprehension (Kyöstiö 1980).

The most frequently cited example of the effect of a writing system on reading achievement is that of Japanese. Makita (1976) attributed the low incidence of reading disability in Japan to the nature of the Japanese writing system,[5] which is basically a combination of two types of symbols—Kana[6] and Kanji. In Kana each syllable represents a consonant–vowel syllable. Rarely is a Kana syllable pronounced in more than one way. The Kanji symbols are ideographs borrowed from Chinese. Kana seems fairly easy to learn (Taylor 1981), and because many Japanese preschoolers have informally learned the Kana system at home (Sakamoto 1980, Sheridan 1982), beginning reading materials, which employ only Kana, present little difficulty (Sakamoto 1976). As Kanji is introduced, reading difficulties become more frequent (Barnitz 1978).

The idea that Kana and Kanji are processed differently was supported by Yamadori (1975), who reported a brain-injured adult who could read Kanji but not Kana, and by Shimada (1981), who found there was a left-hemisphere dominance for processing Kana, but Kanji processing could be conducted in both hemispheres. Somewhat similarly, cases have been reported (e.g., Saffran & Marin 1977) in which brain-damaged persons have been able to respond to whole words but have been unable to decode printed words, or vice versa. Although Japanese presents the clearest contrast between phonographic and logographic scripts within a single language, the comparison is complicated by these factors: (1) Kana is learned first; and (2) the Hiragana syllabary is largely restricted to grammatical function words (L. Henderson 1982).

The influence of parents in the success of learning to read in Japan cannot be overlooked. Japanese parents are strongly encouraged to prepare their children for learning to read and apparently do so by giving them books (almost half of the children's publications in Japan are written for preschoolers), answering

---

[5] Tzeng and Hung (1981) cautioned against accepting this cause–effect relationship for a number of stated reasons.

[6] There are two types of Kana: *Hiragana*, which is used with words of Japanese origin; and *Katagana*, which is used with foreign loan words.

questions about reading, and reading to their children by the time they are a year old (Sakamoto 1981).

Stevenson (1984) constructed comparable reading tests in Chinese, Japanese, and English. The tests were given individually to all the fifth-grade children in 20 classrooms selected to be representative of elementary schools in Taipei, Taiwan (956 pupils); Sendai, Japan (775 pupils); and Minneapolis (453 pupils). The percentages reading at or below second-grade level were 8% in Taipei, 2% in Sendai, and 3% in Minneapolis. The percentages in the lowest 10% in reading but at or above the 16th percentile in cognitive tasks were 7.5% in Taipei, 5.4% in Sendai, and 6.3% in Minneapolis. Stevenson concluded: "Although the form of writing used in any language may be an impediment to the efforts of certain children in learning to read, it seems very unlikely that any particular form of writing is especially conducive to the production of severe reading problems."

Recently, China adopted a phonetic alphabet called *pènyin* ("spell sound"). It is now the writing system taught in first grade and introduces the Mandarin pronunciation (Sheridan 1981, Pope 1982). It will be interesting to learn what impact the change will have on literacy and the incidence of reading disability in China.

Reading and Other Language Arts

A number of writers (Strickland 1979, Barnard & Kendrick 1980) suggest that because reading is a language-based ability, it should either be part of a well-balanced language arts program, in which no one aspect of language is over- or underemphasized, or integrated within the language arts curriculum (e.g., Shuy 1981b, 1982; Clay 1979; 1982; Seaver & Botel 1983). The latter viewpoint is held by those who believe in the holistic nature of language. In either case the basic premise is that the various language arts are highly interrelated (Auten 1983) and that children should be made explicitly aware of the relationships. A concomitant, but unproven, belief is that strengthening ability in one language area will have a positive impact on other language abilities. It is believed, for instance, that through reading students will come to recognize how authors use language to communicate. Such knowledge is supposed to aid the students' reading comprehension, as well as their composition skills. Similarly, having to formulate, organize, and express their ideas in writing should provide insight into the ways other writers have done so, thereby aiding reading comprehension. Writing should also improve spelling skills, and in turn increased spelling ability may facilitate word recognition.

Periodically in the past, the concept of an integrated language arts program has been suggested, attempted, and usually abandoned. The reasons for failure to integrate the language arts in most school curriculums has not been determined, but it seems reasonable to speculate that they include the following: (1) The textbooks on which teachers rely heavily are single-subject oriented; (2) integration requires teacher knowledge, careful planning, and monitoring; and (3) past attempts at integration have failed to teach some skills and strategies that are important for success in each language area; it was often erroneously assumed that the skills—strategies would develop "naturally" or transfer automatically from one mode to another.

There is some disagreement as to the extent to which the language arts should be integrated. For example, Squire (1980) warned against attempting to relate spelling and reading instruction beyond using encoding as a check on decoding because by the end of first grade children's reading vocabularies begin to surpass their spelling vocabularies.

Pellegrini, DeStefano, and Thompson (1983) suggested that children's ability to convey information through oral language is a necessary component for success in learning to read and write and therefore should be incorporated into the language arts program. But, despite such occasional mention of the need for oral language development, the three language areas most often associated in the literature with reading are spelling, writing, and listening. The first two are discussed below; the latter in Chapter 13.

Reading and Spelling

Children usually are good readers and spellers or poor readers and spellers. There are also good readers who are poor spellers (Boder 1973, Frith & Frith 1980); rarely are poor spellers good readers.

Spelling is not a low-order psychomotor skill but is a consequence of complex cognitive operations that only now are coming to be understood (Frith 1980). Generally, the acquisition of spelling ability is part of the acquisition of written language skills and is governed by the cognitive processes involved in language development (Hodges 1982). Spelling ability develops as the child progresses from initial awareness of print as a form of language toward greater understanding of the relationships between spelling and written language.

Children's early attempts at spelling have revealed information regarding the nature and development of spelling ability. Some young children invent their own spellings even before they learn to read (Read 1971, 1975; C. Chomsky 1971, 1979a). Their invented spellings reveal that these children apparently detect and use the phonetic relationships represented in English orthography. Intuitively, they devise a logical system for relating English phonology and orthography, using the letters of the alphabet to do so. There seem to be five stages in invented spelling; each representing a different conceptualization of English orthography (Zutell 1981, Gentry 1982, Wood 1982):

1. *Deviant spelling stage.* Children use letters of the alphabet to represent words, but the children's spelling attempts are not readable because they do not understand the relationships of letters, letter names, and the sounds letters represent.

2. *Prephonetic stage.* The spellings begin to represent grapheme—phoneme relationships. One or more letters are used to represent a word, and a letter—name strategy is employed (e.g., R = are; LEFT = elephant).

3. *Phonetic stage.* Phonetic spellings are quite regular and all the sound features of the word are represented in the spelling.

4. *Transitional stage.* There is a marked movement toward standard spellings; a situation fostered by reading and spelling instruction. Their spellings adhere to the basic conventions of English orthography. Vowels and consonants replace the letter–name strategy (e.g., ELEFANT), common English sequences are employed (e.g., YOUNITED = united), and there is a move from phonological to morphological and visual spelling (e.g., *eighty* is spelled EIGHTEE rather than ATE as in the second stage).

5. *Standard spelling stage.* Knowledge of the English orthographic system and its basic rules is firmly established. Children exhibit correct spellings for words that are appropriate for their grade levels.

Some writers maintain that children who invent spelling learn to read and spell more easily than through direct instruction (Clay 1975). However, longitudinal data regarding the possible influence of invented spelling on learning to read are not extensive enough for a conclusive answer (Wood 1982).

Evidence from studies of the development of spelling ability led Hodges (1982) to conclude:

1. Children make few, if any, random spelling errors. Therefore, observing and analyzing their spelling errors can reveal information about their development of spelling ability and about a child's own logical scheme for spelling words at a given point in development.
2. Efficient spellers seem to have visual, morphophonemic, phonetic, and semantic information about words and to use this knowledge in attempting to spell unfamiliar words. Learning to spell is, to a large degree, learning about both the phonological and the graphic structure of words.
3. Learning to spell is part of general language development and both draws on and is constrained by cognitive and linguistic factors inherent in the acquisition of language. Knowledge of English orthography and other writing conventions is learned continuously by an interaction with written language.
4. In learning to spell, children do not move from one aspect of the orthography to the next—from sounds and letters to syllables to words. Rather, learning to spell involves developing an understanding of the total framework of English orthography and of the interrelatedness among phonological, morphological, and other language factors that the orthography reflects.
5. There are a number of unresolved issues regarding spelling instruction.

Reading and Writing

For many years (and in most curriculums today), instructional programs were based on a linear view of language development—listening precedes speaking, which precedes reading, which develops before writing (authorship). Recently, however, there have been some suggestions that writing activities should precede or occur simultaneously with reading instruction (DeFord 1981). Because reading and writing are related, learning in one mode is believed to have a positive effect on the other (M. Wilson 1981). The more experience children have in structuring their own writing and rereading their drafts, the better prepared they will be for interpreting the written structures of others, and vice versa (Squire 1980; Lehr 1981b, 1984; Auten 1983; Dionesio 1983). But, as Birnbaum (1982) cautioned, despite the recent interest in the relationship between reading and writing, research findings are limited and raise more questions than they answer.

Because writing and reading require attention to language forms not used in spoken language, attempts should be made to increase children's linguistic sensitivity and awareness by helping them deal with language objectively. This is done by bringing what children know implicitly about language to a conscious level. Linguistic consciousness raising can be fostered by using exercises that involve combining short sentences into longer, more complex ones. It is theorized that manipulating sentence structures provides insights into the internal workings of sentences, thereby improving writing ability and reading comprehension. Klein (1980) and C. Chomsky (1981) have provided suggestions for sentence combining. The results of studies regarding the effect of such exercises on reading comprehension are inconclusive (Stotsky 1982).

Before preparing to write, students should consider the purpose of their written message and their intended audience. The steps in producing a written message include generating ideas, drafting, revising, and editing; but these steps are not strictly sequential. Writing a draft may produce new ideas, and editing may indicate the need for revision. In addition to understanding the purposes for writing and the strategies that can be employed in producing a written message, students must be able to manage the conventions of written English (spelling, grammar, punctuation, and sentence construction) that will allow them to communicate (NAEP 1983c).

Ideas for demonstrating the functional communicative nature of reading and writing have been presented by Blass, Jurenka, and Zirzow (1981). Other suggestions for integrating reading and writing or for teaching writing may be found in Rubin (1980a), Gold (1981), Hennings (1982), Trosky and Wood (1982), Oliver (1982), and Glatthorn (1982).

IV. READING DISABILITY

A Brief Historical Overview[7]

Reading failure and attempts to remediate it date back to the beginning of the seventeenth century (Pelosi 1977). Morgan, a British ophthalmologist, published the first report of a case of reading disability in 1896. He described a 14-year-old boy who had not learned to read, although he seemed otherwise intelligent.

[7] Historical developments in reading diagnosis and remediation may be found in Critchley (1970), Thompson (1966), A. J. Harris (1968b), and Pelosi (1981). Refer to Hallahan and Cruickshank (1973) for a historical account of learning disabilities and to Monaghan (1980) for a history of dyslexia and its treatment. A history of remedial reading in the secondary school may be found in Cowan (1977). Cook (1977) traced the history of adult literacy education in America.

Morgan used the term "congenital word blindness," a term that continued to be popular in Europe for many years. Prominent among the early investigators in Great Britain was Hinshelwood (1900, 1917), a Glasgow eye surgeon, whose monographs attracted international attention. The early interest in reading problems on the part of medical men in Great Britain attracted relatively little notice from psychologists and educators.

Uhl (1916) published the first report in the United States of an attempt to diagnose individual reading problems and prescribe treatment. The following year, Bronner (1917) made some interesting observations about reading problems. Schmitt (1918) described a practical phonic method for teaching nonreaders, and Fernald and Keller (1921) outlined the kinesthetic method. C. T. Gray (1922) and W. S. Gray (1922) published the first two books on reading disability in America, and Gates (1927) developed the first battery of diagnostic reading tests.

At schools like the University of Chicago and Boston University, clinics specializing in reading difficulties became the first centers for the training of reading specialists and remedial teachers. New York City began the first large-scale remedial reading program in a public school system in the mid-1930s, as a federal work project of the depression era. Some secondary schools initiated remedial reading programs after World War II when they became aware of the large number of illiterates in the military forces; remedial reading programs dominated at this level during the late 1940s and early 1950s (Cowan 1977).

Although reading disability received a little notice from American physicians as early as 1906, the work of S. T. Orton (1937), a neurologist, first attracted wide attention. Orton recognized that there were multiple causes for delays in learning to read, but he was mainly interested in "*the* reading disability." He considered the primary symptom to be a severe reversal tendency, based on a failure to establish clear dominance of one cerebral hemisphere over the other. Orton coined the term *strephosymbolia* ("twisted symbols") to describe the condition and recommended a systematic sounding–blending method of phonics teaching.

Two opposing tendencies have existed since the beginning of the study of reading disability. Physicians have postulated a basic constitutional condition, often hereditary and usually accompanied by other communication difficulties (e.g., in speech, spelling, handwriting, composition). While they admit that cases of reading disability can stem from other causes, physicians have preferred to concentrate on the constitutional issue.

Educational psychologists, on the other hand, have tended to be impressed by the wide range of physical, psychological, emotional, sociological, linguistic, and educational handicaps that may be seen in poor readers and have tended to favor a pluralistic theory of causation. Without denying the possibility of specific subgroups, they have emphasized the wide range of handicaps to be found in school and clinic populations and the continuity of problems from mild to most severe disabilities.

From about 1935 to 1955, many psychoanalysts and clinical psychologists sought to explain reading disability as a symptom of emotional disturbance and tended to recommend psychotherapy as the preferred mode of treatment. There is little doubt that the great majority of children with reading disabilities who come to the attention of psychologists and psychiatrists have emotional symptoms and problems. In individual cases, however, it is often difficult to determine whether the emotional problem is a cause of the reading disability or a result of it. Psychotherapy alone seems to be an adequate method of treatment in only a small minority of cases.

Since 1955, there has been an accelerating interest in reading disabilities in the United States. This has resulted in a vast expansion of remedial programs and an upsurge in research; federal funding has been largely responsible for such efforts.

During the 1960s, neurologists and special educators proposed causal theories of reading disability that tended to be neurological and physiological in nature; these theorists placed less emphasis on emotional and educational causes. Terms such as *dyslexia* and *learning disability* emerged, and there was a renewed interest in determining the nature of the disability. Most of these theorists believed that reading disability was a symptom of some underlying defect within the learner.

The late 1970s and early 1980s have been highlighted by the contributions of linguists, cognitive psychologists, and neuropsychologists in their attempts to understand the reading process and thereby gain insights into the factors that contribute to reading disability.

The Incidence of Reading Disability

For several reasons, definitive information on the prevalence of reading disability is not available. First, the definitions (e.g., reading retardation, dyslexia, specific reading disability) used to indicate the populations vary considerably. Second, even when similar terms are employed, the criterion used to set a cutoff point has varied from one investigator to another. Finally, populations differ somewhat, and age of school entrance, socioeconomic background, method of teaching, and degree of regularity in the symbol–sound relationships of the language produce variations. Moreover, rarely are the reported percentages based on adequate samples. As Pulliam (1975) discovered, the incidence of disability has increased as the defining criteria were broadened and as the level of severity assumed to be disabling decreased.

Estimates of reading disability reported for various countries range from virtually none in Taiwan (Kuo 1978) and Korea (Taylor 1980) to 1% in Japan (Makita 1968), 2% in Czechoslovakia (Matějček 1976), 2–3% in Russia (Chabe 1983), approximately 5% in Denmark (Jansen *et al.* 1976) and Norway (Vik 1976), 8% in Sweden (Malmquist 1958) and West Germany (Weinschenk *et al.* 1970), 10% in England (Newton 1970) and Finland (Syvälahti 1976), 13% in Israel (Gross 1978), 14% in Argentina (de Quirós & Della Cella 1959), 15% in Scotland (Clark 1979), 16% in Ireland (Swan 1978), and as high as 22% (4% having "severe dyslexia") in Austria (Schenk-Danziger 1960). That such estimates are open to question can be illustrated by the varying percentages reported for the same countries by other authors. For example, instead of 8% in West Germany, Klasen (1976) reported estimates of from 2% to 20%; Gorriti and Muñiz (1976) reported 10% to 25% for Argentina rather than 14%; and Hulme (1981b) concluded that less than 4% of English children experience severe reading problems as compared with the 10% reported by Newton (1970).

A comprehensive survey of available evidence of the incidence of reading disabilities in the United States concluded that about 10% to 15% of American schoolchildren have reading disabilities. "Eight million children in America's elementary and secondary schools today will not learn to read adequately. One child in seven is handicapped in his ability to acquire essential reading skills. This phenomenon pervades all segments of our society—black and white, boys and girls, the poor and the affluent" (National Advisory Committee on Dyslexia and Related Disorders 1969, p. 7).

Legislation, Legal Rulings, and Reading

Legislation, particularly at the federal level, and court rulings have had an increasing impact on reading instruction and reading disability over the past two decades.

Legislation

Title I of the ESEA Act (Public Law 95–561) is the largest federal aid program for elementary and secondary education in the United States. Its funding grew from $959 million in 1966 to over $3 billion in 1980. About 81% of all school districts use Title I funds. About 79% of the students in Title I schools received compensatory reading instruction in 1979–80.[8] Between 1976 and 1980, Title I students narrowed the gap between themselves and their counterparts in schools not receiving such funding (NAEP 1981a). Primary-grade Title I students gained more in reading than similar students who did not receive such services; intermediate-grade children did not. Overall, growth in reading achievement has been modest, ranging from a loss of 2 percentile points to a gain of 5 (Stonehill & Anderson 1982).

ESEA Title I has been reauthorized and substantially amended by Title V (The Educational Improvement Act) of the Omnibus Budget Reconsideration Act of 1981 under the "Financial Assistance to Meet Special Education Needs of Disadvantaged Children" section that went into effect in October 1982 (Stonehill & Anderson 1982).

Section 504 of the Vocational Rehabilitation Act of 1973 provided that a handicapped person may not be "excluded from, deprived the benefit of, or be subjected to discrimination because of his or her handicap by any program which receives federal funds." The Family Education Rights and Privacy Act of 1974 (the Buckley Amendment) allows children and their parents access to the children's school records, to challenge any information in those records, and for the parents to control who has access to those records. Under the Developmentally

---

[8] See Calfee and Drum (1979) and Gordon (1979) for discussions of compensatory reading programs, and Becker and Gersten (1982) for an evaluation of follow-through programs. In the last decade, enthusiasm for compensatory education has waned considerably (Good & Stipek 1983).

Disabled Assistance and Bill of Rights Act of 1977 (PL 94–103), state educational agencies are required to assure that the developmentally disabled are not inappropriately placed in residential institutions, to facilitate their return to a more "normalized" setting once released from an institution, and to provide for their educational needs.

Two recent Supreme Court decisions have suggested a reduced federal role in determining what constitutes appropriate programs and service for the handicapped. For example, the Court ruled that the Education for Handicapped Children Act does not place an obligation on the states to provide a particular level of education or equal educational opportunities for such children (McCarthy 1983).

The Education for Handicapped Children Act of 1975 (PL 94–142) mandated, and provided financial support for, services for children with a broad range of learning disabilities. It required each state to identify all such handicapped children in need of special education, provide free and appropriate public education for them, submit an Individual Educational Program (IEP) for each learning-disabled student, and protect their rights by assuring due process, confidentiality of their records, and parental involvement in the IEP process (Bierly 1978).

Although PL 94–142 does not mandate *mainstreaming*, there has been a trend toward placing handicapped children in regular classes and integrating them into regular school programs while providing support from resource teachers, instead of providing for them in special classes (A. J. Harris 1980a, b). The law simply calls for providing "the least restrictive educational environment"; that is, the program that is best suited to the child's special needs and is as close as possible to the educational program provided for other students. It does not rule out special segregated classes. There is little research evidence favoring any particular educational setting. Educational practices rather than setting per se are likely to be the more important in the success of any reading program (Leinhardt & Pallay 1982; Goldberg, Shiffman, & Bender 1983).

Has PL 94–142 been effective? A recent Rand Corporation report (*Albany Times Union* 1983) concluded that school officials have been paying more attention to handicapped students' legal rights and the design of special education programs as a result of PL 94–142. As for its impact on academic achievement, the answer varies with the specific programs under consideration. But the more important questions remain unanswered—which programs are effective under what conditions; and what is more important, why? (Light & Pillemer 1982).

There have been problems in the identification and treatment of learning-disabled students. Particularly vexing has been the interpretation of the federal definition of learning disability. For example, it is difficult, if not impossible, to determine whether children's learning problems are the result of environmental, cultural, or economic disadvantage, any of which would exclude them under the federal definition. Many children formerly labeled "reading disabled" have been labeled "learning disabled" to make them eligible for funding.

The cost of the identifiction process also has come under fire. A study in Colorado (Shepard *et al.* 1981) revealed that although the average candidate was given an average of 6.6 tests by an average of 7.6 professionals, between 59% and 74% of those identified as perceptually communicative disordered (learning disabled) did not match legal definitions or those found in the literature. Even more damaging was the finding that there was little agreement among the clinicians as to who had the disorder. Further, it cost almost as much to identify a learning-disabled child as to treat him for a year.

Although there were attempts to change the major provisions of PL 94–142 (da Silva 1983), such efforts ceased as of 1984. In addition, Congress passed PL 98–199, which reaffirmed the federal role in special education.

Legal Rulings

In addition to the legal rulings on minimal competency (see pp. 6–7), the courts have made a number of rulings in recent years that have bearing on the teaching of reading (Harper & Kilarr 1977). For instance, several relatively recent cases have suggested that students have a right to instruction appropriate to their educational needs and that they cannot be excluded from free public education because of organic or linguistic deficiencies (Schork & Miller 1978).

Accountability, in which educators are held responsible for the effectiveness of reading instruction (Ruddell 1973, Aaron 1976), has taken on new meaning. Educational malpractice suits have claimed that the school was to blame for a student's illiteracy. As of 1981 the courts had rejected all claims of educational malpractice based on alleged negligent instruction by teachers. The courts, however, did not excuse the teachers from responsibility; rather, they found that the instructional-learning process was not their sole responsibility (P. Williams 1981).

The courts are becoming increasingly assertive in assessing classification practices, requiring schools to produce evidence that they are attempting to meet the needs of variously classified students, and ordering specific instructional programs and procedural safeguards to protect students' interests (McCarthy 1979). The situation has reached a point where the International Reading Association (1982a) passed a resolution opposing extending the role of the courts in dealing with issues involving reading achievement in those areas of decision making (curriculum, methodology, and tests) that ought to be the responsibility of professionals.

Adapted, Enriched, Corrective, and Remedial Programs

Most students make normal progress in developing their reading ability, but some require programs that differ from those found under the label "developmental reading." These include slow learners, the intellectually gifted, and students who are not making as much progress in reading as can be reasonably expected. It is beyond the scope of this book to discuss teaching reading to those with severe visual or auditory defects and those who are emotionally disturbed.

Adapted Programs

The number of children with limited intellectual ability depends on how retardation is defined and the degree of retardation under consideration. The American Association of Mental Deficiency now uses an IQ of 68 as the cutoff point, but the literature indicates a wide variety of practices. In addition, it should be realized that not all children who score very low on an IQ test (particularly on a group test) are mentally retarded. Severe reading disability, emotional or medical problems, sensory defects (e.g., a severe hearing loss), or language handicaps may contribute to low IQ scores or teachers' judgments of limited learning aptitude.

Slow learners need a reading program geared to their abilities, one that accepts their limitations, sets reasonable expectations, and is designed to meet their needs and interests. Such an adapted reading program should differ from the typical developmental reading program mainly in its slower pace and its use of different materials. The materials should more closely resemble those found in remedial reading programs than typical basal readers because slow learners' interests are often more mature than their reading ability. Although no conclusive evidence shows that any one reading method is most effective for slow learners (Blanton, Sitko, & Gillespie 1976), supplemental instruction that provides additional time to learn and is paced properly through a sequence of tasks tends to be beneficial (Singer 1978b). Teaching slow learners to read is covered more thoroughly by Harris and Sipay (1979, pp. 481–486). A good adapted program includes adjustments in the slow learner's entire academic program, not just in reading.

Enriched Programs

At the other end of the intellectual continuum are the gifted—the 7% of our students who have IQs between 120 and 130 and the additional 3% with IQs over 130. Gifted students tend to be 1 to 3 years ahead of their age peers in academic achievement. These students need assistance in continuing their accelerated growth in reading abilities and interests. Suggestions for helping them to do so may be found in Harris and Sipay (1979, pp. 486–491), Trezise (1984), Lehr (1983), Bates (1984), and Moller (1984).

Corrective and Remedial Programs

Children who are reading significantly below their potential should have reading programs that are planned to teach them the reading skills and strategies not yet mastered, using the best methodology, materials, and motivation possible. Efforts to help these children are broadly described as remedial reading. Under this broad heading there is a distinction between corrective and remedial reading programs. Theoretically, the two differ in four respects: (1) where the treatment takes place; (2) who provides the treatment; (3) the number of children treated in a session; and (4) the severity of the problems treated.

Corrective reading occurs within the framework of regular class instruction and is conducted by the classroom teacher for groups or subgroups whose reading-skill weaknesses are uncovered in the daily or periodic assessment of skill development. Remedial reading occurs away from the regular classroom, in or outside the school, and is conducted by a teacher with special training in reading (or by tutors supervised by a reading specialist) for small groups or on a one-to-one basis.

In actuality, the distinction between corrective and remedial reading is somewhat artificial. The problems treated are more likely to differ in degree than in kind, and whether a child receives corrective or remedial reading help may depend more on the resources available than on the nature of the reading problem or the instruction best suited to the child's needs (Clymer 1967).

There can be no quarrel with the proposition that major efforts should be devoted to improving the general efficiency of classroom teaching. As this takes place, the frequency of reading disabilities will diminish somewhat. Nevertheless, with the best of teachers, children will continue to be handicapped by physical defects, to be emotionally upset, to miss school because of illness, and for these or other reasons to fall behind. Detecting weak points in achievement and helping the child overcome these weaknesses are integral parts of effective classroom teaching. Corrective instruction is a sort of educational first aid. It is, of course, remedial teaching, but remedial teaching conceived of without capital letters, as a normal part of good methodology. As corrective teaching in its simpler forms becomes taken for granted because it is part of every good teacher's procedure, the need for calling it by a special name diminishes. In this sense, remedial reading is losing its distinctive character by becoming normal rather than unusual procedure.

Finally, a small percentage of children will continue to have special handicaps in reading that require the application of refined diagnostic procedures by experts and individual teaching by skilled remedial teachers. There is, then, no conflict among the three phases of a good reading program: (1) superior first teaching adapted to the needs and individual abilities of children; (2) frequent classroom use of simple corrective procedures as needed; and (3) careful diagnosis and special remedial help for the seriously disabled reader.

2

Readiness for Reading

This chapter is concerned with reading readiness, the foundation on which accomplishment in reading is based. The chapter has three main sections. The first section explores the nature of reading readiness and describes the main characteristics involved. The second section discusses the several ways to evaluate reading readiness. The final section considers the implications of readiness for practices in kindergarten and first grade.

I. THE NATURE OF READING READINESS

The idea of reading readiness arose from concern over the formerly very high rate of nonpromotion in the elementary schools. In the 1920s, reading failure accounted for 99% of the retentions in Grade 1, 90% in Grade 2, and 70% in Grade 3 (Gates 1927). Schools became aware that there were great differences within the 6-year-old population; some were not as mature as typical kindergartners, while others were far ahead of their age group in some respects.

Readiness for reading is a complex concept involving many different contributing factors and developing through the intimate interplay of learning with biological growth. It depends also, in part, on the fit between the children's abilities and the way they are taught. Children of below-average intelligence may fail in a fast-moving group or succeed in a group taught slowly and patiently.

Learning to read requires both a high level of general growth and cognitive and linguistic development, as well as a host of specific learnings. The intimate interplay of inner growth and environmental stimulation is present in all aspects of child development, and readiness for reading is no exception.

Reading readiness may be defined as a state of general maturity, based on aptitudes and learned knowledge and skills, that allows a child to learn to read under given instructional conditions. Readiness is not an all-or-none characteristic, and all degrees of readiness are found from very low to very high. It is better to ask what the child is ready to learn, and at what rate, than to conceive of readiness as a fixed state. Many factors are involved in reading readiness, and no single factor guarantees success or failure.

The cognitive, physical and physiological, and environmental characteristics related to reading readiness are to a large extent the same as those that distinguish good from poor readers at later ages. These characteristics, as they relate to reading readiness, are discussed briefly here, leaving a more thorough treatment for later chapters.

A number of variables have been shown to be related to success in learning to read and thus are often considered in reading readiness programs or tests. Their exact relationship to reading acquisition, however, is not clear because the data are primarily correlational. There are four possible relationships (Ehri 1979). First, the factor might be a *prerequisite* without which reading acquisition would be impossible or at least highly improbable. Therefore it would be important to teach the skill, as needed, before attempting to teach the child to read. Second, the skill, or knowledge, could be a *facilitator* that allows the student to learn more quickly or easily; although its absence would not prevent learning to read, one would be justified in teaching the skill to those who had not acquired it. Third, the skill or knowledge may be a *consequence* of learning to read; that is, it is acquired in the course of learning to read without any direct instruction. Fourth, the skill and reading ability may be *correlates* of a common underlying variable. In the last two possibilities, teaching the skill would serve little purpose. It is possible that a variable may be both a consequence of what has occurred and a facilitator for future progress.

Chronological Age

In most American school systems, children are accepted into the first grade once a year, and there is a minimum age limit (usually the minimum age is 5 years 9 months when school opens); but there is a range of 5 calendar months among entrance-age requirements in the United States (Langer, Kalk, & Searls 1984). The entering class is likely to vary almost a full year in age, from the child who is barely old enough to the child who was almost old enough the year before. For a child whose rate of development is below average, it is an advantage to be one of the older children. For the rapidly developing child, it makes little difference. Although differences in achievement decrease by age 13 and disappear by age 17, children who are older at age of admission perform significantly better than younger children at age 9, and younger children are retained more often (Langer, Kalk, & Searls 1984).

In studies in which characteristics measurable before reading instruction are correlated with degree of success in beginning reading, chronological age (CA) is one of the poorest predictors of reading. Wide differences in reading achievement are found whether reading instruction is begun at age 5, as in Great Britain, age 6, as in the United States, or age 7, as in Sweden.

Gender

Young boys and girls do about equally well on reading readiness tests (Bond and Dykstra 1967), but American girls tend to get off to a better start in reading and have fewer failures. In Germany, on the other hand, elementary school boys read as well as girls (Preston 1979), suggesting that gender differences in early reading are more the result of school-related and cultural factors than biological factors. Gender, CA, and height and weight were found to be poor predictors in identifying "at risk" kindergartners (Davies 1980).

Cognitive Factors

General Intelligence

General intelligence is an average of many interrelated phases of mental growth. The results are usually expressed in terms of the level of maturity (mental age, or MA) and relative brightness (intelligence quotient, or IQ). The MA increases fairly steadily until mid-adolescence, while the IQ remains fairly stable in most children. About 25% of children have IQs in the bright to superior range (110 and up), about 50% are average (90 to 110), and about 25% are slow learners (below 90); children in the bottom 3% are generally regarded as mentally retarded.

Correlations between intelligence scores and reading achievement in first grade tend to be substantial but not high, with a median r of about .50 for the combined results of 15 large-scale coordinated research studies (Bond & Dykstra 1967). While predictions of reading achievement can be made for groups, the success or failure of individual children cannot be predicted with much accuracy from their intelligence scores.

It is not true that a minimum mental age of 6 years is necessary for learning to read. It has been known for a long time that with individual instruction and much patience, even children with MAs of 4 years can be taught to recognize some words (Davidson 1931). A given degree of intelligence does not guarantee success or failure, but it does influence the rate at which a child can learn. Progress in learning to read is only partly dependent on intellectual ability; the difficulty of the material, the pace of instruction, the specific instructional methods used, and the amount of individual help given all influence progress (Gates 1937).

The relation of MA to both chronological age (CA) and IQ is shown in Table 2.1. From the table one can see that the lower an IQ, the older a child

Table 2.1 Reading Readiness: Relation of Mental Age to Chronological Age and Intelligence Quotient

	INTELLIGENCE QUOTIENT						
	70	80	90	100	110	120	130
Chronological age	Corresponding mental age						
4 yrs. 9 mos.	3–4	3–10	4–4	4–9	5–3	5–9	6–2
5 yrs. 3 mos.	3–8	4–2	4–9	5–3	5–9	6–4	6–10
5 yrs. 9 mos.	4–0	4–7	5–3	5–9	6–4	6–11	7–6
6 yrs. 3 mos.	4–5	5–0	5–8	6–3	6–9	7–6	8–2
6 yrs. 9 mos.	4–9	5–5	6–1	6–9	7–5	8–1	8–9
7 yrs. 3 mos.	5–1	5–10	6–6	7–3	8–0	8–8	9–5
7 yrs. 9 mos.	5–5	6–2	7–0	7–9	8–6	9–4	10–1

Note: Mental ages for other chronological ages and IQs may be computed with the formula Mental Age = Chronological Age times IQ. One must remember that the IQ is really a decimal fraction. For example: To find the MA of a child who is 6 years 6 months old (6–6) and has an IQ of 85, 78 mos. × .85 equals 66.3 mos., which equals 5 years 6 months (5–6).

must be to reach an MA that is adequate for learning to read. If we assume that an MA of 5 years 0 months is minimally adequate, beginning kindergartners with IQs of at least 110 have already reached it, whereas those with IQs below 80 are at least 6 years 3 months when they reach it. Assuming that an MA of 6 years is desirable (but not essential), bright children reach it before or during kindergarten, average children during first grade, and slow learners late in first grade or during second grade.

Logical Thinking
According to Piaget (1963), children in kindergarten and first grade are in the process of transition from the preoperational stage (ages 2 to 6) to the stage of concrete operations (ages 6 to 11). Preoperational children show four kinds of immaturity in reasoning: (1) egocentricity (the child does not understand that his viewpoint may be different from that of other people and is possibly incorrect); (2) limited understanding of cause–effect relationships; (3) centration (focusing attention on only a limited part of a complex stimulus and ignoring the rest of it); and (4) inability to solve conservation problems (in which the quantity of something remains constant when its size or position is changed). Another preoperational characteristic is a lack of seriation (arranging items in order of ascending or descending amounts or determining where an item belongs in a series). Young children also have difficulty understanding how items can be arranged in classes and that an item can belong to two or more classes at the same time (e.g., American, Democratic, Catholic) (Cleland 1981).

These abilities develop gradually during the period of concrete operations—"concrete" because the child can reason successfully about a present situation but cannot imagine a hypothetical situation and reason logically about it. According to Waller (1977), relationships between the attainment of concrete operational thought and reading attainment are low to moderate and are reduced when intelligence is held constant. The attainment of concrete operations is apparently not a prerequisite for learning to read (Robeck 1981).

Specific Cognitive Disabilities

Children who fail to learn to read despite apparently adequate general intelligence may have some specific cognitive deficit, dysfunction, or delay that makes learning to read difficult for them. The best available evidence indicates that in most young children such traits as memory and problem solving are closely interrelated, but that does not rule out the possibility of finding an occasional child who shows very poor memory, perceptual difficulty, inability to concentrate and pay attention, difficulty in following directions, or language disability that is in marked contrast to otherwise satisfactory abilities.

Visual Discrimination

Even with normal visual acuity a child may have immature visual discrimination. Some young children pay attention only to the main characteristics of visual stimuli—size, shape, and color—and ignore details. They may notice the height of a letter and ignore its other distinguishing features. When asked to match letters or words, they make many errors because they do not notice differences that are obvious to older children.

The tendency to make *reversal errors* is common among immature children. To such children, *b, d, p,* and *q* are the same; differences in orientation are ignored. Pairs of words such as *on* and *no*, and *saw* and *was*, also tend to be confused. Reversal errors tend to decrease with age, and first graders with marked reversal tendencies make less than normal progress (Goins 1958, Jansky & de Hirsch 1972).

The ability to perceive visual similarities and differences is consistently related to progress in reading, and items to measure this ability are included in practically all reading readiness tests. Barrett (1965), in a thorough review of the research, concluded that visual discrimination of letters and words has better predictive value than discrimination of pictures and geometric designs.

Visual–Motor Ability

Both visual discrimination and fine motor coordination are involved in the copying of designs, which may be geometric forms, irregular patterns of lines, dots or circles, or letters of the alphabet. Correlations between visual–motor scores and success in beginning reading are only moderate, around .40, and are not highly correlated with visual-discrimination scores.

Auditory Discrimination

Many aspects of auditory discrimination are more closely related to music than to reading (e.g., pitch, loudness, rhythmic patterns). The aspects of auditory discrimination directly related to reading involve comparisons of speech sounds. Two kinds of auditory-discrimination tests for speech sounds have been developed. The first involves listening to two words or pseudowords that are either identical or differ in only one phoneme and deciding if they are the same or different. The second (used in group tests) involves the use of pictures to represent words; the examiner says a word, which is pictured, then names three or four other pictures; each child marks the picture for the word that resembles the first word in a particular way (first sound or rhyming ending). This obviously makes demands on attention, verbal comprehension, and memory, as well as auditory discrimination.

Hammill and Larsen (1974b) found that correlations among different auditory-discrimination tests tend to be low and correlations with beginning reading tend to be low to moderate. However, the Auditory Discrimination subtest of the *Macmillan Reading Readiness Test* correlated .65 with the reading scores of first graders (Harris & Sipay 1970). Auditory discrimination seems more relevant when the beginning reading instruction stresses phonics and less relevant when a visual method of word recognition is stressed.

Several linguists have pointed out that a child who pronounces most words correctly must have adequate auditory discrimination. This is true but beside the point; understandings are involved. The ability to abstract a beginning sound from a heard word and compare it with the beginning sound of another word is a cognitive ability that many 5- and 6-year-olds have not yet developed; in Piaget's terms, it requires "decentration."

Children who speak a divergent dialect or have a foreign-language background tend to score poorly on auditory-discrimination tests. This results from the children's tendency to hear words as they pronounce them. Speakers of black English, for example, may not hear a difference between /bit/ and /bet/ because short /i/ and short /e/ are not differentiated in that dialect. The language background of the child must be taken into account when interpreting auditory-discrimination test scores (Bryen 1976).

Auditory Blending

Auditory blending involves synthesizing speech sounds; the stimuli are auditory, but the skill is cognitive. After the examiner pronounces the parts of a word with a pause between each two sounds, the child has to indicate the spoken word. Auditory blending requires understanding that a spoken word has discernible sounds within it, that it can be spoken part by part, and that a listener can put the parts together mentally to form a recognizable approximation of the spoken word.

Auditory Segmentation

Auditory segmentation involves the understanding that sentences are made up of words (then the concept of *word* would appear to be a prerequisite) and that words are made up of syllables and syllables of sounds. Children are asked to demonstrate these understandings by indicating how many words there are in a spoken sentence, the number of syllables or phonemes (sounds) in a spoken word, or both.

Liberman *et al.* (1977) found that kindergarten children who had the greatest difficulty segmenting words into phonemes also had the greatest difficulty in learning to read. By age 4, nearly half of the children studied by Liberman and Shankweiler (1979) could segment spoken words into syllables, but none could segment by phonemes. At age 5, almost half could segment by syllables and less than 20% by phonemes. By age 6, the percentages increased to 90% and 70%, respectively.

Reading instruction may facilitate auditory segmentation ability. For example, all 20 of the reading-disabled children who had marked deficits in phonemic segmentation in first grade were proficient at phonemic analysis when tested 3 years later (Fox & Routh 1983). Many of them had spelling difficulties, however.

Elkonin (1973) developed a procedure for teaching young Russian children that words are made up of phonemes in a particular sequence. His procedure was adapted to English by Ollila, Johnson, and Downing (1974), who found it more effective than two other programs for helping kindergarteners develop auditory discrimination and the ability to tell the number of sounds heard in a word. The progress, however, did not have a positive impact on reading achievement.

Associative Learning

The ability to learn associations is essential in learning to read. Such ability is demonstrated by learning to associate printed letters with their names or the sounds represented by the letters, or to associate printed words with their spoken equivalents.

Letter-name knowledge has ranked among the best single predictors of reading achievement (Bond & Dykstra 1967). This is why almost every reading readiness test has a letter-name subtest. But while it continues to be a good predictor for kindergarten children, its predictive validity has lessened for first graders because most children now enter first grade already knowing most letter names (Nurss 1979a).

Predictive validity, however, does not necessarily indicate a cause–effect relationship. In fact, a number of studies have indicated that teaching the names of the letters did not have a positive impact on learning to read (Groff 1984). Ehri (1983) has argued that the studies were flawed and that learning the names of the letters can facilitate learning to read. On the other hand, a child who can learn letter names may simply be demonstrating that he has adequate auditory and visual discrimination and memory, adequate associative learning ability, can profit from instruction, and is motivated to learn. The same factors in learning letter names are also important in learning to read. This is not to say that children should not be taught letter names, but simply that doing so may not result in easier acquisition of reading ability. Letter-name knowledge has value (e.g., having verbal labels for letters makes it easier to refer to them), but it is not a prerequisite for learning to read.

Attention

At any given moment, a child receives a tremendous amount of sensory stimulation—visual, auditory, touch, internal sensations—and can attend to only a small part of it. Typically, a child focuses on one main whole or pattern, within which four to seven subunits can be distinguished. The rest is background, vaguely perceived and marginally noticed or totally ignored. Difficulty in attending and maintaining concentration has been identified as significantly related to failure in first-grade reading (Malmquist 1958; Kinsbourne & Caplan 1979). This is not specific to reading; a child who cannot maintain attention to the task at hand may do poorly on any test or in any learning situation.

General and Specific Concepts

The store of concepts a child has developed, and the words that provide labels for these concepts, are essential for carrying out verbal reasoning. Therefore a child's conceptual development is related to success in learning to read. Most novice readers have had real or vicarious experiences from which they have gained information, concepts, and vocabulary that are sufficient for understanding the material being used for reading instruction.

Clay (1979) and others believe that it is important for children to understand (1) the communication purposes of written language; (2) concepts about print (e.g., that a printed word is comprised of a single letter or group of letters sequenced in a way that parallels the sounds in its spoken counterpart); and (3) such conventions as reading from left to right and top to bottom (in most languages). Most preschoolers acquire information about the purposes and use of print (print awareness), and such understandings increase with age (Hiebert 1981) and with learning to read (Ehri 1979, J. Mason 1982a).

Because young children cannot see what a reader does while reading (except perhaps for such motor activities as turning the page), they may not understand the purpose and use of reading and how it is done. When first confronted by reading, many children perceive it as a mysterious activity (P. Moore 1981), but under reasonably good conditions children work themselves increasingly out of a state of *cognitive confusion* into one of *cognitive clarity* whereby they understand that written language has communication purposes and represents features of spoken language (Downing 1979, 1980).

A similar viewpoint is held by Mattingly (1979), who used the term *linguistic awareness* to refer to concepts about language that are important for reading.[1] Ayers and Downing (1979) reported that their test of linguistic awareness had a predictive validity of .80 for reading achievement. However, lower correlations are reported in the test manual (Downing, Ayers, & Schaefer 1983).

According to J. Mason (1981), three aspects of concept and language development are particularly significant before and during learning to read: (1) understanding that spoken language consists of words and sentences that correspond to similar units of print; (2) becoming able to segment speech into abstract phonemic units that correspond to letters and letter groups; and (3) acquiring a variety of labels, rules, and procedures needed to describe and carry out reading tasks. J. Mason (1982a) postulated a three-stage theory of prereading that suggests that learning about reading is best explained in terms of changes in young children's conceptualizations about the forms and functions of print.

Children must understand the technical terms needed for reasoning about the relationship between written and spoken language (Downing 1980). Knowledge of terms is also important in understanding reading instruction. Thus, un-

---

[1] Not all writers define *linguistic awareness* in the same way. For example, Liberman *et al.* (1980) use the term to refer primarily to auditory segmentation.

derstanding concepts such as *word* is important in learning to read. The concept of *word*, as it occurs in both written and spoken language, is poorly understood by many young children (Johns 1980a, b; Hare 1984), is not fully stabilized by most until age 8 (Wood 1982), and is highly related to reading ability (Morris 1980; Horne, Powers, & Makabub 1983). It may be necessary to help some children distinguish between words and nonwords (Robeck 1982), and there are activities for doing so (see Sulzby 1980). Experience with printed language and learning to read may help to develop the concept of *word*. There are also a number of instructional terms, such as *top, letter, right*, that teachers may incorrectly assume are understood by young children.

Physical and Physiological Development

Physical Fitness

The physical defects that interfere most frequently with beginning reading are poor vision and poor hearing. Benger (1968) found about 1 in 11 first graders had a hearing deficiency and 1 in 9 had a visual defect, all previously undetected.

Any marked departure from normal vision may give a child hazy or incorrect images when he or she looks at words. Comparatively few first graders are near-sighted, but many are farsighted and tend to outgrow the condition as they get older (Shaw 1964). Astigmatism and poor eye coordination are also fairly common in 6-year-olds.

A comprehensive examination by a physician for every entering first grader is a desirable practice that should be more widely followed. When a medical examination is not possible, an alert teacher can notice many signs that suggest physical problems. A child whose eyes water and turn pink in the classroom may need glasses. The child who looks stupid may have a hearing defect. Marked clumsiness suggests the desirability of a neurological examination. Listlessness, laziness, and lack of effort may be related to anemia, malnutrition, or a focal infection.

Lateral Dominance

The importance of cerebral dominance in relation to progress in reading is a controversial issue (see pp. 277–285). Part of the issue is an ambiguous terminology. *Mixed dominance* has been used to include three different conditions: directional confusion, shown in inability to identify left and right correctly; mixed or incomplete handiness, ranging from ambidexterity in which both hands seem equally proficient and are equally preferred, to a partial preference for one hand; and crossed dominance, in which the dominant hand and dominant eye are on opposite sides. Directional confusion and delay in establishing a consistent preference for one hand seem to be significantly related to difficulty in learning to read (Cohen & Glass 1968, A. J. Harris 1957), but crossed dominance is not.

Sociocultural Factors

Experience

The general cultural level of the home is the most important determiner of the child's background of knowledge and experience. Young children with educated parents grow up in a home that provides many opportunities for favorable development. Such children, surrounded by adults who speak standard English with a rich vocabulary, tend to develop the same kind of language. Trips and excursions provide broadening experiences. Books and magazines in the home attract with their bright pictures, and listening to stories read or told helps develop an early interest in reading. Such a home is valuable in providing children with a background of experience and knowledge that will help in reading.

Starting in the early 1960s, a great interest developed in educational handicaps related to socioeconomic disadvantages. Special emphasis has been placed on compensatory education for disadvantaged preschool children. Head Start has provided federal support for preschool education for a great many disadvantaged youngsters, and TV programs such as "Sesame Street" provide stimulation for hundreds of thousands of children of all social classes.

Evaluations tend to show that effective prekindergarten programs can result in significant gains in intelligence, language proficiency, and reading readiness and that the most effective prekindergarten programs are those with specific and structured cognitive activities (Stanley 1972).

Language

Studies by R. Gray *et al.* (1980) and Garman (1981) suggest that reading readiness and early reading achievement are not closely related to oral language development. Such findings, however, do not mean that language abilities are not important in learning to read. Rather, the low relationship may reflect the fact that the linguistic demands made on the majority of the children by the instructional programs did not exceed the language abilities of the pupils.

Adequate language development is one of the most important factors in reading readiness. Two major aspects of oral language development are (1) the child's vocabulary, which is very important in both listening comprehension and expressing one's thoughts; and (2) mastery of sentence structure or syntax, shown most clearly in children's spontaneous conversation. Typical first-grade reading material employs only a few hundred words; most 6-year-olds understand the meanings of several thousand words, so a restricted vocabulary is less likely than deficiencies in sentence structure to be a handicap at the beginning reading level.

Of the many factors that influence language development the most important are intelligence, auditory acuity (hearing), and home environment. The generally dull child is slow at learning to talk and understand speech because language is a highly intellectual acquisition. There is, in general, a close relationship between intelligence and mastery of oral language. Delayed or impaired development of language or in the production of speech sounds may be the result of a hearing impairment or the environment in which the child was raised.

Labov (1973) challenged the idea that nonstandard black English is less grammatical or less suitable for logical reasoning than standard English. He and other linguists (Baratz & Shuy 1969) argue that black English is a legitimate dialect with its own rules of grammar and pronunciation. Difficulties arise when a teacher makes it clear that she considers such speech to be incorrect and the child stops trying to communicate in class, or when teacher and child fail to understand each other because of "mismatches" between their dialects. Even more severe problems may arise when children enter school with very limited knowledge of English.

Emotional and Social Maturity

The emotional and social development of first-grade children is as varied as their intellectual development. Some are cheerful, stable, self-reliant children who adapt to the new routines without difficulty. Others are immature in a great variety of ways: They need help taking off or putting on their outer clothing; they need help in the toilet; they cannot play independently; they do not know how to get along with other children; they are too shy to speak up in class; they have not learned to take orders or obey; they are crybabies; they still talk baby talk; they try to monopolize the teacher's attention. These and many other forms of immature behavior may be found in many combinations and in varying degrees of severity. Some bright children are immature in nonintellectual traits and consequently make less progress than one would expect from their IQs.

Three aspects of emotional and social maturity are especially significant in reading readiness. The first of these is emotional stability. Emotional volatility is characteristic of nursery school children, with rapid changes of mood, crying at little provocation, or tantrums. Similar behavior in a first grader is inappropriate. Marked instability at that age usually reflects difficulties in the home situation.

Self-reliance is another aspect of social maturity that is significant for school adjustment. Some parents have wisely encouraged their children's first fumbling efforts at feeding, dressing, and washing themselves; choosing playthings and activities; and solving their own problems. Some neglected children become self-reliant through necessity. Other children are still helpless when they enter school, in many cases because they have been babied at home.

The ability to participate actively and cooperatively in group activities is a third extremely important aspect of social development. So much of the learning in the primary grades is done in groups that a child who is too shy, too restless, or too egocentric to take a normal part in group activities is bound to miss a great deal.

Children who are socially or emotionally immature can learn to read in a classroom if the teacher understands their problems and makes special adjustments for them.

Interest in Books

The desire to learn to read is one of the important aspects of reading readiness. Children who have spent many pleasurable hours listening to stories and looking through picture books usually look forward to learning to read with eager anticipation. One study (Lomax 1977) found that all the children who had strong interest in books had considerable experience with stories at home, whereas only some of the low-interest children had similar experiences. Another study (Flood 1975) found that parental reading to the child and parental encouragement of watching educational TV programs were positively related to reading readiness.

Children's expectations about reading are strongly influenced by what they hear at home. In a pioneer study (Brumbaugh 1940) 700 kindergarten children were interviewed. More children expected reading to be hard than expected it to be easy. Many expectations were based on what they had been told by older brothers or sisters. Some were discouraged before they even started. "You make mistakes and the teacher hollers at you."

The attitudes that the child brings to first grade are quickly modified by experiences in school. A good first-grade program satisfies those who expect to like reading and want to read and changes the attitudes of those whose attitudes are negative or indifferent.

II. METHODS FOR EVALUATING READING READINESS

In the preceding section it was pointed out that reading readiness is a combination of many different characteristics. Some of them can be measured by standardized tests, some can be judged from information obtained from the child's family, and some can be noted only by observing the child's daily behavior.

The Use of Intelligence Tests[2]

Since general intelligence is one of the most important factors in readiness for reading, it is obvious that intelligence tests are useful for appraising certain phases of readiness to read.

Most schools rely on group intelligence tests because they are comparatively economical and can be given and scored by a classroom teacher. Group intelligence tests for first-grade children are all somewhat alike. Directions are given orally, and no reading ability is involved. Items commonly included are intended to measure such abilities as range of information, understanding of single words and sentences, memory, ability to follow directions, recognition of similarities and differences, and logical reasoning. In comparative studies, group tests have sometimes shown higher correlations with first-grade achievement than have individual intelligence tests. This is probably because children's ability to conform to the group situation influences both classroom learning and their scores on a group test.

An individual intelligence test can provide a more reliable measure of mental ability than can a group test. The examiner can observe and judge such things as the child's attentiveness and effort and has a better chance to keep the child doing his best throughout the test. The individual intelligence tests most widely used for children in kindergarten or first grade are the *Revised Stanford–Binet Intelligence Scale* and the *Wechsler Intelligence Scale for Children Revised* (WISC-R) or the *Wechsler Preschool and Primary Scale of Intelligence* (WPPSI),

[2] A descriptive list of tests can be found in Appendix A.

which provide separate Verbal and Performance IQs as well as a Total IQ. These tests should always be administered by a person with special training.

The *Slosson Intelligence Test* and the *Peabody Picture Vocabulary Test* are individual tests that are comparatively quick and do not require a trained examiner. Although not as accurate as the *Stanford–Binet* or WPPSI, they can be used to rule out mental retardation; if the score is close to borderline, a more accurate test should follow.

Tests of Specific Abilities

During the 1960s and 1970s, many people in the field of learning disabilities were committed to the policy that (1) learning disabilities result from specific deficiencies in basic cognitive skills and abilities; (2) one should test the underlying skills and give specific training in those that are weak; and (3) once the underlying skills have been learned, academic learning will improve.

The two tests that were most widely used by those wishing to diagnose and train underlying cognitive skills were the *Illinois Test of Psycholinguistic Abilities,* Revised Edition (ITPA) and the *Frostig Developmental Test of Visual Perception* (DTVP). The ITPA contains 12 subtests measuring aspects of receiving information (decoding), association, and expressing information (encoding). The *Frostig* test contains 5 subtests intended to measure specific aspects of visual perception.

Critical reviews of the ITPA by Carroll (1972b) and Chase (1972) pointed out that the test is heavily loaded with vocabulary and general information, has a middle-class bias, probably taps only three or four interpretable factors, and has some subtests with low reliability. Factor-analysis studies of the *Frostig* show that it measures one main factor and possibly a second factor (Hammill, Colarusso, & Wiederholt 1970), and the diagnostic value of differences among subtest scores is questionable (Mann 1972).

The main reason why use of these tests has been declining, however, is an accumulation of evidence that the training of basic cognitive skills is not an effective way to improve academic performance of young children. This issue is discussed in greater detail on page 141.

Reading Readiness Tests

A number of tests designed to measure readiness for learning to read are available. In some respects, readiness tests are similar to intelligence tests at this age level, but there are important differences. Whereas intelligence tests attempt to measure general mental ability, reading readiness tests attempt to sample the particular phases of mental functioning that are most closely related to success in learning to read. Some readiness subtests measure acquired information, such as letter-name knowledge.

Reading readiness tests sample skills and knowledge that have been shown to correlate significantly with later success in reading. These factors include auditory discrimination, visual discrimination, general concept development (word meaning), understanding spoken language, visual–motor skills, and letter-name knowledge.

The total scores of most readiness tests correlate between .50 and .70 with reading achievement at the end of first grade.[3] Correlations of this size allow fairly good predictions for a group but do not provide accurate predictions for individual children. Care should be exercised in using subtest performance as a basis for "remediation," especially for individuals, for four reasons: (1) Subtest reliability is often not sufficient (below .90) for use with individuals; (2) the skills needed to perform the task required by the subtest may not be the same as those needed in learning to read; (3) there is little evidence regarding the level of a particular skill that is necessary for learning to read (this also may vary with the instructional approach); and (4) there is little evidence that improving a particular skill or knowledge base will, in and of itself, have a positive impact on learning to read. There is also the possibility that unrecognized variables (e.g., ability to follow oral directions, attending behavior) can influence test performance.

A few readiness tests sample the ability to learn through a whole-word approach (e.g., *Murphy–Durrell Reading Readiness Analysis, Canadian Readiness Test*) and some sample the ability to recognize words (match spoken words with their printed counterparts). Durrell and Murphy (1978) developed a *Prereading Phonics Inventory*, and a few tests measure sound–symbol association ability, auditory blending, or both. Some contain subtests that sample the child's understanding of concepts such as *letter* and *word* (e.g., *Canadian Readiness Test*) or primarily measure such concepts and/or the understanding of the functions and conventions of written language (e.g., *Linguistic Awareness in Reading Readiness, Concepts of Print Tests*).

Although standardized readiness tests have been criticized as being biased against minority-group and disadvantaged children, one study found that the *Metropolitan Readiness Test* correlated .76 with end-of-first-grade reading scores for a population of rural first-grade children, one third of whom were black, and continued to have good prediction for second-grade reading scores (Lessler & Bridges 1973). The cutoff point for failure was lower than for a middle-class population, however. One study found that Spanish-surname children did not score higher on a Spanish translation of the *Metropolitan Readiness Test* than on the regular version (Davis & Personke 1968), and another study found that the regular *Metropolitan* given before reading instruction had substantial predictive value for third-grade reading for Mexican-American children (Mishura & Hurt 1970). Reynolds (1980) concluded that various tests used to predict success in first-grade were not racially biased. The case against readiness tests has been exaggerated.

---

[3] Correlations between test performances tend to decrease as the time between test administrations increase. Predictions of success or failure in learning to read are likely to be influenced by what is done, or not done, to help the child, and what instructional methodology is employed.

Predicting Failure in Reading

Efforts have been made to develop procedures that can detect children who are likely to fail in learning to read. The emphasis is on locating children who are "at risk" and distinguishing them from children likely to succeed. Lindsay and Wedell (1982) examined the basic assumptions underlying the early identification of at-risk children and the effectiveness of screening measures for doing so. They concluded that there is a general lack of evidence for the usefulness of such screening instruments.

The changes in performance across time are much greater for disabled readers than for normal readers. This instability makes the prediction of later performance of individual disabled readers even more tenuous. However, adding data about the child's parents to the prediction equation can significantly improve long-term prediction (De Fries & Baker 1983).

In an important pioneering study (de Hirsch, Jansky, & Langford 1966), 39 tests were given individually to kindergarten children. Failure by the end of the second grade was the main criterion. In their first study, they developed a *Screening Index* of 10 tests, which predicted the failures in a middle-class population quite well. In a second study, in which disadvantaged children were also used, they cut the *Screening Index* to 5 tests: Letter Naming, Picture Naming, Gates Word Matching, Bender Gestalt, and Binet Sentence Memory (Jansky & de Hirsch 1972). This Index predicted failure for 77% of the children who did fail and for 19% of those who passed. They also developed a Diagnostic Battery of 19 tests covering 4 factors determined by factor analysis: visuo-motor organization, oral language, pattern matching, and pattern memory.

The original *Predictive Index* has been compared with the *Metropolitan Readiness Tests* in two studies. In one study, in which reading tests were given late in the first grade, the two procedures did not differ significantly in predictive power; the *Metropolitan* correctly classified 89% of the children, while the *Predictive Index* correctly classified 87% (Zaeske 1970). Using end-of-second-grade reading test results, the *Predictive Index* did slightly better than the *Metropolitan* in identifying future failures, but the authors doubted that the slight increase in accuracy justified the expense of individual testing (Askov, Otto, & Smith 1972). Jansky and de Hirsch (1972) have recommended that the *Predictive Index* be used with a flexible pass–fail cutoff that depends on local school standards and in conjunction with teachers' ratings. Satz and Fletcher (1979) pointed out that even with a high overall hit rate, the *Predictive Index* had "little usefulness in detecting those high-risk children who would most benefit from an early intervention program."

SEARCH is described as an individually adminstered scanning instrument for the identification of potential learning disability (Silver & Hagin 1981). Subtests include visual discrimination and memory, visual–motor copying of designs, rote sequencing, auditory discrimination, articulation of speech, directionality, finger schema, and pencil grip. According to the manual, subtest reliabilities range from .23 to .95 with four subtests below .75, and retest reliability for the total score is .80 (.90 or over is desirable). The correlation of .62

between SEARCH scores at end of kindergarten and oral reading a year later is .62, slightly lower than comparable correlations for several group readiness tests.

The *Florida Kindergarten Screening Battery* was developed by Satz and his associates on the basis of a large-scale longitudinal study in which all of the boys in the kindergartens of a Florida school district were tested and reexamined at intervals through fifth grade (Satz *et al.* 1978). The five subtests were selected on the basis of good correlations with later success in reading and a minimum number of false negatives (failure predicted for those who succeed) and false positives (success predicted for those who fail). The main limitation of this battery is the need for individual administration.

Two other tests batteries intended to identify probable failures in reading are the *Slingerland Prereading Screening Procedure* and the *Meeting Street School Screening Test*. According to one comparative study (Kapelis 1975), the *Slingerland* correlated .66 to .68 with first-grade reading and the *Meeting Street* correlated .58 to .62. This makes them about as good predictors as the group readiness tests mentioned in the preceding section.

Hoffman (1971) developed a *Learning Problem Indication Index* by comparing parental information on the early development of 100 children with severe learning disabilities and 200 controls. Large differences were found on the following items: difficult delivery, prolonged labor, cyanosis, prematurity, blood incompatibility, adoption, late or abnormal creeping, late walking, tiptoe walking for more than 1 month, late or abnormal speech, and ambidexterity after age 7. A criterion of two or more signs was present for 72% of the disability group and only 6.5% of the controls. It seems evident that this index selects mainly children whose learning problems have neurological correlates.

Teacher Judgment

Teachers have always tended to form judgments about the rate of progress different pupils would achieve. With the development of standardized intelligence and reading readiness tests, some first-grade teachers have become hesitant to trust their opinions about pupils. The judgment of a competent teacher who has had a few weeks in which to observe the daily behavior of her pupils is by no means to be disregarded.

This should not be taken to mean that all teachers are perfect judges or that tests are useless. The tests provide the teacher with a quick, convenient, standardized basis for judging children's status in certain highly important intellectual abilities. Tests help the teacher to locate quickly most of the pupils who require further careful study. When test results and teacher observations agree, the teacher naturally feels more confident in her opinion; when they disagree, the need for further consideration is shown. Moreover, there are some aspects of reading readiness that tests do not measure, for which teacher judgment, based on observation and interviews, is needed.

It is comparatively easy to form a general overall impression of a child. It is somewhat more difficult, but also more rewarding, to try to analyze the child's strong and weak points. The teacher who does that can determine what specific handicaps may interfere with the child's progress and in many instances can take measures to strengthen the weak abilities.

Banks developed a *Kindergarten Behavioural Index* (KBI) based on a follow-up study of 2304 Australian children. Out of 63 items tried, 37 differentiated poor readers from good readers. These 37 items, which are reproduced in Figure 2.1, "represent a diffuse syndrome of developmental functions involving sensorimotor abilities, language, perception, cognitive abilities, social attributes, and behavioral patternings" (Banks 1970). In two samples, a cutoff score of more than three checks correctly identified 78% and 82% of those who became poor readers in the first grade and misidentified 15.5% and 10% of the successful readers. The Banks KBI seems promising as a screening instrument. It can be filled out by a kindergarten teacher near the end of the year, or by a first-grade teacher 3 or 4 weeks after the beginning of the school year. A follow-up study of the children tested by Banks has shown that the KBI has a substantial correlation with failure in Grades 1–4 (J. Miles, Foreman, & Anderson 1973).

A readiness rating scale that can be used in kindergarten or early first grade is shown in Figure 2.2. While the total score of −5 indicates that Henry is slightly below average in general readiness, the most helpful feature of the rating scale is calling attention to the specific items on which he was rated −1 or −2. The rating scale also points up Henry's advantages: good IQ and language development and a favorable home environment. Teachers are welcome to reproduce this rating scale without special permission.

Whether the teacher records her opinions on a form or keeps them in her head, it is advisable to reconsider them and revise ratings that are no longer correct. Many changes will result from growth or improvement in pupils. Some changes may involve the revision of an opinion that proved to be incorrect. By amending ratings as the children overcome or outgrow their difficulties, the teacher can keep track of the progress of her pupils and at any time can get a bird's-eye view of her readiness problems. When teachers have had several weeks to observe their children, both kindergarten and first-grade teacher ratings show substantial correlations with first-grade reading performance (Feshbach, Adelman, & Fuller 1974).

Glazzard (1979) found that teacher ratings on a 5-point scale were better predictors of school achievement after 1 year but that reading readiness tests were better predictors after 2 to 3 years. Both measures were equally predictive after 4 years.

The *Infant Rating Scale* contains 25 items on which teachers rate children on a 5-point scale. It has a test–retest reliability of .96, and a predictive validity with reading scores 2 years later of .45. This British rating scale samples four factors: language, behavior, aspects of learning, and social integration (Lindsay 1980).

A *School Entrance Check List* compiled by McLeod (1968) provides a quick and convenient questionnaire to be filled out by parents. The 18 items in it were selected on the basis that each tends to differentiate children who are likely to develop reading disabilities from normal learners.

Kindergarten Behavioural Index

Enid M. Banks

INDIVIDUAL RECORD

Name..

Date of Birth.. Age.................... Date of Recording.......................

- [ ] 1 Does not know own age
- [ ] 2 Is ambidextrous—uses left hand for some activities, right hand for others
- [ ] 3 Puts shoes on wrong feet
- [ ] 4 Has difficulty in hopping, changing from one foot to another
- [ ] 5 Reverses letters and numbers when copying or writing
- [ ] 6 Slow and fumbling putting on shoes, coat, etc.
- [ ] 7 Has difficulty doing up buttons
- [ ] 8 Clumsy—trips over, bumps into, knocks over, objects
- [ ] 9 Holds pencil awkwardly
- [ ] 10 Has difficulty controlling pencil—presses hard—messy work
- [ ] 11 Cannot keep within lines when colouring in
- [ ] 12 Has difficulty using scissors
- [ ] 13 Lacks sense of rhythm—keeping in time with music in running, clapping, etc.
- [ ] 14 Has difficulty pronouncing all sounds, e.g. 'wed'–'red', 'fink'–'think', 'muver'–'mother', etc.
- [ ] 15 Uses 'baby talk', e.g. 'me'–'I', 'runned'–'ran', 'dood'–'did'
- [ ] 16 Lacks verbal fluency—speaks mainly in words or phrases
- [ ] 17 Mixes up words, e.g. 'applepine' for 'pineapple'
- [ ] 18 Mixes up order of words in a sentence
- [ ] 19 Stutters
- [ ] 20 Has difficulty ordering thoughts when describing or discussing a topic
- [ ] 21 Loses main thread and goes into irrelevant details when telling a story or talking
- [ ] 22 Forgets an instruction or message and has to ask again
- [ ] 23 Cannot write own name correctly from memory
- [ ] 24 Has difficulty remembering poems, rhymes, etc.
- [ ] 25 Cannot count up to 20
- [ ] 26 Confuses names of colours
- [ ] 27 Avoids talking in front of class
- [ ] 28 Cries easily
- [ ] 29 Appears to be shy
- [ ] 30 Daydreams
- [ ] 31 Slow in carrying out commands
- [ ] 32 Overactive—always on the move
- [ ] 33 Has difficulty sitting still for very long
- [ ] 34 Fidgets with things
- [ ] 35 Lacks concentration—does not pay attention
- [ ] 36 Loses interest quickly—moves from one activity to another
- [ ] 37 Frequently loses belongings
- [ ] TOTAL

Comments..
....

Figure 2.1 The Banks Kindergarten Behavioural Index. Reproduced by permission of *The Slow Learning Child* and Enid M. Banks. Published by Australian Council for Educational Research, Frederick Street, Hawthorn, Victoria 3122. Copyright © Enid M. Banks 1972.

Name: _Henry_   Age: _5–10_   Rated by _____   On: _9/20_   Total Score: _−5_

	Rating				
	Low		Average		High
Factor	−2	−1	0	+1	+2
Cognitive					
MA			X		
IQ				X	
Attention			X		
Specific concepts				X	
General conceptual background				X	
Letter-name knowledge		X			
Auditory discrimination		X			
Visual discrimination	X				
Visual perception		X			
Language					
Vocabulary				X	
Sentence structure				X	
Listening comprehension			X		
Speech production		X			
Physical–Physiological					
Ability to identify left and right		X			
Consistent hand preference	X				
	None	left	right		
Muscular coordination		X			
Visual acuity			?		
Auditory acuity			?		
General health		X			
Social–Emotional–Cultural					
Self-reliance		X			
Self-control		X			
Group participation			X		
Interest in being read to				X	
Interest in learning to read			X		
General cultural level of the home				X	
Intellectual stimulation of the home				X	
Column totals	−4	−9		8	0

Figure 2.2. A reading readiness rating scale. From A. J. Harris and E. R. Sipay, _How to teach reading_ (New York: Longman, 1979), p. 61. Used with permission.

Planning the Evaluation of Reading Readiness

Many schools routinely test all children for readiness. Although it is possible to give the tests near the end of kindergarten and might be advantageous to do so in some schools, it is better to wait until the children are in first grade if a substantial number of children enter school without having attended kindergarten (or if there is a high degree of pupil turnover). The best time for a readiness test is 2 or 3 weeks after the beginning of the school year. This allows time for the children to get accustomed to classroom activities and teacher directions and at the same time is early enough to make the results useful in decisions about such matters as how to group the children and when to start reading instruction.

For this testing, either a group intelligence test or a group readiness test can be used, preferably the latter. Not more than 10 or 12 first-grade children should be tested as a group, and so arrangements need to be made to take care of part of the class while the rest are being tested. The test should be administered by the teacher or a person known to the children, and the directions in the manual should be followed as closely as possible. After the tests have been scored, at least a sampling of them should be rescored by another person; scoring errors are made with deplorable frequency even by experienced scorers.

In most cases, an accurate estimate of each child's readiness can be made by using test results in combination with teacher observation. If test and teacher judgment disagree, further study of the child is needed and further testing may be arranged. Individual testing by a school psychologist is desirable for children whose scores on two or more group tests are very low.

It may be noted that the more efficiently a teacher helps a child to improve in readiness for reading, the more inaccurate a low readiness score will be. The presence of children who succeed in learning to read despite predicted failure may show good teaching rather than a shortcoming in the test. Similarly, when children do well on a readiness test but subsequently fail to learn to read, poor instruction rather than inaccurate measurement may be responsible. This applies to any measure of reading readiness.

III. FROM READINESS INTO READING

A Brief Look Backward

Educators' opinions about the implications of readiness for beginning reading instruction have gone through a series of stages. Before 1930 most schools began reading instruction a few days after school opened, there was little or no adjustment to individual differences, and those who could not keep up with the pace (30–40% in some school systems) had to repeat the first grade (Caswell 1933). Early in the 1930s the idea of readiness was widely adopted and influenced practice.

Three misinterpretations of the readiness idea dominated curricular planning in a great many American kindergartens and first grades. The first was the idea that a minimum mental age of 6 years or 6 years 6 months was essential for success in beginning reading. This led to unnecessary postponement of reading instruction for untold numbers of children. The second misinterpretation, related to the first, was an excessive reliance on maturation. "The inescapable nature of human growth controls what can be learned, and when. . . . But 'building' and 'readiness' are uncongenial terms. They clash. They contradict each other" (Hymes 1958, pp. 9–11). This viewpoint denied the possible value of teaching specific prereading skills. The third fallacy was that if reading readiness activities were good for some children, they should be good for all children. This led to a requirement that particular readiness activities be completed (often one or more readiness workbooks) before starting reading, even if many of the children were ready to read and some were already reading. These three notions prevailed in many school systems for over 30 years, and still prevail in some schools.

The 1960s saw new points of view. One trend was the development of new readiness programs, which were sometimes used in kindergarten, sometimes in first grade. A second trend was moving both readiness activities and beginning reading instruction back into kindergarten in some schools. The 1970s and 1980s continued the trends of the 1960s. A new viewpoint regarded readiness not as something distinct from reading that prepares the way for it, but as the teaching of specific prereading skills that merge gradually into reading.

Special Readiness Procedures

Kephart, developing his principles out of a background of work with brain-injured children, emphasized the desirability of helping children to achieve mastery over basic perceptual–motor skills as a prerequisite for academic learning. His program involved practice in coordinated acts such as hopping, skipping, and balancing while walking on a narrow plank; training to improve laterality and directionality; and training in ocular control and visual perception (Kephart 1960; Ebersole, Kephart, & Ebersole 1968).

Kavale and Mattson (1983) applied the sophisticated statistical technique of meta-analysis to 180 studies of the effects of perceptual–motor training, involving 637 comparisons between trained and control groups. They found that most comparisons resulted in small differences that were not significantly different from zero. There was little evidence of benefit in the perceptual–motor activities that were directly trained, and the effects on reading and other academic skills were predominantly negative. This appeared at all levels of schooling from preschool through high school, and in normal pupils and several types of exceptional children. When the studies were graded for quality, the largest effects were in the poorest studies; trained subjects showed no treatment effects in medium-rated studies and negative treatment effects in high-rated studies. The results failed to supply justification for the use of any perceptual–motor training program, including those by Kephart, Frostig, Getman, and Delacato, among others. "These findings fail to provide support for perceptual–motor training as a feasible intervention technique. . . ."

Special emphasis on language enrichment has not shown a real advantage in reading readiness work with disadvantaged children. Use of the *Peabody Language Development Kit* has been found to improve some language skills of disadvantaged children but does not improve reading performance in the primary grades (Dunn, Pochanart, Pfost, & Bruininks 1968). A kindergarten program intended to improve black children's mastery of speaking as well as listening to standard English did not show an advantage in readiness scores over a program confined to listening (Strickland 1973b). Common sense would indicate that improving the language proficiency of children should benefit their reading, but each technique for doing so needs to be evaluated carefully.

Training in visual and auditory discrimination was emphasized years ago by Durrell and Murphy (1953) as important for first-grade reading success and now forms an important part of the readiness procedures of most basal reader programs. It seems probable that when this training uses letter and word forms, and spoken words from the beginning reading vocabulary, its transfer value to reading is enhanced. It is doubtful that intensive auditory-discrimination training beyond what is provided in conventional programs benefits early reading attainment for most children, although it can improve auditory-discrimination scores (Jeffares & Cosens 1970, Rosner 1973). McNeil (1967) found that Mexican-American and black children trained to hear phonemes within words did show some gain in reading, however. More evidence is needed on the value of training in auditory segmentation as a readiness activity.

In general, the research reviewed above is in harmony with long-established findings about transfer of training, which have shown that the more closely a learning activity resembles the activity to which transfer of learning is desired, the more likely it is for useful transfer to take place. Thus visual-discrimination practice using letters and words is more transferable to reading than is discrimination of geometric forms. Auditory discrimination of words and phonemes is more transferable to reading than is discrimination of nonverbal sounds. The transfer to reading of gaining skill in large-muscle and small-muscle activities is doubtful. Developing listening comprehension seems more relevant to reading than becoming a competent speaker of standard English is. Viewed in the light of transfer, the research on what pays off in readiness training makes sense.

Reading Readiness Workbooks

Most conventional readiness programs, whether in first grade or kindergarten, center on the use of readiness workbooks that are part of the basal reader series used in first grade. These workbooks provide colorful pictures that can serve as a basis for description, discussion, storytelling, and learning new concepts and vocabulary. They also contain series of exercises for making visual and auditory discriminations and observing in a left-to-right sequence. Some workbooks stress visual discrimination of letters and words, and auditory discrimination of words and sounds within words (e.g., initial consonants and rhyming endings). Learning the names of alphabet letters is included in some workbooks, as well as some letter–sound associations.

The use of readiness workbooks has been subject to much criticism. One valid complaint is that many teachers regard the workbooks as the whole of their readiness program, restricting the program to a narrow range of exercises. Teachers can find a wealth of suggestions for enrichment in the teachers' guides that accompany the workbooks, but some ignore them. A second serious criticism is that many exercises in readiness workbooks are either unrelated to reading or unnecessary because most children already have developed the abilities the exercises require. Paradis (1974), for example, gave representative exercises for visual discrimination of pictures, letters, and words, chosen from 7 basal reader series, to 440 kindergarten and 128 preschool middle-class children. About 97% of the kindergartners and 69% of the preschoolers were successful on 80 or more percent of the items. Obviously most of the children had little to learn from these exercises. If a readiness workbook is used, it should be used with children who show some readiness deficiency and then only for skills on which the children need additional learning.

Specific Prereading Instruction

Auditory Segmentation and Blending

Earlier in this chapter auditory segmentation and blending were discussed as factors involved in reading readiness. Understanding that a spoken sentence is composed of separable words and that a word contains distinguishable sounds are important parts of what has been called "cognitive clarity" (Downing 1973b) or "linguistic awareness" (Mattingly 1972). Auditory blending is also related to success in beginning reading.

Understanding the segmentation of sentences into words probably develops as a concomitant of any of the current methods of teaching beginning reading. The segmentation of words into sounds and the blending of sounds into words are taught in some beginning methods and not in others. Specific procedures for teaching auditory segmentation have been developed by Lindamood and Lindamood (1969) and by Rosner (1976). There is insufficient evidence at present to judge the value of these procedures either as prereading skills or as a possible addition to beginning reading instruction.

Letter Discrimination

Children should be able to distinguish alphabet letters from one another with accuracy. Some first graders need help with these visual discriminations, although many kindergartners do not.

The following principles about letter discrimination are fairly well established:

1. It is important to help children to notice the specific distinctive features (e.g., tall–short, open–closed, curved–straight) that make each letter unique (Gibson & Levin 1975).
2. One effective way to do this is to color in red the parts of two letters that differ, then gradually fade out the color cue (Egeland 1975).
3. Another effective way is to use transparent overlays so that, for example, a child placing a *b* over a *d* can immediately see the difference (Copple 1975).
4. Visual discrimination training has more transfer effect than practice in copying, although both are useful (Williams 1975).
5. Three-dimensional letters whose shapes can be fingered and played with can be helpful (Towner & Evans 1974).

6. For sequence, it is probably desirable to begin with pairs of unlike letters and proceed to progressively more difficult discriminations, although the sequence is not very important (Nelson & Wein 1976).

A Gradual Start

The notion that when children do not seem ready to read, one should just wait until they show a spontaneous desire to begin reading has unduly delayed the start of reading for many children. Similarly, there is little justification for an extended readiness period for those who are definitely ready. Much of the criticism of the readiness idea in recent years has resulted from unnecessary delays in the beginning of systematic instruction. The combination of the improvement of beginning reading materials with improved methods of instruction, aided perhaps by the stimulating effect of television, makes extended delays less necessary than they seemed 30 years ago.

Beginning reading can be started gradually and informally with children who do not seem ready; this is preferable to outright postponement. For example, place labels on a child's desk, chair, coat hook, and so on. Display colorful pictures with a brief title below each. Keep a bulletin board with weather reports, special events, and messages for individual children; what they cannot read themselves can be read to them. Informal experience stories provide an interesting and easy introduction to reading (see p. 66) and can be used with all the children. Gradually the immature ones begin to recognize some words, and this indicates that they are becoming ready. Meanwhile, they have had the feeling of being part of the reading program and do not feel excluded from reading. Readiness activities can go on after as well as before these reading activities begin.

Durkin (1974–1975) summarized her 6-year study of children taught to read at age 4 and also the research of others on the effects of teaching reading before first grade. In general, the experimental groups have had significantly higher reading scores than have control groups in first and second grades, with the differences becoming nonsignificant in third and fourth grades. Durkin suggested that the failure of teachers to provide appropriate instruction for superior readers is at least partially responsible for the fading out of the initial advantage. She concluded that "since there is no guarantee that a kindergarten start in reading will lead to greater success in later years, no school should introduce reading instruction into its kindergartens unless that instruction can be of a kind that will add enjoyment and greater self-esteem to the fifth year of a child's life" (p. 60).

A summary of the characteristics of the kindergarten child emphasized the importance of incorporating physical activity, opportunities for manipulating materials, extensive practice in both expressive and receptive oral language, and combining learning activities with play (V. Robinson, Strickland, & Cullinan 1977). These authors also pointed up the limitations of 5-year-olds' reasoning and ability to understand and apply rules. If reading is to be taught to kinder-

garten children, the procedure should be adapted to the kindergartner's intellectual and emotional stages of development.

MacGinitie (1976) stated that "meaningful reading readiness instruction
means a slow and gentle introduction to reading itself—often gamelike, often
hidden in other activities." By beginning reading instruction earlier than first
grade and going as slowly as necessary, the child has more time to learn; a child
who makes little or no progress can always start at the beginning again in first
grade. The program for pre-first-grade children should be informal, individualized, devoid of pressure, and more like play than work. This point of view challenges the conventional idea of postponing reading instruction for the less ready
until they have completed a readiness program in first grade. A similar viewpoint
has been expressed by Pikulski (1978), who advocated starting instruction near
the beginning of kindergarten with an informal language-experience approach
to reading.

Mason conducted a series of studies on 4-year-olds—white, middle-class
children who attended a preschool or day-care center. For such children, the
sequence of skill acquisition began with the recognition and printing of letters,
followed closely by reading signs and labels and learning letter sounds, then
on to a recognition of short words in stories.

> At home children have their own alphabet books, they are read to frequently
> and hear story records, they use the library, they watch educational television,
> and they discuss the television programs with their parents. They are en-
> couraged to print their names, write headings on their pictures, and read labels
> and simple stories. . . . A reading program, ideally, should lead the children
> to an understanding of print by making reading a very familiar experience,
> providing positively reinforcing situations for success in printing and reading,
> and setting up situations where learning occurs through a need to use letters
> and printed words. This favorable environment is not difficult to implement
> at home and in preschool and kindergarten settings where reading activities
> can be fostered through play, art, music, field trips, story telling, reading, and
> talking about letters and words. (1977a, p. 30).

King (1978) summarized the results of 10 studies in which direct instruction
of prereading skills at the kindergarten level was compared with incidental
teaching. Direct instruction involves setting specific objectives, a division of
tasks to achieve the objectives into sequences of small steps, and teaching skills
at set times and by a systematic method. Incidental teaching involves teaching
skills as the need for them occurs in connection with other schoolwork or with
pupils' activities and interests; the classroom environment is planned so that
pupils can experiment, manipulate, inquire, and communicate freely. The majority of the studies showed some advantage for a structured, sequential program
on readiness test scores, but there is little evidence as yet that the advantage
persists through beginning reading instruction. King advocated a blend of direct
and incidental instruction.

Smilanski (1978) studied the results of informal teaching of reading in kindergarten to disadvantaged children in Israel, individually and in small groups,

compared with starting their reading instruction in first grade. Two methods were employed, one stressing phonics, the other beginning with whole words. Fifty-seven kindergarten classes were involved, and achievement was measured at the end of first and second grades. There were two control groups, one using experimental teaching methods in first grade, the other using conventional first-grade methodology. The experimental classes were significantly ahead of both control groups at the end of second grade, and there was no significant difference between whole-word and phonic methods. These results seem to favor early, slow, gradual, and nonpressuring beginning reading instruction for disadvantaged children.

A special class, called a "transition class," for first-grade entrants who are lacking in readiness, was tried out successfully in some large cities around 1940 but has not been widely adopted. A transition class should have a specially trained teacher, be limited in size, and have a carefully planned readiness program leading gradually into reading. In such a class the majority usually are promoted to first grade, although some do so well that they can enter second grade after it.

Dolan (1982) reported a 6-year follow-up of children who had not seemed ready for first grade after a year in kindergarten and had been placed in a transition class. Results showed a gradual blending of transition students with regular peers. However, when parents rejected transition class placement, the need for special services later was increased.

The transition class as a way of providing for unready children has been strongly recommended by Ilg and Ames (1964), who found a large percentage of middle-class children to be lacking in some aspects of readiness, even though of at least average intelligence. In our opinion, the transition class deserves a wider tryout.

An alternative for children whose IQ is normal or higher, but who seem unready for reading in certain respects, is to organize special first-grade classrooms in which reading is taught by methods similar to those used with severe reading-disability cases. East (1969) reported a third-grade follow-up on children with a mean IQ of 110 who had been placed in Specific Language Disability first grades and taught by the Slingerland adaptation of the Orton-Gillingham methods (for description, see Chap. 12). By the end of third grade this goup achieved as well in reading as a control group of equivalent age, sex, and IQ.

The trend seems to favor a slow, gradual start in beginning reading instruction with readiness skills embedded in the context of reading, rather than readiness first and reading afterward (Nurss & Telepak 1980). When to begin reading instruction is still an open question, but there is strong support for an easy, relaxed introduction of reading in kindergarten for children who are ready. For the unready and the disadvantaged, some recent research supports a slow, gradual, nonpressuring introduction of reading at kindergarten level; this important issue is in need of more research. For those who are still unready as they begin first grade, a transition class or special first grade for "at risk" children provides a better alternative than a year of frustration and failure in first grade.

3

Beginning Reading Instruction

This is the second of three chapters devoted to a description of the total reading program. Chapter 2 discussed readiness for learning to read; Chapter 4 covers reading instruction beyond the initial stages. In this chapter, a brief historical review of past methods is followed by a discussion of more recent and current beginning reading approaches; teaching reading to dialect-speaking, limited-English-speaking, and non-English-speaking children; and an evaluative comparison of beginning reading approaches.

I. A BRIEF LOOK AT THE PAST

Over the centuries, many methods for teaching children to read have been introduced. Some gained wide acceptance, only to be replaced by other methods. Many of the changes stemmed from dissatisfaction with a prevailing method, and at times excesses in one direction were replaced by equally objectionable swings to an opposite extreme. Detailed historical accounts of reading methodology may be found in Huey (1908), N. B. Smith (1965), and Mathews (1966). For less detailed but more recent accounts, refer to H. A. Robinson (1977), Ollila and Nurss (1981), and H. Singer (1981a, b).

Reading methods and programs may be classified as synthetic or analytic. The synthetic methods of old are now referred to as code-emphasis methods. Except for some words-to-letters methods, analytic methods are now labeled as meaning-emphasis methods.

Synthetic Methods

Methods that start with letters and move to larger units (syllables, words, phrases, sentences) are called *synthetic* methods.

The alphabet-spelling method was universally used from ancient times well into the nineteenth century. Weeks were spent in memorizing the alphabet. Then two-letter combinations were drilled, with the letters named and the unit pronounced, and eventually the child got to words and sentences. In studying a word the letters were named in sequence, then the word was pronounced over and over until it was learned. In some languages this is an effective procedure because the letter names are essentially the same as their sounds. In English, however, naming the letters of *cat* and putting them together gives something like *seeaytee*. The alphabet-spelling method was mechanical, uninteresting, and difficult. "The value of the practice in learning to spell doubtless had much to do with blinding centuries of teachers to its uselessness for the reading of words and sentences" (Huey 1908, p. 266).

A number of phonic methods were developed during the nineteenth century. Their common characteristic was that they started with the sounds (rather than the names) represented by the letters and then proceeded to the sounding of consonant–vowel and vowel–consonant combinations—*ba, ca, da . . . ab, ac, ad*—then proceeded to syllables and on to words. A child who came to a new word was expected to sound it letter by letter (or by letter groups) and fuse or blend the sounds mentally to get the sound of the whole word.

Two points are often made by critics of synthetic methods: (1) Because there are so many irregularities and complexities of English symbol–sound correspondences, an adequate phonics[1] system would have to be complicated and difficult to learn; and (2) synthetic methods encourage attention to the mechanics of word recognition and do not give enough attention to reading comprehension. To these criticisms, advocates of synthetic methods would answer: (1) English is not as irregular as commonly believed—there is sufficient regularity to allow learners to approximate closely words whose meanings they know; and (2) there is no evidence that early stressing of decoding adversely influences comprehension.

One effort to standardize the symbol–sound relationship was to employ diacritical markings, similar to those in the pronunciation keys of dictionaries.

---

[1] *Phonology* is the scientific study of speech sounds and includes phonetics and phonemics. *Phonetics* deals with the study of the sounds of speech, including their production, combination, description, and representation by written symbols. *Phonemics* is the study of the sounds (phonemes) of a particular language. *Phonics* is the study of the relationship of phonemes to the printed or written symbols that represent them (graphemes) and their use in discovering the pronunciation of printed and written words. Phonics is, therefore, the part of phonology and phonetics most involved in reading instruction.

Long vowels and silent letters were marked as long ago as 1644 (Mathews 1966). Around the beginning of the twentieth century, diacritical markings were used in the popular Ward Readers and Pollard Readers.

Another effort to reduce phonic difficulties was to modify the alphabet by adding new letter forms in order to have a separate letter to represent each sound. A modified alphabet devised by Isaac Pitman was tried in a few American school systems during the mid-nineteenth century; although reports of its results were favorable, it failed to gain acceptance and died out. This was the ancestor of the Initial Teaching Alphabet (see p. 71). A "scientific alphabet" was used for many years in readers and dictionaries published by Funk and Wagnalls.

Analytic Methods

Methods that start from larger units than letters and proceed to the study of parts are generally called *analytic* methods; they are sometimes referred to as *global* methods. They include word, sentence, and story methods.

Horace Mann advocated the word method before the middle of the nine-teenth century, and primers using this method began to be used in some schools around 1850. The usual procedure was for the teacher to print or write a word on the board, pronounce it, and then combine it with other words to form various sentences. The method employed word–picture associations and used flash cards for drill.

Mathews (1966) pointed out that there were two main variations of the word method: a words-to-letters method, in which words were analyzed and studied sound by sound shortly after they were introduced; and a words-to-reading method, in which word analysis was postponed for varying periods of time, and analysis was often not begun until a substantial sight vocabulary had been learned. Most basal reader systems relied heavily on the words-to-reading method until the mid-1960s when the pendulum again began to swing toward use of the words-to-letters method.

The sentence method was first advocated in the United States around 1870. Its proponents argued that since the sentence is the smallest complete unit of meaning, the child should first be taught a whole sentence at a time. The same words were presented in many different sentence arrangements, but the need for continuity of meaning from one sentence to the next was ignored in some of these systems.

The story method attempted to correct the weakness of the sentence method by introducing a whole story at a time. The teacher would read a story, usually a cumulative folktale like "The Gingerbread Boy," over and over to the children until many of them memorized it. She would then present the first few sentences in print and have the children recite the memorized lines as they looked at the print; in this way, word recognition developed. This method assumed that the child would look at the words in proper sequence and in time with the story; failure to do this produced many cases of pseudoreading in which children were able to recite a story perfectly, page by page, without having learned to recognize individual words.

Synthetic methods stressed the need to be able to work out the pronunciations of printed words. Analytic methods emphasized the need for meaningful reading and immediate recognition of words and phrases. Most current methods try to utilize the good features of these older methods and combine them into a comprehensive, flexible program that is adaptable to individual differences.

II. CURRENT APPROACHES TO TEACHING BEGINNING READING

In 1971 Aukerman described more than 100 beginning reading programs; in 1984 his revised book contained 165 descriptions. Various influences have converged to make the past 25 years, and particularly the last decade, a period of change and innovation: dissatisfaction with existing programs; the contributions of cognitive and experimental psychologists, psycholinguists, linguists, and information-processing theorists; agitation by pressure groups for a return to the "basics," or to promote a particular program that will "cure the reading problem"; legal rulings; and federal funding for research, materials, and intervention programs. To those acquainted with the history of reading instruction, some of the "new" ideas and programs seem familiar.

Although the lines of distinction among commercially published reading programs have tended to blur in that they now place more stress on areas formerly emphasized by contrasting programs, most programs can be classified into one of three categories: (1) meaning-emphasis approaches; (2) code-emphasis approaches; and (3) individualized skills-emphasis approaches.

More complete discussions of the approaches and various programs may be found in Harris and Sipay (1979), Aukerman (1971, 1981), Laffey (1971), and Popp (1975). Nurss (1979b) discussed beginning reading instruction in England. The philosophy and methodology of a given program are best understood through studying the teachers' manuals and accompanying materials.

Basically, the approaches differ in the following ways: (1) initial and continuing emphasis on comprehension or decoding; (2) the basis on which words are selected for inclusion in the program; (3) the number of words used at a given level and in the entire program, and the rate at which these words are introduced and repeated in the selections; (4) how a child is first taught to recognize words; (5) the materials used as vehicles for developing reading skills and strategies; (6) instructional methodology; and (7) preplanned structure. Not only are there marked differences as to basic philosophy, methodology, and materials among approaches, but wide variations also exist among programs classified within the same category.

Beck (1981) enumerated specific ways in which meaning-emphasis and code-emphasis approaches differ, and the pros and cons of highly, moderately, and lightly structured programs were presented by T. Johnson, Mayfield, and

Quorm (1980). Criteria for selecting a reading series have been presented by Erickson (1978) and Aukerman (1981).

Meaning-Emphasis Approaches

In basal reader programs, language-experience programs, natural approaches, writing–reading approaches, and individualized developmental reading programs, primary emphasis is placed on reading for meaning. One of these approaches may be used in combination with any of the others.

Basal Reader Programs

Basal reader programs, which are the programs most often used in North America (Ollila & Nurss 1981; Britton, Lumpkin, & Britton 1984), are preplanned, sequentially organized, detailed materials and methods to teach developmental reading skills systematically. For the past 65 years, most basal reader series have been eclectic, trying to provide a balanced developmental reading program with a broad and varied set of objectives. Most of these programs initially teach word recognition through a whole-word approach in which children learn to associate printed words with their spoken counterparts. The rationale for this procedure is that the recognition of whole words permits a quick introduction to meaningful sentences and stories. Before the mid-1960s, decoding skills were introduced very gradually, mainly in second- and third-grade readers. Since then, there has been a decided trend toward more and earlier emphasis on decoding skills (Chall & Conrad 1984). There is considerable variation among basal series, although they have features in common.

Materials. A representative series starts with one or more readiness books, usually in workbook form. The first actual reading materials are usually two or three thin paperbacks, called pre-primers. To dispel the mistaken idea that a given book should be used only in a particular grade, many series number their books by levels. For example, a first pre-primer that follows two readiness books would be labeled Level 3. Pre-primers (Levels 3, 4, and 5^2) are followed by the first hardcover book (primer, or Level 6), and by a first reader (Level 7), which completes the program covered by most first graders. There are usually two second readers (2^1 and 2^2, or Levels 8 and 9), two third readers (3^1 and 3^2, or Levels 10 and 11) and one text each for the fourth, fifth, and sixth reader levels (Levels 12, 13, and 14). A few series have seventh and eighth reader levels (Levels 15 and 16). Some series also have transition books between reader levels or designate the text for possible use at two levels. Since the mid-1960s, there have been some departures from this traditional format, such as a choice between a conventional hardcover reader and the same content bound in two or more paperback units. The average difficulty of a basal reader may be higher than the level designated by the publisher (Crawley 1975), and readers designated for

---

[2] The numbering of levels varies from series to series depending on the number of books in the program. In this text, we will continue to use the older terms pre-primer, primer, first reader, and so on. Greenlinger-Harless (1984a,b) presented a cross-referenced index that may be used to identify the levels of K–8 reading materials.

the same level may differ considerably in average difficulty and in range of difficulty within each book (Bradley & Ames 1978). Stories do not systematically increase in difficulty from the beginning to the end of a text.

Each book in the series is accompanied by a consumable workbook. Some workbooks provide self-help cues at the tops of pages or have recorded directions and answers for self-correction. Other accessory materials may include exercises printed on duplicating stencils; large cards for group practice with phonic elements, words, and phrases; introductory story cards or charts; correlated filmstrips and recordings; and supplementary paperback storybooks. The trend in enrichment is to provide the kinds of materials just mentioned in convenient packages as optional supplements.

Teachers tend to use the components of a commercially published reading program as a package, and their instructional procedures and materials derive primarily from those provided by the publisher rather than from what they may have learned about teaching reading from their college professors (J. Osburn 1981, 1984a). There is little evidence as to why teachers rely so heavily on commercial reading materials (Shannon 1982). Most teachers, however, do not follow the suggested lesson plans exactly.

There is very little information regarding the relationship of workbook content to the objectives of reading lessons, the instructional quality of workbooks, the relevance of workbook activities to the acquisition of reading ability, or the task demands that workbook exercises make on students (J. Osburn 1984a).

Well-designated workbooks can be useful, but if a study by J. Mason (1982b) indicates typical classroom practice, they are greatly overused—far more time was spent giving directions, supervising the completion of exercises, and checking workbooks than in reading or reading instruction. Workbook tasks should be evaluated carefully before being assigned to students (J. Osburn 1984b).

Each basal reader comes with a guide or manual that details the teaching method. Most manuals present a general plan and then give a detailed lesson plan for each selection. Manuals usually provide more suggestions for skill development and enrichment than are needed for most children. The teacher must therefore select activities judiciously, based on the children's needs, as well as determine the appropriate rate of presentation for different groups. The teachers observed by Durkin (1984) and J. Mason (1983) generally did not follow the instructional plans suggested by the manual closely; instruction in reading comprehension was noticeably lacking.

The trend toward progressively smaller vocabularies in basal readers extended from the 1920s through the 1950s but has now been reversed. Current basal readers contain a much more diverse set of words than in previous years (A. J. Harris & Jacobson 1982). The number of new words per story and the number of running words has increased, and the words are repeated less often (Chall 1983a). This increase in vocabulary load may create problems for some beginning readers.

There is considerable variation among basal readers in the number of new words introduced per level, the rate at which they are introduced, the number of times the words are repeated, and the total number of words employed (Willows, Borwick, & Hayvren 1981). Many words are unique to a particular series, and the vocabulary overlap between two series at a given reader level may be limited.

The language of first-grade basal readers has often been criticized as artificial, stilted, monotonous, and unduly repetitious. "Oh, oh, look, look" has been the subject of many jokes. This criticism, although aimed at basal readers in general, has always taken its examples from pre-primers, in which vocabulary restrictions are the most severe. Similar criticism can be leveled at phonic and linguistic programs that control the vocabulary on the basis of phonic regularity or spelling patterns.

Regardless of which approach is used, a limited vocabulary is employed in the initial stages of instruction. This may create some comprehension problems for novice readers (Beck, McKeown, & McCaslin 1981; Pearson 1984). Because the restricted vocabulary cannot carry the story line alone, meaning must be constructed through a combination of print, picture clues, and information provided by the pupil or teacher. Moreover, delimiting the vocabulary necessitates the use of indirect language and expressions that are semantically ambiguous and thus places additional inference burdens on young children. This is especially true in the use of first- and second-person pronouns, locational references (e.g., *here*), and demonstrative pronouns (e.g., *this*).

Basal readers in the 1980s have better balance in racial and ethnic characters; male and female characters; urban, suburban, and rural settings; and geographic locations compared to those in previous years. They include more handicapped characters and senior citizens who are depicted favorably, and their literary quality has improved, as has the artwork. Violence seems to have been deleted from the stories (Aukerman 1981).

Basal readers and children's books have been attacked as being sexist or because of insufficient cultural or ethnic pluralism. An implicit assumption of these charges is that changes in the content of reading material will result in more positive attitudes toward sex roles and minorities. As desirable as such content changes are, we cannot rely on them alone to modify attitudes. Children enter school with attitudes that have been developed over the years, and the influence of the child's family and peers continues to have a strong impact on these attitudes.

Methodology.   The typical directed reading activity (DRA) in a basal series consists essentially of three steps: (1) preparation; (2) reading the selection; and (3) follow-up activities. Although designed to facilitate and develop comprehension, some practices suggested in DRAs can inadvertently block comprehension (Beck 1984). Swaby (1982) suggested ways to vary these steps to prevent boredom, and Spiegel (1981b, 1984) presented a procedure for determining which of six alternatives to the DRA is best suited for a particular instructional purpose.

Preparation.   Preparing to read a new story involves three main phases. First is interest arousal, which can be accomplished by choosing the most effective suggestion(s) from among the many presented in the teacher's manual.

Next is the presentation and teaching of new words. The words may be taught through a whole-word method, or the children may be asked to apply previously taught decoding skills. In some series, much of the phonics teaching and practice occurs at this point. Third is the teaching and clarification of concepts that may be unfamiliar to some children. As demonstrated in a study by Hansen and Pearson (1982), activities should be included that require the pupils to activate their existing schemata and relate them to the reading material. Children can be asked to tell what they know about the topic. Previewing the story may help them to relate their prior knowledge to the selection, and they can be asked to predict what will happen in the story.

Guided Reading and Rereading. Usually the teacher leads some discussion of the story title and first illustration and then asks one or two purpose-setting questions. The children then read silently. The amount read should be geared to the ability of the readers, with capable readers being allowed to read more than the manual suggests. Beck, McCaslin, and McKeown (1981) have suggested that rather than set questions designed to elicit one or two bits of information, the teacher should get the students thinking along the direction the story will take.

After a first silent reading, followed by some discussion, there is often oral rereading. Oral rereading may be done for many reasons: to show how different characters felt, to read sad or funny parts that can be shared, to take parts in dramatizing the story, as a diagnostic tool, and so forth. When every story is reread orally in its entirety, every day, oral reading becomes a drudgery and valuable instructional time is wasted.

Follow-Up Activities. Follow-up activities are of two main kinds: skills development and enrichment activities. In some basal reader programs the major parts of instruction in decoding skills are located after reading and discussion. Additional practice in specific comprehension skills and using workbook pages that incorporate a variety of skills also usually come after reading and rereading.

Most manuals provide suggestions for enrichment. There are recommendations for stories that the teacher can read to the children, songs that can be sung (the music may be provided), poems with related themes, jingles and rhymes, and related art and handiwork. As children become able to do some independent reading, specific supplementary reading selections may be recommended.

If teachers do not have time to cover all parts of the DRA, the follow-up activities are most likely to be neglected (Rosecky 1978). Thus, although a basal manual recommends teaching or practicing skills, the plans may not be carried out in some classrooms. Similarly, enrichment activities may be omitted by teachers who are anxious to keep to preset schedules.

J. Mason (1982b, 1983) found that reading lessons seldom followed the presumed minimal sequence of preparation, directed reading, and discussion. More often, a hurried introduction to a story was sandwiched between workbook exercises and the pupils reading the story at their seats; often, either an introduction or follow-up discussion of the story was omitted. The reading lessons of the observed teachers often lacked a coherent ordering of instructional activities. Durkin (1984) reported similar findings.

Language-Experience Approaches

As early as the 1890s, some experimental schools used short stories dictated by the children and written down by the teacher as beginning reading materials (A. J. Harris 1964). Such "experience stories" have been widely used for decades to provide an informal introduction for basal readers. They have also been incorporated by many teachers in supplementary reading material, with particular reference to experiences in science and social studies. The experience method, now renamed the language-experience approach (LEA), rarely has the preplanned structure associated with other approaches. Generally, a language-experience approach is one in which

> . . . emphasis is placed on the teaching of reading in close correlation with the related activities of listening, speaking, and writing. Children are encouraged to express their thoughts, ideas, and feelings, often stimulated by a specific experience guided and developed by the teacher. The verbal productions of the children are written down by the teacher in the early stages, and are used as the earliest reading materials. Pupil expression is encouraged through the use of a variety of media such as painting, speaking, and writing. Gradually, the program moves from exclusive use of reading material that is developed out of the oral language of the children, into a program of reading in which increasing emphasis is placed upon a variety of children's books. (A. J. Harris & Serwer 1966a)

Current LEA programs attempt to integrate writing, reading, listening, and speaking skills. Their implementation requires a great deal of teacher initiative, creativity, and planning. Helpful suggestions for conducting an LEA program can be found in a number of sources (Hall 1970, Stauffer 1980, Allen 1976, Gans 1979, Allen & Allen 1982, Veatch *et al.* 1979, D. White 1980). Commercially available language-experience programs are not based on interests that originate with the children and tend to be highly structured (Wartenberg 1976). Themes for experience stories can be developed from trips, science, social studies topics, and interesting happenings at home, at school, or in the neighborhood. The topics may be selected and developed by individuals or groups of pupils.

The initial teaching method resembles that of the old story-memory method, going from the teacher's reading of the entire story to the reading of single lines to phrases and words. Word-recognition and decoding skills are developed from words used in the experience stories and usually are introduced as the teacher perceives a need and an opportunity rather than in any preplanned sequence. Compared to basal reader stories, experience stories may be of higher reading difficulty and contain more syntactically complex sentences and words (Sampson 1982). Gradually, as word recognition grows, easy first-grade books can be introduced in an LEA program and a transition made either to a basal reader program or an individualized reading program. See Reimer (1983) and Homan (1983) for suggestions on doing so.

The Natural Approach to Learning to Read

Some writers (e.g., F. Smith 1976, Clay 1982, Y. Goodman 1983) suggest that reading ability can, and should, be acquired just as naturally as spoken language. Basically, they contend that you do not teach children to read; rather, you provide them with the tools with which to teach themselves and the means for them to learn. Because of the nature of our language system, the tools include knowing the letters of our alphabet and learning to relate spellings to the spoken forms of words. The "means" include the necessary background information and an environment that allows children to understand the task in their own terms.

Clay (1979) described her pioneering project in New Zealand in which, during the first 2 years of instruction, the students learned how to teach themselves to read. They learned the aspects of print to which they must attend (e.g., how letters are sequenced within printed words), the aspects of oral language that can be related to print (e.g., sound segments within words), strategies that maintain fluency (e.g., conceptualization of what could follow), strategies that explore detail (e.g., discriminating between words that differ by only one letter), strategies that increase understanding (e.g., phrasing and using relationships between sentences), and strategies for detecting and correcting errors (e.g., cross-relating language and visual cues). They also learned how to relate new information to what they already knew (a strategy that schema theorists would highly endorse). In the process of learning how to learn, the children mastered a reading vocabulary of familiar words, the set of letters used to record language, and the sound equivalents of printed letters and common spelling patterns.

F. Smith (1983) stated that children can learn to write (compose written material) like a writer from what they read by "reading like a writer." Goodman and Goodman (1983), who agree with Smith, also pointed out that readers need not write during reading, but writers must read and reread during writing. So writing experiences are likely to have a positive impact on reading comprehension because "all of the schemata for predicting texts in reading are essentially the same as those used in constructing texts during writing."

According to Tierney and Pearson (1983), one must view reading and writing as essentially similar processes of meaning construction in order to understand the connection between them; both are acts of composing. A somewhat similar viewpoint was presented by Wittrock (1983), who believed that good reading and effective writing involve similar processes that create meaning by building relationships between the text and what we know, believe, and experience.

Despite such theoretical viewpoints, little is known regarding the exact nature of the reading and writing relationship. Her review of the literature led Stotsky (1983) to conclude the following:

1. Correlational studies almost consistently show that better writers tend to be better readers and to read more than poor writers, and better readers tend to produce more syntactically mature writing than poorer readers.

2. Experimental studies that used writing exercises primarily to improve writing did not tend to produce significant effects on reading. But almost all studies that used such procedures specifically to improve reading comprehension found small but significant gains in reading.
3. Studies that attempted to improve writing by providing reading experiences in place of grammar study or additional writing practice found reading to be as beneficial as, or more beneficial than, the experiences they replaced. But almost all studies that sought to improve writing through reading instruction were ineffective.

Individualized Developmental Reading

Individualized developmental reading (IDR) is characterized by the elimination of systematic instruction with a basal series and the use of individual reading in a variety of reading materials as the core rather than a supplement (see Hunt 1971). Each child selects the material that he or she wishes to read, sometimes with help from the teacher. During reading periods the child reads ahead silently, getting help from the teacher or another pupil when needed. At intervals (usually once or twice a week), there is a pupil–teacher conference that may involve discussion of what has been read, some oral reading, and perhaps some skills teaching. Preparation for reading is almost eliminated. Although some children are taught to set their own purposes for reading, reading is usually not guided by any specifically stated purposes except interest in the book. Comprehension is usually checked on the general plot. Rereading is often eliminated in favor of doing a large amount of varied reading. Word-recognition and decoding instruction usually consists of help given to a child as opportunities occur during the conferences, but sometimes temporary groups are formed for those children who need help on specific reading skills.

Three words often repeated by exponents of IDR are seeking, self-selection, and pacing. These concepts imply that children explore a wide range of available reading materials, choose their own reading, and proceed at their own pace. Great stress is placed on the importance of these factors in developing a spontaneous love for reading and in allowing reading to fit harmoniously into the unique pattern of growth of each child. The gradual, steady introduction of new words that can be obtained by reading a series of readers in sequence is considered unnecessary.

Many differences of opinion arise over the details of individualized developmental reading, but a knowledgeable, well-organized teacher would seem to be an absolute necessity. Some of the important issues involved in the use of IDR were discussed by Harris and Sipay (1979, pp. 89–95).

A large number of studies involving IDR have appeared, but many of them are faulty. "Much of the reported research suffers from poor research design, inadequate sampling, careless measurement, and a biased attitude on the part of the investigator" (Duker 1968). The following quotation seems to be a fair evaluation of results of research on IDR:

An examination of the research reports leads to these tentative conclusions about individualized reading instruction: (1) Individualized reading can be somewhat successful under certain conditions. (2) It requires highly competent teachers, and those who are not particularly capable should not be asked to adopt it. (3) Children usually enjoy the personal attention of the individual conference and, as a result, develop favorable attitudes toward reading. (4) They often, but not always, read more books. (5) The less capable pupils and those having special problems are likely to be less successful in individualized reading than in more structured programs. (6) The lack of a sequential skills program and opportunities for readiness causes teachers to feel doubtful about the adequacy of skills learning. (7) Teachers are constantly pressed for time to provide conferences that pupils should have. (Sartain 1969)

It seems unlikely that the kind of individualized developmental reading discussed above will ever achieve wide acceptance, especially at the first-grade level where the children depend heavily on teacher guidance and structure. Seeking, self-selection, and pacing are well adapted to recreational reading; an individualized, free-reading approach to recreational reading should be an integral part of any total reading program. Little has been written about IDR in recent years.

Code-Emphasis Approaches

Code-emphasis programs place initial stress on teaching decoding skills. Phonics programs, teaching by syllables, linguistic programs, and special alphabet and color programs are code-emphasis approaches.

Phonics Programs

Phonics programs stress learning grapheme–phoneme correspondences, tend to stress phonic generalizations and ignore exceptions, tend to provide instruction in blending phonemes, and tend to provide practice in applying decoding skills to words in context. Most phonics programs use a synthetic (parts-to-whole) approach. There are wide variations among phonics programs in content and methodology. Among the differences are the sequence in which symbol–sound associations are taught, the rate at which phonic principles are introduced, the number of generalizations taught, the opportunities for reading connected discourse, and the length and content of the connected discourse to be read.

There are phonics programs intended as preliminary or supplementary materials; these usually appear in consumable workbook form. Other phonics programs are designed to be total developmental reading programs, starting with readiness material and usually going through at least the sixth reader level. In these programs, most of the decoding skills are introduced in the first-grade materials. Beck (1977) described in detail a program that attempts to combine the code- and meaning-emphasis approaches.

Teaching by Syllables

Based on the belief that the syllable is more easily discernible than the phoneme within a spoken word, some authors advocate teaching reading by syllables rather than by grapheme–phoneme correspondences. Rozin and Gleitman (1977) offered a detailed discussion of their 22-element syllabary approach that has been reported to be successful (Gleitman & Rozin 1973, Harrigan 1976). It is difficult to evaluate the Gleitman and Rozin study, however, because of the absence of a large number of necessary controls and the probability that their curriculum was highly motivating, independent of the scripts employed (L. Henderson 1982). A syllabary approach may be useful for children who have difficulty learning phonics.

Linguistic Approaches

Bloomfield, a noted linguist, became interested in the teaching of reading in the late 1930s and wrote an essay on the subject in 1942. However, materials based on his ideas were not published for almost 20 years (Bloomfield & Barnhart 1961). Bloomfield was highly critical of phonic methods, particularly those using a synthetic sounding–blending procedure, and even more critical of the whole-word method, which he likened to the study of Chinese ideographs. Very briefly, his recommended procedure included the following ideas: (1) Start with teaching identification of all alphabet letters by name (not by sound); (2) begin with words in which each letter represents only one phonemic value, avoiding words with silent letters or less common sounds, so that the beginning words consist of three-letter words with a consonant-vowel-consonant pattern containing only short vowel sounds; (3) use the principle of minimal variation, employing a list of words that are alike except for one letter, such as *ban, can, Dan, fan, man, tan*; (4) do not teach rules about letter–sound correspondences, as the children will evolve their own generalizations when sound and spelling correspond in regular fashion; and (5) employ learned words in sentences, such as "Nan can fan Dan."

Since 1961, a number of reading series based on the above principles have appeared. They agree that decoding, or translating the printed words into their spoken equivalents, is the first and most important goal of a beginning reading program. Most of them also use a whole-word method and the principle of minimal variation instead of teaching decoding skills directly. Programs differ on such factors as the use and teaching of high-frequency words (e.g., *the*) that are not phonemically regular. Some use illustrations from the beginning; others consider them distracting and harmful. No two linguistic series agree very closely on details.

There is some question as to how well young children abstract letter–sound associations without direct instruction (Bishop 1962), and there are possible adverse effects of not establishing a "set for diversity" caused by the use of a tightly controlled vocabulary based on a one-to-one letter–sound correspondence in set spelling patterns (Levin & Watson 1962). Questions regarding linguistic reading programs also have been raised by linguists (Wardhaugh 1969) and psycholinguists (Smith & Goodman 1971, K. Goodman 1972), who stated that there is no such thing as a linguistic reading program but only reading programs written by linguists. Linguistic principles have been translated into diametrically opposed ideas as to how reading should be taught (Pikulski 1976).

Special-Alphabet Programs

Based on the belief that the irregularities in the English symbol–sound system are sufficient to cause difficulty for children learning to read, there have been efforts to promote a phonemically regular alphabet for English since the middle 1800s. The idea is that a one-to-one correspondence, in which each grapheme always represented the same phoneme (and vice versa), would make it much easier to "break the code" and thus facilitate the acquisition of reading ability. Supporters of simplified and regularized spelling do not agree on details, but most advocate supplementing our 26-letter alphabet.

The best known of the special alphabets, the Initial Teaching Alphabet (i.t.a.), has 44 characters in which (1) capitals are like lowercase letters in shape, but larger; (2) there is a separate symbol for each of 44 consonant and vowel sounds; and (3) many present letters are retained, and new characters are designed to facilitate transition to traditional orthography (T.O.). The Initial Teaching Alphabet is not an instructional method but an augmented alphabet. The most widely used i.t.a. readers in Great Britain employed an eclectic methodology similar to that of most American basal series, whereas the i.t.a. series most used in the United States followed an alphabet–phonic procedure. Although fairly popular at one time, the use of i.t.a. has markedly declined in the United States, where i.t.a. materials are no longer published.

Other special-alphabet systems employed color cues rather than additional graphemes (e.g., *Words in Color*). Each phoneme, regardless of its spelling, was printed in a particular hue; color cues were gradually phased out. Research did not reveal such programs to be any more effective than programs with which they were compared. They are rarely mentioned in the current literature.

Individualized Skills-Emphasis Programs

Programmed Materials

Programmed materials are designed so that the user (1) encounters a series of small tasks on which success is very likely; (2) is involved in the learning process through actively responding; and (3) receives immediate feedback as to the correctness of each response. In theory, programmed materials should greatly facilitate individualized instruction because they allow each student to work almost independently with material suitable for his or her needs, proceeding at a pace commensurate with ability and interest.

Programmed reading series usually consist of consumable workbook-like texts with accompanying manuals and accessory materials. Their basic method is best described as a phonic–linguistic one.

Programmed readers were found wanting by Beck (1977) for the following reasons: (1) The "missing letter technique" (the user fills in the blank space) is insufficient for developing decoding skills because it does not incorporate an auditory model or auditory feedback; (2) comprehension is interrupted because the child must stop to fill in a response, often in the middle of a sentence; (3) much of the connected discourse that surrounds the target word can be ignored, since the missing letter can be supplied from memory or by finding a copy of the complete word; and (4) very little text must be read to answer the questions correctly.

Skills Management Systems

Skills management systems (also referred to as diagnostic–prescriptive teaching, objective-based instruction, or criterion-referenced systems) place stress on diagnosing each learner's status and needs and on individualizing skill development based on diagnostic findings. Such programs usually have these characteristics: (1) a list of sequenced behavioral objectives for one or more skill areas (e.g., word recognition, comprehension); (2) criterion-referenced tests for each objective; (3) sources of instructional materials; and (4) recordkeeping procedures. A subskills orientation is believed to make learning more meaningful and easier by reducing the information load, simplifying the learning act, and allowing mastery learning (Carnine 1982).

A placement test or a series of pretests places the child along a skills continuum (perhaps at different levels in various skill areas). If the criterion for mastery is not met, the child receives instructional materials and works independently until the teacher thinks that the skill has been mastered. A posttest is then administered. If the posttest is passed, the child takes the next pretest in the sequence; if failed, additional practice is provided. Periodic mastery tests cover broader skill areas.

The teacher's role is to select, administer, and score the diagnostic instruments; arrive at diagnostic conclusions; assign appropriate practice; give individual or group assistance as needed; secure, organize, and keep track of materials; maintain motivation; and keep adequate records.

Although there are basic similarities, skills management systems differ considerably. A number of skills management systems have been described (Prager & Mann 1973, Thompson & Dziuben 1973, Rude 1974, Lawrence & Simmons 1978).

Theoretically, skills management systems promote specific individualized instruction and efficient use of time (children are not required to practice skills they have already mastered). Individualized curriculums relying largely on a test–teach–retest model to guide students through a planned sequence of materials place a considerable strain on teachers' recordkeeping and decision-making skills (Calfee & Brown 1979). Unless teacher aides or computer assistance for test scoring and recordkeeping are available, there may be little time for direct instruction. Such assistance involves additional expense, which many school systems cannot afford. The most frequently cited reasons for discarding skills management systems are their cost (Eveland 1975) and the demands of recordkeeping (Wirt 1976).

As with any program, there are potential disadvantages. Assigning a child to a particular exercise without determining why the pretest was failed can lead to blind repetition of the same kind of error. Instruction also may become too rigid; children do not all learn in the same way nor are all skills equally important. Then, too, there is a strong temptation to teach easily testable skills and slight higher-level skills that are more difficult to measure. Most important, there is the danger that teaching is left solely to the practice exercises; many children need direct instruction by competent teachers.

According to Duffy (1978), objective-based instruction is not a total approach to reading instruction nor does its use dictate a particular instructional method. Rather, it is designed to help teachers organize the reading curriculum and present reading in small, logically sequenced increments. A skills hierarchy should be used as a guide; it is not infallible. Moreover, no skill is truly mastered until the student uses it consistently in independent reading. Therefore skills management systems should provide transfer activities and time for independent reading.

A term frequently associated with skills management systems is mastery learning. *Mastery learning* advocates contend that almost all pupils could learn well *if* instruction was systematic, students were helped when and where they had learning difficulties, sufficient time was provided for achieving mastery, and a clear criterion of what constituted mastery was available. Many of the tenets of mastery learning have been attributed to Bloom (1976, 1981).

Computers and Reading

Computers have been used in two ways in the teaching of reading: computer-assisted instruction (CAI) and computer-managed instruction (CMI). In the pioneering CAI work of Atkinson and Fletcher (1972), the emphasis was on a decoding program to supplement classroom instruction. Recently many kinds of CAI programs have come on the market. Several of the skills management systems utilize computers to score tests and exercises and keep a detailed record on each student.

The advent of the microcomputer has brought about an extremely rapid increase in the availability of computers in school; by 1983 half of the nation's schools offered computer access to some students (Gerrell & Mason 1983). Microcomputer hardware is better developed than the software; most of the reading software we have seen does little that could not be done without a computer. Most of the available software is of the drill and practice type and devoted to specific skills and subskills; few types deal with language at the level of sentences and whole texts (Chall & Conrad 1984, Rubin & Bruce 1984). This situation may only be temporary, however.

Because this field is changing so rapidly, we are not attempting to summarize what is available at present. Geoffrion and Geoffrion (1983) explain how a computer works and its use in teaching reading and provide sources of software and guidelines for evaluating them. Guidelines for evaluating software also may be found in Devall (1983), Chall and Conrad (1984), or obtained from the International Reading Association, and guidelines for purchasing a microcomputer are provided by Auten (1982). Refer to G. Mason, Blanchard, and Daniel (1983) for an annotated bibliography covering a wide range of topics on computer applications in reading. Publications dealing with microcomputers that may be of interest to reading teachers have been listed by Rude (1982). Journals such as

PIRT and the *Journal of Learning Disabilities* regularly devote space to the use of computers in school, and the October 1983 issue of *Exceptional Children* was devoted to the place of microcomputers in special education. The new *Journal of Computers, Reading and Language Arts* may also be of interest.

III. ADJUSTING TO THE NEEDS OF DIALECT, LIMITED-ENGLISH, AND NON-ENGLISH SPEAKERS

Pupils who speak a dialect that differs from standard English (SE) or who speak or understand little or no English tend not only to get off to a poor start in learning to read but also to fall farther behind their age peers as they proceed through school.

A number of large-scale studies have consistently shown that, on the average, low-income minority children are usually at the 20th to 28th percentile in reading by the third grade, approximately a year below grade level. Educational efforts to improve this situation have not been particularly effective, especially in inner-city schools (Meyer, Gersten, & Gutkin 1983). One explanation offered for the reading problems of these pupils is that the disparity between their dialect or language and SE (standard English) creates linguistic barriers that interfere with learning to read and reading comprehension. Certainly, not understanding English has an adverse impact on learning to read, but there may be other variables equally as important as a linguistic mismatch.

Dialect Speakers

The dialect given the most attention in the literature is black English (BE). It is not spoken by all blacks, and there are variations of BE in different communities. Most linguists believe that BE is a well-ordered, cohesive linguistic system. It has some unique features that differ from SE and have been listed as possible sources of interference for dialect speakers. These possible sources are phonological, grammatical, and lexical.[3]

The evidence for phonological interference is not convincing. In fact, Shuy (1979) flatly stated that a phonological mismatch is not a cause of reading difficulty. Even though dialect speakers may pronounce words differently, they evidently obtain meaning (Torrey 1983). Counting dialect renditions as word-recognition errors, however, may depress *scores* on reading tests. For instance, when dialect miscues were not counted as errors in scoring three commonly used oral reading tests, the reading scores of dialect speakers increased more than half a grade level on all three tests (Burke, Pflaum, & Knafle 1982).

Expressive proficiency in SE and BE does not seem to affect the reading performance of older students. Apparently as pupils get older the influence of linguistic factors decreases and the influence of cognitive factors increases (Harber 1982).

---

[3] Refer to A. J. Harris and Sipay (1979, pp. 459–481) for specific information concerning differences between SE and the language of BE, Spanish, and Chinese speakers.

The syntax of BE could interfere with reading comprehension at times. For example, there are certain differences in the ways BE and SE speakers structure prepositions (e.g., BE = "John, sit *to* the table"; SE = John, sit *at* the table." Hall & Guthrie 1982).

Lexical differences (e.g., *tote* for *carry*) are not likely to create serious comprehension problems when reading connected discourse. It is more likely that a restricted store of concepts and the labels for those concepts will create comprehension problems for dialect speakers.

The listening comprehension of dialect speakers does not differ significantly when material is presented in SE or BE (Phillips 1976, Cagney 1977). Nor are BE speakers more successful comprehending material written in their dialect than in SE (Hall & Turner 1974, Simons & Johnson 1974, Liu 1975–1976). It seems that most dialect speakers learn to derive meaning from selections written in SE despite surface-structure differences between their dialect and SE. Speaking SE does not seem vital for reading comprehension, although it has possible social and economic values.

Yet, although the linguistic-mismatch theory does not appear to offer a viable explanation for the relatively poor reading achievement of dialect speakers, it cannot be totally rejected. Our knowledge concerning the possible effect of dialect interference during the crucial period of beginning reading is meager (Seitz 1977).

A spoken dialect or lack of English proficiency may be symptomatic of economic and sociocultural factors that are contributing to the reading problems. Most dialect, limited-English, and non-English speakers are economically disadvantaged. The effects of poverty on reading achievement are pervasive, and because all the factors associated with poverty and its environment are highly interrelated, it may be impossible to isolate any single variable as *the* cause of the reading problem of non-standard-English speakers.

There is also the possibility of an indirect interference of dialect on learning to read. Cultural variations in the function and use of language can have important consequences for dialect speakers (Hall & Guthrie 1982), as can inadequate communication skills (Carroll & Walton 1979) and not knowing the implicit rules of when and how to communicate in the classroom (Brause & Mayher 1982). Teachers may consider the children's dialect or language inferior and denigrate them and their cultures. Teachers' attitudes can also influence their judgments about dialect speakers' learning and reading abilities. This in turn can affect the expectations held for the pupils and communicated to them, the reading group in which they are placed, and so forth.

The reader's prior knowledge is conditioned by cultural factors, and prior knowledge is an important variable in reading comprehension. Low-SES (socioeconomic status) children are less likely than more advantaged children to have prior knowledge of the topics encountered in school material.

McDermott (1976, 1977) has theorized that the reading failure of many minority or culturally different American students is best explained by the cultural makeup of the classroom.[4] When the children's culture and that of the teacher are different enough so that they are unable to make sense of each other, a cultural communication conflict emerges in the classroom. Patterns of selective attention and inattention to reading represent the culturally different child's adaptation to the politics of everyday life in the class. One takes sides by attending or not, depending on whether the child chooses to adhere to the peer group or to the teacher.

Another theory involves a social organizational hypothesis that postulates that the school achievement of many minority children is related to how closely the presentation of the material and the nature of responses allowed approximates their cultural values and norms. In a preliminary test of their hypothesis, Au and Mason (1981) found that Hawaiian 7-year-olds displayed much higher levels of achievement-related behaviors when the teacher allowed them to enter the discussion whenever they wished and to share turns in joint performance than when they were allowed only to respond singly when called on.

Various proposals have been made as to how best to teach dialect speakers to read. There is, however, no conclusive evidence that any of them is more effective than the others (Sommerville 1975).

Some low-income minority children can and do succeed in reading (Wilder 1977; Harber & Beatty 1978; Morgan, Meeks, & Laffey 1982; McPhail 1982; Durkin 1982; L. Meyer, Gersten, & Gutkin 1983). In our opinion, a viable reading program for dialect speakers might incorporate the following: making teachers more knowledgeable about, accepting of, and sensitive to the students' dialects and cultures; making teachers aware of how their often unrecognized attitudes can influence the reading achievement of dialect speakers; initial use of an LEA coupled with a structured skill-development program—all under the direction of skilled, effective teachers who understand and accept the children and who have the support of the school principal and the cooperation of the home. The magnitude of the correlations between third- and ninth-grade reading achievement (.78 and .81) suggests that the success or failure of primary-grade reading instruction has long-term consequences for minority students (L. Meyer 1983).

Attempts are also being made to lessen failure in learning to read by children whose native or strongest language is not English. In the past, most programs simply employed English as the language of instruction and utilized materials in English that depicted a culture foreign to these children. The limitations of such an approach are obvious. Instructional reading materials conceptually attuned to some of the cultures of these children have been developed in the hope that the content will be more understandable and interesting to the learners, as well as reflect their cultural heritage. Research regarding the effect of such materials is still lacking.

Initial reading instruction for limited-English and non-English speakers has usually taken either of two approaches: (1) teaching them to understand and speak English before initiating reading instruction in English; or (2) teaching

---

[4] For a review of the use of ethnography in studying reading, refer to Green and Bloome (1983).

them to read their native language, concurrently teaching receptive and expressive English, then teaching them to read English. Early research did not clearly support either approach (Hatch 1974), but an increasing amount of evidence indicates that literacy should be taught first in the child's primary language (R. Miller 1982).

According to Gonzales (1981b), primary-grade children who have limited command of English should not be taught to read English until they can comprehend the syntactic and semantic structures in the reading text. He presented procedures for assessing a child's level of competence in English and the structural level of reading material. Ortiz (1984) discussed the wide range of communication–language skills that may be found in minority children.

The language of children who come from non-English-speaking backgrounds frequently signals cultural differences that the teacher must consider in order to avoid misunderstandings and problems. For example, there are cultural variations as to what constitutes acceptable or desirable behavior. Thus Anglo teachers should be especially sensitive to situations in which Native American children are likely to be silent, in accord with their culture, and not misperceive their silence as a sign of insolence, ignorance, or disinterest (Sherzer 1977). Cultural differences can result in miscommunication between teachers and pupils (Philips 1983). R. Henderson (1980) reviewed suggestions for meeting the social and emotional needs of culturally diverse children.

Teaching reading to limited-English and non-English speakers is covered more fully in Harris and Sipay (1979, pp. 457–481). Suggestions for teaching reading and other English language skills to such students may be found in Gonzales (1981a, b), Carter (1982), and Feeley (1983). Problems in learning to read English as a second language have been discussed by Barnitz (1982).

IV. AN EVALUATION OF BEGINNING READING APPROACHES

A comparative evaluation of beginning reading approaches is not easy. The majority of children can learn to read by a variety of methods. Approaches may vary in effectiveness depending on local conditions, making it dangerous to generalize from a limited sample; procedures that work well in a prosperous suburb may not suit the needs of children in an impoverished neighborhood.

A review of the studies completed before the mid-1960s led Chall to conclude:

> It would seem, at our present state of knowledge, that a code emphasis—one that combines control of words on spelling regularity (although not complete control of one sound for one symbol), some direct teaching of letter-sound correspondences, as well as the use of writing, tracing, or typing—produces better results with unselected groups of beginners than a meaning emphasis, the kind incorporated in most of the conventional basal-reading series used in the schools in the late 1950's and early 1960's. (Chall 1967, pp. 178–179)

She also concluded that there was no experimental basis for preferring one code-emphasis method over another. Also, it should be noted that Chall's major conclusion was stated cautiously, to the effect that methods that paid more and earlier attention to word-identification skills than did basal readers of the 1950s and early 1960s tended, on the whole, to come out with better results than the basal readers. It was not an endorsement of procedures that ignore meaning for weeks while drilling on letters and words.

Chall also carefully discussed the great variations in results that different teachers obtain with the same method, the favorable but transient effect of novelty, the significance of the effort put forth by teachers volunteering to use a new method, the tendency to spend extra time with a new method, and other complicating factors. Accepting her main conclusion without carefully studying the many qualifications can produce a dangerously inaccurate oversimplification of a complex problem.

Chall cautioned against an overemphasis on decoding when she wrote: "In their enthusiasm, many authors, publishers, and teachers may be extending the decoding practice too far, and students may be spending too much time on it. This may be so both for the highly programmed decoding materials and for teacher-made exercises. Thus, stories and books, the true vehicles for reading for meaning, may be neglected in the zeal for mastery of decoding. Moderation here, as in all of life, should be valued" (1977, p. 12). Still, Chall (1983a) favors direct instruction of synthetic phonics accompanied by the teaching of blending during the initial stages of reading acquisition, with emphasis switching to the meaning and language aspects of reading after third grade.

The U.S. Office of Education supported 27 coordinated first-grade studies in 1964–1965. Summaries of all the projects appeared in *The Reading Teacher* (May & October 1966, May & October 1967) and have been gathered together in a paperback (Stauffer 1967). Results from the projects that utilized representative children and studied methods also employed in other projects were drawn together in a composite statistical analysis, summarized in two reports. The first covers 15 first-grade studies; the second, 13 studies that continued through the second grade. In the summary of the first-grade report, 15 numbered conclusions were offered. Of these, the following seem most significant:

1. Word study skills must be emphasized and taught systematically regardless of what approach to initial reading instruction is utilized.
2. Combinations of programs, such as a basal program with supplementary phonics materials, often are superior to single approaches. . . . The addition of language experiences to any kind of reading can be expected to make a contribution.
3. It is likely that basal programs should develop a more intensive word study skills element, while programs which put major emphasis on word recognition should increase attention paid to other reading skills.
6. Reading programs are not equally effective in all situations. Evidently factors other than method, within a particular learning situation influence pupil success in reading. . . .

9. . . . The tremendous range among classrooms within any method points out the importance of elements in the learning situation other than the methods employed. To improve reading instruction, it is necessary to train better teachers of reading rather than to expect a panacea in the form of materials.

10. Children learn to read by a variety of materials and methods. Furthermore, pupils experienced difficulty in each of the programs utilized. No one approach is so distinctly better in all situations and respects than the others that it should be considered the one best method and the one to be used exclusively.

13. A writing component is likely to be an effective addition to a primary program.

14. It is impossible to assess the relative effectiveness of programs unless they are used in the same project. Project differences are so great even when readiness for reading is controlled that a program utilized in a favored project would demonstrate a distinct advantage over one used in a less favored project regardless of the effectiveness of the program. (Bond & Dykstra 1967, pp. 210–212)

The second-grade report from the Coordinating Center essentially supported and repeated the conclusions of the first-grade report (Dykstra 1968a). Limitations of these studies have been pointed out (Sipay 1968, Lohnes & Gray 1972, Lohnes 1973).

Although at the end of the second year these studies seemed to support Chall's conclusion concerning the superiority of code-emphasis programs, Dykstra (1968b) cautioned about the absence of any clear evidence that the early emphasis on code per se was the only or even the primary reason for the relative effectiveness of code-emphasis approaches. Other characteristics of these programs may have been more crucial in determining pupil achievement. Dykstra later wrote: "We can summarize the results of 60 years of research dealing with beginning reading instruction by stating that early systematic instruction in phonics provides the child with the skills necessary to become an independent reader at an earlier age than is likely if phonics instruction is delayed and less systematic" (1974, p. 397). Beck (1981) drew a similar conclusion. It seems that current publishers have responded to this need.

The early advantage of code-emphasis programs may relate to factors other than their heavy teaching of decoding. In such programs there is a great deal of direct instruction (Resnick 1979a). Instruction is more systematic and focused (Pflaum *et al.* 1980), and lessons are more structured, provide more systematic feedback, allocate more time to reading, and maintain higher levels of time on task (R. Anderson, Mason, & Shirley 1983). Guthrie (1981d) warned that attributing effects to a particular instructional method was unwarranted unless certain variables (e.g., the amount of learning time, unusual teacher characteristics) were held constant.

Of the original 27 projects, 8 followed their pupils through the third grade. In 7 of these projects, which included a variety of methods, the reading test results at the end of the third grade showed no consistent and statistically significant superiority for any method (Fry 1967, A. J. Harris *et al.* 1968, Ruddell 1968, Schneyer & Cowen 1968, Vilscek & Cleland 1968, Sheldon *et al.* 1967, Stauffer & Hammond 1969). In the eighth project, the meaning of the results is obscured by the fact that the phonic–linguistic method that achieved the highest mean-adjusted reading scores in second and third grades also had markedly higher nonpromotion rates in first and second grades; removal of the poorest readers in that method by nonpromotion would seem to have affected the results (Hayes & Wuest 1967).

Thus the largest-scale studies done in America indicate no consistent advantages for any method studied when pupils are followed through the third grade. Similar conclusions were drawn in Great Britain by Morris (1966) and by the Bullock Commission (Department of Education & Science 1975). There is strong evidence that the qualities of the school system, of administrative leadership, of the particular school, of the principal, of the teacher, and of the pupils (in turn related to characteristics of home and neighborhood) far outweigh differences in methodology and materials in their influences on reading achievement.

Overall, the research suggests that when skill in word recognition is the most important objective, code-emphasis programs tend to produce better results than meaning-emphasis programs, especially for low-SES students and low achievers. When comprehension is the criterion, there is no clear advantage for either approach. What is needed is a proper balance between systematic decoding instruction and attention to developing reading comprehension (Resnick 1979a).

There is also evidence that none of the methods studied was able to lessen significantly the proportion of children who make disappointing progress in learning to read, let alone eliminate failure. This does not mean that all beginning reading programs are equally suitable for all children. Not all children seem able to learn through a whole-word method; others cannot learn through a phonics method. Programs also vary considerably in the conceptual demands they place on children. For instance, some first-grade programs are relatively easy in that they introduce fewer words and phonic principles; others introduce many more words and phonic principles at a more rapid pace (Barr 1982a). Factors such as these should be considered in evaluating research studies and in selecting commercially published reading series.

The time has come to end the quest for *the* best method of teaching reading. Gross comparisons of beginning reading approaches have yielded little useful information. Efforts should concentrate on determining which aspects of a program are most effective for particular children when used by certain teachers under given conditions, and what is more important, why.

Attempts to match learner characteristics with instructional methods that supposedly facilitate the acquisition of reading skills because they "play to" the child's strength have not been particularly successful. Matching visual or auditory modality preference with a whole-word or phonic method does not result in better achievement in learning to read (Larrivee 1981). Negative results also have been reported for attempts to match sensory-integration abilities (matching stimuli presented in different modalities) with beginning reading methods (Thom 1971, Pressman 1973).

Until more evidence is available, it seems that for most children a balanced eclectic approach that uses varied sensory cues in combination and that gives balanced attention to word recognition and comprehension seems advisable. When a child continues to fail in a particular reading program, consideration should be given to employing a program that utilizes a different methodology and makes different demands on the learner.

4

An Overview of Reading Instruction

This is the third of three chapters that provide a survey of the total program of reading instruction. Readiness for reading was discussed in Chapter 2 and beginning reading in Chapter 3. The present chapter provides a brief summary of the stages of reading instruction, summarizes the objectives of the reading program, discusses some special issues in the teaching of reading, and considers factors that influence the effectiveness of reading instruction.

I. STAGES OF READING INSTRUCTION

Over half a century ago the National Committee on Reading proposed a five-stage process of learning to read: (1) readiness for reading; (2) beginning to read; (3) rapid development of reading skills (Grades 2 and 3); (4) wide reading (Grades 4–8); and (5) refinement of reading (high school and college) (W. S. Gray 1925). Recently, a six-stage classification has been proposed by Chall (1983c), who described the stages somewhat differently.

According to Chall, *Stage 0* is the *Prereading Stage*, during which understandings about reading are unsystematically accumulated gradually and over a period of years, including preschool and kindergarten.

Stage 1 is the *Initial Reading or Decoding Stage: Grades 1–2, Ages 6–7.* Learning the arbitrary set of letters and associating them with the corresponding parts of spoken words is the central task of this stage. In this stage children (and adults) acquire cognitive knowledge about reading, such as what the letters are for, how to know that *bun* is not *bug*, and how to know when the reader has made a mistake. By the end of this stage the learner experiences a qualitative change as he develops insight about the nature of the spelling system and becomes able to decode words not met before.

Stage 2, Confirmation, Fluency, Ungluing from Print: Grades 2–3, Ages 7–8. In Stage 2 there is a consolidation of what was learned in Stage 1, through reading what is familiar and already known. Stage 2 reading is not for gaining new information but for confirming what the reader already knows. Most children in Stage 2 learn to use their decoding skills along with the repetitions inherent in the language and stories read, gaining competence in using context and consequently improving in fluency and rate. The proper development of Stage 2 requires the reading of many easy and familiar books.

In this stage developmental reading lessons still form the major part of the reading program, although functional reading and recreational reading gradually increase in importance. For developmental reading the class is usually divided into groups reading at different levels of difficulty.

Basal readers for these grades generally are collections of short stories arranged in groups with similar themes. Some basal readers put major emphasis on enjoyable fiction, while others stress the social studies value of their content. Supplementary readers, phonics workbooks, tapes, recordings, filmstrips, a class library for individualized reading, textbooks in other curriculum areas, and informational books related to units or special projects are desirable in addition to the basal readers.

For those using basal readers, the general structure of lesson planning remains basically the same as at first-grade level. In preparatory work, developing the meanings of unfamiliar ideas increases in importance, although providing motivation and presenting new words continue to be essential. Silent reading is usually a few pages at a time, followed by answering questions (which may be provided in the workbook), oral discussion, and oral rereading. Systematic teaching of decoding techniques is a very important related activity. Enrichment activities are expanded in scope by the growing ability of the children to read independently.

Functional reading increases in importance in these grades. This mainly takes the form of the reading of textbooks in various subjects, or it consists chiefly of reading in varied sources to obtain the information needed in the carrying on of units or projects. Weekly newspapers provide a basis for current events and other phases of the social studies in many schools.

As children become better able to read, the range of possible recreational material increases markedly. At first-grade level the classroom library consists mainly of picture books; books at pre-primer, primer, and first reader levels; and books for the teacher to read to the class. At second-grade level many children can read simple story books for pleasure, and at third-grade level there is a wide range of books and stories suitable for individual reading.

Stage 3. Reading for Learning the New: A First Step—Grades 4–8, Ages 9–13.[1] Entering *Stage 3* fits the traditional conception that in the primary grades children learn to read, and in the higher grades they read to learn. Around the beginning of *Stage 3* reading begins to compete with other means of acquiring knowledge. Readers must bring their knowledge and experience to their reading if they are to learn from it. *Stage 3* is essentially for facts, for concepts, for how to do things. At this stage, nuances and varied points of view are found only in the reading of fiction.

Developmental reading activities are concerned primarily with the further refinement and improvement of skills already well started. Time devoted to developmental reading lessons decreases as more time is spent on developing functional reading skills and strategies. While the basic outline of a complete reading activity persists as a desirable general plan, considerable flexibility is in order. Preparation and oral reading usually take proportionally less time than in the primary grades. Word study is concerned more with meanings than with recognition or decoding. Decoding skills involve review of the primary-grade decoding program and systematic teaching of the use of the dictionary for both pronunciation and meanings. Silent reading is done in large units, often a complete story or selection, and comprehension questions may be given either before or after the first reading. Comprehension may be checked by written answers to questions as well as in oral discussion, and an attempt is made to develop skill in answering different kinds of questions and in reading for different purposes. Practice to speed up silent reading may be appropriate for those who have reached an adequate level in other reading skills.

In these grades the basal reader is still the primary focus of developmental reading. The readers are typically collections of selections that have been shortened and adapted from the original or written expressly for the reader. An increasing amount of expository material may be included.

Stage 4. Multiple Viewpoints: High School, Ages 14–18. Whereas in Stage 3 the reader has to deal primarily with one point of view at a time, secondary school texts require dealing with a variety of viewpoints, and thus the texts are more difficult to comprehend. Stage 4 skills are acquired mainly through reading and studying materials that vary widely in type, content, and style. Doing so provides practice in acquiring increasingly difficult concepts and in learning how to learn new concepts and points of view through reading.

Concern about reading in the secondary school first took the form of remedial programs, and in the 1960s and early 1970s there was a dramatic growth in secondary corrective and remedial reading programs (Cowan 1977). By the mid-1970s the need for more comprehensive reading programs in the high school was widely accepted (Early 1977), but secondary school reading programs have changed very little in the past 25 years (Sager 1980, Greenlaw & Moore 1982).

---

[1] Chall did not designate grade or age levels for this stage. Those indicated are our estimates.

The remedial–corrective model is still dominant. There are often small remedial classes for severely disabled readers, large corrective classes for those reading 1 to 2 years below grade level, or both. Occasionally there are developmental classes for students who are reading at or above grade level—to refine present skills and develop more advanced reading and study skills. Reading instruction as part of the instruction in the content subject is rare (Nelson & Herber 1982).

A comprehensive secondary school reading program should include instruction in the reading and study skills and strategies needed for success in whatever courses the pupils are taking. Herber and Nelson-Herber (1984) proposed a program in which the central focus is on reading instruction in the content areas. Reading would be taught functionally; as the students read their texts they are taught how to apply reading to them. If general reading and study skills are taught in a separate course, instruction and guided practice in applying them to the demands of each subject should be provided. The content-subject teachers should be involved in planning and conducting this aspect of the program, under the direction of a reading specialist who would offer the necessary inservice work. Provision also should be made for good readers who want to become superior readers or wish to increase their reading rate or flexibility and for students who have moderate or severe reading problems.

Reading in the content subjects is covered more fully on pages 509–532. Other suggestions may be found in Berger and Robinson (1982), Moore and Readence (1983), and in texts devoted entirely to the teaching of reading in the middle, junior, or senior high school. Farr and Wolf (1984) presented a comprehensive plan for evaluating a secondary school reading program.

Stage 5. Construction and Reconstruction—A World View: College, Ages 18 and Above. Remedial and developmental reading programs for adults who are in and out of school have taken a number of forms. Many junior and senior colleges provide remedial programs for students who are lacking in reading or study skills thought to be necessary for success in college. For those whose general reading and study skills are adequate, fewer colleges offer elective developmental reading courses that may focus on increasing reading rate, efficiency of reading and study skills and habits, and reading selectivity and critically. Out-of-school adults whose reading ability is average or above but is deemed inadequate for their purposes often enroll in commercial programs that emphasize the development of similar skills.

The longest-existing adult programs have dealt with teaching basic literacy and survival skills to out-of-school adults (Reed & Ward 1982). Such programs vary greatly (Mocker 1980), but most fall under the rubric of Adult Basic Education (ABE). Not all segments of our population value the literacy skills that educators and politicians value. For as yet undetermined reasons, only 2% of the target population participate in ABE programs (Park 1981). How to motivate adults to take advantage of opportunities to acquire literacy is a problem. As Cook lamented (1977, p. 128), "millions of Americans will remain functionally illiterate by choice and their children may grow up assimilating this same indifference." A review of the literature led Kavale and Lindsey (1977) to conclude that the ABE movement had made little progress in increasing adult literacy. Perhaps its failure is the result, at least in part, of the short duration of the programs (many ABE programs last only 16 to 20 weeks), inadequately prepared teachers, and inadequate funding. The International Reading Association (1981) presented a checklist for evaluating ABE programs.

A relatively recent interest has developed in the reading abilities, interests, and needs of senior citizens. Senior citizens reported that reading provided them with relaxation, with topics to discuss, and with suggestions for strengthening their inner resources and coping with the problems of aging (Wolf 1980). Senior citizens are likely to be overrepresented in illiteracy studies. Perhaps this is the result of fewer educational opportunities in the past, but senior citizens are the least likely to participate in literacy programs (Park 1981).

II. OBJECTIVES OF READING INSTRUCTION

It is important to be definite about educational objectives. Teachers who make the development of a love for reading as a form of recreation a major objective can find many different ways of working toward it, and each can achieve substantial success. But if developing a love for reading is not one of the teacher's goals, it is unlikely that her pupils will acquire such an attitude as a result of her efforts. Having the right goals and knowing what they are is the necessary first step in developing a sound reading program.

Teachers of reading want their pupils to be able to read, to use reading effectively as a learning tool, and to enjoy and appreciate reading. Using somewhat more technical language, we can talk about developmental reading, functional reading, and recreational reading. Developmental reading activities are those in which the teacher's main purpose is to bring about an improvement in reading skills—activities in which the primary aim is learning to read. Functional reading includes all reading in which the primary aim is to obtain information; in other words, reading to learn. Some writers prefer to call it study-type reading or work-type reading. Recreational reading consists of reading activities that have enjoyment, entertainment, and appreciation as their major purposes.

A somewhat more detailed analysis of these three kinds of reading, stated as general outcomes in terms of learner behavior, is as follows:

I. Developmental reading
   A. Basic or facilitating skills. The learner
      1. Has a large sight vocabulary
      2. Flexibly uses a variety of skills to recognize and decode words
      3. Reads silently with speed and fluency
      4. Coordinates rate with comprehension
      5. Reads orally with proper phrasing, expression, pitch, volume, and enunciation

B. Reading comprehension
1. Vocabulary. The learner
   a. Has an extensive and accurate reading vocabulary
   b. Uses context effectively to
      (1) determine the meaning of an unfamiliar word
      (2) choose the appropriate meaning of a word
   c. Interprets figurative and nonliteral language
2. Literal comprehension. The learner
   a. Grasps the meaning and interrelatedness of increasingly larger units: phrase, sentence, paragraph, whole selection
   b. Understands and recalls stated main ideas
   c. Notes and recalls significant stated details
   d. Recognizes and recalls a stated series of events in correct sequence
   e. Notes and explains stated cause–effect relationships
   f. Finds answers to specific questions
   g. Follows printed directions accurately
   h. Skims to obtain a total expression
3. Inferential comprehension. The learner
   a. Understands and recalls inferred main ideas
   b. Notes and recalls significant inferred details
   c. Recognizes and recalls an inferred series of events in correct sequence
   d. Notes and explains inferred cause–effect relationships
   e. Anticipates and predicts outcomes
   f. Grasps the author's plan and intent
   g. Identifies the techniques authors use to create desired effects
4. Critical reading. The learner critically evaluates what is read.
5. Creative reading. The learner extrapolates from what is read to reach new ideas and conclusions.

II. Functional reading
A. Locates needed reading material. The learner
   1. Uses indexes
   2. Uses tables of contents
   3. Uses dictionaries
   4. Uses encyclopedias
   5. Uses other bibliographic aids
   6. Skims in search for information
B. Comprehends informational material. The learner
   1. Understands technical and specific vocabulary
   2. Applies the general comprehension skills listed above
   3. Uses the specific skills needed by special subject matter, e.g.,
      a. Reading of arithmetic problems
      b. Reading of maps, charts, and graphs
      c. Conducting a science experiment from printed directions

           4. Interprets headings, subheadings, marginal notes, and other study aids

           5. Reads independently in the content subjects

      C. Selects the material needed for a purpose

      D. Records and organizes what is read. The learner

           1. Takes useful notes

           2. Summarizes

           3. Outlines

      E. Displays appropriate study skills and habits

   III. Recreational reading

      A. Displays an interest in reading. The learner

           1. Enjoys reading as a voluntary leisure-time activity

           2. Selects appropriate reading matter

           3. Satisfies interests and needs through reading

      B. Improves and refines reading interests. The learner

           1. Reads different kinds of material on a variety of topics

           2. Reads materials that reflect mature interests

           3. Achieves personal development through reading

      C. Refines literary judgment and taste. The learner

           1. Applies differential criteria for various literary forms

           2. Appreciates style and beauty of language

           3. Seeks for deeper symbolic messages

These three major kinds of reading cannot and should not be kept entirely separate. In a developmental lesson children must read material that is either recreational or functional in character. An enjoyable story may be used for the cultivation of particular reading skills, and developmental lessons should be planned to help pupils in their reading of content-subject material.

A sound reading program must have balance among the major kinds of reading. If the desire to read for fun is killed by an overemphasis on drills and exercises, one of the major aims of reading instruction is defeated and the result is the pathetic graduate who never opens a book after commencement. The relative balance changes grade by grade. For the beginner, nearly all reading activities are primarily developmental; by the upper elementary grades, functional reading is most important and developmental lessons take the least amount of time.

The general learning objectives stated above are anticipated general outcomes of a reading program. These general objectives may be subdivided and stated in varying degrees of specificity. Such specific objectives are commonly known as "behavioral" or "performance" objectives, the writing of which has been described in detail (e.g., Mager 1962, Gronlund 1970). Although there are variations in style, a behavioral objective usually states the condition under which a specified behavior will occur (external conditions), the behavior that is to occur as a result of planned instruction (terminal behavior), and the performance level that will be accepted (acceptable performance). Some writers do not suggest stating external conditions. A behavioral objective is the result that is to follow from instruction, not the instructional activity itself. That is, the behavioral objective should be stated in terms of learner behavior (the anticipated product or outcome) rather than in terms of teacher behavior (the process of what the teacher does with the learner).

To illustrate, the general objective "Evaluates what is read" is a complex objective that calls for the use of critical thinking in reading. A number of more specific learning outcomes can be listed under this general objective:

1. Distinguishes between facts and opinions
2. Distinguishes between facts and inferences
3. Identifies cause–effect relations
4. Identifies errors in reasoning
5. Distinguishes between relevant and irrelevant arguments
6. Distinguishes between warranted and unwarranted generalizations
7. Formulates a valid conclusion from written material
8. Specifies assumptions needed to make conclusions true (Gronlund 1970, p. 14)

How a behavioral objective can be developed may be illustrated with outcome 1 above. Adding external conditions to it would result in the following: Given an editorial, the learner can underline statements of opinion. Then, adding a criterion for mastery, the objective would read: Given an editorial, the learner can underline at least 9 of the 10 statements of opinion without misidentifying any statements of fact. More specificity could be added; for example, the qualifier "written at the sixth reader level" might be added after "editorial."

It is easier to determine when cognitive objectives have been met than it is to evaluate affective objectives. Nevertheless, as Strickler (1977) has illustrated, the latter can be stated and assessed through observation and discussion.

The sequence in using behavioral objectives is (1) to state the objectives; (2) to select and use appropriate instructional procedures, content, and methods; (3) to test to determine if the criterion for mastery has been met; and (4) to reteach if necessary. By clearly stating what a learner should be able to do under given conditions when he or she has achieved the objective, the teacher can determine the extent to which a given specific skill or ability has been mastered.

Care must be exercised, lest reading instruction be fragmented into hundreds of discrete objectives whose mastery becomes the core of the reading program. Skills can be taught and learned in isolation, but ample opportunities must be provided for utilizing them in reading connected discourse.

III. SOME SPECIAL PROBLEMS AND ISSUES

Although each stage of reading instruction has distinct features, certain problems and issues are present at all levels and stages. A few of them are now discussed.

Oral Reading

Many years ago, instruction in reading was predominantly oral. When research showed that children taught in this way tended to be slow, laborious readers, silent reading became the vogue. In many schools the pendulum swung so far that oral reading was almost completely neglected above the first grade. This tendency in turn had its bad effects, among which was inaccurate word recognition.

The traditional oral reading lesson was one in which all the pupils had the book open at the same place and were expected to follow along as each one rose in turn and read two or three sentences. Such a procedure has limited utility as a rapid method of testing. Each oral reading lesson should have a specific goal and should be planned to contribute a definite value to the reading program.

It is now recognized that oral reading contributes to the total development of the child in many ways. Among them, the following are noteworthy: (1) Oral reading gives the teacher a quick and valid way to evaluate progress in important reading skills, particularly those of word recognition and phrasing, and to discover specific instructional needs; (2) oral reading provides practice in oral communication for the reader and in listening skills for the audience; (3) oral reading aids in the development of effective speech patterns; (4) oral reading provides a vehicle for dramatization and effective portrayal of stories in situations where memorization would not be practical; and (5) oral reading provides a medium in which the teacher, by wise guidance, can work to improve the social adjustment of children, particularly those who are shy and retiring (Shane 1955).

Oral reading lessons that seem worthwhile include the following (Taubenheim & Christensen 1978):

1. *Taking turns in small groups.* Oral reading, especially when one's peers are listening, often is a stressful and anxiety-producing situation for poor readers (Hoffman *et al.* 1982). Self-consciousness on the part of the poor reader is less likely when other members of the group are not markedly better readers than he is. The rest of the group should not be required to follow along in their texts; rather, they should provide an audience.

2. *Individual reading to the teacher.* Oral reading gives the teacher an opportunity to observe and note pupils' errors and reading habits that need correction. Having the child read a fairly long, representative selection out loud is an important phase of checking up on the pupil's reading abilities.

3. *Finding and reading answers to questions.* After the silent reading of a selection, some kind of check-up on comprehension has become a nearly universal practice. One procedure that brings in oral reading in a natural and significant way is to ask the children to locate in the selection the answers to specific questions. The answers are then read aloud. This provides purposeful review in silent reading and desirable practice in oral reading and can serve as a stimulus for interesting discussions about the correctness of the answers.

4. *Audience reading.* Each pupil is given a chance to choose and carefully prepare a selection to read to the class, preferably from material that is *not* familiar to the other pupils. After considerable practice and, if possible, a preliminary rehearsal with the teacher, the child reads the selection to classmates. Since the material is new to them and well presented, the interest of the class is usually well sustained, and the pupil experiences satisfaction from a job well

done. Many good teachers of reading make a period of audience reading a weekly event.

5. *Choral reading.* Certain definite values can be derived from occasional periods in which the class reads aloud in unison. The better readers carry along the poorer ones, who may gain a better appreciation of pronunciation, phrasing, rhythm, and interpretation. This kind of oral reading is especially suitable for poetry and other strongly rhythmical material.

6. *Reading parts in radio or TV scripts or plays.* No oral reading is more interesting to children or helps them more to read with natural expression than reading a part in a play. When children are allowed to read their parts from the script, plays can be prepared and presented in a fraction of the time required for memorizing. See Manna (1984) for suggestions on using plays.

7. *Reading with varied intonation patterns.* To get across the idea of how meaning varies with intonation, and how the same sequence of words can convey quite different meanings, it is desirable occasionally to have children read a sentence, placing stress on different words and changing the intonation pattern and then explaining what the specific meaning of each rendition is. For example, *What* am I doing? What *am* I doing? What am *I* doing? What am I *doing*?

The Eye–Voice Span

The eye–voice span (EVS) is the amount by which the reader's eyes are ahead of his voice. A rough measure of a person's EVS is obtained by suddenly covering the material while the person is reading orally; the EVS is the number of words that the reader can say after the text has been covered. The eye–voice span, which is normally the amount the person can read in 1 second (Geyer 1968), shows that material already perceived is stored in short-term memory until the vocal response is made. The eye–voice span is longer for sentences than for unrelated words, and with meaningful material the span tends to stop at a phrase boundary rather than within a phrase, showing that it is controlled somewhat by the grasp of meaning (Levin & Kaplan 1970). A large eye–voice span tends to accompany superior reading; a small span often goes with slow, choppy, word-by-word reading. This is in harmony with evidence that good readers tend to respond to cues at the intersentence, sentence, phrase, and word levels; poor readers tend to respond mainly to part-word and word cues (Clay & Imlach 1971).

The length of the eye–voice span also has been studied in terms of the number of words. For example, Levin and Turner (1966) found the average eye–voice span was approximately 3.0 words for second graders and 4.5 words for fourth graders. The eye–voice span tends to increase with age (Buswell 1922, Levin & Cohn 1968) and is influenced by the meaningfulness of the material (Lawson 1961, Morton 1964) and by linguistic constraints (Wanat & Levin 1970, Fusaro 1974). Thoughtful reviews of the research on eye–voice span have been given by Gibson and Levin (1975) and Levin and Addis (1979).

Silent Reading

Changes have also taken place in the teaching of silent reading. One change is the tendency to think in terms of specific kinds of reading and to plan lessons designed to improve a particular reading skill. One lesson is designed to give practice in finding the central idea of a selection, another to improve ability at locating answers to specific questions, a third to develop ability to remember the sequence of events, and so on. Each lesson should have a definite aim or aims. Reading for appreciation and pleasure is clearly distinguished from work reading or study. Dissection of plot and characters is avoided in pleasure reading because of its tendency to spoil enjoyment, whereas habits of careful and accurate reading are built up with carefully planned exercises in the reading of informational material.

Another trend in silent reading has been toward increasing the amount and broadening the scope of the reading done in the schools. The use of basal readers is supplemented by wide reading in a variety of sources. Magazines, pamphlets, and newspapers are brought into the classroom and used as instructional materials. The "classics" have had to make room for a large amount of reading intimately related to contemporary life. Functional reading of many kinds absorbs a major part of the total time spent in school.

In *sustained silent reading* the teacher and each student select something to read, and then the student reads it without being interrupted for a definite time period. There are no reports, comprehension checks, or records kept. Suggestions for using this procedure may be found in Hunt (1971, 1984), Efta (1978, 1984), and Berglund and Johns (1983). The research evidence regarding the effect of sustained silent reading on reading achievement is mixed, but it does seem to foster interest in, and positive attitudes toward, reading (Sadowski 1980, Levine 1984).

Comprehension after Silent and Oral Reading and Listening

Whether one comprehends better in oral reading, silent reading, or listening seems to be related to how well one can read. In Grades 2, 3, and 4, below-average readers tend to comprehend best after listening, next best after oral reading, and worst after silent reading (Swalm 1972). Average readers may comprehend better in oral than in silent reading (Morris 1970) or do about equally well in both (Swalm 1972). E. Rowell (1976) found that, on the average, both third and fifth graders obtained higher comprehension scores when reading orally than in silent reading. Above fifth grade, one should not be surprised to find that poor readers do best in listening, below-average readers are helped to comprehend by oral reading, and good readers read with better comprehension and more rapidly in silent reading.

Word Identification

Efficient, fluent reading requires both an extensive sight vocabulary (words that are recognized immediately) and the ability to work out the pronunciation and meaning of unfamiliar words met while reading. The greater the emphasis on wide independent reading, the more urgent it is for children to be able to identify unknown words without help from the teacher. Skilled readers have a number of techniques from which they select the most appropriate to identify words that are not recognized at sight.

Modern word-identification programs teach four main strategies, the first three of which can be used in combination. First, children are taught to make intelligent use of the context in which the unknown word appears. Second, pupils learn to apply morphemic and structural analysis techniques—recognition of root words and affixes (*play-ing, re-play*), separation of a word into known parts (*play-thing*), and syllabication (*rab-bit*). Third, phonics is taught because knowledge of the sounds represented by letters and letter combinations is essential. Finally, the use of the dictionary is taught as a dependable aid in determining the pronunciation, meaning, and spelling of words.

Words are to be decoded when they are not recognized as wholes, and the decoding need be carried out only as far as necessary to recognize the word. Thus it would be inefficient to decode *schoolmaster* one phonic element at a time if the words *school* and *master* are in the child's sight vocabulary. At times, decoding only part of the unknown word (e.g., the first syllable) and the use of context clues is sufficient for recognition to occur. Structural and phonic clues should be used in combination with the context. Therefore word-identification instruction should not be concerned primarily with words presented in isolation but should emphasize use of the skills and strategies while reading meaningful material.

When a child has done very poorly with the word-identification skills taught in a developmental program, it is often desirable to use a different method of instruction in remediation. Thus the remedial teacher needs to understand and be able to teach a number of approaches and select the most effective one for a given child.

Reading in Content Areas

Some children whose reading is satisfactory in basal readers and in self-chosen library books run into difficulty in applying their reading skills in content areas such as science, mathematics, and social studies. This is sometimes caused by a misfit between book difficulty and reader competence. Many content textbooks are substantially more difficult than basal readers intended for the same grade level, and children for whom the basal reader is at their instructional level may run into frustration when trying to read a difficult text or reference book. Sometimes children attempt to read the content textbook in the same way that they read a story in a reader, resulting in superficial comprehension and poor retention.

Recognition of Individual Differences

There has been an increased awareness of the importance of individual differences as a factor in reading. Yet some teachers still seem to believe that if their teaching is good, it should bring all or nearly all their pupils up to a fairly uniform level of achievement. The schools are realizing more and more the falsity of this belief. When children enter school, they differ widely in their abilities and in their potentialities for future development. With efficient instruction these differences should increase rather than decrease as they progress through school. Even when the truly dull child is brought by highly efficient instruction up to the highest level that his capacity allows, he will still be far behind his bright classmates. Uniformity of achievement in a class is more apt to indicate neglect of the abler pupils than generally effective teaching.

Recognition of the significance of individual differences has brought about all sorts of attempts to adjust the school program to the varying abilities of the pupils. These have included plans for classifying pupils into instructional groups on the basis of general reading ability and plans that attempt to provide complete individualization of the reading program (see Chapter 5). Realization of the importance of meeting the needs of each pupil has brought remedial instruction into the foreground.

IV. EFFECTIVENESS IN TEACHING READING

Many attempts have been made to discover why teachers who ostensibly use the same methods and materials get different results. From the mid-1950s into the early 1960s, research on teacher effectiveness focused on instructional methods and materials, as well as on teacher characteristics. But no one best method or materials were identified, and effective teachers were found to possess the same characteristics as most well-adjusted people. During the late 1960s and early 1970s, research began to focus on process–product relationships[2] (how teacher behaviors influence student achievement). More recently, research has been concerned not only with teacher behaviors but also with student characteristics (Brophy & Evertson 1981), the interactions between teacher and student behaviors and attitudes (Natriello & Dornbush 1983), and the social system in which they occur (Rupley & Blair 1980; Duffy 1981, 1982).

In interpreting the teacher-effectiveness research, three points must be remembered. First, few, if any, specific teacher behaviors are appropriate in all teaching contexts. For example, different patterns of instruction generally appear to be more effective with different students. Teachers working with high-SES, high-ability pupils are most successful if pacing is rapid, students are given challenging tasks, high expectations are continually communicated, high standards are enforced, and inferior work is not accepted. Teachers who are more successful with low-SES, low-ability students are equally determined to get the most out of their students but usually do so by being warmer and more encouraging, and less business-like and demanding than teachers of high-SES, high-ability pupils. They take more time to motivate their pupils and to deal with their concerns. Effective teachers of low-SES, low-ability students praise more often, minimize criticism of poor work, pace instruction more slowly, and allow more time for practice and overlearning. More time is allowed to respond

[2] Soar (1978), Good (1979), and Duffy and Roehler (1982a, b) discussed the problems involved in analyzing and interpreting teacher-effectiveness studies.

to questions, hints are provided for unanswered questions, or questions are re-phrased (Brophy 1979b).

Second, although variables are discussed separately, they are often highly interrelated. Classrooms take on their characteristics as teachers and pupils alternately influence, and are influenced by, one another (Copeland 1980). Not only do effective teachers know a variety of procedures for teaching reading and possess a wide range of skills, but they also are able to orchestrate their knowledge and skills and adapt their behaviors in response to continually shifting needs (Bennett 1978).

Third, the findings of most of the research on teacher effectiveness are limited to basic skills instruction in Grades 1–5.

Allocated Instructional Time

From the late 1960s to the late 1970s, the average amount of time allocated to reading instruction in American primary classrooms doubled to almost 2 hours (Squire 1980). But the amount of allocated time varies greatly (Guthrie 1980). For example, one study found that second-grade teachers scheduled from 36 to 118 minutes daily (average = 99 minutes) for reading; fifth-grade teachers from approximately 60 to 135 minutes (average = 74 minutes).

Correlations between learning time and reading achievement have been demonstrated repeatedly (A. J. Harris & Serwer 1966; Guthrie, Martuza, & Seifort 1979). In fact, "time to learn" correlates higher than IQ with reading achievement (Gettinger & White 1979). Generally, the more time allocated for reading, the greater the reading achievement. Allotted time alone does not account for reading gains, however. Claims of significant gains by increasing reading instructional time by as little as 5 minutes daily probably are misleading. It is the quality of what occurs during that time, how much of that time is used well, that is important. Also, the amount of time scheduled for reading may reflect the teacher's attitude toward the importance of reading, which itself can have an effect on reading achievement. Increased time alone will do little to help children learn what far exceeds their level of ability. Moreover, instructional time must be spent on relevant tasks (Hiebert 1983).

Apparently, the time available for teaching is not used efficiently by many teachers. Leinhardt, Zigmond, and Cooley (1981), for instance, found that learning-disabled children spent more time daily waiting (21 minutes) and preparing for or wrapping up activities (34 minutes) than in receiving reading instruction (16 minutes). More time could be devoted to reading if teachers decreased the time that children spend waiting and making transitions from one activity to another, and in the time spent coping with disruptive behavior. Improved classroom management often helps to lessen unproductive use of time. Even though the sources of "lost time" may differ from class to class, making teachers aware of how time gets eroded may enable them to adjust their activities so that there is more time available for learning.

The time students spend learning is a consequence of multiple factors—the amount of time allocated to instruction, teacher competence, student aptitude, and the percentage of the allotted time that the students attend to a lesson (Karweit & Slavin 1981).

Academic Engaged Time

According to Rosenshine (1978b), *academic engaged time* (AET) is the time a student spends in academically relevant activities that are at an appropriate, moderate level of difficulty. In general, the higher the academic engaged time, the higher the achievement. When students have the same rate of AET, brighter students are likely to learn more than less capable students. Reading done out of school by middle- and upper-SES pupils probably adds significantly to their total AET; low-SES students are less likely to benefit in this way (Rosenshine & Berliner 1977).

Of the variables related to academic engaged time, two have yielded the highest and most consistent correlations with achievement: the amount of content covered and *time-on-task* (the time students are actually involved in the learning task). Content coverage depends on the amount of allotted time, instructional pacing, the materials employed, and student attention (Barr 1982a).

Time-on-task rates vary but are reportedly higher when the teacher is working with the whole class or with large groups than when there is individual instruction or instruction in very small groups (Brophy 1979a). This finding may reflect teachers' inability to monitor the students with whom they were not working directly or that the seatwork was inappropriate. It does not indicate that all instruction should be whole-class or large-group instruction or that there is no need to individualize instruction. At times it may be appropriate to make initial presentations to the whole class or large groups, especially when follow-up activities are individualized. But organizing the class into reading groups can be effective primarily because it allows for the use of appropriate materials and for an appropriate pace of instruction for each group (Karweit 1983). Somewhat similarly, care should be taken not to misinterpret the finding that time-on-task and reading achievement are higher when children use material that is "easy" for them. Although success rate is an important factor in reading achievement, students should not spend all their reading time on materials with which they are highly successful. A balance is needed between high success and the use of challenging materials (Berliner 1981).

On-task behaviors increase in well-managed classes in which the teacher interacts with students, provides material, and paces instruction that promotes student success, and provides feedback as to their success. Teacher enthusiasm also can influence on-task behavior (Bettencourt *et al.* 1983). If students are already persevering to the extent needed for learning, incentives may increase time-on-task but not the degree or rate of learning (Millman *et al.* 1983).

The fact that pupils learn when they are on-task and do not learn when their attention is elsewhere does not tell us how to get them to pay attention. To some extent, chronic inattention may be constitutional or psychological. But this does not explain why whole groups or classes attend most of the time during reading lessons and others do not. Attending behavior may be a very desirable by-product of effective teaching; inattention may be a signal that teaching is ineffective.

Formal Versus Informal Programs

Formal educational programs are teacher centered; the teacher plans the instructional sequence and guides it step by step. Direct instruction (see below) is closely associated with formal programs. Informal programs tend to be learner centered and stress learner choices and inquiry, with the teacher functioning largely as a facilitator and resource person.

Although research has generally shown that reading gains tend to be greater in highly structured classes, the degree of structure should vary with the cognitive and social maturity of the students (Good 1979). Low-ability students and those low in self-confidence learn better under more structured conditions. High-ability and highly confident students learn better when given some choices (Greene 1980). There is marked variability in results within formal and informal programs, so it is necessary to look for specific factors that influence the effectiveness of reading teachers in both kinds of programs.

Direct Instruction

Direct instruction refers to teaching activities in which the instructional goals are made clear to the students, the time allocated for instruction is sufficient, the content covered is extensive, student performance is monitored, questions are at a low cognitive level and produce many correct responses, and feedback to students is immediate and academically oriented. The teacher controls the instructional goals, chooses appropriate material, and paces instruction (Rosenshine 1978b). Merlin and Rogers (1981) described a number of direct instruction strategies, and Roehler and Duffy (1982) stressed the need for matching direct instruction to desired outcomes. Direct instruction benefits primary-grade children who have not learned to read as well as their peers and older elementary school students from low-SES backgrounds (Guthrie, Martuza, & Seifort 1979). A meta-analysis by Peterson (1982) suggested that although direct instruction tended to produce higher academic achievement, students in less-structured classes were more creative and had better attitudes toward school. The size of the effects for all three variables was small. Based on their analysis of 54 studies, Lysakowski and Walberg (1982) concluded that the following factors had strong effects on learning: (1) *cues* (instruction as to what is to be learned and what the student is to do in the learning process); (2) *participation* (the extent to which students actually are engaged in the learning process); and (3) *corrective feedback* (applying corrective measures as soon as a problem becomes apparent).

Rosenshine and Berliner (1977) stated that direct teacher-centered instruction is usually more effective than student-centered programs because it provides more academic engaged time per hour of instruction. They pointed out, however, that the lower academic engaged time in informal classrooms can be compensated for by additional instructional time. Rosenshine (1978a) warned against the unthinking application of the findings on direct instruction when he wrote: "To many of us, some of the results seem grim and overbearing, and it may be possible, with due reflection, to devise instructional alternatives which are more appealing but equally effective. Furthermore, we do not know whether these direct instruction prinicples are sufficient to the tasks of emotional development, creativity, and enquiry skills."

Classroom Management

Good classroom management underlies all the other principles of effective teaching. It results in more academic engaged time and is thus related to student achievement. Studies suggest that classroom management skills correlate with student gains in learning not only because skilled managers maximize student time-on-task but also because good classroom managers tend to be good instructors, and vice versa. Both aspects of teaching involve similar elements of the ability to prepare and organize, and many elements of classroom management are essentially instructional tasks that require teachers to show pupils what to do (Brophy 1979b).

Effective classroom managers have rules and procedures integrated into a workable system that is taught early to the students (Emmer, Evertson, & Anderson 1980). They clearly establish themselves as classroom leaders. Good managers stress socialization into the classroom system during the first few weeks of school. Good managers manage time well, with smoother, shorter transitions. They give directions and instructions clearly, and once pupils have finished their work, they know what to do. Good managers work out systems for managing instruction that avoid problems. They closely and consistently monitor pupil behavior and work, and they hold students accountable. Effective managers seem to sense the needs of children and react quickly and positively to them. They do not treat inappropriate behavior differently from other teachers, but they stop it sooner. The consequences of inappropriate behavior are known by the students, and they are applied consistently, but with some degree of flexibility, by the teacher. Good managers are aware of individual differences and adjust instruction to them. Their instructional activities are of appropriate duration and pacing. Students expect teachers to manage their classrooms effectively, and when teachers do, children learn more easily (Brophy & Putnam 1979).

Further suggestions for effective classroom management may be found in Duke (1979), Lapp (1980), and Gardino (1981). Ideas for developing self-management skills in pupils are provided by Wang (1979).

Attention to Pupil Needs

Effective teachers are perceptive of individual and group needs, plan and conduct instruction that meets these needs, keep a close watch on pupil progress, and provide help promptly when difficulty arises. Such teacher behaviors exist not only in teacher-directed activities but also in independent activities. When pupils are assigned independent work, effective teachers actively supervise them, giving careful attention to those who need it. Ineffective teachers assign seatwork and leave the children pretty much on their own; anyone who needs help must seek it (Medley 1977). Teacher planning greatly influences academic outcomes (Stern & Shavelson 1983).

Difficulty of Material

Reading materials may be used under a teacher's direction or independently by pupils. Usually the materials in teacher-directed activities can be more difficult than those students use on their own. In either case, the material should be neither so difficult as to make learning or enjoyment impossible nor so easy that there is little to learn or to hold the children's interest. Some teachers do not seem to realize how few unknown words it takes to make a selection difficult for a child or how difficult comprehension is when the pupils lack important prior knowledge.

There is a relationship between the difficulty of the reading material assigned to children and their progress in reading. For example, Cooper (1952) found that primary-grade children who made fewer than 3 word-recognition errors in 100 words made the greatest progress in reading during the year. Those with 95 to 98 correct word recognition on samples taken from their basal readers tended to make smaller gains, and those whose word recognition fell below 95% made very small gains. Slightly lower word-recognition percentages were associated with the reading progress of intermediate-grade pupils.

Attending behavior is also influenced by the difficulty of the material. There is more off-task behavior when the material is too difficult or too easy for the learner.

Basal readers are not always at the levels of readability indicated by the publisher's grade-level designations. In fact, Britton and Lumpkin (1978) found that 70% of the stories in middle-grade basals were written above the publisher's grade-level designation for that text. The problem of choosing material of appropriate difficulty is complicated even further by the fact that the selections in a given basal reader can range considerably in difficulty (Bradley & Ames 1977). Thus a child for whom most of the selections in a book are appropriate may encounter some selections that are frustratingly difficult.

Pacing

Pacing refers to how much is introduced in a lesson and the speed at which children are moved through that lesson. It also has to do with the rate at which new learnings are introduced over time. As such, it influences content coverage. Adjusting the pace of instruction to the abilities of the students can influence reading achievement. Reading instruction should be paced in accordance with the child's ability to assimilate the material (Barr 1982a). More capable groups and individuals respond well to being challenged; therefore the pace of instruction should require them to work fairly continuously at a brisk pace. Slower-learning children respond better when a slower instructional pace is employed and there is more time for learning and review.

Borko, Shavelson, and Stern (1981) reported that high reading groups are paced 2 to 15 times faster than low groups. And, according to Shavelson and Borko (1979), teachers often adjust the pace at which the group moves to those who would fall between the 10th and 25th percentile in ability in that group.

Motivation

Increased motivation also contributes to more academic engaged time. Children are motivated to attend and learn when they achieve success, receive feedback regarding their responses and work, and are encouraged to involve themselves in the learning process. Effective teachers use praise and encouragement more than ineffective teachers do, and they avoid harsh criticism, sarcasm, or other expressions of strong disapproval (Medley 1977). If children are experiencing difficulty in learning and therefore are likely to be discouraged, praise is more meaningful and motivating. Praise needs to be used *well* rather than often. Brophy (1981) provided suggestions for the effective use of praise.

Feedback other than praise also may motivate children or keep them on-task. The teacher's verbal or nonverbal feedback provides information to the students about the effectiveness or quality of their responses, thereby allowing them to adjust and modify future responses. While some writers believe that feedback serves as a reinforcer, others hold that it simply confirms or denies the appropriateness of a response or behavior.

As students process written or spoken language they need to know if they are proceeding appropriately. Skilled readers and listeners are able to monitor their own comprehension efforts, but many less-skilled or novice readers have not developed self-monitoring strategies and require feedback from the teacher. This may involve explaining answers, discussing clues to be used in arriving at an appropriate response, and encouraging clarification of thought (Ribovich 1978). Pupils can be taught strategies for monitoring reading comprehension (Brown, Campione, & Day 1981, 1984).

Teacher Attitudes and Expectations

Since the publication of *Pygmalion in the Classroom* (Rosenthal & Jacobson 1968), there have been frequent claims that teachers' attitudes toward pupils influence teacher expectations and thus how they treat and instruct pupils, which in turn determines how well the pupils achieve. Numerous studies, however, have not supported Rosenthal and Jacobson's findings (Braun 1976). Although teacher bias may influence individual or small-group performance, the evidence that teacher expectations in general become self-fulfilling prophecies (teachers expect children to achieve at a certain level, treat them accordingly, and thus influence how well they achieve) is not compelling.

Research findings suggest that although teachers may prefer to teach good readers (Miller & Hering 1975), their observed behaviors do not indicate favoritism for the top reading groups (Weinstein 1976). In fact, teachers are more likely to make accommodations in assigning reading materials for less-skilled readers than for students reading above grade level (Rubin 1975), provide more attention to learning-disabled children (Chapman 1975), and provide more instructional time and individualized instruction for low-performing pupils (Kiesling 1977–1978, Brophy 1983). Low reading groups receive more instruction with the teacher at their side than do middle or high groups (Ysseldyke & Algozzine 1983).

Expectations based on rigid, inaccurate stereotypes (e.g., obese children are lazy) may distort a teacher's perceptions of children to the point of inducing a self-fulfilling prophecy. The teacher with low expectations may give the misperceived child fewer instructional opportunities, fewer opportunities to take part in discussions, less encouragement, and more criticism. Such treatment can adversely influence the child's motivation and behavior, thus "confirming" the teacher's expectation. Teachers with low opinions of the learning abilities of minority children are likely to find the slow learning rate expected; teachers who believe otherwise encourage them to learn and find that they can learn.

In general, however, teacher expectations do not have much effect (5–10% at most) on student achievement because (1) their expectations are generally accurate and based on the best available information; and (2) their expectations are open to corrective feedback (i.e., they correct inaccurate perceptions as more accurate information becomes available). Students also differ in their susceptibility to being conditioned by expectations (Brophy 1983).

Teacher expectations also can influence their own performance and effectiveness. Teachers who believe that instructing children is basic to their role, who fully expect to conduct such instruction, and who set about doing so are more successful than teachers who do not (Brophy 1979a). Teachers must believe in their ability to help students learn, and must exhibit that confidence to the pupils (Guzzetti & Marzano 1984).

Summary

Knowledgeable teachers are likely to be effective when they
1. Plan well
   a. Schedule enough instructional time to accomplish mastery of the reading program's objectives.
   b. Vary the degree of teacher-imposed structure with the cognitive and social maturity of the students.
   c. Pay close attention to pupil and group needs.
2. Manage well
   a. Provide classroom conditions that are conducive to concentration and sustained attention.
   b. Take steps to ensure high academic engaged time.
      (1) Reinforce students for paying attention during teacher-directed and independent activities.
      (2) Decrease waiting and transition time and time spent on maintaining order.
      (3) Consistently monitor learning activities.

3. Teach well
    a. Are alert to signs of pupil difficulties and provide help promptly when it is needed.
    b. Make it clear to students what they are to learn and how they will be expected to demonstrate that learning.
    c. Model and demonstrate learning behaviors.
    d. Provide instructional materials and utilize instructional procedures that allow students to succeed frequently.
    e. Pace the instruction to differences in the learning rates of groups and individuals.
4. Motivate well
    a. Show a warm interest in students and interact with them often.
    b. Use praise, criticism, and challenge judiciously and provide feedback to students regarding their efforts and the appropriateness of their responses.
    c. Are optimistic about the learning potentials of their pupils and communicate that attitude to them.
    d. Do not allow their perceptions of individual differences to influence their behavior so as to affect the morale and efforts of some pupils adversely (A. J. Harris 1979b, Wyne 1981).

5

Adapting Reading
Instruction to Individual
Differences

There are marked individual differences in reading ability within every school population. Such differences are not surprising in view of the fact that reading ability in particular and learning in general are influenced by a number of interrelated factors that vary among students—learning aptitude, the knowledge gained from prior experiences, motivation, persistence, sensory and perceptual abilities, and so on. Coping with these individual differences presents a challenge because no one as yet has devised a fully satisfactory solution to the problem (Artley 1981).

Most attempts to accommodate instruction to individual differences involve (1) administrative procedures that attempt to make it easier for the teacher to deal with individual needs; (2) classroom procedures that involve the unit of instruction (large group, small group, individual); and (3) instructional procedures that attempt to match learner characteristics with instructional treatments or to vary the pace at which learning occurs. The three are not mutually exclusive.

The effects of various classroom situations and instructional procedures on reading achievement are exceedingly complex and far from being fully understood. Variations in teacher and student abilities and in what is to be taught necessarily dictate differing strategies for optimal learning. Individual and group

Table 5.1   Grade-Equivalent Scores on the Gates–MacGinitie Reading Tests, Second Edition, Form 1 (total score, October norms), Corresponding to Selected Percentile Ranks

	GRADE-EQUIVALENT SCORES		
Percentile ranks	Level C (Grade 3)	Level D (grade 5)	Level E (Grade 7)
99	7.6	11.3	12.9+
90	5.4	8.2	11.2
80	4.4	7.2	9.8
70	3.8	6.3	8.7
60	3.5	5.6	7.6
50	3.1	5.1	7.1
40	2.6	4.5	6.4
30	2.4	4.0	5.7
20	2.1	3.5	4.9
10	1.7	2.6	3.9
1	a	b	c

Source: Adapted from Teachers' Manuals for Levels C, D, and E, *Gates–MacGinitie Reading Tests, Second Edition*, © 1978 and is reproduced with the permission of The Riverside Publishing Company, 8420 Bryn Mawr Avenue, Chicago, IL 60631.
[a] Lowest possible score = 1.6 (percentile rank = 7).
[b] Lowest possible score = 2.3 (percentile rank = 4).
[c] Lowest possible score = 3.2 (percentile rank = 4).

nneds can be accommodated only as the result of careful planning, monitoring, and revising of instruction and curriculum by school personnel as they consider the goals of their reading program, the strengths and needs of their students, and the specific contexts in which instruction occurs (Good & Stipek 1983).

This chapter opens with establishing the fact that children vary widely in reading ability. Next, we present the goals of any plan for accommodating the wide range in reading ability. We follow this with sections on administrative, classroom, and instructional procedures that attempt to help the teacher cope with the range of needs. Then we offer a plan for combining whole-class, group, and individual instruction.

I. INDIVIDUAL DIFFERENCES IN READING ABILITY

Table 5.1 shows the range of grade-equivalent scores on a standardized reading achievement test. In October of fith grade, the scores can range from 2.3 to 12.5, a span of 10 years. Even if only the middle 80% are considered, the range is still over 5 years. The spread of scores is similar for seventh grade; for third grade, it is narrower but still large. The true range may be even larger than shown, since those who attain the lowest possible scores may be totally unable to read.

The actual median and range of reading comprehension scores obtained by first through fifth graders on a standardized reading achievement test are shown in Table 5.2. Also indicated are the average level of reading text and

Table 5.2   Range of Reading Abilities and Assigned Reading Texts

Grade	N	Percentage reading below grade level	Percentage reading above midpoint of next higher grade level	PARAGRAPH MEANING GRADE-EQUIVALENT SCORE		ASSIGNED TEXT	
				Median	Range	Median	Range
1	1,135	3.7	16.3	1.8	1.0–4.0+	P	PP–3²
2	894	18.1	29.4	2.8	1.0–4.0+	2²	PP–5
3	607	24.1	28.3	3.7	1.0–7.7+	3²	PP–6
4	342	25.1	37.1	4.8	1.8–9.5+	4	PP–JH
5	147	23.8	40.1	6.0	1.8–9.5+	5	1–JH

Source: Rosalyn Rubin, Reading ability and assigned materials: accommodations for the slow but not the accelerated, *Elementary School Journal*, March 1975.

Abbreviations: PP = pre-primer, P = primer, 1 = first reader, 2² = high second reader, 3² = high third reader, 4, 5, 6 = fourth reader, etc., JH = junior high school.

range of texts assigned to the children. Both sets of data show a wide range of reading ability at a given grade.

These illustrations only indicate the range of the general level of reading achievement attained by children in a given grade level. Children reading at a given reader level do not all have the same strengths and weaknesses, nor do they learn best in the same ways. Such differences make it all the more difficult to optimize learning.

II. GOALS OF ANY PLAN TO ACCOMMODATE INDIVIDUAL DIFFERENCES

Before discussing various attempts to accommodate the wide individual differences in reading ability, it is desirable to consider the objectives for any plan that tries to do so. Such goals fall into four categories.

First is the objective of providing for the maximum growth of each pupil in three general reading areas. A plan concerned only with developmental reading is too limited; recreational and functional reading must also be given careful consideration.

Second, a sound plan must consider the personal and social adjustment of all the students. Procedures that may lead to social ostracism, poor self-concepts, or poor attitudes toward school should be avoided. The plan should be acceptable to administrators, teachers, pupils, and parents. It should not only help children to become better readers but also to enjoy reading, and to feel happy and secure.

Third, the plan should be one that can be carried out by teachers. Some plans need exceptionally able and creative teachers. Exhorting average teachers to adopt such a plan may discourage them from trying anything new; they may feel unable to meet the requirements. Realistic plans must be usable by most teachers and at the same time allow freedom for excellent teachers.

Finally, a good plan should fit the school and its pupils. Some good plans work well only in schools with hundreds of pupils. Others require a variety of materials beyond what the school can afford. Each school has to appraise its own situation and work out solutions to fit its needs.

III. ADMINISTRATIVE PROCEDURES

Various administrative procedures have been proposed in order to accommodate individual differences. These include promotional policies, school-age entry, attempts to limit the number of children or range of abilities with which a teacher has to cope, and the ways in which schools are organized and instruction is implemented. As one reads about the various administrative plans that have been tried, the striking fact is that all of them seem to have produced favorable results in the local situations in which they were developed. Probably the enthusiasm and ability of the people who operate the plan and the appeal of novelty give any sensible innovation a temporary advantage over what was done before. In this, as in many other important questions about reading instruction, research has produced no final answers.

Retention and Acceleration

Acceleration (skipping a grade) has never been a widespread practice in the United States, but grade retention was fairly common in the elementary school, particularly in first grade, in the early part of this century. By 1950 many school systems were promoting children regardless of achievement because research suggested that nonpromotion neither improved achievement nor reduced the range of individual differences; and nonpromoted children were more likely to be discipline problems, to have social difficulties, and to drop out of school (Anderson & Ritsher 1969). More recent research has resulted in similar findings (Bocks 1977), except for compensatory education where retention in the elementary school (but not in junior high) may have beneficial effects (McAfee 1981). Neither general plans of retention nor "100% promotion" has been particularly successful (Jackson 1975). Findings do suggest, however, that retaining low-achieving students and using the holdover time to develop needed skills may increase their chances of later academic success (Meyer 1983). Only fairly recently have there been attempts (Sandoval & Hughes 1981) to determine the factors involved in successful and unsuccessful retentions.

Each case should be decided individually by determining whether retention, promotion, or acceleration would be in the best interest of the child. Children should be placed where they are most likely to make the best total adjustment, socially and educationally. This is usually, but not always, with their own age group.

Postponing Reading for All Children

In 1898 John Dewey, one of the earliest proponents of the idea that reading is taught when children are too young, stated that "present physiological knowledge points to the age of about eight years as early enough for anything more than an incidental attention to visual and written language-forms" (quoted in Huey 1908, p. 306). Considering the difficulty of phonic methods popular at that time and the high rate of failure then prevalent, his proposal does not sound unreasonable; but methods of instruction have changed. In Sweden, beginning reading instruction at age 7 has not prevented the occurrence of reading disabilities (Malmquist 1958, 1969). Postponing reading for all children does not abolish or even lessen individual differences; it simply delays the time at which adjustment to varied learning rates will have to be made.

Homogeneous Classes

Homogeneous classes narrow the range of ability and achievement in a classroom. Among the arguments presented for homogeneous classes are that smaller individual differences result in more effective teaching and learning, the most capable students can move ahead rapidly, and the least capable are not embarrassed or stigmatized by their inability to compete. Critics of the plan argue that the less able or lower-achieving students are deprived of the stimulation provided by more able or higher-achieving pupils; homogeneous classes adversely affect pupils' perception of themselves and school, and teachers' perceptions and, thus, treatment of them; homogeneous grouping is elitist, and amounts to *de facto* segregation, since low-SES and minority groups are overrepresented in the low classes or tracks.

Gross comparisons between homogeneous and heterogeneous classes reveal only slight mean differences in achievement. There is some evidence, however, that high-ability students achieve better when grouped with others of comparable ability than when they work alone or with lower-ability students. Average-ability students tend to do better in relatively homogeneous classes than when placed with both high and low achievers. Low-ability pupils benefit more from being in classes with higher-ability students than from being in homogeneous classes (Good & Stipek 1983). The effects on achievement are not particularly strong or consistent, however (Leinhardt & Pallay 1982).

Homogeneous classes are much more prevalent in junior and senior high schools than in elementary schools. When reading ability is one of the primary selection factors, the lowest classes usually contain considerably more behavior problems and academic failures than higher-ability classes. Often slow learners, average-aptitude students with some reading problems, and bright adolescents with serious reading problems are placed in the same classroom. Such classes are far from being homogeneous, and the teacher may be unaware of the different reasons for their low reading achievement.

Evertson, Stanford and Emmer (1981) found that junior high school teachers coped with wide ranges of reading ability by (1) providing special attention and assistance in class to low-ability students; (2) limited use of in-class grouping, differentiation of material or assignments, and peer tutoring; and (3) providing frequent academic feedback and maintaining high levels of student accountability.

Homogeneous classes may have failed to solve the problem of individual differences in rate of learning because they did not improve the teachability of groups (Good & Stipek 1983). A group based on one characteristic will probably vary on other variables that influence learning, so true homogeneity is impossible. Extremely heterogeneous classes place extraordinary demands on teachers' time, attention, and skill, but good classroom managers are able to overcome most of the problems and meet individual needs (Evertson, Stanford, & Emmer 1981).

Cross-Grade and Cross-Class Grouping for Reading

Plans in which children are grouped homogeneously only for reading instruction have been in operation for over 40 years. On the basis of test results and teacher judgment the pupils are divided into reading classes with a restricted range of reading ability, all of which are scheduled for reading at the same time. When the bell rings, the children go to their reading teachers; when the reading period is over, they return to their homerooms. Plans of this sort are often referred to as *Joplin Plans.*

In a small school with one class per grade, such a plan would require cross-grade grouping with, for example, the reading scores for all pupils in Grades 4, 5, and 6 placed in a single rank order. The sixth-grade teacher could have the upper range for reading, the fifth-grade teacher the middle range, and the fourth-grade teacher the lowest range (which might be a little smaller in number than the other two). In a large school with several classes at each grade, it is possible to have cross-class grouping for reading within each grade.

In a plan of this sort, the range of reading scores is reduced from about 6 years to 2 or 3 years. It is still far from real homogeneity; not only is there still a 2-year-or-more span of reading levels but also individual pupils with similar scores may have different needs.

Based on a review of the literature, Cushenbery (1967) concluded that the advantages of the Joplin Plan appeared to outweigh its limitations, particularly when procedures were introduced in a careful, systematic manner. On the other hand, two reviewers concluded that once the newness of the plan wears off, the improved reading found during the first year or two tends to disappear (Newport 1967, W. Miller 1971).

In recent years declining school enrollments and budget problems have led some schools to set up multigrade or multiage classes. The limited research that has compared such classes with more typical grade or age arrangements in self-contained classrooms indicates that there is no significant difference in reading achievement (Lincoln 1982) or self-concept (Way 1981).

Split-Half Classes

Some schools have half the class begin and end school an hour or so earlier than their classmates. Reading is taught to one half in the morning hour and to the other half in the afternoon, thus reducing the number of children to whom the teacher must teach reading at a given time. In Denmark favorable results have been obtained with this plan (Lundahl 1976).

Theoretically, under this program teachers should individualize instruction to a greater extent than formerly because they have to deal with fewer children. But, as in any situation, what the teacher does with the time is important. If the reading instruction is the same as when many more children are in the class, the purpose for reducing class size for a given time period is defeated.

Departmentalization

Departmentalization, in which a teacher instructs only one subject or curricular area, is almost universal above the sixth grade and occurs in some middle grades. Among its claimed advantages are these: (1) Having a reading class assures that reading is taught, something that might not normally be part of the curriculum; and (2) reading teachers should be highly proficient because they are not responsible for other subjects. Lamme (1976b) found that teachers could exert more influence on children's reading habits (e.g., amount read, use of book recommendations) in a self-contained class than in a departmentalized structure.

Team Teaching

In team teaching two or more teachers, working together, are responsible for all or most of the instruction provided for the same students (a greater number of students than would be assigned to one teacher). Among the advantages claimed for team teaching over the traditional classroom are more extensive diagnosis, flexible grouping, and provisions for independent study. Although few adequately controlled evaluations have been made, the findings suggest the following directional trends regarding reading achievement and student adjustment: (1) Reading achievement in traditional classrooms was usually significantly higher; and (2) the students' personal–social adjustment was similar under both team teaching and traditional teaching conditions (Townsend 1976).

The Nongraded School

The ideas that children should be able to move ahead in school at their individual rates of learning and that yearly grades are too coarse a basis for pupil classification resulted in nongraded plans of organization, usually restricted to the primary years (Goodlad & Anderson 1959). The primary reading curriculum is divided into 8 to 12 instructional levels. Usually the child's assignment to a level is based mainly on informal reading tests and teacher judgment, tempered by considerations of age, social maturity, and progress in other curricular areas. Each teacher usually has no more than three adjacent levels in a self-contained classroom. A child may move to the next higher level at any time during the year, whenever he or she completes the program for the present level. There is continuous progress in that no child is ever required to repeat a level, although children move through the levels at different speeds. Thus, most children complete the primary program in 3 years; some take 4 years; a few may complete it in 2 years.

Because children who are at the same instructional level may have different patterns of reading skills and needs, a considerable amount of individualization is necessary. Careful diagnosis and planning for individuals are important in any plan for reading instruction; the need seems to be more clearly recognized and more vital for success in a nongraded plan than in a conventional school.

Early research failed to demonstrate improved reading achievement in nongraded schools compared to conventional schools (Di Lorenzo & Salter 1965, McLoughlin 1967). Later studies, however, indicated that, in general, nongraded groups achieved as well as, and often better than, graded groups (Martin & Pavan 1976).

Open Schools and Classrooms[1]

Open or informal schools have the common element of replacing preplanned curriculum sequences with child-centered and, to a large extent, child-initiated learning activities. The ideal classroom is seen as an active place where children choose activities and engage in them individually or in small, temporary groups. The teacher's role is one of helper and resource person rather than director of learning (Downing 1975). Much of the American interest in open schools was generated by a desire to emulate the British informal infant and junior schools.

Usually classes are nongraded and often include children with an age range of 2 or 3 years. Team teaching and open work areas are other features commonly included. Reading instruction in open schools tends to be a combination of language experience and individualized reading approaches, with relatively little systematic attention to skills development (Watters 1971, Moss 1972). In some schools, however, diagnosis and individually prescribed instruction are stressed (Klausmeier, Sorenson, & Quilling 1971), or teachers have reading groups and use a basal series or programmed readers (Wiener 1974, Rogers 1976).

The overall findings regarding the effect of open classrooms on academic achievement and affective outcomes are mixed. Horwitz (1979) concluded that there was enough evidence to defend the concept as a viable alternative when teachers and parents were interested in its use. A meta-analysis, however, led Peterson (1982) to conclude that although open education had positive effects on affective factors, traditional teacher-directed programs had a slight advantage in reading achievement.

IV. CLASSROOM PROCEDURES

A reading teacher must expect that no one way of organizing the class will serve all purposes equally well. A well-rounded reading program includes different kinds of class organization, each used in reading activities for which it is best suited. The question is not one of choosing between individualization and grouping but one of how to combine whole-class, individualized, and group activities into a harmonious whole. When well implemented and suited to the learning

[1] Also see the discussion of formal versus informal programs on p. 97.

situation, individual, small-group, and large-group instruction can have a positive effect on learning; once again, the teacher is the key. Even for whole-class instruction, there are systematic differences between relatively effective and ineffective teachers (Good & Stipek 1983).

Before discussing the various kinds of classroom activities, it is important to clarify a few points. Individualizing instruction means that the activity is tailored to optimize the learning of an individual; the most appropriate material and methodology are employed, instruction is paced to maximize the likelihood of learning, only what the child needs to learn is introduced, and so on. Individualization of instruction is not an either/or proposition; most often, it is a matter of degree. Theoretically, the more instruction is individualized, the more likely it is that learning will be effective and efficient. Individualization is not an exclusive concomitant of any one instructional approach or system of classroom organization.

Instruction can be individualized for a child working alone or in any size group. It is the appropriateness of the instruction and not the number of children working on an activity or the fact that each child is doing something different during the reading period that determines if instruction is individualized. The degree to which individualization occurs still rests with the skill of the teacher.

A fundamental necessity for effective individualization is a teacher or specialist who can diagnose pupil needs, abilities, and interests and can plan appropriate learning activities based on her findings. Unfortunately, the level of diagnostic proficiency among classroom teachers, and even reading specialists, leaves much to be desired.

Whole-Class Reading Activities

Whole-class direct instruction is often maligned, but it survives because it has advantages. It is easier to plan and manage, and it provides more modeling of correct thinking and responses for the less able students (Brophy 1979a).

Several kinds of reading activities can profitably be carried on with the entire class. They include audience situations, choral reading, common new learnings, current events reading, and "open-book" textbook sessions. Each has a legitimate place in the total reading program. The first two activities can be used in either developmental or recreational reading, the third in any of the three strands of a total reading program, and the last two in functional reading.

Audience Situations

An oral reading selection that has been prepared and rehearsed can be presented to the class. Materials can include poems, jokes, selections from stories and books, radio or TV scripts, or short plays. The presentation may be made by an individual or by a small group. Sessions in which children give oral book reports or present reports based on individual or committee reading also can provide whole-class audience situations. Two important requirements are (1) advance preparation so that the performance is reasonably good; and (2) the class does not read along silently, but is a real audience.

Choral Reading

The occasional use of choral reading not only is helpful for the appreciation of poetry and rhythm but also assists in developing a spirit of belongingness and group cohesion in the class.

Common New Learnings

On many occasions a new reading or study skill can be introduced to the whole class, even though not all will learn it with equal rapidity. Alphabetizing, the use of such aids as the table of contents, index, dictionary, and encyclopedia, and new phonic principles and word meanings are among the reading skills that can be introduced in this way.

Current Events

School newspapers provide opportunities for current events periods in which all can participate. Weekly graded editions make it possible for all to do the same kind of reading together, although some may be reading an advanced edition and others an edition intended for lower grades. In the primary grades, experience stories can be used for the same purpose.

Textbook Reading

When a textbook is the focus of a particular curriculum area, it may be necessary to have open-book sessions in which the textbook is used as a basal reader. Often the unavailability of simpler textbooks makes it necessary to use one book with the entire class. The less able readers get the content mainly by listening and are called on only for comparatively easy passages or questions. Better ways to take care of the needs of pupils for whom the content textbook is frustratingly difficult are discussed on pages 531–532.

Individualized Reading Activities

Even though whole-class, group, and individualized activities can be employed in achieving similar general objectives of the three aspects of a total reading program, individualized reading activities differ from the other two types in the number of pupils working on a particular activity. An entire class, a group, or an individual may be involved in an individualized reading activity. Individualized procedures have been developed for developmental, recreational, and functional reading, and for skills practice.

Developmental Reading

There are complete or partial developmental reading programs that attempt to individualize instruction to varying degrees. Many of these were discussed in Chapter 3.

Individualized Developmental Reading (IDR) within a Group

A teacher who generally organizes reading instruction on a group basis might consider the use of IDR with one group rather than with the entire class. For example, it might be impossible to make group lessons profitable for a low group of six children, none of whom is reading at the same reader level. An IDR approach should be beneficial for these six. In a 35-minute period, the teacher could spend 3 to 5 minutes with each child, while the others worked on their own, asking for help as needed. The remaining time could be used for group discussions, motivation, skill development for several children, and the like. Each child could progress at his or her own rate. Whenever the range of individual reading abilities in a group is so large that it is impossible to choose a reading text that is reasonably satisfactory for all group members (and transferring the extremes to another group would not solve the problem), the possible advantages of using IDR with that group should be given serious consideration.

Individualized Progress in Basal Readers

Individualized progress through sequential levels of a basal program is common in nongraded schools. Several programs in which individualized use of a basal reader was combined with other reading activities were briefly described by Sucher (1969).

Bruton (1972) demonstrated how a modified systems approach could be applied to basal readers. Since then, some publishers have incorporated similar ideas into their basal series.

Recreational Reading

Periods for recreational reading, in which children are free to read what they please (within reason), are called free-reading, or independent reading, periods. At such times the teacher can circulate among the students, spending 2 minutes with one child and 5 minutes with another. These individual contacts can be spent in discussing a book already finished, considering with the child what he or she might like to read next, finding out more about the child's interests or problems, providing help on a specific difficulty, and so on.

Since in a free-reading program pupils read what they like, there are great possibilities for developing and broadening a pupil's interest in reading. Extensive reading will bring about enrichment of vocabulary and improvement in reading fluency, rate, and comprehension. It is necessary, of course, to have books of suitable difficulty available on a wide variety of subjects. Arrangements can often be made to borrow an appropriate collection of books from the school library or from a public library; librarians are ordinarily glad to cooperate with teachers. A given amount of money goes farther if much of it is spent on paperbacks.

Functional Reading

Modern teaching procedures create many occasions for a child to read alone to find needed information. For capable readers, this highly motivating reading provides multiple opportunities for intellectual enrichment and personal development. Less able readers who find the on-grade content-subject text frustratingly difficult can be directed to material more in keeping with their reading ability.

Individualized Skills Practice

There can be a place in the schedule for periods in which each child works on the particular reading skills in need of improvement. For this to be effective, one must have ways of determining individual needs; making individual assignments; and providing practice materials set up with clear, self-administering directions and scoring keys. Computer-assisted instruction offers great promise in this area.

Group Reading Activities

The range of individual differences in reading proficiency is wide at every age level and increases as children get older. One way of dealing with these differences is to group for reading instruction. Apparently, teachers prefer group over individualized activities because the major part of reading instruction in American elementary schools is carried out in groups (Hiebert 1983), with from 3 to 5 groups per classroom and usually with from 6 to 10 pupils in a group (Cazden 1982).

Group instruction can be an efficient use of time. Usually, the group receives the same instruction initially, with all the group members using the same material. However, a skill or concept may be presented in more than one way in the lesson in order to reach as many children as possible. Groups may be set up according to reading level, specific needs, or interests; the activity may be carried out with a teacher or other adult, with a pupil leader or tutor, may be self-directed, or may involve supervised seatwork. Because children and teachers differ considerably, no one plan for grouping fits every situation; various group activities may be used concurrently. Whatever the grouping plans, it should be remembered that grouping for reading instruction is a means for facilitating learning; it is not an end in itself.

Kinds of Reading Groups

There are basically four kinds of reading groups, with the first being by far the most common.

General Level of Reading Ability. When the range of reading ability is wide, it is usually advisable to set up reading groups on the basis of general level of reading ability. Ability-level groups are the primary instructional units, but other kinds of reading groups should be used concurrently. Use of a variety of groups also helps lessen the stigma of being in the low group. At times, students may be temporary members of more than one ability-level group. For instance, to determine whether a pupil should be placed in a higher group, the teacher may have the child participate with both groups. Or one or more children who need to acquire a skill may temporarily join the group being taught that skill. Another alternative is *open grouping* in which students are allowed to meet with any group of their choosing in addition to their own (Wilson & Ribovich 1973).

When there is some doubt about the best group placement for a pupil, it is advisable to place the child in the lower of the two groups being considered. This usually ensures successful participation, and it is psychologically more sound to move a child from a lower to a higher group than to "demote" him.

Special Needs. Grouping mainly by levels of reading ability can profitably be supplemented by special-needs groups. Successful special-needs grouping requires a teacher who can accurately assess pupils' needs and who continuously monitors pupil progress. Children who are weak in a particular skill or strategy are grouped together. Thus a second grade could have one group working on specific decoding skills, another group developing more fluent oral reading, and still another selecting and recalling main ideas. In sixth grade, special groups might be formed for accurate but slow readers; for rapid, inaccurate readers; for pupils who need to learn how to monitor their understanding of what is being read; and for pupils who have difficulty following printed directions. Any special-needs group might contain one or more good readers, as well as several less capable readers. As the purpose for a particular skills group is accomplished children can be released from it, or the group can be disbanded and a new group set up to focus on another skill area.

Temporary special-needs groups are also used regularly in some Individualized Development Reading programs. Competently employed, they can counteract to a considerable extent the weakness in skill development that is sometimes characteristic of that approach.

Interests.   Some children may have a hobby or interest in common, such as raising tropical fish, collecting stamps, computers, or reading mysteries or the works of a particular author. Such a group can be encouraged to meet, discover common questions, find reading material related to their special interest, read it, exchange information, and report to the class. Several interest groups may be set up in a class, with membership entirely voluntary. Such groups would not have to meet often; once a week or even once in 2 weeks might be sufficient. Interest groups can be tied in with recreational or functional reading.

Committees.   Many projects, units, or activities are organized on a committee basis. Each committee usually takes responsibility for one part of the total project. Questions to be answered are decided on within the committee, and each member has allotted responsibilities. Committees are usually set up by the teacher so that each contains a cross-section of abilities.

When reading is to be done to find answers to questions, a project committee consults as wide a variety of sources as it can. Better readers tackle the more difficult references; less capable readers use sources that they can understand. Those whose reading is very limited can supply information learned from illustrations. Each committee member contributes to the final report.

Practical Issues

A number of practical concerns must be considered in using group activities. Most of these are discussed in this section.

Class Size

Class size is almost always an administrative decision over which teachers have little or no control. Some research indicates that class size does not influence student performance (Bozzomo 1978), but meta-analyses have indicated that compared to larger classes, smaller classes lead to higher pupil achievement, more favorable teacher effects (e.g., morale, attitude toward students), greater attempts to individualize instruction, a better classroom climate, and more favorable student effects (e.g., self-concept, participation) (Smith & Glass 1980, Glass *et al.* 1982).

All else being equal (and it rarely is), the number of pupils the teacher must instruct should influence the quality of teaching and student participation, and thereby influence achievement. However, an often overlooked variable in class-size research is the quality of teaching. Small class size will have little effect unless the teacher takes advantage of the situation.

Number of Groups

There is nothing magical about having three general reading-level groups. This number is frequently employed, however, with the top group either reading more difficult material or proceeding through the material at a faster pace than the other two groups. The middle group usually works on material of inter-mediate difficulty, and the low group uses the easiest material.

It should be remembered that the labels *high, average*, and *low* are relative terms. The low group in a class that has a very high overall level of reading achievement may be reading at the same level as the high group in the same grade in a school where the reading level is low. Yet the students in each school may be perceived by themselves, their peers, and teachers as low-ability readers (Hiebert 1983).

When there is an extremely wide range of reading ability, three groups may not be sufficient. In such cases, well-organized teachers may have as many as five or six groups, administrative procedures may be applied to lessen the range with which the teacher must deal, teacher aides may be employed, or indivi-dualized developmental reading may be employed for one or more groups.

At times, two groups may be appropriate, especially if the grouping is com-bined with some individualized reading. The upper group uses the on-grade reading text; the lower group, a below-grade-level text. If one or two children in the lower group cannot cope with the text, they will need individual instruc-tion. The best readers finish assignments quickly and use the remaining time for independent reading, or they may help one of the poorest readers. The two-group plan is appropriate for classes in which there is a limited range of reading ability or for teachers inexperienced with group management or unskilled at it.

As for groups other than general-ability groups, the number depends not only on the teacher's management skills but also on the needs and interests of the pupils. Such groups can be used in combination with ability groups. It is better to have fewer efficiently functioning groups in which children are learning than to have learning stifled by a large number of groups operating in chaos.

Durrell (1940), an innovator of new patterns of class organization, advocated using five or more reading groups, with many activities led by pupil leaders and with the teacher supplying the plans and materials and exercising general su-pervision. Later he recommended a varied pattern of class organization involving whole-class activities, some individualized reading, heterogeneous groups for projects, small reading groups with pupil leaders, and skill practice in pairs or groups of three (Durrell 1956). Still later, Durrell (1959) reported a project that stressed team learning in groups of three to five pupils.

Size of Groups

Teachers use two strategies in determining group size. Either they establish equal-size groups because they want to be fair (unequal-size groups mean that some pupils get more attention than others), or they form a small low group based on the belief that its members need more attention (Barr 1982a).

It would be undesirable to fix arbitrary rules concerning group size. Some guiding principles can be set down, however. If children require a good deal of individual attention, the group should be small; with children capable of much individual or self-regulated activity, the group can be larger. If a class has two groups, it is generally desirable for the lower group to be the smaller; similarly, the lowest of three groups should usually be smaller than the middle group. Groups set up on the basis of special needs or special interests can be of any size. Groups of two children are effective for such activities as testing each other on word or phrase cards and for some reading games. One of the pair should know the answers or be provided with them. Such "team learning" initially requires teaching direction, with the procedures being demonstrated (Whisler 1976).

Some studies report differences in group size, with the suggestion that children receive more teacher-directed time if there are fewer members in the group. But evidence regarding the relationship of group size to ability level is mixed (Hiebert 1983).

Bases on which Groups Are Formed

Based on the limited research available, Borko, Shavelson, and Stern (1981) concluded:

1. When forming reading groups, many teachers first combine information about student characteristics into estimates of their reading ability.
2. Groups are then formed on the basis of these ability estimates and selected school environmental factors (e.g., availability of resources, class size and composition).
3. The reading group, rather than the individuals within the group, comprises the "information" on which teachers base their planning.
4. These decisions in turn can affect students' learning. Teachers' plans for high and low reading groups differ considerably (Shavelson & Stern 1981), and differences in such practices as pacing are associated with pupil achievement.

Flexibility in Grouping

The composition of reading groups seldom changes; group membership seems to be relatively permanent (Pikulski & Kirsch 1979, Hiebert 1983). There should be some flexibility in grouping, and it can be of two main kinds.

Changing Group Placements. Children should be moved from one group to another whenever it becomes evident that their reading needs can be better met in the new group. Children differ in their rates of progress; some outgrow a low group, while others are unable to keep up with a top group. Sometimes a child who has been floundering as the poorest reader in a group takes on a new lease on life as one of the best readers in a lower group. Similarly, a child who glides through group assignments with a minimum of effort may respond with redoubled energy to the challenge of working at a higher level of difficulty. In making such decisions it is often desirable to consult the children and respect their desires concerning group placement.

Using Different Groupings Simultaneously. At least two different kinds of groupings should be in operation. In classes with a wide range of ability, grouping for developmental reading should be done according to reading level, with some use of special-needs grouping. Grouping for functional reading can often be in heterogeneous groups, especially if a project or activity unit plan is followed. Both recreational and functional reading provide opportunities for setting up interest groupings. When children belong to various groups, the possibility of developing a rigid caste system in which the poorest readers become "untouchables" is held to a minimum.

One must avoid assuming that flexibility is an end in itself, since that leads to changing groupings just for the sake of change. Under such a system, it is hard to see how either the teacher or the children will be able to settle down and get much work done. Flexibility has value when it improves learning conditions and social interrelations, but too much change can be as undesirable as too little.

Effects of Group Placement

Grouping is thought by some to produce adverse affective outcomes, especially for children in low groups, but the causal relationship between reading-group placement and children's self-concepts and attitudes is unresolved (Hiebert 1983). Research has not indicated whether pupils' negative attitude toward reading creates a lack of interest in reading that contributes to lower group placement or whether lower group placement fosters negative attitudes toward self and reading.

It is also argued that reading-ability groups are treated and instructed differently and that such differences influence reading achievement. As evidence of this, some cite the increasing discrepancy between good and poor readers as they progress through school. Apart from the fact that there are alternative explanations for the situation, there is little information as to how this widening gap relates to differences in experiences the reading groups have.

There is evidence that teachers exhibit different behaviors and provide different instruction to high and low reading groups. Flexibility in procedures and assignments and more individualized follow-up tend to mark the lesson for high groups. Low groups tend to get highly structured lessons and assignments (Borko, Shavelson, & Stern 1981; Shavelson & Stern 1981). High groups receive more meaning-related (comprehension) activities, have their attention called to semantic cues when they make word-recognition errors, and do more silent than oral reading. Low groups tend to get more word-recognition and decoding instruction and practice, to have their attention called to grapho-phonemic cues when they err, and to do more oral than silent reading. Some writers suggest that differences in the way high and low achievers are instructed are undesirable and that the low achievers would become better readers if they were instructed in the same manner as good readers. While there is little doubt that good and poor readers are treated differently, differentiated instruction may be appropriate to meet different needs. No research evidence indicates that providing the same instruction for good and poor readers increases the reading achievement of the latter.

Teachers vary the rate at which they pace groups, but the appropriateness of that pacing is open to question. Some studies have found that teachers spend more time with high groups; other studies have not. Other studies have found that (1) teachers allow fewer interruptions when working with high groups; (2) low groups are given less time to respond to questions; (3) low groups are less frequently engaged in assigned tasks; and (4) teachers spend more time dealing with behavior and attention problems in low groups (Hiebert 1983). The latter two findings often are interpreted to indicate that children in low groups have shorter attention spans and more behavior problems. But other explanations are possible. Some pupils are in low groups because they have behavior or attention problems rather than low reading ability. Also, off-task behavior is influenced by the difficulty of the material for the child, and there is some evidence that poor readers are often given material that is comparatively more difficult for them to read than is the case for good readers.

Group Dynamics

The manner in which group members interact with one another and the teacher can influence learning (Webb 1982). It is therefore important that the teacher understands the nature of these interactions and attempts to assure that each member plays an active, fulfilling role. The ways in which the teacher treats the group overall and its members individually, as well as her attitude toward them, can affect group participation and how children feel about themselves and others.

Equipment and Materials

A classroom should be large enough so that the groups can be separated physically, and classroom furniture should be movable so that it can be arranged in different patterns. For any group activity involving intercommunication, the group should be seated so that everyone can see everyone else; a rectangular arrangement with desks pushed together as if to make a large table and a circle or semicircle of chairs are often used. A large area of chalkboard and bulletin board is desirable. There should be convenient shelving for books and supplies. A library corner should have in it not only space for books but also a table and chairs to encourage browsing and a colorful display of books or book jackets. These are desirable features, but none is absolutely essential.

Materials for a rich, well-rounded reading program should include the following:

1. Sets of basal readers or other materials, in numbers appropriate for the groups using them, ranging in difficulty appropriate for the lowest to the highest group.

2. Workbooks that accompany the reading series and others not correlated with the series. Without these, the teacher has the additional burden of creating or duplicating seatwork.
3. Special teacher-devised materials, to fill gaps in the available commercial materials.
4. Materials that are self-administering and/or self-correcting. These may include programmed materials, computer software, boxes of exercises with answer keys, and commercial or teacher-prepared lessons on tape.
5. Individual and group reading games that can be used when an assignment is finished early.
6. A classroom library of at least 50 books, covering a wide range in difficulty and interest appeal and changed at least several times during the year. Children's magazines should also be part of the classroom library.
7. Reference works, including picture dictionaries and various dictionaries. Above the primary grades, there also should be an encyclopedia set, atlases, an almanac, and the like.
8. Related pictures, filmstrips, slides, tapes, recordings, and movies to help provide ideational background.

In a school where supplies are meager, the teacher can provide some differentiated instruction in reading, but it is unquestionably easiest to do so with sufficient materials.

Choosing Reading Materials.   In most plans for grouping by reading levels, at least two different reading texts are required: one of below-grade difficulty and one of normal difficulty for the grade. The below-grade book should be at an instructional level appropriate for the low group. If there are middle and high groups, it is probably better for them to use different books, with the high group using either a comparatively difficult reading text intended for that grade or a reader intended for the next higher grade. It is also possible to teach effectively with the middle and high groups using the same text. In that case, the high group is given less preparation, works more independently, moves more rapidly, and has more time for supplementary and independent reading.

Some school systems use one reading series for low groups, another for middle groups, and a third series for high groups, through the grades. This has the advantage that no group has heard a story read and discussed by another group before getting to it. In such a plan, the teacher has to keep track of the skills covered in each group so that children who change groups will not miss any important reading skills. In the lower grades the frequent lack of overlapping vocabulary among reading series must be considered when a child changes groups.

Some teachers lose practically all the potential benefits of grouping by levels by having all groups use the same reading text. This is probably even less efficient than whole-class instruction, for not only are most of the children using material too easy or too hard for best results but the amount of direct instruction each child receives is less than in whole-class instruction. For ability grouping to be reasonably effective, the reader must be suitable in difficulty for at least a majority of the group.

One of the major sources of difficulty in group management arises from giving a group a basal reader that is too difficult. This encourages restlessness, inattention, excessive requests for help, and misbehavior; what is more important, children are much less likely to progress in reading achievement.

Assignments

While the teacher is working directly with one group, the other groups must have definite assignments that they can carry on without help from the teacher.

In the earliest grades, one or more groups often are unable to carry on any kind of reading activity without the active participation of the teacher. When this is the case, it is desirable to alternate reading with other activities that the children are able to carry on independently (e.g., weaving, coloring, or cutting out pictures). These can be combined with reading in a rotating plan so that the group reads only when the teacher is with them and engages in quiet self-directed activities when the teacher is with another group. This procedure is essential in first grade and is sometimes needed in higher grades for one or more groups.

Before starting the group activities of the day, it is helpful to take a few minutes to clarify the specific assignments for each group. Members of a group should always have supplementary activities to which they can turn if they finish an assignment before the end of a period. For each group, it is advisable to have a chart that the group members can consult if they forget what to do next. With such a plan, it should be easy for the group to keep busy for a 30- or 40-minute period.

Interference between groups should be kept at a minimum. When working with a group, teachers should keep their voices low; the children soon learn to speak and work quietly also. Routines for distributing and collecting books, workbooks, paper, and other supplies quietly and efficiently need to be developed and practiced.

Time Schedule

It is necessary to consider with care the total amount of time to be devoted to the reading program each day and each week, the duration of reading periods, and appropriate spacing of reading periods in the school day. In the primary grades the developmental reading program should take about 90 to 120 minutes a day. From fourth grade on, the amount of time specifically scheduled for developmental and recreational reading decreases grade by grade, but the amount of time spent in functional reading in a variety of curricular fields more than makes up the differences.

Each teacher has to experiment to determine the length of time that seems to work best with a particular group. When periods are too short, so much time is spent in getting materials out, warming up to the task, and putting things away again that inefficiency results. When periods are too long, children get fatigued or bored, and their increasing restlessness and noise signal to an alert teacher that effective learning has stopped. Young children need somewhat shorter periods than older children. In consequence, the teacher may find it desirable to have two or three short periods a day with a group, rather than one long one. Periods devoted to easy, pleasurable activities can be relatively prolonged; periods requiring intense concentration on difficult tasks should be comparatively brief. Reading can be scheduled for both morning and afternoon.

The psychology of learning indicates that it is efficient to separate periods of similar activity by periods in which different activities are carried on. In the planning of a reading program it would seem desirable to interpolate nonreading activities between reading periods or to follow one reading activity by a quite different kind of reading activity.

Many teachers plan their reading as a solid block of an hour or more, during which they work with each group in turn, but reading instruction can be provided for a group while the rest of the class is working independently on other curricular activities.

There is disagreement as to whether differential amounts of time should be allotted to groups of varying abilities. Some argue that all should get approximately equal time, others that low-ability groups should receive the most instructional time because without it they will not reach their potential. Yet others contend that the best readers should have the most instructional time, since they are our future leaders. The debate is based on opinion, and any decisions about differential time allotments reflect value judgments and not research evidence.

Group Names

Some teachers are concerned about what to call their groups. They think of them as "the high group" or "the low group," but they realize it would be bad for morale to use such terms with the children. Numbering groups is not desirable for the same reason. The assignment of names that imply relative size, speed, or competence is to be avoided. Teachers should be sensitive to the feelings of children about the traits implied by group names. Children are aware of the comparative proficiencies of groups. "The teacher calls us the red, white, and blue groups, but she might as well call us the fruits, vegetables, and nuts." Choosing names wisely does not eliminate this awareness; it merely avoids rubbing it in.

One way to select group names is to allow each group to choose its own name. During a unit on American Indians, for example, the groups may wish to choose the names of Indian tribes. This procedure avoids the dangers cited above.

Perhaps the best way of treating this problem is to make it as casual as possible. Thus, groups with chairpersons can be referred to as Billy's group or Annette's group, or the group can be named according to the title or the color of the cover of the book it is currently using. The less fuss made about group names, the better.

Individualizing Instruction within a Group

Even though the children in a group may be reading at the same general level and using the same material, it is possible to individualize instruction, albeit to a lesser extent than under other procedures. Apart from the use of various other kinds of groups, the teacher can tailor instruction before, during, and after the lesson. Before the lesson, the teacher can develop the necessary background experience for reading a story only for those who need it or excuse those who have met the objective(s) of the lesson. During the lesson, she can match question difficulty to individual children's reading and reasoning ability. The time given to respond also can be adjusted. In the follow-up stage, the teacher can make differing assignments in skill development and enrichment activities and allow varying amounts of time to complete the assignments.

Use of Student and Adult Assistants

Students within the class, older students, and teacher aides may be used to assist teachers in individualizing instruction.

Chairpersons, Helpers, and Tutors.   In many group activities pupils can act as group leaders, making it unnecessary for the teacher to be with the group for that activity. Often a few of the best readers are assigned to be leaders of less capable groups. Sometimes this privilege is rotated among several children so that no child gets conceited or misses too much of his or her own group's reading activities. An alternative is to let each group select its own chairperson, or to have the privilege rotate among members of the group, with each child having a turn. A chairperson who is a member of a group is often accepted with better grace than a leader who comes from another group. When a group is not yet able to function without help, it may be possible to have a chairperson from within the group, who assigns turns to read and keeps order, and a helper from a higher group who can supply assistance.

Helpers can be used during silent reading or workbook practice, as well as during oral reading. One child can be the helper for a group, or each child who needs help may be allowed to select another child as a personal helper; the helper and the child helped may be assigned adjacent seats.

Children do not naturally know how to be effective chairpersons or helpers. Sometimes they give too much help or too little, or they become officious or sarcastic. It is desirable to train helpers or chairpersons for their jobs, and it is certainly necessary to keep an eye on how they carry out their functions.

A study of peer-directed groups (Wilkinson & Calculator 1982) revealed that, in general, first graders were effective in making requests and receiving appropriate responses. Typically their requests were direct, sincere, on-task, and to a designated listener. However, the system worked less well for low-ability children.

Capable students also may be used to tutor other pupils. Peer tutoring has been shown to be effective.

Teacher Aides.   Sometimes it is possible to have two or more adults present during reading instruction. The extra people may be student teachers, volunteers, or paid teaching aides. Team teaching also makes possible situations in which more than one group at a time has adult leadership. Careful planning and supervision are necessary to ensure that what teacher aides and paraprofessionals do is beneficial to the learning of the children.

Suggestions for the Effective Teaching of Groups

Among the research-supported techniques for working with groups are the following (Brophy 1979a; Anderson, Evertson, & Brophy 1979):

1. Use a standard and predictable signal to obtain the group's attention.
2. Seat the pupils in the group with their backs to the rest of the class; the teacher should face all the class members.
3. In order to prepare the students for the presentation, the introduction to the lesson should contain an overview of what is to come.
4. Demonstrate or explain any new activity before asking the children to do it.
5. Work with one child at a time in having students practice the new skill or apply a new concept; make sure everyone is checked and receives feedback during the lesson.
6. After asking a question, wait for the student to respond, and make sure that the other pupils also wait and do not call out the answer. If the child does not respond within a reasonable time, indicate that some response is expected. In such instances, and when the answer is unacceptable (the child should be so informed), a simplification procedure should be used (see 7). Do not ask another child to give the answer.
7. The simplification procedure depends on the task involved. If the question asks for directly stated information (no reasoning is involved), give the child the answer. If reasoning is involved, simplify the question (and the task) and provide needed clues. Give the child the answer if this does not help.
8. When call-outs occur, remind the offender that everyone gets a turn and that he must wait for his.

McKenzie (1975, 1984) suggested ways to personalize group teaching, such as making eye contact and commenting favorably on a child's response or participation. He also provided ways to involve all the group members in responding nonverbally to a question. For example, after a child responds, the teacher can say, "If you agree, raise your hand," or the children can hold up "Agree" or "Disagree" cards. In either case, it is important for the teacher to look at each child to see if a response has been made.

Reading Stations

Reading or learning stations also may be employed in differentiating reading instruction. Each station that provides for a different activity usually accommodates a maximum of five or six pupils at once, all of whom need not be working on exactly the same activity. Activities are geared to the needs and interests of individual students and need not all be directly related to reading. Whenever possible, materials used at a station should be self-administering and self-scoring. Assignments may be made according to a rotational schedule, as shown in Figure 5.1.

Figure 5.1. Rotational scheduling. The rotating outer circle indicates the assignment; the inner circle shows the students selected for that activity. Adapted from E. Duval, R. Johnson, and J. Litcher, Learning stations and the reading class, in R. A. Earle (Ed.), *Classroom practice in reading* (Newark, DE: International Reading Association, 1977). The authors also provided sample forms for student recordkeeping and self-evaluations. Reproduced by permission of the authors and the International Reading Association.

Teacher assignments (e.g., guided reading in a text or workbook, teacher–pupil conference), free choice by students (e.g., recreational reading, reading games), and random assignments (e.g., using the school library) may be combined (Vacca & Vacca 1976). Practical suggestions for conducting reading stations are provided by Thompson and Merritt (1975), and by Meints (1977), who described adapting the learning-station concept for use in high school.

V. INSTRUCTIONAL PROCEDURES

There are a number of instructional procedures that attempt to accommodate individual differences to varying degress. Many of these were discussed in Chapter 3. For example, Individualized Developmental Reading attempts to individualize every aspect of the reading program. Linear programmed materials vary the pace at which children proceed through the program; computer-assisted instruction may allow for greater individualization through branching (e.g., when an incorrect response is made, the computer explains why the answer is wrong, what the correct answer is and why, and presents material designed to help the child learn the skill or strategy). Skills management systems try to individualize instruction by having the pupils work only on skills they have not mastered; pacing is also an individual matter.

Two other instructional procedures are discussed here—mastery learning and aptitude–treatment interactions.

Mastery Learning

Mastery learning is basically what Resnick (1979a) referred to as a "readiness approach" in which instruction is withheld until the learner is ready to acquire some new skill, strategy, or concept. In mastery learning the instructional pace is fully individualized and performance is evaluated according to each child's personal standard. All the students receive basically the same kind of instruction. In mastery learning only the rate at which the pupils progress through the instructional sequence varies. As such, it is similar in philosophy to linearly programmed instruction and a number of skills-system programs. There is some evidence that mastery learning is effective for low-ability pupils (Good & Stipek 1983).

Aptitude–Treatment Interaction

Another attempt at accommodating individual differences involves matching instruction (treatment) to the individual's particular style of learning. Effective matching should result in a positive interaction between the measured aptitude and the instructional treatment. Thus, the term *aptitude–treatment interaction* (ATI). ATI assumes that individuals have characteristic differences in abilities or approaches to learning that can be measured and that different tasks make differing demands on the learner. Instruction is adapted by capitalizing on the individual's strengths and minimizing reliance on weaknesses.

One dimension frequently investigated in ATI studies is *cognitive style*, which refers to the tendency to prefer certain ways of dealing with cognitive tasks. The preference may be a relatively strong aptitude or a fairly consistent behavioral tendency. Three aspects of cognitive style are described in a later chapter (see pp. 264–265).

VI. COMBINING WHOLE-CLASS, GROUP, AND INDIVIDUALIZED READING

The plans described below suggest ways in which a sequential program of reading instruction in groups based on reading level can be combined with whole-class activities, groups based on special needs, groups based on common interests, and periods of individualized reading. Teachers who want to try more individualization than is provided in these plans can do it in more than one way. For example:

1. The reading activities of one group can be individualized. This is easiest to do with the best readers. They can often finish the on-grade reading text(s) early in the spring; for the rest of the year they can be given individualized reading. Sometimes the poorest readers are just too different from one another to be taught as a group, requiring that their reading be individualized.
2. Additional periods of individualized reading can be provided for the entire class, devoting more total time to the reading program.
3. It is possible to alternate days of group instruction with days of individualized reading. This plan, maintaining the program of systematic instruction but incorporating much more individualized reading than is common at present, deserves serious consideration.

Illustrative One-Week Plans

Classes at the same grade level vary tremendously, and so it is impossible to present a plan for a given grade that will suit all classes. The plans described below are intended to be used as sources for ideas, not as specifications to be followed exactly.

In these specimen plans an attempt has been made to adhere to five basic principles: (1) Each plan combines reading by groups with some whole-class and some individualized or independent reading; (2) the teacher is with the group for those activities for which she is most needed; (3) expectancy concerning what a group may be able to do without the teacher (but with a chairman or helper) is realistic; (4) length of periods has some relationship to the maturity of the children; and (5) all groups get a reasonable share of the teacher's attention.

Figure 5.2 shows a sample plan for the middle of the first grade. In the figure are three periods for group work or team learning and one whole-class period every day. Both developmental reading activities and some other kinds of reading and nonreading activities are included. The plan assumes that the high group can do some independent reading in easy books that are below their instructional level but that the low and middle groups require teacher guidance for nearly all reading activities. Some workbook and seatwork periods are scheduled without the teacher, on the assumption that a teacher aide or pupil helper can be with the group; if this is not possible, there would need to be additional periods of nonreading activities for these groups, and it would take a day or two longer to complete each story.

Directions should be given to all groups at the beginning of the school day. At the start of each group period the teacher should spend a short time with each group making sure that they have the right materials and know what to do.

The low group is guided by the teacher through the essential steps of a typical basal reader developmental teaching plan: preparation, guided reading and discussion, oral rereading, and related skills. The group has several periods of nonreading activities but may be able to do workbook and seatwork pages with an aide or helper.

Low Group (pre-primer)	Middle Group (primer)	High Group (first reader)

Whole Class: Directions and assignments to each group daily.

MONDAY

Low Group (pre-primer)	Middle Group (primer)	High Group (first reader)
Nonreading activities	*T* Preparation for new story	Independent reading
T Preparation for new story	Teacher-prepared seatwork or workbook	Workbook
Teacher-prepared seatwork or nonreading activities	Cut pictures from old magazines for picture dictionary	*T* Check workbook; preparations for new story

Whole Class: Teach symbol–sound association *m* = /m/. Teacher reads story.

TUESDAY

Low Group (pre-primer)	Middle Group (primer)	High Group (first reader)
Visual-discrimination seatwork	*T* Guided reading and discussion	Silent reading of story-workbook
T Guided reading and discussion	Workbook	Supplementary reading or nonreading activities
Workbook or nonreading activities	Paste pictures in picture dictionary	*T* Check workbook; discussion of story and selective oral reading

Whole Class: Teacher reads a poem. Children volunteer poems and rhymes. Children listen for rhyming words that teacher lists.

WEDNESDAY

Low Group (pre-primer)	Middle Group (primer)	High Group (first reader)
Nonreading activities	*T* Oral rereading; check workbook	Independent reading; word games
T Oral rereading; check workbook	Duplicated seatwork	Nonreading activities
Word games or nonreading activities	Draw a picture about the story	*T* Preparation for new story

Whole Class: Review symbol–sound association of *m*. Introduce symbol–sound association *p* = /p/. Choral reading of duplicated poem read by teacher on Tuesday.

Figure 5.2. A three-group plan for the middle of the first grade. *T* indicates the group with which the teacher is working. Each of the three daily periods is scheduled for 20–30 minutes; the whole-class period lasts about 30 minutes.

Low Group (pre-primer)		Middle Group (primer)		High Group (first reader)
		THURSDAY		
	Cut pictures from magazines	*T* Check seatwork; related skills: decoding, ·comprehension		Independent reading workbook
T Related skills: decoding, comprehension		Labeling pictures for picture dictionary		Word games or nonreading activities
	Draw a picture about the story	Duplicated seatwork	*T*	Check workbook; discussion of story and selective oral reading

Whole Class: Develop experience story; practice reading it. Review the two new symbol–sound associations.

Low Group (pre-primer)		Middle Group (primer)		High Group (first reader)
		FRIDAY		
	High-utility word games with high group	*T* Check seatwork; preparation for new story		Team with low group for high-utility word games
T Preparation for new story		Nonreading activities		Word games or nonreading activities
	Visual-discrimination seatwork	Silent rereading in preparation for dramatization	*T*	Check seatwork; preparation for new story

Whole Class: Review the two symbol–sound associations introduced during the week. One group dramatizes a story; teacher reads a story.

Figure 5.2. *(continued)*

The middle group also has teacher direction through the cycle of preparation, guided reading and discussion, oral rereading, and related skills. Without the teacher, this group does workbook pages and cuts, pastes, and labels entries for a picture dictionary. The group probably needs a helper for these activities. Nonreading activities fill in the gaps.

The high group has teacher guidance for preparation, discussion of story and oral reading, and checking workbook and seatwork pages. On its own, this group does silent reading in the reader, workbook exercises, and seatwork, as well as some individualized independent reading.

Whole-class activities include decoding skills, the teacher reading to the class, choral reading, experience stories, and dramatization of stories. Decoding skills introduced and reviewed with the whole class have additional review during "related skills" periods for the low and middle groups.

Very Low Group	Low Group	Middle Group	High Group

Whole Class: Directions and assignments given to each group daily as needed.

MONDAY

Very Low Group	Low Group	Middle Group	High Group
Individualized developmental reading	Silent reading of story introduced Friday	*T* Discussion and purposeful rereading of story read silently on Friday	Related workbook *GC* Check workbook
	T Discussion and purposeful rereading	Related workbook	Indendependent reading

Whole Class: Read and discuss different editions (levels) of weekly newspaper.

TUESDAY

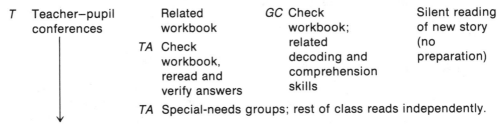

Very Low Group	Low Group	Middle Group	High Group
T Teacher–pupil conferences	Related workbook *TA* Check workbook, reread and verify answers	*GC* Check workbook; related decoding and comprehension skills	Silent reading of new story (no preparation)
	TA Special-needs groups; rest of class reads independently.		

Whole Class: Independent reading; teacher and aide circulate, providing help as needed.

WEDNESDAY

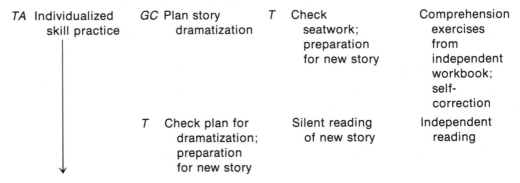

Very Low Group	Low Group	Middle Group	High Group
TA Individualized skill practice	*GC* Plan story dramatization	*T* Check seatwork; preparation for new story	Comprehension exercises from independent workbook; self-correction
	T Check plan for dramatization; preparation for new story	Silent reading of new story	Independent reading

Whole Class: Using dictionary guide words.

Figure 5.3. A four-group plan for a heterogeneous middle grade. Periods are 20–30 minutes each. *T* = teacher works with group; *TA* = teacher aide works with group; *GC* = activity led by group chairperson.

Very Low Group	Low Group	Middle Group	High Group

THURSDAY

Very Low Group	Low Group	Middle Group	High Group
Individualized developmental reading	Silent reading of new story	*T* Discussion and purposeful reading	Independent reading
↓	*TA* Discussion and purposeful rereading	Related workbook	*T* Discussion of two stories

Whole Class: Special-interest and research groups.

FRIDAY

Very Low Group	Low Group	Middle Group	High Group
T Teacher–pupil conferences	*TA* Rehearse dramatization	*GC* Check workbook; reread to verify answers	Critical reading exercises
Word-recognition and vocabulary games (team learning)			*T* Discussion of critical reading exercises

Whole Class (afternoon): Book Club meeting, audience reading, choral reading of poetry, dramatization, group reports.

Figure 5.3. *(continued)*

A plan appropriate for an intermediate-grade class with a wide range of reading ability is shown in Figure 5.3. There are two daily periods for group or individualized activities and one whole-class period. The plan covers developmental reading; much additional time should be scheduled for reading in other curricular areas. Independent (recreational) reading is scheduled for all four groups. This plan makes use of a teacher aide who is available 3 days a week and group chairpersons. If a teacher aide is not available, the plan will need to be adjusted. The teacher or teacher aide works with the lowest group three times a week, with the low group four times, the middle group three times, and the high group twice a week.

Because the reading levels of the lowest group are so diverse, an individualized developmental reading approach is used. Emphasis is placed on developing needed basic skills in both individual teacher-pupil conferences and skill-practice activities.

The low group uses a below-grade-level reading text, and most of the group's work is closely supervised. Group members do not require the teacher's direct supervision for silent reading or for workbook and seatwork pages. The privilege of presenting a story dramatization should rotate among the groups.

The middle group, which uses the on-grade text, is scheduled for somewhat more self-directed reading than the low group. The teacher is with the group for preparation, discussion, and purposeful rereading. Group members in the top three groups are expected to carry on certain activities with a group chairperson and to fill in with independent reading or other quiet activities when they complete an assignment early.

The high group uses an above-grade-level reader. Group members are expected to be able to read a selection silently without teacher-directed preparation or with a very abbreviated preparation during the giving of assignments. Workbooks are corrected by group members, either independently or under the direction of the group chairperson.

The whole-class periods accommodate a wide range of activities, not all of which can be shown in one plan and not all of which would be scheduled every week. This plan shows current events reading. Special-needs groups and special-interest groups can be fitted into periods when most of the class are doing independent reading or other self-directed activities, or are at reading stations.

A wide range of suggestions has been presented in this chapter for accommodating individual differences in reading ability. Each school and teacher will have to decide what combination of procedures best produces the desired results. Whatever plan is adopted, its success will depend on the effectiveness of the teacher and her understanding of students as individuals; the support and cooperation of the school administration, parents, and community; and the desire of the students to learn.

6

Identifying
Reading Disabilities

This chapter is the first of several concerned with the diagnosis of reading disabilities. It begins with a discussion of the meaning of diagnosis. A brief glossary explains commonly used terms, with particular attention to *dyslexia* and *learning disabilities*. The final section describes and explains various objective ways to define reading disability.

I. THE NATURE OF DIAGNOSIS

Diagnosis is a word that comes from two Greek roots, *dia*, meaning "through" or "across," and *gnosis*, meaning "knowledge." Its literal meaning is "to know thoroughly." Its medical meaning is "the process of determining the nature of a disease by examination and observation." For the study of reading disabilities, a more suitable definition is "the act, or result, of identifying disorders from their symptoms" (T. L. Harris & Hodges 1981).

Because reading is an extremely complex ability comprised of many interrelated factors, making an accurate diagnosis is not easy. Reading problems may reflect inadequate development in one or more of a multiplicity of perceptual, linguistic, or cognitive processes or a difficulty in coordinating them (Adams 1980). In making a diagnosis, one must determine if the student's reading difficulties are specific to reading, are common to both listening and reading, or are evidence of a more general deficiency in problem-solving ability (Rubin 1980b). It is also important to determine the causes of the reading problems and the extent to which various factors are currently influencing the pupil's reading ability.

Diagnosis can be carried out to different degrees of completeness by classroom teachers, reading specialists, and special clinic centers. A classroom teacher should not be expected to make a thorough diagnosis of every pupil; this would leave little time or energy for teaching. Fortunately, many of the less complex reading difficulties can be corrected by direct teaching, without an intensive search for the reasons why the skills were not learned previously. Nevertheless, teachers should know the factors that can contribute to reading difficulties and should be able to carry out the less complex parts of a diagnosis.

It is necessary to collect facts in making a diagnosis, and tests can contribute many of the needed facts. But the heart of diagnosis is not testing. It is, rather, the intelligent interpretation of information by a person who has both the theoretical knowledge and the practical experience to know what questions to ask, to select procedures that can best supply the needed information, to interpret the meaning of the findings correctly, and to comprehend the interrelationships of these facts and meanings. The natural outcome of a diagnosis is a plan for treatment that involves two parts: a plan for correcting or minimizing the factors that are still interfering with learning, and a plan for remedial instruction that is most likely to be successful in light of the data obtained from the diagnosis. But the first step in making a diagnosis is determining if the pupil is a disabled reader.

II. TERMINOLOGY

A Glossary of Terms[1]

The following glossary, although it is not exhaustive, illustrates the confusion that exists in the literature. It also may serve as a useful reference. The terms used in this book are defined on page 142.

- *Alexia:* (1) complete inability to read; (2) partial or total loss of ability to read, usually as a result of brain injury or disease; a form of aphasia.
- *Aphasia:* any receptive or expressive language disorder of neurological origin.
- *Backward reader:* an individual whose reading age (based on test scores) falls below the average performance of pupils of the same chronological age; intelligence or learning potential is *not* considered (Vernon 1960).
- *Brain damage, brain injury, organic brain damage, brain lesion:* any injury to the brain structure (Strang 1968).

---

[1] Refer to T. L. Harris and Hodges (1981) for a comprehensive listing and definitions of terms found in the reading and reading-related literature.

- *Congenital alexia:* synonym for developmental dyslexia.
- *Congenital word blindness, word blindness:* synonym for dyslexia once favored by some medical writers (e.g., Hinshelwood 1917, Hermann 1964).
- *Dyslexia:* severe reading disability that may represent loss of reading competency following brain injury or degeneration, or it may represent a developmental failure to profit from reading instruction. Also employed broadly as a synonym for reading disability.
- *Dyssymbolia:* term proposed to replace "learning disability" (Kass 1977).
- *Hyperlexia:* condition characterized by word-recognition and decoding ability before age 5, word recognition and decoding notably superior to reading comprehension, and disordered cognitive and linguistic development (Healy 1982).
- *Learning disability:* significant difficulty in the acquisition of listening, speaking, reading, spelling, writing, or arithmetic skills. Causation usually attributed to central nervous system deficits or dysfunctions. The disability is not the result of sensory impairment, mental retardation, emotional disturbance, or environmental influences.
- *Maturational lag:* slowness in certain specialized aspects of neurological development; concept introduced by Bender (1957).
- *Minimal brain damage* or *cerebral damage* or *dysfunction:* implies that causation is brain damage or disordered brain functioning, although clear evidence of damage or dysfunction is not present (Clements 1966). Diagnosis is often based on "soft neurological signs" that are of doubtful validity.
- *Perceptually handicapped:* indicates a learning problem resulting from a perceptual disorder, most often noted as visual or auditory, or to a combination of disorders such as visual–motor.
- *Psycholinguistic learning disability:* weakness in processes believed necessary for learning to occur, as assessed by the *Illinois Test of Psycholinguistic Ability* (Kirk & Kirk 1971).
- *Psychoneurological learning disability:* learning disability caused by a combination of psychological and neurological factors. It includes speech, writing, and nonverbal disabilities, as well as reading disabilities, and represents conditions in which the central nervous system is not functioning efficiently in sensorimotor, perceptual–motor, or language functions, whether because of genetic, maturational, or traumatic conditions; sociocultural deprivation; emotional problems; or a combination of some of these (D. J. Johnson & Myklebust 1967).
- *Reading difficulty* or *disorder:* synonym for reading disability; it may signify a mild to moderate degree of disability. Also used to refer to deficiency in a specific reading skill or strategy.
- *Reading disability:* reading achievement is significantly below expectancy for both age and learning potential and is disparate with the learner's cultural, linguistic, and educational experience.

- *Reading retardation:* in the United States, reading achievement that is significantly below age and grade norms regardless of such factors as learning potential. In England and for some medical writers, a synonym for reading disability as defined above.
- *Specific language disability:* concept similar to *dyslexia* but broadened to include spelling, writing, and speech problems referable to the same constitutional origin. Term often found in the Orton Dyslexia Society literature.

Cautions in Using Labels

Labeling a child *may* result in lowered self-concept, rejection by peers, lowered level of academic aspiration, biased responding by teachers and parents, or poor postschool adjustment (Palmer 1983). Although there are times when a child must be labeled (e.g., so that he or she may receive necessary treatment), it is wise to consider Samuel's admonition regarding labels as pseudoexplanations:

> By identifying the problem, giving it a name, and putting the students into a diagnostic category, many educators and psychologists delude themselves into believing that they have gained insight into the causes of the problem. If we ask, "Why is the student failing in reading?" we often get the answer, "He is unable to learn because he has a learning disorder." This answer tells us nothing about the actual sources of difficulty the students are experiencing. In fact, the answer implies circular reasoning since it is largely because of the presence of academic retardation that the label is ascribed.
>
> Actually, labels such as learning disorder, dyslexia, etc., provide no useful information as to why students are failing. . . . The labels do not in any way indicate where the student is having trouble, nor do they provide a clue as to how the difficulty may be overcome. (Samuels 1973b, p. 203).

Dyslexia

There is no unanimity concerning the meaning of *dyslexia* (T. L. Harris & Hodges 1981). The medical community and neuropsychologists tend to regard it as a severe reading–language disability for which there is a constitutional, often inherited, basis. Educational psychologists usually define it as a severe reading disability of unspecified origin. Educators tend to waver between these two positions.

Some writers (e.g., Klasen 1972) employ the term *dyslexia* broadly as a synonym for reading disability. Others offer a variety of definitions that include one or more of the following: behavioral manifestations of central nervous system deficits or dysfunctions, genetic or inherited causation, inclusion of other language disabilities along with poor reading, presence of a syndrome of maturational lag, and inability to learn to read through regular classroom methods.

One of the more widely cited definitions is that of Critchley, a neurologist, who defined developmental dyslexia as follows:

. . . a learning-disability which initially shows itself by difficulty in learning to read, and later by erratic spelling and by lack of facility in manipulating written as opposed to spoken words. The condition is cognitive in essence, and usually genetically determined. It is not due to intellectual inadequacy or to lack of socio-cultural opportunity, or to faults in the technique of teaching, or to any known structural brain defect. It probably represents a specific maturational defect which tends to lessen as the child gets older, and is capable of considerable improvement, especially when appropriate remedial help is offered at the earliest opportunity. (Critchley 1981, pp. 1–2)

Among the symptoms of dyslexia cited by Critchley (1981) were (1) overall slowness of performance, punctuated by hesitation when unfamiliar or polysyllabic words are met; (2) confusion of mirror-opposite letters; (3) omissions of short words (articles, conjunctions, prepositions); (4) pluralization or omission of singular nouns; (5) abbreviation of lengthy words (e.g., *adolescent* is read as *adolent*); (6) overreliance on initial letter cues; and (7) substitution of synonyms.

Dyslexia has been qualified as *specific* to distinguish reading failure from general learning failure, and *developmental dyslexia* (reading ability has been poor from the start) is contrasted with *acquired dyslexia* (loss of previously acquired reading skills). Distinctions also are made between deep and surface dyslexia[2] (e.g., Jorm 1979a, b; Patterson 1981). *Deep* or *phonetic dyslexia* involves a severe impairment in decoding printed words; the ability to recognize and obtain meaning from whole words remains largely intact. In *surface* or *semantic dyslexia*, irregularly spelled (nonphonemic) words are misread in a way that suggests the inappropriate application of phonic principles (e.g., *one* is decoded as /ōn/) or the use of an analogy strategy (e.g., *put* is pronounced as rhyming with *but*).

Taylor, Satz, and Friel (1979–1980) compared 40 boys who met all the criteria for dyslexia, as defined by the World Federation of Neurology, with 40 who failed to meet at least one of the criteria and were therefore classified as nondyslexic. Although these 80 poor readers as a group were deficient in many neurodevelopmental skills, comparisons between the dyslexics and nondyslexics revealed no differences of any consequence. The authors thus concluded that there was a need for a substantial revision of the concept of dyslexia.

There are some (e.g., Morris 1966) who doubt the existence of a condition such as dyslexia. Evidence exists, however, that regardless of the label attached, there is a group of disabled readers that lies outside the normal range of variation (Vernon 1971, Yule & Rutter 1976).

Although committees in the United States (National Advisory Committee on Dyslexia and Related Reading Disorders 1969) and England (Tizard *et al.* 1972) concluded years ago that *dyslexia* was not a useful term, and despite the disagreements and ambiguities involved in its definitions, use of the term has grown in recent years. Readers must be careful to determine which of the many definitions of dyslexia a particular author is using. In this book, the term *reading disability* is preferred because of its relative clarity of meaning.

---

[2] This distinction was questioned by Kremin (1982).

Our knowledge of dyslexia has not improved enough to invalidate Vernon's summary of the situation some 15 years ago:

> As to the precise nature of the disability we know little, and much further experimental investigation is required to define this and to demonstrate exactly how it operates in creating reading difficulties. And as to the ultimate cause of the disability, the evidence is too weak and conflicting to do more than suggest certain highly speculative hypotheses. . . .
> It is difficult in the present state of our knowledge to differentiate dyslexia from non-dyslexic backward readers. Indeed it may be impossible to do so with any precision. (Vernon 1971, pp. 176–178)

Learning Disabilities

During the 1960s and early 1970s groups such as the Council for Exceptional Children and the Association for Children with Learning Disabilities were successful in obtaining legal recognition of a group of children with academic difficulties who were not covered by other categories of exceptionality. By 1974 many states had laws requiring special education for such children and providing financial support for it. These state laws used various terms—perceptually handicapped, educationally handicapped, minimally brain damaged, learning disabled—and there was no uniformity in definitions used or criteria specified (Gillespie, Miller, & Fielder 1975). A similar situation exists today.

A legally binding definition of learning disability was included in Public Law 94–142:

> "Specific learning disability" means a disorder in one or more of the basic psychological processes involved in understanding or in using language, spoken or written, which may manifest itself in an imperfect ability to listen, speak, read, write, spell, or to do mathematical calculations. The term includes such conditions as perceptual handicaps, brain injury, minimal brain dysfunction, dyslexia, and developmental aphasia. The term does not include children who have learning problems which are primarily the result of visual, hearing, or motor handicaps, of mental retardation, of emotional disturbance, or of environmental, cultural, or economic disadvantage. (Federal Register 42, no. 250 (December 29, 1977); 65083)

> . . . For the purpose of these regulations, when a severe discrepancy between ability and achievement exists which cannot be explained by the presence of other known factors that lead to such a discrepancy, the cause is believed to be a specific learning disability. (*Ibid.*, p. 65085)

Specific criteria for defining "learning disability" were not indicated. The federal guidelines are very general, simply indicating that children are learning disabled (LD) if there is a severe discrepancy between their learning potential and their performance in one or more of the following areas: written expression (handwriting, spelling, composition), oral expression, listening comprehension, basic reading skills, reading comprehension, mathematics calculation, or mathematics reasoning. The excluded groups—the sensorily impaired, mentally retarded, emotionally disturbed, and disadvantaged—are covered either by other parts of the Education of the Handicapped Act or by Title I of the Elementary and Secondary Education Act.

The requirements of PL 94–142 state that evaluation of a child suspected of being learning disabled is to be made by a multidisciplinary team including the child's teacher and at least one person "qualified to conduct individual diagnostic examinations of children, such as a school psychologist, speech-language pathologist, or remedial reading teacher." The team must determine if a child is learning disabled and must file a written report stating the evidence on which its conclusions were based. This evidence must include an individually administered intelligence test. A preliminary version of the rules specified that the child's achievement had to be less than half of the child's potential achievement, and set an upper limit of 2% of the school population; these provisions were deleted from the final rules. They suggest, however, rough guidelines for the team. According to Messick (1984), 2.3% of American students are in learning-disability programs.

As exemplified by the diversity of opinions expressed in the January 1983 issue of the *Journal of Learning Disabilities*, there are numerous other definitions of learning disability;[3] none is commonly accepted.[4] Definitions of LD contain one or more of four concepts:

1. A severe discrepancy exists between the child's apparent potential for learning and a very low level of academic achievement.
2. Causation is constitutional (and sometimes hereditary) rather than environmental.
3. The low academic achievement is based on deficits or dysfunction in basic psychological processes thought to be necessary for successful academic performance. Depending on the writer's opinion of causation, the deficits may be specified as perceptual, perceptual–motor, attentional, conceptual, or linguistic.
4. Specific groups of children are automatically excluded.

Some writers have suggested that LD almost defies definition. Sabatino and Miller (1980) went so far as to state that, at best, LD is "an expression, not a diagnostic entity" and that current definitions are incapable of describing a meaningful population for research or providing data useful for placement or instruction. Yet others (e.g., Myklebust 1983) insist that LD can be defined usefully.

Six professional organizations, dissatisfied with the definition in PL 94–142, formed a National Joint Committee on Learning Disabilities that formulated a new definition (NJCLD 1981, 1983):

[3] Kirk and Kirk (1983) discussed the definition of learning disability from a historical perspective.

[4] Except for the fact that learning disabilities take in more academic areas, some definitions of dyslexia and learning disability are similar.

Learning disability is a generic term that refers to a heterogeneous group of disorders manifested by significant difficulties in the acquisition and use of listening, speaking, reading, writing, reasoning, or mathematical abilities. These disorders are intrinsic to the individual and presumed to be due to central nervous system dysfunction.

Even though a learning disability may occur concomitantly with other handicapping conditions (e.g., sensory impairment, mental retardation, social and emotional disturbance) or environmental influences (e.g., cultural differences, insufficient/inappropriate instruction, psychogenic factors), it is not the direct result of those conditions or influences.

This definition, discussed by McLoughlin and Netick (1983) and McLeod (1983), is an improvement in that it emphasizes the varied nature of learning disabilities, does not exclude adults, and recognizes that a learning disability may be accompanied by other handicapping conditions.

The identification of LD students is quite inaccurate. Ysseldyke (1983) reported that over two thirds of the students in a private school for LDs had an ability–achievement discrepancy of less than one standard deviation (suggesting that the discrepancy was not meaningful) and that psychologists and LD teachers were correct only 55% of the time in differentiating between LD students and other low achievers.

Warner *et al.* (1980) and Shepard (1983) reported that, as a group, children labeled as LD were indistinguishable from other low achievers. Fewer than half of the LD students in Colorado showed characteristics consistent with the federal definition, while slightly more than half showed language interference, emotional disorders, or mild mental retardation (Shepard, Smith, & Vojir 1983). Many of those labeled as LD were not achieving below grade level as measured by standardized tests. Even the Child Service Demonstration Centers set up under PL 91–230 did not abide by the federal definition of LD (Mann *et al.* 1983). O'Donnell (1980) found that discrepancies between potential and achievement comparable to those for learning disabilities were also present in many children classified as sensorily impaired or behavior disordered. A significant potential–achievement discrepancy is a necessary characteristic of LD, but it is to be found in other groups of handicapped children also.

The term "learning disability" serves to identify a population, but that population is far from homogeneous. While the majority of them read and spell poorly, there are good readers who are poor spellers, those who are good in math computation but poor in composition, and so forth. They may or may not show emotional or behavioral disturbances or sensory defects severe enough to be considered primary causes. Especially for research, the practice of comparing a heterogeneous group of children labeled "learning disabled" with a group of normally achieving children—an all too common procedure—does little to advance the understanding of school failure (Valtin 1978–1979).

As McCarthy (1969, p. 36) indicated, the field of learning disabilities has experienced a rapid shifting of emphases:

Methodologically, we started with visual perception, then went to sensori-motor training, then to ocular pursuit, then to the establishment of cerebral dominance, then to stimulus reduction, then to auditory perceptual or language training, then to multisensory training, then to integration of sensory stimuli, then to an analytic approach, and then to behavior modification. Academically, we have gone from Orton to Fernald to Gillingham to Spaulding to SRA to BRL, to Phonovisual, to the Language Master, to ITA, and now to any reading method which has a decoding emphasis. The focus of remediation has been passed from the social worker to the pediatrician to the psychiatrist to the psychologist to the neurologist to the endocrinologist and now back to the teachers.

Until fairly recently, a common belief in the field of learning disabilities was that the reading and other weak abilities were caused by deficits of dysfunctions in processes underlying these academic abilities. Any processing weaknesses had to be improved before the learning disability could be overcome. A concomitant belief was that the problem lay within the child, instead of being the result of any environmental or educational factors. It was commonly assumed that such processing problems could be identified and successfully treated, and that successful treatment would result in improved academic abilities or at least would facilitate the acquisition of abilities such as reading. These assumptions have been severely challenged (Arter & Jenkins 1979). The reliability and validity of tests commonly used in identifying LD also have been questioned (Coles 1978), and although process training might result in higher scores on posttests measuring those factors, such improvement does not often result in increased academic abilities.

At present, as in the past, the field of learning disabilities is replete with conflict—beginning with the conceptual framework underlying the various theories (Wong 1979) to its lack of an agreed definition, and thus necessarily to how the entity should be diagnosed and treated. In our opinion, the term "learning disability" is greatly in need of clarification.

Implications for Reading Specialists

Many reading specialists have been worried about the effects of PL 94–142 on their activities and job opportunities (A. J. Harris 1980b, Artley 1980). The availability of federal funds to subsidize programs for the learning disabled, and the absence of similar support for remedial reading programs, has caused some schools to reduce or eliminate remedial reading or to shift personnel to programs for the disadvantaged that do have federal support. In some school districts learning-disability teachers are being hired instead of reading specialists, especially where certified special-education teachers must be employed to be in compliance with funding requirements. With reduced school budgets, fewer specialists of any kind are being hired. In some places this situation has led to conflicts between LD and reading specialists.

There need not be territorial conflicts if the situation is put on the level of making the best possible use of staff members by enabling them to do what they do best on behalf of the students. This involves spelling out the kinds of services needed and the professional capabilities best suited to meet those needs (L. Lieberman 1980).

Reading specialists are likely to be involved in the diagnosis and treatment of LD pupils who have reading problems or in advising classroom, resource room, or LD teachers as to suitable methods and materials. Since most children labeled "learning disabled" have reading problems and reading specialists are by far best prepared to deal with reading difficulties, reading teachers need to demonstrate to decision makers that their expertise is valuable and effective in helping disabled readers no matter what they are labeled. The need is there; parents, school boards, and administrators have to be convinced. Suggestions for running effective "public relations" campaigns were made by Gaus (1983) and Landsman (1983). It also may be prudent for reading specialists to become certified in learning disabilities or special education.

Terms Used in This Book

The following terms are used in this book:

- *Disabled reader* or *reading disability:* designates individuals whose general level of reading ability is significantly below expectancy for their age and intelligence and is disparate with their cultural, linguistic, and educational experience. The latter part of the definition suggests that factors other than chronological age and intelligence must be considered.
- *Severely disabled reader* or *severe reading disability:* refers to disabled readers whose general level of reading ability is extremely below expectancy. Some writers apply labels such as *dyslexia* or *learning disability* to these cases.
- *Slow learner in reading:* indicates children who, although reading below age level, are generally functioning in reading close to their somewhat limited learning potential.
- *Underachiever in reading:* applies to children who, although reading at or above age or grade level, are reading significantly below their potential or expectancy level, which is often well above average.
- *Reading skill deficiency* or *difficulty:* indicates that, regardless of a child's general level of reading ability, he or she is weak in one or more reading skills. In some cases, the deficiency may be specific and may not lower the general level of reading ability. Naturally, if there are a number of skill deficiencies, if they are in basic skills, or if the skills are severely deficient, the child's general level of reading ability will be adversely influenced.

Both the disabled reader and the underachiever in reading are working below capacity. The basic difference between the two is that the disabled reader is functioning below age level, whereas the underachiever in reading is not. Children of below-average intelligence can also be disabled readers if their general level of reading ability is significantly below potential.

Moreover, some children do not achieve in school despite adequate reading ability. Their inability to function academically in school therefore cannot be attributed to a reading disability. There may be a lack of positive motivation or interference from emotional problems. These are cases for the psychologist or counselor rather than for the reading specialist.

The terms *disabled reader, underachiever in reading,* and *slow learner in reading* can be useful in that they draw attention to three kinds of learners who generally need differing treatment. Disabled readers often need intensive specialized treatment. Underachievers in reading usually need either to be better motivated or to be allowed to use "above grade level" materials. They rarely receive attention because they are functioning at grade level. Slow learners should not be expected to reach grade level in reading, nor should they be written off as unable to learn. All three types can be misclassified by test scores; expert judgment must also be given consideration. Whatever their classification, most children, including truly slow learners, can learn more if we can determine how to teach them; and often we do not gain such information unless we *attempt* to teach them and analyze these attempts in order to improve our efforts.

III. OBJECTIVE DEFINITIONS OF READING DISABILITY

Since the cause of a reading disability varies and (for a given individual) is often impossible to determine accurately, most current definitions of reading disability are based on the concept of determining whether the individual shows a significant disparity between general potential or aptitude for learning, which we may call *reading expectancy,* and actual achievement in reading. This involves making four decisions: (1) choosing an appropriate measure of reading expectancy, (2) choosing an appropriate measure of reading achievement, (3) choosing a way of comparing expectancy with achievement, and (4) deciding how large the discrepancy must be in order to be considered significant.

Even if agreement existed regarding what tests and formula to use and the amount of difference that indicates a disability, a number of unsolved measurement problems must be considered:

1. No test is a perfectly reliable measure. A test score should be considered as falling within a range of scores estimated by using the test's standard error of measurement rather than as a specific and exact point on a scale.
2. Use of different tests probably will influence decisions, particularly when scores are close to whatever cutoff criterion is used to indicate a disability.
3. A difference between scores on two tests with acceptable reliability may have substantially lower reliability than either of the tests taken individually.
4. The validity of a test (the degree to which it actually measures what it is intended to measure) is always lower than its reliability; this applies both to measures of potential and measures of reading. Because of the

margin of error in all procedures for measuring reading disability, such procedures should not be employed as the sole basis for determining whether efforts should be made to assist an individual to improve his or her reading skills.

5. Regardless of the general reliability and validity of a test, the score of a pupil who did not understand the directions or was not motivated to exert effort on the test cannot be valid.

There are instances when the evidence for the presence of a reading disability is so clear as to be self-evident. For example, a fourth grader who is known to have at least average intelligence and is reading 3 years below grade level is unquestionably disabled in reading. No computation is needed to arrive at this decision. But more exact procedures are necessary for a variety of purposes, such as (1) to arrange a number of children in order of severity of reading disability; (2) to assist in determining eligibility for inclusion in a remedial program; (3) to make statistical studies of the frequency of occurrence of reading disability; (4) to match groups of disabled readers for experimental purposes; and (5) to determine the need for remedial personnel in a school system.

Measures of Reading Expectancy

There are two commonly used measures of reading expectancy: intelligence tests and listening-comprehension tests.

Intelligence Tests[5]

The correlation between mental ability and reading comprehension is substantial at all ages. Correlations are generally in the .40s and .50s in the first grade (Bond & Dykstra 1967), rise into the .70s by fourth grade (Allen 1944), and tend to remain at about .70 for group verbal tests into the freshman year of college (Thorndike 1963). Verbal-ability tests correlate more highly with reading comprehension than they do with average achievement scores or school marks.

Nonverbal intelligence tests or subtests tend to have lower correlations with reading than verbal IQ tests do. For example, the WISC Verbal IQs of 113 disadvantaged seventh graders correlated .78 with their scores on the *Metropolitan Reading Test*. Their WISC Performance IQs and scores on the *Cattell Culture Fair* test (a nonverbal group test) correlated .53 and .56 respectively with the same reading test (G. Downing *et al.* 1965).

Pupils who cannot read the IQ test items cannot score well on such tests and are thus unable to demonstrate their potential for learning. Underestimates of potential may prevent poor readers from receiving remedial assistance, either because they obtained an IQ score below the minimum set for admission to the special program or because the depressed score results in the incorrect conclusion that they are working up to their expected level. Therefore, in testing children with reading difficulties, the use of intelligence tests that require reading

[5] Most recently published tests do not use "intelligence" in their titles; rather, terms such as "cognitive abilities" or "school aptitude" are employed. We use the term "intelligence test" because it is more likely to be familiar to our readers.

ability should be avoided. Children who have the potential to learn may not score well even on individual intelligence tests, for reasons such as expressive language deficits or poor motivation. If there is reason to believe that pupils have the potential to improve their reading ability, they should be given the opportunity to do so regardless of intelligence test scores.

Individuals who have trouble learning to read sometimes show marked differences between their scores on verbal and nonverbal intelligence tests or subtests. Some score substantially higher on nonverbal measures; for others, the reverse is true. There is some opinion that when a discrepancy of this sort exists, the higher of the two scores, whether verbal or nonverbal, should be used as an indicator of reading potential (Myklebust 1968). The rationale is that, although this may sometimes result in overestimating reading expectancy, such errors are less serious than underestimating it.

Nevertheless, because verbal scores tend to correlate much higher than nonverbal scores with reading achievement, they generally are better predictors of reading potential. Reading is a highly verbal ability; therefore it may be unrealistic to expect the individual to achieve at a level in reading commensurate with a high nonverbal score. Nonverbal tests may not adequately measure the mental abilities related to success in learning to read. On the other hand, a high nonverbal IQ shows the presence of some good abilities, which may compensate to some extent for verbal weaknesses . For these reasons, we recommend using the average of verbal and nonverbal scores, or a total score based on both, in determining reading potential.

The type of IQ score used can affect the number of pupils reported as reading disabled and which students are selected. For example, Reed (1970) found that 19 children were identified as disabled readers when the WISC Full Scale IQ was used; 29 were so identified when the Performance IQ was employed.

Tests that contain both verbal and nonverbal subtests include (1) individual tests such as Wechsler's WPPSI, WISC-R, and WAIS; (2) group tests such as the *Cognitive Abilities Test, Differential Aptitude Tests,* and *Tests of Cognitive Ability;* and (3) group tests for primary grades that present verbal and nonverbal tasks without requiring any reading, such as the *Otis-Lennon School Ability Test.*

The Kaufmann Assessment Battery for Children, which assesses the ability to process information and solve problems, yields scores for Sequential Processing (tasks involving repetition of material in some specific order), Simultaneous Processing (tasks that require the child to attend to several aspects of a task at one time; tasks are usually spatial in nature), and Composite Mental Processing. This individually administered battery also yields separate scores for Reading Decoding and Comprehension. All subtests were normed on the same population. When a reading test and an intelligence test have been normed on the same population, the chances are minimized that a difference between a person's scores on the two tests might be the result of differences in test standardization.

Predominately verbal individual tests of intelligence include the *Stanford–Binet Intelligence Scale*, the *Slosson Intelligence Test* (a shorter test using *Stanford–Binet* items), and vocabulary tests such as the *Peabody Picture Vocabulary Test—Revised* and the *Full Range Picture Vocabulary Test*.

Usable nonverbal tests include (1) individually administed measures, such as the Performance parts of the *Weschler* scales, the *Arthur Point Scale of Performance*, and the *Raven Progressive Matrices* (can be used with small groups above age 8); (2) group nonverbal tests, such as the *Cattell Culture Fair Series: Scales 1, 2, 3* and the *Nonverbal Test of Cognitive Skills;* and for younger children, the *Goodenough–Harris Drawing Test*.

Listening Comprehension

Listening comprehension (*auding, capacity level*) is recommended by some as the most satisfactory measure of reading potential. The general technique is to find the highest level at which the child can comprehend material read to him and compare that with his reading level on similar material.

> This ability to understand spoken English demonstrates that the child has the intelligence and perceptual abilities to handle words and sentences, the basis for all later communication skills. . . . Listening comprehension is more directly related to reading than are most tests of intelligence. Intelligence tests measure a variety of mental functions which have varying degrees of relationship to reading. Listening comprehension measures *language* acquisition, the knowledge of the very same words and sentences which are to appear later in reading. (Durrell & Hayes 1969, p. 12)

The rationale for checking listening comprehension is that if the pupil understands orally presented material at a particular level, he should be able to comprehend similar printed material at that level if he does not have difficulties with the special skills required in reading.

There are standardized tests of listening comprehension, such as the *Durrell Listening–Reading Series*, and some standardized reading achievement tests include listening-comprehension subtests. Such tests should measure understanding of connected discourse beyond that of the sentence or brief paragraph level in order to be used for the purpose suggested here. Listening-comprehension scores also may be obtained from informal or published reading inventories, or from standardized measures such as the *Diagnostic Reading Scales*.

Sticht *et al.* (1974) summarized the correlations between auding and reading obtained by many researchers. The average *r* starts low at Grade 1 (.35) and increases steadily to about .60 at Grade 4, remaining at about that level through secondary school and college. Ruddell (1979) found that primary-grade listening-comprehension scores were better than reading-comprehension scores for predicting reading comprehension in Grades 8, 9, and 10. Thus there is some justification for using auding as a measure of reading potential.

There are limitations with using listening comprehension as an indicator of reading expectancy. Auditory handicaps and unfamiliarity with standard English may lower a listening-comprehension score, as may fatigue or inattention. Performance also may be influenced by factors such as learning experiences (or lack of them), the stimulation in a pupil's environment, and how well (or poorly) the material is read by the examiner. On the other hand, scores may be inflated if the examiner emphasizes words or phrases that provide answers to the comprehension check. A child should not be excluded from a remedial program because of a low listening-comprehension score alone.

Determining General Level of Reading Ability

Standardized reading tests, well-constructed informal or published reading inventories, or cloze tests may be used to estimate an individual's present general level of reading ability. The obtained reading score should represent, as accurately as possible, the individual's instructional level. The uses and limitations of such tests for this purpose are discussed in Chapter 7.

For children who are reading below fourth reader level and seem to have problems in reading, equal weight should be given to silent reading and oral reading in arriving at a composite reading score. For those reading at or above fourth reader level, only a silent reading score may be used, but oral reading should be given at least qualitative consideration. "It is better for two reasons to use a composite of oral reading and silent reading scores, rather than silent reading alone. The first is that difficulties in word identification are central in many reading disabilities, and low comprehension scores may be the result of inability to recognize the words. The other is that poor readers tend to get many of their correct answers on multiple-choice tests by guessing, making their scores on such tests less dependable than the scores of normal readers" (A. J. Harris 1971a).

Reading Age

Most reading tests provide grade norms but not age norms. For some of the computational procedures described below it is necessary to have a reading-age score. Since the typical child in American public schools enters first grade at the age of 6.2 years (the usual minimum is 5 years 8 or 9 months) and is promoted regularly, there tends to be a regular difference of 5.2 years between chronological age and grade placement. When a reading test does not provide age norms, grade-equivalent scores may, for the purpose of these computations, be changed into reading-age scores by adding 5.2 years. Because tests such as the informal reading inventory do not yield grade-equivalent scores, the following arbitrary grade-equivalent scores may be assigned to the instructional reading or auding level derived from these tests in order to compute the pupil's reading age or listening age:

Pre-primer = 1.2	low third reader = 3.2
primer = 1.5	higher third reader = 3.7
first reader = 1.8	fourth reader = 4.5
low second reader = 2.2	fifth reader = 5.5
high second reader = 2.7	sixth reader = 6.5; and so on

Estimating Present Mental Age or Listening Age

Unless the measure of potential was obtained recently, it is necessary to estimate a present mental age (MA) or listening age (LA) because MA and LA change with age (until about age 16 for MA). For children under age 16, MA can be estimated with the formula

$$MA = \frac{CA \times IQ}{100}$$

For those 16 and older:

$$MA = \frac{16 \times IQ}{100}$$

(Finucci *et al*. 1982). CA must be converted from twelfths to tenths; simply divide the number of months by 12 (e.g., 8 years 6 months = 8.5 because 6 ÷ 12 = .5). When a listening-comprehension score is in grade equivalents, it can be converted to an LA by adding 5.2 years and adjusting for the length of time since the measure was obtained.

Comparing Expectancy with Reading Achievement

At least six procedures are employed in comparing reading achievement with expectancy: years below grade level, mental age minus reading age, expectancy formulas, standard-score procedures, procedures using quotients, and regression equations.

Years below Grade-Level Procedure

The use of a given number of years below grade level as a sole criterion for reading disability has at least two serious flaws. First, it does not consider the child's potential for learning. Thus slow learners, although reading reasonably close to their potentials, would be classified as disabled readers. Second, the distribution of achievement scores spreads out in the higher grades, so it is likely that more students will fall 1, 2, or 3 years below grade level on norm-referenced tests. The meaning of the differences also changes. For example, a second grader scoring 1 year below grade level might be at the 10th percentile; an eleventh grader scoring 3 years below grade level may be at the 25th to 30th percentile (Shepard, Smith, & Vojir 1983). Mainly as a result of the use of grade-equivalent scores, this method substantially overestimates disability in the upper grades and underestimates the severity of difficulties in the early grades (Reynolds 1981a).

Direct Comparison of Mental Age with Reading Age

The first four editions of this book recommended the direct comparison of MA with RA. But this procedure has two major faults. First, an age scale does not have equal intervals. For example, a difference of 1 year at age 7 may be comparable to a difference of 2 years at age 12. To overcome this, sliding scales were recommended as a guideline in determining when a discrepancy between MA and RA indicated reading disability: at least a 6-month difference in Grades 1–3, a 9-month difference in Grades 4 and 5, and a 12-month difference above fifth grade. Other authors have suggested larger minimum differences, such as 1 year in Grades 2 and 3 and 2 years from Grade 4 up. Second, the MA minus RA procedure ignores the regression effect.

Expectancy Formulas

Reading expectancy formulas are actually variations of a general linear regression model that have been simplified by weighting the variables used in the formulas. Thus they are based on certain assumptions, such as the size of the correlation between the measures of learning potential and reading. Such reading expectancy formulas will be in error depending on the degree to which the correlation between reading and potential and/or the standard deviation of reading achievement is misestimated (Burns 1982b).

The Bond and Tinker formula (Bond, Tinker, Wasson, & Wasson 1984) employs years in school (YIS), IQ, and a constant of 1. Their formula may be expressed as follows:

$$\text{Reading Expectancy (RE)} = \frac{\text{YIS} \times \text{IQ}}{100} + 1$$

Applying this formula to a child with an IQ of 75 at the end of the second grade would result in an RE of 2.5 $\left(\dfrac{2 \times 75}{100} + 1\right)$. The same RE score would result if the child had spent 2 years in first grade. To determine if the child is a disabled reader, his reading achievement score is subtracted from his reading expectancy score. Then this difference score is compared against suggested "minimal grade score discrepancies" that range from .50 for Grade 1 to 2.0 for Grade 7 and above (these increase slightly as the grade levels get higher). There is no indication as to how these criteria were established.

According to Burns (1982b), the Bond and Tinker formula assumes an unrealistically low correlation between IQ and reading achievement. In our opinion, the formula works well for children who are close to average intelligence but sets unduly high expectations for the mentally slow and unduly low expectations for the very bright.

A. Horn (1941) developed four reading expectancy formulas based on correlation between particular intelligence and reading tests administered in Los Angeles. The weighting of MA and CA suggests an increase in the correlations between potential and reading as the pupils got older (.50, .60, .67, and .75 respectively). Horn's RE formulas are as follows:

1. For CAs 6–0 to 8–5, $\dfrac{\text{MA} + \text{CA}}{2}$

2. For CAs 8–6 to 9–11, $\dfrac{3\text{MA} + 2\text{CA}}{5}$

3. For CAs 10–0 to 11–11, $\dfrac{2\text{MA} + \text{CA}}{3}$

4. For CAs 12 and up, $\dfrac{3\text{MA} + \text{CA}}{4}$

A constant of 5 is subtracted from the resulting formula score to provide a RE score in grade-equivalent form. For the previously cited case, application of the Horn formula 1 would result in an RE of 2.0 $\left[\left(\dfrac{6 + 8}{2}\right) - 5\right]$. The reading expectancy formula employed is very likely to influence who is designated as a disabled reader. As with the MA minus CA procedure and Bond and Tinker formula, the problem with the Horn formulas is knowing how much of a difference between expectancy and achievement constitutes a disability.

Difference scores, the result of subtracting one test score from another, are often criticized as being unreliable. This viewpoint has been challenged by Rogosa and Willett (1983). Berk (1984) suggested a procedure in which the reliability and validity of the ability–achievement discrepancy score are calculated and used in deciding whether a disability exists. A formula for determining whether a discrepancy score is significant was offered by Reynolds (1981a), who noted that the size of a discrepancy score needed to indicate a real difference is a function of the reliability and standard deviations of the tests involved. Burns (1982b) presented procedures for developing a confidence band about a true score that may be used to determine how much confidence can be placed in the predicted score.

Standard-Score Procedures

In order to overcome the problems created by use of the grade or age scores, some writers have suggested using standard scores that express the pupil's scores in distance from the mean in standard deviation units.

Erickson (1975) suggested using Z-scores for determining reading disability. Raw scores from the two tests are transformed to Z-scores, and each pupil's Z-score for reading is subtracted from his potential Z-score. Erickson defined the 10% of students with the largest negative discrepancies as having a reading disability.

Winkley (1962) recommended using stanine scores obtained from reading and intelligence tests. The score for the intelligence test had to be at least two stanines higher than that for the reading test in order to indicate that a child had a reading disability.

Hanna, Dyck, and Holen (1979) recommended using nationally standardized tests of aptitude and achievement and converting the test scores into T-scores (normalized standard scores with a mean of 100 and a standard deviation of 10). The reading T-score is subtracted from the aptitude test T-score, with a difference of 8 or more points indicating fairly sure evidence of a disability, and 4 to 8 points a doubtful range. While the T-score has some statistical advantage over age or grade scores, the recommended procedure ignores the size of the correlation between aptitude and achievement scores, as well as the regression effect.

Procedures Using Quotients

Although the idea of an accomplishment quotient in which a measure of achievement is divided by a measure of potential dates back almost to the beginning of standardized testing, its first major application to reading disability was in Monroe's classical study (1932). The Monroe expectancy formula gives weight to MA, CA, and Arithmetic Age (AA). An Expected Reading Grade (ERG) is determined by applying the following formula:

$$ERG = \frac{MA + CA + AA}{3} - 5$$

Monroe developed a Reading Index (RI) quotient in which the Observed Reading Grade (ORG) is divided by the ERG and multiplied by 100 to get rid of the decimal:

$$RI = \frac{ORG}{ERG} \times 100$$

Clinically referred poor readers had an average RI of only 49, while an unselected school population had a mean RI of 102. The RIs for the two groups intersected at about 80, which Monroe recommended as a reasonable cutoff quotient for identifying reading disability. Use of an RI quotient of 80 identified 12% of the unselected group as disabled readers.

Myklebust (1968) recommended use of a Learning Quotient (LQ). In reading, the LQ is reading age divided by expectancy age. The expectancy age is the average of MA, CA, and Grade Age (GA = the child's grade level in years and months). The MA used is the higher of verbal or nonverbal. He explained the inclusion of CA as representing physiological maturity and GA as representing opportunity for school learning. The rationale for including both CA and GA is not convincing, since the correlation between those two variables is very high. Myklebust considered LQs below 90 to indicate disability; mild or borderline if between 85 and 89, and severe if below 85. Because it assumes a correlation of .33 between reading and MA, the Mykleburst formula probably overestimates reading expectancy for pupils with IQs under 100 and underestimates it for those over 100 (Burns 1982b).

Yule and Rutter criticized the use of quotients on the basis that it does not provide for the regression effect. "Thus, any measure of achievement that fails to allow for the statistical effects of regression will end up with a group of 'underachievers' in which bright children are overrepresented and dull children are underrepresented" (1976, p. 28). They overlooked the fact that in using an expectancy measure that is the average of three variables, the effect is similar to that of a multiple regression procedure. A more valid criticism is that both Monroe and Myklebust chose their variables on the basis of armchair reasoning and weighted them in an essentially arbitrary fashion.

Regression Equations

Regression procedures adjust for the phenomenon of regression toward the mean. Predicted scores for high scorers on the measure from which the prediction is made will be lower than if the regression effect had not been considered; the predicted scores of low scorers will be higher. In other words, unless the regression effect is considered, expectancy scores generally will be too high for bright students and too low for children with below-average IQ. This will result in overidentifying high-IQ students and underidentifying lower-IQ students. The higher the correlation between the test of potential and the reading test, the closer the predicted score will be to the potential score; the lower the correlation, the closer it will be to the mean.

R. L. Thorndike (1963) suggested using a regression-based discrepancy procedure in which the regression line is determined empirically. Aptitude and reading tests are administered to a representative sample. Then the average reading score is determined for each IQ score, and a smoothed line is made connecting each IQ point. The individual's predicted reading score is compared with his or her obtained reading score. If the discrepancy is at least as large as its standard error, the chances are at least five to one that the difference between the predicted and obtained scores is significant, thereby indicating failure to read up to expectancy. The advantages of using a regression equation may be offset by the practical problems involved (Cone & Wilson 1981).

McLeod (1979) advocated using data from several sources to develop a statistical model of the regression in the population under consideration. But this approach used a potential–achievement correlation of .5, which is too low for older students, and the cutoff values were too stringent. Later, McLeod (1981) suggested expressing discrepancy scores as Z-scores to overcome the problems caused by the nonnormality of score distributions. A critical value of Z (cutoff score) could be set which would identify a desired percentage of the population as disabled. McLeod's procedures do not exclude slow learners.

Regression procedures were used in several large-scale studies (Yule & Rutter 1976). Using nonverbal group IQ tests, the reality of the regression effect was demonstrated. For those with IQs above the average, the mean reading scores were less above average than the mean IQs; for those with below-average IQs, the mean reading scores were not as low as their mean IQs. A separate regression was used for each age group. "Specific reading retardation" (reading disability) was defined as a reading score two or more standard errors of prediction below the predicted score (Yule *et al.* 1974). This corresponded to a disparity of at least 28 months between the predicted and obtained reading comprehension score and included only 2.3% to 5.4% of the populations. Such a criterion is considerably more severe than ordinarily used in determining reading disability.

There are several problems with the regression procedure. A regression equation is specific for the measures of potential and reading used in obtaining it and the characteristics of the population used. Certain statistical requirements about the normality of the distributions and so on should be met (Cronbach 1971). The correlation should be obtained from one population and cross-validated on other populations to check its generalizability. Application of a regression procedure requires having staff sufficiently well versed in statistics to understand the procedure and apply it correctly. Shepard (1980), who critiqued the regression-discrepancy method, concluded that it should not be used as the sole criterion for identifying reading-disability students.

A Recommended Procedure for Identifying Reading Disabilities

Starting with the Fifth Edition of this book, we have recommended a procedure for identifying reading disabilities that uses a ratio or quotient procedure but has the effect of a regression procedure. It uses the concepts of Reading Expectancy Age, Reading Expectancy Quotient, and Reading Quotient.

General intelligence, or listening comprehension, is only one of many factors that are relevant to an individual's progress in reading. The average correlation between intelligence and reading comprehension (between .60 and .75 at most grade levels) provides a little less than half of the information needed to predict reading performance with complete accuracy. Other factors that influence reading expectancy include errors of measurement and a variety of traits or abilities that improve or grow with increasing age, such as general and specific information, linguistic competence, vocabulary, and reading skills. An estimate of reading expectancy based only on intelligence or listening comprehension is likely to be less accurate than one that also gives some weight to general maturing.

Although chronological age (CA) is not in itself closely correlated with growth in reading when other factors are held constant, CA provides a time dimension within which a variety of maturing traits have the opportunity to develop. Thus CA can function as a common denominator for a variety of factors which influence growth in reading and which develop as children get older.

Reading Expectancy Age

A simple formula that gives priority to the importance of intelligence but also recognizes the presence of other age-related characteristics in reading expectancy involves giving mental age twice the weight of chronological age. The formula may be written:

$$\text{Reading Expectancy Age (R Exp A)} = \frac{2MA + CA}{3}$$

In this formula MA and CA should be expressed in years and tenths, giving R Exp A also in years and tenths.

This R Exp A formula yields essentially the same results as a simple regression equation for predicting reading age from mental age alone, assuming an average correlation of .67 between MA and RA. It is the same as one of the Horn formulas (see p. 149) but applied to a broader age range, from 8 to 14 years. The assumed correlation of .67 does not differ considerably from .61, which was the median of 486 correlations between intelligence and reading reported by Hammill and McNutt (1981).[6]

For children under age 8, the use of any expectancy formula is somewhat dubious. But, if one is to be used, the Horn formula $\frac{MA + CA}{2}$ may provide a closer approximation to what one would find with a regression procedure. It assumes a correlation of .50 between intelligence and reading, which is not far from the .45 that is the median of 60 correlations for Grades 1 to 3 reported by

---

[6] Calculations using all four Horn formulas were made for hypothetical cases of children with CAs of 7, 9, 11, and 13 and with MAs 1 year below, at, and 1 year above their CAs, placing their IQ in the 90–110 range approximately. As would be expected, there were no differences in R Exp As at any age level when MA equaled CA. As the assumed correlations between IQ and reading increased from .50 to .67, the R Exp As decreased by one tenth of a year when MA was 1 year lower than CA; formulas that assumed correlations of .67 and .75 essentially yielded the same R Exp As for below-average IQ children. When MA exceeded CA by 1 year, the R Exp As increased by one tenth of a year as the assumed correlations increased. It would thus seem that for most children, it would make only a slight difference as to which formula was used.

Stanovich, Cunningham, and Feeman (1984). This same formula is preferable when the correlation between the intelligence and reading tests being used is close to .50. Determining reading disability for pupils over age 15 is covered on page 157.

Reading Expectancy Quotient

A quotient that expresses how a pupil's present level of reading ability compares with his expected reading level can be obtained by dividing reading age by reading expectancy and multiplying by 100 to avoid use of decimals. In formula form:

$$\text{Reading Expectancy Quotient (R Exp Q)} = \frac{RA}{R \text{ Exp } A} \times 100$$

Reading Expectancy Quotients that fall between 90 and 110 are considered to fall within normal limits. A cutoff score of 90 takes into account that part of any obtained difference may be an artifact based on chance errors of measurement. An R Exp Q below 90 indicates failure to read up to expectancy and therefore the strong likelihood of a disability or underachievement. The lower the R Exp Q, the more likely the presence of a disability and the more severe the disability. R Exp Qs below 80 almost certainly indicate disability. Finucci *et al.* (1982) empirically validated a zone of achievement quotients from .81 to .90 as the borderline region below which readers are "disabled" and above which they are "normal." A child with an IQ of 100 who was totally unable to read (Reading grade = 1.0, RA = 6.2) at CA 7.7, would have an R Exp Q of 81. If he remained a nonreader, it would fall to 64 at age 9.7 and 53 at age 11.7. Unless a child's reading ability improves, his disability becomes progressively more severe with age.

Quotients above 110 indicate that reading is above expectancy. This may be a sign of great effort and practice, or of very superior instruction; or it may be an artifact of the tests employed (Maginnis 1972).

Distinguishing among Disabled Readers, Underachievers, and Slow Learners

It is worthwhile to make as accurate a distinction as possible among (1) disabled readers who are unable to function academically at grade level because of their poor reading ability, (2) underachievers whose reading ability is sufficient for grade-level requirements although well below their own expectancy, and (3) slow learners whose reading ability is below age level but is in keeping with their somewhat limited learning capacity. This may be accomplished by using both the Reading Expectancy Quotient and the Reading Quotient. The Reading Quotient is simply RA divided by CA, multiplied by 100 to eliminate the decimal point. Thus the formula for comparing the individual's present level of reading performance with that of others of his chronological age is:

$$\text{Reading Quotient (RQ)} = \frac{RA}{CA} \times 100$$

When children's R Exp Q and RQ are both below 90, they are reading significantly below both their own expectancy and the normal performance for

Table 6.1. Summary of Objective Definitions of Reading Ability and Disability

Classification	R Exp Q[a]	RQ[b]
Normal reader	90 or above	90 or above
Disabled reader	below 90	below 90
Underachiever in reading	below 90	90 or above
Slow learner in reading	90 or above	below 90

[a] Expresses how a learner's present general level of reading ability compares with *his* expected reading level.

[b] Expresses how a learner's present level of reading ability compares with that of *others of his chronological age.*

their age group. Therefore they are properly classified as cases of reading disability. Those whose R Exp Q is below 90 but whose RQ is 90 or above are usually able to cope with their reading assignments in school, although they are not making full use of above-average or superior potential; for them, the term "underachiever" seems preferable. An individual whose R Exp Q is 90 or above, but whose RQ is below 90, is reading generally about as well as can be expected of one with somewhat limited potential. An individual with below-average intelligence may more properly be classified as a disabled reader than as a slow learner in reading when he or she is functioning significantly below potential.

An Example. John is 10 years 7 months old (CA = 10.6), has an IQ of 105, and is in the fifth grade. His reading grade-equivalent scores are silent reading 4.3, oral reading 3.1; he therefore has an average reading grade of 3.7, which yields a RA of 8.9 (3.7 + 5.2).

$$\text{MA} = \frac{10.6 \times 105}{100} = 11.1$$

$$\text{R Exp A} = \frac{2(11.1) + 10.6}{3} = 10.9$$

$$\text{R Exp Q} = \frac{8.9}{10.9} \times 100 = 82$$

$$\text{RQ} = \frac{8.9}{10.6} \times 100 = 84$$

Since John is well below the critical value of 90 on both R Exp Q and RQ, there should be no hesitancy in classifying him as having a reading disability.

Using a Reading Expectancy Age Table

The computations explained and illustrated above can be greatly shortened by the use of Table 6.1. If you know the IQ and CA of a child, his or her R Exp A can be read from Table 6.2. If the IQ or CA falls between two values given in the table, use the nearest value and the result will usually be correct within .2 of a year. For greater accuracy, you can interpolate or do the arithmetic as explained above. The use of the table may be illustrated with the example given above. For John, CA 10.6 and IQ 105, the nearest CA column is 10.7 and there is an IQ 105 row; these intersect to give the value of R Exp A as 11.0, only .1 year different from the 10.9 computed with the formula.

Table 6.2. Reading Expectancy Ages for Selected Combinations of Chronological Age and Intelligence Quotient

	CHRONOLOGICAL AGE												
IQ	7.2	7.7	8.2	8.7	9.2	9.7	10.2	10.7	11.2	11.7	12.2	12.7	13.2
140	9.1	9.6	10.3	10.9	11.6	12.1	12.9	13.4	14.1	14.7	15.4	15.9	16.7
135	8.8	9.4	10.1	10.6	11.3	11.8	12.5	13.1	13.8	14.3	15.0	15.5	16.2
130	8.6	9.1	9.8	10.3	11.0	11.5	12.2	12.7	13.4	13.9	14.6	15.1	15.8
125	8.4	8.8	9.5	10.0	10.7	11.2	11.9	12.3	13.0	13.5	14.2	14.7	15.4
120	8.1	8.6	9.3	9.7	10.4	10.9	11.5	12.0	12.7	13.1	13.8	14.3	14.9
115	7.9	8.3	9.0	9.4	10.1	10.5	11.2	11.7	12.3	12.7	13.4	13.8	14.5
110	7.6	8.1	8.7	9.2	9.8	10.2	10.9	11.3	11.9	12.4	13.0	13.4	14.0
105	7.4	7.9	8.4	8.9	9.5	9.9	10.5	11.0	11.5	12.0	12.6	13.0	13.6
100	7.2	7.7	8.2	8.7	9.2	9.7	10.2	10.7	11.2	11.7	12.2	12.7	13.2
95	6.9	7.4	7.9	8.3	8.9	9.3	9.7	10.4	10.8	11.3	11.8	12.2	12.7
90	6.7	7.1	7.6	8.0	8.6	8.9	9.5	9.9	10.4	10.8	11.4	11.7	12.3
85	6.4	6.8	7.4	7.7	8.2	8.6	9.1	9.5	10.0	10.4	10.9	11.3	11.8
80	6.2	6.6	7.1	7.4	7.9	8.3	8.8	9.2	9.7	10.0	10.5	10.9	11.4
75	6.0	6.3	6.8	7.2	7.6	8.0	8.5	8.8	9.3	9.7	10.1	10.5	11.0
70	5.7	6.1	6.5	6.9	7.3	7.7	8.1	8.5	8.9	9.3	9.7	10.1	10.5
65	5.5	5.9	6.3	6.6	7.0	7.3	7.8	8.1	8.6	8.9	9.3	9.6	10.1
60	5.3	5.6	6.0	6.3	6.7	7.0	7.5	7.8	8.2	8.5	8.9	9.2	9.8

Note: Any expectancy age in the table can be changed into an expectancy grade equivalent by subtracting 5.2 years.

Using a Reading Expectancy Quotient Table

Finding Reading Expectancy Quotients can be speeded up by using Table 6.3. In the left-hand column, find the number nearest to the child's RA. Read across on that line to where it meets the vertical column closest to the child's R Exp A; the number at that intersection shows his approximate R Exp Q. The numbers in bold type fall within the normal range of 90 to 110. Numbers below

Table 6.3. Reading Expectancy Quotients for Selected Combinations of Reading Expectancy Age and Reading Age

Reading age	READING EXPECTANCY AGE											
	6.7	7.2	7.7	8.2	8.7	9.2	9.7	10.2	10.7	11.2	11.7	12.2
6.2	**92**	86	80	75	71	67	63	60	57	55	52	50
6.7	**100**	**93**	87	81	77	72	69	65	62	59	57	54
7.2	107	**100**	**93**	87	82	78	74	70	67	64	61	59
7.7	114	**106**	**100**	**93**	88	83	79	75	71	68	65	63
8.2	122	113	**106**	**100**	**94**	89	84	80	76	73	70	67
8.7	129	120	112	**106**	**100**	**94**	**90**	85	81	78	74	71
9.2	137	128	119	112	**106**	**100**	**95**	**90**	86	82	79	75
9.7	145	135	126	118	111	**105**	**100**	**95**	91	87	83	80
10.2	152	142	132	124	117	111	**105**	**100**	**95**	91	87	84
10.7	160	149	139	130	123	116	**110**	**105**	**100**	**96**	91	88
11.2	167	156	145	137	129	122	115	**110**	**105**	**100**	**96**	92
11.7	175	163	152	143	134	127	121	115	**109**	**104**	**100**	**96**
12.2	182	169	158	149	140	133	128	120	114	**109**	**104**	**100**

90, in the upper-right section, indicate that reading is significantly below expectancy. Numbers in the lower-left section, from 111 up, indicate that reading is significantly above expectancy. When the R Exp Q obtained from the table is close to 90, it is advisable to go through the arithmetic operations to get a more accurate result.

Reading Quotients (RQ) can also be read directly from Table 6.3. Interpret the heading *Reading Expectancy Age* to mean *Chronological Age*. Find the number in the left-hand column that is closest to the child's RA and read across horizontally to where the row intersects the CA column closest to the child's CA; at the intersection one finds the number closest to the child's RQ.

Determining Reading Disability for Adolescents and Adults

The procedures described above do not apply well above the age of 15 because mental ability does not continue to grow in approximately linear fashion during adolescence. When the reading-grade score is below eighth grade and a satisfactory IQ is available, however, the procedures described above will not be greatly in error if the CA is used up to the age of 15 and a CA of 16 is used for all ages above that.

When secondary school and college aptitude and reading tests do not have age or grade norms, it is more appropriate to use a regression equation based on the correlation between the particular aptitude and reading tests employed (see p. 151) than just to compare percentile or standard scores on the two tests (R. L. Thorndike 1963). Another method that will work above age 15 is to take the difference between stanines on tests of reading and potential, with a disability indicated when potential is two or more stanines higher than reading.

Some Questions about Objective Measures of Reading Disabilities

Since different procedures for identifying disabled readers can result in considerable differences as to how many and which individuals are selected (Algozzine, Ysseldyke, & Shinn 1982), some consideration of issues concerning the application of objective measures of reading disability is desirable.

1. What is the best measure of intelligence to use? The question of using verbal, nonverbal, or a total score, or alternatively a measure of listening comprehension, has been considered on pages 145–147. Most of the formulas described use MA rather than IQ. If the MA is corrected for present age and the CA is also used, the difference between using MA or IQ should be inconsequential.

2. Which is better to use, age scores or grade scores? The use of grade scores seems to assume that children are equal in readiness at the beginning of first grade and start there from zero. Age scores take into consideration that children have been maturing and learning for about 6 years before reading instruction begins. The advantage is with age scores.

3. Should children of below-average intelligence be excluded? For research purposes, it is legitimate to delimit an experimental population in whatever way needed to check the validity of the hypotheses being studied. For school practice, other considerations should apply. Children who are below average in intelligence, but are not slow enough to be classified as mentally retarded, find it difficult or impossible to achieve at grade level. Many of them try hard, and some of them achieve quite well in relation to their somewhat limited learning abilities. Slow learners who are not eligible for special education should be considered for remedial instruction on the same basis of potential above achievement that applies to brighter children.

4. *What does research show about the relative value of the several formulas?* There is, unfortunately, little research on the comparative merits of the several procedures available. One study (Dore-Boyce, Misner, & McGuire 1975) compared the Bond and Tinker formula, Harris 1 (MA minus RA), Harris 2 (R Exp A), and the Horn formulas. The *Otis-Lennon Mental Ability Test* was used to predict SRA Total Reading scores of 733 fourth- and fifth-grade pupils. Correlations between the formula scores and the obtained reading scores were as follows: Harris 1, .69; Harris 2, .62; Horn, .61; Bond and Tinker, .47. The Bond and Tinker formula was significantly the poorest in all comparisons. The main contributor was found to be MA, with CA adding a little to the accuracy of the prediction; grade placement and gender added nothing. This study's results are limited in generalizability for two reasons: The intelligence test used required reading, making the validity of low scores questionable; and the limited age range of 2 years restricted the possible contribution of CA.

Honel (1973) compared eight reading expectancy formulas and concluded that "the R Exp Q (Harris) appeared to have the broadest application and consequently was deemed to be the preferred formula." It is questionable, however, if breadth of application is the best criterion to use. Burns (1982b) concluded that the Horn formula, which we use, provides the best simplified estimate of reading expectancy.

5. *How accurate are reading expectancy formulas?* Dore-Boyce, Misner, and McGuire (1975) reported standard errors of estimate of 1.3 to 1.5 grades for the formulas they studied. Yule (1967), using different tests, found the standard error of estimate to be 1.3 years for reading accuracy and comprehension. This means that there is a considerable margin of error in a computed reading expectancy score, and this should be kept in mind if a child's expectancy score is close to the cutoff point.

Reading specialists should not rely exclusively on a numerical formula but should give serious consideration to teacher recommendations and the child's academic performance. If the child's reading shows very little growth each year, that reinforces the formula score in indicating a need for special remedial help.

6. *What is the best cutoff point?* For research, any cutoff score may be selected that fits the purpose of the researcher; it may be set low so as to include only severe disabilities or high to include mild disabilities as well.

In school practice a cutoff score is usually not needed. Children are arranged in a rank order of need, considering formula scores and teacher recommendations and school policies, which may favor selecting children from certain grades. The children are chosen from the rank order until the total number that can be accommodated in the remedial reading program are selected;

the rest go on the waiting list. However, if the last child chosen has an R Exp Q well below 85, the remedial reading program is not reaching all the children who need it.

For more complete explanations and critiques of the various procedures for determining reading disability, refer to Cone and Wilson (1981), Burns (1982b), and Berk (1984).

7. *Is it better to use regression procedures or simplified estimates of reading expectancy?* A regression procedure provides more accurate estimates of reading expectancy, but reading expectancy formulas are quicker and easier to utilize. Each user must decide the merits of both procedures and select the most appropriate. When pupils take an intelligence test and a reading test offered by the same publisher, the publisher may be able to provide anticipated reading scores based on the measure of learning potential.

7

Assessing Reading Performance

Information concerning children's reading skills, abilities, levels of achievement, interests, and attitudes can be useful in determining if instructional objectives are being achieved and in program planning. Of course, these two uses are not mutually exclusive.

In the first instance, data from tests, teacher observations, and pupil performance during reading activities are used in assessing pupil progress and evaluating the reading program. The second use, program planning, can involve various degrees of complexity. For most classroom teachers, and as a first stage of diagnosis, data are gathered to answer two questions: (1) At what general level(s) of reading achievement is this child functioning at present? (2) What specific reading skills has the child mastered? The emphasis is on understanding the strengths and needs of individual children. Such information results in assigning appropriate materials for instructional purposes or independent reading and teaching only those skills that have not been mastered and that the child is ready to learn. Thus reading instruction can be adjusted to individual and group needs.

I. SOURCES OF INFORMATION

Information regarding students' reading abilities may be obtained from norm-referenced, criterion-referenced, or informal measures. Each source can provide useful information, and information from a variety of sources over time provides a more complete and reliable assessment of a pupil's reading skills and abilities than a single testing does.

Norm-Referenced Tests

The material in a standardized test is selected after a careful analysis of the reading a pupil in the grades for which the test is intended may be called on to do. Since the test is designed for use in a wide variety of school systems, it must not parallel too closely the content, style, or vocabulary of any one published reading program. It must also include a wide enough range of difficulty so that poor readers in the lowest grade for which the test is intended can get some answers right and the better readers in the highest grade for which the test is intended probably cannot get a perfect score. Nearly always, two or more forms are provided; they are comparable in kind of question and level of difficulty. This makes it possible to retest a pupil without using the same material.

Every standardized test is accompanied by a manual of directions that tells in detail how the test should be given and scored. It is essential to follow these directions closely. If this is not done, the norms will not be applicable because norms are based on performances under standard conditions.

Test users should understand three concepts: reliability, validity, and norms. *Reliability* indicates the degree to which the test yields consistent results, or how sure one can be that the obtained score does not vary greatly from the learner's true score. Test reliability is usually stated as a correlation coefficient or as a standard error of measurement. Split-half reliability coefficients are usually higher than test–retest coefficients.

Test reliability is affected by such factors as the number of items in a test (generally longer tests are more reliable), the range of achievement of the sample in the variable being measured (the more restricted the range, the lower the reliability coefficient), and the characteristics of the group tested. Although the total score of a standardized test usually is highly reliable, subtests may not have sufficient reliability for diagnostic use with individuals.

No test is a perfectly reliable measure; chance errors in measurement and fluctuations in individual performance preclude this. For any test, average scores of groups are more reliable than scores for individuals. For individual assessment, a test or subtest should have a reliability coefficient of at least .90 for a single age or grade level (coefficients based on a wide range of ages or grades tend to be spuriously high), or a standard error of measurement of not more than 3 months for grade-equivalent scores.

The *standard error of measurement* indicates the variation in test scores to be expected if that test were given repeatedly to the individual. By adding and subtracting the standard error of measurement to the obtained score, one can determine the range of scores in which the individual's true score probably lies. Thus, if a learner obtained a grade-equivalent score of 4.3 on a test with a standard error of measurement of 0.2, the chances are about 2 to 1 that his "true" score lies somewhere between 4.1 and 4.5 (4.3 ± 0.2) and about 19 to 1 that it is between 3.9 and 4.7 (4.3 ± twice the standard error). The smaller the standard error of measurement, the more reliable the test.

Validity is the degree of accuracy with which a test measures what it is intended to measure. There are different kinds of validity, each of which answers a somewhat different question about the test.

A test with low reliability cannot be valid, but high reliability does not ensure validity. Evidence about the reliability and validity of a test should be given in the test manual.

Norms are statistics that describe the test performance of the groups on whom the test was standardized. After a test has been constructed, it is given to large numbers of pupils, chosen to be representative of those for whom the test is intended.[1] Norms are simply statements of the results obtained in this initial testing and may be used as a basis for interpreting results on the test when given to other pupils. Norms never should be considered a desired standard of achievement. The kinds of norms used in reading tests are grade-equivalent scores, percentiles, standard scores, normal-curve equivalent scores, scaled scores, extended scale scores, and stanines.

Grade-equivalent scores are based on raw scores, usually the number of correct responses. Few tests use a correction formula for guessing, although many tests have a minimum score below which no norms are assigned. A grade equivalent indicates the grade level for which the raw score was the median score actually obtained by the norming population. By definition, half the children can be expected to score above and half below the median. Grade-equivalent scores are given in years and tenths because there are usually 10 months in the school year (September = .0 and June = .9). Thus, if the average raw score obtained by the norming sample that was in the second month of third grade was 10, any pupil getting 10 correct answers is assigned a grade-equivalent score of 3.1. It makes no difference which 10 items were answered correctly.

Among the limitations of grade-equivalent scores enumerated by Berk (1981), Baumann and Stevenson (1982) and Hills (1983) are the following:

1. They assume that (*a*) the rate of growth is constant throughout the school year (i.e., equal gains are made each month); (*b*) there is no growth, or one month's growth, during the summer; (*c*) the amount of gain is the same from one grade level to the next.
2. They are not directly comparable across tests or subtests.
3. They are not equally spaced in terms of raw scores (e.g., 10 raw score points may separate grade scores of 1.0 and 2.0, but only 4 points may

---

[1] Nationally normed tests, however, may not be as representative as test manuals suggest. A self-selection bias enters in determining which schools participate in the norming. This results in schools with certain characteristics being overrepresented (Baglin 1981).

separate 4.0 from 5.0). At times a small number of correct answers can greatly influence the GE score.

4. They are prone to misinterpretation. A grade-equivalent score usually does not indicate that reading material at that level is suitable for instruction, nor that the child has mastered all the reading skills taught in the reading program up to the grade level indicated by the test score.

5. The grade-equivalent scale reflects the yearly growth of achievement for average students; it is less accurate in doing so for children who are considerably above or below average in reading ability and who therefore are more likely to make yearly growth of more or less than one grade level (MacGinitie *et al.* 1978).

Because grade-equivalent scores have been so badly misinterpreted, the International Reading Association (1982b) has advocated abandoning their use.

Percentiles or *percentile ranks* indicate how a pupil compares with other children in the same grade or age level. These scores range from 1 to 99, with a median of 50. A percentile score of 89 means that the student did as well as or better than 89% of the group with whom the comparison is being made. It does not represent the percentage of correct responses. The distances between percentiles do not represent equal units across the entire percentile range, and so they should not be averaged. A student has to answer more questions correctly in order to obtain a higher percentile in the middle range of scores than at the extremes. For instance, it might take five additional correct answers to move from the 50th to the 55th percentile, whereas one more correct response can move a pupil from the 90th to the 95th percentile or from the 1st to the 5th percentile (Plas 1977).

Standard scores or *T-scores* are normalized scores; that is, they have been transformed to a normal distribution, the mean (usually 50 or 100) and the standard deviation (usually 10 or 15) being preassigned. A standard score of 50 (or 100) indicates average performance. Because standard scores represent equal units, they can be averaged and used to compare performances on different tests.

Normal-curve equivalent scores (NCE) are based on percentile ranks that have been transformed into a normalized scale representing equal units (e.g., a difference of 10 NCE units represents the same difference in reading achievement between any 2 points along the scale). NCEs, which resemble standard scores, range from 1 to 99 with a mean of 50, and describe a pupil's performance in relation to a group of pupils at the same grade level.

Scaled scores (SS) express the results of tests at various levels within a test battery on a single common scale. Thus, scaled scores can be compared from form to form and from level to level, and are useful in measuring change in achievement over time. Scaled scores, however, are not directly comparable from one subject to another (Prescott *et al.* 1978).

Extended scale scores (ESS), also referred to as *expanded standard scores* or a *growth scale*, provide a single continuous scale by which a child's or a group's progress can be followed during the school years. Because ESSs represent equal units, growth in a student's or group's reading achievement can be compared with that of other students or groups even when the initial level of achievement is not the same (MacGinitie *et al.* 1978).

Stanines are normalized standard-score scales divided into 9 segments, ranging from a low of 1 to a high of 9. Stanines 4, 5, and 6 indicate average performance. Each stanine represents a range of scaled scores, thus avoiding some of the implied precision of other kinds of scores. However, even stanines are not perfectly reliable. When comparing stanines for an individual, at least a 2-stanine difference is needed in order to be reasonably certain that a real difference exists between the skills or abilities tested.

Criterion-Referenced Tests

Whereas norm-referenced (NR) tests relate test performance to relative standards (the performance of the one tested is compared with that of the norming population), criterion-referenced (CR) tests relate test performance to absolute standards (the performance of the one tested is compared to a predetermined criterion). NR tests are usually global measures of reading ability, yielding scores in general areas such as word recognition, vocabulary, and comprehension; most CR tests measure mastery of specific skills (e.g., given 10 paragraphs written at fourth reader level, the learner can correctly select from four choices the implied main idea of at least 8 paragraphs). The NR tests are constructed so as not to be biased for or against any particular reading program. The CR tests may be deliberately constructed to assess the skills taught in a given program, with each subtest measuring mastery of a particular instructional objective.

Theoretically, CR tests can be useful in individualizing reading instruction. Of course, those who believe that reading is a unitary ability (see Chapter 1), would not use typical CR tests because they "break up" reading into a number of discrete skills.

Tests That Accompany Reading Programs

Most basal reader programs provide tests that are specifically geared to that program. Some provide oral reading tests to assist in placing the learner in the appropriate text. Such oral reading tests are most often (1) a single selection to determine whether the book from which the selection is taken is suitable for the child's reading instruction, or (2) what amounts to an informal reading inventory based on that reading series. Almost all published programs have silent group mastery tests that are administered after each book has been completed. Validity and reliability of these tests is rarely reported. Some teachers' manuals contain CR tests for assessing skill development. Turner (1984) has provided forms that may be used in evaluating the quality and appropriateness of the test components of a basal reading series.

Informal Assessment

Informal assessment is needed to obtain information unavailable from other sources or to supplement available data. The NR and CR tests do not always yield the desired information, nor is any one measure a perfect indicator of a learner's reading ability. An important aspect, the functional and realistic application of reading skills, can be measured only through informal testing (Bliesmer 1972). Informal assessments are often more valid measures than standardized reading tests because they employ a wide variety of procedures to assess reading performance over a number of different occasions (Farr 1969). The more behaviors sampled, the more likely the assessment is to be accurate.

Ottot (1973) outlined the following steps for informal assessment: (1) Decide exactly what information is desired and what this means in terms of observable behavior; (2) devise new test items, materials, or situations to sample the behavior to be evaluated, or adapt existing ones; (3) keep a record of the child's behavior and responses; (4) analyze the obtained information; and (5) make judgments as to how the information fits the total picture and how well it fills the gap for which it was intended.

Informal assessment may take many forms—observations, teacher-made tests, brief skill tests found in teachers' manuals or in reading materials such as workbooks, checklists that provide for systematized behavioral observations, and anecdotal records. Teacher-made tests may be brief or as extensive as an informal reading inventory.

Some information can be obtained only through skilled observation. For example, because motivation and attention influence reading performance, these two factors should be observed over time while the child is reading in differing situations. Pupils may behave differently when reading in a relaxed one-to-one testing situation than in a tense classroom among peers, or when reading one kind of material as opposed to another. Suggestions for employing behavioral observations in making diagnostic decisions have been provided by Elliot and Piersal (1982).

Correlations between teachers' estimates of children's reading ability and their actual scores on various reading tests fall into the low–moderate range, usually in the .30s to .40s (Brown & Sherbenou 1981). Pupils' evaluations of their own reading abilities have not proven to be a useful source of information (Farr 1969, Jason & Dubnow 1973).

Minimal Competency Tests

Minimal competency tests have taken many forms. There are NR, CR, and informal tests; some are designed for national use, others for particular states, and yet others for specific populations. What they measure and how the skills are sampled also vary considerably. Descriptions of some minimal competency tests appear in Appendix A.

The situation does not seem to have changed since the late 1970s when the literature tended to be pessimistic about the adequacy of the procedures for determining the level of test performance that indicates minimal proficiency (Clearinghouse for Applied Performance Testing 1977). There are various opinions as to how to set standards and establish the reliability and validity of competency tests (see Conaway 1979, Jaeger 1979, Linn 1979a, b, Hambleton &

Eignor 1980). It appears that the one factor common to approaches for setting standards is that they are all judgmental; there is little agreement among cutoff-score methods (Koffler 1980). Guthrie (1981b) stated that minimal competency tests do not possess proven predictive validity. That is, it has not been demonstrated that students who pass these tests are more effective than those who fail the test in meeting society's literacy demands. Perhaps this situation led to the International Reading Association's (1979a) position that "no single measure or method of minimum competencies should ever be the sole criterion for graduation or promotion of a student."

Test Selection and Interpretation

Selecting Reading Tests

Norm-referenced tests can be used to compare the relative reading performance of students. An NR test also can be used to determine the average and range of reading ability in a class or school, to assist in forming reading ability groups, to determine if the child is a disabled reader, and to measure reading growth over time. Criterion-referenced tests are more useful in determining which specific program objectives have been met and by whom, as an aid in establishing special-needs groups, and in measuring individual progress over a short time period. The use of NR and CR tests should not be an either/or proposition. Both have utility, and the information gained from one type should be used to complement that derived from the other.

First decide which type of test, if any, will best provide the desired information. Then narrow the choices by comparing the following information about the available tests: skills measured, how the skills are measured, congruency of test and reading program content, validity, reliability, cost, and time needed for administration and scoring.

Before ordering any test in quantity, it is advisable to consult such sources as Buros (1972, 1975, 1978), Walker (1979), Schell (1981), Mitchell (1983), and Compton (1984) for reviews and opinions about tests. Test reviews also appear from time to time in professional journals, and news about new tests and recent test reviews appear in *News on Tests* (ETS). Test bibliographies and computerized literature searches are available from ERIC/TM at Educational Testing Service. Select a few tests that seem most suitable and order a specimen set of each.

The Proper Use of Reading Tests

Standardized achievement test results are increasingly being used in making policy decisions involving such matters as educational equality and the effectiveness of teachers, schools, and programs. The appropriateness of their use for such purposes is questionable (Haertel & Calfee 1983, Airasian & Madaus 1983).

Most teachers report that they make use of standardized test scores for diagnosing strengths and weaknesses, and for planning instruction for individuals and groups (Stetz & Beck 1981). The prevailing belief, however, is that present testing programs are largely extraneous to daily classroom instruction

(Linn 1983). This is not surprising because standardized tests are not designed to provide much assistance in planning classroom instruction.

Tables that indicate which skills are measured by different reading tests, such as the one presented by Ysseldyke and Marston (1982), can be very misleading. Some educators may mistakenly believe that these tests will actually yield diagnostic information about reading subskills, when all they can indicate is the pupil's relative performances. Most tests cannot reveal why a child gets an item wrong or performs poorly overall. One might also incorrectly assume that certain tests can be used interchangeably because they have similar names. Analysis of the tests usually reveals this to be untrue.

Possible Test Bias

Standardized reading tests have been accused of being biased against minority children. While, in general, minority children score lower than other children on reading tests, the exact reasons for this situation have not been determined. Dialect versions of tests have not proven to be useful in assessment because dialect speakers have not scored higher on such tests than on the original standard English versions (Hockman 1973, Marwit & Neumann 1974, Walker 1975).

There is also the possibility that certain test items are culturally loaded (Royer & Cunningham 1981). But test publishers attempt to keep cultural loading to a minimum, and Veale and Foreman (1983) found little evidence that distractors on multiple-choice items are a source of cultural bias. Only 3 of the 45 items in the comprehension subtest of the *Metropolitan Reading Test* were found to be biased (functioned differently for black students and white students), one of which was biased in favor of blacks (Linn *et al.* 1980). These researchers concluded that (1) there were no generalized principles for guiding the construction of reading comprehension tests that would be useful in avoiding biased items; (2) test bias does not explain differences between the scores of blacks and whites; and (3) it is probably more meaningful to speak of possible bias in the interpretation and use of test results than bias in tests per se. Research evidence does not support the thesis that tests systematically underestimate the performance of minority-group members (Wigdor 1982).

A reading test written in English is invalid for students who have little or no proficiency in English. Many points must be considered in assessing the reading abilities of children with limited English proficiency (Argulewicz & Sanchez 1982), but it seems logical that any such assessment should include a measure of the child's ability to understand or speak English (there is some disagreement over which is a better indicator of language proficiency). An oral language index such as the one developed by Gonzales (1981b, 1984) can be used to assess English language proficiency.

Tests that contain many items that are conceptually alien to the pupils should not be selected, nor should tests be used if they were normed on populations whose attributes differ greatly from those who will be taking the test.

Test scores do not indicate why pupils performed as they did. If a child has difficulty understanding a passage, the possible reasons for this difficulty should be sought. With minority children, particular attention should be paid to a possible lack of task-relevant prior knowledge, syntactic structures with which they may not be familiar, and words that may represent unfamiliar concepts.

Test bias also may be influenced by the extent to which the test measures what the children have been taught. Although standardized achievement tests usually consist of items thought to reflect the important aspects of widely used curriculum materials, they may or may not match the instruction in a particular class or school (Linn 1983).

Out-of-Level Testing

There is some question regarding how accurately standardized tests measure the reading ability of pupils who read way below or way above the grade levels for which the test is intended. The ability of disabled readers may be overestimated because, successfully guessing, they obtain close to the lowest possible score on that level of the test. Gifted readers' ability may be underestimated because it is impossible to score higher than the maximum score obtainable on a given level of a test.

One solution is *out-of-level testing*; that is, pupils are given the level of test commensurate with their estimated present level of reading ability rather than the test usually administered at their grade level. For instance, a fifth grader reading at the second reader level would be given the primary level (usually given in Grades 1–3) rather than the intermediate level (usually given in Grades 4–6) of the test.

Studies of out-of-level testing (Wick 1983, L. Smith *et al.* 1983) have indicated that (1) chance scores were reduced dramatically, and (2) average scores were lower than when in-level tests were administered. Such scores probably reflect the student's achievement more accurately. Some NR tests provide norms for out-of-level testing, and the availability of extended scale scores allows one to convert raw scores from out-of-level testing to in-level scaled scores (L. Smith *et al.* 1983).

Comparing Performance on Subtests or Different Tests

Stanines can be used to compare an individual's performance on reading subtests, with a difference of at least 2 stanines necessary to indicate a real difference. Percentile bands are the most appropriate statistic for assessing student performance across tests. Standard scores are the most appropriate for assessing student growth across test forms and levels for a particular skill area (Iwanicki 1980). Normal-curve equivalents can be used for either individuals or groups, but small differences between NCE scores may not indicate real differences in achievement (MacGinitie *et al.* 1978).

There is also the question whether subtests of NR tests or CR tests really measure discrete reading abilities. Perhaps, as Calfee (1977) commented, differential assessment of specific reading skills may be impossible because reading may be a complex network of interacting systems that cannot be analyzed into simple components. The high correlations among reading subtests, reading and intelligence, and reading and mathematics suggest the possibility that reading, language, and problem solving depend on a single complex cognitive system.

Measuring Reading Gains

A number of unresolved problems in measuring gains in reading achievement (Rankin & Eberwein 1976, Linn & Slinde 1977, Kasdon 1977) go beyond the scope of this book. Suffice it to say that simply subtracting pretest from posttest scores is fraught with problems. Moreover, there is evidence that the majority of children show fluctuations in test performance, at times showing improvement and at other times obtaining lower ratings. Belmont and Belmont stated: "These preliminary findings lend support to the view that individual reading ability is not an even steadily learned function, but rather that it develops in spurts, with rapid advances, backslidings, and slow advances occurring at different times and for different periods of growth" (1978, p. 87).

It should also be realized that a child cannot demonstrate growth if the test does not sample the skills learned. Thus a test that does not reliably measure inferential comprehension would not allow a child to show gains in this area. Many tests are not sensitive enough to reflect small gains in achievement, especially when a short time elapses between pretest and posttesting (e.g., a 4-week summer session). This is particularly important when working with severely disabled readers. A nonreader, for example, may learn to recognize 10 to 15 high-utility words in a month or learn to apply 5 symbol–sound associations in decoding unknown words, but the test score might not show such small gains. When working with disabled readers, it is suggested that baseline data be obtained (e.g., child could not recognize any words in the Harris-Jacobson pre-primer list) so that the gains made can be reported (e.g., at the end of 2 weeks, the child can recognize the following 15 words from the H-J pre-primer list).

Factors That May Influence Test Performance

A number of factors may influence test performance. Factors that cut across various aspects of reading ability are mentioned here; others are considered in the separate sections on assessing comprehension, vocabulary, word recognition, and decoding.

Test-Wiseness. This is the ability to use test-taking skills to their fullest in order to obtain the highest score possible. Students differ widely in their test-wiseness. For example, some students are much better than others in taking multiple-choice tests because they use principles that help them select the most probable correct choice (J. Smith 1982). Because test-wiseness can influence test scores differentially, test-taking skills should be taught. Suggestions for doing so may be found in McPhail (1981), Lange (1981), Stewart and Green (1983), Gordon (1983), and Summers and Shobe (1983).

Passage Dependent–Independent Test Items. Students may correctly answer some reading comprehension items without reading the test passages because (1) the items can be answered from past experience alone; (2) the answer may be revealed in previous questions on the same selection; or (3) the correct answer stands out because it is longer, more precise, or otherwise distinctive (Tuinman

1973–1974, Pyrczak & Axelrod 1976). Test items designed to measure the ability to determine word meaning from context may be similarly influenced (Pyrczak 1976). Such test items are said to lack *passage dependency*.

A number of studies have found that tests vary considerably in their percentages of passage dependent and independent questions. Marr and Lyon (1981) found that good and poor readers did not differ significantly in their ability to respond correctly to passage-independent questions.

Although passage dependency may not be of as much practical significance as commonly believed (Hanna & Scherich 1981), it merits attention in the development of reading tests and in the evaluation of reading comprehension.

Task Demands.   The demands a test places on pupils may differ considerably from test to test, and from those placed on students by their daily reading in school. Comprehension tests, for example, differ in the ways in which comprehension is to be demonstrated (see p. 208–209).

The skills required by the test may not be the same as those needed for daily classroom performance. For example, test-wise children realize that there is no need to remember the information in a test passage for more than a brief time. They also read the accompanying test questions before they read the passage. In the classroom, information often has to be remembered over time, and rarely does the reader know what is important before he reads the material.

Response Accuracy.   Accuracy refers to the proportion of correct answers to the total number of items attempted. Noting test response accuracy may yield information useful in interpreting a child's performance. For instance, two children can obtain the same raw score on an NR test, but do so for different reasons. The child who responds to only the first 10 items on a 50-item test, and gets them all correct, may be an extremely compulsive pupil who is overly concerned with getting everything right; or he may be an extremely slow reader. At the other extreme is the pupil who attempts all 50 items, with his 10 correct responses scattered throughout the test. Such a score is apt to be highly influenced by guessing. How a child arrives at an answer is often more revealing than the correctness of the answer. This is why careful observation during testing and daily activities is strongly recommended.

Other Factors.   Any test performance can be influenced by guessing, inattention, lack of motivation, or just having a "bad day." Factors associated with test administration can also influence test scores. Pupils who know the purpose of the test and have a positive perception of the examiner tend to obtain higher test scores.

II. DETERMINING GENERAL LEVEL OF READING ABILITY

One of the most important questions to answer about a learner's reading ability is this: What level of reading material is appropriate for a given purpose? Answering this question aids not only in forming instructional groups but also in selecting material appropriate for an individual. Moreover, the answer should assist in choosing material that the learner can read independently and may help to determine whether the pupil can profit from using a particular content subject text.

The answer to this question varies somewhat according to the kind of reading done and the degree of proficiency in reading expected. In general, material to be read under the guidance of the teacher can be somewhat more difficult than material the child is to read independently.

More Than One Level of Reading Ability

Levels of reading competence originally described by Betts (1946) are functionally useful. The *independent reading level* is the highest level at which a child can read easily and fluently, without assistance, with few word-recognition errors, and with good comprehension and recall. The *instructional level* is the highest level at which a child can do satisfactory reading provided he or she receives preparation and supervision from a teacher; word-recognition errors are not frequent, and comprehension and recall are satisfactory. The *frustration level* is the level at which a child's reading skills break down: Fluency disappears, word-recognition errors are numerous, comprehension is faulty, recall is sketchy, and signs of emotional tension and discomfort become evident.

This is a useful set of concepts and has helped to clarify thinking about the meaning of "reading level." For example, a child may be able to read fifth reader material with considerable strain, difficulty, and inaccuracy (frustration level); fourth reader material with acceptable accuracy and comprehension after the teacher explains new words and concepts and provides guiding questions (instructional level); and third reader material with ease, fluency, and almost complete accuracy (independent level). If the teacher assigns the child to a group using a fifth reader and expects him to do supplementary reading in fourth reader material, his effort and accomplishment are likely to be disappointing. If he is placed in a group using a fourth reader and encouraged to read independently in material of third reader level, the results are apt to be gratifying. If all his reading is at fourth reader level, he will probably do reasonably well in group lessons but engage in a minimum of other reading. If all his reading material is third reader in difficulty, he may complain about a lack of challenge in his basal reader, while enjoying storybooks at that level. Gickling and Armstrong's study (1978) indicated that when reading assignments were too difficult, on-task behavior, task completion, and comprehension were relatively low; when the assignment was easy, there was a high percentage of off-task behavior.

Assessing Reading Levels

Criterion-referenced tests such as informal reading inventories (IRI), published reading inventories, and cloze tests make it possible to differentiate among a pupil's independent, instructional, and frustration reading levels. Grade-equivalent scores on standardized silent reading tests tend to overestimate the instructional reading level, particularly for poor readers whose scores may be based largely on guessing. A well-constructed, well-administered, and well-interpreted informal reading inventory based on the reading series used locally is apt to indicate a child's instructional reading level more accurately than a standardized norm-referenced test.

Two standardized tests provide scores that resemble an IRI in certain respects. The *Metropolitan Reading Test* provides an Instructional Reading Level (IRL) based on the number of correct answers to a series of paragraphs of increasing difficulty. Smith and Beck (1980) found that, on the average, IRL scores were about 1 year lower than the pupil's instructional levels as determined by published IRIs. The *Degrees of Reading Power* purports to show the level of reading text that is most suitable for pupils scoring within particular ranges.

A Quick Class Survey

Dolch (1953) suggested a quick way to use a basal reader to locate the poor readers in a class. His procedure involves having the children take turns reading a sentence as fast as they can. "Then several things may happen. First, some child may refuse to read. The teacher will cheerfully say, 'All right. Next one read on.' Or a child will read with great hesitation and difficulty. To him the teacher will instantly supply any word that stops him, say 'Good,' and go on. Since each reads but one sentence, there will be little embarrassment."

One sentence is a very brief and unreliable sample from which to attempt to evaluate a child's reading, even in such a rough, preliminary way. We would prefer to have each child read two or three sentences; in other respects, this Dolch procedure seems practical and effective as a quick screening test. Since it does not include any check on comprehension, it can disclose only one side of the reading picture.

One-minute tests of reading words orally in isolation or context were found to correlate from .81 to .87 with cloze test performance and even higher with standardized reading comprehension tests (Deno, Mirkin, & Chiang 1982). However, their claim that a 1-minute sample of word recognition can be used for estimating a child's reading level is open to question. Correlations only indicate how closely two tests rank-order students; they cannot reveal the extent to which the two measures placed children at the same reading level.

For a quick check on comprehension, one can choose a short selection (four or five pages) from near the beginning of the book and ask the children to read it silently. As each child finishes, he or she closes the book and looks up; in this way, the slowest readers are spotted quickly. When all have finished, the teacher can read a list of questions, to which the pupils write their answers. The children who score below 60% are likely to have difficulty understanding the book; the 60% scorers are marginal.

Combining a quick oral screening test with a silent comprehension test not only discloses the children for whom the book is unsuitable but also indicates the book's suitability for the majority of the class. If teachers will take the trouble to "try the book on for size" (Chall 1953), not only with basal readers but also with content textbooks, many frustrating learning experiences can be prevented.

III. GROUP MEASURES

Silent reading ability is far more frequently measured than oral reading because silent reading tests, which can be given to groups, are less time-consuming and require less expertise to administer and score. However, they yield less useful diagnostic information than do oral reading tests. Nevertheless, silent reading ability, especially comprehension, is important to assess.

Standardized Silent Reading Tests[2]

Standardized silent reading tests may be classified according to the reading functions that they purportedly measure. Some measure single functions, such as reading vocabulary or rate; others measure two or more aspects of reading. This section is concerned only with the latter. Single-purpose tests are considered under appropriate headings elsewhere.

There are two major kinds of norm-referenced silent reading tests. *Survey tests* sample skills and abilities that are usually taught in the grade levels for which the tests are intended. Survey tests generally have sufficient time limits so that reading rate is not an important factor in the resulting test scores. Nearly all NR survey tests have two or more forms, making it possible to retest children on comparable forms.

All survey tests contain a comprehension subtest that requires the child to read single sentences (primary grades) or paragraphs. A few primary-grade tests sample both sentence and paragraph meaning. In addition to a comprehension subtest, first- and second-grade tests often have a word-recognition subtest and may include a decoding subtest. Third-grade tests are more likely to measure word meaning than word recognition. From the fourth grade on, the commonly used survey tests have reading vocabulary and comprehension subtests. Some also have subtests of work–study skills, reading rate, or both. A few intermediate-grade tests contain a measure of decoding.

Diagnostic reading tests provide profiles of a student's reading skills from which relatively strong and weak areas may be discovered. These tests are not diagnostic in the true sense because they do not reveal *why* the child responded as he did. They often contain more subtests than do survey tests, with each subtest also containing more items. The number of subtests in group-administered diagnostic tests varies from test to test. Some cover a wide variety of decoding skills, while others attempt to measure different kinds of reading comprehension.

In reviewing *any* test that has subtests, the following points should be considered, but they are particularly pertinent when interpreting diagnostic tests:

1. Each subtest should sample a relatively independent skill. Intercorrelations among subtests should be below .65; the higher the correlation

_____

[2] Reading and reading-related tests are described in Appendix A.

between two subtests, the more likely that they are measuring similar abilities.

2. For use with an individual, the subtest reliability should be .90 or above. Although the reliability of the total test score may be above .90, subtest reliability often falls below this criterion.

3. Time limits on subtests may be so brief as to place an unwarranted premium on reading rate.

4. A subtest label does not necessarily indicate what is really being measured. For example, a task analysis may reveal that items in a literal comprehension subtest actually require reasoning ability or rely heavily on prior knowledge.

Evaluation of Diagnostic Reading Tests

Ramsey (1967) suggested several criteria for judging diagnostic reading tests. *Reality* implies that an ability should be tested in much the same manner as it is used in reading. *Guessing* means that correct guessing should not be possible; this is a general objection to multiple-choice items. *Active* describes the pupil who responds with overt, observable behavior. *Specificity* means that success or failure on an item should be attributable to one ability rather than a combination of abilities. *Comprehension* implies that questions on comprehension should require understanding and interpretation rather than mere recall of directly stated details. According to these criteria, none of the present diagnostic reading test batteries is fully satisfactory. Nevertheless, this does not prevent them from being helpful to those who understand the tests' uses and limitations.

Criterion-Referenced Tests

Group-administered criterion-referenced tests differ widely in the number of objectives covered, the specificity of their objectives, the number of test items per objective, and what constitutes mastery (Horne 1979). For the most part, CR group tests use the same format as NR tests—sentences or brief passages followed by multiple-choice questions. However, most CR group tests are shorter than standardized tests.

There are commercially published CR tests, and many mastery learning, systems approach, and diagnostic–prescriptive reading programs employ CR tests (Stallard 1977). To construct tailor-made CR tests, appropriate items can be chosen from banks of CR tests items available from state education departments, universities, and publishers. Or test users may wish to construct their own tests by employing the suggestions of such authors as Popham (1978b) and Gronlund (1978). Lyons (1984) warned, however, that matching CR test items to skills does not automatically produce a valid measure of a domain. Tests like the cloze and informal reading inventory are CR tests, and brief CR tests may be found in manuals that accompany some basal reading programs.

Guidelines for evaluating CR tests have been suggested by Walker (1978) and Hambleton and Eignor (1978), who evaluated five CR reading tests and found that most fell short of the technical quality necessary to accomplish their intended purposes.

Criterion-referenced tests have their limitations and unresolved problems. Often the criterion for mastery is arbitrarily set at 80% or 90%; however, there is little empirical evidence to substantiate such a standard. It may be that the relative importance of the skills measured varies, and thus varying standards should be employed. Hambleton (1978) offered suggestions for setting cutoff scores. The reliability of CR tests is also a problem. Berk (1980) recommended that 5 to 10 items per behavioral objective should be used for most classroom tests, and 10 to 20 items per objective for school-level tests. Few, if any, CR tests come close to meeting this requirement. Conventional measures of test reliability require variability in scores (a range of scores), but CR tests are designed to produce low variability. Therefore, new measures of reliability have had to be developed for CR tests, but there is little consensus as to which should be used (Hambleton *et al.* 1978).

Among the factors to consider in selecting, constructing, or interpreting CR tests are these:

1. Good tests will not overcome the problem of poor objectives.
2. There is a danger that factors in the affective domain (e.g., appreciation or attitudes) might be overlooked because they are difficult to measure.
3. Ojbectives involving retention and transfer of what is learned may become secondary to the one-time demonstration of mastery (Otto 1973).
4. There is some question whether all measured skills are equally important, and if having to go through a specified skill sequence helps or hinders reading development (Popp 1975).
5. The skills sampled may not be relevant to reading achievement; for example, McNeil (1974) found that three skills supposedly prerequisite for decoding ability were not mastered by 75% of the best readers.

Cloze Procedure

The *cloze* procedure requires the reader to supply words that have been deleted from the passage (see Fig. 7.1). Invented by Ebbinghaus in 1897, the technique gained popularity with its introduction as a measure of readability by Taylor (1953), and soon was also used as a measure of reading comprehension. Only its use as a measure of reading ability is considered here. Its use as a teaching device is discussed on page 495, and as a measure of readability on page 603.

Construction

A passage for a cloze test on a particular book may be randomly selected; this, however, assumes that the selected passage is representative of the text's difficulty. Representative samples may be selected in the same way as selections for an IRI (see p. 193). Or a number of passages can be chosen randomly, made into cloze tests, and administered to students similar to those for whom the material is intended. The passage whose score (percentage of correct responses) comes closest to the average of the passage scores is used for the cloze test.

Immediately the two birds changed their tactics. In an instant they _____ in front of me, _____ before my face almost _____ flycatchers, still uttering their _____ *chink* note. I stopped _____ to watch them. It _____ have been impossible to _____ fishing with that flurry _____ wings going on almost _____ my face. Once more _____ flew to a bush _____, but the minute I _____ downstream again, they _____ back around my head.

_____ put my rod down, _____ it against a bush, _____ watched them. They quieted, _____ continued to flutter their _____. It came to me, _____ I do not know, _____ they were not trying _____ lead me *from* something. _____ wanted me to come _____ them.

Deleted words in order of deletion: were, fluttering, like, distressed, again, would, continue, of, in, they, upstream, faced, were, I, leaning, and, but, wings, how, that, to, They, with.

Figure 7.1.   Part of a cloze test. Reprinted from *The Gift of Reason* by Walter D. Edmonds by permission of *Cricket* magazine and the author, copyright © 1977 by Walter D. Edmonds. Taken from *Visions and Revisions*, p. 54. Copyright © The Economy Company, 1980. Reproduced by permission of the publishers.

Because a minimum of 50 deletions[3] is needed for high reliability, a cloze passage in which every fifth word is deleted (the typical procedure) should be at least 250 words in length. Correspondingly longer passages are needed if the deletions occur less frequently. Often the first and last sentences are left intact to supply necessary clues. Usually deletions are made randomly (e.g., every fifth word beginning with the second word). Random word deletions provide a better measure of reading ability than do deletions of specific kinds of words (C. Robinson 1981). Studies have shown that cloze tests that delete only content words (nouns, verbs, adjectives, adverbs) measure different processes than tests in which only function words are deleted. Content words are the most difficult words to replace (Warwick 1978).

The selections are duplicated with equal-length lines replacing the deleted words. Use of a dash for each letter yields significantly higher scores than use of lines of equal length (Rush & Klare 1978). The purpose for testing dictates the range of selections to be used.

Administration

As with any test, children should be given guided practice in how to perform the task before a cloze test is used. The students are told to read the whole selection silently, and while doing so, to think of words that could best complete the blanks. Then they are to reread the selection silently and write in the missing words. Further rereading is allowed. A generous amount of time should be allotted to complete the test.

Scoring and Interpretation

Because examiners may differ as to which synonyms are acceptable (thus reducing reliability), most authors suggest that only the exact deleted word

[3] A 50-item cloze yields a reliability coefficient of about .85 (Bormuth 1975a).

should be counted as a correct response. However, based on the belief that the ability to supply synonyms indicates comprehension, some examiners may wish to accept them or to score the cloze test in both ways (exact word replacements and exact word plus acceptable synonym replacements). There are, however, no criteria for determining functional reading levels when synonyms are accepted. The cloze score is the number of correct responses divided by the number of deleted items, expressed as a percentage.

According to Bormuth (1968a), the instructional level is indicated by a cloze score of between 44% and 57%; scores below 44% indicate the frustration level; scores above 57%, the independent level. Very similar results with subjects of various ages were reported by Rankin (1971) and Peterson, Paradis, and Peters (1973). In these studies, every fifth word was deleted and only exact word replacements were scored as correct. Therefore, if these criteria are used, these same procedures must be followed.

There is not a consensus as to cloze criteria. For instance, Bormuth (1975a) also presented criteria that vary with grade level and kind of reading material; and Pikulski and Tobin (1982) suggested the following: Instructional level = 30% to 50%; frustration level = below 30%; independent level = above 50%. Most criteria are suggested for use with all pupils, regardless of their level of reading ability, but Peterson and Carroll (1974) reported that a cloze score of between 38% and 44% indicated the instructional level of disabled readers.

Advantages

The main advantage claimed for the cloze procedure over other measures of reading ability is that no extraneous questions of unknown difficulty act as unassessed variables. Its other advantages include: (1) It is easier and quicker to construct, administer, score, and interpret than the IRI; (2) its use requires less expertise; (3) it can be given to groups; (4) it provides a good measurement of the ability to use semantic and syntactic cues; and (5) research findings regarding its reliability and validity for children over age 8 are impressive (Warwick 1978). Additional information concerning cloze procedures may be found in Rankin (1974, 1978) and Pikulski and Tobin (1982).

Possible Limitations

All tests have limitations, and the cloze is no exception. An as yet unidentified minimum level of reading ability is necessary to employ the linguistic skills required by the cloze. Time should be spent in preparing young children to take a cloze test because they are unfamiliar with the task involved and are likely to find it difficult. Young children, and even older children, may have difficulty spelling or writing their answers. Accepting approximate spellings, spelling words for them, or administering the test individually with the answers given orally can help to overcome these possible limitations. It is often suggested that an every tenth-word deletion pattern be used with young children because they find an every fifth-word deletion too difficult. But it is difficult even to find a 250-word selection below the second reader level. Therefore, when used with young children, shorter and less reliable cloze tests may have to be employed.

Cloze tests provide only limited diagnostic information. They do not yield information regarding the child's word-recognition skills, decoding skills, and other reading behaviors or the pupil's strength or weakness in certain reading comprehension skills (e.g., factual or inferential). The fact that a reader can do well on a cloze test does not guarantee an overall understanding of the passage or the ability to identify the main idea (Grundin *et al.* 1978). Performance on the cloze is influenced by two potent variables: (1) the reader's familiarity with the content presented in the passage; and (2) the reader's ability to use language, which is a combination of language development and reading ability (W. L. Smith 1978).

Some researchers (e.g., Kibby 1980; Shanahan, Kamil, & Tobin 1982; Shanahan & Kamil 1983; Leys *et al.* 1983) believe that the cloze does not measure the integration of information across sentences and that therefore the cloze is not a valid measure of reading comprehension. Others, such as Warwick (1978), Rankin (1978), Henk (1982), and Cziko (1983), disagree with this point of view.

Cloze results may be influenced by the literary style of the author (Johnston 1983), and familiarity with the topic may make it easy to predict what words are likely to occur in the passage.

Cloze tests do not closely approximate the functional reading levels estimated by other procedures (Sauer 1969, Hodges 1972, Entin & Klare 1978b, Smith & Beck 1980), and cloze scores have been found to correlate only .63 with free recall (Shanahan & Kamil 1982).

Modifications of the Cloze

One modification of the cloze is the *maze test* in which each deletion is accompanied by three choices. Detailed instructions for constructing and interpreting a modified maze test have been presented by Dieterich, Freeman and Griffen (1978). The criteria suggested by Guthrie *et al.* (1974) indicate that scores of 60% to 70% indicate the maze instructional level for disabled readers. These criteria, however, may be too low for use with children who are making normal progress in reading (Pikulski & Tobin 1982).

In the *matching cloze test*, the deleted words are clustered and placed next to the selection. This would seem to make the task easier than the normal cloze but more difficult than the maze. There are, however, no criteria established for interpreting matching cloze tests.

Informal Measures

Published reading tests make demands on children that differ from those they face in their daily school programs. In order to obtain a reliable measure of silent reading ability, silent reading skills must be monitored by the teacher during daily reading activities, not just during reading instruction.

Children's understanding of what they have read is often checked by means of oral questions and answers. Oral questioning has several advantages over written questions and responses: (1) The question can allow freedom of response; (2) misunderstood questions can be detected immediately and clarified; (3) follow-up probes to incomplete or inaccurate responses are possible; and (4) socialized discussions and exchanges of opinion can occur. The major disadvantage is that usually only one child has a chance to answer a particular question.

Written comprehension checks are also desirable at times, particularly when the teacher assigns a selection for silent reading by one group while she is working with another group. Usually the teacher provides the group that is working independently with a set of questions to answer.

Observations that should be made while children are reading silently are discussed on pages 180–182.

Measuring Rate of Reading

Silent reading rate can be measured on a series of short paragraphs of increasing difficulty or of equivalent difficulty; we prefer the latter. Or rate can be measured on one long passage of several hundred words. In either case, if the material is too difficult for the child to comprehend, an accurate measure of reading rate cannot be obtained. Either a predetermined time limit is imposed for reading the passage(s) or the time required to complete the task is determined. On many rate tests, comprehension is checked.

A number of standardized reading tests provide measures of silent reading rate on those levels intended for use above the intermediate-grade level; a few have rate tests at the intermediate-grade level. The *Iowa Silent Reading Test* for Grades 6 to 9 provides a reading efficiency score that is based on rate and accuracy. Most rate scores on multipurpose standardized reading tests are based on reading for only a very short time period.

Informal tests of reading rate are easy to give and should be administered form time to time as a routine procedure in reading instruction above the primary grades. Selections should be easy for the students. To obtain a fairly accurate measure, a selection should take the child 5 to 7 minutes to read.

The simplest way to measure rate is to start all pupils together and measure the time necessary for each child to finish reading the selection. Pupils should be encouraged to read as fast as they can, but informed that they will be questioned about the selection. They should be told to look up as soon as they finish reading the selection and to copy on their papers the number displayed by the teacher. The teacher should change the number at regular intervals; every 10 seconds gives sufficient accuracy. Knowing the number of words in the selection, the teacher can prepare in advance a table that gives in words per minute the rate corresponding to each number. If the number is changed 6 times a minute (e.g., 1 = 10 seconds has elapsed, 4 = 40 seconds, and so forth), the rate in WPM for any number is obtained by multiplying the number of words read by 6 and dividing by the number copied down (e.g., 200 words read $\times$ 6 $\div$ 8 = 150 WPM).

Another technique is to say "Mark" at the end of each minute and have the pupils mark the last word they read before the signal. The number of words read in each minute can be counted and averaged. This technique may reveal which parts of the selection are difficult for the child, and whether or not he is adjusting his reading rate to the difficulty. Another variation is to give only one signal to mark and then divide the number of words read by the number of minutes allowed. This procedure is especially suitable with selections on which the cumulative total of words is given at the end of each line. After this type of rate test is over, slower readers should be allowed to finish the selection so as to have a fair chance on the comprehension test.

When a pupil is tested individually, the time taken to complete the selection can be obtained with a stopwatch, or a watch with a second hand, and the WPM computed. Norms for rate of reading are given in Table 14.1 on page 533. Since rate of reading varies according to the reader's purpose, the material read, and the reader's knowledge of the topic, any norms for rate must be considered rough approximations.

A comparision of a pupil's reading rate and comprehension may reveal various combinations ranging from very rapid rate–very accurate comprehension to very slow rate–very weak comprehension. Assuming that the tests reflect what the pupil does typically, such a comparison may suggest what needs to be done to help the student (see pp. 536–538).

At times, it is also useful to measure oral reading rates. Beyond the initial stages of reading acquisition, reading rates are increasingy slower for oral than silent reading. Nevertheless, a very slow oral reading rate can indicate a lack of automatic word recognition. Although a child may meet the word-recognition and comprehension criteria at a particular reader level, the material may be judged inappropriate for him because it took much too long to read.

IV. INDIVIDUAL MEASURES

Having the child read orally allows the examiner an opportunity to gain some insights in the learner's reading behaviors that are not observable during silent reading. Oral reading is a more difficult task than silent reading because not only must the learner understand the material but he must have the additional skills that allow him to transmit that understanding too others.

General Behavioral Observations

Observing the behaviors manifested by students as they are reading often provides useful diagnostic information. Some behaviors may appear whether the student is reading orally or silently; others are manifested only during one mode.

Silent or Oral Reading Behaviors
Several behaviors may occur when the child is reading either orally or silently. The following are the more frequently noted of these behaviors.

Lateral Head Movements.   These movements may interfere with speed of reading because the eyes can move much more rapidly than the head. If head movements are pronounced or are continued during long periods of reading, the back neck muscles may become fatigued. The learner may unconsciously associate the discomfort with reading and thus avoid reading.

Finger Pointing.   The pointing may be manifested in various ways that may have different meanings. Some students point to each word. If word-by-word reading is also observed, the examiner should determine whether the word-by-word reading is the cause or the effect of the word-by-word pointing or if both behaviors are caused by a factor such as weak word recognition or difficulty in keeping the place. Other kinds of finger pointing include moving the finger or an object under one phrase at a time as an aid in phrasing, moving the finger under the line of print without pausing, using the hand or finger as a marker under each line of print, or marking the beginning of each line with the finger. All may indicate that the learner is having difficulty keeping the place on the page. Such behaviors may be helpful in avoiding faulty return eye sweeps and omissions of phrases or lines.

Finger pointing is often a needed crutch, and insistence that the child stop the behavior may have adverse effects. No effort should be made to stop the pointing while reversal errors or losing the place continue. When it is time to wean the child from finger pointing, allow the use of a marker and then gradually reduce its use.

Inappropriate Rate.   A child may read either too slowly or too rapidly. In either case, the reasons should be investigated. Excessively slow reading may result from weak word recognition, poor comprehension, inattention to the task, a compulsion to obtain perfect comprehension, or simply never having been instructed in reading faster. Reading too rapidly is probably either a result of the desire to get through the material as quickly as possible or the learner's mistaken belief that all reading should be done as rapidly as possible. Excessively rapid reading often results in poor comprehension and recall. It is difficult to determine the extent to which lack of attention or concentration plays a role in either too slow or too rapid silent reading. In cases where oral reading comprehension is markedly better than silent reading comprehension, it may well be that there is a lack of attention or concentration when reading silently.

Concentration–Task Orientation.   The reading difficulties of some children are aggravated by their inability to concentrate on the reading matter. Such behavior may be a natural result of giving children reading matter that is uninteresting or too difficult and may disappear when more appropriate materials are used.

Inability to maintain attention to the task also may be caused by physiological or emotional problems. A child who is worried about something may find his mind wandering because at the time a problem is much more important than reading. Other children are not task oriented; rather, they avoid any self-investment in the learning situation. Still others have never learned to assume the responsibility required in learning.

Tension Signs.   These signs may take many forms: facial tics, voice tense or tremulous or almost inaudible, wiggling and squirming, shuffling of the feet, body rigidity, crying, and an outright refusal to continue. Such signs are most often indications that the pupil finds it difficult to cope with the material or with the situation in general.

Personality Variables.   Impulsive children may respond quickly without giving any thought to their answers, whereas compulsive children may perform poorly because they do not move ahead unless they are certain that all their answers are correct. Strong anxiety can interfere with performance on tests or in classroom activities. The relation of personality problems to reading disability is discussed in Chapter 10.

Vision.   While the student is reading, the distance from the eyes to the book should be noted. Normal reading distance is approximately 12 to 18 inches. Holding the book nearer or farther than this distance may indicate a visual problem. Note also such behaviors as moving the book forward and backward from the eyes, reading with the head markedly tilted to one side, holding the book at unusual angles, and covering one eye. Even if children's reading is adequate, their vision may need professional care. Vision is discussed in greater detail in Chapter 9.

Posture and Lighting.   It is important for general hygiene, and particularly to avoid eyestrain, that the child sit or stand in a natural, easy posture while reading, with the back reasonably straight and the book held firmly or supported a proper distance from the eyes, on a proper level, and with adequate light that is devoid of glare.

Silent Reading Behaviors

Two behaviors can be observed only during silent reading. *Lip movements* (the "silent" pronunciation of words) and *vocalizations* (which may range from audible whispering to reading orally) are most often either indications that the child is making the transition from oral to silent reading or that the material is difficult for the child.

When children first learn to read, oral reading is usually emphasized. During the transition from reading orally to learning to read silently, it is usual to find that "silent" reading is quiet oral reading. Usually there is a gradual reduction from complete oral pronunciation to lip movements to silent reading, although *inner speech* ("hearing" the words in one's head) still occurs when reading silently. These behaviors, especially lip movements, may persist long after the transition stage.

Frequent lip movements or vocalizations beyond the transition stage usually are symptoms that the material is too difficult for the pupil. Occasional lip movements or vocalization suggest that the student is having difficulty with only that part of the text.

Oral Reading Behaviors

Several behaviors are readily observable when the child is reading orally. The following are the more frequently noted of these behaviors.

Fluency.   Jerkiness, hesitations, and repetitions are defects in fluency that are easily detected. In some children the lack of ease and smoothness in reading is an indication of nervousness or self-consciousness. In many cases, however, hesitations and repetitions are accompaniments of difficulty or slowness in word recognition or problems with comprehension.

Word-by-Word Reading.   The word-by-word reader plods along slowly, tending to pause noticeably after almost every word. When attempting to phrase, the wrong words may be grouped together, and punctuation may be ignored or misinterpreted. Finger pointing often accompanies word-by-word reading, as do lip movements during silent reading and a monotonous voice during oral reading. Word recognition, though slow, may be fairly accurate, particularly on easy materials. Some word-by-word readers have marked deficiencies in their word-recognition techniques; others have learned these strategies fairly well, but have not overcome the habit of reading one word at a time.

Word-by-word readers usually do better on vocabulary or sentence comprehension tests than on tests of paragraph meaning. Their reading rate is understandably very slow, and reading may become a distasteful activity. Understanding and recall of connected discourse is frequently poor, and often material has to be reread in order to comprehend it. Although comprehension may be adequate on material that is conceptually familiar to the child, word-by-word reading puts a strain on short-term memory and may interfere with comprehension of more difficult material.

Word-by-word reading and inadequate phrasing (see below) may result from reading orally at sight. This possibility may be checked after testing by having the child preread appropriate material silently and then reread it orally. If the undesirable behavior lessens greatly, there is no need to be concerned about it. If it persists, the causes should be determined and appropriate action taken. Some word-by-word readers need to increase their word-recognition accuracy or automaticity, or to expand their sight vocabularies. Others will need to learn to group printed words into meaningful phrases.

When word-by-word reading occurs only, or primarily, on material that is frustratingly difficult for the pupil, it need not be treated directly. Providing the child with material of more appropriate difficulty will suffice.

Inadequate Phrasing.   Although the ways in which the words in a sentence may be grouped into phrases can vary slightly, each phrase usually represents a thought unit. Inadequate phrasing means that the reader is not grouping words into meaningful units. Grouping words into thought units facilitates comprehension by placing less of a strain on the reader's information processing capacity. For example, a 15-word sentence chunked into three phrases means that only three bits of information need be held in short-term memory. Lack of comprehension may contribute to inadequate phrasing, or vice versa.

Ignoring or Misinterpreting Punctuation.   Ignoring or misinterpreting punctuation marks may adversely affect comprehension, especially when phrases, clauses, or sentences are run together. Such behaviors usually reflect a lack of training in the use of punctuation marks or an anxiety manifested by rushing through the reading material.

Slow, Halting Reading. This suggests that the learner's phrasing is adequate but that the oral reading is drawn out by elongated pronunciation of the words or pauses between the phrases. Such behavior is usually habitual and may reflect the learner's oral speaking pattern or dialect.

Inadequate Use of Voice. This may take many forms: reading in monotone, volume too loud or too soft, poor enunciation, lack of expression, not speeding up or slowing down to portray the tempo of the story, or tense or high-pitched voice. The latter is usually a symptom of the difficulty of the material. Most of the other behaviors can be attributed to a lack of training, tenseness when reading orally, or the fact that reading is done at sight.

Speech. The classroom or reading teacher cannot help noticing salient facts about children's clarity of speech and use of voice while listening to them read. Major speech faults such as stuttering, stammering, and lisping are, of course, easily detected. Unclear enunciation and faulty pronunciation should also be noted. The quality, pitch, and intensity of the child's voice also deserve attention. A weak, tense, strained, or high-pitched voice may be a highly significant indication that the child is nervous in the reading situation. Excessively loud, nasal, and singsong voices may also be encountered. The former may indicate a hearing loss.

The above behaviors are not mutually exclusive; they often occur together. A child may read word by word in a voice almost too soft to be heard. These behaviors may occur only when the child is reading before a group, particularly one composed of peers. Such a situation usually suggests that something in the classroom situation is inducing anxiety.

Context Readers. Using context clues as an aid to word recognition and meaning is a desirable reading strategy that is frequently and effectively used by skilled readers. Some pupils, however, rely excessively on the general context of the passage. These *context readers* tend to read fairly fluently orally, but their word recognition is inaccurate. They go merrily along, skipping and adding words, or substituting one word for another. When there are too many unknown words or when they are no longer able to make good use of the general context, they may invent a new story that bears little resemblance to the printed text. Context readers tend to score higher on silent than oral reading tests and on tests that involve finding the general meaning of a selection than on tests calling for painstaking attention to details.

There are two general types of context raaders. First are those who have the ability to read more accurately but choose not to. Often their excessive reliance on context has become habitual. They can usually reread sentences accurately after being told that they were misread. Within this first type are two subtypes, those who can read for significant details but who are content with obtaining the gist of the material, and those who do not know how to read for details.

The other type of context reader has decoding problems. Because he has no other word-recognition strategies, he must rely mainly on context for any word that is not in his sight vocabulary. If the child has sufficient cognitive and linguistic competence or can relate a great deal of prior knowledge to the passage, his guesses will often be accurate or at least acceptable. When too many unknown words are met or when the context is not potent enough, his guesses become inaccurate and disruptive. This second type of context reader needs to improve his decoding skills and learn to use them in combination with context clues.

Word-Recognition Errors–Miscues

Deviations from the printed text are commonly referred to as *word-recognition errors*. The term *miscue* (K. Goodman 1969) is more appropriate because the deviations may reflect the reader's attempt to make sense of what is being read.

There is no consensus as to which behaviors should be classified as errors. More important, most scoring systems do not consider the seriousness of the error. Typically, all miscues are given equal weight in scoring a child's oral reading performance (e.g., a response of either *cat* or *go* to the stimulus *kitten* is counted as one error).[4] Simply counting the number of miscues only has value in determining whether a given criterion has been met. Even then, the seriousness of the miscues should be considered in judging the suitability of the material for instructional purposes or in determining the child's general level of reading ability.

In analyzing miscues, it should be realized that reading behaviors may change with the level of difficulty of the material. The child may not employ the same strategies at his instructional and frustration levels and thus may make different kinds of miscues. Also, the quality of the miscues may change. For example, the miscues may indicate that the student had semantic and syntactic control over the material at and below his instructional level but not at his frustration level.

A single sample of reading behaviors may not be reliable. Therefore we recommend that, whenever possible, an analysis of a student's reading behaviors be based on a number of samples over a period of time.

Mispronunciations

Mispronunciations may involve whole words (*dog* and *cat*), word parts in various positions (*cap* for *cat* or *cut* for *cat*), or a combination of word parts (*cup* for *cat*). Some writers distinguish between *mispronunciations* and *substitutions*, the latter indicating that the response made sense in the sentence. Mispronunciations may be caused by inadequate word recognition, inadequate use of context clues, weak decoding skills, overreliance on the initial elements of words, overreliance on context, or inattention to word parts. Responses that are semantically and/or syntactically inappropriate indicate that the pupil is not using context or language clues. Substitutions and mispronunciations are often found to be the most frequent kinds of miscues (M. Kaufman 1976, D'Angelo & Wilson 1979).

---

[4] A scoring procedure that considers the relative seriousness of miscues is described on page 202.

To determine if a mispronunciation is caused by the inability to recognize or decode the word, present the mispronounced word and ask the child to pronounce it. If the attempt is unsuccessful, and if the word is decodable, ask him to figure it out. Inability to decode the word may suggest a decoding problem or that the child has the necessary decoding skills but is reluctant to use them. Encouraging the child to try may help to resolve the issue. Focusing the child's attention on the mispronounced part will help to determine if inattention to word parts may be a problem. Under- or overreliance on context can be determined by examining the contextual appropriateness of the mispronunciations.

Some readers observe the first one or two letters of a word and then guess or infer the rest of it. Intelligent context readers are often surprisingly successful in their use of this strategy because their prior knowledge and facility with language allows them to predict words. Duller or less experienced children and those with limited linguistic ability also attempt to use this technique, but their predictions are often inappropriate. Among the commonest errors made by those who rely on this strategy are confusions of words that begin with *wh* (e.g., *when, where, which*) or *th* (*them, then, there*). Substitutions such as *then* for *when* often result in sentences that remain syntactically acceptable.

Errors on the middles and ends of words are more common than errors in the initial position. The middles of words are especially apt to be misread.

Dialect Variations

We do not all pronounce words in the same way. These variations reflect our exposure to regional and cultural dialects and our personal idiosyncracies. Most dialect differences occur on vowel sounds. For example, *I* /ī/ is commonly pronounced as /ah/ in the South. In many parts of the United States, *path* is pronounced with a short vowel sound /ă/. Many New Englanders, however, pronounce *path* with an /ä/ as in *father*, while no *r* is heard in their pronunciation of words like *yard*. Short /ĕ/ is indistinguishable from short /ă/ in some regions and from short /ĭ/ in others. Sometimes words that rhyme in standard English do not rhyme in a particular dialect.

Few published oral reading tests take dialect renditions into consideration in scoring. This can influence test scores. For example, not counting dialect miscues as word-recognition errors increased the average scores on the *Spache, Gilmore,* and *Gray* tests by slightly over a half year (Burke, Pflaum, & Knafle 1982). Dialect speakers are sometimes inconsistent in their use of dialect while reading, using a dialect rendition in one sentence and standard English in the next (Bean 1978). When a pupil reads orally in accordance with his dialect, the deviations from SE should not be considered to be word-recognition errors. To decide if a response is a dialect variation, one must be familiar with the characteristics of the dialect and how they deviate from SE. Such information about three dialects spoken by minority children can be found in Harris and Sipay (1979, pp. 459–465, 469–472, 479–481).

Words Aided

Some oral reading tests forbid pronouncing unknown words for the pupil. The number of mispronunciations or omissions is likely to be higher on such tests than on tests that allow words to be pronounced for the child. When part of the scoring system, words are usually pronounced for the pupil after a 5-second hesitation. The possible effect of pronouncing words for the child should be considered in interpreting his comprehension score. It may be inflated because without such assistance, comprehension would have been hindered.

Omissions

While reading, a child may omit whole words, word parts, groups of words, or entire lines of print. Omissions may or may not be deliberate, may be caused by inattention, or may suggest a visual anomaly.

Goodman and Gollasch (1980) contended that there are two kinds of word omissions. *Deliberate omissions* are those that the reader, after consideration, chooses to make rather than make a response or ask for the teacher's help. Words that the child cannot recognize or decode may be deliberately omitted. *Nondeliberate omissions*, of which readers are often unaware, include dialect and first-language renditions, omissions of words that the author could have left out without influencing the intended meaning (e.g., noun and clause markers such as *that* in "Rob told his father that the cat was ill"), and omissions dictated by other miscues (e.g., "the dog sits . . . " is rendered as "the dogs sit . . . "). According to Goodman and Gollasch (1981), omissions do not occur frequently (about 10% of the miscues made); nondeliberate omissions are much more frequent than deliberate omissions; and comprehension is rarely affected by omissions.

Of course, if the child correctly responds to the omitted words most of the time, word-recognition problems are not causing the omissions. At times, the pupil may not be attending to the task or to word parts, most often word endings or the middle syllable of polysyllabic words. The occasional omission of groups of words or a whole line of print may be the result of inattention to the task. Frequent omissions of whole lines of print suggest that the child has difficulty keeping his place on the page. Allowing the child to use a marker will help the examiner to decide if such is the case.

Additions

At times while reading, students add words or word parts that are not in the printed text. Most often, *additions*, or *insertions* as they are sometimes called, are in line with a previous miscue or happen because the reader has anticipated words occurring in certain patterns. Additions do not occur frequently and seldom distort the intended meaning (D'Angelo & Wilson 1979, D'Angelo & Maklios 1983). Despite this, it is still important to examine all reading behaviors because a particular type may be disruptive for a given child.

Reversals

There are four kinds of reversals: (1) whole word (*was* for *saw*); (2) single letter (*big* for *dig*); (3) letter order (*clam* for *calm*); and (4) word order (*I was* for *Was I*). Reversals almost always affect the meaning adversely and therefore are usually serious miscues. The possible causes of reversals are discussed on pages 410–411.

Repetitions

Word parts, single words, or groups of words may be repeated. In most scoring systems, repetitions of less than two words are not counted as errors. Repetitions may be made (1) to correct a miscue, (2) to aid comprehension, (3) to regain the train of thought, (4) to stall for time while attempting to recognize or decode a word. Any of the four possible causes, if they occur frequently, may be an indication that the material is too difficult for the pupil. Repetitions may be habitual in that the behavior persists after the original causes are no longer present. Extreme nervousness when reading orally or being tested may cause repetitions. Repetitions also occur during silent reading but can be noted only by careful observation or through the use of eye-movement photography.

Other Behaviors Scored as Errors

In some scoring systems, not responding to a word immediately is countered as a *hesitation* error. Each time a punctuation mark is ignored or misinterpreted also may be counted as one error. And in a few systems, each self-correction is considered to be an error. Whether or not such behaviors are considered errors may affect test scores.

Self-Corrections

A reader may or may not correct a deviation from the printed text. At times, self-corrections occur almost immediately following a child's miscue; at other times, only after material further in the text provides information that something was wrong with the response. Pupils are more likely to correct miscues that are semantically or syntactically inappropriate than those that make sense and are grammatically correct. Self-correction behavior may range from correcting every miscue to rarely, if ever, making a self-correction. Both extremes are undesirble. The former suggests that the reader may be overly concerned with accurate word recognition; the latter that he is not monitoring his comprehension. Generally, an analysis of when children self-correct (and when they do not) provides information about their use of semantic and syntactic cues. However, when most of the uncorrected miscues occur at the frustration level, it may simply indicate that the material was too difficult for the child. It is difficult to self-correct when the story makes little or no sense. Also, some children choose not to self-correct even though they are aware that the miscues are disruptive. Even though they do not self-correct overtly, they may do so covertly. This may be one reason why some children can answer a comprehension question correctly, even though they have mispronounced or omitted a key word. It is also possible that such responses have been gained from redundant information in the text or from prior knowledge.

Self-corrections require a number of control strategies including awareness that meaning or syntax has been disturbed, ability to reassess the context, ability to reexamine and vary word-recognition procedures, and ability to judge the success of the attempt (Pflaum & Bryan 1979).

Relative Frequency of Oral Reading Behaviors

The frequency with which various reading behaviors occur varies with reading ability, grade level, and teaching methodology employed. Individual pupils may differ considerably from the average number of occurrences. Relative frequency also varies with the error classification used. Weber (1968), who analyzed over 50 studies of oral reading errors, pointed out that lack of agreement in the categories used by different investigators makes it difficult to compare their results.

Despite these difficulties, it is safe to conclude that the most frequent oral reading difficulty is inadequate word recognition. Other common faults include poor enunciation, inadequate phrasing (including word-by-word reading), errors on common little words (*a, the,* and others), lack of expression, and habitual repetition.

Informal Assessment

In the typical reading lesson, preparation is usually followed by guided silent reading, and oral reading is usually a form of rereading for a definite purpose. The teacher may, for example, ask a child to read orally the sentence that contains the answer to a specific question. Under these conditions, teacher and pupil are likely to focus their attention on the appropriateness of the child's choice more than on the qualities of the oral reading. When one wishes to evaluate oral reading behaviors as such, the testing situation should be planned to provide optimum conditions for a careful appraisal. While one child is reading to the teacher, the rest of the class can be engaged in other activities.

The teacher should survey the major strengths and weaknesses each child shows in oral reading. For this purpose, a checklist like the one given in Figure 7.2 can be conveniently used. Copies of the checklist can be duplicated and as the child reads, or immediately after he has finished, the teacher runs down the checklist, marking items that are characteristic of the child's reading.

Some teachers prefer to use a briefer checklist so that the results from the group or whole class can be summarized on one sheet. A form convenient for this purpose is shown in Figure 7.3. Particular weaknesses are marked with checks, or with double checks for severe problems, in the appropriate column. A record like this makes it easy to select children who have a similar weakness and can be placed together in a special-needs group.

Many teachers are skeptical of the value of systematically recording oral reading behaviors. They are confident in their ability to remember important facts about their pupils without a written record. Using the checklist system often points out to such skeptics that they have either overlooked or have forgotten a number of specific points about pupils during weeks or months of work.

For a more detailed study of oral reading behaviors and miscues, it is preferable to have a duplicate copy of the reading material on which the information can be recorded. Such a procedure is described in detail on pages 193–203. With experience, a fairly accurate list of the child's miscues can be recorded as shown in Figure 7.5 on page 197. Methods of analyzing word recognition are taken up later in this chapter.

A careful appraisal of each student's oral reading at intervals during the year tends to make the teacher more sensitive to the oral reading characteristics

I. Word recognition, general
____ 1. Inadequate sight vocabulary
____ 2. Errors on high-utility words
____ 3. Omits: ____ whole words; ____ word elements: ____ initial, ____ medial,
        ____ final
____ 4. Inserts: ____ whole words; ____ word elements: ____ initial, ____ medial,
        ____ final
____ 5. Doesn't attempt to decode unknown words
____ 6. Tends to guess unknown words; ____ overrelies on initial elements
____ 7. Tends to respond rapidly, with most responses being ____ appropriate
        ____ inappropriate
II. Use of context–language
____ A. Relies heavily on context
            ____ 1. Substitutes words of similar meaning
            ____ 2. Substitutes words that are grammatically correct
            ____ 3. Reads words correctly in context that are misread in isolation
____ B. Inadequate use of context
            ____ 1. Substitutes words of similar appearance but different meaning
            ____ 2. Substitutes words that spoil or change meaning
            ____ 3. Makes errors that produce nonsense
            ____ 4. Rarely self-corrects
III. Decoding procedures
____ 1. No apparent decoding strategies
____ 2. Unsuccessfully attempts to decode
____ 3. Breaks words into useful parts, such as spelling patterns and syllables
____ 4. Uses morphemic analysis: ____ inflected endings, ____ compound words,
        ____ prefixes, ____ root words, ____ suffixes
____ 5. Looks for little words in big words
____ 6. Spells unknown words
____ 7. Attempts to sound out: ____ single letters, ____ phonograms,
        ____ syllables
____ 8. Overrelies on configuration, size, and shape
____ 9. Attends mainly to one part of word: ____ initial, ____ medial, ____ final
____ 10. Lacks flexibility in decoding
____ 11. Overrelies on decoding

Figure 7.2.   An oral reading checklist. This checklist does not attempt to provide an exhaustive list of oral reading behaviors. Also note that it stresses undesirable behaviors. A single check can be used to indicate the presence of a strength or weakness; a double check, a marked presence. This form may be copied without permission.

that appear during daily reading activities. The informal appraisal recommended here is a supplement to, not a replacement of, the teacher's daily observations. The frequency with which fairly thorough oral reading appraisals are made should vary according to the circumstances, but a 2-month interval will prove sufficient for most pupils. Children whose progress is poor need to be checked more often and more carefully than those who are making good progress. Once a high level of oral reading fluency is reached, thorough periodic rechecks may be a waste of time.

IV. Possible specific decoding difficulties
    ____ 1. Visual analysis skills: ____ monosyllabic words, ____ polysyllabic words
    ____ 2. Symbol–sound association skills: ____ consonants: ____ single,
           ____ blends, ____ digraphs; ____ vowels: ____ single, ____ short,
           ____ long; ____ final silent *e*; ____ vowel digraphs; ____ diphthongs
    ____ 3. Blending: ____ sounds into syllables, ____ syllables into words
    ____ 4. Reversal tendency
    ____ 5. Letter confusions (list them)
V. Comprehension
    ____ 1. Main ideas: ____ strength, ____ weakness
    ____ 2. Facts: ____ strength, ____ weakness
    ____ 3. Inferences: ____ strength, ____ weakness
VI. Fluency
    ____ 1. Word-by-word reading
    ____ 2. Phrases poorly
    ____ 3. Hesitations
    ____ 4. Repetitions
    ____ 5. Ignores–misinterprets punctuation: ____ commas, ____ periods,
           ____ question marks, ____ other
    ____ 6. Inappropriate speed: ____ too fast, ____ too slow
    ____ 7. Rapid and jerky
VII. Use of voice
    ____ 1. Monotone: lack of meaningful inflection
    ____ 2. Enunciation generally poor
    ____ 3. Slurs and runs words together
    ____ 4. Sound substitutions
    ____ 5. Stuttering or cluttered speech
    ____ 6. Nervous or strained voice
    ____ 7. Volume: ____ too loud, ____ too soft
    ____ 8. Pitch: ____ too high, ____ too low
    ____ 9. Peculiar cadence
VIII. Other behaviors
    ____ 1. Finger pointing: ____ word-by-word, ____ by phrases, ____ by lines,
           ____ line marker
    ____ 2. Head movements
    ____ 3. Tension signs
    ____ 4. Vision: holds book ____ too close, ____ too far away, ____ at odd angle;
           ____ covers left/right eye; ____ loses place often; ____ skips lines
    ____ 5. Poor concentration
    ____ 6. Poor task orientation
    ____ 7. Impulsive behavior
    ____ 8. Compulsive behavior
    ____ 9. Lack of motivation
    ____ 10. Unwillingness to try
    ____ 11. Possible emotional problems
    ____ 12. Poor reading posture

Figure 7.2. (*continued*)

Name	Bob	Mary	Jane	Jim	Eric	Judy	Barb	Tony	Dave
Comprehension									
Literal									
Inferential									
Word Recognition–Decoding									
Inadequate sight vocabulary									
Words aided									
Mispronunciations									
Omissions									
Additions									
Inadequate use of context									
Overdepends on context									
High-utility words									
Visual analysis									
Symbol–sound associations									
Blending sounds									
Fluency									
Hesitations									
Repetitions									
Phrasing									
Word-by-word reading									
Ignores punctuation									
Inappropriate rate									
Loses place									
Use of voice									
enunciation									
expression									
volume									
Observations									
Tensions signs									
Finger pointing									
Head movements									
Concentration									
Book held too close/far									

Comments:

Figure 7.3. A checklist for recording oral reading characteristics. This form may be copied without permission.

The Informal Reading Inventory

An *informal reading inventory* (IRI), whose origin and development has been traced by Johns and Lunn (1983), is a series of graded representative selections taken from each reader level in a published reading series and used as a criterion-referenced test. It can be employed to determine a child's general level of reading ability and to yield diagnostic information. The range of the selections may be restricted to cover a limited span (e.g., five reader levels—the on-grade level and two levels below and above it); or the concept may be adapted to test the suitability of any materials, including content subject texts. Because reading series and materials vary considerably in such factors as vocabulary, story content, difficulty, and instructional approaches, the IRI should be based on the material being considered for use by the pupil.

Construction

A word-recognition test for determining the reader level at which to initiate testing (it also may yield information regarding the pupil's ability to recognize or decode words in isolation) may be formulated by randomly selecting 10 to 20 words introduced in each reader level to be tested. Such "new words" are usually listed by the publisher at the back of the book. The words can be typed or printed on separate cards or can be organized as word lists (see Fig. 7.7 on p. 214).

Use the following procedures to select the test passages: Scan each text and choose at least five passages[5] that seem representative of the book in content and language. To these apply a readability formula (see pp. 598–599), which will assist in selecting samples that are representative of the book's difficulty. Application of readability formulas has revealed substantial intrabook variability, frequent disagreement with the publisher's grade-level disignation, and the fact that books in a series are not always scaled from easy to difficult (Bradley 1976, Bradley & Ames 1977). The readability formula may also reveal whether there is a narrow or a wide spread of difficulty within the text and whether the selections progress from "easy" to "more difficult" from the beginning to the end of the book.

From the selections whose readability has been determined, choose at least two selections that approximate the average readability score. One selection is to be used for oral reading and the other or others for obtaining further information about the child's oral reading ability, silent reading, or listening comprehension.

Using the average readability score means that if that text is used for instruction, the children will encounter some selections that are easy and some that are difficult for them. For example, the average sample from a text might be at the fifth reader level; however, the range of readability of the entire text might be from the low third reader to the seventh reader level.

[5] Based on their study, Bradley and Ames (1977) concluded that 24 samples were necessary to adequately predict the readability values of a basal reader. According to Bormuth (1975a), little can be gained by using more than 12 samples.

Selections of 50–75 words usually suffice at pre-primer level. At primer and first reader levels, 100–125 word selections are appropriate, as are 200–250 word selections above that level. The selection chosen should end with a complete sentence. If narrative material is employed, it is preferable that the passage constitute an event that has a beginning, middle, and end.

For each IRI selection, prepare a short introduction that provides the background necessary for understanding the selection, directions regarding how much to read and how (out loud or to yourself, orally or silently), and a motivating or purpose-setting question. Such an introduction might read: "In this story, a boy has ignored the warnings of the older men in the village. Read orally from here to here to find our what happened to him as a result." Below third reader level, the characters' names should be told; the same is true for unusual names (e.g., Amyntas, Sioux) at any reader level.

Some examiners believe that unaided recall is the best way to measure reading comprehension. Thus they prefer to use a free-response comprehension check ("Tell me the story in your own words"). The major concepts and events in the selection should be listed in advance and checked off as the child relates the story. If the pupil does not mention key ideas, the examiner may ask specific questions on them. Some criterion should be set to judge whether the student successfully understood the selection; the categories *good, fair,* and *unsatisfactory* will usually be sufficient.

If specific comprehension questions are to be asked, 5 to 10 relevant questions should be prepared in advance. Both factual and inferential questions should be used, with fewer inferential questions occurring at lower reader levels. The wording of questions should be clearly understood by the pupils; trick questions should be avoided. Questions that can be answered with a simple yes or no should be followed with a "How do you know?" question, the two parts being counted as one test item. Care should be exercised in the formulation of test questions because they can greatly influence IRI results (Peterson, Greenlaw, & Tierney 1978). Any IRI passage or comprehension-check item that proves unsuitable should be replaced.

Classification of Comprehension Question

A number of classification systems have been presented for specifying the type of comprehension involved in answers to questions. In addition to those cited on pages 477–478 and 491, others have been described and illustrated by Pearson and Johnson (1978) and Lucas and McConkie (1980); in both these approaches, the relationship of the question to the information source is considered.

That the effect of the classification system employed can influence the findings of a study is exemplified by Hare and Pulliam (1980). They found that when using Guzak's classification (1967), the question formulated by teachers were classified as 74.4% literal, 10.4% inferential, and 15.2% evaluation. But when using Pearson and Johnson's system, the results were 27.3% literal (textually explicit) and 72.7% inferential.

Use of a Story Grammar to Formulate Questions

A story grammar is a description of the typical elements, and their relationships, frequently found in narratives. To determine the reader's understanding and recall of these events, it is helpful to think of the story as providing answers to five general questions (Sadow 1982):

1. Where and when did the events in the story take place, and who was involved in them? (Setting)
2. What started the chain of events in the story? (Initiating events)
3. What was the main character's reaction to this event? (Reaction)
4. What did the main character do about it? (Action)
5. What happened as a result of what the main character did? (Consequence)

To get at an understanding of the relationship among these events requires posing other questions that create a "causal chain" in which one event leads to another (Pearson 1982, 1984). This necessitates asking *why* questions, such as, "What happened because . . . ?" or, "What did _____ have to do before she could _____?"

Recording Performance

A student's IRI performance can be recorded in one of three ways, the choice depending on the purpose for testing and the amount of information desired. A detailed record form is not necessary if one is interested only in determining which book, or which level of material, is suitable for that child's instruction. A sheet of paper indicating the child's name, the date of testing, and reader-level designation will suffice. Next to each reader-level designation, the examiner tallies the word-recognition errors or miscues as they occur, as well as the number of correctly answered comprehension questions. Later she determines if the criteria have been met.

If more detailed information is desired, either of two forms that allow for an analysis of the child's performance may be used. On a Listing/Tally Form, similar to the one shown in Figure 7.4, are recorded the student's name, date of testing, the student's reading levels (which are filled in *after* testing is completed), the reader levels tested, the pages on which they are located, the total number of words in each selection, and the criteria to be applied (the number of word-recognition errors and the number of correct comprehension questions are filled in at the end of each selection). Mispronunciations or miscues (see p. 185) are recorded under the *Said* column, with the stimulus word under the *For* column. Space is also provided to record words pronounced for the child (*Told*), omissions, additions, repetitions, and comments regarding fluency. If a parallel silent reading selection is administered, the reading rate, comprehension score, and qualitative observations should be recorded.

The other form is a duplicated copy of the selection on which the child's performance is directly recorded (see Fig. 7.5). Double-spaced copy is used to allow room for recording. Placing the answers you are willing to accept in parentheses after each comprehension question encourages more consistent scor-

Name _Susie_   Date _3/29_

Reading Levels: Independent _2_ (Low)   Instructional _2_ (High)   Frustration _3_ (Low)

Low second reader, pp. 18–20 (120 words)   WRE (6) _3_   Comp. (7) _10_

Said	For	Told	Omissions	Reversals
bag	bug	pony		
brown	black			

Fluency: _Very fluent_

High second reader, pp. 56–58 (201 words)   WRE (10) ___   Comp. (7) ___

Said	For	Told	Omissions	Reversals
later	last	every	giant	
covered	come			
our	the			
friends	family			
garden	yard			

Fluency: _Some misphrasing and hesitations_

Low third reader, pp. 31–33 (225 words)   WRE (11) _14_   Comp. (7) _5_

Said	For	Told	Omissions	Reversals
terror	terrible	patient	loose	girl-grill
begin	begun	anxious		
faster	fasten	during		
writing	written	shiny		
wake	weak	stomach		
ton	tongue			
screen	scream			

Fluency: _Word-by-word reading at times. Voice showed tension._

Figure 7.4. A listing–tally form for recording oral reading performance. Cooper's (1952) definition of word-recognition errors and his criteria for the most suitable material (instructional level) were employed (see p. 201). The number in parentheses after *WRE* indicates the maximum number of allowable word-recognition errors. The number after *Comp.* indicates the minimum number of comprehension questions the child must answer to correctly to meet the criterion.

ing. Of course, good answers that were not anticipated should be accepted. Indicating the kind of comprehension questions (e.g., inferred main idea) or what the pupil must know or understand in order to be able to answer the question will aid later interpretation. A duplicated copy saves time because, if the expected responses are given by the child, they need only be checked off rather than written out. Also, knowing where miscues occurred can aid interpretation. Later, listing miscues (as in Fig. 7.4) can help in analyzing the child's performance. Recording the pupil's answers to the comprehension check can help in determining such things as whether the comprehension score was inflated by words pronounced for the child, inability to answer a question was

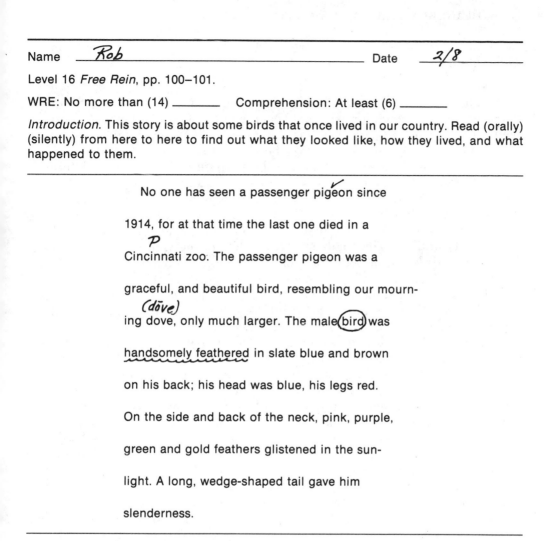

Name __Rob__   Date __2/8__

Level 16 *Free Rein*, pp. 100–101.

WRE: No more than (14) _____   Comprehension: At least (6) _____

Introduction. This story is about some birds that once lived in our country. Read (orally) (silently) from here to here to find out what they looked like, how they lived, and what happened to them.

No one has seen a passenger pigeon since

1914, for at that time the last one died in a

P

Cincinnati zoo. The passenger pigeon was a

graceful, and beautiful bird, resembling our mourn-

(dōve)

ing dove, only much larger. The male bird was

handsomely feathered in slate blue and brown

on his back; his head was blue, his legs red.

On the side and back of the neck, pink, purple,

green and gold feathers glistened in the sun-

light. A long, wedge-shaped tail gave him

slenderness.

1. What happened to the passenger pigeon? (died out; became extinct)

2. Describe the male passenger pigeon. (For full credit, must give at least 2 of 3: 1) graceful or beautiful, or larger than mourning dove; 2) at least 4 of 8 colors; 3) long and/or wedge-shaped tail.

Figure 7.5. Oral reading performance recorded on a mimeographed form. Only one paragraph of the 279-word selection and two of the comprehension questions are shown. The performance was recorded according to the modified procedures shown on p. 199. The content was reproduced from *Free Rein*, Level 16. Published by Allyn & Bacon, 1978. Reprinted by permission of Coward, McCann & Geoghegan, Inc. from *Wildlife in Danger* by Ivah Green. Copyright © 1960 by Ivah Green.

caused by a word-recognition error, or if faulty reasoning may be contributing to the child's comprehension difficulties.

Administration

Select about 30 minutes during which there will be no interruptions and a setting where other children cannot hear the testing (a student may not perform well if he believes his peers can hear him). Have the necessary materials available, and sit where you can observe the child. Take time to establish rapport and put the child at ease. Explain that the purpose of the test is to determine how he reads so that he can be helped to become a better reader.

If a word-recognition test is used, begin with a list below the child's estimated level of functioning (e.g., if the child is using a low second reader in class, being with the primer or first reader). Present each list in increasing level of difficulty until the child fails more than 20% of the words on the list. A response is considered correct if the word is acceptably pronounced within 3 seconds of initial exposure. Self-corrections are accepted as correct.

Initiate oral reading testing at the reader level below the highest-level list on which the child met the criterion on the word-recognition test. Thus, if the highest word list on which the criterion was met is of fourth reader level, oral reading would begin at high third reader level. If a word-recognition test is not employed, begin oral reading at least two reader levels below the reader level the child is using for reading instruction. Starting with an easy selection (1) helps the child overcome initial nervousness and settle down in performance before reaching levels at which a challenge is met, and (2) takes into consideration the possibility that the child's word-recognition ability exceeds his reading comprehension skills. Oral reading is done at sight because preparatory silent reading might conceal some of the child's problems and the strategies employed when he encounters difficulty.

Before the child begins to read, tell him that when he finishes reading you will ask some questions about what has just been read (or will ask him to retell the story). Give the introduction, and as the child reads orally from the book, record his reading using the symbols shown in Figure 7.6 and your observations.

When the child finishes the selection, take the material from him and present the comprehension check. Questions are read to the child, or he is asked to retell the story; the oral responses are recorded. If word-recognition and comprehension criteria are both met (see below), the next higher level is presented.

After the child fails either or both criteria for oral reading, drop back two reader levels and initiate silent reading. For example, if oral reading is terminated at the sixth reader level, begin testing silently at the fourth reader level. Silent reading should be timed,[6] and testing continued at each higher level until the comprehension criterion is not met. Questions are asked and answered orally, or retelling is requested, after the reading of each selection.

---

[6] Timing oral reading also is advisable because it can be helpful in deciding the suitability of material. For instance, although word recognition may be accurate, it may be extremely slow. Rate of oral reading also can be compared with silent reading rate. After about the second reader level, silent reading should be faster.

Behavior	Symbol	Sample
Hesitation	Check mark over word	✓ social
Word pronounced by examiner after 5-second hesitation by child	P over pronounced word; check may be changed to	P social
Mispronunciation; substitution	Child's response over printed stimulus	*buf* bough
Dialectal rendition	Child's response over printed stimulus; add Ⓓ	*des*Ⓓ *be* Ⓓ desk He is here
Reversal	Child's response over printed stimulus; may be letter, complete letter sequence; partial letter sequence; word order	*big* *clam* dig calm *was* *he was* saw was he
Omission	Encircle omitted word(s) or word part(s)	⊙are⊙ pant⊙s⊙
Addition	Child's response over caret, which indicates where insertion occurred	a *big* cat ∧
Self-correction within 5 seconds	Parentheses around correction	*(dog)* puppy
Repetition	Wavy line under repeated material, with bar at left to show where repetition began	⌐the tiny tot 〰〰〰
Punctuation ignored or misinterpreted	× through punctuation mark	He did X
Inadequate phrasing	Slash at pause indicating misphrasing; when frequent, IP in margin	into / the room *IP*
Word-by-word reading	W/W in margin	*w/w*
Finger pointing	FP in margin; indicate type (e.g., word-by-word)	*FP (w/w)*
Head movements	HM in margin	*HM*
Inappropriate rate	Too fast; too slow in margin	*Too fast*
Concentration–task orientation	Behavior that indicates inattention noted in margin (e.g., easily distracted by noise)	*Easily distracted by noise*
Tension signs	Tension sign noted in margin (e.g., facial tics)	*Facial tics*
Vision	Possible signs of visual problem noted in margin	*Held book 4" from eyes*
Personality–emotional problems	Possible symptoms noted in margin	*Bizarre answers to number of comp questions*

Figure 7.6. Symbols for recording oral reading behaviors.

The IRI can also be employed to estimate the child's listening-comprehension level. After testing silent reading, the examiner reads selections to the child, beginning at the level at which the silent reading criterion was failed. Comprehension is checked in the same manner as if the child had read the selection, and testing continues until the comprehension criterion is not met.

Scoring and Interpretation

Material at the child's *independent level* is generally suitable for recreational reading. Of course, at times the child should be allowed to read independently material that is below and above this level. Material at the independent level may also be used for certain instructional purposes. For example, if the child is weak at phrasing or mechanical skills such as the proper use of the voice in oral reading, material at the independent level would be suitable for instruction because the child could concentrate on these skills; word recognition and comprehension should not create any problems. The *instructional level* indicates that the material is suitable for use under the teacher's direction. The material presents some challenge so that new skills can be acquired. Material at the *frustration level* is too difficult. Some examiners determine separate functional reading levels for oral and silent reading; others prefer only one score per functional level, taking into consideration the child's performance in both oral and silent reading.

There is no agreement on the criteria that should be used for determining these functional levels. The main criteria proposed by Betts (1946) were

1. Independent level = (*a*) more than 99% correct word recognition; (*b*) at least 90% comprehension for oral reading, and for silent reading "a rate of comprehension higher than that for oral reading": (*c*) freedom from tension; (*d*) fluent reading.
2. Instructional Level = (*a*) at least 75% comprehension for oral reading and for silent reading "a rate of comprehension substantially higher than that for oral reading"; (*b*) at least 95% correct word recognition; (*c*) ability to anticipate meaning; and (*d*) freedom from tension.
3. Frustration level = (*a*) comprehension below 50%; (*b*) 90% or less correct word recognition; (*c*) slow, halting reading; and (*d*) signs of tension. (1946, pp. 449 ff.)

Some studies seem to support the 95% word-recognition criterion (E. Davis & Ekwall 1976, Leslie & Osol 1978, Hoffman *et al.* 1984). For the instructional level, Powell (1973) suggested the following criteria: (*a*) at least 70% comprehension at all grade levels; and (*b*) correct word recognition: 87–94% for pre-primer to Grade 2, 92–96% for Grades 3–5, and 94–97% for Grades 6 and up.

To date, the best study for determining IRI criteria has been conducted by Cooper (1952). His criteria for determining the instructional level were

1. Second and third grades = (*a*) 99% word recognition (most suitable material) or 95% to 98% word recognition (material of questionable suitability);[7] and (*b*) a minimum of 70% comprehension.
2. Intermediate grades = (*a*) 97% to 99% word recognition (most suitable material) or 91% to 96% word recognition (material of questionable suitability); and (*b*) a minimum of 60% comprehension.

Word-recognition errors included only substitutions, mispronunciations, words pronounced by the examiner after a hesitation of 5 seconds, omissions, and reversals. Additions, hesitations, repetitions, and ignoring punctuation were not counted as word-recognition errors. In addition to the quantitative criteria cited above, Cooper also considered qualitative symptoms in decision making. Any two of the following behaviors combined with a borderline performance, or the presence of more than two behaviors even when criteria were met, were considered indicative of the frustration level: word-by-word reading; inadequate phrasing; slow, halting reading; ignoring punctuation, finger pointing; visible tension; and a strained, high-pitched voice.

In applying any such criteria, one must examine (and use) what the author counted as a word-recognition error. For example, Betts (1946) did not specify specific word-recognition errors. Nor did he indicate whether words could or should be pronounced for the child; and repetitions, insertions, reversals, and omissions seem to be treated as symptoms that were to be considered in making a judgment.

There is not consensus as to what behaviors should be counted as errors in scoring an oral reading test. But Dunkeld (1970) found that a word-recognition score based on a count of mispronunciations, substitutions, words pronounced for the pupil, insertions, and reversals showed a higher correlation with reading comprehension than any other combination of miscues.

Apart from the fact that there is not complete agreement as to what constitutes a word-recognition error, there is some evidence that personality variables such as impulsivity and reflectiveness may influence the kind and number of miscues a child makes (Hood & Kendall 1975, Fisher 1977). In two studies reported by Pikulski (1974) one supported the use of Betts's criteria, the other supported Powell's (Cooper's criteria were not considered). The approach used for teaching reading may influence IRI results, and the student's level of reading ability may influence the balance of word-recognition and comprehension scores.

In almost all scoring procedures suggested for IRIs and published oral reading tests, all word-perception errors are given equal weight. Thus, both a completely mispronounced word that disrupts meaning and an omission of *the* are each counted as one error. Because a distinction between serious and minor

[7] The "questionably suitable" category probably indicates the instructional level of most students, but its upper limits may suggest the frustration level for some.

responses and behaviors should be made, we recommend the following scoring procedure:

1. Count as one error; (*a*) each response that deviates from the printed text and disrupts the intended meaning; (*b*) each word pronounced for the child after a 5-second hesitation.
2. Count as one half error: each response that deviates from the printed text but does not disrupt the intended meaning.
3. Count as a total of one error, regardless of the number of times the behavior occurs: (*a*) repeated substitutions, such as *a* for *the* (except when a distinction between *a* and *the* is important to obtaining the meaning intended by the author); (*b*) repetitions; (*c*) repeated errors on the same word, regardless of the error made.
4. Do not count as an error: (*a*) responses that conform to cultural, regional, or social dialects; (*b*) self-corrections made within 5 seconds; (*c*) hesitations; (*d*) ignoring or misinterpreting punctuation marks.

Use of the above suggestions probably will result in a lower total number of word-recognition errors than would occur using Cooper's scoring procedure. The comprehension score and the presence or absence of symptoms of frustration should be considered. Specific behaviors observed and recorded during testing provide information for a qualitative analysis of the pupil's reading ability. Suggestions on how to make such an analysis are found on pages 217–219.

One can draw some conclusions about the child's relative rate and comprehension in oral and silent reading if comprehension has been checked with similar questions on oral and silent reading selections of comparable difficulty and content, and if the reading of selections is timed.

Estimates of a child's reading level, based on a series of short samples, should be recognized as approximations. Short selections do not yield extremely reliable results. A child's performance in a test situation can be influenced by a number of variables and therefore may not be truly representative of his or her reading ability, and there are marked variations in readability within a given text. Because a student can successfully read one selection written on a certain topic in a particular style does not necessarily mean that he or she will be as successful with material that may be of the same level of difficulty but that differs in content and writing style. The child's subsequent degree of success in reading the assigned book should be monitored, and more appropriate material substituted if necessary.

The examiner's ability can greatly influence IRI results. When 17 reading specialists were asked to rate the same performance, 6 rated it at the independent level, 6 at the frustration level, and 5 at the instructional level (Page & Carlson 1975). Even when provided with information that should have led to a fairly consistent interpretation of a pupil's test performance, the participants in a study by Schell (1982) did not agree in interpreting the data. Approximately 65% of the college professors and 25% of the graduate students judged the performance to be at the instructional level; the others, at the frustration level. Because teachers are exposed to a wide variety of training programs, they may score and interpret IRIs differently. But similarly trained clinicians can obtain very similar results if they use agreed-upon procedures and criteria (Pikulski & Shanahan 1982).

Criteria for determining the instructional level may be adjusted for defensible reasons. For example, with children of limited experiential background, it may be advisable to use a 50% or 60% comprehension criterion rather than 70%; the rationale is that more time than usual will be spent developing the concepts and vocabulary necessary for understanding the stories. On the other hand, if the children are to be placed with highly skilled readers, a more stringent criterion may be selected.

There is also some difference of opinion whether students should be allowed to preread or reread selections and what impact this has on test results and interpretation. Research in this area is limited and has employed only small samples; therefore any resulting suggestions must be considered to be tentative (Gonzales & Elijah 1975, 1978; Brecht 1977; Kender & Rubenstein 1977; Nicholson, Pearson, & Dykstra 1979). Until prereading or rereading procedures are used in establishing new criteria for the instructional level, currently available criteria should be employed in administering and scoring an IRI.

Comparison of IRI Results with Standardized Test Scores

Since Sipay (1964) reported his findings, several studies have found that some standardized reading achievement tests tend to give grade-equivalent scores higher than the instructional level determined by an IRI. It should be realized, however, that the results of such comparisons will be influenced by (1) the standardized test used; (2) the material on which the IRI is based; (3) how well the IRI is constructed, administered, scored, and interpreted; and (4) the criteria used to determine the functional reading levels.

As for other than standardized silent reading tests, Bradley (1976), who compared children's performances on IRIs based on two different basal series with their performances on the WRAT, *Botel*, and *Gilmore*, found, first, that over 75% of the children obtained higher scores on the WRAT and *Gilmore* than on the basal IRIs. Second, even when scores on two tests are highly correlated, they do not necessarily yield similar results. For example, although the *Gilmore* Accuracy score correlated .91 with the *Macmillan* IRI, they agreed in placement on only slightly more than 10% of the students.

Some writers suggest subtracting a constant (e.g., 1 year) from grade-equivalent scores to estimate the learner's instructional level. Such a procedure is not accurate, however (MacGinitie 1973a, Bradley 1976).

Published Reading Inventories

A number of published reading inventories are program independent. Most of these are described in Appendix A. They are very similar in organization, administration, and scoring to an informal reading inventory, but differ widely in such matters as passage content, what is considered to be a word-recognition error, scoring criteria, and the kinds of comprehension questions posed. Almost all lack published data on reliability and validity.

Care should be taken in accepting the labels placed on the comprehension questions as to what kind of comprehension is being sampled, and using such information in making a diagnosis. Schell and Hanna (1981) concluded that the six published inventories they analyzed should not be used to determine strengths and weaknesses in reading comprehension.

In one of the few studies comparing test scores from published inventories and NR tests, W. E. Smith and Beck (1980) found that, on the average, the *Sucher–Allred* and *Rand McNally* scores were a year higher than the grade-equivalent scores on the *Metropolitan Reading Test*. Some children scored higher on the published inventory; others, on the standardized test.

Standardized Oral Reading Tests and Test Batteries

Two commonly used standardized oral reading tests are the *Gray* and the *Gilmore*. The *Gray Oral Reading Test* yields a single score based on word-recognition errors and reading time. Although comprehension is measured, it is not considered in the test score. The latest edition of the *Gray*, published in 1963, evolved from the *Gray Standardized Oral Reading Paragraphs*, first published in 1915. The *Gilmore Oral Reading Test*, whose most recent forms were published in 1968, provides separate scores for accuracy, comprehension, and rate. The scores on the *Gray* and the *Gilmore* are based on the student's performance across selections of increasing length and difficulty.

Measures of the ability to read connected discourse orally also are part of some diagnostic reading test batteries, each of which measures a variety of reading skills in addition to oral reading. The *Gates–McKillop–Horowitz Reading Diagnostic Tests* contain an oral reading test whose score is based only on word recognition; comprehension is not even checked. Oral and silent reading as well as listening comprehension are sampled by the *Durrell Analysis of Reading Difficulty* and the *Spache Diagnostic Reading Scales*. The instructional and potential (listening comprehension) levels from the *Botel Reading Inventory* are based only on word recognition and knowledge of word meaning (the words are presented in isolation).

According to Davis and Shepard (1983), two of the most widely used individually administered NR reading tests are the *Woodcock Reading Mastery Test* and the *Peabody Individual Achievement Test* (PIAT). The former has five subtests; the latter contains two reading subtests. Reading comprehension scores on both tests are based on the reading of very brief passages; the PIAT samples only sentence comprehension. The use of both tests for diagnostic purposes is very limited.

An oral reading test's scoring system should distinguish between miscues that disrupt meaning and those that do not (see p. 202). As yet, no published oral reading test has done so. If a large number of word-recognition errors are nondisruptive, the resulting test score probably underestimates the reading level at which the child is capable of functioning. However, if one is using a *stand-*

ardized test, it must be scored according to the directions in the manual if the norms are to be used.

Learning to Give Oral Diagnostic Tests

Recording a child's performance as he or she reads orally requires speed in the use of a variety of symbols that represent different kinds of errors. Beginners usually cannot record as fast as the child reads, and so their records are often incomplete and only partially accurate. For the inexperienced tester, it is highly advisable that the child's oral reading be recorded and scored later at leisure, when parts of the recording can be replayed as necessary to resolve questions. The use of a tape recorder may allow even an experienced examiner to pay more attention to the child's behavior during reading without distracting the child, who may try to watch what the examiner is writing. A tape recording provides more accurate recording and scoring of errors. It also allows children to listen to their performances and, by comparing them with recordings made after remedial help, to note their progress. Nevertheless, if a child seems upset by the presence of a tape recorder, do the best you can without it.

Comparison of Oral and Silent Reading Ability

As yet, no study has been conducted to show the comparability of widely used oral and silent reading tests for individuals. One way to alleviate the problem of noncomparability of existing tests is to use an informal reading inventory that has two comparable passages at each reader level (realizing, of course, that prior knowledge is always a variable). One set of passages is read orally and the other silently until the comprehension criterion is not met. At times, this will necessitate having the child read passages at levels above which he failed to meet the word-recognition criterion. A difference of at least two reader levels would have to occur before one could reasonably conclude that a child's oral and silent reading levels differed significantly. This two-reader-level criterion is an estimate.

When silent reading seems significantly better than oral reading, the following possibilities, which can occur singly or in combination, should be considered: (1) The reader makes numerous minor miscues that cause him to fail the word-recognition criterion, although do not greatly hamper comprehension; (2) the reader can reread at will in silent reading but is penalized for repetitions in oral reading; (3) the reader has good language skills and is expert at using context, thus achieving sufficient comprehension despite word-recognition weaknesses; (4) the reader is self-conscious or extremely anxious when reading orally but is more relaxed when reading silently; (5) the reader is so concerned about word recognition and "expression" in oral reading that his comprehension suffers; (6) the reader has benefited from extensive guessing when taking the silent reading test (which very often uses multiple-choice questions), artificially raising his score.

Oral reading may be significantly better than silent reading in some cases. This may be the result of the child's having had much more practice reading orally than silently, or being aided by the aural feedback (hearing the words makes it easier for the reader to understand the material). For older readers, the more likely reason is that they must attend to the task when reading orally, but need not when reading silently or listening.

V. ASSESSING READING COMPREHENSION

How well children understand what they read is the most important aspect of reading ability to assess. But as will be indicated in this section, assessing it is not an easy matter.

All measures of reading comprehension are indirect because we cannot directly observe the actual process in the reader's mind. Procedures for testing reading comprehension may be classified as product or process measures. *Product measures* test comprehension after the child has read. *Process measures* attempt to sample comprehension as it is taking place. There are four main kinds of product measures: retelling, questions–answers using unaided recall, multiple-choice questions, and true–false items; and three process measures; cloze, miscue analysis, and eye movements. Johnston (1983) and Chang (1983) discussed each measure, indicating their cognitive demands, advantages, and limitations.

Children's reading comprehension is often described in terms such as being at the "fourth grade" or "fourth reader" level. Such descriptors are derived from one or more of the following sources: an NR grade-equivalent score, the highest reader level at which the criteria were met on a CR test, or the level of text being used with the child for reading instruction. All have limitations, but for the present such general statements will have to suffice.

What tests measure and how test scores are derived differ widely. So do the demands placed on pupils by what they are required to read in school. What constitutes acceptable comprehension differs from teacher to teacher. Therefore one cannot rely on a single test score to predict how well a group, let along a child, will read in various classroom situations. How well children can comprehend the materials used daily in school must be assessed using samples from those materials, and over time.

Narratives often require the reader to supply details and main ideas or to recall them at intervals throughout the story. Readers of narratives also are required to draw on their own experiences and relate present to previous events in order to obtain meaning. Connotative meanings and literary usages of words and phrases often characterize narratives. Since writing styles differ among authors even within the same genre, different narratives may cause problems for different students.

Expository material is usually nonfictional prose in which the events and objects are readily identifiable. Different types of paragraph structures appear in different content-subject material (see Harris & Sipay 1979, pp. 369, 371). Denotative meanings and literal statements characterize expository material; often, less inferencing is needed to obtain meaning than with narratives.

What Should a Reading-Comprehension Test Measure?

The answer to this question may seem obvious, but there are differences of opinion. Some writers (e.g., Carroll 1977, Royer & Cunningham 1981) have suggested developing reading tests that would reduce the effects of reasoning ability and prior knowledge on reading-comprehension test scores. Thus the tests would measure only literal comprehension using only passage-dependent questions. Such "purer" measures of reading might be more sensitive to gains in reading ability, as some authors suggest, but the question remains as to how well such tests would reflect normal reading in which reasoning and prior knowledge often play important roles. T. Carr (1981) stated that comprehension normally involves inferences that may be based on information in the text or on prior knowlege. Both kinds of inferences are central to the comprehension process.

The differences of opinion as to what reading tests measure or how reading comprehension should be measured are illustrated by comparing the work of two writers. On one hand, Spearritt (1980) concluded that cloze and multiple-choice reading-comprehension tests measured much the same skills. Johnston (1983), on the other hand, indicated that the various procedures for measuring reading comprehension place different demands on the testee. Spearritt based his conclusion on factor-analysis studies; Johnston's point of view is based on cognitive psychology and information processing theory.

Prior Knowledge

There is increasing evidence that prior knowledge plays a major role in reading comprehension. Prior knowledge influences comprehension at all levels of processing (Johnston & Pearson 1982). At the decoding and word-recognition level, it operates by limiting the set of words that could possibly appear in a sentence slot. At the short-term memory level, it influences the amount that can be stored in working memory. During the inference stage, it determines which, if any, inferences should be made. And at the storage level, it determines which information will be stored, in what format it will be stored, and whether it will be retrieved.

One way that test constructors have attempted to lessen the possible bias created by prior knowledge is the use of a number of short passages on a variety of topics. The net effect, however, has been that readers with broader general knowledge are likely to do better on the tests.

When word recognition is automatic but comprehension is weak, lack of prior knowledge may be a contributing factor. One way to assess topical knowledge is to present three key content words from the passage to the student, who is asked to free-associate whatever comes to mind when hearing each word. The child's associations are scored as indicating much, some, or little prior knowledge (Langer 1980). Langer's qualitative measure and a quantitative measure (a count of the number of associations made with a word) both successfully predicted overall recall, independent of intelligence and reading level; with the quantitative measure being the better predictor (Hare 1982b).

Text Content and Structure

Various factors within the text can influence reading comprehension (Johnston & Pearson 1982, Johnston 1983, Samuels 1983), such as the quantity of information (often indicated by passage length), the density of information, the density of *new* information, the number of modifiers in clauses, sentence complexity, the familiarity of the vocabulary to the reader, the use of anaphoric terms and cohesive ties.

Differences between test content and classroom reading materials can influence the predictive validity of a test. Test passages are usually shorter and have less obvious structure than classroom reading materials, for example.

Possible Influence of Question Wording

There are two broad categories of question wording: verbatim and paraphrased. *Verbatim questions* use the same, or very nearly the same, wording and sentence structure as the text from which they are derived. For instance, if the text read "The regent's diadem glistened resplendently," a verbatim question would be "Whose diadem glistened resplendently?" It is possible to answer verbatim questions simply by matching the wording of the question and text. The reader being tested can provide the correct answer without understanding the text (e.g., the testee need not know what a regent is or understand that the crown shone brilliantly). One of the limitations of verbatim questions is that you cannot be sure if an acceptable response indicates *recall* or *comprehension*. Therefore, except when the wording of the text is the only acceptable response, it is advisable to ask pupils to put their responses in their own words.

In *paraphrased* or *transformed questions*, the words and/or the syntactic structure differ noticeably from that of the text. Paraphrased questions can be easier or more difficult to answer depending on the wording of the text and question. One of the limitations of paraphrased questions is that the student may understand the text but not the question.

Although most tests give equal weight to all test items, the importance of the concept(s) measured by the test item to understanding the passage should be considered. Some test questions focus on insignificant details.

Production Requirements

The requirements imposed by the manner in which pupils have to demonstrate their reading comprehension are often overlooked in analyzing test performance. Test performance may be influenced by such factors as whether the questions are posed orally or in written form, whether the responses must be given orally or in written form, the format of the comprehension check, and the availability of the text.

Oral questions may be easier to understand than written ones, especially for poor readers, who may not be able to read the questions; they also allow for follow-up by the examiner. Similarly, many children find it easier to respond orally than in writing. Written responses require additional skills — written language production and spelling — so that difficulty in responding in written form may indicate problems other than reading comprehension.

Reading comprehension may be checked by free recall (retelling); open-ended, multiple-choice, true–false questions; or cloze or maze tests. Each of these places differing cognitive demands on the student (Johnston 1983). Probably the most demanding is retelling, followed by cloze tests, open-ended (unaided recall) questions, multiple-choice questions, maze tests, and true–false items. Kendall, Mason, and Hunter (1979) found that fifth graders scored consistently higher on maze and multiple-choice tests than on cloze or unaided recall items. The wording of multiple-choice items can influence the responses of pupils, especially if they are test-wise (Levin *et al.* 1978).

In the *retelling* procedure, the testee is asked to relate the content of what has just been read. Some writers suggest not cuing the pupil at all; more writers, however, recommend either cuing or the use of probe questions if the telling is incomplete. Points are usually assigned subjectively to reflect the relative importance of the elements in the material (e.g., see Clark 1982), but understanding the relationships of the separate points may not be considered. A procedure for assessing the richness of retellings has been developed by Irwin and Mitchell (1983).

Two other points about the use of retellings should be considered. First, retellings place a heavier demand on the ability to retrieve and organize the required information than do other assessment procedures. Second, children's retellings to an examiner or teacher may not indicate their complete understanding or recall of the material. When children think the person to whom they are retelling the story has already read the story (an assumption likely to be made of an examiner or teacher), their retellings are less complete than when relating the story to children who have not read it (Johnston & Pearson 1982).

Many classroom activities and group tests allow the student to refer to the reading material during the comprehension check. This makes the task easier than if the text is not available. When the text is not available to the pupil during the comprehension check, the question whether the inability to respond correctly reflects difficulty in comprehension or in recall can be resolved by allowing the student to refer to the text to find the answers to incorrectly answered questions. If the student is then able to answer the item, or can supply the information omitted from his retelling, comprehension is not the problem.

When Is an Answer Correct?

The responses to comprehension-check questions indicated by test publishers or teachers' manuals are not always the only acceptable answers. A careful analysis of the text may reveal that the child's response is just as plausible as the "correct" one(s). For instance, the text might read "The trip by boat was pleasant, but Adam was thrilled to be on land again." Rather than say "pleasant" in response to the question "What kind of trip did Adam have?" the pupil might say "a boat trip" (which the examiner may follow with a probe) or "long," which is based on an inference — it must have been long because he was thrilled to be on land again (the examiner should follow this response with "How do you know?"). Because pupils draw on their existing knowledge, their answers to questions or their retellings may include elaborations on what is stated in the text. Cultural differences also may influence the interpretation of text.

"Incorrect" responses that are plausible, that indicate possible misconceptions, that indicate faulty reasoning, or that are not completely acceptable should be followed up with probes.

Reading Orally at Sight

Prereading material silently before reading it orally allows the student the opportunity to work on unknown words and obtain at least a general idea of the content of the passage. Even then it is possible that the amount of attention that must be devoted to fluent oral reading may lessen the processing capacity available for comprehension. When children are required to read at sight orally, as is usually the case in testing, even more processing capacity may have to be devoted to word recognition and reading fluently. Word-recognition weaknesses may interfere with the activation of prior knowledge by reducing the amount of attention available for comprehending.

Assessing Comprehension of Spoken Language

If the child is very weak in reading comprehension and if word recognition is not a problem, it is advisable to determine how well he understands similar material read to him. To prevent confounding, the measures of reading and listening comprehension should make similar conceptual and linguistic demands on the pupil. Reading and listening comprehension are compared to determine if the problem is one of language comprehension in general or of reading comprehension only. If the student is attending to the tasks and if his listening comprehension is as weak as his reading comprehension, he probably has a general language-comprehension problem. If listening comprehension is *significantly* higher than reading comprehension, the comprehension problem is centered in reading.

If difficulty understanding syntactic structures is suspected, the child may be asked to paraphrase sentences containing such structures or asked questions that will reveal his understanding of them. For further suggestions on formal and informal tests of spoken language and the problems in devising such measures, refer to Swisher and Aten (1981) and Vellutino and Shub (1982).

VI. ASSESSING READING VOCABULARY

Reading vocabulary refers to the ability to determine the most appropriate meanings of printed words. Although word recognition is usually subsumed under this term, a pupil can sometimes determine the meaning of a word without being able to recognize it or decode it if the context in which the unknown word appears is sufficiently revealing. Conversely, the ability to provide the oral counterpart of a printed word does not assure that the child knows its meaning.

Group-Administered Tests

Almost all published tests intended for use above the second grade sample understanding of word meanings. They do so in a variety of ways. The vocabulary subtest may require students to select synonyms, antonyms, or word classifications for words that appear either in isolation or in varying amounts of context. Some tests include vocabulary items in their comprehension subtests.

Apart from the comparative data they provide and the indication as to whether or not reading vocabulary is a problem area, NR vocabulary tests provide little useful diagnostic information. The words used in NR tests vary greatly from test to test and may not adequately sample the reading vocabulary to which the child has been exposed. The same is true for published CR tests. In almost all cases, only the most common meaning of the word is measured. But many English words have multiple meanings, and the ability to determine which meaning is appropriate in a particular context is an important reading-comprehension skill.

Group-administered vocabulary tests require, at a minimum, that the child recognize the stimulus word and the correct answer, and the meanings of both. An incorrect response to a test item may reflect an inability to recognize or decode the printed words, not knowing the meaning of the stimulus word or the correct response, or any combination of these factors. Only an individual follow-up can provide such information. Having the child read the incorrectly answered test items orally will reveal if word recognition or decoding contributed to the poor test performance. Asking the child to define the stimulus words and the correct responses will indicate if lack of word meaning was a contributing factor. It is also advisable to ask the pupil why he selected his answers. He may have an acceptable, though unexpected, rationale, or he may reveal faulty reasoning.

If word meaning is identified as an area of weakness, the child's understanding vocabulary should be sampled more thoroughly. If the pupil's understanding vocabulary proves meager, the causes for this handicapping condition should be explored. Limited experiential background and learning potential are often associated with limited understanding vocabulary.

Individually Administered Tests

Few individually administered reading tests contain a word-meaning subtest, but some have vocabulary items in their comprehension checks. Care should be exercised in interpreting the Word Comprehension subtest of the *Woodcock Reading Mastery Tests* because it requires the child to make analogies, a skill that heavily involves reasoning ability.

Informal Tests

In most directed reading activities, the children's knowledge of the meanings of key words in the story they are about to read is checked by the teacher. Workbooks that accompany published reading programs often contain word-meaning exercises. Unfortunately, students' knowledge of the vocabulary employed in their content-subject texts is much less frequently assessed.

VII. APPRAISING WORD RECOGNITION

Word recognition is defined here as the ability to determine the oral equivalent of a printed word. It does not involve determining word meaning, although word recognition usually leads to word meaning. A word can be recognized or decoded without knowing its meaning.

Word-recognition scores correlate highly (around .80) with reading comprehension in the primary grades and less highly (around .65) with comprehension in the upper grades. But although word-recognition test scores can be used to estimate an individual's level of reading ability, they cannot substitute for measures of the ability to comprehend connected discourse. Some children are much better at word recognition than reading comprehension, and studies show that word-recognition scores often do not place children at the same levels as do IRIs or NR tests (Froese 1976, Ruggieri & Purnell 1976, Marzano *et al.* 1978).

Assessing Word Recognition

Two aspects of word recognition should be measured: accuracy and automaticity (Samuels 1983). Word-recognition *accuracy* can be measured by having the pupil read orally words presented in isolation or in context. Ability to recognize words in isolation is a purer measure of word-recognition accuracy because the pupil must rely solely on graphic information. Word-recognition accuracy should also be checked while reading connected discourse to find out about the student's use of context clues. Most students' word recognition is better in context than in isolation.

Automaticity means recognizing words with no hesitation and with minimal attention. Samuels (1983) suggested that automaticity can be tested by having the child orally read a previously unread passage (tell the child he will be asked about his comprehension of the material). One indicator of automaticity is the degree of expression used in reading the passage. Another is the accuracy of recall, because in order to comprehend while reading orally, little attention can be devoted to word recognition. Of course, factors such as inadequate prior knowledge or syntactic complexity may also hamper comprehension, even though word recognition is automatic.

The simplest technique for measuring automaticity is to time how long it takes the child to read a list of words. Only words recognized accurately should be counted in computing the average time per word. Since there are no norms for such tests, the average time it takes good readers to read the list can be used as a guideline. When word recognition is automatic, less attention need be devoted to word recognition, but it does not assure comprehension.

Group-Administered Tests

Most NR and CR reading tests designed for use in the primary grades contain word-recognition subtests. These tests vary in the degree to which they sample the words that have been taught to a particular group of children. Tests that accompany basal reading programs sample only the words used in their programs.

Group-administered word-recognition tests may fail to detect children with word-recognition problems because of the manner in which the skill is measured. Word recognition is usually sampled by having the child match one of three or four printed words with a picture or with a word spoken by the examiner. Scores on such tests are influenced by the degree to which the distractors (incorrect answers) resemble the correct response (Baumann, Walker, & Johnson

1981). If the distractors differ greatly (e.g., *ox, elephant, dog* when the correct response is *cat*), the child need rely only on certain cues (e.g., the initial sound–symbol association) in order to arrive at the correct response. In such cases, some children who score well on the test are unable to recognize the same words in isolation or in context when reading orally (Kibby 1979a).

If the above situation is suspected or if a child does poorly on a group test, a follow-up procedure can be employed. Point to each correct answer and ask the child to pronounce it. A comparison of the child's performance on both formats will reveal if the initial results were accurate. An analysis of the errors may provide clues to the child's problem.

Individually Administered Tests

Individually administered word-recognition tests make different and more revealing demands on the testee than do group tests in that they require the child to pronounce the word. The ability to recognize words in context is measured by standardized oral reading tests and informal and published reading inventories. Most oral reading tests do not yield separate scores for words recognized in context; the *Gilmore* does. The *Gray Oral Reading Test* score is based only on word recognition and the time taken to read the passages.

There are also standardized tests that measure only the ability to recognize words presented in isolation. The two most commonly used are the *Wide Range Achievement Test* (WRAT), which also tests math and spelling, and the *Slosson Oral Reading Test* (SORT). WRAT reading scores tend to overestimate the instructional levels of children (Bradley 1976, Pikulski & Shanahan 1982).

Informal Tests

The ability to recognize words in context is frequently checked during classroom instruction, but there are times when the ability to recognize words in isolation should be checked. Such tests are easy to construct. A random sampling of words can be selected from the desired source. To obtain a quick estimate of the suitability of a reading text, a 20-word sample drawn from the new words introduced in that text will suffice (these words are usually indicated in the back of the text or in the teacher's manual). A child who has difficulty with more than 6 of the 20 words is likely to have difficulty reading the book from which the sample was drawn.

Word-recognition tests that are more broadly indicative of word-recognition ability may be constructed by drawing 10-word samples per level from a graded word list. Such a test is shown in Figure 7.7. A brief test of this type also can be used to estimate the ability to recognize high-frequency words or to determine which level of words should be checked out more thoroughly.

Some clinicians test disabled readers on all 220 words in the *Dolch Basic Sight Vocabulary* (see p. 375). Testing all 220 *Dolch* words or any list of such length is unnecessarily tedious and frustrating for most disabled readers, especially if it is done in one session. We prefer to try only a sample of any list of high-frequency words to determine if work on those words will be needed, leaving to remediation the identification of specific words that need to be learned.

Sample Graded Word Lists

Pre-primer	Primer	1st Reader	2nd Reader	3rd Reader
no	box	store	zoom	peel
help	take	another	hope	depend
all	happy	flower	peek	helpless
stop	over	hop	block	apron
up	father	pan	feather	rowboat
for	saw	try	wind	trust
red	would	bone	crack	being
jump	mouse	mean	speak	ceiling
book	into	should	market	split
come	under	dark	trunk	flop

4th Reader	5th Reader	6th Reader	7th Reader	8th Reader
gulf	resign	baron	quail	yacht
tense	haze	torment	ignorant	electrified
recent	socket	originate	wrath	barnacle
occasional	admirer	soundless	bribe	spacious
coward	pianist	cruelty	solitary	obnoxious
snare	cupboard	hesitation	cultivate	trivial
broad	unaware	yield	traverse	deficiency
launch	expand	recreation	factual	legislation
exhibit	mature	locomotive	absurd	geometric
whirlwind	broth	existence	maroon	radiance

Figure 7.7.   Ten-word lists at 10 reader levels. The difficulty levels are not indicated on copies presented to the pupil. The highest level at which the pupil can recognize at least 7 of the words is suggestive of his instructional level. These words were taken from the Harris–Jacobson Basic Lists by Levels (1982).

Testing for both quick recognition (timed exposure) and decoding (untimed exposure) is a good idea. The words must either be placed on individual cards or exposed in a quick-flash device. Presenting only one word at a time and keeping the remaining cards from view helps the child to focus attention on the word. A word card may be exposed briefly or covered with a blank card, which is lifted quickly to expose the stimulus card and then replaced. In either case it is somewhat difficult to keep the exposure time constant. This problem is overcome by using a tachistoscopic device or lessened by using a simple hand tachistoscope, such as the one shown in Figure 7.8.

Multiple copies of the test can be run off so that the examiner can use a fresh copy for each pupil. What is recorded will depend on the information desired.

Miscue Analysis

Procedures for analyzing and interpreting reading miscues, called *miscue analysis*, have been developed by K. Goodman (1969) and Y. Goodman and Burke

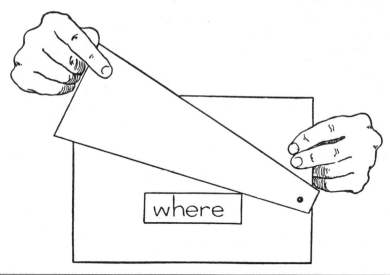

Figure 7.8. A simple hand tachistoscope. This can be made in sizes to fit the use of 4 × 6-in. or 3 × 5-in. index cards. The shield and shutter can be cut out of stiff cardboard or the sides of a grocery carton with a sharp razor blade. To use, hold the shield upright on table top with the left hand. Pick up a card with the right hand and place it against the shield, with the bottom of the card resting on the table, so that the material to be exposed is in the opening. Place the left thumb against the card, holding it in place. With the right hand lift the shutter quickly until its lower corner is level with the top of the shield and let go; this gives a fairly rapid exposure. Very rapid exposures can be obtained by placing the left index finger across the top of the shield and bouncing the shutter against it.

(1972). The latter, less complex *Reading Miscue Inventory* has been reviewed by Anastasiow (1978) and Singer (1978a).

Miscue analysis is based on K. Goodman's model of reading as a psycholinguistic guessing game. Basically, miscue analysis is a procedure for analyzing oral reading. The selection read orally by the pupil must be (1) new to the pupil; (2) a complete story or passage (have a beginning, middle, and end); (3) one grade level *above* the material used by the child in class; and (4) of sufficient length and difficulty to generate a minimum of 25 miscues. Assistance in word recognition is not provided by the examiner, except for urging the reader to guess the word after a 30-second hesitation; if hesitations are continuous, the reader is told to continue reading even if it means skipping a word or phrase. Following the oral reading, the child retells the story, with some general guiding questions posed by the examiner if necessary. Comprehension is scored subjectively by the examiner, who can award up to 100 points for the retelling. The procedure does not yield a reading-level score; rather, it provides insights into the reading strategies employed by the reader.

Sims (1979) presented a simplified set of questions to be asked about each miscue:

1. Does it look and/or sound like the expected response?
2. Does it make sense in the sentence?

3. Does the sentence make sense up to and including the miscue?
4. Does it fit grammatically?
5. Does the sentence make a grammatical fit up to and including the miscue?
6. Has it been influenced by the reader's dialect; is it correct in his own dialect?
7. Was it corrected?
8. How much change was caused by the miscue? How close to the original meaning does the sentence with the miscue come?

Miscue analysis is time-consuming even when a simplified version is used. Hood (1978) pointed out other limitations of miscue analysis:

1. Some miscue scores have questionable reliability because the classification of miscues varies among examiners.
2. Classification of some miscues as "good" or "bad" seems to differ with the reader's age and reading ability.
3. The relationship between passage content and the reader's background seems to influence test results (the same is true for most tests).
4. Miscues made by a given reader are related to the overall accuracy level at which they were made. For example, when word-recognition accuracy was 90% or less and the passage was less related to the reader's experience, there were proportionally more nonsense-word responses or no responses and fewer serious errors were self-corrected. At and above the 95% level of accuracy, proportionally more minor errors occurred.
5. Examiner's opinions regarding the contextual appropriateness of miscues vary tremendously.

According to Weber (1977), not all miscue categories are equally useful. Goldsmith, Nicolich and Haupt (1982) presented an adaptation of the usual miscue taxonomy that attempts to separate the information sources employed by the reader.

There is increasing evidence that the reader's patterns of errors and strategies change with the difficulty of the reading material. The more difficult the material, the less likely is the child to employ semantic and syntactic cues and to correct miscues that disrupt meaning (Christie & Alonso 1980, Pikulski & Shanahan 1982). This suggests that Goodman's recommendation to use only difficult material in making a miscue analysis is questionable and that miscues should be analyzed at both the child's frustration level and instructional level.

Miscue analysis has provided a useful research tool and has forced educators to reconsider beliefs about oral reading behaviors and their meaning. Research on miscue analysis has suggested the following (Wixson 1979):

1. Regardless of age or reading proficiency, most readers make a greater number of semantically and syntactically acceptable miscues than graphophonemically similar miscues.
   a. The majority of miscues are syntactically acceptable.

    b. Most readers average about 20% more syntactically acceptable miscues than semantically acceptable miscues.

    c. The proportion of semantically and syntactically acceptable miscues increases with reading proficiency.

2. Novice readers' miscues tend to include a large number of real word substitutions (often words that have been previously taught) and "no response" omissions.

3. As readers mature, the percentage of graphophonemically similar miscues tends to increase initially and then stabilizes at some point (at least for good readers).

    a. The percentage of "no response" omissions tends to decrease with age.

    b. Older readers tend to substitute nonwords or real words that may not have been previously taught.

4. Compared to proficient readers, less proficient readers

    a. tend to make a relatively higher percentage of graphophonemically similar miscues.

    b. make fewer attempts to self-correct.

    c. tend to correct acceptable and unacceptable miscues at an almost equal rate.

5. Proficient readers

    a. omit words that are not essential to comprehension.

    b. correct unacceptable miscues at a higher rate than acceptable miscues.

6. Many of the miscue patterns that appear to reflect developmental trends actually vary as a function of the complex interaction among instructional methodology; the child's reading skills, background, and purpose for reading; and the nature and content of the written material.

Some Suggestions and Examples

If a child's word-recognition errors or miscues are going to be analyzed, it is advisable to present the words on which the child erred after the test has been administered. If the word has been pronounced correctly most of the time, it should not be included in the analysis. When given a second chance to try a word, children can often correct their errors (Cohn & D'Alessandro 1978, Leibert 1982).

The student's miscues should be carefully analyzed for information about (1) use of semantic, syntactic, and graphic cues; (2) which word-recognition and decoding skills and strategies were employed, and how well they were utilized; (3) particular words, types of words, or word parts that may be causing problems; and (4) the impact of the word-recognition errors on comprehension.

A note of caution seems warranted in analyzing miscues that occurred across a series of graded paragraphs. Passage difficulty can have a significant effect on qualitative error patterns. At their frustration level, children tend to make fewer semantically acceptable miscues and self-corrections, but more graphically similar and gramatically acceptable miscues (Christie & Alonso 1980). Reading ability may play a role in the use of graphophonemic cues. As proficient readers mature, they tend to rely less on such cues; less proficient readers continue to rely on graphic cues (Christie 1981).

A few cases are presented at this point to illustrate different cases and how to interpret their performances.

Susie's oral reading performance (see Fig. 7.4 on p. 196) indicates that at the low second reader level she made very few miscues and had excellent comprehension. At the high second reader level, both word-recognition and comprehension criteria were met. Susie made adequate use of context at the second reader levels, at times combining graphic and context cues to keep the meaning essentially correct. At the low third reader level, however, almost all her miscues were serious, and five words had to be pronounced for her. When many words are unknown or mispronounced, or if the material is not understood, it is difficult to predict words and anticipate meaning. At this level Susie was unable to make much use of context cues as an aid to word recognition. Her miscues suggest little difficulty making symbol–sound associations, except possibly for vowel combinations (e.g., *weak, loose*). Most of her mispronunciations occurred on the final parts of words, but these were more likely the result of inattention to word endings and her overall difficulty with the passage than an inability to decode these elements. These hypotheses can be checked out by presenting the words in isolation and focusing her attention on the ends of the words. Susie's main word-recognition difficulties seem to be with words that contain elements that cannot be decoded by applying phonic principles (e.g., *giant, tongue, patient, stomach*) and decoding words of more than one syllable. These weaknesses should be checked further.

Maria, a third grader, scored 3.1 on the *Gates–MacGinitie Reading Test*. Her teacher, however, reported that Maria was having difficulty reading the third-grade basal reader. Her oral reading was slow and inaccurate. She responded to every word, but nearly all of her miscues were mispronunciations, and many of them were semantically and syntactically inapproproate. A representative sample of her miscues on monosyllabic words follows:

	Stimulus	Response		Stimulus	Response
1.	front	first	11.	flow	few
2.	bread	bag	12.	cold	cool
3.	silt	sit	13.	shall	shell
4.	glass	guess	14.	goat	game
5.	spent	sped	15.	shawl	shade
6.	blank	back	16.	gulp	gal
7.	snip	snag	17.	chart	champ
8.	rigs	rags	18.	these	that
9.	there	that	19.	hear	her
10.	noon	neck	20.	stood	stone

The above sample suggests the following: (1) Maria was overrelying on the initial letter or two and making little use of context. (2) She had difficulty making symbol–sound associations for *r* and *l* blends in the initial position (items 1, 2, 4, 6, 11) but not *s* blends (items 5, 7, 20). (3) She had difficulty making the symbol–sound associations for final blends (items 1, 3, 5, 6, 12,

16) and vowel combinations (items 2, 10, 11, 14, 15, 20). (4) She had no difficulty making symbol–sound associations for single consonants (items 3, 8, 10, 12, 14, 16, 19), the first consonant of each initial blend, and consonant digraphs (items 9, 13, 15, 17, 18). The errors on final single consonants were probably caused by her overreliance on the initial letters and difficulty with vowel combinations. The fact that Maria had no difficulty with single consonants in the initial position reinforces this interpretation. (5) Maria may have difficulty with symbol–sound associations for single vowels, but her overreliance on initial consonants may be strongly contributing to such errors, and three of the single vowels (items 1, 12, 13) are nonphonemic elements. Follow-up testing with the appropriate SWAT tests indicated that Maria did not have problems making symbol–sound associations for initial blends when her attention was focused on the graphemes, but did for vowel combinations and consonant blends that appear only in the final position. Follow-up testing also revealed that she had no problem with visual analysis of monosyllables or with blending.

These findings led to the recommendations that Maria's remedial program should include getting her to develop the habit of attending to the whole word rather than just the beginning; teaching her to monitor her word-recognition responses and make more effective use of meaning clues; and teaching her only those symbol–sound associations she needed to learn.

Rob, a fifth grader, obtained a score of 4.8 on the *Metropolitan Reading Test*. In oral reading, his performance was at third reader level in comprehension and second reader level in word recognition. His miscues showed considerable variety, but for the most part were semantically and syntactically appropriate. Follow-up testing indicated that Rob had little trouble recognizing the words on which he miscued in context when they were presented in isolation and that he could decode difficult polysyllabic words. When reading connected discourse, however, his tendency was to rely too much on context. Rob had to be convinced that, although at times it is not necessary to recognize all the printed words, it is very important to do so at other times. He also needed to learn when this is so, be shown that he had the skills to do so, and be convinced that there is a payoff for making the effort to recognize words accurately. A well-established ineffective reading strategy needed to be replaced with more effective ones.

Relationship between Miscues/Word-Recognition Errors and Reading Comprehension

Pflaum (1980) found that, for disabled readers, higher rates of errors that change meaning were associated with lower comprehension; higher rates of phonic-cue use with higher comprehension. Also, a study by Beebe (1979–1980) revealed that although substitution miscues generally detracted from comprehension and recall, only uncorrected unacceptable substitutions had a negative impact on comprehension and recall. Self-corrections and acceptable substitutions were associated with higher comprehension and retelling scores. It is not surprising that contextually appropriate miscues occur when comprehension is high, since comprehension can influence word recognition and the appropriateness of miscues. But miscues do not always reflect the reader's comprehension. Some children's miscue patterns suggest weak comprehension, but their retellings indicate good comprehension. Other readers produce miscue patterns that indicate adequate comprehension, but they demonstrate minimal comprehension (Wixson 1979).

When word recognition and comprehension are both inadequate on a passage, one of three situations may exist: (1) Weak word recognition is contributing to the inadequate comprehension; (2) inadequate comprehension is contributing to the weak word recognition; or (3) weaknesses in both areas are contributing to each other. Inability to recognize many of the printed words is a very strong contributor to inadequate reading comprehension. To determine if poor word recognition is contributing to inadequate comprehension, the unknown words can be pronounced for the child and the impact on comprehension determined.

III. ASSESSING DECODING SKILLS

Several methods may be used by a child in attempting to decode a word that is not immediately recognized. The word may be guessed from the context in which it is found. If it has been taught in spelling lessons, or if the child has been taught to read through a linguistic approach, spelling the word may stimulate recall. The sounds represented by the graphemes may be determined and then blended to get the pronunciation. The size and shape of the word may serve as clues, or the resemblance of the word to an already known word may be noticed. Good readers are resourceful. If one method does not succeed, they try another. They know how to utilize the context, how to make symbol–sound associations, how to blend, and how to employ visual resemblances. Poor readers often restrict themselves to one method of decoding and employ even that method poorly. It is important to find out what method or methods a child tries to use, as well as how successfully these strategies are employed.

Some children have apparently never learned any decoding technique thoroughly enough to use it successfully. They know the sounds represented by only a few letters, or they cannot blend phonemes even when they succeed in making the symbol–sound associations. They do not look for common recognizable parts or phonograms in a word, or for resemblances to words they know. They have laboriously acquired a small stock of sight words that is inadequate for their needs. They may or may not try to make use of context and language cues. In these cases, remedial teaching must necessarily start near the beginning and should include a thorough and systematic teaching of the necessary decoding skills.

Aside from the use of context, there are three main subskill areas of decoding: visual analysis, phonic analysis, and blending.[8] Good readers usually inspect an unknown word for parts they can utilize, make necessary symbol–sound associations, blend the parts into a whole word, and check for appropri-

_____

[8] These skill areas are discussed more fully on pages 395–401.

ateness. It is possible for different learners to employ different processes and information to arrive at the same final response (Sipay 1971).

A learner who cannot decode words may be deficient in any or all of the skill areas, with symbol–sound association weaknesses occurring most frequently. The examiner's task is to determine which weaknesses are creating most of the problem.

Nonwords, often referred to as nonsense words or syllables, are often employed in decoding tests to rule out the possibility that the pupil might recognize the words at sight and thus not have to utilize any decoding skills. This use of nonwords has been criticized by Cunningham (1977), who suggested that a more valid assessment of decoding skills could be obtained by first flashing real words and then allowing the child time to decode those words not recognized initially.

In assessing decoding ability, two points should be considered. First, it is easier to decode words that are in your listening vocabulary. Second, words in context are easier to recognize and decode than words in isolation because additional cues are available. These two points lead to the conclusion that a test employing nonwords in isolation requires a higher degree of decoding ability than is necessary for decoding real words in context. On such tests, therefore, one should be willing to accept a mastery level below that which might be desirable if real words were used.

Published Group-Administered Decoding Tests

A number of NR survey tests and CR tests contain decoding subtests (using an assortment of titles) at the primary level or at the primary and intermediate levels. Some NR diagnostic tests, such as the *Stanford Diagnostic Reading Test*, even sample decoding skills at the upper grade levels. Tests that accompany commercially published reading programs sample only those decoding skills taught at a given point in the program.

All group-administered decoding tests have a number of limitations. The tasks they require should be examined carefully, giving consideration to the following points:

1. Subtests having the same label may make different demands on the learner.
2. The skill required to accomplish the test task may not be relevant to reading ability.
3. In group-administered decoding tests, it is not possible to measure the same decoding skills as in individual tests.
4. Subtest titles can be very misleading. One "Whole Word Recognition" subtest only requires visual discrimination.
5. Most group tests contain too few items to provide a reliable measure of a specific skill (e.g., ability to make the sound–symbol association /t/ = *t*).
6. It is extremely difficult to measure blending skills realistically on a group test.

7. Group tests do not measure ability to combine all the skills needed for decoding. Usually a subtest measures just one aspect (e.g., syllabication).

Published Individually Administered Decoding Tests

There are several published individually administered decoding tests. Some are part of a diagnostic test battery, such as the *Spache Diagnostic Reading Scales* (DRS), *Gates–McKillip–Horowitz, Durrell*, or *Woodcock*. Others are single-purpose tests, such as the comprehensive *Sipay Word Analysis Tests* (SWAT) and the much briefer *Roswell–Chall Diagnostic Reading Test*. These individual tests also vary considerably as to which decoding skills are measured, and how. Care must be exercised in interpreting test performance, For instance, if the task only asks the pupil to pronounce a printed polysyllabic word (this may be an item on a test labeled "syllabication"), the inability to respond acceptably may be caused by a number of reasons. The child may not know how or where to syllabicate, be unable to decode one or more of the syllables, or be unable to blend the phonemes into syllables or the syllables into words. Also, although the manual gives only one acceptable response, others may be just as permissible, especially if contrived words are used. For example, *prodisla* (a stimulus from a published test) may be "syllabicated" into *pro-dis-la, pro-di-sla, prod-is-la*, or *prod-i-sla*, with the resulting vowel sounds varying in accordance with whether they appear in open or closed syllables.

Informal Tests

Information regarding a learner's decoding skills can be obtained by analyzing their word-recognition errors (see p. 218). Such analyses may reveal possible weaknesses or strengths in a subskill area (e.g., making vowel symbol–sound associations). The analysis can narrow down the areas requiring further investigation. For instance, it may indicate that it is necessary to check the child's ability to make symbol–sound associations for vowel digraphs and diphthongs but not for single vowels.

A pupil may be able to verbalize a phonic generalization but be unable to apply it. On the other hand, some children can apply generalizations but choose not to; some can apply phonic principles without being able to verbalize them. Many phonic generalizations involve a two-step process. The pupil must determine (1) what principle applies (e.g., the single vowel letter probably represents its long sound because it is in an open syllable; the child must know what an open syllable is); and (2) what that sound is (e.g., long vowels say their names). A breakdown in either step can produce an error.

An informal check of visual-analysis skills can be made by presenting unknown words to the child and asking where he would divide them and why. In some cases it is preferable to ask the child what he would do first in attempting to "figure out" what the word says. Some children do not know where to begin.

Symbol–sound associations may be tested by presenting letters in isolation or in words. If words are used, they should not be in the child's sight vocabulary, since there is no need to make symbol–sound associations if the words are rec-

TEST OF PHONIC KNOWLEDGE

A	h	s	v	c	z	k	w	r	f	t
	g	l	b	m	d	n	y	p	j	
B	bl	st	ch	dr	wh	fr	th	pl	sh	
	qu	str	scr	spl	spr	thr	ph	kn	wr	
C	e	o	a	u	i					
D	ee	ai	ay	oa	ou	oi	oy			
	aw	au	ea	oo	ow	ew	ey			
E	weed	dote	pan	jut	bide					
	wed	dot	pane	jute	bid					
F	de	un	re	im	pre	trans				
	tion	ful	ly	ous	ment	ance				

Figure 7.9. A brief test of phonic knowledge. *Directions:* As the child reads from one copy, the examiner records on another. The child points to each stimulus as he gives a response. For the single consonants (*A*) and consonant clusters (*B*), the child may give the sound in isolation or a word beginning with the sound represented by the grapheme. The child may be asked for the alternate sounds represented by *c* and *g*. For the single vowel letters (*C*), the child may be asked what sounds each letter can make, or be asked to give a word containing the corresponding sounds. The alternate sounds represented by *ea, oo,* and *ow* (*D*) may be requested. The two lines of words testing some spelling patterns (*E*) are read horizontally in pairs (e.g., *weed, wed*). This subtest is not given if the child had difficulty making the symbol–sound associations for single consonants and vowels. For children who do well, a few common affixes (*F*) are given.

ognized immediately. A brief test of symbol–sound knowledge is presented in Figure 7.9.

Blending skills should be tested. Depending on which skills one wishes to sample, single letters (*g a m*), a single letter and a phonogram (*g am*), or syllables (*gam ble*) may be presented. Probably it is easiest to blend syllables into whole words, followed by blending a consonant with a phonogram.

Sounds are blended in the testee's mind regardless of whether the original stimuli are visual or auditory. Some children have difficulty blending auditorily even if the test is well administered.

Informal auditory-blending tests can be constructed, or a brief standardized test like the *Roswell–Chall Auditory Blending Test* or a blending test such as the one in the *Gates–McKillop–Horowitz* may be used. In an auditory-blending test, the parts of the word are spoken by the examiner with a brief pause ($\frac{1}{2}$ to 1 second) between each segment. The pupil's task is to blend the parts into a whole word and then say the word. The words that are used, the manner in which they are segmented (e.g., /b/-/a/-/g/ is easier to say and synthesize than /s/-/t/-/r/-/i/-/p/), the enunciation of the examiner, especially how well she can "leave out" extraneous vowel sounds (e.g., /b/ instead of /buh/), and whether or not the word is in the child's lexicon are among the variables that can influence performance on an auditory-blending test.

The Use of Context and Language Clues

The use of context and language clues can aid word recognition and decoding. Minimal visual input may be sufficient to determine an unknown word if the context and the sentence structure offer strong clues as to what the word is. In both cases experiental background plays a role. In the sentence, "The bone was eaten by the ————," the child's knowledge about animals will suggest possibilities for the final word. Experience with language suggests that only certain words are likely to occur in a given pattern. Thus, the unknown word is likely to be a noun. Context and language clues often are combined with other word-recognition or decoding skills.

If the ability to use context or language clues is to be measured, the cloze test material should be at or below the child's instructional level. It is difficult to use context clues if a number of words are not recognized and impossible to do so if most words are unknown.

Follow-Up to Decoding Tests

The best way to determine if a child needs to, or can, learn skills in which tests or observations have shown him to be deficient is to try to teach him these skills. If the initial lessons indicate that the tests were in error, there is no need to continue teaching a skill for which a child already demonstrates mastery. If a child cannot learn the skill after a reasonable length of time, the teacher should attempt to determine what factors are contributing to the problem. These factors may be external or within the child. Emotional stress caused by events at home or in school may be curtailing his ability or desire to learn in general. Or, something within the way in which the skill is being presented may be a factor. Perhaps the child does not understand the directions, or there is an attempt to teach too much at once, or the pace of the lessons is too rapid, or there is a need for additional reinforcement. A child who cannot learn to make symbol–sound associations may be weak in underlying skills. In such cases it is advisable to check the child's auditory and visual discrimination, acuity, and memory. Suggestions for doing so have been provided by Sipay (1971).

IX DIAGNOSTIC USE OF SAMPLE LESSONS

In some of the early approaches to diagnosing reading disabilities, tests of associative learning were used to try to give a clear picture of why the child had trouble learning to recognize words. Tests involved the associating of nonsense syllables with geometric forms, meaningful words with geometric forms, real words with squiggles that looked something like printed words, and so on (Gates 1927). These tests fell into disuse because the test results were of little help in planning a remedial approach. Nevertheless, the idea that it is desirable to test children's ability to learn by trying them on genuine learning tasks has real merit.

The idea of using sample lessons as a diagnostic procedure for reading was developed by A. J. Harris and Roswell (1953). It is now sometimes known as trial teaching and may be used to select an approach for teaching word-recognition or decoding skills to severely disabled readers; it may also be adapted to determine which beginning reading approach is more likely to succeed for which children. Directions for five different methods follow.

DIRECTIONS

The entire session is informal and permissive, with a considerable amount of give-and-take. The examiner notes qualitative observations about the child's ability to profit from reading instruction. Factors like quick or slow grasp, tempo of work, need for repetition of instructions, degree of motivation required, resistance to specific materials, and ability to exert effort, give sustained attention, and recall what is taught are significant in interpreting the results of sample lessons.

Several procedures are tried until success with at least one method is clearly apparent. If time allows, a variety of materials is presented so as to obtain some impression of the child's reactions to readers, workbooks, and game-type devices. Any success is liberally praised and failure is minimized. In one such period it is possible to demonstrate to many children that they have the ability to learn to read. In most cases, this experience is a powerful motivating force for future reading instruction.

The procedures described below should be used at the discretion of the examiner, following careful analysis of the diagnostic reading test results. Thus, which methods to use and at what level to begin the sample lessons should be based on an appraisal of the child's basic reading skills as indicated on the tests.

1. Whole-Word Method. For the child who is a nonreader or almost a nonreader it is advisable to begin with a simple whole-word approach, which is essentially one of learning to associate printed words with their oral counterparts. Words that the child wants to learn may be used, thus supplying additional motivation.

You will need several cards, each with a picture illustrating a well-known object (e.g., a cake, a window, a table, a book). Print or type the name of the object under the picture. On another set of cards, print the words without the corresponding pictures. Make sure that no marks or smudges that could look like cues are on the cards. Test the child to make sure the words are not already known, then select five words for teaching. Note that follow-up may indicate that this is too many for the child to learn and recall in one session.

Present the first picture card, point to the word, and tell the child the word. Ask him to say the word several times while looking carefully at the card. Then ask him to find the nonillustrated card with the same word on it. When the child thinks he has learned the word, proceed to the next illustrated word card. After that has been studied, present the two test cards in random order. Teach a third word, followed by mixed practice with the previously taught words. Follow a similar procedure until all five words have been taught. Then shuffle the five nonillustrated cards and present each three times in random order, prompting if necessary. If the child is successful, retest about 30 minutes later. If possible, check retention 1, 3, and 7 days later; long-term memory is vital in the use of a whole-word approach.

It may be desirable to follow up by teaching a few words from the material being considered for instructional use, followed by reading the corresponding material. If the child objects to this material, it may be necessary to avoid using any book in the early stages of remedial instruction.

Some children are distracted by the use of pictures in learning to recognize words through a whole-word approach. If use of the preceding procedure suggests this, it may be well to repeat the lesson with different words and without the use of pictures.

2. Synthetic Phonic Method. The ability to synthesize or blend sounds into whole words is vital to this method. If the child shows some auditory-blending skill, it is safe to try synthetic phonics. Auditory blending may be checked with one of the available tests or informally by presenting five one-syllable words in the following manner: Tell the child that you are going to pronounce the parts of a word and that you want him to listen carefully so that he can tell what word you said. No visual stimuli are employed. Pronounce the sounds separately with about a half-second pause between each sound (e.g., /o/-/n/, /b/-/a/-/t/, distorting the consonants as little as possible. After each presentation, ask the child to tell what word he heard. A reasonable criterion for adequate performance is 80% correct, but any correct responses indicate that a method relying on blending is not impossible.

Teach or review the symbol–sound associations of four or five consonants and one short vowel (e.g., *m, c, t, s, d,* and *a*). Each symbol–sound association is presented singly as follows: Show the letter *m* (use lowercase letters). "This is *m* (use letter name) and the sound it makes is /m/, the sound that you hear at the beginning of *man* (slightly emphasize the /m/). Listen for the /m/ sound at the beginning of each of these words: *meat, my, milk.* Can you hear the /m/? Now give me some words that begin with /m/." Offer suggestions if necessary. Auditory discrimination (an important subskill in this method) may be informally checked by pronouncing sets of three words and having the child raise his hand when he hears a word that does not begin with the sound being taught. Proceed the same way with *c, d, t, s,* and *a*. Probably the child knows some consonant symbol–sound associations.

"Now I'm going to say a word, then its parts slowly, and the whole word again. Listen carefully. Mat; /m/-/a/-/t/; mat. This is how the word *mat* looks." Use separate large letter cards to form the word, first saying the whole word, then each sound as the letter is put in place, and finally the whole word again. Repeat the word, sound by sound, moving your finger under each letter in the word as the sound is pronounced. Hand the child the appropriate letters and say. "Put these together to make 'mat,'" Ask him to sound out the word as he does so. Help him, if necessary. Then show him how to change *mat* to *cat* and *sat*.

Write a sentence containing the words, such as "The cat sat on the mat," and have him read it, providing help as necessary.

Show him how to change the final elements to form new words: *mat* to *mad, sat* to *sad*. Then provide practice in using the symbol–sound associations to form the five words taught.

Present the five words in random order three times in a manner similar to that described for the whole-word method. If the child reads four of the words successfully, he is likely to succeed with a phonic program that employs a similar method.

With a child who is weak in auditory discrimination, blending ability, or learning symbol–sound associations, it is advisable to postpone phonic instruction. The number of associations presented in one session and the way in which the associations are taught are variables that can influence the success or failure of this method.

3. Linguistic Method. This technique of word recognition or analysis is especially useful with pupils who possess only rudimentary blending ability and are unable to cope with the synthetic phonic method described above. Used solely, however, it affords only a limited degree of independence in word analysis.

Present a well-known word like *man.* Then teach or review separately three consonant symbol–sound associations (e.g., *r, f, p*) that can be used in the initial position to form other common words. Demonstrate how initial consonants may be substituted to form or recognize new words. Provide practice in utilizing this technique, followed by mixed practice with the three words formed with the introduced consonants. Repeat the procedure for a different spelling pattern (e.g., *at* or *un*) and the same initial consonants. Learning and retention may be checked using the procedure described above for the whole-word method.

As with the other methods, teaching variations may be tried to determine their possible effect on learning. For example, instead of using a word like *man* as a starting point, a phonogram that is a commonly known word (e.g., *an*) may be employed, and the child taught to form new words by appending initial consonants. Most linguistic reading programs do not provide direct teaching of symbol–sound associations.

4. Visual–Motor Method. Choose about three words with which the child is unfamiliar (about 5 to 8 letters in length), such as *friend, airplane, pilot.* Present each word separately. Print the word clearly on a card. Say, "This word is 'friend.' Take a good look at it. What is the word? Now close your eyes. Can you see it with your eyes closed? Look again. What is the word?" Remove the word and ask the child to write it. Have him compare his word with the word on the card. If he is incorrect, repeat the above procedure, present the word, pronounce it, have him try to visualize it, and then write it again. Sometimes it is necessary to show the card several times before the child is able to write it. If he reproduces the word correctly, have him write it again, covering up his previous writing so as to be sure that he is recalling the word from memory rather than merely copying it. Check each time to see that it is done correctly. Teach the three words. After a period of time has elapsed, test the words. A more detailed description of this procedure appears on page 435.

5. Kinesthetic Method. The brief summary given below is based on the method fully described by Fernald (see p. 432). Only the initial stages used in teaching by kinesthetic procedure are presented here.

A short period of orientation is suggested. Tell the child that you are going to teach him to read by means of an entirely new method. Assure him as to its value by telling him that other people who have had difficulty with reading learned in this way. Describe the procedure to him. Ask him to suggest a word he would like to learn.

Write the word with a crayon on paper in large-size script (letters approximately 2 inches high). The child traces the word with his index finger (or index finger and thumb, if he wishes), saying the word as he traces it. He repeats this as many times as necessary in order to write the word without looking at the original one. When he seems to know the word, he writes it on another sheet of paper. In case of error, or if the child hesitates and seems unable to complete the word, he retraces the word as a whole. He is not permitted to erase in order to correct errors. If he has difficulty recalling the word, he should be encouraged to trace it over and over and then to write it without consulting the original writing. Teach five words, then test them in random order.

It is evident that any of these approaches may be used successfully as a starting point in learning to read. Before long, however, any procedure must be supplemented by others because successful readers must have a variety of techniques at their command. It is not necessary to try all five methods listed above. Most children can learn by at least one of the first four methods. Thus it is usually unnecessary to try Procedure 5. Nevertheless, in cases of severe disability where children cannot learn by a whole-word approach and cannot synthesize sounds as required in a phonic procedure, the kinesthetic method should be tried. Trial lessons may be used similarly at all levels and should be varied according to the particular case.

The principle of sample word-study lessons has been developed into a standardized technique by Mills (1956). Four methods are used: visual, phonic, kinesthetic, and combined. The examiner spends 15 minutes with each method, teaching 10 words. Mills's adaptation seems to us to be time-consuming and fatiguing for the child, but reading clinics and remedial teachers may find it a real addition to available diagnostic procedures.

The essence of the sample lesson is a situation in which the child's behavior as a learner can be carefully observed and evaluated. Qualitative observation and interpretation are more important than numerical scores or ratings. Such characteristics as interest, attentiveness, distractibility, perseverance, effort, reaction to success and failure, anxiety, discouragement, and efforts to evade the task are some characteristics that may be observed and judged. A standardized procedure and scoring may not draw one's attention away from these qualitative factors, but the temptation to rely on scores is strong. For these reasons it is preferable to use sample lessons in a flexible, unstandardized way.

8

Correlates of
Reading Disability, I:
Cognitive Factors

This chapter is the first of three that discuss the many factors related to reading disability. It starts with a discussion of the purpose of diagnosis, compares the concepts of correlation and causation, and contrasts single and plural views of causation. The fourth section summarizes efforts to identify subtypes of reading disability. The next two sections discuss models of reading disability and some of the problems with reading-disability research. The seventh section deals with the relationship of intelligence to reading disability and the eighth treats language abilities. The final section takes up specific areas of cognition, such as perception, attention, memory, and cognitive style.

I. DIAGNOSIS

The purpose of a reading diagnosis is to determine how best to assist the child to improve his reading ability. Making such a determination requires a person who knows what relevant information to obtain; how that information can be obtained most reliably, validly, and efficaciously; and how to interpret the data intelligently. The first phase of a diagnosis involves determining the student's reading status, skills, strategies, and needs. Procedures for doing so were described in Chapter 7. Sometimes the diagnosis need go no further because such information is sufficient for planning and conducting a successful remedial program. In other cases, it may be important to consider variables that may be interfering with the child's progress in reading. This does not mean that the original or basic cause of the reading disability must be determined. It is not always possible to make this determination; even if it were, there are certain variables about which little can be done.

The hope for years has been to determine the cause(s) of reading disability. Efforts have been based on the belief that knowledge of the cause will dictate the treatment; they have primarily followed a medical model of diagnosis. But, at present, opinions about causation remain largely in the realm of unproven hypotheses, and thus differential diagnosis is very unreliable. Therefore, reading specialists and teachers would be well advised to employ the following sequence in making a diagnosis: (1) Determine the individual's general level of reading achievement and compare it with the child's potential; if a reading problem exists, (2) determine the learner's specific reading strengths and weaknesses; (3) determine which factors, if any, are probably hampering the child's ability to learn at this time; (4) remove or lessen those factors that can be controlled or corrected, either before or during remedial treatment; (5) select the most efficient and effective way to teach the needed skills and strategies; (6) teach the needed skills and strategies until they are mastered, making certain that the child applies them; and (7) refer to an appropriate clinic or agency any pupil who does not respond to treatment after a reasonable period of time. Time spent on attempting to determine causation can often be more profitably spent helping students overcome their present problems. "The focus of diagnostic teaching is not on causation but on the here and now of what the child can and cannot do, what skills he has and what skills he needs, and on matching this information with appropriate opportunities for learning" (A. J. Harris 1977a).

II. CORRELATION AND CAUSATION

Over the years a large number of traits have been found to be significantly correlated with reading disability. Reading-disabled pupils have shown weaker performance than good readers on a large number of tasks. Cognitive, neurological, physical, physiological, educational, socioeconomic, and psychological–emotional factors have been implicated. But no one syndrome of reading disability has been found.

No disabled reader has all, or even most, of the characteristics shown to be related to reading disability, and normally developing readers often display many of the same traits. Nor do most disabled readers have any one characteristic in common aside from the disability.

This situation may exist for a number of reasons. There is the strong probability that reading disability is not a homogeneous entity; rather, it is composed of a number of subgroups each with differing characteristics. Also, many studies have investigated average differences between good and poor readers. When such differences are found, it does not necessarily indicate that the trait is the cause of the differences in reading ability. On the other hand, a trait may have been quite prominently present in a few children, but not in enough of them to have any impact on the mean score of the group.

Differences between good and poor readers may be (1) a symptom of the actual underlying component (e.g., poor eye movements usually do not cause reading disability, but do reflect underlying cognitive processes); (2) caused by the reading problem, rather than causing it; (3) indicative that the reading problem and the other deficits cyclically reinforce one another (e.g., poor vocabulary knowledge may be contributing to the reading problem; but, in turn, poor reading ability cuts off the child from opportunities to increase his vocabulary) (Kleiman 1982).

Many of the factors associated with reading disability have been identified from correlational data. However, correlation—the fact that two or more measurable characteristics tend to be found together—does not prove causation. Correlations simply indicate relationships between variables; the higher the correlation, the stronger the implied relationship. Although a cause–effect relationship may exist, causation cannot be inferred directly from a correlation coefficient; much more direct evidence needs to be established.

Even when there is a strong presumption of a cause–effect relationship, one cannot be sure which is the cause and which the effect. Furthermore, the correlation may be the result of another factor or factors. To illustrate these points, consider the following: In a broad age range of children there is very likely to be a high correlation between height and reading achievement, with shorter children tending to be less capable readers than taller children. But height does not cause reading ability, or vice versa. The correlation between height and reading achievement reflects the fact that taller children tend to be older than shorter children; as such, they have not only had more opportunity to improve their reading ability but also have attained greater cognitive and linguistic maturity. For these reasons we use the term "correlate" rather than "cause" when discussing factors associated with reading disability.

Another issue that complicates determining causation is the possible influence of *compensation*: the probability that strength in one trait related to reading ability can make up for a weakness in another relevant trait. It is also possible that a combination of weak abilities may have a combined causal effect that no one of the weaknesses could produce by itself.

Thus we are often faced with the situation of having a child who displays several characteristics that have been shown to be related to reading disability, but we cannot be certain that any of them caused, or are even contributing to, the child's reading problems. Yet there are logical and theoretical reasons to suspect that certain factors *might* be contributors. This apparent dilemma is not as hopeless as it might seem. The reading ability of many pupils who are disabled in reading often can be improved through direct instruction. When remedial efforts are successful, there is little need to determine what originally caused the problem. Also, there are some variables over which we have little or no control. In other instances, knowing the cause would be of little use because, as yet, that information does not tell us how best to instruct the pupil.

Something can be done about certain factors (e.g., visual problems, dietary deficiencies) that inhibit a child's progress in learning to read. If a condition cannot be corrected, it possibly can be circumvented. Even if immediate use cannot be made of the information, reading teachers should be aware of the factors that *may* contribute to some reading problems, if for no other reason than to understand the theoretical bases for particular remedial procedures and to appreciate the efforts being made toward differential diagnosis.

III. VIEWS OF CAUSATION

Single-Factor Theories

The earliest literature on reading disability (Morgan 1896; Hinshelwood 1900, 1917) indicated that the cause of *congenital word blindness* was a deficiency in the local area of the brain where visual images are stored. Since that time, various writers have suggested that all or most cases of reading disability are attributable to a single cause. Most of these single-factor theories seem to refer to the seriously disabled reader and imply a cognitive or neurological basis for the reading disability. Thus we have theories involving deficits, deficiencies, or dysfunctions in perceptual, visual–motor, linguistic, and psycholinguistic functioning, as well as in auditory–visual integration, memory and attention. Similarly, there are theories that implicate hemispheric rivalry, incomplete hemispheric lateralization, the presence of a function in a hemisphere not best suited to subserve that function, or a problem in the coordination between, or the exchange of information between, the two hemispheres of the brain. Other theories involve frank or implied brain damage, vestibular disorders, or a lack of neurological organization. A few theories are related to neurological hypotheses, for example, the chemical imbalance hypothesis of Smith and Carrigan (1959). And rather than implying damage or dysfunction, the maturational-lag theories of Bender (1957, 1975) and Satz and his associates (1978) suggest a specialized slowness in certain aspects of neurological development. In these theories, factors such as poorly established hemispheric dominance and reading disability are thought to be the result of the developmental lag. A somewhat similar developmental view holds that the main cause of school failure is general immaturity (Ames 1968, 1983).

Still others argue that reading or learning disability is caused, directly or indirectly, by one or more physical or physiological factors, such as visual or auditory sensory defects, glandular disturbances, or dietary deficiencies or inclusions (that which is included or not found in what children eat or drink).

Few specific theories involving educational, socioeconomic, and emotional problems have been offered. Rather, the theories in these areas have been rather diffuse, citing such general variables as inadequate or inappropriate teaching, poverty, and emotional blocks to learning.

To us, it seems probable that each of the single-cause advocates has emphasized one part of what is really a very complex situation.

Multiple-Causation Theories

For many years, the majority of educators and psychologists have favored the view that there are many possible causes of reading disability. As Monroe (1932, p. 80) stated over 50 years ago, "In considering the causes for a child's failure to read, we must inquire into a number of possible impeding factors, both in his constitutional organization and in his environment."

Studies of disabled readers have revealed a variety of possible causal or contributing factors. One of the most intensive studies of causal or contributing factors in reading disability to date is H. M. Robinson's study (1946) of 30 cases of severe reading disability. A social case history was taken by a trained social worker, and the child was examined by a psychologist, a psychiatrist, a pediatrician, a neurologist, an ophthalmologist, an otolaryngologist, a speech pathologist, and an endocrinologist. After the examinations had been completed, a case conference was held on each child, at which the specialists came to a group decision concerning which factors were probably causal and which were merely concomitants of the reading problem. Treatment was supervised in 22 of these cases. After the results of treatment were known, another conference was held at which the conclusions previously reached about causation were reviewed and sometimes changed. A summary of causal factors was then made, based on both diagnosis and remediation. The number of probable causal factors ranged from one to four. The most frequent were social problems and visual difficulties, followed by emotional maladjustment, neurological difficulties, speech or discrimination difficulties, school methods, auditory difficulties, endocrine disturbances, and general physical difficulty. Each handicap was present more often than it was judged to have causal significance, and each handicap was considered by the specialists to be a possible cause before remediation in more cases than it was judged to be a probable cause after remedial treatment.

A study of 34 very poor readers in Swedish first grades led Malmquist (1958) to write:

> On the basis of our results, it appears reasonable to draw the important conclusion that to attempt to find a single factor which will entirely explain the occurrence of reading errors is, in the great majority of cases, a vain endeavor. Most frequently there appear to be several factors in constellation which are related to reading failure. Many of these factors seem to be closely interrelated. There appears to be an interplay between the child's general physical, intellectual, emotional and social development, and the development of his reading ability. (1958, p. 390)

The factors that seemed most significant to Malmquist were intelligence; ability to concentrate, persistence, self-confidence, and emotional stability; spelling ability; visual perception; social status and educational level of the parents; and the teaching experience of the child's teacher.

The multiple-causation point of view contends that there is more than one cause of reading disability. As such, it is closely related to the belief that there are probably a number of types of reading disability.

IV. SUBTYPES OF READING DISABILITY[1]

Two main approaches have been used in attempts to identify subtypes of reading disability. Representative studies of each type are summarized below.

Clinical–Inferential Classification[2]

When this general procedure is used, the classification may be based on presumed causation (often based on the belief that the cause of the reading disability is an intrinsic constitutional deficit), on different performance patterns on various neuropsychological measures (nonreading variables), or on reading achievement variables. Diagnosis is often by exclusion. The subtypes were derived from visual inspection of complex, multidimensional data.

Ingram and Reid (1956) studied reading-disabled children who had differences of 20 or more points between their Verbal and Performance IQs. Those with higher Verbal IQs more often showed visuospatial reading and spelling errors; this subtype was labeled *visuospatial dyslexia. Audiophonic dyslexics* had higher Performance IQs and tended to have difficulty with auditory discrimination, blending, and letter–sound associations. Based on his study of speech-retarded children, Ingram (1969) concluded that the more severe the reading disability, the more likely the occurrence of both visuospatial and audiophonic symptoms in the same child. A mixed category was added later (Ingram, Mason, & Blackburn 1970).

Rabinovitch (1968) proposed a three-group classification that attempted to distinguish neurological dysfunctioning from brain damage. The *primary reading retardation* group had basic neurological disturbances without evidence of definite brain damage. This subtype is similar to *developmental dyslexia* as defined by Critchley (1970). *Secondary reading retardation* included cases whose reading problems were not caused primarily by nervous system disorders but were the result of such varied nonneurological factors as impaired vision, emotional maladjustment, and environmental deprivation. Rabinovitch (1962), however, admitted that it was often difficult to find a pure case of either type; thus, in effect, his classification also included a "mixed" category. His third subtype was *brain damage with reading retardation.*

A viewpoint similar to that of Rabinovitch was expressed by Matějcěk (1977). He distinguished between severe disabilities whose cause was constitutional in nature and mild disabilities that had variable causation influenced by teaching methods, educational pressures, and aggravating factors such as sociocultural problems, poor motivation, or poor health.

---

[1] Studies in which the samples were identified as reading disabled, learning disabled in reading, and dyslexic are used in this discussion. We feel justified in including the latter two designations because most children classified as learning disabled have a reading disability, and dyslexics could not be differentiated from disabled readers on a number of variables (Taylor, Satz, & Friel 1979–1980). In most cases, we have used the term employed by the researcher–author.

[2] This classification was suggested by Satz and Morris (1981). Other reviews of the literature regarding subtypes of reading disability may be found in Doehring *et al.* (1981); Malatesha and Dougan (1982); Rosenthal, Boder, and Callaway (1982); A. J. Harris (1982); and Lyon (1983).

Bannatyne (1971) differed from Rabinovitch in not attempting to distinguish neurological dysfunction from brain damage and in his inclusion of an inherited cause. He listed four main categories of dyslexia: (1) *primary emotional communicative* (e.g., parental rejection or neglect); (2) *minimal neurological dysfunction*, involving a disorder in one or more of visual–spatial, auditory, integrative, conceptual, or tactual and kinesthetic functioning; (3) *social, cultural or educational deprivation*; and (4) *genetic dyslexia*, which is characterized by a strong tendency to run in families.

Kinsbourne and Warrington (1963, 1966), like Ingram, identified two subgroups of disabled readers who had large differences between their Verbal and Performance IQs. The *language-retarded* group were characterized by a late onset of language, significantly lower Verbal than Performance IQs, phonetically inappropriate spelling errors, and adequate performance on math and finger localization tests.[3] The *Gerstman syndrome* group had lower Performance IQs than Verbal IQs, directional confusion, and poor performance in writing and on arithmetic and finger localization tests. These researchers concluded that a cerebral deficit may delay the acquisition of reading and writing in different ways.

Denckla (1972) attempted to classify 190 disabled readers through an "extended neurological examination." Only 30% fitted clearly into one of three categories: (1) those with *specific language disabilities* without perceptual deficits but with "poor visuomotor and audiovisual circuits" (15%); (2) *dyscontrol syndrome*, characterized as impulsive, "sweet, silly, and sloppy" (10%); and (3) *specific visuospatial difficulties* similar to the Gerstmann syndrome, with left–right confusion, poor finger localization, low Performance IQ, more difficulty with arithmetic and writing than with reading and oral spelling, and emotional problems (5%).

Mattis, French, and Rapin (1975) utilized a control group of brain-injured children who could read normally in order to eliminate psychological deficits that do not interfere with learning to read. They reported that most of their dyslexic children fell into three groups: (1) *language disorder*, involving difficulty in naming, along with poor auding, poor imitation, or poor speech-sound discrimination (28%); (2) *articulatory and graphomotor*, with poor sound blending and incoordinated writing, but normal auding (48%); and (3) a small *visuospatial* group with low Performance IQ and difficulty in visual perception and memory (14%). Mattis (1978) reported a cross-validation study that verified the three groups and added a fourth. In this sample of 165 dyslexic children, mainly from disadvantaged minority backgrounds, he found the following proportions: language-disorder syndrome, 63%; articulatory and graphomotor syndrome, 10%; visuoperceptual disorder, 5%; combination of two syndromes, 9%; and a sequencing disorder, with poor auditory memory span and difficulty with the concepts of before–behind and left–right, 10%.

Boder (1973) used patterns of performance on a graded word-recognition test and written spelling of words that were and were not in the children's sight

[3] See page 271 for a description of finger localization tests.

vocabularies to classify 107 children with developmental dyslexia. She was able to place 100 of them into one of three subtypes. Children in the *dysphonetic* group (*N* = 67) had some sight vocabulary but lacked word-analysis skills and were unable to make symbol–sound associations and blend phonemes into words. Those in the *diseidetic* group (*N* = 10) were deficient in the ability to perceive words as wholes or visual gestalts and tended to employ a phonic-analysis approach to word recognition. The most severe cases were those who were both dysphonetic and diseidetic (*N* = 23). Her research led to the development of *The Boder Test of Reading-Spelling Patterns* (Boder & Jarrico 1982).

Myklebust (1978) hypothesized five subtypes: (1) *inner-language dyslexia* in which deficits in both auditory and visual verbal processing prevent children from understanding written language, even though they can recognize and pronounce printed words (a severe form of *word calling*); (2) *auditory dyslexia,* which involves the inability to "symbolize auditory information" and relate phonemes to graphemes; (3) *visual dyslexia (visual–verbal agnosia)* in which the child cannot attain symbolic meaning from print because of visual perceptual deficits; (4) *intermodal dyslexia,* which is the inability to integrate visual and auditory information; and (5) a neurological deficit in storage and retrieval (a memory deficit).

Pirozzolo (1979) and his associates (Pirozzolo, Dunn, & Zetusky 1983) identified two subtypes, the first being by far the more prevalent. *Auditory–linguistic dyslexics* have language disorders such as impaired expressive language, lower Verbal IQs than Performance IQs, agrammatism, anomia, and faulty grapheme to phoneme matching. *Verbal–spatial dyslexics* are weak in visual perceptual, spatial, and occulomotor skills as indicated by their directional disorientation, spatial dysgraphia, dyscalculia, and finger agnosia. Pirozzolo attributed the difficulty of auditory–linguistic dyslexics on tasks requiring rapid, complex linguistic processing to the late maturation of the nerve-fiber pathways involved in these left hemispheric functions. He further hypothesized that visual–spatial dyslexics were impaired on tasks requiring visual discrimination, analysis, and memory because of late maturation of the fiber pathways in the brain's visual association areas, and possibly the corpus callosum.

Pennington and Smith (1983) reported that, in a study primarily concerned with the genetic basis of reading and other language disorders, 91% of the 125 disabled readers fell into one of four subtypes: (1) a deficit only in reading (41%); (2) spatial–reasoning deficit (23%); (3) coding–speed deficit (18%); and (4) deficits in all three factors—a mixed category (9%).

Other researchers have also attributed the causes of different subtypes of reading disability to brain or neural dysfunctions. For example, Smith and Carrigan (1959) attempted to explain different types of reading disability—the context reader, the word caller, and so on—in terms of an imbalance between two chemicals that influence the transmission of nerve impulses in the brain; the symptoms would vary according to patterns of excess and deficiency in the chemicals. And Rosenthal, Boder, and Callaway (1982) claimed that their *language-symbolic dyslexia* has its origins in the left hemisphere, and their *spatial–gestalt* subtype had a dysfunction in the right hemisphere.[4] Indeed, Gaddes (1980, p. 242) stated: "The reading circuits in the brain are extremely complex, including specific centers usually in the left hemispheric cortex, with thalamic connections to other subcortical areas. There are most likely as many types of dyslexia as there are loci of cerebral lesions in this circuit and its contiguous brain tissue."

Based on observed differences in the strategies used by children with reading-comprehension problems, Maria and MacGinitie (1982) suggested that poor comprehenders could be categorized into three subgroups: (1) those who interpret each sentence separately and who seem unaware of the contradictions that arise when they do not maintain a common schema for what they are reading: (2) those using a *fixed-hypothesis strategy*, who form an interpretation of one or more of the first sentences in the text and try to interpret the remainder of the text to conform with their original hypothesis; and (3) poor comprehenders who employ a *nonaccommodating strategy* and overrely on prior knowledge. They use a few words in the text to call up related background knowledge but are little influenced by the information in the text.

Statistical Classification

In contrast to the clinical–inferential approaches, statistical classification approaches use cluster analysis and factor-analytic techniques to identify subtypes of reading disability. Cluster analysis is a procedure that groups subjects into clusters based on each individual's pattern of performance on the tests used. The Q technique is a kind of inverted factor analysis that analyzes correlations between individuals to classify them into groups with similar characteristics. Achievement and/or neuropsychological variables are used to make the classifications.

Among the limitations of some studies using statistical classification are the use of narrow and sometimes questionable measures of reading ability and the apparently subjective manner in which clustered strengths and weaknesses are interpreted (Satz & Morris 1981). The results of any statistical classification are highly influenced by the number of tests employed and the demands they really place on the testee (not necessarily the ones they assumedly require). Therefore, in reading the literature in this area, careful attention should be paid to how reading is defined and the tasks required by both the reading and the neuropsychological tests.

A statistical and case-study analysis of severely reading-disabled boys aged 10 to 14 by Doehring (1968) revealed three possible subtypes: language, perceptual, and mixed (having both linguistic and perceptual deficits). Two later studies (Doehring & Hoshko 1977; Doehring, Hoshko, & Bryans 1979), which used the Q technique, identified three groups: (1) a *language deficit* type who performed poorly on the syllable and word reading tasks but had normal scores on all visual matching and most auditory–visual matching tests; (2) a *phonological deficit* type marked by low auditory–visual matching; and (3) an *intersen-*

---

[4] Hemispheric specialization and its relationship to reading disability is considered on pages 277–290.

sory-integration deficit type who were almost normal in auditory–visual matching of letters but not of syllables and words.

More recently, Doehring *et al.* (1981), who stressed the interaction of reading, language, and neurological deficits, were able to classify 82% of 88 disabled
readers into one of three subtypes. The *oral reading disability* cases tended to
perform much more poorly on the oral reading of letters, syllables, and words
than on "silent reading" tasks (visual and auditory–visual matching of letters,
syllables, and words). Children in the *associational reading disability* group
tended to perform very poorly on all auditory–visual matching and oral reading
tasks. Those with a *sequencing reading disability* tended to be very weak on all
tasks using syllables and words, but not when single letters were used. It should
be noted, however, that from 30% to 60% of the subjects scored within the normal
range on the oral reading tasks and that the three subtypes were not distinct,
since a number of the classified subjects exhibited some of the same characteristics displayed by those in another subtype.

Using the Q technique, Petrauskas and Rourke (1979) were able to place
about 50% of their disabled readers aged 8 to 10 into one of three subgroups.
Those with a *language disorder* ($N = 40$) were mainly characterized by impaired
verbal fluency and sentence memory. The *impaired verbal coding* group ($N =
13$) was mildly or moderately impaired in finger localization, verbal fluency,
sentence memory, and visual–spatial (sequencing) memory, and moderately to
severely impaired in concept formation. The third subtype ($N = 26$, 92% males)
showed moderate to severe impairment in sentence memory, finger localization,
and visual–spatial memory. Three similar, but not as discrete, subtypes were
also identified in a multivariate analysis study by Fisk and Rourke (1979) with
children aged 9–14.

Two factor analytic studies by Hicks and Spurgeon (1982) revealed two
subtypes of dyslexia: one with deficits in auditory processing marked by bizarre
spelling, poor sound blending, and poor auditory discrimination; and the other
with verbal problems characterized by poor visual memory, phonic errors, left–
right confusion, and sequencing and vocabulary weaknesses.

Satz and Morris (1981) first used a cluster analysis of the achievement patterns in reading, spelling, and arithmetic (as measured by the WRAT) to classify
236 fifth-grade boys into subgroups. The data from the 89 boys in the two lowest
groups were then subjected to cluster-analytic techniques based on their scores
on four neuropsychological tests. Five subtypes ($N = 86$) emerged: (1) an *unexpected learning disability* type ($N = 12$) who did not show any neuropsychological deficits; (2) a *global language impairment* type ($N = 27$) who scored
very low on both language measures but in the average range on nonlanguage
perceptual tests; (3) a *specific language (naming)* type ($N = 14$) who were impaired on only the verbal fluency test; (4) a *visual–perceptual–motor impaired*
type ($N = 23$) whose performance was deficient on the perceptual, but not the
language, tests; and (5) a *mixed* type ($N = 10$) who performed poorly on all four
tests but who probably should not be classified as reading or learning disabled
because they all scored poorly on the IQ test.

Taylor, Fletcher, and Satz (1982) believed that it would be more fruitful to attempt to relate cognitive deficits to groups of children who were disabled in different areas of reading ability. From a group of 45 disabled readers who had been given a battery of reading and neuropsychological tests, they were able to classify 18 (40%) into one of three subtypes. However, data on only eight cases were reported. The three cases with a *deficit in word recognition* had fairly intact language skills but were deficient on some visually related tasks (although there was variability among the kinds of deficits displayed). These cases were similar to Boder's dyseidetic and Mattis *et al.*'s visual–perceptual disorder subtypes. Relatively few neuropsychological impairments marked the two cases with *reading-comprehension problems*. The only defect they had in common was their inability to retrieve words from a memorized list. The three disabled readers with *word-attack deficits* were characterized by selective difficulty in lower-order language skills such as naming and phonemic analysis. This group was like Boder's dysphonetic and Myklebust's auditory dyslexic subtypes. As with the other studies, the three subtypes were not distinct groups; the disabled readers in one group evidenced some of the neuropsychological deficits displayed by children in another classification.

Lyon (1983), who also used cluster analyses, reported two studies, which revealed six subgroups. One group had minimal sight vocabularies and deficient decoding skills and were deficient in receptive-language comprehension, sound blending, visual–motor integration, visual–spatial skills, and auditory and visual memory. A second group had deficits in receptive-language comprehension, auditory memory, and visual–motor integration. A third group had problems in receptive-language comprehension and sound blending. The fourth subtype was impaired in visual perception, but without language deficits. A fifth subtype had global language problems, and the sixth group was comprised of poor readers who had normal neuropsychological profiles (unexpected learning disability). Lyon also reported a pilot study that indicated differentiated effects, in the expected manner, of a 26-week synthetic phonics remedial program.

Other Evidence of Subtypes

Possible anatomical evidence of reading-disability subtypes was obtained by Hier *et al.* (1978), who analyzed the computerized brain tomograms of 24 developmental dyslexics. Eight subjects exhibited normal hemispheric asymmetry (a wider left than right parieto-occipital region). Ten displayed a reversed pattern, and there was no difference between the left and right hemispheric areas in 6 cases.

There also is some electrophysiological evidence. Fried *et al.* (1981) used event-related potentials (ERPs) to study word and musical-chord processing in the right and left hemispheres. They concluded that dysphonetic subjects (those with auditory–verbal deficits) had failed to develop normal left-hemisphere specialization for processing auditory–linguistic material.

Summary

Despite its promise, the subtyping research reported to date has had significant limitations (Satz & Morris 1981; Taylor, Fletcher, & Satz 1982). The subtypes are not homogeneous; cases within a subtype do not manifest exactly the same profiles; and there is overlap among subgroups. Furthermore, some good readers display some of the same deficits as disabled readers. More important, reading is often defined by tests that measure only basic skills.

A number of investigators, using a variety of selection criteria, tests, and approaches to data analysis, have reported the existence of from two to six subgroups, with three being by far the most frequent.

A. J. Harris (1982, p. 459) reviewed the research on subtypes and concluded:

> . . . the recent studies demonstrate that there are at least three subtypes or syndromes within the disabled reader populations that have been used. The first and most common shows a general deficiency in language skills (coupled with normal visual and visual-motor skills) and a lower Verbal IQ than Performance IQ. The language deficit is shown in poor listening comprehension, limited vocabulary, difficulty in verbal expression, limited grasp of sentence structure, poor auditory discrimination and memory, and poor blending ability.
>
> A second pattern involves difficulty with visual perception and visual-motor tasks, coupled with relatively normal language abilities and a Verbal IQ higher than Performance IQ. Benton (1978) has described this group as follows: "Reversal errors, the cardinal feature of a visuo-spatial type of disability, have been found to be associated with right-left confusion in body schema performances, with left-handedness and mixed laterality, with a more generalized learning disabiity extending beyond reading, and with signs of neurological abnormality."
>
> A third pattern is what Satz and Morris (1981) called an "unexpected" subtype whose cognitive abilities fail to show any significant deficits that could account for the reading failure. It may be that this group has predominantly environmental problems. The size of this group probably varies greatly according to the economic, cultural, and linguistic conditions of the family and neighborhood, and it may include as high as 70% of some disabled reader populations (Denckla 1972).
>
> A fourth type found in some but not all of the recent studies involves normal verbal comprehension and vocabulary but a deficiency in verbal fluency. These children are slow in naming tasks and have marked difficulty in segmenting spoken words and blending phonemes into words.
>
> There are a number of less frequent findings that may indicate the reality of small but nevertheless significant subgroups. One of these is the group with difficulty in finger localization. Another such group has difficulty in identifying tactile patterns. Levinson's insistence on the importance of cerebellar and vestibular difficulties may apply to a subgroup.
>
> The question of a genetic type of reading disability has not been resolved. Unquestionably there are some families with several disabled readers,

but the degree to which this is inherited or learned within the home environment is still uncertain.

It may be that each case of reading disability involves a unique constellation of handicapping conditions—constitutional, environmental, and motivational—and that the search for a relatively small number of subtypes into which they can be pigeon-holed is futile.

One of the main reasons why we have been unable to find a satisfactory explanation for reading disabilities may be the extremely complex interactive nature of cognition, language, and reading, each of which in itself is a complex process. It may well be that we will have to await a more complete understanding of each area before we can understand how deficits in any of them can interact to cause reading disabilities of various subtypes (Doehring, Backman, & Waters 1983).

V. MODELS OF READING DISABILITY

The plan of a research study depends on the researcher's notions or expectations concerning the nature of reading disability and its causation. Wiener and Cromer (1967) described several kinds of relationships, starting with a single cause—single effect and increasing to multiple causes—multiple effects. They also postulated the existence of four different types of causal relationships, each having a different kind of etiology and remediation: (1) *defect* attributable to some malfunction (e.g., sensory–physiological factors) that prevents the learner from benefiting from his experience; (2) *deficiency* attributable to the absence or low level of some function; (3) *disruption*, which suggests that something (e.g., anxiety) is interfering with reading; and (4) *difference*, in which there are mismatches between the learner's characteristics and the expectations of the environment.

Guthrie (1973) pointed out that the degree of integration or interrelatedness among relevant abilities may be significant. He described two kinds of relationships: an assembly model, which assumes that the skills involved in reading are independent and can be isolated both in diagnosis and in remedial teaching; and a systems model, in which reading is viewed as involving interdependent components so that one or two severely deficient abilities could prevent the development of other needed abilities. Guthrie presented results that suggested that the systems model applied to normal readers, for whom a variety of reading tests were substantially intercorrelated, but that the assembly model fitted disabled readers better, since they showed low intercorrelations.

Vernon (1977) argued that reading disability can result from a variety of pyschological dysfunctions that can induce breakdown at critical points in learning to read. She described four main types: (1) in the initial phases of letter and word perception, deficiencies in the capacity to analyze complex, sequential visual and/or auditory–linguistic structures; (2) deficiencies in the linking of visual with auditory–linguistic symbols; (3) inability to establish regularities in variable grapheme–phoneme correspondences, which may involve what Mattingly (1972) has called a lack of linguistic awareness; and (4) inability to group recognized words into meaningful phrases.

Valtin (1980) described five different assessment approaches (which could serve as models of reading disability) and their limitations:

1. In the *etiological approach*, attempts are made to identify the physical, environmental, or educational factors that may impede reading progress.
2. The *cognitive approach* attempts to isolate various types of reading problems by determining cognitive deficits. In this *functional model* of reading disability, the causes are primarily attributed to the child's lack of capabilities, not to the instructional process.
3. The *symptoms approach* attempts to analyze errors that may provide hints regarding the specific difficulty in the reading process.
4. The *process-oriented approach* attempts to identify the partial processes of reading in which the reading disabled are deficient.
5. The *task-analysis,* or *subskills, approach* suggests that one source of reading disability is a lack of integration and interfacilitation among reading subskills (e.g., see Guthrie (1973) above).

Doehring, Backman, and Waters (1983) listed three types of models: (1) a direct, simple cause–effect model; (2) an intermediate, three-stage cause–effect model in which a specific brain deficit results in the deficient development of a nonreading ability that is essential to reading, and in turn, this specific nonreading deficit prevents normal reading acquisition; and (3) models suggesting that reading disability is not a unitary disorder.

Kinsbourne (1983) described a number of models of learning disability that are also applicable to reading disability. Kleiman (1982) summarized, and discussed the limitations of, various reading-disability models.

VI. SOME PROBLEMS WITH RESEARCH ON READING AND LEARNING DISABILITIES

Although hundreds of studies comparing reading- or learning-disabled students with those who are making normal progress in reading have been reported, most have been flawed (Doehring 1978, Valtin 1978–1979, Kleiman 1982). A major problem has been with the selection of the disabled sample, which can vary in number and characteristics depending on the selection criteria. As Valtin (1980) pointed out, observed differences between good and poor readers can be artifacts of research methodology. If truly representative samples of good and poor readers are drawn, the groups will differ in variables such as IQ and SES. Consequently, they also will differ on factors that are correlated with these variables (e.g., memory, language abilities, prior knowledge). Therefore poor readers will show a number of cognitive deficits. But if only cases in which reading ability is not commensurate with potential are included in the study, the deficits will vary depending on whether a Verbal IQ (VIQ), Performance IQ (PIQ), or Full

Scale (FS) is used. Whereas both the average VIQs and PIQs of good readers approximate 110, the majority of disabled readers show a significantly higher PIQ (about 105) than VIQ (about 95). Therefore, if good and poor readers are matched on PIQ, poor readers will have lower VIQs and FS scores and will show deficits in factors related to verbal ability, especially language. If VIQ is used, these differences tend to disappear. If FS is used, poor readers will show better results in visual tasks. Group selection also may be influenced by the reading test employed (Silberberg & Silberberg 1977).

A second problem is the representativeness of the groups. Normally developing readers in many studies have average IQs of about 115, while disabled readers tend to have average IQs of 10 to 20 points lower. In order to match good and poor readers on intelligence, one has to choose from the higher end of the disabled readers' IQ distribution and the lower end of the good readers' distribution; thus neither sample is truly representative of the population from which they were selected.

The selection of control groups is also important. Usually the control group is similar in age and IQ (and sometimes SES and gender) and much better in reading than the disabled group. Guthrie (1973) pointed out some advantages of using two comparison groups: a group of similar age but much better in reading ability than the disabled group; and a younger group with reading achievement equal to that of the disabled group. Mattis, French, and Rapin (1975) used three groups: disabled readers with brain damage, disabled readers without brain damage, and good readers with brain damage. The latter group served to eliminate from consideration deficient abilities that do not prevent brain-damaged children from learning to read.

Another problem is the washing-out effect. When two or more subgroups exist within the reading-disabled sample, the high scores of one subgroup on a particular skill or attribute may offset the low scores of another subgroup.

It is commonly accepted that there is an interaction between constitutional and environmental variables. So there is no way of completely ruling out the possible effects of past differences in experience on the characteristics displayed by the subjects in a study (Doehring, Backman, & Waters 1983).

VII. INTELLIGENCE AND READING

Intelligence has been defined as "the aggregate or global capacity of the individual to act purposefully, to think rationally and to deal effectively with his environment" (Wechsler 1944). Most intelligence tests include several different subtests (e.g. verbal, numerical, and spatial materials) requiring different kinds of responses. By including a variety of tasks, the possibility of the result being strongly influenced by a special talent or deficit is minimized. Factor-analysis studies have shown that a common factor underlies all kinds of intelligent performances, and this is usually labeled g; there are also several broad areas of somewhat special abilities and numerous highly specialized abilities that in some cases have only low correlations with g. Most psychologists believe that the intellectual functioning of an individual involves the intimate interplay between an inborn potential for development, which varies from one person to another, with environmental conditions that strongly influence the degree to which this potential is realized.

Individually administered intelligence tests are generally considered more valid than group tests, partly because the examiner is better able to motivate the child or to note behavior that casts doubt on the validity of the results, and partly because such tests are less dependent on scholastic skills than most group tests are. The most widely used individual intelligence tests for children are the *Revised Stanford–Binet Intelligence Scale* and the *Wechsler Intelligence Scale for Children* (WISC-R). The latter allows scoring for three IQs, Verbal, Performance, and Full Scale, and also permits analysis of patterns of high or low scores on specific subtests. Despite the popularity of the WISC, some psychologists insist that the *Stanford–Binet* is superior in coverage of abilities relevant to learning to read. The *Wechsler Preschool and Primary Scale of Intelligence* (WPPSI) is similar to the WISC but is for ages 4 through 6. *The Wechsler Adult Intelligence Scale* (WAIS) is a similarly organized test for older adolescents and adults.

Most intelligence tests can be scored both for mental age (MA) and intelligence quotient (IQ). Mental age is a measure of the level of mental maturity reached at the time of measurement. A bright child, an average child, and a dull child could all have the same mental age of 9 years, but the bright child would reach it in less than 9 years, the average child would take 9 years, and the dull child would take more than 9 years. The IQ therefore shows the average rate of mental development, or brightness. The mental age is the better measure for indicating present expectancy and short-term prediction; the IQ is the better measure for prediction over a period of years.

The *Stanford–Binet* and *Wechsler* tests require trained examiners and are relatively time-consuming. In the search for brief individual tests that can be administered by teachers without special training, the *Slosson Intelligence Test* seems to have greater validity than the *Peabody Picture Vocabulary Test* or the *Quick Test* (Jerrolds, Callaway, & Gwaltney 1971; Buros 1972, vol. I, pp. 764–767). The *Slosson* is based largely on items from the *Stanford–Binet*. One report found the PPVT and SIT to correlate equally well with WISC for children with reading disabilities (Pikulski 1973). Gensemer, Walker, and Cadman (1976) found that the *Peabody* IQs of learning-disabled children tended to be 5 to 10 points higher than their WISC IQs.

Group intelligence tests for the primary grades usually present questions in pictorial form and so are not influenced directly by reading ability. Such tests have substantial but not high correlations with reading in the primary grades. From the fourth grade up, most group mental-ability tests present their questions in printed form that must be read and understood before they can be answered. One study found that children in the intermediate grades with reading-grade scores below 4.0 were handicapped an average of 10 IQ points on a typical group mental-ability test (Neville 1965). Such tests are therefore of little value in differentiating between low reading ability and low mental ability. Below the age of 10, group verbal tests have less stability of IQ scores than the *Stanford–Binet*, and nonverbal group test IQs are less stable than group verbal IQs (Hopkins & Bracht 1975). Group tests that are usable with poor readers are listed in Appendix A.

Many children with reading disabilities have average or above-average general intelligence. In 13 studies summarized by Belmont and Birch (1966), the average WISC IQs for disabled readers ranged from 91.8 to 109.8. When they studied children who scored in the bottom 10% in reading, those with IQs below 90 were generally reading at a level commensurate with expectancy, while those with IQs of 90 and above generally were a year or more below expectancy. However, even a mentally retarded child may be considered to have a reading disability if he has reached a level of mental maturity substantially above his reading level.

The WISC is the intelligence test most often used in the clinical examination of retarded readers, and opinions differ as to which of the three WISC IQs (Verbal, Performance, or Full Scale) one should rely on as the best indicator of reading expectancy. Some researchers have used the Performance IQ; others suggest that one should use either the Verbal or the Performance IQ, whichever is higher. Since children with disparities of 10 or more points between Verbal and Performance IQs are common, and disparities of 30 or more points are sometimes found in children with reading disabilities, it makes a difference which IQ one uses. Using the highest IQ optimistically assumes that the child's abilities in the lower area of functioning can be substantially improved, an assumption that often is not borne out. Depending on which IQ one uses, the children one will identify as having disabilities will be somewhat different populations, and their common characteristics will vary accordingly. "The modality deficiencies, the cognitive defects, the aptitude weaknesses and the relation of verbal to performance abilities will vary according to the method of identifying the retarded reader" (Reed 1970). At the present time it is probable that fewer mistakes will be made by relying on the Full Scale IQ rather than the Performance IQ alone or the higher of the Verbal or Performance. Whether IQ is or is not related to reading for members of a particular age group depends on such variables as the nature and difficulty of the task, the capabilities of the reader, the time allowed for learning, the quality of instruction, and the nature of the tests used for assessing intelligence and reading (H. Singer 1973).

Patterns of Abilities on the WISC

There is a belief that the WISC-score patterns of reading- or learning-disabled children differ from those of pupils who are making normal progress in reading and that such differences have diagnostic value. The patterns most frequently mentioned are significant discrepancies between Verbal and Performance IQs, subtest score scatter (variability), and characteristic test profiles.

Verbal–Performance IQ differences are common in reading- or learning-disabled children, but the same is also true of children without such problems (Dudley-Marling, Kaufman, & Tarver 1981). In fact, 25% of normal children have differences of at least 15 points between their VIQs and PIQs. The diagnostic value of such discrepancies, as well as patterns of abilities on the WISC, is further weakened by the fact that low scores on the Information and Arithmetic subtests often distort the meaning of the VIQs of reading- or learning-disabled pupils, who consistently score low on these two subtests, which are highly related to schooling (A. Kaufman 1981). Furthermore, Klasen (1972) reported that in 488 cases of reading disability, 22% had significantly higher VIQs than PIQS, 19% had significantly higher PIQs, and the scores did not differ significantly in 59%.

Subtest scatter (widely differing standard scores on the subtests) is supposedly typical of reading- or learning-disabled children. However, the average difference between the lowest and highest scores was seven standard score points in the sample upon whom the WISC-R was normed (A. Kaufman 1976). So it is not unusual for normal children to exhibit considerable subtest scatter (A. Kaufman 1981; Dudley-Marling, Kaufman, & Tarver 1981). Nor does WISC-R subtest scatter differentiate among mentally retarded, learning-disabled, and behaviorally disordered children (Thompson 1980) or among learning-disabled, emotionally disturbed, or nonhandicapped children (Berk 1983).

Bannatyne (1971, 1974) recommended summing the scaled scores from the WISC subtests to form four categories: conceptual ability (Comprehension, Similarities, and Vocabulary), spatial ability (Block Design, Object Assembly, and Picture Completion), sequencing ability (Picture Arrangement, Digit Span, and Coding), and acquired knowledge (Information, Arithmetic, and Vocabulary). Bannatyne's recategorizations were found to be of little value in distinguishing among learning-disabled, mentally retarded, and emotionally disturbed children (Webster & Lafayette 1979) or between learning-disabled and normally achieving children (Henry & Wittman 1981).

WISC-R profile analysis has been recommended (e.g., Vance, Wallbrown, & Blaha 1978; Wallbrown, Blaha & Vance, 1980). But there is no one profile that characterizes all reading- or learning-disabled children (Dudley-Marling, Kaufman, & Tarver 1981) or common characteristic across all reading- or learning-disabled pupils (Ryckman 1981).

VIII. PSYCHOLINGUISTIC AND LANGUAGE ABILITIES

Psycholinguistic Abilities

Psycholinguistics is the "interdisciplinary field of psychology and linguistics in which language behavior is examined" (T. L. Harris & Hodges 1981). Thus, in its broad definition, psycholinguistic ability refers to one's use of language. In practice, however, the term is most frequently operationally defined by the *Illinois Test of Psycholinguistic Abilities* (ITPA). Since the advent of the ITPA, the relationship between psycholinguistic abilities and reading ability and disability has received considerable attention.

Reviews of the ITPA by Carroll (1972) and Chase (1972) indicated the following: (1) Only half of the subtests involve the use of language; (2) ITPA total scores are highly related to intelligence; (3) the 12 subtests do not measure discrete abilities; (4) the norms are based on middle-class children; (5) several subtests penalize dialect speakers; (6) the test has good internal reliability but only fair retest reliability; and (7) there is no particular pattern of high and low subtest scores that characterizes the reading disabled.

An analysis of 28 studies in which ITPA subtests were correlated with reading (Newcomer & Hammill 1975) revealed that only the Sound Blending (auditory blending) subtest correlated significantly (.38) with reading ability, and no subtest consistently distinguished between disabled readers and those progressing normally in reading development. Newcomer and Hammill (1975) concluded: "There appears little doubt that, when used with schoolaged children, . . . its [the ITPA's] use for individual diagnosis is neither supported nor recommended."

Language

As T. L. Harris and Hodges (1981) stated, "defining *language* is both a difficult and controversial effort, and a definition . . . is conditioned by the theoretical or subjective views of the definer." At the risk of oversimplification, *language* is defined here as a system of communication that employs spoken or written symbols. Or, as Benson (1983) defined it, language is the capacity to recognize and produce symbols that convey meaning among individuals who understand that signal system.

Given the important role of language in reading ability, it is not surprising that their interrelationships have been studied and that language deficits or dysfunctions have been identified as causes of reading problems. Bottom–up theories suggest that printed words are almost always phonologically recoded (pronounced overtly or in inner speech), with all subsequent language processing occurring through the spoken language system. These code-emphasis theories predict that any specific effect of language deficiencies on reading ability would involve language abilities at or below the level of phonological recoding (see p. 370); lexical, syntactic, and semantic level deficiencies would occur in both spoken and written language. Top–down theories postulate that in reading there is direct access to meaning. Therefore, effects of language deficiencies on reading ability would involve language deficits at or above the lexical level. Top–down theorists also postulate that poor readers fail to use their linguistic knowledge to increase unitization (chunking information into fewer units); or fail to use context clues to make better predictions concerning the information that is likely to be coming up next (Morrison & Manis 1982). As for interactive models, Roth and Perfetti (1980) suggested that the severity of language dysfunctions within a complex processing system (such as in reading) may be a matter of the degree to which the dysfunction has affected other subsystems and the degree of compensatory processing that has emerged.

Numerous studies have found that disabled readers are less proficient than good readers on a wide variety of language skills ranging from phonemic segmentation to the use of syntactic and semantic information (Wiig, Lapointe, & Semel 1977; T. Bryan 1979; Godfrey *et al.*, 1981; Willows & Ryan 1981; Morrison

& Manis 1982). But disabled readers do not always have language deficits (Newcomer & Magee 1977), and there may be developmental changes in the linguistic correlates of reading achievement. Fletcher, Satz and Scholes (1981) reported that, on the average, disabled and good readers differed significantly at ages $5\frac{1}{2}$, $8\frac{1}{2}$, and 11 on language skills that develop early and are thought to be important for the early phases of reading acquisition. Differences on later-developing language skills were significant between good and poor readers only for the older children.

Children who are slow in language development are likely to encounter problems in learning to read (de Hirsch, Jansky, & Langford 1966; Ingram 1969). However, since language development usually is measured by the understanding and use of spoken language, it may well be that the slow development of such skills and reading ability are all related to underlying linguistic deficiencies.

Doehring *et al.* (1981) gave 22 language measures, which sampled phonemic segmentation and blending, short-term verbal memory, following oral directions, use of morphophonemic rules, use of syntactic structures, paradigmatic word associations, and knowledge of complex syntactic–semantic relationships, to 88 disabled readers. Many of them showed marked weaknesses in phonemic segmentation and blending, serial naming, morphophonemic knowledge, syntactic usage, and following spoken instructions. However, half the subjects scored within the normal range on these language tests, and there was considerable variability from test to test and from subject to subject. Nor could any of Doehring's three identified subtypes of reading disability be clearly differentiated solely on the basis of the language skills measured. Doehring *et al.* (1981) cautioned that although their findings supported a language-deficit hypothesis, the relatively milder impairment on high-level semantic and syntactic skills suggests that their reading-disabled subjects did not have a generalized language disorder. Also, Denckla (1983) reported that as they got older, some children initially diagnosed as "language impaired" displayed linguistic competence on all but the more subtle aspects of syntactic comprehension. Thus it would seem that deficient language ability as a whole is not the cause of reading disability; rather, linguistic skills may be factors in some cases of reading disability.

Language, Oral Language Production, and Speech Defects

Distinctions need to be drawn among language (which is a much more encompassing term), oral language production, and speech defects.

There is a difference between language *competence* and the *production* of oral language. Individuals may have the competence necessary to process spoken language, but they do not necessarily produce those aspects of language in their spoken language. For example, children understand the meanings of many spoken words and syntactic structures that they do not commonly use in speaking to others. Moreover, students with language deficits often will not be classified as having oral language problems because linguistic deficiencies in such abilities as phonemic segmentation may hamper reading acquisition but may not noticeably influence spoken language (Doehring *et al.* 1981).

Speech refers to the neuromuscular activities that produce communication activities. Speech can be significantly abnormal without any concomitant disturbance of language or thought (Benson 1983). There is some evidence (e.g., Lyle 1970) of a relationship between early articulatory speech defects and later reading problems, and the speech of some disabled readers is indistinct with blurred consonants and a generally "thick" quality; or it is rapid, jerky, and stumbling (sometimes referred to as *cluttering*). Others may stutter, speak with a lisp, or slur their words. But it should not be assumed that all children with speech defects also have a reading disability or that the speech defect is the cause of the child's reading problem. Speech-disabled children are often incorrectly diagnosed as having a reading problem based on their oral reading, with their mispronounced words being considered to be word-recognition errors. In the latter case, for instance, a hearing loss may be the cause of the speech problem, and difficulty in hearing the teacher's instruction is likely to hamper reading acquisition. Any speech defect may produce embarrassment in attempting to communicate verbally, thus adversely influencing language development and creating personality problems. It also may produce a dislike of oral reading, especially if the child is asked to read in front of his peers. Decoding skills may be difficult to learn for the child with a marked speech problem, especially if a synthetic phonics approach is employed with a child who is also hearing impaired.

Verbal Processing

Verbal processing ability includes vocabulary, knowledge of the contextual meaning of words, mastery of syntax, awareness of the phonological attributes of spoken and printed words, sensitivity to language, and, especially, the verbal coding[5] of information (Kagan 1983).

Verbal processing plays a key role in Vellutino's verbal-deficit hypothesis (1979, 1983), which suggests that disabled readers have difficulty using semantic, syntactic, or phonological codes to store and retrieve information. More specifically, he considers difficulties with identifying whole words to be caused by limited semantic and syntactic development; he believes that problems with phonetic analysis (decoding) are the result of limited phonological development. His theory also considers lexical development, word retrieval, and metalinguistic skills. Such processing difficulties can disrupt word identification and reading in general (Vellutino & Scanlon 1982). Thus Vellutino's verbal-deficit hypothesis suggests that a reading problem may be associated with one or more of several types of linguistic dysfunction or inefficiency. It is not a single-factor theory; the cause is linguistic in nature, but the language impairment can be of a variety of types and is often subtle rather than obvious.

---

[5] The term *coding* refers to the "abstract, internal representation in memory of events and relations between events. It relates to the structure of memory, its components and their organizations within a system" (Haines & Leong 1983, p. 67).

Denckla (1983) cautioned against complete acceptance of any linguistic-deficit hypothesis because reading also requires a type of visual information processing that is not considered in the typical perceptual-deficit hypotheses. The verbal-deficit hypothesis has been questioned by M. Singer (1982a), but Kagan (1983) interpreted his findings as being in support of it.

Vocabulary Knowledge

As concepts are learned, verbal labels (word names) are attached to them. Words are stored in our lexicons (mental dictionaries) from which they can be retrieved.

Spoken words have semantic, syntactic, and phonological features (Vellutino & Shub 1982). A word's semantic features are the concepts it represents. The quality of a child's verbal concepts may be revealed by his definition of a word. Preschool children usually explain words in terms of their function or use—a ball is to throw. Primary-grade pupils are apt to add some description—a ball is a round thing you play with. Intelligent older students usually state a category to which the item belongs and then indicate one or more ways the item can be distinguished from other members of that category—a ball is a plaything and is usually round; it can be thrown, caught, or kicked. As children get older and have more experiences, concepts are refined and broadened. Brighter children usually acquire concepts more rapidly and have larger vocabularies. Thus vocabulary knowledge is a good indicator of learning ability in general and of probable success in school. Breadth and depth of word meaning is also important for reading comprehension.

Words also have syntactic features; that is, they serve as parts of speech. Some words have only one grammatical function; others more than one (e.g., *can* may be either a noun or verb). Through experience with language, children acquire implicit knowledge of a word's syntactic features.

The phonological features of a word are defined by the unique sequence of phonemes that comprise the word. These phonological features can aid word identification because many English words contain regular grapheme–phoneme correspondences.

As the child is exposed to printed words, the word's graphic and orthographic features come into play. A word's graphic features are the visual patterns formed by the letters that make up the word. These graphic features are abstracted and stored in memory.

Orthographic features refer to a word's internal structure and are characterized by letter sequences that occur frequently in print, letter sequences that are allowable in English (*ble* is a legal sequence, *grt* is not), and letter–sound associations. Discovering the regularities in our orthographic system assists the learner in discriminating among visually similar words and in reducing the amount of visual information that must be processed in reading.

Rapid Automatic Naming

Rapid Automatic Naming (RAN), or *word-finding ability*, refers to the ability to name things (e.g., pictured objects, colors) accurately and quickly. Its use as a measure of verbal ability evolved from the common finding of *anomia* (difficulty with word finding and picture naming) in adults with the acquired reading disability known as *alexia without agraphia* (Denckla 1983). Learning-disabled pupils have been found to be impaired on a number of word-finding, naming, and speed-of-naming tasks (Wiig, Lapointe, & Semel 1977; Rudel, Denckla, & Broman 1981; Denckla, Rudel, & Broman 1981; Wiig, Semel & Nystrom 1982). Rudel (1980) also found that in RAN tasks, learning-disabled children tended to circumlocute (give the function rather than the name—e.g., *temperature* for *thermometer*), reverse syllables (e.g., *shoehorse* for *horseshoe*), or name another object in the same category (e.g., *sink* for *faucet*).

Based on the belief that verbal summaries ("single or other brief classificatory schemata that 'hold' and elicit other related information") appear to be essential for encoding information, Denckla, Rudel, and Broman (1981) postulated that the root of reading disability is the incapacity to utilize organizing principles actively. That is, the reading-disabled appear to fail to seek or to find the appropriate single word or phrase for encapsulating information.

Ackerman and Dykman (1982) contended that effortful semantic processing depends on more than naming facility and that the failure of other studies to find naming-speed differences between learning-disabled and other clinical groups who read normally weakened the hypothesis. They did, however, indicate that compared to normally achieving students, reading-disabled children tended to name more slowly, to scan the stimuli more slowly, and to be less appreciative of rhyme. These deficiencies, singly or in combination, may make memorization difficult for disabled readers.

Semantic Coding and Processing

Many poor readers have semantic coding difficulties. *Semantic coding* involves the use of words, phrases, and sentences to code meaningful information. Difficulties in semantic coding may be caused by dysfunction or inefficiency in the storage or retrieval of lexical information. Whether such difficulties reflect problems in syntactic or phonological coding or limited lexical development is unknown, but it is likely that both types of deficits are involved in some interrelated manner (Vellutino & Scanlon 1982).

Without semantic processing (abstracting meaning from verbal stimuli), it would be impossible to remember the words in a sentence or the sentences in a paragraph clearly enough to extract the intended meaning. Some disabled readers may be deficient in the use of semantic processing (Ceci 1982).

Syntactic Coding and Processing

Syntactic coding refers to the application of implicitly known grammatical rules that constrain the contexts in which words can appear, as well as the ways in which they can be combined to form meaningful sentences (Vellutino 1983). The use of these syntactic rules allows the reader to process increasingly large units of information, which in turn reduces the load on short-term memory and enables more efficient extraction of information from text (Fletcher 1981).

The syntactic characteristics of first grader's oral language do not correlate significantly with their reading achievement, but the relationship increases at later grade levels (Fletcher 1981). Studies imply that some poor readers are not as proficient as good readers in the comprehension and use of syntactically complex structures (e.g., embedded relative clauses, conjunctions, and passives); in their knowledge and use of prefixes, suffixes, and inflectional endings; and in their use of linguistic context to assist in word identification and linguistic functioning in general (Morrison & Manis 1982; Vellutino 1983). The relatively weak syntactic development of poor readers is more likely a cause rather than a result of reading difficulties, since syntactic weaknesses appear before or during the initial stage of learning to read (Vellutino 1983).

It has been hypothesized by some writers that the syntactic structures of sentences found in children's reading material create comprehension problems. There is some evidence that children can better comprehend material when it is written to match their oral language patterns (Ruddell 1974). Inability to understand syntactic structures may be a cause of poor reading comprehension, especially when the structure is not commonly found in oral language.

Phonemic Coding

Phonemic coding is the ability to internalize the phonological representation (pronunciation) of a word's graphic and orthographic components as a means for recovering its name and meaning when it appears in print. It is the process whereby words, phrases, and sentences are encoded phonologically. Some writers have suggested that short-term memory relies on the phonemic coding of information in order to hold a sufficient number of individual words and their sequences in memory long enough to process each sentence.

Deficiencies in phonological processing as a source of reading disability are postulated in auditory discrimination deficiency theories and the phonemic segmentation theory. Good readers more consistently apply phonemic coding strategies (Fletcher 1981), and less skilled readers are less efficient in phonological coding (Shankweiler, Liberman, & Mark 1982; Haines & Leong 1983). Nevertheless, the data indicate that lack of phonemic coding cannot be the sole source of reading disability; rather, results of studies suggest a more general problem (involving not only verbal stimuli) in rapid encoding (Morrison & Manis 1982).

Cognitive Clarity and Linguistic Awareness

Cognitive clarity and linguistic awareness theories attempt to explain reading disability in terms of the pupil's lack of understanding of important concepts about language.

According to the *cognitive clarity theory* (Downing 1979a, b; Downing & Leong 1982), the learning-to-read process requires novice readers to understand the purposes of reading (reading is a communicative process) and the concepts needed for reasoning about the relationships between speech and writing. They must have clear concepts of *word* and *sentence*, be aware of their constituent parts—*letters, sounds, syllables,* and *phrases*—and be able to associate the written word with the spoken word. The theory holds that young children normally approach reading instruction in a state of cognitive confusion about the purposes and features of language, and children gradually achieve the cognitive clarity that allows them to profit from reading instruction and reading experiences.

Downing (1979a) credited Vernon (1957) with having proposed that "the fundamental and basic characteristic of reading disability appears to be cognitive confusion." Later, Vernon (1971, p. 79) stated: "It would seem that in learning to read, it is essential for the child to realize and understand the fundamental generalizations that in alphabetic writing all words are represented by combinations of a limited number of visual symbols. . . . But a thorough grasp of this principle necessitates a fairly advanced stage of conceptual reasoning." This again suggests the interrelationship of cognitive and linguistic development.

Research on cognitive clarity has emphasized the importance of the understanding of the concepts of *word, sound,* and *letter.*[6] There are other terms, often used by teachers, which some children may not understand, such as *page, line, first, last, third, middle, right, before, after* (A. J. Harris 1979a). Other concepts thought to be important are those involved with *print awareness* (Clay 1976, 1979), which refers to an understanding of the uses of written language to communicate and how print is used for such purposes. A similar construct involves the *conventions of print* (Samuels 1983), which refers to knowledge that certain graphic information is used to represent some aspects of spoken language. These concepts include the use of spaces between words and wider spaces between sentences, the role of punctuation marks, and the meaning of underlined or italicized words.

In addition to understanding the terms used in reading instruction, children must also contend with the language forms used for instruction. Styles of language usage, called *registers,* may range from highly formal to highly informal and colloquial (De Stefano 1973). A register is a set of linguistic forms (pronunciation, vocabulary, sentence structure) used in a given circumstance. An informal register is used in conversing with friends and relatives, but most school instruction in given in a formal style called the *Language Instruction Register.* Children's familiarity with the Language Instruction Register varies, but most first graders have some knowledge of it. As pupils progress through the grades, their understanding of the Language Instruction Register generally increases. The extent to which lack of familiarity with this formal style of language interferes with the acquisition of reading ability is unknown, but it seems plausible that it may be an important factor in some cases.

Linguistic, or *metalinguistic, awareness* is the ability to deliberately bring to bear one's phonological and grammatical knowledge (particularly the former) in the course of reading (Mattingly 1972, 1979). Research into linguistic awareness has concentrated on *auditory segmentation*—the ability to segment sentences into words and words into sounds. Since such abilities require an understanding of the concepts *word* and *sound,* a relationship between cognitive clarity and linguistic awareness is obvious.

The strongest advocates of the importance of auditory segmentation, and in particular *phonemic segmentation* (that a spoken word is comprised of phonemes arranged in a given order), are I. Liberman and her associates. Basically their position is that although auditory segmentation is intuitive and automatic

---

[6] Children's understanding of these concepts is discussed on page 39–40.

in speech perception, it must be explicit and fully conscious in learning to read. Similarly, they believe that lack of phonemic segmentation ability is one of the main causes of reading disability because it makes it difficult to encode words into short-term memory and interferes with learning to make the symbol–sound associations necessary for decoding unknown words. They assume that written language must be transformed into its spoken form in order for meaning to be processed. Therefore, in order to learn to "map" the written word onto its spoken counterpart, children must understand the phonetic nature of our alphabetic writing system; that is, how the orthography represents our language. Not only must the child understand that spoken words are comprised of sounds, but they also must be able to divide spoken words into their constituent segments that are represented by the letters of our alphabet. In an alphabetic language, such as English, the orthography does not represent the speech sounds; rather, it is an abstraction from speech. The orthography bears a regular relation to speech, but the nature of that relationship is difficult for children to understand. It is their lack of *phonological maturity*, which is common in young children, that prevents them from taking full advantage of the more abstract aspects of English orthography. The more one reads, the greater the phonological maturity; but only if one attends to the relationship between printed words and the phonology of their spoken counterparts (I. Liberman 1983).

I. Liberman *et al*. (1977) have demonstrated that vowels and consonants in words do not have invariant sound-wave patterns; the /b/ in *bed* represents a somewhat different pattern from the /b/ in *boat* or in *rob*. The sound-wave pattern depends on the sequence of sounds, not just on a single phoneme. It is difficult for a young child to hear that the spoken word *bed* contains three phonemes, since the sound-wave pattern has no breaks; and the concept of the sound of /b/ is an abstraction from somewhat variable patterns that the sound has in different words. Syllables are more invariant than phonemes and are easier units to identify in spoken words.

Evidence that insensitivity to the phonetic structure of English contributes significanty to reading disability is only indirect (Vellutino & Scanlon 1982). Nor is it clear that cognitive clarity, linguistic awareness, or phonological maturity is a cause or a result of reading disability, or whether they simply co-occur. For kindergarten children who had not yet learned to read, sound awareness tasks, especially the segmentation task, were reported by Huba (1984) to be good predictors of learning through a whole-word approach and in learning initial consonant substitution.

IX. SPECIFIC COGNITIVE FACTORS

Perception

Stimulation of our sense organs, such as the eyes and ears, produces sensations. *Perception* is the interpretation of these incoming sensory data by the brain, which selects, groups, organizes, and sequences them. Meaningful interpretation can then lead to appropriate responses. The perceptual aspects of reading are complex because the mind must act on a succession of stimuli in which both spatial and temporal patterns must be perceived. "Reading is a continuing cycle of excitation and reaction in which each moment of perception produces a feedback effect which sets the person for the following perception. In this rapidly repeating cycle the sequential perceptions are apprehended as forming linguistic sequences that convey large units of meaning" (A. J. Harris 1961b).

The following terms are frequently encountered in the literature on perception and reading:

1. *Figure-ground.* Normally, one major unit or group of units is perceived clearly against a background that is more vaguely perceived. In reading, the print is the figure that stands out from the white background of the page.

2. *Closure.* There is a strong tendency to perceive wholes; one tends to fill in parts that are missing. Examples of closure as related to reading are the ability to understand the meaning of a sentence that contains one or more unknown words, the ability to fill in the deleted items on a cloze test, the ability to recognize or pronounce correctly a word from which some letters are missing, and the ability to recognize incompletely heard words or words from which phonemes have been deleted.

3. *Sequence.* In listening, sequence is inherent in the sensory input; in reading, the sequence of the visual stimuli must be imposed by the reader. The left-to-right sequence of letters in words and words across the page, as well as the top-to-bottom arrangement of written English, are arbitrary conventions that children must learn.

4. *Discrimination.* The ability to distinguish among stimuli increases with age and experience. As skills develop there is a change from vague perception of wholes to reliance on prominent details toward mature perception in which the whole is perceived sharply and the details within it are also clearly discerned.

5. *Mind Set.* One's immediate mind set provides an anticipation of what is likely to occur next. Such anticipations can be helpful in predicting what words or concepts are likely to occur in the next portion of a text. On the other hand, it can lead to errors when the anticipation is incorrect.

Visual Perception[7]

Most often, visual perception is defined by test performance, but visual-perception tests vary widely as to what they measure (some actually sample visual–motor skills) and how reliably they do so (see Colarusso & Gill 1975–1976).

The most widely used perceptual test in the past was the *Frostig Developmental Test of Visual Perception* (DTVP) whose five subtests supposedly measured discrete skills. Remedial programs to overcome weaknesses indicated by the subtest scores were employed, particularly in the field of special education. Factor-analysis studies tended to show that the DTVP measured one main factor—*visual-perception maturity* (P. Smith & Marx 1972) or *perceptual read-*

[7] Those interested in this topic may wish to refer to the annotated bibliography by Weintraub and Cowan (1982).

iness (Olson 1980), and its usefulness in discriminating poor from good readers was challenged (Larsen & Hammill 1975). The consensus of researchers strongly suggests that the content validity of the DTVP should be seriously questioned (Olson 1980). Visual perceptual training has resulted in higher scores on the DTVP, but not in significant increases in reading achievement (Coles 1978). Other visual perceptual tests are described in Appendix A.

Satz *et al.* (1978) found that performance on an unpublished perceptual test was one of the three best predictors of reading disability in Grades 2, 3, and 4. They theorized that perception and perceptual–motor abilities change rapidly from ages 5 to 8 and therefore can be good short-term predictors of reading failure around those age levels, but that language and conceptual abilities increase in importance as children get older.

Kavale (1982b) performed a meta-analysis of visual-perception studies. He concluded that visual perception is an important correlate of reading achievement but that the proportion of explained variance in reading skills was contingent on the combination of visual and reading variables considered. Correlations between the perceptual and reading variables ranged from .01 to .89 with a mean of .37 and a median of .48. Visual memory and visual discrimination appeared to have a greater association with reading ability than visual closure, spatial relationships, visual–motor integration, visual association, figure-ground, and visual–auditory integration. Only the Visual Sequential Memory subtest of the ITPA correlated significantly with reading (.40), but that correlation is too low for making predictions. Only the Form Constancy subtest of the *Frostig* correlated significantly with reading (.30); also too low for use as a predictor. When IQ was partialed out, the magnitude of the correlations decreased and only six correlations ranging from .16 to .34 were found to be significant; those are too low to be used as predictors.

Meares (1980) reported that some disabled readers seemed to have a visual-ground difficulty, which was due to perceptual instability induced by the black print on a white page. These children reported experiencing print as blurring, moving, jumping, and flickering in the absence of visual defects. Meares stated that the effect was reduced and reading became easier for them with the use of light print on a darker background (reduced brightness contrast), with small rather than large print, and with a minimum of space between words and lines. Her claims need to be researched, but it is not unusual for severely disabled readers to report such symptoms.

Visual–Motor Performance

For many years, psychologists have used tests of the ability to copy visual designs (visual–motor coordination) as diagnostic tools. The most frequently used of these is the *Bender Visual–Motor Gestalt Test* (BVMGT). A series of designs is presented, one at a time, which the student is asked to copy. The stimuli are available to the child, so visual memory is not a factor. While the test yields an age-level score, the qualitative features of the child's productions (e.g., rotations, difficulty with diagonals, form distortions) are felt to be of more diagnostic significance (Bender 1938, Koppitz 1964). In interpreting the *Bender*, the examiner cannot always be sure if poor performance results from perceptual difficulty, poor motor control, or the linking of motor behavior to perception.

The use of the *Bender* in the diagnosis of learning disabilities has been reviewed by Keogh (1969) and Bender (1970). There is, however, no clear agreement as to its predictive value. On the average, the *Bender* correlates approximately .31 with reading achievement; but the magnitude of the relationship decreases significantly when intelligence is partialed out (Kavale 1982b). This suggests that *Bender* scores do not provide much improvement over chance in predicting the reading scores of individuals. The notion that reading problems are primarily caused by malfunctioning in visual–motor perception that can be measured by the *Bender* is incorrect. The *Bender* is sensitive to emotional problems as well as neurological development and dysfunction (Coles 1978).

The Perceptual-Deficit Hypothesis

Vellutino (1977, 1979) grouped various theories dealing with the possible role of visual perception in reading disability and used the term *perceptual-deficit hypothesis* to indicate the general premise of these theories. Essentially, the perceptual-deficit hypothesis states that reading disability is caused by visual–spatial confusions stemming from a neurological dysfunction or deficiency. These constitutional disorders, which are believed to disrupt visual perception and then visual memory, are manifested in orientation and sequencing errors (e.g., reversals). But according to Vellutino and Scanlon (1982), the perceptual-deficit hypothesis can be criticized on empirical grounds (data indicating that disabled readers do perceive printed words accurately). Other writers, such as Carr (1981) and Kagan and Moore (1981), have also rejected the visual perceptual-deficit hypothesis. A more cautious stance was taken by Olson (1980), who stated that perceptual deficiencies may contribute to, but not cause, reading disability.

Auditory Perception

The three aspects of auditory perception most commonly associated with reading disability are segmentation (discussed on p. 391), discrimination, and blending.

Auditory discrimination, which is the ability to perceive differences among spoken stimuli, has been cited as a strong contributor to reading disability (e.g., Wepman 1961, Johnson & Myklebust 1967). The assumption is that an auditory-discrimination disorder indicates either a neurological problem or maturational lag and creates problems with learning in general. It is measured in varying ways by different tests. The *Wepman Auditory Discrimination Test* requires the pupil to listen to pairs of words, most of which differ on one minimally contrasting phoneme (e.g., *thin–fin*), and respond as to whether each pair sounds the same or different. In the *Goldman–Fristoe–Woodcock Test of Auditory Discrimination*, the child selects one of four pictures (e.g., *cap, cab, cat, catch*) that represents the word spoken by the examiner. Reading readiness tests commonly ask the child to indicate which of a number of pictured words begin or end with the same sound as the word spoken by the examiner. That different auditory-discrimination tests actually sample different skills, at least for young children, was demonstrated by Dykstra (1966).

The findings are mixed as to whether the *Wepman* can be used to distinguish learning- or reading-disabled children from those without such problems (Coles 1978). Tallal (1980) found that good and poor readers did not differ on auditory discrimination and temporal-order perception tasks when verbal and nonberbal stimuli were presented at slow rates, but the reading-disabled subjects performed more poorly when the stimuli were presented more rapidly. She interpreted her findings as suggesting that some reading-disabled children have a primary perceptual deficit that influences the rate at which they can process information. Such a deficit could lead to difficulty with phonemic segmentation and could partially account for the difficulties poor readers have in segmenting and recoding phonemically.

Vellutino (1983) and others have pointed out that children who fail auditory-discrimination tests often can verbally repeat the stimuli presented by the examiner, thereby demonstrating adequate discrimination (e.g., they could not say the word pairs exactly as given if they were unable to distinguish between the minimally contrasting phonemes). It is also suggested that children who speak clearly cannot have auditory-discrimination problems. The counterargument is that the types of auditory discrimination needed for oral language and reading differ.

A literature review led Hammill and Larsen (1974b) to conclude that auditory discrimination, memory, sound blending, and auditory–visual integration are not essential for successful reading. Nevertheless, failure to find average differences between good and poor readers does not negate the possibility that some disabled readers have marked deficits in one or more aspects of auditory perception that may be contributing to their reading problems.

Kavale (1981b) concluded that auditory perception was an important correlate of reading ability (correlations ranged from .02 to .81, with a mean of .358 and a median of .328) and of some use in predicting reading achievement. However, he also noted that intelligence appeared to be a major component of all auditory perceptual skills and that only auditory discrimination maintained some independence from intelligence in its relationship to reading ability.

In interpreting performance on auditory-discrimination tests the following points should be considered: (1) Dialect speakers and nonnative speakers of English may do poorly on tests of phoneme discrimination because the sounds under consideration may differ in their dialect or first language from standard English; (2) performance on any auditory test can be greatly influenced by attending behavior; (3) the speech of the examiner can affect test scores; and (4) tests often require skills or concepts in addition to those suggested by the test title (e.g., the child must understand the concepts *same* and *different*).

Auditory blending is the ability to synthesize sounds mentally into syllables and syllables into words. Auditory blending differs from visual blending in that in the former, the sounds are presented by an examiner; in the latter, the pupil must first recognize units of the printed word, whose sounds are then blended into a recognizable whole. At times, children are diagnosed as having blending problems when in fact their problem is their inability to make the necessary symbol–sound associations in decoding unknown words. To rule out such possible misdiagnoses, auditory-blending tests are given. Performance on auditory-blending tests can be greatly influenced by the manner in which the words are broken up and the skill of the examiner in not distorting the separate sounds (see p. 223). Apparent blending problems also may reflect poor memory for individual sounds when more than four sounds must be blended (Moore *et al.* 1982).

The *Roswell–Chall Auditory Blending Test* correlates significantly with reading (Chall, Roswell, & Blumenthal 1963). Richardson *et al.* (1980) reported that ITPA auditory-blending scores were significantly related to reading achievement even when IQ was partialed out. Kavale (1981b), however, did not find this to be so.

Memory

One of the most consistent characteristics of reading disability is poor memory (Kagan 1983). It seems reasonable to relate memory deficits or dysfunctions to reading difficulty because, logically, memory must somehow be involved in the reading process. If nothing else, the reader must retain at the end of the sentence, paragraph, or page, the meaning of what was read before that point. Many reading-disabled children perform poorly on short-term memory (STM) tasks (Torgesen & Greenstein 1982).

There are several stages in the visual memory process. First, there is a *sensory visual trace* in which the visual image of the input from an eye fixation is stored very briefly (about .25 seconds). Typically, this sensory trace is erased or masked by the next visual input. If information is to be remembered, it must be processed beyond this point. In the *iconic store*, the visual input is matched to a stored visual image. This iconic image lasts from 1 to 2 seconds, allowing enough time for the visual information to be coded verbally. Because an iconic image can hold several inputs simultaneously, it helps create the context effects needed for deriving meaning from sequentially presented inputs. Some information from the iconic store is transferred to the next stage of the memory system.

Short-term memory (STM) is the working memory used by skilled readers for sentence comprehension. Verbally encoded information is stored for a few seconds while the sentence is being processed for meaning. For novice readers, STM provides a "working area" for synthesizing small parts of words into whole words (Torgesen 1978–1979). The fact that working memory decays after a brief time is compatible with the assumption that because poor readers do too much slow attention-demanding processing, encoded information decays before it can be utilized, at least part of the time (Lesgold & Perfetti 1981). STM is a limited capacity system, but information can be maintained for longer than a few seconds through rehearsal (see below). There may be two STM stores, one for acoustic (phonetic) information and another for visual information.

Some information from STM is passed on to *long-term memory* (LTM). To a large extent, elaborative encoding strategies (rehearsal, clustering, grouping, and reorganizing the material) determine the amount of information transferred to LTM (Bauer 1982). LTM involves relatively permanent storage, usually semantic in nature. When information reaches LTM, meaning is realized. Findings regarding which, if any, of these levels of memory is deficient in disabled readers are equivocal (Aaron & Baker 1983).

Theories: Memory and Reading Disability

The short-term memory theory of reading disability holds that the recoding difficulty of disabled readers is a by-product of a fundamental deficit in STM. An extreme view was held by Jorm (1979a), who contended that an STM deficit causes severe reading disability. Jorm's theory has been challenged by Byrne (1983). Some STM theorists postulate a generalized memory deficit; but this point of view is undermined by the fact that disabled readers are deficient only on certain kinds of memory tasks (Sternberg & Wagner 1982). Others implicate only *serial memory* (maintaining the order in which items or events occurred). Yet others suggest that slow and inefficient encoding of new items into STM and the clearing of old items out of it creates a backlog in short-term store. This "traffic jam" interferes with comprehension (T. Carr 1981).

The *abstractive memory* model states that remembering is an abstractive process in which certain information is selectively filtered out and forgotten; other information is designated "to be remembered." The *central-incidental hypothesis* aspect of this model of memory states that the importance of material determines what is attended to and recalled. Unskilled readers may select what is to be remembered on factors other than the importance of the information, or may attempt to remember everything. The latter results in a memory overload, which in turn creates weak recall. Skilled readers screen out incidental and irrelevant information and store important information in LTM (Luftig 1983). Thus this model leads to the conclusion that it is the inability to differentiate relevant from irrelevant information, rather than a deficient memory per se, that contributes to the reading problem.

It is difficult to determine exactly where memory is breaking down because memory is not a unitary ability. Rather, it involves encoding, retention, and retrieval processes. For example, Shankweiler *et al.* (1979) suggested that a number of supposedly memory-related problems of poor readers were really manifestations of phonetic-coding deficiencies because working memory relies on phonetic coding of the information to be retained while interpreting a written sentence. A similar viewpoint was expressed by Doehring *et al.* (1981).

There is also some question as to whether memory can be studied apart from other cognitive functions (Torgesen 1978–1979). Furthermore, poor recall could result from test anxiety; inefficient strategies in the coding, rehearsal, or organization of information; unfamiliarity with the material; or inefficiency in gaining access to stored information (Kagan 1983). An apparent auditory-memory problem may be the result of such factors as an unrecognized defect in auditory acuity, inattention, or failure to comprehend the task instructions.

Sequential Memory

Deficits in *sequential memory* (the ability to recall items in the sequence in which they were presented) as a cause of reading disability is intuitively appealing for at least two reasons. First, the order in which the letters appeared in the word is important in word recognition, as is the order in which phonemes are blended during decoding. Second, the sequence of words and phrases in sentences has a bearing on sentence meaning, and the sequence in which information is processed influences comprehension.

Auditory sequential memory is often measured by the digit-span subtest of the WISC-R or ITPA. There are some interpretation problems when such tasks are used (Torgesen 1978–1979). Black (1983) found that the WISC digit spans of learning-disabled children did not differ significantly from what would be expected on the basis of intelligence and that those LD pupils whose forward digit spans were at least three digits higher than their backward spans did not have a higher incidence of neurological disorder than those with normal discrepancies. Both groups performed similarly on a variety of academic and psychological measures. Visual sequential memory is frequently measured by the ITPA subtest of the same name. It requires the child to reconstruct abstract designs, each shown for 5 seconds.

The finding that poor readers tend to perform more poorly than good readers on serial memory tasks has been interpreted by some to mean that inefficient or deficient sequential memory (e.g., Bakker & Schroots 1981, Moore et al. 1982), or an insensitivity to order information (M. Singer 1982b), is a cause of reading problems. Such serial memory deficit theories are based on the assumption that general memory ability and the ability to recall the order in which stimuli were presented are supported by neurologically separate memory systems. Research evidence does not confirm the view that reading-disabled pupils suffer from a fundamental and independent deficit in serial ordering ability (Vellutino & Scanlon 1982, Morrison & Manis 1982). Although performance on serial memory tasks is a good predictor of reading achievement, such information tells us little about which memory processes are deficient (Torgesen 1978–1979).

A number of researchers have suggested that sequential-memory difficulties are probably the result of deficient coding: either phonological recoding, which is believed to be STM's best hedge against loss of serial order information (e.g., Liberman et al. 1980; Katz, Shankweiler, & Liberman 1981; T. Carr 1981), or verbal coding (e.g. Vellutino 1979, Torgesen & Houck 1980, Vellutino & Scanlon 1982, Stanovich 1982a,c).

In a series of four studies, Hicks (1980) found that good and poor readers differed in the use of verbal labeling strategies. Good readers usually named the visual stimuli and retained them in acoustic memory storage; but when their verbal labeling was suppressed, their performance on visual sequential-memory tasks was no better than that of the poor readers. Poor readers attempted to recall the stimuli on the basis of visual memory alone; but when they learned to use rehearsal strategies (repeating the items), their retention of serially ordered visual stimuli increased significantly. Thus, inadequate performance on visual STM memory tasks appears to depend on the ability to label items and to store them in some form of *verbal* rather than visual memory (Hicks & Spurgeon 1982).

Rehearsal strategies (e.g., repeating the sequence of items to oneself) can be taught to disabled readers (Naylor 1980), and such instruction results in their increased use (Haines & Torgesen 1979). Use of rehearsal strategies can improve recall (Bauserman & Obrzut 1981, Moore *et al.* 1982). Similarly, children with reading problems tend not to use organizational strategies (e.g., clustering items into categories) (Wong 1978, 1982), but they can be trained to do so (Torgesen, Murphy, & Ivey 1979). However, although STM performance can be improved by inducing poor readers to use mnemonic strategies, such devices do not suffice when STM processing must occur rapidly and automatically as a component of a complex cognitive task like reading (Torgesen & Greenstein 1982).

Integration between Modalities

Reading appears to require the integration of information from the auditory and visual sensory systems—the association between graphemes and phonemes, between printed and spoken words, between the written and spoken forms of language. The ability to integrate sensory information is also known as auditory–visual integration (AVI), cross-modal transfer, or intersensory integration.

Birch and his colleagues (Birch & Lefford 1963, Birch & Belmont 1964) explored the idea that the major cause of reading disability was difficulty in integrating sensory information. But basic deficits in sensory integration as a cause of reading disability have received little support over the past two decades. Research has indicated that AVI is significantly related to reading achievement, but AVI does not add much to its prediction (Rodenborn 1970–1971, J. P. Jones 1970). Although AVI skill tends to increase with age through approximately age 10 for children with normal intelligence, its actual relationship to the development of reading skills is unknown (Silverston & Deichmann 1975). The degree of the relationship is highly dependent on the subject's developmental level, gender, SES, and task requirements. Furthermore, poor readers perform as poorly on intramodal (auditory–auditory, visual–visual) tasks as they do on AVI (Van de Voort, Senf, & Benton 1972).

On the other hand, Kavale (1980) somewhat cautiously concluded, based on his meta-analysis, that AVI was sufficiently associated with reading ability to be considered in the prediction of reading achievement. AVI correlated about .34 with various measures of reading, except for vocabulary (.13). The correlation was higher for good readers (.35) than for disabled readers (.21). Intelligence appeared to be a component of AVI.

A number of factors have been suggested as influencing AVI performance. Blank and Bridger (1966) implicated attention and verbal labeling, but Drader (1975) failed to find evidence of a verbal labeling deficiency. Rudel and Denckla (1976) found that whether the stimulus pattern was simultaneous or successive was more important than whether the sequence of stimuli was auditory to visual or visual to auditory. Badian (1977) interpreted her data as indicating that poor AVI was the result of inferior auditory sequential memory. But poor performance on a sequential-memory test may reflect a number of factors, as indicated above. More recently, Vellutino and Scanlon (1982) suggested that apparent AVI deficits may reflect the difficulty poor readers have in dealing with tasks that draw heavily on verbal ability.

At present it appears that although AVI ability is related to reading ability, a cause–effect relationship has not been established. There is no evidence that AVI training has any benefit for growth in reading skills (Calfee & Drum 1978).

Attention

A distinction should be drawn among *attention*, which in the broad sense refers to noticing stimuli; *sustained attention*, which involves concentrating over a period of time; and *selective attention*, which means the ability to maintain focus on particular stimuli and disregard or suppress other stimuli. Selective attention is basic to efficiency in perception, learning, memory, and information processing.

There is not complete agreement on the components of attention. For example, Wittrock (1983) stated that attention consists of two components: a short-term, orienting response; and a long-term or sustained voluntary response. Keogh and Margolis (1976) indicated that attention has three partially independent but interactive aspects: coming to attention, decision making, and maintaining attention. According to Elliot and Piersal (1982), attending behavior has three components: (1) capacity—the amount of information a learner can manage effectively at a given time; (2) selectivity—the process of identifying and processing a small portion of the available information; and (3) vigilance, or on-task behavior—the capacity to maintain attention to a relevant portion of the task over a period of time. Assuming the existence of such components of attention, attentional deficits could conceivably occur at any point in the reading process.

A distinction also should be drawn between selective attention and the extreme distractibility associated with brain damage (Strauss & Lehtinen 1947, Cruickshank *et al.* 1961). The attention problem for such neurologically impaired children is suppressing distracting external stimuli and maintaining attention to relevant rather than irrelevant visual or auditory stimuli. Distractibility is also commonly listed as a symptom of hyperactivity. Although the evidence indicates some degree of attentional deficit in LD children, it does not necessarily imply brain damage or dysfunction (Dykman *et al.* 1983).

The few studies on sustained attention have not revealed major deficits in the ability of disabled readers to maintain attention over reasonably long periods (Morrison & Manis 1982). R. Brown (1982) found that normally achieving students increased with age in sustained attention to both auditory and visual stimuli; the ability of hyperactive children increased only in response to auditory stimuli.

Learning-disabled children perform more poorly than normally achieving students in their selective attention to both visual stimuli (Long, McIntyre, & Murray 1982) and auditory stimuli (Cherry & Kruger 1983). Tarver *et al.* (1977) related the inattention of the learning disabled to their lack of verbal rehearsal; in other words, they tended not to remind themselves of what they were supposed to be doing.

Although, on the average, disabled readers exhibit poorer selective attention than do good readers on reading tasks (Moore *et al.* 1982), the two groups perform similarly when nonreading tasks are used (Vellutino & Scanlon 1982). The poorer performance of disabled readers on reading tasks may be result from (1) their reading disability, which causes them to disengage from reading; (2) looking at other words or pictures in an attempt to find clues to unknown words; or (3) attempts to escape the frustration and anxiety caused by repeated failures in reading (Morrison & Manis 1982). Or differences in attention between good and poor readers may be due, at least partially, to differences in rapid, automatically functioning information-processing skills (Torgesen 1978–1979). As a group, disabled readers do not exhibit basic or pervasive deficits in selective attention. There is little evidence to support an attentional-deficit hypothesis (Bauer 1982). Koppell (1979) concluded that there was no basis for favoring an attentional-deficit hypothesis over either the diminished-capacity explanation (reading-disabled children have less processing capacity to allocate to any task) or the specific-processing-deficit notion (disabled readers have a dysfunction in some stage of information processing).

There are many uncertainties concerning attention and its measurement (L. P. Harris 1976). Nevertheless, it seems clear that getting the learner to focus attention on the task at hand is an important responsibility of any teacher and is particularly vital in remediation. Selective attention can be improved by teaching children to use verbal rehearsal (Tarver et al. 1977), by using a reward system (Hallahan et al. 1978), or by teaching them self-monitoring strategies (Hallahan, Marshall, & Lloyd 1981).

Lack of attention can be situational or created by external factors, such as educational practices. As Wittrock (1983) stated, attention is influenced by the questions teachers ask, the texts they use, and the direction provided pupils regarding the relationships pupils need to construct between the text and their prior knowledge. The appropriateness of the difficulty level of the material used for reading instruction also influences attending behavior (Gambrell, Wilson, & Ganitt 1981).

Cognitive Style

Cognitive style has been characterized in a number of ways, but all deal with individual differences in the ways in which information and experiences are organized and processed (Messiak 1982). Guilford (1980) believed that cognitive styles are personality traits regarding preferences for information processing. Three aspects of cognitive style that are relevant to reading are field dependence–independence, reflectiveness–impulsiveness, and modality perference.

Field dependence–independence refers to a dimension at one end of which are the field dependent, who are socially sensitive, conforming, and easily influenced. At the other end are the field independent, who tend to be impersonal, analytical, and not easily influenced. Most people fall between the extremes and are somewhat variable according to the situation (Witkin 1977). Keogh and Donlon (1972) found LD boys to be highly field dependent, but no direct relation to reading disability has been established, and the implications of this dimension for teaching are not clear.

Conceptual tempo (reflectiveness–impulsiveness) refers to a dimension with the reflective (slow but accurate) at one end and the impulsive (fast but inaccurate) at the other. Most people fall between the extremes, and many are slow and inaccurate or fast and accurate. Although some studies have shown that field-independent pupils scored higher on standardized reading tests than did field-dependent students, other studies have found no significant differences between the two groups; the effect of intelligence has been ignored in most of these studies. Recommendations concerning use of reading approaches that are congruent with a student's cognitive style are premature (Roberge & Flexer 1984). Impulsiveness and reflectiveness may influence the kind and number of miscues a child makes; impulsive children in the early grades tend to rely on the first letter of a short word or the first or last syllable of a long word (Fisher 1977).

Modality preference, the idea of matching a child's strongest learning aptitude with a corresponding teaching method, has been noted in Chapter 3 as not supported by the research thus far (see p. 80). Most children do not show a marked discrepancy between their visual skills and their auditory skills. For the few who do, those with strong visual preferences do not do better with a whole-word method than with phonics, and those with strong auditory abilities show no special advantages in a phonics method (H. M. Robinson 1972). Among the possible reasons for a lack of significant findings are these: The tests for modality preferences may be inadequate; both auditory and visual abilities are required for reading; and it is extremely difficult to control the modality through which students learn.

Learning Styles

In contrast to cognitive style, which involves the ways in which individuals process information, *learning style* deals with the way that pupils respond to the environmental, sociological, and physical stimuli around them. Learning style is the aggregate of a student's opinion regarding the conditions under which he or she learns best. Some writers (Dunn 1981, Dunn *et al.* 1981) believe that some pupils learn more easily in a cool, quiet school setting; other students respond better in a warm, well-lighted room. Carbo (1983) claimed that, compared to good readers, disabled readers tend to have a greater need for quiet, mobility, structure, and interaction with peers and teachers. They had more difficult learning in the early morning than at other times during the school day. There is, however, no agreement as to what constitutes learning style, and research on its identification and use in reading instruction is still in its infancy (White 1983).

9

Correlates of Reading Disability, II: Neurological, Physiological, and Physical Factors

This is the second of three chapters on the correlates of reading disabilities. The main topics discussed are hemispheric specialization, neurological damage and dysfunction, laterality and lateralization, sensory defects, and other physical conditions that may contribute to reading disability.

I. NEUROLOGICAL FACTORS

The Brain and Reading[1]

The brain is an incredibly complex organ, and knowledge of its functioning in learning to read and reading disability is far from complete. But since reading is one of the most difficult, abstract, and symbolic human activities, it is reasonable to assume that reading requires a brain that is functioning within normal limits and that deviations from these limits may result in reading problems.

The human brain, which contains billions of nerve cells interconnected in incredibly complicated ways, is divided into two cerebral hemispheres connected mainly by a large band of nerve tissue called the *corpus callosum*. The

---

[1] For more complete information on the brain and its functioning, refer to Wittrock (1978), Taylor (1978), Masland (1981), Downing and Leong (1982), Benson (1983), or Kirk (1983).

hemispheres are not exactly the same structurally, and each usually plays a dominant role in performing certain functions.

Each hemisphere controls motor and sensory functions on the opposite (contralateral) side of the body. So, for example, damage to certain areas of the left hemisphere results in paralysis of the right arm, hand, or leg. This connection is the basis for the assessment of handedness in studying cerebral lateralization.

The role of each hemisphere in congnitive functioning is much less clearly established. There are a variety of theories regarding lateral asymmetries (Cohen 1982). *Structural models* postulate that each hemisphere is specialized for processing certain kinds of cognitive functions. The belief is that performance is superior when the processing takes place in the hemisphere whose structure is specialized to perform that function.

Some theories propose that there is hemispheric specialization for particular stages of processing. Others hold that each hemisphere specializes in a characteristic type of processing, irrespective of the stimuli. Thus, left-hemispheric processing is characterized as sequential, serial, temporal, or analytic; right-hemispheric processing is parallel, gestalt, or holistic.

In about 95% of right-handed and 70% of left-handed persons, the left hemisphere appears to be dominant for linguistic functions. The right hemisphere seems to specialize in numerous perceptual skills. However, existing data regarding the functions of the left and right hemispheres lack convergent validity; different methods and samples have not led to consistent findings (Hiscock & Kinsbourne 1982).

There are opposing viewpoints concerning when cerebral lateralization for language occurs. One view holds that, early in life, both hemispheres have equal potentiality for assuming language functions and that hemispheric specialization develops as the child develops (Trevarthen 1983). The other viewpoint argues that the left hemisphere is specialized for language at or before birth.

The right hemisphere's capacity to mediate language following early left-hemisphere damage or removal is cited by equipotentiality theorists as evidence for their belief. But Leong (1980) contended that such an occurrence is due to the plasticity of the right hemisphere rather than to hemispheric equipotentiality; and Pirozzolo *et al.* (1981) noted that the nature of the recovery process in children does not rule out the possibility that language functions are lateralized early in development.

There are also opposing views concerning the areas of the brain that serve specific language functions. The *structural localization* theory states that specific language functions are located within specific areas of the brain. The *holistic* view holds that language is so complex that most of the brain is used in normal language functions. Neither conceptualization is entirely correct (Benson 1983), and there is considerable individual variability in the exact location of language processes in the cortex (Ojemann 1983).

Two areas within the left hemisphere are frequently associated with language functions (see Fig. 9.1). *Broca's area* is important for speaking; *Wernicke's area* is important in understanding language. It is unlikely that Broca's area is involved in reading disability because damage in that area does not disrupt the

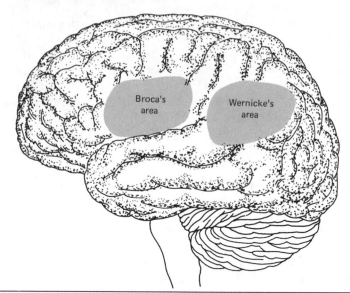

Figure 9.1. Speech areas of the cortex in the left hemisphere of the human brain. From T. Teyler, *A primer of psychobiology: brain and behavior* (San Francisco: W. H. Freeman, 1975). Used by permission of the author and publisher.

ability to comprehend spoken or written language. Damage in Wernicke's area does adversely affect the ability to understand spoken and written language (Hanley & Sklar 1976).

The left hemisphere appears to be the better equipped anatomically for language development and functioning. The language region in the left hemisphere is larger than the corresponding area in the right hemisphere[2] (Pirozzolo & Hansch 1982) and the left hemisphere has a number of components specialized for processing spoken and written language (Trevarthen 1983).

Even when language functions are primarily lateralized in the left hemisphere and there has been no brain damage, the right hemisphere participates, although in a limited manner, in the comprehension of oral and written language and in acoustic–verbal memory (Tzavaras, Kaprinis, & Gatzoyas 1981; Moscovitch 1981). Leong (1980) suggested that word recognition involves reciprocal contributions from both hemispheres: feature analysis by the right hemisphere and decoding and naming by the left.

If the left hemisphere is severely damaged or is surgically removed early in life, language abilities develop in the right hemisphere. Masland (1981) suggested that the cutoff point for this plasticity is around ages 8 to 12, but it may be much earlier; according to Benson (1983), brain lateralization is well under way by age 5. When the right hemisphere takes over language functions, it apparently does not serve reading and spelling skills as well as the left hemisphere (Masland 1981; Dennis, Lovett, & Wiegel-Crump 1981; Greenblatt 1983).

[2] It is not known, however, whether the larger size of a sector of the cortex implies better functioning (Kinsbourne 1983).

According to L. Henderson (1982), the idea that all reading competence is restricted to the left hemisphere is based on the false equation of all reading as oral reading. A fair amount of reading comprehension can be mediated by the right hemisphere after surgical removal of the left. Apparently what the right hemisphere cannot do readily is convert print to sound.

The presence of language functions primarily in the right hemisphere, or the lack of lateralization for language in either hemisphere, is interpreted by some to be strongly related to reading disability. Right-hemispheric specialization of language as a causal factor is based on the belief that it is normal to have language centered in the left hemisphere and that any deviation from this situation is due to some brain damage or dysfunction. The lack of hemispheric dominance for language in either hemisphere is most often attributed to maturational or neurological lag.

Neurological Damage, Deficits, and Abnormalities

Various hypotheses attempt to relate brain deficits to reading disability; the following illustrate some of them. Geschwind's (1965) disconnection theory proposed that a lesion within the *corpus callosum* disconnected the right visual cortex region from the left angular gyrus. Jorm (1979a) stated that severe reading disability was the result of a genetically based dysfunction of the inferior parietal lobe, the region believed important for short-term memory and reading. Another hypothesis (Denckla 1983, p. 41) suggested that a "pure dyslexic, with no deficit in spoken language, appears to have some subset of general verbal learning deficits associated with left convexity frontal lobe." And Tarnopol and Tarnopol (1979) argued, rather unconvincingly, that learning to read may be adversely influenced by dysfunction in the sensorimotor areas of the brain. Other theories contend that reading disability is caused by delayed development of the angular gyrus. All of these hypotheses lack conclusive empirical evidence.

There is medical evidence, primarily from postmortem examinations, for the neuroanatomical bases for various forms of *alexia* (loss of already acquired reading ability). These have been well described by Benson (1981) and Greenblatt (1983). Basically, the findings indicate that damage to given areas of the brain results in the predictable loss of certain language, cognitive, and motor functions in particular combinations (e.g., alexia without agraphia). Such findings have led some authorities to infer that the inability to acquire reading ability must be due to similar deficits or to subtle brain damage in the language areas. Rare cases of congenital and acquired brain deficits of a specialized kind have also been diagnosed in living persons. For example, skull x-rays revealed a large undeveloped area in one part of the brain (*porencephaly*) of a dull–normal teenage nonreader who had been referred to one of the authors.

Structural abnormalities also have been discovered in the brains of some disabled readers. Half of the 20 disabled readers studied by Hier *et al.* (1978) had a larger right than left tempero–parieto–occipital region. This reversed structural pattern, however, also occurs in 10% to 12% of the general population. Only in certain vulnerable children does it interact with other factors to produce reading disability (Hier *et al.* 1978). Galaburda (1983) contended that this reverse pattern is more common in severely disabled readers, especially those with delayed speech development, than it is in the general population.

Galaburda and Kemper (1979) studied the brain of a 20-year-old accident victim who had been diagnosed as dyslexic at age 6. They found abnormalities in the ways in which the cells were arranged in the language areas of the left hemisphere. Galaburda (1983) stated that both subtle and more obvious distortions of cortical cell arrangement probably occur sometime between the sixteenth and twenty-fourth weeks of gestation. He also suggested that the right hemisphere develops more fully in the dyslexic than in the nondyslexic child.

Some form of cerebral damage or abnormality may be the cause of reading disability in some children, and the number of such children probably has increased over the years. The number of children who survive brain injury at birth or brain tissue damage during childhood from high-fever diseases such as encephalitis has increased greatly with improved medical knowledge and care. There are many varieties of brain damage, and its functional consequences can range from such observable difficulties as cerebral palsy, complete or partial paralysis, or profound mental deficiency to a lack of any discernible abnormality. It is possible, therefore, that the acquisition of language and reading ability is hampered by subclinical damage in some children who do not show any overt signs of neurological damage. Pirozzolo *et al.* (1981) reviewed some of the basic causes of cerebral dysfunction in children and their consequences.

In spite of the probability that more children than formerly may now have neurological impairments, there is little evidence that it is a major cause of reading disability. Actual injury in particular areas of the cortex occurs in only a few cases (Vernon 1971, Denckla & Rudel 1976), and cerebral lesions and firm neurological signs are not apparent in most reading-disabled pupils (Fletcher 1981).

An examination of the literature on teaching reading to brain-injured children led Reed, Rabe, and Mankinen (1970) to conclude that the criteria for diagnosing brain damage were generally inadequate. Medical verdicts on the presence or absence of brain damage or dysfunction are not always made on the firmest of grounds, and the younger the child, the more difficult it is to distinguish between damage and immaturity that will be outgrown. Follow-up studies of newborns with indications of brain damage at birth have found that a large proportion of these at-risk children are completely normal and free of symptoms by age 7 (Spreen 1982).

The typical neurological examination does not reveal much about the neurological basis of higher mental processes. Nevertheless, there are times when a child should be referred to a pediatric neurologist. Symptoms that suggest the need for such a referral include a history of difficult birth as indicated by prolonged labor, instrument delivery, marked head deformity, difficulty in starting breathing, cyanosis, difficulty sucking or swallowing, and so on; prematurity or low birth weight; poor equilibrium and general awkwardness; delayed speech development in the presence of otherwise normal mental ability; a history of convulsive seizures or lapses of consciousness; and extreme restlessness or distractibility. *Petit mal*, a mild form of epilepsy, may not be detected because the overt signs are subtle (unconsciousness is momentary and there are no convulsions).

One neurological test often mentioned in the literature is *finger localization*, the ability to detect which finger has been touched when the examinee cannot see the touching taking place. In adults, failure in finger localization is a symptom of Gerstmann's syndrome, which is thought to be indicative of neurological dysfunctioning. In children it has been found to be characteristic of disabled readers with low Performance IQs (Kinsbourne & Warrington 1966). Satz *et al.* (1978) reported that kindergarten finger-localization scores (based partly on number knowledge) were the best predictors (in their battery) of reading disability in Grades 2, 3, 4, and 5. Fletcher *et al.* (1982), however, reported that finger localization did not have any specific relationship to reading achievement.

Minimal Brain Dysfunction

Minimal brain dysfunction (MBD) is a suspected neurological problem the existence of which cannot be proven by existing medical tests. There are two main concepts of MBD: It is (1) a lesser variant of brain damage; and (2) it is a hyperkinetic syndrome in which MBD results from a genetically determined disorder rather than from any brain injury (Rutter 1982). Diagnoses of MBD are based on *soft signs*, which are physical characteristics and responses considered to be developmentally abnormal. Such soft signs include fine and gross deficiencies in motor coordination, defective or delayed speech, short attention span, poor balance, gait disturbance, inadequate muscle tone, and general awkwardness. Children with Strauss syndrome, which is thought to be indicative of MBD or brain damage, are described as being hyperactive, impulsive, distractible, emotionally very changeable, perserverative, and perceptually disordered.

Diagnoses of MBD are based on inferences using criteria that are of questionable validity. In addition to the fact that some soft signs also appear in some normally developing readers, research has not supported the use of soft signs as indicators of neurological dysfunctioning (Coles 1978). Spreen (1982), however, has argued that soft signs are of diagnostic significance.

Some clinical and school psychologists and neuropsychologists have interpreted certain kinds of performance on various psychological tests as indicating brain damage or dysfunction. Such interpretations should always be regarded as suggestive, not conclusive. Similarly, some physicians suggest that the paradoxical effect of a stimulant drug on a hyperactive child demonstrates neurological etiology; a contention not fully supported by the evidence (Coles 1978). Even when evidence pointing to neurological dysfunctioning is strong, psychological testing cannot as yet distinguish accurately between MBD and delayed and irregular neurological development.

Practitioners in the relatively recent field of neuropsychology are particularly prone to diagnose neurological dysfunctions on the basis of psychological tests. The theoretical position of many neuropsychologists appears to stem from Luria (1973, 1978). Basically, Luria believed that reading ability is dependent upon a complicated "functionalization of cooperating zones of the cerebral cortex and subcortical structures. Accordingly, a deficit in any one, or several of these zones may impede the learning and/or performance of fluent reading behavior" (Lyon 1983, p. 104).

Doehring *et al.* (1981) found quite low correlations (none exceeding .41) between 37 neuropsychological tests and reading test scores. Even lower and less significant correlations were found between their neuropsychological tests and reading-related skills. Reynolds (1982) correctly cautioned against drawing unwarranted conclusions from neuropsychological tests.

Vestibular Disorders

According to de Quiros and Schrager (1978), the automatic control of balance and posture is deficient in one form of dyslexia. Balance is dependent on sensory impressions from the vestibular canals of the inner ear and from muscles in the neck, coordinated by the cerebellum and other brain centers below the level of the cerebral cortex. When the automatic-reflex control of balance is deficient, eye movements are also affected, and reading activities are disrupted. They stated that the requirement of conscious effort for postural control and balance puts an added burden on the cerebral cortex and interferes with its efficiency in processing language and thought.

Frank and Levinson (1975–1976) used a test of "blurring speed" to diagnose a condition they labeled "dysmetric dyslexia and dyspraxia." This condition is indicated when moving targets against a fixed background are seen as blurring at a comparatively low speed; they regarded it as an indicator of cerebellar–vestibular dysfunction. Frank and Levinson reported finding this condition in 97% of 250 consecutively referred cases of dyslexia. In a later paper (1976), however, they reported that the condition tends to be outgrown during preadolescence and that some "dysmetric dyslexia" cases are good readers; this they regarded as showing successful compensation for a defect. They have also reported (1977) some success in treating the condition with anti-motion-sickness medication. Their choice of terminology is unfortunate, and they have not yet issued detailed statistical data on their findings. Levinson's book (1980) provided little useful information.

Ayres (1972, 1977, 1978) developed a sensory-integration theory that holds that reading and other learning disabilities are the result of the failure to integrate proprioceptive, kinesthetic, visual, and auditory information at the brain-stem level. She devised a battery of tests to identify such problems and a treatment program to remedy them through carefully controlled stimulation of the vestibular and positional awareness systems. There is no firm evidence to support Ayres's theory (Vellutino 1983) and no independent confirmation that mastering such postural skills carries over into academic skills such as reading (L. B. Silver 1975, Sieben 1977).

Until more conclusive evidence is available to support the above theories, reading clinicians should rely on neurologists for interpretation of the meaning of deviations in posture, balance, and oculomotor reflexes.

Hyperactivity

The primary symptoms of *hyperactivity* (*hyperkinesis*) are overactivity, inattention, impulsivity, and distractibility. The term can refer to a number of very different behaviors, and many of the symptoms of hyperactivity also are manifested in childhood depression or anxiety; other symptoms may be acquired as the result of the social or familial milieu in which the child is raised (Levine & Oberklaid 1980). Most hyperactivity scales have moderate reliability and validity but are subject to rater bias, often contain vague leading questions, and primarily cover negative symptoms (Prout & Ingram 1982).

Some believe that hyperactivity, or *attention-deficit disorder*,[3] as it is increasingly labeled, causes inability to sustain attention, which in turn has a negative effect on academic performance. However, hyperactivity is a relative condition—what is considered to be excessive activity by some is thought to be within the normal limits by others. Futhermore, hyperactivity is often situational. The term is best reserved for that small percentage of children whose activity levels are excessive across all settings and situations (Hartlage & Telzrow 1982).

It is likely that there is multiple causation of hyperactivity (J. Johnson 1981). Keogh (1971) proposed three main types of hyperactivity: (1) an accompaniment of cerebral dysfunction; (2) excessive activity that disrupts attention and interferes with learning, without any evidence of cerebral dysfunction; and (3) impulsiveness in decision making, similar to Kagan's impulsivity dimension in cognitive style. She proposed that the first type be treated by medication; the other two, by behavior management. A study by Keogh and Glover (1980) found differential effects of medication, behavioral modification, and cognitive control training on the behavior of hyperactive children.

Some professionals differentiate between impulsivity, which is a kind of "driven" behavior that is internally determined and does not seem to be triggered by particular stimuli, and the kind of hyperactivity and distractibility that involves excessive responses to stimuli most children can ignore. The former corresponds to Keogh's Type I and is the more serious.

There is an extensive body of literature on hyperactivity, which cannot be adequately summarized here. For a summary of the research findings and a discussion of the causes, diagnosis, and treatment of hyperactivity, refer to Schworm (1982), who noted that efforts to determine the cause of, diagnose, and prescribe treatment for hyperactivity have been fraught with inconsistencies and confusion. Sandoval (1982) has suggested ways to help hyperactive children in the classroom.

There is some indication that many children outgrow their hyperactivity by adolescence. But Hartlage and Telzrow (1982) cautioned that many hyperactive adolescents can inhibit excessive activity but continue to experience attentional difficulties. This may be one reason why, although many parents and physicians believe that the adolescents have outgrown their hyperactivity, teachers continue to report academic difficulty. It is also quite possible that the poor

---

[3] The American Psychiatric Association (1980) differentiates between attention-deficit disorders with and without hyperactivity.

academic performance reflects reading-skill deficiencies and conceptual gaps that are the result of earlier learning difficulties.

According to a meta-analysis involving 135 studies (Kavale 1982a), stimulant drugs (e.g., Ritalin, thorazine, and dextroamphetamine), which have a paradoxical effect on children, are effective treatments for hyperactivity. All of the major drugs employed in the studies were equally effective; caffeine was less effective. Possible side effects of stimulant medication include appetite loss, insomnia, irritability, depression, and headaches. Although the effects are less evident as the child reaches adulthood, there is reasonable evidence that such therapy, especially when administered in high-normal doses, moderately suppresses growth (Roche, Lipman, & Oaerall 1980). The overall effects of treatment during pubescence and early adolescence are unknown, but drug therapy does not lead to drug abuse in adolescence (O'Donnell 1982).

While agreeing that stimulant drugs are effective in reducing excessive motor activity, improving the ability to attend, and reducing aggressiveness in grossly hyperactive children, Aman (1980, 1982) and Gittelman, Klein and Feingold (1983) concluded that recent studies have failed to demonstrate drug effects on reading and other scholastic achievement. On the other hand, Kavale (1982a) found that drug-treated children showed moderate gains on the WRAT and *Gray Oral Reading Test.*

Thirty-four of our states do not have any laws or regulations dealing with the use of medication in schools. In these states, school personnel involved in drug therapy are open to a number of legal risks (Courtnage 1982). Standardized evaluation instruments for assessing the effects of pharmacotherapy are rarely used, and communication between the school and physicians is almost nonexistent (Gadow 1982, Sindelar & Meisel 1982). We believe that drug therapy should be carefully considered before it is initiated; and if it is employed, its effectiveness should be objectively measured and medical supervision is necessary to monitor undesirable side effects and adjust dosage as necessary.

Prenatal Conditions and Prematurity

Since the pioneer study by Kawi and Pasamanick (1958) that found poor prenatal conditions and prematurity to be more common among disabled readers than normal readers, many other studies of conditions before, during, and soon after birth have been made. Reading difficulties are comparatively frequent when there is a history of such problems during pregnancy as pre-eclampsia, hypertension, and bleeding; forced labor and difficult birth; and low birth weight (Smith & Wilborn 1977). It seems probable that such factors can influence reading several years later only to the extent that they damage neurological functioning (Balow, Rubin, & Rosen 1975–1976). Prematurity and other complications can be associated with deficient oxygen for the fetus or newborn and thus can induce brain damage. Questions about early development should be included when taking a case history.

Delayed and Irregular Neurological Development

There is substantial medical opinion to the effect that severe reading disability is often the result of some delay in the maturing of the central nervous system, slight enough to allow the development of normal general intelligence, but enough to slow the development of certain cerebral areas that are critical for acquiring reading ability. Developmental-lag theories have been expressed by Bender (1957), Rabinovitch (1962), and Critchley (1970), among others. Maturational lags would not necessarily all be alike, so the concept allows for more than one pattern of deficits.

Satz *et al.* (1978) interpreted the results of their longitudinal studies as showing that severe reading disabilities are related to a lag in brain maturation that differentially delays those skills that normally develop during a certain period. The skills in which disabled readers are deficient change as the children get older. Perceptual skills tend to be delayed in young reading-disabled pupils. As the disabled readers get older, their perceptual skills develop, but they are likely to show lags in linguistic and conceptual skills. Satz *et al.*'s findings have been inconsistent, but they provide some support for their theory. Their analyses lumped together all reading-disability cases; significant differences within the reading-disability group may have canceled out one another in the process of averaging.

A corollary of the developmental-lag theory is that, as children with irregular neurological development get older (around age 10 or so), some or all of the lagging areas will have developed sufficiently to allow improved reading ability. It was on this basis that the hypothesis was challenged by Rourke (1976). He concluded that "until it is shown that retarded readers, either as a group or individually, eventually 'catch up' in those abilities thought to subserve the reading function—and, for that matter until it is actually shown that they 'catch up' in reading ability itself—the weight of the evidence would appear to favor a deficit rather than a developmental lag position" (p. 136). A study by Rourke and Orr (1977) revealed that about one quarter of the poor readers showed enough improvement over 4 years to be considered possible cases of delayed maturation; the others remained poor readers, thereby giving support to the permanent-deficit hypothesis. According to Doehring *et al.* (1981), Satz *et al.*'s own data (1978) did not support the hypothesis that disabled readers overcome their developmental lag, since the majority of Satz's subjects did not show improvement by the fifth grade. More recently, Fletcher and Satz (1980) indicated that the data from their longitudinal study should not be interpreted as supporting a developmental-lag hypothesis. Less than 6% of their subjects attained age-appropriate achievement levels after 6 years of school.

If we assume that there are subtypes of reading disability, it seems probable that some disabled readers have maturational lags and others have permanent deficits. But as yet we are unable to distinguish the "late bloomers" from those with more lasting handicaps, prior to remediation.

Heredity

Some writers (Hinshelwood 1917, Hallgren 1950, Hermann 1964, Critchley 1981) believe that severe reading disability is inherited. Others suggest that there is a genetic basis for only one type of reading disability (Bannatyne 1971) or for a right-hemisphere asymmetry (H. Gordon 1983). One must distinguish, however, between familial incidence and inheritability.

There is evidence that reading disability tends to run in certain families and that it is more frequent in the male members[4] (Walker & Cole 1965, Finucci *et al.* 1976, Decker & DeFries 1980, DeFries & Decker 1982). On the other hand, other studies have failed to find significant evidence of familial reading disability (de Hirsch, Jansky, & Langford 1966; Clark 1970). These conflicting results may be due to a number of reasons, including the possibility that the incidence of such families varies in different populations, and in some populations is too small to be statistically significant.

Twin, family, and pedigree studies have demonstrated the familial nature of severe reading disability, even when environmental influences have been controlled (Finucci 1978). But, although familial incidence argues for a genetic determination, it does not provide sufficient evidence (Masland 1981, DeFries & Decker 1982). Familial cultural transmission remains a possibility (Thomas 1973, Benton 1978). The question at present remains open.

DeFries and Decker's extensive study (1982) failed to identify any single-gene model that adequately accounted for the transmission of reading disability in the 125 families they studied. Perhaps there are different kinds of reading disability, each involving a different mode of transmission (Doehring *et al.* 1981, Pennington & Smith 1983). Hier, Atkins, and Perlo (1980) did not detect any sex-chromosome aberrations in 20 reading-disabled male adults; but learning, speech, and attentional disorders were frequent in 69 subjects with known sex-chromosome aberrations. Children with particular chromosome patterns were prone to delayed speech development and later academic problems in the language arts. The results of a study by S. D. Smith *et al.* (1983) strongly suggested that a gene playing a major causal role in one form of reading disability is on chromosome 15.

Biochemical Bases

There may be inadequate brain functioning as a result of some biochemical imbalance, without any structural defect in the brain, D. E. P. Smith and Carrigan (1959) attempted to explain various disabled readers—the context reader, the word-caller, and others—in terms of an imbalance between two chemicals (acetycholine and cholinesterase) that are probably involved in the conduction of nerve impulses in the brain. Using a special battery of tests, they differentiated five subtypes and provided a physiological explanation of each. They also tried, unsuccessfully, to demonstrate a relationship of these patterns to endocrine functioning. Although their research is open to criticism and their explanations fall in the realm of unproved hypotheses, Smith and Carrigan opened up a new area for research that may yet prove fruitful (A. J. Harris 1960).

Biochemical bases for MBD also have been hypothesized. Wender (1977) cited an abnormality in monoamine metabolism (a genetically transmitted problem), and Buckley (1981) proposed that the integration of two neurochemical

---

[4] Although more boys than girls are diagnosed as having severe reading disabilities, there does not appear to be evidence for a sex-linked inheritance (Pennington & Smith 1983).

transmitters (dopamine and norepinephrine) is disrupted in MBD. According to Brase and Loh (1978), blood serotonin levels are typically lower than normal in MBD children. Further research is needed for a firm conclusion regarding the biochemistry of reading or learning disabilities (Pirozzolo & Hansch 1982).

II. LATERALITY AND LATERALIZATION

The following definitions, taken mainly from Hiscock and Kinsbourne (1982), are used in this book. However, the reader should be aware that not all authors define the terms similarly.

- *Laterality* (or lateral dominance) refers to the degree to which a receptor or effector organ on one side of the body is superior to, or used in preference to, its counterpart on the other side. Laterality is measurable and is manifested by handedness, ear advantage, and so forth.
- *Lateralization* is the state of cerebral organization in which there are qualitative and quantitative differences in functions between the two hemispheres. It is now generally agreed that lateralization refers to hemispheric specialization rather than to one hemisphere exercising control over the other (Leong 1980).
- *Cerebral dominance* implies the general mastery of one hemisphere over the other, but it is more accurate to think of each hemisphere as being dominant for certain functions. Thus, the term "hemispheric specialization" is preferable.

Lateral dominance was once widely defined as the preferred or superior functioning of one side of the body over the other. It was assumed that if the dominant hand and eye (or perhaps also the ear and/or foot) were on the same side of the body, the child had achieved hemispheric dominance or a high level of neurological organization. This definition and its assumptions are inaccurate.

Theories Regarding the Relationship of Lateralization to Reading Disability

A thorough presentation of the various viewpoints regarding the relationship of hemispheric lateralization or specialization to reading is not possible in a few pages. A number of reviews were noted in the Seventh Edition of this book on page 288; more recent reviews have been written by Leong (1980), Naylor (1980), Hiscock and Kinsbourne (1982) and Hiscock (1983). The following summaries illustrate the diverse hypotheses.

Dearborn (1933) emphasized a motor conflict when he indicated that we tend to pivot at the elbow and find it easier to move outward from the middle of the body than across its midline. Dearborn believed that when a person was not definitely right- or left-sided, competing motor tendencies developed. These, in turn, produced inconsistent eye movements and confused visual perception, which resulted in reading difficulties.

Orton (1937) assumed that sensory impulses were received simultaneously by both hemispheres and that each received a memory trace (engram) that was the mirror image of the other. If one hemisphere was clearly dominant, the memory trace in the nondominant hemisphere would be suppressed, and normal perception would result. But if dominance was incomplete, control could alternate between the two hemispheres and would result in shifting or inconsistent perception and therefore many reversal errors. Orton considered laterality to reflect hemispheric dominance and stated that poorly established hand preference would accompany poor reading.

Zangwill (1962) theorized that children who lacked strong and consistent lateral dominance may be particularly vulnerable to stress. Somewhat similarly, Leong (1980) noted that poorly established laterality patterns in combination with other factors may make the pupil more vulnerable to learning disorders.

Witelson (1977) claimed that disabled readers have normal left-hemisphere linguistic functions but that spatial functions (normally right-hemisphere functions) are represented in both hemispheres. She argued that this bilateral representation of spatial functions interfered with the left hemisphere's ability to carry out its language functions. She also thought that it caused disabled readers to read with a predominately spatial–holistic strategy and to neglect a phonetic–sequential strategy.

Yeni-Komshian, Isenberg, and Goldberg (1975) concluded that reading disability was related to a right-hemisphere processing dysfunction or to impaired transmission of information from the right to the left hemisphere.

Hynd and Obrzut (1981) stated that differences between reading-disabled and good readers on laterality tests were caused by the attentional deficits of the disabled readers. According to Kershner (1983), learning disability appears to involve reduced left-hemisphere processing capacity, severe right-hemisphere-directed attentional disorders, and the inability to coordinate the simultaneous processing of linguistic information between the hemispheres.

Hiscock and Kinsbourne (1982) identified four classes of hemispheric-related models of reading disability:

1. *Translocation models* presuppose that an otherwise normal processor may perform inadequately if it is located in the wrong hemisphere (e.g., language functions being centered in the right rather than left hemisphere), if it must share its territory with another processor (e.g., Witelson's theory), or if it is spread too thinly across the cortex.

2. *Unilateral-deficit models* suggest that reading disability is due to a deficit in one hemisphere. Right-hemisphere deficit theories hold that the left hemisphere participates sufficiently in information processing, but that the right hemisphere is deficient (Keefe & Swinney 1979). Such theories, however, have not received much research support (Pirozzolo & Rayner 1979).

3. *Callosal models* hold that there is a deficit in the *corpus callosum*, resulting in too little or too much information being transferred between the hemispheres, distortion of information, or transmission of information to the wrong region in the opposite hemisphere. Some authors believe that since bilateral

integration is mainly subserved by the *corpus callosum*, which is a relatively late maturing structure, problems may arise when its growth is delayed (Bakker 1982).

4. *Output competition models* suggest a conflict between the hemispheres. They are exemplified by Orton's theory of incomplete dominance.

To the above may be added theories involving maturational lag in hemispheric development.

Methods of Determining Cerebral Lateralization

Both invasive and noninvasive procedures have been used to study brain lateralization.

Invasive Methods

Early direct methods involved noting the particular behavioral changes that followed brain damage from a stroke or wound and comparing them with autopsy findings. Such medical research helped identify the brain areas in which language, sensations, or movements are located. But such studies dealt with centers of destruction and not centers of function.

Penfield and Roberts (1959) developed the technique of opening the skull and electrically stimulating tiny areas of the cerebral surface to determine the possible effects of surgical removal of these areas. Their results agreed with those of the Wada test (see below) in showing that the left hemisphere is usually dominant for language regardless of the individual's handedness.

In the 1960s a few patients with severe intractable epilepsy were treated by severing the nerve fibers that connect the two hemispheres (commissurotomy), thus in effect producing "two brains." Studies of these split-brain patients (Gazzaniga & Sperry 1967; Sperry, Gazzaniga, & Bogen 1969; Searleman 1977) revealed that, usually, (1) receptive and expressive language, analytic reasoning, and sequential processing are left-hemisphere functions; (2) simultaneous perception of visual forms, such as faces or geometric figures, are functions of the right hemisphere; and (3) the right hemisphere is not wholly nonverbal, but it cannot produce connected speech once speech has been firmly lateralized in the left hemisphere (see Fig. 9.2). While noting that information from split-brain studies has provided valuable information (the data are largely in accord with that of studies involving normal subjects), Beaumont (1982c) warned that there are considerable problems of interpretation of the data. For example, there are extensive data on only seven subjects, of whom two have provided most of the data from which conclusions were drawn.

The Wada test (Wada & Rasmussen 1960) involves injecting sodium amytal into the carotid artery that conveys blood from the aorta to the cerebral hemisphere on the same side of the body. If the injection produces a temporary aphasia, loss of speech or reading ability, that hemisphere is specialized for language functions; if not, the language functions are assumed to be centered in the other hemisphere. Wada test results have shown that language is centered in the left hemisphere in over 95% of right-handers and about 70% of all others.

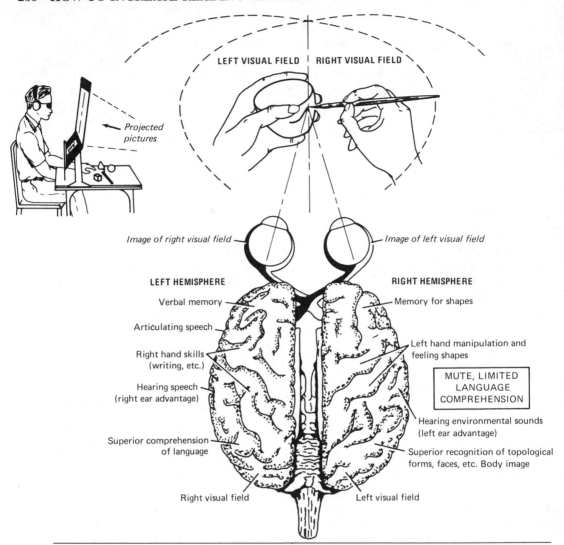

Figure 9.2. Hemispheric functions revealed by psychological tests of commissurotomy patients, carried out with orientation controlled as shown on the left. From C. Trevarthen, Development of the cerebral mechanism for language, in U. Kirk (Ed.), *Neuropsychology of language, reading, and spelling* (New York: Academic Press, 1983). Used with permission of the author and publisher.

In only about 2% to 3% of the general population is language centered in the right hemisphere or in both hemispheres (Rasmussen & Milner 1975).

Hiscock and Kinsbourne (1982) warned, however, that findings based on pathology, temporary incapacitation of most of one hemisphere (Wada test), electrical stimulation of cortical regions, and so forth are not generalizable. Such invasive techniques are not used to study normal brains.

Noninvasive Methods

Noninvasive, or indirect, techniques are commonly used to study brain functioning and determine laterality from which cerebral specialization is inferred.

Because each hemisphere controls motor functions and sensations on the opposite side of the body, preference or superiority of the hand, eye, ear, and foot has been assumed to indicate that the hemisphere on the opposite side is dominant. What is often further assumed is that deviations from the left-hemisphere–right-side pattern are abnormal.

Handedness. Handedness is usually tested by asking the child to perform certain tasks (e.g., use a toy hammer) or by observing which hand is used more commonly. The more frequently used hand is said to be the preferred, or dominant, hand. Many studies use only one measure, or a few brief measures, of handedness. A more reliable estimate can be made with tests such as those in the *Harris Tests of Lateral Dominance*, which include measures of knowledge of left and right, hand preferences, simultaneous writing with both hands, and speed and coordination in writing, tapping and dealing cards, as well as tests of eye and foot dominance.

Studies of general school populations do not indicate a significant relationship between handedness and reading achievement (Hiscock 1983), while studies based on clinic populations have tended to show a significantly large number of children with mixed handedness, often accompanied by directional confusion (A. J. Harris 1957, Zangwill 1962, Heacaen & de Ajuriaguerra 1964, Ingram 1969). *Mixed handedness*, or *mixed hand dominance*, refers to a lack of consistent preference for either hand. The term includes ambidexterity and individuals with a slight preference for one hand.

An explanation sometimes offered as a cause of reading disability is the changing of a child's handedness from left to right by the use of coercion, punishment, or ridicule. Supposedly, the way in which the change was made and not the fact of changed handedness produced an emotional block that disrupted learning. There is little data to confirm this hypothesis.

Eyedness. Whereas each hand is controlled by the hemisphere on the opposite side, each eye is connected to both hemispheres (see Fig. 9.3). Because each eye sends signals to both hemispheres, eye-preference tests (e.g., sighting a gun, looking through a cone, acuity tests, retinal-rivalry tests, and tests of the controlling eye) are of no use in determining brain lateralization. This fact of anatomy also questions the practice of patching one eye to establish "eye dominance" on the same side of the body as the preferred hand.

Visual Half-Fields. It is possible to present visual information to either the right or left hemisphere. The left half of the visual field of each eye is connected to the visual area in the right hemisphere; the right half-fields with the left hemisphere (see Fig. 9.3). In the *visual half-field* (VHF) technique, a stimulus can be directed to one hemisphere by arranging things so that the simulus ap-

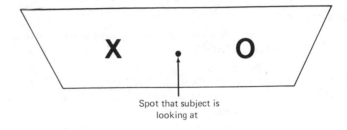

Spot that subject is
looking at

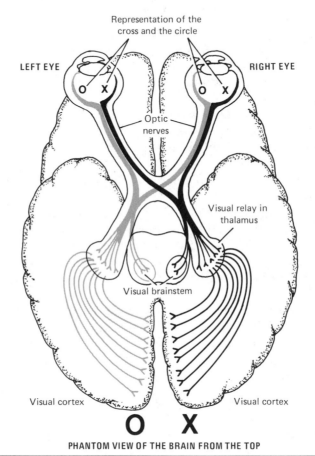

Representation of the
cross and the circle

LEFT EYE   RIGHT EYE

O   X   O   X

Optic
nerves

Visual relay in
thalamus

Visual brainstem

Visual cortex   Visual cortex

O X

PHANTOM VIEW OF THE BRAIN FROM THE TOP

Figure 9.3. The visual pathway of man. Images from the right half of the visual field are focused on the left side of each retina. The information from these two left sides travels to the left hemisphere of the brain via a relay in the thalamus. Similarly, images from the left half of the visual field are processed in the right cerebral cortex. The retina also sends axons into the visual area of the brainstem. Adapted from "The Neurophysiology of Binocular Vision" by J. D. Pettigrew. Copyright © 1972 by Scientific American, Inc. All rights reserved.

pears in only the left or right visual field. This is done by having the subject fix his gaze on a dot on the screen. Visual stimuli are then flashed very quickly to the left or right of the fixation point. Visual stimuli to the left of the point of fixation (left visual field) are transmitted via both eyes to the visual cortex of the right hemisphere. Those to the right of fixation go to the left hemisphere (Beaumont 1982b). This allows comparison of the processing of the stimuli by the hemispheres. In VHF studies, only about 70% of the individuals who have a left-hemisphere dominance for language on the basis of the Wada test exhibit a right VHF advantage (Cohen 1982).

Results of VHF studies are somewhat inconsistent, but they generally indicate that words are perceived better in the right VHF (left hemisphere); the results are less clear for other verbal stimuli such as letters. With nonverbal stimuli, only faces yield a consistent left VHF superiority; when geometric forms, etc., are used, the evidence is less certain (Beaumont 1982a).

There are many methodological problems in arranging for presentation of the stimuli at a specific locus in one of the visual fields, and there are problems interpreting the data because of the variety of theories as to what happens after the information is received by the visual cortex (Beaumont 1982a). Hiscock and Kinsbourne (1982) suggested that performance on VHF measures, as well as other measures of laterality, can be influenced by attentional biases. And Leong (1980) indicated that hemispheric differences in VHF studies may reflect differences in the processing strategies adopted by the subjects. Similarly, Young and Ellis (1981) cautioned that differences in hemispheric asymmetry between good and poor readers may reflect differences in the ways in which the task was approached and accomplished rather than differences in cerebral organization of function. L. Henderson (1982) stated that the mechanisms relating hemispheric specialization and VHF effects are not well understood. The low reliability (typically .50 to .65) of VHF and dichotic listening tests limits the faith one can place in their use to determine lateralized functions (Reynolds 1982). The relationship of lateralization as inferred from VHF studies to reading disability is inconclusive.

Crossed Eye–Hand Dominance.   *Crossed dominance* refers to the preferred eye and preferred hand being on opposite sides of the body. Such a finding is thought by some (e.g., Gaddes 1980) to indicate incomplete cerebral lateralization that is related to reading disability; but it is not. Many normal readers show mixed eye–hand dominance, since about one third of the population is left-eyed and about 90% are right-handed (Hiscock & Kinsbourne 1982). It is no surprise, therefore, that most studies have not found a significant relationship between crossed eye–hand dominance and reading disability.

Ear Advantage.   As shown in Figure 9.4, not all of the auditory pathways to the brain are crossed, but the most powerful auditory input goes to the opposite hemisphere (Teyler 1975). Ear advantage is measured by the *dichotic listening technique* in which different simuli are presented simultaneously to each ear through stereophonic earphones. The stimuli may be verbal (e.g., phonemes, words) or nonverbal (e.g., musical notes, two-note melodies). Scoring can be

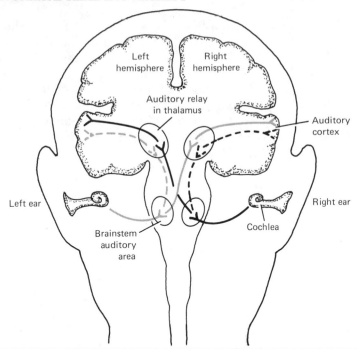

Figure 9.4. Auditory pathways in the brain. All of these pathways are not crossed (notice dashed lines), but the most powerful auditory input goes to the opposite hemisphere, that is, right ear to left hemisphere. Adapted from "The Asymmetry of the Human Brain" by D. Kimura. Copyright © 1973 by Scientific American, Inc. All rights reserved. Taken from T. Teyler, *A primer of psychobiology: brain and behavior* (San Francisco: W. H. Freeman, 1975). Used by permission of the author and publisher.

based on which stimuli are heard first, the completeness and accuracy of reporting of the stimuli presented to each ear, and so forth. The ear with the higher score (ear advantage) is assumed to indicate that the opposite hemisphere is dominant for the class of stimuli used. In general, dichotic listening studies have shown a right-ear advantage and left-hemisphere lateralization for verbal material and left-ear advantage for nonverbal stimuli.

Among the perplexing things about the results of dichotic listening tests is that only 65% to 85% of the subjects show a left-hemisphere lateralization for verbal stimuli (Cohen 1982) compared to the 90–98% revealed by other measures. There are also a number of inconsistencies among the results of the various studies (Satz 1976). For example, whereas Dutch children do not show a right-ear advantage (REA) for verbal stimuli until age 9, many preschool American children do (Piazza 1977). The reliability of the dichotic listening technique has been questioned by Kinsbourne and Hiscock (1978), and there have been methodological problems with dichotic listening studies (Leong 1980, Naylor 1980). Reading-disabled students often do not show the usual REA effect (Cummins & Das 1977, Pirozzolo & Hansch 1982), but ear asymmetry, as measured by a dichotic REA, did not differentiate between disabled and good readers in a study by Obrzut (1979).

Bakker (1973, 1982) and his associates (Bakker, Teunisson, & Bosch 1976) speculated that the ear asymmetry–reading ability relationship changes with the level of reading ability. They thought that not having a dominant hemisphere was an advantage in the initial stage of reading acquisition. The right hemisphere could handle the perceptual processes needed for word recognition. At later stages of reading, when linguistic processing becomes more important, left-hemisphere (REA) lateralization for language functions is desirable. Bakker's theory implies a change of hemisphere tied to reading strategies during the development of reading ability.[5] Although it is plausible that reading draws differentially on the specialized skills of each hemisphere at different stages of reading proficiency, there is no satisfactory empirical basis for such a claim (Hiscock & Kinsbourne 1982).

Footedness. At times foot preference is used as a measure of laterality. The rationale for determining footedness is the same as for handedness. But, unlike handedness, foot preference is not likely to be subject to use or change by cultural pressures. The limited available findings on footedness approximate those for handedness; and the correlation between footedness and handedness is positive (Hiscock & Kinsbourne 1982).

Electroencephalography

By placing electrodes on various parts of the scalp, the electrical activity of the brain nearest these points can be measured. The resulting electrical bursts and rhythmic waves are amplified and traced on moving graph paper, resulting in an *electroencephalogram* (EEG), as shown in Figure 9.5. Four types of EEG findings indicate abnormality: (1) positive spikes; (2) excessive occipital slow waves; (3) temporal-lobe sharp waves or spikes; and (4) generalized or diffuse abnormality (Hughes 1982). According to Corning, Steffy, and Chaprin (1982), diffuse EEG slow frequency reflects maturational lag.

There is a difference of opinion regarding the usefulness of an EEG in determining hemispheric specialization. For instance, Hughes (1982) stated that some studies had indicated its usefulness, but Doehring *et al.* (1981) wrote that EEG evidence regarding hemispheric specialization was inconclusive.

A specific association between EEG findings and reading or learning disabilities has not been equivocally demonstrated (Benton 1975). The EEG results of learning-disabled children are usually within normal limits (Boyle 1982).

It is difficult to put much faith in EEG findings when the incidence of positive findings (supposedly indicating abnormality) is 20% to 30% in normally

---

[5] Bakker (1982) also postulated two hemispheric-related etiologies of reading disability. In the L-type, the basic problem is that the language-mediating left hemisphere is overdeveloped. The P-type of disabled reader is overly sensitive to the perceptual aspects of script and continues to rely on reading strategies generated by the right hemisphere.

achieving children (Hughes 1971). An EEG should be part of a reading diagnosis only when specifically requested by a neurologist.

Recent modifications of the EEG have employed computers to analyze the results. Duffy *et al.* (1980a, b) used a "brain electrical activity mapping" (BEAM) technique that achieved 80% to 90% accuracy in distinguishing normal from dyslexic children. Hanley and Sklar (1976) used another computerized EEG procedure for which they reported 76% accuracy in classifying an unselected group.

Neurometrics is a quantitative method that uses an EEG and evoked potentials in a standard test intended to provide information about brain functions, especially in patients with cognitive dysfunctions. The scores of the child being diagnosed are compared against norms based on normally functioning individuals (Roy 1981).

Other Recent Techniques for Studying the Brain

Evoked responses involve taking EEG recordings while the person tested is exposed to auditory or visual stimuli.[6] Evoked-response studies of disabled readers have indicated abnormal readings in the left angular gyrus (the cerebral cortex area usually involved when adults lose the ability to read as a result of brain injury or stroke) in some cases. However, there are discrepancies in the reported findings (Pirozzolo & Hansch 1982), and the brain mechanisms responsible for evoked responses are not yet well understood (Mirsky 1978). There is a paucity of knowledge concerning the neurophysiological and cognitive concomitants of evoked potentials (Rugg 1982).

Computer-assisted tomography (CAT scan) employs multiple x-ray beams and computer processing of the data to produce three-dimensional images of the body (Fincher 1984). The relative size of certain areas in the left and right hemispheres differs in some disabled readers from what is typical of normal readers (Downing & Leong 1982, Le May 1981, Pirozzolo & Hansch 1982). On the other hand, Hiscock and Kinsbourne (1982) stated that CAT scans provide information about anatomy but not about brain functioning, and there is no reason to expect that substantial numbers of disabled readers have gross abnormalities of brain structure.

Three other recently developed techniques are positron emission tomography, which records changes in the body's biochemistry; nuclear magnetic resonance spectroscopy (Fincher 1984); and cerebral arteriography (Lassen, Ingvar, & Skinkøj 1978). Although these techniques have not yet been used with disabled readers, they may contribute useful information about reading disability in the future.

Other Measures of Laterality

Silver and Hagin (1982) claimed that the arm-extension test can be used to determine if hemispheric dominance has been established. The arm-extension procedure suffers from the same limitations as does handedness as a measure of lateralization.

---

[6] See Evans *et al.* (1982) or Rugg (1982) for a description of the nature and methodology of evoked responses.

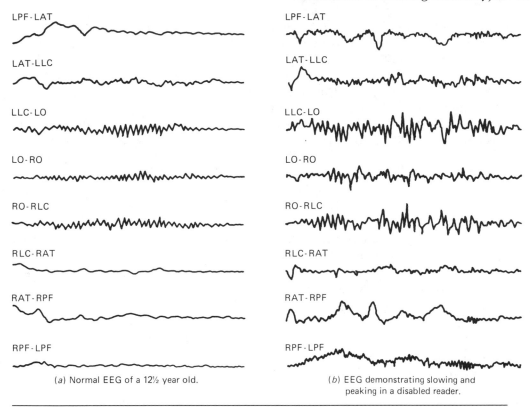

LPF-LAT

LAT-LLC

LLC-LO

LO-RO

RO-RLC

RLC-RAT

RAT-RPF

RPF-LPF

LPF-LAT

LAT-LLC

LLC-LO

LO-RO

RO-RLC

RLC-RAT

RAT-RPF

RPF-LPF

(a) Normal EEG of a 12½ year old.

(b) EEG demonstrating slowing and peaking in a disabled reader.

Figure 9.5. Examples of normal and abnormal EEGs. From H. Goldberg, G. Schiffman, and M. Bender, *Dyslexia: interdisciplinary approaches to reading* (New York: Grune & Stratton, 1983). Reproduced by permission of the authors and publisher.

Hiscock and Kinsbourne (1982) briefly described a dual-task measure of functional lateralization that requires the child to perform motor tasks with either the right or left hand while reading. Little information concerning the efficacy of their procedure is available.

Laterality, Cerebral Lateralization, and Reading Disability

Various measures of laterality have been used in attempts to relate hemispheric lateralization or dominance to reading disability. According to one theory, a person who does not show a right hand (ear, foot, eye) preference or superiority is likely to be a disabled reader. The notion is that any deviation from right-sidedness indicates that some form of damage or dysfunction in the left hemisphere resulted in language functions being centered in the right hemisphere, which is not as well suited as the left hemisphere for performing language functions.

There are a number of problems with the theory, not the least of which is the fact that language functions are centered in the left hemisphere in approximately 95% of right-handers and 70% of left-handers. Non-right-handers are considered at risk for cognitive deficits for a number of reasons, but the percentage of left-handers who are disabled readers is not significantly greater than for right-handers (Clark 1979, Hiscock 1983). Knowledge of handedness will not improve our ability to predict language lateralization until we are able to distinguish between those left-handers who have left-lateralized speech and those who do not (Hiscock & Kinsbourne 1982).

The observation that left-handed persons had more immune disorders led Geschwind (1983) to speculate that both the immune disorder and reading disabilty are the result of a hormonal imbalance. He suggested that an elevated quantity of testosterone in the developing fetal brain slows the growth of the left hemisphere and also accounts for the higher incidence of reading disability in males.

VHF and dichotic listening techniques are also employed in inferring hemispheric specialization. It is hypothesized that disabled readers will demonstrate less than normal language lateralization in the left hemisphere as indicated by a smaller left VHF or right-ear advantage. But such differences have not been consistently found between disabled readers and children making normal progress in reading (Doehring *et al.* 1981).

Mixed handedness is believed by some to indicate a lack of cerebral dominance, neurological lag, or incomplete neurological organization. But even though mixed handedness is found frequently among disabled readers, many individuals who do not show a consistent hand preference or superiority make normal progress in reading.

Most recent reviewers have noted the inconclusive findings regarding the relationship of cerebral lateralization and reading disability, and have questioned the role of lateralization as an important factor in reading or learning disabilities. Hiscock and Kinsbourne (1982) believed that even when students are classified into more homogeneous subgroups, it is as yet unclear how the characteristics of any subgroup may be related to cerebral lateralization. It is also possible that the degree of reading disability may be a variable contributing to the inconclusive findings. For example, Garren (1980) found that a significant relationship between reading disability and lateralization did not occur unless the subjects were 18 months or more below their expected reading level.

Gender, Reading Disability, and Cerebral Lateralization

It has been hypothesized by some that differences in cerebral lateralization may account for the larger number of males who are reading disabled. According to Bakker, Teunissen, and Bosch (1976), girls pass through the successive laterality–reading stages faster than boys. As a consequence, boys run the risk of getting stuck in the early reading strategies generated by the right hemisphere.

Hier (1979) stated that sex differences in hemispheric specialization for verbal and spatial processing underlie the prevalence of reading disability in boys. Males show a strong left-hemisphere specialization for verbal processing, whereas females show greater bihemispheric participation in both verbal and spatial processing.

According to Masland (1981), certain male characteristics might predispose them more than females to reading disability: (1) less well developed left-hemisphere language functions; (2) greater specialization of spatial skills in the right hemisphere; (3) a lesser degree of left-hemisphere dominance; and (4) an earlier lateralization of functions but, in general, a slower maturation of them.

Remedial Procedures Based on Lateral Dominance

Delacato (1959, 1963, 1966) theorized that in some children poor intellectual and educational development resulted from a failure to achieve neurological integration at a subcortical level of the brain. For such children he advocated a treatment program that emphasized such activities as sleeping in a particular position and creeping and crawling. For children who had achieved subcortical integration, he attributed reading disability to a lack of clear and consistent cerebral dominance, shown usually by crossed eye–hand dominance. For them he recommended treatment procedures to compel the child to rely on the eye on the same side as the dominant hand by occluding the other eye, eliminating music, etc. Apart from the fact that his theoretical basis is open to serious question, independent research evidence does not support the Doman–Delacato treatment (Yarborough 1964, Anderson 1965, Robbins 1966, Kohlmorgen 1971). In fact, "without exception, the empirical studies cited by Delacato as a 'scientific appraisal' of his theories of neurological organization are shown to be of dubious value" (Glass & Robbins 1967). Eight major medical and health organizations issued a joint report that described the theory underlying the approach as being without merit and charged Delacato and Doman with making undocumented claims of cures (*New York Times* 1968). Reading specialists can safely ignore the Delacato–Doman approach.

Van den Honert (1977) reported a procedure based on the assumption that the disabled reader's left hemisphere has insufficient dominance over the right hemisphere. Using stereophonic earphones, she directed reading instruction to the right ear (left hemisphere) and popular music to the left ear in order to keep the right hemisphere busy and prevent it from interfering with the left hemisphere's control of reading. She used a blackened eyeglass to block out the vision of the left eye. She reported a great improvement in her pupil's rate of learning to read, although the instructional procedure (intensive phonics) was the same as before. In response to an inquiry from the senior author, van den Honert wrote: "If I use either the glasses alone or the auditory setup alone, nothing much happens. It is only when I do both over a period of time that I begin to get dramatic results." Nothing has appeared in the literature concerning this technique since 1977, to the best of our knowledge. The visual part of the procedure does not make theoretical sense. Nevertheless, this procedure deserves to be researched.

Directional Confusion

There is evidence to support a relationship between confused knowledge of left and right and reading disability, at least in young children (A. J. Harris 1957,

Benton 1959, Belmont & Birch 1965) or in specific subtypes of reading disability (Mattis 1978). Inability to differentiate right and left should not be regarded as clinically significant before age 8, however (Clark 1979). For knowledge of left and right, the brief tests of the *Harris Tests of Lateral Dominance* are sufficient for young children; for older pupils, the more comprehensive tests developed by Benton (1959) are more satisfactory. Directional confusion is most likely to occur in children with mixed handedness as measured by the *Harris* tests.

When children enter school, directional confusion is typically shown by reversals in reading but also may appear in spelling, writing, or in producing arabic numbers. Some directional confusion accompanied by reversal tendencies is so common among preschool children, especially with letters such as *b* and *d*, that it has to be considered a normal characteristic up to age 6 or 7. It is only when such confusion persists after considerable instruction in the left-to-right direction in reading and writing that it requires careful consideration.

The cause of directional confusion is unknown. At times a physiological basis for its is inferred from a history of difficult birth, delayed or irregular maturation, or a familial growth pattern characterized by a delay in establishing handedness, a strong reversal tendency, some speech difficulty, and early difficulty in learning to read.

III. SENSORY DEFECTS

Kinds of Visual Defects

There are many different kinds if visual defects, some of which seem to be more important than others in the causation of reading difficulties.

The three defects best known to the layman are nearsightedness (myopia), farsightedness (hypermetropia), and astigmatism. All are usually caused by structural deviations from the normal shape of the eye. The myopic eye is too long from front to back, and so light focuses in front of the retina and tends to produce a blurred impression. The farsignted eye is too short from front to back; light coming from a source near the eye focuses behind the retina. It is possible for the moderately farsighted person to get near objects into clear focus, but long-continued attention to near objects, as in reading, tends to produce eyestrain with accompanying fatigue and headaches. Astigmatism is usually the result of uneven curvature of the front part of the eye so that light rays coming into the eye are not evenly distributed over the retina; the results are blurred or distorted images and eyestrain. All three conditions can be corrected with prescription lenses.

The eyes have to make four major adjustments for clear vision. There is an automatic reflex adjustment of the size of the pupillary opening to the amount of illumination (*pupillary reflex*); this permits a larger amount of light to enter in dim light and protects the eye against the dazzling effect of bright illumination. Second, there is an automatic reflex adjustment of the shape of the lens to the distance of the object being looked at; this *accommodation reflex* acts like the adjustment for distance in a camera. Third, there is an automatic reflex control of the degree to which the eyes turn in so that both focus on the same spot (the *convergence reflex*); the eyes are almost parallel when viewing an object more than 10 feet away but turn in noticeably when aimed at a target a foot away. Fourth, the eyes must be aimed so that the objects we wish to see most clearly are in the center of the visual field, where acuity is greatest. This requires smooth, continuous movement when following a moving object, and quick, jerky movements (*saccadic movements*) with intervening pauses (*fixations*) when observing stationary objects. These movements are not easily seen in casual observation but are easily noted in eye-movement photography or when making special observations of eye movement.

Some defects cannot be detected when each eye is tested separately but do appear when the eyes are used together. For normal binocular vision, both eyes must be focused accurately on the same target. This allows a fusion in the brain of the slightly different images from two eyes. Fusion difficulty is often the result of paralysis of an eye muscle. When there is no fusion, the person sometimes see double (as when under the influence of alcohol), but more commonly the image from one eye is ignored or suppressed. Continued suppression of the vision of one eye for a period of years may eventually produce loss of vision in that eye, and the person will have to depend completely on the preferred eye. It is therefore very important to detect cases of visual suppression early.

Partial or imperfect fusion is more apt to interfere with clear vision than a complete absence of fusion. When fusion is incomplete, a blurred image is likely, even though the person may see clearly with either eye separately. Some people can fuse the images but do it slowly. This may not be a handicap in the ordinary use of the eyes but may interfere with clear vision when rapid, precise focusing is needed, as in reading (Brod & Hamilton 1973). There has been no research follow-up on the finding by Witty and Kopel (1936) that slow visual fusion was present in 29% of 100 poor readers and in only 1% of the control group of normal readers.

Poor fusion is often associated with a lack of proper balance among the six pairs of muscles that turn the eyeballs. When the lack of balance is extreme, the condition is called *strabismus* (*cross-eyed* or *walleyed*). The person with strabismus usually ignores one eye completely and so has no interference with the vision of the other eye. Milder cases of poor muscle balance (*heterophoria*) occur in which one eye turns in too much (*esophoria*), turns out (*exophoria*), or focuses a little higher than the other (*hyperphoria*). Most people with these defects are able to obtain proper fusion when the eyes are not tired but get blurred vision after extended reading or other close and exacting visual work. When the eyes are tired, they may get blurred images, may see a combination of the things each eye is looking at, or may see objects in reverse order. There also may be a complete suppression of one eye.

Color blindness of the usual type, which involves difficulty or inability in distinguishing reds from greens, is found in 4% to 8% of boys and is rare in girls. There is no evidence to indicate that it has any effect on reading ability. Weakness in the ability to perceive depth (*astereopsis*) has been mentioned as possibly being involved in reading-disability cases; it is related to poor fusion. *Aniseikonia*, a condition in which one eye forms a larger image of the object than the other eye, has been found to cause visual disturbances in some individuals; it would seem to be a reasonable cause for poor fusion is some cases.

As yet little is known about the possible importance for reading of the speed and precision with which the pupillary, accommodation, and convergence reflexes adapt the eyes to new targets or to a changing target. Vision tests currently in use do not attempt to measure these factors.

The Significance of Visual Defects for Reading[7]

Although many studies have investigated the relationship of visual defects to reading ability, an exact statement on the degree to which poor reading is caused by poor vision cannot yet be made. Studies can be found to support or deny (1) the contention that a particular visual defect is more prevalent in disabled readers than in a random group; and (2) the hypothesis that remediation of a particular visual dysfunction has a positive effect on reading achievement (Suchoff 1981).

There is general agreement that myopia and astigmatism are not more prevalent in disabled readers than in good readers; myopia actually occurs more frequently in good readers. Hyperopia appears to be more frequent in poor readers. Low to moderate astigmatism does not cause sufficiently blurred vision to interfere with reading; high amounts of astigmatism may. Total lack of binocular vision, as evidenced by strabismus, does not appear to be characteristic of reading disability. In general, research has demonstrated few one-to-one relationships between particular visual conditions and reading (Suchoff 1981). Refractive errors (near- and farsightedness, astigmatism) are correctible with lenses; rarely are they responsible for impaired reading (W. Smith 1984).

There are three possible reasons for the inconclusive findings. First, it is difficult to compare findings because the subjects and tests employed in the studies frequently are not comparable. Second, and more fundamentally, people vary in their ability to adapt to handicaps. For instance, two people can have the same moderate degree of exophoria, but the condition may not cause a problem for the person who is able to compensate. Third, poor vision is only one of the handicaps that may interfere with reading. If poor vision is the only handicap, the child may be able to become a good reader in spite of it; if he has several additional handicaps, the combined effects may be too much for him.

There is a tendency for ophthalmologists to minimize the significance of visual problems in the causation of reading disability (e.g., Martin 1971; Goldberg, Shiffman, & Bender 1983; Werner 1984). Optometrists, on the other hand, tend to stress the importance of binocular vision, accommodation, convergence, and ocular motility (e.g., Flax 1970, Allen 1977, W. Smith 1984). Optometrists schooled in developmental vision emphasize the value of *orthoptic training*

[7] Research on this topic is too extensive to review here. Those interested may wish to refer to the annotated bibliography by Weintraub and Cowan (1982, pp. 13–26), with particular attention to the early summaries by H. M. Robinson (1946), Cleland (1953), and Rosen (1965). More recent summaries have been written by Hartlage (1976) and Suchoff (1981).

(e.g., Ludlam 1981, Solan 1981, W. Smith 1984), the idea being that specialized visual exercises will improve visual and perceptual abilities, thereby making it easier to learn to read. Keogh (1974), who made a comprehensive review of the relevant literature, concluded that inadequacies of research methodology precluded any conclusive finding regarding the value of orthoptic training for developing school readiness and for the remediation of learning disabilities. Little has appeared in the last decade to alter this conclusion.

At least part of this professional difference of opinion reflects differences in the way vision is defined and in the education of each type of visual specialist. Nevertheless, their disagreement makes it difficult to know to whom a child with suspected visual problems should be referred.

The truth regarding the relationship of visual defects and reading probably lies somewhere between two extreme points of view—absolutely no relationship versus a major cause. The answer awaits future research that is conceived and conducted better than in the past. For the present, it seems reasonable to conclude that visual defects may contribute to the reading problems of some children. But even if definitive evidence indicated that there was no relationship between vision and reading, it would still be prudent to suggest that teachers should be alert to possible signs of visual problems and that children should be screened and referred to visual specialists when necessary.

The Detection of Visual Defects

Schools commonly give simple visual screening tests to select children whose vision requires careful professional examination. Usually this is done with the Snellen Chart or some similar test. The child stands 20 feet from the chart and tries to name letters of different sizes, with one eye covered. Thus the Snellen measures monocular acuity at far point. In addition to the fact that reading is normally done at 12 to 18 inches, using both eyes, the Snellen has other drawbacks: (1) It is possible for a child to memorize the chart and thus simulate adequate distance vision; (2) it fails to detect moderate degrees of farsightedness or astigmatism; and (3) it fails completely to detect even severe cases of poor fusion and eye-muscle imbalance. Eames (1942) reported that Snellen tests had suggested the presence of defective vision in only 48 of 100 children who had visual defects as determined by an ophthalmological examination.

Visual screening tests that include measures of acuity for both near and distance vision, eye-muscle balance, and binocular coordination are available. These tests, which use stereoscopic instruments, include the *Massachussetts Vision Test* (Welch–Allyn, American Optical, Keystone), *Keystone Visual Survey Tests* (Keystone), *School Vision Tester* (Baush & Lomb), *Sight Screener* (American Optical) and *Titmus School Vision Tester* (Titmus). The *Modififed Telebinocular Technique*, which does not call for specialized training, supposedly provides superior results (Schubert & Walton 1980), but independent verification has not been made of their claim.

Jobe (1976) explained why the results of screening tests may not agree with the findings of vision specialists. Ophthalmologists, whose background is medical, tend to emphasize far-point measurements and structural eye defects. Optometrists tend to put greater emphasis on near-point measurements and disorders of function and coordination. Some tests depend on the subjective judgment of the examiner. The lack of agreement in findings also may result from errors in administering and scoring the screening tests or from inherent differences between stereoscopic and clinical testing procedures. Jobe recommended that if a school vision screening program is to be set up, a committee including optometrists, ophthalmologists, and parents should settle in advance the questions of what procedures to use, how to train the examiners, and how to interpret the results in order to make appropriate referrals.

Teachers should always be alert to signs of visual discomfort in the children's appearance or behavior. Among the things to look for are bloodshot, swollen, teary, or discharging eyes; inflamed eyelids; complaints of sleepiness, fatigue, headache, nausea, dizziness; blurred, double, or distorted vision; pain, or a feeling of dryness, itching, burning or grittiness in the eyes; strained or tense facial expressions; rapid blinking or facial twitchings; and such habits as holding the book very close or far from the eyes, or off to one side; moving the reading material alternately toward and away from the eyes; holding the head to one side of the book; or occluding one eye while reading.

No matter how complete school vision tests may be, no teacher, nurse, or psychologist should attempt to diagnose visual defects or prescribe treatment for them. Their responsibility is to identify those children who probably need expert attention and to refer them to a vision specialist.

Two tests have had some use in reading clinics; both use stereoscopic slides and are available from Keystone. The *Keystone Binocular Skills Test*, an adaptation of the *Gray Oral Reading Check Tests*, can be used to compare the relative efficiency of the two eyes in reading. In the *Spache Binocular Reading Test*, different words are omitted from the version of the reading selection shown each eye. It can be used to determine whether each eye is contributing its share while reading.

Hearing

The degree to which poor hearing is a handicap in learning to read depends on the amount of emphasis given to oral instruction in reading. In a careful study, Bond (1935) found significant differences in hearing between good and poor readers in the second and third grades and reported that partly deaf children were seriously handicapped in classes where oral-phonetic methods were stressed but made normal progress in classes that stressed visual teaching materials and silent reading. This is another impressive bit of evidence to demonstrate that teaching methods must be adapted to the learning abilities and disabilities of the individual child. A British study found that even a relatively slight impairment of hearing frequently has marked effects on communication skills and verbal knowledge, and those with defects in both ears are more handicapped than those with defective hearing in one ear (Owrid 1970). Embrey

(1971) found that children with mild hearing loss tended to be 6 months to 1 year retarded in achievement.

Middle-ear effusion (fluid in the middle-ear space) during the formative years from birth to age 6 may have adverse effects on the development of language and cognitive skills (Denk-Glass, Laber, & Brewer 1981). Such problems often go undetected.

Testing Hearing

By far the most satisfactory way to measure hearing in the schools is to use an audiometer. For the purpose of singling out pupils who need careful medical examination of their hearing, audiometers are available that can be used to test as many as 40 children at one time. In such a test, each child listens thorugh an earphone and writes down the numbers he or she hears. The numbers, spoken with different degrees of loudness, are played on a special phonograph, and from the child's written answers the degree of hearing loss can be readily calculated. For individual testing, an audiometer that measures amount of hearing loss for pure tones of low, medium, and high pitches should be used.[8]

Frequency (HZ), or pitch, is the number of vibrations per second produced by the sound source. The range of human hearing is 20 to 20,000 HZ; audiologists typically test the 25 to 8000 HZ range. *Intensity* or loudness is measured in decibels. A loss of over 25 decibels on an audiometer is almost certain to handicap a child in hearing in classroom situations and is usually accompanied by some indistinctness in speech. Because ear infections and other temporary conditions can cause a transitory hearing loss, an audiometer retest 2 months after a failing performance is advisable.

The handicapping effect of a partial hearing loss is much greater for some people than for others. Some make up for their sensory weaknesses by concentrating intently and getting the greatest possible meaning out of what they do hear; others, combining inattention or disregard for small differences with their sensory loss, seem greatly handicapped.

While the majority of children with somewhat impaired hearing show lessened acuity across the full range of pitch represented by the piano keyboard, there are otheres whose deficiency is concentrated in the higher frequencies. An example of high-frequency hearing loss is shown in Figure 9.6.

Raymond was a 10-year-old boy, barely able to read a primer. His Stanford–Binet IQ was 85, but his Performance IQ was 120, showing inferior verbal ability but superior ability in nonverbal situations. His speech was marked by a lisp and indistinctness in the pronunciation of *s, sh, z, th, f,* and *v* sounds; he also spoke very jerkily. His father, a mechanic, had the same speech pattern. It seems probable that Raymond's inability to hear high-frequency sounds clearly was responsible for his inability to pronounce them well and resulted in confusing him in reading because words that sounded alike to him had different letters in them and different meanings.

[8] Good audiometers are marketed under the following names: Beltone, Maico, and Zenith.

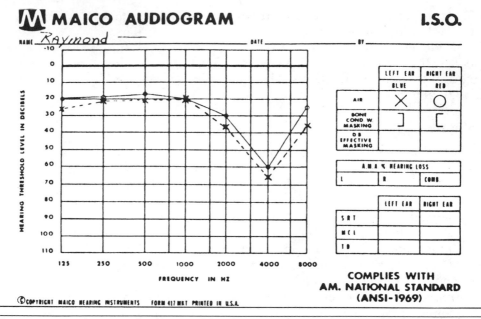

Figure 9.6. Audiogram of a 10-year-old with a severe reading disability. The chart shows an impairment of acuity in the higher frequencies in both ears, with the left ear slightly poorer than the right. Reproduced by permission of Maico Hearing Instruments.

Some conditions that lead to progressively increasing deafness can be cured if treated early enough, and careful periodic tests of hearing should be part of the routine health procedure in every school. Teachers should watch for signs of poor hearing in a child's general behavior. Children with inflamed or running ears should of course be referred for medical treatment. Poor hearing should be suspected if a child asks to have statements repeated, cups a hand behind his ear, scowls or otherwise shows intense effort in listening, confuses words of somewhat similar sounds, or has indistinct speech. Teachers sometimes mistakenly decide that a child is stupid because his face has a blank expression because of his inability to hear.

IV. OTHER PHYSICAL CONDITIONS

Illness

There is no evidence that surgical operations or the common infectious diseases of childhood are directly related to reading disability. Prolonged illness of any kind may influence reading ability if the child is out of school for a long period of time and misses important work. A history of a series of long absences in the first and second grades is found fairly often among children with severe reading handicaps. Many children show no lasting scholastic effects of such absences, either because they were ahead of the class or because their mothers and teachers gave them special help to make up the lost ground. When neither of these conditions is present, the child may not catch up.

Certain chronic conditions lower a child's general vitality so that he or she tires quickly and cannot put forth a normal amount of effort. Rheumatic fever, asthma, heart trouble, sinus trouble, other chronic infections, and malnutrition are conditions that cause intermittent absence and lower the child's energy output. Lack of energy can also be the result of insufficient sleep.

Coordination

A number of poor readers are generally clumsy. They are below average in athletic skill, are awkward in walking and running, and make poorly formed letters and numbers in writing. While there does not seem to be any direct causal connection between awkwardness and poor reading, in some cases they may both result from the same condition. Mild injuries to the brain or delayed neurological maturation may be responsible both for poor muscular coordination and for speech and reading disabilities.

Kephart (1960) emphasized the importance of basic motor skills and eye–hand coordination in slow learners, and Frostig and Maslow (1979) stressed movement training for the learning disabled.

Glandular Disturbances

The endocrine or ductless glands are small organs that have tremendous influence on human growth and efficiency. Marked thyroid deficiency is usually accompanied by obesity and mental sluggishness; an overactive thyroid gland may cause loss of weight, fatigue, and nervous irritability. Abnormalities of the pituitary gland may cause dwarfism and gigantism, obesity, or sexual immaturity. Each of the endocrine glands has important regulative functions, and medical authorities are still far from a complete understanding of them. Among the poor readers seen by the writers, the frequency of endocrine deviations has been greater than in the normal child population. Most of these children have been overweight, with signs of either thyroid deficiency or a general endocrine disturbance involving the thyroid, pituitary, and sex glands (Eames 1960). Many of these children have shown marked improvement in mental alertness, effort, and learning ability after appropriate endocrine treatment. Park and Schneider (1975) reported markedly elevated thyroxine levels in 53 children with severe reading disabilities. However, controlled experimentation has generally resulted in frustration when attempting to apply biochemical therapy to learning (Green & Perlman 1971).

Diet, Nutrition, and Malnutrition

Feingold (1976) asserted that the use of synthetic food colors and flavors is responsible for many cases of hyperactivity and learning disability. The Feingold diet eliminates all foods containing additives, dyes, and natural salicylates. Other physicians criticized Feingold's claims as being based on faulty or insufficient evidence and called for a moratorium on use of the diet (Spring & Sandoval 1976, Sieben 1977). In rebuttal, Feingold (1977) pointed out that one questioned food at a time could be eliminated to determine its effect and that his limited diet is not harmful. The research findings on the diet's effects on hyperactivity are mixed; however, the situation is best summarized by Connors (1980), who concluded that the efficacy of the Feingold diet is poorly substantiated but not refuted; and by E. Taylor (1979), who stated that eliminating additives from the diet might prove helpful for a minority of children, particularly those under age 6.

Powers (1975) stated that the caffeine in coffee, tea, and cola drinks tends to make children overwrought and overstimulated, especially when combined with excessive intake of sugar and carbohydrates. His evidence consisted mainly of his private cases. More conclusive evidence on this is desirable, although eliminating caffeine and reducing sugar in children's diets seem desirable as general health measures. However, Firestone *et al.* (1978) reported that caffeine given to hyperactive children tended to reduce their impulsivity and improved their general behavior.

There are indirect and direct relationships between nutrition and learning (Pertz & Putnam 1982). Examples of an indirect relationship are the possibility that poor nutrition leads to absenteeism and that an iron-deficient diet and its consequent anemia reduces the child's energy level. An example of a direct relationship is the research finding that protein-poor diets produce children who have lower IQs, are less able to learn, and have poor language development. The nutrition of pregnant women is vitally important because the child's brain begins to develop long before birth.

It is difficult to establish a direct relationship between an inadequate diet and academic achievement because moderate malnutrition is so closely bound up with the environmental effects of poverty. Severe malnutrition during prenatal life and/or infancy adversely affects brain development and behavior (Read 1976) and negatively affects both mental and physical growth (Perkins 1977).

Orthomolecular or megavitamin therapy, a controversial medical issue, involves giving massive doses of vitamins and minerals to hyperactive or learning-disabled children. The aim is to produce optimum concentrations of certain substances normally present in the human body. For the pros and cons on this issue, see Cott (1977), Philpott (1977), Sieben (1977), and Adler (1979). In response to Sieben's criticism, Cott wrote: "The efficacy of these various treatment modalities has not been supported overall by incontrovertible evidence. But that is not reason to dismiss the possibilities." Brenner (1982) concluded from his review of controlled, long-term follow-up studies that megadoses of selected B-complex vitamins may benefit some hyperactive children. According to Dunn (1976), cholinesterase requires calcium, magnesium, and vitamins C and E for proper functioning in its relationship to acetylcholine (see p. 276).

Another controversial issue is the analysis of trace minerals in the hair to detect deficiencies in necessary minerals like potassium and the presence of excessive toxic metals like lead in the human body (Pihl & Parkes 1977). This diagnostic procedure is used in orthomolecular therapy (Dunn 1976), but there is little or no evidence of the effect of treatment to modify mineral concentrations on learning disabilities (Sieben 1977).

Controversial medical issues such as the above and the possible effects of allergies on learning and behavior (Mayron 1979) are not for the reading specialist to decide. Parents are responsible for choosing their physicians and for following or not following the medical advice received. When asked, however, the reading specialist may wish to relate both sides of the issue and the research findings on the topic to parents and educators.

Care should be taken in reading the literature. Favorable articles on a health topic are likely to appear in popular magazines and in some journals aimed at educators. Fewer research studies testing the hypothesis and conducted by objective researchers are likely to be published.

10

Correlates of Reading Disability, III: Educational, Sociocultural, and Emotional Factors

The preceding two chapters explored the cognitive, neurological, and physical factors that may be correlates of reading disability. This chapter discusses educational, sociocultural, and emotional factors. The chapter concludes with a consideration of the interrelationships of factors as they may occur in a disabled reader, and with directions for making a case study.

I. EDUCATIONAL FACTORS

Information from School Records

Cumulative school records can provide useful information, such as the child's age on entering school; when poor academic progress was first noted and what, if anything, was done about it; which grades, if any, were repeated; and how often there was a change of school or teacher. Attendance records can indicate if learning opportunities were disrupted by frequent or prolonged absences and raise the question of illness or truancy. Ratings year by year on conduct, effort, and personality may be highly significant. Scores on achievement and intelligence tests should be noted, although low IQs based on group tests may show only that the child could not read the test. A clear health record, including vision, should not be taken at face value; a thorough physical examination should, if possible, be part of the diagnostic study whenever physical or neurological problems are suspected.

Teachers who have previously had the child in their classes should be consulted for information not entered on records. It is important to try to find out what methods of teaching reading have been used with the child, especially in first grade. The child's former teachers can also contribute information about behavior in class, attitude toward reading, home conditions, and their impression of the child's intelligence and language facility. Attempts also should be made to determine the child's academic values. Students who do not value school, who see little purpose in reading, or who enjoy other activities in preference to reading are unlikely to develop a high level of reading achievement (Athey 1982).

Instructional History

An instructional history can cast light on how a reading disability started and developed, but it is usually impossible to obtain an accurate history. Parents can recall what they thought of the first-grade teacher, but they never knew the details of what went on day by day in class. The child's recollections of early schooling are apt to be vague, and many children are unwilling to confide information about their true feelings to an inquisitive adult. The teacher's view of the child may have been biased, and teachers rarely realize their own possible contributions to the failure of children.

Teacher effectiveness has a strong effect on how well children learn to read (Bond & Dykstra 1967; A. J. Harris 1969, 1979b).[1] It seems reasonable to conclude that some children who have become disabled readers might have fared better with different teachers. But if most children learn reasonably well with a particular teacher, the child who does not may have handicaps that prevent him from responding to instruction.

Teacher Practices That Contribute to Failure

According to McDermott (1976, 1977), communicative barriers between teachers and pupils can create hindrances to learning: ". . . any kind of classroom talk can do the instructional job as long as mutual trust and mutual accountability between the teacher and the child are achieved." Children "respond most often not to the activity but to the feeling that the adult displays about them in the course of asking them to do whatever it is the adult has in mind."

A similar point of view was expressed by Larsen and Ehly (1978), who discussed the damaging effect that can be created by inaccurate and inflexible opinions about children's capabilities. The danger is the creation of a self-fulfilling prophecy, which can be especially damaging when it is based on a stereotype of an ethnic or racial group as capable only of inferior learning. Negative labels can influence teachers' perceptions of children and their expectations for them (Foster, Schmidt, & Sabatino 1976).

Teacher practices that aggravate the learning problems of pupils include (1) failing to ensure readiness for learning a new skill or strategy; (2) using

[1] See pages 94–102.

materials that are too difficult for the child; (3) instructing the child or group at a pace that is too fast for acquiring new learnings; (4) ignoring unsatisfactory reading behaviors until they become well-learned habits; (5) rarely calling on a child; (6) failing to give recognition and approval when the child makes a correct response or makes an effort to complete a task; (7) expressing disapproval or even sarcasm when the child makes mistakes; (8) allowing or encouraging other children to express disdain or derision for the child's efforts; (9) expecting a child to perform poorly because his or her older brothers and sisters did so. When a child senses that he habitually fails to satisfy the teacher's standards, and he receives more disapproval than approval, his attitude and effort are likely to deteriorate.

Spelling

The correlations between reading and spelling ability range from approximately .5 to .8 (Malmquist 1958), indicating a moderate to high relationship. Frith and Frith (1980) indicated three major patterns of reading–spelling ability relationships: (1) good reader and speller; (2) poor reader and speller; and (3) good reader but poor speller. Apparently children who are good spellers but poor readers are rare.

Spelling tests are used by many European and some North American researchers as part of the diagnostic testing for determining dyslexia. Also, types of spelling errors are used in some procedures for delineating subtypes of reading disability. Boder, for example, classified disabled readers as dysphonetic or diseidetic on the basis of the kinds of spelling errors they made (see p. 235). Reading specialists may want to determine a child's spelling ability, as well as his writing and computational skills, in order to assess the pupil's level of literacy or to obtain information against which to compare the pupil's progress in reading.

Carpenter (1983) found that disabled readers made more unrecognizable spellings of regular and irregular (nonphonetic) words than good readers did. Similarly, most of the poor readers studied by Fox and Routh (1983) made nonphonetic and bizarre spelling errors, whereas the misspellings of good readers tended to be phonetic equivalents of the stimulus words. Frith (1980) reported that the misspellings of good readers who were poor spellers (estimated to be approximately 2% of the population) were consistently phonetic, whereas a sizeable proportion of the misspellings by those who were poor in both reading and spelling were inconsistent and often nonphonetic.

As for the possible effect of poor reading ability on the acquisition of spelling ability, Nelson (1980, p. 492) wrote that poor reading ability will "inevitably have some effect on the development of spelling ability both by limiting the opportunity for learning and by affecting the ability of the child to accurately monitor his own work. But it is unlikely that what can often be a very severe spelling retardation could be accounted for merely in terms of a secondary effect of the reading retardation."

Handwriting

Poor penmanship occurs frequently among disabled poor readers. Much of the difficulty results from failure to learn letter forms and inability to spell correctly. In order to test handwriting independently of spelling, it is advisable to present a printed or typed selection to be copied. Since writing words may be used in teaching word recognition as well as spelling, it is desirable to include some attention to improved handwriting in a remedial reading program. One should not overlook the possibility that poor penmanship may be an expression of a dislike for reading and everything that goes with it. On the other hand, poor penmanship may be a sign of an underlying visual–motor deficit or of neurologically based poor coordination.

Arithmetic

Children with reading disabilities are often below average in arithmetic also, although not as much as in reading and spelling. As part of a reading diagnosis, it is not necessary to use an elaborate battery of tests such as the *Key Math Diagnostic Arithmetic Test*. A selection of examples ranging from simple two-digit addition to computations taught at the child's grade will usually disclose any weaknesses. Asking the child to do each incorrectly answered example out loud will often pinpoint specific difficulties, such as gaps in knowledge of basic number combinations, adding or subtracting starting at the left instead of the right, saying a correct number but writing it incorrectly (saying 71 and writing 17), or using the wrong operation (adding when the example calls for multiplying).

The child who is poor at solving written arithmetic problems should be asked to explain his or her procedure step by step. It is then possible to identify specific sources of difficulty, such as incorrect word recognition, lack of understanding of vocabulary, careless errors in reading, choice of a wrong operation, skipping an essential step, errors of computation, or failure to check for reasonableness of the answer.

II. SOCIOCULTURAL FACTORS

Three topics are discussed in this section. First, various opinions as to why girls are initially better readers than boys are presented. This is followed by the role of the family in promoting reading achievement. Last is a discussion of the relationship of socioeconomic status and minority-group membership to reading disability.

Gender Differences in Reading Ability and Disability

In the United States, girls 17 years of age and younger generally score higher on the NAEP reading tests than do boys of the same ages (NAEP 1982).[2] They

---

[2] According to Downing and Ollila (1982), when girls reach the secondary school, they lose any significant superiority in reading achievement that they may have had in the elementary school.

receive higher grades in reading than boys do (Johnson & Greenbaum 1980); boys constitute 70–75% of reading-disability cases (Asher 1977); and the preponderance of children classified as learning disabled are males (Leinhardt, Seewald, & Zigmond 1982). Such data have led to various speculations as to the cause of the apparent gender differences in reading achievement.

Research findings suggest that maturational or biological explanations are not viable because similar female superiority does not exist in other countries (Preston 1979, Downing 1982). Nor can the apparent female superiority in reading be attributed to the feminization of American schools because, on the whole, male and female teachers do not differ significantly in their perception or treatment of boys and girls (Lahaderne 1976, Stake & Katz 1982). There are also no bases for the beliefs that (1) the contents of basal readers favor the interest of girls; (2) boys achieve higher when taught by males; and (3) female teachers structure classroom situations in ways that alienate boys (Johnson & Greenbaum 1980). It may be that, at least in the elementary school, girls are more motivated to succeed academically, try harder, complete their assignments, are less disruptive, and so forth, thus accounting for the higher grades in reading assigned by teachers. It does not, however, account for the female superiority on standardized reading tests; and the question why girls are more motivated or conforming than boys remains unanswered.

Cultural and sex-role expectations probably contribute to gender differences in reading achievement. School-age girls in North America view reading as femininely appropriate. Young North American boys accept reading as an appropriate masculine activity (Downing *et al.* 1979, May & Ollila 1981), but they rapidly learn to perceive reading as feminine. In other countries, males perceive reading as an appropriate masculine activity throughout school. But because of methodological difficulties, the findings of cross-cultural studies have not offered definitive evidence that cultural differences are the main cause of gender differences in reading achievement (Downing, May, & Ollila 1982).

Cultural influences appear to begin early in sex-role expectations. For instance, in one study girls obtained higher scores than boys on the *Preschool Inventory*, a difference Laosa (1981) attributed to differential home instruction at age 3; parents involved girls more than boys in school-relevant activities. When children enter school, they are expected to act in the "appropriate" student role that typically emphasizes obedience, conformity, and learning by listening and reading rather than by active participation. These expected behaviors fit the traditional female sex role better; young boys who are highly accepting of the traditional masculine sex role are more likely to experience conflict and stress in school (Johnson & Greenbaum 1980).

There are various neurological and biochemical hypotheses as to why more boys than girls are disabled readers (see pp. 282–289). Additionally, Goldberg *et al.* (1983) suggested that one reason for the higher proportion of reading disability in males is the greater incidence of trauma of the central nervous system experienced by males. But, contrary to what would be expected from theoretical speculation regarding gender differences in hemispheric organization and structure, Canning, Orr, and Rourke (1980) found that male and female disabled readers did not differ significantly on a number of perceptual, visual–motor, language, and concept-formation abilities. There also may be a referral bias, as suggested by Naiden (1976), who found the ratio of intermediate-grade boys to girls who were reading at least 2 years below grade level was only 3 to 2. This contrasts sharply with reported ratios of as high as 10 to 1.

The reasons for gender differences in reading ability are of interest for a number of reasons; however, the issue may be irrelevant for classrooms and reading teachers because the range of individual differences in reading ability within each sex is so wide that average differences between the sexes are almost meaningless for educational planning. Each learner should be treated as an individual.

Contributions of the Family to Reading Achievement

A major influence on differences in academic achievement among children is the family. Variables within the home that are related to school learning fall into two categories (Kifer 1977, Fotheringham & Creal 1980): (1) status variables (e.g., SES), which, although positively correlated with school achievement, are of limited value in explaining how the effects of the family are passed on to the child; and (2) process variables (e.g., achievement press, providing rich language environments), which indicate what parents do to encourage and support academic achievement for their children.

Familial influence seems to operate through the initial level of learning ability with which the child enters school, which is partly inherited, and through opportunities for learning and attitudes toward education (Fotheringham & Creal 1980). Child-rearing attitudes and practices can influence preschool children's intellectual development (Laosa 1981) and their later academic achievement (Banner 1979), as can helping the child with his reading at home (Hewison & Tizard 1980; Shuck, Ulsh, & Platt 1983). British inner-city children whose parents listened to them read books sent home by the school over a 2-year period made significant gains in reading (Tizard, Schofield, & Hewison 1982).

Sartain (1981) summarized the research on the family's contribution to reading achievement: (1) Many pupils probably gain somewhat more functional knowledge from the home and community than from the school; (2) good readers tend to come from home environments that are psychologically comfortable, foster positive attitudes toward reading and learning, and provide stimulating cultural and language experiences; (3) parents who are encouraged or trained to do so can be effective in providing cultural and learning experiences; and (4) siblings and relatives can make valuable contributions through informal tutoring. The home environment is a better predicter than SES of students' attitudes toward reading (Wigfield & Asher 1984).

Reading to preschoolers is linked with children's awareness of print and success in learning to read. It seems that important competencies are more likely to develop if, in reading to the child, adults or older siblings (1) interact verbally with the child; (2) make references to the child's experiental background before reading and relate them to the story content; (3) provide positive reinforcement for involvement; (4) answer the child's questions, and (5) present and discuss evaluative questions after the reading (Teale 1981, Shanahan & Hogan 1983).

Most parents are interested in their children's reading ability and are concerned about their progress in reading (Nicholson 1980). Parents need to know what the school is attempting to accomplish for their children, how it is trying to do so, and how they can assist the school. Practical suggestions for getting parents involved and communicating with them were presented by Criscuolo (1980a), Granowsky, Rose, and Barton (1981), and Vukelich (1984), and for conducting effective parent conferences by B. Barron and Calvin (1983). M. Harris (1981) offered suggestions that families can use to help their children in language and reading development, and Noonan (1978, 1984) enumerated a number of ways to foster a school–home partnership.

Socioeconomic Status and Reading Achievement

The correlations reported between socioeconomic status (SES) and academic achievement range from about .35 to .50 (Fotheringham & Creal 1980), and a large proportion of children who do not perform well academically come from low-SES families. Low-SES pupils are likely to experience learning problems; and when they do develop learning difficulties, their academic prognosis is worse than for middle- and upper-SES students with the same difficulties (Schonhaut & Satz 1983).

There are a number of minority groups in America. Primarily they are non-white, although Caucasians in some inner-city and isolated rural areas also form minority groups. Minority-group members who also have low-SES status (as defined commonly by income, parental occupation, residence, and other related variables) are often termed "disadvantaged." Disadvantaged minority groups often speak a dialect that deviates from standard English or have a native language other than English. Their cultures often differ from that of "mainstream America."

There is ample evidence that disadvantaged children tend to have low reading achievement. Barton (1963) concluded that, on the average, upper-middle-class children were reading 1 year above grade level from the end of first grade, whereas the average for disadvantaged children was 1 or more years below grade level by the time they reached the intermediate grades. The gap tends to widen as they progress through the grades. For instance, G. Downing *et al.* (1965) found that only 18% of the black seventh graders in their study were reading at or above grade level; 57% were reading more than 2 years below grade level. Their average Reading Expectancy Quotient (see p. 154) was only 79; this means that the majority of these seventh graders were functioning well below their potential levels. The causes for this situation are probably multiple and varied (M. Fry & Lagomarsino 1982).

Differences in parental involvement in reading activities and the value parents place on school success probably give rise to differences in achievement motivation, which in turn influences effort and achievement (Wigfield & Asher 1984). Wigfield and Asher also pointed out that middle- and upper-SES children are more likely to enter school with the idea that reading is important, and to have been exposed to parental teaching that fosters school-relevant cognitive skills and motivational styles. They also noted that although there is little difference in the early grades between SES groups regarding their self-concepts, the self-concepts of low-SES children declined more quickly.

Minority-group children can become satisfactory readers, as illustrated by the CRAFT Project (A. J. Harris *et al.* 1968). At the beginning of first grade, the median reading readiness score of the 20,000 inner-city children in their study was at the 20th percentile, but with experimental teacher training and motivation, these children scored close to national norms in reading comprehension in second and third grades. There is also recent evidence that minority children have increased their reading achievement (see p. 4).

When disadvantaged children's reading achievement is significantly below the norm for their own group, one must recognize the possibility that factors that induce reading disabilities in middle- and upper-class children can also be present. In such cases, very severe reading disabilities may result because disadvantaged children often have additional factors working against them.

Family Influences

Children from the same cultural, ethnic, or racial background who live in the same neighborhood and attend the same school can vary widely in reading achievement. A study in England (G. Miller 1970) revealed that social class was less closely related to reading ability than each of the following: a dominant parent–submissive child relationship, general deprivation, desire for education, intellectual enterprise, confidence, and parental support. In a sample of Mexican American children, the highest correlation (.61) with reading scores after 3 years in school was for achievement press (Henderson 1972). It seems noteworthy that parental pressure for their child's achievement predicted third-grade reading achievement a little more accurately than most readiness and intelligence tests can. Henderson also found significant correlations between reading achievement and language models, academic guidance, range of social interaction, intellectuality in the home, identification with models, and perceived value of education.

Factors such as parental desire for their children to be educated, guidance without strict domination, emotional support, and parental intellectuality and interest in reading help to determine which economically disadvantaged children will succeed in school. Indeed, blanket use of the term "disadvantaged" is open to question; some low-SES children seem to be advantaged in many significant characteristics and disadvantaged only in family income and social-class membership.

Language: Deficit or Difference?

Bernstein (1964) described lower-class language as a restricted code that was less abstract, less flexible, and less subtle than middle-class language and attributed the poor school progress of lower-class children to a lack of the linguistic tools needed for abstract reasoning. His theory that lower-class and dialect-speaking children are deficient in language has been challenged by many American linguists (e.g., Adler 1972, Labov 1973).

The degree to which oral language differences may interfere with academic achievement is still a matter of debate. Spoken language is inextricably associated with cultural differences and perhaps with racial prejudice. Teacher expectations may also be a variable (see p. 101). Differences between the oral language of the children and the teacher can create misunderstandings and communication problems, as illustrated by Griese (1971) for Eskimo and Indian (Native American) children.

Concise summaries of the differences between standard English and black English, Spanish-influenced English, and Chinese-influenced English can be found in A. J. Harris and Sipay (1979, pp. 457–481). Articles on teaching reading to dialect-speaking children and to children whose first language is not English can be found in Horn (1970), Laffey and Shuy (1973), Cullinan (1974) and Thonis (1976). Ching (1976) prepared an annotated bibliography on bilingual children, and Feitelson (1979) edited a publication on teaching reading in multilingual societies.

Peer Influences

As children move through the grades, peer systems become important influences on student's learning (Hiebert 1983). Peer influence can be positive, but if the pupil belongs to a gang or club whose code is antagonistic to school and derogates school success, it becomes almost obligatory for a member to neglect learning. Peer groups exert a negative influence on the school achievement of low-SES students (Wigfield & Asher 1984). According to Labov (1973, p. 36), "inner city children who are rejected by the peer group are quite likely to succeed in school. In middle-class suburban areas, many children do fail in school because of their personal deficiencies; in ghetto areas, it is the healthy, vigorous, popular child with normal intelligence who cannot read and fails all along the line. . . . Many children, particularly those who are not doing well in school, show a sudden downturn in the fourth or fifth grades. It is at the same age, at nine or ten years old, that the influence of the vernacular peer group becomes predominant."

It may be, as Labov suggests, that such children will continue to fall further behind in reading as they get older unless the aims of the peer group and school are brought into harmony, or until peer-group antagonism to schooling is neutralized. Labov's viewpoint is limited in application, however. Some gang members learn to read well, and others remain nonreaders. This would not happen if gang influence was the only important factor.

Health Factors and SES

In general, health problems of many kinds tend to be more common among the poor, and when there is a health problem, it is more likely to be neglected or receive poor attention and treatment. One might expect, for example, that poor maternal health during pregnancy, and the resulting possibility of neurological damage to the baby, is more common among the poor than in the general population. In a study of 2000 black children in Chicago, prematurity and poor maternal health during pregnancy were significantly related to later school adjustment (Kellam & Schiff 1969). Intensive clinical studies were made of 29 children chosen as the poorest readers at the end of first grade in a school with mainly black and Puerto Rican children, living in a low-income neighborhood. "A comparatively large proportion of the first-grade children in this study gave evidence of constitutional difficulties or developmental lag. The difficulties discovered were of several types and the etiology in most cases was not clear. Emotional and social factors compounded the difficulties in almost every case and complicated the diagnosis" (Fite & Schwartz 1965). A multidisciplinary study of 306 disadvantaged children with learning disorders indicated that over half showed indications of neurological problems (Kappleman, Kaplan, & Ganter 1969).

When a disadvantaged child functions in reading well below the norm for his peers, as well as below his own expectancy, a seach for persisting handicaps and inhibiting factors beyond those common to the group is important.

III. EMOTIONAL AND SOCIAL PROBLEMS

Disabled readers are usually studied a few years after their troubles have started, and because of the time that has passed and the difficulty of getting accurate information about the past, it is always hard to determine what part emotional problems may have played in causing the reading problem. Usually there are evidences of other handicaps also, and the relative importance of the different handicaps is frequently impossible to determine. Estimates of the significance of emotional factors in the causation of reading disabilities vary widely. Most children with reading disabilities show signs of emotional maladjustment, which may be mild or severe. The percentage of maladjustment reported by a particular investigator varies with the standard used, the community from which the cases come, the bases used in making referrals, and the biases of the clinicians.

Some time ago, Gates (1941) estimated that among cases of severe reading disabilities, about 75% show personality maladjustment, and in about 25% the emotional difficulty is a contributing cause of the reading failure. More recently, a study of 399 Swedish children resulted in the conclusion that nervous traits were probably contributing causes in 23% (Malmquist 1967); and in 306 disadvantaged children, 25% were diagnosed as having emotional disturbances as predominating causes (Kappleman, Kaplan, & Ganter 1969). "Every poor reader is at risk for psychological disturbance, almost always as one result of, rarely as the cause of, and frequently as a further contribution to, the poor reading" (Eisenberg 1975, p. 219). It is also possible that some other factor is responsible for both the emotional problem and the reading disability.

Among children with reading problems, one finds some emotionally healthy children, some very inhibited "good" children, some children with definite neurotic symptoms, some children whose misbehavior is conspicuous, some predelinquents, and some prepsychotic and psychotic children. Reading disability is not a unique entity; rather, it is found in combination with practically all other forms of child maladjustment. Whereas case studies of children often reveal intimate connections between their emotional difficulties and reading difficulties, research studies comparing the personalities of poor readers with good readers have failed to reveal any consistent group differences. This probably reflects the mistaken attempt to find a common personality type or problem in the reading-disability cases (A. J. Harris 1954a, b; 1971b).

Behavior problems and dreamers, extroverts and introverts, show-offs and self-effacing, all can be found among disabled readers. When they are lumped together, the resulting average is meaningless. Thus, much of the research comparing the personalities of disabled readers with those of normal readers has been a waste of time and effort.

Personality Theories and Reading Disability

There is no one unified theory of personality; there are many theories, and each theory expresses a point of view that may help the reading specialist to understand some children. Athey (1976) provided an excellent short summary of several personality theories and indicated, for each theory, some implications for reading and the results of research relating the theory to reading problems. The brief descriptions below are oversimplified versions of theories. To be understood fully, each theory must be carefully studied in far greater detail.

Lecky's (1951) self-consistency theory explains resistance to learning to read as a conflict between the child's belief structure as to what he wants to be (and how he wants to act) and what the school expects of him. For example, a first-grade boy's notions of how a boy should behave (e.g., based on playing cowboy and other aggressive games) may cause him to reject the story content he finds in first-grade readers.

Developmental-task theory (Erikson 1950, Havighurst 1953) states that at each stage of development the accomplishment of certain tasks is central to healthy personality growth. "In American society learning to read is the *major* developmental task of the elementary school years" (Athey 1976, p. 363). Those who succeed tend to develop feelings of autonomy, mastery of their environment, accurate perception of reality, positive attitude toward learning, and low anxiety; those who fail tend to show the opposite traits. But the correlations do not show whether poor progress in reading is the result or the cause of negative personality traits.

Expectancy theory emphasizes the importance of the teacher's beliefs about children's abilities. It emphasizes that pupil's self-perceptions tend to be influenced by their perceptions of the teacher's feelings toward them. It is necessary to note that the teacher's perception may be accurate or inaccurate, flexible or fixed. An inaccurate, fixed opinion about a child can do real damage.

Psychoanalytic theory has developed several theoretical explanations of ways in which personality dynamics can influence learning. For example, inhibition of sexual curiosity as a result of real or imagined parental threats can be overgeneralized by the child to an emotionally based inhibition of intellectual curiosity in general (Strickler 1969).

Self-Concept, Attribution, and Learned Helplessness

According to self-concept theory, children with feelings of adequacy, self-confidence, and self-reliance tend to be good readers; poor readers tend to have negative feelings about themselves, particularly in relation to school achievement. Correlational studies, however, indicate that the relationship between self-concept and reading achievement is low (Hansford & Hattie 1982). The relationship between self-concept and reading achievement is not clear. A child's self-concept may both influence success and be influenced by it; it can be cause, effect, or both (Lang 1976). The relationship is also likely to be influenced by factors such as personal and familial aspirations, peer accomplishments, and teacher and school expectations (Serafica & Harway 1979).

In addition to experiencing academic failure, reading- and learning-disabled pupils tend to be rejected by their teachers and classmates (Horne 1982), a situation about which they are keenly aware (Siperstein *et al.* 1978). Many also assume that they are stupid. It is therefore not surprising that many disabled readers rate high in school-related anxiety (Neville, Pfost, & Dobbs 1967) and low in self-esteem (Thomson & Hartley 1980, Athey 1982). There is also a significant negative relationship between self-esteem and general anxiety (Patten 1983). High anxiety has a debilitating effect on school performance (Willig *et al.* 1983), but anxiety has differential effects on children. For some, it causes distress that disrupts performance; for others it presents a challenge that enhances performance (Eisenberg 1975). Research suggests that anxiety interferes with learning by causing some anxious children to divide their attention between the task and their preoccupation with how well they are doing (Wigfield & Asher 1984).

Although research suggests that school success increases the probability that students will develop positive self-images and that repeated failure or low performance increases the likelihood of low self-concepts (Braun, Neilson, & Dykstra 1976), the evidence strongly suggests that attempts to enhance students' feelings about themselves may not lead to improved academic achievement (Scheirer & Kraut 1979). It may be that in addition to improving self-concept, the intervention must also improve the child's reading ability. In our experience, the disabled reader's self-concept often improves as a result of improving in reading.

Attribution theory holds that an individual's motivation and behaviors are influenced by what the person attributes success or failure to. *Locus of control* refers to whether a person believes that outcomes are the result of one's own effort or ability (internal control) or factors beyond one's control, such as the actions of others, task difficulty, or luck (external control). High reading achievement scores are significantly related to high self-concept and internal locus of control; low reading scores to low self-concept and external locus of control (Eldredge 1981).

According to attribution theory, attributing success to ability and failure to lack of effort leads to willingness to try more challenging tasks. It also leads to task persistence and continuing motivation because the student believes that effort will result in success (Willig *et al.* 1983). Children who attribute outcome to effort are likely to work harder and longer than those who attribute outcome mainly to ability. Students who attribute failure to lack of ability are likely to be less persistent at tasks (the feeling is that effort will not make much difference), and the less persistent the child, the greater the tendency to take less personal responsibility for both success and failure (Thomas 1979). Attributing one's academic failure to poor ability is significantly related to expectancy of poor achievement.

Compared to children who are making normal progress in reading, disabled readers tend to believe that success is caused by external factors (Hiebert 1983) and reflects more a lack of ability than a lack of effort (Hill and Hill 1982). They are also less likely to attribute failure to a lack of effort than to task difficulty or luck (Pearl, Bryan, & Donahue 1980). Johnston and Winograd (1983) argued that many of the problems evidenced by poor readers are the result of their passive participation in reading.

Learned helplessness is the phenomenon by which children learn, over time, that they have no control over outcomes. Attribution play a key role in learned-helplessness theory. The belief that their efforts have little effect on outcomes results in passivity, decreased effort and persistence, anxiety, a depressed affect, lower self-esteem, and self-blame (Greer & Wethered 1984). But, for learned helplessness to develop, the child must also experience failure (Thomas 1979).

Children who develop learned helplessness may react with impaired performance even when success is clearly within their capabilities and in areas in which they do not have a specific disability. They are generally pessimistic regarding their ability to influence outcomes (Pearl, Bryan, & Donohue 1980). Children assessed as having learned helplessness tend to place significantly less emphasis than achieving children on the amount of effort required for success (Thomas 1979).

Although many remedial approaches suggest providing students with opportunities to experience success as a means of improving their self-concepts and developing a more positive attitude toward tasks, such experiences can be ineffective with children who underplay the role of their effort in success. According to Willig et al. (1983), the negative attribution involved in learned helplessness can be reversed through attribution retraining, but such attempts are not always successful (e.g., Pflaum & Pascarella 1982). Performance is optimized when pupils accept responsibility for their success or failure and understand that effort and persistence may help to overcome failure (Stipek & Weisz 1981). A successful procedure involves directly inducing children with negative attribution, who also possess the skills necessary for success, to change their attitudes by suggesting to them that they can overcome failure by persisting and by assuring them that success can be achieved through further effort (Pearl, Bryan, & Donohue 1980; Fowler & Peterson 1981).

Relationship of Constructs

A possible oversimplification of the theoretical relationships among self-concept, attribution, and learned helplessness is as follows: Children with poor self-concepts tend to attribute their failures to lack of ability or to factors beyond their control. The belief that they cannot do anything to overcome their failures leads to decreased effort and eventually to a feeling of helplessness. Poor self-concept, external locus of control, negative attribution, and learned helplessness are associated with poor reading achievement. What is not known, however, is the direction of the relationship. Are, for example, poor self-esteem, negative attribution, and lack of effort a cause or an effect of reading disability? Or are the conditions mutually reinforcing?

Emotional Problems as Causes of Reading Disabilities

Some authors and teachers blame reading problems on "emotional blocking." Unfortunately the term "emotional block" is a vague one and is only the beginning of the description of what is wrong. There are different kinds of emotional blocking, and corrective procedures should differ according to the kind of blocking that has taken place. Even when an emotional problem has been identified and seems to have a causal relationship to the reading difficulty, one must remember that other children with similar emotional problems read well. Often it is the combination of an emotional problem with a visual defect, a directional confusion, absence at crucial times for learning, or a particularly disliked or ineffectual teacher that centers the focus of the problem on reading.

Because reading is the first of the three Rs to be systematically taught to children and is the one with which parents and teachers are most deeply concerned, it naturally becomes the first major educational issue around which problems of reluctance to grow up, resistance to going to school, or defiance of adult authority may be worked out. And because successful reading requires application and sustained concentration, emotional problems that prevent a child from concentrating and paying attention during reading lessons also prevent him from learning to read.

The attempt to describe carefully and accurately the different emotional problems that can be contributory causes in reading disabilities is just in its early stages. Nevertheless, several different problems can already be distinguished.

1. Conscious refusal to learn. The child feels real hostility to parents or teachers or both—hostility consciously realized and readily expressed—and rejects reading because it is identified with the adult or adults against whom these feelings are directed. This frequently occurs when there is a conflict between the cultural values of teacher and pupil; the child from a minority background may not be willing to accept the goals that teachers approve. To do so might jeopardize the child's social standing in the gang. Or the child may be imitating an admired parent who frequently voices contempt for "book learning."

2. Overt hostility. In some children, self-control is hard to maintain because they have built up intense feelings of resentment, and their angry feelings are apt to break out with relatively little provocation. Such children are generally regarded as "bad," and school tends to become for them a continuing series of skirmishes and battles, interrupted by punishments. For these children the teacher–pupil relationship is rarely conducive to good conditions for learning.

3. *Negative conditioning to reading.* The child has built up a negative emotional response to reading (fear, anger, dislike) through the normal working of learning by association. Reading, having been present with someone or something already feared or disliked, becomes capable by itself of producing negative emotional reactions. As an example, one child had a first-grade teacher who walked around the room rapping knuckles with a ruler, and this teacher placed great stress on reading. The child's paniclike reaction to the teacher continued in response to reading lessons from other teachers in later years.

4. *Displacement of hostility.* The child may be jealous of a favored brother or sister who is good in reading, and the child's hostility becomes transferred to the act of reading, which is the sibling's strong point. Another pattern is that of the child whose parent is an avid reader and the child is unable to express hostility toward the parent in any open and direct fashion. The hostility may be expressed indirectly by failure in reading, which is so important to the parent. Displaced hostility is rarely recognized as such by either parent or child.

5. *Resistance to pressure.* Mothers who are overanxious about a child's eating and try during early childhood to cram as much food as possible into the child often find their children becoming feeding problems. Similarly, the overambitious parent who wants Jimmy to be a genius can develop a resistance to pressure for intellectual attainment that may take the form of lack of interest in reading. Reading in such cases become the main battleground on which the child fights for his rights.

6. *Clinging to dependency.* The child who is overprotected and babied may, consciously or unconsciously, prefer to remain infantile and get attention through helplessness. Learning to read may mean growing up and becoming self-reliant, which the child is not yet ready to attempt. This is a common pattern among children who were the only child for 4 or 5 years, the first brother or sister arriving while they were in kindergarten or first grade. Such children may interpret being sent to school as an attempt to get them out of the house so mother can give her full attention to the baby.

7. *Quick discouragement.* Some children start off with a desire to learn to read but meet with initial difficulty and quickly give up and stop trying. These children, as a rule, come to school with marked feelings of inferiority and insecurity already well established. Their home life fails to provide them with security and affection. Often they come from broken homes or homes in which much quarreling goes on. Many of them have the feeling (justified or unjustified) that their parents do not care for them. In various ways their lives have failed to give them wholesome feelings of self-confidence and self-respect. Because of this, they are easily convinced that they are stupid and accept their inferior status in reading as natural, when other, more self-confident children would exert extra effort.

8. *Success is dangerous.* In some children with deep-lying emotional problems almost any successful form of self-expression may stir up feelings of intense anxiety and distress, related to unconscious fears of destruction or damage. For such a child, success in reading may symbolize entering into an adult activity and therefore attempting to compete as a rival with a parent; such competition,

in turn, implies the possibility of dreadful forms of retaliation. On an unconscious level such a child feels that safety lies in self-restriction and passivity. This reaction, based on deep-lying unconscious conflicts, tends to be resistive to remedial help unless psychotherapy is also provided.

9. *Extreme distractibility or restlessness.* A high degree of tension in a child may build up an uncontrollable need for relief in the form of physical activity. The child who is unable to sit still is likely to fall behind in learning, and once he is aware of being behind, quick discouragement is likely to set in. Distractibility is often closely related to restlessness and complicates the picture, since the child's attention is pulled away from the reading task by almost any stimulus. In cases of neurological deviation, distractibility is one of the main problems to be overcome and often requires that the remedial work be completely individual, be conducted in a bare, distraction-free place, and be done calmly, since high motivation may bring about disorganization.

10. *Absorption in a private world.* Some children are absorbed in their own thoughts to such an extent that they can give only intermittent attention to their environments and cannot devote to reading the sustained attention needed for good learning. Many of their daydreams and reveries are of a wish-fulfilling type in which they hit home runs, score touchdowns, and achieve other romantic ambitions. Sometimes their ruminations are of a morbid character. In either case, their inner preoccupation interferes with the attentive concentration that good reading requires. When retreat into fantasy is severe enough to interfere with progress in a good remedial situation, referral for study by a clinical psychologist or psychiatrist is desirable. Some children who seem merely to be inattentive insofar as the teacher is concerned are found to have severe mental disturbances (obsessive-ruminative psychoneuroses or schizoid states) for which intensive psychotherapy is urgently needed. If the condition is very severe (autism or childhood schizophrenia), residential care may be required. But some schizophrenic children can respond to remedial reading help on an outpatient basis (Levison 1970).

11. *Depression.* Depression in children may not be recognized by teachers, and depressed students may be misdiagnosed as having specific learning problems (Brumback & Staton 1983). The number of depressed children may be greater than generally believed. Colbert *et al.* (1982), for instance, found that 54% of their 282 cases had two or more symptoms of depression, and 38% had three or more. Only 11 children (7.2%) had specific learning problems, although many more had been previously diagnosed as learning disabled. The incidence in this study may be higher than normal because their clients had been referred to a clinic. The incidence of severe depression in elementary school children is uncertain, but Brumback and Staton (1983) estimated it to be 1.5% to 2.0%. Indicators of depression include hopelessness, loss of appetite, sleep disturbance, loss of pleasure, low self-esteem, decreased concentration, crying spells, social withdrawal, aggressive behavior, guilt, somatic complaints (headaches, abdominal pain), separation anxiety, sulkiness, and irritability. The overlap of these symptoms with other conditions mentioned in this chapter is apparent.

In describing emotional reactions found in disabled readers, an attempt has been made to make them understandable. More technical descriptions have been given by Pearson (1952), and Kaye (1982) reviewed the literature on the psychoanalytic perspectives of learning disability. Not all cases fit neatly into any of these categories. According to Eisenberg (1975), psychiatric disorders per se can interfere with reading. In addition to the neurotic and personality disorders mentioned above, there are childhood psychoses (e.g., autism, childhood schizophrenia, disintegrative psychosis). Psychotic children often perform poorly on cognitive and information processing measures so that their reading failure may mistakenly be attributed to mental deficiency. Some of these emotionally disordered children do read well, and others have excellent word recognition but little comprehension (hyperlexia). Still others can understand what they read but are so impaired in their social relationships that their idiosyncratic responses to questions may make teachers doubt their reading comprehension.

Although successful remedial reading can improve the adjustment of many children with emotional problems, it is not sufficient for psychotic children; psychiatric intervention is needed. Emotional problems that are secondary to reading failure may require professional treatment in addition to reading remediation. The parents of children with severe, long-standing reading problems may require counseling to deal with their own feelings of guilt and despair (Eisenberg 1975).

The Juvenile Delinquency–Reading- and Learning-Disability Relationship

Reports of a high incidence (approximately 60–65%) of reading or learning disability in delinquent children and adolescents are fairly common (e.g., Wilgosh & Paitich 1982). Dunwant (1982) found that learning disability and juvenile delinquency were significantly related even when differences in sociodemographic backgrounds were controlled. A causal relationship has neither been established (Lane 1980) nor disproven (Keilitz, Zaremba, & Broder 1979). Lane (1980) summarized the range of relationships suggested by the research. There seem to be three possibilities: (1) The learning difficulty leads to classroom failure, which in turn results in delinquency; (2) many reading- or learning-disabled children possess antisocial characteristics that at least contribute to, if not cause, their academic problems; and (3) both the antisocial behavior and school failure are the consequences of adverse family backgrounds (Schonhaut & Satz 1983).

There is also the possibility that somewhere in the juvenile justice system, learning-disabled children are treated differently for the same delinquent behaviors manifested by non-learning-disabled children, since Keilitz, Zaremba, and Broder (1979) did not find any difference between the two groups in the number or type of delinquent activities. Unlike other studies, Sturge (1982) found that children with both disorders did not resemble (in current behavior and family background) either those with only reading-disability or only antisocial problems.

Effect of Reading Failure on Personality

Any child outdistanced by other children is apt to be disturbed by lack of progress. At first he is likely to try harder. If his efforts are misdirected and fail to bring improvement, eventually a strong feeling of frustration develops. He becomes convinced that he is "dumb" or stupid. When called on to read, he is apt to become tense and emotionally upset, which makes his performance even worse. He generally builds up a strong dislike for reading and takes every opportunity to avoid it. As he falls farther and farther behind in school he loses interest in much of the classwork and becomes inattentive, at least during reading lessons. His parents are likely to show strong disappointment because of poor report cards and may nag, threaten, or punish him. This in turn tends to intensify his emotional difficulties and increase his dislike for school. Thus a vicious cycle becomes established.

The child with a reading difficulty is very sensitive to the opinions of others and usually feels keenly the criticism of teachers, classmates, and parents, even when the critical attitude is not stated plainly in words but only implied in actions and facial expressions. If the teacher is lacking in sympathetic understanding of the child's problem, the child is likely to become bitterly resentful.

Different children react to feelings of failure in different ways. Some attempt to make themselves as inconspicuous as possible and develop a meek, timid attitude that seems to say that they hope nobody will notice them. These children often acquire the habit of daydreaming to excess. Nervous habits such as twitching, nail biting, stuttering, and general fidgetiness appear in reading-disability cases who showed no signs of nervousness when they entered school. Some complain of headaches and dizziness or resort to vomiting spells in order to be sent home frequently. One youngster played hooky whenever he had a little money and would ride up and back on the subway until he was caught or hunger got the best of him. Fairly satisfactory compensations are achieved by some children through becoming highly proficient in such school subjects as arithmetic and art or by becoming outstanding in mechanical work or athletics. A few attempt to compenstate for their shortcomings by boasting, bluffing, and exaggeration. One remedial case was described by his teacher as "a suitable prospect for the Tall Story Club." Still others adopt a truculent, defiant pose, as if to dare anyone—teacher included— to make fun of their weakness. The meaning of their behavior can be understood only by one who is willing to look for the reasons behind the behavior before taking disciplinary measures.

Even if children are emotionally well adjusted when they enter school, continued failure in the most important part of schoolwork is very likely to have unfavorable effects on personality.

Parental Reactions

Some children react negatively to reading in response to a home situation for which the parents are primarily responsible. Going beyond that, it is important to inquire how parents react to the discovery that their child has a reading problem.

In a follow-up study of over 200 cases, it was concluded that severe reading disabilities caused emotional problems in families more often than family emotional problems caused reading disabilities. The parents were especially hurt by three problems: (1) frustration in the attempt to find good diagnostic and treatment resources; (2) the ignorance, hostility, and defensiveness of some teachers and principals; and (3) actual cruelty to the child in the classroom (Kline & Kline 1973).

Efforts to get accurate information from parents, and to convey diagnostic conclusions and recommendations to them, sometimes fail because the parents are unable to respond.

> Parental reactions of denial, projection, helplessness, and hopelessness are equally common and equally deterrents to adjustment. Denial is a basic form of self-protection against painful realities. Some parents are unable to face the facts; they cannot "hear" the diagnostic interpretation; they "shop around" for magical cures; they acknowledge physical defects but are oblivious to mental disability. . . . The tendency of some parents to project blame elsewhere for the child's shortcomings is further symptomatic of stress. The obstetrician is blamed for inducing labor prematurely, the pediatrician is blamed for improper treatment of infection and injury, and sometimes parents blame each other. When the teacher is included as a target for blame, an effective partnership with the parent is difficult to achieve. In denial or projection, the child is the ultimate loser. (Begab 1967)

Abrams and Kaslow (1977) pointed out that family dynamics can play a significant role in reading disabilities and that different family constellations provide clues to the best kind of intervention for each family. They discussed seven intervention strategies, ranging from educational help only to psychotherapy involving both the child and the parents, and suggested criteria for deciding which intervention may be best in each case. Kronick (1976) lived with the families of three learning-disabled children and described the sometimes destructive interaction among the family members. The parents' perception of and reaction to the child's reading difficulty may be contributing to the child's problem and therefore may have to be attended to while the child is receiving remedial instruction (Rourke & Fisk 1981).

Investigating Emotional and Social Conditions

An understanding of the child's emotional makeup comes best from learning his past history and from day-to-day contact with him. The first and perhaps the most important phase of remedial procedure is to gain the child's friendship. A teacher who is accepted as a friend can usually get the child to talk with some freedom about himself, his likes and dislikes, fears and hopes, hobbies and interests, friends and enemies, family—in fact, about nearly anything. Since many of these children regard themselves as friendless, the remedial teacher is in an ideal position to become a sympathetic listener.

Personality tests of the paper-and-pencil questionnaire type are often not very helpful with reading-disability cases. Frequently it is necessary to read the questions to the child—a procedure that is time-consuming and probably less revealing than the information one can obtain by using the same time for informal talks. Some children find it difficult to talk about their feelings but have less difficulty answering the more impersonal printed questions. An incomplete-sentence test like the one in Figure 15.2 on page 580 may be very revealing.

The psychologist who has only a limited time in which to try to understand the child relies on interviews and observation of the child's behavior during testing, supplemented by case-history material and possibly by the use of projective tests.

Parents are important sources of information, and their opinions and information should be sought. With both children and parents it is important to be understanding, sympathetic, and noncritical if true feelings are to be expressed. Even when a cordial relationship has been established, one must remember that self-protection and self-deception are both prevalent, and so what one is told must be interpreted with discriminating judgment.

Among the questions one should try to answer are the following:

1. Who are the other people in the home? What are their ages? How much education have they had? Which ones work? What are their outstanding traits?

2. What is the social and economic status of the family? How large is the family income? What sort of house or apartment and what sort of neighborhood do they live in? Are they living at a poverty, marginal, adequate, comfortable, or luxurious level? Has the status of the family changed markedly since the child's birth?

3. How adequate is the physical care given the child? Is he provided with suitable food and clothing? Does he get proper attention when sick? Have physical defects been corrected?

4. What intellectual stimulation is provided in the home? What language(s) is spoken? What newspapers, magazines, and books are available in the home? How much has the child been encouraged to read?

5. How is the child treated by his parents? Do they love him, or are there indications of rejection or of marked preference for other children? What disciplinary procedures do they use? Do they compare him unfavorably with other children or regard him as stupid? Are they greatly disappointed in him?

6. How is the child treated by his brothers and sisters? What do they think of him? Do they boss him or tease him about his poor reading ability?

7. How does the child feel about his family? Does he feel neglected or mistreated? Has he feelings of hatred or resentment against family members? Does he resort to undesirable behavior in order to get attention?

8. What efforts have been made to help at home with his schoolwork? Who has worked with him? What methods have been used? How has the child responded to this help? What have the results been?

9. How does the child spend his spare time? What interests does he show? Does he have any hobbies? Does he show any special talent? What are his goals for the future?

10. Who are his friends, what are they like, and how does he get along with them? Does he play by himself? Does he prefer younger children? Is he a leader or a follower?

11. What signs of emotional maladjustment does he show? Has he any specific nervous habits? Is he a poor eater or poor sleeper? What variations from normal emotional behavior does he show?

12. How does he feel about himself? Has he resigned himself to being stupid? Does he give evidence of open feelings of inferiority and discouragement? If not, what substitute forms of behavior has he adopted? Does he engage in lying, stealing, fire-setting, or vandalism?

13. How does the child feel about school? Classmates? Teacher? Which subject does he like best? Least? How does he think the teacher(s) feels about him? The way his classmates feel about him? Does he try to evade going to school?

14. How does the teacher feel about the child? His learning ability? His effort? His conduct? His status among his classmates? Does the teacher try to provide help? In what way? Has the school provided remedial help? If so, how, when, by whom, and with what results?

When there seems to be evidence of a marked emotional disturbance, the teacher should not try to analyze this, but should take the initiative to call the child to the attention of the person responsible for working with such problems in the school system. This may be the school guidance counselor, school psychologist, prinicipal, visiting teacher, or school social worker. Intensive study in a child guidance clinic or examination by a clinical psychologist or psychiatrist is probably needed. Decisions on what kind of treatment should be started first, and whether or not to proceed with remedial teaching, should preferably be made by the specialist or the clinic. If, however, there will have to be a delay of several months before the special diagnostic study can be carried out, it is better to try remedial instruction than just to wait and do nothing.

Those who are interested in delving further into the relations between reading disability and social and emotional problems will find helpful integrative summaries and discussions, accompanied by useful bibliographies, by Connolly (1971), A. J. Harris (1971b), and Athey (1976).

IV. INTERRELATIONSHIPS OF CAUSAL FACTORS

The diagnostic problem would be comparatively easy if one could expect to find only one important handicap in each reading-disability problem. That would be a mistaken expectation. Most children who develop severe disabilities labor under the burden of several handicaps, any one of which could be an important drawback to progress in reading.

Mitchell was 7½ years old and had just completed second grade in a private school. His teacher did not think that his reading was very poor, but his mother was worried about it. During a morning of testing and interviewing, the following significant facts were discovered:

(1) Mitchell has slightly above-average general intelligence. (2) His speech was somewhat indistinct, and a slight hearing loss was suspected. (3) He had entered the first grade in public school when only 5½ years old. His teacher rated him as immature and inattentive, and in addition he missed several weeks because of scarlet fever. He was transferred to a private school and entered the high first grade with zero reading ability. Lack of reading readiness was obvious. (4) The *Keystone Visual Survey* showed marked difficulty in binocular vision, with both vertical and horizontal eye-muscle imbalance. He had been taken to an eye specialist, who prescribed stereoscopic exercises to correct the condition, but Mitchell's mother had had difficulty getting him to do the exercises and had discontinued them. (5) Mitchell could not remember which was his right hand and which his left and could be considered a case of directional confusion. (6) The combination of indistinct speech, immaturity, inattentiveness, poor eye coordination, and directional confusion strongly suggested delayed and irregular neurological maturation. (7) He had been exposed to teaching that was undoubtedly ineffective and unsuited to his needs. Although the class was small, there was no individualization of work. The teacher used the now outmoded story-memory method; one day the teacher would read a selection to the class, and the next day the pupils would take turns in oral reading of the same selection. Mitchell had good auditory memory, and by listening carefully he had been able to "read" well without paying attention to the printed words. Actually he was unable to read primer material satisfactorily, but he had been trying to read first and second readers. No training in decoding had been given. (8) There were several sources of emotional difficulty. Mitchell had been a nervous, overactive child since babyhood. His mother had taken him to a child guidance clinic when he was 4 years old because she had such trouble trying to get him to mind. He had one older sister whose good behavior and excellent schoolwork were frequently held up to him as examples. His father had been in the army for 3 years, stationed away from home. Since Mitchell was much more attached to his father than to his mother, this separation was undoubtedly a source of anxiety. (9) Mitchell had never shown evidence of a strong desire to learn to read.

In Mitchell's case, as in so many others, there was more than enough causation to create a severe reading disability, and it was impossible to determine the relative contribution of each handicap to the total outcome. Was Mitchell reacting with immaturity to the loss of his father's attention and his mother's favoritism toward his sister? Would he have developed a reading disability because of delayed and irregular neurological maturation regardless of the family picture? We will never know. The number of different, possibly contributing factors he displayed is not unusual in severe cases of reading disability.

From a practical standpoint, the aim of a thorough diagnosis is not to fix the blame for the child's difficulties but to discover each of the many conditions that may require correction. A person who develops an enthusiasm for any theory of causation can frequently find evidence of the handicap he looks for but is likely to overlook many other significant complications while doing so. An unbiased search for every possible handicap is needed for a really comprehenisve and satisfactory diagnosis. This usually requires the combined efforts of several different professions.

It is satisfying to a diagnostician to be able to come out with a definite conclusion about causation in each case, but from a practical viewpoint this is unnecessary. The practical value of an intensive diagnostic study depends on the degree to which answers are provided to the following questions: (1) What persisting and present handicaps are likely to interfere with responsiveness to remedial instruction? (2) What can be done to eliminate these handicaps or lessen their impact? (3) Should remediation be started as soon as possible, or should it be delayed until other forms of treatment help the child to be more responsive to instruction?

Among the forms of noneducational treatment to be considered are correction or control of medical conditions; correction of visual problems; speech correction; drug treatment to control hyperactivity; social service assistance to the family; and counseling or psychotherapy for the child, the parents, or the family. Aside from remedial instruction, educational recommendations may involve a change of school, class, teacher, or program and may require providing information about the child to the school staff in a way that should improve their treatment of him.

V. HOW TO MAKE A CASE STUDY

After a child has been selected for intensive study, the teacher should spend the first remedial period or two getting acquainted with him and leading him into the proper frame of mind for the diagnostic and remedial work. The school records should naturally be consulted as soon as possible. Testing may be started as soon as the child seems ready to cooperate. One should be careful not to give too many tests at once; the testing program can be spread over several periods, and some tests can be given after remedial work has been started. It may take weeks before one has an adequate picture of the child's emotional makeup and home background. It is advisable to begin the remedial work as soon as possible, even though the remedial procedures may have to be changed as soon as a more complete diagnosis has been made. The literature suggests that many psychoeducational recommendations are never implemented. The causes of this and ways of overcoming such problems were discussed by Williams and Coleman (1982).

After the diagnostic evidence has been collected, it is necessary to consider the complete picture and arrive at conclusions about what the child's major difficulties in reading are, what seems to be the most reasonable explanation of how these difficulties have come about, what persisting handicaps may impede progress, and what remedial procedures should be employed to overcome them.

After the remedial work is under way one should check up periodically with informal and standardized tests to determine the effectiveness of the procedures being used and find out if a shift in methods should be instituted. Before finishing work with a case, one should, of course, retest to find out how much progress the pupil has made.

All the factors that need to be considered in the diagnostic phase of a case study have been discussed in this chapter and the chapters preceding this one. The selection of appropriate remedial methods and materials will be considered in the chapters that follow. The task of the person making a case study, after the separate data have been obtained, is to get an overall picture of the child and his needs. This task, never easy, is simplified somewhat if all the relevant information is briefly summarized in such a way that the interrelations can be seen. Such a summary form is shown in Figure 10.1.

If a formal case report is to be submitted, it is desirable to follow a definite outline. This is fairly good insurance against omitting important information, as well as an aid to a person reading the report. The outline that follows can be useful to teachers as a guide in writing up remedial reading cases. The amount of space given to a heading does not indicate its comparative importance; headings G, H, and I should be much more important in a case report than the space allocated to them in the outline would suggest.

A. Objective data
1. Child's name
2. Date of birth and age at beginning of study
3. School grade at beginning of study
4. Intelligence test data, including name of test and form, date of administration, MA, and IQ
5. Silent reading test scores, including name of test and form, date of administration, reading age, and reading grade
    When separate norms are available for parts of the test, the scores on the parts should be listed as well as the total score
6. Oral reading test scores, including name of test and form, date, and reading grade
7. Results of standardized tests in other school subjects if such tests have been given
8. Results of informal testing
B. Health data
1. Results of vision tests and other evidence about vision
2. Results of hearing tests and other evidence about hearing
3. Summary of child's present health status
4. Summary of child's health history
5. Laterality
C. Home background
    The questions listed on pages 319–320 may be used as a guide in summarizing information about home background

SUMMARY OF READING DIAGNOSIS

Name _____ Date of Birth _____ CA _____ Grade, Class _____

Teacher _____ School _____ Examiner _____ Date _____

Reading Levels   Oral   Silent
   Independent   _____   _____
   Instructional   _____   _____
   Frustration   _____   _____
Listening Comprehension Level _____

Reading Expectancy Quotient _____ Reading Quotient _____
Classification: Normal Progress _____ Disabled Reader _____
Severely Disabled Reader _____ Underachiever _____
Slow Learner _____

Test Results

Reading Test	Form	Date	Scores
_____	_____	_____	_____
_____	_____	_____	_____
_____	_____	_____	_____
_____	_____	_____	_____

Intelligence Test	Form	Date	MA	IQ	Subscores
_____	_____	_____	____	____	_____
_____	_____	_____	____	____	_____
_____	_____	_____	____	____	_____

Other Tests	Form	Date	Results
_____	_____	_____	_____
_____	_____	_____	_____
_____	_____	_____	_____

Comments on test results: _____
_____
_____

Reading Skill Strengths and Weaknesses
Word recognition _____
_____

Decoding _____
_____

Vocabulary _____
_____

Comprehension _____

Figure 10.1. A two-page record form for summarizing briefly the results of a reading-disability case study.

Rate _____

Oral Reading _____

Silent Reading _____

Health: Vision _____
Hearing _____
Present physical condition _____
Health History _____
Home Background: Cultural _____
Socioeconomic _____
Family _____
Siblings _____
Treatment of child _____

Personality: Personality traits (temperament, mood)
Self-esteem _____
Interests _____
Emotionality _____
Attitude toward reading _____
Relationship w/adults _____
Relationship w/peers _____
Remarks _____
School History: Grade progress _____
Attendance _____
Marks in reading _____
Methods of reading instruction _____
Marks in other subjects _____
Conduct & behavior _____
Possible Contributing–Causal Factors: _____

Recommendations
Reading _____

_____

_____

School adjustment _____

Advice to parents _____

Other exams or treatment _____

Figure 10.1 (*continued*). Form for a case study.

D. Child's personality
  1. Statement of outstanding personality traits, with illustrations
  2. Child's interests in reading, school, and play
  3. Child's attitudes toward teachers, playmates, and family
E. School history
  1. Record of progress through the grades
  2. Marks in reading and other subjects
  3. Attendance record
  4. Notations about conduct and general behavior
  5. Methods of teaching reading used by former teachers
F. Interpretation of reading results
  1. Interpretation of silent reading performance
  2. Interpretation of oral reading performance
G. Summary of diagnosis
  1. Summary of outstanding strengths and difficulties in reading
  2. Summary of factors related to the child's difficulties
H. Recommendations for remedial treatment
  1. Recommendations concerning reading instruction
  2. Other recommendations for school adjustment
  3. Recommendations to the parents
  4. Recommendations for medical examination or treatment
  5. Other recommendations
I. Description of remedial treatment
    The description of treatment should be given in detail. Preferably a chronological order should be followed, describing procedures used at the beginning and explaining changes made in procedure as the remedial work progressed. Methods should be described in sufficient detail to allow others to reproduce them. Materials used should be indicated.
J. Evaluation of results
  1. Tabular summary of initial test scores and retest scores
  2. Evaluation of progress shown by formal and informal tests
  3. Evidence of change shown in the child's general schoolwork
  4. Evidence of change shown in the child's personality and behavior

Rigid adherence to an outline such as this is not absolutely necessary, but a systematic procedure should be followed. Some cases are more complex than others and need to be described in greater detail.

11

Basic Principles of Remedial Reading

The suggestions for differentiating and individualizing reading instruction discussed in Chapter 5 are based on the assumption that a good developmental reading program must provide for marked differences in rate of learning. Those plans also included provisions for giving specific corrective help as needed. In this way, much of what formerly was considered as corrective or remedial activity is now provided for within the framework of the regular classroom program. Helping children with reading difficulties is much the same whether the help is given within or outside of the regular classroom. For this reason, the term "remedial" is used in this chapter as applying both to corrective reading in classrooms and remedial reading in out-of-class situations. Remedial reading, then, means giving special help to students whose progress in learning to read is not commensurate with reasonable expectations.

In many ways, remedial reading resembles good classroom teaching. Both have the same desired outcomes, and both involve application of the same basic principles of learning and motivation. Many of the factors that contribute to teacher effectiveness (see pp. 94–102) also contribute to effective remediation.

The main differences between classroom instruction and remedial teaching are in opportunity and competence. Remedial teaching allows for diagnosis of individual needs and instruction tailored to fit those needs to a degree that few classroom teachers can match. Skilled remedial teachers are more expert at both diagnosis and at individualized instruction than are most classroom teachers.

Even in schools where well-differentiated reading programs are in operation, the need for special remedial help for some pupils is not eliminated. The program of the lowest reading group in the class may still be frustrating for the least capable readers, and the teacher may find it impossible to give them enough individual attention to meet their needs. There is also the necessity for detailed diagnoses when dealing with severe cases of reading disability. A classroom teacher, even when capable of conducting such a diagnosis, may not be able to spare the time required.

A good total reading program needs to provide special services for the reading disabled. Provisions for diagnoses should be made. At a first level, a reading specialist can make an analysis of the child's reading performance and can outline a specific remedial program. At a second level, the student may be referred to a psychologist for testing of intellectual and personality characteristics or to other specialists for sensory or medical evaluation and possible treatment. At a third level, it should be possible to refer the child to a clinical facility where an intensive diagnostic study can be made.

I. GENERAL CHARACTERISTICS OF REMEDIAL TEACHING

Basing Remedial Instruction on Needs and Strengths

A "teach, test, reteach" pattern is commonly used in good classroom instruction. This points up the importance of determining whether new skills have been mastered and providing review or reteaching for what was not learned. In remediation, however, the more common pattern is "test, teach, retest, reteach." Since the pupils have been exposed to a number of reading skills and strategies, the remedial teacher starts by determining what has been mastered and what needs to be improved. Not only can such determinations make more efficient use of the time available for remediation, but they also prevent needless repetition that might bore the child. On the basis of test results, observations, and discussions with the child[1] and professionals who can offer pertinent information, the reading specialist formulates a plan of teaching to overcome difficulties and make use of strengths. After proceeding with this instructional plan for a while, it is necessary to determine whether the instruction has been effective. If it has been, new skills or strategies can be introduced; if not, additional instruction and practice is probably necessary, or a different instructional approach may be needed.

Starting from What the Pupil Knows

Laying the foundation before putting up the superstructure is as important in remedial reading as it is in building construction. A 12-year-old who is reading

---

[1] Indrisano (1982) outlined an interview procedure for eliciting information about themselves from children.

at the first reader level needs instruction in basic reading skills. Marked weaknesses in word recognition must be overcome before one can expect satisfactory results from instruction designed to improve reading comprehension. On the other hand, if the child does not have a word-recognition problem, it would be foolish to drill him on high-frequency words. Similarly, if the pupil already knows and can use three short-vowel symbol–sound associations, it is not necessary to reteach all five.

Selecting Appropriate Materials and Methods

Selecting appropriate materials and methods is just as important as starting at the appropriate level in skill development. Three points should be considered in selecting material for remediation: (1) the difficulty level of the material; (2) the interest of the material; and (3) whether the material lends itself to the teaching and learning of desired skills and strategies.

Early in the remedial program, material near the easy end of the child's instructional level works well for most students. At times, material below the pupil's instructional level is needed. Such times include the need to be absolutely certain the child will achieve success, and when one does not want word-recognition or comprehension problems to interfere with the acquisition of particular skills (e.g., phrasing, use of voice during oral reading, reasoning to make an inference). The necessity of providing materials that the pupil can read successfully cannot be overemphasized.

Also important is the interest value of the content, particularly for older students, who often express disdain for books written for young children. In such cases, the "high interest–low vocabulary" books are valuable (see Appendix B). The use of interesting material not only helps motivate the child but also makes it more likely that he will have prior knowledge that helps in comprehending the material.

Reading skills are often introduced initially in isolation in order to allow the learner to focus attention on the specific task. While this is an acceptable practice, it is not sufficient. The real test of mastery is whether the child applies that skill or strategy in reading connected discourse. After the skill has been introduced, the pupil should have a number of opportunities to apply it in a meaningful task. Thus, once the child has been taught to infer important details, he should be presented with reading materials that require him to do so. Similarly, if the symbol–sound association for a particular vowel digraph has been introduced, some of the material the child reads should contain unknown words that can be decoded by applying that skill. Other guidelines for selecting and developing instructional materials have been provided by Cohen, Alberto and Troutman (1979), Roberts (1980), and Cunningham (1981).

When selecting practice materials, the teacher should analyze them to determine the actual demands made on the user, rather than simply accept the title of the exercise or the objective stated by the publisher. Such an analysis may reveal that the exercise is inappropriate or that other skills are necessary for successful completion of the task.

A number of remedial techniques or methods are available. From these, the teacher must select the one(s) that she believes will probably be the most effective. Trial teaching may help to narrow the choices (see p. 224). If the technique or methodology does not promote the desired effects after a reasonable time, another should be employed. Pelosi (1982) suggested and illustrated a method for classifying remedial reading techniques.

Pacing, Practice, and Review

In remediation, particularly during the early stages, it is important to present instruction in steps small enough for the child to understand and master, and to pace instruction at a rate that will facilitate learning. Pacing not only involves how much is taught at once but also the rate at which new skills are introduced. A skill should be practiced until the child can utilize it with a comfortable degree of facility before new related skills are introduced. One factor contributing to the child's problem may be that someone has tried to teach him too much too rapidly. On the other hand, neither should pacing be too slow.

Once a skill has been taught, it should be practiced and integrated with previously taught skills. One would, therefore, teach only one short-vowel symbol–sound association in an introductory lesson, rather than attempt to teach all five at once. After the child is fairly secure with the first, another symbol–sound association can be taught. This would be followed by practice involving both skills, and so forth. There should also be periodic spaced review of previously taught skills.

II. PRINCIPLES OF EFFECTIVE MOTIVATION

The child whose efforts to read have been unsuccessful gets caught in a vicious circle. Because his experiences in reading have been unpleasant, he has learned to dislike reading. Because he dislikes reading, he avoids it when he can. By doing a minimum of practice he achieves a minimum of improvement. Meanwhile, children who like to read keep on improving, and the poor reader's handicap keeps on increasing.

The main task for remedial teaching is to arouse and maintain the will to learn. This is not easy, particularly when some of the things to be learned are neither easy nor particularly interesting.

The poor reader feels his inadequacy not only in reading lessons but also in all other phases of schoolwork in which reading is done. One can accept limited failure, such as being unable to sing in tune or write very legibly, without being hurt deeply or having one's self-estimate badly impaired. The stress placed on reading as a criterion of general competence in school—by teachers, parents, and fellow pupils—often causes the poor reader to feel that he is stupid.

From this standpoint, one of the main tasks in remedial reading is to help the learner change his feelings about his competence to learn to read, and raise his self-esteem. A program aimed at this goal has four main aspects: (1) The poor reader should be helped to feel that he is liked, appreciated, and understood;

(2) success experiences are essential, and so the child has to see that he is beginning to make progress; (3) active effort must be stimulated and sustained by use of both intrinsically interesting reading material and extrinsic or somewhat artificial incentives; (4) the learner can be involved in an analysis of the reading problem, the planning of reading activities, and the evaluation of progress.

Acceptance, Approval, and Understanding

In general, the best way to raise children's self-esteem is to have them experience success (Scheirer & Kraut 1979); but some children are so deeply discouraged that they have given up trying and have resigned themselves to chronic failure (see discussion of learned helplessness, p. 312). This attitude may be limited to the classroom or may extend to general social relationships. Daydreaming may take the place of any attempt at real accomplishment. For such children, it may be wise to delay a new start on reading until they have found at least one other activity in which they feel successful and for which they have received merited approval and recognition. It makes sense to attack total discouragement first by building success in an area where good results can be obtained more quickly than in reading.

The poor reader's needs go beyond being liked; he desperately wants to be understood. He often feels hurt, discouraged, or angry. The teacher who recognizes these feelings can get across to the child that the teacher's friendly interest is not shaken by awareness of the child's upset; this can help the child to get his emotions under control.

One feeling that is prevalent among poor readers is that they are not like other children, that their troubles are strange and unusual. The teacher should try to convey that one can be bright in many ways and still have trouble with reading, that many children have trouble learning to read, and that it is a difficulty that is neither unusual nor impossible to overcome. Axelrod (1975) provided suggestions for dispelling misconceptions that disabled readers have about themselves and remediation.

During the course of a remedial program there are inevitable downs as well as ups; discouragement returns and effort slackens. These periods may be induced by events outside the remedial program, such as a quarrel at home, insufficient sleep, a sarcastic remark by another teacher, or being excluded from a game. At these times the remedial teacher can provide invaluable support by slowing the pace and maintaining a steady faith in the child. Being a sympathetic listener occasionally for a child who wants to pour out his troubles also can serve a useful purpose, provided the teacher remains a friendly teacher and does not trespass into psychotherapy.

Nothing Succeeds Like Success

It is essential to begin a remedial program at a level, and with specific tasks, that are easy enough so that successful performance is virtually certain. The inexperienced remedial teacher often fails to recognize fully the extent of a child's deficiency and tends to overestimate the level at which he or she can experience success. Grade-equivalent scores on standardized tests are not a safe guide to selecting remedial material. Such scores tend to show the level at which comprehension can be achieved with some difficulty rather than the level at which fluency and reasonable accuracy can be expected. If this is the only information available, it is wise to begin 1 or 2 years below the level indicated by test scores. An informal tryout of sample pages from books of different difficulty levels is a safer basis for selecting material.

After a child has tasted the delightful flavor of an auspicious beginning, good judgment is needed in estimating how much to try to cover, how fast to go, and how soon to move to a higher level of difficulty. The child's responses to the material and the pace of instruction provide cues to the alert teacher. The teacher who is willing to proceed very slowly at first is often rewarded by accelerated progress later.

Dramatizing Progress

Since most poor readers are insecure and lack self-confidence, visible concrete evidence of their improvement is more important than it is with normal readers. The principle of celebrating a child's successes is essential in remedial teaching. At first, every little improvement should be noted and praised. As the child becomes more accustomed to success, procedures for recognizing progress that work over weeks and months become more important.

Progress records and charts can be devised to record progress in any phase of reading. Different charts can be constructed for number of pages, stories, or books read; number of new words learned; number of phonic elements mastered; decrease in frequency of errors in oral reading; increased accuracy of comprehension; gradual elimination of a specific fault, such as confusing *then* with *when*; rate of reading; and so on. It is desirable to have a separate record for each objective being emphasized, and at any one time a remedial pupil should be keeping track of improvement toward three or four major objectives. After these objectives have been attained, new objectives should be selected.

There are many kinds of progress records. With young children, colored stars, a rubber stamp that says *Good*, paper bunnies, or pine trees can be used. Older children require more sophisticated rewards.

Some charts that have been used successfully include the following:

1. *The thermometer chart.* As the cumulative total goes up, the red moves up the center of the thermometer. Useful for cumulative results such as number of words learned or stories read. A variation attractive to many children is a rocket chart. A small cutout paper rocket is fastened to the chart by tape that is sticky on both sides and can be lifted up and replaced higher on the scale.

2. *The skyscraper chart.* As a unit of work is completed, the child adds a window.

3. *The race-track chart.* Progress is recorded by moving a tiny auto or horse around the track. A variant is completing laps back and forth across a swimming pool.

4. *A map chart.* A trip across country, the world, or outer space is divided into units, and each completed exercise is noted by filling in another unit until the trip is completed.
5. *A bar graph.* This can be used for a group, with each child having a column, which is filled in as another unit is completed.
6. *A bookcase chart.* Used mainly for independent reading, the child adds another book to the bookcase each time he or she finishes a book.
7. *The airplane or ship chart.* The outline of a plane or ship is fastened to a cardboard base so as to make a pocket. The child records progress by adding "passengers" (slips of paper).
8. *The line graph.* This type of graph, which takes note of decreases as well as increases, is most useful for recording rate and comprehension scores.

Frequently it is advisable to allow the child to choose, and to make, the progress chart rather than use a more polished chart made by the teacher. Although the child's chart may be less attractive and cruder, it will mean more to the child.

Units of improvement to be recorded on the progress chart should be small enough so that progress can be recorded at frequent intervals. It is more desirable to have a child compete with his or her own record than compete with other children. If a group is fairly homogeneous, however, a chart that compares the progress of all children in the group sometimes aids motivation.

Social Recognition

Social recognition is very important. Opportunities can be created for the poor reader to demonstrate his growing competence before classmates whose generosity in commending him for improvement can usually be counted on to bolster his shaky self-esteem and serve as a further incentive. The school principal and other teachers may provide appreciative audiences. It is especially valuable to keep parents well informed about the child's progress and to send commendatory notes home at frequent intervals. For many children, the anxiety of parents, shown in nagging, threats, punishment, and ineffectual attempts at tutoring, is a major deterrent to progress. When parents relax such pressures at home, the child is able to function better in school.

The Interest Factor

The desirability of making reading interesting is not a controversial issue in theory, but in practice it is often ignored as teachers rely too much on drill and repetition. There are two main ways to make reading interesting: (1) Employ reading material that is intrinsically capable of attracting and holding the reader's interest; and (2) use material in ways that foster interest. These are not alternatives; rather, they are two aspects that can be combined to produce excellent results.

The teacher who has seen the magical effects obtainable when just the right book is placed in a child's hands cannot ever again disregard the importance of matching the book to the child. To find the right book one must know both the child and the books. This issue is treated in detail in Chapter 15.

When unable to find material to fit the child's known interests, the resourceful teacher is sometimes able to stimulate interest in material that is available. In attempting to sell a book in a new category it is advisable to use stories and books known to have wide appeal for many children.

Using the Language-Experience Approach in Remedial Reading

Some poor readers confront the teacher with a dilemma: They reject material easy enough for them to read on the ground that it is "baby stuff," and the books they are willing to try are all too difficult for them. These children are usually trying hard to give the impression that they are grown up. Their inner insecurity makes it very difficult for them to acknowledge and accept the low level at which they actually can function in reading.

Creative writing can be both a way of building self-respect and an avenue to reading for these children. The emphasis placed by Fernald (1943) on the use of stories created by the child was probably as great a contribution to remedial procedure as the kinesthetic procedures she advocated.

The procedure is an adaptation of the language-experience approach used in beginning reading instruction. The child is encouraged to talk about his recreational outlets—sports, pets, hobbies, or favorite radio or TV programs—and the teacher notes topics about which the child shows enthusiasm. Selecting one such topic, the teacher suggests that maybe he would like to make up a little story about it, which the teacher will write down. With inarticulate or inhibited children it may be necessary to have pictures that can serve as the basis of brief descriptive statements. It is advisable to use the child's exact words, even if they are somewhat ungrammatical. As the child becomes more secure, he can select a favorite story for "editing" into correct spelling and usage. No effort should be made to simplify the vocabulary; the child is using language he understands, and perhaps is proud of any long or unusual words he is able to employ. Early selections should be kept short.

Once dictated, the story is printed in manuscript or typed by the teacher, and the child reads it. He is taught each word that he cannot recognize and rereads the selection until he reads it well enough to read it to his parents and classroom teacher.

It is important to avoid rote repetition without sufficient attention to the copy. Transfer of responsibility for writing the story to the child may be made as soon as he has enough of a writing vocabulary to feel like trying it; help with many words will continue to be needed. After a while, the child will usually express a wish to start reading in a book, and a gradual transition to book reading can be begun.

The priceless ingredient of this approach is its ability to motivate children who are resistive or antagonistic to easy printed materials. Its drawbacks are fairly obvious. It makes heavy demands on the teacher, who must prepare the reading material and provide close supervision during the child's reading. It is also deficient in amount of reading and cannot provide the extensive practice necessary to develop fluency.

Fortunately, many poor readers are not so resistant to the use of easy and not too exciting books. For many, the experience of being able to read anything with ease and fluency more than makes up for the immature content; success itself generates and maintains interest. Some of these children are emotionally immature enough to really enjoy stories written for children several years younger. Others can be given the incentive and face-saving purpose of preparing simple little stories to read to a younger brother or sister, or to a first-grade or kindergarten class. High-interest, low-vocabulary books are often acceptable to poor readers.

The Begin-Over Approach

With older children, the teacher can explain the reasons for going back to very easy books. The importance of learning the bothersome little first- and second-grade words can be pointed out. The fact that the child is older and smarter than when he tried such books before can be emphasized. If the child is willing to start over, things will come much more easily and quickly than they did before, and a foundation can be built for progressing to reading matter that is more appropriate for his age as soon as he is ready.

The begin-over approach seems to work best with those who are willing to do almost anything if it will help them. For such children, the carefully controlled vocabularies and well-spaced repetition of good modern basal readers can help speed up the learning of fundamental reading skills. However, such materials should not be paced as slowly as in a developmental program once basic skills have been mastered; nor must every story be read.

Avoiding Monotony

Variety adds spice to the remedial program. Children often get tired of doing the same thing again and again, even if they are highly motivated to improve their reading. Each lesson should be subdivided into at least three different activities; some teachers like to break an hour-long session into five or six different activities. It is also desirable to have some variation in the plan from lesson to lesson and to introduce a surprise occasionally.

Another reason for variety during a remedial lesson is the desirability of keeping *retroactive inhibition* to a minimum. When the same kind of learning activity is continued for some time, the material learned last tends to blot out or inhibit memory for what was learned earlier in that lesson. Otto (1966) summarized research evidence relating retroactive inhibition to learning difficulties and indicating that poor readers show more of it than good readers. As a poor reader continues uninterrupted with the same learning task, the effect of more practice is increasingly canceled by retroactive inhibition, and the net gain may be very little. Retroactive inhibition can be held to a minimum by introducing short rest perods and by shifting from one learning task to a quite different one.

The duration of the task should be geared to the child. Some children welcome frequent shifts of activity, and others are bothered by them.

Transforming Drills into Games

Many kinds of drill that are not particularly interesting in themselves can be disguised as games, thus becoming play rather than distasteful work. Adaptations of Bingo are easily constructed or can be purchased ready-made. Card games such as rummy and poker are adaptable as word or phrase cards. A magnet on a string can catch "fish" (word cards decorated with paper clips) from a "pond" (desk top). The rules of baseball, football, and basketball can provide scoring systems for competitive contests between two players or two teams, or between pupil and teacher. Other ideas for reading games may be found in Wagner and Hosier (1970), Thompson (1973), Vail (1976), E. Spache (1976), McCormick and Collins (1981), and in the "Classroom Reading Teacher" section of *The Reading Teacher*. Snyder (1981) discussed the pros and cons of teacher-made and commercially published games.

The learner's competitive urge to improve his own record can be a most effective form of motivation. This is what give such motivating power to activities in which the learner can keep his score in comparable units, lesson after lesson. The magic of the *G-score* (grade-equivalent score on one exercise) keeps the McCall–Crabbs exercises popular after 50 years of use (see p. 549). The graphing of rate and comprehension scores is effective both in increasing the rate of excessively slow readers and in improving the accuracy of fast but careless readers.

The Remedial Teacher as a Person

The most important characteristic of a good remedial teacher is a real liking for children. The liking must be genuine; children are quick to detect the difference between a warm, friendly person and one who puts on a show of friendliness without really feeling that way. Appearance, dress, age, speech, theoretical knowledge, experience—all these are less important that a genuine fondness for children as they are, complete with their faults and annoying habits.

Good remedial teachers convey a note of optimism and good cheer to children. The teachers may be full of contagious enthusiasm, or they may be quiet people who create a calm, relaxed atmosphere. They try to avoid any display of vexation or irritation with the children, They create opportunities to praise and try to make criticism kindly and constructive.

Good remedial teachers are sensitive to the emotional needs of children. They try to provide settings in which children feel that they are appreciated and that their ideas and feelings are respected. The teachers seek to build up children's self-confidence and enhance their shaky feelings of personal worth. They do not ask embarrassing questions but accept confidences with friendly interest. They try to avoid confrontations by arranging situations in which the child will do willingly what the teacher wants.

A few people seem to be naturally endowed with warmth, tact, and sympathetic understanding. Such people usually get good results in remedial work even if the methods they employ are far from the best. A few others seem to be completely insensitive to children as people; these should avoid all branches of teaching. The rest, and they constitute the majority, can greatly improve their relationships with children.

Each teacher who succeeds with poor readers finds ways of dealing with the children that are compatible with her personality. A quiet teacher who creates a calm and relaxed atmosphere, a vivacious teacher who stirs children up, and a strong teacher whose self-assurance conveys a sense of security to children may all get fine results although their ways are different.

Behavior Modification

Behavior-modification techniques attempt to change behaviors by systematically rewarding desirable behaviors and either disregarding or punishing undesirable ones. They are based on operant conditioning, the learning model from which B. F. Skinner developed teaching machines and programmed instruction.

A general description of the steps to be taken includes the following: (1) Specify carefully the behavior to be modified and the outcomes desired, in the form of behavioral objectives; (2) collect data on the occurrence of this behavior under present conditions (often called "establishing a baseline"); (3) change the environmental setting, using stimulus change and reinforcement, to induce behavior change in the desired direction; (4) continue to collect data to show degree and direction of change until the objective is reached; (5) if the change is insufficient, modify the program (Knowles 1970).

A token system is often used. One or more tokens (chips, beans, pennies, checks on a record card) are earned for a desired response or series of responses; when enough tokens have been earned, they can be exchanged for a prize. The prizes can be material (candy, money) or take the form of privileges (e.g., having a specified number of minutes of free time). The reinforcement schedule is changed as learning progresses. Near the start, every desired response may be reinforced. As the child improves, reinforcement is given for larger numbers of correct responses and intermittently; intermittent reinforcement seems to have more lasting effects than consistent reinforcement. The reinforcement may be based on the performance of the individual child or the performance of a group.

A list of procedures consistent with behavior-modification principles includes the following:

1. Make specific rules as to what is expected of the children.
2. Communicate rules to the children as clearly as possible.
3. Find out what rewards seem to be strong for this child or these children.
4. Use rewards that are as potent as feasible.
5. Reinforce behavior that facilitates learning.
6. Administer reinforcement with minimum delay at first, and make it clear to the child why he is being rewarded.
7. Determine the maximum delay between a token reward and the actual reward that the children can tolerate, then gradually increase it.

8. Ignore behaviors that interfere with learning and teaching; do not punish them.
9. Reinforce behaviors that are incompatible with the behaviors you wish to decrease.
10. Bring peer pressure to bear on nonconformers by giving some rewards only when all members of the group are complying.
11. Make it clear to the children that the reward system is an objective one which they are free to accept or ignore and that it is not based on pleasing the teacher.

Reinforcement

Near the beginning of a program, and particularly with children who have received little reinforcement in their previous school experiences, the more frequent the reinforcement, the better (Heitzman 1970). Among the effective reinforcers are tokens exchangeable for prizes or privileges, feedback on progress, praise and encouragement, free time, and rewards based on the behavior of the whole group. Bannatyne (1972a) provided a list of reinforcers that are useful to remedial teachers.

The kind of reinforcement may operate differentially with various individuals. For instance, Brent and Routh (1978) found that a response–cost procedure (5 cents was taken away for every incorrect word on the first response) was more effective than positive reinforcement (5 cents and verbal praise was given for each correct initial response) in reducing the number of word-recognition errors made by impulsive children. Other studies have shown that positive reinforcement is more effective with reflective children.

The importance of social reinforcers was stressed by Kuypers, Becker, and O'Leary (1968). They favored giving praise and privileges for improvement in behavior as well as for academic learnings. Deviant behaviors should be ignored unless someone is being hurt or prevented from learning, in which case the offender is simply removed temporarily. It is important to find something the child does that can be rewarded, even if in the beginning, this "something" is nothing more than staying in his seat. Not talking to his neighbor, having the right materials in front of him, paying attention, and working can all be reinforced even if the child is not yet showing much academic progress.

It is important to choose the right behaviors for reinforcement. Deaton (1975) compared the results of reinforcing poor readers for accuracy with reinforcing a comparable group for percentage of time-on-task. The accuracy group became more accurate and also remained on-task 97.5% of the time. The on-task group improved its on-task time to 99.7% but decreased in accuracy to 88%. Programmed material was used, and the author commented that "the problem of cheating is prevalent and offers a challenge to those who teach problem readers with programmed materials." Apparently an unintended result of the reinforcement procedure was to reinforce cheating as an easy way to get 100% accuracy.

Stott (1978) described a procedure for classifying faulty learning patterns found in learning-disabled children and outlined a treatment program for each maladjustment pattern based on behavioral-modification procedures.

It is evident that reinforcement theory provides one theoretical explanation for the strong emphasis that good remedial teachers placed on motivation long before the concepts of behavioral modification were developed. Teachers emphasized starting at low enough levels and with small enough steps to ensure success. They made the work interesting with games and carefully chosen materials. They provided frequent feedback on successful tries ("That's fine!" "OK!" "Terrific!" "Very good!") and provided encouragement and praise for effort when the going was hard. They arranged for social reinforcement through praise from classroom teachers, parents, classmates, the principal, and so on. They used progress charts and records to make progress vividly visible. To them, behavior modification is just a new terminology for long-established practices.

Some cautions about behavior modification have been expressed. Although token economies are usually successful while in operation, the continuation of gains afterward, and the generalization of gains to other learning situations, often have not been checked (Kazdin & Bootzin 1972). The concept of "classroom engineering" or "precision teaching" may lead to a coldly mechanical application of reinforcement. Instead, the use of specific reinforcements should take place in an atmosphere that focuses on trust, positive attitudes, and empathy toward the child (Griffiths 1970–1971). According to Rose, Koorland, and Epstein (1982), most of the studies of reinforcement strategies have been methodologically flawed.

The teacher who wants to develop a more complete understanding of behavior modification can gain much from a book by Axelrod (1977). But knowing about a technique does not provide skill in applying it. It is helpful to be able to try behavior modification with the aid of an expert consultant (Rosenfeld 1979). Without such help, trial-and-error learning may contain serious errors, and a teacher without guidance may not be able to recognize and correct the errors.

Cognitive Behavior Modification

Following the lead of Bandura (1969), a new trend in behavior therapy stresses modeling and modification of "internal dialog." Modeling means giving the learner the opportunity to observe a demonstrator performing the desired action in the correct way. This is, of course, followed by opportunities to imitate the demonstrator. Modification of inner speech involves learning to recognize negative self-statements and images ("It's too hard; I might as well not try") and replace them with more positive self-statements and with coping behavior ("It's hard, but I can do it if I try hard enough"). Meichenbaum (1977) has described in detail many variations in cognitive behavior therapy; unfortunately none of his examples comes from work with disabled readers. Abikoff (1979) reviewed 14 studies of cognitive behavior modification and concluded that the verdict is not yet in concerning the effectiveness of this kind of treatment. He noted the need for larger-scale studies, conducted for considerably longer periods of time.

(Meichenbaum (1980) outlined guidelines for maximizing the generalization effects of cognitive behavior modification.

Carlton, Hummer and Rainey (1984) proposed a four-stage strategy in which children are taught to (1) think through what must be done before attempting a task ("I must do _____ to get ready for this assignment"); (2) think statements that help to analyze the task ("First, I must do _____, then etc."); (3) think statements that guide them through the task ("I still have to _____") or that provide self-corrections ("That's not right, I need to go back and do _____"); and (4) praise themselves after completing a subtask or task ("I've done a great job").

Cooperation between Teacher and Learner

One vital ingredient of a well-motivated remedial approach is the learner's feeling that the program is his program, not something imposed on him by somebody else. This can be achieved if the reading problem is approached as something on which teacher and pupil can work together. For this to succeed, there must be a teacher–learner relationship in which the learner trusts the teacher's good intentions and wants to help himself. Under these conditions the learner can take an active part in discussing his problems in reading, in trying to select the particular weaknesses that are most urgently in need of attention, in the selection of materials to be used, and in evaluating progress. This is particularly true with adolescents.

The degree of insight some children possess into their own difficulties is amazing. Sometimes they not only can pick out the major weak points in their reading skills but also have intelligent ideas about how they came to be poor readers. Such children often can be given wide latitude in selecting their own materials. They delight in devising ways of checking their work and in constructing charts to record their progress.

This does not mean that the teacher adopts a passive role. On the contrary, the teacher is responsible for the entire process. She encourages the learner to make suggestions, but is obligated to point out important issues the learner may have overlooked, to correct erroneous interpretations and proposals, and to provide helpful guidance at every stage. Encouraging the learner to help in planning does not mean abdication of responsibility but the creation of an atmosphere of truly cooperative work.

Occasionally a pupil resents the implication that anything is wrong with his reading. "Why pick on me? I can read all right," is a familiar complaint, particularly to junior high school teachers. In a way, many of these pupils are right. They can read enough to plow through a passable portion of the assigned reading. But their reading is likely to be laborious, halting, slow, full of minor inaccuracies and misunderstood words, and only partially understood. On standardized tests these pupils usually rate 2 or more years below grade placement. They are aware that they are not particularly good readers, but usually do not realize how faulty their reading actually is.

Rob, an eighth grader, was resentful about having been singled out of his class for special help in reading. "Maybe you are right," said the teacher. "You can take a reading test if you want to, and we can score it together. After that you can decide whether or not you want to work on your reading." Rob took the *Iowa Silent Reading Test*, on which his subtest grade scores ranged from 3.3 in Rate to 7.6 in Use of Index. A bright boy of 13, he was quite shocked at his poor showing. But he had checked the scoring himself, and soon he and the teacher were discussing possible reasons why his reading was so slow and listing some of the things he could do to increase his rate.

Learning exactly where one stands is not a good stimulus for some poor readers. To a sensitive, easily discouraged child it may be disheartening. It is also inadvisable for those who are already reading about up to capacity. For them, emphasizing their retardation may be a form of needless cruelty. For pupils like Rob, however, the opportunity to learn just where they stand on objective standardized tests may be exactly what is needed to break through the crust of real or assumed indifference. One of the potential values of standardized tests often overlooked in schools is the function of helping the pupil, as well as the teacher, appraise progress and become aware of needs.

Children sometimes develop the notion that the main reason for learning to read is to please the teacher. The teacher shows pleasure when one reads well and shows or implies displeasure when one reads poorly. If the child wants to retaliate against the teacher, it may seem logical to get even by not reading or by reading poorly.

Such an attitude is usually a transfer to the classroom of attitudes learned at home. Many children eat, not because they are hungry, but to please mother. Such children can often beat their mothers in a contest of wills by refusing to eat. If a child who has learned this technique has a mother who is quite concerned over his reading, he is likely to experiment to find out if rejecting reading can be used in the same way as rejecting food. Often the experiment is successful. Not progressing in reading can become a way of keeping mother's attention centered on the child, and this may be more important to the child than the satisfactions of successful learning. Since teachers are to a large extent substitute parents, the child may be attempting to capture a larger share of the teacher's attention by not trying to read.

If the child is refusing to read because he thinks he can control his mother and teacher that way, obviously the first step is to demonstrate to him that it will not work. Mother and teacher must both switch over to the attitude that they are not going to try to make Johnny read—if he does not learn, he is the one who will be hurt—and must maintain this attitude steadily for a period long enough to convince him. This plan should not be attempted unless there is good reason to believe that it will be carried through without faltering. In class, the teacher must be able to put across the idea that Johnny doesn't have to read if he doesn't want to, and that while she likes him and would like to see him succeed, Johnny himself is the only one who loses out if he doesn't learn to read.

Since the need for attention underlying such a problem will persist, a really satisfactory solution must involve providing the child with better ways of obtaining the attention and affection he craves. Approval must be given for commendable things that the child does if he is to give up less praiseworthy means of attracting notice. When resistance to reading arises out of the child's fundamental emotional needs, more than a change in teaching technique is required.

Remedial Reading and Psychotherapy

Good remedial teaching has some characteristics of good psychotherapy. It is based on the development of a friendly, warm, comfortable relationship between teacher and pupil, for which the term *rapport* is used. It employs reassurance to express the teacher's faith in the child's ability to improve. It provides the child with the security of feeling that the adult knows what she is doing and can be relied on, and at the same time the child is offered some choice of activities. It requires that the teacher be clear about what kinds and degrees of freedom the child can be allowed, and that she be pleasantly firm in maintaining the particular limits she feels it necessary to employ. It requires sufficient objectivity on the teacher's part to avoid becoming involved as a partisan in the child's struggles with parents or complaints about teachers. It is intended to strengthen the child's self-respect so that he or she becomes able to attack problems with courage, energy, and persistence.

There are, however, some important differences. A remedial situation must have a definite structure of planned activities, and the freedom allowed is to choose among approved learning activities, whereas in psychotherapy a much wider freedom of action is permitted (especially in play therapy). The major difference, though, is in regard to interpretation. A major goal of most forms of psychotherapy is the development of insight and self-understanding through the therapist's interpretations of remarks and actions. The remedial teacher should in general avoid interpreting to the child what she thinks the true significance of the child's remarks or conduct may be, or giving advice outside the field of reading and schoolwork.

If a child wants to spend some of the lesson time talking about the problems or pleasant experiences, it is usually advisable to allow this. "If the child chooses to do so, the tutor should listen respectfully and make natural comments, expressing sympathy, understanding, happiness for the child's triumphs, or whatever would be appropriate between any two people who respect one another and have something in common" (Dahlberg, Roswell, & Chall 1952). When in doubt, the safest procedure is to say, "You think that . . ."or "You feel that . . ." and to complete the sentence by restating the gist of the child's statement to you. This is one way to use the technique called "reflection of feeling" by C. R. Rogers (1942), whose nondirective methods of handling interview material can be very useful to remedial teachers.

Many remedial pupils do not accept their remedial teachers at face value but test them again and again to try to find out what they are really like. As a guarded, conforming, polite child begins to be less suspicious of the teacher, he may let a bit of hostility show or may become critical or argumentative. It is important to recognize this for what it is: a venture in the direction of self-assertion and the overcoming of shackling inhibitions. It is important for the child to feel that he can be liked even when he wants to do objectionable things; this helps to set the teacher's response, which should be to show liking for the child while drawing the line firmly against unacceptable behavior. Expressions of jealousy of other pupils point to a need for reassurance about the teacher's interest in the jealous one. Attempts to prolong lessons beyond their time limits should be understood as partly a play for more teacher attention and partly a challenge of the limit set. The setting of limits in a kindly but firm and consistent manner is in itself a therapeutic process, which provides some children with a feeling of security and safety that they have lacked in their relationships with other adults.

Some psychologists have explored the possibilities of a therapeutically oriented remedial setting in which the teacher is very permissive and the child may choose freely among reading and play activities and is encouraged to express his feelings about reading, school, and his family. A skillful and well-trained psychotherapist may be able to get good results with such a combined approach. Our limited observations of such efforts lead us to believe that results in both reading improvement and better adjustment come faster when remediation and psychotherapy are carried on concurrently by different people and are coordinated.

There have been relatively few controlled research studies on the value of counseling or psychotherapy with disabled readers, and most of them are limited in applicability because of small groups, the difficulty of matching groups, and the difficulty of trying to control the quality of treatment. Pumfrey and Elliott (1970) reviewed the evidence on the value of psychotherapy as a treatment for reading failure and concluded that unequivocal proof of effects on adjustment and reading skills had not been shown. Michielutte (1977) compared four matched groups of underachieving sixth-grade boys: a group-counseling group, a tutored group (also in groups of four or five), "contact control group," and a no-contact control group. The first three groups improved; the no-contact group did not. There was a slight advantage for the counseling group, but the number of remedial tutoring sessions was too small (16) to be fair to that procedure. It can be concluded that several kinds of special attention given to such children may show some beneficial effects; results will depend on the quality as well as the kind of intervention.

Printed case reports describe various ways to combine remedial instruction with individual or group counseling or psychotherapy (A. J. Harris 1970, Cases 1, 5, 6, 7, 14; Edelstein 1970; Krasnow 1971–1972; Wright & McKenzie 1970). Such case reports provide persuasive evidence of the value of combined approaches in specific cases.

Hypnosis

The use of hypnosis has been recommended as an aid to improving study habits, improving concentration, reducing test anxiety, increasing motivation, and facilitating learning (Krippner 1970, 1971). Self-hypnosis can be taught to highly susceptible subjects and can be used to improve rate and comprehension (Willis 1972). However, not all people are hypnotizable; the value of hypnosis in treating cases of severe reading disability has not been explored sufficiently; and even if further results should be favorable, properly trained hypnotists are scarce. In a small-scale study (Oldridge 1982), disabled readers who received hypnotic or nonhypnotic suggestion did not score higher in reading achievement than a control group.

Suggestopedia

The terms *suggestopedia* and *suggestology* are alternative names for a system of instruction developed by Lozanov (1975). The system assumes that most individuals have a great potential for improved learning and that a combination of positive suggestion and relaxation can overcome barriers to high-speed learning. The key components of suggestopedia are (1) suggestions that emphasize the worthiness of the individual; (2) relaxation and imagery (breathing exercises, progressive muscle relaxation, tension-release exercises, imagining a pleasant place, and so forth); (3) exciting presentations of lessons, and active learning; and (4) music and environmental sounds (Brownlee 1982). Pritchard and Taylor (1978) described the application of suggestopedia to 17 poor readers ranging in age from 8 to 13. After 4 months of instruction, most of the group improved a year or more in oral and silent reading; less in word recognition. Their statistical treatment was meager, and there was no control group other than the same teacher's previous results with (possibly) similar children. This is a development to be watched, but it needs to be researched by nonpartisans.

Reality Therapy

Reality therapy is a nonpunitive approach designed to help reading- and learning-disabled students acquire strategies that will assist them in dealing with their social and emotional hurts and rejections. It focuses on personal interaction. Fuller and Fuller (1982) described a 10-step approach to reality therapy.

Relaxation Training

As the term implies, relaxation therapy attempts to help the individual to relax, usually by employing self-suggestion. Biofeedback-induced relaxation training decreased impulsivity and increased attention to task for 32 8-to-11-year-olds who were learning disabled (Omizo & Michael 1982). Frey (1980) reported that relaxation therapy lowered the anxiety of German disabled readers in the elementary school and improved their reading performance.

It is likely that such therapies do not directly improve reading ability. Rather, they probably allow the child to be better able to demonstrate his reading ability.

The Parents' Role in a Remedial Program

The importance of home conditions in the causation of reading disabilities was discussed in Chapter 10. When children enter a remedial program, the continuing behavior of the parents toward the child is a significant influence on the child's progress.

It is a reasonable assumption that the parents of most disabled readers have tried to help them. With the best of intentions, however, parents can aggravate the problem, particularly by inappropriate efforts at motivation.

> William (IQ 105) was a difficult problem when he entered Grade 3 after repeating the preceding grade. He was totally uninterested and created disorder by bothering the children around him. His teacher devoted a great deal of attention to him and succeeded in getting him to work hard at his reading and other studies. After a few weeks she noticed that his work was growing worse again and that he was getting increasingly nervous and restless. The mother was invited to come to school. She told the teacher that she and her husband were trying their best to help. She kept William in the house studying every afternoon, and his father quizzed him every night and beat him when he did not know his lessons.

William's parents were not unusual; they reacted in the way that many parents do when they try to help in remedial work. They are so anxious for success that they lack the patience to allow the child to learn at his own rate. In consequence, they become easily discouraged and emotionally tense, and sometimes resort to severe punishment in an attempt to spur the child on to better work.

In talking with the parents of a child who has a reading disability, it is advisable first to inquire about their ideas concerning the causes of his difficulty. Sometimes they bring out many complaints about the child—he is lazy, he will not work, he must be stupid. Sometimes they blame the school or a particular teacher. Very often their attitude is defensive, and they attempt to prove that his poor work is not their fault. After the parents have made their suggestions, one can try to correct their misconceptions. In general, an attempt should be made to restore the parents' confidence in the child and to convey the impression that neither the parents nor the child should be blamed for his failure.

Most children with reading disabilities have already had a great deal of "help" at home. If this had succeeded, they would no longer be disabled. It is a fairly safe assumption that the family efforts were not helpful. Parents are usually unskilled at teaching, and their procedures are often at variance with what the school is teaching and therefore confusing to the child. They expect too much and lose patience quickly. Often these sessions end with the parent angry and the child crying. Many parents nag, scold, punish, and exhort the poor reader to be more like a scholastically more successful brother or sister. Siblings often make things worse by sarcastic comments and uncomplimentary remarks. The problem of how to discuss these issues with parents without antagonizing them requires more understanding than could be imparted in a sentence or two here (see Lieben 1958). Perhaps the main idea to remember is that the parents have been trying to do the right thing.

On the positive side, parents should be given encouragement to believe that there are important things they can do to help the remedial program. Particularly with younger children, the importance of continuing (or resuming) the reading and telling of stories to the child can be stressed. Many parents do not realize the value of conversation, visits to places of interest, and trips in helping the child to enrich ideas, expand vocabulary, and provide a base for improved comprehension. Sharing these and other activities with the child may improve the parent–child relationship.

Many overanxious parents are unable to stop their attempts to teach the child to read, even when they have agreed to do so. When this seems likely, it is often better to give them a very limited job to do than to ask them to step out of the reading instruction entirely. The job should be one that can be completed in 5 to 10 minutes and consist more of review than of new learning. The exact procedure the parent is expected to use must be explained in detail and demonstrated in a sample lesson.

As the child progresses in remedial work, it is desirable to send notes home at frequent intervals, praising the child's effort and mentioning some new achievements. Sometimes a lessening of parental dissatisfaction with a child induces further helpful changes in the home situation.

Group counseling for parents can be helpful. One program is a structured series of parent meetings, each starting with a short lecture, followed by discussion, and concluding with instruction about specific activities the parents are encouraged to engage in with their children (McWhirter 1976). Another program is more like group psychotherapy. Parents are encouraged to talk about their feelings about school, teachers, their spouses, and the child. They learn that their child's problems are by no means unique, and after giving vent to feelings of frustration and anger, they can begin to explore with other parents ways in which they can become more helpful (Bricklin 1970). Unfortunately, many parents are unable to participate in such programs because of jobs or small children at home, and some refuse to get involved.

III. ROLES AND RESPONSIBILITIES OF READING SPECIALISTS

The "Guidelines for the Professional Preparation of Reading Teachers" (International Reading Association 1978) recognized three categories of reading specialist position: clinical–remedial, consultative, and directive–supervisory. These guidelines recommended specific professional preparation and indicated specific attitudes, concepts, and skills that should characterize the competent practitioner in these three specialties, as well as the classroom teacher. Data on state certification requirements for administrative and reading specialist positions have also been published by the International Reading Association (1979b). The IRA Code of Ethics may be found in the October 1980 issues of *The Reading Teacher* and the *Journal of Reading*.

Attempts to standardize titles and define roles and responsibilities have not been successful (Pertz *et al.* 1979). Reading specialists with the same title can be performing very different functions, just as those with different titles can be fulfilling very similar duties.

Structuring the Position

Before accepting a new position, the reading specialist should determine what roles and responsibilities are expected of her. These should be in the form of a written job description. It is also advisable to determine if expectations differ from those stated in writing. Classroom teachers often perceive reading specialists as important, even necessary personnel who spend most of their time working directly with children but who are available for consultation (Pikulski & Ross 1979). Reading specialists and school administrators may differ widely in their perceptions of the specialist's role. For instance, administrators indicated that reading consultants should spend most of their time making diagnoses and providing reading instruction and the least time as inservice leaders and resource persons. Reading consultants saw their roles as being just the opposite (Mangieri & Heimberger 1980). Conflicting expectations can lead to serious misunderstandings. It is important to determine how other school personnel (including teachers, administrators, and supervisors) envision the role and responsibilities of the reading specialist, and how open to change their ideas are.

Reading specialists also need to know what written and unwritten policies have been established and how specific they are. Policies cover such items as the objectives of the remedial program, pupil referral and selection procedures, evaluation procedures, caseload, restrictions as to how many children a teacher can work with during a remedial period, the length of time a child can stay in the program, and so forth. These policies may be district-wide or may differ from school to school within the district. It is also prudent to determine the extent to which established policies are followed. In a new situation it is advisable to adhere to existing policies until one is fairly secure in the position before working for policy changes.

Closely related to the policy issue is the need for a clear understanding of the lines of authority. The reading teacher is usually supervised by the school principal but may be directly answerable to an assistant principal, the district reading consultant or supervisor, a director of pupil personnel services, or the person in charge of special services or special education. Optimally, there will not be clashes among personnel with whom the reading teacher must deal; if there are, the reading specialist needs tactfully to avoid taking sides or being caught in the middle.

Other things the reading specialist needs to know include which reading program(s) is employed in the school; the availability and usefulness of existing records; the use made of tutors and aides; the availability of space, supplies, and equipment; and how previous reading teachers related to other school personnel.

Making an Inventory

One of the first steps is to inventory available space and materials. There may be books, workbooks, games, and audiovisual equipment in the reading room or elsewhere in the school. A simple coding system can be employed to indicate the approximate difficulty of an item, the specific purpose(s) for which it can be used, and whether it requires teacher direction or can be used independently.

Using a Preparatory Period

An experienced reading teacher may need 1 week to prepare for the coming school year; new teachers may require a 2- or 3-week preparatory period. Pupil selection always takes time. Even if selection was done during the previous term or semester, vacancies may have occurred; filling them will probably involve studying pupil records, some diagnostic testing, and conferring with teachers and parents. Record folders have to be started for newly admitted pupils, and the records of continuing pupils must be updated. Groups need to be organized, sessions scheduled, and lesson plans developed.

The physical setup of the reading room or center also must be organized. Instructional materials should be arranged for easy access and convenient use. Space must be planned for individual and group activities, a listening center, a visual-aids center, and a comfortable browsing area. Volunteer helpers can be useful during this aspect of the preparatory period.

Pupil Selection

In selecting students for the remedial program it is not desirable to set a minimum IQ as a criterion for two reasons. The chances that the IQ score is inaccurate are far greater for a disabled reader than for a pupil who is making normal progress in reading. Moreover, the correlation between IQ and ability to profit from remedial help, while positive, is low (Chansky 1963, Frost 1963). The objective measure of reading disability described on pages 152–157 can be used to rank referred students as to the severity of their reading disability. However, use of statistical procedures such as the R Exp Q should be tempered by giving consideration to the child's age and grade placement, teacher recommendations, and so forth.

When a remedial program is started, it is probably desirable to take the most serious cases first, regardless of grade level. Admission to the program should not be limited to the beginning of the school year or semester; rather, it should be on a need–space availability basis throughout the school year. In deciding how many and whom to admit, slots must be reserved for continuing pupils. Some places should also be left open for newly admitted students who need help in reading and for children whose problems have become more acute because they have not received remedial help.

School policies may give priority to children in specific grades. Some remedial programs concentrate on second and third graders, hoping to overcome problems before they become too serious. Above the primary-grade level, remedial efforts are often concentrated on students in the first year of a particular school: for example, seventh graders in a junior high school and freshmen in a four-year high school.

Efficient Use of the Remedial Teacher's Time

Instructional Blocks

Many remedial teachers have found it useful to divide the school year into 4 blocks or terms of approximately equal duration. In a typical school year of 38 weeks, there can be 4 teaching blocks of 8 weeks each, with a nonteaching week for preparation, testing, conferring, recordkeeping, and planning before each block and 2 nonteaching weeks at the end of the year. Alternatively there can be 2 preparatory weeks at the beginning and 1 week at the end.

The Remedial Teacher's Schedule

Remedial periods usually last from 30 to 45 minutes, depending on the school situation. In departmentalized schools or grades the remedial period conforms to the school-wide schedule. When there are self-contained classrooms, shorter periods can be used for younger children and somewhat longer periods for older children. The usual result will provide the remedial teacher with five teaching periods a day plus a lunch period and a nonteaching period (usually the last one) for correction of tests and exercises, recordkeeping, instructional planning, and conferences. Often the completion of the jobs for the nonteaching period will keep the remedial teacher busy until well after school.

Five teaching periods a day, or 25 periods a week, can best be utilized by having some groups twice a week and other groups three times a week. There does not seem to be any dependable evidence that more than three remedial periods a week produces faster learning than three periods do. Having five groups on three days and another five groups on the two intervening days is possible whether the teacher is located in one school or divides time between two schools. The scheduling of children should be cleared with classroom teachers to try to make sure that no child will miss too much of another important subject. Sometimes neatness of scheduling has to be sacrificed in order to minimize the inroads into children's other schoolwork.

Highly individualized remedial teaching becomes increasingly difficult as the size of the group is increased. Reviewing 15 "good" studies of the results of remedial reading, Guthrie, Seifert, and Kline (1978) found that although groups of 4 to 8 pupils achieved good results, groups of 1 to 3 pupils produced still better results. This comparison was, however, confounded with IQ; the schools that provided smaller groups tended to have brighter children in the program. If one assumes that the total caseload of a remedial teacher should not be more than 40 children, this can be achieved by having 10 instructional groups averaging 4 children each.

Duration of remediation is also important. Guthrie, Seifert, and Kline (1978) found that a minimum of about 50 instructional hours seemed necessary if improvement is to be significant and lasting. While rate of improvement is not closely related to age, older pupils usually have greater disparities between their initial performance and normal performance than younger children do, and therefore require longer duration of remedial help in order to come up to grade level.

Group Management

It is natural for members of a newly formed group to be highly competitive with one another. Some have learned previously that the only way they can win is by cheating, and some try to establish their superiority by calling attention to the blunders made by other group members.

The teacher should repeatedly point out that all of us have had trouble in learning to read, and what counts is each one's progress, not who makes mistakes. Making mistakes is a normal part of learning. Each group member keeps records of his or her progress and the teacher praises each child's improvement, showing no interest in comparing one child's record with another's.

It is advisable also to praise any group member who encourages or supports or helps another, and to ignore derogatory remarks. Gradually the group will tend to become mutually supportive. It is also helpful to include some games in which chance rather than ability determines the winner so that the slowest learner in the group will sometimes win.

Utilizing the Remedial Period

In an efficiently planned remedial period every child is doing something useful nearly all the time. A plan for a 40- to 45-minute period that has worked well is as follows:

5 min.:	Assignments, getting materials, clearing up at end.
10 min.:	Teacher-led group lesson, often introducing a new subskill.
15 min.:	Follow-up practice in applying the group lesson subskill. Teacher uses time to work individually with 2–3 children.
10–15 min.:	Children finishing the follow-up exercise move to an individual activity, often self-chosen.

Such a plan allows considerable flexibility. A child who does not need the group lesson may use the time for individual activities. Five minutes may be reserved for the teacher to read from an exciting story that is above the reading level, but within the listening level, of the group. Group games may replace all or part of the time for individual activities.

The Use of Tutors and Paraprofessionals

Classroom and remedial teachers who have one or more assistants can provide more individual help than they could single-handed. Peer and cross-age tutoring by other pupils has positive effects on the reading achievement and attitudes of both the tutored and tutors, particularly when the programs are structured (Cohen, Kulik, & Kulik 1981; Lehr 1984). There is wide speculation as to why tutors improve their academic skills as much as, or more than, the tutees. These ideas have been reviewed and critiqued by Nevi (1983).

Student tutors can help provide the individual attention needed by pupils; the student tutors must be trained in tutoring skills and techniques, must clearly understand what is to be done and how it is to be accomplished, and must be supervised carefully (King 1982). The same is no less true for adult volunteers or paid paraprofessionals. According to Ellson (1976), the critical conditions for successful tutoring by nonprofessionals are intensive training and supervision by professionals in unstructured tutoring programs or highly structured programs that tutors are required to follow in detail. Boomer (1980) presented ideas for interviewing, selecting, training, and using paraprofessionals. Other suggestions for tutoring programs may be found in Mavrogenes and Galen (1979) and Koskinen and Wilson (1982 a, b, c).

The introduction of nonteachers into the instructional–social structure can create problems. One of the potential dangers in tutoring programs is that the tutee and tutor may come to believe that the child being tutored is incapable of being taught if some real progress is not shown. On the other hand, tutees who make progress are likely to attribute the outcomes to their ability, resulting in an improved self-concept (Medway & Lowe 1980).

Individual Remediation

It is expensive from the standpoint of both financial cost and professional time to tutor a child on a one-to-one basis. Yet, at times individual tutoring is the only way to produce results. Some disabled readers cannot work in even a small group; they need intensive, highly individualized instruction over a period of time by a skilled teacher who can keep them on-task. Unfortunately, few schools are able to provide such remediation. Parents must often turn to remedial reading teachers who are in private practice or to privately operated clinics. Some private tutors are well trained in diagnostic and remedial procedures and work closely with the school or referring agency, but their competence varies greatly.

Out-of-School Assignments

Children become better readers by reading. Often those who like to read do more reading outside of school than in school, and this voluntary reading is a very important factor in their continued improvement. If poor readers can be induced to read extensively between lessons, their progress will very likely be accelerated.

It is not advisable, however, to insist that children read at home, especially at the start of a remedial program. One should wait until children demonstrate confidence in their reading ability and find that they can get pleasure from it. Then one can suggest that the child might like to do some reading between lessons. The importance of doing as much reading as possible can be discussed and a progress chart for outside reading can be started. At first these stories should be short, of interest to the pupil, and well within the child's independent reading level. Reports on outside reading should be kept to a minimum; when used, they should be required only from the standpoint of discussing what the child enjoyed about the story. As a check on progress, the child can be asked to read a particularly enjoyable or interesting part of the story to the teacher.

Workbook exercises are less interesting than stories and usually should not be assigned for completion outside the tutoring situation unless the child enjoys doing them. The same principle—that the pupil should want extra practice—should govern decisions about any homework assignment.

Recordkeeping

Keeping useful records is important in any phase of a total reading program, but it is vital for a successful remedial reading program. Well-kept records help in making instructional decisions and provide feedback on program management, a concrete measure of accountability, and a record of each pupil's program and progress. A basic recordkeeping system should be manageable by the teacher, fairly easy to use, provide only for the collection of useful data, and give a simple means of displaying the data (Lund, Schnaps, & Bijou 1983). Records should indicate student strengths and needs, exactly what activities have been attempted, how successful they were (along with any changes that should be made), and the need for any follow-up (Memory 1980). Many of these requirements can be met by use of a form such as that shown in Figure 11.1.

Different kinds of records can be kept. Records kept by the teacher include checklists or other summaries, such as those found in cumulative records, detailed profiles as found in a case study (see pp. 322–326), anecdotal notes, and comments written on lesson plans. If children in the remedial group are working on different activities during the allotted time, the teacher needs to have a master schedule of what each pupil is doing.

In individual tutoring it is desirable to keep a day-by-day diary that contains notations about children's behavior and feelings as well as their reading. If such a detailed record is impractical, significant changes in performance, unusual behavior, the effectiveness of a particular technique, and so on can be noted briefly on a handy pad and dated. These notes should be placed in the child's file and be reread periodically. Each child's records (including diagnostic summaries and recommendations, an outline of the teaching plan, and notations about progress) should be kept in a separate file folder or envelope. Use of abbreviations and checklists can reduce the amount of writing necessary.

Records also should be kept of the assignments given to each child. These should contain notations as to when they were begun and finished and comments about how well they were accomplished (see Fig. 11.2). Each child should have a notebook in which to do written work and a large envelope in which to keep notebook, assignment sheets, progress charts, word cards, and so on.

Individualized Educational Programs

Public Law 94–142 mandates that an Individualized Educational Program (IEP) be written for each handicapped student. Although there is some evidence that reading teachers are not perceived as contributing much to, or exerting much influence on, IEP committee decisions (Gilliam & Coleman 1981), they should be involved in the development, conduct, and evaluation of IEPs for handicapped children who have reading problems. Even if a disabled reader is not

PROGRESS REPORT

Name _Marcia_

Objective _Will recognize, within 1 second each, 3 of the Harris - Jacobson Core pre-primer words (list attached)_

Date	Method–Material	Evaluation
9/9	1. T: a. Show ball printed on card — no time limit b. "This word says _ball_." c. "Look carefully at this word." d. Repeat a + b. e. "What does this word say?"	c. S has difficulty maintaining attention
	2. S: Responds orally	2. ball
	3. T: Repeat 1a—e	
	4. S: Repeat 2	4. ball
	5. Repeat 1–4 with _can_.	5. Still difficulty with attention. Correctly responded to _can_ on both trials.
	6. Provide mixed practice with _ball_ and _can_.	6. Responded correctly to both words on first 3 trials.
	7. Repeat 1–4 with _play_.	7. Attention slightly better. Correctly responded to _play_ on both trials.
	8. Provide mixed practice with all 3 words.	8. Unable to respond correctly to all 3 words in 3 trials. Responses suggest S isn't using initial consonants as cues.
9/10	1. Repeat 9/9 plan, but call S's attention to use of initial consonants as aid to word recognition.	1. S responded to all 3 words correctly on first 3 trials.
	2. Combine _ball_, _can_, _play_ with previously learned words _I_, _big_, _my_, _a_, _have_, _is_ in sentences.	
	Have S read a. I can play ball. b. I have a big ball. c. My ball is big.	a. Responded correctly to all words. b. Ditto c. Ditto

Figure 11.1. A form for a progress report. A separate set of forms is used for each objective. The form also may be modified for use as a daily lesson plan. If so, then all the objectives for a lesson would be stated and the plan laid out in the sequence in which the lesson would be presented. T = Teacher, S = Student.

READING ASSIGNMENT SHEET

Name _____

Date Assigned	Assignment	Date Completed	Comments

Figure 11.2.   A form for individual reading assignments.

classified as handicapped, reading specialists may want to use IEPs to help plan and evaluate their remediation.

Apparently there is some confusion over what constitutes an acceptable IEP (Kammerlohr, Henderson, & Rock 1983), as well as some question as to its utility (Calfee 1982). Each IEP must include (1) a statement of the student's present level of educational performance; (2) annual goals and short-term instructional objectives that lead to the attainment of the annual goals; (3) the specific educational services the child will receive to achieve those goals; (4) the duration of services; and (5) a method of determining if the goals are attained (Bierly 1978). There is no standard IEP form, and a new IEP need not be written annually; however, it must be revised as needed and kept up to date.

Trumbell, Strickland, and Hammer (1978a, b) provided a concise description of the PL 94–142 regulations pertaining to IEPs and described how to formulate IEPs that are in compliance with the legal requirements. There are also suggestions for developing data-based IEPs (Deno, Mirkin, & Wesson 1983), developing IEPs based on a "whole-language" model (Hassilriis 1982), evaluating IEPs (Freasier 1983), involving students in the formulation of their own IEPs (Salend 1983), and using microcomputers in writing IEPs (Gore & Vance 1983). The aforementioned should be read carefully and critically. For example, the contention by Salend that students can determine their own instructional levels accurately is open to question; and although computers may be useful in developing and monitoring IEPs, presenting a menu from which goals are to be selected may lead to stilted, mechanical procedures that bypass the thought that is often necessary to formulate a useful IEP.

Discharging Students from a Remedial Program

Discharging pupils from a remedial reading program before they are ready may in the long run defeat the aims of the program. Setting an arbitrary time limit for which a child may receive remediation creates the danger that many children will stop improving when the program stops. Remedial reading programs must show that they can provide lasting benefits.

Two criteria should be applied for judging when a child is ready to leave the remedial program: (1) Does he have the ability to read classroom assignments with adequate comprehension? (2) Has he established the habit of reading for pleasure? The first criterion implies that the remedial teacher must know what demands will be placed on the child in the regular classroom and prepares him to meet these demands. The second criterion induces the child to practice newly acquired skills. Failure to meet either criterion may mean that progress in reading will come to a halt when special help is stopped.

If pressure from a long waiting list makes it necessary to discontinue children before they are ready, the remedial teacher should confer with the classroom teacher and provide both teaching suggestions and appropriate materials. Allowing the child to return to the remedial room for an occasional visit also helps.

Providing Support in Other Curricular Areas

Sometimes a child makes good progress in a remedial program and gains confidence as he experiences successful learning only to be crushed when, at the end of the year, he fails in other subjects and is required to repeat. The remedial teacher should try to prevent this from happening. Conferring with the child's teacher or teachers may make it possible for him to receive shorter and more appropriate homework assignments. Arrangements can be made to have his assignments read to him, by a student volunteer, by a member of his family, or by providing him with a taped recording of the textbook. Tests can be given and answered orally. When the reading tasks required are well above a child's frustration level, it seems reasonable to give him the same opportunities to learn that one would give a child with severely defective vision. Further suggestions about content-subject instruction for disabled readers may be found on pages 531–532.

Consultation

When a reading specialist is employed as a reading consultant, it is expected that the main responsibility will be working with and through classroom teachers. The reading consultant may carry out diagnostic studies of individual children in order to make specific instructional recommendations for the teacher to carry out, may demonstrate how to teach a group of poor readers, or may provide individual help to a small number of children to get them started. But the main responsibility for teaching the child to read rests with the classroom teachers.

Specialists employed as remedial reading teachers sometimes find themselves isolated from the rest of the school (Cohen, Intili, & Robbins 1978). Robinson and Pettit (1978) discussed ways in which a remedial teacher can expand her role in the school's total reading program. Of course, skill in human relations is a prerequisite. At Level 1, acceptance by classroom teachers is improved by volunteering to share such chores as lunchroom duty, conferring regularly with teachers who have children in the remedial program, and offering to demonstrate new reading materials and techniques. At Level 2, the remedial teacher accepts an invitation from a teacher to visit her classroom during reading instruction in order to suggest ways of improving that teacher's reading program, and serves on such faculty committees as curriculum, textbook selection, and library committees. At Level 3, the remedial teacher, with administrative approval, serves at least half-time as a reading consultant.

Dworkin (1979) described a program in which a consultant demonstrated for a group of teachers how to apply certain principles of learning and how to establish an instructional sequence in which a disabled child was practically guaranteed success. Each teacher then set limited goals for a specific child for a period of 2 to 4 weeks. On an attitude scale given as a pretest and posttest, the teachers' expectations became significantly more positive.

Supervision and Staff Development

Some reading specialists are responsible for a school or district-wide reading program and thus have to supervise classroom and reading teachers. Space does not allow these topics to be treated adequately here, but some references are indicated for those interested.

Rauch (1982) discussed the characteristics of a good directed reading lesson, Sanacore (1981) presented a checklist for observing remedial reading lessons, Bagford (1981) developed a procedure for evaluating the teaching of developmental and functional reading, and Bell (1982) put forth a five-stage model for helping teachers to analyze and improve their teaching of reading. Staff development is the subject of publications by Griffen (1983), Shanker (1982), and J. L. Vacca (1983). Suggestions for conducting inservice programs were made by Conley (1983) and by Lindsey and Runquist (1983). Ideas as to how a reading specialist can effect changes in existing reading programs were offered by Bean and Wilson (1981) and Horn (1982).

Accountability and Remedial Reading

With increasing frequency, reading specialists are being asked to demonstrate the worth of their remedial programs. Retesting at appropriate intervals is one way to determine how much children have improved. What is measured, and how, will depend on what has been taught, test content and demands, and the purpose of testing.

Norm-referenced tests are not appropriate for measuring gains over short periods of time, especially for individuals. They are not sensitive to small but meaningful changes in reading skills or behaviors. The NR tests may not measure the skills taught or may sample them in a way that differs from that in which the skills were practiced. The NR tests may provide reliable measures of change for groups over a fairly long period, but growth in general level of reading ability is perhaps better demonstrated through the use of individually administered tests.

Informal or criterion-referenced tests are more likely to be useful in evaluating the effectiveness of a remedial program. The development of particular skills or strategies also can be documented through recordkeeping. It is advisable to obtain baseline data on each child and compare progress against these starting points. For example, a child may recognize at sight only eight words from a list of high-frequency words. If he learns one additional word a day over a 6-week period (30 days), the child will have almost quadrupled his sight vocabulary, but such gains may not result in significant gains on an NR test.

"Rate of progress" scores can be used to obtain a rough approximation of program effectiveness. The gains made by the child before and after remediation are changed to percentages and compared. For example, if Susie had a reading score of 1.5 in September of the third grade, she would have made a half-year (5 months) of progress in 2 years of instruction (grade-equivalent scores start at 1.0). Her rate of progress was only 25% of normal. If, after 10 months of remedial help, she scored 2.8 on the posttest, her gain would be 1.3 years. This indicates a rate of progress of 130%. Put another way, during regular classroom instruction she made an average gain of a quarter of a month for each month of instruction. With remediation, she made an average gain of 1.3 months for each month of remediation.

Another usable procedure is to compute a Reading Expectancy Quotient for the pupil before and after remediation. If Susie's IQ was 100 and her MA and CA were both 8.2, her R Exp Q before remediation would have been 81.7 (6.7 ÷ 8.2). After 10 months of remediation, it would have been 87.9 (8.0 ÷ 9.1), showing progress toward normal reading but still a somewhat disabled reader.

Another way to evaluate growth as a result of remediation is to use single-subject, multiple-baseline data (Johnston & Afflerbach 1983). Or the number of children who have been successfully returned to the regular classroom program can be used.

Use of "rate of progress" scores and the R Exp Q have been criticized (Yule & Rutter 1976, McLeod 1979) on the grounds that they do not allow for regression effects. Usually when a group is retested with an equivalent test, the average score for those who were very low at the first testing tends to be somewhat closer to the average; it regresses toward the mean. This should occur regardless of whether remediation was provided. Yule and Rutter recommended computing a regression equation, using it to find an expected score for each child, and then comparing the obtained score with the expected score. The trouble with this is that disabled readers who do not receive remediation do not as a group regress toward the mean. Instead, they tend to fall farther behind each year. The expected score from a regression equation sets an unrealistically high expectation, and in some cases actually converts a real gain in reading into a theoretical loss.

Effectiveness of Remediation

The evidence on the effectiveness of remediation is mixed. For instance, Gittelman and Feingold (1983) found that remediation produced significant improvement. Ito (1980) reported that resource-room intervention had a significant positive effect on reading achievement but that these gains were not maintained in the regular classroom one year later. In Raim's (1983) study there were no significant differences in reading gains among a control group and groups of disabled readers who were (1) tutored by graduate students at a clinic; (2) assigned homework that was checked by graduate students; (3) tutored by older students in their school; and (4) helped at home by their parents. Some studies on pull-out programs (see p. 362) also questioned the effectiveness of remedial programs. Guthrie, Seifert, and Kline (1978) identified conditions needed for significant and lasting improvement (see p. 359).

How much reading improvement can be reasonably expected probably depends on many variables and their interactions. Among these factors are (1) the severity of the reading disability; (2) the child's intellectual ability; (3) the accuracy of the diagnosis; (4) the appropriateness of the remediation; (5) the quality of the reading teacher; (6) the intensity of the remediation (two 15-minute periods per week for a seriously disabled reader is almost a waste of time, and may have a negative effect if the child does not improve); (7) the duration of remediation; (8) whether the child was taught to transfer skills to his regular school program; and (9) the child's desire to improve his reading ability.

Long-Term Effects of Reading Disability and Remediation

Many intelligent pupils who received high-quality remedial help long enough to enable them to handle school reading assignments have completed high school, college, and even graduate school (H. M. Robinson & H. K. Smith 1962; Rawson 1978; Newman 1982). However, they tended to concentrate in academic areas that did not require extensive reading, and they often had residual problems such as slow reading and poor spelling. Others are not as fortunate. Compared to a control group, young adults who had been diagnosed as learning disabled when younger had jobs with significantly lower status, were less active socially and recreationally, and were more likely to have been convicted of a crime (White et al. 1982). What appears to account for the differences in many cases are the family's SES (and the myriad of interrelated factors associated with it); the learning potential of the child; the quality, intensity, and duration of the remediation; and the adjustments made for the child after being discharged from the remedial program.

In the British follow-up studies summarized by H. C. M. Carroll (1972), the general result was a slowing down or complete loss of reading gains after remediation was discontinued. Carroll pointed out that these results may have in part reflected the fact that many of these children continued to remain in the same environmental conditions that were causal initially, or to the failure of the schools to provide for students whose reading ability was marginal when they were discharged from the remedial program.

A longitudinal study (Balow & Blomquist 1965) also casts some light on why the positive effects of remediation sometimes do not last. Children given remedial help for long periods (2 to 3 years) tended to continue to improve; those given short-term remediation (e.g., summer school) did not. Those whose remediation tapered off gradually, with opportunities to see the remedial teacher about once a month, were more likely to have continued improving than were those whose remediation ended abruptly.

Kline and Kline (1975) reported that private tutoring four to five times weekly resulted in improved reading for 95% of the 92 dyslexics studied. Most of them required from 1 to 3 years of treatment, with the amount of reading gain positively related to the length of treatment. In contrast to several other studies, older children improved more than younger pupils.

In order to make the results of the 15 studies in their analysis comparable, Guthrie, Seifert, and Kline (1978) changed all the results to learning gains (gains in months divided by the number of months of remedial help). Using only studies with satisfactory control groups, they found that the tutored groups showed significantly greater improvement in reading. Under favorable conditions, a learning rate double that of normal children with classroom instruction was obtained in several studies. The following characteristics were found in programs that had both high learning rates during remediation and continued improvement at least at a normal rate for 2 years after remedial help was stopped: pupils of elementary school age; middle-class-SES students; students with IQs of 90 or over; more than 50 hours of remedial help; certified, experienced remedial teachers or trained, supervised tutors. Secondary students learned at about the same rate as did elementary school children, but the former had much more to learn and so needed much more time.

According to Spreen (1982), most pupils referred to a clinic for reading or learning disabilities never catch up, and their disabilities are more likely to worsen over time. Spreen claimed that the effects of remediation were minimal at best, except for high-SES, high Verbal IQ students who attended private schools. He also stated that although reading-disabled students may make continual progress in reading and academic subjects up to the adult years, they still have problems with academic subjects throughout their school careers, which are often cut short, with early entry into jobs with low pay and status. As young adults they may have occupational, social, or personal problems (these are strongly associated with SES), but few have psychiatric disorders. There is, however, a great deal of variability in how such students turn out in later years.

In the 18 follow-up studies reviewed by Schonhaut and Satz (1983), 4 showed favorable gains in reading, 12 did not, and the findings of 2 were mixed. They summarized the findings of these studies as follows: (1) The academic outlook for children with early learning problems is poor, unless the pupil comes from a high-SES family and/or is exposed to an intensive remedial program such as the Orton–Gillingham (see p. 437), in which case the outlook is good; (2) children with early learning disabilities are probably more likely to drop out of school; (3) with the exception of high-SES students, few learning-disabled children will enter occupations demanding extensive education; (4) whether early identification and treatment improves the prognosis is still unanswered; and (5) the reported connection between early learning disabilities and later antisocial behavior or emotional disorder is uncertain.

IV. TYPES OF REMEDIAL READING ORGANIZATIONS

Model Programs

From the remedial reading programs financed by the federal government from about 1965 to 1970, the American Institute for Research in the Behavioral Sciences selected those with superior results that might serve as models. These descriptive reports are available through the ERIC system in microfiche or photocopy; in the brief mentions that follow, their ERIC order numbers are given instead of the usual citations. The model programs were of many kinds and included the following: programmed tutoring of disadvantaged first graders by paraprofessionals individually, a few minutes each day (ED 053 883); a reading center for each elementary school in a large district, which provided both small-group remedial instruction for children and inservice training and consultations for teachers (ED 053 885); Intensive Reading Centers providing concentrated instruction for disadvantaged first graders in groups of 10 or 11, for a full morning each day for 10 weeks (ED 053 886); a remedial reading program for Spanish American children in Grades 2–4, 30 minutes a day in small groups (ED 053 890); summer sessions providing individualized and small-group instruction, elementary (ED 053 884) and junior high (ED 053 882); a county reading–learning center to which children were bused for hour-long lessons 4 days a week, and in which classroom teachers were trained as reading specialists (ED 053 887); a multilevel program including a diagnostic clinic, small-group remedial reading instruction in the schools, and inservice teacher training (ED 053 888); and a high school program including a reading clinic, a reading laboratory open to good readers as well as poor readers, and a program of individually prescribed study (ED 053 881). Other innovative programs have included the use of fully equipped reading clinics or laboratories in buses that travel from school to school; programs to train and use volunteers, high school pupils, or paraprofessional teacher aides as reading tutors; after-school study centers, some of them located in churches or empty stores; and the like. Remedial reading services in secondary schools have been described by Palmer and Brannock (1982) and E. Webber (1984).

Remediation in Regular Classrooms

Within the regular classroom, remediation may be provided by a classroom teacher or a tutor who receives consultation and direction from the reading specialist. Disabled readers placed in this option are likely to have relatively minor reading problems. The teacher or tutor must have the ability, time, and inclination to follow through on the reading specialist's recommendations.

Remediation also can be conducted in the classroom by the reading specialist. This plan may facilitate coordination of the child's remedial reading program and his classroom program. Lack of coordination can confuse the child who is given different and perhaps conflicting reading programs by the reading specialist and classroom teacher.

Having the reading specialist come to the classroom to provide remediation also has some potential drawbacks. It takes more of the specialist's time in getting from classroom to classroom, and there may not be children within the classroom who have similar needs and thus can be grouped for instruction. Also, some children are unable to concentrate in the face of the many stimulations and distractions present in the typical classroom. For some disabled readers, the embarrassment of being watched or overheard by their classmates is a severely inhibiting factor.

Mainstreaming

As a result of PL 94–142, more handicapped children with learning, physical, and emotional problems are now in regular classrooms on a full-time or part-time basis than formerly. Research findings favor the placement of learning-disabled students in regular classrooms using individualized instruction or supplemented by well-designed resource programs (Madden & Slavin 1983). But mainstreaming has occasioned a number of problems for the teacher, as well as for the students (Horne 1985). In addition to the need to provide educational programs for handicapped pupils, there is also the need to be concerned about their social and emotional well-being. Little attention has been paid to the mainstreamed child's ability to function socially in the classroom, and to prepare nonhandicapped children and the regular classroom teacher for accepting and interacting with handicapped children (Lipson & Alden 1983). The results of a study by Thompson, White, and Morgan (1982), however, did not support the view that mildly handicapped students who are mainstreamed will be at a serious disadvantage because of preferential teacher interactions with the nonhandicapped.

The practical problems that may be created by mainstreaming are similar to those for any pull-out program (see p. 362). Such problems can be greatly lessened, if not overcome, by planning and coordination. Cooperative planning by the reading teacher, special educators, and the regular classroom teacher is essential for effective mainstreaming (Riegel 1983).

Remediation Outside the Regular Classroom

More commonly, remedial reading services are provided outside the regular classroom setting.

Reading Room

Many schools have remedial reading teachers who primarily work with students in one or more schools. A special room is set aside, and the reading teacher works with a small group or one child at a time. As pupils become able to function in their regular classrooms they are discharged and replaced by other students with reading problems.

Resource Room

In some schools, handicapped children receive instruction in one or more subjects in a location outside their regular classroom. This resource room is run by a teacher trained to provide the special education needed by these children.

According to Leinhardt and Pallay (1982), the resource room seems to be the easiest to implement of the alternatives for providing the "least restrictive environment" for handicapped children and reduces some of the negative features while supporting some of the positive features. Ideas for developing and operating resource rooms can be found in Cohen (1982); and Cheyney and Strichart (1981) outlined a plan for using learning stations in a resource room.

In order for a resource-room program to be effective, the pupil must invest himself in the learning task and be willing to make the necessary effort to achieve. As the child becomes more secure he should be encouraged and taught how to set goals for himself and plan purposeful behavior toward the attainment of a goal. Pupils must be encouraged to take responsibility for their achievement, and reasonable expectations must be maintained. Before the child is to be discharged from the reading or resource room, the teacher should make an effort to wean him away from any dependency on her and convince him that he can be successful in the regular classroom program. It is also advisable to plan the transition with the classroom teacher.

Taking children out of their regular classroom for remediation is sometimes referred to as "pull-out" instruction. The most frequently cited shortcomings of pull-out programs are scheduling problems, the time children lose in getting from the classroom to the reading resource room or clinic and back again, the other academic instruction children miss when they are out of the classroom (and the difficulty of making up such losses), and lack of coordination between the child's reading instruction in his classroom and remedial programs. Many of these potential problems can at least be minimized by careful planning.

Some schools have found it efficient to combine remedial reading with enrichment for normal readers in one setting, which is sometimes called a reading resource room or a reading laboratory. In an interesting example from a middle school (Grades 6–8), each of two reading labs was staffed by a reading specialist and a corps of student volunteer aides. The lab offered three kinds of programs: a remedial program for those who needed it; minicourses in specific reading and study skills, for average and above-average readers; and a recreational reading program, open to all students (Crawford & Conley 1971). This kind of program deserves emulation.

Reading Clinics, Centers, and Laboratories

Children with severe reading disabilities and those who fail to respond to remedial efforts in their schools should, when possible, be referred for more intensive and complete diagnosis to a reading clinic, center, or laboratory. The differences among these terms are based more on preferences in choosing a name than on actual differences in organization and program. Many of these facilities are run by universities and colleges and combine training of graduate students as reading specialists with research and service to clients. Some are outpatient clinics located in the neurological, psychiatric, or pediatric services of a hospital. Others are organized within the pupil personnel services of a school system. A few are privately operated. Many children with reading disabilities are also seen in child guidance clinics, in which a psychiatric orientation usually predominates. Several clinics and their procedures were described in the May 1982 issue of the *Journal of Learning Disabilities*.

In addition to a director and one or more reading specialists, a clinic or center should have on its staff representatives of professions such as clinical psychology, psychiatry, neurology, pediatrics, social work, ophthalmology or optometry, and speech correction, or should refer to such specialists for examinations or consultations that seem desirable. After the clinical findings have been interpreted and integrated, recommendations are made both about the treatment of handicaps that interfere with learning and about the kind of remedial instruction the child needs. Treatment is often given in the same clinic. Muia and Connors (1978) provided a very useful discussion of legal requirements concerning confidentiality and obtaining client permissions.

Remedial Schools

A few full-time schools take children with very severe reading disabilities. Some of them are sponsored by universities; others are under private auspices. There are also schools for children who need special education that include learning disabilities among the groups served. Unless a remedial school is heavily endowed, tuition is necessarily high. A partial listing of such resources is published annually (*Directory of Educational Facilities* 1985).

Summer Programs

That some pupils show a decline in reading skills over the summer is fairly well established. Summer reading programs may prove helpful (Cornelius & Semmel 1982), if for no other reason than they get the children to practice their reading skills. Well-designed and operated summer remedial programs may help some children make significant gains in reading. Summer reading programs have been described by Zeller (1980) and Gambrell and Jarrell (1980). However, the permanence of gains from programs lasting only a few weeks is questionable.

12

Developing Word-Recognition Skills and Dealing with Word-Recognition Problems

In this text *word recognition* means that the reader can either directly associate a printed word with its oral counterpart or indirectly determine its pronunciation. Understanding the meaning of the word is not implied in this definition; however, if the appropriate word meaning is in the reader's lexicon, word recognition is likely to lead to word identification. *Word identification* indicates that the reader both recognizes and understands the intended meaning of a printed word (the development of word meaning is taken up in Chapter 13). This distinction is made because a word can be pronounced without understanding even its most common meaning. For example, most readers could arrive at the correct pronunciation of *kine* the first time they see it in print, but not necessarily know its meaning. On the other hand, word meaning can be obtained from a previously unencountered word without knowing or determining its pronunciation if the context in which the word occurs is sufficiently potent and the reader uses the available clue(s). For instance, one would not necessarily need to determine the pronunciation of *kine* to determine its meaning in "The *kine*, or cattle as we call them, were eating grass."

This chapter opens with definitions of terms that should be helpful in understanding the text. Next, the importance of word recognition in the reading process is discussed; our basic conclusion is that word recognition is necessary but not sufficient for reading comprehension. The third section deals with theoretical issues—the process by which words are recognized and the lexicon (mental dictionary) accessed. Sections IV through X are concerned primarily with the development of word recognition and the correction of relatively minor problems, although many of the ideas presented could also be useful in remedial reading.

Section IV contains discussions of points that should be considered in making instructional decisions—which factors influence word recognition, which cues can be used to recognize words, and which words should be taught. Sections V and VI deal with the two most commonly used methods for teaching children to recognize words. These are followed by a detailed discussion of decoding, a suggested scope and sequence in teaching decoding skills, a section in which ways to understand and deal with specific word-recognition problems are suggested, and a description of materials that can be used to improve word-recognition skills.

Some children find it extremely difficult to learn to recognize printed words through conventional teaching methods. The rest of the chapter is devoted to helping such students.

I. TERMINOLOGY

In the literature on reading, different terms are sometimes used to label the same, or similar, phenomena; and the same term can have different meanings, depending on the author. We use the following definitions in this text; other terms are defined at appropriate places in the chapters:

- *Grapheme*: the letter(s) that represents a speech sound. A grapheme is indicated by italics (e.g., *b*, *th*).
- *Phoneme*: a sound in a language. A phoneme is indicated by slashes (e.g., /a/).
- *Grapheme–phoneme correspondence* (symbol–sound association): the association between a letter(s) and the sound it represents.
- *Phoneme–grapheme correspondence* (sound–symbol association): the association between a sound and the grapheme that represents it.
- *Phonics*: the study of grapheme–phoneme relationships; the use of symbol–sound associations in decoding.
- *Decoding*: using a variety of skills, including phonics, to determine the spoken equivalent of a printed word. Some authors use the term *decoding* to mean comprehending written language and *encoding* to mean translating written to spoken language or processing information. *Recoding* may refer to changing information from one code to another or may have the same meaning that we use for *decoding*.
- *Whole-word method*: an instructional method that emphasizes learning to associate printed whole words with their spoken counterparts.

- *Sight vocabulary*: all the words a reader can recognize immediately. The words may have been learned originally through a whole-word, phonic, or any other instructional approach.
- *Lexicon*: all the words that an individual can identify, including their meanings and syntactic functions; a person's mental dictionary.

II. THE IMPORTANCE OF WORD RECOGNITION

Word recognition provides a necessary foundation for reading comprehension, but word recognition alone is not sufficient for reading comprehension. Yet, despite its importance, relatively little is known about the word-recognition process (Juel & Roper-Schneider 1982) or how it develops in children (Barron 1981a). It is likely, however, that word recognition is not a unitary process but is comprised of a number of interrelated subprocesses (Venezky & Massaro 1979, Schadler & Thissen 1981, Rumelhart & McClelland 1981, Stanovich 1982a).

Novice readers must learn to identify printed words accurately, rapidly, and completely in the sense that the word's meaning, as well as its oral counterpart, is apparent to the child when the printed word is seen (Ehri & Wilce 1980). The reading comprehension of even skilled readers is likely to be disrupted or impaired if most of the printed words are not recognized and identified accurately and rapidly.

There are various theories as to why rapid, accurate word identification is important for reading comprehension. Often, short-term memory (STM) is implicated (e.g., Gough 1972). The belief is that words cannot be organized into meaningful groups unless word recognition is accurate and fast enough to avoid exceeding the limits of STM.

Vellutino (1982) advocated a three-stage model of memory as applied to word recognition. The *sensory register* involves the processes that record the physical stimuli in raw uncoded forms for very brief durations (200–300 milliseconds). During this first stage, the visual features of letters and words are analyzed and encoded. During the short-term memory (STM) stage, five to nine chunks of information can be retained for up to approximately 30 seconds. The type of lexical information processed during STM varies with the skill of the reader and the nature of the reading task. For novice readers, letters and letter clusters might be the processing units. For more skilled readers, STM is used for the temporary storage of words and phrases while processing the constituents of a sentence. Long-term memory (LTM) is an unlimited capacity system that retains information indefinitely, but the retrieval of particular items depends on the ability to set up a "mental filing system" that facilitates efficient search and location for all of the information contained about a printed word—its oral counterpart, graphic (visual) features, orthographic (structural) components, phonological (auditory) characteristics, and semantic and syntactic properties.

The limited-attention model (LaBerge & Samuels 1976) and limited-capacity model (Perfetti 1976, Perfetti & Lesgold 1977, 1979) both hold that the amount of attentional or processing capacity devoted to word recognition limits the resources available for processing meaning. Or, as Stanovich, Cunningham, and Feeman (1984) put it, words must be recognized rapidly in order to provide sufficient word meaning for comprehension, and automatically in order to free cognitive capacity for allocation to comprehension rather than word-recognition processes. Whereas skilled readers need to allocate only minimal attentional resources to word recognition because they are so automatic, novice readers must allocate considerably larger amounts of their attentional resources to word recognition (West 1979).

Word-Recognition Accuracy and Reading Comprehension

Correlations between word-recognition accuracy and reading comprehension tend to be higher in the primary grades (about .80) than at upper grade levels (about .65). This is not surprising, since the number of words used in beginning reading materials is limited, the meanings of nearly all these words are understood by most children, the story concepts are usually within their semantic competence, and most sentence patterns are within their syntactic competence. As factors such as sentence complexity become more important influences on reading comprehension, the relationship between word recognition and comprehension decreases.

Word-Recognition Speed and Reading Comprehension

Studies of *word-recognition latency* (the time taken to respond to a printed word) have indicated a relationship between word-recognition speed and reading comprehension. The more rapid the word recognition, the higher the comprehension (Perfetti, Finger, & Hogaboam 1978; McCormick & Samuels 1979; Stanovich, Cunningham, & West 1981; Marr & Kamil 1981). Correlations between word-recognition speed (as measured by various means) and reading ability range from about .50 to .80 (Stanovich 1982c).

Research findings regarding the influence of rapid single-word-recognition training on reading comprehension are mixed. Blanchard and McNinch (1980) cited five studies that reported positive effects. Three studies failed to show such an effect (Fleisher, Jenkins & Pany 1979; Spring, Blunden, & Gatheral 1981; Piggens & Barron 1983). Lyon's findings (1984) did not support the hypothesis that rapid, accurate word-recognition training would improve the reading comprehension of only those disabled readers who had the linguistic competence necessary to understand the material (those whose listening comprehension was significantly higher than their reading comprehension). Apparently, although automatic word recognition is a facilitator, it alone is not sufficient for reading comprehension. Perhaps, as Resnick (1979b) suggested, instruction in any single subskill, such as rapid word recognition, is unlikely by itself to change poor readers into good ones because the observed skill difference is actually just one indicator of many differences between good and poor readers.

Studies have indicated that word-recognition speed usually increases with age; that the word-recognition speed of good readers is significantly faster than that of poor readers, except perhaps for high-frequency words; and that word recognition is faster in context than in isolation, especially for poor readers (Lyon 1984). According to Juel and Roper-Schneider (1982), mastery of context-free word recognition appears to be one of the major factors that separate good from poor readers. Successful readers usually have gained automatic word-processing skills by second or third grade.

It is possible that word-recognition ability is a consequence of, as well as a cause of, good reading ability. Good readers read a great deal, and since reading improves word recognition, good readers develop excellent word recognition. Poor readers often do not read much, so they cut themselves off from a major source of word-recognition development.

III. THEORETICAL ISSUES

The Word-Recognition Process

Obtaining reliable information about how words are recognized is extremely difficult, for as J. C. Johnston (1981) pointed out, our minds tend to make only the final product of their processing available to conscious awareness; the intermediate processing steps are usually hidden from us. As yet, the process of word recognition is not well understood. Although there is some commonality, theorists are not in complete agreement as to what is involved in word recognition. For example, compare Venezky and Massaro (1979), Ehri (1980), Rumelhart and McClelland (1981), Vellutino and Scanlon (1982), L. Henderson (1982), and Juel (1983). There are, for instance, considerable differences of opinion regarding the unit of perception in reading. The various theories fall into one of four categories: (1) theories in which the featural components of letters are believed to be the units of perceptual analysis; (2) letter-based hypotheses, in which word recognition involves processing the word's component letters; (3) letter-cluster hypotheses, in which the unit of perception is a group of letters; or (4) whole-word hypotheses (Adams 1978, Juola *et al.* 1979).

Early studies by Cattell (1885, 1886) and Huey (1908) are often cited as evidence that the word is the unit of perception in reading.[1] Their data, however, do not support this contention (Kamil 1980). Nor do the findings which indicate that individuals *can* use letter and letter-cluster information in recognizing words (e.g., Mewhort & Campbell 1981) support the belief that such units are actually used during normal reading (N. F. Johnson 1981).

Vellutino (1982) summarized and critiqued feature analysis, component letter, letter-group, and whole-word theories of word recognition and concluded that the unit of perception in reading is relative. He stated that all the visual information contained in a printed word is apprehended by the reader but that the unit in focal attention at the time when word identification is finalized is variable and depends on the nature of the stimulus, the context in which the word is perceived, and the information available to and typically used by the reader. For example, words that are easily discriminated from others (*hippopotamus*) or words that are highly constrained by context may be identified at

---

[1] These studies also are cited as early justifications for use of the whole-word method of instruction.

the level of salient word features. Less easily discriminated words must be processed more carefully, especially when they appear in isolation or in ambiguous or uncertain contexts.

The word-recognition strategies employed by novice readers may depend on the instruction methodology employed, but beginners also may employ strategies other than these taught (Barr 1974–1975). Word-recognition strategies also may change with reading experience (Patberg, Dewitz, & Samuels 1981). Novice readers may use units smaller than the word in word recognition. Increasingly, units larger than the letter may be employed as students unitize smaller into larger units of perception (Samuels 1981).

Vellutino and Scanlon (1982) presented the following theory of word recognition: The initial processing of a word involves the analysis of its visual characteristics. Precise word recognition requires attention to the word's salient or global features (e.g., configuration, length), sensitivity to subtle differences that distinguish it from visually similar words (e.g., the letter sequences that define the word), and a sensitivity to the letter sequences that are permissible in English orthography. After the visual analysis is completed, an attempt is made to match the printed word with an item in the lexicon. This may be done through a direct-access route using the whole word or via a mediated route involving phonological recoding (see below).

The learner gradually builds a complicated associational network in which various word features are interrelated and synthesized. Once established, each of these representations is activated whenever the printed word is seen, thereby constituting alternative means by which the word may be recognized.

Identities and Features of Words

According to Ehri (1980), the words in one's lexicon that have been acquired through experiences with spoken language have a (1) *semantic identity*, which specifies the word's meaning in various contexts; (2) *syntactic identity*, which indicates its characteristic grammatical function(s); and (3) *phonological identity*, which specifies its acoustic, articulatory, and phonemic structure. When one learns to read, an *orthographic identity* is added; orthographic images are learned as sequences of letters bearing systematic relationships to acoustic or articulatory segments already stored in lexical memory. A word's orthographic form is secured to its phonological form when at least some of the letters come to represent phonetic segments. When all of the word's identities have been amalgamated to form a single unit in one's lexicon, its printed form comes to symbolize the word's other identities, and the word is processed as a single unit rather than as a sequence of letters. At this point the printed word becomes a symbol of meaning, as well as sound, and replaces the sound as the "address" used for locating a word in the lexicon; word meaning can be accessed directly rather than only through phonological recoding.

Vellutino (Vellutino *et al.* 1981, Vellutino & Shub 1982, Vellutino 1983) also discussed the featural information in words. Vellutino's viewpoint differs from that of Ehri mainly in his definitions of phonological features (the unique ordering of phonemes comprising a word) and orthographic features (the word's internal structure).

Lexical Access

Information about a word stored in the lexicon (primarily its semantic and syntactic identities) has to be accessed in order for reading comprehension to occur. Two forms of lexical access have been theorized. In *direct access*, words are identified by finding a direct match between the visual stimulus and a lexical entry, or printed words are converted to a visual code that is spatially defined and involves word shape and length, letter features, and the features of letter sequences and groupings (Katz & Feldman 1981). In the latter case, the visual-orthographic code is matched with the lexical entry. In *phonological access*, the printed words are first converted to a phonological code (the sound of the word), which is then used to search the lexicon until a match is made.

Once orthographic images are established as word symbols in the lexicon, this mediated function ceases and from then on, orthographic images are used to identify words from their printed forms.

Some writers (e.g., Mitterer 1981) have suggested that there are two types of poor readers—"recoding poor readers," who rely heavily on phonological recoding, and "whole-word poor readers," who make little use of it. Others (e.g., Shankweiler *et al.* 1979) have stated that disabled readers are unable to make adequate use of the phonological route. Ellis (1981), on the other hand, was of the opinion that severely disabled readers were deficient in the use of both routes for lexical access.

Disagreement among theorists concerning lexical access seems to center on two main areas: (1) whether or not phonolocial recoding is necessary for lexical access; and (2) when the phonological identities of words are determined.

Authorities such as Gough (1972) argue that a phonological code is essential. One of the reasons given for the importance of phonological recoding is that phonologically coded linguistic information can be retained longer in STM (through rehearsal) than can orthographic information. Because the information is available longer, it is more likely that meaning can be obtained (Nickerson 1981; Foster 1981; Tanenhaus, Flanagan, & Seidenberg 1980; Stanovich 1982a). Others (e.g., Venezky 1981) point out weaknesses in the phonological mediation hypothesis. In dual-process, independent-channel models of word identification, both routes are activated simultaneously, with the first to produce a match in the lexicon being acted on by the reader.

There is growing evidence that either pathway may be utilized, with the choice depending on various factors (Haines & Leong 1983). Novice readers may be more reliant on visual than phonological information when reading familiar words (Katz & Feldman 1981, Stanovich 1981a) or when they have been instructed through a whole-word method or have not had much instruction and practice in decoding (Barron 1981a). Recent research strongly supports the position that direct access is possible for skilled readers but that they use mediated access when confronted by unknown words (Kleiman & Humphrey (1982).

The second point of disagreement involves whether phonological recoding occurs before or after lexical access. On one hand, Allport (1979) and others have argued that the pronunciation of a word must depend on postlexical phonology, otherwise how could a reader determine differences in pronunciation of such words as *dough* versus *cough* and the pronunciations and meanings of words like *bow* and *lead*. On the other hand, Doctor (1981) and others have concluded that phonological encoding is prelexical for pronunciation tasks involving single words in isolation but postlexical (if it occurs) when reading words in context.

IV. METHODOLOGICAL CONSIDERATIONS

Factors That Influence Word Recognition

Many factors influence the recognition and retention of printed words. One is teaching methodology. Children initially taught with a phonic method (1) are less likely to guess unfamiliar words; (2) are more likely to recognize phonemically regular words than irregular words; (3) are likely to make mispronunciations that are graphically or phonemically similar to the stimuli but may be semantically inappropriate; and (4) are likely to make little use of semantic and syntactic cues (Barr 1972, 1974–1975, 1975; Dank 1977). Children taught initially with a whole-word method (1) are likely to guess unfamiliar words; (2) rely heavily at first on context clues, at times disregarding graphic cues; (3) often substitute a previously taught word for the stimulus; (4) tend to apply decoding skills as they are acquired; and (5) increasingly combine contextual and graphic cues as reading ability improves (Biemiller 1970).

Based on an intensive case history of 50 first graders, most of whom were economically disadvantaged, Calfee and Piontkowski (1981) concluded that children learn what they are taught. Those in meaning-emphasis programs performed far better on reading passages than on recognizing words in isolation; those in code-emphasis programs became proficient decoders but were less successful at reading passages. Decoding-skills emphasis seemed to lead to comprehension more often than emphasis on meaning led to better decoding performance.

Some words tend to be learned more easily by children.[2] These include words that children want to learn and are meaningful to them (Brescia & Braun 1977), have strong emotional overtones (Adams 1974), or evoke imagery (Hargis & Gickling 1978, Kolker & Terwilliger 1981, Terwilliger & Kolker 1982). Van der Veur (1975) listed the imagery ratings of 1000 high-frequency words. The majority of studies found that concrete words such as nouns are learned more readily than abstract words (e.g., Ehri 1976; Arnold, McNinch, & Miller 1978; Ollila & Chamberlin 1979). Jorm (1977) found that high-frequency words were easier to learn; Horodezky (1979) did not.

---

[2] Even the words used in musical TV commericals can be used to generate interest and to learn to read words (Klink 1976, Hirst & O'Such 1979). Dalzell (1976) found that use of TV scripts and programs was highly motivating and resulted in increased reading-test scores.

Function words (prepositions, conjunctions, relative pronouns, auxiliary and linking verbs, and articles) often are troublesome because they have no clear lexical meaning and because of the similarity of their physical features (e.g., they begin with *th*—*that, this, there*; or *wh*—*what, which, why*). Yet function words must be mastered because they occur so frequently in print. Jolly (1981, 1984) presented suggestions for teaching function words.

Repetition and Reinforcement

Practice does not necessarily make perfect. Mere repetition is not a sufficient basis for learning. Nevertheless, repetition has some relevance. Children differ greatly in how quickly they learn to recognize printed words. Some children can remember a word easily after one or two exposures; others need many repetitions. To be effective, repetition should not be monotonous drill but should be presented so as to maintain the child's interest and encourage accurate perception. After a word is introduced in a reading series, it usually is repeated a number of times in differing contexts in the reading text. Correlated workbooks can furnish additional repetitions; and an abundance of easy, pleasurable reading provides an excellent way to practice word recognition.

Although flash cards[3] are widely used to provide word-recognition practice, such cards sometimes encourage dependence on the wrong cues, such as a smudge on the card or a dog-eared corner. When used for first teaching, word cards not only encourage dependence on accidental and incidental cues but also may result in little transfer to recognition of the words in meaningful context. Word cards can be used to build sentences, to test words after they have been taught, and in quick-exposure techniques to develop speed of recognition after the words have been fairly well learned by the child.

Picture—word cards that can be used for independent study and self-teaching can be made by the teacher or pupils. The word is printed on one side of an opaque card, and an illustrative picture with the word below it is on the other side. Clipping one corner makes it easier to keep the cards right side up. After studying the picture—word side of a few cards, the cards are turned over and the child tests himself, checking the correctness of each response by looking again at the picture.

Nouns are easiest to depict. Action verbs (*run*) and direction words (*above, to, from*) may be represented by using stick figures, arrows, and so forth. Abstract words (e.g., *an, is*) are difficult to picture and usually must be placed in a phrase or sentence in which context is the main cue to the underlined word (e.g., The girl *is* running).

Word cards such as *The Dolch Basic Sight Vocabulary Cards* (Garrard) are also in wide use. Printed word cards based on the vocabulary found in beginning reading materials are available from the publishers of most reading series. Teacher-made word cards can be used to provide practice on words that need special attention. Auditory cues can also be provided by special machines (see Fig. 12.1). The *Language Master* (Bell & Howell), VOXCOM (ETA), *Electric*

---

[3] The term *word card* is more appropriate since the card can be displayed for any length of time and can be used for other than quick exposures.

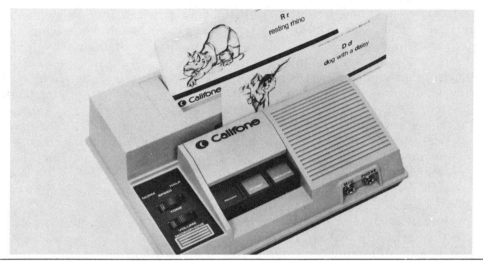

Figure 12.1. A card reader. Reproduced by permission of Califone International, Inc.

Card Reader (Mast), and others employ cards on which strips of magnetic tape are mounted. The child can look at the card; attempt to read the word, phrase, or sentence; then place it on the machine and listen as a recorded voice provides the oral counterpart. The child's response also can be recorded and compared with the recorded voice. Both printed, prerecorded magnetic cards and blank cards can be purchased.

Regardless of the initial teaching method, as the words are encountered repeatedly in print they become sight words; that is, they are recognized immediately. If slow word recognition persists and becomes a real handicap, a child may need special training.

Which Words Should Be Taught?

When a particular reading series is used in developmental reading, it is more important for children to recognize the words used in their instructional materials than those that appear on a given word list. The words introduced in a reading series do not occur equally as often in those materials or in any printed material. Some words may appear only once, or at best a few times; others occur repeatedly.

K. Goodman and Bird (1984) found that high-frequency words fall into two groups. Words that occur frequently across texts are function words (words that have grammatical but not lexical meaning—these include noun determiners, verb markers, conjunctions, and prepositions), pronouns, and copulas (forms of the verb *be*). Such words occur frequently because English syntax requires them and because only a few words can fulfill each function. Function words are the "glue" that cements communication (D. Johnson & Pearson 1984). Pronouns are among the most frequently occurring words in print because writing style requires their use once the referents have been established (repeated use of a proper noun would make the material stilted and uninteresting). Pronouns provide a great deal of text cohesion by providing chains of reference. Therefore, recognizing function words as well as pronouns and identifying their referents are important aspects of reading comprehension.

The other group are words common to a particular text. Nouns, especially proper nouns, are the only content words likely to appear often in a particular text. Other content words (verbs, adjectives, and adverbs) are rarely repeated more than a few times for pragmatic and stylistic reasons, and because more words with similar meaning are available to fill the slots within each class of content words. Cohesion can be maintained without repeating the same words.

K. Goodman and Bird (1984) found that approximaterly 55% of the words occurred only once. A small set of words appeared very frequently (e.g., 25 words accounted for 36% to 40% of the running words).

More instruction and practice should be provided for frequently occurring words than for those that rarely appear in the instructional materials. If information about word frequency is not available from the publisher, a list of high-frequency words can be used as a guideline.

One of the basic tenets of the language-experience approach is that the students should be taught the words they want to use in creating their stories. The belief that words that carry high emotional charges and interest for the children are easier for them to learn was the basis for the development of an "organic vocabulary" first advocated by Ashton-Warner (1959) and later systematically developed by Veatch *et al.* (1979).

In remedial reading the teacher has a number of options. She may choose to teach first the words the child wants to learn and then gradually introduce other words. Or she may opt to start with high-utility words and a few content words in order to get the child quickly into reading meaningful material containing words that are likely to have high transfer value. At times, high-frequency words containing the same phonetic element may be taught together and then used as a basis for teaching through an analytic phonics method. If the teacher has determined that a phonics method is advisable to use with a child, she may first teach those phonic elements that will allow the child to decode orthographically regular words.

Word Lists

A relatively small number of the over 600,000 English words appear frequently in print. Johns (1981) stated that 13 words (*a, and, for, he, is, in, it, of, that, the, to, was, you*) account for over 25% of the words in print. Fry, Polk, and Fountoukidis (1984) estimated that 100 words make up half of all the words in written material, and 1000 words account for over 90%. High-frequency word lists are not in complete agreement as to the rank order of such words, nor do they all contain the same words.

Since E. L. Thorndike (1921) compiled the first word list, numerous others have appeared.[4] The most recent comprehensive lists are based on Grade 1–8

[4] Refer to A. J. Harris and Jacobson (1982) for a brief history of reading vocabulary lists.

textbooks (A. J. Harris & Jacobson 1982; the pre-primer, primer, and first reader lists of which are shown in Fig. 12.2). Other comprehensive lists include one based on a wide variety of materials used in Grades 3–9 (Carroll, Davies, & Richman 1971),[5] and one based on adult reading materials (Kučera & Francis 1967). A 9000-word list that includes 6530 words with multiple meanings and 86 homographs was compiled by Johnson, Moe, and Baumann (1983). A book of lists (Fry, Polk, & Fountoukidis 1984) presents lists covering such areas as high-utility words, words found in content subjects, homophones, homograms, and word families.

Many shorter lists have been developed for specific purposes. For instance, Reich and Reich (1979) published a 200-word list of the vocabulary of Canadian primary-grade children, and an oral vocabulary of 6442 words used by first graders was determined by Moe, Hopkins, and Rush (1982). There are also lists of survival words and phrases (e.g., DANGER, DON'T WALK) (Polloway & Polloway 1981), and road and traffic-sign words (McWilliams 1979) that can be successfully taught to disabled readers (Test & Heward 1983). Otto and Stallard (1976) compiled a list of 100 words that appear in 16 other word lists. For descriptions and comparisons of word lists, see A. J. Harris and Jacobson (1973–1974), Hillerich (1974), and Monteith (1976).

The old but still frequently used *Dolch Basic Sight Vocabulary* contains 220 words exclusive of nouns. The fact that after over 40 years these words still account for over 50% of the words found in reading materials (Johns 1976) attests to their high utility. Johns (1981) used four word lists published between 1957 and 1971 to update the Dolch list. He eliminated 31 and added 37 words. These 226 words accounted for over 55% of the vocabulary in four basal series.

Dolch (1939) suggested that the "easiest" 110 words on his list should be mastered by the middle of second grade and the "harder" 110 by third grade. A few years ago, approximately 80 of the 220 words were on the H–J first-grade list; about 20% were on the second-grade list; and a few were at the third-grade level (A. J. Harris & Sipay 1980, pp. 372–374). Now, as shown in Figure 12.2, over 90% are at the first reader level (many more on the H–J pre-primer and primer lists than in 1980), and the rest are second reader words (see Fig. 12.3). In setting up an instructional sequence from any alphabetized word list, it may be helpful to compare it against the words introduced at the various reader levels in the materials from which the child is being instructed.

Because words appear on a word list or are called "basic" does not mean that a particular child can recognize them. Neither should it be assumed that children know the meanings of high-frequency words. Such words may have multiple meanings and function as different parts of speech. Although the multiple meanings of a given word rarely occur in the same text (K. Goodman & Bird 1984), shifts in word meaning can cause comprehension problems for the reader, especially when common words represent uncommon meanings.

---

[5] The Carroll *et al. Word Frequency Book* was used by Fry (1980b) to develop a 300-word list and by Walker (1979) to produce a 1000-word list.

PRE-PRIMER LIST

a*	come*	here*	of*	the*
all*	day	hide	old*	they*
am*	did*	home	on*	thing
and*	do*	I*	out*	this*
are*	dog	in*	pet	time
at*	don't*	is*	pig	to*
be*	down*	it*	play*	too*
bear	fish	it's	read*	up*
big*	fly*	jump*	red*	want*
blue*	for*	let*	ride*	we*
book	from*	like*	run*	what*
boy	game	little*	said*	where*
but*	get*	look*	say*	who*
by*	girl	make*	see*	will*
came*	go*	man	she*	with*
can*	good*	me*	sit*	yes*
can't	have*	my*	so*	you*
car	he*	no*	stop*	your*
cat	help*	not*	that*	

PRIMER LIST

about*	cut*	frog	how*	mother
after*	dad	fun	I'll	mouse
an*	didn't	funny*	I'm	Mr.
animal	does*	good-by	if*	Mrs.
as*	door	got*	into*	much*
ask*	duck	green*	just*	must*
away*	each	grow*	know*	name
back	eat*	had*	lake	need
bad	end	happy	last	new*
bag	every*	has*	laugh*	next
ball	fall*	hat	liked	night
bat	fast*	hello	lion	nothing
bed	father	hen	live*	now*
bee	feel	her*	lived	oh
bird	feet	hid	lost	one*
bob	find*	high	lot	open*
box	fire	hill	made*	or*
call*	fix	him*	many*	other
city	found*	his*	may*	over*
could*	fox	hot*	maybe	paper
cow	friend	house	more	park

Figure 12.2. Harris–Jacobson word lists for first grade. From *Basic reading vocabularies* by Albert J. Harris and Milton D. Jacobson. Copyright © 1982 by Macmillan Publishing Co. Reproduced by permission of the authors and publisher. Words that are also in the Dolch Basic Sight Vocabulary List are marked with an asterisk. Note that many of the words in the H–J but not the Dolch list are nouns; the Dolch 220 does not contain any nouns.

pat	saw*	sun	today*	water
people	school	surprise	took	way
pick*	seed	swim	top	well*
place	show*	take*	tree	went*
plant	sing*	talk	trick	were*
put*	sky	tell*	truck	when*
rabbit	sleep*	thank*	turtle	why*
rain	slow	that's	two*	window
ran*	small*	them*	under*	woman
road	some*	then*	us*	won't
rock	something	there*	very*	work*
sad	sometime	think*	wait	would*
same	still	thought	walk*	you're
sat	street	three*	was*	youth

FIRST READER LIST

again*	bone	draw*	great	let's
ago	breakfast	drink*	grew	letter
alone	brother	drove	ground	light*
along	brown*	even	guess	line
always*	bus	ever*	hand	long*
another	cake	everyone	he's	love
ant	care	everything	head	lunch
any*	cave	everywhere	hear	making
anything	chair	eye	heard	mayor
apple	children	face	helper	mean
aren't	class	family	herself	men
around*	clean*	far*	hi	might
ate*	close	faster	hold*	miss
bake	cloud	feed	hole	mix
bark	clown	fell	hop	mom
beautiful	coat	fill	horse	money
because*	cold*	fine	hungry	morning
been*	color	first*	hurt*	most
began	coming	floor	I've	move
begin	cook	flower	inside	moved
being	couldn't	food	isn't	myself*
best*	country	gave*	jay	named
better*	cry	give*	keep*	near
bike	dance	glad	kind*	never*
birthday	dark	glass	king	nice
bit	dinner	gold	kite	noise
bite	doctor	gone	kitten	nose
black*	doesn't	grandma	leave	note
boat	don	grass	leg	off*

Figure 12.2. (continued)

only*	sang	someone	teacher	until
our*	sea	song	than	use*
outside	seat	soon*	their*	wasn't
paint	secret	sorry	there's	watch
pan	seen	sound	these*	we'll
part	sheep	squirrel	those*	wet
party	shoe	stand	tiger	what's
picture	shop	star	tire	which*
plan	should	start*	together*	while
please*	shout	stay	told	white*
pot	side	step	tonight	wind
pound	sign	stick	town	winter
pretty*	sister	stone	toy	wish*
push	six*	store	track	without
quiet	smell	story	train	wood
ready	smile	stuck	tried	word
real	smiled	sure	trip	worker
right*	snake	table	try*	yell
room	snow	tail	turn	yellow*
rope	someday	tall	TV	zoo
sandy				

Figure 12.2.   (*continued*)

Word-Recognition Cues

There are basically four sources of information that aid word recognition. Although discussed separately, such cues are likely to be used in combination, particularly by skilled readers. Children should be made aware of these cue systems and instructed in using them effectively and efficiently.

Visual–Graphic Cues

Printing conventions[6] dictate that printed words are separated by spaces wider than those used between letters but narrower than spacing between sentences. Once aware of this convention, visual segmentation of sentences into words should no longer be a problem for children with normal vision.

Word length does not seem to be a significant factor in word recognition (Cogar 1974, Jorm 1977). But at times it may provide a visual cue to the reader by helping to delimit the possible choices, especially when the words begin with the same letter (e.g., *me, mean, morning*).

Configuration

The outline, or general shape, of the word may be of some assistance if the visual differences are significant, such as between dog and cat, and when word length is also a factor (egg, elephant). Word-shape information, when combined with other cues, can help reduce the number of alternatives from which

---

[6] Other printing conventions provide visual information to the reader. For instance, sentence boundaries are also marked by capital letters and punctuation marks; and quotation marks aid in determining who is saying what. See R. Haber and Haber (1981b).

before	eight	its*	shall
both	five	once	ten
bring	four	own	upon
buy	full	pull	warm
carry	goes*	round	wash
done	going*	seven	write

Figure 12.3. Dolch Basic Sight Vocabulary words that are not in the Harris–Jacobson first-grade lists. Words marked with an asterisk are inflected forms of words on the H–J pre-primer list. The remaining 21 words are on the H–J second-grade list.

the reader has to choose. For example, in "The cat drank the m⬚", the initial letter plus the configuration rule out semantic and syntactic possibilities like *water*. And although both words begin with the same letter and have similar shapes, the answer is more likely *milk* than *meat* because of prior knowledge. Words similar in shape, length, and component letters (*want–went, saw–was*) can cause problems for novice readers who do not notice small visual differences and are relatively insensitive to letter sequence in words. Calling their attention to the sequences of letters in such word pairs may help them to overcome such confusions, and as a general practice when introducing new words may help novice readers to rely less on initial letters and more on orthographic structure as an aid to word recognition. Terwilliger and Kolker (1982) found that the subsequent learning of words was faster for first graders who were first taught words that begin with similar initial letters than for children who first learned to recognize words beginning with different letters.

There are differences of opinion regarding the value of configuration in word recognition. Some researchers have concluded that configuration is an ineffective and seldom-used cue (Timko 1970; Williams, Blumberg, & Williams 1970). Since their studies used only words of equal length, the findings cannot be generalized to normal reading where word length is a major factor in configuration. Groff (1975) argued that the number of words represented by unique shapes is too small to provide enough visual information for accurate word recognition. But R. Haber and Haber (1981a, b) contended that the shapes of high-frequency words differ sufficiently to provide useful visual information, especially when combined with context and other cues. A few studies (J. Williams 1977; Haber, Haber, & Furlin 1983) have shown that adult readers can make use of configuration and word-length cues, but they have not revealed how important such information is to skilled readers. Barron (1981a), and Ehri and Wilce (1982) believed that specific letter information provides more useful information than does configuration.

It is not advisable to encourage children to rely heavily on word shape or length as word-recognition cues. The same is true for certain letters in words (e.g., "The *oo* looks like two eyes, so that should help you to remember *look*") because the cue is not generalizable (e.g., the cue would have little value in recognizing words like *tool*).

Research has indicated that initial letters are frequently used visual cues in word recognition, more so than final letters, which are more frequently relied on than medial letters. This may be due to the fact that initial letters in words are more predictable. Also, initial and final letters in words are less subject to lateral masking because they are not completely surrounded by other letters (Barron 1981a). Word endings may receive attention because they convey linguistic information (e.g., pluralization) (Gibson & Levin 1975). Partial graphic information (e.g., initial letter, configuration) may be very salient, though insufficient for word recognition, for novice readers who lack more reliable graphic information (Barron 1981a).

Information from Letters

Theories regarding how readers extract and use letter-shape information fall into two general categories (R. Haber & Haber 1981b). *Template* or *prototype* models suggest that the description of a letter is holistic and gestalt-like. In *feature models*, the description of a letter is a list of the features that make the letter unique and different from all other letters. R. Haber and Haber (1981b) believed feature models to be more tenable and that only one or two features of a letter were often sufficient to identify a letter. But L. Henderson (1982) was of the opinion that the wide acceptance of the distinctive feature theory has prevented us from learning more about the initial stage of letter or word analysis.

The physical properties of letters, such as the ascending and descending features of some lowercase letters, assist word recognition in a limited way. There are more visual cues in lowercase than in capital letters, so words printed in lowercase are easier to recognize. The upper halves of lowercase letters provide more visual information than the lower halves do. It is easier to read with vowels omitted than with consonants deleted (Carroll and Walton 1979):

Th __ f __ t d __ g __ t __ __ b __ n __.
__ __ e __ a __ __ o __ a __ e a __ o __ e.

Orthographic Knowledge

The spellings of English words are constrained by the positions in which letters can occur (e.g., *ck* can occur in the final but not initial position) and the allowable sequences of letters (e.g., *sm* is a legal sequence, *sx* is not) (Venezky 1981). There is also a high likelihood of certain letters following others (e.g., only three consonants, *h*, *r*, and *w*, can follow an initial *t*, and *h* occurs 65% of the time) (L. Haber & Haber 1981). Orthographic knowledge facilitates word recognition because less visual information is required (Samuels 1981). Expectations for letter sequences develop over time from repeated experiences with printed words (Venezky 1979b).

The degree to which letter strings conform to the rules of English spelling influences the perception and processing of the stimuli (E. Smith & Kleiman 1979; Barron 1981a). Regularly spelled letter strings (*blost*) are better perceived than those that violate spelling rules (*stobl*), which are more readily recognized than letter strings that greatly violate spelling regularity (*tsxbl*). The degree to which the stimuli are similar to known words also influences their decodability.

It is difficult to establish precisely what aspects of orthographic regularity are used in word recognition, and the overall impact of sensitivity to orthographic knowledge on various experimental tasks has been relatively small (Juel 1983). The apparent developmental nature of sensitivity to orthographic structure and high correlations between it and word-recognition ability (e.g., .80 by Leslie & Shannon 1981) suggest that orthographic knowledge is a consequence rather than a cause of word-recognition ability (Henderson & Chard 1980, Leslie & Shannon 1981).

English orthography may present the reader with information about the sounds that constitute the word's spoken equivalent, as well as providing linguistic information. Our spellings preserve morphophonemic information (e.g., pluralization is marked by *s* in both *cats* and *dogs*, even though *s* represents different sounds in each). Spellings also assist in distinguishing between homophones (*hare* vs. *hair*, *band* vs. *banned*).

Graphophonemic Cues

In our writing system, letters are used to construct words which represent their spoken counterparts. Although the relationship between graphemes and the phonemes they represent is not entirely consistent, the letters in words can provide information useful in word recognition. Knowledge of grapheme–phoneme relationships may be acquired informally or as a result of direct instruction. These symbol–sound association skills can be used as an aid in recognizing a word that is not firmly fixed in one's sight vocabulary, especially if used in conjunction with other cues. For instance, determining the sound of the initial letter or so and the use of context may be all that is needed to recognize a word. When a word is met for the first time in print, it may be necessary to decode it more fully.

Syntactic Cues

Syntactic or grammatical cues involve implicit knowledge of word order and the functions of words. Only certain word sequences are allowable in English, and only certain kinds of words fit into particular slots in our sentence patterns. In "the baseball player _____ the ball," the missing words must be a verb, and the alternatives are restricted to such verbs as *saw, threw, caught* and *hit*. Additional visual cues could further restrict the possibilities, as could other cues within the sentence. Thus, if *yesterday* appeared at the end of the sentence, only a past tense verb could be used; and the addition of "with his bat" would exclude such words as *saw, threw*, or *caught*.

Changes in word order can influence meaning greatly (Susie saw Rob. vs. Rob saw Susie) or subtly as a change in emphasis (Rob saw Susie vs. Susie was seen by Rob).

Most children enter school with the ability to understand most English syntactic structures, and they understand more of these structures than they use in their oral language. The formal syntactic patterns that often occur in written material differ from those commonly used in spoken language and may cause problems for some novice readers. But children learn early to expect that what they find in print differs from their oral language (Y. Goodman & Greene 1977).

Children continue to make substantial gains in their ability to understand syntactic structures until about age 13 (M. Adams 1977), and many continue to refine these skills through extended experiences with spoken and written language.

Context Effects

Semantic and syntactic cues usually function together and often are referred to as *context clues*. Studies have generally indicated that word recognition is usually more accurate and faster in context than in isolation (Lyon 1984).

The most prevalent explanation for context effects is that what has been read reduces uncertainty as to what is likely to follow. The preceding context allows the reader to predict what is coming. The ability to make use of context requires word-recognition skills, grammatical knowledge, semantic knowledge, and topical knowledge. Apparent inability to use context may reflect weaknesses in one or more of these areas (Potter 1982). Accurate but very slow word recognition also may be disruptive.

Context effects arise primarily from within the sentence containing the target word (West *et al.* 1983), and the effect of global context (e.g., the chapter in which the word appears) is probably semantic, whereas the effect of local context (the immediately surrounding phrase or sentence) probably has an important syntactic component (Gough, Alford, & Holley-Wilcox 1981). But exactly how context facilitates word recognition is largely unknown, and theories are vague as to what is predicted.

Young unskilled readers may not make maximum use of context clues because (1) their word-recognition skills are just developing, so they must focus their attention on visual information rather than on obtaining meaning; (2) they do not yet understand how to apply the skills they use to understand spoken language as an aid to comprehending written language; and (3) the semantic and syntactic cues available in beginning reading texts may not be potent enough to facilitate word recognition or comprehension. Samuels (1980) suggested that novice readers have great difficulty in using context as an aid to word recognition because their attention is focused on elements smaller than the word. This results in the STM's being filled with nonmeaningful parts of words, so meaningful context cannot be used.

Skilled readers are sensitive to, and can use, context clues to predict a set of possible alternatives within a given class of words, although probably not the precise word (Wildman & Kling 1978–1979; I. Taylor 1981; Gough, Alford, & Holley-Wilcox 1983). Ehrlich (1981) concluded that the reader's dependence on context for word recognition decreases with age, although sensitivity to contextual constraints increases. It may be that the automatic word recognition of skilled readers allows them to rely less on context for recognition of the vast majority of words but that, when needed, they become increasingly able to use context clues to aid in identifying unknown words.

It is commonly believed that good readers make more, and better, use of context than do poor readers, but there are those who dispute this viewpoint (Kleiman 1982, M. Singer 1981a). Biemiller (1977–1978) found that good and poor readers in Grades 2 through 6 did not differ significantly in the effectiveness with which they used context clues. Another study using poor readers (Perfetti and Roth 1981) determined that their use of context was sufficient to provide significant help in word identification.

Stanovich (1980, 1982c) proposed an interactive–compensatory model in which both visual and contextual information contribute to word recognition, which predicts that a deficiency in either information source results in greater reliance on the other source. Thus, readers who are unable to process visual–graphic information rapidly have to compensate by relying more on context to achieve word identification.

The difficulty of the material for the reader may well influence the use that can be made of context. When first graders were faced with increasingly difficult material, there was an increase in their use of graphic information (Biemiller 1979). Kibby (1979b) found that approximately 75% of 46 disabled readers who demonstrated adequate use of context on easier material could not do so on a more difficult passage. Kibby concluded that such children do not need to be taught how to use contextual strategies but need to learn other skills that will decrease the number of unfamiliar words in the material.

Leslie (1980) reported that as miscue rates increased, syntactically inappropriate miscues increased. Below-average readers made proportionally more meaning-change miscues and showed greater dependence on graphic cues (although such dependence did not result in successfully recognizing more unknown words). Average readers made proportionally more semantically appropriate miscues. Leslie concluded that miscue rates affect the use of contextual information.

Schwantes (1981) reported that context had a greater effect on the word-recognition speed of third graders than sixth graders, a finding that he interpreted as support for Stanovich's interactive–compensatory model (1980). He also found that difficult material had a more negative impact on the use of context by younger than older pupils.

Illustrations

The rationale for using illustrations is that they (1) aid in the initial acquisition of new words and later in recognizing words in context; (2) facilitate comprehension; or (3) arouse interest and motivate children to read. Grinnell (1982) found that first graders used pictures mainly to aid word recognition, but research findings are mixed regarding the contributions of illustrations in the learning of new words. Some studies have found that more words were learned and retained when they were presented in isolation than when accompanied by pictures (Harzem, Lee, & Miles 1976; Samuels 1977a; Dollenger & Walker 1978; Ehri & Wilce 1980; Willows, Borwick, & Hayvren 1981). Such findings are often interpreted as supporting the *focal attention hypothesis*, which states that the word-alone presentation is more effective because it forces the child to focus attention on graphic cues that provide for greater transfer to word recognition. Those who agree with this point of view hold that although pictures and context ease the initial learning task, their use results in inferior transfer because the child focuses attention on cues that are not present in the transfer task (H. Singer 1980b).

Other researchers have reported that pictures are helpful in learning to recognize words (Denburg 1976; Montare, Elman, & Cohen 1977; Arlin, Scott, & Webster 1978–1979). Ceprano (1981b) concluded that the learning of printed words was best facilitated by a procedure that focuses the child's attention on printed words and at the same time enhances word meaning through picture clues. This suggestion is in line with the viewpoint that printed words are best learned when all of their identities are called into play.

Beginning reading materials usually have many illustrations that carry the story line because only a limited number of words are used in the stories they contain. Pictures can also provide information as to how the story characters probably would say the written text. They also may provide word-recognition cues (e.g., pictures of the story characters may aid in the recognition of their printed names). In later reading materials, illustrations may be used to make vague or abstract ideas more concrete.

Some reviewers (Grinnell 1982, O'Donnell 1983) have concluded that the evidence regarding the influence of illustrations on reading comprehension is generally inconclusive. Schallert (1980), however, concluded that illustrations are helpful in learning from text, especially if they represent spatial information or information important to the total message, and when information to be derived from pictures is explicitly repeated in the text. Levin (1981) wrote that the effects of visual illustrations on children's comprehension of narratives are "positive, potent, and pervasive," especially when they are constructed to be relevant to the story content. He also concluded that illustrations may be helpful in learning history and science, depending on the type of passage and kind of illustration.

Some children misinterpret illustrations and therefore receive information that hinders comprehension (O'Donnell 1983). Grinnell (1982) found that basal reader pictures containing information contradictory to that in the basal reader hindered literal comprehension. Thus it would seem that teachers should monitor children's interpretation of illustrations and help them deal with contradictory information.

Line drawings are more effective than realistic illustrations in promoting reading comprehension (Rusted & Coltheart 1979, O'Donnell 1983). However, abstract or elaborate stylization may increase the task demands for identifying an important picture element (Beck 1984). The ability to learn from pictures increases with age (O'Donnell 1983).

In general, illustrations have little motivational effect (Levin 1981b; Willows, Borwick, & Hayvren 1981). As long as the material itself is sufficiently interesting there is no reason to believe that illustrations will increase interest. However, there is little doubt that children like pictures in books (O'Donnell 1983).

V. THE WHOLE-WORD METHOD

Children can be taught to recognize words in a variety of ways. Usually, children are initially taught to read through either a whole-word method or a phonic method (see Chapter 3), but rarely does a program rely solely on either methodology. Regardless of how words are initially taught, if the words are seen in print often enough, eventually they will be recognized immediately and thus become part of the individual's sight vocabulary.

The *whole-word method* is a teaching procedure that initially emphasizes learning to associate whole printed words with their oral equivalents and with the concepts represented by the words. It is the predominant method of introducing printed words in meaning-emphasis approaches. Most basal reader series combine whole-word methodology with decoding and other word-recognition skills from the beginning or introduce other word-recognition skills shortly thereafter.

The rationale for use of a whole-word method is that (1) most children can learn to read by it; (2) words can be taught quickly and then used to construct meaningful context—children read for meaning sooner than if a phonic method is employed; (3) some young children find it difficult to learn through a phonic method, especially one that depends on phonemic analysis and synthesis; and (4) a number of high-utility words are phonemically irregular (e.g., *said, of*), and therefore must be learned as wholes.

New words[7] may be introduced in context or in isolation. Some authorities believe that introducing words in context will aid word recognition; the meaning of the word will be more apparent, and it will encourage later use of context as a word-recognition cue. Researchers like Biemiller (1970), however, advise against the early use of context and picture cues because they do not allow the child to focus on the use of graphic information.

Ceprano (1981a) reported that kindergarten children who were taught words in isolation recognized significantly more words than those who were taught words in context when the posttest involved words in isolation. On the posttest of words in context, there were no significant differences between the two groups. Each method appears to offer unique advantages and disadvantages, and what gets learned depends on how the words are introduced and practiced. First graders who learned words embedded in sentences learned more about the semantic and syntactic identities of words, whereas those who learned words in isolation remembered their orthographic identities better and could pronounce the words faster and more accurately in isolation (Ehri & Roberts 1979; Ehri & Wilce 1980).

One probably should not use one procedure to the exclusion of the other. Use of both procedures may be more productive. Rather than choose between the two, the choice should be which to use initially. Such decisions can be based on the purpose of the instruction and the nature of the words. Abstract words and homographs are best presented first in context because it aids word meaning (Durkin 1978). Whether polysemous words are introduced in context or not may depend on the meaning of the word the teacher wants the children to understand. On the other hand, if the word can be guessed so easily in context that there

---

[7] "New" means that the word is introduced for the first time in that particular reading program. Some "new" words may already be in some children's sight vocabulary.

would be little need to focus on its graphic information, it might be best to introduce it first in isolation. Any potential harm may be lessened considerably by combining both procedures.

A printed word may be presented initially in isolation, may be shown to the pupils as it is being spoken in an oral context, and soon thereafter may be presented in a printed phrase or sentence. Practice in recognizing the word in isolation may precede and follow its presentation in printed context. Words first introduced in isolation must be read in connected discourse shortly thereafter if the child is to learn that reading is a meaning-getting process (Ceprano 1981b).

When words are presented in isolation, the oral form is spoken by a person or audio device ("This word says _____") while the printed form is shown. A picture may accompany the word. Whether the word is shown in isolation or context, the children should be instructed to look at the word carefully while saying it.

New words presented in context can be highlighted (e.g., underlined or color coded), printed in isolation above the word in the sentence or near the sentence, or the word can be shown in isolation immediately following its presentation in context. When new words are presented in context, all or almost all the other words in the printed sentence should be in the children's sight vocabulary so they can concentrate on learning the new word. The context should be rich enough so that the intended meaning of the new word is abundantly clear.

There are two other considerations involved in formulating contextually potent sentences (Duffelmeyer 1982b): (1) Use language structures that are within the child's repetoire and concepts to which the child can relate his prior knowledge; and (2) it is better to embed the new word in the middle or end of the sentence in order to provide more semantic and syntactic information before the target word is met. The sentence may be read first by the teacher and then orally by some pupils, or it may be read silently first by all the children, then orally by a few. Pupils may be asked how they "figured out" the new words, and the teacher may point out how previously taught skills can be used to aid in recognizing the new word. She also can demonstrate how the new word is similar to or different from previously taught words, especially if such words are likely to be confused. Children also can be asked to note the sequence of letters within the word.

Practice with new words may involve selecting the word spoken by the teacher from several word cards, matching the word card with the word in a phrase or sentence, or arranging word cards to form different sentences. In the first two types of exercise, the child should say the word while making his choice. Workbook exercises may involve matching the word to a picture, selecting the sentence containing the new word that matches a picture, writing the word into an incomplete sentence, selecting which of two or three words best completes a sentence, reading the word in a question that can be answered very briefly, or reading the word in a context that differs from that in which the word was introduced. Children may keep packs of cards on which the words they have mastered have been printed, or they may construct their own picture dictionaries and learn how to use them.

In the "every pupil" response technique (Hopkins 1979), each child in the group responds simultaneously to the teacher's oral question by displaying the appropriate response from a set of manipulative materials, such as a pair of cards with YES and NO printed on them. The technique encourages active participation; increases the number of responses a child makes in a given amount of time; and, by scanning the raised cards, the teacher can immediately detect which children are responding correctly or are slow to respond. When used to reinforce word recognition, the teacher may present an oral context and ask the children to show the appropriate word when she pauses, ask them to show the same card that she shows, or to show the card in response to a spoken word, and so forth. The technique also can be used in teaching decoding skills.

For most children, recognition of a word becomes automatic as a result of reading the word in a wide variety of contexts. If a child has difficulty learning through a whole-word method, such variables as the number of words introduced in a session and the amount of reinforcement and spaced practice provided should be considered. Trying to accomplish too much too quickly can prevent learning. Or it may be necessary to try another instructional method. Poor readers often need to overlearn the recognition of all the words they encounter in print (Lesgold & Curtis 1981).

VI. DECODING METHODS[8]

In this text, *decoding* means determining the spoken equivalent of a printed word through the application of various skills but relying heavily on the ability to make symbol–sound associations. Decoding can refer to an instructional method (we use the term *phonic method*) or to the strategy employed by a reader in attempting to determine the pronunciation (and perhaps the meaning) of a printed word that is not recognized at sight.

In addition to its uses as a beginning reading method and as a word-recognition strategy, learning to decode printed words provides the reader with some insight into the alphabetic nature of written English and the regularities of English orthography. Decoding instruction also calls children's attention to the sequence of letters and phonemes within words, thereby helping them to acquire the orthographic and phonological identities of words. Learning early that letters represent sounds encourages children to seek out other such regularities and independently discover other grapheme–phoneme correspondences (Carroll & Walton 1979).

Goodman and Goodman (1982) claimed there is no need for phonic instruction because children will learn their own rules for relating print to speech as they read meaningful text. A less extreme view was taken by F. Smith (1978),

---

[8] Johnson and Pearson (1984, p. 14) summarized various instructional programs as to their use of analytic or synthetic phonics, early and intensive teaching or gradual introduction of decoding skills, whether or not generalizations are taught, and if an inductive or deductive approach is used.

who stated that children should be expected to learn phonics only to the extent to which they can make sense out of such instruction. Other psycholinguists, such as Shuy (1981c), felt that knowing letter-sound correspondences is useful to novice readers. It may be that the only way to become a skilled reader (one who can bypass phonological recoding) is to learn the process of phonemic translation first (Resnick 1979b).

Moderate to high correlations (.49 to .86) have been reported between decoding ability and reading achievement in the primary grades (Venezky & Johnson 1973; Baron & Treiman 1980; Fletcher 1981; Calfee & Piontkowski 1981; Juel & Roper-Schneider 1982). The relationship diminishes after the primary grades (Rosso & Emans 1981), but mastery of letter-sound correspondences is still positively related to reading ability in the secondary school (Ryder & Graves 1980).

There is no compelling evidence that children taught through a decoding-emphasis method become either slow readers (Carroll & Walton 1979) or poor comprehenders (Lesgold & Perfetti 1981). On the other hand, decoding should not be overemphasized because it may encourage children to focus on visual or phonological information at the expense of contextual information (Barron 1981a).

Code-emphasis beginning reading approaches initially stress decoding and primarily teach symbol–sound associations and blending skills. In meaning-emphasis approaches, less early emphasis is placed on teaching decoding. For most children, it matters little which methodology is emphasized initially. Regardless of the instructional program employed, children are likely to be taught some words through a whole-word method and how to decode printed words. The differences among programs lie in when the skills are taught and the emphasis placed on them. Certain words must be taught as wholes because they are not decodable (e.g., *was*). For example, only 41% of 334 high-utility words were found to be completely phonetically regular (Lewandowski 1979). Yet children cannot be pretaught all the words they will ever encounter in reading; they must learn how to decode unknown words in order to become self-reliant readers.

According to Snowling (1980), normally developing readers are characterized by a developmental increase in decoding ability and an increase in the size of their sight vocabularies. Some severely disabled readers, however, seem to lack the decoding skills that normally accompany a given reading level. They seem to have a selective impairment in use of the phonological access route to the lexicon.

Readiness for Decoding Skills

A study by Dolch and Bloomster (1937) had a great effect on phonic instruction for many years. They found that first and second graders with mental ages below 7 years performed very poorly on the phonic test that required the application of phonic principles to uncommon monosyllabic words presented in isolation. This led Dolch and Bloomster to conclude that the ability to learn and apply phonic principles requires a higher level of mental maturity than needed for learning through a whole-word approach. They recommended that the major part of phonic instruction be placed in the second and third grades because the majority of first-grade pupils were not ready to profit from such instruction. But the Dolch–Bloomster phonics test presented the children with a more difficult task than they face in reading connected meaningful material, and thus their findings underestimated the phonic readiness of first graders. More recent research demonstrated that code-emphasis programs can be used successfully with first graders.

Auditory and Visual Discrimination

Children who have difficulty discriminating among letter forms (visual discrimination) or phonemes (auditory discrimination) may have difficulty learning phonics. For example, not being able to distinguish between *m* and *n* makes it difficult to learn with which letter the sound /m/ should be associated.

Training in visual discrimination for those who need it may involve exercises that require the child to mark the letter or word that is the same or different from a target letter or word. There are differences of opinion as to whether visual-discrimination training should employ letters that are highly similar visually in order to help children to learn the distinctive features of each letter (Samuels 1976b) or whether initially to use maximally constrastive letters and later those that require more demanding discriminations (M. Singer 1982c). Research indicates that it is desirable to point out to the child the specific feature or features that distinguish that letter from all others (Guralnick 1972, Samuels 1973a).

Auditory discrimination of speech sounds can be weak even when auditory acuity is normal. As with visual discrimination, it is not a matter of sensory acuity but of hearing selectively the beginning, middle, or end of a word and comparing it with the sounds of the corresponding parts of other words, thus providing the basis for comparison and the recognition of both similarities and differences.

Poor auditory discrimination is often accompanied by inaccurate or indistinct speech. The child who pronounces *with* as /wiv/ is not likely to notice any difference between final /v/ and /th/ in words. It is hard for many children to discriminate among short-vowel sounds because those sounds do not differ greatly. Dialect speakers may not perform well on an auditory-discrimination test given in standard English, and poor test or exercise performance may be the result of not understanding the directions or concepts (e.g., "same" and "different") or a lack of attention.

The aspects of phonic readiness, listed roughly in order of increasing difficulty, appear to be the ability to (1) discriminate between printed words and letters; (2) determine whether a difference exists between two spoken words that may differ in only one phoneme (/had/–/had/, /had/–/hat/, /had/–/hid/); (3) detect whether two words begin with the same sound; (4) listen to a word and supply two or three words that begin with the same sound; (5) determine whether two words rhyme; (6) supply a word that rhymes with a spoken word (numbers 5 and 6 are important in teaching the use of vowel–consonant phonograms or word families); (7) detect similarities and differences in the ends of spoken words; (8) detect similarities and differences in the middle of spoken words; and (9) auditorily blend word parts. All these abilities can be improved somewhat through direct instruction and practice, but the impact of such improvement on decoding ability has not been established.

In developing auditory discrimination, a variety of procedures can be used. The general technique is to provide a list of spoken words containing (usually beginning with) the element to be taught, to focus the children's attention on that particular sound in the words, to get them to compare words and determine which words contain the target sound, and to encourage them to think of additional words that contain the sound in a particular position. In teaching auditory discrimination involving /f/, for example, the technique would encompass the following:

1. Have the children listen carefully to a short list of words (fun, fox, field) and explain how they are alike.
2. Play listening games in which the children signal in some way which words begin with the same sound (teacher says /fat/, /fur/; children respond to /fun/, /make/, /toy/, /fig/.
3. Ask the children to suggest words that begin like /fat/ and /fur/. To make this more challenging, the words may have to fit a category, such as the name of a person or animal.
4. Give incomplete oral sentences or riddles that the children are to finish or answer with a word that begins like /fat/ and /fur/. For example, Susie's cat is skinny, but Rob's cat is _____. Or, what pets can you keep in water? (fish)

Sound–Symbol Associations

Instruction and practice in making sound–symbol associations (hearing a phoneme and associating its sound with the grapheme) may precede learning symbol–sound associations, or sound–symbol associations may be given concurrently to reinforce symbol–sound associations. Learning sound–symbol associations can help make children aware that the sounds in spoken words can be represented by letters. It is more helpful for spelling than for reading. This concept also can be developed by pronouncing a whole word normally. Then, as each phoneme is said with very brief pauses between them, its grapheme is printed on the board.

On the average, children score higher on phoneme–grapheme tests than on grapheme–phoneme tests (Filp 1975). Both skills were well developed and mastered almost equally by the second graders studied by Fusaro (1978). To introduce a sound–symbol association:

1. Tell the children that all the words you are going to say begin with the same sound (or end with, or are the same in the middle).
2. Pronounce three words, slightly emphasizing the target sound (/fig/, /fur/, /fat/). It may be necessary to separate or isolate the target sound slightly in order for some children to understand the concept.

3. Print the letter that represents the sound on the board (f) and tell the children that the sound they hear at the beginning of the cue words is "made by"[9] this letter, which you point to and name. ("This sound that you hear at the beginning of *fig, fur,* and *fat* is made by this letter, whose name is /ef/.") The teacher may add: "The sound /f/ is made by this letter" while pointing to it.

Practice in making sound–symbol associations can be given by having children hold up the appropriate letter card, write the letter, or say the letter name when asked what letter makes the sound heard in a particular position in the stimulus words. Other exercises can have the children place appropriate pictures on a peg, below which the letter is printed, or select the letter that "makes the sound" at the beginning of a pictured word.

Segmentation Skills

Both visual- and auditory-segmentation skills have been found to be related to reading ability. Visual-segmentation studies have dealt mainly with the ability to determine the spatial boundaries of words, an ability related to the concept of the printed word (see p. 40). Children who have been exposed to print (have been read to, etc.) are likely to be aware that a printed word is marked by spaces on either side of it, especially after receiving reading instruction. In a whole-word method, words are often introduced or shown in isolation or are highlighted. Difficulty with visual segmentation as it pertains to the recognition of printed words is not likely to be a problem.

Auditory segmentation as it relates to reading readiness was discussed on pages 37–38. Many of the beliefs regarding the importance of phonemic-segmentation ability would seem to have relevance for learning to decode printed words. I. Liberman and her associates (Liberman & Shankweiler 1979, I. Liberman *et al.* 1980) believed that the unique advantage of our alphabetic writing system is that it enables the reader to generate the pronunciation of an unknown printed word from its spelling but that in order to take full advantage of an alphabetic writing system, one must (1) realize that speech can be segmented into phonemes; (2) know how many phonemes are contained in words in one's lexicon and the order in which these phonemes occur within the word; and (3) know that letters represent phonemes rather than syllables or some other unit of speech. Stanovich, Cunningham, and Feeman (1984) interpreted their data as indicating that phonemic awareness underlies the ability to segment and analyze speech, and is therefore causally related to decoding ability.

Other writers suggest that auditory-segmentation ability is related to blending ability. The belief is that before children can synthesize sounds and recognize the result as a specific spoken word, they must grasp the concept that a spoken word, heard as an unbroken continuous pattern, can be segmented into phonemes.

[9] Letters do not "make" sounds, but the terms "stand for" and "represent" are not understood by many children.

Vellutino and Scanlon (1982) reported that training improved the phonemic-segmentation ability of both poor and good readers in the second and sixth grades (poor readers were less proficient than good readers before and after training) and that the segmentation training allowed the poor readers to perform as well as the good readers on a transfer task—learning to associate printed nonsense words with their oral counterparts. Their findings suggest that phonemic segmentation is amenable to training and that it may facilitate learning through a whole-word method as well as through a phonic method.

Children probably should be familiarized with speech sounds in isolation before being asked to detect sounds in words. Then the concept that words are comprised of phonemes can be demonstrated to them. To do so, first say the word as a whole, then pronounce each phoneme in the word (distorting each as little as possible) with about a half-second pause between each, and lastly say the word again. The children should repeat the process because understanding the concept requires attention to articulatory as well as to auditory clues. For those who have difficulty grasping the concept, it may be necessary to start with segmenting only the initial sound from the word. Later, consonant–vowel and vowel–consonant words can be introduced.

Letter-Name Knowledge

Although letter-name knowledge correlates quite highly with success in learning to read in first grade (see p. 38), training experiments have indicated that it does not facilitate the acquisition of word-recognition or decoding skills (Beck 1981). On the other hand, Durrell (1980) has defended the value of letter-name knowledge in learning to read and spell. He pointed out that the awareness of letter names at the beginning of spoken words is among the earliest developmental abilities on which reading acquisition is based (e.g., the young child hears "bee" in "beaver" and expects the word to begin with *b*). Durrell also cited as evidence the use of letters containing their names in children's invented spellings (e.g., ENGINE = NJN). Durrell and Murphy (1978) stated that except for *h,q,w*, and *y*, consonant letter names are made up of the basic phoneme plus a vowel (e.g. /b/ + /ē/, /ĕ/ + /f/, /j/ + /ā/), and that the names of the vowels are their "long sounds." Venezky (1975, 1979b) disputed their contention.

There is also disagreement about whether letter names should be used in teaching phonics. Some writers contend that learning the letter names and symbol–sound associations ("This letter is bee and it makes the sound /b/") places an additional burden on the child. Others suggest that the concurrent use of the letter name and sound confuses the child as to which is which. Since most children already know the letter names before being taught to decode, their use is not likely to provide an additional learning task. Because children have such knowledge, it is important to make clear to them the distinction between letter names and the sounds that letters represent.

Nevins (1972) found that presenting letter names and sounds concurrently facilitated learning word-recognition skills. But if their combined use produces a problem for the child, the name of the letter simply can be deleted ("This letter makes the sound /b/").

Regardless of the various disagreements, there is no evidence that teaching letter names is harmful. Furthermore, even if such knowledge were completely unrelated or even useless in learning to read, letter-name knowledge can serve other useful purposes.

Decoding Instruction in Meaning-Emphasis Approaches

In meaning-emphasis programs, phonics is taught along with other decoding strategies, but less initial emphasis is placed on sounding and blending techniques. The procedure most frequently used is *analytic phonics*, in which children are helped to understand the relationship of letters and phonograms to the sounds they represent and to use that knowledge to decode unknown words by comparing and contrasting whole words. Rather than learn, for example, that "*M* says /m/," pupils are taught that the letter stands for the sound heard at the beginning of *mother* and *me*—words that are already in their sight vocabulary.

The teacher may emphasize the target sound in the words while pronouncing them or may slightly segment the sound from the rest of the word. Although some analytic phonic proponents oppose ever mentioning the phoneme in isolation, such a prohibition is decidedly questionable. Pointing out to children that *bus, book,* and *boat* all sound alike at the beginning and all start with the letter *b* may lead them to think "bee say buh" if they are not told that "bee says /b/ as in /book/ and /bus/. Furthermore, some children have difficulty segmenting the target sound or letter from the rest of the word. The teacher has no control over what the children are thinking or saying to themselves, and so the children are better off if given a model to imitate.

Cue words also may be used in teaching symbol–sound associations (e.g., "Em, /m/, is for milk"). A picture of the cue word (a milk carton) accompanied by the lowercase, and perhaps the uppercase, letter can be shown and then displayed in the room so that the children can refer to it as needed. Simply thinking of the cue word may help some children to remember the sound represented by the letter. But being able to think of the sound without referring to a cue word is preferable.

The following substitution procedure may be taught: (1) Think of known words that begin and end like the unknown word; (2) use the known parts to determine the sounds represented by the similar elements in the unknown word; (3) mentally blend the parts; and (4) say the word aloud or to yourself. Thus, if the unfamiliar word was *mast*, the child might think: *milk* and *last*; /m/, /ast/, /mast/. Or the child may quickly perceive the parts, be aware of their sounds, and decode the word without having to think of known words that are similar in some respect. As decoding skills grow, the new part is substituted immediately. The substitution technique also can be used for final consonants and medial vowels. Substitution seems to work satisfactorily for a majority of children, but experimental comparisons of the relative effectiveness of different kinds of phonic methods are not available. It is probably much easier for children to respond correctly to a "new word" when the teacher changes the initial consonant (*last* is shown; the *l* is erased and replaced with *m*) than to use substitutions on their own.

Decoding Instruction in Code-Emphasis Approaches

Three major types of methods are used in code-emphasis reading programs. Each has certain advantages and limitations.

Single-Letter Phonics

Probably the oldest of these approaches is letter-by-letter sounding and blending, as /k/ /a/ /t/ = /cat/.[10] This *single-letter phonics* method teaches a systematic left-to-right sequence in decoding the word and requires initially teaching a relatively small number of phonic elements. Its four main possible disadvantages are these: (1) Extraneous sounds added to the phonemes (e.g., /ə/ is added to certain consonants) may hamper recognition of the oral word (e.g., the result of blending /cuh/-/a/-/tuh/ does not sound like /cat/); (2) blending single phonemes is comparatively difficult for young children, even when extra sounds are minimized; (3) a number of words are not amenable to single-letter phonics (e.g., *elephant*); and (4) it may be more useful for short words because in longer words the child may forget the symbol–sound associations made for graphemes at the beginning of the word. Successive blending of each phoneme with the preceding sound or group of sounds might lessen the latter problem.

Initial Consonant Plus Phonogram[11]

The initial consonant is sounded and the rest of the word is sounded as a phonogram unit or spelling pattern of two or more graphemes, usually a vowel and consonant (e.g., /k/ /at/ = /cat/; /p/ /ik/ = /pick/). Word families, such as *at, bat, cat, fat, hat, mat, pat, rat, sat*, are taught. Because many one-syllable words belong to such word families, this has been a popular procedure. Blending is easier than in single-letter phonics because only two parts need to be fused together. Use of this procedure can result in these problems: (1) improper eye movements resulting from looking at the word ending before the beginning; (2) adding /ə/ (schwa) to the initial consonant, thus making if difficult to blend; (3) practice on word families in list form may have little transfer to recognition of these words in context; and (4) many commonly taught phonograms (*ap, end, ist, ong*) are infrequent in words of more than one syllable.

Phonogram Plus Final Consonant

The initial consonant and following vowel are sounded as a unit, and the final consonant is added, as /ka/ /t/ = /cat/, /pi/ /k/ = /pick/. Cordts (1955) claimed that this procedure avoids adding extraneous sounds, makes blending comparatively easy, and prepares the way for syllabication of longer words. Critics have pointed out that (1) a very large number of consonant-vowel combinations would have to be taught; (2) it is difficult to know whether to give the vowel its long

---

[10] Slashes are not usually used to indicate a spoken word, but they are used here for consistency. Whole words are not phonetically respelled so that they can be recognized more easily.

[11] Lists of word families may be found in D. Johnson and Pearson (1984) and Fry, Polk, and Fountoukidis (1984).

or short sound because that depends on what follows the vowel; and (3) if followed exclusively, the method prevents teaching such phonograms as *ight, ind, ound,* and *old,* which are best learned as units.

Since a good reader needs flexibility in decoding, exclusive devotion to any of these three procedures is less desirable than a varied approach.

A few important points greatly influence the success or failure of sounding and blending techniques:

1. Attention should be given to the development of adequate auditory and visual discrimination.
2. Try to avoid adding extraneous sounds to the phonemes.
3. Words should be sounded continuously, with the sound of one phoneme running into the next phoneme. If it is necessary to pronounce the phonemes separately, the time interval between the sounds should be as short as possible.
4. When a child has difficulty blending, the teacher should pronounce the whole word, then pronounce it successively more slowly until the individual sounds are given separately. Then the process is reversed, starting with the separate sounds and speeding up gradually so that the relation between the separate sounds and the pronunciation of the word as a whole can be understood more clearly. The same procedure can be used to demonstrate auditory segmentation.
5. If the skills developed in phonic lessons are to function in connected reading, abundant practice should be provided in the application of the skills to unknown words in reading easy interesting material.

VII. SKILL AREAS IN DECODING

In order to decode a word completely, children must be able (1) to divide it mentally into usable parts; (2) to determine the sounds each part represents; and (3) to blend the sounds mentally in correct sequence into a recognizable whole word. These three areas are referred to as visual analysis, symbol–sound association, and visual blending.

Visual Analysis

A competent reader meeting unfamiliar printed words tries to analyze them into some component parts that he or she recognizes or finds useful in decoding. Although the term *visual analysis* is used, it should be realized that, except when words are broken at the end of a line, the stimuli are seen as whole words. The stimuli are visual, the process is mental. The term is used to distinguish it from auditory analysis, in which no printed stimuli occur.

Monosyllables

Children instructed in single-letter phonics or the use of phonograms or spelling patterns are likely to receive instruction in how to analyze one-syllable words. Depending on the instructional methodology employed, they may separate the word into single letters; a consonant and vowel–consonant phonogram; a consonant–vowel phonogram and final consonant; or grapheme and spelling pattern (*m all*). Although phonograms and spelling patterns are fairly consistent in the sounds they represent in monosyllabic words, looking for that part, or looking for the "little word" in the "big word," can be misleading (*all*igator, *father*, *fin*al).

Morphemic Analysis

Morphemic analysis means analyzing words into their morphemes, or meaning units. There are *free morphemes*, whole words that cannot be further divided into meaning-bearing elements, and *bound morphemes*, ones that must be combined with a free morpheme to change meaning. Children are taught early to recognize such endings (bound morphemes) as *s, es, ed, er, est*, and *ing*. Unknown words divided into their meaningful parts can often be decoded quickly because the parts are already familiar. Morphemic analysis should be tried before other analysis skills are attempted.

Dividing compound words into their component words is another form of morphemic analysis that is taught early. This technique should be limited to words that naturally separate into known meaningful words (e.g., *cowgirl*, *something*). Exercises for teaching compound words appear in D. Johnson and Pearson (1984, pp. 132–136).

A third form of morphemic analysis involves the use of familiar or decodable prefixes, root words, and suffixes (*repay, excitement, untruthful*). Instruction in the recognition and meaning of common affixes usually begins with third-grade materials. Polysyllabic words are typically composed of monosyllabic content words to which affixes have been added (L. Haber & Haber 1981).

There are two useful morphemic-analysis generalizations:

1. Divide between the words that form a compound; other divisions may occur in either or both parts.
2. Divide between the root word and an affix; other divisions may occur in the root or affix.

Syllabication

A syllable is an uninterrupted unit of speech that contains one vowel phoneme, forming either a whole word or part of a word; also the grapheme(s) that represents the spoken syllable. A syllable may consist of a vowel only or a vowel preceded and/or followed by one or more consonants.

By second or third grade the child meets many printed words of more than one syllable. By at least second grade the children's attention should be called to the fact that some words are made up of more than one syllable; they can be given practice in noting the number of syllables heard in a word.

Children can learn to recognize a word that has been divided into syllables for them long before they can make independent use of syllabication generalizations. Often children who have difficulty blending single phonemes find it easier to blend syllables to make a spoken word. It is not necessary, therefore, to wait until generalizations are taught before using syllabication as an aid in word recognition.

Syllabication generalizations should be worded as clearly as possible, and their application rather than recitation should be stressed. Only generalizations that have wide application and relatively few exceptions should be taught. These include the following:

1. Usually divide between two consonants that are not a digraph or a blend (e.g., meth od).
2. A single consonant between two single vowels may go with either syllable.[12]
3. Final *le* and the preceding consonant usually form the final syllable.
4. Final *ed* may be a separate syllable.

Although teaching syllabication generalizations has been criticized (Groff 1971, Waugh & Hovell 1975), the fact remains that, when properly taught and utilized, they can provide guidelines for dividing "big words" into decodable units. Children can divide the same word in various ways and still closely approximate its oral equivalent. For example, *treaty* may be analyzed as *treat-y*, *trea-ty*, or *tr-ea-ty* (but the *ea* must be treated as a unit) and the word correctly decoded. The fewer parts into which the word is analyzed, the more efficient the decoding.

The research findings regarding the value of teaching syllabication are mixed; for example, compare Canney and Schreiner (1976–1977) with Scheerer-Neumann (1981).

Use of Compare–Contrast or Analogy Strategies

Some evidence suggests that rather than use phonic and syllabication generalizations when decoding or attempting to recognize unknown words, children may search for familiar letter clusters or word parts (Glass & Burton 1973; Hardy, Stennett, & Smythe 1973b) or compare the unknown word to known words or word parts (P. Cunningham 1975–1976). Glass (1973) has developed a teaching procedure using letter clusters as a decoding strategy.

According to P. Cunningham (1979, 1984), children should be taught to segment an unknown word into the largest manageable parts derived by using the compare–contrast strategy. Her suggestions do not differ greatly from our recommendations that morphemic analysis should be applied first and that the largest possible units be employed in decoding. Use of compare–contrast or analogy strategy would seem to require a store of word identities in the lexicon on which to draw, so its use requires a certain level of reading ability.

Compare–contrast strategies are applicable to phonemically regular words but may result in incorrect responses with irregular words (e.g., *put* pronounced

---

[12] D. McFeeley (1981) reported that the first vowel in over 2000 VCV spellings represented its long sound 55% of the time; in 95% of the rest of the items, it represented its short sound. It would seem that the child should be told to try the long sound first, and if the result does not make sense, to try its short sound.

as rhyming with *but* or *abroad* pronounced with an /ō/ sound because it was compared to *road*.

Accenting

Accent, or stress, is the emphasis given to a syllable in a word (or to a word in a sentence) that makes it stand out in comparison to adjacent syllables (or words). In most two-syllable words, one of the syllables is accented. In words of three or more syllables, one syllable has primary accent ('); there is sometimes a secondary accent (') on another syllable. Shifts in accent can influence word pronunciation and meaning (*rec'-ord, re-cord'*).

Only two accenting generalizations merit being taught: (1) Usually the first syllable of a two-syllable word is accented; and (2) affixes usually are not accented. Resourceful readers try to accent one syllable to see if this results in a word they know that fits the meaning of the sentence; if it does not, they try accenting another syllable.

Symbol–Sound Associations

Our alphabetic writing system attempts to codify the relevant sounds of English into distinctive graphic symbols. Knowledge of these grapheme–phoneme correspondences can be quite useful. At times it may be necessary to determine all or most of the grapheme–phoneme relationships in an unknown word; at other times, only one or two such associations will trigger recognition.

Letter–sound patterns of English may be classified as invariant, variant-predictable, and variant unpredictable (Venezky 1981).[13] Symbol–sound associations that are invariant or for which there are few exceptions are the consonants *f, j, ph, qu* (which usually represents /kw/), *sh, v, wh*, and *z*. The variant-predictable class includes most of the other consonants and a few vowels. The position of the letter, adjacent letters, and morphemic identification influence letter–sound associations.

There are two types of consonant combinations: consonant blends or clusters (e.g., *bl, st, cr, spl*) and consonant digraphs (*ch, sh, th, wh* and *ph*). Although it is more efficient to treat a blend as a unit, it is possible to decode a word successfully by making an appropriate symbol–sound association for each letter in the blend. But because a digraph represents a single sound, it must be treated as a unit. In some programs the term *silent consonants* is used, and symbol–sound associations are taught for them (e.g., *kn, wr, mb*). In other programs such graphemes are referred to as consonant digraphs. Some "silent letters" are not always silent. For instance, the *b* in *mb* is silent in the base word (*bomb*) and before inflectional suffixes (*bombed*), but not before other letters (*bombard*) (L. Henderson 1982).

For historical reasons, vowel symbol–sound associations are more variable than those for consonants (Calfee 1982). Single-vowel letters usually represent either their long or short sounds, but they may represent other sounds when

---

[13] Refer to Venezky (1970) or Sipay (1973) for a more complete discussion of the frequency with which graphemes represent particular sounds.

followed by *r* (e.g., *car*) or *l* (e.g., *call*). There is sufficient consistency in these spelling patterns to be useful in decoding. Vowel digraphs are two letters that represent one phoneme (which usually could be represented by one of the letters in the digraph). In *diphthongs*, the vowel sound could not be represented by either of the letters alone. Only four vowel digraphs (*ai, ay, ee,* and *oa*) are very consistent in their symbol–sound associations and occur relatively frequently. The common diphthongs (*au, aw; oi, oy;* and *ou*) are also very consistent. The "two-vowel rule" (the first letter says its name and the second is silent) is of little value and could be very misleading. A few common vowel combinations (*ea, oo, ow*) most likely represent one of two sounds; others, such as *ew, ey,* and *ie,* although fairly common, are much more inconsistent in their symbol–sound associations. Some vowel combinations are fairly consistent but appear infrequently (e.g., *oe*); yet others are neither consistent nor common (e.g., *ui*). In our opinion, only the common and at least fairly consistent associations should be taught.

Research studies have shown that many of the once commonly taught phonic generalizations are not very useful (Clymer 1963; Emans 1967; Burmeister 1968, 1971; McFeeley 1974). There are, however, four phonic principles that may be useful. They regard the effect of position on vowel symbol–sound associations and often are taught in conjunction with syllabication and accenting generalizations:

1. A single-vowel letter at the end of an accented syllable usually represents its long sound. Syllables that end with a vowel are called *open syllables.*
2. A single-vowel letter followed by a single consonant other than *r* usually represents its short sound in an accented syllable. Syllables that end with consonants are called *closed syllables.*
3. A single-vowel letter followed by a single consonant (other than *v*) and a final *e* usually represents its long sound and the *e* is silent.
4. Vowel letters in many unaccented syllables represent a schwa sound (/ə/ or /ŭ/).[14]

Few phonic generalizations deal with consonants, but children are commonly taught that *c* and *g* usually represent their "soft sounds" (/s/ and /j/ respectively) when followed by *e, i,* or *y.* When followed by any other letter or when they end a syllable, *c* and *g* usually represent their "hard sounds" (/k/ and /g/). According to Venezky (1979b), children and adults have a strong bias toward associating *c* with /k/ regardless of the spelling pattern in which it occurs.

There is no evidence that the ability to state a decoding generalization facilitates the ability to apply it (Beck 1981), and many children can apply decoding generalizations without being able to verbalize them (Rosso & Emans 1981). Some children abstract and apply phonic generalizations before such skills

---

[14] The schwa can be represented by any single-vowel letter and some vowel combinations (e.g., fam*ou*s).

are taught, but reading-disabled students are much less likely to do so. The inability to make vowel symbol–sound associations is more common among poor than good readers (Smiley, Pasquale, & Chandler 1976; J. Mason 1976).

After a decoding generalization or principle has been taught, practice in applying it to unknown words in context should be provided. This may be done by using single sentences containing the target word. Children can be asked if the sentence makes sense (e.g., The mane ate the food"); to indicate yes or no to such sentences as "A bug can run" or "A rug can run"; to select, then write in, the word that best makes sense ("The man used his _____to help him walk" [*can* or *cane*]).

Heavy emphasis on phonic generalizations does not seem justified. It is more advisable (1) to teach the phoneme most commonly represented by a grapheme; and (2) to teach the second-most-likely sound for those letters that can represent more than one sound with some degree of frequency. Children who have difficulty learning or applying even a few generalizations may be taught the long and short sounds of the vowels and the alternate sounds represented by *c* and *g*, and may be instructed that if their first attempt does not result in a satisfactory response, "Try the other sound."

Blending

Two terms are used in reference to the ability to blend or synthesize phonemes into syllables and syllables into words. In *auditory blending* the examiner or teacher provides the sounds to be fused; there are no visual stimuli. In *visual blending* the pupil must first make the appropriate symbol–sound associations and then blend the results into a recognizable whole.

Auditory-blending ability is significantly related to scores on reading readiness tests (Rohrlack, Bell, & McLaughlin 1982) and to reading ability (Richardson, Di Benedetto, & Bradley 1977). The correlations in the 21 studies reviewed by Whaley and Kibby (1979) ranged from .19 to .67. There is a trend for sound blending to be more highly correlated with decoding and word-recognition skills than with reading comprehension (Backman 1983).

Roberts (1979) reported that of 168 English 5-year-olds, 36% were competent in auditory blending (got at least 16 of the 20 items correct), 46% were not competent (4 or fewer correct responses), and the rest were in a state of transition. She also found that using voiced consonants (*b* = *buh*) did not necessarily affect performance negatively; so did Haddock (1978). Sound-blending ability increases quickly in the primary grades (Backman 1983).

Haddock's suggestion (1976) that teaching children to blend auditorily might facilitate acquisition of visual-blending ability seems logical since once the grapheme–phoneme correspondences have been made, the same cognitive tasks come into play. Suggestions for teaching auditory blending may be found in Liberman and Shankweiler (1979), Samuels (1981), and some phonics manuals.

Despite Groff's doubts (1976a) about the usefulness of teaching children to blend, blending is an important decoding skill that may require direct teaching for some children. Few meaning-emphasis programs and only some decoding-emphasis programs attempt to develop blending skills in any consistent or systematic manner (Beck 1981). Whaley (1975) indicated how blending was taught in a number of different reading programs and offered suggestions for teaching blending.

In single-letter phonics programs children are usually taught to make all the necessary symbol–sound associations and then to blend them into a word (*c* = /k/, *a* = /a/, *t* = /t/; /k/ + /a/ + /t/ = /kat/). This creates problems for some children because it puts a strain on their short-term memory, especially when more than four or five phonemes are involved. The child may forget the symbol–sound associations he made for the beginning of the word. Use of a successive blending procedure (Resnick & Beck 1976) may be more useful for many children because the readers need only hold two bits of information in STM at any one time. As soon as two sounds are produced they are blended together, and each additional phoneme is blended to what has already been fused. For example, *cat* would be decoded and synthesized as follows: *c* = /k/, *a* = /a/; /k/ + /a/ = /ka/; *t* = /t/; /ka/ + /t/ = /kat/.

Durkin (1976) recommended a blending technique in which the vowel in a syllable is pronounced first, then the preceding consonant is added to it, and finally the final consonant is added (/a/, /ka/, /cat/). The serious drawback of this procedure is that it disrupts a systematic left-to-right sequence.

Some children who have difficulty in grasping the concepts of segmentation and blending are helped by constructing a word with separate alphabet letters. For segmentation, place a word like *man* on the table. Explain that you are going to show how the word can be taken apart. "This word says /man/. I am going to show you how you can take it apart." Move the *m* to the left and say /m/, /an/. For blending, "Now we can put the sounds together again; /m/, /an/." Move the *m* to the right and as you do so say, "/m/, /an/, /man/." Have the child imitate the whole procedure. For initial consonants it is desirable to begin with those that are easy to blend with vowels, such as *f, l, m, n*, and *r*, postponing the stop consonants until the child is getting the idea. Repeat the procedure, changing the initial consonant and final phonogram, and continue until the child can sound and blend without the help of the movable letters.

Spelling as a Word-Recognition Strategy

In many linguistic reading programs (see p. 70) children are encouraged to spell, letter by letter, any word that they do not recognize. Apparently it is hoped that spelling the word will help the child recognize the spelling pattern, which is fairly tightly controlled in these programs (e.g., Nan can fan Dan).

According to Durrell (1980), spelling out an unknown word is usually more effective than "sounding it out" (1) because spelling forces close examination of the word with every letter being noted; and (2) because most letter names contain their phonemes. Durrell and Murphy have published START (Curriculum Associates), a beginning reading program that contains 400 pictured words in which letter names are easily heard. In our opinion, spelling is a relatively ineffective word-recognition strategy, especially with words of more than four letters, and it interferes with the use of more effective word-recognition strategies.

VIII. SCOPE AND SEQUENCE IN TEACHING DECODING SKILLS

Many different sequences are used in teaching decoding skills, particularly phonic skills. There is no conclusive evidence on which is the most effective. In attempting to devise a sensible sequence for introducing decoding skills, the major guiding principles are to introduce early those skills met frequently in primary-grade words, and to teach those skills most readily learned and useful in decoding a reasonable number of words. If one adheres to these common-sense ideas, a number of different sequences can achieve satisfactory results.

Probably the ideal time to introduce a new decoding skill is when the child has a need for it and is ready to learn it. If these conditions are met, teachers should not hesitate to teach a new skill, even though it deviates from a previously planned sequence.

In our judgment, Table 12.1 suggests a resonable sequence of skills and reader levels by which these skills should be acquired. No attempt has been made to indicate a sequence in which the skills should be taught at a particular reader level. This table is intended to provide a list from which behavioral objectives can be derived or a checklist to determine what needs to be reviewed or first taught, rather than to provide an instructional sequence. Many children will not master a particular decoding skill the first time it is introduced; therefore, spaced review at that and higher reader levels is a necessity. No attempt has been made to indicate specific readiness activities at the different levels.

IX. DEALING WITH SPECIFIC WORD-RECOGNITION PROBLEMS

Most children who need corrective help in reading have only a few specific word-recognition weaknesses. One pupil may have a reversal tendency; another, difficulty making vowel symbol–sound associations. Yet other students may need help in recognizing certain high-frequency words or in making better use of context clues.

A child's word-recognition strengths and needs are usually based on an analysis of his oral reading. For this reason, the headings in this section use the terms that correspond to these behaviors.

General Comments

Rather than repeat a comment a number of times or suggest the same procedure each time it may be applied to treat a word-recognition problem, some general comments will simply be enumerated in this section.

1. There is no need to be concerned about
    a. an occasional error or miscue that disrupts comprehension
    b. relatively infrequent miscues that do not disrupt comprehension
    c. dialectal renditions

2. There is a need to treat frequent miscues that disrupt comprehension.
3. Although, in general, remedial techniques may not differ greatly from classroom procedures, the following suggestions tend to make learning more effective: Teach only one or two skills at a time, introduce skills at a pace that allows for mastery, reinforce initial learning in a variety of ways, teach the skill until it is overlearned, provide guided application of the skill to words in context, and have periodic spaced reviews.

Before attempting to teach a skill, an effort should be made to determine if the student really is weak in that area or simply is not using a skill that he has in his repetoire. If the former, the skill needs to be taught and practiced; if the latter, an attitude change is needed.

Refusal to Attempt Words

A fairly common oral reading behavior is reluctance or refusal to try to read an unknown word. The child may stop and wait for a teacher reaction, may try to omit the word without the omission being noticed, or may simply say that he does not know that word. The majority of refusals are caused by inadequate word-recognition skills or strategies; they diminish in frequency as word-recognition skill improves.

Some children, however, do not try words even when they have the skills to recognize or decode them. This may reflect a lack of confidence in their own ability that is the result of a long period of frustrated effort. Other pupils are not risk-takers, do not want to assume the responsibility needed for learning, or have other personality traits that lead to such behaviors. Lack of confidence can be overcome by demonstrating to the child that he can be successful. Some children do not attempt unknown words because they have learned that the teacher will provide the word for them.

Decoding Skills

Many pupils have inadequate knowledge of symbol–sound associations. They may know the majority of correspondences for single consonants but have difficulty with consonant blends and vowels. Knowledge of common phonograms may be uneven, and a strategy for decoding multisyllabic words is often unknown territory. Some of these gaps represent deficiencies in previous instruction, but many of them are the aftereffects of teaching for which the child was not yet ready. It is desirable to find out by preliminary testing and observation which associations are known and which need to be taught; those that seem most urgently needed should be given priority in the teaching sequence.

Vivid Cues

For children who have difficulty in remembering sounds, it is important to provide vivid associations that can be used to recall the sound. Picture cards representing cue words are often helpful. If a child comes to the word *met* and has difficulty remembering the short *e* sound, he can look at the picture of the egg (accompanied by *egg* and *e*). Saying "egg" to himself can remind him of the

Table 12.1 Desirable Decoding Skills by Reader Level

Pre-primer

Grapheme–phoneme associations for consonants: *b, c /k/, d, f, g /g/, h,* j, *l, m, n, p, r, s, t, w*

Substitution: substituting initial and final consonants in known words

Context cues: using context and consonants to recognize unknown words

Morphemic analysis: inflectional endings *s* (plural marker—*dogs*) and *ed* (*called*)

Primer

Grapheme–phoneme associations:

    consonants: *k, v, y, z*

    consonant digraphs: *ch, sh, th*

    consonant blends: *pl, st, tr*

    short vowels: *a, e, i, o, u*

    spelling patterns: *er, or, ur, ar, ow, et, an, ight, at, ay, all*

Substitution: using grapheme–phoneme assoications and parts of known words to recognize unknown words

Context cues: using semantic and syntactic cues to monitor responses to unknown printed words

Morphemic analysis:

    inflectional endings: *s* (3rd person singular verbs—*eats*), *d* (*liked*), *es* (*boxes*), *'s* (possessive—*Ann's*), *er* (comparative—*faster*)

    suffix: *er* (as agent—*farmer*)

First Reader

Grapheme–phoneme associations

    consonant: *x*

    consonant digraphs:[a] *wh, kn /n/, wr /r/, ck /k/*

    consonant blends: *br, cr, dr, fr, gr, bl, cl, fl, sl, sc, tw, ld, nd*

    short vowels: *y*

    long vowels: *a, e, i, o, u, y*

    vowel digraphs: *ay, ea /ē/ & /ĕ/, ee, oa, ow /ō/*

    vowel diphthongs: *oi, oy, ow /ou/*

    spelling patterns: *alk, eigh, ind, old, ook*

    generalization: In the initial position, *y* represents a consonant sound; in other positions, a vowel sound

Morphemic analysis:

    inflectional endings: *ing* (*walking*), *est* (*fastest*)

    compound words: compounds comprised of 2 known words

    contractions: *not = n't* (*doesn't*), *will/shall = 'll* (*I'll*)[b]

Structural analysis:

    separating monosyllables into parts

    counting the number of vowel sounds in a word as a clue to the number of syllables

Synthesis: blending sounds into syllables; syllables into words

---

Second Reader

Grapheme–phoneme associations:

    consonants: *c /s/, g /j/*

    consonant digraphs: *ph /f/, tch /ch/, gn /n/, mb /m/, dge /j/*

    consonant blends: *gl, pr, qu /kw/, sk, sm, sn, sp, sw, scr, sch, str, squ, thr, lk, nk*

    vowel digraphs: *ai, oo /ōō/ & /oo/, ey, ew, ei, ie, ue*

    vowel diphthongs: *ou, au, aw*

    schwa: /ə/ as represented by an initial vowel (*ago*)

Table 12.1 (continued)

Second Reader

r- controlled vowels: *ar, er, ir, or, ur, oor (door, poor) ear (year, earn, bear, heart), our (hour, four)*

spelling pattern: *ough (through, though, thought, rough)*

generalizations:
1. When *c* and *g* are followed by *e, i,* or *y* they usually represent soft sounds
2. A single vowel letter at the end of an accented syllable usually represents its long sound
3. A single vowel letter followed by a consonant other than *r* usually represents its short sound in an accented syllable
4. A single vowel letter followed by a single consonant, other than *v,* and a final *e* usually represents its long sound and the *e* is silent

Morphemic analysis:

inflectional endings: *s' (boys'), en (beaten)*

prefix: *un*

suffixes: *ful, fully, ish, less, ly, ness, self, y*

contraction: *have = 've (I've)*[b]

generalizations:
1. Divide between the words that form a compound; other divisions may occur in either or both parts
2. Divide between the root word and an affix; other divisions may occur in either the root or affix

recognizing words with spelling changes made by adding suffixes when: the final *e* has been dropped (*hide—hiding*), *y* has been changed to *i* (*baby—babies*), and a final consonant has been doubled (*sit—sitting*)

Accenting: hearing and marking accented syllables

Third Reader

Grapheme–phoneme associations:

consonant blends: *spl, spr, ng, nt*

generalization: A single vowel letter or vowel combination (dang*er*ous) represents a schwa sound in many unaccented syllables

Morphemic analysis

prefixes: *dis, ex, im, in, post, pre, re, sub, super, trans*

suffixes: *or* (as agent—*actor*), *ous, tion, sion, ment, ty, ic, al, able*

contractions: *are = 're (they're),*[b] *would/had = 'd (I'd)*[c]

Structural analysis: Syllabicating words of more than 2 syllables

Accenting generalizations:
1. Usually the first syllable in a 2-syllable word is accented
2. Usually affixes are not accented

---

[a] Silent consonants are included under consonant digraphs.

[b] More words with this contraction are likely to be encountered at higher reader levels.

[c] Most contractions of *would/should* ('d) and *is/has* ('s) are likely to be encountered above the third reader level.

sound. Cue cards like this can be mounted above the chalkboard for reference, or each child can have a personal set. Sometimes cue cards made by the children are more effective than commercially available ones.

It is sometimes effective to dramatize sounds. Each sound can be associated with a situation in which the sound is made, as /s/—the hissing of steam or a snake; /t/—the tick of a clock; /ō/—what we say when we are surprised; and so on. Tracing and writing the letter can be used for reinforcement. Schmitt (1918) advocated teaching letter sounds in this way. She employed a continued story, in which cows mooed /m/, for example; one new sound was added each day. This was followed by practice in which the teacher pronounced unblended parts of words (/r/ /un/ to me; /f/ /old/ your hands) as a preliminary to training in blending.

Letter or Word Confusion

Monroe (1932) pointed out that many children who confuse letters do not hear the differences between sounds clearly. She therefore advocated preliminary training in auditory discrimination, which started by presenting pictures of several objects, some of whose names begin with the sound. The child was taught to discriminate sounds in the following way: The child looks at the pictures and says, "/s/—soap, yes, soap sounds like /s/; /s/—man, no, man doesn't sound like /s/," and so on. A child who had difficulty in pronunciation with such sounds as /d/, /t/, and /th/; /s/ and /sh/; /r/, /l/, and /w/; or /f/ and /v/ was taught the differences in the lip, tongue, and throat movements involved in making the sounds. After the phonemes could be distinguished and pronounced correctly, they were associated with the printed letters.

A persistent tendency to confuse two letters or letter combinations can be treated by following a sequence of five steps:

1. Point out the visual differences in the letters.
2. Present a printed list of words, all of which contain one letter to be taught. For consonants, use words beginning with the letter; for vowels, use one-syllable words with the vowel at the beginning or in the middle. Present a similar list for the other letter. Have the child read each list; help him when necessary.
3. Use the principle of minimal variation to present pairs of words that are alike except for one grapheme as *hill, bill; hat, hit; can, cam.*
4. Give the child silent reading exercises of a multiple-choice or completion type: The cat ran after the (house, mouse); The cat ran after the __ ouse (or m __ __ __ __).
5. Give the child sentences to read orally that contain many words in which the two letters are used.

As an example of this procedure, assume that a child confuses *m* and *n*. The letter *m* is presented, and the fact that it has two humps is pointed out. The *n* is presented, and the fact that it has only one hump is noted. The two letters are compared, sounded, and written. The fact that /m/ is pronounced with lips closed and /n/ with lips open is demonstrated. Next a list of words such as *mat*, *milk*, and *make* is presented and read, followed by a list such as *not*, *nip*, and *nut*. Then pairs of words are introduced, such as *map* and *nap*, *mail* and *nail*. Sentences are then employed, such as: A boy grows into a (*man*, *nan*); We get light from the (*moon*, *noon*) and the (*sum*, *sun*); A ___ouse ran across the roo___.

Students should learn to monitor their decoding efforts by asking themselves three questions: (1) Does it sound like a word I know? (2) Does it make sense in this sentence? (3) Does the sentence sound right with this word in it? In short, they should learn to use their lexical, semantic, and syntactic knowledge.

Difficulties with Words of More Than One Syllable

Above the second- or third-grade level, difficulties in word recognition are apt to involve words of more than one syllable. The word-recognition skills that have been successful in learning such words as *went* and *their* do not seem to work when employed on such words as *migration*, *provocative*, *theoretical*, and *constitutionally*. In fact, difficulties in word recognition may arise during the middle grades in children who have previously had little difficulty with reading.

Many of these children have few decoding skills or do not employ those they do possess. They developed satisfactory sight vocabularies as long as the new words were taught to them; and their sight vocabularies, aided by guessing from the context, keep them going fairly well. Nevertheless, their lack of decoding knowledge makes it impossible for them to work out the correct pronunciation of the separate syllables in a long, unfamiliar word. They may not know how to analyze the word into usable parts. They soon form the habit of guessing from the context, aided by the general appearance of the word with perhaps a more careful inspection of the word's beginning. Sometimes they form the habit of skipping long words altogether, filling in during oral reading with a vague mumble. Analysis of the words on which the errors occurred and follow-up testing will suggest what needs to be taught.

The ability to recognize polysyllabic words may be more of a problem than commonly recognized. P. Cunningham (1980) found that only 37 of 117 fourth and fifth graders were able to correctly decode 12 or more of the 15 polysyllabic words in a screening test.

In some programs children are asked to indicate the number of syllables heard in words pronounced by the teacher. This is done either as an exercise in auditory segmentation or because it is believed to be a readiness skill for learning to syllabicate words.

Procedural Plans

Schell (1978) developed a PPARR cycle for teaching decoding to poor readers:

1. *Present* the skill using an inductive approach and tying in the skill to prior knowledge.

2. *Practice* is structured to assure success and transfer to actual reading. Immediate feedback about the appropriateness of his responses is supplied to the child.
3. *Apply* means the teacher repeatedly shows the student how learned skills can be used in reading.
4. *Review* recognizes that overlearning requires an adequate number of varied repetitions and the opportunity to practice the skill in a variety of contexts.
5. *Re-review* provides for cumulative review of two or more skills in a practice session.

Bryant (1980, 1981) outlined a nine-step plan for using a whole-word or phonic method. It is based on direct teaching of specific skills, controlling the amount to be learned in one lesson, reducing response competition (words or phonic elements are dropped out of a lesson as they are mastered so the child need concentrate on fewer items), providing immediate feedback, providing immediate and distributed review, mastery learning, and teaching for transfer.

Positional Errors in Words

Errors on the beginnings of words are relatively infrequent. Those that do occur are likely to be letter reversals (*b–d*), confusion of similar words (*when, then*), words beginning with single vowels that represent a schwa sound (*again, other*), or as one phase of a serious general weakness in word recognition. Helping children to overcome reversal tendencies is discussed below. Pupils who consistently err on initial consonants need to learn these symbol–sound associations and how to combine this knowledge with other cues to recognize unknown words. Calling attention to the fact that certain high-utility words begin with a schwa sound (which they do not expect to hear for that vowel letter) may help children overcome such errors. When the errors are caused by inattention to the beginnings of words, forced-choice exercises that draw attention to the initial word elements may help. Exercises in alphabetizing and the use of dictionaries also call attention to the beginning of the word.

Many unskilled readers observe only the beginning of an unfamiliar word and guess at the rest. This behavior is common in context readers and is found in children who get little or no help from the context. In either case, such errors may alter the intended meaning of a passage.

Medial errors usually involve an inability to make vowel symbol–sound associations; therefore, unknown correspondences should be taught and practiced. After the associations are taught, provide practice in reading words that are alike except for their medial vowels (e.g., The sun is (*hat, hot, hut*).

A form of medial error found in individuals of fairly advanced reading ability is the confusion of multisyllabic words that have similar beginnings and endings, such as *commission* and *communion* or *precision* and *procession*. These pupils must be taught to make better use of context and how to decode such words systematically. It is often helpful to insert vertical lines between the syllables, or to emphasize the part omitted or misread by underlining it.

Some errors on word endings are caused by a failure to note inflected endings or suffixes. Usually specific practice is sufficient to overcome such behaviors. After pointing out how the ending can change the meaning of a word, provide practice in reading sentences like these: There are many (*horse, horses*) in the barn; I can run (*fast, fastest, faster*) than you. Multiple-choice exercises that compel the child to pay careful attention to the total word also can be employed: The lady put her money in the (*benk, bank, balk*). In other cases, the behavior indicates the child cannot recognize the element as a unit (e.g., *tion*) or does not possess the skills necessary to decode it. In some cases, the miscue merely reflects the reader's dialect (see A. J. Harris & Sipay 1979, pp. 459–481).

Mispronunciations and Substitutions

The term *mispronunciation* usually implies that the response violated the context (*dog* for *dig*); *substitution* implies that the replacement made sense (*cat* for *kitten*). In both cases, the response differs from the stimulus. An analysis of the child's mispronunciations and substitutions may reveal a pattern to the responses (e.g., phonemically irregular high-utility words or errors on words containing vowel combinations). The appropriate word-recognition skills should be taught. If testing also reveals that the child is not making use of context and needs to learn those skills, appropriate treatment can be given.

Mispronunciations and substitutions also may indicate that the pupil is reading too rapidly or carelessly. In these situations there is a need to change the pupil's attitude and reading habits. Frequent mispronunciations also can be the result of using material beyond the child's instructional level. In such cases, the cure is to provide more appropriate material and analyze the performance to determine the causes of the mispronunciations.

Children may be able to obtain meaning from a selection in which they make fairly frequent substitutions, particularly if the content is within their experiential background. It may not be the meaning intended by the author, however, or subtle differences in meaning may not be comprehended. Pronouncing *pup* as *dog* may prevent the child from fully understanding the story; if *pup* means a baby seal, the meaning is lost entirely. As the reading material becomes further removed from the child's experiential background, substitutions are more likely to hamper obtaining full meaning; and there are times when exact reading (e.g., in science or math problems) is very important. Children who make frequent substitutions, especially when the miscue begins with the same letter as the stimulus, may be relying excessively on context or may not have the skills necessary to decode the unknown word. In the former case, the possible danger of such overreliance should be pointed out to the pupil, and more exact word recognition required of him. In the latter case, the needed skills should be taught.

Additions and Omissions

Additions occur less frequently than omissions, and most often do not disrupt meaning. Additions may be inserted to make the sentence flow more easily for the reader, or to make it more grammatically acceptable or more in keeping with the child's oral language pattern.

Omissions of whole words indicate that the child is (1) "editing out" words that are not needed to obtain meaning; or (2) translating the passage into his dialect. In either case there is no need for concern. Words also may be omitted because they are not recognized or the child lacks the necessary skills or inclination to decode them. In these cases the treatment is obvious.

Letters and syllables are more likely to be omitted at the end or middle of a word than in the initial position. Such errors may result from inattention, reading too rapidly, the inability to recognize or decode that element, or a dialectal rendition. As the inattention, recognition, or decoding problem is overcome such omissions and additions usually disappear. Frequent omissions of whole lines of print may indicate a problem with return sweep (see p. 544) or with keeping one's place on the page. The use of a marker, which is moved down one line at a time, provides "first aid" until the basic cause is overcome.

Reversals

The term *reversal* may refer to (1) a confusion of single letters (*b–d, p–g, n–u*); (2) a complete reversal of letter sequence in a word (*on–no, saw–was*); (3) a partial reversal of letter sequences or transposition of letters (*ram–arm, ate–tea, girl–grill*); or (4) a reversal of the word order in a sentence ("The boy saw the dog" for "The dog saw the boy"). Bannatyne (1972b) distinguished three types of letter-orientation reversals: (1) mirror images (*b–d*); (2) inversions (*u–n*); and (3) rotations (*b–p*).

Reversals are fairly common among young children, who apparently tend to think that differences in the spatial orientation of letters or the order of letters in words are relatively unimportant. They take the same attitude as they do toward a picture of a person, which they can recognize about as well when it is sideways or upside down as when it is right side up (Jackson 1972). Or, as Downing and Thackray (1971) put it, before entering school, children have learned to ignore such things as mirror images—a stick is a stick no matter in which direction it is presented. Children must learn that, in reading, direction does matter.

Preschool children, particularly those under age 5, have great difficulty discriminating among visual stimuli that differ only in orientation, whether the stimuli are horseshoes or letters like *b-d-p*. Ability to discriminate between *up* and *down* improves with age, but differentiating between left and right continues to be a problem until about age 6 (Ross 1976). Thus first graders will be less likely to confuse *b* and *p* than *b* and *d*. Only when reversals persist much beyond age 7 is there need for concern.

Reversals usually do not occur in reading with much frequency beyond the initial stages of acquisition. They tend to occur more frequently with certain letters and words (Liberman *et al.* 1971) and are influenced by context (Y. Goodman 1976), being less likely to occur when they violate context.

For years, reversals have been considered symptomatic of, or associated with, reading disability. But, as a proportion of total word-recognition errors, reversals are no higher in poor than in good readers (Fischer, Liberman, & Shankweiler 1978; Stanovich 1982a). Although there are a number of theories about the cause of reversals (lack of cerebral dominance, directional confusion, sequencing problems), all lack firm research evidence (Stone 1976). One of the earliest theories to appear in the United States was that of S. T. Orton (1937), who postulated that reversals were the prime symptom of "the reading disability," which he termed *strephosymbolia* (twisted symbols). According to Orton's theory, reversals reflected the failure to develop a clear dominance of one cerebral hemisphere. When the less-dominant hemisphere took over sporadically, reversals occurred. Since not all reversals involve mirror images, Orton's theory cannot be considered definitive, and the exact role of hemispheric dominance in reading ability is still unresolved. There is some evidence that reversals are not caused by inadequate perception or a neurological deficit (Fischer, Liberman, & Shankweiler 1978; Cohn & Strickler 1979). When Deno and Chiang (1979) provided incentives for accurate responses, there was a rapid decrease in reversals by children who previously made such errors. Other studies (Liberman *et al.* 1971, Lyle 1968) found that letter-orientation reversals were not significantly correlated with letter-sequence reversals, suggesting that the two may have different causes.

Factors other than immaturity may cause reversals. Failure to develop consistent left-to-right eye movements in reading may result in reversals. Because of regressive movements, the letters or parts of the word may be interpreted in the wrong direction or order, or words may be scanned in the wrong direction or order. Other possible causes of reversals are difficulty with fusion and eye coordination and directional confusion.

The general principles described in this chapter for overcoming letter confusions will usually suffice to overcome letter reversals. The need for tracing and writing letters is greater for children who reverse letters than it is for those who make other letter errors, and more intensive drill is usually necessary before reversals are eliminated.

Reversals of words, parts of words, and the order of words in sentences usually indicate that the child needs training to develop a consistent left-to-right sequence in reading. The need for such a consistent direction should first be explained to the child, with illustrations of how the words and meanings are changed when the correct order is not maintained. Then various methods may be employed to build up proper directional habits. Among the devices found to work well in overcoming reversal tendencies are the following:

1. Tracing, writing, and sounding words that are frequently confused. These procedures automatically enforce using the correct sequence of letters. Cursive writing is more helpful than manuscript writing.
2. Covering a word with a card and moving the card slowly to the right so that the letters are exposed in proper sequence.

3. Underlining the first letter in the word. Sometimes underlining the first letter in green and the last letter in red—"traffic lights"—is effective. The child is told to start on green and stop on red.
4. Encouraging the child to use a finger or pencil as a guide in reading along a line. This practice is very helpful as a means of teaching the proper direction for eye movements.
5. Exposing a line of print a little at a time by means of a card or an opening cut in a card, by opening a zipper, or by use of a controlled reader set at slow speed.
6. Drawing an arrow pointing to the right under words that are frequently reversed.
7. Allowing the child to use a typewriter. This has favorable effects on spelling and composition, as well as on word recognition.

Fernald (1943, p. 89) stated that reversals quickly disappeared when children were taught by the kinesthetic method, making sure that they started to write at the left edge of the paper. Monroe (1932, p. 127) found that systematic letter-by-letter phonic training, combined with tracing, had a similarly beneficial effect on the reversal tendency.

Teaching the use of context to monitor responses while reading also can aid children with reversal tendencies. A child with *b–d* problems who monitors the appropriateness of his responses is not likely to accept /done/ for *bone* in the sentence "The dog ate the bone." Forced-choice exercises in which the context is very revealing also can be used for this purpose. When letter reversals do not seem amenable to training, the child can be taught a compensation strategy that may help. Knowing, for example, that he confuses *b* and *d*, he says to himself, "If the word isn't *bump,* it must be dump." Wearing a ring on the left hand and starting from the ring can also be helpful.

Repetitions

The oral reading of some children is marred by frequent repetitions. These may be repetitions of part of a word, a whole word, a phrase, or the entire sentence. For example, a child may read "The boy went for a walk with his spotted dog" as follows: "The boy—the boy want for—the boy went for a—a walk—with his stop—spotted dog."

Some repetitions are caused by slowness in word recognition; the child repeats a preceding word or two, or part of a word, to have more time for decoding. These repetitions will drop out as greater skill in word recognition is attained. Another cause of repetitions is the realization that the first reading did not make sense; two instances of this type, involving *want* for *went* and *stop* for *spotted,* are in the example above. Although repetitions caused by self-corrections are desirable behaviors, their frequent occurrence indicates a need for more automatic word recognition. Sometimes a child loses the trend of thought and goes back in order to pick up the meaning. As comprehension improves, the need for repetitions of this sort lessens. Frequent repetitions may also indicate that the material is too difficult for the child. Regressive eye movements accompany repetitions, but usually the need to repeat causes the regressive movements, rather than vice versa.

Many children repeat words because of nervousness in oral reading. They need to have their confidence built up and then their hesitations and repetitions will diminish. These children should be given opportunities to rehearse easy selections carefully and then read the selections to children who are unfamiliar with the story. They also need large doses of encouragement and praise.

Occasionally a child will tend to overcorrect; that is, the child compulsively corrects every miscue, even minor ones. Again, a balance needs to be struck. The child needs to learn that, at times, 100% correct word recognition is not necessary.

Lack of Fluency

Some children's oral reading lacks fluency. Their reading is marked by such behaviors as hesitations, word-by-word reading, improper phrasing, repetitions, and an inadequate use of voice. Lack of fluency is sometimes the result of reading at sight and abates if the material is preread silently. Hesitations, word-by-word reading, and repetitions usually are caused by inadequate word recognition; once these problems are overcome, work can proceed on developing fluency.

Some children need to learn how to group words into meaningful phrases (see pp. 473–475). Modeling by the teacher, followed by guided practice, can improve phrasing and use of voice. Listening to taped stories while following along a printed copy may also help. D. D. Smith (1979) reported that reading stories to children at approximately 100 words per minute improved the word recognition of her three subjects.

Samuels (1979) suggested using a method of *repeated readings* to develop fluency. The method consists of reading a short, meaningful selection again and again until fluency is satisfactory; then the procedure is repeated with a different selection. Reading speed, rather than word-recognition accuracy, is stressed. Reading rates are said to increase with each new selection, and fewer rereadings become necessary to achieve fluency. B. Anderson (1981) suggested that a criterion of 85 WPM be used in determining adequate fluency, but this may be too slow.

A useful modification of the repeated readings technique is to have the child read along silently with a taped story, then read the story alone silently until he can read it orally with fluency (Samuels & Eisenberg 1981). Bos (1982) and Kann (1983) recommended combining the technique with the Neurological Impress Method (see p. 441), and Lauritzen (1982) described how the technique could be used with groups.

According to Schreiber (1980), repeated reading and similar methods are effective either because they help children discover the appropriate prosodic pattern of the material or because the massive practice helps them to transfer the assignment of the appropriate prosodic features to novel passages.

Repeated readings can result in gains in fluency, but the technique may be productive only for those who are reading up to about the fifth- or sixth-grade level. And whatever skills are acquired may transfer only to the same type of material as the practice task (Carver & Hoffman 1981).

Slow Word Recognition

Some children recognize words slowly. This is apparent on tests using words in isolation, when a number of their correct responses are made very close to the time limit allowed (often 3 seconds), or they can recognize the words when given additional time. Lack of automatic word recognition also can be noted when reading in context; reading rate is slow and often word by word. Slow word recognition can adversely affect both fluency and comprehension (Stanovich 1980, Beck 1981).

Slow word recognition is not unusual in children who are just learning to read. Word-recognition accuracy may be acquired rather quickly; but rapid, automatic recognition follows a slow developmental trend (Samuels 1981). With progress in reading, word recogniton becomes faster and more automatic. Reading a great deal of easy, interesting material also tends to increase word-recognition speed. Repeated readings also may help.

Some children who have been given intensive phonic training develop the habit of trying to sound out most words. This behavior, referred to as an over-analytical set, keeps their speed far below what it would be if they responded immediately to words as wholes. Even some fairly skilled readers have to sound out many multisyllabic words, although they have no difficulty with monosyllabic or two-syllable words. Although they attempt to decode almost every word, these children often can recognize a number of these words when they are presented quickly. Quick-flash techniques can be used to demonstrate to them that they need not decode every word. The advantage of recognizing words at sight should be discussed.

Another helpful procedure for increasing word-recognition speed is the use of flash cards (see p. 372) or a tachistoscope (see p. 546). One should start with one-syllable, high-utility words to which the child has already been exposed. At first the words should be of different shapes, such as *all, father, house,* and *they.* Longer and more visually similar words can be introduced gradually. If phrases (*to the store*) are shown, more time should be allowed because even excellent readers do not usually take in more than two or three words with one fixation.

Since high-utility words make up more than half the running words of most reading material, speeding up their recognition often improves reading fluency, rate, and perhaps comprehension; the attention previously spent on recognizing or decoding words can be shifted to attaining meaning. The emphasis in quick-exposure drills should be on changing "two look" words to "one look" words.

Use of Context Clues

Research findings suggest the following text-processing differences between good and poor readers: (1) Poor readers make proportionally more meaning-change miscues than do good readers; (2) poor readers do not use context as effectively as good readers to make predictions and to self-correct disruptive miscues; and (3) poor readers above the primary grades use graphic cues as effectively as good readers do, but they do not coordinate the use of graphic cues with other cues as well as good readers do. In short, poor readers make more miscues, are less aware of the extent to which their miscues disrupt meaning, and are less effective in using multiple cues and alternative strategies in preserving the meaning of the text (Aulls 1981).

Overreliance on Context

Stanovich (1990, 1982c) theorized that some poor readers rely heavily on context to compensate for their inadequate word recognition. If such is the case, the treatment would involve increasing word-recognition accuracy and speed.

Some students seem to have gotten into the habit of overrelying on context, even though they possess adequate word recognition. They make frequent substitutions which often begin with the same letters as the stimuli and which, although contextually appropriate, vary in the degree to which they alter the author's intended meaning. Very often they can supply the word when their attention is called to it. While such behavior may not be too disruptive when reading only to get an overview or the gist of the material, or when reading for pleasure, it could be quite disruptive when close, careful reading is required by the task. Treatment for context readers should begin with changing a habit that may be well ingrained. Context readers should be told that at times it is important to read all, or almost all, of the words accurately; this fact also needs to be demonstrated to them. Pointing out how certain miscues change meaning, providing practice in reading for specific details, and having them read to carry out specific directions may help.

Inadequate Use of Context

Pupils cannot or do not use context clues to their advantage for a number of reasons. If many of the words are not recognized, little or no context is available to the reader. The treatment for such cases is obvious. Use of context also requires the availability and use of semantic and syntactic knowledge. A temporary solution for such situations would be to simply provide easier material or to supply the needed information to the pupil before he reads the material. Reasoning ability is also needed in the use of context clues. Some truly slow learners will have difficulty for this reason.

Use of context as a self-monitoring device necessitates that the reader be aware when a miscue is disruptive and know some self-correction strategies. Children who are reading at least at the second reader level can be taught to distinguish between disruptive and nondisruptive miscues and how to use a self-correction procedure (Pflaum & Pascarella 1980). K. D'Angelo (1982) made suggestions for developing self-correction behaviors.

Pupils can be helped to become aware of disruptive miscues by having them listen to material containing semantic and syntactically inappropriate miscues and by having them compare the correct printed version with one containing the disruptive miscue. The child's task is to indicate where such errors occur.

Taylor and Nosbush (1983) recommended a four-step procedure for encouraging students to correct their disruptive miscues: (1) The child, on a one-to-one basis, reads a 100–300 word passage at his instructional level to the teacher, who provides as little feedback as possible; (2) the teacher praises the child for something done well in oral reading, especially for self-correcting disruptive miscues; (3) one or two uncorrected disruptive miscues are pointed out to the child by reading his rendition to him and having him tell what word did not make sense or sound right; and (4) the child is helped to recognize the words on which the errors were made by demonstrating how graphic and context clues could be employed.

As the occasions arise during reading lessons, the teacher can model how to use context as an aid to word identification by saying out loud the thoughts that occur in her mind as she goes through the process. Specifically constructed cloze or maze exercises or sentences containing nonsense words (e.g., "I knew the girls were happy because they were plinking") also could be provided, and the pupils asked to explain the bases on which their responses were made. If their choices are unacceptable, the teacher should explain how to arrive at a better prediction. Strategy lessons based on an analysis of pupils miscues may be found in Goodman and Goodman (1982), Y. Goodman (1970, 1984), and Y. Goodman and Burke (1980).

Dahl and Samuels (1977) presented a hypothesis–test strategy for using context to aid word recognition. The steps in the strategy are as follows: (1) Use information from the passage (and, we would add, from conceptual background and language cues); (2) make a prediction (the hypothesis) as to which word is most likely to occur; (3) compare the printed and predicted words (testing the hypothesis) for goodness of fit; and (4) accept or reject the prediction. Rejection should lead to another attempt.

Samuels (1981) suggested teaching the hypothesis–test strategy after the child is fairly proficient in decoding. His rationale was that knowledge of symbol–sound associations could be combined with context to make more accurate predictions.

The first strategy the child should employ when encountering an unknown word is to finish reading the sentence because it may provide additional information. The unknown word should be checked for graphic cues that could be combined with context clues. If the word is important to meaning, an attempt should be made to decode it. Rereading the sentence also may help.

If completing or rereading the sentence does not clear up meaning or cue an important unknown word, rereading some of the preceding text may provide useful information or reveal a previously undetected error. At times, reading more of the text following the disruption may prove helpful.

Combining Context Cues, Graphic Cues, and Phonic Skills

Because the goal is to recognize words as quickly and efficiently as possible, the less the child has to do, the better. Thus, instantaneous recognition of the whole word is quickest and most satisfactory.

When the first look does not result in word recognition, the combination of an intelligent prediction based on context and whatever familiar part(s) of the unknown word are immediately discernible is often sufficient. The general category of the unfamiliar word may be suggested by the rest of the sentence, or the preceding sentence (e.g., Henry went into the _____ to buy some candy). Use of synatactic cues indicates that the unknown word is almost certainly a noun. The term *noun* need not be known, but the child's past experience with spoken language suggests the kind of word that grammatically fits the sentence. Past experience and semantic cues further limit the words that can make sense in this sentence. And uncertainty about the specific noun in question can be reduced further by employing as many additional cues as necessary. The initial letter (e.g., *s*) alone may narrow the possibilities, but the reader may need to go to the second letter (e.g., *st*) or beyond to rule out *shop*. Word length and configuration clues may rule out some possibilities (e.g., *stadium*).

If the use of context and partial graphic information is not sufficient (context is not always potent enough to cue the reader, or a number of words in the sentence are unfamiliar and thus make it difficult to use context clues), the reader needs to be able to apply additional decoding skills, going only as far as necessary to achieve word recognition. Skilled readers use only as many cues as necessary to recognize words, but they possess highly developed decoding skills and employ them flexibly.

Morphemic analysis may be sufficient when all or most parts of the word are already known at sight. However, morphemic analysis is frequently used in combination with context and phonic cues beyond the initial stage of learning to read. The unknown word is divided into reasonable parts; the parts are sounded and blended. The resulting response is then tested to determine its appropriateness in the sentence. At this point, the child's listening and speaking vocabulary becomes important. If the unfamiliar printed word is one the child has heard or uses, a close approximation of the spoken equivalent, or even a partial decoding of the word, often is sufficient for recognition. If the word is completely new, the child has to infer both its pronunciation and meaning, and neither is any help in determining the other. Thus, a word like *incognito* may be correctly divided into syllables, each of which is sounded in a reasonable way. But the wrong syllable may be accented, and wrong vowel sounds may be tried, because the word is entirely unfamiliar to the reader.

As a last resort, the interested reader may turn to a dictionary or glossary to determine the pronunciation of the unfamiliar printed word. This requires the ability to understand the phonetic respelling code used in that dictionary. At times, readers are surprised to find in the dictionary that they have heard or used that word before and know its meaning but have never encountered it before in print (e.g., *island, depot*).

Reading skills usually are taught separately but used in combination. Skill in combining various word-recognition skills can be developed by the use of materials that demand careful attention to both meaning and word details. This exercise, in its many variations, requires the reader to understand the sentence as a whole to predict what word to expect and choose correctly among words that look very much alike. A modified cloze procedure in which various graphic cues are provided is another method for helping children combine cues (e.g., It is foolish to go into the pool if you can't sw__ __).

An effective word-recognition program teaches children to employ a variety of skills flexibly; no one strategy is overemphasized. The goal is to equip learners with a variety of strategies and let them select the ones that work best for them in a given situation.

Teacher Correction Behavior

A recent area of interest is the possible influence of teacher behavior on the word recognition and reading comprehension of children. A basic premise of many of these studies is that correcting word-recognition errors, especially those that are not semantically disruptive, will have an adverse effect on reading comprehension because it focuses the child's attention on the graphic input rather than on obtaining meaning. The evidence in this regard is mixed. For example, Furniss (1980) interpreted his findings as indicating that corrective feedback may be detrimental to reading comprehension; Pany, McCoy, and Peters (1981) did not.

The data regarding the relationship between teacher behavior and the oral reading of students are largely correlational. Some studies, however, have experimentally examined the effects. Simply acknowledging correct responses and correcting errors had little effect on the number of words learned by first graders who had word-recognition problems (Kibby 1979a). McNaughton (1981) found that second graders were less prone to respond, self-corrected fewer miscues, were less sensitive to disruptions in meaning, and were less accurate in word recognition when the teacher provided correction within 5 seconds than when the correction was received after 5 seconds or when the student reached a sentence boundary. Apparently, immediate error correction interferes with learning to monitor one's responses. There were no significant differences in oral reading accuracy between two groups of poor readers who were either encouraged to use previously taught decoding skills or were supplied unknown words (L. Meyer 1982).

Hoffman, O'Neal, and Baker (1981) reported that the teachers in their study made overt responses to only 37% of the children's miscues. They were more likely to respond to miscues made in material that was difficult for the child or that disrupted meaning, or when pupils made repeated unsuccessful attempts to respond to a word. In general, teacher responses were early and fast, but were evenly divided between terminal feedback (telling the word to the child) and sustaining feedback (aiding the child by pointing out cues that should help him recognize the word).

Somewhat similarly, Lass (1984) found that teachers individualize their responses to match variations in miscues. These teachers tended to disregard nondisruptive miscues, provided feedback when the use of graphic cues would be helpful, and provided instruction or supplied the word when the child refused to attempt a word or made unsuccessful attempts. The "read it again" strategy was useful only if the child was cued. Hoffman et al. (1984) also found that teachers seem to adjust their manner of responding to the qualitative characteristics of miscues rather than simply responding to any error. These researchers also found that a hesitation followed by the teacher's supplying the word led to a situation in which the next time an unknown word was encountered, the more likely the child was to wait for the teacher's immediate feedback, and the teacher to oblige. Thus, a vicious cycle was established.

To break the cycle, Hoffman *et al.* (1984) suggested: (1) Use reading material of appropriate difficulty; (2) teach the children to continue reading following a miscue (this puts the primary monitoring burden on them); (3) teach explicit strategies for dealing with miscues; (4) make no responses to nondisruptive miscues; and (5) provide delayed sustaining feedback as needed.

Hoffman *et al.* (1984) concluded that the timing of the feedback (both in terms of point of interruption and elapsed time) seems to be potentially more important than the actual form of the teacher response; delayed feedback is more beneficial than immediate feedback.

The Importance of Accurate Word Recognition

On the basis of three related studies, Nicholson, Pearson, and Dykstra (1979) concluded:

1. The necessity for accurate word recognition depends on the comprehension one considers important. Accurate word recognition is important for precise comprehension but relatively unimportant for global interpretation.
2. Because semantically acceptable errors (e.g., *giant* for *gorilla*) seem reasonable, they are likely to disrupt precise comprehension more than unacceptable errors (e.g., *wall* for *gorilla*).
3. Comprehension questions that required the child to relate the ideas in two sentences were affected by the error rate in one study, but questions primarily requiring prior knowledge were not.

These authors stated that although there is a natural temptation to prefer global interpretation over precise comprehension, there are many times (particularly in instructional settings) when gross semantically acceptable responses will not suffice. "No matter how sincere the reader's attempt to impose meaning into a text that seems to defy interpretation, he or she will quite often answer detail questions incorrectly" (p. 19).

X. MATERIALS FOR IMPROVING WORD-RECOGNITION SKILLS

Manipulative Devices and Games

Many manipulative devices and games can be used to add variety and interest to word-recognition and decoding programs. They serve to break the monotony that may otherwise cause a pupil's effort to slacken. Depending on the task set

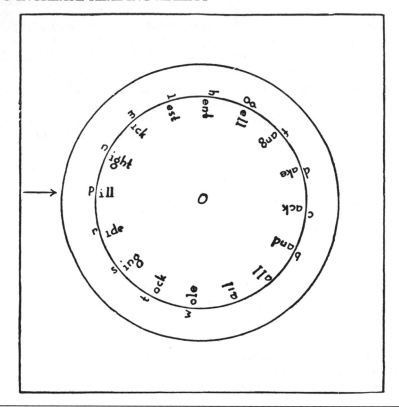

Figure 12.4. "Lucky Wheel" for phonic practice. Both outer and inner circles can be rotated.

for the learner and the nature of the stimuli, most of these devices can be used for teaching or reinforcing word-recognition or decoding skills. The following descriptions are representative of materials that may be made or purchased. Blank or reusable game boards are available from Childcraft and Ideal.

Use of games can improve word recognition (Kirby, Holborn, & Bushby 1981). Physically active games (e.g., Word Toss) were found to be more effective than passive games (e.g., Go Fish) in increasing the word recognition of inner-city children (Dickerson 1982).

DIRECTIONS FOR USING GAMES

1. Lucky Wheel. Two circles, one smaller than the other, are fastened together through their centers so that each can be rotated freely without disturbing the other (see Fig. 12.4). Initial consonants or consonant clusters are printed around the outer circle, and phonograms are printed around the edge of the inner circle; in this way, different words can be formed. By rotating the outer circle, different initial elements can be combined with the same phonogram; and by rotating the inner circle, the same initial elements can be combined with different phonograms. Many variations of this general idea have been devised. Such a wheel can be used as a basis for competitive games. Commercial materials include the 63 *Webster Word Wheels* (Webster); the *Phonetic Word Analyzer* (Milton Bradley), which has wheels with interchangeable disks; and the wooden *Turn and Read*

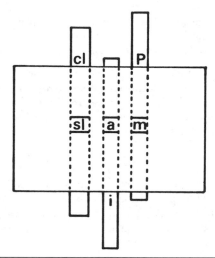

Figure 12.5.   A phonic card, showing how strip inserts can be used to form a variety of words.

(Childcraft) in which initial consonant or blend wheels are inserted into blocks with various phonograms printed on them. Some, such as *Vowel Wheels* (Milton Bradley), are designed only for particular phonic elements.

2. Phonic Strips. Three horizontal slits, close together and in line, are made across a 4 × 6-inch index card. Three other slits are made directly below them. A number of thin strips are prepared (by cutting up another index card); the strips should be of a proper width so that they can be threaded through the slits in such a way as to expose only a small part of the strip. On one strip a number of initial consonants can be printed, one below the other; on a second strip, middle vowels; on a third strip, common word endings; and so on. By inserting the strips and moving them up and down, a large number of different words can be formed (see Fig. 12.5). This device can be adapted for practice on word beginnings, middles, or endings and can be used with phonograms as well as single letters.

An interesting variation of phonic strips are the *Sort and Sound Word-Making* and *Vowel Diagraph Word-Making Cards* (ETA). The cards are cut into strips that contain a picture and a three- or four-letter word. In assembling the picture, the corresponding word is formed automatically.

3. Rhyme Making. Lines from several verses are printed on separate strips. The child picks out all the lines that end in the same sound and assembles them into a little poem. High poetic standards are not necessary.

4. Darts. An inexpensive dart-and-target set is used. Small cards, each with a single phonogram, are pasted to the target, and an initial consonant is pasted on each dart. If the word formed when the dart hits a phonogram is read correctly, a point is scored. A beanbag toss game may be substituted for the dart set.

5. Word-O. Game cards, modeled after Bingo or Lotto, can be made, using words instead of numbers, and the usual rules for such games can be used or modified. The leader says the word and holds up the card, or the word is said but not shown. The players look for the word on their cards and cover it if they find it. The first player who covers five words in a row, column or in a diagonal and can identify them correctly wins.

Commercial materials of this type include the *Group Word Teaching Game, Consonant Lotto, Vowel Lotto*, and the *Group Sounding Game* (Garrard), *Phonetic Quizmo* (Milton Bradley), *Wingo Wordo* (EPS), and *Primary Phonics* (SVE).

6. Anagrams. An inexpensive anagram set can be purchased, or letters can be printed on small pasteboard squares. Word-building games of several kinds can be played. *Word Builders* (Kenworthy) includes both capital and small letters. The phonic elements are color coded (e.g., consonants on white cards, vowels on blue) in the *Rainbow Word Builders* (Kenworthy). Plastic letters that can be linked together are found in *Link Letters* (Milton Bradley).

7. Spin the Pointer. Words are arranged around the outside of a circle, and the child tries to read the word at which the pointer stops. Failures and successes can be scored according to the rules of games like baseball and football. In baseball, for example, correctly recognizing the word is a hit and failure to do so is an out; the score is kept in terms of runs. By making slits into which word cards may be inserted, the same circle and pointer can be used indefinitely.

8. Fishing. One word, phrase, or sentence is printed on each of a number of cardboard cutouts in the shape of fish, to which paper clips are attached. The child picks up a fish by means of a horseshoe magnet on a string, and keeps the fish if the word is read correctly. Similar games can be devised involving pulling leaves off a tree and so on.

9. Racing. A large racetrack is drawn and divided into boxes, in each of which a word is placed. Each child has a car, horse, etc., of a different color. Each player, in turn, spins a pointer, which indicates a move of one, two, three, or four boxes. If the word is read correctly, the marker is advanced that many spaces; if not, the player waits for his next turn. *Road Race* (Curriculum Associates), *Word Trek-Blends and Digraphs* (DLM), and *Ron the Python* (Childcraft) also require blending skills.

10. Word Hospital. Words that cause persistent difficulty are called "sick" words, and the child, as doctor, puts them to bed in a word hospital until they are cured (see Fig. 12.6).

11. This to That. Starting with one word, one of the letters in the word is changed each time, making a series of words: *his, him, ham, ram*. The game can also be played with the changing of two-letter combinations allowed: *shook, spook, spoke, broke*. Reading such a sequence is a welcome change from the monotony of word families and provides an interesting form of review.

12. Word Tic-Tac-Toe.[15] One of nine practice words is printed into each space on a blank form, or word cards are fitted into slots cut into a form made of oak tag. The game is played like Tic-Tac-Toe, but the player must acceptably pronounce the word in the square in order to place his X or O in that space.

13. Alphabet Pyramid. A word beginning with *a* is written by the first player. The next player must add a word that begins with the next letter of the alphabet. The player who is able to add the last word is the winner.

14. Card Games. Packs of blank playing cards, with decorative backs but no printing on the face side, are available from some playing-card manufacturers, or oak tag cut into

---

[15] This game and *Alphabet Pyramid, Change Over*, and *Synonyms/Antonyms* were adapted from ideas found in PIRT.

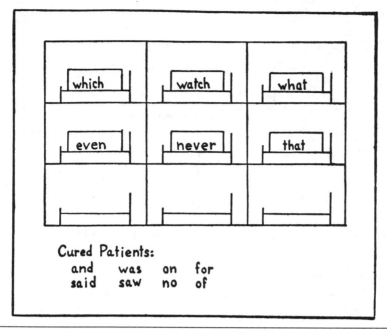

Figure 12.6. A "hospital" for "sick" words. A word with which the child has persistent difficulty is printed on a small card and is put to bed (inserted in the slit corresponding to the mattress of the bed). When a sick word is cured, its name is entered at the bottom of the chart.

rectangles of appropriate size can be used. By printing the same word on four cards, it is possible to make a "rummy" deck containing a given number of words or adapt the deck to the rules of other simple card games (e.g., casino). Commercially available sets of cards that can be used to teach or reinforce sight vocabulary or decoding skills include the following:

Basic Sight Vocabulary Cards (Garrard). The Dolch 220 high-utility words are printed on individual cards. The same words on slightly larger cards are available as *Popper Words*, Set 1 and Set 2, each containing 110 words.

Picture Word Builder (Milton Bradley). Pictures of 36 familiar objects are on cards die-cut so that only the correct word can be inserted to complete the word-picture matching. *Phonic Couplets* (ETA) is a similar set of materials containing 20 cards. In such exercises, it is important that the child associate the printed word with the correct name of the picture and not just rely on the die cut for matching. Such cards and other self-correcting materials are illustrated in Fig. 12.7.

Build It (Kingsbury). A challenging word-recognition game that requires quick visual perception of the similarities and differences within words. Four decks, two with short vowels (#1 with single consonants, #2 with blends) and two with long vowels (#3 with single consonants, #4 with blends).

Phonic Rummy Card Games (Kenworthy). Six sets, each containing 108 word cards, can be used to develop recognition of high-utility words and various phonic skills.

Big Deal (EPS). Six card games (*Concentration, War, Sourpuss, Go Fish, Rummy,* and *I Doubt It*) can be played using sets of words at ten levels of spelling complexity.

Take (Garrard). This card game involves matching the sounds of beginnings, middles, or endings of words.

Figure 12.7. Examples of self-checking materials. Adapted from C. Mercer and A. Mercer, The development and use of self-correcting material with exceptional children, *Teaching Exceptional Children*, Fall 1978.

The Syllable Game (Garrard). Three decks of 64 cards are designed to teach use of syllabication in the middle and upper grades.

Syllabo and Super Syllabo (Curriculum Associates). Each player tries to make as many words as possible from a set of syllable cards; more than 25 words can be formed from a single set.

Go Fish (Kingsbury). This interesting card game is well liked by remedial pupils and can be used in reinforcing phonic skills; one deck for initial consonants, another for initial blends.

Vowel Dominoes (Kingsbury). This game, played something like dominoes, involves matching short vowel sounds.

Blend Dominoes (Ideal). Players use domino-like cards containing consonants, blends, digraphs, and phonograms to construct words.

ABC Skill Builder (Kenworthy). This matching game, similar to *Old Maid*, is played with cards on which each card has a letter, a cue word, and a picture for the cue word.

Doghouse Game (Kenworthy). Initial consonants and blends are added to 12 cards, each with 35 word-ending spelling patterns.

New Phonics We Use Learning Games Kits (Rand McNally). Ten different games are in each kit: one kit for primary and one for intermediate grades.

Reading Laboratory 1: Word Games (SRA). The kit contains 44 word games, a Phonics Survey, pupil workbooks, a teachers' handbook, and check tests.

Change Over. In this teacher-made game, which is played like *Crazy Eight*, each card has a word that contains one or more symbol–sound associations to be practiced; the same word may appear as more than one card in the deck. Five cards have "Change Over" printed on them; these may be used to change the choice to any other consonant or vowel sound. Each player is dealt eight or fewer cards and the top card from the remaining deck is turned over; the rest of the deck is face down. The first player attempts to match a word in his hand with either the initial consonant or vowel sound in the word on the turned-up card. The rules may require the player to say the words on the target card and the word chosen from his hand or just to place his choice on top of the turned-up card. If the player makes an appropriate match the card from his hand is placed over the turned-up card. If the player cannot make a match with a word in his hand, he continues to draw from the deck until he can, or until the cards are used up. Then the next player takes a turn. The first player to get rid of all his cards is the winner.

Synonyms/Antonyms. Target words are printed on cards and placed in a deck. When a card is turned over, the first player attempts to provide orally an acceptable synonym or antonym and must tell if his response is the same or opposite in meaning. If an acceptable response is made, the player picks up the card. A new card is turned up, and the next player takes a turn. If the player cannot make an acceptable response, the next player tries. If none of the players can "win the card," a new one is turned up. The winner is the child who has the most cards when the deck is depleted or no more acceptable responses can be made.

15. *Crossword Puzzles.* Crossword puzzles can be constructed to provide practice in either word recognition or decoding or to develop word meaning. Published crossword puzzles include *Phonic Crossword Puzzles* (McCormick-Mathers); *Crossword Puzzles* (Ideal), which are reusable; *Crossword Puzzles for Phonics* (Continental); *My Puzzle Book 1 & 2* (Garrard), which uses the Dolch 220; and *Across and Down* (Scholastic), which is suitable for older students reading at fourth- to sixth-grade levels.

16. *Letter–Word Cubes.* Letters, phonograms, word parts, or words may be attached to, or printed on, the side of 1-inch or larger cubes. The cubes are cast like dice; the learner's task is to form as many words or sentences as possible. Task difficulty can be controlled by limiting or increasing the possible number of responses. For example, if practice with only three initial consonants is desired, each consonant letter would appear twice on the cube, thus limiting the number of words that can be formed when added to the vowel–consonant phonogram(s) on the other block(s). Among the activities for which cubes can be used are (1) single letter and/or multiple letters (e.g., blends, digraphs, diphthongs) on all the cubes, to form as many words as the player can think of; (2) single consonants and/or consonant clusters in some blocks, and vowel–consonant and/or consonant–vowel phonograms on the others, to practice substituting initial and final consonants to form

words; (3) root words on some blocks, affixes on the others, to practice use of prefixes and suffixes (this can be made into a vocabulary exercise by having the learner define the words constructed); and (4) words on all the cubes, to practice word recognition, "sentence sense," or comprehension. Commercially prepared cubes under various trade names are available.

17. Flip Cards. Cards that have flip folds can be used for practice in substituting word beginnings and endings or to aid morphemic analysis. One part of the card can be folded over to form a new word. Examples of published flip-fold cards are *Phonetic Drill Cards* (Milton Bradley), *Word Prefixes and Word Suffixes* (Kenworthy), *Consonant Flip Book* (DLM).

18. Concentration. Pairs of words, one per card, are printed on 3 x 5-inch cards. The cards are shuffled and placed facedown on a hard surface. Each player (2 to 4 can play) takes a turn exposing two cards. If the words match and are pronounced acceptably, the player keeps the cards and takes another turn. If the words do not match, or the word is not pronounced acceptably, the cards are returned to their original place. When all the cards are gone, the player with the most cards is the winner.

Intensive practice in the application of phonic skills may be provided by using materials in which the vocabulary contains only certain phonic elements (e.g., consonant–short vowel–consonant trigrams; single consonants and particular vowel combinations that represent certain long vowel sounds). In addition to the texts found in linguistic reading programs (see p. 70), other available materials include *Snoopy Snake and other Stories* (Word Making), *Primary Readers* and *V²/Vowels and Values* (MCP), *Windows on Reading* (Follett) and *Phonetic Reader Series* (EPS).

Many other teacher-made games and devices for developing reading skills, particularly word-recognition and decoding skills, can be found in Wagner and Hosier (1970); Dorsey (1972); Mattleman (1973); R. Thompson (1973); Russell, Karp, and Mueser (1975); The Reading Development Centre (1976a, b); Herr (1977); and Burns and Roe (1979). Canney (1978) has suggested ways for turning commercial games into reading games, and M. McGinnis (1978) has developed an annotated bibliography of published materials for use in Grades 7–12.

Workbooks and Texts

The workbooks that accompany commercial reading programs have many pages of practice material on word-recognition and decoding skills. Independent workbook material can be helpful in remedial and corrective work and in teaching children who seem to need a more systematic phonic procedure than a meaning-emphasis approach may provide. It should be clearly understood, however, that simply having a learner complete workbook pages or exercises does not constitute teaching. The child who can complete the task successfully probably has whatever skills are required to perform that task. For the child who cannot perform the task, the teacher must seek to determine *why* he cannot, if it is an important skill to learn. Even when the student can demonstrate skills in workbook or other exercises, the teacher cannot be assured that the child will apply the new skills in the actual reading act. Opportunities for doing so must be provided, and monitored with guided practice provided as necessary. Periodic checks must be made to determine if the skills are being employed. The same is true in teaching vocabulary, comprehension, and study skills. The output of workbooks, boxed sets of phonic practice materials, and phonic texts has been so great in recent years that a comprehensive listing would run on for pages.

Even if a lack of funds prohibits the purchase of consumable workbooks, the resourceful teacher is still not entirely prevented from making some use of them. From single copies, which are generally inexpensive, the teacher can get ideas that can be incorporated in board work or developed in duplicated worksheets of her own construction. Note, however, that imitation is permissible, but outright copying is plagiarism and is a violation of the law.

Many successful remedial teachers have developed files of useful practice exercises. They order two copies of each of a number of workbooks and cut them up (since pages are printed on both sides, two copies are needed). Each page is mounted on heavy paper or oak tag and can be covered with transparent plastic for permanence. Large plastic envelopes and markers are available from Ideal and Imperial. By assembling pages from several workbooks, a comprehensive series of exercises can be built up. Exercises constructed by the teacher can be inserted into the series at any time. A carton or box can be used as a file drawer. The exercises should be classified by type and number within each type. Care in classifying and numbering exercises makes it possible for a pupil–librarian to keep the collection in order and select for each pupil the exercises assigned by the teacher. A separate file of answer keys, corresponding to the exercises, makes it possible for the teacher to correct written work quickly, or for pupils to correct their own work.

Programs and Kits

Programs and kits primarily designed for developmental reading also contain material and procedures that may be used in corrective or remedial work. It should be realized, however, that the pace suggested by the manuals may be inappropriate, the materials may provide too little or too much skill practice, and the materials require reading ability. Unless the student is very deficient, it is more efficient to work only on the skills in which he is weak, rather than take him through an entire program. The Reading Teacher Staff (1978) found that middle-grade high-ability students performed reasonably well with self-teaching kits; low-ability students did not.

Multimedia Materials

An increasing number of programs use two or more media. Most of these combine tapes or records with one or more forms of reading material. New multimedia learning packages will unquestionably continue to be placed on the market faster than their usefulness can be determined. Since the cost of such materials tends to run high, it is desirable to arrange for a careful local evaluation and, if possible, for a trial use on approval before investing in such programs. When trained remedial personnel is scarce, however, materials that allow the teacher to give remedial help to more children by providng self-directing and self-checking learning experiences may justify their cost.

There are also films, filmstrips, and recordings based on children's books, a number of which have been annotated and evaluated by Greene and Schoenfeld (1977). Their main purpose is to motivate children to read. Some tapes are dramatizations of parts of the stories; others have taped parts of the whole selection with which the children are to read along. Although they are apparently used widely, there is a lack of information regarding how and why taped books are being used in the classroom and how effective they are (Monteith 1978).

XI. WORD-RECOGNITION METHODS FOR SEVERE DISABILITIES[16]

Some children have serious, pervasive word-recognition difficulties. After a number of years of schooling, they can recognize or decode a small number of printed words; a few nonreaders cannot even recognize their names in print. Disabled readers, especially the seriously disabled, are much more likely to have weak word-recognition skills than have difficulty comprehending written language. Once they "break the code," most disabled readers show progress in reading comprehension.

Choice of Methodology

Cumulative records and interviews should reveal what method(s) of teaching word recognition has been used with the child. Such information and diagnostic testing may indicate that the method was inappropriate for the child or that so many different, often conflicting, methods were used that the child became confused. In the latter situation, it is not uncommon to find that if one method was unsuccessful after a short time, another was initiated. Often there has been no coordination between classroom and remedial reading instruction.

What cumulative records and interviews are not likely to reveal is that (1) the pace of the program was too rapid to allow the child to learn and retain the skills; (2) the teacher attempted to present too much for the child to absorb in a lesson; (3) skills were not reinforced or periodically reviewed to check maintenance; (4) opportunities were not provided for the child to apply the skills in reading interesting connected discourse; and (5) the child simply was not ready to learn the skill at the time it was introduced. For the most part, diagnosis and remediation should be concerned with the child's present abilities and needs. Unfortunately, at present no theory of reading disability from which instructional methods can be derived has been sufficiently confirmed by research (Doehring *et al.* 1981).

---

[16] According to Pelosi (1982), most current remedial techniques are actually only slight adaptations of those recommended years ago. For example, Huey (1908) mentioned "imitation reading" long before the Visual Impress Method became popular.

Basic Remedial Strategies

Broadly speaking, there are two basic strategies for teaching individuals who have had difficulty learning word-recognition skills. The chief difference between the two strategies is that word-recognition skills are taught immediately in the direct-treatment strategy. In the indirect-treatment strategy, enabling processes are developed before word-recognition skills are introduced.

Each basic strategy is based on assumptions. In the immediate teaching of word-recognition skills it is assumed that the acquisition of the skills and strategies thought to be needed for success in reading will result in improved reading ability. Often a task analysis is used to determine which reading skills are important, and a determination of the disabled reader's strengths and weaknesses in these areas is made.

Process-oriented advocates make two conflicting assumptions. Those who favor the training of nonreading deficits before initiating reading instruction assume that these process deficits are amenable to training and that their improvement will facilitate the acquisition of reading. Those who advocate teaching of reading by matching instruction to the disabled reader's strong or intact perceptual, psycholinguistic, or cognitive abilities seem to assume that nonreading deficiencies of neurological origin are irreversible and cannot be improved by training (Doehring *et al.* 1981) or that it is more efficient to play to the strengths and bypass the weak processes.

A view that differs from most others was voiced by P. G. Aaron and Baker (1983), who contended that whether weaknesses should be remediated or existing strengths used depends largely on the pupil's age. They stated that weaknesses in reading skills should be remediated for preadolescents, but existing cognitive strengths should be used in treating adolescents for whom the goal is satisfactory academic achievement and not reading improvement.

Immediately Teach Word Recognition

There are two types of direct treatment. In one, instruction is based on measured strengths, bypassing or minimizing the need for weak abilities. For instance, an attempt is made to match modality preference or strength with a teaching method. Thus, a child thought to have a strong visual preference or strength (a visual learner) or weak auditory skills (e.g., an auditory dyslexic—see D. J. Johnson 1979) or a child with an "articulation and graphomotor dyscoordination syndrome" (see Mattis 1981) would be taught initially through a whole-word approach. A pupil deemed to have strong auditory skills (an audile learner), weak visual skills (e.g., a visual dyslexic), or with a "language-disorder syndrome" would be given a phonic program. A student strong in kinesthetic abilities or with a visual–perceptual disorder would be taught through a VAK or VAKT method (see p. 432–436). Little or no attempt is made to develop weak abilities initially, although such training may occur later.

This type of direct treatment is based on three unproven interrelated assumptions: (1) We can validly measure the abilities and distinguish among various types of learners; (2) specific ability strengths are needed for success with a particular instructional method; and (3) different instructional methods make differing demands on the learner.

There are measurement problems in distinguishing among various types of learners, and relatively few children can be so classified (E. Miller 1974). Both auditory and visual abilities seem important in almost all methods of teaching word recognition. For example, printed words are visual stimuli, but auditory skills are also required in learning through a whole-word method because an association must be made between the visual and auditory forms of the word. A phonic method may require a high degree of auditory abilities, but visual skills also must be used because letters must be associated with sounds. Whether or not there is an interaction between a learner's traits and the instructional method or treatment is still open to question. Aptitude-treatment (ATI) studies are methodologically complex and fraught with interpretation problems (Cronbach & Snow 1977, pp. 217–244, 491–524). P. G. Aaron, Grantham, and Campbell (1982) claimed that a phonic method was more effective than a whole-word method with diseidetics (see p. 236). However, most ATI studies have not supported basing instruction on modality preference (see pp. 80, 265). Perhaps the modality model is invalid, or it may be that the available assessment and instructional procedures are inadequate (Zigmond, Vallecorsa, & Leinhardt 1980). Or perhaps significant results were not obtained because the treatment worked for only a few children, and so any positive results were washed out in a comparison of mean scores (J. Wiliams 1977). Reynolds (1981b) contended that the important variable in ATI is not the sensory modality through which the information is received but the method used to process that information. Examples of different processing styles are sequential and simultaneous processing. Gunnison, Kaufman, and Kaufman (1982) discussed the hypothesized neuropsychological bases for each type, how they can be assessed, and made recommendations for matching word-recognition instruction to processing style. Their rationale for the latter is difficult for us to accept.

In the other variation of this strategy, a method the child is able to employ with some success is used. As soon as a successful method is determined through trial lessons (see pp. 224–228), word-recognition instruction is begun. When utilizing trial teaching, the more common and less time-consuming methods (i.e., whole-word phonic) should be tried first. While most children could learn through a tracing technique, its use is less preferable because it is slow and time-consuming. Many children can be helped by using a visual—motor method; relatively few require a systematic kinesthetic procedure (see pp. 432–435). In choosing the method, it is also wise to consider the possibility that the child has developed an aversion to the method in which he or she has failed.

This version differs from other types of direct-treatment strategy in that no assumptions are made about the abilities needed for success with a particular method, and remediation of deficient abilities can take place concurrently with the teaching of word recognition (but takes up only a minor part of the remedial period). Readiness activities are as closely related to reading activities as possible. Visual-discrimination exercises emphasize noting similarities and differences in the letters, letter groups, and words being taught. Auditory-discrimination practice utilizes the phonemes and words used in word recognition instruction. Kinesthetic reinforcement is provided by practice in writing the graphemes and words being studied.

After initial success with a method, other word-recognition skills are taught. For example, if a phonic method is employed initially, a whole-word method is introduced later. If the child cannot learn through a whole-word method, either a visual–motor or kinesthetic method is used to teach the child to recognize phonemically irregular words.

Process Training First

The second basic strategy, the *indirect-treatment strategy*, involves training certain prerequisite or facilitative abilities *before* attempting to teach word recognition. The belief is that training perceptual, psycholinguistic, or cognitive abilities will either alleviate the reading problem directly or set the stage for learning to read (Zigmond, Vallecorsa, & Leinhardt 1980; Wiederholt & Hale 1982). The basic problem is seen as existing within the child, rather than in the reading instruction, so initial treatment emphasizes the development of deficient processing abilities. There appears to be a shift away from process-oriented treatment in the field of learning disabilities.

It is of interest to note that Frostig (1972), whose name is highly associated with the perceptual-deficit hypothesis, also advocated the simultaneous teaching of specific reading skills according to whatever abilities the child could use, as well as activities to strengthen weak perceptual abilities.

Weaknesses in the process-oriented viewpoint have been pointed out by Coles (1978), Arter and Jenkins (1979), and Wong (1979) (see p. 141). It is difficult to obtain valid measures of the processes thought to be the causes of reading disability and to specify the relationship between deficit processes and reading disability because most of the processes cannot be observed directly (Doehring *et al.* 1981). The empirical evidence to support these programs is not convincing (Zigmond, Vallecorsa, & Leinhardt 1980). None of the reviewers of the research in this area found that emphasis on perceptual, perceptual–motor, or motor training had any advantage over direct teaching of needed reading skills (Balow 1971; H. M Robinson 1972a; Klesius 1972; Hammill, Goodman, & Wiederholt 1974). As Wiederholt and Hale (1982) concluded, research findings have not provided sufficient evidence that any of the indirect methods improve reading ability. If better reading is the goal of treatment, then reading should be taught directly.

It is possible that process training may be a valid procedure for a limited number of individuals. However, it should be coordinated with direct reading instruction (Clements & Barnes 1978). Or it may be that process-oriented remediation has not been successful because the tests and treatments were based on theoretical constructs which have not been adequately defined or whose validity has not been well established (Doehring *et al.* 1981).

One of the few studies on the effect of auditory perceptual remediation on reading ability (Wilson, Harris, & Harris 1976) found that it was not effective in developing word recognition.

Since the advent of the *Illinois Test of Psycholinguistic Ability* (ITPA), the relationship between psycholinguistic abilities and reading ability has received considerable attention. The effectiveness of training psycholinguistic skills was questioned by Hammill and Larsen (1974a). More recently, the general conclusion reached by Kavale (1981a) on the basis of a meta-analysis was that psycholinguistic training was effective. But Sternberg and Taylor (1982) found several serious methodological and interpretive flaws in Kavale's study and noted that even though the differences reached statistical significance, the impact of psycholinguistic training lacked practical significance (the effect was small, especially in light of the amount of time devoted to such instruction). A meta-analysis using six additional studies to those employed by Kavale led Larsen, Parker, and Hammil (1982) to reaffirm their position: "To date, the cumulative results of the relevant research (no matter how they are statistically analyzed) have failed to demonstrate clearly that psycholinguistic training has value. Consequently, programs and techniques designed to improve ITPA-based skills should continue to be viewed with caution and monitored with care."

Multisensory Techniques

When a pupil is unable to remember words after painstaking teaching efforts, the teacher is apt to wonder what is wrong with the child's memory. Severe word-recognition problems are more likely the result of failure to develop a mental image of the word that can be recalled at a later time. Many severely disabled readers first perceive a word in a very incomplete and hazy fashion, and additional exposures to the printed word do little to improve their first impression. In some cases the initial perception is fairly good, but the child has little or no visual image when he closes his eyes and tries to "see" the word mentally.

Methods that have generally succeeded with such severe cases all involve the combined use of additional sensory and perceptual cues that lend vividness to the visual image of the word so that it can be stored and retrieved from memory.

The Kinesthetic Method

In 1921 Grace M. Fernald and Helen B. Keller described a method that emphasizes tracing and writing as basic procedures for teaching nonreaders. The following description of the method is based on the account given in Fernald's book (1943):

DESCRIPTION

At first the child is asked to tell the teacher a few words he would like to learn. These are taught one by one. As soon as a few words have been learned, the child is encouraged to compose a little story and is taught any words in the story that are not already known. The compositions are at first dictated to the teacher and later written by the child. After the story has been read in written form, it is typed so that the child can read it the next day in type. The child's own compositions are the only materials used until a fairly large sight vocabulary has been learned.

The method of teaching words changes as the child's ability to learn words improves. Four stages are distinguished.

Stage 1. Tracing. The word is written for the child on a strip of paper about 4 inches by 10 inches, preferably in large cursive writing. The child traces the word with his finger in contact with the paper, saying each syllable of the word as it is traced. This is repeated until the child can reproduce the motions of writing the word from memory. He writes it on scrap paper and then in his story. Later the story is typed and read in typed form. Each new word that is learned is placed by the child in an alphabetical file. The following points of technique are stressed: (1) Finger contact is important; tracing in the air or with a pencil is less useful. (2) The child should never copy a word, but always writes from memory. (3) The word should always be written as a unit. (4) The child must say each syllable of the word either to himself or out loud as he traces it and writes it. (5) Whatever he writes must be typed and read before too long an interval; this provides transfer from the written to the printed form.

Stage 2. Writing without tracing. After a while (days in some cases, weeks in others) the child does not need to trace most new words. He looks at the word in script, says it to himself several times, tries to "see" the word with his eyes shut, and writes it from memory. If he makes an error, he compares his result with the model, paying particular attention to the part or parts he missed. This is repeated until he can write the word correctly from memory. Index cards with the words in both script and print form are substituted for the large word strips and are filed alphabetically. Essentially this is the same procedure as the VAK method described on page 435.

Stage 3. Recognition in print. It becomes unnecessary to write each new word on a card. The child looks at the word in print, is told what it says, pronounces it once or twice, and writes it from memory. Reading in books is usually started about the time that this stage is reached.

Stage 4. Word analysis. The child begins to identify new words by noting their resemblance to known words, and it is no longer necessary to teach each new word. Although phonic sounding of single letters is not taught, skill in word analysis gradually develops through noticing grapheme–phoneme correspondences that are met repeatedly.

Total nonreaders are started at Stage 1; children with partial disabilities are often started at Stage 2. No special techniques are used to overcome such difficulties as reversals or omissions; these are said to drop out without special attention, since the tracing–writing process enforces a consistent left-to-right direction and requires correct reproduction of the entire word.

Unique features in Fernald's method are the great emphasis on tracing and writing, the teaching of difficult as well as easy words from the beginning, the use of the child's own compositions as the only reading material in the early stages, and the beginning of book reading at a fairly difficult level.

Although research evidence regarding its effectiveness is equivocal and inconclusive (J. Williams 1977), the kinesthetic method has produced successful results with many severe disability cases who had histories of repeated failure (Myers 1978). In addition to the many cases in Fernald's book, cases using the

Fernald approach have been described by Kress and Johnson (1970), Berres and Eyer (1970), Enstrom (1970), and Cotterell (1972).

The approach has several desirable features: (1) It enforces careful and systematic observation and study of words; (2) it makes necessary a consistent left-to-right direction in reading; (3) it provides adequate repetition; (4) errors are immediately noted and corrected; (5) progress can be noted by the child at practically every lesson; and (6) the sensory impressions from tracing, writing, and saying the words reinforce visual impressions.

Nevertheless, there are several limitations to the use of the kinesthetic method as outlined by Fernald:

1. The teacher has to direct and check every step in the child's work and teach every new word until the child has progressed far along the road to skilled reading. During the early stages, the child is unable to do any independent reading. The method is well suited for use in a special clinic school such as the one supervised by Fernald, in which the children were with the remedial teacher for a full school day 5 days a week, but is not so well adapted to a remedial setup in which the child has only a small number of remedial periods each week.
2. The majority of nonreaders can learn to recognize words by methods that are faster than the rather cumbersome tracing–writing procedure. The VAK method of word study (Fernald's Stage 2) is, however, often helpful.
3. We see no advantage in avoiding the use of easy books in the early stages of remedial work unless the child has a strong resistance to them. It is desirable to start reading in books as early as possible, even if pre-primers must be used, provided the child's cooperation can be obtained and the words are pretaught.

It has become customary to call tracing methods VAKT (visual–auditory–kinesthetic–tactual) methods (M. S. Johnson 1966). Actually the child (1) sees the teacher write the word; (2) hears the teacher say the word; (3) says the word; (4) hears himself say the word; (5) feels the movements made as he traces the word; (6) feels the surface with his fingertips as he traces; (7) sees his hand move as he traces; and (8) says and hears himself say the word (or syllables) as he traces.

Witman and Riley (1978) described a method that differed from Fernald's in a number of ways including tracing the word written in chalk (thereby allowing easy detection of faulty tracing) and spelling the word after pronouncing it. Other authors have suggested such variations as tracing over the raised effect created by writing the word on a screen with a crayon, tracing the word in the air with the eyes opened or closed, and tracing the word in a sand tray. No data suggest which variation is likely to work best, but observational reports suggest the VAKT is more successful with children aged 8 and above (Miccinati 1979) than with younger children. Knowing a number of variations and ways to reinforce initial learnings increases the likelihood of success with the VAKT method.

Two theories have been offered as to why a VAKT approach is effective for some learners. Based on three studies, Hulme (1981a) concluded that tracing verbal material benefits disabled readers because they are reluctant or unable to use phonological coding and instead rely heavily on a visual code. Tracing is thought to improve visual memory processes. Peters (1981) hypothesized that a VAKT method could work with children who do not have clearly defined functional lateralization of the hemispheres for the processes involved in reading and spelling. His reasoning was that use of kinesthetic and tactile components forces a clear lateralization of the visual and auditory processes. Whereas the auditory and visual sensory channels provide information to both hemispheres simultaneously, kinesthetic and tactile information is transmitted to only the contralateral hemisphere. Thus, when the left hand is stimulated kinesthetically and/or by touch, the information is registered in the right hemisphere.

Visual–Motor Method

Many children do not need extensive practice in tracing but are helped greatly by a visual–motor, or VAK (visual–auditory–kinesthetic), method that combines visual observation while saying the word with writing the word from memory. The procedure is as follows:

1. Select a few unknown words to teach. Words may be from the story about to be read, from an experience story, or simply words that the child wants to learn.
2. Introduce each word in meaningful context; check the child's understanding of its meaning(s) (it may be used in a less common manner); and teach the meaning if necessary.
3. Present the word in a sentence on the board; emphasize the word as in the whole-word method.
4. While holding up a word card, pronounce the word. As the children look carefully at the word, they pronounce it aloud softly and then a few times to themselves. Caution the children not to spell the word letter by letter.
5. Tell the children to shut their eyes and try to "make a picture" (visual image) of the printed word (not the object it represents). Tell them to open their eyes and compare their mental images with the original model on the card.
6. Cover or remove the word card and tell the children to print (or write) the word *from memory*.
7. Expose the word card and have the children compare their reproductions with the original, paying particular attention to any parts not reproduced accurately.
8. Repeat the process until the children can reproduce the word correctly from memory.
9. Teach the other words in the same way.
10. Shuffle the word cards and use them to provide practice in recognizing the new words, and later to develop speed of recognition.

11. Have the children read the words in meaningful context.

After using the VAK method for a month or so, children usually no longer need to write the word in order to remember it. At this point, the whole-word method may be introduced. Gradually, phonic skills also should be developed.

The VAK, or VAKT, method also may be used to teach specific words (e.g., *when–then*) that are causing problems for the child. Some workbooks provide large copies of the words for tracing as part of their regular instructional procedures.

According to Fernald, who originated it, the VAK method is a modified kinesthetic procedure in which the motor imagery of the movements involved in writing the word reinforces the auditory–visual association between the sound of the word and its printed form. Probably the kinesthetic element is of minor importance. Instead, it seems likely that writing helps the child remember the word because the printed form must be perceived correctly in all its details in order to reproduce it accurately. The method seems to work as well whether the child prints the word, writes it, or types it. Whatever the true explanation may turn out to be, many children who have difficulty learning through a whole-word or phonic method can learn and remember words when a visual–motor method is employed.

Roberts and Coleman (1958) found that poor readers who had normal visual perception were not aided by kinesthetic cues. Berres (1967) found that motoric reinforcement did not help disadvantaged disabled readers in speed of learning but did improve their long-time retention; tracing and writing helped more than writing without tracing, and both improved retention over visual study without motor reinforcement. On the other hand, Vandever and Neville (1972–1973) reported that poor readers tended to learn more words when visual and auditory cues were stressed than when tracing cues were emphasized. Ofman and Schaevitz (1963) compared two tracing methods with learning nonsense syllables through a whole-word method. Tracing with the eye was as effective as tracing with the finger; both were superior to "look-and-say." They speculated that enforced attention to details in sequence rather than tactual-kinesthetic sensation is the significant aid to learning. This would seem to explain the success of VAK for many children; it does not rule out the need for VAKT by a few.

Zorotovich (1979) reported the unique case of a left-handed child who seemed unable to learn by tracing with his left hand. She tried having him trace with his right hand, which was easy for him; but he could not write legibly with that hand. He began to make real progress when she had him trace with the right hand and write with the left.

"Blind" Tracing and Writing

A little-researched variation involves tracing three-dimensional letters while blindfolded and drawing letters on the child's back (Blau & Blau 1968, 1969). The rationale offered for this auditory, kinesthetic, tactile (AKT) "modality blocking" technique is that it allows development of clear kinesthetic perception, imagery, and memory without interference from deficient or distorted visual perception. Blau and Loveless (1982) suggested use of the tactile modality with severely disabled spellers. Based on the assumption that it makes use of right-hemisphere processing, two fingers on the left hand are used to trace the letters while blindfolded. Such a procedure *might* work in some cases because it avoids neurological overloading, which may happen in an immature or damaged brain when several sensory avenues are stimulated simultaneously (D. J. Johnson 1979). Of course, after the "feel" of the word has been learned, it will still be necessary to build a visual–kinesthetic association. Frostig (1965) also recommended a "blind writing" procedure for use with children who have inferior visual perception.

A comparison of VAKT, AKT, and other methods did not indicate any superiority for any of the methods with children in a special education class (Koepsel 1974). But this procedure deserves further study, particularly in very severe cases in which progress with VAKT or with phonics is extremely slow.

Methods Based on Sounding and Blending

Synthetic phonic methods based on learning the phonemes represented by letters, sounding them, and blending the sounds, supplemented by some use of kinesthetic procedures, have been advocated by many remedial specialists, particularly those influenced by S. T. Orton. A clear and relatively brief summary of the Orton point of view has been given by J. Orton (1966). A lengthy and detailed manual of procedure by Gillingham and Stillman (1966) has been the main training textbook for followers of the Orton school. A detailed manual adapting the approach for classroom use by primary-grade teachers has been prepared by Slingerland (1976) and Traub (1982) has developed a somewhat similar program. Somewhat briefer manuals have been prepared by J. Orton (1976) and by Cox (1977). A guide for teaching spelling in a way consistent with Orton's procedures has been written by Childs and Childs (1971). Research on the Orton–Gillingham approach has been extremely limited (Ansara 1982).

The basic common features of the approach used by followers of Orton have been briefly summarized by J. Orton as follows:

> Their common conceptual background can usually be seen in their introduction of the kinesthetic element to reinforce the visual-auditory language associations and to establish left-to-right habits of progression. Their phonetic approach is generally the same; teaching the phonic units in isolation but giving special training in blending; introducing the consonants and the short sounds of the vowels first and building three-letter words with them for reading and spelling; programming the material in easy, orderly, cumulative steps. (1966, p. 144)

According to Gillingham, the method requires five lessons a week for a minimum of 2 years. Drill on letter sounds and blending is the main activity for many weeks. The first group of letters taught includes *a, b, f, h, i, j, k, m, p, t.* After these have been learned (usually not more than one new letter a day) and used in blending and spelling short words, simple sentences using only words containing these letters may be introduced. One way of teaching blending has been described earlier in a sample lesson procedure (see pp. 400–001). Gillingham preferred to sound the initial consonant and vowel together, then add the final consonant (/ba/-/t/). She emphasized the importance of simultaneous oral spelling (saying the sounds in sequence, then saying the letter names in sequence while writing them). Kinesthetic procedures were used to teach words with irregular grapheme–phoneme relationships. Other points stressed by Gillingham included the following: (1) Parents were advised to read all homework to the pupil until he became able not only to read but to read with reasonable fluency; (2) teachers were asked to excuse the child from written tests and test him orally; and (3) independent reading was not allowed until the major part of the phonic program had been covered.

If, on the basis of diagnostic testing and sample lesson tryouts, it seems likely that a child may make more rapid progress with a systematic phonic approach than with a whole-word or kinesthetic method, many different phonic systems can be used with success. The considerations that apply when phonics is used for remedial work are no different from those that apply in developmental instruction. At this point, therefore, it is desirable to review pages 395–401. Auditory-discrimination training is important. Rigid adherence to any phonic method will inevitably produce difficulties because of the irregularity of the grapheme–phoneme relationships of the language. As much as possible, practice should be given in applying phonic skills in meaningful context rather than concentrating on drill with isolated words. As soon as it is feasible, words that have to be sounded out should be practiced for immediate sight recognition.

For the majority of reading disability cases, phonic instruction is more effective when it is used in combination with other procedures than when it is made the almost exclusive method of learning words. With some children, however, previously disappointing progress becomes very rapid when they are changed to a systematic phonic method and when instruction is paced to their ability to master the skills.

Methods Stressing Visual Analysis and Visualizing

In addition to the kinesthetic and phonic methods just described, there is a third basic method that emphasizes visual analysis and visualizing. Such a procedure was described and advocated by Gates (1947). Words are taught as wholes, and illustrations are used freely as ways of introducing and giving clues to words. Workbook exercises present new words and give practice in word recognition and comprehension. The pupil is encouraged to close his eyes and visualize words, first part by part in left-to-right order and then as a whole. Then he is asked to pronounce the word softly, part by part, while writing it; this is essentially the VAK procedure. Phonic work and writing are used as supplementary devices when pupils seem not to be progressing satisfactorily without them. Familiarity with word elements is developed through finding similarities and differences in words already learned.

Essentially this program is similar to that used for teaching normal beginners with most basal readers. It differs mainly in that the pupil's learning is more carefully supervised and more attention is devoted to making sure that new words are really learned than is the case in most classroom teaching. It is a program which assumes that the child has the capacity to learn as normal readers do, but has been handicapped by such factors as immaturity when first exposed to reading instruction, inefficient teaching, or something else that does not affect the child's present learning ability.

A Combination Method

The majority of children with reading disabilities do not have special cognitive or neurological defects; the disability results from such causes as lack of reading readiness when first exposed to reading instruction, uncorrected sensory defects, discouragement, emotional problems, and poor teaching that is sometimes aggravated by linguistic and cultural mismatches between teachers and pupils. If that is so, remedial work with those cases should not be radically different from general methods used with primary-grade children.

The majority of severe cases of reading disability (those with less than second-grade reading ability) show inattention to details in visual perception and have poor phonic aptitude. Such children can be started at the beginning of the easiest pre-primer in an unfamiliar set of readers, accompanying workbook, using the "begin-over" explanation to make the easy materials acceptable.

These children need to be carefully pretaught the new words that they will meet in the next few pages of connected reading. Each new word is printed on a card. It is studied by a whole-word or by the VAK method, whichever seems to suit the child better. After a few words have been taught, the cards are shuffled and reviewed. Then the child reads the connected material in which the new words appear and reviews the new word cards again. The workbook provides practice in matching the few words in the pre-primer vocabulary with pictures; and between the repetition in the workbook and that in the pre-primer, the child learns the words by being prompted every time he stumbles or forgets. The number of repetitions needed to learn new words gradually lessens. The cards are reviewed in the next few lessons. When the child recognizes a word without prompting, a little checkmark is made on the back of the card. Three checks, on different days, indicate that the word has been learned.

Rather than depend exclusively or primarily on a whole-word method, phonics is taught early and systematically. However, the majority of reading-disabled children require a good deal of phonic readiness work before they can begin to apply phonics in word recognition. By the time the child has completed reading one or two pre-primers, he has usually become sound conscious and pays attention to initial consonants. Auditory-discrimination exercises are continued throughout the phonics program. Systematic teaching of phonics accompanies the use of a primer and first and second readers, with adaptations for individual differences. Some children catch on to blending and can be given a systematic covering of symbol–sound associations with the letter-by-letter sounding technique. Others never become proficient at blending and are taught phonics through the use of a large number of phonograms or by initial consonant–vowel combinations.

On the other hand, some children seem, right from the start, to have excellent phonic aptitude. With such children, it seems sensible to follow a synthetic phonic procedure with emphasis on the teaching of symbol–sound associations and blending. Nonphonetic words have to be learned by these children also, and many of them need the VAK method because of their lack of success with a whole-word method. With some children, a hard part of the remedial job is to persuade them to give up the practice of spelling words letter by letter, in favor of a sounding procedure.

Few children seen by us have seemed to need tracing of the sort emphasized by Fernald. The VAK method of word study has been very helpful to many, however, and supplementary practice in writing words from dictation on paper and at the board has been used considerably.

When resistance to the use of first- and second-grade readers is strong, it is advisable to give up the books entirely for the time being, using instead a combination of experience stories and teacher-devised material. In such cases, much time can be spent in the early stages playing word-recognition or decoding games. If a typewriter is available, the opportunity to use it is welcomed by most children. Children are started on easy books as soon as they are receptive to their use.

Other Materials and Methods

Linguistic basal reader programs stress regularity of spelling patterns and avoid the use of words with irregular grapheme–phoneme relationships in beginning reading material (see p. 70). Such materials can be used with disabled readers, with emphasis on spelling patterns in whole words. They also can be employed as supplementary reading in a synthetic phonics program. Their possible value in the initial stages of instruction lies in the consistency of the symbol–sound association in the words employed, particularly vowels. The child does not have to decide which of the possible sounds a letter represents, and massive practice on the associations is provided. Contrary to their use in developmental reading, many remedial teachers provide direct instruction in symbol–sound association *before* the element is met in the program. The disadvantages are: (1) Some children are confused by the repetitiveness of only short-vowel words; (2) the language structure and story content are restricted and often artificial; and (3) no set for diversity is established. As yet no research on the value of linguistic readers in remedial reading has appeared.

A "massive oral decoding technique" makes simultaneous use of several series of linguistic readers (R. J. Johnson, Johnson, & Kerfoot 1972). After a spelling pattern has been introduced with one series, the pages emphasizing the same pattern in several other series are read before introducing a new pattern. The teacher guides oral reading of selection after selection, providing reinforcement of correct decoding responses. No phonic generalizations are taught, and no comprehension questions are asked. R. J. Johnson *et al.* (1972) indicated that the procedure was effective across a considerable range of disabled readers. Janicke (1981) reported that the technique was successful with 10 disabled readers in the seventh and eight grades.

Material printed in i.t.a. has also been used in remedial reading. Gardner (1966) reported that it worked better with disabled readers with at least average intelligence than with mentally slower children. Mazurkiewicz (1966) recommended the use of i.t.a. in remedial reading but presented little evidence in support of his claims. The problems that can arise when disabled readers learn to read in i.t.a. and then must transfer to the conventional alphabet have not been studied sufficiently.

Two systems that use color as a clue to grapheme–phoneme relationships have been described and advocated for use as remedial materials by their originators (Bannatyne 1966, Gattegno & Hinman 1966). There is as yet no well-controlled research on the value of these color systems in remedial teaching. Other authors, such as Frostig (1965, 1972), recommended color coding the letters to aid learning symbol–sound associations. Attention can be focused on a grapheme by coloring it differently from the rest of the word.

Programmed instruction would seem to have considerable promise in remedial reading, particularly in providing self-correcting work that the pupil can do while the teacher is working with another child or group. The principle is attractive, but the remedial value of any particular set of programmed materials still needs to be verified. Programmed tutoring, shown to be effective with slow first graders when provided by paraprofessionals (Ellson, P. Harris, & Barber 1968), can be helpful when volunteers or aides can be trained to employ it.

In the Neurological Impress Method (NIM) (Heckelman 1966, 1969), the teacher and student read aloud simultaneously for 15 minutes daily. The teacher, who is slightly behind the child, directs her voice into the student's ear. As the words are spoken, the teacher, and later the child, slides her finger along smoothly under the words. No attention is called to the pictures, no direct attempt is made to teach word recognition or decoding, and comprehension is not checked. The material is reread until fluency is attained by the pupil. The simultaneous seeing of the printed word and hearing the spoken word supposedly produces a neurological memory trace.

According to Kann (1983), research findings regarding the effectiveness of NIM are mixed; but Bos (1982) stated that, for the most part, its use has resulted in significant gains in both word recognition and comprehension for disabled readers. Bos also indicated, however, that the studies often lacked control groups and used small samples, and that NIM may be more effective for severely than moderately disabled readers. Henk (1983) suggested replacing the guided silent reading step in the Directed Reading Activity with NIM.

Other "listening–reading" or "read along" or "imitative reading" techniques have three elements in common: (1) The reading is modeled either by a person or tape; (2) the line of print is tracked by the child with a finger or marker; and (3) the child reads the same material to which he has listened (Janiak 1983). In *Prime-O-Tec* (Jordan 1967), which is an adaptation of NIM, individuals or groups listen to a taped story through earphones while following the written text with their finger. *Echo reading* (B. Anderson 1981) involves the teacher first reading the material to the child, who then repeats (echoes) it; later the child listens to a taped story while reading it. In C. Chomsky's technique (1978), the child listens to a tape while reading and rereads the story until it can be read fluently to the teacher. Stage 1 of *assisted reading* is like echo reading. In Stage 2 the teacher reads to the child and omits words that she thinks the child can recognize; the child is instructed to pronounce the word when the teacher pauses. During Stage 3, the child reads orally and the teacher supplies help as needed. Assisted reading has been promoted by Hoskisson (1975, 1979) as a supplementary procedure for initial reading instruction. Advocates often believe that such methods improve reading ability because a global approach rather than a skills approach is employed.

These techniques reportedly improve word recognition, reading comprehension, and fluency. Words are supposedly learned because the child is looking at the printed word as it is being spoken. This assumption may be incorrect in some cases because where the child is looking is not controlled. Comprehension may be improved for the same reasons given for the success of repeated readings (see p. 413), or because fluency is increased. Fluency is likely to increase because of the model provided by the teacher or tape and because of the practice provided.

Use of Braille has been reported to be successful in teaching reading to two severely disabled readers (Cronin 1972, McCoy 1975), and a Braille phonic technique was found to increase phonic skills (Fishbein 1979), but the study was apparently methodologically flawed. The use of sign language and finger spelling to remediate reading disabilities has been advocated (Vernon & Coley 1978; Vernon, Coley, & DuBois 1980); and McKnight (1979) and Stein (1982) strongly recommended finger spelling to teach phonics. Techniques usually employed with sensory-impaired children may have value in teaching some disabled readers, but at present evidence of their successful use is based primarily on testimonials rather than firm research evidence.

The Choice of Method

Although we may have knowledge of individual differences among children, possession of such knowledge is not particularly helpful in selecting the best instructional procedure in advance of actual tutoring. Currently there are no reliable guidelines to determine how student characteristics will interact with a particular method (Zigmond, Vallecorsa, & Leinhardt 1980). With many children, it is helpful to try brief sample lessons with each of several word-recognition procedures (see pp. 224–228) in order to determine which method should be used initially. As lessons proceed, the child's rate of learning and emotional responsiveness should guide the teacher in modifying instruction.

The remedial teacher must be resourseful. If the pupil has not made adequate.progress after a fair attempt to utilize one method, she must be willing to try something else. Adapting to the pupil's needs is far more important than devotion to a particular procedure. For most cases, the preferable strategy is to use a method that takes advantage of the child's relatively strong abilities and minimizes use of his weak ones and at the same time provides training to develop the weak abilities without postponing reading instruction.

It seems likely that any remedial program in word recognition that provides good motivation, ensures careful observation of words and word parts, and enforces consistent left-to-right habits in reading will succeed with most cases. The specific details of the method are less important than the fact that the major objectives are attained in one way or another.

13

Improving Reading Comprehension

Reading is comprehending; it is the meaningful interpretation of the written form of language. Reading comprehension is the result of the interaction among the reader's perception of the graphic symbols that represent language, linguistic skills, cognitive skills, and knowledge of the world. A wide range of factors can influence children's reading comprehension ability and their interpretations of what they read. Word recognition, which was considered in Chapter 12, is a prerequisite for reading comprehension. However, the ability to recognize words alone is insufficient; readers must use their word-recognition ability to reconstruct the meaning intended by the author. Once a person understands the intended meaning of the written text, he or she can think critically about that information.

In this chapter attention is devoted to vocabulary development because knowledge of word meaning influences reading comprehension; to sentence comprehension because understanding single sentences and the relationships between sentences can influence comprehension of longer written discourse; and to reading comprehension. Learning from or through reading—studying—is taken up in Chapter 14. Word recognition, word meaning, and various other components of reading comprehension are considered separately simply because it is easier to do so for sake of discussion. They actually function in highly complex interactive ways in the reading process.

I. VOCABULARY DEVELOPMENT

In our highly verbal culture an accurate understanding of the meanings of words is a necessary prerequisite for reading with meaning. A minimum essential for comprehension in reading is an understanding of the words used by the author. The development of a reading vocabulary that is both extensive and accurate is necessary for good comprehension.

Words and Concepts

A word is a verbal label that represents a concept or idea. As children mature, the concept represented by the word gradually becomes more refined and accurate. The concept represented by *dog*, for example, is usually vague and overgeneralized by tots beginning to talk, who may apply it to any four-footed animal. The child learns to exclude large animals, such as horses and cattle, then develops criteria (wags tail, barks, etc.) that include dogs of various sizes and exclude cats and other animals whose sizes overlap the range of dog sizes. Rentel (1971) recommended the following principles for the teaching of concepts: (1) Establish the proper word label for the concept or attribute; (2) place emphasis on significant differentiating characteristics; (3) provide examples and instances of a concept in an appropriate sequence; (4) encourage and guide student discovery of the essence of the concept; and (5) provide for application of the concept. Providing children with experiences from which a concept can be developed may not be enough. The teacher can help children to extract the generalized characteristic, clarify it, and codify it (Frazier 1970).

Concepts representing things (nouns) or actions (verbs) or observable qualities (adjectives, adverbs) are comparatively easy to develop; concepts representing relationships (function words such as conjunctions and prepositions) are more difficult.

Types of Vocabulary

The first vocabulary a person acquires is a listening vocabulary. Most babies show that they can respond correctly to spoken words before they are able to use those words in their own speech. Listening vocabulary develops earlier than speaking vocabulary, and throughout life the number of words to which people can react appropriately when they hear them remains larger than the number they employ correctly in their speech or writing. When children start to read, they begin to acquire a reading vocabulary (words they both recognize and understand). Gradually they begin to learn the meanings of words that occur in their reading but have not been in their previous vocabularies; they begin to acquire new meaningful vocabulary in reading. They also learn, through composition and spelling, to use a large number of words in their writing; these words, which are nearly always fewer in number than the speaking, hearing, or reading vocabularies, can be called a writing vocabulary. A child's total meaningful vocabulary is the sum of all the words he or she can understand or use correctly, whether in listening, speaking, reading, or writing.

Vocabulary Knowledge and Reading Comprehension

The relationship between vocabulary knowledge and reading comprehension has been documented in factor-analytic and readability studies (Carnine, Kameenui, & Coyle 1984). Factor-analytic studies have consistently found that vocabulary knowledge accounts for substantial proportions (.41 to .93) of the variance in reading comprehension (Mezynski 1983). There are also moderate to high correlations (.41 to .93) between vocabulary and reading comprehension, and robust correlations (.71 to .98) between word knowledge and general intelligence (R. Anderson & Freebody 1981). Vocabulary is so closely related to comprehension and reasoning that a good vocabulary test can serve effectively as a measure of general intelligence, and most intelligence tests contain vocabulary subtests.

The instrumentalist theory (a causal relationship) leads to two predictions: (1) The use of less difficult vocabulary should improve the comprehension of that material; and (2) teaching the meanings of the words that appear in the material should result in increases in reading comprehension.

Anderson and Freebody (1982) concluded that although the evidence strongly suggests that vocabulary difficulty does influence reading comprehension, its effects are not as strong as might be expected from the research on readability.

Research findings regarding the second prediction also have been mixed (Mezynski 1983). Some studies have found that preteaching the meanings of words that appear in sentences or passages the students are asked to read has produced significantly higher scores on measures of reading (Kameenui *et al.* 1982; Roser & Juel 1982; Beck, Perfetti, & McKeown 1982; Stahl 1983; McKeown *et al.* 1983[1]). Other studies have not (Jenkins, Pany, & Schreck 1978).[2]

There is some belief that one problem some poor readers have is slowness in activating stored information (Chabot, Petros, & McCord 1983; Kagan 1983). The belief is that inefficiency in this stage of information processing makes it difficult to maintain information long enough in STM to integrate semantic information or that difficulty in accessing word meaning interferes with comprehension because attention must be diverted. Vocabulary instruction over a period of time can result in more rapid access of semantic information and improved reading comprehension (Beck, Perfetti, & McKeown 1982).

Estimates of Vocabulary Size

Dale (1965) summarized the best available evidence at that time regarding vocabulary size as follows: "If we assume that children finish the first grade with an average vocabulary of 3,000 words, it is likely that they will add about 1,000 a year from then on. The average high school senior will know about 14,000 to 15,000 words, the college senior 18,000 to 20,000." But estimates of the number

---

[1] The vocabulary program used in these studies was described by Beck and McKeown (1983).

[2] This study is often cited as evidence that vocabulary instruction does not result in improved reading comprehension. However, the experimental group did score significantly higher than the control group on answering comprehension questions, but not on the cloze or retelling measures.

of words whose meanings individuals can understand vary widely. For instance, estimates range from 2562 to 26,000 words in first grade; 2000 to 25,000 in third grade; and from 4760 to 51,000 words in seventh grade (R. Anderson & Freebody 1981). There is a substantial lack of agreement as to vocabulary size at any given age or level or development, but previous low estimates are probably in error (Nagy & Anderson 1982, 1984). It appears that vocabulary size approximately doubles between Grades 3 and 7 (Jenkins & Dixon 1983).

A number of reasons may account for the diversity of findings regarding vocabulary size. The definition of *word* differs among studies. Some use only root words in their counts; others count inflected and derived forms of the root as separate words. A second factor involves differences in what is meant by "knowing the meaning of a word." Many English words have a number of meanings, and some serve different syntactical functions. Is a word known if the child knows its most common meaning or any of its possible meanings, or must more meanings be known; and if so, how many? A related variable is the manner in which vocabulary knowledge is measured. At times a multiple-choice test is used, or students are asked to define a word in writing or orally, or they are simply asked to indicate (yes–no) whether they know a word.[3] Most vocabulary studies consider a word "known" if one meaning is correctly identified on a multiple-choice test; hardly a complete measure.

Three dimensions of vocabulary are significantly related to comprehension (Roekle 1969). *Extensiveness* (number of words for which a correct synonym is chosen) is most highly related to reading comprehension. Then comes *intensiveness* or *breadth of vocabulary* (number of meanings known per word) and *flexibility* (selection of the particular meaning that fits a given context). In these terms, most reading vocabulary tests sample extensiveness only.

Differences also occur in the manner in which estimates of vocabulary size are made from a sample (Nagy & Anderson 1982, 1984). Moreover, there may be marked differences among children according to their SES. For example, M. Graves, Brunetti, and Slater (1982) estimated that the reading vocabularies of 183 primary-grade middle-class children were 2711, 4038, and 4656 words for Grades 1, 2, and 3, respectively. The estimates for "disadvantaged" children in these three grades were 1791, 2800, and 2842 words.

Despite differences in estimates of vocabulary size, there appears to be a rapid growth in vocabulary knowledge during the elementary school years. Word meanings may be acquired as a result of direct instruction (children are told definitions and/or labeled examples are provided), self-instruction (e.g., looking up the word in a dictionary), or "indirect" learning through the use of oral or written context or morphological analysis (e.g., having learned the meaning of refer, the learner can deduce the meaning of *reference, referendum, referent, referral*, and so forth). These various means of acquisition are not mutually exclusive, and vocabulary learning usually involves their combined use. Exactly

---

[3] When asked to indicate which words they knew, good readers were able to define about half the words they indicated as "known." Poor readers greatly overestimated the number of words they could define but were accurate in indicating which words they did not know (Drum 1983).

how each means of acquisition contributes to vocabulary knowledge is largely unknown (Jenkins & Dixon 1983).

Direct vocabulary instruction can neither account for all the word meanings that children learn nor cover more than a modest proportion of the words they encounter in the materials they read in school (Nagy & Anderson 1982, 1984). The time required to produce vocabulary learning and the available instructional time would preclude learning a large number of word meanings through direct instruction. Moreover, direct vocabulary instruction in school seems to be sparse and not particularly effective (Jenkins & Dixon 1983).

Learning word meanings from context does occur, but apparently not to the degree that would be needed to explain the rapid growth in vocabulary knowledge. Most elementary school children are not particularly adept at deriving word meanings from context, and there is some question as to how well pupils are taught to use contextual information to infer word meanings.

Therefore, it seems that (1) estimates of vocabulary growth are seriously exaggerated; or (2) effective vocabulary growth takes place outside of direct instruction; or (3) students are far better at learning from context than the data suggest; or (4) large numbers of word meanings are learned incidentally through oral language contacts (e.g., conversations, television). Probably no single source accounts for most of the variance in vocabulary learning (Jenkins & Dixon 1983).

Factors That Influence Vocabulary Size

Intelligence or learning aptitude is highly related to the rate of acquisition and size of one's vocabulary. While some pupils score low on intelligence tests for reasons other than limited ability to learn, it seems reasonable to conclude that low verbal intelligence leads to delayed and limited language development and difficulty in understanding and acquiring word meanings, particularly those that represent abstract concepts. Compared to those who truly have limited learning capacity, bright pupils are likely to know the meanings of more words (vocabulary breadth) and more meanings for a word (vocabulary depth), to make more effective use of context to learn new word meanings, and to select the most appropriate meaning of a multiple-meaning word because of their greater reasoning ability. On oral vocabulary tests, bright children tend to give abstract or generalized definitions of words; slow learners tend to define words in terms of use or function if they can respond acceptably at all.

Words have meaning only when they are related to things one has experienced or knows about. Individuals who have been intellectually stimulated, exposed to a rich and varied vocabulary and to a variety of experiences, and who have had practice in the use of language are likely to know the meanings of more words and more meanings of a word. Those who have not had such experiences tend to have much smaller vocabularies. Speech defects and defective hearing also can interfere with vocabulary acquisition because they cut off many opportunities to learn from oral language experiences.

Methods of Increasing Vocabulary Knowledge

A well-conceived and delivered vocabulary program should be an important part of a reading or language arts curriculum. The need for planned systematic vocabulary development was well elaborated by Dale and O'Rourke (1971, 1984). Vocabulary development must go far beyond simply teaching the meanings of words that will be needed to understand some material to be read shortly by the pupils. Increasing vocabulary knowledge involves providing experiential background, developing an interest in words, directly teaching some word meanings, explaining and illustrating verbal relationships, developing the means needed to deduce word meanings on one's own, and providing materials and time for wide reading.

Providing a Background of Experience

The first essential in a program of vocabulary development is to provide children with a background of meaningful experience. Vivid firsthand sensory experience is the best basis for the development of accurate concepts. For this reason, trips and excursions, when intelligently planned, are excellent for broadening children's horizons. The main difficulty with them is that in most schools they occur too infrequently to make a real dent in the problem. Also, when a trip is made, the teacher often feels that she has done well if she gets the children back safely. The opportunities for developing meaningful concepts and vocabulary are too frequently neglected. When firsthand experience is not available, visual teaching materials such as movies, videotapes, filmstrips, slides, pictures, and charts are the best substitutes. Storytelling and oral reading by the teacher are also valuable ways of imparting experience, especially in the lower grades. Practice in the use of language is highly important. Natural opportunities for intelligent listening and speaking arise in discussions, reports, informal conversation, and dramatics.

Motivation

Motivation is probably as important as any other variable in increasing word knowledge. As in many endeavors, interest determines the allocation of one's time and efforts. Teachers should not hesitate to talk about the importance of words and should employ various ways of impressing on their pupils the importance of using the best word to fit each idea. The teacher's own enthusiasm for words helps to initiate and sustain an interest in vocabulary knowledge.

Sometimes enthusiasm for learning new words can be whipped up by staging contests, using word puns, or playing word games (see Lake 1967, 1972; Wise, 1972) or by personalizing vocabulary development (see Bourgere 1968, 1972; Haggard 1982). Other children get "turned on to words" by being introduced to and studying euphenisms, word origins[4], palindromes (words and phrases that are spelled the same way forward and backward—e.g., *radar*, "Madam I'm Adam") coined words (*blurb*), portmanteau words (*smog*), slide words (*jeep*),

---

[4] Refer to Pilon (1978, 1984), Gold (1981), or D. Johnson and Pearson (1984) for lists of children's books on etymology.

acronyms, and so forth (see Pilon, 1978, 1984). Specially designed vocabulary tests can be used to demonstrate to highly motivated pupils the need to increase their word knowledge. The use of a variety of motivational techniques is more likely to be effective overall than the use of any one.

Direct Teaching

For previously stated reasons, it would be impossible to teach the meanings of all of the words children will encounter in print. This suggests that the words to be taught must be well chosen and their meanings well developed. It appears that at present, however, direct vocabulary instruction is sparse and ineffective. Studies have revealed that the level of vocabulary teaching prescribed in commercially published reading programs ranges from virtually zero to modest at best, and that most overlook some basic training and learning principles (Jenkins & Dixon 1983). On the basis of classroom observations in Grades 3 through 6, Durkin (1978–1979) concluded that all too many teachers are "mentioners"; they mention the meaning of a new word in a single-sentence explanation, often without any example, and go on to the next word without trying to find out if the children understood the explanation and without giving any practice in using the word. As a result, the children show little sign of benefiting from this kind of inadequate vocabulary presentation.

One difficulty with the explanation and discussion procedure is the danger of relying on superficial verbalizations. Meanings that are clear to the teacher may be quite hazy to the child. Many of the classical boners result from a superficial and inadequate grasp of word meanings. It is not sufficient to tell a child that *frantic* means *wild* or that *athletic* means *strong*; the child may try to pick frantic flowers, or pour athletic vinegar into a salad dressing.

The other main difficulty with this procedure is the danger of spending too much time on word study. This can be avoided if the reading material is not overloaded with new words.

Deciding Which Word Meanings to Teach

Teachers must decide which word meanings should be taught. Words may be classified into four types for the purposes of instructional planning (M. Graves 1984). Type 1 words are decodable using the skills possessed by the reader. As a child's ability to recognize and decode words independently increases, the number of Type 1 words that need to be taught directly decreases.

Type 2 words are those for which the pupil must learn an additional meaning for a word already in his reading vocabulary (the printed form can be recognized and a meaning, usually its most common meaning, is known). There are many *polysemous* words in English. For example, about one third of the words in the *Living Word Vocabulary* (Dale & O'Rourke 1981) and over 70% of the 9000 words in the *Ginn Word Book for Teachers* (D. Johnson, Moe, and Baumann 1983) have more than one meaning. There are two kinds of Type 2 words: those that have more than one common meaning (and possibly, a number of uncommon ones, e.g., *run*) and common words that have a different restricted meaning when used in a content subject (e.g., *bar* as in a bar graph [arithmetic], *sand bar* [social studies], "Crossing the Bar" [Literature]). If the child knows more than one meaning for the first kind of Type 2 word, he may be able to use available context to determine its most appropriate meaning. With the second kind of Type 2 word, it is usually necessary to teach the specific word meaning.

Type 3 words are not in the child's understanding or reading vocabularies, but the concepts they represent are fairly easily developed. Both word recognition and word meaning must be taught for Type 3 words.

Type 4 words are neither in the pupil's understanding nor reading vocabularies, and the concepts that they represent are not easily established (e.g., *democracy*). Understanding such concepts adequately takes a considerable period of time; simply teaching them as "new words" may only confuse students. M. Graves (1984) listed sources that suggest how to teach the different types of words.

When a child is reading and says, "I don't know that word," there are three possible explanations: (1) The meaning would be known if the child could recognize the word (Type 1 words); (2) the printed form is recognized, but its meaning is unknown (Type 2 words) and (3) the printed form is not recognized and the meaning is unknown (Type 3 and Type 4 words). If the first situation occurs frequently, emphasis should be placed on developing word-recognition skills. Frequent occurrences of the second type suggest the need to build up the child's understanding vocabulary; and of the third type, the need for both kinds of treatment.

Some teachers prefer to have a group of pupils read the selection first and then ask the students what new words caused them trouble. These words can then be explained in the usual way. Two advantages are claimed for this procedure: (1) The number of words pupils will ask about is nearly always less than the number that the teacher would have selected for preliminary teaching; and (2) the teaching arises from a need felt by the pupils and therefore is more apt to be well motivated and to produce effective learning. This procedure can work well with motivated children who are good readers; poor readers fail to ask about many of the words they do not know, either because they are unaware that they do not know them or because they are too embarrassed to admit they do not know them.

Numerous attempts have been made to establish a specific grade-by-grade list of words that definitely should be taught. But almost all these lists, such as those mentioned on pages 374–375, are based on the frequency with which the words appear in print. Only *The Living Word Vocabulary* (Dale & O'Rourke 1981) deals with word meaning in that it indicates the percentage of students at various grade levels who knew the meanings of words, including alternative meanings of the same word. Word-frequency lists, however, may be of some use in determining the likelihood that *a meaning* (not necessarily the intended meaning) of a word is known. It is quite probable that at least the most common meanings of high-frequency words are known; knowledge of their less common meanings will depend on the child's age and linguistic competence. As the frequency with which a word is used in print decreases, so does the probability that its meaning is known. A word-frequency list can provide a rough estimate for gauging whether a word meaning is likely to be known and thereby can serve as an aid in determining the possible need to teach that word.

The Keyword Method

The *keyword method* involves a two-stage mnemonic process whereby the students are taught first to link a familiar word that is visually or acoustically similar to the unfamiliar word and then to create or use a thematic relationship (an interactive image between the two terms) as an aid in remembering the meaning of the new word. It was originally designed for teaching foreign-language vocabulary; so, for example, to learn the Spanish word *carta* ("letter"), the student would think of *cart* and then imagine a letter being transported in a shopping cart.

J. Levin (1981a) has defended the use of this mnemonic technique, and according to Merry (1980), and Guthrie (1984), it is an effective technique for learning word meanings. Pressley, Levin, and Miller (1981) cautioned, however, that use of the keyword method with children age 10 and under may require more than just instructing the child to use visual imagery. The teacher will probably have to provide illustrations of the keyword and definition referents, and maximum facilitation may occur only if the child is provided with illustrations in which the interaction between the keyword and definition referent is made explicit.

Illustrating Verbal Relationships

The meanings of words develop as pupils understand the relationships among concepts more clearly and accept the need for more precise language to express meaning in the most accurate way possible. There are many activities that can be used to provide practice in clarifying word meaning through bringing out various relationships between and among words. As students grasp these relationships, their understanding of words becomes more accurate. Many of the suggested ideas can be adapted for use either orally or as reading exercises.

Synonyms.   The study and use of synonyms can help pupils make fine discriminations between word meanings and understand the relationships among words grouped together by meaning.

Sample synonym exercises are these:

1. What word means the same as *attractive*?
2. Underline the word that means the same as *quiet*: pretty, still, yet, leave.
3. A *courteous* remark is: (*a*) rude (*b*) polite (*c*) deceitful (*d*) intact.
4. List all the words that mean about the same as *happy*.

Use of *synonymic webs* (see Fig. 13.1) and *semantic maps* (see Fig. 13.2) also can serve the above purposes. Their construction and use requires the active participation of the students (see D. Johnson & Pearson 1984).

Antonyms.   D. Johnson and Pearson (1984) indicated that there are over a dozen categories of antonyms. Learning about antonyms helps children to understand that no two words have exactly the same meaning.

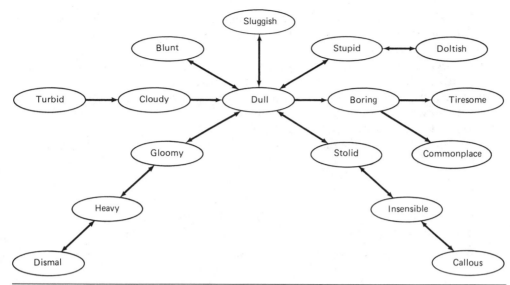

Figure 13.1. Synonymic web of relationship. From Joseph P. O'Rourke, *Toward a science of vocabulary development* (The Hague: Mouton, 1974), p. 75. Reproduced by permission of the author and the Mouton Publishing Co.

Examples of antonym exercises are these:

1. What word is the opposite of *big*?
2. Underline the word that means the opposite of *curved*: twisted, bumpy, straight, round.
3. A *compulsory* act is not: (*a*) optional (*b*) contagious (*c*) necessary (*d*) repulsive.
4. *Animated–lethargic* Same Opposite (Underline one).

Categorization.   Categorization exercises require the systematic arrangement of objects, pictures, or words into groups or categories in accordance with some predetermined criteria (e.g., things that fly). A modification of this technique involves placing the items into as many different categories as possible (e.g., a *fork* may be classified under "things to eat with," "metal objects," "sharp objects," etc.).

Sample categorization or classification exercises include the following:

1. Name the parts of an automobile.
2. A *wing* is a part of: (*a*) an animal (*b*) a bird (*c*) a fish (*d*) a plant.
3. Place the following words under either *vegetables* or *fruits*: orange, potato, pineapple, lettuce.
4. List all the words you can under the following headings: *Clothing–Food–Animals.*

Many other types of vocabulary practice also require classification skills. Readence and Searfoss (1980) described a three-component categorization technique that might prove useful.

Analogies.   Of all the techniques for increasing vocabularies, analogy exercises are probably the most difficult for children to use. They are problem-solving activities that require reasoning ability and prior knowledge. Analogy exercises may appear in different formats: (1) *Foot* is to *hand* as *show* is to ___; (2) *good* is to *bad* as *light* is to: (*a*) bright (*b*) naughty (*c*) dark (*d*) happy; (3) *governor* of a state: *mayor* of a: (*a*) city (*b*) country (*c*) president (*d*) county. Exercises may also involve various types of analysis (Ignoffo 1980):

Part to whole	lead:pencil::ink:_____
Object to function	refrigerator:cold::oven:_____
Object and its composition	car:metal::book:_____
Worker and tools	mechanic:pliers::sculptor:_____
Size or degree	stream:river::sea:_____

Denotations–Connotations.   A *denotation* is the literal meaning of a word (yellow = color); a *connotation* refers to an implied nonliteral meaning (yellow = cowardly). Children can be helped to distinguish between literal and emotional tones of words by using exercises such as those suggested by D. Johnson and Pearson (1984) and Baldwin, Ford, and Readence (1981).

Learning Fine Shades of Meaning.   Many children fall victim to the insidious use of a small number of stock words rather than attempt to state an idea as clearly or descriptively as possible. Some children are unaware of fine shades of word meanings; others have the necessary vocabulary to distinguish nuances but opt not to.

One of the best ways to awaken children to the desirability of stating their meanings with precision is to take advantage of a pupil's use of a word whose generalized meaning has been worked to death. If a student describes a party as being "lousy," the teacher might ask, "Was it boring, dull, disappointing? Were the refreshments insufficient, unappetizing? Were the people covered with lice?" Discussion of this sort can lead to exercises such as the construction of a *word line*, which depicts the relationships among words in a single category on a graduated line. For example, a word line dealing with size might have the words *minuscule* and *colossal* printed at the ends, with various words indicating changes in size in between the extremes. Pictures rather than printed words can be used in the lower grades; it can be a group or individual effort. Hofler (1981) discussed how word lines can be used to develop word knowledge. The *concept attainment strategy* (Thelen 1982) also stresses the hierarchical arrangement of words. Capable students in the upper grades should be shown how to use an appropriate-level thesaurus and be encouraged to do so.

Homographs, Homonyms, and Homophones.   *Homographs* are words that are spelled the same but that have different pronunciations and meanings (e.g.,

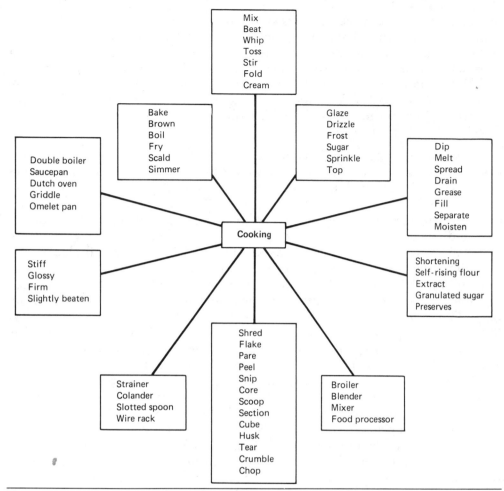

Figure 13.2. Semantic map for cooking. From *Teaching reading vocabulary*, 2d Ed. by Dale D. Johnson and P. David Pearson. Copyright © 1984 by CBS College Publishing. Reprinted by permission of Holt, Rinehart and Winston, CBS College Publishing.

bow, lead). A list of 86 homographs appears in D. Johnson, Moe, and Baumann (1982, p. 8). *Homonyms* are spelled and sound alike but have different meanings; many English words have more than one meaning (e.g., *pool* can mean a place to swim, a game of billiards, or to combine resources). *Homophones* are words that are pronounced alike but are spelled differently and have different meanings (e.g., *you, yew, ewe*). Refer to D. Johnson and Pearson (1984, p. 184) or to Fry, Polk, and Fountoukidis (1984, pp. 2–7) for lists of homophones.

The above-mentioned types of words can cause meaning problems for children, particularly homonyms (the different spellings of homophones is an aid to word meaning). The key to successful instruction is to focus the pupil's attention on the differences in spelling and meaning of homophones, on the differences in pronunciation and meaning of homographs, and on the differences in meaning of homonyms, and to develop the meanings of words that the child needs to learn. Multiple-meaning words are best learned when they are encountered in a variety of contexts. Pupils are often confused more by a familiar word used in an unfamiliar sense than by a word that is totally new to them. A child who knows *strike* means "to hit" may need help understanding its use in such expressions as "strike it lucky," "to go on strike," or "to strike a camp." The learning of new meanings for "old" words is an important part of vocabulary development.

Learning to Understand Figurative Language.   Authors frequently use words and phrases whose intended meanings differ from the obvious literal meanings of the words. These figurative expressions include idioms, unusual secondary meanings of words, similes, metaphors, personification (attributing human characteristics to a nonhuman), and hyperbole (great exaggeration: the suitcase weighed a ton).

Amelia Bedelia (Parish 1963) is a book in which the central character is very literal minded: She "trims" a steak with ribbons and "dresses" a chicken in clothing. This book has been greatly enjoyed by middle-grade children and provides an excellent steppingstone to the study of uncommon secondary meanings, idioms, and other figurative language. For many suggestions about ways to teach children to be interested in and understand figurative language, see Turner (1976, 1984) on figurative language; Forester (1974), Edwards (1975), and May (1979) on idioms; Sherer (1977) on metaphors; and Ortony (1978) and Readence, Baldwin, and Rickelman (1983a) on similes, metaphors, and analogies. McKenna (1978) is a good reference on "portmanteau words" (words formed by merging portions of other words, such as *smog* and *brunch*). The interpretation of proverbs has been discussed by Saltz (1979).

To some extent the ability to interpret ideas when they are presented through analogies, similes, metaphors, euphemisms, and circumlocutions grows from meeting such forms of expression again and again in settings that make their meaning clear. It does not take a young man long to realize that the plea of a headache, used to break a date, is usually a polite evasion. Few people are deceived by the "great regret" with which a public official's resignation is received by his superior.

Sensitivity to implied meanings also requires a fairly high level of verbal intelligence. The person who easily recognizes analogies and readily notes similarities and differences in concepts is likely to enjoy discovering the implied meanings in what he reads. The person who lacks facility in understanding verbal relationships is likely to grasp only the obvious stated meanings.

Probably the best way to develop a real understanding of figurative or indirect language is through practice in paraphrasing. The attempt to restate another's thoughts in clear, unambiguous language of one's own is a crucial test of whether the thought has really been understood. Erroneous interpretations can be discovered, and correct interpretation can be explained.

Of the various kinds of figurative language, metaphors have received the most research attention. According to Reynolds and Ortony (1980), much of this research has been flawed. Pupils may fail to understand a specific metaphor because they (1) interpret it literally; (2) fail to identify the appropriate matching attribute(s); or (3) have insufficient word knowledge to identify the critical matching attribute. The latter is most likely the cause in older students (Ortony 1980b; Pearson *et al.* 1981; Readence, Baldwin, and Rickelman 1983b). For example, to understand "the man ran like a cheetah," the person must know that a cheetah is extremely fast and therefore the man is a fast runner.

Ortony (1980a) suggested that young children usually do not understand the nonliteral nature of metaphors, but there is some evidence that they can comprehend metaphorical language under certain conditions (Pearson *et al.* 1981, Vosniadou *et al.* 1983).

The ability of young blacks to understand and engage in ritual insults that require a high degree of skill with figurative language, especially metaphors, suggests that comprehending figurative language may depend largely on having sufficient appropriate experiences (M. Taylor & Ortony 1981; Taylor-DeLain, Pearson, & Anderson 1983). For a discussion of children's understanding of figurative language, see Ortony (1984).

Helping Students to Learn Word Meanings on Their Own

When pupils are reading independently, there are four strategies that they can employ when they encounter a word whose meaning is not readily apparent. They may simply ignore the word, and if this disrupts meaning, they may attempt another strategy. A second strategy is to ask someone what the word means. Children, especially poor readers, who are more likely to encounter unknown words, are reluctant to do so. Or the students can consult a glossary or dictionary if they know how to use one and one is available. This strategy is likely to disrupt their train of thought, and few students or adults consult either source while reading. But learning to use a dictionary and glossary provides pupils with another means for learning word meanings independently. The best strategy to employ while reading is to make use of whatever contextual or morphological information is available. In order to make use of contextual and morphological cues to increase their vocabulary knowledge, students must read widely.

Use of Context Clues

In general, studies have indicated that children are not particularly adept at using context clues to infer word meaning. H. A. Robinson (1963) reported that fourth graders could determine the meaning of a word from context only from 10% to 61% of the time. Rankin and Overholser (1969) found that the success rate ranged from 43% in fourth grade to 62% in sixth grade. Another study (Carnine, Kameenui, & Coyle 1984) revealed that sixth graders could determine the meaning of only about 40% of the words from context.

As Deighton (1959) pointed out, context determines word meaning but only infrequently reveals the meaning of an unknown word. When children are taught to use context clues, the target words are set in a *pedagogical context*, that is, one contrived to illustrate clearly how a particular kind of context clue can be used to deduce the meaning of an unknown word. But pupils read words much more often in a natural context. Because *natural context* is used primarily to communicate ideas, the contextual information may not provide appropriate cues to word meaning (Beck, McKeown, & McCaslin 1983). According to Beck (1984), basal reader programs rely on the children to derive word meaning from context or from a glossary independently. She concluded, however, that the extent to which context in modern basals is likely to lead to the meaning of a target word depended more on chance than design. Yet, at times authors do employ various kinds of clues to word meaning, and children should be taught to be aware of and to use them.

Illustrating, discussing (not only the answers, but how they were arrived at), and providing guided practice in use of the following context cues should help children to utilize them.

1. *Synonym.* A more common synonym for the unfamiliar word may (1) appear in parentheses—*avarice* (greed); (2) appear in apposition—He did not *repent*, regret, his actions; (3) be embedded in a sentence—Tom was *exhausted* and Fred was tired too. At times the use of a synonym is too subtle for children to apprehend easily—Rare books cost more because they are *scarce* and in demand.

2. *Antonyms.* The unfamiliar word is contrasted with an antonym whose meaning is more likely to be known—Dolores *hastened* to complete the job, but Alice did not hurry. A key to the use of this technique is recognition of such "thought reversing" cues as *but*. An author who thinks a word meaning is quite important may employ a synonym–antonym technique—Mary's speech was *concise*; it was brief, but John's speech was too long.

3. *Definition.* The unfamiliar word is defined: (1) in parentheses—The *caboose* (the last car on the train); (2) in apposition—*Polygamy*, the custom of having more than one wife at a time, is still practiced; (3) embedded in a sentence—The male principal of a private school often is called the *headmaster*, or in a subsequent sentence—Blood flowed from the *lesion*. This wound, etc.; (4) by supplying examples (usually introduced by such words as "such as")—*Odd numbers*, such as 1, 3, 9; (5) by a restatement (often introduced by "that is")—She was *wan*; that is, very pale; and (6) in a footnote.

4. *Experiential background.* The cue is based on the child's past experiences, either with life in general (The horselike animal with black and white stripes is a *zebra*) or language (Nickie was as quiet as a *mouse*). Past experience with language also leads the reader to anticipate words occurring in certain positions, or in a given sequence, or in conjunction with other words.

5. *Summary.* The preceding information is summarized by the unfamiliar word—First they saw an elephant. Then they saw lions and tigers in cages. Adam liked the *zoo*.

6. *Reflection.* The general situation or mood of the sentence or paragraph provides the cue—The eerie music made me shudder. And when the candle went out, a strong feeling of *trepidation* came over me (A. J. Harris & Sipay 1979).

Studies have suggested the following information regarding the use of contextual information in determining the meaning of words: (1) Contextual information can assist in deducing word meaning under certain conditions, but these conditions do not occur frequently in natural context; (2) instruction in the use of context clues has a positive effect on the use of clues; (3) the closer the cue to the target word, the more likely it is to be helpful; (4) the ability to use context clues increases with age and reading ability; and (5) good readers are more sensitive than poor readers to contextual information and make more effective use of it (Madison, Carroll, & Drum 1982; B. Carroll & Drum 1982; Jenkins & Dixon 1983; Carnine, Kameenui, & Coyle 1984).

According to Jenkins and Dixon (1983), learning word meanings from context probably depends on such other variables as the number of occurrences of the unknown word in the material being read and the contexts in which the word appears. Generally, multiple occurrences in variable contexts increase the number of meaning clues available to the reader. This in turn increases the likelihood that the meaning of the word will be apprehended. The higher the proportion of unknown words, the less likely the context is to provide information regarding the meaning of any single word. Prior knowledge about the topic may be of assistance in determining the meaning of an unknown word.

Cloze exercises are often used to develop the use of contextual information. Their use is based on the premise that the information surrounding the deleted words may allow the reader to predict the missing word. The use of cloze exercises, however, is not likely to increase a child's vocabulary knowledge because in order to fill in the blank, the word must already be in the reader's understanding vocabulary. The potential value of these exercises lies in learning to use whatever contextual information is available. Students should be informed as to how what they learn from cloze exercises can be useful in determining the meaning of an unknown printed word.

Exercises for teaching the use of context clues may be found in D. Johnson and Pearson (1984, pp. 114–147). Many of the prediction and verification exercises suggested by Goodman and Burke (1980) also may be helpful.

One final point needs to be made regarding the use of context clues as a way of increasing vocabulary knowledge. Jenkins and Dixon (1983) made an important distinction between *deriving* the meaning of an unfamiliar word from context and *learning* that meaning. A student can successfully infer a word meaning and utilize it to understand the text; however, he may promptly forget that word meaning. Therefore, several encounters are needed to learn the word's meaning.

The Use of Morphological Cues

The use of morphological clues involves employing meaningful units as an aid in determining the probable meaning of a word. These units include the words that form a compound word, base words or Latin or Greek roots, and the prefixes and/or suffixes that have been added to them. Morphological clues are best used in conjunction with context clues.

Nagy and Anderson (1982, 1984) estimated that for every word a pupil learns, there are from one to three additional words that he should understand, depending on his ability to use morphological and context clues. The number of derived words whose meanings should be fairly readily apparent increases as one goes toward the lower end of a frequency continuum.

Children are usually taught compound words fairly early in their reading programs. There are three kinds of compound words: (1) The meaning is the sum of its parts (*houseboat*); the meaning is related to but not completely represented by the meaning of its components (*shipyard*); and (3) the meaning is not literally related to the meaning of its parts (*moonstruck*) or the compound has more than one meaning (*doghouse*) (Moretz & Davey 1974). So, if a child encounters *doghouse* for the first time in print, dividing it into *dog* and *house* will very likely reveal its meaning quickly, since its most common meaning (a place where a dog lives) is probably already known. However, one of its nonliteral meanings (to be in disfavor) will not be readily apparent from morphological clues alone. But when combined with the use of contextual clues, it may (e.g., The man was in the *doghouse*. His wife was angry at him for not mowing the lawn).

Inflectional endings (*s, es, d, ed, ing, er, est, ly, y*) are understood in speech by practically all children entering first grade. Children are usually taught to recognize their printed forms and interpret them in first and second grades.

Many English words start with prefixes. Stauffer (1942) found that 24% of the first 20,000 words in the Thorndike list have prefixes. While there are many different prefixes, Stauffer indicated that 15 prefixes accounted for 82% of all the prefixed words. These 15 and some other ones probably worth teaching are shown in Table 13.1.

Deighton (1959) recommended teaching 11 commonly used prefixes that have invariant meanings: *apo, circum, com, equi, extra, intra, intro, mal, mis, non*, and *syn*. Of these, only *mis* is found with any degree of frequency in the Harris–Jacobson list (1982). The three letters *com* at the beginning of a word often do not signal a prefix. Of the additional 9 prefixes having more than one meaning worth teaching, according to Deighton only *fore* and *semi* do not appear in the list shown in Table 13.1. To these, Stotsky (1978) has added *anti, counter, inter, mid*, and *semi*.

The fact that some prefixes have more than one meaning and that some meanings are represented by more than one prefix can cause problems in the use of prefixes. The former is much less of a problem because the meanings do not differ that greatly. But the alternative spellings of some prefixes are not likely to be recognized by students (or even many adults). Because of the phonetic structure of English, the final sound of some prefixes is absorbed or "assimilated" into the word or root to which it is attached (Hodges 1982). So, instead of *ad-pear* (to + become visible), we have *appear; different* rather than *different*; and *illegal*, not *in-legal*. Some children may overgeneralize, which can lead to such errors as thinking that *invaluable* means *not valuable*.

Most pupils probably will find it difficult to make use of prefixes attached to Latin or Greek roots, especially when the prefix has a less common spelling.

Table 13.1. A Recommended List of Prefixes

Prefix	Meaning(s)	Examples
ab	away from	abnormal
ad, ap, at	to, toward, nearness or addition to	admit, appear, attract adjoin, adrenal
be	by	beside
com, con, col, co	with, together	combine, concur, collect, cohere
de	from	detract
	reverse, undo	defrost
dis, dif	not	dishonest
	reversal	disappear
	cause to be the opposite of	disable
em, en	in, into	embrace, enclose
	cause to make to be	endanger
ex	out	expel
	former	ex-boxer
	beyond	excess
in, im	in, into	infuse
	not	incorrect, impure
mono*	one	monochrome
bi*	two, happening every two or twice during	biped, biweekly, bimonthly
tri*	three	triangle
ob,* of,* op*	against	obnoxious, offend, oppress
	to, toward	object
post*	after	postdate, postpone
pre	before	prewar
	in front of	predict
pro	in favor of	pro-labor
	before, ahead of	promote, prologue
re	back	repay, refer
	again	reappear
sub	under	subsoil
	to a lesser degree	subtropical
super*	over, above	superscribe
	higher in rank	supervisor
	surpassing, greater than normal	superhuman
trans*	across	transport, transatlantic
un	not	unhappy
	do the opposite of	untie

Not all of the alternate spelling or meanings are indicated; they may be found in a dictionary. Prefixes with an asterisk were not among the 15 cited by Stauffer (1942).

Prefixes are more likely to be useful when they have been added to a word that the child already knows. For instance, it is much easier to perceive the meaningful units in *unhappy* and *remake* than in *appear* or *collect*. It is easier to build on prior knowledge, and teachers should take advantage of this fact. Therefore it is advisable to introduce prefixes in connection with known words, to teach those that have the most transfer value (the most frequently occurring and consistent in meaning), and to leave the more difficult prefixes for individual

Table 13.2   The Most Common Latin Roots in the Vocabulary of Children

Root	Meanings	Examples
fac, fact (facere)	to make or do	facile, factory
fer (ferre)	to bear, carry	transfer, ferry
mis, mit (mittere)	to send	admissible, transmit
mov, mot (movere, motus)	to move	movement, motion
par (parpare)	to get ready	prepare, repair
port (portare)	to carry	export, portable
pos, pon (posito, ponere)	to place, put	position, opponent
spect, spic (specere)	to look	inspect, conspicuous
stat, sta (stare)	to stand	station, stanza
tend, tens (tendere, tensus)	to stretch	extend, tension
ven, vent (venire)	to come	convention, event
vid, vis (videre, visus)	to see	provide, vision

SOURCE: L. C. Breen, Vocabulary development by teaching prefixes, suffixes and root derivations, *The Reading Teacher*, November 1960.

study by the most capable students in the upper grades. Suggestions for teaching prefixes may be found in M. Graves and Hammond (1980) and D. Johnson and Pearson (1984).

Knowledge of the meanings of the more common Latin roots shown in Table 13.2 can help mature, bright students determine the meanings of unknown words and thus increase their word knowledge. Only 82 Latin roots and 6 Greek roots occur 10 or more times each in children's vocabulary (Breen 1960). Roots like *port* (to carry) and *fac, fact, fic* (to make or do) are fairly easy to learn and use; for example, the meaning of *export* is easily perceived. Templeton (1983) suggested that the study of roots should begin with those whose meaning is relatively constant. These roots are *spect* (to look), *press* (to press), *port*, (carry), *form* (shape), *pose* (to put or place), *tract* (draw or pull), *spir* (to breathe), and *dict* (to say). O'Rourke (1974) listed 21 roots having at least 5 applications. But the use of roots and affixes as an aid to word meaning requires a fairly high level of reasoning ability and even then the meanings of many words are not easily determined (e.g., con spic uous = together—look—full of = easy to see).

Rather than teach the meanings of roots in some abstract fashion, it may be preferable to demonstrate to students how some words are related, and how their commonality can be helpful in determining word meaning. This can be done by building a "word family"[5] (a group of morphologically related words). Start with a word whose meaning is known (e.g., *porter*) and have the pupils add to the list (e.g., *import, export, report, reporter, transport, portable*), pointing out the visual spelling cue that is common to all the words and discussing the word meanings as they are affected by their affixes.

Teaching words together as a family has advantages (Nagy & Anderson 1982, 1984): (1) If the most frequent words in the family are already known, bridges can be built between the old and the new; (2) it calls attention to the word-formation process that relates different words within the family, so students

[5] The term *word family* more commonly refers to such spelling patterns as *an* and *ight*.

Table 13.3   Fairly Common Suffixes That Have a Reasonably Consistent Meaning

Suffix	Meanings	Examples
er, or	one who does	teacher, sailor
ist	one who does or practices	pianist, dentist
	one who believes in	abolitionist
ian	one who is expert in	musician, statistician
tion, sion	act of	creation, decision
ment	result of	judgment
	act of	management
ence, ance, ancy	act of	persistence
	state of	repentance, truancy
ness	state of being	sadness
ty, ity	condition of, quality of	safety, purity
al	pertaining to	musical
ic, ical	pertaining to	historic, historical
	like	angelic
ous, ious	like	laborious
	full of	joyous
ful	full of	painful
	pertaining to, tending to	forgetful
ly, y	in the manner of	truly, windy
ble, able, ible	capable of being	adaptable, permissible
less	without	homeless
ward	in the direction of	westward

NOTE: Some of these suffixes have other meanings in addition to those indicated.

are more likely to take advantage of such relationships on their own; and (3) it familiarizes students with the kinds of meaning changes that often occur between related words.

There are many suffixes in English, but the majority of them have more than one meaning, so teaching only the most common meaning may create some confusion. Suffixes that are both fairly common and have a reasonably constant meaning are shown in Table 13.3.

Developing Vocabulary through Wide Reading

About 50 years ago, E. L. Thorndike (1936–1937) concluded that it would be impossible to teach all the words that children encounter in reading. He recommended that the best way to solve this problem was to have children read a variety of interesting books that were easy enough so that new ideas and words could be learned from them. According to Nagy and Anderson (1982, 1984), a major factor in vocabulary acquisition after third grade is the amount of independent reading done by students.

Wide reading is a pleasant way to extend vocabulary knowledge, and it should be greatly encouraged. Its influence on vocabulary acquisition, however, will vary depending on the amount of reading done, the number of words in the material whose meanings are unknown to the reader, how well context reveals meaning, and the child's ability to infer word meaning from whatever contextual information is available. Bright, motivated students who read well and enjoy reading are apt to read a wide variety of materials and have the ability and desire to deduce word meanings, so they will profit the most. Poor or reluctant readers are much less likely to increase their vocabulary knowledge through wide reading. Word-by-word readers have difficulty using context to aid word meaning. Those most in need of increasing their vocabulary are least likely to avail themselves of the opportunity to do so through reading, thus establishing a vicious cycle. Limited reading restricts the opportunity to learn new words, and failure to build up vocabulary knowledge hampers reading improvement.

Use of the Dictionary

Even though readers may not use a glossary or dictionary while reading to determine the meaning of an unknown word, the fact remains that the dictionary is an excellent source of word meaning, as well as other useful information. Picture dictionaries can be used as early as the first grade and are helpful additions to the library table through the primary grades and in remedial work beyond that level. Meyer (1980) critically reviewed 16 children's dictionaries and presented criteria that can be used in selecting one.

A good dictionary definition usually has two elements: (1) It states a class or category to which the concept belongs, and (2) it gives one or more descriptive characteristics that distinguish this concept from other members of the category. Thus, a *fanatic* is defined as "a person with an extreme and unreasoning enthusiasm or zeal, especially in religious matters." The category is "person"; the rest tells how fanatics differ from other persons. Children can be helped to analyze definitions, to construct their own definitions for familiar words, and to compare their definitions with the definitions in the dictionary.

Synonyms are often given as definitions. This is fine when the synonym is already understood or is clearly and understandably defined. Learning synonyms is a good way to enlarge one's vocabulary, especially when the dictionary explains fine distinctions, as among *ancient, antique, antiquated,* and *old-fashioned.* Fortunately, circular definitions (fantasy—hallucination; hallucination—a form of fantasy) are rare in today's dictionaries.

A dictionary is a complex work, and in order to get children to use it willingly, it is advisable to prepare a planned sequence of lessons to teach elementary dictionary skills. The following outline lists the major dictionary skills. The simplest ones can be started in first grade; the more difficult ones can be made the objective of planned lessons in fourth, fifth, and sixth grades.

1. Location of words in alphabetical order
   a. Learning the sequence of the alphabet
   b. Practice in determining which letter comes before and which comes after a given letter
   c. Arrangement of a list of words alphabetically by first letter
   d. Arrangement of words having same first letter in alphabetical order according to second, third, and fourth letters
   e. Practice in opening the dictionary at a point near the word
   f. Practice in the use of a thumb index
   g. Learning how to use the guide at the top of a page

2. Finding out the pronunciation of words
   a. Practice in reading words by syllables
   b. Interpretation and use of the accent mark
   c. Understanding of phonetic respelling
   d. Understanding and use of diacritical marks
   e. Location and use of the guide to pronunciation
3. Finding out the meaning of words
   a. Ability to interpret typical dictionary definitions
   b. Ability to select from several meanings listed in the dictionary the one that fits the present context
   c. Ability to find synonyms for a word
   d. Ability to relate derived forms of a word to the basic form
   e. Ability to distinguish current usage from obsolete or slang usage

Practice exercises in the use of the dictionary can be found in a number of reading workbooks for the middle and upper grades (Laughlin 1978). Various dictionary exercises can be found in D. Jones (1980), Criscuolo (1980b), and D. Johnson and Pearson (1984). E. F. Miller (1962, 1984) discussed ways to use a dictionary to stimulate reading.

Effectiveness of Instructional Approaches

Over 15 years ago, Petty, Herold and Stoll (1968) concluded that the research comparing the effectiveness of different methods of teaching vocabulary was inconclusive. The situation does not seem to have changed. Introducing words in meaningful context has been shown to be more effective than other techniques in some studies (e.g., Gipe 1980). Other studies (e.g., Pany, Jenkins & Schreck 1982) show that teaching synonyms and definitions resulted in learning more word meanings. However, J. Levin et al. (1982) stated that there were no significant differences between teaching word meaning in context versus a definition technique when instructional time was controlled, and Stahl (1983) found that a combined use of both techniques was more effective than a definitional treatment alone, on one posttreatment measure but not the other.

Based on their review of the literature, Jenkins and Dixon (1983) concluded that the keyword method, massed practice, and expanded teaching with reviews have been more effective in increasing vocabulary knowledge than have informal references to meaning, categorization and dictionary exercises, and the use of specially constructed sentences from which the children had to derive word meaning. But they also indicated that their conclusion must be tempered by the noticeable lack of long-term studies. The success of the vocabulary program used in the studies reported by Beck, Perfetti, and McKeown (1982) and McKeown et al. (1983) was attributed to the provision of a variety of opportunities to learn and use new words, and to challenging the students to explore and extend newly learned concepts in a lively, verbal environment.

Mezynski (1983) stated that the effectiveness of vocabulary instruction on reading comprehension is determined largely by three variables: (1) the amount of practice provided; (2) the breadth of training in the use of word meanings; and (3) the degree to which active processing by the students is encouraged. The failure of some vocabulary programs to improve reading comprehension may have been the result of the word meanings not having been learned well enough to be understood in a novel context. In general, vocabulary programs that stress breadth of knowledge and provide multiple examples of concepts seem to have a positive impact on reading comprehension. The same is true when students are actively involved in the learning of new words.

One of the vocabulary techniques that has been successful in improving reading comprehension involves teaching the words in the context of a unifying theme. This *category clustered* procedure helps pupils to understand the relationships among words and integrate them with prior knowledge.

Materials and Suggestions for Vocabulary Development

Many vocabulary-building activities are provided in workbooks correlated with basal readers and independent workbooks designed to develop only vocabulary or reading comprehension in general. Multimedia materials and computer software are also available. Each set of materials should be evaluated before it is used with students. M. Graves (1984) noted that many commercially published vocabulary programs teach rather obscure words instead of the word meanings that most children need to learn.

Many of the games suggested on pages 419–426 for developing word recognition can be adapted for vocabulary development. The following games can also be used to provide enjoyable practice with word meanings:

Fun with Words (Dexter & Westbrook). The series of gamelike aids at six levels generates interest in word meanings.

Synonimbles and Phantonyms (Curriculum Associates). In *Synonimbles*, games for intermediate-grade children, students must relate two given synonyms to an unknown third; 125 puzzles with clues at five levels. In *Phantonyms*, the players must find a mystery word (antonym) concealed in the clue sentence; 110 puzzles at five levels.

Homonym Cards, Antonym Cards, Homophone Cards (DLM). In each of these games the basic task is to match pairs of pictured words; other tasks also may be required of the players in order to score points. Similar cards are published by Milton Bradley.

Press and Check Bingo Games (Milton Bradley). There are four games: *Prefixes and Suffixes, Homonyms, Synonyms and Antonyms*, and *Abbreviations and Contractions*. In response to questions, the players push the tab above a possible answer and are able to see the answer–question relationship.

Pronoun Pinch Hitter (DLM). This game emphasizes understanding pronouns in sentences. The player must insert the appropriate pronoun for an underlined noun to move one base; worksheets for reinforcement.

A variety of vocabulary games and exercises can be found in Platts (1970); Dale and O'Rourke (1971); O'Rourke (1974), Wagner, Hosier, and Cesinger (1972); Criscuolo (1981, 1984); Hodges (1982); and D. Johnson and Pearson (1984).

II. SENTENCE COMPREHENSION

The importance of accurate, automatic word recognition and knowledge of word meanings for reading comprehension have already been discussed. This section deals with the factors that influence sentence difficulty and how to improve sentence comprehension.

Factors That May Influence Sentence Difficulty

Some sentences are more difficult than others to understand. In this section some of the factors that influence the comprehensibility of sentences are discussed.

Surface Versus Deep Structure

Transformational-generative linguists stress the idea that every sentence has a surface structure and a deep structure. A *surface structure* refers to what is actually written, a *deep structure* to what the sentence means. A sentence is said to be understood when the meaning of its deep structure is grasped.

Two sentences may have very similar surface structures but different meanings (as in sentences *a* and *b* below). Or two sentences may have different surface structures and have the same meaning (as in sentences *b* and *c* below).

> *a.* He painted the house red.
> *b.* He painted the red house.
> *c.* He painted the house that was red.

The deep structure of a sentence may not be apparent from its surface structure. The closer the match between the surface and deep structures of a sentence, the fewer transformations the reader has to make and therefore the easier the sentence is to understand (McNeil 1984). "Judy fed the dog" is easy to understand because it is clear as to who did what for or to whom, and because children have had numerous experiences with such simple active sentences of the subject–verb–object type. Other kinds of sentences require the reader to carry out special mental operations to make the transformation. For example, passive sentences (e.g., The dog was fed by Judy) can cause problems because the sequence of words in the sentence is an inversion of the basic subject–verb–object word order, and a form of *be* is introduced. Who did what to or for whom is less clear. Passive sentences are usually more difficult for children to comprehend, all else being equal. Passive sentences focus attention on the recipient of the action; active sentences focus on the subject of the sentence. Many readers, even those who are fairly skilled, fail to understand this subtle difference in meaning.

There also may be a discrepancy between the surface and deep *semantic* structure of a sentence (McNeil 1984). An author may intend an entirely different meaning for a sentence than its surface structure suggests. Thus, "That's nice" can be a positive comment by a story character, or it can be a sarcastic remark. The alert reader infers the meaning from the context.

Sentence Length

In and of itself, sentence length is not a factor in sentence difficulty. Long sentences are often more difficult to understand than short sentences because they contain one or more dependent clauses, embedded phrases or clauses, or plural subjects or predicates. Such constructions increase the syntactic complexity of the sentence. It is the syntactic and semantic complexity of the sentence and not its length per se that makes it difficult to understand.

Short sentences are not necessarily easy to understand. For example, in early reading materials that contain a great deal of dialogue, the speaker of a sentence is often not clearly marked (e.g., "Jane said" is not continuously repeated). Other short sentences require the reader to infer missing words (e.g., in "'Shut the door,' said Mother," the reader must infer to whom Mother was speaking). Or sentences may have a number of possible meanings. For example, "It is hot in here" may be a simple statement of fact or a subtle request to open a window.

A series of short sentences is not necessarily easier to understand than a longer sentence expressing the same idea(s). For instance, "The tired fisherman caught a huge sailfish" is probably easier to understand than "The fisherman was tired. The fisherman caught a sailfish. The sailfish was huge." The longer sentence is easier to process because the information is chunked into two phrases and the relationships among the ideas are more explicit. Somewhat similarly, it is easier to grasp the meaning of "The machine stopped due to an electrical power failure" (even though the effect precedes the cause) than "The electrical power failed. The machine stopped." The cause–effect relationship is explicitly marked by *due to* in the longer sentence; the reader must infer *due to* in order to understand the relationship between the two short sentences.

Concept Density

Sentences of relatively equal length may vary considerably in the number of concepts they contain. Densely packed idea units are difficult to understand because they place more of a burden on limited cognitive processing systems (Samuels & Eisenberg 1981). Children who lack adequate reading fluency may find it difficult to retain enough incoming information to establish a relationship among the concepts.

Syntactic Complexity

Syntax is the primary means by which the intended relations among words are specified. So, understanding the syntactic structure of a sentence is important to reading comprehension.

In most cases, the reader's level of syntactic competence exceeds the level of syntactic complexity used in the material being read. But it should be remembered that, for the most part, syntactic competence is based on experience with oral language, especially for novice readers. The syntactic structures found in written material tend to be more complex than those used in the informal oral language experiences of children. Some written syntactic structures rarely occur in spoken language. For example, one does not frequently encounter spoken sentences that contain a number of embedded clauses. A student may not have a particular syntactic structure in his linguistic competence. The large amount of attention devoted to word recognition also detracts from the novice reader's use of phrase and sentence structure (E. Ryan 1981).

In general, the more syntactically complex the sentence, the more difficult it is to understand. However, a potentially difficult syntactic structure may not cause a problem if the reader's topical knowledge matches the sentence content (Barnitz 1979, 1984). Syntax can also be a problem when complex syntactic structures are needed to express semantic relationships that are too advanced for the reader (Huggins & Adams 1980). As noted earlier, sentence comprehension can be limited by the reader's lack of familiarity with the syntactic structure and with the concept(s) it is attempting to reveal.

Direct measures of sentence complexity or depth have been devised (Yngve 1962, R. L. Allen 1966, Botel & Granowsky 1972), but they are not commonly used. Another measure of sentence difficulty is the *kernel distance theory* (Fry, Weber, & DePierro 1978). It suggests that the farther apart the subject, predicate, and object of a sentence are, the more difficult the sentence is to understand. Sentences with fewer words between the subject and verb and between the verb and the object are supposedly easier to understand.

Some students have difficulty understanding negative or complex verbs (Hildyard & Olson 1982). Mathewson (1984) provided examples of typical negative sentence structures (e.g., We never want to go; None of us wants to go; We are unable to go), discussed why children find them difficult to comprehend, and offered suggestions for helping pupils grasp their meaning.

Other pupils have difficulty understanding dependent or subordinate clauses in general. Many of these problems are caused by a lack of understanding of the *signal words* that introduce, connect, order, and relate ideas to larger concepts; they can occur within a sentence or act as cohesive ties between sentences. Among the signal words likely to be encountered by children are the following:

- *More information to follow:* also, and, another, as well as, besides, finally, furthermore, in addition to, in conclusion, moreover
- *Opposite idea to follow:* although, as a matter of fact, but, either . . . or (implies alternative), even if, however, in spite of, instead of, nevertheless, on the other hand, rather, still, yet
- *Cause indicated:* as a result of, because, due to, in order to, on account of, since
- *Effect indicated:* as a consequence, as a result, consequently, so, so as to, so that, therefore
- *Exceptions to follow:* all but, except
- *Conditions to be met:* after, as soon as, before, following, if (also may indicate a supposition), provided that, should, while, without, unless, until
- *Comparison to be made:* as, before . . . after, like, once . . . now, some . . . others, than

- *Examples to follow* (these words are often followed by is or are): examples, for example, kinds, ordinal numbers (e.g., (1) . . .; (2) . . .), others, several, some, such as, the following, types, ways.

Stoodt (1972) reported that the best-understood signal words through fourth grade were *and, for,* and *as;* those that were comparatively difficult were *when, so, but, or, where, while, how, that,* and *if.* Robertson (1968) found that sentences containing clauses introduced by *however, thus, which, although,* and *yet* were difficult for intermediate-grade children; understanding of these connectives was closely related to intelligence and listening comprehension, and correlated .83 with reading comprehension. Differences in the mastery of conjunctions among age and ethnic groups were revealed in a study by McClure and Steffenson (1980); however, such differences are often highly related to language background and SES.

Primary-grade children are better able to understand time relationships when the sequence of events in the surface structure matches the natural sequence in which the events occurred (e.g., I ate lunch before I went out to play) than when the time sequence is reversed in the printed sentence (Before I went out to play, I ate lunch) (Distad & Paradis 1983, McNeil 1984). Irwin (1979) found that fifth graders of average reading ability generally had problems understanding cause–effect relationships marked by *because* but not with time sequence indicated by *after.* There is growing evidence that implicit connectives are more difficult to understand than explicitly stated connectives (Irwin 1980). Irwin suggested that work on understanding implicit connectives could begin in the middle grades by discussing the necessity for looking for such relationships and focusing questions and discussions on implicit connective relationships.

Anaphora[6]

Anaphora involves the use of a word or group of words that substitute for another word or group of words. The use of anaphoric terms provides a way for authors to avoid repetition. But its use also can create comprehension problems for the reader because it requires inferencing or reasoning ability, as demonstrated by Nash-Webber (1978), to relate the anaphoric term with its referent. The clarity of the relationship between any form of anaphora and its referent influences the comprehensibility of the sentence(s).

Personal pronouns are the most commonly recognized form of anaphora. In general, it is more difficult to infer the relationship between a pronoun and its referent when more than one pronoun or other anaphoric term occurs in the material, the pronoun precedes its referent, there are many words between the two, and the pronoun and its referent are in different sentences. But such generalizations must be tempered by the fact that other variables also influence the ease with which the relationship can be understood. In the sentence "John saw

---

[6] Linguists distinguish between *anaphora* and *cataphora*. In the former, the referent comes before the substitution; in the latter, it comes after it. We use *anaphora* to refer to the relationship regardless of direction because it is more commonly used in that way.

Mary and he said hello to her," the parallel construction of the two clauses and the gender differences in the pronouns make it comparatively easy to relate the pronouns to their referents, even though the antecedent closest to *he* is *Mary*. Because the referents are not clear in "John saw Tom and he said hello to him," the sentence is ambiguous.

There are also locative pronouns (*here, there*) that often refer to phrases (Julia eats *in the kitchen*. It is warm *there*). And at times a pronoun may refer to a whole sentence (*Helen eats noisily. This* annoys Ben). Except for a few structures, most pupils are able to comprehend pronouns by the sixth grade (Barnitz 1981). Disabled readers, however, may not be as skilled in this area, as suggested by the finding that learning-disabled adolescents could correctly select fewer than two thirds of the 22 pronoun referents in short paragraphs (Fayne 1981).

Some structures require readers to make even more difficult inferences. For example, one or more words may be omitted from a sentence. A pronoun may have to be inferred (e.g., in "John saw Mary and said hello to her," *he* must be inferred as occurring between "and" and "said"). More than one word is omitted in other structures (e.g., "No one else would wash the floor, so Barbara did). Or a verb may have a verb-phrase referent (e.g., Marshall *eats too much*. Marge knows that he *does*). Refer to Bormuth (1975c) for other examples. Pearson and Johnson (1978) also suggested how to use questioning to determine if anaphoric relations were understood and offered suggestions for teaching anaphoric relations, as did McNeil (1984). Kachuck (1981) discussed how to help children overcome problems in understanding relative clauses.

Other possible use of referring terms that may cause comprehension difficulty, especially for novice readers, include (1) temporal references (e.g., the *next* day); (2) locational references (e.g., *under* the table); and (3) discourse references in which third-person pronouns represent those in the passage (e.g., Give *this* to *them*) (Samuels & Eisenberg 1981).

Improving Sentence Comprehension Ability

When young children are learning to read, they should be provided with oral reading exercises that emphasize reading the material using the same intonations that they use in speaking. It may be necessary for the teacher to demonstrate this. Since many of the early stories contain dialogue, the children can be encouraged to "read it, just like＿＿＿ would say it," and urged to take their cues from the action in the story or accompanying pictures. At this level of development, weak word recognition is most likely to interfere with sentence comprehension.

Practice in sentence comprehension is often based on workbook or worksheet exercises. These can be helpful if teachers determine why children made wrong answers and then teach the needed skill or strategy. Children who consistently make few errors on such exercises should be excused from them; otherwise their use can become boring busywork and lead to disinterest in reading.

Specific questioning about each misunderstood sentence should vary according to the nature of the sentence. The child's understanding of the essential factual content of most sentences can be checked by questions asking *who, what, where, when,* or *how.* Comprehension of causal relations can be assessed by asking *why.* Questions such as "Who did _____ ?" "What did _____ do?" and "To whom (or to what) did _____ do it?" can be used to check the child's understanding of the relationships among subject, verb, and object. When an incorrect answer is received, a general question such as "How do you know?" or "Why do you think so?" may reveal the source of the difficulty. Or further probing may be needed. Once a source of difficulty is located, it is the teacher's responsibility to provide the necessary instruction and guided practice.

Comprehension of written sentences of increasing length and complexity is limited by the child's linguistic competence. Exposure to oral language that is richer and more complex than the child's speech may provide a background for reading material of similar complexity. Learning to write increasingly complex sentences also may aid sentence comprehension. Research on teaching children to understand syntactic structures is sparse (Jenkins & Pany 1981).

One of the reasons why children have difficulty understanding clauses is that they are not accustomed to hearing or using oral language that makes much use of them. This is especially true of certain connectives. Practice in the construction of sentences employing these clauses and connectives is one good way to clarify their meanings so that they can be understood when met in reading. Having children paraphrase sentences or express them in their own words also can facilitate sentence comprehension. Weaver (1979) found that use of sentence anagrams (the children formed sentences from words) and a word-grouping strategy (which is clearly outlined in the article) resulted in improving the reading comprehension of third graders. "Sentence sense" or "sentence organization" skills also can be developed by having students manipulate phrase cards to make meaningful sentences (Greenewald & Pederson 1983).

Sentence combining and decomposing exercises may help some children understand complex or compound sentences. The use of such exercises has been shown to increase the syntactic complexity of student's writing (W. L. Smith & Combs 1980). Sentence-combining ability seems to improve with age; nevertheless, on a national assessment test, only 20% of the 13-year-olds and 44% of the 17-year-olds were able to respond correctly to the more difficult sentence-combining task items (NAEP 1982a). The findings regarding the impact of sentence-combining exercises on reading comprehension are mixed. For example, Greenewald and Pederson (1983) cited four studies that indicated positive results, and Straw and Schreiner (1982) found that the sentence-combining and sentence-reduction groups scored higher than the control group on the cloze but not the standardized reading comprehension test. Noyce and Christie (1981) and Tierney and Cunningham (1984) stated that such programs have not been particularly effective in improving reading comprehension. Tierney and Cunningham suggested that such findings may in part reflect the use of measures that are not sensitive to sentence-combining or sentence-reduction improvement, and to the fact that such training can only help those who need it.

Suggestions for improving sentence comprehension may be found in Barnitz (1979, 1984) and McNeil (1984).

Teaching the Use of Punctuation Marks

Some children become confused in reading connected material because they do not make use of the clues provided by punctuation. They have not learned to recognize a capital letter as a sign of the beginning of a sentence, a period or question mark as the end of a sentence, or a comma as a "partial stop" separating parts of a sentence. Children of somewhat higher reading ability may need assistance in the interpretation of semicolons, colons, and dashes. Simple explanation and supervised practice in noticing punctuation marks will usually overcome difficulties of this sort. If errors persist, coloring the first letter of a sentence in green, commas in yellow, and periods in red is an effective way to emphasize the punctuation.

Improving the Ability to Read in Phrases

One reason why spoken language is easier to understand than written language is that the speaker often pauses between phrases, thus separating the message into thought units. In reading, the reader has to "chunk" the printed words into phrases. It is easier and more efficient to process language by thought units than by single words, because fewer bits of information must be held in STM and reading by phrases forces the reader to look for relationships between words and larger units of meaning.

Processing by phrases means that the individual words in a phrase are held in STM, with varying degrees of partial processing, until the entire phrase is completed. This is an efficient processing method because the meaning, pronunciation, and syntactic function of an individual word are sometimes ambiguous until the other words in the phrase provide a context (I. Taylor 1981). Children who are making normal progress in reading do not need much special practice in reading phrases. Reading words in meaningful groups develops as part of the total pattern of reading ability. Most children learn to read by phrases as a result of teacher modeling (the teacher reads orally to them), by being encouraged to read orally with natural expression, and by practice exercises in which phrases are employed.

New words are often introduced in phrases or sentences. Teachers can use phrase cards in various ways, such as in assembling sentences or in answering questions by selecting the proper phrase card. If phrase cards are used to develop speed of word recognition, the exposure time should be longer than that used for single words. Few elementary school children can perceive a phrase as a unit in a single visual fixation, so more view time must be allowed.

Children's attention can be directed to phrases by posing oral questions that require the reading of phrases as meaningful units. For example, if the written sentence was "Nora bought the door at the lumberyard," the teacher may ask, "Where did Nora buy the door?" Written exercises that require the pupil to write in or select the correct phrase also may be employed. For example, the following items could be generated from the preceding sample sentence:

> Nora bought the door _____ .
>
> Nora bought the door
>
> | in the woods | at the grocery store |
> |---|---|
> | at the lumberyard | from her father |

Some pupils do not read in phrases long after reading instruction has been initiated. Most often, this is the result of inaccurate or slow word recognition. For these children, the treatment will depend on the severity of the word-recognition problem. If the child can recognize few words, there is little sense in working on phrasing until the child's sight vocabulary is adequate. If word recognition is accurate but slow, efforts can be made to speed up word recognition, and work on phrasing can be given concurrently. Two other points should be considered. First, inadequate phrasing or word-by-word reading may persist as a habit even after a word-recognition problem is overcome, unless efforts are made to help the pupil read in phrases. Second, phrasing may be inadequate when children read orally at sight simply because they are reading the material for the first time. The need for special work in phrase reading should not be considered unless inadequate phrasing persists after the child has had a chance to preread silently. If inadequate phrasing or word-by-word reading occurs only on material that is difficult for the child, the treatment is simply to provide more appropriate reading material.

The most extreme case of inadequate phrasing is word-by-word reading. Unless the material is conceptually easy for the pupil, word-by-word reading is likely to have an adverse influence on reading comprehension. Reading with perceptible pauses between each two words places a strain on one's information-processing system. Only a limited amount of information can be held in STM at one time. Treating each word individually makes it difficult to make use of syntactic and semantic information (Perfetti & Lesgold 1979).

There is some research evidence that teaching children to read in phrases is possible and that improvement in phrase reading is durable (Amble 1967). Cromer (1970) distinguished between two kinds of poor comprehenders. His "deficit" group was poor in both reading vocabulary and paragraph comprehension; the "difference" group was poor in comprehension but had normal reading vocabularies. When reading material was marked off in phrases, the reading comprehension of the "difference" group improved, but not that of the "deficit" group. Segmenting written text into phrases has been shown to improve the reading comprehension of 9-year-old disabled readers (McBride 1976), slow but accurate readers (O'Shea & Sindelar 1983), and high school sophomores (K. Stevens 1981).

Many different procedures can be helpful in overcoming word-by-word reading and faulty phrasing. Among the most helpful are the following:

1. In order to allow the child to concentrate on the phrasing and meaning, reading matter used for practice in phrasing should present few or no difficulties in word recognition and word meaning.
2. It is helpful to provide a good model for the pupils to imitate. The teacher can read a sentence orally with somewhat exaggerated phrasing and then have the children imitate her reading of the sentence. Reading of alternate sentences by teacher and pupils is also helpful. Some children gain considerable benefit from reading in unison with the teacher.
3. Practice can be given in reading printed material in which the phrases have been marked off by the teacher. A vertical line can be made in pencil between each two phrases, or each phrase can be underlined. The following sentence is shown with the phrases marked off in three different ways:

    The boy|is going|to the store|for some milk.

    The boy is going to the store for some milk.

    The boy is going to the store for some milk.

4. When special material is typed, mimeographed, or printed by hand, perhaps the best way to set off phrases is to leave additional space between them. For example:

    The boy   is going   to the store   for some milk.

5. Material can be typed with one phrase on a line, as in Figure 13.3. A piece of stiff paper or cardboard with an opening the length of a full line is moved at a steady rate down the page, exposing one phrase at a time. Some remedial teachers prefer to keep the opening stationary and pull the page up. In the latter case, it is usually necessary to paste several pages together so as to form a continuous strip.
6. After the pupil has developed some skill in the use of marked reading material, he can be given an unmarked selection to mark off the phrases. His ability to group words properly can be evaluated quickly, and faulty grouping can be corrected.
7. Practice can be given in the recognition of phrases as units during brief, but sufficient, exposure. Phrase cards can be shown in isolation, or phrases can be presented in teacher-made tachistoscopes (see p. 215) or commercially produced devices, many of which have phrase materials to go along with them.

It is important for children to try to use their new phrasing skills in their everyday reading. Unless the results of special practice are carried over into general reading, the time spent on them is wasted.

III. READING COMPREHENSION BEYOND THE SENTENCE LEVEL

In this section we discuss beliefs about the nature of reading comprehension; the relationship of prior knowledge to reading comprehension, and how knowl-

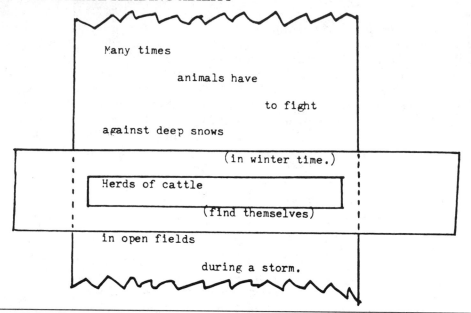

Figure 13.3. One type of practice material for reading in phrases. A strip of paper with one phrase typed per line is placed flat on the reading surface and a strip of stiff paper with a rectangular opening is moved steadily down the page, exposing one phrase at a time. Phrases in parentheses are concealed by the strip.

edge is represented in the mind (schema theory); whether reading comprehension is taught in the schools; and general and specific suggestions for developing reading comprehension.

The Nature of Reading Comprehension

As indicated by H. Singer (1981b) in his historical account, research on reading comprehension and ways of improving it had been going on for a century. But the period between 1978 and 1982 witnessed more research on basic reading comprehension processes and instructional practices than any previous time period, however long. There has been a virtual barrage of new theories that attempt to explain the comprehension process, and a wealth of new terminology, which, if not representing totally new concepts, at least provides more detailed descriptions than their often vague predecessors (Pearson & Gallagher 1983).

The various theories regarding the nature of the reading process were covered in Chapter 1 and will not be considered here. Rather, the emphasis is on differences of opinion as to whether reading comprehension is a unitary process or can be thought of as consisting of distinguishable skills or subprocesses.

Statistical Analysis of Reading Comprehension

The technique of factor analysis has been applied to try to determine whether reading comprehension is unitary or if there are distinct comprehension subskills. F. B. Davis (1968, 1971, 1972) analyzed a large battery of tests given to high school students and concluded that the following subskills were identifiable: recalling word meanings and drawing inferences about a word from context; getting the literal sense of details and weaving together ideas in the content; drawing inferences from the content; and recognizing an author's purpose, attitude, tone, mood, and techniques.

Spearritt (1972) reanalyzed Davis's data with different factor-analytic procedures and identified four distinguishable skills; recalling word meanings; drawing inferences from the content; following the structure of a passage; and recognizing a writer's purpose, attitude, tone, and mood. He concluded, however, that aside from word knowledge, which accounted for most of the variance, comprehension tests are so highly intercorrelated that they mainly measure "reasoning in reading." R. L. Thorndike (1973–1974) also reanalyzed Davis's data and concluded that, aside from word knowledge, none of the other skills was separately distinguishable and all could be described as "reasoning in reading." In a later study, Spearritt (1977) gave a large battery of tests to sixth graders and found three subskills: knowledge of word meanings, sentence comprehension, and grasp of semantic content. He found no difference between literal and implied meanings or between cloze tests and multiple-choice tests.

These studies left open the question of how important word recognition is for comprehension, since failure on a vocabulary test item could be the result of inability to decode the word, lack of knowledge of its meaning, or both. They showed that word meaning is a very important determiner of comprehension and questioned whether the many comprehension subskills discussed below are genuinely distinct from one another.

There are a number of problems with the use of factor analysis in an attempt to solve the holistic–subskill debate (P. Johnston 1981). The findings revealed by factor analysis are highly influenced by the items chosen to measure the traits and the intercorrelations among those traits. As Johnston pointed out, the search has attempted to find *independent* comprehension skills, but there is no reason to suppose that different comprehension skills should not be correlated. In fact, Guthrie's study (1973) suggested that there is an interfacilitation among reading subskills. Furthermore, there is some reason to doubt that the test items supposedly measuring literal or inferential comprehension were "pure" measures of these traits.

Logical Analysis of Reading Comprehension

The *Taxonomy of Educational Objectives: Cognitive Domain* (Bloom 1956) is a classification of objectives designed to systematize the desired intellectual outcomes of education in a comprehensive and logically sound hierarchical arrangement. Barrett adapted the Bloom taxonomy to produce a classification of reading objectives (R. J. Smith & Barrett 1974). Barrett used four main headings (literal recognition and recall, inferential comprehension, evaluation, and appreciation), each of which had subheadings and finer subdivision.

Another widely used classification employs four main headings: (1) literal comprehension, the skill of getting the primary, literal meaning; (2) interpre-

Skill Competencies	COMPREHENSION LEVELS		
	Factual	Interpretive	Applicative
1. Details			
a. Identifying	✓	✓	
b. Comparing	✓	✓	✓
c. Classifying		✓	✓
2. Sequence	✓	✓	✓
3. Cause and Effect	✓	✓	✓
4. Main Idea	✓	✓	✓
5. Predicting Outcome		✓	✓
6. Valuing			
a. Personal judgment	✓	✓	✓
b. Character trait identification	✓	✓	✓
c. Author's motive identification		✓	✓
7. Problem solving			✓

Figure 13.4. Classification of reading comprehension subskills. From R. B. Ruddell, Developing comprehension abilities: implications from research for an instructional framework, in S. J. Samuels (Ed.), *What research has to say about reading instruction* (Newark, DE: International Reading Association, 1978), p. 112. Used by permission of the author and the International Reading Association.

tation, the probing for greater depths of meaning; (3) critical reading, the evaluating and passing of personal judgment; and (4) creative reading, which starts with an inquiry and goes beyond implications derived from the text (N. B. Smith 1972). Still another classification identifies three levels of comprehension: literal, interpretive, and applied—students read to find out what the author said, what the author meant, and how to use the ideas (Herber 1978). It is evident that inferential comprehension means the same as interpretation, evaluative and critical are synonyms, and creative reading and application are somewhat alike but not identical.

Ruddell (1978) revised the Barrett classification as shown in Figure 13.4 Most of the seven main subskills of comprehension skill can be addressed at a factual, an interpretive, or an applicative level. This classification is a practical one. It does not, however, include two useful and necessary distinctions: (1) between factual questions that can be answered using the exact wording of the book and those requiring that the child restate the idea in his own words (paraphrase or translation); and (2) between questions that allow rereading to find the answer and those that require recall. A third useful distinction not included is between items in which the child chooses among given possible answers and those in which he has to produce the answer.

Granted that correlations among reading comprehension tests are high and that there is not complete agreement as to how to classify the skills involved, it still makes sense to provide practice in answering many different kinds of questions. When this is done, students can improve their ability to reason while reading many kinds of materials with a variety of specific purposes. They can also learn what questions to ask themselves while reading different materials.

Carroll (1977) discussed three bases for reading comprehension: cognition, language comprehension, and reading skill. The three are interrelated but need to be distinguished from one another. Cognition (knowing, reasoning, inferencing, and the like; intelligence) cannot be taught directly but sets limits to the individual's ability to develop language comprehension and reading comprehension. Language comprehension is teachable but is limited by the individual's cognitive development, which in turn limits the degree of reading comprehension possible. Carroll recommended the use of parallel auding and reading comprehension tests to distinguish between comprehension difficulties that reflect a lack of sufficient language competence and those that are caused by a lack of reading skills.

Reading Comprehension within a Theoretical Framework

A number of writers believe that reading comprehension is not a unitary process but a complex process comprised of a number of interacting subprocesses. Or, as Perfetti and Lesgold (1979) put it, these components are not functionally independent; rather, they are mutually facilitative. The subprocesses can be isolated in principle, but they are interrelated in practice. In order to specify the effect of any of the myriad of factors involved in the reading process, one would have to know how that factor interacts with all the other factors. At present, it is impossible to describe all these interactions (Samuels & Eisenberg 1981), so it seems that the complexity of the reading process and the interactive nature of the subprocesses almost preclude the identification of separate comprehension skills. They may exist, but we simply cannot separate them out.

These subprocess theories suggest that gains in one subprocess allow for gains in others and that insufficiently developed or dysfunctioning subprocesses may limit development of other subskills. Following this line of reasoning, attempts to improve reading comprehension would involve improving the various subcomponents, as well as the abilities and knowledge needed to perform them.

Two Key Factors in Reading Comprehension

A wide range of variables can influence reading comprehension. These cognitive, linguistic, neurophysiological, and sociocultural factors have been discussed in detail in other chapters. Reading is often described as an interactive process involving what is in the reader's head and what is on the printed page. This section is concerned with two key factors involved in this interaction—the reader's prior knowledge (and how that knowledge is organized), and text coherence and structure.

Prior Knowledge

That a reader's knowledge base is an important factor in reading comprehension is not a recent discovery (e.g., see W. S. Gray 1948). For years it has been referred to as *background knowledge*, and for years the importance of prior knowledge has been recognized. What is relatively recent is the research attention devoted to prior knowledge.

Prior knowledge may be defined as all the information an individual has in her or his long-term memory. A distinction is sometimes made between *world knowledge*, which is a more encompassing term, and *topical knowledge*, which refers to the information an individual has concerning the specific topic.

According to Adams and Bruce (1982), comprehension is the use of prior knowledge to create new knowledge; for without prior knowledge, written material would be meaningless. The more knowledge the reader can bring to bear (prior knowledge must be activated to be useful), the more likely it is that the material will be understood. The influence of prior knowledge is readily demonstrable by reading an article on a very familiar topic and another dealing with something one knows nothing about.

A study by Langer and Nicolich (1981) indicated that level of prior knowledge was highly related to passage recall, independent of IQ. Other studies (Marr & Gormley 1982, D. Hayes & Tierney 1982) have found that prior knowledge does account for differences in reading comprehension. There is also research evidence that poor readers do not use their prior knowledge as well as good readers do, especially when learning from expository text (B. Holmes 1983b); cultural knowledge influences reading comprehension (Pratt, Krane, & Kendall 1981; R. Reynolds *et al.*, 1982); and young pupils may have difficulty comprehending material when the textual information conflicts with their prior knowledge (Lipson 1984). Making explicit the connection between prior knowledge and text content improves reading comprehension (Beck, Omanson, & McKeown 1982), and teaching topical knowledge can improve reading comprehension (K. Stevens 1982).

If the child's topical knowledge is extremely deficient, the teacher can switch materials or attempt to raise the child's prior knowledge to a level that will allow him to understand the text. Often, neither choice offers a viable solution. Whether switching materials is an option depends on how necessary it is for the child to read that particular work and the availability of more suitable material. Whether or not one tries to raise the child's topical knowledge depends on how deficient that knowledge base is (it may take too long to develop adequate knowledge), how important that knowledge may be in the future, the availability of sufficient time to develop the necessary concepts, and the interest and motivation of the pupil.

There are no very specific guidelines for how to develop background knowledge (Tierney & Cunningham 1984). This should not deter teachers from attempting to develop background knowledge. Preteaching vocabulary and associated concepts may help, and children can learn new information through listening (tapes, discussion) or from movies or filmstrips. At times it is possible to find reading material of appropriate reading difficulty that explains or clarifies concepts or events. A fairly new technique, and one that may have some transfer value, involves providing analogies to the children. An analogy is used to help students understand the new and possibly difficult-to-understand information by comparing and/or contrasting it with something they already know. The few studies that have employed the technique (D. Hayes & Tierney 1982, Vosniadou & Ortony 1983) suggest that it shows promise.

Schema Theory

Because prior knowledge is vital in comprehension, it becomes important to understand how knowledge is stored in the mind and retrieved. *Schema theory* attempts to explain how knowledge is represented in the mind and how those representations facilitate the use of knowledge. According to schema theory, all knowledge is packed into units referred to as schemata.[7] A *schema* is more than just a definition of a word. Each schema is a "packet of knowledge"; it summarizes what one knows about the concept and how these pieces of information are related. In addition to the generic concept itself, a schema includes other information related to that concept and how this knowledge is to be used (Rumelhart 1984). For example, a schema for *giraffe* may include knowledge of what it eats, where it lives, how it is able to drink, and so forth. Or a schema may represent all we know about an event (e.g., a parade), or a situation (e.g., what it feels like to experience physical or emotional pain), or a sequence of actions (e.g., eating in a restaurant involves being seated, receiving a menu, reading the menu, making a decision, and so forth), or a role (e.g., mother). Schemata are thought to be hierarchically arranged networks of concepts (Durkin 1981b, 1984). Pieces of information may be missing in a schema ("empty slots" are said to exist), so new information can be added to it. A schema also can be modified by new information. Any one schema is not likely to contain all the information that would be useful in a particular situation, so more than one schema can be evoked concurrently (Samuels & Eisenberg 1981). The reader's task is to determine which schemata are needed to understand the text.

There are two types of schemata (Mavrogenes 1983). *Contextual schemata* refer to the person's knowledge of real or imaginary worlds. Contextual schemata are used by the reader during reading and after reading to help recall what has been read. *Textual schemata* involve knowledge of discourse conventions.

A schema is developed from experiences through a process of abstracting the common characteristics of the events. Schemata contain information generalized from events that one has experienced. Therefore, since few people have had exactly the same experiences, schemata are apt to be idiosyncratic. This is thought to be the reason why two people reading the same material can have widely differing interpretations of it. But, for the most part, there are enough similarities among people to permit communication.

According to schema theory, the reader constructs hypotheses about the interaction between his schemata and the textual information, and these hypotheses are progressively refined, modified, or discarded (Mason *et al.* 1984). Words mentioning any component of a schema will probably bring to mind the schema as a whole, and once the schema is activated, the reader will probably be reminded of other parts (R. Anderson & Pearson 1984). A text is said to be

---

[7] *Schemata* is the plural form; *schema*, the singular. Some writers use the term *frame* or *script* rather than *schema*. The notion of schema is not new; Bartlett (1932) used the term in its present meaning over 50 years ago.

understood when the reader is able to form a schema that offers a coherent account of the written text (Rumelhart 1984). Thus, schema theory suggests that reading comprehension depends on the information in the reader's mind, as well as that in the text, and upon the reader's ability to put together information from these two sources.

Not only does prior knowledge help us to comprehend what is written, but it also is vital in making inferences and predictions. Schemata allow the reader to "understand" far beyond what is stated in the text. They allow us to fill in the information not provided by the author, as well as to infer what the author means by use of certain words or phrases (e.g., figurative language). Readers are not consciously aware of the *inferential elaboration* they make while reading. That we can and do make such elaborations can be demonstrated by reading the following sentences:

> *a.* The punter kicked the ball.
> *b.* The golfer kicked the ball.

Assuming that one has the necessary topical knowledge, the differences in the size and shape of the ball in each sentence are known to the reader and can be used in understanding the sentence and later parts of the text. Moreover, the reader can infer that (1) the game being played in sentence *a* is football; (2) the punter's team has failed to make a first down or is using the punt as a defensive strategy; (3) it probably is not a field-goal attempt because place kickers, not punters, are used in such situations; and (4) this is a routine occurrence in a football game.

In sentence *b* the reader will probably infer that the golfer had some reason for kicking the ball, since such behavior is not the way in which the game is played. For instance, one might infer that the golfer missed an easy putt, got angry, and kicked the ball in anger or that the ball was lying in an disadvantageous spot so the golfer kicked it to give himself an advantage. His cheating allows one to infer something about the golfer's character.

Research findings have suggested that both the ability to make inferences and the nature of those inferences depend on prior knowledge. Durkin (1981b, 1984) contended, however, that schema theory offered nothing new for the teaching of reading. But as Strange (1980, 1984) pointed out, the use of a coherent theory may allow us to understand more clearly what we know and observe. Barr (1982b) was of the opinion that although schema theory might have considerable value in sensitizing teachers to the importance of prior knowledge for reading comprehension, it had little direct relevance regarding how pupils should be guided in reading expository material.

Prior Knowledge and Reading Comprehension Failure

Reading comprehension may be hampered because readers lack sufficient topical knowledge or fail to activate the relevant knowledge that they possess. Or they may have an impoverished understanding of the relationships among the facts that they do know about a topic. It is also possible that the author failed to provide enough clues to activate the pupil's prior knowledge (L. Baker & Brown 1984b).

Comprehension problems also can occur when the reader fails to maintain a proper balance between the information in his head and that in the written text. Some pupils rely too much on text-based information and fail to use their world knowledge to guide their text processing (Spiro 1979). Other readers rely much too heavily on their prior knowledge and fail to consider textual information.

MacGinitie and his associates (MacGinitie, Kimmel, & Maria 1980; Maria & MacGinitie 1982) identified two types of poor comprehenders who overly relied on top–down processing. Type 1 readers employ a *fixed-hypothesis strategy*. They form an initial interpretation based on an early portion of the text and then try to interpret the rest of the text to conform to their initial hypothesis. Often, Type 1 readers give far-fetched interpretations of later portions of the text or may change the details in the text to make them conform with their initial interpretation. They lack flexibility.

Type 2 readers use a *nonaccommodating strategy*. They read the text as though it were simply repeating what they already know and fail to take account of the textual information or fail to use it to modify their existing schema. When the text does not conform to their prior knowledge, they may ignore or misinterpret that textual information. Thus, Type 2 readers may find it difficult to learn well from text that contains new information. This type of comprehension problem is compounded by the fact that the reader often does not know that he doesn't know.

To help children who rely too heavily on prior knowledge, the teacher can (1) demonstrate to the pupil the need to read more carefully; (2) teach the pupil some strategies for monitoring comprehension; (3) have the pupil read material that has to be read carefully in order to perform some activity successfully; (4) provide the pupil with activities that require careful reading, such as outlining and notetaking; and (5) force the student to construct the author's intended meaning through the use of teacher questioning (Tierney & Spiro 1979). It also may help to show the pupil what he is doing and how it can cause comprehension problems.

Kimmel and MacGinitie (1984) also identified a group of children who use a perseverative text-processing strategy. They employed either an inductive or deductive strategy, regardless of the task demands. There are also pupils who have comprehension difficulties when the text contradicts their prior knowledge or beliefs (Lipson 1984). Such children have inaccurate notions that they are reluctant to relinquish in favor of textual information. Like MacGinitie's Type 1 readers, they are likely to distort textual information to bring it into line with their previous knowledge.

Text Coherence and Structure

The degree to which material is comprehended depends not only on the reader's levels of reading, cognitive and linguistic skills, and prior knowledge but also on how well the text is written. If written text is to communicate, it must be organized by authors in a manner that will facilitate the acquisition of their message by the reader. A text must be coherent in order to be understood. *Coherence* refers to how smoothly the ideas in a text are woven together. In coherent material the relationships among the ideas are clear enough to allow a logical connection or flow of meaning from one idea to another. Coherent discourse makes it easier for the reader to process the information as an integrated unit (Armbruster & Anderson 1984).

Coherence, or *cohesion*, as it is sometimes called, operates at both local and global levels. At the local level (the level of the individual sentence) various features related to coherence help the reader to interpret information within and between sentences. Cohesive ties, which are discussed below, make explicit the relationships between ideas (Armbruster & Anderson 1984). Cohesive chains are often built by an author by using pronouns, key content words, and a varied set of terms all semantically related to the content of the story (K. Goodman & Bird 1984).

At the global level, text is coherent to the extent that it facilitates the integration of high-level ideas across the entire discourse. Global coherence is a function of the overall structure or organization of the text (Armbruster & Anderson 1984). Text structure is discussed below.

Research findings support the contention that text coherence affects its comprehensibility. Among the aspects of coherence that make material less comprehensible are (1) use of terms whose referents are ambiguous, distant, or indirect; (2) inclusion of concepts unfamiliar to the reader; (3) lack of a clear relationship between story events; and (4) inclusion of irrelevant ideas or events (Beck *et al.* 1984). For a further discussion of coherence, refer to L. Chapman (1983, 1984).

Cohesive Ties

Intrasentence cohesion is determined primarily by syntactic structure, but relationships within the sentence may be marked by cohesive ties. Intersentence cohesion is achieved by cohesive ties that integrate semantic relationships between sentences. *Referential ties* involve a relationship between a term and its referent. The three kinds of referential ties (personal, demonstrative, and comparative) are usually expressed as pronouns, comparative adjectives, and adverbs. *Conjunctions* differ from the other cohesive ties in that they represent logical relationships between items in the text instead of requiring the reader to search the text for a referent. In ellipses, a part of the message is omitted but can be inferred from the text (e.g., Did you find the book? Yes, I did [find the book]).

The ability to understand cohesive ties is still being acquired long after the initial stages of learning to read and is not achieved by some students until they are in secondary school (L. Chapman 1984). Bridge and Winograd (1982) found that ninth-grade good and poor readers were generally able to understand cohesive ties. Their ability to understand intra- and intersentence information varied with the kind of cohesive tie involved. Conjunctive relationships gave poor readers the most difficulty.

Some studies have indicated that the presence of linguistic connectives facilitates comprehension; others have not revealed any significant difference related to the presence or absence of connectives. Poor readers, however, find it more difficult to infer implied relationships than to understand those marked by connectives (McKenzie, Neilsen, & Braun 1981). The density of cohesive ties and the distance between them does not seem to affect reading comprehension or recall (Neilsen 1981).

Text Structure

Text structure refers to how the ideas in a text are interrelated to convey the author's message to the reader. Text structure specifies the logical connection among ideas, as well as the subordination of some ideas to other concepts. Text structure may be analyzed at three primary levels: (1) the sentence level; (2) the paragraph level; and (3) the top level structure. An analysis of the content structure of a text shows how some ideas are superordinate to others. Some concepts (main ideas) are located at the top level of content structure. Ideas at the middle level correspond to supporting details. Lower-level ideas correspond to very specific deatails. Top-level ideas dominate the subordinate ideas; each of the other levels of ideas provides further information regarding the ideas in the level above them in the structure. Text structure provides an organizational structure that can be used during reading for understanding information, judging its importance, and aiding recall (B. Meyer 1984). But the ability to capitalize fully on text structure is probably a late-developing skill (L. Baker & Brown 1984b).

Three of the most widely used prose analysis systems (those of Fredericksen, Kintsch, and Meyer) were described, compared, and critiqued by Meyer and Rice (1984). Tierney and Mosenthal (1982) and Tierney, Mosenthal, and Kantor (1984) also described various types of text analysis.

Organizational Patterns in Textbooks

An analysis of 142 middle school content-subject textbooks (Cheek & Cheek 1983) revealed four main organizational patterns: (1) *enumeration*—the topic was immediately followed by additional information to expand the topic (e.g., a main idea followed by an explanation); (2) *relationships*—including cause–effect (often found in social studies textbooks), compare–contrast (often found in science textbooks), and classification; (3) *persuasive*—use of propaganda techniques; and, (4) *problem solving*—a problem is presented and the reader is to solve it to demonstrate his understanding of a concept (used in mathematics, science, business education, and vocational education textbooks). Another analysis of six junior high school science and social studies textbooks indicated that cause–effect, compare–contrast, and a simple listing were the most frequent text structures (Colwell & Helfeldt 1983). According to MacGinitie, Kimmel, and Maria (1980), many third- through sixth-grade texts are written using an inductive style—several sentences lead up to a main point in the paragraph. Among the subtypes of this inductive structure are (1) negation—an initially stated idea is later said to be false; (2) analogy—an idea is explained by comparing or contrasting it with an analog; (3) example–explicit topic—an example is followed by a concluding statement; and (4) example–implicit topic—an example is not followed by a unifying statement.

According to Meyer and Rice (1984), five groups of rhetorical relations may hold segments of text together.:

1. Antecedent–consequence: causal relations between topics are shown.
2. Response: use of question–answer and problem–solution formats.
3. Comparison: differences and similarities between two or more topics are pointed out.
4. Collection: grouping together ideas or events on the basis of some commonality (includes a sequence of events).
5. Description: more information regarding the topic is given by presenting attributes, explanations, setting, or specifics.

Calfee and Curley (1984) presented the more comprehensive listing of rhetorical styles shown in Table 13.4. As readers have repeated encounters with each of these rhetorical structures, they usually develop a schema for each type of structure.

Although the use of text structure seems to be a significant factor in the recall of expository material, most intermediate-grade pupils are unaware of how ideas are organized in a text (S. Elliott 1980, B. Taylor & Samuels 1983). Fifth-grade good readers were found to be more aware of text structure and to make better use of it than were fifth-grade poor readers and third-grade good readers (L. McGee 1982a). At the junior high school level, good readers were better than poor readers in using text structure to organize their recalls (Pearson & Gallagher 1983). There seems to be a developmental trend from the sixth grade thorugh college in the use of the structure of expository text to facilitate comprehension and recall (L. McGee 1982b).

A successful strategy for using text structure is employed by skilled older readers but by few younger children. It involves searching for the author's theses (the main ideas) and identifying the relationships among the primary theses and the major supporting details (L. McGee 1982b, B. Meyer 1984). Training in the use of top-level structure significantly improved the recall of tenth-grade poor readers but not of good readers, who apparently were already using an effective strategy (Siedow & Fox 1984). There is no empirical evidence to support instructional programs or materials based on any one method of text analysis (Ringler & Weber 1982).

Research on text structure has revealed the following: (1) Top-level ideas are retained and recalled better than are lower-level ideas; (2) the types of relationships among ideas greatly influence recall when they occur at the top level of content structure, but the same is not true at the lower levels; (3) different types of relationships at top-level structures affect recall differentially; (4) students who can identify and use top-level structure remember more of what they read than do students who cannot or do not; (5) students can be taught to identify top-level structure (the writing plan used by the author); (6) training in use of top-level structure increases reading comprehension as measured by free recall;

Table 13.4   Categories of Rhetorical Style

Description

Definition	Definition elaborates on the meaning of a term. It may identify features, uses, or relationships with other known objects, events, or ideas.
Division of classification	Division distinguishes the parts or members of an object or class. Classification relates groups of objects, events, or ideas according to a principle of similarity.
Comparison and contrast	Comparison generally highlights similarities among two or more entities, while contrast emphasizes differences

Illustration

Analogy	"Illustrative analogy is . . . a comparison between two different things or activities for the purpose of explanation" (p. 72).
Example	Illustration through a sample of typical or outstanding instances.

Sequence

Process	"Process is a series of connected instances, each developing from the preceding one, that result in something: a decision, a product, an effort or some kind" (p. 81).
Cause and effect	A sequence of events which is related in a causal chain.

Argument and persuasion

Deductive reasoning	An argument from generalities to particulars, where the conclusion necessarily follows from the premises.
Inductive reasoning	An argument from particulars to generalities. A given outcome may be "characterized as more or less probable depending on the strength of the evidence in relation to the conclusion" (p. 354).
Persuasion	A line of argument laid out so as to present the ideas in the most *convincing* manner. The correctness of the argument is not necessarily a criterion.

Functional

Introduction	An opening statement in which the author "will indicate a point of view and perhaps also [the] ways the subject is to be developed" (p. 246).
Transition	Establishes a framework for integrating prior information with forthcoming information. Emphasizes relationships among ideas or explains changes in theme.
Conclusion	Generally includes review of thematic material. Ties together any lines of thought left uncompleted.

SOURCE: R. Calfee and R. Curley, Structure of prose in the content areas. In J. Flood (Ed.), *Understanding reading comprehension* (Newark, DE: International Reading Association, 1984). Adapted from the work of G. Levin (1978). Reprinted by permission of the authors and The International Reading Association.

and (7) failure to use top-level structure has a more negative impact when the topic of the material is unfamiliar than when it is familiar (B. Meyer 1984).

B. Meyer (1984) suggested that the following steps be used in teaching pupils to use text organization or structure: (1) Ask the students to identify relationships (e.g., cause–effect) that occur in real-life situations; (2) explain how these relationships also are used to organize information in textbooks; (3) teach the pupil to look for signal words that explicitly signal relationships; (4) ask questions that encourage pupils to infer how ideas are interrelated; (5) teach pupils to ask themselves the same kinds of questions; and (6) provide guided practice. Well-organized text should be used at first; less well-organized material can be used after children become more proficient in the use of text structure.

Story Grammar and Story Schema

A story is a series of events related to one another in specified ways (Sadow 1982). Theorists have described the common components of a story and how these relate to one another. The resulting *story grammars* indicate that well-formed stories from Western cultures[8] have all or most of the following key elements: (1) setting (time, place, major characters); (2) an initiating event (the problem is identified); (3) the protagonist's reaction to the problem and his or her goal; (4) the protagonist's attempts(s) to achieve the goal; and (5) the resolution, or lack of resolution, of the problem. An example of a basic story structure is shown in Figure 13.5.

Hearing and reading stories enables children to develop a *story schema,*[9] which consists of an internal representation or general framework that includes a hierarchical ordering of story elements, with the basic components of a story being causally or temporally related (Rand 1984). As children mature, their concept of "story" becomes more sophisticated and more fully developed (Applebee 1978, Whaley 1981a, b). Kindergartners have a great deal of knowledge about stories, but children are unable to recall stories completely until about age 8 (Pellegrini & Galda 1982). Older pupils have better defined schemata for story than do younger children, but it still is not clear how and under what conditions this develops (Rand 1984).

Children use their story schemata as a framework for comprehending a story by setting up expectations for certain content occurring in a particular sequence. It also is believed to help them determine what information is most important in understanding a story so that they can focus their attention on those elements (McConaughy 1982). If the story being read does not conform to the reader's story schema, comprehension is likely to be decreased or seriously impaired (Calfee & Spector 1981). How easily a young child understands a story depends on how well formed the story is, but is also dependent on how well the social

[8] Japanese folktales differ significantly from the structure of Western stories (Matsuyama 1983).

[9] Gates (1947) stressed the value of "story sense" to comprehension almost 40 years ago. But not until fairly recently have story grammars been described and their influence on comprehension tested empirically.

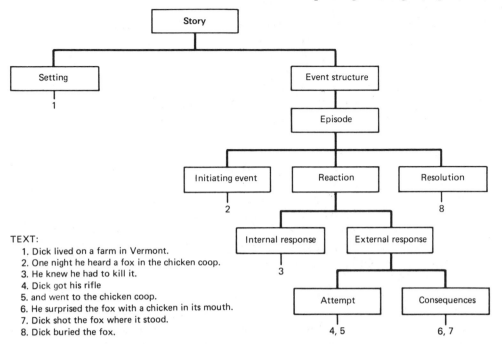

Figure 13.5. An example of a basic story structure. From R. Tierney, J. Mosenthal, and R. Kantor, Classroom applications of text analyses: toward improving text selection and use, in J. Flood (Ed.), *Promoting reading comprehension* (Newark, DE: International Reading Association, 1984). Reproduced with permission of the authors and the International Reading Association.

situations and interactions in the story are understood by the child (Stein & Trabasso 1981).

Research findings indicate that story grammar instruction does not necessarily improve the ability to comprehend stories. Pupils who already have a keen sense of story content and structure are not likely to benefit from such instruction, but it may help students who are poor comprehenders of narratives (Marshall 1983, Tierney & Cunningham 1984).

Suggestions for helping children develop or refine their story schemata and make use of them to aid their understanding of narratives have been offered by Rubin (1980a), Whaley (1981b), Beck and McKeown (1981), G. Fowler (1982), M. Smith and Bean (1983), and Gordon and Braun (1983). M. Olson (1984) presented guidelines for teaching children how to use a story grammar to write book reports.

General Procedures for Developing Reading Comprehension

Is Reading Comprehension Taught in the Schools?

When reading instruction was defined as explaining, illustrating, or questioning to clarify, extend, or raise the level of comprehension, observations of third- through sixth-grade classes indicated that reading comprehension instruction was rare (Durkin 1978–1979). Rather than teach relevant skills and strategies and help children understand how their application could facilitate reading comprehension, comprehension activities were found to consist mainly of assessing how well the reading material was understood and providing massive doses of often unguided practice in the form of completing workbook pages and duplicated exercises. Social studies lessons concentrated on acquiring the facts to be learned, with much oral reading by the good readers of text materials deemed too difficult for the poor readers. Hardly any effort was made to teach comprehension or study skills during these social studies periods. Similar findings were reported by Neilsen, Rennie, and Connell (1982). It would thus seem that in both reading and social studies periods the emphasis was on the *product*, rather than the *process*, of reading comprehension (Pearson 1984).

Durkin's study (1978–1979) has been criticized on methodological grounds by Heap (1982) and for its use of too narrow a definition of reading instruction. Using Durkin's data, but a broader definition of reading instruction, C. Hodges (1981) found that approximately 23% (as opposed to the much less than 1% reported by Durkin) of the reading period was devoted to the teaching of reading comprehension.

Analyses of basal reader manuals (Durkin 1981a, P. Johnston & Byrd 1983) have revealed that they provide little guidance to teachers in how to develop reading comprehension in children. Teacher's manuals devote far more attention to suggestions for assessing and practicing reading comprehension. On the other hand, D. Johnson and Barrett (1980) reported that some of the current thinking on reading comprehension had been translated into instructional terms in the basal reader manuals and teacher-education texts they examined.

That little has been done to teach reading comprehension is not surprising. Until fairly recently, very little has been known about the reading comprehension process that could be translated into instructional practices.

Teachers' Questions

Questioning children about what they have read is the most extensively used form of comprehension guidance (Beck & McKeown 1981). Comprehension questions can serve two purposes. First, they can be used to assess comprehension; this is by far their more common usage. Second, questions can be employed as an instructional device to help students clarify meaning or organize and integrate textual information. Questioning also can be a means for activating a reader's prior knowledge or helping the child make use of topical knowledge.

The kinds of questions posed by teachers may influence how children come to define reading (decoding vs. a meaning-getting process) as well as what they learn to consider as being important when they read (McGrade 1983). Repeatedly asking the same kinds of questions focuses students' attention on the text segments containing the information needed to answer the questions, and they learn to allocate their attention accordingly (Pearson 1982, 1984).

The kinds of comprehension practice pupils receive is largely determined by the kinds of comprehension questions asked of them. In most directed-reading activities, reading is usually preceded by a question that alerts the children to look for a main idea. At various points during the reading of the selection, the teacher may ask questions to determine whether the children have understood the material and may attempt to clear up any lack of comprehension or misunderstandings before reading continues. Or the teacher may pose a question that asks the pupils to predict what will happen next and then to read and check their hypotheses.

The questions found in basal reader manuals vary from series to series in the degree to which they emphasize literal comprehension or making inferences and judgments (Hare 1982a). The same is true of the workbooks and worksheets so frequently used in classrooms.

Some teachers prefer to formulate their own comprehension questions. But studies show that teachers' questions largely call for literal comprehension (Guszak 1966, 1967; Hare & Pulliam 1980; Raphael & Gavelek 1984). High reading groups are more likely to be asked questions calling for evaluation, explanation, or conjecture. Low reading groups are mainly asked recognition and recall questions. According to Medley (1977), this adjustment to pupil abilities is helpful to both the high and low reading groups. Others would contend that unless you ask high-level questions of poor readers, you will never raise their level of reading comprehension.

Literal comprehension is the simplest level of comprehension because it makes the least cognitive demands on the reader. There should be an equitable balance between literal and inferential questions. Literal comprehension questions may need to be asked because factual information is the main focus of the reading material (e.g., science material), and at times it is necessary to establish whether the child's inability to make an inference is based on his lack of literal comprehension. As Pearson (1982, 1984) pointed out, details are crucial to building a coherent representation of text.

Andre (1979) concluded that the use of higher-level questions facilitates reading comprehension. Winnie (1979), however, concluded that no study had documented that the use of higher cognitive questions actually promoted the assumed cognitive processes in pupils and that the literature suggested that whether teachers used predominantly higher cognitive or predominantly factual questions had little effect on school achievement.

Teachers have been observed to accept most of the answers they receive to their questions (McGrade 1983). When they follow up on unacceptable responses, teachers are likely to provide additional information or simply repeat the question. Providing additional information results in many more acceptable answers.

Ruddell (1978, p. 115) considered four kinds of questions to be most useful for developing comprehension. "*Focusing* enables the teacher to immediately establish a mental set, a purpose for reading. *Extending* allows the teacher to elicit additional information at the same comprehension level. *Clarifying* enables the teacher to encourage returning to a previous response for further clarification, explanation or redefinition. *Raising* allows the teacher to obtain additional information on the same subject but at a higher comprehension level."

Teachers are prone to allow very little time for children to think about their responses before answering a question. The evidence suggests that allowing children 5 seconds or more of "think time" results in higher-level thinking and an increase in appropriate responses (Gambrell 1980). Gambrell suggested that teachers should refrain from providing feedback immediately following a response because doing so cuts off children's thinking.

Suggestions for formulating and using comprehension questions may be found in Spiegel (1980), Pearson (1982, 1984), Lange (1982), Christenburg and Kelly (1983), McNeil (1984), and Ruddell (1984).

Teachers should remember that in order to answer the oral questions they pose, children must (1) understand the question; (2) remember the question; (3) determine where the information to the question may be found; (4) retrieve the information; and (5) have some criteria for determining when the obtained information is sufficient for answering the question adequately (Raphael & Gavelek 1984). In the *QAR procedure* developed by Raphael (1982a, b), children are taught to identify the kinds of information required to answer questions and the sources of that information—explicitly stated in the text, implicity indicated in the text, or primarily in one's knowledge base. Research has indicated that teaching the QAR strategy to students improved the quality of their answers to questions and was of most benefit to average and low-average students. Children in Grades 4 and 5 need 1 week of intensive training plus 6 to 8 weeks of practice. Only the week of training is needed by sixth graders, and a 10-minute orientation regarding the concepts is all that is necessary for older students to learn to employ the strategy (Raphael 1984).

Herber and Nelson (1975, 1984) stated that if students do not possess a particular reading skill, asking them questions that require the skill does not help them to learn it. They proposed a sequence in which the teacher at first gives students a statement (answer to a question) and the location of the supporting evidence, which the students have to identify; next step, statements without locations; third step, questions with locations where answers are given; fourth step, questions without locations; final step, students formulate their own questions.

Student-Generated Questions

Getting pupils to generate their own questions while reading can serve three useful purposes. First, it can place the responsibility for learning on the pupil. Formulating one's own questions while reading increases the student's active attention; and if the students find that they cannot answer their questions, they should be alerted to the need for taking some corrective action.

There are two kinds of student-generated questions (Raphael & Gavelek 1984). *Reflective questions* involve asking oneself how well previously read material was understood. Such questions could be asked of any material (e.g., Who are the main characters?) *Prospective questions* are more content specific and are generally of a predictive nature (e.g., "What is _____ trying to accomplish?"). Meichenbaum and Asarnow (1979) successfully taught children to carry on an internal dialogue to monitor their reading comprehension while reading.

H. Singer (1978, 1980a) recommended a sequence of steps to transfer the formulation of questions from teachers to pupils and provided a sample lesson to illustrate the process. Palinscar (1984) reported that an eight-step reciprocal teaching procedure (which is described in the article) significantly improved the reading comprehension of the students and that the effects of the training were durable. Student-generated questions are an integral part of the Directed Reading–Thinking Activity (Stauffer 1969) and the ReQuest procedure (Manzo 1969).

Reviewers differ in their conclusions regarding the value of student-generated questions. H. Singer (1981a) and Palinscar (1984) concluded that its value had been documented. But according to Bean (1983), the research regarding the effectiveness of self-questioning while reading was limited and the findings conflicting. T. Anderson and Armbruster (1984b) reported that three studies showed positive findings, and five studies indicated that the treatment was not effective.

The Placement of Questions

Questions may be posed before or after the material is read or while the material is being read. The basic assumptions underlying the use of prereading questions are that it provides the pupil with a purpose for reading, thereby helping to maintain attention, or that knowing what to look for facilitates comprehension. Research indicates that prequestions can have a facilitative effect *if* the material is difficult for the student and *if* the information on which the questions focus is important. The use of prequestions results in the acquisition of the information sought by the questions at the expense of other information in the text (Tierney & Cunningham 1984, Raphael & Gavelek 1984). Massed prequestions rarely enhance the learning of the desired information (Memory 1982).

Self-questioning while reading was discussed above. Providing students with questions during reading is a fairly common practice. Teachers frequently stop students and pose questions either to check on their understanding of previously read material or provide some guidance for what is about to be read. According to J. L. Vaughn (1982a), research findings consistently favor the use of inserted questions over pre- and postreading questions. However, Tierney and Cunningham (1984) stated that research findings generally confirm that inserted questions facilitate the recall of factual information, but when application of textual information is required, students perform better when they have to respond to both inserted and postquestions.

Postreading questions can serve as a measure of comprehension or as a means for organizing and interpreting what has just been read (Beck 1984). They can also serve as a summary. Research findings suggest that postquestions create the need for a review of the text and that this review strengthens recall (Raphael & Gavelek 1984). Different kinds of postquestions result in different kinds of processing. In general, higher-level questions result in a general review of the material; lower-order questions require only a review of the questioned information (Wixson 1984). When using postquestions, teachers typically provide feedback that lets the students know how well they have responded. In general, research supports this practice. Feedback following incorrect answers has the greatest impact on learning; but if the material is too difficult for the child, questioning and feedback are likely to have little value (Tierney & Cunningham 1984).

ReQuest

Manzo's ReQuest procedure (1969) is a form of reciprocal questioning. The teacher models questioning behavior, and as sections of the text are read silently the teacher and pupil(s) take turns asking and answering questions. A test of the effectiveness of ReQuest was inconclusive (Ankney & McClurg 1981).

Reciprocal teaching also may be used to foster reading comprehension. The teacher models appropriate comprehension activities, and the pupils participate at whatever level they can. The teacher assigns a segment of text (usually a paragraph) to be read. After it is read silently, the teacher summarizes the content, discusses and clarifies any points of difficulty, poses questions to check if comprehension took place, and then makes a prediction as to future content in the material. Later, students take the role of the teacher (L. Baker & Brown 1984b). Reciprocal teaching was used as the vehicle for successfully teaching comprehension-monitoring strategy to seventh-grade poor readers (Palincsar & Brown 1983).

Listening Comprehension

The correlation between reading and listening comprehension increases from .35 in first grade to about .60 in fourth grade and remains fairly constant thereafter (Sticht & James 1984). This change in relationship has led some to believe that once word recognition has been mastered, both reading and listening are controlled by very similar cognitive process. Others hold that different cognitive processes are required because of the large differences in grammar, vocabulary, and style between written and spoken language. The present data are insufficient to resolve the issue (Danks 1980). Nevertheless, a prevailing belief is that comprehension skills acquired in one mode should transfer to the other mode. Most frequently, the training occurs in the auditory mode because of the belief that aural comprehension skills are more advanced than reading comprehension skills.

Boodt (1984) found that a critical-listening program improved the ability of disabled readers to read critically, and Sticht and James (1984) stated that 10 of 12 studies reported a successful transfer of skills from auding to reading. Pearson and Fielding (1982, 1984) indicated that it was fairly safe to conclude that (1) direct instruction resulted in the improvement of specific listening comprehension skills at almost any age level, but there was not much transfer from one listening skill to another; and (2) after students became mature readers, whatever training benefited listening comprehension also benefited reading comprehension, and vice versa; but prior to that stage, transfer from one mode to the other was possible but less likely. P. Cunningham (1975) provided suggestions for helping children transfer comprehension skills from listening to reading. The differences between comprehending spoken and written language were enumerated on pages 14–16 and should be considered in any attempt to transfer any comprehension skill from listening to reading.

We are in firm agreement with those who suggest that schools should place more emphasis on developing listening comprehension. Even if its development did not improve reading comprehension, listening comprehension ability is important.

Cloze as an Instructional Tool

The use of cloze as a technique for helping children improve their reading comprehension skills is based on the belief that filling in the blanks forces the reader to process the information surrounding the deletion and that doing so requires very similar cognitive processes to those used in reading unmutilated text. Its use further assumes that the skills learned in completing cloze tasks will transfer to normal reading.

On the basis of a literature review, Jongsma (1980) concluded the following: (1) Cloze can be an effective teaching technique but is no more nor less effective than many other widely used instructional methods; (2) cloze is most effective in developing some comprehension skills and least effective in developing word-meaning knowledge; (3) there is no evidence that the cloze is more effective with narrative or expository text; (4) cloze is not more effective for any one age or grade level or for any level of reading ability; (5) although findings are mixed, cloze instruction is likely to be more effective when discussion is focused on clues that signal appropriate responses; (6) cloze materials that are carefully sequenced as to difficulty are more effective than undifferentiated exercises; (7) the quality of cloze instruction is more important than the length of the program; (8) there is no firm evidence regarding the minimum amount of instruction needed before cloze instruction is effective; (9) selective deletion systems aimed at particular contextual relationships are more effective than semirandom deletion systems; and (10) semantically acceptable responses should be encouraged (there is no need to demand exact word replacements for instructional purposes).

For further suggestions on using the cloze for instructional purposes, refer to Thomas (1978), Gunn and Elkins (1979, 1984), and McKenna and Robinson (1980).

Improving Reading Comprehension through Writing Activities

The author–reader relationship has been well described by Tierney and Pearson (1983) and Tierney et al. (1983). Basically, they stress that reading (comprehending text) and writing (authoring text) involve essentially similar processes in the construction and reconstruction of meaning.

The basic premise underlying most attempts to improve reading comprehension through writing is that expressing one's thoughts clearly in writing requires the ability to organize and relate information in an understandable manner. It is hoped that having to use such skills in writing will improve the pupil's ability to "read like a writer." There is only limited evidence that there is a transfer of skills between writing and reading.

Suggestions for using writing activities to develop reading comprehension can be found in Hennings (1982) and Sanacore (1983), as well as in some of the articles in Jensen (1984).

Illustrations and Imagery

Some reviewers (Grinnell 1982, O'Donnell 1983, McNeil 1984) have concluded that the evidence regarding the influence of illustrations on reading comprehension is generally inconclusive. Schallert (1980), however, concluded that illustrations are helpful in learning from text, especially if they represent spatial information or information important to the total message, and when information to be derived from pictures is explicitly repeated in the text. J. Levin (1981b) wrote that the effects of visual illustrations in books on children's comprehension of narratives are "positive, potent, and pervasive." He also concluded that illustrations may be facilitative in learning history and science, depending on the type of passage and kind of illustration. Levin believed that pictures were more likely to improve comprehension if they (1) made information more specific; (2) helped organize textual information; and (3) made difficult material more understandable.

J. Levin (1981b) stated that visual imagery (self-generated images in the mind) usually does not improve reading comprehension or recall and that when positive effects do occur, they are small or limited in generalizability. Tierney and Cunningham (1984) concurred with Levin. However, Levin did indicate that some pupils seem to profit substantially from visual imagery instruction. For example, it may be just the organizational strategy needed by students who have adequate word recognition but poor comprehension.

One of the problems with much of the research on imagery is the failure of the researcher to provide evidence that imagery actually occurred. A number of studies suggest that attempting to read and image at the same time presents difficulties for both children and adults and that reading may supress imagery. A study by Sadowski (1983), however, found that imagery seemed to occur in fifth graders who were reading in a natural situation and that reported imagery was positively related to reading comprehension.

Some children misinterpret illustrations and therefore receive information that hinders comprehension (O'Donnell 1983). Thus it would seem that teachers should monitor children's interpretation of illustrations and help them deal with contradictory information.

Line drawings are more effective than realistic illustrations in promoting reading comprehension (Rusted & Coltheart 1979, O'Donnell 1983). However, abstract or elaborate stylization may increase the task demands for identifying an important picture element (Beck 1984). The ability to learn from pictures increases with age (O'Donnell 1983).

Other Suggestions for Improving Reading Comprehension

For young children, acting out the events of a story produced better comprehension of basal reader selections than did use of the comprehension exercises in the basal reader workbooks (Henderson & Shanker 1978, Galda 1982b). Tharp (1982) described the KEEP program, which improved the reading comprehension of high-risk Hawaiian children, and Carlisle (1983) discussed the components of a reading comprehension program for middle school students. Another plan for developing comprehension is the Reflective Reading–Thinking

Activities used in the Junior Great Books program. The teacher starts with factual questions, proceeds to interpretative questions, and concludes with evaluative questions (Biskin, Hoskisson, & Modin 1976).

Refer to Roehler and Duffy (1982, 1984) and Mason, Roehler, and Duffy (1984) for a model of how to use direct instruction in the development of reading comprehension processes. Teaching strategies for improving reading comprehension also were suggested by Pearson and Johnson (1978), DuBois and Stice (1980), Eeds (1981), and Baumann (1983b)

Developing Specific Comprehension Skills

Although some doubt exists about the statistical independence of types of comprehension, there is evidence that specific practice tends to produce improved performance in the skill practiced. For example, fourth graders given systematic practice in following printed directions made more improvement in the following printed directions than a control group given regular basal reader instruction (Calder & Zalatimo 1970).

Such special practice will not work, however, if the material is so difficult that decoding the words, phrases, and sentences is a frustrating task. For the development of comprehension skills, it is essential to use materials that are within the pupil's instruction level.

There is not enough space in this chapter to discuss all the specific comprehension skills. A few of them are considered below.

Reading for Main Ideas or the Central Thought

One of the most valuable comprehension skills is the ability to find the main idea or central thought. To be able to select the most important thought from a mass of words calls for an ability to distinguish between essentials and nonessentials, between the most important idea and subordinate details. It is a form of reasoning that involves comparison and selection. It is not strange, therefore, that children of below-average intelligence often have more trouble with this kind of comprehension than they do in reading and understanding details.

Children are not particularly adept at understanding main ideas (Baumann 1982), but this is not surprising since sensitivity to gradation in the importance of ideas is very poor in novice readers and increases only gradually with reading experience (M. Adams 1980). L. McGee (1981) reported that fifth-grade good readers were better able to determine important textual information than were fifth-grade poor readers or third-grade good readers.

Activities that may help children select and understand main ideas include the following:

1. Have the pupils choose the most satisfactory title from two or more choices. At first, use short selections. Later they can be asked to make up their own titles, which is a more difficult task.
2. Ask pupils to find the main idea in paragraphs of expository material. The teacher and students must have the same understanding of what is meant by a main idea. There is clearly a difference between a topic

sentence, topic, theme, and so forth. If the pupils do not respond, they may be given two or more choices from which to select and the reasons for their choices discussed.

Pupils are often urged to find the topic sentence in a paragraph and told that it contains the main idea. Clear topic sentences are rare in general prose (Moore & Readence 1980), and they occur in less than half the paragraphs in social studies textbooks (Baumann & Serra 1984). When a paragraph does contain a topic sentence, it most often is the first or last sentence. Many paragraphs do not have topic sentences, so the main idea must be inferred.

After skill has been attained in finding the central thought in a single paragraph, similar activities can be used with increasingly longer selections.

3. Have the students write headlines for selections, as though they were preparing a newspaper article. Actual newspaper articles with their headlines removed can be used, and the children can compare their headlines to the originals.

4. Ask questions about and discuss what emotion was felt by the main story character during or after a significant incident in a narrative.

5. Request a one-sentence summary of a story event or later of the whole story.

6. Discuss the use of the headings, subheadings, marginal notes, introductory statements, and final summaries used by the authors of their textbooks.

7. Have readers pay special attention to introductory and summary paragraphs.

8. Have the students outline well-organized material. This and similar activities also can be used as informal measures of the children's sensitivity to the relative importance of ideas.

One of the most consistent research findings is that important text elements are more likely than less important ones to be learned and remembered. The selective-attention hypothesis (readers selectively attend to important elements) appears to be the most promising explanation for this finding (R. Anderson & Pearson 1984). The following is a simple version of this theory: (1) A gauge for judging the importance of upcoming text elements is provided by the schema to which the text is being assimilated, already processed text information, and an analysis of task demands; (2) as each text element is encountered, it is processed to some minimal level and then graded for importance; (3) extra attention is devoted to text elements that surpass a criterion of expectation; and (4) because of the attention they receive, important text elements are learned and remembered better than other text information.

Skimming to Get a Total Impression

Skimming involves superficial, rapid reading to get a general overall impression. Some of the situations in which skimming is useful are these:

1. Previewing a textbook chapter prior to serious study in order to get an idea of its general scope
2. Sampling a few pages to decide whether the material is worth reading
3. Going quickly through an article on a controversial issue to find the author's point of view, without bothering to note his specific arguments
4. Looking through reading material to judge if it is likely to contain the kind of information one is seeking
5. Examining reading material to decide if it is comprehensible

In this kind of skimming the reader must have a specific purpose. The teacher may suggest reading activities such as the following: "John, look this book over and let me know if you think you would enjoy reading it." "Phyllis, look over these three books and decide which one will help you most in your selection of an Indian legend that the class could make into a play." "Harold, look through the section on mining in this book to see if it is too hard for you to read." As with other reading skills, improved efficiency in this kind of reading comes gradually with motivated practice. One useful skimming technique involves reading only the first sentence of each paragraph while reading the introduction and conclusion or summary more carefully.

In one study (Kobasigawa, Ransom, & Holland 1980) virtually all the eighth graders but only two-thirds of the sixth graders and half the fourth graders were able to describe "how to skim." The pupils at all three grade levels could skim when explicitly instructed to do so, but skimming as a spontaneous strategy based on an implicit task assignment did not occur until eighth grade. D. McGee (1979) and Memory and Moore (1981) offered suggestions for developing skimming skills.

Reading to Note and Recall Details

In many reading situations it is just as important to note and remember significant details as it is to understand the main ideas. This is especially true in the functional reading called *study*, in which the purpose is to assimilate as thoroughly as possible the material presented by the author. Some pupils who are expert, rapid readers in fiction and who get the main thoughts easily in factual material seem to have little or no interest in details, do not notice them as they read, and cannot remember them later. Balanced training in reading should include practice in reading for details.

It is probable that in American education too much attention has been paid to details as such, standing alone and unrelated to the situations in which they have significance. This tendency is sometimes encouraged by teachers who make up tests consisting mainly of questions on minor points. A general fondness and esteem for the ability to recall isolated, unrelated bits of information is glorified in many TV quiz programs. Too many questions ask who, what, where, and when; too few questions call for meaning, significance, or analysis of relationships.

Ideally, children should be taught to see details in their relation to the major ideas they support. Details have many functions in expository material:

they provide concrete illustrations that make a generalization more meaningful; they provide evidence in support of a conclusion; or they show ways in which an idea can be applied. What is needed is not so much a disparagement of attention to details as encouragement of the ability to relate the details to the major ideas.

Some of the kinds of practice in noting and recalling details in reading are as follows:

1. In informal discussion after oral or silent reading, the main thought should first be discussed. Then attention can be called to the details by such questions as

   What are the ways in which this is shown?
   What evidence of the truth of this statement is presented?
   What applications of this idea are given?
   What are the places where this holds true?
2. An incomplete outline of a selection can be presented, with the main ideas filled in and blank spaces left for the details. After reading, the pupils complete the outline.
3. Straightforward questions about details also have their uses. Questions can be put in multiple-choice, completion, or short-answer form. The multiple-choice question is quicker to mark, but the other forms encourage a more attentive attitude while reading because they require recall rather than simple recognition.

Ability to Find Answers to Specific Questions

In many reading situations the pupil reads to find an answer to a specific question he has in mind. Sometimes the question requires careful reading and analytical reasoning; for example, reading to find out why oxygen is essential for combustion. In such reading the question provides point, purpose, and a way for the reader to determine if his reading was satisfactory: Does he have an answer? Children who have not had practice in reading to find answers to definite questions are likely to have difficulty in selecting the relevant from the irrelevant; even superior readers in the middle grades have difficulty in distinguishing between paragraphs that are helpful in providing information on a specific question and paragraphs that are somewhat related, but provide no information on that question. At times, therefore, questions should precede reading, and the reading should be for the purpose of answering those particular questions. Written or oral answers, followed by discussion, provide a means for judging success and correcting errors.

Scanning

One of the most important comprehension skills is the ability to skim rapidly over reading material. Two kinds of skimming can be distinguished (Fleming 1968). One kind involves rapid reading to find the answer to a very specific question, such as a name, a date, a telephone number, and so on. This is often called *scanning*.

Practice in learning how to scan for a specific item of information can be best provided through use of the kinds of material that are normally scanned in functional reading. Some questions to which answers are found by scanning are as follows:

1. What is the largest wheat-producing state?
2. What are the leading industries in Boston?
3. What is Mr. John X. Smith's telephone number?
4. At what theater is a particular moving picture playing?

To give practice in scanning, the teacher can prepare a list of questions based on the reading matter to be used. The questions should be presented to the pupils before they read the selection, and they should be encouraged to find the answers as quickly as possible and write them. After the pupils have finished, there can be discussion of the answers, with oral reading of the sentences that contain the answers, or the written answers can be collected and scored as a test. Material of many different sorts can be used. There is no reason why schools should not make use of such reading materials as daily newspapers and phone books for practice in skimming. Textbooks in the various content subjects can also be used to good effect.

Experts at scanning for specific information have developed a distinctive skill that is quite different from other reading. As they run their eyes rapidly over the material, they do not absorb the meaning but merely notice that what they are looking for is not there. When they come to the desired item, it seems to stand out as if in boldface type. Some people are able to achieve almost incredible speed in scanning.

Making Inferences

Inferencing refers to the application of reasoning ability to understand ideas or relationships that are not explicitly stated. Readers may either have to find a relationship between ideas or events expressed in the written text or they may have to fill in missing information necessary for making such connections (Trabasso 1981). As mentioned throughout this chapter, the reader often has to make inferences. The meaning of a word may need to be inferred, or the reader may have to infer what the author meant by a particular phrase or sentence.

The ability to make inferences requires (1) background knowledge; (2) vocabulary knowledge; (3) knowledge of text structure; (4) knowledge of social interactions and the motives behind human actions; and (5) knowledge of causal relationships. How the process of inferencing is accomplished is largely unknown (Trabasso 1981).

Inference training can have a positive effect on children's reading comprehension, but it takes time to develop inferential comprehension skills (E. Carr, Dewitz, & Patberg 1983). Techniques that focus on helping second graders make spontaneous connections between what they already know and what is in the text can help them make inferences, but the transfer to new situations is weak (Hansen 1981). Poor readers in the fourth grade tended to benefit more than good readers from a program designed to improve inferential comprehension; both groups scored higher than the control group on the postmeasure (Hansen & Pearson 1982). Suggestions for teaching inferencing in the primary grades were offered by K. Carr (1983), and Hansen and Hubbard (1984) described how to help poor readers learn to make inferences while reading. Holmes (1983a) related a procedure for helping poor readers improve their ability to answer inference questions. Older students draw more spontaneous inferences than do younger children, but the reason for this difference is not well understood (Pearson & Gallagher 1983).

Understanding Cause–Effect Relationships

Cause–effect statements may appear in single sentences or separate sentences. The relationship may be explicitly marked or have to be inferred. Either the cause or effect can come first, but usually the cause comes first in inferred statements. Cause–effect relations expressed through subject and predicate may be difficult for children to understand, especially if the passive form is used (e.g., Irene's inability to concentrate caused her to fail the test). Even when the relationship is marked, certain constructions seem to cause difficulty for children. For example, a construction with an "effect" marker (*so, then*, etc.) in the middle of a sentence is more difficult to comprehend because the reader must wait to be informed that the second clause is an effect (e.g., Bill left, so Zeb put down his rifle).

Other statements, similar to those of cause–effect, also create comprehension problems for pupils. These include *conditionals* (If I run fast [then] I will win; Unless I run fast, I will not win) and *concession*, which often indicates a lack of cause–effect (She wept, but she was not sad). Refer to Cronnell (1981) for further information on cause–effect statements.

Providing open-ended *why* questions that require pupils to identify the cause(s) in short paragraphs helped low-average but not good readers learn to understand such relationships better (Memory 1983a, b).

Reading to Follow a Sequence of Events

An essential part of the understanding of narrative material, whether fictional or historical, is the ability to note the sequence of events, to grasp the cause–effect relationships involved, and to anticipate the rest of the story. Practice in this kind of comprehension can be given in many ways, of which the following are examples:

1. The most effective and most natural procedure is to ask for a retelling of the story. Omissions of significant events, changes in the order of events, and misunderstandings can easily be noted and corrected through discussion and rereading.
2. As a group or class exercise following silent reading, the major events described in the selection can be listed in scrambled order on the board or in mimeographed form, and the pupils can be asked to number them in the order in which they happened, or to rewrite the list in correct order.

3. The habit of thinking ahead while reading, and trying to anticipate the story, can be developed by presenting brief unfinished stories and asking the pupils to make up a suitable ending for each, or to select the most plausible of several suggested endings. In a longer story, the teacher can stop at a critical point and ask the pupils what they think will happen next.

Refer to D. Baker (1982) for practical activities that can be used to develop sequence skills.

Following Printed Directions

One of the most important uses for reading in everyday life is to find out how to do things. People must rely more and more on printed directions and manuals of procedure. The auto mechanic with printed specifications for different makes and models, the surgeon reading an account of a new operation, the worker filling out a social security application—all need to be able to read carefully and accurately and to follow a series of directions precisely and in correct order. During World War II, the armed forces were able to train millions of men to become hundreds of different kinds of specialists largely because the men could teach themselves by following directions in printed manuals.

Practice in reading and following directions is best provided in relation to activities that children wish to carry out or skills that they want to learn. Many content-subject textbooks contain directions that can be used for reading practice. This is particularly true in arithmetic and science. Directions for handwork activities can also be used to good effect. If the task is one easily corrected or repeated, the children can attempt to carry it out with no preliminary discussion, and the teacher can judge by the results whether the directions were properly read. If the task is a long one or involves expensive materials, it is desirable first to discuss the directions and clarify any misconceptions through rereading and further discussion.

Many different sources of material can be used. Children like to work on directions from the *Scout Handbook,* magazines like *Popular Mechanics,* books such as *How to Make Toys,* directions for performing scientific experiments, and so on. Or they can be interested in cooking recipes and directions for sewing, playing a game, making marionettes, and the like. When additional practice in following directions seems to be needed, workbook exercises can be employed.

Written directions can provide unique problems for children. There are often no explicit links between the steps, and directions often contain telegraphic sentences, implied procedures, and abbreviations. Teachers can help students learn to read directions by asking questions that both focus on the unique characteristics of directions and provide information that facilitates comprehension. Marshall (1984) has provided suggestions for doing so. Other useful suggestions may be found in A. Wolf (1982).

Grasping the Author's Plan

Good writing is organized writing, in which the author starts with something he wants to say, thinks out the sequence, relative importance, and interrelatedness of the specific ideas he intends to convey, and plans his exposition accordingly. In fiction there are characters to be introduced, a setting to be described, and a line of action that, if well planned, leads up to a climax. In informational or factual writing there are usually an introduction, a body, and a conclusion or summary. There are differences between exposition and argument, between writing intended to inform and writing intended to persuade. The particular pattern a writer uses can vary greatly, but in well-written material the pattern should be discernible.

In books written for children, many clues are provided and can be used to discover the author's plan. A chapter may start with an overview and end with summary and questions for application. In between there are headings, subheadings, material in bold type, marginal notes, and so on, which help the reader to determine what a particular section is about. Although the utility of these devices seems obvious and the purpose clear, many children need specific guidance in how to used these aids.

Development of Critical Reading Ability

An important kind of critical reading involves comparison of two or more sources of information. Children are usually amazed when they first find two authorities contradicting each other. An experience like that can serve as a preliminary to discussion of such questions as the reputation and prestige of each author, his impartiality or bias, the comparative recency of the two sources, and so on. Reading experiences of this sort develop naturally when children do wide reading to find data on a problem. The teacher should be alert and should make use of such occasions as steppingstones toward a more mature attitude on the credibility of reading matter. In the study of current events, comparison of the treatment of an event by two newspapers or magazines of opposing points of view can form an effective point of departure.

A second kind of critical reading involves considering new ideas or information in the light of one's previous knowledge and beliefs. The thoughtful reader asks himself, Is it reasonable? Is it possible? He does not, of course, automatically reject the unfamiliar idea or challenging conclusion. But he becomes doubly alert when he finds disagreements with what he has previously accepted as true.

One of the most important aspects of critical reading is the ability to detect and resist the influences of undesirable propaganda. In recent years, the molding of public opinion has become tremendously important in political and social affairs. While the term *propaganda* has sometimes been defined to include all activities intended to influence people in a given direction, concern has been centered mainly on attempts to persuade people to believe or act in a biased fashion.

There is reason to believe that teachers, by the kinds of discussions they lead, influence the degree to which children read critically (Davidson 1967). It is not easy, however, for teachers to change their established personal habits of questioning, especially when it comes to critical reading (Wolf, King, & Huck 1968).

Refer to the following for teaching suggestions regarding the indicated topics: propaganda analysis (A. J. Harris & Sipay 1979); use of advertisements to teach critical reading (Tutolo 1981); checking the reliability of a source of information (E. Ross 1981); distinguishing fact from opinion, identifying bias and slant (Hillerich 1980a, b); and judging the authenticity and accuracy of fictionalized biographies (Storey 1982).

Encouraging Creativity in Reading

Creative readig may be described as going beyond understanding of reading matter to arrive at new ideas or conclusions. The encouragement of creativity has been a major goal for some psychologists and educators in recent years. They contrast convergent thinking (arriving at a specific correct answer) with divergent thinking (in which the individual can develop alternative answers, none of which is incorrect); divergent thinking is a synonym for creative thinking.

Reading teachers can encourage creative by a number of procedures. Some of them are as follows:

1. Stop the children at a given point in the story and ask each one to think of an ending for the story. Compare the endings developed with one another and with the one provided by the author.
2. After finishing a story, ask children to devise endings for it that are different from the author's ending. Let each child devise as many different endings as he can.
3. Ask children to use the plot of a given story but to change the setting to a different time and place. What changes will have to be made?
4. Stop a story at a given point and change a specific event (e.g., a character finds money instead of losing it). How will this change the rest of the story?

Procedures such as the ones just described can enliven the reading period and provide needed practice in applying creative thinking to reading. Other ideas for developing creativity through reading were discussed by Martin, Cramond, and Safter (1982).

Poor Comprehension Resulting from Inappropriate Rate

Comprehension may suffer when the rate of reading is either too fast or too slow. Some inaccurate readers need to be temporarily slowed down until they reach a satisfactory standard of accuracy; when that result has been attained, they can gradually speed up again while maintaining the newly achieved precision. Some very slow readers do poorly in comprehension because their many repetitions and hesitations break up the continuity of thought. The relation between rate and comprehension, and the procedures that are effective in coordinating them, are treated in detail in Chapter 14. For practice materials, timed reading exercises with thorough comprehension checks are usually desirable.

Poor Concentration

The inability to concentrate on the meaning of what one is reading is a frequent cause of poor comprehension. But inability to concentrate is not an explanation for poor reading comprehension; it is iteslf a result of causes. The individual is unable to adjust to the requirements of the reading situation. Before taking practical measures, one should try to find out what makes it difficult for the person to concentrate. The causes will usually be found in the answers to one or more of the following questions:

1. Does the person suffer from eyestrain? Eyestrain is a frequent and often unsuspected cause of concentration difficulties. Examination by an eye specialist is a desirable routine procedure.
2. Is the pupil physically below par? Many physical conditions lower vitality and impair the ability to exert effort.
3. Is the student generally overworked? Accumulating fatigue resulting from an effort to carry too heavy a load may bring on a decline in ability to concentrate.
4. Is the material the child is trying to read much too difficult or much too easy? Providing material of more suitable difficulty may improve concentration.
5. Is the pupil interested in what he is trying to read? A marked improvement in concentration sometimes occurs when more interesting material is provided.
6. Does the pupil read in suitable physical conditions? For most efficient reading, one should sit upright or bending slightly forward in a straight-backed chair, with good, glareless lighting, in surroundings free from distracting sights and sounds. While some people can read well in unfavorable surroundings, poor readers should give themselves the benefit of good working conditions.
7. Do other thoughts keep running through the reader's mind? One's attention can be focused well on only one thing at a time. To read well, one must be able to exclude other thoughts for the time being. When questioning discloses that the reader's mind runs off on other things when he or she is supposed to be reading, one has to try to determine whether this is a superficial habit that can be broken or a symptom of a deep-lying emotional difficulty that needs expert treatment.

In helping a child to develop better concentration, it is sometimes desirable to start with very small units. For example, 2 or 3 minutes of intensive silent reading are followed by discussion of the meaning of the material and then a brief period of relaxation before another practice exercise is tried. For work of this type, exercises such as are found in *Standard Test Lessons in Reading* (Teachers) can be used to good advantage. When proficiency is attained in handling brief assignments, longer selections can be introduced gradually.

Remembering What One Has Read
Children and adults complain that they understand what they read when they read it, but cannot remember it later. This is a serious complaint and one that deserves careful consideration.

There are, of course, large individual differences both in speed of assimilation and permanence of retention. Some people have naturally better memories than others. However, the correct application of known and generally accepted principles of learning would enable most of these complainers to remember what they read far better than they do at present.

The principles listed below are not original but can be found in almost every textbook of educational psychology.

1. Material is easy to remember in proportion as it is meaningful. It is very difficult to recall ideas that have been only partially understood.
2. Material that is well organized in the reader's mind is easier to remember than material that is unorganized. The efficient reader tries to grasp the author's plan and understand the relationships between ideas and the relations between the major ideas and the facts or details that give them definite meaning.
3. Many people are aided in remembering what they read by outlining, summarizing, or taking notes as they read. Others obtain similar benefits from underlining significant points or writing comments in the margin.
4. An active intention to remember is an aid to recall. When one is determined to remember, one's attention seems better concentrated and one tends to read more effectively.
5. Recall should be selective. One cannot hope to remember everything one reads. The points that one really wants to remember should be singled out for special attention.
6. A single reading is rarely enough. Most people have to do some reviewing and rereading if they want to remember for any length of time.
7. After reading, one should try to recall the points worth remembering and recite them to oneself. If there is time, it is desirable to check one's recall by rereading and then reciting again. At least half the time spent (after the first reading) in trying to fix the material in memory should be spent in active recitation. Omission of this procedure is one of the most frequent errors of those who complain about their poor memories.
8. What we learn but never review or use is gradually forgotten. What we really want to remember must be refreshed by review from time to time.

Poor memory for what one has read, then, results from unselective, passive reading in the first place, followed by an overoptimistic failure to review and recite to oneself the points one wishes to remember. Both of these major faults are correctible.

Some teachers encourage reading without the intent to recall by the kinds of reading practice they give and the kinds of questions they ask. In most workbook exercises, the child is free to look back into the material if he cannot remember the answer. Unless some practice is given in answering questions with the book closed or the page covered, the child may become excessively dependent on rereading. He may also learn to read the questions first and then read for the answers, a desirable procedure in many situations, but not suitable when one is trying to stimulate the ability to recall. Excessive reliance on multiple-choice or true–false questions may also be harmful to recall, since such questions require only recognition of the correct answer, and pupils may become quite skillful at recognizing what they cannot remember. It is therefore important to ask recall questions and provide at least some practice in reading with the intent to reproduce the gist of the material.

Elaboration

Elaboration refers to the formation of a relationship between previously learned information and new, unfamiliar material by means of mental images (as in the Keyword method, see p. 452) or verbal elaborations such as inferences and analogies. The attempt is to make the information more memorable by embellishing what is presented in the text. For example, "The woman bought the food" could be elaborated by thinking that the woman must have been very kind because she was buying the food for a hungry child. Only precise information will facilitate comprehension and recall. For further information on elaboration, refer to Bransford, Stein, and Vye (1982); R. Anderson, Mason, and Shirley (1983); and Bransford, Vye, and Stein (1984). See Reder (1980) for a critical review of the research on the role of elaboration in the comprehension and retention of information. Three studies dealing with elaboration as a study technique have produced mixed findings (T. Anderson & Armbruster 1984b).

14

Learning through Reading and Learning to Read Rapidly and Flexibly

This chapter considers two related topics. The first section deals with how to help children learn from written text. Studying is defined, the variables that affect studying are discussed, and ways of helping children learn from their textbooks are presented.

The second part of this chapter is devoted to improving the ability of pupils to read rapidly and flexibly. Subsections consider the relationship of rate and comprehension, eye movements, eliminating behaviors that reduce reading rate, and increasing reading rate through direct practice.

I. HELPING STUDENTS LEARN THROUGH READING: STUDYING

Studying is a special form of reading.[1] It differs from other forms of reading in that students are expected to learn something specific that they will have to apply to a test or discussion (T. Anderson 1980). The outcomes of studying are a function of the interaction between status variables (the status of the student and the reading material) and processing variables. Student status variables include the reader's knowledge of the criterion task, topical knowledge, and mo-

[1] Unless otherwise indicated, this section was based on T. Anderson & Armbruster (1984b).

509

tivation. Among the important text variables are the organization or structure of the text, other features that affect its comprehensibility, and the content covered. Processing variables include the initial focusing of attention, encoding the information to which attention is directed, and the retrieval of the information as required by the criterion task. The variables not covered elsewhere in this book are briefly discussed next.

Knowledge of the Criterion Task

The underlying assumption is that the better students understand what needs to be known in order to perform a task successfully (e.g., pass a test, participate in a discussion) prior to reading, the more likely they will be to spend more time and effect on relevant segments of text, and therefore the better they will learn. This belief is generally supported by research; however, knowledge of the criterion task will not affect performance unless students adjust their study strategies.

Processing Variables

In order to learn, students must understand the material and assimilate the new information into their existing knowledge. The processing demands required by this can be quite heavy. For instance, it is not unusual for a page of expository text to contain at least 50 idea units that could be interrelated in a vast number of ways. Students cannot, nor should they, attempt to remember everything or even most of the information found in textbooks and related materials. Therefore, one of the primary tasks in studying is to focus attention on the important information and ensure that these ideas are well understood and likely to be remembered.

Focusing Attention

The little research available suggests that there is a positive relationship between the amount of time spent on important text segments and measures of achievement. It is not clear, however, whether this behavior is a cause or an effect. That is, do good comprehenders know what is important, or does knowing what is important make one a good comprehender?

Encoding Activities

Performance of school-related learning tasks is determined by the extent that students attend to, interact with, and elaborate on the underlying meaning of the text. Students can and do engage in activities believed to help them comprehend and remember information. Research, however, has failed to confirm many of the purported benefits of commonly used studying techniques. No particular studying strategy has been shown to be superior to others. But good students know when to employ deep-processing strategies and when not to. Their purpose for reading dictates whether skimming will suffice or whether reading in depth is required (Pauk 1982). They also know whether their comprehension is adequate. Instruction in studying strategies is most effective when it includes training in metacognitive skills. Metacognition is discussed below.

Almost any study technique can be effective if its use is accompanied by focused attention and encoding of information in a form and manner compatible with the requirements of the criterion task. Some techniques, however, have a greater potential for promoting the deep processing suited to criterion tasks that require greater comprehension and/or recall. These include outlining, networking, mapping, and schematizing, which all force the student to identify the relative importance of information and the relationships within that information. Such study procedures probably yield the highest benefits, but they also entail the greatest cost in time and effort.

The prime comprehension-fostering activities (and cognitive activities in which good readers engage) include (1) clarifying the purposes for reading (understanding the explicit and implicit task demands); (2) setting goals; (3) activating relevant prior knowledge; (4) allocating attention to important information; (5) critically evaluating the text content for internal consistency and for compatibility with prior knowledge and common sense; (6) monitoring ongoing activities to determine how well comprehension is occurring (the goals are being met); and (7) applying necessary "fix up" strategies (Palinscar & Brown 1983, Tierney & Cunningham 1984). These activities are important for reading in general, but their importance increases when studying.

Appropriate instruction can help students acquire, and learn to apply independently, reading strategies that will enhance reading comprehension. In such instruction, the strategies are carefully defined, the strategies are modeled for the students, ample guided instruction and feedback are provided, and students are encouraged and allowed to practice the strategies on their own. A useful instructional cycle involves explanation, guided practice, corrective feedback, independent practice, and application (Pearson & Gallagher 1983).

Before a content-subject lesson, teachers need to decide the kind and amount of prereading instruction or assistance to provide. After the lesson, they must decide which types of questions to ask and of whom, which application activities are called for, and how much time should be spent in review (Frager 1984). In planning the lesson teachers also must decide if what they want the students to learn differs from what the author thinks is important. If so, teachers must employ techniques that will direct the students to what they consider to be important.

The status of the teaching of reading and study skills in the classroom appears to be at the same low level as the teaching of reading comprehension in general (see pp. 489–490). The main purpose for content-subject lessons is "getting the content from the book into the pupil's heads." The most common practices are (1) round-robin oral reading of about a textbook page by a student (usually a good reader), which is interspersed by numerous low-level questions by the teacher; (2) the students read a textbook chapter on their own, followed by teacher questions, the answers to which are equally as likely to require prior knowledge, picture or illustration interpretation, or recall of isolated details; and (3) after the students read the text, the teacher paraphrases it for them, emphasizing what is important to remember. The universal justification for such practices is that most of the students cannot read the text, so something must be done to help them acquire the information. Few teachers teach children how to read their textbooks (Pearson & Gallagher 1983).

Instructional and Learning Activities

There are a number of activities that teachers can use to help students learn from text, many of which also can be used by students as self-directed strategies. A number of these are described below. They are divided into prereading, during-reading, and postreading activities, but some may be used at various times.

Prereading Activities

The major purpose for prereading activities is to increase the probability that the reading material will be understood by the pupils. Prereading activities may be grouped into general study strategies, procedures for relating prior knowledge to upcoming textual information, and graphic representations; these activities are not mutually exclusive.

General Study Procedures

The five-step SQ3R procedure (F. P. Robinson 1970) is widely used. *Survey* involves quickly reading the table of contents, the introductory and summary paragraphs, the headings and side headings, marginal notes, and pictorial aids. The purpose is to obtain an overview of the author's purpose(s) and the structure used to transmit that message. It should also serve to activate topical knowledge. *Question* means to turn each heading and side heading into a question before that section is read; where such typographical aids are not present, the topic sentence may be used. Generating questions provides a purpose for reading, helps readers focus their attention, and supplies a means for self-monitoring comprehension. *Reading* must be an active process in which the reader relates what he or she already knows to textual information in order to answer the questions. Care must be taken, however, not to overlook any important information not covered by the self-generated questions. *Recite* means stating the obtained information to yourself, subvocally, or in some more permanent form such as underlining, note taking, or informal outlining. Recitation allows one to check how well the material was understood and recalled, and may suggest the need to reread. Understanding can be checked by expressing the author's ideas in one's own words. This immediate review helps to store the information in memory. Written forms of recitation require the pupil to determine the relative importance of information and organize it in some fashion that can be used later as a review. *Review* involves spending appropriate amounts of time to go over the material immediately after reading and at appropriate intervals thereafter. The review not only helps to retain information over time but also provides a continual check as to how well the material is still understood.

The SQ3R procedure seems well grounded in the psychology of learning; and as indicated above, it can accommodate many of the more recent ideas on cognition and metacognition. It has not, however, been subjected to much careful empirical scrutiny (J. L. Vaughn 1982). Johns and McNamara (1980) cited six studies that found the SQ3R method to be as effective as, but no more effective than, other studying procedures. A. Adams, Carnine, and Gersten (1982) reported a study in which fifth graders who were taught a modified SQ3R method for 4 days scored higher than a control group on short-answer questions involving factual information. The two groups did not differ in their retellings.

A number of minor modifications of the SQ3R have been developed. Pauk (1962) proposed an OK4R system: Overview, determine Key Ideas, Read, Recall, Reflect, and Review. More recently, Pauk (1984) suggested an SQ4R technique: Survey to get started, Question to focus attention, Read with concentration, Record by taking succinct notes, Recite by covering the whole page except for your marginal notes and then reciting aloud using the notes as a cue, and Reflect by thinking about the information. G. Powell and Zalud (1982) described an adaptation for use with older poor readers. It uses a worksheet that the students complete. A S2RAT technique was developed by J. Lange (1983), and a PQ5R study method was proposed by Graham and Robinson (1984).

PReP is a three-step study procedure developed by Langer (1981, 1982). First, the students free-associate with key words, phrases, or pictures from the text. This serves to activate relevant prior knowledge and allows the teacher to assess the extent of that prior knowledge and thereby judge the need for establishing additional background knowledge before having the pupils read the material. This first step is similar to the *brainstorming* technique discussed by H. A. Robinson and Schatzberg (1984) and Tierney, Mosenthal, and Kantor (1984). Next, the teacher encourages the students to reflect on their initial associations by asking such questions as "What made you think of _____?" This allows the students to become aware of their network of associations and to evaluate and monitor the adequacy of their topical knowledge. Lastly, the students are encouraged to reformulate their ideas by questions such as "Based on our discussion, what new ideas do you have?" The PReP activity has been shown to help increase the comprehension of a particular text (Langer 1984).

Another instructional technique involves presenting the students with clearly stated objectives before they read. The assumption is that knowing what one is expected to learn and how that learning will be assessed will allow a pupil to study more systematically. Just as with prequestions, objectives seem to focus the students' attention on the targeted information but have a negative effect on the acquisition of untargeted information (Tierney & Cunningham 1984). The influence of objectives on the acquisition of targeted information decreases as the reading material increases in length, and objectives are less effective than prequestions (Klauer 1984).

Procedures to Relate Prior Knowledge to New Information

The most likely known activity in which attempts are made to get children to relate prior knowledge and new information is the Directed Reading–Thinking Activity (Stauffer 1969). Preteaching of the meanings of key vocabulary items also may serve to activate prior knowledge.

Advance organizers are short introductory passages intended to facilitate learning. They are based on Ausubel's theory (1960), which holds that "cognitive structure is highly organized in terms of highly inclusive concepts under which are assumed less inclusive subconcepts and informational data." In other words, knowledge is organized hierarchically. Ausubel's theory is generally consistent with schema theory (Ausubel 1980) in that it assumes that new information is learned and retained to the extent that it can be related to one's existing cognitive structure. The function of advance organizers is to encourage the development of the ideational or organizational framework needed to facilitate comprehension and learning (C. Clark & Bean 1982).

Most studies of the effectiveness of advance organizers have used college students. High school students have been used occasionally; elementary school children, rarely. Since 1975, there have been at least seven literature reviews, but their conclusions have differed widely. About all that one can safely say about advance organizers is that they tend to help some readers, but their effects vary (Pearson & Gallagher 1983). An even less positive conclusion was rendered by Tierney and Cunningham (1984). The most comprehensive of the reviews, a meta-analysis of 135 studies (Luiten, Ames, & Acherson 1980), indicated that the average advance organizer study shows a small but facilitative effect on learning and retention of content-subject material and with pupils of all grade and ability levels (although they are generally more beneficial to lower-ability students). The short duration of many of the studies (one or two class periods) may have contributed to the small treatment effects. Other possible explanations are that the advance organizers used in the studies did not assist the pupils to relate new information to existing knowledge or that the pupils already had the knowledge developed by the advance organizer (Jenkins & Pany 1981). It would seem that a single advance organizer may not be appropriate for use with a group simply because of wide individual differences in prior knowledge, reading ability, and reasoning ability. The major problems seem to be the lack of a clearly specified definition of an advance organizer and the global nature of the questions researchers have tended to ask (Tierney & Cunningham 1984). Mayer (1979) provided a checklist that may be used to produce effective advance organizers.

A technique that combines pre- and postreading activities involves having students predict the contents of the material (from various cues presented by the teacher) and then having the pupils evaluate their predictions after they have read the material (J. Nichols 1983, K. Wood & Robinson 1983). This procedure seems best suited for use with narratives. The construction and use of an *anticipation guide* may be found in Herber (1978); Moore, Readence, and Rickelman (1982); and K. Wood and Mateja (1983). Unlike the typical study guide, in this method students are asked to react to statements, not all of which are supported by the text.

Thelen (1982) presented a procedure that combines the format of a structured overview (see below) and a model of concept attainment. It is designed to help guide students to organize their prior knowledge into a conceptual framework, to fill in informational gaps in the student's background knowledge, and to blend past experiences with the new content.

Graphic Representations
Graphic representations attempt to depict key concepts and their relationships visually. As a prereading activity, their purpose is to help students com-

prehend the material by clarifying new ideas and indicating the structure of the text. As a postreading activity, they can serve to help students learn to organize textual information, and the finished product can be used as a review aid. When used before reading, graphic representation is a teacher-directed activity, although pupils may participate. When employed after reading, the students may play a major or independent role in their construction. In either case, the hope is that the graphic representations and the accompanying discussions will help students acquire comprehension skills that will transfer to new situations. There is some belief that diagrammatic representations transform the information into a symbolic representation that more closely represents the way in which knowledge is stored in memory and thus make it easier to activate prior knowledge and incorporate new information into existing knowledge (T. Anderson & Armbruster 1984). The following are examples of the various graphic organizers currently in use.

A *structured overview* (Herber 1978, Vacca 1981) attempts to provide cognitive readiness by presenting key terms in a schematic diagram that conveys their relationship (see Fig. 14.1). The vocabulary is taught and the relationships among the concepts are discussed (Readence & Moore 1979). Research findings suggest that structured overviews are effective under certain conditions with certain students. In general, students with high Verbal IQs seem to benefit the most (Tierney & Cunningham 1984), and the overviews appear to be more effective when the students participate in their construction (J. L. Vaughn 1982). Studies have not adequately addressed the influence of the quality of structured overviews.

Mapping (see Fig. 14.2) involves visually displaying key textual concepts so that the relationships among them are made explicit. Differing symbols and shapes can be used to demonstrate how the ideas are linked to each other and also to show the organizational pattern of the text (Armbruster & Anderson 1982). The cognitive maps can take a variety of shapes and designs, but usually the information is arranged in hierarchical order, and words are kept to a minimum. Mapping procedures also have been described and illustrated by Ryder (1982), J. Davidson (1982), Atwood and Malena (1984), and McNeil (1984). Studies have revealed only modest transfer effects, but mapping has been shown to be more effective than rereading and note taking (Pearson & Gallagher 1983, Tierney & Cunningham 1984).

Webbing is a graphic way of showing the important relationships that define the text structure (see Fig. 14.3). At the center of the web is the topic or main idea (selected by the teacher), and its spokes contain the related ideas (generated by the pupils). The procedure can be used to demonstrate or identify specific text (rhetorical) structures such as cause–effect (Clewell & Haidemenos 1983). The web also may contain "*strand ties*," which depict the relationships between and among strands. Webbing procedures also can be found in Widomski (1983). Friedman and Reynolds (1980) illustrated the use of webbing with basal reader stories.

In *pyramiding*, the levels of information (main ideas, middle-level ideas, specific details) are shown graphically. Pyramiding can be used to illustrate

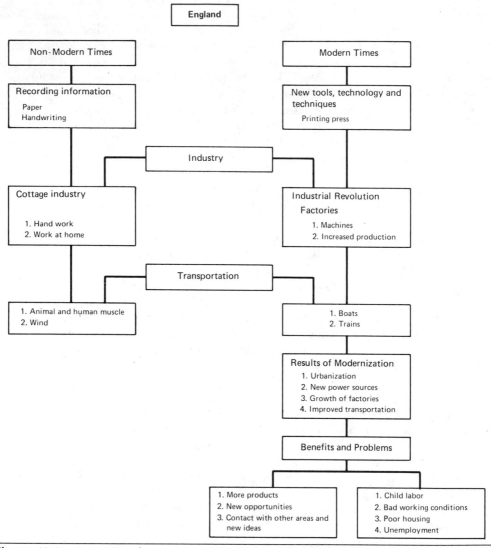

Figure 14.1. A structured overview. From E. Carr, P. Dewitz, and J. Patberg, The effect of inference training on children's comprehension of expository text, *Journal of Reading Behavior* 1983, *15,* 3. Reprinted by permission of the authors and the National Reading Conference.

superordinate and subordinate information, to help students become more sensitive to the relative importance of information, as a review of content, and to prepare students for learning to outline or to take notes (Clewell & Haidemenos 1983).

Other prereading activities may be found in Holbrook (1984) and in Moore, Readence, and Rickelman (1982), who also offered guidelines for selecting the most appropriate activity for a particular purpose.

Reading selection

The snake plant is very easy to grow. It has erect long leaves that grow 12"–18" tall. It is usually dark green with bands of light green. One variety has a gold band.

The snake plant is easy to take care of. It will grow in any part of the home that has a window. Don't water it a lot. It should be kept dry. It grows in soil of loam, sand, and peat moss. To propagate the snake plant, divide clumps of older plants or take leaf cuttings.

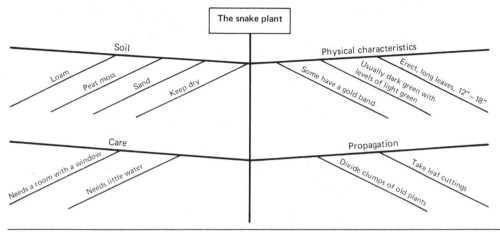

Figure 14.2. An example of mapping. From P. Gold, Cognitive mapping, *Academic Therapy*, January 1984, *19*. Reprinted by permission of the author and *Academic Therapy*.

During-Reading Activities

A *study guide* is a teaching aid prepared by the teacher and used by students. Its purpose is twofold: to facilitate the student's comprehension of the text, and to develop comprehension skills. It is usually a typewritten copy, keyed to the textbook, that can be placed beside the textbook and referred to while studying. The study guide identifies a reading task and presents a plan or strategy for the student to follow. The assumption is that comprehension will be enhanced when the directions that stipulate goals are in clear proximity to the textual material containing the relevant information (Tutolo 1977, 1984). Other suggestions for developing and using study guides can be found in Herber (1978), McClain (1981) and M. Olson and Longion (1982). Few studies have evaluated the effectiveness of study guides, but the available evidence generally suggests they facilitate comprehension (J. L. Vaughn 1982, Tierney & Cunningham 1984).

Because students do not often apply skills learned in isolation, Otto, White, and Camperell (1980) developed the *gloss* procedure. It uses marginal and other notations to tell the students how to apply specific skills and strategies. Gloss directs the students' attention to places in the text where certain kinds of thinking would facilitate comprehension. The dual focus on content and process acts as a guide for integrating new with known information. A detailed description of the technique and examples of gloss appear in Otto *et al.* (1981), and guidelines for preparing gloss may be found in Richgels and Hansen (1984) and Richgels and Mateja (1984). An example of gloss is shown in Figure 14.4.

A *Guide-o-Rama* can be used to help students process major points in a text by highlighting significant ideas (K. Wood & Mateja 1983).

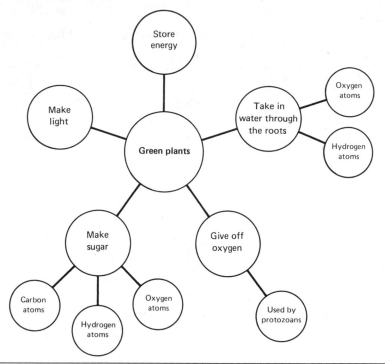

Figure 14.3.   An example of webbing. From S. Clewell and J. Haidemos, Organizational strategies to increase comprehension, *Reading World*, May 1983. Reproduced by permission of the authors and the College Reading Association.

Postreading Activities

Summarizations

In today's elementary schools, summarizing occurs as part of the reading program from the first grade on. Each experience story is a little summary. In planning a unit or project, the results of class discussion are often summarized on charts. When they reach the higher grades, these children are familiar with the concept of an organized summary. This makes it easier to teach them to apply the concept in studying.

A. Brown, Campione, and Day (1981) identified six rules essential to summarization: (1) delete unnecessary or trivial information; (2) delete material that is important but redundant; (3) substitute a superordinate term for a list of items (e.g., *pets* for *cats, dogs, goldfish,* etc.); (4) substitute a superordinate term for the components of an action (e.g., "Carol went to New York" for "Carol left the house. She got on the bus, etc."); (5) select a topic sentence; and (6) invent a topic sentence if one is not given. Children are able to use the two deletion rules (Rules 1 and 2) at a relatively early age, but fifth and seventh graders have problems with the generalization and integration rules (Rules 3 and 4) and with the topic-sentences rule (Rule 5). The invention rule (Rule 6) is the last to develop and is the most difficult to apply even for junior college students (A. Brown & Day 1983).

Gloss	Text
1. Notice that the topic of this passage is given in the heading and by the bold print word *oxidation*. You need to find out what oxidation is.	21:1 Oxidation (a)

The term *oxidation* was first applied (b) to the combining of oxygen with other elements. There were many known |
| 2. This sentence gives you a defintion of oxidation. Oxidation is _____ . But notice the word *first*—there must be a second or later definition of oxidation. | instances of this. Iron rusts and   (c) carbon burns. In rusting, oxygen combines slowly with iron to form Fe_2O_3. In burning, oxygen unites rapidly with carbon to form CO_2. Observations of these reactions gave |
| 3. The final, better definition is going to be similar to the first, but that means that it will not be exactly the same, but also what is changed in the later definition of oxidation. | rise to the terms "slow" and "rapid" oxidation.

Chemists recognize, however, that   (d) other nonmetallic elements unite with substances in a manner similar to that |
| 4. This sentence tells what observations led to the later definition of oxidation. What is the same is that something is _____ . What is different is that there is no _____ | of oxygen. Hydrogen, antimony, and sodium all burn in chlorine, and iron   (e) will burn in fluorine. Since these reactions were similar, chemists formed a more general definition of oxidation. Electrons were removed from each free element by reactants O_2 or Cl_2. |
| 5. Since oxygen is not always involved, you will end up with a "more general" definition of oxidation. The more general definition is given in this sentence. It is that oxidation is _____ | Thus, oxidation was defined as the   (f) process by which electrons are apparently removed from an atom or ion. |

Figure 14.4. Text and accompanying gloss sheet with example of developmental gloss. Text from R. C. Smoot, J. Price, and R. G. Smith, *Chemistry: a modern course*, 5th Ed. (Columbus, OH: Charles E. Merrill Publishing Co., 1979), p. 488. Reprinted by permission. Figure taken from D. Richgels and J. Mateja, Gloss II: integrating content and process for independence, *Journal of Reading*, February 1984. Reproduced by permission of the authors and the International Reading Association.

Teaching fifth graders to understand and use the rules of summarization had a positive effect on their reading comprehension (McNeil & Donant 1982), as did teaching a hierarchical summary procedure to intermediate-grade students (B. Taylor 1982). Winograd (1984) found that most eighth graders knew what should be included in a summary. In Winograd's study, the problems encountered by poor readers in producing summaries were caused by their inability to select what was important and in condensing information.

There are developmental differences in the production of summaries between fifth grade and college, and summarization is a relatively late-developing skill. Overall, the research regarding the effectiveness of summarization as a study technique has been sparse, and its findings mixed (A. Brown, Campione, & Day 1981, 1984). There is a modest transfer of summarization ability within a content area but not across content subjects (Tierney & Cunningham 1984). Summarization is more likely to become an effective study strategy when students receive instruction on how to produce summaries, and the criterion task demands reflect the kind of processing used in producing a summary (T. Anderson & Armbruster 1984b).

K. Taylor (1984) suggested that pupils be taught the following strategy in writing summaries: (1) Read carefully to identify the structure and content of the material; (2) check your comprehension of the material; (3) write a first draft; (4) check the first draft against the original article; (5) write a second draft; and (6) check the second draft against the original article. Ideas for helping students with précis writing were offered by K. D'Angelo (1983).

Self-directed summarization can be an excellent comprehension-monitoring activity. As the student goes along, he or she attempts to summarize what has been read. Inability to produce an adequate synopsis should be a clear sign to the reader that comprehension is not proceeding smoothly and that corrective action is called for. Poor readers do not readily engage in self-directed summarization or questioning (Palinscar & Brown 1983).

Underlining

Underlining is one of the most popular studying techniques. Like other strategies, the ability to underline requires knowing what is worth underlining. It has been our experience that pupils underline too much. To verify this, one has but to look at the almost complete change in page color to yellow when students underline a textbook with a yellow felt-tip pen. Among other things, students should be told not to underline until they have finished reading a headed section because waiting may reveal a summary statement that only need be underlined. They also should be taught to develop at least a two-tiered system of differentiating between important (use of a star or double underscoring) and less important information. Refer to McAndrew (1983) and Podstay (1984) for ideas on teaching underlining. Most studies have not shown outlining to be any more or less effective than other studying procedures.

Note Taking

Note taking is a form of summarizing. Taking notes on what one reads can be a useful study strategy, and it has to be used rather than underlining when one does not own the reading material. Notes can be taken on separate sheets of paper as one reads. Or a notation may be delayed until a section of the text has been read. Note taking becomes a very important skill when one has to consult a number of sources from which information has to be obtained and retained.

In addition to its value for review or in preparing a report, note taking performs a useful function in enforcing selective, thoughtful reading. To take good notes, one must select what is worth recording by separating major from minor points, must consider the relation of one idea to another, and must condense the author's ideas into an accurate restatement in one's own words. Passive reading is impossible when one is taking good notes.

Learning to take efficient notes is not easy. Many students leave out so much important information that the notes could not be substituted for a re-reading of the material. Other pupils take such voluminous notes that they are difficult to use. In both cases, the cause is usually the inability to determine what information is important. In the latter situation, the child also may need to learn that "more is not better."

The overall research literature, which deals primarily with taking notes from lectures, suggest that note taking can be a useful learning strategy, especially when notes are reviewed before taking a test (Rickards 1979b, 1984; Hale 1982). The few studies dealing with reading and note taking have produced mixed findings, with most showing note taking to be no more or less effective than other studying strategies.

Outlining

When first introducing outlining, the teacher should discuss the importance of being able to outline what one reads. She can point out that an outline shows the relative importance of each idea, its relation to other ideas in the material, and its place in the whole selection; that it is, in effect, the skeleton or framework of ideas that the writer has "dressed up" by expressing them in well-written sentences and paragraphs. Then the teacher can demonstrate the procedure by outlining some well-organized expository text that the children have read. She should model how and why she selects certain ideas to place in the outline, and how the outline format signals the importance of ideas and relationships between them. This demonstration outline should not be very complex.

Once motivation has been established, the teacher can present a series of graded exercises in outlining, in which pupils are initially given a great deal of help. For the first two or three sessions, the teacher should display a complete outline of the material. After the students read the text, the outline is discussed, and the teacher answers any questions that are raised. In this meaningful setting it is easy to explain the system of progressive indentation, the sequence of roman numerals, capital letters, and so on. When the plan of a formal outline has been learned, the second stage is to assign outlines on which the complete skeleton is shown, but only part of the outline itself is provided. Some of these incomplete outlines contain only the main headings, and the details are to be filled in. In others, the details are provided and the headings have to be inserted. After reading the accompanying material, the children complete the outline, and discussion follows. In the third stage, the structure of the outline is given, but no slots are filled in by the teacher. In the fourth stage, only the number of main headings is given, and in the final stages the pupils produce a complete outline without assistance.

Learning how to condense a sentence into a few words can be achieved through discussion of the most satisfactory way to state a given part of the outline. Different statements can be compared as to clarity and conciseness and the best ones selected. The writing of acceptable incomplete sentences in a telegraphic style can be taught in a meaningful situation.

It is desirable to teach the use of the formal outline before teaching children to use informal outlines. The basic difference between the two forms is the absence of the number-and-letter scheme in the informal outline. Once one has learned to think in outline terms, the trappings can be discarded without losing the ability to reduce what has been read to its essential structure.

A teacher-prepared outline can serve to activate students' prior knowledge, to develop expectations, and to provide a structure that can be used to guide the pupils' reading. As a postreading activity it can help students learn to separate important from less important information and to organize information. The outline can also be used as a study aid.

In two studies in which students were trained to outline, outlining was more effective than the strategies to which it was compared. In none of the four studies that showed no significant difference between treatments were the pupils trained to outline (T. Anderson & Armbruster 1984b).

Metacognition[2]

If students are to become successful comprehenders, they must actively participate in reading; and if they are to become independent learners, they must accept responsibility for their learning. Therefore, an additional role of the teachers is to get the children actively involved in the comprehension process and assure that they take increasingly greater responsibility for their learning. Pupils are more likely to take active participation in comprehending and learning if they understand the significance of their participation and understand that what they know (or do not know) or do (or do not do) can and does influence how well they comprehend and learn. Furthermore, they must understand that they can control learning outcomes. As Tierney (1982) put it, "helping students learn from text for themselves involves bringing students to the point at which they can self-initiate and self-regulate their reading behaviors." This is where metacognitive skills enter in.

The term *metacognition* has been used to refer to many aspects of active comprehension, but two broad but closely related categories of metacognition can be distinguished (Brown & Palinscar 1982). *Knowledge about cognition* involves reflection on one's own cognitive operations. Because this kind of knowledge requires learners to step back and consider their own cognitive processes as objects of thought and reflection, it is probably a late-developing skill. *Regulation of cognition* involves control of cognitive processes. Prime executive

---

[2] In developmental reading the teacher primarily directs the learning, and basal reader stories are read as a means of acquiring and practicing word-recognition, word-meaning, and comprehension skills. There is no need to remember the story content for more than a day or so, and usually for a much shorter time. When students begin reading to learn (i.e., to use reading as a vehicle for acquiring knowledge), they should also start to accept increasing responsibility for their learning, and they also must retain information from their textbooks over a period of time. For these reasons, metacognition is considered in this chapter and not in Chapter 13.

functions include *planning* activities before and during reading, *monitoring* activities during reading, and *checking* outcomes.

Essentially, metacognitive skills, as they relate to reading comprehension and learning from written text, involve *awareness* of what is to be learned and why, how the learning can best be accomplished, how well one is equipped to accomplish the learning, how well comprehension is proceeding and what can be done if comprehension falters, and how to determine if comprehension–learning has been adequate. Metacognitive skills involve the monitoring of one's cognitive processes before, during, and after reading. Once *aware of* these factors, the reader must *control* them, but self-awareness is a prerequisite for self-regulation.

The following example of purposeful reading illustrates how metacognitive skills operate during reading–studying. First, the pupil identifies the explicit and implicit task demands. This involves determining the purpose for which the material is to be read. Knowledge of why the material is to be read and whether or not comprehension of that material is to be assessed (and if so, how) allows the student to set a goal, which in turn suggests the initial reading strategy to employ (e.g., if obtaining the gist of the passage is the goal, then skimming will probably suffice). Doing so also sets a criterion by which he can monitor his comprehension (e.g., "I still don't understand the process of photosynthesis") and helps him judge what information in the text is most important. Also, before reading, the pupil will obtain an idea of the text content and organization, by previewing typographical aids. Having done so, he continues his plan for learning by activating relevant prior knowledge. The learner also will assess his own competence to perform the tasks necessary to accomplish the goal.

While reading, the student uses the organization of the text to guide his reading, the text structure plus his purpose for reading to help separate important from less important information, and he allots his attention accordingly and relates ideas within the text to his prior knowledge. He may attempt to use imagery to enhance comprehension, and periodically he monitors his comprehension by self-questioning, summarizing, or taking notes. If comprehension is inadequate, corrective action will be taken. As he reads he attempts to organize the information so that the interrelations among ideas are clear.

When reading is completed, the pupil assesses how well the goal has been met (e.g., uses his notes to see how well he understands them and can elaborate on them), and decides what further action, if any, needs to be taken (e.g., re-reading a portion of the text). If he is going to have to demonstrate his comprehension at some later time, the learner may utilize a study strategy (e.g., outlining, semantic webbing). This study strategy also may serve as a check on how well the text was understood, and determine his readiness to be tested on that information. The choice of study strategy may depend in part on its cost effectiveness (is it worth the time it takes?). Or it may be unnecessary to employ any study technique because the goal was simply to understand the author's point of view or purpose for writing the material.

Studies have indicated that young and poor readers tend to be deficient in both their knowledge of and control over metacognitive skills. Research findings also indicate that comprehension monitoring is usually a late-developing meta-cognitive skill, one that generally does not emerge fully until late adolescence. Some researchers have concluded that comprehension monitoring can be strengthened through explicit instruction and practice and that the effects of such instruction are large, durable, and transferable (Palinscar & Brown 1983) and result in improved reading comprehension (Mier 1984).

Good teachers focus the pupil's attention on important textual information, get the pupils to monitor their comprehension by asking questions about the degree to which they understand the material, and help the students understand how new information can be related to prior knowledge. Children can be taught to engage in these activities on their own while reading. Successful cognitive skills training programs have three main aspects: (1) training and practice in the use of task-specific strategies (skill development); (2) instruction in overseeing and monitoring these skills (self-regulation training); and (3) information regarding when these skills should be used and the positive impact they can achieve (awareness training) (Baker & Brown 1984b).

Activities for developing metacognition skills can be found in the articles cited in this section and in J. Fitzgerald (1983), Babbs and Moe (1983) and Sanacore (1984). The *Reading Comprehension Interview* (Wixson *et al.* 1984) can be used to assess how well pupils understand reading tasks, the demands such tasks place on them, and which strategies can be used to accomplish the tasks (see Fig. 14.5).

Other Factors That Affect Learning from Text

In addition to reading, cognitive, and metacognitive skills, successful comprehension monitoring also may depend on personality and affective factors. Some pupils are unwilling to admit, even to themselves, that they do not understand something. Often such children are reluctant to ask questions for fear of appearing "stupid." Other personality variables, such as differences in field dependency–independency and reflection–impulsivity (see pp. 264–265), may enter in, just as might such factors as dogmatism and closed-mindedness (Athey 1982, L. Baker & Brown 1984b). Affective factors such as self-image, peer pressure, and the teacher's empathy also can influence learning (A. Brown *et al.* 1982). Any affective factor that diminishes or rules out students' active involvement in their own learning is likely to result in weaker use of metacognitive skills and poorer academic performance (Athey 1982, Johnston & Winograd 1983).

At present, a conclusion that ineffective monitoring of one's cognitive processes is the major cause of poor reading comprehension would be premature. Nevertheless, instruction in cognitive monitoring should help those pupils whose comprehension problems are due to a lack of awareness and use of cognitive monitoring skills and strategies (Baker & Brown 1984b).

Strategies a Reader May Employ in Dealing With a Comprehension Problem

Assuming that the reader is aware that his comprehension is not proceeding smoothly, there are basically six strategies he might employ (Collins & Smith 1982, Baker & Brown 1984b): (1) Ignore it and continue reading; (2) suspend

Name: Date:

Classroom teacher: Reading level:

                                                 Grade:

Directions: Introduce the procedure by explaining that you are interested in finding out what children think about various reading activities. Tell the student that he or she will be asked questions about his/her reading; that there are no right or wrong answers, and that you are only interested in knowing what s/he thinks. Tell the student that if s/he does not know how to answer a question s/he should say so and you will go on to the next one.

General probes such as "Can you tell me more about that?" or "Anything else?" may be used. Keep in mind that the interview is an informal diagnostic measure and you should feel free to probe to elicit useful information.

1. What hobbies or interests do you have that you like to read about?
2. a. How often do you read in school?
   b. How often do you read at home?
3. What school subjects do you like to read about?

Introduce reading and social studies books.

Directions: For this section use the child's classroom basal reader and a content area textbook (social studies, science, etc.). Place these texts in front of the student. Ask each question twice, once with reference to the basal reader and once with reference to the content area textbook. Randomly vary the order of presentation (basal, content). As each question is asked, open the appropriate text in front of the student to help provide a point of reference for the question.

4. What is the most important reason for reading this kind of material?
   Why does your teacher want you to read this book?
5. a. Who's the best reader you know in _____?
   b. What does he/she do that makes him/her such a good reader?
6. a. How good are *you* at reading this kind of material?
   b. How do you know?
7. What do you have to do to get a good grade in _____in your class?
8. a. If the teacher told you to remember the information in this story/chapter, what would be the best way to do this?
   b. Have you ever tried _____?
9. a. If your teacher told you to find the answers to the questions in this book, what would be the best way to do this? Why?
   b. Have you ever tried _____?
10. a. What is the hardest part about answering questions like the ones in this book?
    b. Does that mean you do anything differently?

Introduce at least two comprehension worksheets.

Directions: Present the worksheets to the child and ask questions 11 and 12. Ask the child to complete portions of each worksheet. Then ask questions 13 and 14. Next, show the child a worksheet designed to simulate the work of another child. Then ask question 15.

11. Why would your teacher want you to do worksheets like these (for what purpose)?
12. What would your teacher say you must do to get a good mark on worksheets like these? (What does your teacher look for?)

Ask the child to complete portions of at least two worksheets.

13. Did you do this one differently from the way you did that one? How or in what way?
14. Did you have to work harder on one of these worksheets than the other?
    (Does one make you think more?)

Present the simulated worksheet.

15. a. Look over this worksheet. If you were the teacher, what kind of mark would you give the worksheet? Why?
    b. If you were the teacher, what would you ask this person to do differently next time?

Figure 14.5. Reading comprehension overview. From K. Wixson et al., An interview for assessing students' perceptions of classroom reading tasks, *The Reading Teacher*, January 1984, *37*. Reprinted by permission of the authors and the International Reading Association.

judgment and continue reading; (3) form a tenative hypothesis and continue reading; (4) reread the current sentence; (5) reread the previous context; or (6) go to an expert source. The degree to which each of these strategies disrupts the flow of reading increases from the first to the sixth strategy, but the numbering does not indicate the order of desirability or effectiveness.

As a disruption in comprehension occurs, the reader must decide what, if anything, to do. These decisions will depend on one's reason(s) for reading and one's investment in the reading–learning task.

Discussing the use of these strategies and their advantages and disadvantages with students may help the students to use them. Teachers can encourage their use as the occasions arise.

A "think aloud" modeling of how to monitor comprehension, as well as use of the above "fix-up" strategies, may help to improve student's use of metacognitive strategies (Davey 1983). The teacher may read orally and mention a point at which her comprehension begins to lag (or may read silently and verbalize the confusing point). She then "thinks" the option(s) out loud and demonstrates a strategy (e.g., form a tentative hypothesis, reread the sentence), explaining why the choice was made.

Content-Subject Textbooks

Most content-subject material requires special adaptations of general reading skills and specialized reading and study skills. Although the ideal situation would be to have each content-area teacher instruct her students in how to read the materials in that subject, this is not likely to occur. Reading teachers and content-subject areas can work together, however, to develop and deliver an effective reading–study program. If a remedial teacher finds that a pupil is failing in a content area in which the classroom teacher has not provided guidance in how to read the subject matter, she should provide the needed instruction, and should use the child's textbook in doing so.

Content-subject textbooks often are difficult to comprehend because of the use of technical vocabulary, high concept load and density, complex syntactic structures, abstract nature of the content, and varied and changing structural organization. Some textbooks are not clearly written (T. Anderson, Armbruster, & Kantor 1980).

Guidelines for examining the comprehensibility of textbooks were provided by Clewell and Cliffton (1983), and a Textbook Evaluation Checklist and accompanying discussion may be found in T. Anderson and Armbruster (1984a). Armbruster and Anderson (1984) developed a textbook chapter based on the notion of "considerate text"; that is, the chapter was written to maximize its comprehensibility.

Vocabulary Burden in Textbooks

Beginning reading materials usually contain only words whose meanings are already familiar to children or that can be explained easily. Therefore word meaning is rarely a problem for novice readers. As the levels of the basal reader materials get higher, progressively more new words and ideas are introduced, and more meanings of a particular word are employed.

The vocabulary burden is more acute in content-subject textbooks than in general reading materials. Each content area has an extensive specialized vocabulary that must be learned if one is to understand the content. Successful teachers take pains to introduce new concepts and the verbal labels that represent them with meaningful illustrations and examples, guide the formulation of a statement of what the term means, and then check carefully to see if the concept has been understood and the printed word recognized. Technical vocabulary is of two main kinds: (1) words that are specific to that content field, such as *divisor* and *longitude*; and (2) words whose meanings change from subject to subject, such as *group* in biology (a large number of plants or animals related to each other because of a common similarity) or in social studies (a number of persons gathered together and forming a unit) or in chemistry (a radical—a group of two or more atoms that acts as a single atom and goes through a reaction unchanged or is replaced by a single atom). Teachers also must be aware of the semantic confusions many pupils experience when a high-frequency word has an uncommon, technical meaning: *left* meaning *remainder* and not a direction, *coast* meaning a *shore* and not something done with a sled, or *subject* used as a verb.

Lists of content-subject words are available. Subject-area vocabularies are listed by broad grade ranges (e.g., primary, intermediate, secondary) by Fry, Polk, and Fountoukidis (1984). A. J. Harris and Jacobson (1972) provided lists of the technical vocabularies in four subject areas. The *EDL Core Vocabularies* (S. Taylor *et al.* 1979) have mathematical word lists for Grades 1–3 and 4–6, and social studies and science lists for Grades 3–6. Swett (1978) presented a brief list of essential math terms, and O'Mara (1981) listed mathematical words and terms. Reutzel (1983) indicated the words that signal the types of computations required to solve a word problem. These lists may be helpful in identifying the important technical terms in each subject area. Dupuis and Snyder (1983) described and illustrated an approach to teaching technical vocabulary as a part of concept development. J. Cox and Wiebe (1984) developed a test of the important vocabulary and concepts used in primary-grade mathematics.

Research indicates that the material used in mathematics is more difficult to read than for any other content area (V. Schell 1982). Dunlap and McKnight (1978) demonstrated with many examples the difficulties that children experience in trying to translate mathematical language into their everyday language so as to comprehend it. They also showed how drawings and diagrams can be used to clear up many of the problems.

One of the biggest problems children have in mathematics is solving word problems. Usually the difficulty lies in comprehending the written problem and not in performing the calculations. Earp (1970) suggested the following five-step pattern for reading math problems: (1) Read to visualize or grasp the situation presented; (2) reread to note the specific facts given; (3) note any difficult concepts or terminology and get help if needed; (4) reread to select the operations to be used and to plan the solution; (5) after finding an answer, reread again to check the process chosen and the reasonableness of the solution. Other plans were offered by Cassidy (1984) and Kreese (1984). Word problems can be made more understandable by simplifying the syntax and resequencing the information in the problem to match the order in which it will be needed to solve the problem (O'Mara 1981). When sixth graders were taught to resequence in this manner and to delete extraneous material from word problems, their ability to solve written math problems improved significantly (S. A. Cohen & Stover 1981). McCabe (1981) reported that ninth graders performed significantly better when math problems were rewritten to match the syntax of their oral language. Presenting word problems in telegraphic form (e.g., Had 16¢. Lost 10¢. How much left?) does not help either good or poor readers (Sowder-Threadgill et al. 1984).

Science is another area in which exactingly slow, careful reading is necessary. Suggestions for how to read science material may be found in Ferguson (1969) and the Metropolitan School Study Council (1960, 1972). Teachers should be aware that students' comprehension of science material is often adversely affected by their prior beliefs and preconceptions that are at odds with accepted scientific thinking (C. Anderson & Smith 1984).

Many social studies textbooks are difficult to read because they are not well written (Armbruster & Gudbrandsen 1984). Suggestions for teaching reading in the social studies may be found in Lunstrum and Taylor (1978). Armbruster et al. (1984), who found that many questions found in history texts were hard to understand, presented a taxonomy of American History questions and gave examples of what students must know or be able to do in order to answer each type of question.

Research has indicated that providing reading- and study-skill instruction in the social studies can raise achievement scores in both reading and social studies to levels higher than those attained by students who did not receive such instruction. The successful instructional programs were the ones in which (1) the teachers played an important role in designing the program; (2) there were more than just a few activities and materials employed; and (3) the teachers played an active role in instruction, rather than rely on written overviews and exercises (Wade 1983).

Hillocks and Ludlow (1984) developed and validated a hierarchically ordered taxonomy of the comprehension skills needed to comprehend fiction. Their taxonomy, beginning with the lowest level of skills, is (1) basic stated information; (2) key details; (3) stated relationships; (4) simple implied relationships; (5) complex implied relationships; (6) the author's generalizations; and (7) structural generalizations (how parts of a story operate together to achieve certain effects). The first three levels involve literal comprehension; the last four, inferential comprehension.

Questioning and practice in understanding apparent versus true motivation improved the ability of intermediate-grade children to read narratives (Carnine et al. 1982). Use of fairly detailed previews significantly increased the ability of poor readers in the junior high school to comprehend difficult short stories (M. Graves, Cooke, & LaBerge 1983). And high school juniors, who were taught

how to generate story-specific questions while they were reading, comprehended complex short stories better than did the control group (H. Singer &
Donlan 1982).

Questions on narratives should tap information central to the development
of the story. Rather than questions about discrete bits of information, the questions should guide the students in understanding the important story concepts
and highlight the interrelationships of these concepts and events (Beck 1984).
Ringler and Weber (1982) suggested how to help students make the inferences
that are often necessary to comprehend narratives.

Differences between Comprehending Narrative and Expository Text

Schrieber (1983) enumerated the different requirements placed on readers
by narrative and expository text. Narratives often require the reader to supply
main ideas and fill in details from background knowledge. Connotative meanings
and literary usage of words and phrases characterize narratives. Not only do the
writing styles differ among the kinds of narration (e.g., short stories vs. biographies) but there are also differing styles among authors within a genre.

Expository text usually amplifies on a series of concepts. The events and
objects in exposition are readily identifiable, and details and descriptive phrases
are explicit. Denotative and literal statements are characteristic of expository
text.

Different strategies are needed for reading various narrative and expository
materials. These have been discussed by Beach and Appleman (1984). Forgan
and Mangrum (1981) listed the reading skills needed for the various content
areas. Other useful suggestions for developing reading-to-learn skills may be
found in H. Singer and Donlan (1980); Gaskins (1981); Tierney and Schallert
(1982); Roth, Smith, and Anderson (1984); A. J. Harris and Sipay (1979, pp. 359–
395); Dupuis (1984); and Graham and Robinson (1984). A number of textbooks
are devoted entirely to teaching reading in the content areas. Moore, Readence,
and Rickelman (1983) presented a historical account of reading instruction in
the content areas.

Reading Maps, Graphs, Charts, and Tables

It is often possible to present a large amount of material concisely in visual
form by means of a map, a graph, a chart, or a table. Unfortunately, pupils frequently do not make use of this source of information.

There are wide variations as to types and purposes within each of these
four kinds of graphical representations, and learning to use any one of them
requires the acquisition of a number of skills. Teaching children how to interpret
these efficient aids to understanding and encouraging their use is the responsibility of each content-subject teacher. Fry (1981, 1984) offered excellent suggestions for developing graphic literacy.

Learning to Locate Information

Using an index to find information is a great time saver. Instruction in using an
index should begin as soon as one appears in a textbook, and its use should be
taught to upper-grade pupils who lack this skill.

The first index encountered by children is usually one in which the topics are arranged alphabetically by topic and subtopic. This fact should be explained to children, as well as the meaning of the numbers and other notations (e.g., *see also*) that may accompany an entry. By the time indexes appear in their books, most children are fairly advanced in their knowledge of alphabetization. So the instructional emphasis should be on locating information. In an introductory lesson, children can be asked to suggest headings under which information might be classified; the desired information should appear in one of their textbooks. For example, information on the number of cattle raised in Colorado may be found under several headings: Cattle, production of; Colorado, cattle raising in; and so on. After the teacher discusses why some of the suggestions are better than others, the possibilities can be listed on the board, and the pupils check their texts to see if it contains those entries. When the page references are found, pupils can find the information located under the various headings and report it to the group. After the general procedure has been learned, the teacher can provide periodic practice in the use of an index, but its use will probably be best learned as children employ it to find needed information on their own.

After they have mastered the use of a book index fairly well, pupils should learn the value of and how to use reference resources such as encyclopedias, almanacs, atlases, a library card index, and the *Readers Guide to Periodical Literature*. Encouraging them to use their index skills to find information in these references often serves as a good introduction. A suitable teaching sequence should include (1) knowledge of the kinds of information contained in the different reference works; (2) practice in thinking up relevant headings or entries under which the information might be found; (3) how to choose the correct volume when the reference has more than one; and (4) the interpretation of commonly employed abbreviations. M. J. Miller (1979) listed the library skills and understandings that should be developed in the primary grades.

The use of a table of contents is usually introduced early in the primary grades. Once they understand its use, children have little difficulty employing a table of contents to locate a particular story or section in a book.

Study Habits

Students develop habits about the amount of time they spend in studying; the promptness with which they get to, and complete, work; the conditions under which they study; their degree of concentration; and the study strategies they employ. Many students who fail or marginally pass in various content areas have adequate reading skills and perhaps knowledge of appropriate study skills. What they lack is good study habits.

Pupils generally do not perceive their reading assignments to be either meaningful or a necessary activity (F. R. Smith & Feathers 1983). Students report that their textbooks are boring and difficult to understand and that at best they read a textbook assignment only once (J. L. Vaughn 1982, Tierney & Schallert 1982, Chall & Conrad 1984). It is therefore little wonder that they also report that they have difficulty remembering what they "read." Making students aware

of the need to continue to study until they are ready to be tested on their understanding and recall of that information improves study performance (L. Baker
& Brown 1984b).

Allocation of study time is something few students do well. It is a metacognitive skill based on knowing what needs to be learned and how long it will
take one to learn it. Refer to A. J. Harris and Sipay (1979, pp. 390–394) for
suggestions on assessing and developing study habits.

Content-Subject Instruction for Disabled Readers

Some teachers, particularly subject-matter specialists, feel that little can be done
to assist the student to learn if he cannot read on-grade texts. Thus disabled
readers, and at times even average readers, are left to flounder and fail because
they cannot cope with reading assignments. Contrary to such beliefs, things can
be done to assist disabled readers to develop the concepts and attitudes called
for by the curriculum.

Although by no means the only possible program change that can be made,
material more appropriate for the learner's level of reading ability can be obtained. Granted that material on exactly the same topic as in the on-grade text
may not always be available, an increasing amount of material is becoming available for use in the content areas with students reading below grade level. For
example, in the physical sciences Globe has published a series of 12 texts, *Pathways in Science*, for junior and senior high school students who are reading at
the fifth- or sixth-grade level. There are three books each for earth science,
chemistry, physics, and biology. Other reading materials that might be used
include the Reader's Digest *Science Readers* and *Social Studies Readers* (7 each)
whose reading levels go from the third to the sixth grade, and *Science for You*
and *Wonders of Science* (Steck-Vaughn). Some of the materials found in the
series listed in Appendix B may be appropriate.

In the social sciences, there are similar programs such as *American Adventures World History Program* (Scholastic), *America's Story* (Steck-Vaughn),
and *Civics, World History*, and *American History* (Follett). These materials are
intended for use with junior–senior high students who are reading at the fourth-
to eighth-grade level. The *Reading Range Plus* (Macmillan) is an adaptation of
their on-grade social studies series for use with elementary school children who
have reading problems. Other books written at a low level, but with high interest,
are those in series such as *How They Lived* and *Living in Today's World* (Garrard). Both written at the fourth reader level, the former deals with documen-
taries of America's growth and heritage, the latter with people of other cultures.

Similarly, there are programs in English such as *Pathways to the World of
English* (Globe) and *Activity-Concept English* (Scott, Foresman). In the literature area, either other books or paperbacks can be substituted for those called
for by the curriculum, or adapted classics may be read.

There are also materials for other content subjects. For example, the *Pal
Health Books* (Xerox) were written for sixth to ninth graders who are reading at
third or fourth reader level.

It is highly advantageous for disabled readers to receive information through media other than print. Texts may be read to the student at home or by a volunteer during study periods, or lessons may be recorded. If learning is to be primarily auditory, lessons in listening comprehension should be built into the child's program. If "learning through listening" programs were initiated early enough, disabled readers could have more academic success when they finally learn to read because they would have the conceptual and informational background necessary to understand the texts.

Whatever the adjustments made for disabled readers, it is important to allow the learner to display his knowledge. For some severely disabled readers, it is advisable to administer tests orally. If he cannot read the test, the student cannot demonstrate his knowledge—a situation that can be quite frustrating and kill any motivation to learn.

II. HELPING STUDENTS READ RAPIDLY AND FLEXIBLY

There is so much to read today that the ability to read quickly has become an important asset. A literate adult in today's hectic world goes through more reading material in a week than his great-grandfather probably covered in a year.

The average reader wastes a great deal of time in unnecessarily slow reading. We do not know the fastest rate (with comprehension) that students are capable of attaining. Cornell students typically went from about 250 WPM (words per minute) to about 500 WPM with no loss in comprehension (Pauk 1964). Students at the University of Minnesota were reported to have improved from an average of 252 WPM with 63% comprehension to 1548 WPM with 62% comprehension (J. Brown 1976). Many programs have attempted to improve reading rate, with widely varying results. It is certain, however, that most readers are capable of reading material of easy and average difficulty far faster than they do.

Recognizing that to read rapidly is an advantage, it is important always to keep in mind that to go through material without understanding it and without being able to remember what it said is a waste of time, no matter what the speed at which this may be accomplished. A skilled reader is one who not only reads well but also adjusts his reading rate while maintaining comprehension.

The Relation of Rate to Comprehension

How fast readers compare with slow readers in comprehension was one of the early questions that reading researchers tackled, and by 1950 a large number of studies had been completed. The results favored neither those who expected fast readers to be careless and inaccurate nor those who expected the good reader to be both fast and accurate in comprehension.

The relationship between rate and comprehension varies with the age of the readers, the material used, and the methods of measuring the two factors. In the primary grades one would expect to find a fairly high relationship, because slow reading at that level is usually caused by difficulty in word recognition,

Table 14.1 Median Rates of Reading for Different Grades as Determined by Several Standardized Reading Tests

	GRADE								
	2	3	4	5	6	7	8	9	12
Highest test	118	138	170	195	230	246	267	260	295
Median test	86	116	155	177	206	215	237	252	251
Lowest test	35	75	120	145	171	176	188	199	216

NOTE: The number of tests included in the table is 7 for Grades 2, 3; 8 for Grades 4, 5, 6, 7; 6 for Grades 8, 9; and 3 for Grade 12.

which impairs comprehension also. At higher levels, the many research studies show great variations in results. At the secondary and college level most of the correlations tended to be positive but quite low, around .30 (Tinker 1939). Among bright pupils, fast readers tended to comprehend better than slow readers, whereas at lower intelligence levels there was some evidence that the slower readers tended to comprehend better (Shores & Husbands 1950). In mathematics and science, the correlations tended to be low and negative; with many exceptions, the faster pupils read, the less they tended to understand (Blommers & Lindquist 1944). Little research attention has been devoted to this topic in the past 35 years.

Because certain distinctions must be made when discussing reading rate and its relation to comprehension, the following subsections deal with how fast pupils *do*, *can*, and *should* read, whether they *should* and *can* be trained to read faster, and whether students *should* and *can* be taught to read more flexibly.

How Fast Do Pupils Read?

This is the easiest question to answer, but the answers must be qualified. Data from a number of different standardized tests are shown in Table 14.1. Since these data are from norm-referenced tests, each figure represents the median number of words read per minute (WPM). They do not indicate the rates attained by the fastest, average, and slowest reader at each grade level. It should be understood that not only were there individuals who read much slower or faster than the indicated WPMs but also that the task demands differed from test to test. Norms for reading rate can be misleading because they can vary so much according to the nature of the material and the type of comprehension check employed. In short, task demands vary widely. This is one of the reasons why the typical reading rates reported by different investigators can differ markedly. As yet, no one has established rate norms for reading the same kinds of material for different purposes. It also should be understood that the rate at which pupils read under test conditions may not be the same as the rate that they employ in their daily reading in school.

Nevertheless, the data from Table 14.1 provide some useful information. There is a difference of roughly 50 to 80 WPM in the number of words per minute reported between the highest and lowest median WPMs at each grade level. This may reflect such factors as differences in task demands and the subjects on whom the tests were normed, but considering that there were faster and slower readers than the medians indicate, the data suggest that there is a fairly wide range of reading rate at each grade level.

The data in both Tables 14.1 and 14.2 (p. 554) generally indicate a steady upward trend in WPM from the primary grades through Grade 9. They differ, however, in that the data in Table 14.1 indicate a leveling off at 250 WPM in Grades 9 and 12, whereas Table 14.2 shows a continuing increase from Grade 9 (214 WPM) to Grade 12 (250 WPM). The NAEP (1972) results showed the average 17-year-old reading at 195 WPM (material at the tenth-grade level was used), with only 25% of the students reading at 250 WPM or higher (only 10% read at 300 WPM or above) in this national study. It would appear that the average American high school student reads at about 200–250 words per minute.

How Fast Can a Person Read?

The answer to this question depends primarily on how reading rate (and reading) is defined and how it is measured. Opinions vary widely as to how fast an individual can read. There are those who contend that reading rates of 2000–3000 WPM or even higher can be achieved with the proper instruction and practice. Other state that such claims are unfounded because the individuals were actually skimming and not "really reading" or that questionable comprehension measures were employed. It has been argued that it is physiologically impossible to take in every printed word on the page at such high speeds and counterargued that one need not perceive every word in order to comprehend the material.

Sticht (1984) wrote that, although high rates of skimming can be accomplished, there is little or no evidence that people can or typically do read at rates far above those at which they can *aud* (listen with comprehension) or speak. According to Sticht (1984), the maximal auding and reading rates are probably the same because they use the same language base (lexicon and syntax) and conceptual base (semantic memory). Sticht (1984, Sticht *et al.* 1974) concluded that once word recognition has been mastered, speed of reading is limited by the individual's ability to process language and that the maximal rates for auding and reading are both about 250–300 WPM, with comprehension falling off after 300 WPM.

Very similar conclusions were reached by Carver (1982, 1984). In one study, Carver (1982) found that for college students there was a consistent optimal rate at which comprehension efficiency was maximal regardless of the difficulty of the material. Carver also reported that when college students had to read and later estimate the percentage of the total number of complete thought units in the material they understood (reading for general meaning), their comprehension was about 80–90% when reading between 62 and 250 WPM, dropped off to 40% at 500 WPM, fell further to 15–20% at 1000 WPM, and was practically nil above 1000 WPM. When reading to find the missing verb (reading for details), the comprehension scores were even lower at the various rates. Both Sticht and Carver, therefore, would contend that reading faster than 300 WPM is very likely to result in considerable loss in comprehension.

Fullmer (1980) found that the maximum rate, defined as the rate at which comprehension is no better than chance, is around 700 WPM for reading and approximately 500 WPM for auding. Her findings are in contrast with Sticht's hypothesis that one's levels of auding and reading comprehension are basically the same.

Based on their study of college students, Graesser, Hoffman, and Clark (1980) concluded that differences in reading rate can be attributed to differences in the speed with which students analyze the microstructure but not the macrostructure of the text. That is, reading rate is apparently determined by the speed with which skills involved in performing lexical, syntactic, and propositional analyses within sentences are performed. It seems that the question as to how fast individuals can read is still far from being answered.

How Fast Should a Person Read?

Reading rate is often defined by the number of words read per minute, but we think it should be defined as the speed with which a person can gain the desired information from the written text. This definition implies that reading rate is relative and depends on the reader's cognitive and reading skills, his purpose for reading, and the difficulty of the material.

No one rate of reading is appropriate in all situations; rather, the efficient reader varies his rate according to his purposes and the requirements of the task and the material. Yoakam (1955) distinguished four major rates of reading and indicated some of the kinds of reading situations in which they are appropriate.

1. Skimming rate
   a. Work-type reading: to find a reference; to locate new material; to answer a specific question; to get the general idea of a selection
   b. Recreational reading: to go through a book or magazine to get a general idea of the contents; to review a familiar story
2. Rapid Reading
   a. Work-type: to review familiar material; to get the main idea or central thought; to get information for temporary use
   b. Recreational: to read narrative material primarily for the plot; to read information material for pleasure; to reread familiar material
3. Normal rate
   a. Work-type: to find answers to specific questions; to note details; to solve a problem; to grasp relation of details to main ideas; to read material of average difficulty
   b. Recreational: to appreciate beauty of literary style; to keep up with current events; to read with the intention of later retelling the story
4. Careful rate
   a. Work-type: to master content including details; to evaluate material; to get details in sequence, as in following directions; to outline, summarize, or paraphrase; to analyze author's presentation; to solve a problem

b. Recreational: to read material with unusual vocabulary or style; to read poetry; to read with the intent of memorizing; to judge literary values

The choice of an inappropriate rate of reading is sometimes an important factor in comprehension difficulties. Some children, given a reading diet that consists almost entirely of light, easy fiction, become rapid, fluent readers. Later, when they are expected to read materials that require careful study, they try to employ the same reading habits that are effective in their recreational reading. Then their tendency to read rapidly and superficially produces sad results. Other children are drilled carefully for accuracy from the beginning. They find it easy to note details in their reading but may experience difficulty in discovering the central thought of a selection or in following a sequence of events.

An efficient reader should vary his or her rate of reading over a wide range. In reading light fiction or easy nonfiction, a rapid rate is highly advantageous. A superior adult reader should be able to go through material of this sort at a rate of at least 400 WPM; rates of more than 5000 WPM have been reported. A person's normal reading rate, for somewhat more careful reading, may be only two thirds as fast as his or her most rapid reading. In very careful reading it may be sometimes desirable to slow down to less than one third of one's rapid rate.

Should and Can Students Be Taught to Read Faster?

Whether attempts should be made to increase a pupil's rate of reading depends on a number of factors. Students may show one of four patterns in regard to their reading rate and comprehension: (1) adequate rate and at least adequate comprehension; (2) satisfactory comprehension but slow rate; (3) rapid rate and poor comprehension; or (4) slow rate and poor comprehension. These categories assume that this is typical behavior and does not occur only occasionally.

Students falling in the first category are likely to benefit from improving their reading rates. Their comprehension is at least adequate, and almost all of them could increase their rates without decreases in comprehension (unless of course, the material is too difficult for them to understand). They are also likely candidates for learning to read more flexibly.

When reading comprehension is generally satisfactory but rate is well below normal, treatment can *usually* concentrate on increasing reading speed. Often these pupils have to be convinced that they can read faster without a loss of comprehension. Before working on reading rate, it is a good idea to tell them that it is not unusual for comprehension to drop off at first when one attempts to read faster but that comprehension will pick up again in a short time. Charting their rate and comprehension can be used to demonstrate this. Some children read slowly because they have the misconception that every word must be read regardless of one's purpose for reading. These pupils must first be convinced that at times it is not necessary to read every word; they need to become more flexible readers. Exercises in which many of the less important words have been deleted can be used to get across the idea that one can read for meaning without reading every word (see Fig. 14.6). Teaching these children to skim also helps. Once their misconception is cleared up, work on reading rate can begin.

EXERCISE 7

This exercise will show you how much meaning you can get by concentrating on important words. In the selection below, only the important words are given. Skim quickly over the selection. Work for speed.

Directions: Number your paper 1–8. Write the word or words that complete each of the sentences on page 168. Do not write in this book.

_____ coyote _____ always _____ considered _____ villain _____ western plains. _____ recent years, _____ moved east _____ become _____ problem _____ Adirondacks _____ New York State. No one _____ sure _____ coyote _____ travel _____ _____ far _____, but hunters, cattlemen _____ poultry keepers _____ hate _____ animal as _____ westerners _____.

_____ coyote _____ larger _____ fox _____ more crafty. _____ eat _____ anything _____ sheep, calves, chickens _____ mice. _____ everything _____ available. _____ will eat berries, grasshoppers _____ June bugs. _____ hard _____ trap _____ will not rush _____ bait. _____ Conservation Department _____ worried _____ coyotes _____ increasing _____ number.

_____ no one _____ reported _____ coyote _____ harmed _____ human _____. Perhaps _____ coward, or perhaps _____ too smart _____ close _____ man. _____ places, _____ bounty _____ $25 _____ paid _____ killing _____ coyote.

1. The coyote is described as a   ?   .
2.   ?   is now troubled by coyotes.
3. Men who deal with   ?   hate the coyotes.
4. A reward of   ?   is often paid for killing a coyote.
5. A coyote will eat   ?   .
6. In this article he is compared to the   ?   .
7. The   ?   Department is worried about the increasing number of coyotes.
8. Coyotes are not known to attack   ?   .

Figure 14.6.   An exercise giving practice in gaining meaning using only the more important words in a selection. From *Advanced Skills in Reading*, Book 1, 2d Ed., by Joseph C. Gainsburg. Copyright © 1962, 1967 by The Macmillan Co., Inc. Reprinted by permission of the publishers.

There are pupils who read rapidly but with poor comprehension. They may either have the mistaken belief that "fastest is best" or that the rapid rate has little, if anything, to do with their weak comprehension. Therefore, it is first necessary to determine if comprehension would be more adequate if the pupil read more slowly and read more carefully (i.e., focused attention on comprehension rather than speed). A listening-comprehension test may provide useful information, and the child can be asked to read more slowly and told that his comprehension will be checked when he has finished reading. If slowing down the child's rate results in significantly improved comprehension, the first step in treatment has already been initiated—convincing him that speed without comprehension is self-defeating and that he can comprehend better simply by reading more slowly and carefully. This kind of child also needs to learn to be a flexible reader and often needs to learn strategies for monitoring his reading comprehension. Such pupils will require guided practice in the application of their newly acquired skills, and need to have their comprehension checked frequently to make sure the skills are being applied.

If the assessment reveals that trying to read too fast is not causing the comprehension problem, other reasons for the inadequate comprehension must be sought. Some students read rapidly (or even within normal limits) and accurately but have poor comprehension because they have learned that reading is "saying the words right." These word-callers need to learn that reading is comprehending. The recommended diagnosis and treatment is the same as indicated in the preceding paragraph. In any case, care must be exercised so as not to shift reading speed to the other extreme; slow reading is just as undesirable. The stress should be on "read as fast as you can, but make sure you understand what you are reading." It often helps to inform this kind of pupil that as soon as his comprehension improves, he can go back to reading faster. Almost all of these pupils will need to learn to become flexible readers. As students learn the degree of comprehension necessary for different kinds of reading, their ability to adjust rate to the task requirements will improve.

When a pupil's reading speed is slow and his comprehension is poor, the reason(s) for his weak comprehension should be sought. Providing some children with material of more appropriate difficulty solves the problem temporarily. Once the interfering factors are identified, correctible underlying weaknesses should be improved to a point where they can no longer hamper comprehension. Often overcoming basic skill weaknesses results in an increased reading rate. As pupils develop automatic, accurate word recognition, acquire a more extensive word-meaning vocabulary, and learn to read in thought units, reading speed will increase somewhat without any direct attention being paid to reading rate. If poor reading comprehension is the result of limited learning aptitude, the child will require an adjusted reading and academic program.

A child's word recognition may be accurate but not automatic, or he may be reading in a word-by-word fashion. Excessively slow reading can interfere with reading comprehension because it makes it difficult to make use of semantic relationships and syntax, since the needed information is not available in short-term memory. Once slow word recognition or word-by-word reading is overcome, treatment can concentrate on developing fluency and its by-product, rate. One of the best ways to develop fluency is to provide the child with abundant opportunities to read easy, interesting material.

There are numerous accounts of successful reading-speed programs, but the degree to which the increased rates carry over to other reading situations is variable. Not only are there wide individual differences in reading rate, but pupils also differ in their ability to increase their rate. Reading rate is related to rate of thinking. Of two pupils, both reading at 150 WPM, one may be able to improve her or his rate tremendously, while the other may already be close to his or her maximum rate of effective thinking (processing information). Students who were originally faster readers usually gain more than slow readers from reading-rate practice. It is futile to hope to bring all slow readers up to the average.

Should and Can Students Be Taught to Read More Flexibly?

Almost a decade ago, T. L. Harris (1976) bemoaned the fact that reading flexibility was a neglected aspect of reading instruction. To a large extent it still is. Reading flexibility is often defined as adjusting one's rate of reading to one's purpose for reading, to one's prior knowledge, and to the nature of the reading material. But how does the reader know when to adjust his reading rate? The answer is that reading flexibility is a metacognitive skill (see pp. 522–524). It is one aspect of monitoring one's reading comprehension. When one knows the purpose(s) for which the material is to be read (including how comprehension and recall are to be assessed), and how comprehensible the material probably is in light of his level of reading ability and prior knowledge, then one can decide at what overall speed the material probably should be read. The flexible reader adopts a comprehension strategy that will best accommodate all the variables he is aware of and can control. At one extreme of the continuum is the situation where the excellent reader's purpose is simply to obtain the gist of some very familiar material that is to be reported orally to the teacher immediately after the material is read. All the reader probably needs to do is skim the material very rapidly. At the other extreme is the poor reader who knows that he will be asked to produce a detailed account long after he has first read material whose content is unfamiliar to him and poorly written. Such a situation calls for slow, careful reading.

Reading flexibility does not involve only reading different kinds of material at various speeds or reading the same kind of material at different rates for differing purposes. It also means that, despite the overall rate at which one chooses to read, there may be times within that material that one should speed up or slow down. This, in effect, means adopting a different, and usually temporary, reading comprehension strategy. The flexible reader reads as fast or as slowly as needed to comprehend what needs to be understood.

Are students flexible readers? The answer depends on which research one reads. Some studies have indicated that students do not adjust their reading rates. McDonald (1965) found that over 90% of the 3000 readers at various age levels whom he studied tended to maintain a characteristic approach and invariant rate with all types of material, despite being told to read for different purposes and in spite of variations in the difficulty, style, and content of the materials. Carver (1983) interpreted his data on 333 fourth- through twelfth-grade pupils and 102 college students as indicating that they read at a constant rate instead of adjusting their rate for the difficulty of the reading material. Carver (1984) also reported that the comprehension of 102 college students was not substantially affected by the purpose for which they were directed to read.

On the other hand, some studies indicate that readers show some flexibility in modifying rate to purpose. Intermediate-grade children tended to read faster for details than for main ideas, and faster for main ideas than sequence (Otto, Barrett, & Harris 1968), and fourth graders and college students both read faster when reading for general ideas than for details (Samuels & Dahl 1975). Seventh and eighth graders read passages to get an overview faster and with better comprehension than passages that they read to find details (P. DeStefano, Noe, & Valencia 1981). Both disabled and normally achieving readers showed flexibility when reading to answer general as opposed to specific questions at Grades 4 and 7; but at Grade 10, only the good readers varied their rates (Dowdy, Crump & Welch 1982). Rankin (1970–1971) found that college students varied their rates within a selection, slowing down for difficult portions and reading faster when the material was easier.

These differences in findings may be the result of methodological differences among the studies, or students may have reacted differently from study to study. In fact, they may behave very differently under study conditions than in the normal classroom situation. Then again, inflexibility of rate may simply reflect a lack of appropriate instruction; not much effective teaching of reading flexibility takes place in schools. This may be why many adults complain that they read everything with the same slow, careful rate as they do materials in their professions.

To some extent this individually characteristic and relatively invariant rate of reading may be constitutional. Buswell (1951) found a substantial correlation between reading rate and rate of thinking on nonreading tasks. H. Brown (1970) reported that the reaction time and movement time of seventh-grade boys correlated significantly with both oral and silent reading rates. Quickness or slowness may be a characteristic common to reading and many other categories of human responses. There may be an optimal reading rate for reading comprehension beyond which skilled readers do not tend to pass; if true, this may have a ceiling effect in studies of reading flexibility with skilled readers. Both Carver (1982) and Sticht (1984) postulate that reading comprehension tends to deteriorate above 250 to 300 WPM. Carver (1982) further hypothesized that it would not be appropriate for good readers to adjust their rate as the material decreases in difficulty because it would be inefficient for them to do so, since the optimal rate for reading efficiency is constant.

There is evidence that children can be taught to be flexible readers. P. Miller (1978) discussed the complications that have made research on reading flexibility difficult to conduct, and provided sensible suggestions for developing flexibility in the classroom. Other suggestions were offered by Schachter (1978, 1984) and J. Hoffman (1979). The suggestions for developing metacognitive skills also pertain to the development of reading rate flexibility.

Eliminating Reading Behaviors That May Contribute to Slow Reading

Experienced teachers in any area know how important it is to perform correctly and smoothly before trying for speed. Music teachers know how ruinous it is to allow a child to increase tempo too quickly. Golf pros caution their pupils against trying to hit the ball hard. What they want is a smooth, easy swing that sends the ball a satisfactory distance without disrupting coordination. In all complex abilities the basis of a highly expert performance is not the expenditure of a great deal of effort but the attainment of a smooth, graceful, easy, relaxed, well-coordinated performance.

Reading is no exception to the principle that an emphasis on rate should be postponed until good form has been achieved. Before trying to increase a student's reading rate, one should be assured that the pupil can read fluently. A number of reading behaviors can interfere with fluency in reading. These should be eliminated, or at least greatly reduced, before any pressure is exerted for greater speed in reading. It is assumed that word-recognition accuracy and comprehension are adequate.

Excessive Decoding

Occasionally a child reads at an extremely slow rate because he attempts to decode every, or almost every, word encountered. He may inspect each word by syllable or even letter by letter. This is the kind of child that Bond and Tinker (1973) referred to as having an "overanalytical set." Such pupils must be first convinced that they can recognize words as wholes (and many of them can when forced to). This can be demonstrated to them by using quick-flash techniques. Once the child is convinced, work on phrasing can begin.

Slow Word Recognition

Speed of word recognition can be increased gradually by direct practice in recognizing known words that are exposed for only a brief duration. The use of word cards for this purpose was discussed on page 372, and an easily made hand tachistoscope is illustrated in Figure 7.8 on page 215.

Word-by-Word Reading

The harmful effect on comprehension of reading each word as a separate unit was discussed on page 474. Obviously word-by-word reading will also result in a slow reading rate. The usual treatment is to develop the child's ability to group the words into thought units and to read in phrases, as described on pages 473–475.

Increasing Perceptual Span

There is some belief that increasing the amount that one can see in a fixation will result in the need to make fewer fixations and thereby increase reading rate. Such attempts are almost always a waste of time. There is little difference between the perceptual spans of good and poor readers, and even very skilled readers take in only one or two words in a fixation (see p. 554). If a child has an unusually narrow span of perception, work with rapid recognition of single words is just as productive as attempts to increase his span of perception by showing increasingly longer words or a line of numbers in tachistoscopic devices.

Lip Movements and Subvocal Reading

Nearly all children learn to read by associating printed symbols with previously acquired listening and speaking skills. When asked to read to himself, the beginner continues to mouth the words, but barely audibly. Silent reading soon becomes inaudible, but lip movements may continue in silent reading for many years. Early suppression of lip movements may interfere with reading comprehension and retard growth in reading competence.

In silent reading, even superior adult readers show tiny changes in the electrical activity of the muscles involved in speech (Edfeldt 1960). These changes are similar to the ones that occur during overt speech, but at a miniature level, requiring sensitive electrodes to detect them. Thus nearly all people when reading silently go through the motions of speaking the words, but without any externally observable movement or sound. This covert or unobservable behavior is accompanied by "inner speech," which is often termed *subvocal reading* or *silent speech*. The person reports that he "hears" the words as though spoken by an inner voice, similar to the inner speech that occurs during thinking.

The attainment of true silent reading involves a gradual process of the type described as *cue reduction* (Woodworth 1929). This is the process by which a smaller and smaller part of a total stimulus situation becomes adequate to bring about a response that was originally made only to the total situation. Similarly, an original response involving action of the entire body may gradually be reduced until its significance is conveyed by a slight movement of one part of the body; the lifting of one eyebrow, for example, may convey the meaning of a paragraph of comment. In reading, both kinds of cue reduction take place. While the beginner must inspect each word carefully and often has to look at the separate letters, the expert recognizes most words in an almost instantaneous glance and often reacts to a phrase as a unit. On the response side, the beginner has to read aloud to obtain meaning. Gradually he reduces the response to mumbling, to silent lip movement, to subvocal reading with tiny movements that cannot easily be detected, and finally, in a comparatively few exceptionally fast readers, to an instantaneous flash of meaning that seem to have no special motor or sensory accompaniment.

It seems probable that as rate of reading rises significantly above a comfortable rate of speaking (for pupils making normal progress, around fifth- or sixth-grade level), subvocal reading diminishes but does not disappear. The reader still has inner speech and accompanying tiny muscle changes, but not for every word. A kind of "telegram style" pattern develops in which key words represent phrases. By dropping out the less important words, inner speech becomes compressed and silent reading at a rate two or more times oral reading rate becomes possible.

The research on subvocal reading suggests that a natural decrease in subvocalization should take place without teacher intervention in a learning environment which provides ample experience in reading at independent and instructional levels, avoiding frustration (Pomerantz 1971). Subvocal activity may provide needed reinforcement and be beneficial to comprehension. Teachers should regard this as a natural part of the reading act and should not try to suppress it. There is no need to make pupils conscious of such activity. Even lip movements may be needed by the pupil who continues to make them, and attempts to get pupils to stop them should be made only with a cautious appraisal of the probable effects on comprehension. The persistent use of a "crutch" often means that the child still needs it, and premature efforts to stop its use may be harmful (Davies 1972).

Using auditory feedback (electrodes pick up tiny currents from the speech muscles and feed them to an amplifier, and the reader can hear noises when he has speech-muscle activity during subvocal reading), adults can learn to suppress the speech-muscle activity. But opinion is divided (Cloer 1977) whether such suppression is harmful to comprehension (McGuignan 1973) or does not interfere with rate and comprehension (Bergering 1976). Research findings are mixed. Not only is the relationship between subvocalization and reading rate unclear, but its relation to reading comprehension is poorly understood (Riley & Lowe 1981). Research provides no support for trying to suppress subvocalization in elementary school children (Bruinsma 1980). It seems to be a normal part of the reading process, and it is debatable whether it ought to be suppressed at any educational level.

Finger Pointing and Head Movements

Finger pointing is a symptom; the cause needs to be considered. It is not an unusual behavior in novice readers, and they soon outgrow the need to use this crutch as their word recognition and skill in reading from left to right improves. Teachers should not discourage such behavior in young children. When the behavior persists beyond the initial stage of learning to read, the cause for finger pointing should be determined and removed if possible.

But teachers should not be quick to forbid children to use a needed crutch. Once the cause of the finger pointing has been taken care of, pupils can be slowly weaned from finger pointing by allowing them to use a marker (usually a card placed under the line) as an intermediate step. Word-by-word finger pointing is much more likely to be disruptive to both reading rate and comprehension than is moving the finger smoothly under the line of print. The most frequently given reason for eradicating finger pointing in older pupils is that it slows down the reading rate. The validity of this argument is doubtful.

Moving the head from side to side is not necessary for almost all readers. It may help children with mild binocular coordination problems. It may slow down reading rate (the eyes can move across the page much more rapidly than the head can move from left to right), and if used for a long period of time, it may cause the neck muscles to tire. Pointing out the possible negative effects of head movements and providing the readers with ways to remind themselves to stop this head movement often serves to eradicate the behavior.

Regressions

The remedial work needed to reduce the frequency of regressive movements depends on the causes, which have been listed on page 188. Regressions are the eye-movement equivalents of repetitions in oral reading. When they are caused by deficiencies or inaccuracies in word recognition or word meaning, attempting to train the eye movements will obviously be of little or no value. Any reader, no matter how skillful, will make a large number of regressions when reading material heavily loaded with unfamiliar words, peculiar or highly involved sentence structure, or very difficult ideas. If a tendency to excessive

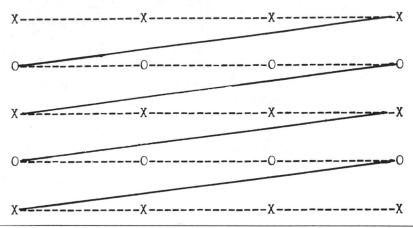

Figure 14.7. Several lines of a cross-line exercise prepared on a typewriter, triple spaced.

regressions persists as a lingering bad habit in a reader whose word recognition and comprehension are at a high level, however, specific exercises to overcome the regressions may be advisable.

A practice that is sometimes helpful in the reduction of unnecessary regressions is the use of *cross-line exercises*. In the beginning, use a page prepared on the typewriter, as shown in Figure 14.7. The instructions are to go across the top line, taking one look at each letter, then follow the diagonal to the second line, and so on down the page. At the beginning of each remedial practice period the reader goes over this page three to five times, gradually speeding up. After the reader has become skillful in using this page, a second page is introduced in which single words replace the meaningless letters. A third stage uses widely spaced phrases, three or four to a line.

One should not expect too great benefits from cross-line exercises. They serve mainly to convince the reader that he can go smoothly across lines without looking back. A direct transfer of the steady, evenly spaced movements built up in this exercise to connected, meaningful reading is not usually achieved.

A second practice that is helpful for reducing regressions is to use a cover card. A blank index card of the 4 × 6-inch size is convenient. The reader starts the card at the top of the page. As he reads, he moves the card gradually down the page so as to cover what he has already read and in that way prevents regressions. The card should be slanted slightly with the left corner a little lower than the right, so as to cover the beginning of each line before the end of the line. This practice, which can be used by the reader himself with any kind of printed reading matter, should have a greater transfer to normal reading than the cross-line exercise because it utilizes a normal reading situation to which only a slight addition has been made.

The elimination of regressions is also one of the purposes of the several kinds of controlled reading practice described in the next section.

Difficulty with the Return Sweep

Some children have difficulty in making a return sweep from the end of one line to the beginning of the next line. This is shown in the observation of

eye movements by the fact that one or two extra fixations are made at the beginning of each line. There are a few children who, after reading a line, look
back along the line and then drop vertically to the beginning of the next line.
This habit results in taking nearly twice as long to read the line as is necessary.
When difficulty in making the return sweep is discovered, one should look for
evidence of eye-muscle difficulty or slow fusion, which at reading distance sometimes is a result of uncorrected farsightedness.

To develop greater skill in making the return sweep, which should be a
single quick diagonal movement, one can use widely spaced lines, with diagonal
lines connecting near the end of each line with near the beginning of the next
line. The child is instructed to try to look along the diagonal when going from
line to line. There is very little prepared material of this sort available, and
usually it is necessary to make up special material on the typewriter, starting
with triple spacing and reducing to double spacing as the child improves (see
Fig. 14.7). Often only a few days of practice are needed. The addition of finger
pointing may make it easier for the child to master the return sweep. Pointing
can continue after the diagonal lines are discontinued, and will eventually be
discontinued without pressure from the teacher. The use of a marker also may
help.

Increasing Reading Rate by Direct Practice

Once the slow reader has reached satisfactory levels in word recognition and
comprehension and has begun to eliminate specific interfering reading behaviors, he is ready for practice aimed directly at speeding up his reading. There
are five main practices for increasing rate of reading: tachistoscopic training,
controlled reading, timed reading, the so-called dynamics method, and extensive
reading without specific emphasis on speed.

Mechanical Pacing Devices

Three mechanical pacing devices have been designed to increase reading
rate—motion pictures, specialized projectors, and pacers. All three attempt to
increase rate by forcing the students to read as fast as the print is exposed; all
employ continuous discourse. The rate at which the material is exposed can be
adjusted but remains uniform for the entire selection to be read, and the typical
procedure is to start at a fairly comfortable speed and decrease the viewing time
(increase the number of words shown per minute) as the students become proficient at a given speed.

Motion pictures present one phrase at a time brilliantly lit against a fainter
background of the rest of the page. Two such sets of films have been produced.
One is the *Harvard University Reading Films* (Harvard); the other, the *Iowa
High School Training Films* (Iowa State University). The levels for which they
are intended are indicated by their titles.

Specialized projectors project material from filmstrips or special slides at
varying speeds, a line or a part of a line at a time. Devices for group use may
be purchased from EDL, Psychotechnics, Cenco, and PDL, and for individual

practice from Craig and EDL.[3] Each machine has its own accompanying reading materials, which adds to their expense.

A method for controlling reading rate without imposing a set pattern of phrasing was worked out by Buswell (1939). It involved the simple principle of a shutter that gradually covered a page from top to bottom at a speed that could be regulated. Reading pacers are sold by AVR, SRA, and Psychotechnics. They provide individualized practice in which the learner can set his own rate at each practice session and can use his own reading material, including his school textbooks (which could be a big advantage). When the practice is followed by adequate comprehension checks, they provide what seems like a well-motivated procedure for guiding the learner toward gradually increased rate without sacrificing comprehension. The same could be true of other specialized devices if used individually.

One of the main problems with using mechanical pacing devices with groups is that it is impossible for a reading selection to be of suitable difficulty and be set at a speed suitable for every member of the group. Another possible problem with all these devices is presenting an entire selection at the same rate. This makes it impossible for the reader to slow down when he meets with difficulty or reread as one might under normal reading conditions. This is somewhat less of a problem when the equipment is used by an individual who can stop the machine or reset the rate. On the other hand, their value may lie in forcing students to attend to the task, since they know that they will not get a second chance to read something; and if left on their own, some students might not push themselves to read faster. Another problem is that there is often little carryover to natural reading situations. There is likely to be more carryover if the pupil's own materials are used with the pacing devices.[4] It also may be helpful to have students attempt to read material of their choice at the speed just imposed by the pacing device, immediately after the paced exercise ends. How much of any favorable effect is the result of controlling the rate and how much is due to motivation that could be secured by nonmechanical procedures is impossible to estimate at present. Some students are intrigued with the machinery and motivated by its use. Other students will increase their reading rate only if a reading speed is imposed on them. The machine does this for them. It is still too soon to comment on the use of the computer to increase reading rate, although the possibilities seem exciting.

Tachistoscopic Training

A *tachistoscope* is a device that allows the presentation of visual material for brief intervals of time ranging usually from one second to 1/100 of a second. Some have a fixed exposure time, but most have variable exposure times. They can range from a simple handmade device (see Fig. 7.8 on p. 215) to complex instruments for controlling the exposure time. Inexpensive small tachistoscopes

[3] The addresses of companies mentioned in the book appear in Appendix C.

[4] A desirable aspect of the *Shadowscope* (Psychotechnics) is its use of a beam of light to pace the reader. The illumination of the beam can be reduced until it is barely perceptible, thereby producing an almost natural situation.

for individuals are available from the Reading Institute, EDL, Reading Laboratory, and AVR. Projection tachistoscopes have two parts: a slide or filmstrip
projector and a shutter-like device that can be set for different exposure speeds.
These devices, which range widely in cost, can be obtained from Keystone, SVE,
EDL, PDL, Psychotechnics, Califone, and Lafayette.

Research findings have failed to indicate any positive impact of tachistoscope training on reading speed or comprehension (Cleland 1950, Manolakes
1952, Kleinberg 1970). Learning to recognize words in less than 1/25 of a second
is irrelevant to continuous reading because most of the fixation time in reading
is required for the brain to process the incoming visual information. Attempts
to increase the span of perception or to develop the ability to recognize complete
phrases at high speeds are questionable, since even skilled readers usually take
in only one or two words in a fixation. The value of tachistoscope training lies
mainly in its effects on motivation and attention.

Increasing Rate through Motivated Reading

In contrast to the point of view that favors controlled reading is one that puts
major emphasis on increased motivation in natural reading situations. The major
causes of slow reading are considered to be lack of enough practice in reading
easy, interesting material and lack of motivation to improve speed. From this
point of view, a program for increasing rate of reading should have three major
components. The first consists of overcoming specific interfering reading behaviors, as described on pages 540–545.

The second involves motivating the reader to do a large amount of easy
reading. This provides the abundant practice needed to develop fluency. The
absence of vocabulary and comprehension difficulties in such material allows
the reader to read easily, without the need to hesitate and reread that is created
by difficult reading matter. If the subject matter is sufficiently interesting, the
desire to find out what comes next provides natural motivation to read quickly,
while the absence of pressure to read at a rate set by someone else eliminates
strain and tension. Methods for developing greater interest in voluntary reading
are discussed in Chapter 15.

Rereading a favorite story or book over and over again should be encouraged. Rereading provides a background of relevant knowledge that effectively
improves use of context and ability to anticipate what comes next. With each
rereading an improvement in fluency and accuracy is likely. As the child finds
himself reading easily and fluently, his self-confidence and motivation are bound
to be favorably affected. This procedure is particularly important with primary-
age children, who generally enjoy hearing the same story over and over, but it
can be effective at any age.

The third phase of the program involves a series of timed silent reading
exercises with comprehension checks. For these, one can use either published
workbook selections or general reading matter of a comparatively easy nature.
The timed exercises strengthen motivation to keep the rate going up, provide a

definite record of progress, and at the same time ensure that comprehension does not suffer in the process.

Several workbooks can be used for timed reading in the upper grades and secondary school. The McCall–Crabbs *Standard Test Lessons in Reading* have been used successfully in many programs (see Fig. 14.8). Each page consists of a brief selection followed by several multiple-choice questions. Three minutes are allowed for reading the selection and answering the questions. If the reader goes too slowly, he cannot answer enough of the questions; if he reads carelessly or too rapidly, he gets too many answers wrong. In successive exercises he learns to read so as to increase his scores. Approximate grade scores are given for each exercise. These grade scores are a powerful incentive, as practically every reader strives to raise his grade scores. Provided that one is willing to count or estimate the number of words, almost any suitable selection for which a good method of checking comprehension can be devised can be adapted for use as a timed reading exercise. Green (1971) trained ninth graders on McCall–Crabbs and similar materials and found a greatly improved balance between rate and comprehension, as well as an improvement in total reading scores.

The "Dynamics" Method

A method widely advertised by a commercial organization has never been revealed to educators in detail, so the description here is necessarily sketchy. The "dynamics" method attempts to replace the usual reading pattern of reading across each line in a series of fixations by a variety of patterns in which the reader's eyes follow his finger down the page. The Evelyn Wood organization's advertising asserts that the typical graduate reads at 1200 W. P. M. with 70% comprehension. The materials used for testing are easy, or of moderate difficulty, usually taken from general adult nonfiction. It is not clear whether time spent in previewing before reading the selection is counted in the computation of rate.

Because no detailed description of the "dynamics" approach has ever been made public, we have asked Charlotte Harris Wiener to write a brief description of her procedures. She taught the Evelyn Wood method for 3 years, and for several years gave a course entitled "Faster and More Effective Reading" at a unit of the State University of New York. Her account follows:

> My work with about a thousand students over the last decade has convinced me that speed reading is an invaluable technique, although it must be used with discretion. Whether my students have been well-educated adults, sixth graders with diverse socioeconomic and racial backgrounds, or "educationally disadvantaged" inmates in prison, the results are strikingly similar. Almost all have learned to speed-read on materials that for them are easily comprehended. Almost all have found that practicing speed techniques has increased their normal reading rate while allowing them a satisfactory level of comprehension.
>
> The following is an outline of one of the basic drills I use for improving rates, and for teaching skimming and scanning:

4

Who would ever have thought that the old trolley car, with its bell clanging for joy, might return to our city streets? Your grandparents could tell you that most trolleys were long ago replaced by buses and cars.

What's wrong with buses and cars? If everyone used private cars, our city streets would become choked with traffic. Both buses and cars produce unhealthy air pollution. The government wants to find a new way to move lots of people quickly, cheaply, and quietly.

Since the trolley car runs on electricity, it is quiet and does not produce clouds of exhaust fumes. Shiny new trolley cars, which are called *light rail vehicles*, are now being built for many cities. Do not be surprised if older folks smile when they see this new "vehicle of the future" clanging down the street.

---

1. **Trolley cars** Ⓐ are a new invention Ⓑ were used many years ago Ⓒ will never be used again Ⓓ are found only in museums
2. **Most trolleys run on** Ⓐ steam Ⓑ coal Ⓒ electricity Ⓓ gasoline
3. **What is the best reason for using trolleys?** Ⓐ they can reduce air pollution Ⓑ they are old Ⓒ they are fun to ride Ⓓ they run on tracks
4. **One problem with using buses is that they** Ⓐ are too small Ⓑ cause traffic jams Ⓒ help cause air pollution Ⓓ do not have a bell
5. **Trolleys are now called** Ⓐ light buses Ⓑ heavy rail vehicles Ⓒ rail buses Ⓓ light rail vehicles
6. **This story says that most old trolleys** Ⓐ remained in use Ⓑ were replaced by buses and cars Ⓒ were painted red Ⓓ were too expensive
7. **Choose the best title:** Ⓐ The End of the Line Ⓑ The Happy Return of the Trolley Ⓒ The History of Railroads Ⓓ Private Cars Are the Answer
8. **According to this story** Ⓐ cities are too large Ⓑ cities should build more parks Ⓒ old ideas sometimes give new solutions Ⓓ older people should own cars

---

No. right	1	2	3	4	5	6	7	8
G score	2.7	3.3	3.7	4.2	4.7	5.4	6.0	6.7

Figure 14.8. A page from the McCall–Crabbs *Standard Test Lessons in Reading*. Reprinted by permission of the publisher from *McCall–Crabbs Standard Test Lessons in Reading*, Book C (New York: Teachers College Press, Copyright © 1979, 1978, 1961, 1950, 1926 by Teachers College Press, Columbia University. All rights reserved.) Reduced in size.

1. Choose an easy novel for beginning practice (in a class it is desirable for all to use the same book).
2. Read about 10 pages, underlining each line with a finger and keeping pace with the eyes.
3. "Practice read" the same 10 pages, using a finger pattern to guide the eyes. The first three times are done at 12 seconds per page, the fourth time at 6 seconds per page, and the fifth at 4 seconds per page. After the first "practice read," write down any words or ideas that you recall. After each subsequent "practice read," add to the notes. Have someone count the seconds until the reader gets the rhythm.
4. Repeat Steps 2 and 3 with consecutive sections of the book for about a half hour daily. Marked improvement in rate of reading and in recall will be noticed within 1 or 2 weeks. Practice should be continued until the reader is satisfied with his performance.

In applying speed reading to nonfiction, previewing the section very briefly before starting to read it and writing a very brief summary after reading are desirable accompaniments of the procedure.

While speed reading is possible without using one's hand, it is easier to learn and maintain if one uses a finger as a pacer and guide for the eyes. A variety of patterns for moving the hand down the page may be used, although the zigzag, curving, and looping patterns seem to be the most popular. The reader is encouraged to keep the eyes relaxed so that he can see an area of the page, not just a portion of a line. It takes hours of practice before one can see all of the words.

Training in speed reading should be combined with training designed to improve flexibility, comprehension, and study skills. A speed reader should adjust his rate according to his purpose; the style and difficulty of the reading material; and the reader's experience with the vocabulary, concepts, and general informational background relevant to the subject matter. He might read a difficult selection in an unfamiliar field at one fifth his rate for easy narrative fiction.

Speed reading feels subjectively different from skimming, although the rates attained may be similar, the scores may be similar on short-answer tests, and skilled readers often use a combination of speed reading and skimming.

Four studies of the "dynamics" method cited by Cranney *et al.* (1982) questioned the claims made of extremely high rates made by advocates of the method. Their study, however, found that the five university students trained in the "Reading Dynamic" program read five to six times as fast but with the same comprehension as the control group when allowed to read at their own pace. When paced at 2600 and 3000 WPM, the "dynamics" group had significantly higher comprehension than the control group. The training program involved (1) using the hand as a pacer, initially line by line and later in a vertical fashion; (2) mapping—the student notes the main idea and fills in other ideas in a diagram fashion (two-tiered notes are taken); and (3) using an add-a-page drill in which the students are extolled to reread very rapidly (double or triple the speed) material that they had just finished reading. Six hours a week were devoted to practice.

Other Speed-Reading Procedures

Schale (1964) described a procedure she called the "2R-OR-ALERT method." The symbols stand for Reinforced Reading, Overview, Read rapidly, Answer questions, Locate mistakes, Examine mistakes, Reread at the same rate (if comprehension unsatisfactory), and Transfer adjustment of comprehension to rate to another article. Emphasis is placed on using "inclusive skimming" (reading only the first sentence of each paragraph horizontally, and skimming the rest vertically for key words). She reported a gain of one group of 24 students from a pretest mean of 506 WPM to a posttest mean of 2313 WPM. This group obviously had very superior rate on the pretest. In a later paper (Schale 1972) she reported two girls who reached speeds of over 20,000 WPM after training in Reinforced Reading; one was able to read vertically, taking in two columns at a time! We have not found reports by other investigators on this procedure, which deserves careful independent evaluation.

Berger (1968) reported a comparison of four methods for increasing rate of reading, used in a one-semester reading-study skills course for college freshmen who were below average on freshmen entrance-test scores. There were four experimental groups of 40–45 students each, and a control group. The four methods were tachistoscopic training, use of the Controlled Reader, controlled pacing, and paperback scanning. In the latter method the reader was required to scan each page vertically under time pressure: first 2 minutes, 8 seconds per page; next 2 minutes, 7 seconds per page; and down to 2 seconds per page; then up to 10 seconds per page. Significant gains were made by all four groups in rate as compared to the control group; the tachistoscopic group made the smallest gains and the paperback scanning group made the largest gains, not only in rate but also in reading flexibility.

Brown (1976, 1984), in discussing techniques for increasing reading rate, emphasized the importance of student and teacher expectancies and attitudes. The instructor's beliefs about how much the students could improve seemed to set limits to how much they did improve. Such student attitudes as "fear of missing something," "lack of confidence," and "the faster you read, the less you comprehend" inhibit progress unless the student is helped to overcome them. Brown emphasized the importance of active self-discoveries and the use of "visual expediters." He reported results from three kinds of courses, each of which carried college credit. In each course rate increased while comprehension remained constant. In a college course with direct student–teacher interaction, rate gained from initial 252 WPM to 1548 WPM; in an independent study-cassette version of the course, from 314 WPM to 889 WPM; and in a TV course of 12 sessions each lasting 30 minutes, from 293 WPM to 903 WPM.

Tinker (1958) concluded that 800 WPM is about the fastest rate possible for genuine reading and that rates faster than that are based on skimming. Spache (1962) insisted that while rates of several thousand WPM can be attained by rapid skimming or scanning, genuine reading (in which most of the words are perceived) cannot proceed faster than 800 to 900 WPM. These calculations were based on the assumption that 10-word lines were read with an average of three fixations per line, of about .25 seconds each, plus the very brief times for moving the eyes from one fixation to the next and from the end of one line to the beginning of the next line.

Whether speeds of over 1000 WPM should be called reading or skimming is still an open question. The fact is that for some reading purposes, and for some material, such speeds are both possible and desirable. But the goal should be flexible adaptation to one's purpose for reading and the nature of the material, not a uniformly very high rate of reading.

Implications for School Practice

At the primary-grade levels it is extremely doubtful that any direct efforts should be made to develop speed in reading, despite an occasional report of good results from the use of tachistoscopic and controlled reading procedures as low as the second grade (R. Rowell 1976). A well-conceived developmental reading program that creates fluent, intelligent reading through balanced attention to word recognition and comprehension, oral and silent reading, careful directed reading and extensive independent reading should result in a satisfactory rate of reading as a by-product.

In third, fourth, and fifth grades, there is also some doubt about the advisability of aiming at greater speed through specific practice. Cason (1943), working with matched groups at the third-grade level, found that extensive free independent reading brought about as good an improvement in rate as either controlled reading with the *Metron-O-Scope* (an early type of controlled reader) or timed silent reading practice. Bridges (1941) compared several methods with pupils in Grades 4, 5, and 6. She concluded that "training that emphasized comprehension and took no account of speed was more effective in developing both speed and comprehension than was training that emphasized speed and minimized comprehension. Undirected daily practice in reading was also more effective at this level than training in rapid reading." These conclusions held for average and below-average pupils, but not for those reading above sixth-grade level. Although these studies were done long ago, they have not been contradicted by more recent research.

Once children have reached the point where recognition of most words is rapid and automatic (usually around sixth-grade reading level) they are probably ready for some instruction in how to read faster while maintaining comprehension. For this, the procedure described above as motivated, timed reading with comprehension checks seems to give as good results as those that require expensive equipment. In terms of transfer of training, procedures that most closely resemble normal reading situations would seem to have an advantage over those that utilize quite artificial conditions.

There are reports, but no controlled experimental studies, that speed-reading procedures can be taught successfully as low as the sixth grade. Considering the practical importance of the possibility of reading at rates several times today's average rates, the scarcity of research in this area is deplorable. After an initial flurry of interest during the 1960s, research workers have ignored this area of investigation.

Training for improved speed of reading should become a definite part of a developmental reading program at and above the sixth grade. Individual pupils may, of course, need remedial help at lower grade levels because of extremely slow reading, but for the majority, rate can be expected to develop as a by-product of a well-rounded developmental reading program until the sixth grade. From then on, specific provisions for speeding up reading seem desirable through high school and at least the first year of college.

Eye Movements

In 1878 Javal published the first account of systematic observations of eye movements during reading. His work stimulated other studies, and when Huey (1908) published the first important book on the psychology of reading, a considerable store of knowledge on eye movements had been gathered. Early investigations were handicapped by clumsy and sometimes painful apparatus. After Dodge invented an eye-movement camera, many important studies were made, notably by Buswell (1922).[5]

As individuals read they have the feeling that their eyes are moving most of the time, but actually such movements take up less than 10% of the reading time. On the average of about four times per second, the eyes make a quick jerky movement known as a *saccade*. An average saccade covers about 8 to 10 letter-character spaces and requires 35 milliseconds[6] (McConkie 1982). Each saccadic movement serves to bring a new region of text into foveal vision[7] for detailed analysis.

The pauses between the saccades are called *fixations*. During a fixation, which lasts an average of a quarter of a second, the eyes are relatively still.[8] It is only during a fixation that the eyes see the print. Although the eyes are still during a fixation, the mind is actively at work. Skilled readers acquire most of the information necessary for reading during the first 50 msec. of a fixation, and the decision where to move the eyes next is based on information acquired early in the fixation (Rayner 1983b).

The duration of a fixation may be influenced by information acquired in previous fixations (Underwood 1982) and is related to the characteristics of the word being fixated. Unusual words receive longer fixations; common words, shorter fixations.[9] On the average, the duration of fixation changes very little from first grade through college (see Table 14.2). Words in the important region

---

[5] A brief history of eye-movement research has been given by Weintraub (1977).

[6] A millisecond is a thousandth of a second. Thus, 250 msec. = $\frac{1}{4}$ of a second, 500 msec. = $\frac{1}{2}$ of a second.

[7] Foveal vision is the area of central vision, where vision is the clearest. Parafoveal vision extends farther out, and stimuli seen in this area are seen less clearly than in foveal vision. In peripheral vision, which extends out even farther than parafoveal vision, vision is the least clear.

[8] The eyes do show small drifts and tremors, which are critical to proper vision. Without them, visual stimuli would appear to fragment and disappear (McConkie 1982).

[9] On a single-word fixation, the duration of fixation is not related to word length in words ranging from 5 to 11 letters and from 1 to 4 syllables in length. Word frequency correlates only .11 with duration of fixation (Kliegl, Olson, & Davidson 1983).

Table 14.2   Eye-Movement Norms

	GRADE												
	1	*2*	*3*	*4*	*5*	*6*	*7*	*8*	*9*	*10*	*11*	*12*	*Col*
Fixations per 100 words (including regressions)	224	174	155	139	129	120	114	109	105	101	96	94	90
Regressions per 100 words	52	40	35	31	28	25	23	21	20	19	18	17	15
Average span of recognition (in words)	.45	.57	.65	.72	.78	.83	.88	.92	.95	.99	1.04	1.06	1.11
Average duration of fixations (in seconds)	.33	.30	.28	.27	.27	.27	.27	.27	.27	.26	.26	.25	.24
Rate with comprehension (words per minute)	80	115	138	158	173	185	195	204	214	224	237	250	280

SOURCE: Sanford E. Taylor, Helen Frackenpohl, and James L. Pettee, *Grade Level Norms for the Components of the Fundamental Reading Skill*, Research Information Bulletin, No. 3 (Huntington, N.Y.: Educational Developmental Laboratories, Inc., a Division of McGraw-Hill Company, 1960), p. 12. Reproduced with permission. These norms are based on students who scored 70% or better in comprehension when reading material of average difficulty for the grade.

of the text tend to be fixated longer. In short, how long a fixation lasts is probably related to both perceptual and psycholinguistic factors (Kliegl, Olson, & Davidson 1983). What is less clear is the extent to which all of the processing activities related to the fixated word are completed before the eyes move from that word.

The amount that a reader sees in one fixation is called a *recognition span*,[10] or, as McConkie (1982) defined it, a *span of perception* is the region from which the reader acquires and uses visual information during a fixation. As shown in Table 14.2, the average span of recognition is about half a word in first grade (the novice reader averages two fixations per word), but is not much greater than one word even at the college level.[11] A recognition span is influenced by such factors as word length and type and purpose for reading.

One school of thought holds that skilled readers rely minimally on visual information from the text, sampling graphic information only as needed to conform their predictions. Eye-movement data, however, indicate that at least when reading carefully, skilled readers perceive no more than one or two words at a time (McConkie 1982). They sample text very frequently, usually fixating adjacent words or skipping no more than one word (Carpenter & Just 1983). Other eye-movement researchers (Shebilske & Fisher 1983) report, however, that readers fixate only one half to two thirds of the words in many situations.

For readers of English,[12] the perceptual span extends from the beginning of the currently fixated word (but no more than 3 to 4 letter spaces to the left

[10] Rayner (1981) described and critiqued various techniques for studying the span of perception.

[11] The fact that good readers have longer eye-voice spans (EVS) than do poor readers is sometimes used to argue that good readers actually see more in a fixation. However, an EVS is probably the result of at least two fixations, since a single fixation lasts only about 250 msec, and an EVS lasts between 640 to 700 msec (Underwood 1982).

[12] den Buurman, Roersema and Gerrissen (1981) reported a perceptual span of from 25 to 31 letter positions for Dutch college students.

of the fixation) to about 15 letter spaces to the right of the center of the fixation (Rayner 1983b). It should be realized, however, that the span of perception is not a fixed constant. Recent findings suggest that the amount of information picked up during a fixation varies from fixation to fixation (Hogaboam 1983).

What information the reader uses for reading in a single fixation is more important than what he sees. Information useful in determining word meaning is obtained from the foveal region (six to eight letters around the center of fixation; one or two words depending on word length) and the beginning of the parafoveal region. Some letter-feature information is obtained from the region slightly further to the right, but it is not used in word identification during that fixation. In many fixations the fixated word along with the first few letters of the upcoming word are processed. This preliminary letter processing of the upcoming word presumably speeds up the reading process. Word-length information, which is useful in guiding the eyes to their next fixation, is acquired out to about 15 letter spaces to the right of the fixation (Rayner 1981, 1983a, b). Therefore, while the reader is processing during a fixation, he has available not only all the information obtained from reading to that point and that which is currently in his foveal vision but at least some information regarding word length and word shape (R. Haber and Haber 1981a, b).

The bases on which the mind decides when to make a saccade and where to make the next fixation are not well understood. There is some disagreement regarding both the nature of the information used in deciding where to send the eyes next and how soon that information is utilized in making the final decision. There seems to be more agreement as to where the next fixation is placed. According to Rayner (1983a, b), information obtained from parafoveal vision regarding word length seems to be the primary determinant as to where to make the next fixation, but some estimate of how far to the right of the present fixation words can be identified is also possible. If the upcoming word is long, the eyes will probably be sent to or very near to the center of the word. If there are two short words, the eyes will be sent beyond the first word (McConkie & Zola (1984). There is also a tendency to avoid blank spaces and not to fixate *the* as often as other three-letter words. Words that are "skipped" tend to be high-frequency words (Hogaboam 1983).

Information as to when to initiate a saccade can be influenced by visual information acquired during the current fixation, but processing of that information is not necessarily completed by the time the decision is made to move the eyes. Some fixations appear to be too short to be affected by any visual information acquired during that fixation, so a decision as to when to make the next saccade must be based on information obtained prior to that fixation (McConkie and Zola 1984).

Each fixation provides a slightly different image of the stimuli to the mind.[13] Yet, although each fixation is discrete and provides overlapping as well as new visual information to the mind, the reader is unaware of any discontinuity from

[13] See L. Haber and Haber (1981) for a schematic representation of this phenomenon.

one fixation to the next. Exactly how the mind integrates these differences in input and maintains continuity across fixations to give the appearance of a single flowing experience is largely unknown (see McConkie 1982, L. Haber & Haber 1981).

Factors such as reading ability, text difficulty, and reading purpose influence saccade length and duration of fixation, but such changes are small in comparison to the variations shown not only between individuals but also by the same person reading a single passage. Saccade length may range from 1 to over 20 letter characters, and fixation duration may range from 1/10 to 1/2 of a second (Rayner 1983a).

When the reader comes to the end of a line of print, there is a smooth continuous left-to-right diagonal movement to the beginning of the next line. This is called a *return sweep* (see Fig. 14.9).

Sometimes the eyes move backward to get another look at something that was not seen or understood clearly (more likely the latter). Such a backward eye movement is known as a *regression*. As shown in Table 14.2, the average number of regressions is quite high in first grade and declines to a fairly constant percentage at about the eighth grade. Regressions in skilled college readers occur on the average about 15% of the time but may vary from 0% to 40% (Rayner 1983a, b).

As reading ability increases, there are fewer fixations per line, fewer regressions and shorter duration fixations (see Table 14.2 and Fig. 14.10). Eye-movement patterns become more regular with increasing reading ability.

Measurement of Eye Movements

There are portable eye-movement cameras available, such as the *Reading Eye II* (EDL) and *Eye-Trac* (Applied Science). An optical system positions images of the reader's eyes on a ground glass screen, and two pairs of photocells monitor eye movements. The photocell signals are amplified and recorded on heat-sensitive paper. The movements of both eyes are monitored simultaneously, and in smooth reading, their parallel movements give a sort of descending staircase effect (see Fig. 14.9). The duration of each fixation is shown by the length of the vertical line. The amount of print taken in during a fixation is indicated by the length of the horizontal line representing the movement between fixations. A regression is shown by a short horizontal movement to the left and a return sweep by a long horizontal movement to the left.

Young and Sheena (1975) reviewed the eye-movement measurement techniques available at that time; but in the last decade, much more sophisticated equipment has become available for research purposes (refer to McConkie 1982; McConkie, Wolverton, & Zola 1984). These make use of scleral or corneal reflection techniques and a computer that continually checks the position of the eyes and can measure eye movements very precisely. The reading material is usually presented on computer-controlled displays, and the text can be altered for various reasons without the reader even being aware of it, even to the point of changing aspects of the text display contingent on the reader's eye movements.

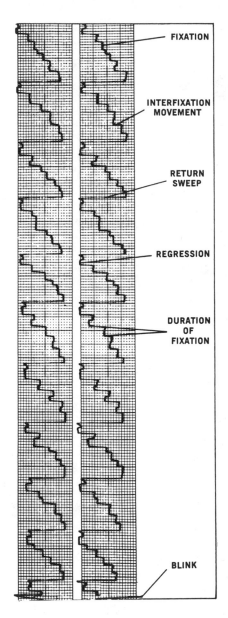

Figure 14.9. Diagram showing how eye-movement characteristics are represented in a Reading Eye II recording. From *Eye-Movement Analysis with the Reading Eye II,* by Helen Frackenpohl Morris. New York: McGraw-Hill Inc., 1973. Reproduced with the permission of EDL/McGraw-Hill, a division of McGraw-Hill Book Company.

There are three informal procedures for observing eye movements. Although none is as revealing or reliable as the procedure described above, they may provide some useful information and certainly should be informative to anyone who has never observed a pupil's eye movements while reading.

In the *mirror method,* the child is seated at a table on which the book is held in a reading position. The observer sits slightly behind and to one side of the child, also facing the table. A rectangular mirror is placed on the table fairly

MATURATION OF READING PERFORMANCE

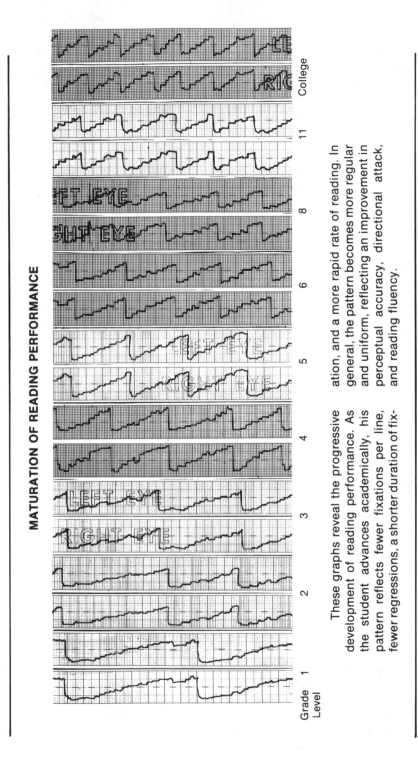

These graphs reveal the progressive development of reading performance. As the student advances academically, his pattern reflects fewer fixations per line, fewer regressions, a shorter duration of fix- ation, and a more rapid rate of reading. In general, the pattern becomes more regular and uniform, reflecting an improvement in perceptual accuracy, directional attack, and reading fluency.

Figure 14.10. Samples of eye-movement photographs, showing development through the school years and in college. From a photograph supplied by Educational Developmental Laboratories and used with their permission.

close to the book and held or propped at an angle so as to allow the child's eyes to be observed.

To use the Miles Peep-Hole Method (Miles & Segel 1929), an appropriate reading selection is mounted on a sheet of pasteboard. A ¼-inch-square opening is made near the middle of the page between two lines. The observer is positioned so that she can look through the opening as the child reads the selection. The peephole method gives a somewhat clearer vision of the eye movements than does the mirror method, but it requires special preparation.

In the procedure that we prefer, the child sits and holds a book on a level with his eyes as he reads. The observer sits across from the child and watches the reader's eyes across the top of the book. Because the reader's eyes begin to be obscured by his eyelashes when he nears the middle of the page, this procedure can be used only for the top half of each page.

Eye Movements, Poor Reading, and Reading Disability

Compared to good readers, poor and disabled readers show longer durations of fixations, shorter saccades, many more regressions, and generally more erratic-looking eye-movement patterns (McConkie 1982).[14]

Data such as the above have been interpreted in diametrically opposed ways. They are believed to be either the cause of reading disability or simply to be an effect. The former viewpoint is discussed first.

Lefton et al. (1979) found that, in addition to the differences mentioned above, disabled readers made significantly more fixations than did good readers and showed relatively unsystematic eye movements, which varied considerably from line to line. They concluded that disabled readers were severely hampered by "chaotic oculomotor control." Somewhat similar, but not as dramatic, conclusions have been reached by Elterman et al. (1980) and Shapira, Jones, and Sherman (1980).

Pavlidis (1981a, b; 1983) claimed that eye-movement performance can be used to differentiate between dyslexics and other disabled readers by requiring them to track light sources that were illuminated sequentially. Pavlidis also reported that the duration of the dyslexics' fixations was highly variable, that they made significantly more right-to-left saccades (and these regressions often occurred in clusters of two or more), that their eye movements were erratic and idiosyncratic, and that the narrow perceptual span of dyslexia was a consequence of their erratic eye movements and excessive regressions. He further claimed that the dyslexics displayed the same eye-movement patterns when reading easy material and when performing nonreading tasks. Although Pavlidis (1983) suggested that it was as yet impossible to tell which of five possible factors caused these erratic eye movements, he appears to favor strongly a malfunctioning oculomotor control system, a general sequencing problem, or an interaction between the two.

Pavlidis's claims are controversial. Three studies have failed to replicate his findings (Rayner 1983a), and his conclusions have been questioned by other

---

[14] Various patterns of eye movements in disabled readers have been reported by Olson, Kliegl, and Davidson 1983).

findings (Olson, Kliegl, & Davidson 1983; A. Jones & Stark 1983). McConkie (1982) wrote that the aberrant eye-movement patterns of disabled readers indicate that processing is not flowing smoothly but that, at present, they do not indicate the nature of the problems. Most studies have found that when given material of appropriate difficulty, the eye movements of poor readers do not differ significantly from those of good readers of the same age (Pirozzolo & Hansch 1982, Rayner 1983a).

Perhaps, as Rayner (1983a) suggested, Pavlidis's subjects were a different subtype of disabled readers than those found in other studies. Only further studies will clarify the issue. There is, however, some evidence of differences in eye movements between two subtypes of disabled readers (Rayner 1983a, Pirozzolo 1983). Whereas audiolinguistic dyslexics do not show evidence of eye-movement disorders, visual–spatial dyslexics do (their eye movements are similar to those reported by Pavlidis). But neither Rayner nor Pirozzolo agree with Pavlidis that such eye movements are causal. Eye-movement patterns reflect the moment-to-moment cognitive changes induced by an interaction of the visual stimuli and the task of comprehending (McConkie & Zola 1984).

The Significance of Eye Movements

When selections of sufficient length are used, eye-movement photography gives reliable and valid measures of reading performance (Tinker 1946). However, the expense of the apparatus and the necessity of having a trained technician to run the machine and interpret the results make the eye-movement camera a luxury that has seemed impractical for most school and clinical situations.

Photography or informal observation of eye movements discloses *what* the eyes do while the person reads; it does not provide an explanation of *why* they move as they do. Reading, like walking, is controlled by the brain. One cannot walk without legs, but the speed and direction of a person's walking are controlled by the central nervous system. In reading, similarly, the eyes are the servants of the brain. Discovering that there are many regressions in a person's reading does not in itself explain the difficulty or indicate the specific nature of the remedial work needed.

In most cases, poor eye movements are not the cause of poor reading; they are symptoms of the fact that the reader is reading poorly. Tinker studied the question of training eye movements for over 30 years and summarized his conclusions as follows:

> Actually, there is no evidence to support the view that eye movements determine reading proficiency. . . . All experimental evidence derived from well-designed studies shows that oculomotor reactions are exceedingly flexible and quickly reflect any change in reading skill and any change in perception and comprehension. . . . Real progress in programs of teaching reading would be achieved if the term and concept of rhythmical eye movements were abandoned, if eye-movement photography were confined to the research laboratory, and if the use of gadgets and other techniques to train eye movements were discarded. (Tinker 1965, pp. 111–112)

The good reader is not aware of what his eyes do when he reads any more than he is aware of what his stomach does when he is digesting a tasty meal. If he tries deliberately to control his eyes while he reads, his concentration on the meaning suffers and his reading efficiency deteriorates. If a reader's comprehension and rate are satisfactory, his eye movements can be safely ignored. If his eye movements are poor, the remedial work should usually stress the basic elements of good comprehension: accurate word recognition, knowledge of word meanings, phrasing, good concentration, and so on. Some people need training to overcome specific bad eye-movement habits, but they are definitely in the minority.

At present, even with the most sophisticated equipment available, there is little diagnostic or remedial information to be gained from eye-movement photography. A number of issues remain to be resolved (see McConkie 1983), but with the emergence of more testable models of the reading process and with the availability of highly sophisticated technology, the future looks promising.

15

Fostering Reading Interests, Attitudes, and Tastes

A recent survey (NAEP 1982b) indicated that voluntary reading and enjoyment of reading decrease with age. The percentage of pupils who reported that they voluntarily read daily dropped from 54% at age 9 to 35% at age 13 to 33% at age 17. Whereas 81% of the 9-year-olds said they enjoyed reading very much, a similar response was given by only half of the 13-year-olds and 42% of the 17-year-olds. In a study by Neuman and Prowada (1982), most of the students reported spending less than 5 hours a week reading for pleasure, and 24–34% (depending on age level) said they spent less than 1 hour a week reading voluntarily. Given a choice between going to a movie, watching television, reading a book, or reading a magazine, half the 9-year-olds and nearly two thirds of the teenagers would rather go to a movie (NAEP 1981b).

Of what value is it to develop skillful readers if the skill is used to little purpose in adulthood? Enormous amounts of time, effort, and money are expended in teaching children how to read, yet we apparently have produced what Huck (1971) referred to as a nation of "illiterate literates." A successful reading program must not only develop children who *can* read but also children who *do* read. Three major objectives of any total reading program should be to build a favorable attitude toward reading, to develop a lasting interest in reading, and to improve reading tastes. A good reading program must create the desire to read and help the individual to find pleasurable recreation in reading. It also should foster the desire to read for personal development, to learn more about the world, and to gain increasing understanding of people and society.

The following statement by the Joint Committee on Reading Development deserves wide attention:

> At all times and with every means at her command, the teacher must learn how best to counteract the attitude that reading is for school only; that reading is a second-hand and, therefore, an inferior form of experience. Reading must be understood and interpreted as a tool of invention, relevance, and creativity, as a sort of depth-perception device that gives dimension to firsthand experience; and as a principal means by which the intellectual inheritance is tested and developed. (Dietrich & Mathews 1968)

I. PLANNED RECREATIONAL READING PROGRAMS

In the elementary school a distinction usually does not exist between recreational or voluntary reading and a literature program. Few literature programs at this level emulate the formal study of literature found in the secondary school. Unfortunately, most recreational reading occurs on an unplanned basis (Hardt 1983). For these reasons, we use the term *planned recreational reading program*, which has as its purposes to develop favorable attitudes toward reading, an interest in reading as a voluntary activity, and an awareness of what is considered to be good children's or adolescent literature. In short, its basic purpose is to motivate children to read and help them to expand their reading interests and tastes. This is accomplished by promoting the concept that reading can be a pleasurable, rewarding activity; by exposing pupils to various kinds of works, writing styles, topics, and authors; and by providing them with abundant, appropriate materials to read and with the time to choose, read, and discuss them. One of the important aspects of a planned recreational reading program is the allocation of time *during* school to conduct the program. If we do not demonstrate that reading is a worthwhile activity by providing school time, how can we expect children to value reading? Allowing children to read material of their choice only after school assignments are completed helps to develop a less than desirable attitude toward reading as a leisure-time activity.

A planned recreational reading program will incorporate the following activities in a flexible overall plan: (1) *free reading periods* in which children are allowed to read materials of their own choice, as in sustained silent reading (see p. 92); (2) the teacher *reading aloud* to the students; (3) *guided supplementary reading* in which the pupils are helped to select materials but during which the teacher does not deaden interest by dominating the choices; (4) *topic units*, which utilize a subject, type of work, style of writing, and so forth as a coordinating theme; and (5) creative *sharing*, which is accomplished through discussion, oral reading, storytelling, and creative activities (Huus 1975, 1984).

According to Odland (1979), four major concentrations should form the framework for a literature program that allows for flexibility in both methods and materials and provides for the direct teaching of literature:

1. *Children's interests* provide excellent motivation for reading and the serious study of literature.
2. *Study of literary types* should include myths and legends, folktales, contemporary and historical fiction, fantasy, science fiction, poetry, biographical fiction, and nonfiction.
3. *Literary elements* should focus on exposure, through listening and reading, to the elements that are part of the composition of a work. Children learn to examine their responses to the material and perceive what it is in the literature that causes these responses.
4. *Creators of books* involves learning about the contributions of authors, illustrators, and others involved in the production of literary works.

Practical ideas for incorporating literature into the total reading program were offered by L. Hopkins (1980); Spiegel (1981a) offered a number of suggestions for getting children to read for pleasure.

Planned recreational reading programs are effective in increasing the quality and quantity of voluntary reading. Children learn to read by reading, and learn to love to read when pleasure is the purpose for reading (Pillar 1983). In what appears to be the only study of its kind, G. Manning and Manning (1984) compared four models of recreational reading regarding their impact on attitudes toward reading. They found that the peer-interaction and teacher–pupil conference groups scored significantly higher on their reading attitude scale than did the sustained-silent-reading and control groups. Perhaps verbal interaction helps develop a more favorable attitude toward reading. The peer-interaction group also scored significantly higher than the other three groups on a measure of reading achievement.

In order to accomplish the aims of a planned recreational reading program, teachers need to know about the reading interests of children, how to determine reading interests and attitudes toward reading, the affective aspects of reading, how and where to locate materials, and how to estimate the difficulty of reading materials.

II. READING INTERESTS[1]

For a variety of reasons, it is difficult to make definitive statements about the reading interests of children and young adults. Marked differences among stud-

[1] Some writers recently attempted to distinguish between *reading interests* and *reading preferences* (Spangler 1983, Summers & Lukasevich 1983), but the distinctions are not universally agreed on, nor are the terms well described. Generally, though, the distinction appears to be that an *interest* is inferred from what has been read, whereas a *preference* pertains to what children say they would like to read but have not read yet.

ies as to the methods through which interests were determined and in the populations studied make it difficult to compare research findings (Huus 1979). "In general, the research into children's reading interests has suffered from, among other things, lack of clear definition and lack of vigor in design, as well as from questionable data-gathering instruments" (Weintraub 1977).

Interest Categories by Age Levels

The limited research dealing with the reading interests of preschool children is inconclusive. It is possible that interests are fleeting and do not stabilize until children can read on their own. Illustrations have as much or more appeal than story content, but very young children like repetition and repeatedly ask to hear familiar stories. An analysis of children's favorite picture storybooks revealed that the story structures children liked best (in descending order of preference) were confrontation and solution of a problem (note the similarity to story grammar); episodic, usually a series of adventures; contrasts in which characters have opposing points of view; plotless (a catchall category for alphabet books and the like); and travel in which the character embarked on an adventure. Young children liked fantasy, humor, and realistic fiction (Abrahamson 1980).

Primary-grade children are strongly interested in make-believe, animals, and children's activities. These preferences were expressed by children in 10 different countries (Kirsch, Pehrsson, & Robinson 1976). Middle-class first graders prefer the pranks theme over the pollyanna theme, peer interaction over parent–child interactions, and activities dealing with their own gender (Rose, Zimet, & Blom 1972). Interest in the fanciful usually increases until the age of 8 or 9 and then gradually declines.

Most preschool and primary-grade children seem to prefer humorous poems, followed by poems about animals and poems related to their own experiences. Although there was a considerable range of opinion expressed when poetry was read to primary-grade children, their order of preference for poetic form was narrative poems, limericks, rhymed verse, free verse, lyric poetry, and haiku. There was a strong preference for poems that rhymed and that used sound (alliteration, onomatopoeia). Poems relying on metaphor, similes, or personification were generally disliked. Traditional poems were preferred over modern ones (M. White 1980, Fisher & Natarella 1982).

Intermediate-grade children have a greater variety of interests than their younger schoolmates. By the age of 9 or 10, definite sex differences are expressed. Boys generally become absorbed in adventure, sports, and mystery tales. They also read fictionalized history and biography, and some of them read extensively on mechanics, science, invention, and material related to hobbies. Girls seem to prefer sentimental stories of home and school life and animals, and usually develop an interest in romantic fiction between the ages of 11 and 14.[2] They share the boys' liking for mystery and adventure, humor and fantasy

---

[2] A phenomenon of the 1980s has been the scores of contemporary teen romance novels, especially planned, written, and marketed for adolescent girls. They have received a great deal of criticism and opposition, but teenage girls read them (Parrish 1983).

(Ross & Fletcher 1980, Summers & Lukasevich 1983), but usually do not care for reading related to science and invention. Boys, on the other hand, tend to ignore human interest stories and in general avoid anything that seems definitely feminine. Intermediate-grade children tend to like exciting and humorous stories (Lauritizen & Cheves 1974) and stories in which the characters have to struggle with problems similar to the ones they face in their own lives (Worley 1967). Jose and Brewer (1983) found that fourth- and sixth-graders' identification with the story character increased their liking for the story, but there was a difference in their preference for story endings. Fourth graders preferred positive outcomes regardless of whether the character was good or bad; sixth graders preferred positive endings for good characters but negative endings for bad characters. Most middle-grade children enjoy comic strips and comic books. They also read magazines and newspapers (A. Miller 1967).

For intermediate-grade children, the most popular poems tend to be those related to children's experiences, those with humor, and those having strong rhythm and rhyme (Bridges 1967). Limericks and narrative poems are popular in the middle grades; haiku, serious or sentimental poems, and poems that are difficult to understand are not (Terry 1974). Children may find poetry difficult because it often requires a high level of thinking but uses devices that make it look easy, thus misleading them (Marston 1975).

The fact that poetry is not popular with children has been well documented (W. S. Gray 1960). Unimaginative, burdensome, and joyless teaching of poetry may contribute to its relative lack of popularity. An observational study by Baskin, Harris, and Salley (1976) revealed three major teaching faults: (1) using poetry to achieve unrelated academic purposes (e.g., a handwriting exercise); (2) overloading children with a certain type of poetry; and (3) assigning poetry memorization as punishment.

At junior and senior high school levels, studies have shown a continuing trend toward individual differentiation. Rough categories for boys include action and adventure, sports and games, science fiction, historical novels, humor, mystery, and war (Stanchfield & Fraim 1979). Girls' interests include books about people and social relationships, romance, humor, and mystery without violence. Adolescents express a strong preference for themes in which the central problem is resolved successfully. Boys' preference for a male protagonist becomes significantly stronger from Grades 7 to 11, girls' preference for female protagonists decreases as grade level increases (Beyard-Tyler & Sullivan 1980). Humor is an important element of what teenagers choose to read (Nilsen & Nilsen 1982). Young people dislike many of the titles considered classics by their English teachers (Norvell 1972), and high school students are generally negative toward poetry (Elliott & Steinkellner 1979).

Voluntary reading usually increases in amount until the age of 12 or 13. In some schools there is a marked decline in voluntary book reading, which coincides in time with both increasing homework and the teaching of literature. In other schools, teachers are successful in maintaining the amount of voluntary reading and helping adolescents toward mature tastes.

Norvell (1966) explored the popularity of magazines with 6000 children. He found marked differences between the preferences of boys and girls, except for *National Geographic*, which was popular with both. Children showed a liking for adult magazines early. Seven of the 10 magazines most popular with children in Grades 4 through 6 were adult magazines. One may wonder to what extent the presence of adult magazines in homes, and the absence of children's magazines, may have contributed to that result. Intermediate-grade children read a wide variety of magazines. They have strong preferences for nonfiction and humor magazines, but there are marked sex differences in interests. Boys read more magazines than girls below Grade 7, but girls read more from Grade 7 up. On the whole, interest in magazine reading was somewhat lower in the 1960s than it had been in the 1930s. Comparable data for the 1970s and early 1980s were not available. It would appear, however, that magazine reading is still popular, since 13 magazines for young people rank among the top 200 magazines in circulation in the United States (Monteith 1981a).

Newspaper readership increases with age until about age 17, with the content reportedly read most often changing substantially with age. There are sex differences as well as age differences. The trend in the direction of acquisition for boys is the comics, sports, and news. For girls, it is the comics, a diversity of personal and social development information, combined with the news (which increases with age). Readership is influenced by availability and being required to read by the teacher (Guthrie 1981a). High school juniors and seniors report a strong interest in newspaper reading (Elliot & Steinkellner 1979). Criscuolo (1981) offered 10 suggestions for creative homework with newspapers. Suggestions for "teaching with newspapers" may be found in the newsletter of the same name (American Newspaper Publishers Association).

Probably the most important finding about reading interests is the tremendous range of individual differences both in amount of voluntary reading and specific interests expressed. Even in a group of children who are similar in intelligence, age, and cultural background, the range of individual preferences is tremendous. While a knowledge of general trends is helpful to teachers in allowing them to anticipate the interests of pupils, it does not relieve them of the responsibility of trying to discover the particular interests of each pupil.

There are frequently marked differences between what children would prefer to read and what teachers and librarians recommend (Nilsen, Peterson, & Searfoss 1980). Many of the books selected as the best of the year by adults have been ignored by children (Terman & Lima 1937, Vandament & Thalman 1956, Taylor & Schneider 1957). Nor do children's choices of the best books published annually agree closely with the interests revealed by various studies (Greenlaw 1983). Similarly, children's poetry preferences do not agree closely with those revealed by research studies (Sebesta 1983).

Personal and Institutional Factors Influencing Reading Interests

A number of factors seem to influence reading interests. None of these factors appears to operate in isolation, but their interrelationships have not been clearly established. As with much research, it is difficult to separate which variables are operative and to what extent they interact. Furthermore, there is some question as to the reliability of the instruments and techniques used to determine reading preferences (McNinch 1970–1971, H. M. Robinson & Weintraub 1973).

Personal Determinants

Personal factors that may influence reading interests are age, sex, intelligence, reading ability, attitudes, and psychological needs. Age-level interests are covered here in broader terms than on pages 565–567.

Reading interests of elementary school children show a definite development by grade level. Students of all ages maintain an interest in stories that have characters of their own age. At an early age there is an identification with fantasy figures (usually animals) who represent childlike experiences. Older elementary school students prefer more realistic stories that portray peers undergoing suspenseful adventures. There is some evidence that the reading interests of children 2 years or so below or above grade level are more influenced by reading age than chronological age (Geeslin & Wilson 1972).

Changing interest patterns appear at the junior and senior high school levels. Seventh and eighth graders display a wider range of interests than younger children do, but by the last 2 years of high school, the interests narrow. At about the eighth and ninth grades adult interests seem to begin, and the motivation for reading shifts from reading for entertainment to reading for self-understanding. After age 16 interests do not change considerably unless drastically affected by education or employment.

Another determinant of reading interests is the sex of the reader. Sex differences are found in reading preference during the primary grades, but they are not very strong (Kirsch 1975). Differences in reading interests between the sexes increase in the intermediate grades (Ross & Fletcher 1980, Summers & Lukasevich 1983). Sex differences in reading interests become more pronounced in junior high school, and lessen during the senior high years.[3]

A somewhat different interpretation of the research literature was offered by C. Johnson and Greenbaum (1982) who concluded that girls will read about boys and their activities, but this finding says nothing about girls' preferences; boys will read about girls and their activities if the story content appeals to them; although girls have a wider variety of interests, there are many overlapping interests between boys and girls; reading interests are unique, so there is no need to be concerned with gender interests in reading; and there is a need to be concerned only with individual interests.

Sex differences in interests seem to be lessening (Feeley 1982), and although sex role stereotypes have not been completely eliminated, there has been quantitative and qualitative improvement in the portrayal of females in children's literature over the past decade or so (Frasher 1982). There has been some progress in this area, but boys and girls still seem to select books in accord with cultural expectations. As cultural attitudes change, children may be given more

---

[3] Elliott and Steinkellner (1979) reported clear sex differences in reading interests in Grades 11 and 12.

encouragement to read in areas previously considered as more appropriate for the opposite sex. As such changes occur, so may expressed reading interests. But, as desirable as these changes may be, it is not likely that reading alone will significantly alter sex-role attitudes, which are fairly well developed before children enter school and are reinforced through the years by family and peer beliefs.

The relationship between intelligence and reading interests has not been clearly established. Generally, bright children read much more than average children, have a wider range of reading interests, and are usually 1 to 2 years ahead of average children in interest maturity. The mentally slow child reads less and usually has preferences that are slightly immature for his age but more mature than those of younger children of his mental level (Lazar 1937, R. L. Thorndike 1941). At the secondary school level, however, little relationship was found between IQ level and liking for specific selections (Norvell 1973).

Although reading ability is related to sophistication of interests, it does not correlate directly with reading interests. Poor readers and high school students of below-average intelligence tend to give high ratings to material in which it is easy for them to identify emotionally with the central character (Emans & Patyk 1967). The same principle probably applies to younger poor readers. Good readers are not necessarily avid readers (Lamme 1976a).

Only a small number of studies have been done on the influence of attitudes on reading interests. On the basis of his study with sixth-grade children, Sauls (1971) concluded that there were significant relationships between the number of books read and the pupil's attitude toward reading, the pupil's reading ability, and home and teacher encouragement. If reading fulfills a need, positive attitudes toward reading usually develop. Attitudes vary with the reader's level of reading ability, background, efforts, and peer influences. They are unique, personal, and highly unpredictable.

Alexander and Filler (1976) concluded: (1) Correlations between favorable attitudes toward reading and reading achievement are not always positive; (2) some instructional procedures can, but do not necessarily, improve attitudes; (3) attitudes toward reading are influenced by the student's self-concept and interests, and by the attitudes and behaviors of parents and teachers; and (4) the child's gender, intelligence, and socioeconomic status do not necessarily influence attitudes toward reading.

In one study (Aaron & Seaton 1976) an attempt to change reading attitudes was not successful. In another (Waller, Trisman, & Wilder 1977), there were some significant gains in positive attitude, but these did not result in improved reading achievement.

One of the major determinants of reading interests is the satisfying of psychological needs. Needs and interests are not synonomous because the same need may find expression in different interests. Among the needs are the need to develop self-concept, intellectual needs, emotional needs, social needs, and aesthetic needs. Whether or not elementary school children read to satisfy their developmental needs remains an unanswered question. For example, the reading interests of children do not seem to correspond very closely to their felt needs. They frequently turn to sources of information other than reading when they need information and regard reading primarily as a recreational activity (Rudman 1955). However, individual differences vary so considerably that it is impossible to generalize about the relationship of needs and interests. Students may turn to other media to satisfy their needs if the expectations of reward from reading are not high.

Institutional Determinants

Purves and Beach (1972) listed the following factors as institutional determinants of reading interests: availability of books; socioeconomic status and ethnic background; peer, parent, and teacher influences; and television and movies.

Much of the research regarding reading interests has been biased in that reading choices have been limited in one way or another. If more choices were available, other results might have been obtained. Books borrowed from public libraries are more often completed than those taken from school libraries, as are books read during "free time" as opposed to those read during school library periods. Students also prefer books from a library or book club to those given to them in class.

Accessibility and availability have a strong influence on children's choices. Study after study has shown that the amount and kind of reading matter in a child's home have a marked relationship to his or her reading habits. The use of a public library by children is directly related to the distance of the library from the child's home and school. Increasing recognition of the importance of accessibility has been one of the major factors in the building up of library collections in schools. Each classroom in a well-equipped school has a library collection of its own. Many elementary schools, a well as most secondary schools, have a central library collection, and the number of librarians in schools has increased. Interest in reading is highest when there are both classroom and school libraries (Schulte 1969). Traveling libraries have been created to provide better library service to rural schools. In cities and towns, loan systems have become common by which a teacher can borrow a large assortment of books from a public library and replace it with different books from time to time.

Most research has concluded that socioeconomic factors do not affect interests significantly. Although differences in amount and range of reading apparently resulting from such factors as intelligence and reading ability do occur, low-, middle-, and upper-class students have similar reading interests. Among the possible explanations for their lack of differences are these: (1) Most studies employed white subjects who were exposed to middle-class-oriented literature; (2) interests usually were inferred from titles known or available to the subjects, thus actual interests may not really have been indicated; (3) until recently, titles on checklists or questionnaires have not included works of ethnic or minority writers; and (4) the response required of the subjects may be biased toward verbal ability. There seems to be little difference in the reading interests of rural, suburban, and metropolitan students (Huus 1979).

Some studies have shown significant differences between ethnic groups at all age levels, with the widest differences occurring in the intermediate grades.

The influence of ethnicity on reading interests may begin early. Lewis (1970) found that black kindergartners strongly favored books about children in ghetto areas, whereas white children disliked such books. It is impossible to state what other factors may have influenced these choices, however. Lickteig (1972) found that although there were some similarities between inner-city and suburban children, such as preference for science fiction at both fourth and sixth grades, inner-city children tended to prefer black fiction more than suburban children did, while white suburban children preferred horse stories more than inner-city children did.

On the other hand, Bouchard (1971) did not find any significant differences among the reading interests of blacks, whites, and Spanish speakers in the intermediate grades. Johns (1973) reported that contrary to the prevailing belief, the intermediate-grade inner-city children in his study, most of whom were black, preferred to read stories or books containing middle-class settings, characters with positive self-concepts, and characters in positive group interactions. In studying the expressed reading interests of Anglo, Negro, American Indian, and Mexican American fifth graders, Barchas (1971) found that in most general reading interests, the four ethnic groups were more alike than different. When reading content provided opportunity for minority-group ethnic identification, however, their expressed interests were more different than alike. Minority-group children expressed a high degree of interest in topics related to their own ethnic group and immediate environment but generally low interest in topics related to other minority groups. Within each minority-culture title collection, certain titles were of high interest to all groups, particularly fiction stories combining minority culture with suspense and adventure, folktales, and certain biographies, sports books, and cookbooks. While the sexes shared many common interests (mystery or adventure, humor, animal stories, and child's immediate environment), sports and science topics were of more interest to boys. A wide range of individual interests was found within each ethnic and gender group, with much overlapping of interests among all groups. Considerable similarity of interests across races and cultures was reported by Asher (1978) and Kirsch, Pehrsson, and Robinson (1976).

Peers, friends, parents, and teachers influence reading interests directly through recommended or assigned reading and indirectly by serving as models. Friends and peers played an important role in why fifth graders selected certain books to read, whereas television and movies did not (Lawson 1972). Next to peer recommendations, teachers' enthusiasm can be an important factor in developing interests.

Effects of Other Media on Reading Interests and Achievement

The effects of other media on reading interests and achievement is very complex and not well understood. Almost all of the current interest in this area is centered on the impact of TV viewing.

In the mid-1960s, elementary school children viewed television an average of 20 hours weekly; slightly less in the primary grades, slightly more in the intermediate grades (Witty & Melis 1965, Witty 1966). In the 1970s and early

1980s, children 6 to 11 years old watched television an average of 24 hours per week; teenagers watched almost 20 hours (Lamb 1976, Larrick 1983). The average amount of time spent watching television during the school week did not differ for good and poor readers in the seventh grade (Moldenhauer & Miller 1980). Viewing time diminishes with age (Neuman & Prowda 1982), but so does the amount of time reading for pleasure (Telfer & Kann 1984). On the average, regardless of age, children spend more time watching television than they spend on homework and recreational reading combined (Gough 1979). In fact, by age 18, children will have spent 50% more time watching televison than they will have spent in school (Carnegie Corporation 1977).

Research findings seem to agree that there is a negative association between the amount of TV viewing and IQ: the more television watched, the lower the IQ. There is a wide variation in IQ scores among those who are light viewers but a narrow range for heavy viewers. For high-IQ students, heavy TV watching is related to low reading comprehension. A cause–effect relationship, however, has not been determined (NIMH 1982).

In general, the amount of time spent watching television either has not been found to be significantly related to reading achievement (Wagner 1980, 1984) or there is a low negative correlation (P. Williams *et al.* 1982). A slightly different picture emerges when students are grouped by the hours of TV viewing time. Moderate viewers (usually defined as 1 to 2 hours daily) tend to have higher reading achievement than light or heavy viewers. Beyond 10 hours per week, achievement scores tend to decrease as the amount of viewing time increases. The correlations are reduced but remain significant even when IQ is controlled (P. Williams *et al.* 1982, NIMH 1982). What these correlational data do not reveal, however, is whether or not increased TV viewing contributes to poor reading achievement (and if so, to what extent). The effects of TV viewing also may differ depending on which kinds of programs are watched (Zuckerman, Singer, & Singer 1980), the conceptual bakground and linguistic level of the viewer, and so forth. There is, for example, some evidence that shows like "Sesame Street" and "The Electric Company" have a positive impact on the acquisition of basic reading skills. Television can expose viewers to experiences they might not otherwise have, and listening to spoken English may help non- or limited-English speakers to acquire the language.

There is little doubt that the borrowing and sale of books related to TV programs increase after their telecasts (Potter 1981, Shoup 1984). But Hornick (1981) concluded that this has no significant effect on the overall amount of recreational reading done and that what interest whetted by television does, at best, is redirect reading choices. Wagner (1980, 1984) concluded that, in general, there was no clear evidence that television had either stimulated or hindered an interest in reading.

The effects of TV on reading performance may be more subtle than the simple displacement of one activity by another. Reading requires perceptual continuity to line after line. Television habituates the mind to short takes and not to the continuity of thought required by reading. Focusing and paying attention to print becomes a strain for the conditioned TV viewer (Purves 1984).

As TV viewing has increased, time spent reading comics and pulp magazines seems to have decreased permanently (Hornick 1981). Over the long run, books, newspapers, and better magazines seem to hold their own as leisure-time activities. Although there is some evidence that television may influence reading choices (Hamilton 1973, 1976; McKenzie 1976), whether or not watching television influences reading tastes is still an open question (Feeley 1973, 1974). There is little relationship between TV viewing and reading preferences in general; but for low-IQ children, the more television they watched, the more different things they liked to read about (NIMH 1982). For the most part, average and superior readers who use one or more media widely also tend to spend more time reading. Children who are inadequate readers have less of an interest in reading than in other media (H. M. Robinson & Weintraub 1973).

Witty (1965, 1966) also inquired about movies, radio, and voluntary reading. The majority of children went to the movies biweekly; about one third went every week. Radio listening (mainly popular music) averaged about 7 hours a week in elementary school and 12 to 14 hours a week in high school. Children in the 1960s were doing a little more voluntary reading than in the 1930s, even though the hours per day for reading were only one third the time spent watching television. Comparable data are not available for the 1970s or the early 1980s, except that in one study eleventh graders reported spending more time watching television than listening to the radio (Telfer & Kann 1984). Perhaps with the advent of MTV (Music Television) teens are turning more to television than to radio to fill their "popular music need."

The attraction of television was beautifully expressed by one youngster: "It gives you stories like a book, pictures like movies, voices like radio, and adventure like a comic. Television has action while you stay in one spot" (Shayon 1951, p. 29). As Witty and Shayon both pointed out, television is filling otherwise unmet needs in a somewhat satisfactory fashion. Regulating the amount of time spent in watching is highly desirable but does not solve the problem completely. A comprehensive approach would require working with parents to develop more active and creative forms of recreation in the home, helping children develop and apply criteria for evaluating and selecting TV programs, and using television for motivating and enriching reading (McDonald 1959). Suggestions for using TV viewing to stimulate reading interests may be found in Becker (1973), Adams and Harrison (1975), and Solomon (1976), and a curriculum guide for developing TV viewing skills appears in Ploghoft and Sheldon (1983). Instructional television programs, which dramatize exciting excerpts from stories and introduce authors to children, are available for motivating children to read (Gough 1979).

Before the advent of television, the failure of many children to read at home was blamed on radio, the movies, and comic books. But these activities have often been replaced by TV watching (Hornick 1981, NIMH 1982). The fact is that children who do not like to read will find other things to do with their spare time, and if they love to read they will find time for reading no matter what competing attractions there are. If children find reading easy, interesting, and accessible, we will not need to blame the mass media for capturing and holding their attention.

Other Factors Influencing Reading Interests

Three other factors may influence reading interests and preferences: illustrations, the reading of comics, and the difficulty of the material.

Illustrations

Marked changes in the illustrations used in books have taken place over the past years. Colorful covers have become general. Boxed-in small pictures have given way to pictures without definite margins, which sometimes spread across facing pages. Line drawings with flat, primary colors have been supplanted by pictures employing shading and a wide range of attractive tints. Illustrations occupy a greater proportion of the total page space and are more carefully integrated with the story. Children prefer illustrations that have a definite center of interest, are colored, depict action, but are realistic (Rudisill 1952, Whipple 1953).

Reading the Comics

Many teachers are concerned over the great interest shown by children in comic books and comic strips, most of which contain adventure tales or portray the exploits of superhuman characters. The appeal of comic books is illustrated by the fact that 113 different titles are released in one month, each with a printing of over 50,000 copies (G. Wright 1979). Comic book popularity increases through the elementary school years and peaks at about age 12 to 14. Although many high school and college students read comics, the major consumers are in the 9- to 13-year-old bracket (Dechant & Smith 1977). Comics are read as frequently by good readers as by poor readers (Swain 1978), and there is no evidence that reading comic books, in and of itself, has a negative impact on reading achievement (Hornick 1981). In Ireland, children who read the comics had relatively good reading achievement, while those with low reading ability devoted little time to reading the comics or books (Greaney 1980).

It is futile, even if it were possible, to try to prevent children from reading the comics. Instead, one should attempt to help them discriminate between the better and poorer types, and to use their comic-book reading as a springboard toward the reading of stories and books that will satisfy the same interests at a higher level. The inclusion of freedom to criticize and compare comic books during a book club meeting provides a basis for developing a group opinion that almost inevitably will frown on the worst specimens. In the upper grades, a skillful teacher can lead the more voracious readers of comics into reading books of the *Tom Swift* and *Tarzan* varieties and later to Jules Verne, H. Rider Haggard, and H. G. Wells.

Comics can be used to teach such reading skills as left-to-right progression, use of picture clues, use of quotation marks, and distinguishing reality from fantasy (Hallenbeck 1976). Comics also can be used to initiate an interest in reading (Koenke 1981). The readability of comic books ranges between 1.8 to 6.4, according to the Fry formula (G. Wright 1979). While comics may provide the needed incentive to read, there is a need for caution in using them. Good readers were found to spend as much time on reading when using either books or comics. Poor readers, however, spent more time on actual reading and made greater gains in reading comprehension when reading books other than comic books (Arlin & Roth 1978).

Interest and Difficulty

Few people, children or adults, can really enjoy reading a book that taxes their skill. One of the reasons why so many children place reading low on their list of leisure-time activities is that, for the most part, the books they have been given to read have been too difficult to allow easy and enjoyable reading.

Many teachers find that the books they have been given to use as texts and readers seem to be much too difficult for their pupils. When that happens, teachers must do the best they can with inadequate materials (see A. J. Harris & Sipay 1979, pp. 378–380). Such a situation is probably one of the reasons why normal development of reading skills is not achieved more commonly. The need for adequate reading materials is even more important for remedial teachers. To handicap them with improperly chosen materials is to saddle them with a burden that they can carry only by the expenditure of a great deal of effort.

Disabled readers should be given reading material that is no more difficult than the level at which they can read successfully. At the beginning of remedial treatment it is often desirable to give them materials that are at their independent reading level rather than their instructional reading level. This ensures successful reading from the beginning of the remedial work and thus tends to stimulate effort. It also gives opportunity for fluent reading and for paying attention to thought getting—something that is overshadowed when much attention has to be devoted to the mastery of new reading vocabulary.

Despite the pressure from teachers for simpler instructional materials, textbooks in the content fields continue to be difficult reading matter for the majority of children in the grades for which they are intended. Even when the vocabulary is not excessively difficult, the tendency to try to cram in as many facts as possible creates a "concept density" that makes for difficult reading, with textbook readability often exceeding the publisher's grade-level designation (Roe 1970, Chester 1974).

Although two studies (Brooks 1972, Schultz 1975) did not find a significant relationship between interest and comprehension, three studies reported by Asher (1980) and the NAEP study (1982) did. Both good and poor readers perform considerably better on high-interest than low-interest material (Asher 1980), but the findings regarding the interaction of reading interest and level of reading ability are mixed. Schnayer (1967) and Vaughn (1975) found that interest had a more positive effect on the reading comprehension of poor than of good readers. Another study (K. Stevens 1979) revealed just the opposite, and Asher (1980) concluded that there was no interaction between these two variables. Girls perform better than boys on low-interest material, but there are no sex differences on high-interest material. Both black pupils and white pupils comprehend more of high-interest than low-interest material, but interest does not differentially affect the reading comprehension of these racial groups (Asher 1980).

Osako and Anders (1983) reported that topic interest was only a marginal predictor of how well ninth graders of average or above-average reading ability were able to comprehend expository text. It also seems that when students are interested in the material, they can satisfactorily comprehend material that would ordinarily be considered above their instructional reading levels (Schnayer 1967, Belloni & Jongsma 1978).

It is difficult, to determine the nature of the cause–effect relationship between interest and comprehension. For one thing, it is hard to attend to dull material. Interest motivates one to read, to attend to the task, and to put forth effort. Then, too, a person usually knows more about a topic in which he or she has an interest, thereby facilitating reading comprehension.

This does not mean that if a selection is sufficiently interesting, its difficulty does not matter. If the selection contains a large number of unknown words, it probably will be difficult to comprehend. Even if the child can grasp the general meaning of the selection, it is unlikely that he will learn and retain many of the new words. Furthermore, interest alone is not always sufficient to overcome the conceptual or syntactic difficulties of a selection.

III. METHODS OF DETERMINING READING INTERESTS AND ATTITUDES TOWARD READING

Many techniques have been used in research studies on reading interests. Circulation data for newspapers and magazines have been compiled, the popularity of books has been studied by counting the number of times each was withdrawn from a library, and elaborate questionnaires have been employed. Most of these methods are too complicated and time-consuming to be practical for the classroom teacher.

One of the simplest and most effective ways of finding out children's interests is to watch their daily behavior and listen to their conversations (Frasher 1978). In schools in which children are encouraged to be spontaneous, they display their preferences in many ways: in conversation, in play, in drawing, and in other activities that encourage self-expression. Donald's absorption in aviation shows in his drawings and in the many airplane models he builds. Lillian's love for playing nurse can lead to reading a biography of Clara Barton. Tommy's devoted care of the class's rabbits suggests the reading of books of animal stories. The alert teacher can find many leads concerning possible reading interests by observing her children.

A second useful procedure is to arrange for a hobby club period or a period in which each child has a chance to tell about the things he or she likes to do in spare time. This not only informs the teacher about the leisure-time activities enjoyed by the pupils but also helps popularize certain interests. An enthusiastic report about stamp collecting, a home aquarium, or some other hobby may start several other children on the same activity. Groups with similar hobbies can be established and special reading matter supplied for each group.

A third useful procedure is to arrange for a quiet interview with each child. During the interview the teacher can encourage the child to talk about his likes and dislikes in games, movies, TV programs, the books he has read, what he wants to be when he grows up, and so on. Naturally, the teacher must be liked and trusted by the children if she wants them to confide in her. The preparation of a mimeographed record form helps to keep such interviews fairly uniform in terms of the questions asked and provides a convenient way of recording information. With large classes, it is often impractical to attempt to interview all the pupils.

Another possible technique is the use of a checklist, such as the one developed by Eberwein (1973) for use in junior high school. As shown in Figure 15.1, the student is asked to read a number of book titles and check those she or he would like to read or use. A simple interest questionnaire appears in A. J. Harris and Sipay (1979, p. 406), and an interest checklist for the middle school was developed by Heathington (1979). The *Dulin-Chester Reading Interests Questionnaire*, for use in the elementary school, appears in Dulin (1979, 1984). Heathington and Koskinen (1982) developed an interest inventory for adults in a literacy program. It assesses the topic about which they would like to read, the preferred format(s) of reading material (e.g., comics, newspapers) and the functional materials the adults need to read in their everyday lives. Such information can be very helpful in planning a reading program and increasing its chances for success.

If a questionnaire study by Mangieri and Corboy (1981) is indicative of what exists nationally, teachers know very little about children's literature (only 9% of 571 respondents could name three children's books written in the past 5 years) or how to promote recreational reading (only 11% could name three or more such activities). There is also evidence that teachers lack knowledge of their pupils' interests (Byers & Evans 1980). Given these two probabilities, it is unlikely that teachers often match children's interests with reading material.

Attitudes toward Reading

Studies generally show that good readers have a more positive attitude toward reading than poor readers, but the correlations are modest, ranging from .20 to .40 (Wigfield & Asher 1984). Not all good readers have a positive attitude toward reading, nor do all poor readers have a negative attitude toward reading. Nevertheless, a child's attitude toward reading can be an important factor in his voluntary reading and reading achievement.

Studies have shown that preschoolers have positive attitudes toward reading but that negative attitudes toward reading develop in the primary grades (Shapiro 1979). A number of opinions have been offered to account for such changes, but there is little hard evidence. One of the reasons may be the fact that primary-grade teachers spend little class time attempting to develop positive attitudes toward reading (Heathington & Alexander 1984). Attitudes toward reading seem to be promoted by a set of variables rather than any one variable (Walberg & Tsai 1983).

Reading Interest Inventory

Directions: Below are the titles of some books that you might like to read or use during the next year. If you think you would like to read or use the book, make a √ mark on the line in front of the title. If you are fairly sure that you would not like to read or use the book, or if you do not know if you would like to read or use the book, leave the line blank. Please be sure to read all the titles and decide if you would, would not, or do not know if you would like to read or use each book during the next year.

_____ 1. Bionics, The Science of Living Machines 001.5

_____ 2. Reference Books, a Brief Guide for Students 016

_____ 3. Books for the Teen-Age 028.52

_____ 4. How to Use the Library 028.7

_____ 5. The World Book Encyclopedia 031

_____ 6. Readers' Guide to Periodical Literature 051

_____ 7. Museum, The Story of America's Treasure Houses 069

_____ 8. Behind the Headlines, The Story of Newspapers 070

_____ 9. Witches 133.4

_____ 10. How to be a Successful Teen-Ager 155.5

_____ 11. The Tree of Life, Selections from the Literature of the World's Religions 208

_____ 12. The Story of the Dead Sea Scrolls 221.4

_____ 13. Jesus of Israel 232.9

_____ 14. Prayers for Young People 242

_____ 15. Religions in America 280

_____ 16. Heroes, Gods and Monsters of Greek Myths 292

_____ 17. Questions Teen-Agers Ask 301.43

_____ 18. Black Pride, A People's Struggle 301.451

_____ 19. Information Please Almanac 317.3

_____ 20. Petticoat Politics, How American Women Won the Right to Vote 324.73

_____ 27. How to Study Better & Get Higher Marks 371.3

_____ 28. For Good Measure, The Story of Modern Measurement 389

_____ 29. Fashion as a Career 391.069

_____ 30. Manners Made Easy 395

_____ 31. King Arthur and His Knights of the Round Table 398.2

_____ 32. All About Language 400

_____ 33. Egyptian Hieroglyphs for Everyone 411

_____ 34. Webster's Third New International Dictionary of the English Language 423

_____ 35. The New Cassell's German Dictionary 433

_____ 36. Mansion's Shorter French and English Dictionary 443

_____ 37. Cassell's Spanish Dictionary 463

_____ 38. Cassell's New Latin Dictionary 473

_____ 39. The Russian Alphabet Book 491.7

_____ 40. 700 Science Experiments for Everyone 507.2

_____ 41. The Wonderful World of Mathematics 510.9

_____ 42. Exploring Mars 523.4

_____ 43. The Riddle of Time 529

_____ 44. Push and Pull, The Story of Energy 531

_____ 45. Inside the Atom 539.7

_____ 46. The A B C's of Chemistry 540.3

_____ 47. World Beneath the Oceans 551.4

_____ 48. Instant Weather Forecasting 551.59

_____ 54. The Wildlife of South America 591.98

_____ 55. Field Book of Insects of the United States and Canada 595.7

_____ 56. The Birds of America 598

_____ 57. The World of the Opossum 599

_____ 58. The Young Inventors' Guide 608

_____ 59. The Wonderful Story of You, Your Body – Your Mind – Your Feelings 612

_____ 60. Human Growth, The Story of How Life Begins and Goes on 612.6

_____ 61. Drugs, Facts on Their Use and Abuse 613.8

_____ 62. Here is Your Hobby, Amateur Radio 621.3841

_____ 63. Motors and Engines and How They Work 621.4

_____ 64. Your Future as a Pilot 629.13

_____ 65. How to Build Hot Rods and Race Them 629.22

_____ 66. Walk in Space, The Story of Project Gemini 629.45

_____ 67. The Book of Horses 636.1

_____ 68. Young America's Cook Book 641.5

_____ 69. Strictly for Secretaries 651

_____ 70. The Story of Glass 666

_____ 71. Cloth from Fiber to Fabric 677

_____ 72. Model Making 688

_____ 73. Careers in the Building Trades 690.69

_____ 74. The World of Art 709

_____ 75. Old Cities and New Towns, The Changing Face of the Nation 711

Figure 15.1. Part of a *Reading Interest Inventory* for use in junior high school. From Lowell Eberwein, What do book choices indicate? *Journal of Reading*, December 1973, *17*, 186–191. Reproduced by permission of the author and the International Reading Association. Approximately two thirds of the items are shown.

An attitude is a disposition to respond in a favorable or unfavorable manner. It is a mental construct that cannot be measured directly but must be inferred. There are three general methods for determining attitudes. Observations are the most useful because they can be used over time. But their reliability and validity are highly dependent on the skill of the observer. Projective techniques (e.g., sentence completions) hold promise because children are less likely to respond in socially desirable ways. Self-reports, which are the most commonly used instruments, can be useful if the scale or questionnaire is reliable and valid. Pupils tend to respond in socially acceptable ways on such instruments, however. The best procedure is to make use of all three (Teale 1980).

The *Incomplete Sentence Projective Test*, reproduced in Figure 15.2, can be used over a wide range of ages. If it is used as a group test, the children write the answers, but the teacher can read the items to them and help them with spelling if necessary. Used individually, it can be given to nonreaders. It is often very revealing of the child's true feelings, especially about reading. The question "I'd read more if _____" has brought such answers as "I liked to read," "books weren't so hard," "I could read better," and so on. In answer to "I'd rather read than _____," Ruth wrote, "I wrath get bet by a snake." Positive ideas and feelings come out just as freely. When children trust the teacher, a device like this can help the teacher greatly in the effort to understand (Boning & Boning 1957).

Among the self-reports available is the *Wisconsin Reading Attitude Inventory* (Dulin 1979, 1984), which was designed for use in the elementary school.[4] Lewis and Teale (1980) contended that secondary school students' attitudes toward reading are multidimensional and suggested that the reason for much of the conflicting research data is that the studies treated "attitude" as unidimensional. Thus, the *Teale-Lewis Attitude Scale* measures three dimensions: the value placed on gaining insight into oneself or others; the value placed on the role of reading for attaining educational success; and reading for pleasure. In a series of studies, Wallbrown and his associates (Wallbrown & Wisneski 1981, 1982; Wallbrown & Cowger 1982) gathered normative and reliability data for the eight-dimensional *Survey of Reading Attitudes*. It is meant for use with intermediate-grade pupils. Another attitude scale was developed by Summers and Lukasevich (1983).

Many measures of attitude toward reading are available and have been described by Alexander and Filler (1975, 1976). A review of the available instruments led Summers (1977) to conclude that (1) most published reports lack sufficient information; (2) information on the assessment of reading attitudes is scanty; (3) few instruments are developed and standardized adequately; (4) results from scale-development studies are often overgeneralized; (5) few studies report more than one reliability check; (6) except for the *Estes Scale*, which the

---

[4] An updated and revised version of the *Estes Attitude Scales*, which is part of the Wisconsin Inventory, is available from the Virginia Research Institute or from Pro-Ed, which publishes separate forms (1981 edition) for use in the elementary and secondary schools.

1. Today I feel _____
2. When I have to read, I _____
3. I get angry when _____
4. To be grown up _____
5. My idea of a good time is _____
6. I wish my parents knew _____
7. School is _____
8. I can't understand why _____
9. I feel bad when _____
10. I wish teachers _____
11. I wish my mother _____
12. Going to college _____
13. To me, books _____
14. People think I _____
15. I like to read about _____
16. On weekends I _____
17. I'd rather read than _____
18. To me, homework _____
19. I hope I'll never _____
20. I wish people wouldn't _____
21. When I finish high school _____
22. I'm afraid _____
23. Comic books _____
24. When I take my report card home _____
25. I am at my best when _____
26. Most brothers and sisters _____
27. I don't know how _____
28. When I read math _____
29. I feel proud when _____
30. The future looks _____
31. I wish my father _____
32. I like to read when _____
33. I would like to be _____
34. For me, studying _____
35. I often worry about _____
36. I wish I could _____
37. Reading science _____
38. I look forward to _____
39. I wish _____
40. I'd read more if _____
41. When I read out loud _____
42. My only regret _____

Figure 15.2. Incomplete Sentence Projective Technique. From Thomas Boning and Richard Boning, I'd rather read than . . ., *The Reading Teacher*, 1957, *10*, 197. Reproduced by permission. The items are adapted from an earlier version by Ruth Strang.

reviewer felt was the best available, attitudinal scales lack validity; and (7) few scales are based on a clear underlying concept.

IV. CREATING AND ENRICHING READING INTERESTS

One of the most crucial tasks in a reading program is the transformation of children's attitudes toward reading from indifference or active dislike to avid reading. As long as progress depends entirely on what the children read under the eyes of the teacher, it is likely to remain slow. Spectacular gains in reading ability often result when the children begin to read a book or two a week, aside from class lessons. The most carefully planned lessons may bring disappointing results unless the teacher is able to ignite a tiny spark of interest and then nurture it carefully into a clear flame of enthusiasm for reading.

The teacher can help to develop a positive attitude toward reading, and an interest in it, by creating lessons and situations that consider the student's personal needs, aspirations, and attitudes. Pupils are motivated to read when the teacher focuses on their areas of greatest interest, matches the material to their levels of reading ability, displays a high regard for reading, and makes the students aware of their success (Betts 1976).

A classroom environment that nurtures an interest in reading is one in which (1) the teacher is enthusiastic about books; (2) the classroom is full of well-selected books to which the children have easy access; (3) the children have time to browse, choose, and read; (4) children get personal introductions to special selections; (5) books are the subject of much comment and discussion; and (6) appreciation for reading is developed through cumulative experiences (Hickman 1983).

Creating Interest in Reading

The basic principles of successful work in developing reading interests have been admirably summarized as consisting of a "a lure and a ladder." The lure may be any of a variety of ways of enticing children to begin pleasurable reading. The ladder involves providing suitable reading matter that will intensify the child's interest in reading and in which he or she can progress gradually to reading material of superior quality.

The first essential is to provide physical surroundings in the classroom that will create an atmosphere favorable to reading. There should be a "reading corner" in every classroom. Its furnishings do not have to be elaborate. A table or two, a few chairs, and bookshelves are the essentials. Interest can be stimulated if, at the beginning of the term, the children build or paint the bookcases, make and hang curtains, place colorful jackets on the books, and so on.

A good class library should contain at least 50 books. They should range in difficulty from easy and interesting enough for the poorest readers in the class to others that will appeal to the most advanced readers. There should be special collections of books of varied difficulty relating to the activity units that are currently engaging the attention of the class. In addition, there should be fairytales and legends, animal stories, adventure tales, stories with foreign settings, humor and nonsense, nature study and science, and some poetry. Current and back isues of the good children's magazines should find a place also. Larrick (1978) critiqued the 45 best-selling children's magazines and provided subscription information. A description of magazines designed for children under age 14, as well as ordering information, can be found in Richardson (1983).

A simple classification scheme makes it easier for children to select books. The books can be arranged under a few simple headings: *Make believe, Real-life stories, Animals, People and places,* and so on. Some teachers use colored tabs, a different color for each reading group in the class, to help the children find books of appropriate difficulty. Of course, the daily class schedule must provide some free time for browsing and independent silent reading if the reading corner is to function properly.

A teacher who makes it a regular practice to read fascinating stories to her class usually has no trouble arousing interest in reading. Pupils of any age love to listen to a lively tale. A good book or story that the teacher has read to the class will find many readers when it is placed in the library collection. Teachers who take the trouble to study the art of telling and reading stories to children reap dividends in improved attention, listening comprehension, and interest in reading (Martin 1968; Thornley 1968; McCormick 1977a, b). Reading to pupils can expose them to the works of different authors and writing styles. It also can provide a model of oral reading and may help young children to develop a story schema. Refer to Butler (1980) and Green and Harker (1982) for suggestions on what to read to children. Trelease (1982) not only provided excellent ideas for reading to children but also a detailed guide to over 300 read-aloud books. Teachers who wish to become good storytellers will profit from reading Farnsworth (1981) and Kingore (1982). Recorded and taped stories can also be used, with the child or group either listening or following in the book while listening. Many commercially prepared taped books are paced too quickly for poor readers. Carbo (1981) related how storybooks can be recorded for use with such children.

Book talks also can interest children in reading voluntarily. The teacher (or librarian) attempts to make reading seem desirable and worthwhile by communicating enthusiasm and providing some honest, low-keyed guidance to well-written books. Following a 20- to 30-minute book talk in which four to eight books are presented, the children are invited to take a book that interests them. Witucke (1979) and Paulin (1982) offered sample book talks and techniques for conducting them.

Children often show great interest in stories that are too difficult for them to read independently. After hearing the story, however, they can often read it with pleasure, since they have become acquainted with the author's style and have learned the meanings of the unfamiliar concepts and vocabulary that would otherwise be stumbling blocks.

Audience reading can be used to very good effect to foster independent reading. The nature of audience reading has been described on page 90. The desire to find and prepare a suitable selection to read to the class is a powerful incentive for many children and creates a natural motive for reading with an evaluative attitude. Through the short selections presented in an audience reading period, the listeners are exposed to samples from many different sources and may have their interests awakened in books and stories that they might otherwise have overlooked.

Many teachers have made excellent use of a book club. Membership is open to the entire class. The usual requirements include possessing a library card and being ready to report on one book. The club elects officers, ordinarily a president and a secretary, and sometimes a treasurer. At each weekly meeting a few members are given the privilege of reporting on books they have read, telling whether or not they recommend the book, and, if they wish to, reading to the club some especially delightful portion. Greatly increased liking for book reading and marked improvement in critical ability and taste are the normal results of a well-run club.

Some book clubs decide to have dues, which are used by a purchasing committee to buy materials for the class library collection. The judgment shown by a pupil committee in selecting materials to buy with club funds is often amazingly good, and the experience the children gain in visiting bookstores and inspecting books for possible purchase is invaluable. The handling of the funds also provides a real situation for the use of functional arithmetic. At the end of the year the purchases can be distributed to the members of the club or left behind for the next class.

The use of paperbacks in the schools has been increasing steadily. These inexpensive books have been employed successfully to stimulate interest in a variety of classrooms (J. Davis 1970) and even in a reform school (Fader 1977).

Reading is Fundamental (RIF), a voluntary national program, has distributed millions of free paperbacks, which children are allowed to choose and keep. Matching funds for purchasing books for a school reading-motivation program are available through a program administered by RIF. Federal funds for paperback libraries also are available under the National Reading Improvement Program and Title IV-B (School Libraries and Instructional Resources) of the Elementary and Secondary Education Act.

There are seven key elements for a good reading-motivation program (Zuckerman 1977): (1) Free books are given to the children; (2) children are allowed to make their own selections; (3) there are related motivational activities before and after the books are distributed; (4) parents are involved in the program; (5) there is a special book-selection committee; (6) there is a wide variety of books; and (7) more than one book is provided for each child.

Most trade book publishers produce paperbacks, some of which are aimed at the reluctant reader. Among the paperback book clubs are those of Scholastic, Weekly Reader, and Xerox Education. A helpful reference found in many libraries is *Paperback Books for Children* (Simmons 1972), which annotates more than 700 books arranged by subject area with suggested grade levels. There are numerous creative ways to use paperbacks in the primary grades (see Dutt 1980) and middle grades (see Hellriegel 1980).

Ideas and techniques for promoting voluntary reading in the junior and senior high school were offered by Blostein (1980). Bishop (1981) described a motivational technique that uses paperbacks related to the topics under consideration in the content areas, and Lunstrum (1981) described how to use controversy to encourage secondary school students to read.

The Child Who Dislikes Reading

The procedures just described are usually successful in creating a classroom atmosphere favorable to recreational reading and work well with the majority of children. With children who have a confirmed dislike for reading, special procedures may be necessary.

In addition to helping reluctant readers develop the reading skills that will allow for more successful reading, the teacher should help them develop their self-concepts. There should be a warm, accepting atmosphere, as well as firm positive control and direction from the teacher (Noland & Craft 1976).

The first step in introducing such a child to pleasurable, voluntary reading is to locate a book that is easy and brief and will attract and hold his interest. For this purpose, it is desirable to try a book that has many pictures, few lines to a page, and comparatively few pages. Naturally, content should be chosen in relation to what is known about the child's interests. Humorous books usually make an excellent start. Few children who can read them can resist the fun in *The Cat in the Hat*, Bennett Cerf's *Book of Riddles, Curious George*, or *Mr. Popper's Penguins*. After a successful first taste, the child is likely to want several more books of the same general type before venturing into a different sort of content. Types of humor that appeal to children of various age levels, and materials that appeal to them, were listed by Gentile and McMillan (1978, 1984). An annotated list of 150 short, light humorous materials (joke books, riddles, puns) was compiled by Moe and Hopkins (1978). Fifty humorous books were listed by Wendelin (1980), who concluded from her study that taste in humor is highly individual. J. E. Bennett and Bennett (1982) found that humorous books appealed to intermediate-grade pupils but that not many of the humorous books suggested for this age group were appropriate for fourth graders, who found the complexities and subtleties too advanced for them.

In introducing such a book it is desirable to show the book, turn a few pages to show the illustrations, and then read enough of the story aloud to arouse a desire to know the rest of it. Then the child can be asked if he would like to continue reading by himself. It may be desirable to suggest that he read ahead 5 or 10 pages. If by the next lesson he has read more than the suggested amount, the teacher knows that the procedure has been successful. From then on, the problem is mainly one of keeping the child supplied with a succession of suitable books.

Sometimes older children are reluctant to take books home because they are afraid that other children will notice the "baby books" and make fun of them. Supplying a large manila envelope in which books can be carried minimizes this difficulty.

After the child has made a good start in voluntary reading, he should be introduced to the school or public library. If possible, the teacher or an aide

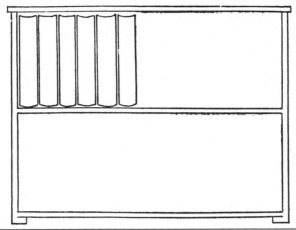

Figure 15.3. A bookcase chart for recording independent reading. As the child finishes a book he draws another book in his bookcase. If the bookcase is made about 6 × 9 inches, the books will be large enough to allow printing the author and title on each, and the date completed. Coloring the books in crayon adds to the attractiveness of the chart.

should accompany him on his first visit, help him through the formalities of getting a library card, and show him where to look for books and how to take them out. For a while, he may need the assistance of a specific list of four or five suggested books to take with him; otherwise, the long rows of books may be bewildering. And if his first few attempts at selecting his own books turn out poorly, he may become discouraged.

One should try to select reading material in accordance with a child's known likes until the habit of voluntary reading is well established. Some children want nothing but fairytales; others disdain anything that is not true; narrow preferences confined to animals or airplanes or blood and thunder should be respected as far as possible.

A children's librarian can be of invaluable help to both teacher and child in suggesting suitable books. A teacher of reading should, however, regard a continually enlarging acquaintance with children's books as an essential part of her own professional equipment. Aids to the location of reading matter of various kinds are discussed in the last part of this chapter.

Although primary motivation in voluntary reading comes from enjoyment of the reading itself, progress charts help here, as in other phases of reading impr   ement. An individual progress chart that appeals to all ages is shown in Figure 15.3; it consists of a bookcase, with books filled in as they are completed. Coloring the books with crayons adds to the attractiveness of such a chart.

Expanding and Improving Reading Interests

While it is vitally important to help children find reading matter closely related to their present interests, teachers should also try to broaden children's reading horizons. Children's interests are not fixed; they change as children get older and are susceptible to many environmental influences, not the least of which is the influence of the teacher. There are many good ways in which children's reading interests can be improved and enriched. The worst way is to assign compulsory readings and detailed book reports.

An ingenious teacher can find many ways of suggesting new fields of reading and awakening curiosity about new books. One teacher reported excellent results from displays of the colorful jackets of books that were added to the class library (Colburn 1944). Another teacher found that her pupils were reading nothing but fiction. To stimulate interest in nonfiction, she asked them to write on slips of paper the topics or questions about which they would like to find information. A card index of topics was set up, with book references listed for each topic. A marked increase in the reading of informational material was the result (Putnam 1941).

An approach tried successfully by a seventh-grade teacher is worth relating. Near the beginning of the term, she gave her class a little talk on "Your Reading Diet." In it she started by reviewing the need of a proper diet of food for proper physical nutrition and growth. Then she drew an analogy to reading. Mystery stories were likened to dessert, and comic books to candy between meals. "What would happen to your digestion if you ate nothing but desserts and candy?" After some discussion, the class, which found the idea novel and stimulating, drew up a plan for a balanced eight-course reading meal: fruit cup—poetry; soup—current events; fish course ("brain food"), science and nature study; meat—biography and history; vegetable—special practice exercises in reading; dessert—fiction; milk—sports and hobbies; after-dinner mints—comics. Each child drew up a menu and filled in the titles of his or her reading as the term progressed. The children could take as many helpings as they wished of the courses they liked best, provided that they ate at least one dish of every kind.

An intelligent interest in current events should be one of the outcomes of education. Some schools develop interest in news events gradually, through the regular reading and discussion of one of the weekly papers prepared for school. Such papers as the series of weekly papers published by Scholastic Magazines and *My Weekly Reader* published by Xerox Education Publications make it possible to introduce reading about current happenings as early as the first grade and continue it with reading matter appropriate to each grade through the elementary and secondary school years. There is even a magazine *Kids* (Kids Publishers), written by children. *World Traveler* (Open Court), which is a monthly written at the primary-grade level using material from *National Geographic*, should interest elementary and junior high school children.

Another procedure that can be used at the upper levels is to devote some of the social studies time to current events periods in which each child is expected to present a brief oral report about some interesting development in the news of the preceding week. This combines motivated independent reading in newspapers and news magazines, critical comparison of possible selections, practice in organizing a summary, and effective oral English work.

Among the other ways for stimulating interests in books and voluntary reading suggested by W. Johnson (1972) and Roeder and Lee (1973) are these: (1) Have the students advertise and sell books, each trying to prove that the book they read is the best; (2) displaying colorful posters to advertise a specific monthly topic; (3) having a read-in in which the child selects a partner and time is set aside for them to read to each other; and (4) teacher reading to the students, stopping at an exciting point, then providing several copies of the book for them to read. Numerous other suggestions have been made by Criscuolo (1978, 1979, 1982), Mason and Mize (1978), P. Ross (1978), M. Johnson (1980), Ciani (1981), L. Cohen (1981), Wilton (1981), and Holbrook (1982). Even book reports need not be deadly dull. Many imaginative ideas for using them to stimulate student involvement in reading have been offered (Fennimore 1977, Pillar 1975, Criscuolo 1977a, Nichols 1978, Fisher 1979, L. Robbins 1981). Many of these suggestions have been summarized by A. J. Harris and Sipay (1979, pp. 420–430). Yet another way of interesting some students in reading books is to allow use of kits such as the *Pilot Library Series* (SRA) that contain short excerpts from books and then provide the books in which they express an interest.

Poetry has become somewhat neglected in reading programs in recent years. The amount of space devoted to poetry in readers has decreased markedly, and the tendency to substitute wide individualized reading for uniform class study of specific selections has lessened the amount of attention devoted to poetry in the upper grades. There are many ways in which the modern teacher can awaken and develop an appreciation of poetry. One of the most important is the reading of well-chosen poems to the class by the teacher. A teacher who loves poetry and can read it well can make poems come alive for children (Jacobs 1959). A second useful procedure is choral reading and speaking. Poems that the children enjoy can be prepared for group presentation. Choral reading is ideally suited to the development of an appreciation of poetry. At a simple level, the whole class can read the poem in unison. As the children become more expert, delightful effects can be achieved through a balancing of solo parts and choral effects. A third way in which interest in poetry can be developed is through encouraging children to prepare poems for presentation in audience reading periods.

With a little planning and effort, the summer can be an ideal time for recreational reading. Aasen (1959) planned a real sales campaign. She worked on two fourth-grade classes, promoting the idea of summer reading, letting each child know what his reading-test scores were, bringing in the librarian, providing a recommended list of books, arranging for Bookmobile service, and setting up a system of recording one's reading. In September these two classes showed a gain of .7 years in reading grade, while a control class, not given this program, showed no change.

The Use of Literature in the Content Subjects

Reading accurate historical fiction not only can make history "come alive" for the student but can also develop concepts that help students to understand their textbooks better. Cianciolo (1981) discussed these and other points. *Notable Children's Trade Books in the Field of Social Studies* (Children's Book Council) contains an annotated bibliography, and guidelines for the selection and use of fictionalized biographies were provided by Storey (1982). A series of annotated bibliographies that focuses on the history and character of different geographic areas of the United States has been published by the American Library Association.

Dole and Johnson (1981) offered a number of suggestions whereby science literature would be read more widely through the cooperative efforts of science teachers, librarians, and the reading teacher. Guerra and Payne (1981) suggested ways in which popular science books and magazines could be used to develop pupils' interest in general science. Smardo (1982) annotated books with reading levels of third reader and below that could be used to clarify science concepts for young children. Radenbaugh (1981) recommended specific books that might be used to develop various math concepts for young children.

Home Environment and Children's Reading

The impact of the home on readiness for reading and the relationship between home conditions and reading disabilities have been discussed earlier in this book. Obviously, the attitudes of parents and older siblings toward books and reading have an impact on young children. Several studies have shown that, in general, good readers have had parents who have provided models for them by reading themselves at home and have read to their children (Goldfield & Snow 1984). Durkin (1982) found that the one common element in the background of low-SES black children who became successful readers was being read to as preschoolers. Home reading environment is a better predictor of children's attitudes toward reading than SES per se (Wigfield & Asher 1984). The research has shown a positive relationship between parents reading to their preschool children and the children's later success in and attitudes toward reading, but most of this research has been correlational (Teale 1981). More definitive research needs to be done to determine the specific causal relationships involved.

Most parents need guidance concerning their role in the development of their children's reading achievement and voluntary reading. Helpful ideas for parents are available in Larrick (1975), and ways of involving parents in their children's voluntary reading were offered by Manley and Simon (1980) and Sittig (1982).

V. AFFECTIVE GROWTH THROUGH READING

As H. M. Robinson and Weintraub (1973) pointed out, few would disagree that reading may change attitudes and behaviors, since reading offers an opportunity to identify with a character or to solve a problem. Yet, most of this "conventional wisdom" is based on opinion. The few studies conducted in this area neither support nor refute these possible values of reading. Perhaps, as Huus (1973) believed, attitudes are changed more often through reading followed by discussion than by reading alone. It is at present difficult to assess attitudinal or behavioral changes because of the apparent complexity of the behaviors themselves and the inadequacies of available instruments to measure change.

Bibliotherapy

One of the possible values of reading is therapeutic. Bibliotherapy is the attempt to promote mental and emotional health by using reading materials to fulfill needs, relieve pressure, or help an individual in his development as a person (Hoagland 1972). Basically the process involves three steps: identification, catharsis, and insight. Supposedly, the reader identifies with the story character, thus lessening his sense of isolation; as the reader vicariously experiences the motivation, conflicts, and emotions of the character, catharsis occurs. Identification and catharsis lead to insight, through which the reader's tensions are relieved (Corman 1975).

Evidence on the value of bibliotherapy is mixed (Tulman 1984), and interpretations of research findings differ. According to Purves and Beach (1972), bibliotherapy can be useful in group psychotherapy, but the results of classroom studies are mixed. Narang (1977), on the other hand, concluded that bibliotherapy, properly conducted with any age level, is likely to produce a positive change in attitudes and self-concept and can lead to improved social and emotional adjustment. Schrank, Engels, and Silke (1983) concluded that the research evidence on bibliotherapy suggests the following:

1. It may change attitudes, but not always.
2. It may help to reduce fears, but not always.
3. The evidence is so contradictory that it is impossible to indicate the impact of bibliotherapy on mental health.
4. It has no effect on school achievement.

There is some evidence that bibliotherapy may have undesired effects. Not only did bibliotherapy *not* reduce fears of second-grade children, but it actually induced them in many of the children who had never thought about such fears before (Newhouse & Loker 1984). As Lehr (1981a) warned, the casual use of bibliotherapy can make a bad situation worse.

Those who wish to learn more about bibliotherapy may refer to Riggs (1971), Schultheis (1972) and *Bibliotherapy: Methods and Materials* (Association of Hospital and Institution Libraries 1971). Books may be used to promote sensitivity and empathy through techniques such as those recommended by Greer (1972) and in *Reading Ladders for Human Relations* (Tway 1981).

Annotated guides and bibliographies, as well as suggestions for using the material, are available on a variety of themes: the handicapped (Baskin & K. Harris 1977, Fein & Ginsburg 1978, Criscuolo 1983), children's needs and problems (Dreyer 1977), troubled or broken homes (Haley 1975), life crises such as death and hospitalization (Hormann 1977), separation and loss (Berstein 1977), divorce (Monteith 1981b), teenage problems (Halpern 1978), the single-parent family (Horner 1978), and aging and the elderly (Storey 1979, Trusty & Link 1980, J. Watson 1981).

Bibliotherapy will not take the place of psychotherapy for those with serious emotional problems. It is probably most effective when combined with discussion and counseling by a knowledgeable, sensitive person.

Improving Attitudes toward Others

Bibliotherapy is directed at individuals who have personal or emotional problems. But untroubled pupils can also benefit from reading about and discussing story characters who differ in some way from them. A better attitude toward others, such as minority groups (Lehr 1981a) and the handicapped (Salend & Moe 1983), can be developed. In the latter case, an increased need for modifying attitudes toward the handicapped has been brought about by mainstreaming. Greenbaum, Varas, and Markel (1980) and Lass and Bromfield (1981) suggested guidelines for evaluating children's books about the handicapped and provided an annotated list of such books. Dobo (1982) listed sources of literature on the handicapped and suggested ways to help nonhandicapped children to understand and accept the handicapped. Refer to Horne (1985) for a comprehensive treatment of attitudes toward the handicapped.

Responding to Literature

Because individuals have had different experiences and because they may focus on different aspects of a story, their responses to literature may differ widely *if* the teacher allows open discussion rather than impose one particular interpretation on the pupils. The ways in which students respond to literature, both verbally and otherwise, have begun to be investigated. Studies have revealed that (1) children can respond to what they read but often cannot document the reasons for their responses; (2) pupils focus on the content when they respond to literature; (3) the better one understands the story, the better she or he is able to comment on it; and (4) different pieces of literature promote different kinds of responses (Galda 1982a).

In underscoring the contention that only after we understand, analyze, and appreciate students' responses to literature will we be able to expand and extend their ability to respond, Galda (1982a) made three major points:

1. Readers should not be penalized when their responses differ from the expected.
2. Teachers should seek the reasons behind their pupils' responses, and should teach them to do so also. Knowing what in the text or in the reader (or oneself) evoked a particular response should result in more flexible and knowledgeable readers.
3. Before assessing any response, the teacher must consider her degree of involvement with her pupils and understanding of them.

Teachers should encourage children to respond and help them to evaluate their responses. This means that teachers should encourage the freedom to question, explore, and make tentative choices and that teachers should provide opportunities to reassess decisions and recognize that ideas and opinions are likely to change (Meagher 1981). Monson (1979) presented ways to get children to respond to what they have read, and Galda (1982a) discussed ways to encourage children to make flexible responses and document them, as well as how to assess these responses. Those interested in the topic may wish to refer to Hickman (1980, 1981), Cianciolo (1982), and M. Benton (1984).

Censorship

In recent years, attempts to censor reading materials and textbooks used in schools have increased markedly (M. Hunt 1982, Micklos 1983). E. Jenkinson (1980) described two of the main censorship efforts in the United States and listed 20 organizations that protested the use of certain books in the schools and the 40 topics they opposed most often.

The National Council of Teachers of English issued a pamphlet, *The Student's Right to Read* (Burress & Jenkinson 1982), which provides a constitutionally based rationale for freedom to read without censorship and suggests a plan of action for dealing with the problem. It stresses the link between freedom to read widely and the breadth of learning needed by students if they are to become informed, thinking citizens. While recognizing the right and responsibility of parents to monitor their children's education, the International Reading Association also opposed policies that deny pupils access to certain reading materials (Mikulecky 1981).

In 1982 the Supreme Court ruled in *Island Tree* vs. *Pico* that while a school board has discretion over curricular matters, including the books assigned for classroom reading, it could not remove books from the school library where "voluntary inquiry holds sway." The Court, however, was split evenly on the issue of whether students had the constitutional right to have specific books available for their use in school libraries. The Court further ruled that the constitutionality of the school board's action rested on their motivation for removing the books from the school library and returned the case to a federal court for a thorough examination of the facts. But, before the matter came to trial, the Island Tree school board dropped its ban on the books and instead required parental notification when those books were checked out by students. The Supreme Court ruling did not set a precedent for future cases, but it seems to have offered some protection against the capricious removal of books from a school library. It also suggested the need for written school policies for evaluating and acting upon challenges to school materials (Micklos 1983).

Suggestions for dealing with attempts at censorship have been offered by W. Palmer (1982) and K. Smith (1982). Basically they deal with developing written policies that specify guidelines for book and material selection, establish a rationale for their use, specify procedures for dealing with legitimate complaints, and indicate a policy for handling censorship efforts. They also suggest the need to promote community support for freedom to read.

The contention of the would-be censor is that certain themes or content are inconsistent with the values of parents or the community at large and that students will acquire wrong values through reading books containing such unacceptable ideas. Behavioral science data, however, suggest that reading about an idea that runs contrary to one's beliefs is not likely to change those beliefs (Guthrie 1983).

VI. LOCATING READING MATERIALS

There is such a wealth of reading matter for children today that the task of selection is by no means easy. The purpose of this section is to acquaint the reader with sources in which she can look up recommended books and materials to meet all sorts of reading needs. The references are grouped in four categories: for elementary school children, for secondary school, for disabled or reluctant readers, and for special purposes.

Book Lists for Elementary School Children

The references that follow are useful primarily for selecting books for children who are average or above-average readers, and for locating books to read to children. The age or grade designations they give are usually quite broad, covering 3 or 4 years, and are more likely to underestimate than overestimate the level of reading ability required to read the books independently.

Suggestions for using trade books to improve language arts skills can be found in Stewig and Sebesta (1978). Somers and Worthington (1979) developed response guides for 27 popular children's books. Each guide includes a summary of the story, identification of the theme, disussion questions, and project suggestions.

Adventuring with Books (NCTE 1981). An annotated list of over 2500 books for preschool to Grade 6 with suggested difficulty and interest levels by category.

A Multimedia Approach to Children's Literature (ALA 1983). Guide to book-related nonprint materials for use in preschool through Grade 6.

Best Books for Children: Preschool through the Middle Grades (Bowker 1981). An annotated bibliography of nearly 9000 books arranged by subject areas and grade levels. Annual supplements.

The Best in Children's Books (Chicago 1980). Contains about 1400 titles of outstanding children's books published from 1973 to 1978.

Bibliography of Books for Children (ACEI 1977). About 2000 books arranged by subject; particularly good for preschool and primary levels.

Booklist (ALA). Bimonthly reviews of children's books and nonprint media recommended for purchase. Once a month it includes reviews of easy-reading books keyed to both reading and interest levels.

Children's Book Review Index (Gale). Series of annual volumes that cite the sources of all reviews of children's books (K–5) published that year.

Children's Catalog (H. W. Wilson 1981). A very comprehensive listing containing reviews of over 5400 titles for preschool to sixth-grade children. Revised every 5 years.

Children's Literature Review (Gale). These three volumes excerpt significant book reviews and commentaries.

Classroom Choices (Children's Book Council). An annual annotated list of books chosen by children. Also appears in *The Reading Teacher*, usually in the October issue. A composite list covering 7 years appears in Roser and Frith (1983).

Literature and Young Children (NCTE 1977). Includes an annotated bibliography of 100 books and suggestions for their use.

Most teachers also will find help in the sources annotated by White and Schulte (1979). Reviews of the most recent books for children can be found in such publications as *Horn Book, Junior Libraries, Language Arts, The Reading Teacher,* the *Bulletin* of the Center for Children's Books (Chicago), and the children's book section of the *New York Times*.

Booklists for the Secondary School

There are several useful book lists for junior and senior high students. The following are representative:

Book Bait (ALA 1979). A detailed annotation of adult books that have immediate and strong appeal to 13- to 16-year-olds.

Books for Secondary School Libraries (Bowker 1976). A computerized list of over 4000 titles; no fiction is included.

Books for the Teen Ager (New York Public Library 1981). Approximately 1250 titles with brief annotations.

Books for You: A Booklist for Senior High Students (NCTE 1982). Nearly 1400 books published or reprinted since 1976 are described. Titles are divided into 35 categories. Designed primarily for student use.

Junior High School Library Catalog (H. W. Wilson 1975). Contains reviews of 3791 books for Grades 7–9. Annual supplements.

Senior High School Library Catalog (H. W. Wilson 1972). Contains reviews of over 4750 titles. Annual supplements.

Your Reading: A Booklist for Junior High and Middle School Students (NCTE 1983). An annotated list of over 3000 books, most of them published since 1975. Titles are classified into 36 categories. Designed for student use.

Book Lists for Disabled and Reluctant Readers

The following references are helpful in selecting materials for disabled and reluctant readers:

Good Reading for Poor Readers by George D. Spache (Garrard 1978). Discusses principles of choosing books. Contains listings on trade books useful with poor readers; adapted and simplified materials; textbooks, workbooks, and games; magazines and newspapers; series books; book clubs, indexes, and reading lists; and programmed materials. Appendix gives directions for the Spache Readability Formula.

High Interest Books for Teens: A Guide to Book Reviews and Biographical Sources (Gale 1981). A list of over 2000 books identified on reading lists and publishers' catalogs as high-interest/low-reading-level books. Information is provided about each title.

High Interest—Easy Reading for Junior and Senior High School Students (NCTE 1984). An annotated list of 283 easy-to-read books for use by reluctant, not disabled, readers, listed by 18 subject categories; broad range of reading levels indicated.

High/Low Handbook: Books, Materials and Services for the Teenage Problem Reader (Bowker 1981). An annotated bibliography of 175 high-interest/low-reading-level titles arranged alphabetically. Each entry includes a plot synopsis, interest level, and reading level. Also annotates 100 other titles for slightly better but reluctant readers.

Read-Ability Books for Junior and Senior High Students (Walch 1978). Briefly annotated list of approximately 2000 books grouped by reading levels (Grades 1–9); interest levels also indicated (Grades 1–12).

Books Written Especially for Disabled Readers

An increasing number of books, including paperbacks, are both easy enough for, and interesting to, disabled readers. A list of "high interest, low vocabulary load series" is given in Appendix B. Other such materials have been annotated by G. Spache (1978); Graves, Boettcher, and Ryder (1979), and in the February 1978 issue of the *Journal of Education* (Boston University).

Many simplified and shortened versions of famous books frequently used at the secondary school level are also available. Appendix B lists some of them. Some of these adaptations are well done; others are poor. They range in difficulty from second to eighth reader levels, and so the fact that a book is a simplified version gives no indication of its actual difficulty. *Treasure Island*, for example, is available in four different versions that range from fourth to eighth reader level in difficulty.

Not all high-interest/low-vocabulary books are well written, so they should be examined carefully before purchase. G. Mason (1981) provided a history of high-interest/low-reading-level books and discussed their future.

Materials Written by Teachers and Pupils

It is often necessary to use stories written especially to appeal to a particular child. The first step is, naturally, to find out what the child would like to talk about. It is easy to get the child's cooperation in such an undertaking, and he is usually very proud to dictate a story to the teacher and later read it in his own words. In addition to their interest value, such stories have an important advantage in that all the words used are from the child's own speaking vocabulary and therefore easy for him to understand; training in word recognition is therefore not hampered by comprehension difficulties. Stories written by one child are often enjoyed by other children. Scrapbooks of stories written by the children themselves have great appeal as supplementary reading in remedial classes. The stories should be typewritten or printed.

A remedial teacher may also find it advisable because of a scarcity of suitable books to rely largely on material prepared by herself. Sometimes stories and selections from advanced books can be rewritten so as to be readable by disabled pupils. Unless a teacher has considerable originality, she will ordinarily be more successful in adapting the writings of others than in attempting to write completely original material. Since writing special materials is very time-con-suming, every effort should be made to utilize the materials that are available in printed form.

Materials written for remedial pupils should be couched in a simple and straightforward style and at a level of complexity within the grasp of the pupil. Compound and complex sentences may be used in moderation, provided that they do not contain many inversions of normal word order or other involved constructions. One should try to use an easy word in place of a more difficult synonym whenever possible. After the material has been written, its vocabulary may be checked against one of the word lists (see pp. 374–375) to make sure that it does not contain an unreasonable number of unusual or difficult words. The best test of the suitability of the story, however, is the ease with which the pupil can read it.

In planning story-type or informational material for disabled readers, it is a good idea to make each unit short enough so that it can be finished in one remedial period. A brief introductory statement may be used to give the pupil suggestions about the way in which the selection should be read. At the end of the selection specific questions should be included, which may be answered in writing or may serve as a basis for oral discussion.

Material on Minority Groups

Although research does not clearly indicate whether or not minority-group students prefer to read material pertaining to their own cultural or ethnic backgrounds, an increasing amount of such material has been published. It is probable that many children do like to read about characters similar to themselves and perhaps about those who are different, so ethnic materials may be of interest to both minority- and majority-group children. A useful source in attempting to extend sensitivity toward others is *Reading Ladders for Human Relations* (Tway 1981), which annotates nearly 2000 books and offers suggestions for their use.

According to Bachner (1969), literature for minority-group adolescents should deal with contemporary problems, employ a writing style that is informal and forceful, and have characters with whom the students can identify. Beauchamp (1970) studied the reading interests of minority ninth graders who were disabled readers. Among his findings were the following: (1) Their reading interests did not vary substantially from those of other children of their age, but they did develop at a later date; (2) these students could and did read books that "ought to be too difficult" for them *if* the books had extremely high interest; (3) they preferred books with fewer characters but without a clear preference for characters similar to themselves; (4) they tended to reject love and romance themes, preferring those of perseverance, physical strength, triumph over adversity and obstacles, and detective stories; and (5) adapted classics were successful provided that description was minimized and action and suspense maximized.

Among the materials published for and about minority groups are the following:

Open Door Books (Children's Press). Thirty-six books that contain realistic autobiographies of minority men and women who have faced modern society and won. Reading level about fifth grade; interest level, Grades 5–12.

Stories of the Inner City (Globe). Twenty-seven contemporary short stories written at the fourth or fifth reader level for junior and senior high school students.

Target Today Series (Benefic). A remedial series of four books, each containing 100 short story lessons that use urban life as the main theme. Reading levels 2–5, interest levels 4–12.

Americans All (Garrard). Biographies of great Americans of all races, creeds, and national origins; emphasis on character and personal determination. Reading level about 4, interest level 3–6.

Living City Adventure Series (Globe). Three collections of short stories that focus on the problems and dreams of multiethnic young people of today. Written at the fourth or fifth reader level, these stories should be of interest to those in Grades 7–12.

We Are Black (SRA). Selections of from 300 to 900 words taken from books and periodicals. A reading-skill program accompanies the materials. Reading levels 2–6, interest levels 4–8.

Selections from the Black (Jamestown). A three-book college-level developmental reading series containing 90 selections by black writers. Reading levels: Olive 6–8, Brown 9–11, Purple 12–college.

Voices from the Bottom (Jamestown). Similar to above, but the selections are by and about Indians, Chicanos, and Puerto Ricans.

Ethnic Reading Series (Book Laboratory). Twenty short booklets focus on the lives of black, Jewish, Italian, and Puerto Rican Americans of both sexes. Reading levels 3–5, interest levels 7–12.

Contributors to American Life Series (Benefic). Three books (Afro-Americans, American Indians, Hispano-Americans), each containing at least 20 biographies, and each with three parts at second, third, and fifth reader levels. Interest levels 4–9.

Indians (Garrard). Factually accurate biographies of Indian men and women, honest and unstereotyped; American history from the Indian's viewpoint. Reading level about 3, interest levels 2–5.

Indian Culture Series (Montana). Authentic, interesting books depicting the life of the Indians before the coming of the white man and present-day life. Reading levels 3–5, interest levels 4–12.

Our American Heritage (Xerox). Present American Indian cultures, their contributions to the country, and current Indian leaders. Reading levels 4–5.

Folk Tales and Legends (Montana). Eleven different titles of the authentic tales and legends from different Indian tribes. Written at reader levels 1–4, the books should interest elementary and junior high school children.

Indian Children's Books (Montana). Annotated list of books judged to be accurate in their interpretation of Indian cultures. Books are listed by tribes, regions, and subject. Interest and reading levels are indicated. One chapter discusses how to use the books.

Indian Reading Series (NWRL). A supplementary reading program containing 142 stories written by Indians of 16 reservations. Organized into 6 levels for the elementary school.

Books of interest to and about minority-group children have been listed by Archer (1972), Weber (1972), Strickland (1973a), and G. Spache (1975). Lass (1980) listed books that use black English (primarily in dialogue) and indicated the interest and reading levels of each. Children's literature dealing with interracial families was discussed and annotated by Long (1978).

Annotated bibliographies of literature by and about American Indians were prepared by Stensland (1979), Westcott (1982), and Gilliland (1982). Vugrenes (1981) listed sources of North American Indian myths and legends, and Blair (1982) examined the readability and content of adolescent literature about the Indians in northern and western Canada. May (1983) described a literature and film approach to promote a better understanding of and appreciation for Native Americans. An annotated listing of over 750 books, each dealing with some aspect of the life of American Indians and Eskimos, was edited by Lass-Woodfin (1978). J. Stott (1983) discussed the folktales of one Eskimo tribe that have been adapted for children.

Schon (1977, 1981) provided critical reviews of the children's literature dealing with the customs, life styles, folklore, and history of Mexicans and Mexican Americans. Wagoner (1982) presented an annotated bibliography of children's books containing Mexican-American characters and discussed the common themes found in them.

Suggestions for using Asian-American children's literature may be found in Aoki. Algarin (1982) presented an annotated bibliography of Japanese myths, legends, and fairytales.

Also available are an annotated bibliography of the biographies of 1100 women (Siegel 1984), an annotated bibliography dealing with Cajun themes (J. Cox & Wallis 1982), and a series of annotated guides to children's fiction (in English) from Czechoslovakia, Hungry, Poland, the Soviet Union, the Ukraine, and Yugoslavia (Povsic 1980a, b, c; 1981a, b; 1982a, b). Auten (1984) annotated ERIC articles on developing an understanding of other cultures through literature.

VII. ESTIMATING THE DIFFICULTY OF READING MATERIAL[5]

The difficulty of reading material can be estimated in three ways: (1) considered judgment; (2) use of a readability formula; or (3) use of a cloze or informal reading test. Judgment and readability formulas are used to predict how readable the material will be in general. These two methods have the advantage of being less time-consuming but are less accurate in determining the difficulty of a given

[5] For comprehensive treatments of readability, see Klare (1974–1975, 1984) and Bormuth (1968b). Refer to Selden (1981) or to A. J. Harris and Jacobson (1979) for historical accounts of readability formulas. Klare (1984) reviewed the "high points" in recent readability research.

selection or book for a particular individual. Because the child must actually read the material in a cloze or an informal reading test such as an IRI, its use is more likely to reflect how well the student can read that material and material similar to it. Direct testing, however, has the disadvantage of being time-consuming. All of the procedures have uses and limitations, and none is perfectly reliable or accurate.

Considered Judgment

Teachers' judgments as to the difficulty of reading materials may vary considerably, as much as six grade levels (Jorgenson 1975). If possible, teachers should check their initial impressions by consulting references that list the difficulty of books (see pp. 592–594). The relationships among the readability ratings of textbooks by teachers, cloze performance, and readability formulas is generally moderate to fairly high. For example, teachers' ratings correlated between .60 and .77 with readbility formula scores, teacher and student ratings correlated between .51 and .69 with cloze test performance, and readability formula scores correlated with cloze ratings from .35 to .61 (C. Harrison 1979).

Readability Formulas

Readability formula developers have examined over 250 variables as possible predictors, but in general two factors have stood out—semantic difficulty and syntactic difficulty—with semantic difficulty typically accounting for more of the variance (i.e., it is the better predictor of the two) (Klare 1984). The most widely used readability formulas employ vocabulary difficulty and sentence length as measures of semantic and syntactic difficulty. Passages with rare words and difficult syntax require more cognitive effort than equivalent passages with common words and simple syntax (Britton *et al.* 1982). These two factors are valid measures of readability (MacGinitie & Tretiak 1971, A. J. Harris 1976, Klare 1976), account for most of the variance in readability measurement (Entin & Klare 1978a, Klare 1984), and suffice except when doing exacting research (Klare 1974–1975). They are also better indicators of learnability (the extent to which new learning results from reading a passage) than are linguistic measures (Guthrie 1972).

Well over 50 readability formulas have been developed (Schuyler 1982). Some are meant for special purposes, such as FORECAST (Sticht 1975) for determining the readability index for job-related reading materials and the ARI (E. Smith & Kincaid 1970) for technical materials. Most formulas, however, are designed to be used across various kinds of materials, although many are applicable only to certain ranges of difficulty.

Among the most widely used formulas are those by Spache (1974) for the primary grades[6] and by Dale and Chall (1948) for Grades 4 through college.[7] The Harris–Jacobson Wide Range Readability Formula yields readability scores from 1.0 to 11.3, is easier to apply than the aforementioned formulas, and is based on basal readers in wide use in 1980. Full directions for using this formula

[6] Burmeister (1976) formulated a table that makes the Spache formula easier to apply.

[7] Tables for rapid determination of Dale–Chall scores were developed by Klare (1952), R. T. Williams (1972), and Layton (1980).

are provided in A. J. Harris and Jacobson (1982) and are reproduced in Appendix D of this book. The Spache tends to rate material at each reader level as somewhat less difficult than does the Harris–Jacobson formula (A. J. Harris & Jacobson 1980).

Fry's Readability Graph (1968, 1972) is also easy to apply and has been extended to cover Grades 1 through 17 (Fry 1977). The Fry Graph overestimated the difficulty of second- and third-grade materials (A. J. Harris & Jacobson 1980) and had very low validity at high school levels (A. J. Harris & Jacobson 1976). Fry (1980a) claimed that other data indicated that his formula compared quite well with the Harris–Jacobson and Spache formulas, and Longo (1982) reported that the Fry yielded scores that compared closely with those of three other formulas when applied to college texts. G. Fitzgerald (1980, 1981) questioned the reliability of Fry scores based on only three samples, as the manual suggests, and indicated that taking even a much larger sample may not increase its reliability sufficiently.

The SEER (Singer 1975) and the Rauding Scale (Carver 1975–1976) do not involve any computations. Rather, the passage of unknown difficulty is compared to passages of known difficulty, and one subjectively decides which of the passages of known difficulty the passage in question most closely represents. Froese (1981) and Duffelmeyer (1982a) disagreed as to how well the SEER and Rauding Scales compared in determining readability. Other easy-to-apply readability formulas are the Rix and Lix (J. Anderson 1983), which Kretschmer (1984) reported as comparing favorably with three other easy-to-apply formulas, and Raygor's formula (1977), which Baldwin and Kaufman (1979) reported as yielding scores within one year of the Spache in over 90% of the comparisons. Two other relatively easy to apply formulas are the Fog Index (Gunning 1979) and the SMOG (McLaughlin 1969), for which Maginnis (1982) developed a table for even quicker use. It should be noted, however, that as Schuyler (1982) pointed out, the easiest formulas to apply also yield the most erratic results.

Criticisms of Readability Formulas

Readability formulas have come under increased attack in the past few years. For example, Davison and Kantor (1982) and Davison (1984) have argued that readability formulas "fail to define readable text"; and Bruce, Rubin, and Starr (1981) claimed that readability formulas "have not fulfilled their promise." R. Anderson, Mason, and Shirley (1983) wrote that readability formulas provide only a superficial indication of the deeper reasons for reading ease or difficulty. Basically these criticisms have centered on two points: (1) Readability formulas do not indicate very well how comprehensible a text is going to be for an individual; and (2) the formulas are poor guides for writing comprehensible material. Many of the points regarding comprehensibility are well taken, but their attacks would often be better directed at misapplication of readability formulas.

As Klare (1984) pointed out, a readability formula is a *predictive* device intended to provide a quantitative, objective estimate of reading difficulty. Much of the controversy reflects a failure to recognize the implication of the term *predictive*. Modern readability formulas have achieved extremely high correlations with their criteria. In other words, they do what they were designed to do—predict how difficult material is likely to be as compared with the criterion measure. Klare (1984) contrasted *prediction* with *production*. In the latter, the goal is to produce more comprehensible reading materials. Prediction research only need show relationship to the criterion. Production research must demonstrate a causal relationship in that a manipulation of variables produces a significant increase in pupils' comprehension. Klare reported that in 36 studies, the more readable versions (those rewritten to make them more comprehensible) produced significant increases in comprehension in only about 60% of the cases.

There are variables within the child (e.g., prior knowledge, motiviation) and within the text (e.g., vocabulary, text structure, cohesion) that must be considered in attempting to select material of suitable difficulty because they interact to determine how comprehensible that material is for a particular pupil. It would be foolhardy simply to match a readability grade score with a child's grade-equivalent score from a standardized test, as some critics (e.g., L. Dreyer 1984) suggest is done.

Attempts to increase the predictive power of readability formulas by adding linguistic measures have not been particularly successful. For instance, adding a measure of syntax increased the predictive power of a readability formula for older readers using more difficult texts but had little effect for younger readers (Selden 1981). Bormuth (1966) found that the number of words per sentence correlated .86 with a formal measure of word depth. And Bamberger and Rabin (1984) reported that in about 70% of the cases, use of their Readability Profile (subjective judgment of text content, organization, print, style, and motivation) did not add to, or detract from, the estimate of difficulty indicated by the readability formula score.

The criteria against which readability formulas have been validated also have come under fire. It has been argued that to use the publisher's grade-level designation is tantamount to circular reasoning because publishers use readability formulas to determine the levels of their basal readers. A number of formulas have used the *McCall–Crabbs Standardized Test Lessons* as their criterion. K. Stevens (1980) claimed that the McCall–Crabbs was not based on extensive testing, that the grade-equivalent scores lacked reliability and comparability, and that complete technical data were not available from the publisher. On the other hand, Selden (1981) wrote that the McCall–Crabbs had the advantage of having been normed on a large population and that there seemed to be some empirical basis for the grade placement of the passages. Furthermore, Selden indicated that although originally normed in 1925, a fairly recent study indicated that the norms were still indicative of performance, except at the twelfth-grade level.

That two formulas may be very highly correlated indicates only that the rank order in which they place the passages shows high agreement. When applied to the same materials, readability formulas consistently disagree as to the levels of difficulty they assign (Schuyler 1982, J. Anderson 1983, Klare 1984). The degree to which formula scores disagree (and they have been shown to disagree from one to six or more grade levels) varies with the formulas used and the materials to which they are applied. Some formulas yield consistently higher scores than do other formulas. For example, when 8 formulas were applied to the same 16 passages, the ARI yielded the lowest ratings in 15 comparisons, and the Fry indicated the highest scores in 9 (Schuyler 1982).

As for the second main criticism, most readability formulas were never meant to provide a guide for readable writing, and most developers of readability formulas have so stated (Chall & Conrad 1984). Readability formulas were intended to be indices of the difficulty of the passage but were never meant to provide specifications of text characteristics that contribute to text difficulty (Selden 1981). As has been demonstrated by Davison and Kantor (1982), attempts to simplify text may well result in less comprehensible material. Replacing a compound or complex sentence with a number of short, simple sentences often makes the relationships that link ideas together more vague, and may require the readers to make additional inferences (e.g., by deleting a connective that signals a cause–effect relationship). Deleting details may not clarify meaning, and replacing low-frequency but precise words with "easy" words may blur the intended meaning. Furthermore, condensing ideas may increase their density to a point that causes conceptual overload for the student (T. Anderson, Armbruster, & Kantor 1980).

Other writers (e.g., Ostertag & Rambeau 1982) still recommend that all one need do to make material "easier to read" is make the sentences shorter and replace the hard words. Such changes will probably reduce the readability formula score, but they may make the material less comprehensible. As Shuy (1981a) pointed out, simplicity is not necessarily equivalent to clarity of writing.

Suggestions for rewriting materials that go beyond the usual ones mentioned above have been provided by Charry (1975), Fry (1975), Craig (1977), and Frenzel (1982). It is of interest to note that comprehension improved most when both word difficulty and sentence length were manipulated, rather than either factor alone (Funkhouser & Maccoby 1971, Shaffer 1977).

Proper Use and Interpretation of Readability Formulas

Readability formulas have value, especially when their limitations are understood. It would be impossible to test directly every potential reader with each piece of reading material, so estimates of difficulty are useful in initially selecting materials. Klare (1984) offered a number of suggestions for the proper use of readability formulas.

Formulas do not necessarily yield similar levels of difficulty when applied to the same material, so the predicted difficulty of any passage or book may well depend on which formula is used. Educators would be well advised to use the formula that best predicts the difficulty of the material being used by their pupils who are reading that material.

It may be advisable to supplement the data provided by a readability formula with information about the text's comprehensibility. A checklist may be used for this purpose. The checklist presented by Clewell and Cliffton (1983) is based on the premise that text comprehensibility is influenced by the reader's prior knowledge, text coherence, the degree to which the author sticks to the topic, and text structure. Irwin and Davis's 5-point rating scale (1980) considers the relationship betwen text information and the reader's conceptual development and prior knowledge, as well as syntax; how clearly main ideas are stated; the inclusion of irrelevant details; and the exclusion of explicit connectives. Among the problems with such checklists are that they require a knowledgeable user and that subjective judgment is used to rate information that is not readily apparent or available (e.g., the reader's prior knowledge). Reliability of such assessments could vary widely.

Among the findings of readability studies summarized by Klare (1976) were the following:

1. At times, motivation can override the effects of readability on comprehension.
2. Easier readability may increase the likelihood that pupils will continue to read, even when it does not result in better comprehension.
3. It is more important to improve the readability of low-preferred than high-preferred material.
4. The grade-equivalent scores provided by readability formulas are not precise values.
5. Readability formulas may (a) underestimate the difficulty of material in which a pupil has limited background information; and (b) overestimate the difficulty for highly intelligent and well-informed readers.

Computer Applications

With the increased availability of microcomputers, it was inevitable that computer programs would be developed to save time in applying readability formulas (see Mason, Blanchard, & Daniel 1983). Keller (1982) developed a prototype readability formula for use with a microcomputer, and Kretschmer (1984) wrote a program for use with the RIX readability index. The most comprehensive treatment to date was that by Schuyler (1982), who covered eight readability formulas. Instructions for how to change Schuyler's Apple programs for use with the TRS-80 may be found in Schilkowsky et al. (1983). Other sources of computer programs for readability were listed by Judd (1981). One of the apparently unanswered questions when using the microcomputer to apply certain formulas is how the application of certain rules is taken into consideration. Readability data on a number of basal readers, supplementary books, and standardized reading tests are available from Britton and Associates.

Current Status of Readability

As indicated by the over 1000 references on the topic, interest in readability is alive and thriving (Klare 1984). This interest has spread to the development of readability formulas for languages other than English. The LIX formula, upon which the RIX formula is based, was developed for Swedish (J. Anderson 1983). There are also readability formulas for Vietnamese (Nguyen & Henkin 1982), and Austrian (Bamberger & Rabin 1984). The Fry has been modified for use with Spanish (Gilliam, Peña, & Mountain 1980).

Interest in readability–comprehensibility is also indicated by publications such as *Simply Stated* (AIR), a monthly newsletter that tells of efforts to make documents more readable. As of 1983, 27 states had laws requiring the use of "plain language" in insurance policies.

In response to the question "Have we gone too far with readability?" Klare (1984) replied in the negative with regard to research. He also indicated that research has clearly begun to move in the direction of attempting to understand how changes in readability can work for individual readers. As for whether the application of readability has gone too far, Klare offered a cautious "sometimes yes, sometimes no." We can go too far in attempts at predicting and producing readable writing, but we need not. If readability formulas are selected and used properly, they can be helpful screening devices. But they cannot serve as guides for readable writing because humans and language are too complex to expect simple cause–effect relationships.

Direct Measures of Comprehensibility

An estimate of how comprehensible a given piece of reading is for a particular child can be obtained by employing an informal reading inventory (see pp. 193–203) or a cloze test (see pp. 175–178).

Cloze scores and readability formulas do not yield similar results (Schlief & Wood 1974, Froese 1975a). The cloze also has limitations. Cloze tests lack face validity; that is, they do not look like measures of comprehensibility. Cloze scores are greatly influenced by the kind and number of deletions. For example, deleted words (nouns, main verbs, and adjectives) are probably more difficult to supply than structure words are; an every-fifth-word deletion may not be suitable for everyone. Also, the ability to complete many items successfully depends more on the reader's experiential background and general language ability than on the content of the material itself (Hittleman 1973, 1978). It also may depend heavily on the reader's verbal problem-solving ability (Selden 1981).

This chapter has stressed the importance of finding "the right book for the right child" as a way of increasing children's interest in reading for pleasure and providing a basis for the gradual maturing and refining of taste and critical standards. The child who reads extensively will make his own comparisons and will, in the long run, prefer sound writing to trash. Even if he does not, an omnivorous reading diet is far superior to none at all. In the face of the competition from mass media such as television, it takes both superior materials and clever salesmanship by teachers to develop the reading habit; without this habit, much of reading instruction is wasted. For the disabled reader, fluency and ease in reading can develop only through much reading of interesting, easy material.

APPENDIX A

A Descriptive Listing of Tests by Types

The lists that follow give pertinent information about the tests mentioned in this book, as well as about tests that are mentioned in the literature or that may be found in diagnostic reports. A few tests are listed because of their historical interest. The exclusion of a test does not mean that we consider it to be an inadequate test, and test inclusion does not indicate our endorsement.

Within each category, the tests are listed alphabetically. When a test is part of an achievement battery, only the reading and reading-related tests are described. Test authors and acronyms are mentioned when such information may be helpful in identifying the test. Information about the test that appears in its title is not repeated in the description. Oral reading tests must be administered individually; therefore the word "individual" is omitted from their descriptions. Unless otherwise indicated, you may assume that in all but obvious cases a test is group-administered, norm-referenced (or interpreted as in the case of projective tests), read silently, and has but one form.

Each description is brief and not evaluative. In order to determine what a test really measures and its adequacy, you must analyze the tasks required by that test or rely on the judgments of others. More detailed descriptions and critical evaluations may be found in journals (many of these are listed in *News on Tests*), and in the volumes edited by Buros (1968, 1972, 1975, 1978). British reading tests and assessment procedures are reviewed by Vincent *et al.* (1983). The ERIC Clearinghouse on Tests is also a useful source of information.

Before deciding which test to use, you should make a tentative selection of a few tests that might be suitable and order a specimen set of each for careful study. For large-scale testing, you also should consider such factors as how well the test measures the objectives of the school's reading program, the practicality and cost of hand-scoring versus machine-scoring (all tests cannot be machine scored), and the test result reports that publishers can provide (and the cost of such).

The names of the test publishers are abbreviated. Their full names and addresses are given in Appendix C.

READINESS AND EARLY IDENTIFICATION OF HIGH-RISK CHILDREN

Analysis of Readiness Skills: Reading and Mathematics (1972). Five scores: visual perception of letters, letter identification, mathematics (identification, counting), total. Directions and norms for both English- and Spanish-speaking children. Grades K–1. Riverside

Anton Brenner Developmental Gestalt Test of School Readiness (1964). Visual–motor copying test. Rating scale yields 2 scores: achievement–ability, social–emotional. Ages 5–6. WPS

Aston Index (1972). Battery of tests designed to identify "at risk" children who have a predisposition to dyslexia-type language difficulties. Verbal and perceptual tasks; family history included. Aston

Basic School Skills Inventory—Screen (1983). Twenty-item measure used to identify high-risk children. Ages 4–6. Pro-Ed

Beginning Assessment Test for Reading (1975). Criterion-referenced. Measures understanding of spoken words, visual and auditory discrimination, classification, rhyming, sequencing, riddles, letter names, sound–symbol associations, picture–word and picture–sentence matching, spelling, sentence completion, oral production and comprehension, and color naming. Placement test measures 12 objectives with 2–6 items for each. Comprehensive test measures 19 objectives with 2–6 items each. Grades K–1. Lippincott

Braun–Neilsen Pre-Reading Inventory (1979). Subtests: conventions of language (basic literacy concepts, speech–print association, spoken word boundaries), semantic-associational relationships (classroom concepts, classification), and grapho-phonemic (letter recognition, visual discrimination, beginning sounds). Supplementary tests: listening for sequence, listening for meaning, auditory discrimination, and rhyming elements. Two forms. Grades K–1. Ginn (Canada)

Brigance Screen for Kindergarten and First Grade (1983). Primarily individual. Brief criterion-referenced battery of 18 tests (only 12 or 13 given to each child). Seven tests given to both kindergarten and first-grade children: personal data (child gives name orally, etc.), color recognition (names 10 colors), picture vocabulary, visual–motor skills (copying 5 geometric shapes), rote counting, numerical comprehension (associating quantities with numerals), and prints personal data. Curriculum Associates

California Achievement Tests: Reading (1978). Level 10 has 6 subtests: listening, letter forms, letter names, letter sounds, visual discrimination, and sound matching. Kindergarten. CTB

CAP Achievement Series: Reading (1980). Level 4 (Age 4) has 10 subtests (96 items): visual matching and oddities, auditory picture closure, picture rhymes, attention, comprehension, silly pictures, generalization, combining information and developmental mathematics. Level 5 (Age 5) has 10 subtests (96 items): letter recognition, picture-to-picture rhymes, sound–picture relations, developmental mathematics, auditory classification, visual synthesis, sequencing, generalization, visual oddities, and negation. Ages 4–5. American Testronics

Circus (1979). Measure of reading and school readiness. Levels A (Grades pre-K to K.5) and B (K.5–1.5) contain 12 or 14 tests covering a variety of areas (e.g., receptive vocabulary, quantitative concepts, perceptual–motor coordination, productive language, visual memory, and problem solving) and 2 or 3 teacher-completed inventories. Levels C (1.5–2.5) and D (2.5–3.5) contain measures of phonetic analysis, oral reading, reading, vocabulary, and sentence and reading comprehension. Two forms. Grades K–3. CTB; PTS

Clymer–Barrett Readiness Test (1983). Six subtests: recognizing letters, matching words (both classified as visual-discrimination tests), auditory discrimination of beginning and ending sounds (matching sounds of spoken and pictured words), completing shapes (completing geometric forms) and copy-a-sentence. Includes a readiness survey that uses a 3-point scale. Two forms. Grades K–1. Chapman

Concepts about Print Test: Sand (1972); *Stones* (1979). Individual. Different from most reading readiness tests, *Sand* and *Stones* are 20-page paperbacks that resemble children's picture books. Used to observe and evaluate child's concepts about book orientation (e.g., when pictures and print are right side up); whether print or pictures carry the message; directionality of lines of print, words, and page sequence; relationships between written and spoken language; words, letters, capitals, space, and punctuation. Ages 5–7. Heinemann

Contemporary School Readiness Test (1970). Subtests other than reading test can be group administered. Subtests: name writing; colors; science, health, and social studies; numbers; handwriting readiness; reading; visual and auditory discrimination; listening comprehension. Grades K–1. Montana Council on Indian Education

CTBS Readiness Test (1977). Six subtests: letter names, letter forms, listening for information, letter sounds, visual discrimination, and sound matching. Grades K–1. CTB

CTBS: Reading (1981). Level A measures letter recognition, visual discrimination, auditory discrimination, vocabulary, and listening comprehension. Kindergarten. CTB

Diagnostic Reading Readiness Tests (1966). Measures relationships, eye–handedness, coordination, visual and auditory discrimination, and vocabulary. Grades K–1. Committee

Dyslexia Schedule (1968). School-entrance questionnaire (89 items) completed by parents. Score based on 23 discriminating items, 21 of which are on *School Entrance Check List*. Also used to elicit information about children referred because of reading disability. EPS

Dyslexia Screening Survey (Valett 1980). Checklist of neuropsychological skills thought to be involved in the reading process. Covers phonetic–auditory, visual, and multisensory processing skills. Grades 1–6. Fearon

First Grade Screening Test (1969). Used to identify children with potential learning difficulties. Includes items on social and emotional adjustment as well as intellectual and perceptual abilities. AGS

Florida Kindergarten Screening Battery (1982). Designed to detect young children "at risk" for subsequent reading disability. Includes *PPVT-R*, recognition–discrimination (visual perception of rotated figures), *Beery Visual–Motor Integration Test*, alphabet recitation, and finger localization. Used in studies by Satz (see p. 275). ATP; PAR

Gesell Preschool Tests (1980). Series of individual test situations that reveal child's relative maturing in 4 basic areas of behavior: motor, adaptive, language, and personal–social. Ages 2½–6. Program for Education

Harrison–Stroud Reading Readiness Profiles (1956). Five subtests: using symbols, visual discrimination, using context, auditory discrimination, and using context and auditory clues. Also includes test of letter names. Grades K–1. Riverside

Iowa Tests of Basic Skills: Reading (1982). Level 5 assesses listening, word analysis, and vocabulary (all tests are administered orally). Grades K–1. Riverside

Kindergarten Behavioural Index: A Screening Technique for Reading Readiness (1972). Behavior rating scale designed to aid in identifying children with potential learning problems. Grades K–1. Australian Council. A copy of the KBI is shown on page 49.

Lee–Clark Reading Readiness Test (1962). Four tests measure visual discrimination of letter forms (2 tests), concepts, and visual discrimination of word forms. Grades K–1. CTB

Let's Look at Children (1981). Procedures for assessing and developing school readiness of children, especially minority children. Based on works of Piaget. Grades K–3. Addison-Wesley

Linguistic Awareness in Reading Readiness Test (LARR) (1983). Group-administered test with 3 subtests: recognizing literacy behavior (measures extent to which child can recognize the kinds of activities involved in reading and writing); understanding literacy functions (measures understanding of the varied purposes of reading and writing); and technical language of literacy (measures knowledge of technical terms such as *letter*, *word*, and *top line*). Two forms. Ages 5–6. NFER–Nelson

Macmillan Reading Readiness Test (1970). Subtests include a quantified rating scale, visual and auditory discrimination, vocabulary and concepts, letter names, and visual–motor skills. Grades K–1. Macmillan

McCarthy Screening Test (1978). Criterion-referenced adaptation of *McCarthy Scales of Children's Abilities*. Six tests: right–left orientation, verbal memory, draw-a-design, numerical memory, conceptual grouping, and leg coordination. Percentile cutoff scores used to identify children "at risk" for learning problems. Ages 4–6½. Psy Corp.

Meeting Street School Screening Test (1969). Individual. Designed to identify children with potential learning problems. Three subtests: motor patterning (bilateral sequential movement patterns and spatial awareness), visual perceptual–motor (visual discrimination, visual memory, eye–hand coordination, spatial and directional concepts), and language (listening comprehension, auditory memory, and language formulation). Also includes behavior rating scale. Ages 5–7½. Meeting Street

Metropolitan Achievement Tests: Reading Instructional Tests (1978). Primer level has 6 subtests: auditory and visual discrimination, letter recognition, phoneme/grapheme—consonants, sight vocabulary, and comprehension. Grades K–1. Psy Corp.

Metropolitan Readiness Tests (1976). Level I (K.0–K.5) has 6 subtests: auditory memory, rhyming, letter recognition, visual matching, school language and listening, and quantitative language; also includes optional copying test. Level II (K.5–early first grade) contains beginning consonants, sound—letter correspondences, visual matching, finding patterns, school language, listening, and 3 optional tests (quantitative concepts and operations, copying). Grades K–1. Psy Corp.

Monroe Reading Aptitude Tests (1936). Group and individual subtests. Measures 5 factors: visual perception and memory, auditory perception and memory, motor control, oral speed and articulation, and language. Grades K–1 and nonreaders to age 9. Riverside

Murphy–Durrell Prereading Phonics Inventory (1978). Five subtests: identifying letters named, letter names in spoken words, phonemes in spoken words, writing letters from dictation, and syntax matching (examiner reads sentence, child points to target word in printed sentence as directed by examiner). Grades K–1. Borg-Warner. Also part of *Durrell Analysis of Reading Difficulty*.

Murphy–Durrell Reading Readiness Analysis (1965). Yields 6 scores: sound recognition, letter names (capitals, lower case, total), and learning rate (ability to learn to recognize printed words). Early first grade. Psy Corp.

Prescriptive Reading Inventory (1976). Criterion-referenced tests covering 10 objectives each for Levels 1 and 2. Level 1 (K.0–1.0): sound discrimination, sound matching, form matching, visual reasoning, sound–symbol correspondence, letter names, oral language, literal comprehension, interpretative comprehension, and attention skills. Level 2 (K.5–2.0): 8 areas. Same as in Level 1; sight vocabulary and initial reading replace form matching and letter names. Grades K–1. CTB

Pupil Rating Scale: Screening for Learning Disabilities (Myklebust 1981). Child's behavioral characteristics rated (5-point scale) on 24 items in 5 areas: auditory comprehension and memory, spoken language, orientation, motor coordination, and personal–social behavior. Ages 5–14. Psy Corp.; WPS

Quickscreen (1981). Brief screening test to identify children with potential learning problems. Kindergarten level: name writing, figure copying, story, and sentence repetition. First-grade level: name writing, figures, words, story, and sentences. Second-grade level: name writing, figures, story, and sentences. Four forms at kindergarten level; 2 forms at others. Cutoff scores used. Grades K–2. WPS

Rhode Island Profile of Early Learning Behavior (1982). Forty items divided into 9 areas of behavior: body perception, sensory–motor coordination, attention, memory for events, self-concept, visual memory, spatial and sequential arrangements of letters and symbols, and memory for symbols. Five-point scale used to rate behaviors over 4 observations. Grades K–2. Jamestown

School Readiness Survey (1975). Administered and scored by parents with school supervision. Yields 8 scores: number concepts, form discrimination, color naming, symbol matching, speaking vocabulary, listening vocabulary, general information, and total. Also includes general readiness checklist. Ages 4–6. Consulting Psychologists

School Readiness Test (1974). Classifies children into 6 levels of readiness based on the total score of 7 subtests: word recognition, identifying letters, visual discrimination, auditory discrimination, comprehension and interpretation, handwriting readiness, and number readiness. Grades K–1. *Spanish Language Edition* (1977). STS

SEARCH (1981). Individual. Designed to identify potential learning-disabled children. Subtests: visual perception (discrimination, recall, visual–motor), auditory perception (discrimination, rote sequencing), intermodal (articulation, auditory segmentation, writing initial consonants), and body image (directionality, finger schema, pencil grip). Ages 5–6. Walker

Slingerland Pre-Reading Screening Procedures (1977). Measures auditory, visual, and kinesthetic skills. Contains 12 subtests: visual perception 1 & 2 (visual discrimination), visual perception and memory (visual memory), near- and far-point copying, auditory–visual association (understanding spoken sentences), letter recognition (letter names), visual–kinesthetic memory (visual–motor integration), auditory perception with comprehension (understanding a short oral story), auditory discrimination, auditory–visual–kinesthetic integration (matching spoken letter name with its printed form and then copying it), and auditory–visual association (sound–symbol association). Grades K–1. EPS

Slingerland Screening Tests for Identifying Children with Specific Language Disability (1974). Attempts to identify children who have or are likely to have disabilities in reading, spelling, speaking, or handwriting. All levels contain 8 subtests: copying from near- and far-point, visual memory, visual discrimination, visual–kinesthetic memory, auditory kinesthetic memory, auditory analysis (with written response, and auditory–visual integration (matching spoken and printed words). Form D also has subtests to identify possible confusion in orientation in time and space and to determine written expression. Three subtests given individually: echolalia (echoing words and phrases), word finding (auditory cloze), and storytelling (retelling of story read by examiner). Prereading form (Kindergarten), Form A (Grades 1–2), B (2–3), C (3–4), D (5–6). EPS

Spanish Reading Criterion Referenced Test: Kindergarten (1971). Measure of readiness to learn to read in Spanish. National Hispanic Center

SRA Achievement Series: Reading (1978). Level A measures visual and auditory discrimination, letters and sounds, listening comprehension, and mathematical concepts. Two forms. Grades K–1. SRA

Stanford Early School Achievement Test (1982). Levels 1 (K.0–K.9) and 2 (K.5–1.9) have subtests: sounds and letters (auditory perception, letter names, sound–symbol associations), word reading (word recognition), and listening to words and stories (understanding vocabulary and listening comprehension). Level 2 also includes sentence-comprehension subtest. Grades K–1. Psy Corp.

Test of Early Reading Ability. Measures reading ability of preschool, kindergarten, and primary-grade children. Yields information about child's letter-name knowledge, conventions of reading (e.g., book orientation and format), and reading comprehension. Ages 3–7. Pro-Ed

Walker Readiness Test for Disadvantaged Preschool Children (1972). Individual. Subtests: likenesses or similarities (visual discrimination), differences (distinguishing size, shapes), numerical analogies, and missing parts (visual closure). Directions available in English, Spanish, and French. Two forms. Ages 4–6. ED 037 253

READING

American School Achievement Tests: Reading (1975). Primary II (Grades 2–3), Intermediate (4–6), Advanced (7–9) levels each yield 4 scores: vocabulary, sentence meaning, paragraph comprehension, and total score. Two forms. Grades 2–9. Bobbs; Pro-Ed

Analysis of Skills (ASK): Reading (1974). Criterion-referenced. Each of 4 levels (Grades 1–2, 3–4, 5–6, 7–8) measures 43–48 objectives of the total of 60 covered by the series. Each skill sampled by 3 items; mastery equals all 3 correct, or 2 of 3 including most difficult item. Three main areas tested; word analysis, comprehension, study skills. Grades 1–8. STS

Analytical Reading Inventory (Woods & Moe 1977). Individual. Criterion-referenced. Commercially published IRI. Each of 3 forms consists of 7 graded 20-word lists (primer– Grade 6) and 11 graded passages (primer–9). Six comprehension questions at primer to second reader level; 8 at others. Questions balanced among main idea, factual, terminology, cause–effect, inference, and conclusions. Instructional level: 95–98% word recognition; 75–89% comprehension. Oral reading and listening comprehension measured; silent reading optional. Grades 1–9. Merrill

Assessment of Reading Growth (1980). Measures reading comprehension, using items released by NAEP. Level/Age 9 measures literal comprehension (word meaning, reference, facts, main ideas and organization) and inferential comprehension (drawing inferences, critical reading). Levels/Ages 13 and 17 sample literal comprehension (same as Level 9 plus written directions) and inferential comprehension. Raw scores converted to percent correct and compared to national norm tables. Grades 3, 7, 11. Jamestown

Bader Reading and Language Inventory (1983). A series of graded 10-word lists (primer– Grade 8) and 4 supplementary word lists (words used in instructional materials, tests, and words encountered in daily living), 3 sets of graded reading passages (pre-primer– Grade 12), 14 phonic and word-analysis subtests, 7 spelling tests, 4 cloze tests (to assess semantic, syntactic, and grammatical processing), visual- and auditory-discrimination tests, an interest test, an estimate of language abilities (receptive and expressive language, handwriting), and a brief arithmetic test. Grades 1–12, adult. Macmillan

Basic Achievement Skills Individual Screener (BASIS): Reading (1983). Individual achievement tests that yield both norm- and criterion-referenced information. Test items grouped in grade-referenced clusters ranging from readiness to Grade 8. Readiness measured by letter identification and visual discrimination. At lower levels, decoding, word recognition, and sentence comprehension assessed. Reading test assesses comprehension of graded passages (primer–8), using a cloze procedure (child reads orally and supplies missing words). Grades 1–12. Psy Corp.

Basic Reading Inventory (Johns 1981). Individual. Criterion-referenced. Commercially published IRI. Each of 3 forms consists of 10 graded 20-word lists (pre-primer–8) and 10 graded passages (pre-primer–8). Words on lists first shown quickly; unknown words presented again untimed. Four comprehension questions at pre-primer level; 10 at others (1 main idea, 5 factual, 2 inference, 1 vocabulary, 1 experience (evaluation). Instructional level: 91–98% word recognition, 55–85% comprehension; preferably 95% word recognition and 75% comprehension. Oral reading measured; silent reading and listening comprehension optional. Grades 1–8. Kendall/Hunt

Basic Reading Rate Scale (Tinker & Carver 1970). Measure of rate when reading very easy material. Yields 3 scores: number correct, number attempted, and percent accuracy. Grades 3–16, adults. Revrac

Basic Word Vocabulary Test (1975). Measure of word-meaning knowledge. Printed words presented in isolation. Testee selects 1 word (4 choices) whose meaning most similar to target word. Number of words range from 55 at Grade 3 to all 123 for adults. Yields

Vocabulary Age score and Vocabulary Development Quotient. Estimated Vocabulary Size score is obtained by multiplying raw score by 100. Grade 3–adult. Jamestown

Boder Test of Reading–Spelling Patterns (1982). Individual. Used to identify 4 subtypes of disabled readers: dysphonetic, diseidetic, dysphonetic and diseidetic, and nonspecific (see p. 236). Reading subtest has 13 graded lists (pre-primer–adult), each containing 10 phonically regular and 10 irregular words. Words are flashed and each unknown word presented again for 10 seconds. Reading level = highest word list with at least 50% words correct when flashed. Reading Quotient = 5 years + reading age + CA × 100. Spelling subtest individualized; 10 words correctly recognized (5 regular, 5 irregular) and 10 words incorrectly recognized on reading subtest. Subtypes determined on basis of RQ, percent of known and unknown words spelled correctly or as good phonic equivalents. Disabled readers of all ages. Grune & Stratton

Brigance Diagnostic Comprehensive Inventory of Basic Skills (1983). Informal, individual battery of criterion-referenced tests covering a wide range of skills. Reading subtests include word recognition, word analysis, vocabulary, and oral reading. Spelling and study skills measured by other tests. Grades K–6. Curriculum Associates

Burt Word Reading Test—New Zealand Revision (1981). Individual. Measures ability to recognize words presented in isolation. Consists of 110 words printed in different-size type and graded in difficulty. Ages 6–13. New Zealand

California Achievement Tests: Reading (1978). Norm-referenced, but yields criterion-referenced information. Level 11 (Grades 1.0–1.9) contains subtests: phonic analysis (sound–symbol associations), reading vocabulary (synonyms, antonyms, and selecting intended meaning of polysemous words), and reading comprehension (literal and interpretive). Levels 12 (Grades 1.6–2.9) and 13 (2.6–3.9) include same subtests as Level 11 plus structural analysis (compound words, root words, affixes). Levels 14–19 (3.6–4.9, 4.6–5.9, 5.6–6.9, 6.6–7.9, 7.6–9.9, 9.6–12.9) have only vocabulary and comprehension subtests; critical reading included at Levels 13–19. Two forms at Levels 13–19. Grades K–12. CTB

Canadian Test of Basic Skills (1981). Levels 5 and 6 (Grades K–1) are readiness tests. Levels 5–8 (K–3) assess listening, word analysis, vocabulary, reading, oral and written language, work–study skills, and math. Levels 9–14 (Grades 4–8) measure vocabulary, reading, writing mechanics, study skills, and math. Levels 15–18 (Grades 9–12) have 4 tests: reading, math, written expression, and using sources of information. Normed on same population as *Canadian Cognitive Abilities Test*. Two forms. Grades K–12. Nelson Canada

CAP Achievement Series: Reading (1980). Level 6 (Grade 1) has 13 subtests: auditory word rhymes, sound–letter relations, adding and taking away sounds, letter recognition, blending, words in sentences, reading comprehension, picture opposites, visual closure, finding causes, and 2 tests on math. Levels 7 (Grade 2) and 8 (3) have 3 subtests: word attack, vocabulary (word meaning in context), and reading (literal and inferential comprehension, defining words through context, and determining main ideas). Levels 9–12 (Grades 4–8) have vocabulary, reading comprehension, and study skills subtests. Levels 13–14 (Grades 9–12) have a reading subtest (literal and inferential comprehension, word meaning from context, antonyms). Two forms for Levels 7–12. Grades 1–12. American Testronics

Carver–Darby Chunked Reading Test (1972). Criterion-referenced. Measures rate and retention. After reading each of 5 passages, student is presented "chunks" (groups of meaningful related words within a sentence). From each set of chunks, the reader marks the one whose meaning has been changed from that of the original text. Yields 3 scores: rate (number of answers given), efficiency (number of correct answers), and accuracy (efficiency ÷ rate × 100). Two forms. Grades 7–16, adults. Revrac

Classroom Reading Inventory (Silvaroli 1979). Individual. Criterion-referenced. Commercially published IRI. Each of 3 forms consists of 8 graded 10-word lists (pre-primer–Grade 6) and 10 graded passages (pre-primer–8). Each passage followed by 5 comprehension questions (factual, inference, vocabulary). Instructional level: 95% word recognition, 75% comprehension. Oral reading measured, silent reading and listening comprehension optional. Also has optional spelling test. Grades 1–8. William C. Brown

Comprehensive Tests of Basic Skills: Reading (1981). Level B (K.6–1.6) has 3 subtests: word attack, vocabulary, and oral comprehension. Levels C (Grades 1.0–1.9), D (1.6–2.9), E (2.6–3.9) measure word attack, vocabulary, and reading comprehension. Levels F–K (3.6–4.9, 4.6–6.9, 6.6–8.9, 8.6–12.9, 11.0–12.9) have vocabulary, reading comprehension, and reference skills subtests. Two forms. CTB

Contemporary Classroom Reading Inventory (Rinsky & de Fossard 1980). Individual. Criterion-referenced. Commercially published IRI. Each of 3 series consists of graded 20-word lists (primer–Grade 7) and graded passages (primer–9). One series each for fiction, social studies, and science. Primer and first-reader passages have 5 comprehension questions; second reader has 6; third reader, 7; fourth reader, 7 or 8; all others have 8. Types of questions: main idea, detail, inference, sequence, vocabulary, reasoning/conclusion, and evaluation. Instructional level: 92–96% word recognition, 60–79% comprehension. Oral reading measured; silent reading not indicated; listening comprehension optional. Also contains cloze tests in the same 3 content areas. Grades 1–9. Gorsuch Scarisbrick

Content Inventories, English, Social Studies, and Science (McWilliams & Rake 1979). Group. Criterion-referenced. Cloze Placement Inventories and Group Reading Inventories in English (Grades 7–12), social studies, and science (Grades 4–12). Instructional level on cloze tests: 37–57% exact replacement. Passage in Group Reading Inventory is read silently, then taken away. Student answers 14 questions in writing (2 main idea, 3 use of context, 5 details, and 4 inference). Unlike other inventories, only 1 passage given. Instructional level: 64–79% comprehension (9–11 answers correct). Also contains study skills assessment (use of book parts, locational skills, note taking, interpreting graphic aids, reading for different purposes, attitudes, habits, and interests). Grades 4–12. Kendall/Hunt

Cooperative English Tests: Reading Comprehension (1965). Provides scores for level of comprehension, rate of comprehension, and vocabulary. Form 1 (Grades 12–14); Form 2 (9–12). Three forms. Grades 9–14. CTB

Cooper-McGuire Diagnostic Word Analysis Tests (1972). Primarily group-administered. Criterion-referenced. Readiness test samples letter names, auditory and visual discrimination, and sound blending. Seventeen phonic analysis tests (e.g., sound–symbol associations, initial consonant with context, auditory perception of vowels, decoding nonsense words) and 10 structural-analysis tests (e.g., inflected endings, root words, number of syllables heard in words). All subtests need not be given. Two forms. Grades 1–6; disabled readers. Croft

Criterion Reading (1971). Criterion-referenced. Five levels (K, 1, 2–3, 4–6, 7–adult) covering 451 overlapping specific-objective subtests. Level 1 has 90 subtests: motor skills, visual matching, and auditory matching. Levels 2–5 have 361 subtests in 5 areas: phonics, structural analysis, verbal information, syntax, and comprehension. Grade K–adult. Random House

Criterion Referenced Curriculum: Reading (1982). Includes 267 objectives for Grades K–6. Merrill

Criterion Test of Basic Skills: Reading (1976). Individual. Criterion-referenced. Measures 18 objectives dealing with letter recognition, letter sounds, writing letters, phonics, and word recognition. Average of 13 items per objective. Grades K–8. ATP

CTBS Espanol. Spanish-language adaptation of 1978 CTBS test battery. Levels 1 (Grades 3–4), 2 (5–6), and 3 (7–8). Grades 3–8. CTB

Davis Reading Test (1958). Provides scores on level of comprehension and rate of comprehension. Series 2 (Grades 8–11); Series 1 (11–13). Two forms. Grades 8–13. Psy Corp. Out of print.

Decoding Inventory (1979). Group screening test used to determine level of test to be administered individually. Criterion-referenced. Level R (Readiness) measures auditory and visual discrimination. Level 1 (Basic) (Grades 1–3) has 10 subtests; Level 2 (Advanced) (Grades 4 and up) has 17 parts. Grades 1 and up. Kendall/Hunt

Degrees of Reading Power (1981). Measure of reading comprehension using maze format. A series of 325-word nonfiction passages arranged in increasing order of difficulty. Each passage contains 7 deletitions for which the pupil selects (from 5 choices) the one that best completes the sentence. Yields 3 scores in DRP units that translate to independent, instructional, and frustration levels. Readability data in DRP units available on reading materials; can match with test performance. College Board

Diagnosis: An Instructional Aid—Reading (1974). Criterion-referenced. Covers 306 objectives at Level A (Grades 1–4) and 224 at Level B (Grades 3–6). Skill areas measured: phonic and structural analysis; comprehension, vocabulary, study skills, and use of sources. Almost three-quarters of the objectives are sampled by only 1 or 2 items. Grades 1–6. SRA

Diagnostic Achievement Battery (1984). Primarily individual. Ten tests provide a profile of strengths and weaknesses in listening, speaking, reading, writing, and math. Ages 6–14; suspected learning-disabled pupils. Pro-Ed

Diagnostic Analysis of Reading Errors (DARE) (1979). The 46 words in the WRAT spelling test (Level II) are read to students, who select the word spoken by the examiner from 4 printed choices. Four scores: number of correct responses, sound substitutions, omissions, and reversals. Ages 12–adult. Jastak

Diagnostic Analysis of Reading Tasks (1976). Criterion-referenced. Uses nonsense words. DART 1 (Grades 2.5 and below) yields 3 scores: encoding (spelling), decoding, and auditory screening (number of syllables heard in a word). DART 2 (Grade 2.5 and above) yields 6 scores: encoding (sections A, B), decoding (sections A, B), medial diphthongs and digraphs, and irregular letter clusters. Grades 1 and up. Slosson

Diagnostic Reading Inventory (Jacobs & Searfoss 1979). Individual. Criterion-referenced. Commercially published IRI. Eight graded 20-word lists (Grades 1–8) and 8 graded passages (1–8), one each for oral reading, silent reading, and listening comprehension. Twelve questions for Grades 1–3; 20 questions for Grades 4–8 (literal, inferential, critical/evaluative, vocabulary). Instructional level: 92–97% word recognition, 60–

89% comprehension. Two levels of a decoding inventory also included. Optional phrase list. Grades 1–8. Kendall/Hunt

Diagnostic Reading Scales (Spache 1981). Individual. Criterion- and norm-referenced battery. Three word lists (40–50 words each), two sets of 11 graded passages (pre-primer–seventh reader) with 7–8 comprehension questions each (primarily literal details) and 12 supplementary decoding tests. Word-recognition criterion for oral reading is norm-referenced (mean plus 1 standard deviation). Comprehension criterion for oral and silent reading, and listening comprehension is criterion-referenced (60%). Instructional level is based on oral reading, independent level on silent reading. Decoding tests yield grade-equivalent scores. Grades 1–7; disabled readers. CTB

Doren Diagnostic Reading Test of Word Recognition Skills (1973). Criterion-referenced. Twelve subtests measure beginning and ending sounds, sight words, rhyming, whole-word recognition, words within words, speech consonants, blending, vowels, discriminate guessing, letter recognition, and spelling. Scoring based on number of incorrect items; 7 or more errors on a subtest indicates need to teach those skills. Grades 1–6. AGS

Durrell Analysis of Reading Difficulty (1980). Battery of individually administered diagnostic tests. Five primary and 3 intermediate-level paragraphs, each followed by 5–9 primarily factual detail questions. Instructional level (oral reading) based primarily on reading time, with comprehension given consideration. Five different primary and 3 intermediate-level passages for silent reading. Independent level (silent reading) based on reading time and recall (comprehension measured by retellings). Six passages (Grades 1–6) available for listening comprehension, each followed by 7–8 questions. Criterion for listening comprehension: no more than 2 incorrect answers (72%, 75%). Word-recognition/word-analysis test consists of 4 50-word lists. Words are first flashed, and unknown words are shown untimed. Listening-vocabulary test consists of 5 15-word lists (same words as in word-recognition test); student indicates in which of 3 categories word belongs. Listening vocabulary also used as measure of reading potential. Sounds-in-isolation test measures symbol–sound associations. Spelling test consists of 2 20-word lists; and 15 words are dictated on the phonic-spelling-of-words test. Also included are visual memory for words and identifying sounds in words, as well as prereading phonic abilities inventories. Grades 1–6; disabled readers. Psy Corp.

Durrell Listening–Reading Series (1970). Vocabulary and sentence comprehension subtests in both reading and listening. Provides for comparison of pupil's reading and listening abilities. Primary level (Grades 1–2); Intermediate (3–6); Advanced (7–9). Two forms. Grades 1–6. Psy Corp.

ECRI Informal Reading Inventory (1981). Individual. Criterion-referenced oral reading test. Separate tests for Grades 1–6 and Grade 7–adult, each with 17 graded passages (pre-primer–Grade 12). Six comprehension questions per passage. Instructional level: 91–95% word recognition, 50–75% comprehension. Grade 1–adult. Cove

Edwards Reading Test (1980). Individual. Criterion-referenced. Commercially published IRI. Eight graded word lists and 8 graded passages (Ages 6–13). Four to 10 questions per passage. Instructional level: 90–95% word recognition, 70% comprehension. Oral reading, silent reading, and listening comprehension measured. Two forms. Heinemann

Ekwall Reading Inventory (1979). Individual. Criterion-referenced. Commercially published IRI. Each of 4 forms consists of 11 graded word lists (primer–Grade 9) and 11 graded passages (pre-primer–9); there is no primer level. Five comprehension questions at pre-primer level; 10 at others (factual, inference, vocabulary). Instructional level: 95–

98% word recognition, 60–89% comprehension. Oral and silent reading measured; listening comprehension optional. Also contains Quick Survey Word List and the El Paso Phonics Survey. Grades 1–9. Allyn & Bacon

Fountain Valley Reading Skills Tests. Criterion-referenced. For Grades 1–6: series of 77 one-page tests covering 367 objectives (number of objectives per test level range from 33 to 125, with 2 to 12 items per objective). Skill areas sampled: phonic and structural analysis, vocabulary, comprehension, and study skills. For Grades 7–12: 61 specific-objective subtests, usually with 4 to 6 items each. Measures vocabulary, comprehension, and study skills. Grades 1–12. Zweig

GAP Reading Comprehension Test (1967, 1970). Cloze technique with approximately every tenth word deleted in each of 7 brief paragraphs. Yields a Reading Age. Australian and British editions. Two forms. Grades 2–7. GAPADOL for ages 10–16. Heinemann

Gates–MacGinitie Reading Tests (1978). Basic R (Grades 1.0–1.9) consists of 4 subtests: letter sounds (primarily sound–symbol associations), vocabulary (word recognition), letter recognition (most letters are embedded in printed words), and sentence comprehension. Levels A (1.5–1.9), B (2), C (3), D (4–6), E (7–9), and F (10–12) have 2 subtests: vocabulary and comprehension (stated and implied). Two or 3 forms. Grades 1–12. Riverside

Gates–McKillop–Horowitz Reading Diagnostic Tests (1981). Test battery contains 15 individually administered tests. Oral reading test has 7 paragraphs; score based on number of word-recognition errors (reading comprehension questions are not even asked). Reading sentences test has 4 sentences that are read orally; score based on word recognition. Words: Flash consists of 4 10-word lists; Words: Untimed uses same words. Knowledge of word parts: Word attack measures syllabication, recognition and blending of common word parts, decoding nonsense words, making symbol–sound associations for single consonants, and naming upper- and lowercase letters. Recognition of visual form of sounds measures sound–symbol association of single vowels. Auditory tests measure blending and discrimination. Spelling and writing skills are sampled by written expression test. Grades 1–6; disabled readers. Teachers College Press

Gillingham–Childs Phonics Proficiency Scales (1967). Individual. Criterion-referenced tests of letter–sound correspondences, syllabication, and decoding of real and nonsense words with different spelling patterns. Series 1 contains 17 subtests each in reading and spelling. Series 2 has 20 subtests in reading. Grades 1–6. EPS

Gilmore Oral Reading Test (1968). Individual. Ten graded passages (pre-primer–high school; 5 literal questions on each. Scores (based on performance across passages) for accuracy (word recognition), comprehension (literal), and rate of reading. Performance ratings (e.g., above average) also provided. Two forms. Grades 1–8. Psy Corp.

Gray Oral Reading (1967). Thirteen graded passages in each of 4 forms. Child continues reading until 7 or more word-recognition errors on 2 consecutive passages. Four factual comprehension questions per passage, but score does not consider comprehension. Score based on time taken to read each passage and number of word-recognition errors per passage; based on performance across passages. Separate norms for girls and boys. Grades 1–12. Bobbs; WPS

Gray Standardized Oral Reading Check Tests (1923–1955). Set 1 (Grade 1); Set 2 (2–3); Set 3 (4–5); Set 4 (6–8). Each set contains 5 passages of approximately equal difficulty (used to measure progress). Yields 2 standard scores: reading rate and accuracy (word recognition). Grades 1–8. Bobbs

Gray Standardized Oral Reading Paragraphs (1915). Twelve graded paragraphs (Grades 1–12). Yields 3 scores: paragraph, total raw, and B-scores (grade equivalents). Comprehension is not measured. Grades 1–12. Bobbs

Group Assessment in Reading (1984). Battery of criterion-referenced tests. Series of graded passages (pre-primer–Grade 12) for silent reading (instructional level = 75–96% comprehension). Cloze tests (primer–Grade 12) require exact word replacement (instructional level = 40–60%). Also measures specific comprehension skills (word meaning, literal and inferential comprehension, critical reading), work–study skills (locating information, reference sources, pictorial and graphic materials, organizing information), attitudes, and interests. Grades 1–12. Prentice-Hall

Group Diagnostic Reading Aptitude and Achievement Tests (Marion Monroe & E. Sherman 1939). Yields 15 scores: reading (paragraph comprehension, rate), word discrimination (vowels, consonants, reversals, additions, and omissions), arithmetic, spelling, visual ability (letter and form memory), auditory ability (letter memory, discrimination, and orientation), motor ability (copying, crossing out letters), and vocabulary. Grades 3–9. Nevins

Group Phonics Analysis Test (1971). Criterion-referenced, 75-item test. Areas measured: number and letter reading, hearing consonants, alphabetization, recognition of vowels, vowel digraph rule, final *e* rule, open and closed syllables, syllabication. Grades 1–3. Jamestown

High-School Subjects Tests: Literature and Vocabulary. Measures literal and inferential comprehension, recognition and application of literary terms, and vocabulary. American Testronics

Individual Evaluation Procedures in Reading (IEP/r) (1983). Criterion-referenced. Battery consists of 9 graded 20-word lists, 11 graded passages (primer–Grade 10) in each of 3 content areas (literature, science, history), 6 visual-discrimination tests, 1 auditory-discrimination test, 2 auditory memory tests, 1 phonic and structural-analysis test, 2 lists of survival words, and an interest inventory (used to determine in which content area to test reading). Separate instructional levels for word recognition in isolation (at least 75% of 20 words correct) and in context (88–90% correct; dialectal renditions *are* deliberately counted as errors), and for oral reading, silent reading, and listening (60% criterion). Of the comprehension items, 20–40% for each passage measure word meaning. PAL score is Projected Achievement Level. Two forms. Grades 1–12. Prentice-Hall

Individual Phonics Criterion Test (1971). Criterion-referenced. Covers 99 phonic skills in 14 areas such as single consonants, long and short vowels, consonant digraphs and blends, and schwa sounds. Grades 1–6. Jamestown

Individual Pupil Monitoring System: Reading (1974). Criterion-referenced, but a mastery level is not suggested in the manual. Separate test booklets for word attack, vocabulary and comprehension, and discrimination/study skills for each grade level (1–6). Each of 343 overlapping objectives measured by a 5-item test. Two forms. Grades 1–6. Riverside

Informal Reading Assessment (Burns & Roe 1980). Individual. Criterion-referenced. Commercially published IRI. Two graded word lists (pre-primer–Grade 12) and 4 sets of graded passages (pre-primer–12). Eight questions at pre-primer–second reader; 10 at others (6 types on each passage—main idea, detail, sequence, cause–effect, inference, and vocabulary). Instructional level: 85–95% word recognition (Grades 1–2) or 95–98% word recognition (Grades 3–12) and 75–89% comprehension. Oral reading measured; silent reading and listening comprehension optional. Grades 1–12. Rand McNally

Instant Words Criterion Test (1980). Individual. Criterion-referenced. Consists of 300 high-frequency words presented in isolation. Quick survey and suffix tests included. Grades K–3. Jamestown

Iowa Silent Reading Tests (1973). Measures ability to apply reading skills to different kinds of reading tasks. Reading Efficiency Index indicates relative effectiveness of reading rate and comprehension. Level 1 (Grades 6–9) and Level 2 (Grades 9–14) include subtests of vocabulary, comprehension (including items on which the student is not allowed to look back at the selection), directed reading (work–study skills including locational skills, skimming, and scanning, and reading efficiency (6 short easy passages)). Level 3 (academically accelerated high school students and college students) does not include a directed reading subtest. Two forms. Grades 6–14. Psy Corp.

Iowa Tests of Basic Skills: Reading (1982). Level 6 (K.8–1.9) measures listening, word analysis, vocabulary, and reading comprehension. Levels 7 (1.7–2.6) and 8 (2.7–3.5) also sample work–study skills. Levels 9–14 (Grades 3–8) measure vocabulary, reading comprehension, and work–study skills. Grades K–8. Riverside (new edition 1985)

IOX Objectives-Based Tests: Reading (1973). Criterion-referenced; mastery level not specified. Consists of 38 word-attack skills tests (objectives) and 40 comprehension tests. Manual does not suggest which tests should be given at a given grade level. Most word-attack tests have 10 items; most comprehension tests, 5. Two forms. Grades 1–6. IOX

Johnson Basic Sight Vocabulary Test (1976). Measures recognition of 300 high-frequency words; 10 30-item subtests. Two forms. Grades 1–3. Personnel

Library Skills Test (1980). Forty-five-item test designed to locate strengths and weaknesses in working with library materials, including terminology, card catalog classification system, filing, parts of a book, indexes, reference tools, and bibliographic forms. Grades 7–13. STS

Kennedy Institute Phonics Test (KIPT). Individual (production) and group (recognition) tests. Measures variety of decoding skills, (symbol–sound associations, blending) and sound–symbol associations. Ages 5 and up. Test Collection

Mastery: An Evaluation Tool: Reading. See SOBAR

Macmillan Diagnostic Reading Pack (1980). Stage 1 (Reading ages 5–6); item scores in 3 areas: visual skills (e.g., 32 key words, letter matching, visual-memory reproduction), auditory skills (e.g., sound values of letters, auditory discrimination), and phonic blending (auditory blending, blending two- and three-letter words). Stage 2 (Reading ages 6–7); item scores in 5 areas: key words (68 and 32), phonic recognition (e.g., blends and digraphs), phonic blending, phonic spelling (two- and three-letter words), and oral reading (accuracy, comprehension). Stage 3 (Reading ages 7–8); 5 areas: key words, phonic recognition, phonic blending, phonic spelling, oral reading. Stage 4 (Reading ages 8–9); 4 areas: phonic recognition, phonic blending, phonic spelling, oral reading. Ages 5–9. Macmillan England

McCullough Word Analysis Test (1963). Seven subtests: initial blends and digraphs, phonetic discrimination (vowels), matching letters to vowel sounds, sounding whole words, interpreting phonetic symbols, syllabication, root words in affixed forms. Remedial work suggested for skills in which subtest score is one standard deviation below mean. Grades 4–6. Personnel; Ginn

McGuire–Bumpus Diagnostic Comprehension Tests (1979). Criterion-referenced. Measures 12 skills in 4 types of comprehension: literal (selecting details, translating details, identifying signal words, selecting main ideas), interpretive (determining implied ideas, identifying organizational patterns, inferring main ideas), analytic (identifying the problem, developing hypotheses, determining relevant details), and critical reading (selecting criteria for judgment, making a judgment). Each type is measured at 3 levels; the level used is dependent on the child's level of reading ability: Early primary (1^2–2^2), Primary (2^2–3^2), and Intermediate (4–6 reader level). Each objective is sampled by 12 multiple-choice questions. Two forms. Grades 1–6. Croft

McLeod Phonic Worksheets (1977). Criterion-referenced. Measures 6 areas: initial and final single consonants, single vowels, consonant blends and digraphs, vowel blends, and auditory discrimination. Grades 1–3. EPS

Metropolitan Achievement Tests: Reading Instructional Test (1978). Primer (Grades K.5–1.4): reading comprehension, sight vocabulary, phoneme/grapheme–consonants, auditory discrimination, visual discrimination, letter recognition. Primary 1 (1.5–2.4): same as first 4 tests in Primer, plus vocabulary in context, word-part clues. Primary 2 (2.5–3.4): same as Primary 1, except phoneme/grapheme–vowels replaces auditory discrimination. Elementary (3.5–4.9): same as Primary 2 plus rate of comprehension. Intermediate (5.0–6.9): comprehension, vocabulary in context, rate, skimming and scanning, phoneme/grapheme–consonants and vowels, word-part clues. Advanced 1 (7.0–9.9): same as first 4 subtests in Intermediate. Survey tests for Primer through Advanced 1 levels are same as reading comprehension subtests of Reading Instructional Tests. Both Survey and Instructional tests are norm-referenced and provide criterion-referenced information. Both also provide an instructional reading level (IRL) based on child's raw score on the reading comprehension subtest. Normed on same population as *Otis–Lennon School Ability Test* (Form R). Two forms at all but Primer level. Grades K–9. Psy Corp.

Mills Learning Methods Test, Revised Edition (1970). Trial teaching procedures. Used to determine comparative effectiveness of 4 methods of teaching word recognition: visual, phonic, kinesthetic, or a combination. Grades K–3; disabled readers. Mills Center

Monroe Diagnostic Reading Test (Marion Monroe 1928). Preliminary tests include *Stanford-Binet, Gray's Oral Reading Paragraphs, Haggerty Reading Examination, Monroe Silent Reading Test, Ayres' Spelling Scale,* and *Stanford Achievement Test in Arithmetic.* Analytic tests include alphabet repeating (alphabetic sequence) and reading (letter-name knowledge), iota word test (recognition of words in isolation), reversible-letters test, mirror reading, mirror writing, number reversals, word discrimination (reversible words), sound blending, and handedness. A profile of word-recognition errors is suggested. Grades 1–4; disabled readers. Stoelting

Monroe's Standardized Silent Reading Test (Walter Monroe 1919). Very brief tests of rate of comprehension. Test I (Grades 3–5): 17 paragraphs each followed by 1 multiple-choice item; Test II (6–8): 16 paragraphs; Test III (9–12): 12 paragraphs each followed by 1 completion item. Tests I and II are self-scoring. Two forms. Grades 3–12. Bobbs

Multilevel Academic Skills Inventory: Reading and Language Arts (1982). Criterion-referenced tests covering 3 broad areas: reading decoding, reading comprehension, and language arts. Designed for use with children having learning problems in Grades 1–8. Merrill

Neal Analysis of Reading Ability (1966). Yields 3 scores: accuracy, comprehension, rate of reading. Three optional tests: names and sounds of letters, auditory discrimination through simple spelling, blending and recognition of syllables. Ages 6–13. Macmillan England

Nelson Reading Skills Tests (1977). All levels measure word meaning and reading comprehension. For Level A (Grades 3.0–4.5): sound–symbol correspondences, root words, and syllabication are optional. For Levels B (4.6–6.9) and C (7.0–9.9), reading rate is optional. Two forms. Grades 3–9. Riverside

Nelson–Denny Reading Test (1981). Measures vocabulary (50 prefixes and 50 nonprefixed words), reading comprehension (8 passages with a total of 36 questions—18 each literal and interpretation), and reading rate based on the first minute of the reading comprehension test. Two forms. Two levels: Grades 9–12, 13–16. Riverside

New Developmental Reading Tests (1968). Lower Primary (Grades 1.0–2.5) and Upper Primary (2.5–3.9) measure word recognition, and comprehension of significant ideas and specific instructions. Intermediate (Grades 4–6) measures reading vocabulary; reading for information, relationships, appreciation, and interpretation. Creative comprehension score based on reading for appreciation and interpretation. Two forms. Grades 1–6. Rand McNally. Out of print.

New Sucher–Allred Reading Placement Inventory (1981). Individual. Criterion-referenced. Commercially published IRI. Each of 2 forms has 12 word lists and 12 oral reading selections. Five comprehension questions per passage (literal, inferential, cause–effect, main idea). Instructional level: 92–96% word recognition, 60–79% comprehension. Economy

Objectives—Referenced Bank of Items and Tests: Reading and Communication Skills (ORBIT) (1980). Customized, criterion-referenced tests (4-item, single-objective subtests) covering up to 50 objectives chosen by the school district to match those of their reading program. Grades 1–12. CTB

Oral Reading Criterion Test (1971). Individual. Criterion-referenced. Consists of 10 brief passages (Grades 1–7). Independent, instructional, and frustration levels based only on word recogniton. Grades 1–7. Jamestown

Peabody Individual Achievement Test (PIAT) (1970). Individual. Wide-range screening test: reading, arithmetic, spelling, and general information. Reading recognition includes 18 readiness skills (e.g., visual discrimination, letter names) and 66 words in isolation that the student attempts to read aloud. Reading comprehension contains 66 sentences that are read silently; after each, the student selects the picture (4 choices) that best illustrates the meaning of the sentence. Grades K–12. AGS

Prescriptive Reading Inventory (PRI) (1976). Criterion-referenced. Covers 30 objectives for Levels 1 (Grades K.0–1.0) and 2 (K.5–2.0) and 90 objectives for Levels A (1.5–2.5), B (2.0–3.5), C (3.0–4.5), and D (4.0–6.5). Reading readiness skills at Levels 1 and 2. Other 4 levels measure phonic and structural analysis; translation (vocabulary); and literal, interpretive, and critical comprehension. Over 80% of pretest objectives are measured by 3–4 items; mastery defined as not more than 1 error. Grades K–6. CTB

Prescriptive Reading Performance Test (1978). Individual. Uses child's performance on graded word lists (Grades 1–12) and spelling of words that are and are not in the child's sight vocabulary to classify students as normal or into 3 subtypes of reading disability. WPS

Primary Reading Profiles (1968). Each level has 5 subtests: aptitude for reading, auditory association, word recognition, word attack, and reading comprehension. Level 1 (Grades 1.5–2.5); Level 2 (2.5–3.5). Grades 1–3. Riverside

PRI/RS (1980). Criterion-referenced. Measures 4 skill areas: oral language at Levels A (Grades K–1) and B (1–2); word attack and usage–word analysis, vocabulary, word usage at Levels A, B, C (Grades 2–3), and D (4–6); comprehension–literal, interpretive, and critical reading at Levels B, C, D, and E (Grades 7–9); and application–study skills, content-area reading at Levels C–E. Measures 171 objectives across the 5 levels. Grades K–9. CTB

Prueba deLectura (1978). Assesses reading comprehension in Spanish. Grades 3 and 6. Test Collection

Primary Reading Test (1981). Assesses ability to apply reading skills to comprehend words and simple sentences. Ages 6–12. NFER–Nelson

PRISM: Reading 1 (1982). Microcomputer-based software. Criterion-referenced test based on diagnostic–prescriptive approach. Item bank contains over 2000 items in 3 skill areas: word identification, comprehension, and study skills. Levels C, D, E: Grades 3, 4, 5. Psy Corp.

Reading Diagnosis: Informal Reading Inventories (Fry 1981). Primarily individual. Criterion-referenced. Battery of informal tests measures oral reading, silent reading comprehension (2 10-item multiple-choice tests: literal and inferential comprehension), phonics (symbol–sound associations of various elements in isolation; decoding nonsense words), recognition of words in isolation, word meaning, letter and number recognition, spelling, handwriting, vision, hearing, and interests. *Oral Reading Criterion Test* has 2 passages for Grades 1–3 and 1 passage for Grades 4–7. Instructional level based only on word recognition (criterion varies from approximately 71% to 97%). *Brief Reading Comprehension Test* read silently; Primary (Grades 1–2) and one test each for 9- and 13-year-olds. Criterion for primary grades is 75% comprehension, 70% for others. Grades 1–6. Jamestown

Reading Placement Inventory. Individual. Criterion-referenced. Commercially published IRI. Consists of 12 graded word lists and passages (primer–Grade 9). All passages taken from *Keys to Reading Program* (Economy). Each passage has 5 comprehension questions; one each: main idea, factual, sequence, inference, and critical thinking. Instructional level: 92–96% word recognition, 60–79% comprehension. Grades 1–9. Economy

Reading Skills Inventory: A Portfolio of Tested Diagnostic and Remedial Techniques (1980). Series of group or individual informal reading inventories in social studies, literature, science, and mathematics. Identifies instructional level and suggests remedial activities. Grades 4–12. Prentice-Hall

Reading Yardsticks (1981). Criterion-referenced but supplemented by NR information. Level 6 (kindergarten) assesses visual and auditory discrimination, letter and word matching (and identification), vocabulary (understanding spoken words or sentences), and literal and interpretative comprehension of phrases, clauses, and sentences. Levels 7 and 8 (Grades 1 and 2) test auditory and visual discrimination, phonic analysis, vocabulary (meanings of printed words), and comprehension. Level 8 also measures structural analysis. Levels 9–14 (Grades 3–8) measure structural analysis, vocabulary, comprehension, and study skills. Reading rate is assessed at Grades 5–8 (average WPM over 2 passages).

Number of subtests in a skill area for a given level range from 4 to 8; number of objectives range from 17 to 46. Specific objectives measured by 3–5 items each. Grades K–8. Riverside

Roswell–Chall Auditory Blending Test (1963). Brief individual test of ability to hear the sounds of a word pronounced separately by the examiner and then blend them into a whole word, which the testee pronounces. Grades K–2; disabled readers. Essay

Roswell–Chall Diagnostic Reading Test of Word Analysis Skills (1978). Individual. Brief measures of fundamental skills. Yields 15 scores: high-frequency words, decoding (10 subtests), letter names (upper and lower case), and spelling (single consonants, phonically regular CVC words). Two forms. Grades 1–6; disabled readers. Essay

San Diego Quick Assessment (n.d.). Individual. Measures ability to recognize (pronounce) words presented in isolation. Grades 1–11. Ramon Ross

SCORE (1977). Criterion-referenced tests customized to match local school programs. Covers reading readiness, sound–symbol associations, word meaning, comprehension, study skills, and classifying and analyzing forms of literature. Grades K–12. Riverside

Sequential Tests of Educational Progress (STEP): Reading, Series III (1979). Measures vocabulary in context and literal and inferential comprehension. Vocabulary test samples knowledge of synonyms. Study skills and listening test measures listening comprehension, following directions, dictionary usage, library skills, and reference skills.) Levels E (Grades 3–5), F (4–6), G (8–12). Two forms. Grades 3–12. CTB

Silent Reading Diagnostic Tests (1976). Eight subtests provide detailed analysis of word recognition and phonic skills. Measure ability to recognize words in isolation and in context; identify root words; syllabicate and apply syllabication rules; blend word parts; distinguish beginning and ending sound, vowels, and consonant sounds. Grades 3–6. Rand McNally

Sipay Word Analysis Tests (SWAT) (1974). Individual. Criterion-referenced. Battery of 16 tests from which examiner selects ones needed to provide desired information (manuals also suggest which to give). Measures decoding ability in 1 or more of 3 areas: visual analysis, symbol–sound associations, and blending; also ability to combine skills. Each specific skill (e.g., symbol–sound association for *t*) is measured by at least 3 items on any test. Answer sheets designed to facilitate detailed analysis of child's performance. Also has report form for each test that specifies for each skill whether it has been mastered, needs to be practiced under the teacher's guidance, or needs to be taught. Grades 1–6; disabled readers. EPS

Slosson Oral Reading Test (SORT) (1981). Very brief individually administered test of ability to recognize (respond orally) words presented in isolation. Grades 1–12. Slosson; AGS

SOBAR (*System for Objective-Based Assessment: Reading*) (1976). Criterion-referenced test for each grade (K–9). Each contains 23 to 35 3-item, single-objective subtests (criterion for mastery usually 100%). Skills areas measured: letter recognition (kindergarten), phonic analysis (K–4), structural analysis (1–9), vocabulary (1–9), comprehension (K–9), and study skills (1–9). Also 9 selected short SOBAR reading tests for Grades 3–9. Tests in either English or Spanish can be customized to fit school objectives. Grades K–9. SRA

Spandafore Diagnostic Reading Tests (1983). Individual. Criterion-referenced. Assesses decoding; word recognition; and oral reading, silent reading, and listening comprehension. Grades 1–12. ATP

Spanish Criterion Referenced Test (1974). Designed to determine mastery of Spanish in reading program for bilinguals. Covers phonics, structural analysis, and comprehension. Grades K–5. Test Collection

Spanish Oral Reading Test (1982). Individual. Designed for use with native Spanish speakers. Consists of 2 word lists, 2 paragraphs at each of 6 grade levels, and 6 phonics tests (includes English sounds frequently distorted by Spanish speakers). Grades 1–6. Paradox

Spanish Reading Comprehension Tests and English Reading Comprehension Tests (1978). Spanish tests standardized and normed in Mexico. English tests translated from Spanish tests. Elementary level (Grades 1–6) consists of 73 items; Secondary level (Grades 7–12, adult) consists of 81 items. Designed to determine degree of bilingualism or to evaluate bilingual programs. Grades 1–12. Moreno Educational

SPIRE Individual Reading Evaluation (1973). Criterion-referenced. Levels I (primer–Grade 6) and II (Grades 4–10) have 2 tests. *Quick Placement Test* has 7 graded word lists and 7 graded silent reading passages. QPT instructional level: highest word list with minimum of 80% correct and highest passage with at least 60% comprehension. *Diagnostic Individual Evaluation* (DIRE) yields independent, frustration, and 3 instructional levels; scores based on a combination of word recognition accuracy as well as oral and silent reading comprehension. Five comprehension questions per passage (vocabulary, inference, detail, and main idea). Grades 1–10. NDE

SRA Achievement Tests: Reading (1978). Levels B (Grades 1–2) and C (2–3) subtests: letters and sounds, listening comprehension, vocabulary, and reading comprehension. Level B also measures auditory discrimination. Levels D (Grades 3–4), E (4–6), F (6–8), G (8–10) and H (9–12) sample only vocabulary (word meaning) and comprehension. Separate reference materials tests in Levels E–H. Two forms. Grades 1–12. SRA

SRA Reading Record (1959). Ten subtests with short time limits: rate, comprehension, paragraph meaning, directory, map–table–graph, advertisement, index, technical and general vocabulary, and sentence meaning. Grades 6–12. SRA

Standard Reading Inventory (McCracken 1966). Individual. Criterion-referenced. Commercially published IRI. Each of 2 forms has 11 graded word lists (preprimer–7), 11 oral reading passages, and 8 silent reading passages. Five comprehension questions at preprimer level; 13–15 at others (literal, inferential, vocabulary). Yields independent, minimum instructional, maximum instructional, and frustration levels. Instruction level can have "no subtest rated as frustration." Also yields 6–9 subtest scores: word recognition in isolation and context, total oral reading errors, recall after oral and silent reading, total comprehension, word meaning, oral and silent speed, as well as various ratings and check lists. Grades 1–7. Klamath

Stanford Achievement Test: Reading (1982). Norm-referenced but provides criterion-referenced information. Levels: Primary 1 (1.5–2.9); Primary 2 (2.5–3.9), Primary 3 (3.5–4.9), Intermediate 1 (4.5–5.9), Intermediate 2 (5.5–7.9), and Advanced (7.0–9.9). Skill areas and grades at which measured: Word–study skills (sound–symbol association, structural analysis)—Grades 1.5–7.9; word reading (matching spoken and printed words or printed words with pictures)—Grades 1.5–3.9; reading comprehension (literal and inferential)—Grades 1.5–9.9; vocabulary (understanding *spoken* words)—Grades 1.5–9.9; and listening comprehension—Grades 1.5–9.9. Normed on same population as *Otis Lennon* (Form S). Two or 3 forms. Grades 1–9. Psy Corp.

Stanford Diagnostic Reading Test (1984). Levels: Red (Grades 1.5–4.5); Green (3.5–6.5); Brown (5.5–8.5); Blue (7.5–13.0). Skill areas and grades at which measured: Auditory discrimination—Grades 1.5–6.5; phonetic analysis (sound–symbol associations)—Grades 1.5–8.5; auditory vocabulary (meanings of spoken words)—Grades 1.5–8.5; word reading (word recognition)—Grades 1.5–4.5; reading comprehension (literal and inferential)— all grades; structural analysis (analysis of word parts)—Grades 3.5–13.0; reading rate (ability to read easy material quickly with comprehension)—Grades 5.5–13.0; word parts (knowledge of affixes and root words), vocabulary (understanding meanings of printed words), and skimming and scanning—Grades 7.5–13. Two forms. Grades 1–3. Psy Corp.

Stanford Test of Academic Skills (TASK): Reading (1982). Measures vocabulary (word meaning) and comprehension. Task I (Grades 8.0–12.9); Task II (Grades 9.0–13.9). Two forms. Grades 8–13. Psy Corp.

STS Analysis of Skills—Reading (1974). Criterion-referenced. Three parts: word analysis (discrimination; phonetic analysis—consonants, vowels; structural analysis; word recognition); comprehension (vocabulary in context; literal, inferential, critical comprehension); and study skills (library and reference, organization, pictorial and graphic material). Grades 1–8. STS

Study Habits Checklist. Yields scores on 37 study skills and habits. Grades 9–14. SRA

Test of Reading Comprehension (TORC) (1978). Three subtests: general vocabulary (ability to identify words related to a common concept), syntactic similarities (understanding semantically similar, but syntactically different sentences), and paragraph reading (understanding storylike paragraphs). Yields Reading Comprehension Quotient (RCQ), with 85–115 being average. Scaled scores for 4 supplementary tests: math, science, and social studies vocabulary; understanding written directions commonly found in schoolwork. Optional sentence-sequencing test (arranging 5 sentences to form a story). Grades 2–12. Pro-Ed

Tests of Achievement and Proficiency: Reading (1978). Reading comprehension test measures ability to define words from context and comprehend prose, poetry, newspaper articles, advertisements, and subject-matter content. Using sources of information test calls for reading maps, graphs, tables, charts, and reference materials. Normed on same population as *Cognitive Abilities Test*. Levels 15–18 (Grades 9–12). Riverside (new edition 1985)

Tests of Individual Needs in Reading (1982). Individual and group. Criterion-referenced. Provides reading level and analysis of reading skills strengths and weaknesses. *Bidwell* form for use with students in western U.S. and Canada; *Red Cloud* form for Native Americans; *Kangaroo* form for use in Australia. *Red Fox* is supplementary group test to evaluate potential for developing word recognition and reading comprehension. Grades 1–7. Council for Indian Education

The 3-R's Test: Reading (1982). Reading comprehension measured at all levels. Levels 8–18 (Grades 2–12) measure main ideas, explicit and implicit details, and logical relationships/inferences. Levels 9–18 also include words in context, literary analysis, and author's purpose. Vocabulary (word meaning in sentences) measured at Levels 8–18; synonyms also at Levels 8–18. Visual discrimination and sound–symbol association at

Levels 6 and 7 (Grades K–1). Study skills at Levels 8–18 (Grades 2–12). Abilities tests (Levels 9–18) measure verbal and quantitative reasoning. Grade-Development Score (GDS) provides estimate of student's level of reading ability. Grades K–12. Riverside

Traxler High School Reading Test (1967). Part I measures rate (number words read in 5 minutes) and comprehension (20 questions) of easy material. Part II samples ability to locate main ideas in paragraphs. Two forms. Grades 9–12. Bobbs

Traxler Silent Reading Test (1969). Yields scores in rate (number of words read in 200 seconds), story comprehension (10 multiple-choice questions based on story used to measure rate), vocabulary (synonyms), and paragraph comprehension. Four forms. Grades 7–10. Bobbs

Valett Developmental Survey of Basic Learning Abilities (1966). Compendium of 233 tasks in 7 areas: motor integration; tactile, auditory, and visual discrimination; visual–motor coordination; and language and conceptual development. Ages 2–7. Consulting; Stoelting

Wide Range Achievement Test (WRAT) (1978). Individual. Three subtests: reading, spelling, and arithmetic. Reading subtest primarily measures ability to recognize words in isolation. Level I (Ages 5–11) samples visual discrimination, letter naming, and recognition of up to 75 words. Level II (Ages 12 and up) has a preword section and 74 words. Ages 5 and up. Jastak; Slosson

Wisconsin Design Tests of Reading Skill Development (1972). Criterion-referenced. Tests measure wide range of word-attack skills at 5 levels: A (Grades K–2), Transition (Grade 1), B (1–3), C (2–4), and D (3–6). Comprehension and study skills measured at 7 levels (K–6). Number of items per subtest greater than found in most CR tests; mastery criterion = 80%. One or 2 forms. Grades K–6. Learning Multi-Systems

Woodcock Reading Mastery Tests (1973). Battery of 5 individually administered tests: letter identification (letter names; mixed script used); word recognition (recognition of words in isolation); word attack (decoding nonsense words); word comprehension (task requires word recognition *and* reasoning ability; analogies format); and passage comprehension (sentence comprehension using a cloze format with key words omitted). Yields easy reading level (level at which probability of success will be 96% mastery); reading grade score (90% mastery); failure reading level (75% mastery); grade level score, and percentiles. Separate sex and SES-adapted norms available. "Best suited for use as a global screening measure for reading disability and not for any precise decisions" (Dwyer 1978, p. 1304). Two forms. Grades K–12. AGS

ADULT BASIC EDUCATION, LITERACY, MINIMAL COMPETENCY

Adult APL Survey (1976). Measures functional literacy at fifth–sixth grade levels. Reading strand has 9 items (of test total of 40) that measure reading in 5 areas of everyday living. Grade 9–adult. American College

Adult Basic Learning Examination (1974). Measures educational achievement of adults who have not completed a formal eighth-grade education. Four subtests: listening vocabulary, reading comprehension, spelling, arithmetic. Levels I (Grades 1–6), II (3–9), III (9–12). Two forms. Ages 17–adult. Psy Corp.

Adult Basic Reading Inventory (1966). Measure of literacy. Subtests: sight words, auditory and visual discrimination, word meaning (both listening and reading), and reading comprehension. Grades 6–12. STS

Basic Skills Assessment: Reading (1979). Minimal-competency test that uses such items as medicine labels, income tax forms, and job applications. Also measures writing and math skills. Entry norms for Grades 8–9; exit norms for Grade 12. Three forms. Grades 7–12. CTB

Everyday Skills Tests: Reading (1975). Criterion-referenced test of functional literacy. Measures ability to read labels, want ads, tax forms, and so forth. Fifteen objectives, each with 3 items. Use of reference and graphical materials subtests are norm-referenced. Grades 6–12. CTB

High School APL Survey (1976). Measures functional competency at fifth–sixth grade level. Reading ability sampled in 5 areas of daily functioning. Grades 11–12. American College

IOX Basic Skill System (1978). Criterion-referenced measures of minimal competency in reading, writing, and math. Elementary level (Grades 5–6), Secondary level (Grades 7–12). Two forms. Grades 5–12. Psy Corp.

Life Skills: Reading (1980). Criterion-referenced minimal-competency test. Measures ability to follow directions (signs, labels, etc.), locating and understanding references (phone books, catalogs, etc.), interpretation and use of information (want ads, lease agreements, etc.), and understanding of forms (taxes, installment purchases). Two forms. Grades 9–12. Riverside

Literacy Assessment Battery. Contains reading- and listening-comprehension tests to determine any discrepancy between the two, a vocabulary test to determine the difference between understanding of spoken and written words, and a decoding test. HumRRO

Minimum Essentials Test (1980). Measures basic skills in reading, language, and math; also, ability to apply these skills to life situations. Reading basic skills section: literal and inferential comprehension, defining words through context, determining main ideas through title selection. Life skills section: reading items in areas of health, safety, nutrition, communication, transportation, finance, government and law, and occupations. Grades 8–12, adult. American Testronics

Performance Assessment in Reading (PAIR) (1981). Criterion-referenced minimal competency test. Seventy-two items sample ability to read warning signs, maps, ads, telephone directory, schedules, and forms. Two forms. Grades 7–9. CTB

Reading/Everyday Activities in Life (R/EAL) (1972). Criterion-referenced measure of functional literacy (criterion = 80% items correct). Consists of 9 stimulus displays of printed materials used in everyday life (45 fill-in items; 5 per display). Two forms. Ages 15–adult. Westwood

Senior High Assessment of Reading Performance (SHARP) (1980). Criterion-referenced minimal-competency test. Measures ability to apply basic reading skills to life-role situations. Consists of 30 displays representing written materials commonly encountered in daily living. Two forms. Grades 10–12. CTB

SRA Survival Skills in Reading and Mathematics (1976). Criterion-referenced functional literacy tests (norm-referenced scoring can be arranged). Reading tests measure such skills as reading a phone book, street signs, and bills. Grade 6 and up. SRA

Tests of Adult Basic Education (1978). Reading test comprised of vocabulary and comprehension subtests adapted from 1970 edition of *California Achievement Tests*. Also includes math, spelling, and language tests. Levels E (upper primary); M (upper elementary); and D (junior high). High school–adult. CTB

INTELLIGENCE, LEARNING, AND SCHOLASTIC APTITUDE

Arthur Point Scale Revised Form II (1947). Individual. Nonlanguage scale of mental ability that includes adaptions of 6 tests: *Knox Cube, Seguin Formboard, Arthur Stencil Design, Healey Picture Completion*, and *Porteus Maze*. Requires trained examiner. Ages 5–15. Psy Corp.; Stoelting

British Ability Scales (1983). Designed to help diagnose learning difficulties. Consists of 23 scales measuring a wide range of cognitive abilities that cover 6 areas: speed of information processing, reasoning, spatial imagery, perceptual matching, short-term memory, and retrieval and application of knowledge. Ages 2½–17. NFER–Nelson

British Picture Vocabulary Scales (1982). Individual. British adaptation of PPVT. Ages 3–18. NFER–Nelson

California Short-Form Test of Mental Maturity (1963). Provides separate language and nonlanguage MAs and IQs as well as total. Eight levels, K–16. CTB. Out of print.

California Test of Mental Maturity Long Form (1963). Reading and nonreading items used for testing memory, attention, spatial relations, reasoning, and vocabulary. Separate MAs and IQs for language, nonlanguage, and total scores. Levels 0 (Grades K–1), 1 (1–3) 2 (4–8), 3 (7–9), 4 (9–12), 5 (12–16). CTB. Out of print.

Canadian Cognitive Abilities Test (1981). Levels 1 and 2 (Grades K–3) measure verbal, quantitative and nonverbal reasoning, and problem solving. Levels A–H (Grades 3–12) measure scholastic aptitude and abstract reasoning ability. Normed on same population as *Canadian Test of Basic Skills*. Grades K–12. Nelson Canada

Cognitive Abilities Test (1982). Levels 1 and 2 (Grades K–3) are single-score, untimed, nonreading tests of general cognitive skills; use pictorial materials and oral instructions. Levels A–H (Grades 3–12) yield 3 separate scores for verbal, quantitative, and nonverbal reasoning abilities. 1985 edition to provide 3 separate scores at all levels, and to be normed concurrently with the ITBS and TAP. Grades K–12. Riverside

Columbia Mental Maturity Scale (1972). Individual. Brief test that does not require verbal responses and only minimal motor responses. Consists of 92 items arranged in 8 overlapping levels. From a series of drawings, child selects one that does not belong. Ages 3½–10. Psy Corp.

Culture Fair Intelligence Test (Cattell 1933–1973). Measure of general intelligence. Does not require reading and is generally free from cultural and educational influences. Scale 1 (Ages 4–8 and mentally retarded adults) not fully group administrable; Scale 2 (Ages 8–14 and average adult); Scale 3 (Ages 14–superior adult). Scales 2 and 3 have 2 forms and Spanish editions. Ages 4–adult. WPS

Detroit Tests of Learning Aptitude (1975). Individual. Battery of 19 subtests measure reasoning and comprehension, practical judgment, verbal ability, time and space relationships, number ability, auditory attention, visual attention, and motor ability. Yields MA for each subtest and for total score. Ages 3–adult. Bobbs

Detroit Tests of Learning Aptitude (DTLA-2) (1984). Individual. Battery of 11 subtests in 4 domains: linguistic, cognitive, attention, and motor. Yields standard scores and percentiles for 8 composite aptitudes: verbal, nonverbal, conceptual, structural, attention-enhanced (STM), attention-reduced (LTM), motor-enhanced (manual dexterity), and motor-reduced (motor-free). General Intelligence Quotient based on total of 11 subtest scores. Ages 6–17. Pro-Ed

Developing Cognitive Abilities Test. Based on premise that academic abilities are flexible, nonstable traits that can be directly affected by instruction. Measures 3 abilities: verbal, quantitative, and spatial. Level 2 (Grade 2); Levels 3–12 (Grades 3–12). Levels 3–12 provide information on 5 levels of Bloom's taxonomy: knowledge, comprehension, application, analysis, and synthesis. Two forms for Levels 5–12. Grades 2–12. American Testronics

Differential Aptitude Tests (1981). Battery of scholastic aptitude tests. Measures 8 abilities: verbal reasoning, numerical ability, abstract reasoning, clerical speed and accuracy, mechanical reasoning, space relations, spelling, and language usage. Index of scholastic ability based only on verbal reasoning and numerical ability scores. Only verbal reasoning test requires reading ability. Two forms. Grades 8–12. Psy Corp.

Expressive One-Word Picture Vocabulary Test (1980). Individual. Measure of verbal intelligence. Testee continues to name picture shown (110 available) until makes 6 consecutive errors. Yields MA, IQ, percentile, and stanine scores. Ages 2–12. Slosson; WPS

Expressive One-Word Picture Vocabulary Test—Upper Extension (1983). Individual. Seventy-item measure of verbal intelligence. Ages 12–16. ATP

Full-Range Picture Vocabulary Test (Ammons & Ammons 1948). Individual. Measure of verbal intelligence. From 4 pictures, testee chooses one that best illustrates meaning of word spoken by examiner or read by himself. Two forms. Ages 2–adult. Psychological Test

Goodenough–Harris Drawing Test (1963). Nonverbal test of mental ability. Child's drawings of human figures compared against 12 ranked drawings or scored for the presence of up to 73 characteristics. Separate norms for boys and girls. Ages 3–15. Psy Corp.

Healey Pictorial Completion Tests (1921). Individual. Based on testee's appreceptive ability. In Test I, testee presented a picture with 10 apertures representing 10 incomplete places in the scene. Testee selects and puts in 10 correct inserts from 50 provided. Test II involves selecting 10 squares from 60 choices to complete each of 10 pictures representing, in sequence, daily situations in the life of a school boy. Ages 5 and up. Stoelting

Henmon–Nelson Test of Mental Ability (1973). Primary battery (Grades K–2) consists of 3 subtests (listening, picture vocabulary, size and number) that measure 9 abilities; does not require reading ability. Tests for Grades 3–6, 6–9, and 9–12 include measures of vocabulary, sentence completion, opposites, general information, verbal analogies, verbal classification, verbal inference, number series, arithmetic reasoning, and figure analogies; reading ability required. Yields IQ (a standard score by age), age and grade percentile ranks, and stanines. Grades K–12. Riverside

Hiskey–Nebraska Test of Learning Aptitude (1966). Individual. Can be administered entirely via pantomimed instructions; requires no verbal response from testee. Consists of series of performance tasks organized in ascending order of difficulty with 12 subscales. Learning-age score determined by median age level of pupil's performance on subscales. Separate norms for deaf and hearing. Ages 3–17. Hiskey

Kaufman Assessment Battery for Children (K–ABC) (1983). Individual. Measures intelligence and achievement. Yields 4 global scores: sequential processing, stimultaneous processing, mental processing composite, and achievement; derived scores for subtests (reading scores only in grade equivalents). Only 13 of 16 subtests given to any child. Intelligence assessed through problem solving using simultaneous and sequential memory processes. Sequential Processing Scale comprised of 3 subtests that require child to solve problems by arranging stimuli in sequential or serial order: hand movement (e.g., child performs series of hand movements in same order as examiner), number recall (digit span), and word order (child touches series of silhouettes of common objects in same sequence as names of objects presented orally by examiner). Simultaneous Scale comprised of 7 subtests that require child to solve problems (usually spatial or analogic) in contexts when the input has to be integrated and synthesized in order to produce the appropriate solution (language ability minimized): magic window (identifying pictures which are only partially visible at any one time), face recognition (visual memory of faces), Gestalt closure (visual closure), triangles (assembling triangles into abstract patterns that match models), matrix analogies (selecting pictures or abstract designs that best complete visual analogies), spatial memory (recalling the places of pictures on a page that was exposed briefly), and photo series (putting photographs of an event in chronological order). Achievement Scale measures expressive vocabulary (naming pictured objects); faces and places (naming depicted well-known persons, fictional characters, or places); arithmetic (number and math concepts, counting, computation); riddles (inferring names of concrete or abstract objects when given its characteristics); reading/decoding (naming letters, reading words in isolation); and reading/understanding (acting-out written commands, some of which are single words). Intelligence and achievement tests normed on same population. Ages $2\frac{1}{2}$–$12\frac{1}{2}$. AGS

Knox's Cube Test. Nonverbal test of mental ability. Measures attention span and short-term memory. KCT Junior (Ages 2–8); KCT Senior (Ages 8–adult). Ages 2–adult. Stoelting

Kohs Block-Design Test (1919). Individual nonverbal intelligence test consisting of 16 colored cubes used to reproduce 17 colored designs depicted on cards. Similar to block design subtest of *Wechsler* tests. Ages 5–20. Stoelting

Kuhlman–Anderson Tests (1982). Measure of academic potential. Consists of 8 subtests: 4 verbal, 4 nonverbal. Levels K (Kindergarten); A (Grade 1), B (2), CD (3–4), D (4–5), EF (5–7), G (7–9), H (9–12). Grades K–12. STS

Leiter International Performance Scale (1969). Nonverbal test of intellectual functioning. Examinee uses blocks to construct designs shown on stimulus cards. Yields MA and IQ scores. Ages 2–18. Slosson; Stoelting

Lorge–Thorndike Intelligence Tests. Multi-Level Edition (1966) (Levels A–H for Grades 3–13) provides 3 scores: verbal, nonverbal, and composite. Separate Levels Edition (1962) yields nonverbal score for Levels 1 (K–1) and 2 (Grades 2–3); verbal and nonverbal scores for Levels 3–5 (Grades 4–6, 7–9, 10–12). Two forms. Riverside

McCarthy Scales of Children's Abilities (1972). Individual measure of general intelligence. Provides 6 scores: verbal, perceptual-performance, quantitative, composite (general cognitive), memory, and motor. Ages $2\frac{1}{2}$–$8\frac{1}{2}$. Psy Corp.

Nonverbal Test of Cognitive Skills (1981). Fourteen subtests measure aspects of reasoning, rote memory, recognition and memory of patterns, visual memory, discrimination, spatial relations, thinking and memory, and visual–motor perception. Instruction can be pantomimed; oral language not required of testee. Ages 6–13. Merrill

Otis–Lennon School Ability Test (1982). Measure of abstract thinking and reasoning ability (scholastic aptitude). Levels : Primary I (Grade 1), Primary II (2–3), Elementary (4–5), Intermediate (6–8), and Advanced (9–12). Reading not required on Primary I and II. Two forms. Grades 1–12. Psy Corp.

Peabody Picture Vocabulary Test—Revised (PPVT–R) (1981). Individual. Measure of verbal intelligence. From 4 choices, child points to picture that best illustrates word spoken by examiner. Two forms. Ages 2½–4. AGS

PMA Readiness Level (1974). Revision of 1962 edition of *Primary Mental Abilities*. Five subtests: auditory discrimination, verbal meaning, perceptual speed, number facility, and spatial relations. Grades K–1. SRA

Porteus Maze (1914–1965). Nonlanguage test of mental ability. Series of 12 mazes of increasing difficulty. Yields qualitative and quantitative scores. Ages 3–14. Psy Corp.; Stoelting

Primary Mental Abilities Test (1962). All 5 levels (K–1, 2–4, 4–6, 6–9, 9–12) sample verbal meaning, number facility, and spatial relations. Perceptual speed tested in K–6 and reasoning ability in 4–12. Grades K–12. SRA

Quick Test (Ammons & Ammons 1962). Individual test of verbal intelligence. Similar to but shorter than (50 items) *Full-Range Picture Vocabulary Test*. Child selects drawing (4 choices) that best illustrate meaning of word spoken by examiner or read by child. Three forms. Ages preschool–adult. Psychological Services

Raven Progressive Matrices (1938–1965). Individually administered nonverbal test of mental ability. Requires examinee to solve problems presented in abstract figures and designs. Standardized in England. Yields percentile scores. Ages 8–65. Psy Corp.

Revised Beta Examination (BETA II) (1978). Measure of mental ability that does not require reading ability. Six subtests: mazes, coding, paper form boards, picture completion, clerical checking, and picture absurdities. Yields IQ scores and percentile ranks. Ages 16–64. Psy Corp.

Short Form Test of Academic Aptitude (1970). Four subtests: vocabulary, analogies, sequences, and memory. Yields language and nonlanguage scores. Level 1 (Grades 1.5–3.4), 2 (3.5–4), 3 (5–6), 4 (7–9), 5 (9–12). Grades 1–12. CTB

School and College Ability Tests (SCAT), Series III (1980). Verbal subtest uses verbal analogies to measure word meaning. Quantitative subtest measures fundamental number operations. Elementary level (Grades 3–6); Intermediate (6–9); Advanced (9–12). Two forms. Grades 3–12. CTB

Slosson Intelligence Test (1981). Individual. Brief measure of verbal intelligence. Many items *very* similar to those on the Stanford–Binet. Ages 2–18. Slosson; Stoelting

SRA Pictorial Reasoning Test (1973). Designed "to measure learning potential of individuals from diverse backgrounds with reading difficulties." Entails reasoning with nonverbal, pictorial materials. Consists of 80 sets of 5 pictures or designs. Task is to select the one that differs from the rest. Ages 14 and over. SRA

SRA Verbal Form (1973). Abbreviated adaptation of *Thurstone Test of Mental Alertness*. Three scores: quantitative, linguistic, and total. Grades 7–16, adults. SRA

Stanford–Binet Intelligence Scale (1972). Individual test of general intelligence (primarily verbal). Test items arranged by age level, with 6 subtests administered at each.

Abilities measured include memory, vocabulary, abstract reasoning, and social competence. Yields MA and IQ scores. Ages 2–adult. Riverside

The 1985 edition to have 15 subtests in 4 areas: verbal reasoning (vocabulary, comprehension, verbal relations, absurdities); abstract/visual reasoning (pattern analysis, matrices, paper folding and cutting, copying), quantitative comprehension (quantitative, number series, equation building); and STM (memory for sentences, digits, objects, and beads). Will yield scores for each subtest, each of the 4 general areas, and a complete score. Requires trained examiner.

STAR: Screening Test of Academic Readiness (1966). Intelligence test that yields 9 scores: picture vocabulary, letters, picture completion, copying, picture description, human figure drawing, relationships, numbers and total. Ages 4–6½. Priority

System of Multicultural Pluralistic Assessment (SOMPA) (1978). Individual and group-administered. Assesses cognitive and sensorimotor abilities and adaptive behaviors. Provides estimate of learning potential (ELP) that takes into account differences in family backgroud, SES, etc. Two major components: Parent Interview (adaptive behavior inventory, sociocultural scales, health history inventories) and Student Assessment (physical dexterity, weight by height, visual and auditory acuity, *Bender*, and WISC-R or WPPSI). Ages 5–11. Psy Corp.

Test of Cognitive Skills (1981). Measure of scholastic aptitude, reflecting such abilities as reasoning, problem solving, evaluating, discovering relationships, and remembering. Four subtests: sequence (ability to comprehend a rule or principle implicit in a pattern or sequence of figures, letters, or numbers); analogies (ability to understand concrete or abstract relationships and to classify objects or concepts according to common attributes); memory (ability to recall previously presented material); and verbal reasoning (ability to discern relationships and to reason logically). Yields subtest and Cognitive Skills Index (total score). Successor to *Short Form Test of Academic Aptitude.* Level 1 (Grades 2–3); Level 2 (3–5); Level 3 (5–7); Level 4 (7–9); Level 5 (9–12). Grades 2–12. CTB; PTS

Test of Nonverbal Intelligence (TONI) (1982). Individual or small-group. Fifty-item language-free measure; examiner pantomimes instructions and testee responds by pointing. Involves abstract problem solving of increasingly more complex tasks. Two forms. Ages 5–85. Pro-Ed; Slosson

Wechsler Adult Intelligence Scale-Revised (WAIS-R) (1981). Individual. Yields verbal, performance, and full-scale IQ scores. Verbal scale subtests: information, digit span, vocabulary, arithmetic, comprehension, and similarities. Performance Scale subtests: picture completion, picture arrangement, block design, object assembly, and digit symbol. Requires trained examiner. Ages 16–74. Psy Corp.

Wechsler Intelligence Scale for Children-Revised (WISC-R) (1974). Individual. Yields verbal, performance, and full-scale IQs. Verbal Scale subtests: information, similarities, arithmetic, vocabulary, comprehension, and digit span (supplementary subtest). Performance Scale subtests: picture completion, picture arrangement, block design, object assembly, coding, and mazes (supplementary subtest). Requires trained examiner. Ages 6–16. Psy Corp.

Wechsler Preschool and Primary Scale of Intelligence (WPPSI) (1967). Individual. Yields verbal, performance, and full-scale IQs. Verbal Scale subtests: information, vocabulary, arithmetic, similarities, comprehension, and sentences (supplementary subtest). Performance Scale subtests: animal house, picture completion, mazes, geometric design, and block design. Requires trained examiner. Ages 4–6½. Psy Corp.

Wide Range Intelligence–Personality Test (1978). Measure of global intelligence and personality variables. Ten subtests measure verbal, pictorial, spatial competency, and so on. Also provides cluster scores for language, reality set, motivation, and psychomotor skills. Ages 9½–adult. Jastak

PERCEPTUAL, PERCEPTUAL–MOTOR, MEMORY, LATERALITY

Auditory Discrimination Test (Wepman 1978). Individual. Forty-item test of ability to distinguish whether two spoken words are exactly the same or differ (in one minimally contrasting phoneme). Two forms. Ages 5–8. Language; WPS

Auditory Memory Span Test (Wepman & Morency 1975). Individual. Requires ability to retain and recall sets of single-syllable words spoken by the examiner. Sets range from 2–6 words. Two forms. Ages 5–8. Language; Stoelting

Auditory Sequential Memory Test (Wepman & Morency 1975). Individual. Brief test in which child tries to repeat increasingly longer series of single digits in exactly the same sequence as spoken by examiner. Two forms. Ages 5–8. PTS; Stoelting

Bender Visual Motor Gestalt Test (1946). Usually individual. Measures perceptual–motor integration. Testee copies, one at a time, 9 abstract designs, which remain in view. Child's reproductions are scored on basis of departures from stimuli. *Bender* often scored using Koppitz system for 5- to 10-year-olds. Pascal and Suttell scoring system often used for older children and adults. AGS; Psy Corp.

Benton Revised Visual Retention Test (1974). Usually individual. Designed to assess visual perception, visual memory, and visual–motor integration. Ten designs, one at a time, shown briefly, and examinee attempts to draw each. Also yields IQ equivalents. Ages 8–adult. Psy Corp.

Bieger Test of Visual Discrimination (1982). Identifies levels of mastery in identifying larger contrasts, lesser contrasts, and almost identical words and letters. Grades 1–6. Stoelting

Bruininks–Oseretsky Test of Motor Development (1978). Individual. Used to assess motor development, neurological development and dysfunction. Measures 8 areas of gross and fine motor proficiency. Yields scores for gross motor, fine motor, and battery composite. Short form consists of 14 of the 46 items that constitute complete battery; yields only a general motor proficiency score. Ages 4½–14½. AGS

Developmental Test of Visual–Motor Integration (VMI) (1967). Usually individual. Measures ability to integrate visual perception and motor behavior. Pupil draws geometric forms, which remain in view. Short and long forms. Ages 2–15. MCP

Frostig Developmental Test of Visual Perception (DTVP) (1966). Five subtests: eye–motor coordination (drawing continuous lines between increasingly narrower boundries, or drawing lines to connect 2 targets); figure–ground (picking out and outlining geometric forms embedded among other forms); constancy of shape (discriminating among geometric forms of differing sizes, shadings, textures, and positions); position in space (distinguishing between figures in the same or reversed or rotated positions); and spatial relations (joining dots to reproduce forms and patterns shown). Ages 7–8. CPS; Stoelting

Goldman–Fristoe–Woodcock Test of Auditory Discrimination (1970). Individual. Measures ability to discriminate speech sounds in quiet and in noise. Testee responds to word (on tape) by pointing to 1 of 4 pictures whose names differ in only one sound. Ages 4–adult. AGS

Goldman–Fristoe–Woodcock Auditory Skills Test Battery (1976). Individual. Battery of 12 tests in four categories: auditory selective attention, auditory discrimination, auditory memory, and sound–symbol tests (which includes measures of auditory analysis, sound blending, and ability to make symbol–sound associations). Age 3–adult. AGS

Halstead–Reitan Neuropsychological Test Battery (1979). Individual. Consists of 3 test batteries. *Reitan–Indiana Neuropsychological Test Battery for Children* (Ages 5–8): 13 tests. *Halstead Neuropsychological Test Battery for Children* (Ages 9–14): 11 tests. *Halstead Neuropsychological Test Battery for Adults* (Age 15 and over): 13 tests. Ages 5–adult. Neuropsychological Laboratory

Harris Tests of Lateral Dominance (1958). Individual. Set of brief tests of knowledge of left and right; hand preferences; simultaneous writing with both hands; speed and coordination in writing, tapping, and dealing cards; monocular and binocular tests of eye dominance; and foot dominance. Ages 7 and up. Psy Corp.

Jordan Left–Right Reversals Test (1980). Consists of series of numbers, letters, and words printed in correct or left–right reversed spatial orientation. Level 1 (Ages 5–8) contains only single numbers and letters. Level 2 (Ages 9–12) consists of words (many contain reversed letters) and short sentences containing reversed words. Ages 5–12. ATP; Slosson

Kindergarten Auditory Screening Test (1971). Individual. Recorded test with 3 subtests: listening for speech against a noise background, sound blending, and auditory discrimination. Grades K–1. Follett

Lincoln–Oseretsky Motor Development Scale (1956). Individual. Consists of 36 items involving a wide variety of motor skills, such as coordination, speed of movement and finger dexterity, eye–hand coordination, and gross activity of the hands, arms, legs, and trunk. Both unilateral and bilateral motor tasks measured. Ages 6–14. Stoelting

Lindamood Auditory Conceptualization Test (1971). Individual. Consists of 4 parts: precheck (understanding of concepts needed to take the test; e.g., same/different); identifying the number of sounds heard and determining if they are the same or different; indicating the sequence of sounds, and determining the number of sounds in a syllable, and changes in the sound pattern when sounds are added, deleted, changed or repeated. Understanding of task indicated by manipulating colored blocks. Two forms. Ages preschool–adult. Teaching Resources

Luria–Nebraska Neuropsychological Battery (1980). Individual. Assesses broad range of neuropsychological functions. Consists of 269 discrete, scored items in 14 scales: motor, rhythm, tactile, visual, receptive and expressive speech, writing, reading, arithmetic, memory, intellectual, pathognomonic, left and right hemisphere. Requires trained examiner. Two forms. Ages 15 and up. WPS

Memory-for-Designs Test (Graham & Kendall 1960). Usually individual. Design is shown for 5 seconds, then testee attempts to draw it from memory. Each of 15 designs scored 0 to 3 by comparing it to a model. Ages 8½–60. Psychological Test

Mertens Visual Perception Test (1974). Individual. Measures 6 areas of visual perception: design copying, design reproduction, framed pictures, design completion, spatial recognition, and visual memory. Grades K–1. WPS

Minnesota Percepto-Diagnostic Test (1969). Usually individual. Measure of visual–motor performance. Six designs copied in different settings. Used to diagnose neurological dysfunctions, emotional problems, and personality disorders. Also used to classify LDs as visual, auditory, or mixed. Ages 5–70. Clinical; WPS

Motor-Free Visual Perception Test (1972). Individual. Brief 36-item test that does not require motor skills other than pointing. Child selects (4 choices) the item that is the same as (or different than) the line drawing shown. Section 3 requires visual memory; Section 4, visual closure. Yields perceptual quotient and perceptual age scores. Ages 4–8. ATP; Slosson

Psychoeducational Inventory of Basic Learning Abilities (1968). Individual. Measures 53 basic learning abilities in 6 areas: gross motor development, sensory–motor integration, perceptual–motor skills, language development, conceptual skills, and social skills. Ages 5–12. Fearon

Purdue Perceptual–Motor Survey (1966). Individual. Series of 11 tasks measuring balance and posture, body image, perceptual–motor skills, ocular control, and form perception. Ages 6–10. Merrill; PTS

Screening Test for Auditory Perception (STAP) (1981). Assesses weaknesses in 5 areas of auditory discrimination: long vs. short vowel sounds, initial single consonants vs. blends, rhyming vs. nonrhyming words, same vs. different rhythmic patterns, and same vs. different words. Grades 1–6. Slosson

Southern California Motor Accuracy Test (Ayres 1980). Individual. Measures degree of, and changes in, sensorimotor integration of upper extremities. Ages 4–8. WPS

Southern California Sensory Integration Tests (Ayres 1980). Individual. Battery of 17 short tests: space visualization, figure–ground perception, design copying, motor accuracy, kinesthesia, manual form perception, finger identification, graphesthesia, localization of tactile stimuli, double tactile stimuli perception, imitation of postures, crossing midline of body, bilateral motor coordination, right–left discrimination, and standing balance, eyes open and eyes closed. Ages 4–8. WPS

Spatial Orientation Memory Test (Wepman & Turaids 1975). Individual. Assesses ability to retain and recall orientation (direction) of visually presented forms. Child responds by pointing to one of a choice of visual stimuli. Two forms. Ages 5–9. WPS; Stoelting

START: Screening Test for the Assignment of Remedial Treatment (1968). Individual. Contains subtests: visual and auditory, memory, visual copying, and visual discrimination. Ages 4–6. Priority

Test of Lateral Awareness and Directionality (1980). Usually individual. Criterion-referenced. Used to identify children with left–right labeling problems. Pupils classified as high, medium, or low risk. Grades 1–2. ATP

Test of Non-Verbal Auditory Discrimination (TENVAD) (1975). Individual. Nonverbal test of auditory discrimination. Subtests: pitch, loudness, rhythm, direction, and timbre. Ages 6–8. Follett

Tree/Bee Test of Auditory Discrimination (1978). Usually individual. Assesses phonetic discrimination in individual words, phrases, word pairs, and same/different comparisons. Scored for initial and final consonants, vowel sounds, auditory memory, and ability to follow oral directions. Two forms. Grades K–8. PTS

Visual Aural Digit Span Test (1978). Individual. Measures short-term memory. Two to 7 digits presented orally or visually for verbal or written repetition. Eleven subtests yield scores for auditory and visual processing, and intrasensory integration. Ages 5½–12. Slosson; ATP

Visual Memory Test (Wepman *et al.* 1975). Individual. Sixteen-item test of ability to recall unfamiliar forms that cannot be readily named. Two forms. Ages 5–8. WPS; Stoelting

Visual Discrimination Test (Wepman *et al.* 1975). Twenty-item test of ability to determine which 2 of 5 nonalphabetic forms are identical. Two forms. Ages 5–8. WPS; Stoelting

SENSORY, EYE MOVEMENTS (All individually administered)

A O Sight Screener (1956). Targets available for both readers and nonreaders of English words and numbers. American Optical

Dvorine Pseudo-Isochromatic Plates (1958). Measure of color blindness. Ages 3 and up. Stoelting; Psy Corp.

Eye-Trac. Eye-movement camera. Can determine number and duration of fixations and regressions, span of recognition, and reading rate. Set of 64 reading selections (Grade 1– college) for use with Eye-Trac. G & W Applied Science

Keystone Tests of Binocular Skill (1938–1949). Adaptation of *Gray Standardized Oral Reading Check Tests* for use with telebinocular. Comparable selections are read orally with each eye separately and with binocular vision. Identifies children who can read better with one eye than with both eyes together. Grades 1–8. Keystone

Keystone Visual Screening Test (1933–1971). Telebinocular (stereoscopic instrument) and 15 stereographs provide measure of binocular near- and far-point acuity, muscle balance, depth perception, fusion, and color vision. Short screening test available. Separate School Vision Tests for Massachusetts, Michigan, and New York. Grades 1 and up. Keystone

Keystone Visual Survey Tests (1933–1961). Uses revision of *Betts Ready to Read Test* with telebinocular. Grade 1 (Grade 2 or 4 for some tests). Keystone

Ortho-Rater (1958). Stereoscopic instrument (various models) and accompanying stereographic slides used for visual screening. Measures binocular near- and far-point acuity, depth perception, visual discrimination, and color vision. Short test for rapid screening. Grades 1 and up. Bausch and Lomb

Picture Spondee Threshold Test (1983). Audiometric test used with individual who cannot function within standard hearing test format that requires them to repeat words. All ages. DLM

Reading Eye II. Portable eye-movement camera. Measures fixations, duration of fixations, regressions, span of recognition, reading rate with comprehension. Provides 3 ratings: grade level of reading, relative efficiency, directional attack. Includes 64 reading selections. Grade 1–adult. EDL

School Vision Tester (1974). Consists of 6 tests; tumbling E acuity (each eye), farsightedness (each eye), muscle balance (far, near). Same instrument as Ortho-Rater. Grades K and up. Bausch & Lomb

Spache Binocular Reading Test (1955). Individual. Measures relative participation of each eye in reading by using stereoscopic slides with different words omitted on each side of the slide. Three levels of difficulty. For use in telebinocular or stereoscope. Test 1 (nonreaders and Grade 1); Test 2 (Grades 1.5–2); Test 3 (Grade 3 and over). Keystone

Titmus Vision Tester (1969). Both School Unit (Grades 1–5) and General Testing Unit (Grades 1–12) duplicate *Massachusetts Vision Test*. Titmus

OTHER TESTS AND MEASURES

Arithmetic

KeyMath Diagnostic Arithmetic Test (1976). Individual. Criterion-referenced. Fourteen subtests. Assesses 3 basic areas of math: content (basic math concepts), operations (basic computations), and applications (use of math skills in daily life). Preschool–Grade 6. AGS

Attitudes

Estes Attitude Scales (1981). Elementary form (Grades 2–6) includes 3 scales for measuring attitudes toward reading, science, and math. Secondary form (7–12) include 5 scales: reading, science, math, English, and social studies. Grades 2–12. Pro-Ed; Slosson

Reading Appraisal Guide (1979). Individual. Interview measure of attitudes toward reading and a form for recording errors during oral reading. Grades 5–12. Australian Council; NWRL

School Attitude Measure. Samples students' stated views of their academic environment and of themselves as learners. Five scales: Motivation for Schooling, Academic Self-Concept—Performance Based, Academic Self-Concept—Reference Based (how others view my school performance), Sense of Control over Performance, and Instructional Mastery (what I need to succeed and learn in school). Levels 4–12 (Grades 4–12). American Testronics

Language, Spelling

Illinois Test of Psycholinguistic Abilities (ITPA) (1969). Individual. Evaluates abilities in 3 dimensions: channels of communication, psycholinguistic processes, and levels of organization. Twelve subtests: auditory reception, visual reception, auditory association, visual association, verbal expression, manual expression, grammatic closure, visual closure, auditory closure, and sound blending. Ages 2–10. Slosson; WPS

Northwestern Syntax Screening Test (1971). Individual. Provides quick estimate of syntactic development in receptive and expressive language. Ages 3–8. Northwestern; Stoelting

Test of Adolescent Language (TOAL) (1980). Individual. Eight subtests provide information about wide range of language abilities including word meaning and syntax used in listening, speaking, reading, and writing. Yields 10 scores plus Adolescent Language Quotient (ALQ). Grades 6–12. Pro-Ed

Test of Language Development (TOLD) (1982). Individual. Primary Edition (Ages 4–8) has 7 subtests that measure various components of spoken language (word meaning and use, grammar, articulation, auditory discrimination). Intermediate Edition (Ages 8–12) has 5 subtests that measure word meaning and use and 3 aspects of grammar. Ages 4–12. Pro-Ed

Test of Written Spelling (1976). Usually individual. Measures ability to spell phonically regular and phonically irregular words. Yields spelling, age, spelling quotient, and grade-equivalent scores. Grades 1–8. Pro-Ed

Learning and Modality Preferences and Styles

Barsch Learning Style Inventory (1980). Informal 24-item self-report that purports to indicate relative strengths and weaknesses in learning through different sensory channels. Grades 9–16. ATP

Kerby Learning Modality Test (1980). Individual. Brief screening test to measure visual, auditory, and motor activity strengths and weaknesses. Eight subtests: visual and auditory discrimination, visual and auditory closure, visual and auditory memory, visual and auditory motor coordination. Ages 5–11. WPS

Learning Style Identification Scale (1981). Identifies 5 learning styles based on testee's internal sources of information (e.g., feelings, beliefs, attitudes) and external sources of information (e.g., other people, events, social institutions). Grades 1–8. PTS

Learning Style Inventory (1979). Uses responses to 100 true–false items to identify students' preferred learning conditions. Grades 3–12. Price

Reading Style Inventory (Carbo 1981). Identifies individual reading style preferences and strengths of pupils as they are reading. Fifty-two items on which student selects from 2 or 3 statements the one that best describes her or him. Considers 30 elements in 4 types of stimuli: environmental (e.g., sound, light, temperature, design), emotional (source of motivation, persistence, responsibility, need for structure), sociological (with whom pupil prefers to read, or if alone), and physical (e.g., time of day prefers to read, modality strengths and weaknesses). Grades 1–12. Learning Research Associates

Medical, Neurological

The Anser System (1981). Integrates health, education, developmental, and behavioral data in order to assess children's school adjustment or learning problems. Parent and School Forms for each of 3 levels: Form 1 (Ages 3–5), Form 2 (Ages 6–11), and Form 3 (Ages 12–18). Form 4 is self-administered profile for students aged 9 and up. Ages 3–18. EPS

Institutes Developmental Profile (1980). Individual. Designed to determine child's neurological age. Covers visual, auditory, manual, and tactile competence; language; and mobility.Used with Doman-Delacato approach. Institutes

Neurological Dysfunctions of Children (1979). Individual. Screening device for deciding whether to refer child for a neurological examination. Series of 18 yes–no (normal–impaired) items. First 16 items require child to perform simple tasks (e.g., walking along a straight line, touching a finger to nose, and following moving object with eyes). Ages 3–10. AGS

Quick Neurological Screening Test (1978). Individual. Brief individual screening test assesses 15 areas of neurological integration. Samples motor development, control of large and small muscles, motor planning and sequencing, sense of rate and rhythm, spatial organization, visual and auditory perception, balance and cerebellar–vestibular function, and attention. Ages 5–adult. Slosson; ATP

Psychiatric and Personality Disorders

Children's Apperception Test (1980). Individual. Projective technique (basic assumption of projective techniques is that testee will reveal motives, fears, interests, etc.). Ten pictures of various situations shown to child, who tells a story about, or describes, each. Requires trained examiner. Ages 3–10. Stoelting; Psy Corp.

Holtzman Inkblot Technique (1973). Individual. Projective test. Testee is shown 45 blots and asked to describe what he sees. Requires trained examiner. Two forms. Ages 5 and over. Psy Corp.

House–Tree–Person Projective Technique (1966). Individual. Testee makes freehand drawings of a house, a person, and a tree and then discusses each. Requires trained examiner. Ages 3–adult. WPS

Michigan Picture Test-Revised (1980). Individual. Projective technique. Child responds to 4 pictures. Measure of emotional maladjustment and various personality factors. Requires trained examiner. Grades 3–9. Greene & Stratton; Psy Corp.

Rorschach Psychodiagnostic Test (1951). Individual. Projective technique. Testee is shown 10 "inkblots" and asked to describe what he sees. Requires trained examiner. Ages 3 and over. Stoelting; Psy Corp.

Stroop Color and Word Test (1978). Individual. Very brief test used to investigate personality, cognition, stress response, psychiatric disorders, and other psychological phenomena. Consists of 3 pages: A Word Page on which the names of colors are printed in black; a Color Page with semantically meaningless symbols (*X*s) printed in various colors; a Word-Color page on which the words on the first page are printed in the colors presented on the second page, but the name of the color and the color in which it is printed do not match. Grades 2 and up. Stoelting

Thematic Apperception Test (1973). Individual. Projective technique. Subject shown series of 20 pictures and asked to tell a story about each. Requires trained examiner. Ages 6–adult. Stoelting; Psy Corp.

APPENDIX B

Series Books for Remedial Reading

Many series have been written specifically to link interest appeal with simplified vocabulary and style. These series have greatly enriched the available resources for corrective and remedial reading. Some of the series have tapes of complete stories, dramatizations of part of the story, or both.

One of the most difficult yet most important things to do when working with a poor reader is to get him interested in reading. Thus it is important to choose reading material with care. In choosing books for a poor or reluctant reader, you should select titles that seem likely to appeal to his interests. These materials should be at or below his independent reading level, at least initially. A teacher who has only a rough idea of a child's independent reading level should start with material that is at least two years below the level of material currently being used for reading instruction. If the first book tried seems too easy or too difficult, an adjustment should be made in making the next choice. The reading grade levels shown below are those indicated by the publishers.

Title	Publisher	Reading Grade Level	Interest Grade Level
ANIMAL ADVENTURE SERIES	Benefic	PP–1	1–4

Action and adventures of animals based on sound scientific knowledge; 12 stories that could actually happen.

| BUTTERNUT BILL SERIES | Benefic | PP–1 | 1–4 |

Adventures of a young boy and his friends in the Ozark Mountains in the 1850s; 8 titles.

Title	Publisher	Reading Grade Level	Interest Grade Level
TOM LOGAN SERIES	Benefic	PP–1	1–6

Ten books that relate the adventures of a boy growing to manhood in the Old West.

COWBOY SAM SERIES	Benefic	PP–3	1–6

Western content of these 15 books appeals to many boys.

MOONBEAM SERIES	Benefic	PP–3	1–6

Ten space-age adventures of a monkey, with adult multiethnic characters as co-stars.

DAN FRONTIER SERIES	Benefic	PP–3	1–6

Ten adventure books depicting early pioneer life in the Midwest.

COWBOYS OF MANY RACES	Benefic	PP–5	1–7

Depicts adventures of black American, Spanish-American, and Indian cowboys on the early western frontier; 7 titles.

MANIA BOOKS	Childrens	1	1–5

Sixteen books on such subjects as clowns, animals, and volcanoes; numerous full-page illustrations.

HELICOPTER ADVENTURE SERIES	Benefic	1–3	1–4

Six adventure stories, some with women in active roles.

FIND OUT ABOUT	Benefic	1–3	1–6

Twelve science books that investigate basic science facts and concepts.

READY, GET SET, GO BOOKS	Childrens	1–3	1–6

Twenty-four books on such topics as dinosaurs, motorcycles, trucks, and dolls.

FIRST READING BOOKS	Garrard	1	2–3

Written with the easier half of the Dolch Basic Sight Words and the 95 common nouns. Content deals with pets, birds, and wild animals.

JIM FOREST READERS	Addison	1–3	2–7

Adventure stories about Jim Forest, young teenager, and his Forest Ranger uncle.

PACESETTERS	Childrens	1–4	4–12

Twenty-four mysteries, suspense stories, science fiction, and adventure stories.

PAL PAPERBACK SERIES	Xerox	1–5	6–12

Eighteen titles in each of 4 kits. Short stories of the supernatural, adventure, and courage.

BREAKTHROUGH	Allyn	1–8	7–12

Series of short paperbacks containing modern stories, articles, biographies, and poetry.

BEGINNER BOOKS	Random	2	1–4

The emphasis is on humor and good plot. Several are in rhyme.

A BOOK ABOUT	Raintree	2	2–4

Sixteen books dealing primarily with science topics.

BASIC VOCABULARY BOOKS	Garrard	2	3–4

Content about folktales, animals, and Indian folklore.

FIRST HOLIDAY BOOKS	Garrard	2	3–5

Folklore and legends from America and other countries woven into holiday stories.

PRIME TIME ADVENTURES	Childrens	2	4–12

Ten mystery and adventure tales with mature formats.

NEW TRUE BOOKS	Childrens	2–3	1–4

Science subjects appealing to most interests; books contain well-organized, constructive information; 100 titles.

Title	Publisher	Reading Grade Level	Interest Grade Level
BOXCAR CHILDREN MYSTERIES	Whitman	2–3	3–8

Series of 19 separate mysteries involving the Alden family, who begin their adventures by making their home in a boxcar in order to stay together.

STEP-UP BOOKS	Random	2–3	3–8

Continuous flow of action will please both the reader who reads beyond his usual age interest and the older reluctant reader who looks for information and an unobtrusively simplified vocabulary.

DISCOVERY	Garrard	2–3	4–6

Over 60 biographies of outstanding women, scientists, explorers, reformers, humanitarians, and statesmen.

READ ABOUT SCIENCE	Raintree	2–3	4–6

Fifteen titles covering such topics as space, light and color, and time and clocks.

INTRIGUE SERIES	Benefic	2–3	4–12

Four tales of mystery and intrigue. Map and chart skills developed in the process of unraveling the plots.

CLASSICS LIBRARY	ETA	2–3	5–12

Shortened adaptations including *The Jungle Book, The Last of the Mohicans*, and *Moonstone.*

TOP FLIGHT READERS	Addison	2–3	5–12

Adventures involving various aviation vehicles. Characters of many ethnic backgrounds.

PACEMAKER TRUE ADVENTURES	Fearon	2–3	5–adult

Eleven true stories in paperback; includes historical figures, escape, spies, and pirates.

PACEMAKER CLASSICS	Fearon	2–3	5–adult

Eight abridged and adapted paperback versions including *The Jungle Book, Two Years Before the Mast*, and *A Tale of Two Cities.*

ADAPTED CLASSICS	Nat. Assn. Deaf	2–3	6–12

Two titles not found elsewhere, *Beowulf* and *The Song of Roland.*

JIM HUNTER BOOKS	Fearon	2–3	6–adult

Adventures of a James Bond-type secret agent; 16 titles.

BESTSELLERS I, II, III	Fearon	2–4	6–adult

Each set contains 10 novelettes with suspense, romance, mystery, or science fiction as themes.

LAURA BREWSTER BOOKS	Fearon	2–3	6–adult

Six fast-paced whodunit mysteries and adventures of Laura Brewster, insurance investigator.

SPECTER	Fearon	2–3	6–adult

Series of eight ghost stories.

SPORTSTELLERS	Fearon	2–3	6–adult

Each of eight books focuses on a major sport; subplots explore conflicts and challenges facing today's athletes.

GALAXY 5	Fearon	2–3	6–adult

Six science-fiction stories.

SPECTER	Fearon	2–3	6–adult

Eight horror and mystery short stories.

Title	Publisher	Reading Grade Level	Interest Grade Level
SPACE POLICE	Fearon	2–3	6–adult

Six space-age "cops and robbers" books.

HI–LO PAPERBACKS	Bantam	2–3	7–12

Series of 14 contemporary adventure, horror, and mystery stories.

INNER CITY SERIES	Benefic	2–4	2–7

Young people solve their problems with imagination, humor, and determination; 5 titles.

EMERGENCY SERIES	Benefic	2–4	2–9

Six adventures of a paramedic team (one team member is a woman).

THE WILDLIFE ADVENTURE SERIES	Addison	2–4	3–7

Books portray true-to-life experiences of different wild animals.

THE MORGAN BAY MYSTERIES	Addison	2–4	3–8

Nine well-illustrated mystery books for remedial, supplementary and individualized reading programs. Includes teenage characters.

GEMINI BOOKS	Childrens	2–4	3–12

Sixteen short books dealing with basic information about topics such as cars, karate, climbing, running, woman's sports.

HORSES AND HEROINES	Benefic	2–4	4–7

Six stories involving the adventures of a young girl and her horse.

SPORTS MYSTERIES SERIES	Benefic	2–4	4–12

Teenage boys and girls meet and overcome problems in sports and school activities; 12 titles.

RACING WHEELS SERIES	Benefic	2–4	4–12

Adventures of an inner-city boy and his friends, who learn about the training, equipment, and driving techniques of auto racing; 12 titles.

CHECKERED FLAG SERIES	Addison	2–4	5–12

Fast-moving stories combine a racing setting with the intrigue of mystery. Different types of cars, races, or motorcycles are featured in each book.

CRISIS SERIES	Fearon	2–4	6–adult

Teenagers are confronted by some unhappy realities of life (e.g. alcoholism, adoption, death) in each of 6 books.

HIWAY BOOKS	Westminister	2–4	7–12

Seventeen titles that have adventure, mystery, racing, and interpersonal relationships as their themes.

TALESPINNERS	Fearon	2–4	7–adult

Eight diverse novels that combine believable characters with cliff-hanging predicaments; history, adventure, mystery, and science fiction.

THE DEEP SEA ADVENTURE SERIES	Addison	2–5	3–8

Twelve adventure and mystery stories about the sea. Mature characters.

ACTION LIBRARIES	Scholastic	2–5	7–12

A number of original paperback novelettes with high-interest plots; characters from various racial and cultural backgrounds.

WORLD OF ADVENTURE SERIES	Benefic	2–6	4–9

Eight suspense stories built around expeditions.

MYSTERY ADVENTURE SERIES	Benefic	2–6	4–12

Young-adult boy and girl solve mysteries through deductive reasoning, courage, and determination; 6 titles.

Title	Publisher	Reading Grade Level	Interest Grade Level
SPACE SCIENCE FICTION SERIES	Benefic	2–6	4–12

Adventures of space travelers who visit alien planets and their inhabitants; 6 titles.

| TURNING POINT | McCormick | 2–6 | 5–10 |

Thirty paperbacks ranging in topics from contemporary teenage experiences to the supernatural.

| NEW KALEIDOSCOPE READERS | Addison | 2–9 | 7–12 |

Eight paperbacks covering topics such as careers, sports, and cars. Aimed at reluctant readers.

| FOLKLORE OF THE WORLD | Garrard | 3 | 4–5 |

Fourteen books covering folktales from around the world.

| FAMOUS ANIMAL STORIES | Garrard | 3 | 4–6 |

Each of the 17 titles highlights an animal that displays heroism, devotion, or intelligence.

| INDIANS | Garrard | 3 | 4–6 |

Thirteen biographies of female and male Indian heroes; history from the American Indian's point of view.

| HOLIDAYS | Garrard | 3 | 4–6 |

History, customs, and traditions in the United States and other lands.

| GOOD EARTH BOOKS | Garrard | 3 | 4–7 |

Science topics dealing with ecology and environmental education.

| JUNIOR SCIENCE BOOKS | Garrard | 3 | 4–7 |

Authentic and well-illustrated books that deal with facts scientifically.

| SCOUT SKILL BOOKS | BSA | 3–4 | 5–8 |

Twelve inexpensive papers on wide variety of topics.

| AMERICAN FOLKTALES | Garrard | 3–4 | 4–5 |

Lively stories about famous folk heroes, regional lore, and exaggerated adventures.

| AMERICAN WEST SERIES | Fearon | 3–4 | 4–adult |

Stories of well- and lesser-known western heroes, outlaws, and Indian chiefs.

| TRUE TALES | Fearon | 3–4 | 6–adult |

Ten paperbacks, each contain short tales of people and events.

| DOOMSDAY JOURNALS | Fearon | 3–4 | 7–adult |

Six suspenseful stories dealing with possible calamities or disasters; contains science facts.

| THAT'S LIFE | Fearon | 3–4 | 9–12 |

Eight worktexts in which one of 4 ethnic families deals with personal or financial problems, such as medical care and buying a used car.

| PLAY THE GAME SERIES | Bowmar | 3–5 | 4–12 |

Eight stories of famous athletes from various sports.

| SEARCH BOOKS | Bowmar | 3–5 | 4–12 |

Twelve 16-page booklets covering a variety of science topics such as weather, telling time, dolphins, and bird migrations.

| SPORTS | Garrard | 5 | 5–7 |

Histories of individual sports and biographies of great names in sports.

| PLEASURE READING BOOKS | Garrard | 4 | 5–7 |

Adaptations of famous stories and legends including Robin Hood, Robinson Crusoe, Aesop, fairytales, and folktales.

Title	Publisher	Reading Grade Level	Interest Grade Level
AMERICANS ALL	Garrard	4	5–7

Biographies emphasize character and personal determination of individuals of many races, creeds, and national origins.

| EXPLORING AND UNDERSTANDING SERIES | Benefic | 4 | 4–9 |

Each of the 13 books explores a subject in depth, with special emphasis on science processes.

| EVERYREADER SERIES | Webster | 4 | 6–8 |

Twenty simplified classics and short-story collections.

| INCREDIBLE SERIES | Barnell–Loft | 4–5 | 7–12 |

Twelve short books that relate unusual historic events.

| FASTBACK MYSTERY BOOKS | Fearon | 4–5 | 7–adult |

Series of 12 32-page paperbacks dealing with suspense and mystery.

| FASTBACK ROMANCE BOOKS | Fearon | 4–5 | 7–adult |

Set of 10 paperbacks, each dealing with events faced by young people in a wide range of romantic adventures.

| YOUNG ADVENTURERS SERIES | Bowmar | 4–6 | 4–12 |

Teenagers of both sexes in various adventures such as surfing and gliding.

| LANDMARK BOOKS | Random | 4–6 | 5–9 |

Over 65 titles concerned with historical events and important people. Many books written by outstanding authors.

| ALLABOUT BOOKS | Random | 4–6 | 5–11 |

Well-written, factual books on many topics of interest to children.

| SUPERSTARS SERIES | Steck–Vaugh | 4–6 | 7–12 |

Each of 6 books contains 15 short stories about music, movies, television, and sports stars.

| ADAPTED CLASSICS | Globe | 4–8 | 5–12 |

Nineteen simplified and shortened versions including *Moby Dick*, *Tom Sawyer*, and *The Scarlet Letter*.

| GREAT UNSOLVED MYSTERIES | Raintree | 5 | 6–adult |

Twenty titles, such as *The Bermuda Triangle*, *Stonehenge*, *UFO's*, and *Killer Bees*.

| MYTHS, MAGIC, AND SUPERSTITIONS | Raintree | 5 | 6–adult |

Twenty books on ghosts, ghouls, haunted houses, great magicians, and so on.

| JAMESTOWN CLASSICS | Jamestown | 5 | 6–12 |

Twenty-four short adapted versions of stories authored by Jack London, Bret Harte, and Arthur Conan Doyle.

| TOP PICKS | Reader's Digest | 5–7 | 5–12 |

Abridged versions of the works of famous authors; 2 or 3 texts on each of 10 topics including comedy, science fiction, sports, and people.

APPENDIX C

A List of Publishers and Their Addresses

The following list contains, in alphabetical order, the names and addresses of publishers mentioned in this book. It also lists producers and distributors of books, tests, games, reading materials, and so on, although their products may not have been mentioned.

Only one office is listed for each publisher. Where an abbreviated name has been used for the publisher, the abbreviated form is listed in italics, followed by the full name and address. The rapidity of publishing mergers, name changes, and changes of address makes it inevitable that some of the entries below will become out of date.

Abelard-Schuman, Ltd., 10 E. 53rd St., New York, NY 10022

Abingdon Press, 201 Eighth Ave., S., Nashville, TN 37202

Academic Press, 111 Fifth Ave., New York, NY 10003

ATP. Academic Therapy Publications, 20 Commercial Blvd., Novato, CA 94947

Addison. Addison-Wesley Publishing Co. Inc., One Jacob Way, Reading, MA 01867. Reading tests formerly published by Addison-Wesley are now available from CTB/McGraw-Hill.

APL. Adult Performance Level Project, Extention Bldg. 202, University of Texas, Austin, TX 78712

Alexander Graham Bell Association for the Deaf, 3417 Volta Pl. N.W., Washington, DC 20007

Allyn. Allyn & Bacon, 7 Wells Ave., Newton, MA 02159

Almqvist & Wiksell International, 26 Gamla Brogatan, S-101 20, Stockholm, Sweden

Ambassador Publications, P.O. Box 4206, Clearwater, FL 33518

American Book Co., 135 W. 50th St., New York, NY 10020

American College Testing Programs, 2201 N. Dodge St., Iowa City, IA 52240

American Council on Education, 1 Dupont Circle, Washington, DC 20036

AERA. American Educational Research Association, 1230 17th St. N.W., Washington, DC 20036

AGS. American Guidance Service, Inc., Publishers Bldg., Circle Pine, MN 55014

AIR. American Institute for Research, 1055 Thomas Jefferson St. N.W., Washington, DC 20007

ALA. American Library Association, 50 E. Huron St., Chicago, IL 60611

American Newspaper Publishers Association Foundation, The Newspaper Center, Box 17407, Dulles International Airport, Washington, DC 20041

American Optical Corp., Industrial Safety Division, Southbridge, MA 01550

American Orthopsychiatric Association, 1775 Broadway, New York, NY 10019

American Psychiatric Association, 1400 K St. N.W., Washington, DC 20005

American Psychological Association, 1200 17th St. N.W., Washington, DC 20036

American Reading Council, 20 West 40th St., New York, NY 10018

American Testronics, P.O. Box 2270, Iowa City, IA 52244

Ann Arbor Publishers, P.O. Box 7249, Naples, FL 33940

Appleton-Century-Crofts. *See* Prentice-Hall.

Aspen Systems Corp., 1600 Research Blvd., Rockville, MD 20850

ACEI. Association for Childhood Education International, 3615 Wisconsin Ave., N.W., Washington, DC 20016

ACLD. Association for Children with Learning Disabilities, 4156 Library Rd., Pittsburgh, PA 15234

Aston. See University of Aston.

AVR. Audio Visual Research Co., P.O. Box 71, Waseca, MN 56093

Australian Council for Educational Research, Ltd., Frederick St., P.O. Box 210, Hawthorne, Victoria, Australia 3122

Avon Books, 1790 Broadway, New York, NY 10019

Baldridge Reading Instruction Materials, Inc., Box 439, Greenwich, CT 06830

Bantam Books, 2451 S. Wolf Rd., Des Plaines, IL 60018

Barnell Loft, Ltd., 958 Church St., Baldwin, NY 11510

Basic Books, Inc., 10 E. 53rd St., New York, NY 10022

Bausch & Lomb Optical Co., Rochester, NY 14602

Beckley-Cardy Co., 114 Gaither Dr., Mt. Laurel, NJ 08054

Beginner Books. *See* Random House.

BRL. Behavioral Research Laboratories, Box 577, Palo Alto, CA 94302

Bell and Howell Co., Audio Visual Products Division, 7100 McCormick Rd., Chicago, IL 60645

Beltone Electronics Corp., 4201 W. Victoria St., Chicago, IL 60646

Benefic Press, 1900 N. Naragansett, Chicago, IL 60639

Berkley Publishing Corp., 200 Madison Ave., New York, NY 10016

Bertamax Inc., 101 Nickerson, Suite 202, Seattle, WA 98109

Bobbs-Merrill Co., Inc., 630 Third Ave., New York, NY 10017

Book Lab Inc., 500 14th St., North Bergen, NJ 07047

Borg-Warner Educational Systems, 600 W. University Dr., Arlington Heights, IL 60004

R. R. Bowker Co., 205 E. 42nd St., New York, NY 10017

Bowmar. Bowmar/Noble Publishers, Inc., 4563 Colorado Blvd., Los Angeles, CA 90039

BSA. Boy Scouts of America, P.O. Box 61030, Dallas/Fort Worth Airport, TX 75261

Milton Bradley Co., 443 Shaker Rd., East Longmeadow, MA 01028

Britton & Associates, Inc., 7549 N.W. Mountain Dr., Corvallis, OR 97330

William C. Brown Co., 2460 Kerper Blvd., Dubuque, IA 52001

Brown University Press, 194 Meeting St., Box 1881, Providence, RI 02912

Burgess Publishing Co., 7108 Ohms Ln., Minneapolis, MN 55435

Buros Institute of Mental Measurements, 135 Bancroft Hall, University of Nebraska, Lincoln, NE 68588

Cadmus Books. *See* E. M. Hale & Co.

Califone International, Inc., 5922 Bowcroft St., Los Angeles, CA 90016

CTB. California Test Bureau/McGraw-Hill, Del Monte Research Park, Monterey, CA 93940

CTB/McGraw-Hill, Ryerson Ltd., 330 Progress Ave., Scarborough, Ontario, Canada MIP225

Cal Press, Inc., 76 Madison Ave., New York, NY 10016

Cambridge University Press, 32 E. 57th St., New York, NY 10022

Career Institute, Inc., 1500 Cardinal Dr., Little Falls, NJ 07424

CBS Television Reading Programs, 51 West 52nd St., New York, NY 10019

CEMREL, Inc., 3120 59th St., St. Louis, MO 63139

Cenco Educational Aids, 2600 S. Kostner Ave., Chicago, IL 60623

Center for Applied Linguistics, 3520 Prospect St. N.W., Washington, DC 10007

Center for Social Organization of Schools, The Johns Hopkins University, 3505 N. Charles St., Baltimore, MD 21218

Center for the Study of Reading, 51 Gerty Dr., University of Illinois, Champaign, IL 61820

Changing Times Education Service, 300 York Ave., St. Paul, MN 55101

Chapman. Chapman, Brook & Kent, 1215 De la Vina St., Suite F, P.O. Box 21008, Santa Barbara, CA 93121

Chicago. See University of Chicago Press.

Childcraft. *See* World Book.

The Children's Book Centre, 229 College St., Toronto, Ontario 1R4, Canada

Children's Book Centre, 140 Kensington Church St., London W8, England

Children's Book Council, Inc., 67 Irving Pl., New York, NY 10003

Childrens. Childrens Press, 1224 W. Van Buren St., Chicago, IL 60607

Chilton Book Co., Chilton Way, Radnor, PA 19089

Citation Press. *See* Scholastic, Inc.

City College Reading Center, School of Education, CUNY, New York, NY 10031

CAPT. Clearinghouse for Applied Performance Testing, 710 S. W. Second Ave., Portland, OR 97204

Clinical. Clinical Psychology Publishing Co., 4 Conant Square, Brandon, VT 05733

The College Board, 888 Seventh Ave., New York, NY 10106

College Reading Association, c/o Dr. James Layton, 3340 S. Danbury Ave., Springfield, MO 65807

College Skills Center, 320 W. 29th St., Baltimore, MD 21211

The Committee on Diagnostic Reading Tests, Inc., Mountain Home, NC 28758

Communicad, Box 541, Wilton, CT 06897

Communication Skill Builders, 3130 N. Dodge Blvd., Tucson, AZ 85733

The Computing Teacher, 1787 Agate St., University of Oregon, Eugene, OR 97403

Consulting. Consulting Psychologists Press, 577 College Ave., Palo Alto, CA 94306

Continental Press, Inc., 520 E. Bainbridge St., Elizabethtown, PA 17022

Council for Educational Development and Research, 1518 K. St., N.W., Washington, DC 20005

CEC. Council for Exceptional Children, 1920 Association Dr., Reston, VA 22091

Council for Indian Education, Box 31215, Billings, MT 59107

Cove Publishers, 3310 S. 2700 E., Salt Lake City, UT 84109

Craig Corp. *See* Creative Curriculum.

Creative Curriculum, Inc., 4302 Rolla Ln., Madison, WI 53711

Croft, Inc., 4601 York Rd., Baltimore, MD 21212

Benjamin Cummings Publishing Co., 2727 Sand Hill Rd., Menlo Park, CA 94025

Curriculum Advisory Service, 500 S. Clinton St., Chicago, IL 60607

Curriculum Associates, Inc., 5 Esquire Rd., North Billerica, MA 01862

Curtis Publishing Co., 1100 Waterway Blvd., Indianapolis, IN 46206

John Day Co. *See* Intext Press.

Delacorte Press. *See* Dell Publishing Co.

Dell Publishing Co., Inc., 245 E. 47th St., New York, NY 10017

Dexter & Westbrook, Ltd. *See* Barnell Loft.

Dial Press, 1 Dag Hammerskjold Plaza, New York, NY 10017

The Directive Teacher, 101 Student Services Bldg., 154 West 12th Ave., The Ohio State University, Columbus, OH 43210

DLM Teaching Resources, One DLM Park, Box 400, Allen TX 75002

Document Design Center. *See* American Institute for Research.

Dodd, Mead & Co., 79 Madison Ave., New York, NY 10016

Dormac, Inc., P.O. Box 752, Beaverton, OR 97005

Doubleday & Co., Inc., 245 Park Ave., New York, NY 10017

Drier. *See* Jamestown Publishers.

E. P. Dutton, 2 Park Ave., New York, NY 10016

ETL. Easier-to-Learn, Box 329, Garden City, NY 11530

The Economy Co., Box 25308, 1901 N. Walnut St., Oklahoma City, OK 73125

Edmark Associates, P.O. Box 3903, Bellevue, WA 98009

Education Commission of the States, Suite 300, 1860 Lincoln St., Denver, CO 80295

Education Department of South Australia, Education Stores Branch, 31 Flanders St., Adelaide, South Australia 5000

EDL/McGraw-Hill, 1221 Avenue of the Americas, New York, NY 10020

Educational. EDITS/Educational and Industrial Testing Service, Box 7234, San Diego, CA 92107

EPA. Educational Performance Associates, Inc., 563 Westview Ave., Ridgefield, NJ 07657

ERB. Educational Records Bureau, Box 619, Princeton, NJ 08541

Educational Service, Inc., Box 219, Stevensville, MI 49127

Educational Solutions, Inc., 80 Fifth Ave., New York, NY 10011

Educational Systems, Inc., 2360 S.W. 170th Ave., Beavorton, OR 97005

ETA. Educational Teaching Aids, 159 W. Kinzie St., Chicago, IL 60610

ETS. Educational Testing Service, Princeton, NJ 08541. Some reading tests formerly published by ETS are now available from CTB/McGraw-Hill.

EPS. Educators Publishing Service, Inc., 75 Moulton St., Cambridge, MA 02238

EBE. Encyclopedia Britannica Educational Corp., 425 W. Michigan Ave., Chicago, IL 60611

Entry Publishing Co., 27 W. 96th St., New York, NY 10025

ERIC/RCS. ERIC Clearinghouse on Reading and Communication Skills, 111 Kenyon Rd., Urbana, IL 61801

ERIC Clearinghouse on Tests, Educational Testing Service, Princeton, NJ 08540

ERIC Document Reproduction Service, P.O. Box 190, Arlington, VA 22210

Essay Press, P.O. Box 2323, La Jolla, CA 92037

ECRI. Exemplary Center for Reading Instruction, 3310 S. 2700 E., Salt Lake City, UT 84109

Exposition Press, Inc., 325 Rabro Dr., Box 2120, Smithtown, NY 11787

Far West Laboratory for Educational Research and Development, 1855 Folsom St., San Francisco, CA 94103

Fearon Education, 19 Davis Dr., Belmont, CA 94002

Field Educational Publishers. *See* Addison-Wesley and Benjamin Cummings.

Follett Publishing Co., 1010 W. Washington Blvd., Chicago, IL 60607

Forum, 582 Baldy Hall, SUNY at Buffalo, Amherst, NY 14260

Free Press. *See* Macmillan Publishing Co.

W. H. Freeman and Co., 660 Market St., San Francisco, CA 94104

Funk & Wagnalls, Inc., c/o Harper & Row Publishers, 10 E. 53rd St., New York, NY 10022

Gale Research Co., Book Tower, Detroit, MI 48226

Garrard Publishing Co., 1607 N. Market St., Champaign, IL 61820

Ginn & Co., 191 Spring St., Lexington, MA 02173

Globe Book Co., Inc., 50 W. 23rd St., New York, NY 10010

Golden Press. *See* Western Publishing Co.

Gorsuch Scarisbrick, Pubs., 576 Central, Dubuque, IA 52001

The Great Books Foundation, 307 N. Michigan Ave., Chicago, IL 60601

Grolier Inc., Sherman Turnpike, Danbury, CT 06816
Grune & Stratton, Inc., 111 Fifth Ave., New York, NY 10003
Gryphon Press, 220 Montgomery St., Highland Park, NJ 08904
The Guilford Press, 200 Park Ave. S., New York, NY 10003
G & W Applied Science Laboratories, 335 Bear Hill Rd., Waltham, MA 02154
Hammond, Inc., 515 Valley St., Maplewood, NJ 07040
HBJ. Harcourt Brace Jovanovich Inc., 757 Third Ave., New York, NY 10017
Harper. Harper & Row, Inc., 10 E. 53rd St., New York, NY 10022
Harvard University Press, 79 Garden St., Cambridge, MA 02138
Harvey House, 20 Waterside Plaza, New York, NY 10010
Hastings House Publishers, Inc., 10 E. 40th St., New York, NY 10016
Hawthorne Center, Northville, MI 48167
D. C. Heath & Co., 125 Spring St., Lexington, MA 02173
Heinemann Educational Books, 4 Front St., Exeter, NH 03833
Marshall Hiskey, 5640 Baldwin, Lincoln, NE 68507
Hoffman Educational Systems, 4423 Arden Dr., El Monte, CA 91734
Holiday House, Inc., 18 E. 53rd St., New York, NY 10022
Holt. Holt, Rinehart & Winston, 383 Madison Ave., New York, NY 10017
The Horn Book, Inc., 31 St. James Ave., Boston, MA 02116
Humanities Press, Inc., Atlantic Highlands, NJ 07716
Houghton. Houghton Mifflin Co., 2 Park St., Boston, MA 02107
HumRRO. Human Resources Research Organization, 300 W. Washington St., Alexandria, VA 22314
Ideal School Supply Co., 11000 S. Lavergne Ave., Oak Lawn, IL 60453
Indiana University Reading Programs, Suite 211, School of Education, Indiana University, Bloomington, IN 47405
The Institute for the Achievement of Human Potential, 8801 Stenton Ave., Philadelphia, PA 19118
IPAT. Institute for Personality and Ability Testing, P.O. Box 188, Champaign, IL 61820
IRT. The Institute for Research on Teaching, College of Education, Michigan State University, East Lansing, MI 48824
I/CT. Instructional Communications Technology, Inc., 10 Stephar Pl., Huntington Station, NY 11746
IOX. Instructional Objectives Exchange, 11411 W. Jefferson Blvd., Culver City, CA 90230
Instructo Corp., Cedar Hollow & Matthews Rds., Paoli, PA 19301
IRA. International Reading Association, 800 Barksdale Rd., Newark, DE 19714
Intext Press, 257 Park Ave. S., New York, NY 10010
Invalid Children's Aid Association, 126 Buckingham Palace Rd., London, SW1W, England
Iowa State University Press, S. State Ave., Ames, IA 50010
Irvington Publishers, Inc., 551 Fifth Ave., New York, NY 10017
JAI Press Inc., 36 Sherwood Pl., Greenwich, CT 06836
Jamestown Publishers, Box 6743, Providence, RI 02904
Janus Book Publishers, 2501 Industrial Pkwy. W., Hayward, CA 94545

Jastak Associates, Inc., 1526 Gilpin Ave., Wilmington, DE 19806
Johns Hopkins University Press, Baltimore, MD 21218
Jones Kenilworth Co., 8801 Ambassador Dr., Dallas, TX 75247
Jossey-Bass, 433 California Ave., San Francisco, CA 94104
Journal of Computers, Reading & Language Arts, P.O. Box 13034, Oakland, CA 94661
Journal of Education, Boston University, 765 Commonwealth Ave., Boston, MA 02215
Judy Publishing Co., Box 5270, Main P.O., Chicago, IL 60608
Kendall/Hunt Publishing Co., 2460 Kerper Blvd., Dubuque, IA 52001
Kenworthy Educational Service, Inc., Box 60, 138 Allen St., Buffalo, NY 14205
Keystone View Co., 2212 E. 12th St., Davenport, IA 52803
King Features, Education Div., Dept. 1286, 235 E. 45th St., New York, NY 10017
Kingsbury. See Remedial Education Press.
Klamath Printing Co., 320 Lowell St., Klamath Falls, OR 97601
Kluwer-Nijhoff Publishing, 190 Old Derby St., Hingham, MA 02043
Alfred A. Knopf, Inc., 201 E. 50th St., New York, NY 10022
Lafayette Instrument Co., Inc., Box 5729, Lafayette, IN 47903
Laidlaw Bros., Thatcher and Madison, River Forest, IL 60305
Lakeshore Curriculum Materials Co., 2695 Dominguez St., P.O. Box 6261, Carson, CA 90749
Language Research Associates, P.O. Box 2085, Palm Springs, CA 92262
Lantern Press, Inc., 354 Hussey Rd., Mount Vernon, NY 10552
LEA. Lawrence Erlbaum Associates, 365 Broadway, Hillsdale, NJ 07642
Learn, Inc., Mt. Laurel Plaza, 113 Gaither Dr., Mt. Laurel, NJ 08054
Learning Multiple Systems, 340 Coyier Ln., Madison, WI 53713
Learning Research Associates, P.O. Box 39, Roslyn Heights, NY 11577
Learning Research and Development Center, University of Pittsburgh, Pittsburgh, PA 15313
Lerner Publication Co., 241 First Ave. N., Minneapolis, MN 55401
Library Professional Publications, 995 Sherman Ave., Hamden, CT 06514
J. B. Lippincott Co., East Washington Sq., Philadephia, PA 19105
Little, Brown & Co., 34 Beacon St., Boston, MA 02106
Longman Inc., 1560 Broadway, New York, NY 10036
Longwood Division of Allyn & Bacon, Link Dr., Rockleigh, NJ 07647
Lothrop, Lee and Shepard Co., Inc., 105 Madison Ave., New York, NY 10016
Love Publishing Co., 1977 S. Ballaire St., Denver, CO 80222
Lyons and Carnahan. *See* Rand McNally.
Macmillan Education, 4 Little Essex St., London WC2R3LF, England
Macmillan Publishing Co., Inc., 866 Third Ave., New York, NY 10022
Maico Hearing Instruments, 7375 Bush Lake Rd., Minneapolis, MN 55435
Massachusetts Dept. of Public Health, Div. of Maternal and Child Health Service, 88 Broad St., Boston, MA 02110
Mast Development Co., 2212 E. 12th St., Davenport, IA 52803
Mastery Education Corp., 85 Main St., Watertown, MA 02172

McCormick. McCormick-Mathers Publishing Co., 135 W. 50th St., New York, NY 10020

McCutchan Publishing Corp., 2526 Grove St., Berkeley, CA 94704

McDougal, Littel & Co., P.O. Box 1667-B, Evanston, IL 60204

McGraw-Hill Book Co., 1221 Avenue of the Americas, New York, NY 10020

McGraw-Hill Ryerson, Ltd., 330 Progress Ave., Scarborough, Ontario, MIP 2Z5 Canada

David McKay Co., Inc., 2 Park Ave., New York, NY 10016

Meeting Street School, 333 Grotto Ave., Providence, RI 02906

Meredith Corp., 1716 Locust, Des Moines, IA 50336

Merrill. Charles E. Merrill Publishing Co., 1300 Alum Creek Dr., Columbus, OH 43216

Julian Messner, 1230 Avenue of the Americas, New York, NY 10020

Michigan State University Press, 1405 S. Harrison Rd., 25 Manly Miles Bldg., East Lansing, MI 48824

Midwest Publications, P.O. Box 448, Pacific Grove, CA 93950

The Mills Center, 203 West State St., P.O. Box 597, Black Mountain, NC 28711

MIT Press, 28 Carleton St., Cambridge, MA 02142

MCP. Modern Curriculum Press, 13900 Prospect Rd., Cleveland, OH 44136

Montana Council for Indian Education, 517 Rimrock Rd., Billings, MT 59107

Montana Reading Publications, 517 Rimrock Rd., Billings, MT 59107

Moreno Educational Co., 7050 Belle Glade Ln., San Diego, CA 92119

Mouton Publishers, 200 Saw Mill River Rd., Hawthorne, NY 10532

William Morrow & Co., Inc., 105 Madison Ave., New York, NY 10016

C. V. Mosby Co., 11830 Westline Industrial Dr., St. Louis, MO 63141

National Academy of Sciences, 2101 Constitution Ave. N.W., Washington, DC 20418

NAEP. National Assessment of Educational Progress, Box 2923, Princeton, NJ 08541

National Association of the Deaf, 814 Thayer Ave., Silver Springs, MD 20910

National Association for the Education of Young Children, 1834 Connecticut Ave., Washington, DC 20009

National Association of School Psychologists, P.O. Box 55, Southfield, MI 48037

National Center for State Courts, 300 Newport Ave., Williamsburg, VA 23185

National Clearinghouse for Bilingual Education, 1300 Wilson Blvd., Suite B2-11, Rosslyn, VA 22209

NCS. National Computer Systems, 4401 W. 76th St., Minneapolis, MN 55435

National Council for the Social Sciences, 1515 Wilson Blvd., Suite 1, Arlington, VA 22209

NCTE. National Council of Teachers of English, 1111 Kenyon Rd., Urbana, IL 61801

NCME. National Council on Measurement in Education, 1230 17th St. N.W., Washington, DC 20036

National Evaluation Systems, P.O. Box 226, Amherst, MA 01002

National Hispanic Center, 255 E. 14th St., Oakland, CA 94606

NIMH. National Institutes of Mental Health, 5600 Fishers Ln., Rockville, MD

NRC. National Reading Conference, 1070 Sibley Tower, Rochester, NY 14604

National Science Teachers Association, 1742 Connecticut Ave. N.W., Washington, DC 20009

Thomas Nelson, Inc., P.O. Box 14100, Nelson Pl. at Elm Hill Pike, Nashville, TN 37214

Thomas Nelson and Sons. *See* Nelson Canada.

Nelson Canada Ltd., 1120 Birchmont Rd., Scarborough, Ontario, M1K 5G4, Canada

Neuropsychology Laboratory, 1338 E. Edison St., University of Arizona, Tucson, AZ 85719

Nevins Printing Co., 311 Bryn Mawr Island, Bayshore Gardens, Bradenton, FL 33507

New Century. *See* Meredith Corp.

NDE. New Dimensions in Education, 83 Keeler Ave., P.O. Box 5080, Norwalk, CT 06856

New England Reading Association Journal, P.O. Box 83, Waterville, ME 04901

New Readers Press, Laubach Literacy International, Box 131, Syracuse, NY 13210

New Zealand Council for Educational Research, Education House, 178 Willis St., Wellington C-2, New Zealand

NFER-Nelson Publishing Co., Ltd., Darville House, 2 Oxford Rd. East, Windsor, Berks, SL4 1DF, England

NWREL. Northwest Regional Educational Laboratory, 300 S.W. Sixth Ave., Portland, OR 97204

Northwestern University Press, 1735 Benson Ave., Evanston, IL 60201

Odyssey Press, 4300 W. 62nd St., P.O. Box 7080, Indianapolis, IN 46206

Ohio State University Press, Hitchcock Hall, Rm. 316, 2070 Neil Ave., Columbus, OH 43210

OISE. Ontario Institute for Studies in Education, 252 Bloor St. W., Toronto, Ontario M5S 1V6, Canada

Ontario Library Association, Suite 402, 73 Richmond St. W., Toronto, Ontario M5M 1Z4, Canada

Open Court Publishing Co., Box 599, La Salle, IL 61301

Optometric Extension Program Foundation, 2912 S. Daimler St., Santa Ana, CA 92705

Orton Dyslexia Society, 724 York Rd., Baltimore, MD 21204

F. A. Owen Publishing Co., 7 Bank St., Dansville, NY 14437

Owen. Richard C. Owen Publishers, Inc., Rockefeller Center, Box 819, New York, NY 10185

Oxford University Press, 200 Madison Ave., New York, NY 10016

Paradox Press, P.O. Box 1438, Los Gatos, CA 95030

Parents Magazine Press, 685 Third Ave., New York, NY 10017

Parker Publishing Co. *See* Prentice-Hall.

Pendulum Press, The Academic Bldg., Saw Mill Rd., West Haven, CT 06516

Penguin Books, 625 Madison Ave., New York, NY 10022

PDL. Perceptual Development Laboratories, Box 1911, Big Spring, TX 79720

Pergamon Press, Inc., Maxwell House, Fairview Park, Elmsford, NY 10523

Personnel Press, 191 Spring St., Lexington, MA 02173

PDK. Phi Delta Kappan, Eighth and Union, Box 789, Bloomington, IN 47402

Phonovisual Products Inc., 12216 Parklawn Dr., Rockville, MD 20852

Pitman Learning, Inc., 6 Davis Dr., Belmont, CA 94002

Plays, Inc., Publishers, P.O. Box 892, Boston, MA 02116

Plenum Publishing Corp., 233 Spring St., New York, NY 10013

PIRT. Practical Ideas for Reading Teachers, c/o TACT, P.O. Box 1052, Doylestown, PA 18901

Praeger Publishers, 383 Madison Ave., New York, NY 10017

Prentice-Hall, Inc., Rte. 9W, Englewood Cliffs, NJ 07632

Price Systems, P.O. Box 3271, Lawrence, KA 66044

Priority Innovations, Inc., Box 792, Skokie, IL 60076

Pro-Ed, 5341 Industrial Oaks Blvd., Austin, TX 78735

Programs for Education, 1200 Broadway, New York, NY 10001

PAR. Psychological Assessment Resources, Inc., P.O. Box 98, Odessa, FL 33556

Psy Corp. The Psychological Corp., 7500 Old Oak Blvd., Cleveland, OH 44130

Psychological Services Inc., 3450 Wilshire Blvd., Suite 1200, Los Angeles, CA 90010

Psychological Test Specialists, Box 9229, Missoula, MT 59807

Psychotechnics, Inc., 1900 Pickwick Ave., Glenview, IL 60025

PTS. Publishers Test Service, 2500 Garden Rd., Monterey, CA 93940

The Putnam Publishers Group, 200 Madison Ave., New York, NY 10016

Raintree Publishers, Ltd., 205 W. Highland Ave., Milwaukee, WI 53203

Rand McNally & Co., Box 7600, Chicago, IL 60680

Random House, Inc., 201 E. 50th St., New York, NY 10022

Reader's Digest, Educational Division, Pleasantville, NY 10570

Reading Institute, 116 Newbury St., Boston, MA 02116

RIF. Reading is Fundamental, L'Enfant 2500, Smithsonian Institute, Washington, DC 20560

Reading Laboratory, Inc., 55 Day St., South Norwalk, CT 06854

Reading Psychology, c/o Dr. Lance Gentile, College of Education, North Texas State University, Denton, TX 76203

Remedial Education Press, Kingsbury Center, 2138 Bancroft Pl. N.W., Washington, DC 20008

Research Institute for the Study of Learning Disabilities, Box 118, Teachers College, Columbia University, New York, NY 10027

Revrac Publications, 10 W. Bridlespur Dr., Kansas City, MO 64114

Frank E. Richards Publishing Co., P.O. Box 66, Phoenix, NY 13135

Right to Read, 400 Maryland Ave. S.W., Washington, DC 20202

Riverside Publishing Co., 8420 Bryn Mawr Ave., Chicago, IL 60631

Ronald Press, 605 Third Ave., New York, NY 10016

Ramon Ross, School of Education, California State University, 5402 College Ave., San Diego, CA 92115

Rotterdam University Press, P.O. Box 66, Groningen, Netherlands

Routledge & Kegan Paul, 9 Park St., Boston, MA 02108

Sage Publications, 275 S. Beverly Dr., Beverly Hills, CA 90212

St. Louis Public Schools, Division of Curriculum Services, 1517 S. Theresa Ave., St. Louis, MO 63104

Scarecrow Press, Inc., 52 Liberty St., Box 656, Metuchen, NJ 08840

Scholastic, Inc., 730 Broadway, New York, NY 10003

Scholastic Book Services, 50 W. 44th St., New York, NY 10036

Scholastic Magazine, 900 Sylvan Ave., Englewood Cliffs, NJ 07637

STS. Scholastic Testing Service, 480 Meyer Rd., Bensenville, IL 60106

SRA. Science Research Associates, Inc., 155 N. Wacker Dr., Chicago, IL 60606

Scott F. Scott, Foresman and Co., 1900 East Lake Ave., Glenview, IL 60025. Test division now part of American Testronics.

Charles Scribner's Sons, 597 Fifth Ave., New York, NY 10017

Seabury Press, Inc., 815 Second Ave., New York, NY 10017

Short Story International, 6 Sheffield Rd., Great Neck, NY 11021

Silver Burdett Div., General Learning Corp., 250 James St., Morristown, NJ 07960

Simon & Schuster, Inc., 1230 Avenue of the Americas, New York, NY 10020

Singer. See Random House.

Singer Education Division, 3750 Monroe Ave., Rochester, NY 14603

Slosson Educational Publications, Inc., P.O. Box 280, East Aurora, NY 14052

Society for Research in Child Development, 5801 S. Ellis Ave., Chicago, IL 60637

SVE. Society for Visual Education, Inc., 1345 Diversey Pkwy., Chicago, IL 60614

SWRL. Southwest Educational Research Laboratory, 4665 Lampson Ave., Los Alamitos, CA 90720

Special Child Publications, P.O. Box 33548, Seattle, WA 98133

Special Learning Corporation, P.O. Box 306, Guilford, CT 06437

Springer-Verlag, 175 Fifth Ave., New York, NY 10010

Steck. Steck-Vaughn Co., 807 Brazos, P.O. Box 2028, Austin, TX 78768

Stoelting Co., 1350 S. Kostner Ave., Chicago, IL 60623

Strine Printing Co., Inc., I-83 Industrial Park, P.O. Box 149, York, PA 17405

Sunburst Communications, 39 Washington Ave., Pleasantville, NY 10510

Syracuse University Press, 1600 Jamesville Ave., Syracuse, NY 13210

Teachers. Teachers College Press, 1234 Amsterdam Ave., New York, NY 10027

Teachers Publishing. *See* Macmillan.

Teaching Resources Corporation, 50 Pond Park Rd., Hingham, MA 02043

Test Collection, Educational Testing Service, Princeton, NJ 08541

Charles C Thomas, Publishers, 2600 S. First St., Springfield, IL 62717

Titmus Optical Vision Testers, 1312 W. Seventh St., Piscataway, NJ 08854

UNIFON, 2021 DeSoto Rd., Sarasota, FL 33580

UKRA. United Kingdom Reading Association, Edge Hill College, St. Helens Rd., Ormshork, Lancaster, England

U.S. Army Research Institute for the Behavioral and Social Sciences, PERI-P, 5001 Eisenhower Ave., Alexandria, VA 22333

U.S. Government Printing Office, Superintendent of Documents, Washington, DC 20402

University of Alabama Press, Box 2877, University, AL 35486

University of Aston, Gosta Green, Birmington B4 7ET, England
University of Chicago Press, 5801 S. Ellis Ave., Chicago, IL 60637
University of Illinois Press, 54 E. Gregory Dr., P.O. Box 5081, Champaign, IL 61820
University of Minnesota Press, 2037 University Ave. S.E., Minneapolis, MN 55455
University of Nebraska Press, 901 N. 17th St., Lincoln, NE 68588
University Park Press, 300 N. Charles St., Baltimore, MD 21201
Vanguard Press, 424 Madison Ave., New York, NY 10017
Viking Press, Inc., 40 W. 23rd St., New York, NY 10010
Virginia Research Associates, Ltd., P.O. Box 5501, Charlottsville, VA 22902
Visible Language, Cleveland Museum of Art, Box 1972 CMA, Cleveland, OH 44106
The Volta Bureau, 1537 35th St. N.W., Washington, DC
Voxcom, P.O. Box 4741, 10 Latta Rd. at River St., Rochester, NY 14612
Harr Wagner. *See* Field Education Publications.
Walch. J. Weston Walch, P.O. Box 658, Portland, ME 04104
Walker Educational Books Corp., 720 Fifth Ave., New York, NY 10019
Frederick Warne & Co., Inc., 2 Park Ave., New York, NY 10016
Washington Square Press, Inc., 1230 Avenue of the Americas, New York, NY 10020
Watts. Franklin Watts, Inc., 387 Park Ave., New York, NY 10016
Wayne State University Press, 5959 Woodward Ave., Detroit, MI 48202
Webster. Webster/McGraw-Hill, 1221 Avenue of the Americas, New York, NY 10020
Weekly Reader, 245 Longhill Rd., Middletown, CT 06457
WPS. Western Psychological Service, 12031 Wilshire Blvd., Los Angeles, CA 90025
Western Publishing Co., 850 Third Ave., New York, NY 10022
Westinghouse Learning Corporation, 5005 110th St., Oak Lawn, IL 60453
Westminister Press, 925 Chestnut St., Philadelphia, PA 19107
Weston Woods, Weston, CT 06883
Westwood Press, Inc., 76 Madison Ave., New York, NY 10016
Whitman. Albert Whitman & Co., 5747 W. Howard St., Niles, IL 60648
Wiley. John Wiley & Sons, Inc., 605 Third Ave., New York, NY 10016
Williams & Wilkins Co., 428 E. Preston St., Baltimore, MD 21202
H. W. Wilson Co., 950 University Ave., Bronx, NY 10452
Winston Press, Inc., 430 Oak Grove, Minneapolis, MN 55403
Winter Haven Lions Research Foundation, Inc., Box 112, Winter Haven, FL 33880
Wisconsin Design. See Learning Multiple-Systems.
World Book Childcraft International, Merchandise Mart Plaza, Chicago, IL 60654
Xerox Education Publications, 245 Long Hill Rd., Middletown, CT 06457
Zaner-Bloser, 612 N. Park, Columbus, OH 43215
Zweig Associates, Inc., 1711 McGraw Ave., Irvine, CA 92714

APPENDIX D

The Harris–Jacobson Wide Range Readability Formula

The readability formula presented here may be used with materials ranging from pre-primer through eighth-reader levels and, by extrapolation, at secondary-school and adult levels. It uses two variables: the percentage of hard words (V1) and sentence length (V2).

PREPARING FOR AND USING THE FORMULA

A worksheet comparable to the one on page 659 is useful for tabulating information and using the formula.

Selecting and Counting Samples.   Readability is estimated on the basis of representative samples. For a short selection, a minimum of three samples should be used and the readability scores averaged. For a book, a minimum of five samples should be used.

The samples should be taken at equal intervals through the selection or book. For three samples, divide the work into rough thirds and open at random to one page in each third. For five samples, choose one page at random from each fifth of the work. Do not use the first two paragraphs of selection, in which there is often a concentration of new vocabulary. Do not count numbers or other nonverbal symbols, or the verbal material in figures and tables as words.

Taken from Albert J. Harris and Milton D. Jacobson, *Basic Reading Vocabularies.* New York: Macmillan, 1982. Pp. 19–37. Reproduced by permission of the authors and the Macmillan Publishing Co.

Start each sample at the beginning of a paragraph, marking the place with a check in the margin. Count 200 consecutive words and continue counting to the end of the sentence that contains the two-hundredth word. (One-hundred-word samples have been shown to be comparatively unreliable.) Record the page number of the sample and the total number of words on Line A of the worksheet. Count and record the number of sentences in the sample. Count each heading and subheading as a sentence. Record the number of sentences on Line C of the worksheet.

Finding Variable 1.   V1 is the percent of hard words in a sample. Hard words are words not on the Readability List. The list is composed of the preprimer through Grade-2 words from the basic Alphabetical List, including the inflectional endings shown. Words in a sample that are not in the list are counted as hard except for proper nouns, which are counted as easy even if they are not on the list. (Numbers, symbols, etc., are not counted at all, as mentioned above.) A hard word is counted as hard only the first time that it occurs in a sample. If a hard word occurs in two samples, it is counted as hard both times. Make a tally mark for each hard word and count the tallies. Record the number of hard words on Line B of the worksheet. The Readability List is found on pages 659–666.

Divide the number of hard words by the number of words in the sample. Multiply the result by 100 to express the result as a percentage. Carry the result to three decimal places. This is the V1 score.

Finding Variable 2.   V2 is average sentence length, or mean number of words per sentence. Divide the number of words in the sample by the number of sentences. Carry the result to three decimal places. This is the V2 score.

How to Use the Formula.   The following equation is used to find the Predicted Raw Score for a sample.

$$\text{Predicted Raw Score} = .245 \text{ V1} + .160 \text{ V2} + .642$$

The following example may be helpful in clarifying the steps that are followed in finding the Predicted Raw Score and the Readability Score.

Steps in Using the Formula[1]

Sample: Page 21
Number of words (A)   207
Number of hard words (B)   8
Number of sentences (C)   24
Step 1. Obtain the V1 score.
              $8 \div 207 = .0386 \times 100 = 3.865$
Step 2. Obtain the V2 score.
              $207 \div 24 = 8.625.$
Step 3. Multiply the V1 score by .245
              $3.865 \times .245 = 0.947$
Step 4. Multiply the V2 score by .160
              $8.625 \times .160 = 1.380$

---

[1] When using a hand calculator, one may wish to do Step 3 before Step 2. This makes it quicker to calculate the formula because V1 and V2 scores need not be erased from and later reentered into the calculator. The data can be recorded on the worksheet as they are obtained.

Steps in Using the Formula (Continued)

Step 5. Add together the result of Step 3, the result of Step 4, and
.642 (a constant).
0.947 + 1.380 + .642 = 2.969 (the Predicted Raw Score)

Step 6. Round off the Predicted Raw Score to one decimal place.
2.969 = 3.0

Step 7. Find the Predicted Raw Score in Table D.1 and record
the Readability Score that corresponds to it.
For 3.0, the Readability Score is 2.9

The Readability Score is an adjustment of the Predicted Raw Score. Table D.1 gives the Readability Scores that correspond to the Predicted Raw Scores. To find the Readability Score for a selection or a book, add the Readability Scores for each sample and divide by the number of samples. This mean constitutes the Readability Score for the selection or book.

Table D.1 Readability Scores Corresponding to Predicted Raw Scores[a]

Raw Score	Readability Score	Raw Score	Readability Score	Raw Score	Readability Score
1.1	1.0	3.4	3.4	5.7	6.7
1.2	1.0	3.5	3.5	5.8	6.9
1.3	1.0	3.6	3.6	5.9	7.1
1.4	1.1	3.7	3.7	6.0	7.3
1.5	1.2	3.8	3.8	6.1	7.5
1.6	1.3	3.9	3.9	6.2	7.7
1.7	1.4	4.0	4.0	6.3	7.9
1.8	1.5	4.1	4.1	6.4	8.1
1.9	1.7	4.2	4.3	6.5	8.3
2.0	1.8	4.3	4.5	6.6	8.5[a]
2.1	1.9	4.4	4.6	6.7	8.7
2.2	2.0	4.5	4.7	6.8	8.9
2.3	2.1	4.6	4.8	6.9	9.1
2.4	2.2	4.7	5.0	7.0	9.2
2.5	2.3	4.8	5.2	7.1	9.4
2.6	2.4	4.9	5.4	7.2	9.6
2.7	2.6	5.0	5.5	7.3	9.8
2.8	2.7	5.1	5.7	7.4	10.1
2.9	2.8	5.2	5.9	7.5	10.3
3.0	2.9	5.3	6.0	7.6	10.5
3.1	3.1	5.4	6.2	7.7	10.7
3.2	3.2	5.5	6.4	7.8	10.9
3.3	3.3	5.6	6.5	7.9	11.1
				8.0	11.3

[a] Readability Scores above 8.5 have been derived by extrapolation.

Worksheet

Book title_____ Author_____

Publisher_____ Copyright date_____ Scored by_____

Sample Number	1	2	3	4	5
Pages of sample	20,21	46,47	. . . .	. . . .	. . . .
A. No. of words	207	205	. . . .	. . . .	. . . .
B. No. of hard words	8	10	. . . .	. . . .	. . . .
C. No. of sentences	24	22	. . . .	. . . .	. . . .

Step

1. $V1 = B \div A \times 100$	3.865	. . . .	. . . .	. . . .	. . . .
2. $V2 = A \div C$	8.625	. . . .	. . . .	. . . .	. . . .
3. $V1 \times .245$	0.947	. . . .	. . . .	. . . .	. . . .
4. $V2 \times .160$	1.380	. . . .	. . . .	. . . .	. . . .
5. Step 3 + Step 4 + .642 = Predicted Raw Score	2.969	. . . .	. . . .	. . . .	. . . .
6. Step 5 rounded	3.0	. . . .	. . . .	. . . .	. . . .
7. Readability Score	2.9	3.3	. . . .	. . . .	. . . .

READABILITY LIST

a	always	as	basket s
able r st	am	ask s ed ing	bat s 's ted ting
about	an	asleep	bath s
above	and	at	be
across	angry ier iest	ate	beach es ed ing
act s ed ing	animal s 's	aunt s 's	bean s
add s ed ing	another 's	awake d	bear s 's ing
afraid	answer s 's ed ing	away s	beat s ing
after	ant s 's	baby ies 's	beautiful ly
afternoon s 's	any	back s ed ing	beaver s 's
again	anybody 's	backyard s	became
against	anymore	bad dest ly	because
age s d ing	anyone 's	bag s ged ging	become s ing
ago	anything	bake s d ing	bed s ded ding
agree s d ing	anyway s	ball s 's ed	bedroom s
ahead	anywhere	balloon s 's ing	bedtime
air s 's ed y ily	apart	band s ed ing	bee s
airplane s 's	apartment s	bang s ed ing	been
alike	apple s 's	bank s 's ed ing	before
all	are	bar s 's red ring	began
alley s	aren't	bare s d ing r st ly	begin s ning
almost	arm s 's ed ing	bark s ed ing	behind
alone	around	barn s 's	being s
along	arrow s ed	base s 's d ing	believe s d ing
already	art s	baseball s 's	bell s 's ed
also	artist s 's	basement s	belong s ed ing

below
belt s ed
bench es ed
bend s ing
beside s
best
bet s ting
better s ed ing
between
beyond
big ger gest
bike s d ing
bill s ed ing
bird s 's
birthday s 's
bit s
bite s ing
black s ed ing er
    est ly
blackberry ies
blanket s ed ing
blew
block s ed ing y
bloom s ed ing
blow s ing
blue s 's r st
board s 's ed ing
boat s 's ed ing
bob s bed bing
body ies 's
bone s d ing
book s 's ed
boot s ed ing y
born
boss es 's ed y
both
bottle s 's d
bottom s
bought
bow s ed ing
bowl s ed ing
box es ed ing y
boy s 's
brace s d ing
branch es ed ing
brave s 's d r st ly
bread s ed
break s ing
breakfast s 's ed
breath s y

breeze s d
bridge s 's d ing
bright er est ly
bring s ing
broke r
broken ly
brook s
brother s 's ly
brought
brown s ed
brush es ed ing y
bug s ged ging
build s ing
buildings
built
bump s ed ing y
bunch es ed ing
bunny ies
burn s ed ing
bus es
bush es ed y ily
busy ied ier iest
but
butter 's ed ing y
butterfly ies 's
button s ed ing
buy s ing
by
cage s d y
cake s 's d ing
call s ed ing
came
camp s 's ed ing y
can s ned ning
can't
candle s
candy ies ied
cannot
cap s ped ping
captain s 's
car s 's
card s ing
care s d ing
careful ly
carrot s y
carry ies ied ing
case s 's d ing
castle s 's
cat s 's
catch es ing y

cattle 's
caught
cave s 's d ing
center s 's ed ing
certain ly
chair s 's ed
chance s d
change s d ing
charge s d ing
chase s d ing
cheer s ed ing ily y
cheese s
cherry ies
chest s y
chew s ed ing y
chicken s 's
chief s 's ly
child 's
children 's
chin s
chirp s ed ing
choose s ing
circle s 's d ing
circus es 's
city ies 's
clap s ped ping
class es ed ing y
classroom s
clay s 's
clean s ed ing est
    ly
clear s ed ing er
    est ly
clever er est ly
click s ed ing
climb s ed ing
clock s 's ed
close s d ing r st ly
cloth s
clothe s d ing
cloud s ed ing y
clown s 's ed ing
clue s 's d
coat s ed ing
cock s ed ing y
coin s 's ed
cold s er est ly
collect s ed ing
color s ed ing
come s

coming
cook s 's ed ing
cookie s
cool s ed ing er est
    ly
copy ies 's ied ing
corn y
corner s ed
cost s ing ly
could
couldn't
count s 's ed ing
country ies 's
course s d ing
cover s ed ing
cow s 's ed
cowboy s 's
coyote s 's
crab s bed bing
crack s ed ing
crash es ed ing
crawl s ed ing y
crayon s ed
cricket s
cross es ed ing er
    ly
crow s 's ed ing
cry ies ied ing
cup s ped ping
curl s ed ing y
cut s ting
dad s 's
daddy 's
dam s med ming
dance s d ing
dandelion s
dark s er est ly
dash es ed ing
daughter s 's
day s 's
daylight s
daytime s
dcar s 's er est ly y
decide s d ing
deep s er est ly
deer 's
desk s
detective s 's
did
didn't

die s d
different ly
dig s ging
dine s d ing
dinner s 's
dirt y
dish es ed ing
dive s d ing
do 's ing
doctor s 's ed ing
does
doesn't
dog s 's ged ging
doghouse s
doll s 's y
dollar s 's
don s ned ning
don't
done
donkey s 's
door s 's
doorbell s
doorway s
dot s ted ting
down s ed ing y
downstairs
Dr.
dragon s 's
draw s ing
dream s ed ing ily
   y
dress es ed ing
drew
drink s ing
drive s ing
driver s 's
drop s ped ping
drove s
drum s med ming
dry ies ied ing ier
   iest ly
duck s 's ed ing y
dug
during
dust s ed ing y
each
ear s
early ier iest
earth 's ly y
east

easy ier iest
eat s ing
eaten
edge s d ing
editor s 's
egg s ing
eight s 's
either
elephant s 's
elevator s 's
else 's
elves
empty ies ied ing
end s ed ing
enemy ies 's
enough
enter s ed ing
even s ed ly
evening s 's
ever
every
everybody 's
everyday
everyone 's
everything 's
everywhere
exact s ing ly
except ing
exchange s d ing
exercise s d ing
explain s ed ing
explore s d ing
extra s
eye s d ing
face s d ing
fact s ly
factory ies
fair s 's er est ly
fall s 's ing
fallen
family ies 's
far
farm s 's ed ing
farmer s 's
farther
fast ed ing est
faster
fat s ter test
father s 's ed ly
favorite s

fear s ed ing
feather s ed ing y
fed s
feed s ing
feel s ing
feelings
feet
fell s ed ing
felt s
fence s d ing
few er est
field s 's ed ing
flight s ing
fill s ed ing
final s ly
find s ing
fine s d r st ly
finger s 's ed ing
finish es ed ing
fire s 's d ing
first s ly
fish es 's ed ing
   ily y
fishermen 's
fit s ted ting ter
five s
fix es ed ing
flap s ped ping
flash es ed ing y
flat s test ly
flew
flip s ped ping
float s ed ing
flood s ed ing
floor s ed ing
flour s y
flower s ed ing y
fly ies 's ied ing
fold s ed ing
follow s ed ing
food s
fool s 's ed ing
foot ing
for
forest s ed
forever
forget s ting
forgot
forgotten
forth

found ed ing
fountain s
four s 's
fox es 's ing y
free s d ing r ly
fresh er est ly
Friday s 's
friend s 's ly
frighten s ed ing
frog s 's
from
front s ed
fruit s ed
full er est y
fun
funny ies ier iest
funny-looking
fur s
fuzz y
gallop s ed ing
game s 's ing ly
garage s
garbage
garden s 's ing
gate s 's
gather s ed ing
gave
geese
geography
get s ting
ghost s 's ing ly
giant s 's
girl s 's
give s ing
given
glad dest ly
glass es ed y
go es ing
goat s 's
gold s
golden
gone
good s 's ly
good-by s
goodness
got
gotten
grab s bed bing
grade s d ing
grandfather s 's ly

grandma s 's
grandmother s 's ly
grass es y
gray s ed ing er
great s er est ly
green s ing er est
grew
ground s 's ed ing
grow s ing
growl s ed ing
grown
guess es ed ing
ha
had
hadn't
hair s 's ed y
half
hall s
hammer s ed ing
hand s 's ed ing y
   ily
hang s ed ing
happen s ed ing
happily
happy ier iest
hard er est ly
has
hat s 's
hate s d ing
have ing
haven't
he
he'd
he'll
he's
head s 's ed ing y
hear s ing
heard
heavy ier iest
held
hello s
help s ed ing
helper s 's
hen s 's
her s
here
here's
herself
hey
hi

hid
hidden
hide s ing
high er est ly
hill s y
him
himself
his
hiss es ed ing
hit s ting
hold s ing
hole s 's d y
home s 's ing ly y
homework 's
honey ed
hop s ped ping
hope s d ing
horn s 's ed y
horse s 's ing y
hose s d
hospital s 's
hot ter test ly
hour s 's ly
house s 's d ing
how
howl s ed ing
hug s ged ging
huge st ly
hum s med ming
hundred s 's
hung
hungry ier
hunt s ed ing
hunter s 's
hurry ies ied ing
hurt s ing
I
I'd
I'll
I'm
I've
ice s d ing
idea s
if
important ly
in
indeed
indoor s
inside s
instead

interest s ed ing
into
invite s d ing
is
island s 's
isn't
it s
it's
itself
jam s 's med ming
jar s 's red ring
jay s 's
jet s ted
job s 's
join s ed ing
joke s d ing
joy s
jump s ed ing y
junk
just ly
keep s ing
kept
key s ed
kick s ed ing
kid s 's ded ding
kill s ed ing
kind s er est ly
king s 's ly
kiss es ed ing
kitchen s 's
kite s 's
kitten s 's
knee s 's d ing
knew
knock s ed ing
knot s 's ted ting
know s ing
known
ladder s 's
lady ies 's
lake s 's
land s 's ed ing
language s
lap s ped ping
large r st ly
last s ed ing ly
late r st ly
laugh s ed ing
lay s ing
lead s ed ing

leaf ed ing y
lean s ed ing er est
leap s ed ing
learn s ed ing
leather y
leave s ing
led
left y
leg s 's ged ging
lemon s ed
lesson s
let s ting
let's
letter s ed ing
library ies 's
lick s ed ing
lie s d
life 's
lift s ed ing
light s 's ed ing er
   ly
like s ing ly
liked
line s d ing
lion s 's
listen s ed ing
little r st
live s ing
lived
lock s 's ed ing
log s ged ging
lonely ier iest
long s ed ing er est
look s ed ing
loose d ing r ly
lose s ing
lost
lot s 's
loud er est ly
love s 's d ing ly
low ing er est ly
luck ily y
lunch es
lunchroom
lunchtime
lying
ma 's
machine s 's d
mad der ly
made

magic 's
mail s ed ing
main ly
make s
making s
mama 's
man s 's ned ly
many
map s 's ped ping
march es ed ing
mark s ed ing
market s ing
marry ies led ing
mask s ed ing
matter s ed
may
maybe
mayor s 's
me
meadow s 's
mean s ing er est
meant
measure s d ing
meat s y
meet s ing
melt s ed ing
men 's
meow s ed ing
message s
met
mice
middle s
might y ily
mile s 's
milk ed ing y
miller 's
mind s 's ed ing
mine s 's d ing
minute s 's ly
mirror s 's ed ing
miss es ed ing
mix es ed ing
moan s ed ing
mom s 's
Monday s 's
money s 's
monkey s 's
monster s 's
month s 's ly
moo s ed ing

moon s 's ing y
moonlight
more
morning s 's
most ly
mother s 's ed ing
    ly
mountain s 's
mouse 's d ing y
mouth s 's ed ing
move s ing
moved
movie s
Mr.
Mrs.
Ms.
much
mud
music
must y
my
myself
nail s ed ing
name s 's ing ly
named
nap s ped ping
near s ed ing er est
    ly
nearby
neck s
need s ed ing y
neighbor s 's ed
    ing ly
neither
nest s ed ing
net s ted ting
never
new s er est ly
newspaper s 's
next
nice r st ly
night s 's ly
nine s 's
no
nobody 's
nod s ded ding
noise s
none
noon
north 's

nose s d ing y
not
note s d ing
nothing 's
notice s d ing
now
nowhere
number s ed ing
nut s ting
o'clock
ocean s 's
of
off ing
office s 's
officer s 's
often
oh
oil s 's ed ing y
OK
old s er est
on
once
one s 's
only
onto
open s ed ing ly
or
orange s
order s ed ing ly
other s 's
our s
out s ing
outdoor s
outside s
oven s 's
over ly
overhead
owl s 's
own s ed ing
pack s 's ed ing
page s d
pail s
paint s ed ing
painter s 's
paintings
pair s ed ing
pan s ning
pant s ed ing
papa 's
paper s 's ed ing y

parade s 's d ing
park s 's ed ing
parrot s 's
part s 's ed ing ly
party ies 's
pass es ed ing
past
paste d ing
pat s ted ting
patch es ed ing y
path s
paw s ed ing
pay s ed ing
pea s
peanut s
peek s ed ing
pen s ned ning
pencil s ed
penny ies
people s 's d
pepper s ed y
perfect ed ly
person s 's
pet s 's ted ting
phone s 's d
piano s
pick s ed ing y
picnic s
picture s 's d ing
pie s
piece s d ing
pig s 's
pile s d ing
pillow s ed
pin s ned ning
pink s er
pipe s d ing
place s 's d ing
plain s er ly
plan s ned ning
plane s 's d
plant s 's ed ing y
plate s d
play s 's ed ing
player s 's
playground s
please s d ing
pocket s ed ing
poem s 's
point s ed ing y

pole s d ing y
police d
pond s 's
pony ies 's
pool s 's ed
poor er est ly
pop s 's ped ping
popcorn
porch es
possum s
pot s 's ted ting
potato es 's
pound s ed ing
pour s ed ing
practice s d ing
present s ed ing ly
press es ed ing
pretend s ed ing
pretty ied ier iest
prince s 's ly
print s ed ing
prize s d
probably
problem s
promise s d ing
proud er est ly
prove s d ing
puff s ed ing y
pull s ed ing
puppy ies 's
purple s d ing st
purr s ed ing
push es ed ing y
put s ting
puzzle s d ing
quack s ed ing
queen s 's
question s ed ing
quick er est ly y
quiet ed ing er est
   ly
quilt s ed ing
quite
rabbit s 's
raccoon s
race s 's d ing
radio s 's ed
rail s ing
rain s 's ed ing y
rainbow s 's

raise s d ing
ran
ranch es 's ing
rang
rat s 's
reach es ed ing
read s ing
ready ied ing
real ly
red s 's der dest ly
remember s ed ing
repair s ed ing
rest s ed ing
return s ed ing
rice ing
rich es er est ly
rid s
ride s ing
right s ed ing ly y
ring s ed ing
river s 's
road s 's
roar s ed ing
robber s
rock s ed ing y
rode
roll s ed ing
roller s
roof s 's ed
room s 's ed ing y
rooster s 's
root s ed ing
rope s 's d ing
rose s
rough s ed ing er
   est ly
round s 's ed ing er
   est
row s ed ing
rub s bed bing
ruler s 's
run ning
runner s 's
rush es ed ing
rustle s d ing
sack s ing
sad der dest ly
safe s r st ly
said
sail s 's ed ing

sale s
salt s ed ing y
same
sand s 's ed ing
sandwich es ed
sandy
sang
sank
sat
Saturday s
save s d ing
saw s 's ed ing
say s ing
scare s d ing
scary ier iest
school s 's ed ing
scientist s 's
scold s ed ing
scream s ed ing
sea s 's
seat s ed ing
second s 's ed ly
secret s ly
see s ing
seed s ed ing
seek s ing
seem s ed ing ly
seen
sell s ing
send s ing
sense s d ing
sent
sentence s d ing
set s 's ting
seven s 's
shade s d ing
shadow s 's ed ing
   y
shake s ing
shall
shape s d ing ly
share s d ing
sharp er est ly
she
she'd
she'll
she's
sheep 's y
sheet s ed
shell s ed ing

shine s d ing
shiny ier iest
ship s 's ped ping
shirt s
shoe s
shook
shoot s ing
shop s ped ping
shore s d ing
short s ing er est ly
   y
shot s
should
shoulder s ed ing
shout s ed ing
show s 's ed ing y
shut s ting
shy ied ing est ly
sick er ly
side s 's d ing
sidewalk s
sigh s ed ing
sight s ed ing ly
sign 's ed ing
signal s ed ied ing
   ling
silly ies ier iest
silver y
since
sing s ing
sink s ing
sir
sister s 's
sit s ting
six es
size s d ing
skate s d ing
sky ies 's
sleep s ing ily y
slept
slid
slide s ing
slip s ped ping
slow s ed ing er est
   ly
small er est
smart s ed ing er
   est ly
smell s ed ing y
smile s ing

smiled
smoke s 's d ing y
smooth s ed ing er
    est ly
snake s 's d ing
snap s ped ping
sneaker s ed
sniff s ed ing y
snow s 's ed ing y
so
soap s ed y
sock s ed
soft er est ly
soil s 's ed
sold
some
someday
somehow
someone 's
something 's
sometime s
somewhere
son s 's
song s
soon er
sorry ier iest
sound s 's ed ing er
    ly
soup s
south 's
space s d ing
spaceship s 's
speak s ing
special s ly
spell s 's ed ing
spend s ing
spent
spill s ed ing
spin s ning
splash es ed ing y
spoke s
spoken
spoon s 's ed ing
spot s ted ting
spread s ing
spring s 's ing y
squirrel s 's
stack s ed ing
stage s d ing
stair s

stand s ing
star s 's red ring
stare s d ing
start s ed ing
state s 's d ing ly
stay s ed ing
step s ped ping
stick s ing y
still s ed er
stomach s 's
stone s 's d
stood
stop s ped ping
store s 's d ing
storm s 's ed ing y
story ies 's ied
stove s 's
straight er ly
strange st ly
stranger s 's
straw s
stream s 's ed ing
street s 's
stretch es ed ing
strike s ing
string s ed ing y
stripe s d
strong er est ly
stuck
stuff s 's ed ing y
such
sudden ly
sue d ing
suit s 's ed ing
summer s 's y
sun s 's ned ning
Sunday s
sunny iest
super
supper s 's
suppose d ing
sure r st ly
surprise s d ing
swam
sweet s er est ly
swim s ming
swing s ing
swung
table s
tag s ged ging

tail s ed ing
take s ing
taken
talk s ed ing
tall er est
tap s ped ping
tape s d ing
taste s d ing
tea s
teach es ing
teacher s 's
team s 's ed
tear s ing y
teeth
telephone s d ing
tell s ing
ten s 's
tent s 's
terrible
test s ed ing
than
thank s ed ing
that
that's
the
their s
them
themselves
then
there
there's
these
they
they'll
they're
thin s ned ning ner
    nest ly
thing s 's
think s ing
third s ly
this
those
though
thought s
three s 's
threw
through
throughout
throw s ing
thumb s ed ing

thump s ed ing
thunder s ed ing
Thursday s 's
tickle s d ing
tie s d
tiger s 's
tight s er est ly
till ed ing
time s 's d ing ly
tinkle s d ing
tiny ier iest
tiptoe s d ing
tire s d ing
to
toad s 's
toast s ed ing y
today s 's
toe s d ing
together
told
tomorrow s 's
tonight 's
too
took
tool s ed
top s 's ped ping
toss es ed ing
touch es ed ing y
toward s
towel s
town s 's
toy s ed ing
track s ed ing
trail s ed ing
train s 's ed ing
trap s ped ping
travel s ed led ing
tree s 's
trick s 's ed ing y
tried
trip s ped ping
trot s ted ting
trouble s 's d ing
truck s 's ed ing
true r st
trunk s
truth s
try ies ing
tub s
Tuesday

tug s ged ging
tuna
turn s 's ed ing
turtle s 's
TV 's
twig s
two s 's
ugly ier iest
umbrella s
uncle s 's
under
understand s ing
understood
unhappy ier iest
unite d ing
untie s d
until
up s ped
upon
upset s ting
upside
upstairs
us
use s d ing
valley s 's
van s 's
vegetable s
very
village s 's
vine s
visit s ed ing
voice s d ing
wag s ged ging
wagon s 's
wait s ed ing
wake s d ing

walk s ed ing
wall s ed
wander s ed ing
want s ed ing
warm s ed ing er
    est ly
was
wash es ed ing
wasn't
watch es ed ing
water s 's ed ing y
wave s d ing
way s 's
we
we'd
we'll
we're
we've
wear s ing
weather s 's ed ing
Wednesday s
weed s ed ing y
week s 's ly
welcome s d ing
well s ed ing
went
were
weren't
west
wet s ting ter ly
what
what's
whatever 's
wheel s 's ed ing
when
whenever

where
where's
wherever
which
while s d
whisper s ed ing
whistle s d ing
white s 's d r st ly
who
who's
whole
why
wide r st ly
wife 's
wild s er est ly
will s ed ing
win s ning
wind s 's ed ing y
window s 's ed
wing s 's ed ing
wink s ed ing
winner s 's
winter s 's ed ing
wire s d ing
wise r st ly
wish es ed ing
with
without
woke
wolf 's ed
woman 's ly
women 's
won
won't
wonder s ed ing

wonderful ly
wood s ed y
wooden ly
wool ly y
word s 's ed ing y
work s ed ing
worker s 's
world s 's ly
worm s ed ing y
worn
worry ies ied ing
worth y ily
would
wouldn't
write s ing
writer s 's
written
wrong s ed ly
wrote
yard s 's
year s 's ly
yell s ed ing
yellow s ed ing er
    est y
yes
yet
you
you'd
you'll
you're
you've
young er est
your s
yourself
youth s 's
zoo s

DEVELOPMENT OF THE WIDE RANGE READABILITY FORMULA

The new basic word list in three arrangements provided an opportunity to develop an improved readability formula. The concept of readability was defined, for this purpose, as those characteristics of reading material which make for ease or difficulty in comprehension.

Establishing the Criterion

It was assumed that the average characteristics of eight new series of basal readers would provide a satisfactory criterion scale for developing the readability formula. Each of the series contained preprimers, a primer, a first reader, two second readers, and two third readers. From fourth grade up, if a series had two readers for a grade, they were combined. There were seven primary levels and five levels from fourth grade up, twelve levels in all.

For books above first grade, a computer program was used to select the samples. It divided the book into five equal sections of lines of text and selected a 200-word sample at random in each section, skipping the first two paragraphs of a story and always beginning a sample at the start of a paragraph. For the first-grade books, the samples were selected manually. This provided 40 samples at each level and a total of 480 samples with about 100,000 running words.

Each sample was given a reading-difficulty score as follows: preprimer, 1.3; primer, 1.5; first reader, 1.8; low second, 2.2; high second, 2.7; low third, 3.2; high third, 3.7; fourth, 4.5; fifth, 5.5; sixth, 6.5; seventh, 7.5; and eighth, 8.5. It was expected that some samples would be easier and some harder than those assigned criterion scores, and that the effect of this would be to lower somewhat the correlation between readability scores and the criterion.

The Variables

On the basis of previous formulas, two variables were chosen for initial tryout. These were percent of hard words and mean number of words per sentence.

Percent of Hard Words.   In developing previous Harris–Jacobson readability formulas, we had found that vocabulary difficulty was the most important variable and that the percent of hard words (words not on a specific list of easy words) was a better measure of vocabulary difficulty than such other measures as mean number of letters per word, mean number of syllables, or percent of words with more than five letters.

In previous formulas we had used either a Short List (first- and second-grade words of the 1972 Core and Additional Lists) or a Long List (first-, second-, and third-grade words). The Short List had a slight advantage at primary levels and the Long List was slightly better at secondary levels. Knowing that the new word list contained substantially more words at first- and second-grade levels than the 1972 list and was intermediate in length between the old Long and Short Lists, we decided to use a Readability List consisting of the roots and inflected forms of first- and second-grade levels in the new word lists. It contains 1462 root words in comparison to 910 roots in the old Short List and 1825 roots in the old Long List.

The VI score (percent of hard words) is the number of words not in the Readability List divided by the number of words in the sample, in percent. The means and standard deviations for V1 at the twelve levels are shown in Table D.2. There is a consistent increase, level by level, with no inversions. The standard deviations also show a gradual increase, with two small inversions.

Mean Words per Sentence.   The V2 means and standard deviations are also shown in Table D.2. The means show a steady increase from level to level with one exception (at high third, the mean V2 score was slightly higher than for fourth grade). The standard deviations for V2 increase gradually from 1.2 to 4.6, with two minor inversions (at high second- and high third-grade levels). There is some overlapping from level to level.

Deriving the Readability Formula

The first step in developing the formula was to find the correlations of V1 and V2 with the criterion, and the correlation of V1 with V2. These Pearson *r*s are shown in Table

Table D.2 Means and Standard Deviations for V1 and V2

	V1		V2	
Criterion	Mean	S.D.	Mean	S.D.
1.3	.30	.441	5.50	1.153
1.5	.37	.377	6.88	1.276
1.8	.87	.972	7.47	1.292
2.2	1.76	1.438	8.40	1.414
2.7	2.91	1.981	8.97	2.052
3.2	4.69	2.822	9.05	1.737
3.7	6.39	2.461	11.10	3.131
4.5	7.94	3.793	10.59	2.810
5.5	9.51	3.517	12.45	3.233
6.5	12.09	4.773	12.57	3.471
7.5	13.54	5.690	14.44	3.783
8.5	14.64	5.168	14.86	4.587

D.3. The V1 scores correlate .831 with the criterion, a very high result. The V2 correlation is .704, a little lower but still good. The correlation between V1 and V2, .679, is fairly high, but low enough to warrant the expectation that the combination of two variables will be an improvement over V1 alone.

Multiple Correlation.   The correlations shown in Table D.3 were entered into an iterative multiple-correlation computer program in order to find the maximum multiple correlation and the corresponding regression equation. As shown in Table D.4, R (the multiple coefficient of correlation) is .930, a very high result. This is an improvement of 6% over the Harris–Jacobson Formulas 1 and 2. The regression equation is as follows:

$$\text{Predicted Raw Score} = .245 \text{ V1} + .160 \text{ V2} + .642$$

The use of this equation in finding the Predicted Raw Score has been explained on pages 657–658.

Obtaining the Readability Score.   After the regression equation had been obtained, Predicted Raw Scores were obtained for all 480 samples. The mean Predicted Raw Score was then found for each reader level. These means are shown in Table D.5. One can note that the Predicted means are higher than the criterion scores below fourth-grade level, and lower than the criterion scores from fourth grade up. This is an example of the regression effect, the tendency for predicted scores to be closer to the mean than the scores are that are used to make the prediction.

The Predicted Raw Score means were plotted graphically against the criterion scores and a line of best fit was drawn. For each possible Predicted Raw Score from 1.1

Table D.3 Correlations Among the Criterion, V1, and V2

Variable	1	2	3
1. Criterion scores	1.000		
2. V1 scores	.831	1.000	
3. V2 scores	.704	.679	1.000

Table D.4 Multiple Coefficient of Correlation (R), R², and Standard Error of Estimate

R	R^2	S.E.est
.930	.864	.501

to 8.0, the corresponding adjusted score was read from the graph. These adjusted scores are called Readability Scores and are shown in Table D.1. When several samples have been taken from a work, the mean of their Readability Scores is the Readability Score of the work.

INTERPRETING THE READABILITY SCORE

If we should obtain a Readability Score for every possible sample of a work, the mean of those scores would be the Readability Score of the work. When we estimate a work's readability on the basis of a small number of samples, we can expect that there may be some disparity between the predicted Readability Score and the true readability of the work. The size of the uncertainty is indicated by the *standard error of estimate* (S.E.est). The higher a correlation, the smaller the S.E.est derived from it; the lower the correlation, the larger the S.E.est.

For the Wide Range Readability Formula, the S.E.est is .501, or half a grade. The S.E.est is really the standard deviation of the differences to be found between the Readability Scores of single samples and the true readability of the work. For a sample with a Readability Score of 3.0, the chances are even that the work is below 3.0 or above 3.0. The chances are 68 in 100 that the true readability of the work is ±.5 from 3.0, in other words, between 2.5 and 3.5. The chances are 95 in 100 that the true readability is ±1.0 from 3.0. One should also note that there are 16 chances in 100 that the true value is below 2.5, and 16 chances in 100 that it is above 3.5. There are only 5 chances in 100 that the true value is below 2.0 or above 4.0.

When the mean is obtained for several samples from a work, the chance fluctuations of single samples tend to cancel out, and the margin of uncertainty is reduced. However,

Table D.5 Criterion Scores and Predicted Raw Scores

Reader Level	Criterion Score	Mean Predicted Raw Score
Preprimer	1.3	1.594
Primer	1.5	1.831
First reader	1.8	2.049
Low second reader	2.2	2.414
High second reader	2.7	2.789
Low third reader	3.2	3.239
High third reader	3.7	3.982
Fourth reader	4.5	4.280
Fifth reader	5.5	4.963
Sixth reader	6.5	5.614
Seventh reader	7.5	6.270
Eighth reader	8.5	6.605

it is better to be too cautious than too confident. We recommend that the user of this formula think of an obtained Readability Score as probably within half a grade of the true readability of the work. If the Readability Scores of the samples fluctuate widely, one should realize that an average Readability Score for the work is relatively meaningless.

VALIDITY AND RELIABILITY

Validity

The process of investigating the validity of a measuring instrument involves determining what the instrument measures and how well it functions in a variety of situations in which it can be used (Cronbach & Quirk 1971).

Predictive Validity.   The predictive validity of an instrument is found by obtaining the correlation between scores on the instrument and scores on an independent measure of the characteristic in question, which is called a *criterion*. For the present formula, the criterion is the scale of grade scores assigned to the twelve basal reader levels. As shown in Table D.4, the multiple correlation between formula scores and the criterion is .930, a very high result.

The degree to which predictions from an instrument are better than pure chance is shown by the square of the multiple correlation (R^2). R^2 for this formula is .864, indicating that scores predicted from this formula are 86% more accurate than chance guesses would be.

Goodness of Fit.   Goodness of fit refers to the degree to which the Readability Scores obtained from a formula place books or selections at the same level of difficulty as the criterion does. It is possible for a formula to place a number of books in the same sequence as the criterion does, and at the same time to overestimate the difficulty of all the books, or underestimate it. For the present Wide Range formula, the Readability Scores have been adjusted so that the average Readability Score for the 40 samples at each criterion level is exactly equal to the criterion score, from preprimer through eighth-reader level. Readability Scores above 8.5 will place samples in the correct sequence of difficulty, but the accuracy of fit of such Readability Scores has not been verified, since they are derived by extrapolation.

As an example of the importance of goodness of fit, we compared three readability formulas to a criterion consisting of two of the eight series (Houghton Mifflin and Economy) used in the present study (Harris & Jacobson 1980). A three-variable Harris–Jacobson formula agreed with the publishers' designations at all primary levels except high first (1.8), where the Harris–Jacobson score was 2.1. The Spache Formula (1974) agreed with the publishers' designations from preprimer through low second, but underestimated the publishers' designations at the high-second, low-third, and high-third levels; the difference was .6 grades at 3^1 and .7 grades at 3^2. The Fry Graph (1968) rated the 2^1 readers as 2.9, the 2^2 readers as 4.0, the 3^1 readers as 4.8, and the 3^2 readers as 6.0. All three formulas placed the books in the correct sequence of difficulty, but there were obvious differences in goodness of fit.

Cross Validation.   As an additional check on validity of the present formula, comprehension scores on exercises taken from the McCall, Crabbs *Standard Test Lessons in*

Reading (1961 Edition) were used as a second criterion. These test lessons had been administered to 22,650 Virginia students, from whom a subsample of 18,000 students was selected to match national norms on aptitude and reading comprehension tests. Using a Latin Square design, 51 exercises were administered to fourth graders; 54 exercises to sixth graders; 53 exercises to ninth graders; and 32 exercises to twelfth graders. About 300 pupils took each exercise, without time limit, each pupil taking five test lessons (Grades 6, 9, and 12) or four test lessons (Grade 4).

The mean number of correct answers to the multiple-choice questions included in each test lesson was computed for each of the fourth-grade lessons, and these means provided a comprehension criterion scale at fourth-grade level. Using the Wide Range Formula, Predicted Raw Scores were computed for all fourth-grade test lessons. The correlation of these Predicted Raw Scores with the criterion is .66, as shown in Table D.6.

The same procedure was followed at the other three grades, with correlations of .53 at sixth grade, .55 at ninth grade, and .65 at twelfth grade (see Table D.6).

Comparisons with Other Readability Formulas.   At each of the four grades, readability scores were computed for each exercise, using the Dale–Chall Readability Formula. The correlations of Dale–Chall scores with the criterion of mean comprehension scores are shown in Table D.6. The Dale–Chall correlations were approximately the same as the Wide Range correlations at Grades 4, 6, and 9. At twelfth grade, the Wide Range was significantly the higher; using R^2, the Wide Range Formula has an 18% advantage at twelfth grade.

It may be noted that the Dale–Chall correlation we have found is a little lower than the .70 reported by Dale and Chall (1948). This may be due to differences between our population and that on which the original McCall–Crabbs grade scores were developed, our use of a more recent edition, or our use of mean comprehension score, whereas Dale and Chall used the grade scores supplied with the test lessons.

A similar procedure was followed for the Fry Readability Formula, with results shown in Table D.6. The Fry Formula had a useful correlation with the criterion only at fourth grade, where it was 10% poorer than both the Wide Range and the Dale–Chall Formulas. At sixth and ninth grade, its correlations with the criterion were low, and at twelfth grade it was not better than chance guessing. These Dale–Chall and Fry results have been previously published (Harris & Jacobson 1976).

We have also correlated two other readability formulas with the McCall–Crabbs criterion, the Wheeler–Smith Formula (1954), and the SMOG Formula (McLaughlin 1969). The results of those two formulas are also shown in Table D.6. These two were

Table D.6 Correlations of the Wide Range Readability Formula and Other Readability Formulas with McCall–Crabbs Comprehension Means[a]

Grade	Wide Range		Dale–Chall		Fry		Wheeler–Smith		SMOG	
	R	R^2	R	R^2	R	R^2	R	R^2	R	R^2
4	.66	.44	.67	.44	.58	.34	.53	.28	.53	.28
6	.53	.28	.53	.28	.30	.09	.43	.18	.41	.17
9	.55	.30	.58	.33	.45	.20	.52	.27	.46	.21
12	.65	.42	.49	.24	.10	.01	.40	.16	.01	.00

[a] Since comprehension is higher when Readability Scores are lower, these correlations are negative. The minus signs have been omitted.

consistently inferior to both the Wide Range and Dale–Chall Formulas at the four grades, and at twelfth grade, SMOG correlated only .01 with the criterion.

Problems with the Criterion.   Stevens (1980) has pointed out that although the McCall–Crabbs test lessons have been used as the criterion in the development of at least twelve readability formulas, these exercises were intended to be used as teaching materials and not as tests or as a criterion for readability formulas. In describing the McCall–Crabbs exercises in 1948, Dale and Chall said: "This material, it should be noted, has serious deficiencies as a criterion, but it is the best we have at the present time."

In our computations we ignored the G (grade) scores provided for the test lessons and used, instead, the average comprehension score for the approximately 300 pupils who took the exercise. Our assumption was that these randomly selected groups of 300 were, at each grade, equal in average reading comprehension so that test lessons with lower average scores could be safely assumed to be more difficult (less readable) than test lessons with higher average comprehension scores. To the extent that this may not be completely true, our criterion is imperfect. However, the effect of such imperfection should be to lower the correlations for all readability formulas equally.

It should be noted, also, that a formula tends to have its highest correlation with the criterion used in developing it and lower correlations with other criterion scales. This is true of the Wide Range Formula, which had a much higher correlation with publishers' designations than with McCall–Crabbs. The Dale–Chall Formula was developed using McCall–Crabbs as the criterion. In equaling Dale–Chall results at three grades and surpassing it at one grade, the Wide Range Formula stands the test of cross-validation very well.

Construct Validity.   The degree to which a measure conforms to a theoretical base is called its *construct validity*. Linguists have emphasized that the ease or difficulty of language is dependent upon word meaning (lexical, semantic) and grammatical (syntactic) factors. Early research by Lorge (1944), Dale and Chall (1948), and Spache (1953) indicated that the most satisfactory measure of vocabulary difficulty is the percent of words that are outside a list of common easy words. In a comprehensive review of research on readability, Klare came to the following conclusions: "A simple 2-variable formula should be sufficient, especially if one of the variables is a word or semantic variable and the other is a sentence or syntactic variable. . . . The word or semantic variable is consistently more highly predictive than the sentence or syntactic variable when each is considered singly. . . . Using a list of familiar words appears to give a slightly more predictive index than counting word length, probably because length is a (secondary) reflection of familiarity" (1974–1975, pp. 96, 97).

The present formula conforms exactly to Klare's specifications. The Readability Word List employed in it is the most up-to-date word list available and contains the first- and second-grade words used in a majority of eight current series of basal readers. By itself, the V1 score (percent of words not in the list) correlates .831 with the criterion, a higher correlation than most formulas that employ two or more variables achieve.

On the average, long sentences are harder to understand than short ones. This does not apply, of course, to single sentences, which may be harder or easier—depending on their word difficulty and syntactic complexity. But when estimating the difficulty of selections or whole books, average sentence length combined with percent of hard words provides as good an estimate of overall readability as can be obtained from two variables.

There have been several attempts in recent years to devise linguistically sound measures of syntactic complexity. MacGinitie and Tretiak (1971) tried out several of them, and reported that none of the measures of sentence depth, when combined with percent of hard words, gave as high a multiple correlation as did the combination of hard words with average sentence length.

It is evident, therefore, that the two variables used in the present formula have strong theoretical as well as statistical justification.

Reliability

As applied to an educational measuring instrument, reliability means the consistency with which the instrument will give the same or closely similar scores on retesting. One way to estimate the reliability of the instrument is to use information concerning its validity. "To be valid a test must be reliable." (Garrett 1958, p. 360). The validity coefficient sets the lower limit of the instrument's reliability, since its correlation with an outside criterion cannot be higher than its self-consistency.

Ordinarily, reliability coefficients of .90 or above are considered to be good. The validity coefficient of the Wide Range Readability Formula is .930 (see Table D.4), and therefore the reliability must be at least .930.

This was checked by dividing the 480 samples into two sets of 240 samples, on an odd-even basis. R was computed for each set, and came out .947 for the first set and .928 for the second set. Thus the results are stable and reliable.

Bibliography

AARON, IRA E. Evaluation and accountability. In J. E. Merritt (Ed.), *New horizons in reading*. Newark, DE: International Reading Association, 1976. Pp. 558–564.

AARON, P. G., & BAKER, CATHERINE. Empirical and heuristic bases for diagnosis. *Topics in Learning and Learning Disabilities*, January 1983, *2*, 27–42.

AARON, P. G., GRANTHAM, SONTRA L., & CAMPBELL, NANCY. Differential treatment of reading disability of diverse etiologies. In R. Malatesha & P. Aaron (Eds.), *Reading disorders: Varieties and treatments*. New York: Academic Press, 1982. Pp. 449–452.

AARON, ROBERT L., & SEATON, HAL W. Modification of pupil attitude toward reading through positive reinforcement scheduling. In W. D. Miller & G. M. McNinch (Eds.), *Reflections and investigations on reading*. Clemson, SC: National Reading Conference, 1976. Pp. 219–220.

AASEN, HELEN B. A summer's growth in reading. *Elementary School Journal*, 1959, *40*, 70–74.

ABIKOFF, HOWARD. Cognitive training interventions in children: Review of a new approach. *Journal of Learning Disabilities*, February 1979, *12*, 123–135.

ABRAHAMSON, RICHARD F. An analysis of children's favorite picture storybooks. *The Reading Teacher*, November 1980, *34*, 167–170.

ABRAMS, JULES C., & KASLOW, FLORENCE. Family stress and the learning disabled child: Intervention and treatment. *Journal of Learning Disabilities*, February 1977, *10*, 86–90.

ACKERMAN, PEGGY T., & DYKMAN, ROSCOE A. Attention and effortful information-processing deficits in children with learning and attention disorders. *Topics in Learning and Learning Disabilities*, July 1982, *2*, 12–22.

ADAMS, ABBY, CARNINE, DOUGLAS, & GERSTEN, RUSSELL. Instructional strategies for studying content area texts in the intermediate grades. *Reading Research Quarterly*, Fall 1982, *18*, 27–55.

ADAMS, ANNE H., & HARRISON, CATHY B. Using television to teach specific reading skills. *The Reading Teacher*, October 1975, *29*, 45–51.

ADAMS, ERNEST. A technique for teaching word identification in the content areas. In G. G. Duffy (Ed.), *Reading in the middle school*. Newark, DE: International Reading Association, 1974. Pp. 112–116.

ADAMS, MARILYN J. Models of word recognition. Technical Report No. 107. Champaign, IL: Center for the Study of Reading, University of Illinois, October 1978.

ADAMS, MARILYN J. Failures to comprehend and levels of processing in reading. In R. Spiro *et al.* (Eds.), *Theoretical issues in reading comprehension*. Hillsdale, NJ: LEA, 1980. Pp. 11–32.

ADAMS, MARILYN, & BRUCE, BERTRAM. Background knowledge and reading comprehension. In J. Langer & M. T. Smith-Burke (Eds.), *Reader meets author/bridging the gap: A psycholinguistic and sociolinguistic perspective*. Newark, DE: International Reading Association, 1982. Pp. 1–25.

ADLER, SOL. Dialectical differences and learning disorders. *Journal of Learning Disabilities*. June/July 1972, 5, 344–350.

ADLER, SOL. Megavitamin treatment for behaviorally disturbed and learning disabled children. *Journal of Learning Disabilities*, December 1979, 12, 678–681.

AIRASIAN, PETER W., & MADAUS, GEORGE F. Linking testing and instruction: Policy issues. *Journal of Educational Measurement*, Summer 1983, 20, 103–118.

Albany Times Union. One in four reads 20 books a year, survey finds. October 23, 1978, 190, 14.

Albany Times Union. Mandated aid to handicapped has large effect on schools. April 26, 1983, 347, A-12.

ALEXANDER, J. ESTILL, & FILLER, RONALD C. Measures of reading attitude. *Elementary English*, March 1975, 52, 376–378.

ALEXANDER, J. ESTILL, & FILLER, RONALD C. *Attitudes and reading*. Newark, DE: International Reading Association, 1976.

ALGARIN, JOANNE P. *Japanese folk literature: A core collection and reference guide*. Ann Arbor, MI: R. R. Bowker, 1982.

ALGOZZINE, BOB, YSSELDYKE, JAMES E., & SCHINN, MARK. Identifying children with learning disabilities: When is a discrepancy severe? *Journal of School Psychology*, Winter 1982, 20, 299–305.

ALLEN, JAMES E. The right to read—target for the 70's. *Elementary English*, April 1970, 47, 487–492.

ALLEN, M. Relationships between Kuhlmann–Anderson Intelligence Tests and academic achievement in grade IV. *Journal of Educational Psychology*, 1944, 44, 229–239.

ALLEN, MERRILL J. The role of vision in learning disorders. *Journal of Learning Disabilities*, August/September 1977, 10, 411–415.

ALLEN, ROACH VAN. *Language experiences in communication*. Boston: Houghton Mifflin, 1976.

ALLEN, ROACH VAN, & ALLEN, CLARYCE. *Language experience activities* (2nd ed.). Boston: Houghton Mifflin, 1982.

ALLEN, ROBERT L. *The verb system of present-day American English*. The Hague: Mouton, 1966.

ALLEN, VERNON L, FELDMAN, ROBERT S., & DEVIN-SHEEHAN, LINDA. Research on children tutoring children: A critical review. *Review of Educational Research*, Summer 1976, 46, 355–386.

ALLPORT, ALAN. Word recognition in reading. In P. Kolers, M. Wrolstad, & H. Bouma (Eds.), *Processing of visible language*. New York: Plenum Press, 1979, Pp. 227–257.

AMAN, MICHAEL G. Psychotropic drugs and learning problems—a selective review. *Journal of Learning Disabilities*, February 1980, 13, 87–97.

AMAN, MICHAEL G. Psychotropic drugs in the treatment of reading disorders. In R. Malatesha & P. Aaron (Eds.), *Reading disorders: Varieties and treatments*. New York: Academic Press, 1982. Pp. 453–471.

AMBLE, BRUCE R. Reading by phrases. *California Journal of Educational Research*, 1967, 18, 116–124.

American heritage dictionary of the English language. New York: American Heritage Publishing, 1969.

AMERICAN PSYCHIATRIC ASSOCIATION. *Diagnostic and statistical manual of mental disorders* (3rd ed.). Washington, DC: APA, 1983.

AMES, LOUISE B. Learning disabilities: The developmental point of view. In H. R. Myklebust (Ed.), *Progress in learning disabilities*, Vol. I. New York: Grune & Stratton, 1968. Pp. 39–74.

AMES, LOUISE B. Learning disability: Truth or trap? *Journal of Learning Disabilities*, January 1983, *16*, 19–20.

ANASTASIOW, NICHOLAS (REVIEWER). Reading miscue inventory. In O.K. Buros (Ed.), *Eighth mental measurements yearbook*, Vol. II. Highland Park, NJ: Gryphon Press, 1978. Pp. 1318–1319.

ANDERSON, BETTY. The missing ingredient: Fluent oral reading. *Elementary School Journal*, January 1981, *81*, 173–177.

ANDERSON, CHARLES W., & SMITH, EDWARD L. Children's preconceptions and content area textbooks. In G. Duffy *et al.* (Eds.), *Comprehension instruction: Perspectives and suggestions*. New York: Longman, 1984. Pp. 187–201.

ANDERSON, JONATHAN. Lix and Rix: Variations on a little-known readability index. *Journal of Reading*, March 1983, *26*, 490–496.

ANDERSON, LINDA M., EVERTSON, CAROLYN M., & BROPHY, JERE E. An experimental study of effective teaching in first-grade reading groups. *Elementary School Journal*, March 1979, 79, 193–223.

ANDERSON, RICHARD C., & FREEBODY, PETER. Vocabulary knowledge. In J. Guthrie (Ed.), *Comprehension and teaching: Research reviews*. Newark, DE: International Reading Association, 1981. Pp. 77–117.

ANDERSON, RICHARD C., & FREEBODY, PETER. Reading comprehension and the assessment and acquisition of word knowledge. Technical Report No. 249. Champaign, IL: Center for the Study of Reading, University of Illinois, June 1982.

ANDERSON, RICHARD C., MASON, JANA, & SHIRLEY, LARRY. The reading group: An experimental investigation of a labyrinth. Technical Report No. 271. Champaign, IL: Center for the Study of Reading, University of Illinois, February 1983.

ANDERSON, RICHARD C., & PEARSON, P. DAVID. A schema-theoretic view of basic processes in reading comprehension. Technical Report No. 306. Champaign, IL: Center for the Study of Reading, University of Illinois, January 1984.

ANDERSON, ROBERT H., & RITSHER, CYNTHIA. Pupil progress. In R. E. Ebel (Ed.), *Encyclopedia of educational research* (4th ed.). New York: Macmillan, 1969. Pp. 1050–1062.

ANDERSON, RUSSELL W. Effects of neuro-psychological techniques on reading achievement. Unpublished doctoral dissertation, Colorado State College, 1965.

ANDERSON, THOMAS H. Study strategies and adjunct aids. In R. Spiro *et al.* (Eds.), *Theoretical issues in reading comprehension*. Hillsdale, NJ: LEA, 1980. Pp. 483–502.

ANDERSON, THOMAS H., & ARMBRUSTER, BONNIE B. Content area textbooks. In R. C. Anderson *et al.* (Eds.), *Learning to read in American schools: Basal readers and content texts*. Hillsdale, NJ: LEA, 1984. Pp. 193–266. (a)

ANDERSON, THOMAS H., & ARMBRUSTER, BONNIE B. Studying. In P. D. Pearson (Ed.), *Handbook of reading research*. New York: Longman, 1984. Pp. 657–679. (b)

ANDERSON, THOMAS H., ARMBRUSTER, BONNIE B., & KANTOR, ROBERT N. How clearly written are children's textbooks? Or, of bladderworts and alfa. Reading Education Report No. 16. Champaign, IL: Center for the Study of Reading, University of Illinois, August 1980.

ANDRE, THOMAS. Does answering higher level questions while reading facilitate productive learning? *Review of Educational Research*, Spring 1979, *49*, 280–318.

ANKNEY, PAUL, & MCCLURG, PAT. Testing Manzo's Guided Reading Procedure. *The Reading Teacher*, March 1981, *34*, 681–685.

ANSARA, ALICE. The Orton–Gillingham approach to remediation in developmental dyslexia. In R. Malatesha & P. Aaron (Eds.), *Reading disorders: Varieties and treatments*. New York: Academic Press, 1982. Pp. 409–433.

AOKI, ELAINE M. "Are you Chinese? Are you Japanese? Or are you just a mixed-up kid?" Using Asian American children's literature. *The Reading Teacher*, January 1981, *34*, 382–385.

APPLEBEE, ARTHUR N. *The child's concept of story: Ages 2–17*. Chicago: University of Chicago Press, 1978.

ARCHER, MARGUERITE P. Minorities in easy reading through third grade. *Elementary English*, May 1972, *49*, 746–749.

ARGULEWICZ, ED W., & SANCHEZ, DAVID T. Considerations in the assessment of reading difficulties in bilingual children. *School Psychology Review*, 1982, *11* (3), 281–289.

ARLIN, MARSHALL, & ROTH, GARRY. Pupil's use of time while reading comics and books. *American Educational Research Journal*, Spring 1978, *15*, 201–216.

ARLIN, MARSHALL, SCOTT, MARY, & WEBSTER, JANET. The effects of pictures on rate of learning sight words: A critique of the focal attention hypothesis. *Reading Research Quarterly*, 1978–1979, *14* (4), 645–660.

ARMBRUSTER, BONNIE B., & ANDERSON, THOMAS H. Idea-mapping: The technique and its use in the classroom or simulating the "ups" and "downs" of reading comprehension. Reading Education Report No. 36. Champaign, IL: Center for the Study of Reading, University of Illinois, October 1982.

ARMBRUSTER, BONNIE B., & ANDERSON, THOMAS H. Producing "considerate" expository text: Or easy reading is damned hard writing. Reading Education Report No. 46. Champaign, IL. Center for the Study of Reading, University of Illinois, January 1984.

ARMBRUSTER, BONNIE B., & GUDBRANDSEN, BETH H. Reading comprehension instruction in social studies programs, or, on making mobiles out of soapsuds. Technical Report No. 309. Champaign IL: Center for the Study of Reading, University of Illinois, February 1984.

ARMBRUSTER, BONNIE B., et al. What did you mean by that question? A taxonomy of American History questions. Technical Report No. 308. Champaign, IL: Center for the Study of Reading, University of Illinois, January 1984.

ARNOLD, ELIZABETH, MCNINCH, GEORGE, & MILLER, WALLACE. Experiments in word learning. In P. D. Pearson & J. Hansen (Eds.), *Reading: Disciplined inquiry in process and practice*. Clemson, SC: National Reading Conference, 1978. Pp. 45–50.

ARTER, JUDITH A., & JENKINS, JOSEPH R. Differential diagnosis-prescriptive teaching: A critical appraisal. *Review of Educational Research*, Fall 1979, *49*, 517–555.

ARTLEY, A. STERL. Learning disabilities versus reading disabilities: A vexing problem. In C. McCullough (Ed.), *Inchworm, inchworm: Persistent problems in reading education*. Newark, DE: International Reading Association, 1980. Pp. 119–124.

ARTLEY, A. STERL. Individual differences and reading instruction. *Elementary School Journal*, November 1981, *82*, 143–151.

ASHER, STEVEN R. Sex differences in reading achievement. Reading Education Report No. 2, Champaign, IL: Center for the Study of Reading, University of Illinois, October 1977.

ASHER, STEVEN R. Influence of topic interest on black children's and white children's reading comprehension. Technical Report No. 99. Champaign, IL: Center for the Study of Reading, University of Illinois, July 1978.

ASHER, STEVEN R. Topic interest and children's reading comprehension. In R. Spiro *et al.* (Eds.), *Theoretical issues in reading comprehension*. Hillsdale, NJ: LEA, 1980. Pp. 525–534.

ASHTON-WARNER, SYLVIA. *Spinster*. New York: Simon and Schuster, 1959.

ASKOV, WARREN, OTTO, WAYNE, & SMITH, RICHARD. Assessment of the de Hirsch Predictive Index tests of reading failure. In R. C. Aukerman (Ed.), *Some persistent questions in beginning reading*. Newark, DE: International Reading Association, 1972. Pp. 33–42.

ASSOCIATION OF HOSPITAL AND INSTITUTIONAL LIBRARIES. *Bibliotherapy: Methods and materials*. Chicago: American Library Association, 1971.

ATHEY, IRENE. Reading research in the affective domain. In H. Singer & R. B. Ruddell (Eds.), *Theoretical models and processes of reading* (2nd ed.). Newark, DE: International Reading Association, 1976. Pp. 352–380.

ATHEY, IRENE. Reading: The affective domain reconceptualized. *Advances in Reading/Language Research*, 1982, *1*, 203–217.

ATKINSON, RICHARD C., & FLETCHER, JOHN D. Teaching children to read with a computer. *The Reading Teacher*, January 1972, *25*, 319–327.

ATWOOD, KAREN J., & MALENA, RICHARD F. Conceptual synonyms: The teacher's graphic organizer and the student's map. *Wisconsin State Reading Association Journal*, Spring 1984, *28*, 6–10.

AU, KATHRYN HU-PEI, & MASON, JANA M. Social organizational factors in learning to read: The balance of rights hypothesis. *Reading Research Quarterly*, 1981, *17* (1), 115–151.

AUKERMAN, ROBERT C. *Approaches to beginning reading*. New York: John Wiley & Sons, 1971.

AUKERMAN, ROBERT C. *The basal reader approach to reading*. New York: John Wiley & Sons, 1981.

AULLS, MARK. Developmental considerations for reading research: Applications to good and poor reader research. In M. Kamil & M. Boswick (Eds.), *Directions in reading: Research and instruction*. Washington, DC: National Reading Conference, 1981. Pp. 83–91.

AUSUBEL, DAVID P. The use of advance organizers in the learning and retention of meaningful verbal material. *Journal of Educational Psychology*, 1960, *51*, 267–272.

AUSUBEL, DAVID P. Schemata, cognitive structure, and advance organizers: A reply to Andersen, Spiro, and Anderson. *American Educational Research Journal*, Fall 1980, *17*, 400–404.

AUTEN, ANNE. A guide to purchasing a microcomputer. *Journal of Reading*, December 1982, *26*, 268–271.

AUTEN, ANNE. Reading and writing: A mutual support system. *Journal of Reading*, January 1983, *26*, 366–368.

AUTEN, ANNE. Understanding other cultures through literature. *The Reading Teacher*, January 1984, *37*, 416–419.

AXELROD, JEROME. Misconceptions some pupils have about remedial reading and themselves. *The English Record*, Fall 1975, *26*, 70–74.

AXELROD, S. *Behavior modification for the classroom teacher*. New York: McGraw-Hill, 1977.

AYERS, DOUGLAS, & DOWNING, JOHN. Children's linguistic awareness and reading achievement. Paper presented at the University of Victoria/IRA Reading Research Seminar, June 1979. Victoria, B.C., Canada.

AYRES, A. JEAN. *Sensory integration and learning disorders*. Los Angeles: Western Psychological Services. 1972.

AYRES, A. JEAN. A response to defensive medicine. *Academic Therapy*, November 1977, *13*, 149–152.

AYRES, A. JEAN. Learning disabilities and the vestibular system. *Journal of Learning Disabilities*, January 1978, *11*, 30–41.

BABBS, PATRICIA J., & MOE, ALDEN J. Metacognition: A key for independent learning from text. *The Reading Teacher*, January 1983, *36*, 422–426.

BACHNER, SAUL. Teaching literature to the disadvantaged. Unpublished doctoral dissertation, Wayne State University, 1969.

BACKMAN, JOAN. The role of psycholinguistic skills in reading acquisition: A look at early readers. *Reading Research Quarterly*, Summer 1983, *18*, 466–479.

BADDELEY, ALAN, & LEWIS, VIVIEN W. Inneractive processes in reading: The inner voice, the inner ear, and the inner eye. In A. Lesgold & C. Perfetti (Eds.), *Interactive processes in reading*. Hillsdale, NJ: LEA 1981. Pp. 107–129.

BADIAN, NATALIE A. Auditory-visual integration, auditory memory, and reading in retarded and adequate readers. *Journal of Reading Disabilities*, February 1977, *10*, 108–114.

BAGFORD, JACK. Evaluating teachers on reading instruction. *The Reading Teacher*, January 1981, *34*, 400–404.

BAGLIN, ROGERT F. Does "nationally" normed really mean nationally? *Journal of Educational Measurement*, Summer 1981, *18*, 97–108.

BAKER, DEBORAH T. What happened when? Activities for teaching sequence skills. *The Reading Teacher*, November 1982, *36*, 216–218.

BAKER, LINDA, & BROWN, ANN L. Cognitive monitoring in reading. In J. Flood (Ed.), *Understanding reading comprehension*. Newark, DE: International Reading Association, 1984. Pp. 21–44. (a)

BAKER, LINDA, & BROWN, ANN L. Metacognitive skills and reading. In P. D. Pearson (Ed.), *Handbook of reading research*. New York: Longman, 1984. Pp. 353–394. (b)

BAKKER, DIRK J. Hemispheric specialization and stages in the learning-to-read processs. *Bulletin of the Orton Society*, 1973, *23*, 15–27.

BAKKER, DIRK J. Cognitive deficits and cerebral asymmetry. *Journal of Research and Development in Education*, Spring 1982, *15*, 48–54.

BAKKER, DIRK J., & SCHROOTS, H. J. Temporal order in normal and disturbed reading. In G. Pavlidis & T. Miles (Eds.), *Dyslexia research and its application to education*. New York: John Wiley & Sons, 1981. Pp. 87–98.

BAKKER, DIRK J., TEUNISSEN, JETTY, & BOSCH, JOOP. Development of laterality-reading patterns. In R. Knights & D. Bakker (Eds.), *The neuropsychology of learning disorders*. Baltimore: University Park Press, 1976. Pp. 207–220.

BALDWIN, R. SCOTT, FORD, JEFF C., & READENCE, JOHN E. Teaching word connotations: An alternative strategy. *Reading World*, December 1981, *21*, 103–108.

BALDWIN, R. SCOTT, & KAUFMAN, RHONDA K. A concurrent validity study of the Raygor Readability Estimate. *Journal of Reading*, November 1979, *23*, 148–153.

BALMUTH, MIRIAM. *The roots of phonics: A historical introduction.* New York: McGraw-Hill, 1982.

BALOW, BRUCE. Perceptual-motor activities in the treatment of severe reading disability. *The Reading Teacher*, March 1971, *24*, 513–525.

BALOW, BRUCE, & BLOMQUIST, M. Young adults ten to fifteen years after severe reading disability. *Elementary School Journal*, 1965, *66*, 44–48.

BALOW, BRUCE, RUBIN, ROSALYN, & ROSEN, MARTHA J. Perinatal events as precursors of reading disabilities. *Reading Research Quarterly*, 1975–1976, *11* (1), 36–71.

BAMBERGER, RICHARD, & RABIN, ANNETTE. New approaches to readability: Austrian research. *The Reading Teacher*, February 1984, *37*, 512–519.

BANDURA, ALBERT. *Principles of behavior modification.* New York: Holt, Rinehart and Winston, 1969.

BANKS, ENID M. The identification of children with potential learning disabilities. *Slow Learning Child*, 1970, *17*, 27–38.

BANNATYNE, ALEXANDER D. The color phonics system. In J. Money (Ed.), *The disabled reader.* Baltimore: Johns Hopkins Press, 1966. Pp. 193–214.

BANNATYNE, ALEXANDER D. *Language, reading and learning disabilities: Psychology, neuropsychology, diagnosis and remediation.* Springfield, IL: Charles C Thomas, 1971.

BANNATYNE, ALEXANDER D. Choosing the best reinforcers. *Academic Therapy*, Summer 1972, *7*, 483–486. (a)

BANNATYNE, ALEXANDER D. Mirror images and reversals. *Academic Therapy*, Fall 1972, *8*, 87–92. (b)

BANNATYNE, ALEXANDER D. Diagnosis: A note on recategorization of the WISC scaled scores. *Journal of Learning Disabilities*, May 1974, *7*, 272–273.

BANNER, C. N. Child-rearing attitudes of mothers of under-, average-, and over-achieving children. *British Journal of Educational Psychology*, June 1979, *49*, 150–155.

BARATZ, JOAN C., & SHUY, ROGER W. *Teaching black children to read.* Washington, DC: Center for Applied Linguistics, 1969.

BARCHAS, SARAH E. Expressed reading interests of children of differing ethnic groups. Unpublished doctoral dissertation, University of Arizona, 1971.

BARNARD, DOUGLAS P., & KENDRICK, ROBIN. A new consciousness for integrating communication arts instruction. Ginn Occasional Papers No. 6. Columbus, OH: Ginn, September 1980.

BARNITZ, JOHN G. Interrelationships of orthography and phonological structure in learning to read. Technical Report No. 57. Champaign, IL: Center for the Study of Reading, University of Illinois, January 1978.

BARNITZ, JOHN G. Developing sentence comprehension in reading. *Language Arts*, November/December 1979, *56*, 902–908, 958. Also in A. J. Harris & E. Sipay (Eds.), *Readings on reading instruction* (3rd ed.), New York: Longman, 1984. Pp. 286–293.

BARNITZ, JOHN G. Linguistic and cultural perspectives on spelling irregularity. *Journal of Reading*, January 1980, *23*, 320–326.

BARNITZ, JOHN G. Syntactic effects on the reading comprehension of pronoun-referent structures by children in grades two, four, and six. *Reading Research Quarterly*, 1981, *15* (2), 268–289.

BARNITZ, JOHN G. Orthographies, bilingualism and learning to read English as a second language. *The Reading Teacher*, February 1982, *35*, 560–567.

BARON, JONATHAN, & TREIMAN, REBECCA. Use of orthography in reading and learning to read. In J. Kavanaugh & R. Venezky (Eds.), *Orthography, reading, and dyslexia.* Baltimore, MD: University Park Press, 1980. Pp. 171–189.

BARON, JONATHAN, et al. Spelling and reading by rules. In U. Frith (Ed.), *Cognitive processes in spelling.* New York: Academic Press, 1980. Pp. 159–194.

BARR, REBECCA C. The influence of instructional conditions on word recognition errors. *Reading Research Quarterly*, Spring 1972, *7*, 509–529.

BARR, REBECCA C. Instructional pace differences and their effect on reading acquisition. *Reading Research Quarterly*, 1973–1974, *9* (4), 526–554.

BARR, REBECCA. The effect of instruction on pupil reading strategies. *Reading Research Quarterly,* 1974–1975, *10* (4), 555–582.

BARR, REBECCA. Influence of reading materials on response to printed words. *Journal of Reading Behavior,* Summer 1975, *7,* 123–135.

BARR, REBECCA. Classroom reading instruction from a sociological perspective. *Journal of Reading Behavior,* 1982, *14* (4), 375–389. (a)

BARR, REBECCA. Reader knowledge and classroom instruction. In W. Otto & S. White (Eds.), *Reading expository text.* New York: Academic Press, 1982. Pp. 75–84. (b)

BARRETT, THOMAS C. The relationship between measures of pre-reading visual discrimination and first-grade achievement: A review of the literature. *Reading Research Quarterly,* Fall 1965, *1,* 51–76.

BARRON, BONNIE G., & COLVIN, JUDY M. How to talk to parents. *Journal of Reading,* February 1983, *26,* 452–453.

BARRON, RODERICK W. Visual and phonological strategies in reading and spelling. In U. Frith (Ed.), *Cognitive processes in spelling.* New York: Academic Press, 1980. Pp. 195–213.

BARRON, RODERICK W. Development of visual word recognition: A review. In G. MacKinnon & T. Waller (Eds.), *Reading research: Advances in theory and practice,* Vol. 3. New York: Academic Press, 1981. Pp. 119–158. (a)

BARRON, RODERICK W. Reading skill and reading strategies. In A. Lesgold & C. Perfetti (Eds.), *Interactive processes in reading.* Hillsdale, NJ: LEA, 1981. Pp. 299–325. (b)

BARTLETT, F. C. *Remembering: A study in experimental and social psychology.* Cambridge, England: Cambridge University Press, 1932.

BARTON, ALLEN H. Reading research and its communication: The Columbia-Carnegie project. In J. A. Figurel (Ed.), *Reading as an intellectual activity.* Newark, DE: International Reading Association, 1963. Pp. 246–250.

BASKIN, BARBARA H., HARRIS, KAREN H., & SALLEY, COLEEN C. Making the poetry connection. *The Reading Teacher,* December 1976, *30,* 259–265.

BASKIN, BARBARA H., & HARRIS, KAREN H. *Notes from a different drummer: A guide to juvenile fiction portraying the handicapped.* New York: R. R. Bowker, 1977.

BATES, GARY W. Developing reading strategies for the gifted: A research-based approach. *Journal of Reading,* April 1984, *27,* 590–593.

BAUER, RICHARD H. Information processing as a way of understanding and diagnosing learning disabilities. *Topics in Learning & Learning Disabilities,* July 1982, *2,* 33–45.

BAUMANN, JAMES F. Research on children's main idea comprehension: A problem of ecological validity. *Reading Psychology,* April–June 1982, *3,* 167–177.

BAUMANN, JAMES F. Children's ability to comprehend main ideas in content textbooks. *Reading World,* May 1983, *22,* 322–331. (a)

BAUMANN, JAMES F. A generic comprehension instructional strategy. *Reading World,* May 1983, *22,* 284–294. (b)

BAUMANN, JAMES F., & SERRA, JUDITH K. The frequency and placement of main ideas in children's social studies textbooks: A modified replication of Braddock's research on topic sentences. *Journal of Reading Behavior,* 1984, *16* (1), 27–40.

BAUMANN, JAMES F., & STEVENSON, JENNIFER A. Understanding standardized reading achievement test scores. *The Reading Teacher,* March 1982, *35,* 648–654.

BAUMANN, JAMES F., WALKER, ROBERT N., & JOHNSON, DALE D. Effect of distractor word variability in children's performance on a word identification test. *Reading Psychology,* Spring 1981, *2,* 88–96.

BAUSERMAN, DEBORAH N., & OBRZUT, JOHN E. Free recall and rehearsal strategies in average and severely disabled readers. *Perceptual & Motor Skills,* April 1981, *52,* 539–545.

BEACH, RICHARD, & APPLEMAN, DEBORAH. Reading strategies for expository and literal text types. In A. Purves & O. Niles (Eds.), *Becoming readers in a complex society.* 83rd Yearbook of the National Society for the Study of Education, Part I. Chicago: University of Chicago Press, 1984. Pp. 115–143.

BEAN, RITA M. Research on teaching reading comprehension. *Reading News,* March 1983, *12,* 1, 4.

BEAN, RITA M., & WILSON, ROBERT M. *Effecting change in school reading programs: The resource role.* Newark, DE: International Reading Association, 1981.

BEAN, THOMAS W. Decoding strategies of Hawaiian Island dialect speakers in grades four, five, and six. *Reading World,* May 1978, *17,* 295–305.

BEAUCHAMP, ROBERT F. Selection of books for the culturally disadvantaged ninth grade student. Unpublished doctoral dissertation, Wayne State University, 1970.

BEAUMONT, J. GRAHAM. Developmental aspects. In J. Beaumont (Ed.), *Divided visual field studies of cerebral organization.* New York: Academic Press, 1982. Pp. 113–128. (a)

BEAUMONT, J. GRAHAM. Introduction. In J. Beaumont (Ed.), *Divided visual field studies of cerebral organization.* New York: Academic Press, 1982. Pp. 1–9. (b).

BEAUMONT, J. GRAHAM. The split-brain studies. In J. Beaumont (Ed.), *Divided visual field studies of cerebral organization.* New York: Academic Press, 1982. Pp. 217–232. (c)

BECK, ISABEL L. Comprehension during the acquisition of decoding skills. In J. T. Guthrie (Ed.), *Cognition, curriculum, and comprehension.* Newark, DE: International Reading Association, 1977. Pp. 113–156.

BECK, ISABEL L. Reading problems and instructional practices. In G. MacKinnon & T. Waller (Eds.), *Reading Research: Advances in theory and practice,* Vol. 2. New York: Academic Press, 1981. Pp. 53–95.

BECK, ISABEL L. Developing comprehension: The impact of the directed reading lesson. In R. Anderson, J. Osburn, & R. Tierney (Eds.), *Learning to read in American schools: Basal readers and content texts.* Hillsdale, NJ: LEA, 1984. Pp. 3–20.

BECK, ISABEL L., MCCASLIN, ELLEN S., & MCKEOWN, MARGARET G. Basal readers' purpose for story reading: Smoothly paving the road or setting up a detour. *Elementary School Journal,* January 1981, *81,* 156–161.

BECK, ISABEL L., & MCKEOWN, MARGARET G. Developing questions that promote comprehension: The story map. *Language Arts,* November/December 1981, *58,* 913–918.

BECK, ISABEL L., & MCKEOWN, MARGARET G. Learning words well—A program to enhance vocabulary and comprehension. *The Reading Teacher,* March 1983, *36,* 622–625.

BECK, ISABEL L., MCKEOWN, MARGARET G., & MCCASLIN, ELLEN S. Does reading make sense? Problems of early readers. *The Reading Teacher,* April 1981, *34,* 780–785.

BECK, ISABEL L., MCKEOWN, MARGARET G., & MCCASLIN, ELLEN S. Vocabulary development: All contexts are not created equal. *Elementary School Journal,* January 1983, *83,* 177–181.

BECK, ISABEL L., OMANSON, RICHARD C., & MCKEOWN, MARGARET G. An instructional redesign of reading lessons: Effects on comprehension. *Reading Research Quarterly,* 1982, *17* (4), 462–481.

BECK, ISABEL L., PERFETTI, CHARLES A., & MCKEOWN, MARGARET G. Effect of long-term vocabulary instruction on lexical access and reading comprehension. *Journal of Educational Psychology,* 1982, *74,* 506–521.

BECK, ISABEL L., *et al.* Improving the comprehensibility of stories: The effects of revisions that improve coherence. *Reading Research Quarterly,* Spring 1984, *19,* 263–277.

BECKER, GEORGE. *Television and the classroom reading program.* Newark, DE: International Reading Association, 1973.

BECKER, WESLEY C., & GERSTEN, RUSSELL. A follow-up of Follow-Through: The later effects of the Direct Instruction Model on children in fifth and sixth grades. *American Educational Research Journal,* Spring 1982, *19,* 75–92.

BEEBE, MONA J. The effect of different types of substitution miscues on reading. *Reading Research Quarterly,* 1979–1980, *15* (3), 324–336.

BEGAB, MICHAEL J. Childhood learning disabilities and family stress. In J. I. Arena (Ed.), *Management of the child with learning disabilities: An interdisciplinary challenge.* San Rafael, CA

BELL, LOUISE C. Supervising reading teachers. *Reading World,* May 1982, *21,* 333–339.

BELLONI, LORETTA F., & JONGSMA, EUGENE A. The effects of interest on reading comprehension of low-achieving students. *Journal of Reading,* November 1978, *22,* 106–109.

BELMONT, IRA, & BELMONT, LILLIAN. Stability or change in reading achievement over time: Developmental and educational implications. *Journal of Learning Disabilities,* February 1978, *11,* 80–88.

BELMONT, LILLIAN, & BIRCH, HERBERT C. Lateral dominance, lateral awareness, and reading disability. *Child Development*, 1965, *34*, 57–71.

BELMONT, LILLIAN, & BIRCH, HERBERT G. The intellectual profile of retarded readers. *Perceptual & Motor Skills*, 1966, *22*, 787–816.

BENDER, LAURETTA. *A visual-motor gestalt test and its clinical use.* Research Monograph No. 3. New York: American Orthopsychiatric Association, 1938.

BENDER, LAURETTA. Use of the visual-motor gestalt test in the diagnosis of learning disabilities. *Journal of Special Education*, Winter 1970, *4*, 29–39.

BENDER, LAURETTA A. A fifty-year review of experiences with dyslexia. *Bulletin of the Orton Society*, 1975, *25*, 5–23.

BENGER, KATHLYN. The relationship of perception, personality, intelligence, and grade one reading achievement. In H. K. Smith (Ed.), *Perception and reading*. Newark, DE: International Reading Association, 1968. Pp. 112–123.

BENNETT, JOHN E., & BENNETT, PRISCILLA. What's so funny? Action research and bibliography of humorous children's books—1975–80. *The Reading Teacher*, May 1982, *35*, 924–927.

BENNETT, NEVILLE. Recent research on teaching: A dream, a belief, and a model. *Journal of Education*, August 1978, *160*, 5–37.

BENSON, D. FRANK. Alexia and the neuroanatomical basis of reading. In F. Pirozzolo & M. Wittrock (Eds.), *Neuropsychological and cognitive processes in reading*. New York: Academic Press, 1981. Pp. 69–92.

BENSON, D. FRANK. Brain processes and language. In H. Myklebust (Ed.), *Progress in learning disabilities*, Vol. 5. New York: Grune & Stratton, 1983. Pp. 3–25.

BENTON, ARTHUR L. *Right-left discrimination and finger localization.* New York: Hoeber, 1959.

BENTON, ARTHUR L. Developmental dyslexia: Neurological aspects. In W. J. Friedlander (Ed.), *Advances in neurology*, Vol. 7. New York: Raven Press, 1975. Pp. 1–47.

BENTON, ARTHUR L. Some conclusions about dyslexia. In A. L. Benton & D. Pearl (Eds.), *Dyslexia: An appraisal of current knowledge*. New York: Oxford University Press, 1978. Pp. 451–476.

BENTON, MICHAEL. The methodology vacuum in teaching literature. *Language Arts*, March 1984, *61*, 265–275.

BERGER, ALLEN. Effectiveness of four methods of increasing reading rate, comprehension, and flexibility. In J. A. Figurel (Ed.), *Forging ahead in reading*. Newark, DE: International Reading Association, 1968. Pp. 588–596.

BERGER, ALLEN, & ROBINSON, H. ALAN (Eds.). *Secondary school reading: What research reveals for classroom practice.* Urbana, IL: National Council for Research in English & ERIC/RCS, 1982.

BERGERING, ANTHONY J. An investigation of laryngeal EMG activity and its relation to reading. *Dissertation Abstracts International*, February 1976, *36* (8-B), 4192.

BERGLUND, ROBERT L., & JOHNS, JERRY L. A primer on uninterrupted sustained silent reading. *The Reading Teacher*, February 1983, *36*, 534–539.

BERK, RONALD A. Practical guidelines for determining the length of objective-based, criterion-referenced tests. *Educational Technology*, November 1980, *20*, 36–41.

BERK, RONALD A. What's wrong with using grade-equivalent scores to identify LD children. *Academic Therapy*, November 1981, *17*, 133–140.

BERK, RONALD A. The value of WISC-R profile analysis for the differential diagnosis of learning disabled students. *Journal of Clinical Psychology*, January 1983, *39*, 133–136.

BERK, RONALD A. An evaluation of procedures for computing an ability-achievement discrepancy score. *Journal of Learning Disabilities*, May 1984, *17*, 262–266.

BERLINER, DAVID C. Academic learning time and reading achievement. In J. Guthrie (Ed.), *Comprehension and teaching: Research reviews*. Newark, DE: International Reading Association, 1981. Pp. 203–226.

BERNSTEIN, BASIL. Elaborated and restricted codes: Their social origins and some consequences. *American Anthropologist*, 1964, *66*, 56.

BERSTEIN, JOANNE E. (Comp.). *Books to help children cope with separation and loss.* New York: R. R. Bowker, 1977.

BERRES, FRANCES B. The effects of varying amounts of motoric involvement on the learning of nonsense syllables by male culturally disadvantaged retarded readers. Unpublished doctoral dissertation, University of California at Los Angeles, 1967.

BERRES, FRANCES, & EYER, JOYCE T. John. In A. J. Harris (Ed.), *Casebook on reading disability.* New York: David McKay, 1970. Pp. 25–47.

BETTENCOURT, EDWARD M., *et al.* Effect of teacher enthusiasm on student on-task behavior and achievement. *American Educational Research Journal,* Fall 1983, *20,* 435–450.

BETTS, EMMETT A. *Foundations of reading instruction.* New York: American Book, 1946.

BETTS, EMMETT A. Capture reading motivation. *Reading Improvement,* 1976, *13,* 41–46.

BEYARD-TYLER, KAREN, & SULLIVAN, HOWARD. Adolescent reading preferences for type of theme and sex of character. *Reading Research Quarterly,* 1980, *16* (1), 104–120.

BIEMILLER, ANDREW. The development of the use of graphic and contextual information as children learn to read. *Reading Research Quarterly,* Fall 1970, *6,* 75–96.

BIEMILLER, ANDREW. Relationships between oral reading rates for letters, words, and sample text in the development of reading achievement. *Reading Research Quarterly,* 1977–1978, *13* (2), 223–253.

BIEMILLER, ANDREW. Changes in the use of graphic and contextual information as functions of passage difficulty and reading achievement level. *Journal of Reading Behavior,* Winter 1979, *11,* 308–318.

BIERLY, KEN. P.L. 94–142: Answers to some questions you're asking. *Instructor,* April 1978, *87,* 63–65, 72–73.

BINGHAM, ADELAIDE. Decoding ability does not make listening and reading comprehension equal. *Wisconsin State Reading Association Journal,* Winter 1983, *27,* 16–18.

BIRCH, HERBERT G., & BELMONT, LILLIAN. Auditory visual integration in normal and retarded readers. *American Journal of Orthopsychiatry,* October 1964, *34,* 852–861.

BIRCH, HERBERT G., & LEFFORD A. Intersensory development in children. *Monographs of the Society for Child Development,* 1963, *28,* 1–47.

BIRNBAUM, JUNE C. The reading and composing of selected fourth- and seventh-grade students. *Research in the Teaching of English,* October 1982, *16,* 241–260.

BISHOP, CAROL. Transfer of word and letter training in reading. Unpublished master's thesis, Cornell University, 1962.

BISHOP, DAVID M. Motivating adolescent readers via starter shelves in content area classes. In A. Ciani (Ed.), *Motivating reluctant readers.* Newark, DE: International Reading Association, 1981. Pp. 44–70.

BISKIN, DONALD S., HOSKISSON, KENNETH, & MODIN, MARJORIE. Prediction, reflection, and comprehension. *Elementary School Journal,* November 1976, *77,* 131–139.

BLACK, F. WILLIAM. Digit repetition in learning-disabled children. *Journal of Clinical Psychology,* March 1983, *39,* 263–267.

BLAIR, HEATHER. Canadian native peoples in adolescent literature. *Journal of Reading,* December 1982, *26,* 217–221.

BLANCHARD, JAY S., & MCNINCH, GEORGE H. Testing the decoding sufficiency hypothesis: A response to Fleisher, Jenkins, and Pany. *Reading Research Quarterly,* 1980, *15* (4), 559–564.

BLANK, MARION, & BRIDGER, WAGNER H. Deficiencies in verbal labelling in retarded readers. *American Journal of Orthopsychiatry,* 1966, *36,* 840–847.

BLANTON, LINDA P., SITKO, MERRILL C., & GILLEPSIE, PATRICIA H. Reading and the mildly retarded: Review of research and implications. In L. Mann & D. Sabatino (Eds.), *The third review of special education.* New York: Grune & Stratton, 1976. Pp. 143–162.

BLASS, ROSANNE J., JURENKA, NANCY A., & ZIRZOW, ELEANOR G. Showing children the communicative nature of reading. *The Reading Teacher,* May 1981, *34,* 926–931.

BLAU, HAROLD, & BLAU, HARRIET. A theory of learning to read. *The Reading Teacher,* November 1968, *22,* 126–129, 144.

BLAU, HAROLD, & BLAU, HARRIET. A theory of learning to read by modality blocking. In J. Arena (Ed.), *Successful programming: Many points of view.* Pittsburgh, PA: Association for Children with Learning Disabilities, 1969.

BLAU, HAROLD, & LOVELESS, EUGENE J. Specific hemispheric routing—TAK/V to teach spelling to dyslexics: VAK and VAKT challenged. *Journal of Learning Disabilities*, October 1982, *15*, 461–466.

BLIESMER, EMERY P. Informal teacher testing in reading. *The Reading Teacher*, December 1972, *26*, 262–272.

BLOMMERS, PAUL J., & LINDQUIST, E. F. Rate of comprehension of reading: Its measurement and its relationship to comprehension. *Journal of Educational Psychology*, November 1944, *34*, 449–473.

BLOOM, BENJAMIN S. (Ed.). *Taxonomy of educational objectives, Handbook I: Cognitive domain.* New York: David McKay, 1956.

BLOOM, BENJAMIN. *Human characteristics and school learning.* New York: McGraw-Hill, 1976.

BLOOM, BENJAMIN S. *All our children learning.* New York: McGraw-Hill, 1981.

BLOOMFIELD, LEONARD, & BARNHART, CLARENCE L. *Let's read: A linguistic approach.* Detroit: Wayne State University Press, 1961.

BLOSTEIN, FAY. *Invitations, celebrations: A handbook of ideas and techniques for promoting reading in junior and senior high schools.* Toronto: Ontario Library Association, 1980.

BOCKS, WILLIAM M. Non-promotion: A year to grow? *Educational Leadership*, February 1977, *34*, 379–383.

BODER, ELENA. Developmental dyslexia: A diagnostic approach based on three atypical reading-spelling patterns. *Developmental Medicine and Child Neurology*, 1973, *15*, 663–687.

BODER, ELENA, & JARRICO, SYLVIA. *The Boder Test of Reading-Spelling Patterns: A Diagnostic Screening Test for Subtypes of Reading Disability.* New York: Grune & Stratton, 1982.

BOND, GUY L. *Auditory and speech characteristics of poor readers.* Contributions to Education No. 657. New York: Teachers College, Columbia University, 1935.

BOND, GUY L., & DYKSTRA, ROBERT. The cooperative research program in first-grade reading instruction. *Reading Research Quarterly*, Summer 1967, *2*, 5–142.

BOND, GUY L., & TINKER, MILES A. *Reading difficulties: Their diagnosis and correction* (3rd ed.). New York: Appleton-Century-Crofts, 1973.

BOND, GUY L., TINKER, MILES A., & WASSON, BARBARA B. *Reading Difficulties: Their diagnosis and correction* (4th ed.). Englewood Cliffs, NJ: Prentice-Hall, 1979.

BOND, GUY L., TINKER, MILES A., WASSON, BARBARA B., & WASSON, JOHN B. *Reading difficulties: Their diagnosis and correction* (5th ed.). Englewood Cliffs, NJ: Prentice-Hall, 1984.

BONING, THOMAS, & BONING, RICHARD. I'd rather read than. . . . *The Reading Teacher*, 1957, *10*, 196–200.

BOODT, GLORIA M. Critical listeners become critical readers in remedial reading class. *The Reading Teacher*, January 1984, *37*, 390–394.

BOOMER, LYMAN W. Special education paraprofessionals: A guide for teachers. *Teaching Exceptional Children,* Summer 1980, *12*, 146–149.

BORKO, HILDA, SHAVELSON, RICHARD J., & STERN, PAULA. Teacher's decisions in the planning of reading instruction. *Reading Research Quarterly*, 1981, *16* (3), 449–466.

BORMUTH, JOHN R. Readability: A new approach. *Reading Research Quarterly*, Spring 1966, *1*, 79–132.

BORMUTH, JOHN R. The cloze readability procedure. In J. R. Bormuth (Ed.), *Readability in 1968.* Urbana, IL: National Council of Teachers of English, 1968. Pp. 40–47. (a)

BORMUTH, JOHN R. (Ed.). *Readability in 1968.* Urbana, IL: National Council of Teachers of English, 1968. (b)

BORMUTH, JOHN R. The cloze procedure: Literacy in the classroom. In W. D. Page (Ed.), *Help for the reading teacher: New directions in research.* Urbana, IL: National Conference on Research in English and ERIC/RCS, March 1975. Pp. 60–89. (a)

BORMUTH, JOHN R. Reading literacy: Its definition and assessment. In J. B. Carroll & J. S. Chall (Eds.), *Toward a literate society.* New York: McGraw-Hill, 1975. Pp. 61–100. (b)

BORMUTH, JOHN R. The anaphora: Its surface manifestations. Paper presented at the Annual Meeting of the American Educational Research Association, 1975. (c)

BORMUTH, JOHN R. Literacy is rising, but so is demand for literacy. In L. Reed & S. Ward (Eds.), *Basic skills: Issues and Choices, 1.* St. Louis: CEMREL, April 1982. Pp. 183–190.

BOS, CANDACE S. Getting past decoding: Assisted and repeating readings as remedial methods for learning disabled students. *Topics in Learning & Learning Disabilities*, January 1982, *1*, 51–57.

BOTEL, MORTON, & GRANOWSKY, ALVIN. A formula for measuring syntactic complexity. *Elementary English*, April 1972, *49*, 513–516.

BOUCHARD, LOUISA-MAY D. A comparative analysis of children's independent reading interests and the content of stories in selected basal reading texts; grades 4–6. Unpublished doctoral dissertation, Marquette University, 1971.

BOUGERE, MARGUERITE B. Vocabulary development in the primary grades. In J. Figurel (Ed.), *Forging ahead in reading*. Newark, DE: International Reading Association, 1968. Pp. 75–85. Also in A. J. Harris & E. Sipay (Eds.), *Readings on reading instruction* (2nd ed.). New York: Longman, 1972. Pp. 244–248.

BOYLE, THERESA. Learning disabilities: Miscellaneous information concerning the complex. *American Journal of EEG Technology*, December 1982, *22*, 187–201.

BOZZOMO, LAWRENCE E. Does class size matter? *The National Elementary Principal*, January 1978, *57*, 78–81.

BRADLEY, JOHN M. Evaluating reading achievement for placement in special education. *The Journal of Special Education*, Fall 1976, *10*, 237–245.

BRADLEY, JOHN M., ACHERSON, GARY, & AMES, WILBUR S. The reliability of the maze procedure. *Journal of Reading Behavior*, Fall 1978, *10*, 291–296.

BRADLEY, JOHN M., & AMES, WILBUR S. Readability parameters of basal readers. *Journal of Reading Behavior*, Summer 1977, *9*, 175–183.

BRADLEY, JOHN M., & AMES, WILBUR S. You can't judge a basal by the number on the cover. *Reading World*, March 1978, *17*, 175–183.

BRANSFORD, JOHN D., STEIN, BARRY S., & VYE, NANCY J. Helping students to learn how to learn from written texts. In M. Singer (Ed.), *Competent reader, disabled reader: Research and application*. Hillsdale, NJ: LEA, 1982. Pp. 141–150.

BRANSFORD, JOHN D., VYE, NANCY J., & STEIN, BARRY S. A comparison of successful and less successful learners: Can we enhance comprehension and mastery skills? In J. Flood (Ed.), *Promoting reading comprehension*. Newark, DE: International Reading Association, 1984. Pp. 216–231.

BRASE, D. A., & LOH, H. H. Possible role of 5-hydroxytryptamine in minimal brain dysfunction. *Life Sciences*, 1975, *16* (7), 1005–1016.

BRAUN, CARL. Teacher expectations: Sociopsychological dynamics. *Review of Educational Research*, Spring 1976, *46*, 185–213.

BRAUN, CARL, NEILSON, ALLAN R., & DYKSTRA, ROBERT. Teacher expectations: Prime mover or inhibitor? In Brother L. Courtney (Ed.), *Reading interaction: The teacher, the pupil, the materials*. Newark, DE: International Reading Association, 1976. Pp. 40–48.

BRAUSE, RITA S., & MAYHER, JOHN S. Teachers, students, and classroom organization. *Research on the Teaching of English*, May 1982, *16*, 131–148.

BRECHT, RICHARD D. Testing format and instructional level with the informal reading inventory. *The Reading Teacher*, October 1977, *31*, 57–59.

BREEN, L. C. Vocabulary development by teaching prefixes, suffixes and root derivations. *The Reading Teacher*, November 1960, *14*, 93–97.

BRENNER, ARNOLD. The effects of megadoses of selected B complex vitamins on children with hyperkinesis: Controlled studies with long-term follow-up. *Journal of Learning Disabilities*, May 1982, *15*, 258–264.

BRENT, DEBORAH E., & ROUTH, DONALD K. Response cost and impulsive word recognition errors in reading-disabled children. *Journal of Abnormal Child Psychology*, June 1978, *6*, 211–219.

BRESCIA, SHELAGH M., & BRAUN, CARL. Associative verbal encoding and sight vocabulary acquisition and retention. *Journal of Reading Behavior*, Fall 1977, *9*, 259–267.

BRICKLIN, PATRICIA M. Counseling parents with learning disabilities. *The Reading Teacher*, January 1970, *23*, 331–338.

BRIDGE, CONNIE A., & WINOGRAD, PETER N. Readers' awareness of cohesive relationships during cloze comprehension. *Journal of Reading Behavior*, 1982, *14* (3), 299–312.

BRIDGES, ETHEL B. Using children's choices of and reactions to poetry as determinants in enriching literary experience in the middle grades. *Dissertation Abstracts International*, 1967, *27*, 3749A.

BRIDGES, L. H. Speed versus comprehension in elementary reading. *Journal of Educational Psychology*, 1941, *32*, 314–320.

BRITTON, BRUCE K. *et al.* Effects of text structure on use of cognitive capacity during reading. *Journal of Educational Psychology*, February 1982, *74* (1), 51–61.

BRITTON, GWYNETH E., & LUMPKIN, MARGARET C. Readability labeling: An answer to the middle grade slump. *Reading Improvement*, Fall 1978, *15*, 162–169.

BRITTON, GWYNETH, LUMPKIN, MARGARET, & BRITTON, ESTHER. The battle to imprint citizens for the 21st century. *The Reading Teacher*, April 1984, *37*, 724–733.

BROD, NATHAN, & HAMILTON, DAVID. Binocularity and reading. *Journal of Learning Disabilities*, November 1973, *6*, 574–576.

BRONNER, AUGUSTA F. *Psychology of special abilities and disabilities.* Boston: Little, Brown, 1917.

BROOKS, R. A. An investigation of the relationship between reading interest and comprehension, 1972. ED 067 625.

BROPHY, JERE E. Teacher behavior and student learning. *Educational Leadership*, October 1979, *37*, 33–38. (a)

BROPHY, JERE E. Teacher behavior and its effects. *Journal of Educational Psychology*, December 1979, *71*, 733–750. (b)

BROPHY, JERE. Teacher praise: A functional analysis. *Review of Educational Research*, Spring 1981, *51*, 5–32.

BROPHY, JERE E. Research on the self-fulfilling prophecy and teacher expectations. *Journal of Educational Psychology*, 1983, *75* (6), 631–661.

BROPHY, JERE E., & EVERTSON, CAROLYN M. *Student characteristics and teaching.* New York: Longman, 1981.

BROPHY, JERE E., & PUTNAM, JOYCE G. Classroom management in the elementary grades. In D. Duke (Ed.), *Classroom management.* 75th Yearbook of the National Society for the Study of Education, Part II. Chicago: University of Chicago Press, 1979. Pp. 182–216.

BROWN, ANN L., CAMPIONE, JOSEPH C., & DAY, JEANNE D. Learning to learn: On training students to learn from texts. *Educational Researcher*, February 1981, *10*, 14–21. Also in A. J. Harris & E. Sipay (Eds.), *Readings on reading instruction* (3rd ed.). New York: Longman, 1984. Pp. 317–326.

BROWN, ANN L., & DAY, JEANNE D. Macrorules for summarizing text: The development of expertise. Technical Report No. 270. Champaign, IL: Center for the Study of Reading, University of Illinois, January 1983.

BROWN, ANN L., & PALINSCAR, ANNEMARIE S. Inducing strategic learning from texts by means of informed, self-control training. Technical Report No. 262. Champaign, IL: Center for the Study of Reading, University of Illinois, September 1982.

BROWN, ANN L., *et al.* Learning, remembering, and understanding. Technical Report No. 244. Champaign, IL: Center for the Study of Reading, University of Illinois, 1982.

BROWN, ERIC R. A theory of reading. *Journal of Communication Disorders*, November 1981, *14*, 443–466.

BROWN, HARRY J. Reaction and movement time as related to oral and silent reading in disabled readers. Unpublished doctoral dissertation, University of Minnesota, 1970.

BROWN, JAMES I. Techniques for increasing reading rate. In J. Merritt (Ed.), *New horizons in reading.* Newark, DE: International Reading Association, 1976. Pp. 158–164. Also in A. J. Harris & E. Sipay (Eds.), *Readings on reading instruction* (3rd ed.). New York: Longman, 1984. Pp. 397–401.

BROWN, LINDA L., & SHERBENOU, RITA J. A comparison of teacher perceptions of student reading ability, reading performance, and classroom behavior. *The Reading Teacher*, February 1981, *34*, 557–560.

BROWN, RONALD T. A developmental analysis of visual and auditory sustained attention and reflection-impulsivity in hyperactive and normal children. *Journal of Learning Disabilities*, December 1982, *15*, 614–618.

BROWNLEE, PHYLISS P. Suggestopedia in the classroom. *Academic Therapy,* March 1982, *17,* 407–414.

BRUCE, BERTRAM, RUBIN, ANDEE, & STARR, KATHLEEN. Why readability formulas fail. Reading Education Report No. 28. Champaign, IL: Center for the Study of Reading, University of Illinois, August 1981.

BRUINSMA, ROBERT. Should lip movements and subvocalization during silent reading be directly remediated? *The Reading Teacher,* December 1980, *34,* 293–295.

BRUMBACK, ROGER A., & STATON, R. DENNIS. Learning disability and childhood depression. *American Journal of Orthopsychiatry,* April 1983, *53,* 269–281.

BRUMBAUGH, F. Reading expectancy. *Elementary English Review,* 1940, *17,* 153–155.

BRUTON, RONALD W. Individualizing a basal reader. *The Reading Teacher,* October 1972, *26,* 59–63.

BRYAN, TANIS H. Communication competence in reading and learning disabilities. *Bulletin of the Orton Society,* 1979, *29,* 172–188.

BRYANT, N. DALE. Modifying instruction to minimize the effects of learning disabilities. *The Forum,* Fall 1980, *6,* 19–20.

BRYANT, N. DALE. A summary of directions for the "LD-Efficient" teaching manual. New York: Research Institute for the Study of Learning Disabilities, Columbia University, 1981.

BRYEN, DIANE N. Speech-sound discrimination ability on linguistically unbiased tests. *Exceptional Children,* January 1976, *42,* 195–201.

BUCKLEY, ROBERT E. The biobasis for distraction and dyslexia. *Academic Therapy,* January 1981, *16,* 289–301.

BUNDA, MARY ANNE, & SANDERS, JAMES R. (Eds.). *Practices and problems in competency-based measurement.* Washington, DC: National Council of Measurement in Education, 1979.

BURKE, SUZZANE M., PFLAUM, SUSANNA W., & KNAFLE, JUNE D. The influence of black English on diagnosis of reading in learning disabled and normal readers. *Journal of Learning Disabilities,* January 1982, *15,* 19–22.

BURMEISTER, LOU E. Usefulness of phonics generalizations. *The Reading Teacher,* January 1968, *21,* 349–356.

BURMEISTER, LOU E. Contents of a phonics program based on particularly useful generalizations. In N. B. Smith (Ed.), *Reading methods and teacher improvement.* Newark, DE: International Reading Association, 1971. Pp. 27–39.

BURMEISTER, LOU E. A chart for the new Spache Formula. *The Reading Teacher,* January 1976, *29,* 384–385.

BURNS, EDWARD. Bivariate normal distribution estimates of the prevalence of reading disabilities. *Journal of Special Education,* Winter 1982, *16,* 431–437. (a)

BURNS, EDWARD. Linear regression and simplified reading expectancy formulas. *Reading Research Quarterly,* 1982, *17* (3), 446–453. (b)

BURNS, EDWARD. The use and interpretation of standardized grade equivalents. *Journal of Learning Disabilities,* January 1982, *15,* 17–18. (c)

BURNS, PAUL C., & ROE, BETTY D. *Reading activities for today's elementary schools.* Chicago: Rand McNally, 1979.

BUROS, OSCAR K. (Ed.). *Reading: Tests and reviews.* New Brunswick, NJ: Gryphon Press, 1968.

BUROS, OSCAR K. (Ed.). *The seventh mental measurements yearbook,* Vols. I & II. Highland Park, NJ: Gryphon Press, 1972.

BUROS, OSCAR K. (Ed.). *Reading Tests and Reviews II.* Highland Park, NJ: Gryphon Press, 1975.

BUROS, OSCAR K. (Ed.). *The eighth mental measurements yearbook,* Vols. I & II. Highland Park, NJ: Gryphon Press, 1978.

BURRES, LEE, & JENKINSON, EDWARD B. *The student's right to know.* Urbana, IL: NCTE, 1982.

BUSWELL, GUY T. *Fundamental reading habits: A study of their development.* Supplementary Educational Monographs No. 21. Chicago: University of Chicago Press, 1922.

BUSWELL, GUY T. *Remedial reading at the college and adult levels.* Supplementary Educational Monographs No. 50. Chicago: University of Chicago Press, 1939.

BUSWELL, GUY T. Relationship between rate of thinking and rate of reading. *School Review,* September 1951, *49,* 339–346.

BUTLER, CYNTHIA. When the pleasurable is measurable: Teachers reading aloud. *Language Arts,* November/December 1980, *57,* 882–885.

BYERS, J. L., & EVANS, T. E. Using a lens-model analysis to identify factors in teacher judgment. Research Series No. 73. East Lansing, MI: Institute for Research on Teaching, Michigan State University, 1980.

BYRNE, BRIAN. Reading disability, linguistic access and short-term memory: Comments prompted by Jorm's review of developmental dyslexia. *Australian Journal of Psychology*, April 1981, *33*, 83–95.

CAHN, STEVEN M. Restoring the house of intellect. *American Educator*, Fall 1981, *5*, 12–13, 37–38.

CALDER, C. R., & ZALATIMO, S. D. Improving children's ability to follow directions. *The Reading Teacher*, December 1970, *24*, 227–231.

CALFEE, ROBERT C. Assessment of independent reading skills: Basic research and practical applications. In A. Reber & D. Scarborough (Eds.), *Toward a psychology of reading*. Hillsdale, NJ: LEA, 1977. Pp. 289–323.

CALFEE, ROBERT. Cognitive models of reading: Implications for assessment and treatment of reading disability. In R. Malatesha & P. Aaron (Eds.), *Reading disorders: Varieties and treatments*. New York: Academic Press, 1982. Pp. 151–176.

CALFEE, ROBERT, & BROWN, ROGER. Grouping students for instruction. In D. Duke (Ed.), *Classroom management*. 78th Yearbook of the National Society for the Study of Education, Part II. Chicago: University of Chicago Press, 1979. Pp. 144–181.

CALFEE, ROBERT C., & CURLEY, ROBERT. Structure of prose in the content areas. In J. Flood (Ed.), *Understanding reading comprehension*. Newark, DE: International Reading Association, 1984. Pp. 161–180.

CALFEE, ROBERT C., & DRUM, PRISCILLA A. Learning to read: Theory, research, and practice. *Curriculum Inquiry*, Fall 1978, 183–249.

CALFEE, ROBERT C., & DRUM, PRISCILLA A. (Eds.). *Teaching reading in compensatory classes*. Newark, DE: International Reading Association, 1979.

CALFEE, ROBERT C., & PIONTKOWSKI, DOROTHY C. The reading diary: Acquisition of decoding. *Reading Research Quarterly*, 1981, *16*, 346–373.

CALFEE, ROBERT C., & SPECTOR, JANET E. Separable processes in reading. In F. Pirozollo & M. Wittrock (Eds.), *Neuropsychological and cognitive processes in reading*. New York: Academic Press, 1981. Pp. 3–29.

CANNEY, GEORGE F. Making games more relevant for reading. *The Reading Teacher*, October 1978, *32*, 10–14.

CANNEY, GEORGE, & SCHREINER, ROBERT. A study of the effectiveness of selected syllabication rules and phonogram patterns for word attack. *Reading Research Quarterly*, 1976–1977, *12* (2), 102–124.

CANNING, PATRICIA M., ORR, R. ROBERT, & ROURKE, BYRON P. Sex differences in the perceptual, visual-motor, linguistic and concept-formation abilities of retarded readers. *Journal of Learning Disabilities*, December 1980, *13*, 563–567.

CARBO, MARIE. Making books talk to children. *The Reading Teacher*, November 1981, *35*, 186–189.

CARBO, MARIE. Research in reading and learning style: Implications for exceptional children. *Exceptional Children*, April 1983, *49*, 486–494.

CARLISLE, JOANNE F. Components of training in reading comprehension for middle school students. *Annals of Dyslexia*, 1983, *33*, 187–202.

CARLTON, GLEN, HUMMER, TERRY, & RAINEY, DAVID. Teaching learning disabled children to help themselves. *The Directive Teacher*, Winter/Spring 1984, *6*, 8–9.

CARNEGIE CORPORATION OF NEW YORK. Making television better for children: The challenge of ACT. *Carnegie Quarterly*, Spring 1977, *25*, 1–3.

CARNINE, DOUGLAS W. Direct instruction: A bottom up skills approach to elementary instruction. In L. Reed & S. Ward (Eds.), *Basic skills: Issues and choices: Approaches to basic skills and instruction 2*. St. Louis: CEMREL, April 1982. Pp. 135–146.

CARNINE, DOUGLAS, KAMEENUI, EDWARD J., & COYLE, GAYLE. Utilization of contextual information in determining the meaning of unfamiliar words. *Reading Research Quarterly*, Winter 1984, *19*, 188–204.

CARNINE, DOUGLAS, *et al.* Effects of facilitative questions and practice on intermediate students' understanding of character motives. *Journal of Reading Behavior*, 1982, *14* (2), 179–190.

CARNINE, LINDA, CARNINE, DOUGLAS, & GERSTEN, RUSSELL. Analysis of oral reading errors made by economically disadvantaged students taught with a synethetic-phonics approach. *Reading Research Quarterly*, Spring 1984, *17*, 343–356.

CARPENTER, DALE. Spelling error profiles of able and disabled readers. *Journal of Learning Disabilities*, February 1983, *16*, 102–104.

CARPENTER, PATRICIA A., & JUST, MARCEL A. Cognitive processes in reading: Models based on readers' eye fixations. In A. Lesgold & C. Perfetti (Eds.), *Interactive processes in reading*. Hillsdale, NJ: LEA, 1981. Pp. 177–213.

CARPENTER, PATRICIA A., & JUST, MARCEL A. What your eyes do while your mind is reading. In K. Rayner (Ed.), *Eye movements in reading: Perceptual and language processes*. New York: Academic Press, 1983. Pp. 275–307.

CARR, EILEEN M., DEWITZ, PETER, & PATBERG, JUDYTHE P. The effect of inference training on children's comprehension of expository text. *Journal of Reading Behavior*, 1983, *15* (3), 1–18.

CARR, KATHRYN. The importance of inference skills in the primary grades. *The Reading Teacher*, February 1983, *36*, 518–522.

CARR, THOMAS H. Building theories of reading ability: On the relationship between individual differences in cognitive skills and reading comprehension. *Cognition*, February 1981, *9*, 73–114.

CARROLL, BONNIE, & DRUM, PRISCILLA A. The effect of context clue type and variation in content on the comprehension of unknown words. In J. Niles & L. A. Harris (Eds.), *New inquiries in reading: Research and instruction*. Rochester, NY: National Reading Conference, 1982. Pp. 89–93.

CARROLL, H. C. M. The remedial teaching of reading: An evaluation. *Remedial Education*, February 1972, *7*, 10–15.

CARROLL, JOHN B. Defining language comprehension: Some speculations. In J. B. Carroll & R. O. Freedle (Eds.), *Language comprehension and the acquisition of knowledge*. Washington, DC: Winston, 1972. Pp. 1–30. (a)

CARROLL, JOHN B. *Review of the Illinois Test of Psycholinguistic Abilities*. In O. K. Buros (Ed.), *Seventh mental measurements yearbook*, Vol. I. Highland Park, NJ: Gryphon Press, 1972. Pp. 819–823. (b)

CARROLL, JOHN B. The nature of the reading process. In H. Singer & R. B. Ruddell (Eds.), *Theoretical models and processes of reading* (2nd ed.). Newark, DE: International Reading Association, 1976. Pp. 8–18.

CARROLL, JOHN B. Developmental parameters in reading comprehension. In J. T. Guthrie (Ed.), *Cognition, curriculum and comprehension*. Newark, DE: International Reading Association, 1977. Pp. 1–15.

CARROLL, JOHN B., & CHALL, JEANNE S. (Eds.). *Toward a literate society*. New York: McGraw-Hill, 1975.

CARROLL, JOHN B., DAVIES, PETER, & RICHMAN, BARRY. *American Heritage word frequency book*. Boston: Houghton Mifflin, 1971.

CARROLL, JOHN B., & WALTON, MARSHA. Has the reel reeding prablum bin lade bear? In L. Resnick & P. Weaver (Eds.), *Theory and practice in early reading*, Vol. I. Hillsdale, NJ: LEA, 1979. Pp. 317–354.

CARTER, CANDY (Chair). *Non-native and nonstandard dialect students: Classroom practice in teaching English, 1982–3*. Urbana, IL: National Council of Teachers of English, 1982.

CARVER, RONALD P. Measuring prose difficulty using the Rauding Scale. *Reading Research Quarterly*, 1975–1976, *11*, 660–684.

CARVER, RONALD P. Optimal rate of reading prose. *Reading Research Quarterly*, 1982, *18* (1), 56–88.

CARVER, RONALD P. Is reading rate constant or flexible? *Reading Research Quarterly*, Winter 1983, *18*, 190–215.

CARVER, RONALD P. Reading theory prediction of amount comprehended under different purposes and speed reading conditions. *Reading Research Quarterly*, Winter 1984, *19*, 205–218.

CARVER, RONALD P., & HOFFMAN, JAMES V. The effect of practice through repeated reading in gains in reading ability using a computer-based instructional system. *Reading Research Quarterly,* 1981, *16* (3), 374–390.

CASON, ELOISE B. *Mechanical methods for increasing the speed of reading.* Contributions to Education No. 878. New York: Teachers College, Columbia University, 1943.

CASSIDY, JACK. Good news about American education. *The Reading Teacher,* December 1978, *32,* 294–296 (a)

CASSIDY, JACK. High school graduation: Exit competencies? *Journal of Reading,* February 1978, *21,* 398–402. (b)

CASSIDY, JACK. Reading mathematics: As easy as ABC or RSTUV. *Reading,* April 1984, *1,* 11.

CASWELL, HOLLIS L. Non-promotion in the elementary school. *Elementary School Journal,* 1933, *33,* 644–647.

CATTELL, J. M. Ueber die Zeit der Erkennung und Benennung von Schriftzeichen, Bildern, und Farben. *Philosophische Studien,* 1885, *2,* 635–650.

CAZDEN, COURTNEY B. *Child language and education.* New York: Holt, Rinehart and Winston, 1972.

CAZDEN, COURTNEY B. Contexts for literacy: In the mind and in the classroom. *Journal of Reading Behavior,* 1982, *14* (4), 413–427.

CECI, STEPHEN J. Extracting meaning from stimuli: Automatic and purposive processing of the language-based learning disabled. *Topics in Learning & Learning Disabilities,* July 1982, *2,* 46–53.

CEPRANO, MARIA A. Context versus isolation methods of word instruction: Efficiency assessed by paralleling assessment modes. *Journal of Reading Behavior,* Winter 1981, *13,* 381–390. (a)

CEPRANO, MARIA A. A review of selected research on methods of teaching sight words. *The Reading Teacher,* December 1981, *35,* 314–322. (b)

CHABE, ALEXANDER M. The Russian reading program: A re-examination. Paper presented at the New York State Reading Association Conference, Kiamisha Lake, NY, November 1983.

CHABOT, ROBERT J., PETROS, THOMAS V., & MCCORD, GARY. Developmental and reading ability differences in accessing information from semantic memory. *Journal of Experimental Child Psychology,* February 1983, *35,* 128–142.

CHALL, JEANNE S. Ask him to try on the book for fit. *The Reading Teacher,* December 1953, *7,* 83–88.

CHALL, JEANNE S. *Learning to read: The great debate: An inquiry into the science, art, and ideology of old and new methods of teaching children to read 1910–1965.* New York: McGraw-Hill, 1967.

CHALL, JEANNE S. *Reading 1967–1977: A decade of change and promise.* Bloomington, IN: Phi Beta Kappa Educational Foundation, 1977.

CHALL, JEANNE S. *Learning to read: The great debate* (Updated ed.). New York: McGraw-Hill, 1983. (a)

CHALL, JEANNE S. Literacy: Trends and explanation. *Educational Researcher,* November 1983, *12,* 3–8. (b)

CHALL, JEANNE S. *Stages of reading development.* New York: McGraw-Hill, 1983. (c)

CHALL, JEANNE S., & CONRAD, SUE S. Resources and their use for reading instruction. In A. Purves & O. Niles (Eds.), *Becoming readers in a complex society.* 83rd Yearbook of the National Society for the Study of Education, Part I. Chicago: University of Chicago Press, 1984. Pp. 209–232.

CHALL, JEANNE S., ROSWELL, FLORENCE C., & BLUMENTHAL, SUSAN H. Auditory blending ability: A factor in success in beginning reading. *The Reading Teacher,* 1963, *17,* 113–118.

CHANG, FREDERICK R. Mental processes in reading. A methodological review. *Reading Research Quarterly,* Winter 1983, *18,* 216–230.

CHANSKY, NORMAN M. Age, IQ, and improvement in reading. *Journal of Educational Research,* 1963, *56,* 439.

CHAPMAN, L. JOHN. *Reading development and cohesion.* Exeter, NH: Heinemann, 1983.

CHAPMAN, L. JOHN. Comprehending and the teacher of reading. In J. Flood (Ed.), *Promoting reading comprehension.* Newark, DE: International Reading Association, 1984. Pp. 261–272.

CHAPMAN, ROBERT B. Differential interactions between classroom teachers and learning disordered children. Unpublished doctoral dissertation, University of Texas at Austin, 1975.

CHARRY, LAURENCE B. Controlling readability factors of teacher-made materials. In B. S. Schulwitz (Ed.), *Teachers, tangibles, and techniques: Comprehension of content in reading.* Newark, DE: International Reading Association, 1975. Pp. 93–99.

CHASE, CLINTON I. Review of the *Illinois Test of Psycholinguistic Abilities.* In O. K. Buros (Ed.), *Seventh mental measurements yearbook,* Vol. I. Highland Park, NJ: Gryphon Press, 1972. Pp. 823–825.

CHEEK, EARL H., & CHEEK, MARTHA C. Organizational patterns: Untapped resources for better reading. *Reading World,* May 1983, *22,* 278–283.

CHERRY, ROCHELLE S., & KRUGER, BARBARA. Selective auditory attention abilities of learning disabled and normal achieving children. *Journal of Learning Disabilities,* April 1983, *16,* 202–205.

CHESTER, ROBERT D. The psychology of reading. *The Journal of Educational Research,* May/June, 1974, *67,* 403–411.

CHEYNEY, WENDY, & STRICHART, STEPHEN S. A learning stations model for the resource room. *Academic Therapy,* January 1981, *16,* 271–279.

CHILDS, SALLY B., & CHILDS, RALPH DE S. *Sound spelling.* Cambridge, MA: Educators Publishing Service, 1971.

CHING, DORIS C. *Reading and the bilingual child.* Newark, DE: International Reading Association, 1976.

CHOMSKY, CAROL. Write first, read later. *Childhood Education,* March 1971, *47,* 296–299.

CHOMSKY, CAROL. When you still can't read in third grade: After decoding, what? In S. J. Samuels (Ed.), *What research has to say about reading instruction.* Newark, DE: International Reading Association, 1978. Pp. 13–30.

CHOMSKY, CAROL. Approaching reading through invented spelling. In L. Resnick & P. Weaver (Eds.), *Theory and practice of early reading,* Vol. 2. Hillsdale, NJ: LEA, 1979. Pp. 43–65. (a)

CHOMSKY, CAROL. Language and reading. In R. Shafer (Ed.), *Applied linguistics and reading..* Newark, DE: International Reading Association, 1979. Pp. 112–128. (b)

CHOMSKY, CAROL. Linguistic consciousness-raising in children. *Language Arts,* May 1981, *58,* 607–612.

CHRISTENBURG, LEILA, & KELLY, PATRICIA P. *Questions: A path to critical thinking.* Urbana, IL: ERIC/RCS & NCTE, 1983.

CHRISTIE, JAMES F. The effects of grade level and reading ability on children's miscue patterns. *Journal of Educational Research,* July/August 1981, *74,* 419–423.

CHRISTIE, JAMES F., & ALONSO, PATRICIA A. Effects of passage difficulty on primary-grade children's oral reading error patterns. *Educational Research Quarterly,* Spring 1980, *5,* 41–49.

CIANCIOLO, PATRICIA. Yesterday comes alive for readers of historical fiction. *Language Arts,* April 1981, *58,* 452–462.

CIANCIOLO, PATRICIA J. Responding to literature as a work of art—An aesthetic literary experience. *Language Arts,* March 1982, *59,* 259–264, 295.

CIANI, ALFRED J. (Ed.). *Motivating reluctant readers.* Newark, DE: International Reading Association, 1981.

CITRON, CHRISTIANE H. Competency testing: Emerging principles. *Educational Measurement: Issues and Practice,* Winter 1982, *1,* 10–11.

CITRON, CHRISTIANE H. Courts provide insight on content validity requirements. *Educational Measurement: Issues and Practice,* Winter 1983, *2,* 6–7.

CLARK, CHARLES H., Assessing free recall. *The Reading Teacher,* January 1982, *35,* 434–439.

CLARK, CHARLES H., & BEAN, THOMAS W. Improving advance organizer research: Persistent problems and future decisions. *Reading World,* October 1982, *22,* 2–10.

CLARK, MARGARET M. *Reading difficulties in schools.* First edition, Baltimore: Penguin Books, 1970. Second edition, Exeter, NH: Heinemann, 1979.

CLAY, MARIE M. *What did I write?* Exeter, NH: Heinemann, 1975.

CLAY, MARIE M. Early childhood and cultural diversity in New Zealand. *The Reading Teacher,* January 1976, *29,* 333–342.

CLAY, MARIE M. *Reading—The patterning of complex behavior* (2nd ed.). Exeter, NH: Heinemann, 1979.

CLAY, MARIE M. Learning and teaching writing: A developmental perspective. *Language Arts*, January 1982, *59*, 65–70.

CLAY, MARIE M., & IMLACH, ROBERT H. Juncture, pitch, and stress as reading behavior variables. *Journal of Verbal Learning and Verbal Behavior*, April 1971, *10*, 133–139.

Clearinghouse for Applied Performance Testing Newsletter. Minimum competency testing: Procedures, impact, and legal issues. November 1977, *3*, 1–3.

CLELAND, CRAIG J. Learning to read: Piagetian perspectives for instruction. *Reading World*, March 1981, *20*, 223–224.

CLELAND, DONALD L. An experimental study of tachistoscopic training as it relates to speed and comprehension in reading. Unpublished doctoral dissertation, University of Pittsburgh, 1950.

CLELAND, DONALD L. Seeing and reading. *American Journal of Optometry*, 1953, *80*, 467–481.

CLEMENTS, SAM D. *Minimal brain dysfunction in children: Terminology and identification.* National Institute of Neurological Diseases, Monograph No. 3, Public Health Service Publications No. 1415, 1966. Washington, DC: Governmental Printing Office, 1966.

CLEMENTS, SAM D., & BARNES, STEPHEN M. The three R's and central processing training. *Academic Therapy*, May 1978, *13*, 535–547.

CLEWELL, SUZANNE F., & CLIFFTON, ANNE M. Examining your textbook for comprehensibility. *Journal of Reading*, December 1983, *27*, 219–224.

CLEWELL, SUZANNE F., & HAIDEMENOS, JULIE. Organizational strategies to increase comprehension. *Reading World*, May 1983, *22*, 314–321.

CLOER, CARL T., JR. Subvocalization—asset, liability, or both? In P. D. Pearson (Ed.), *Reading: Theory, research, and practice.* Clemson, SC: National Reading Conference, 1977. Pp. 209–213.

CLYMER, THEODORE. The utility of phonic generalizations in the primary grades. *The Reading Teacher*, January 1963, *16*, 252–258.

CLYMER, THEODORE. Research in corrective reading: Findings, problems and observations. In M. S. Johnson & R. A. Kress (Eds.), *Corrective reading in the elementary classroom.* Newark, DE: International Reading Association, 1967. Pp. 1–10.

COGAR, ROY L. Comparative difficulty of beginning reading vocabulary: Set III (word length). Unpublished doctoral dissertation, University of Pittsburgh, 1974.

COHEN, ALICE, & GLASS, GERALD G. Lateral dominance and reading ability. *The Reading Teacher*, January 1968, *21*, 343–348.

COHEN, ELIZABETH G., INTILI, JO-ANN K., & ROBBINS, SUSAN H. Teachers and reading specialists: Cooperation or isolation? *The Reading Teacher*, December 1978, *32*, 281–287.

COHEN, GILLIAN. Theoretical interpretations of lateral asymmetries. In J. Beaumont (Ed.), *Divided visual field studies of cerebral organization.* New York: Academic Press, 1982. Pp. 87–111.

COHEN, JUDITH H. *Handbook of resource room teaching.* Rockville, MD: Aspen, 1982.

COHEN, LIBBY. Motivating the reluctant reader: An annotated bibliography. *New England Reading Association Journal*, 1981, *16* (3), 48–50.

COHEN, PETER A., KULIK, JAMES A., & KULIK, CHEN-LIN. Educational outcomes of tutoring: A meta-analysis of findings. *American Educational Research Journal*, Summer 1982, *19*, 237–248.

COHEN, S. ALAN, & STOVER, GEORGIA. Effects of teaching sixth-grade students to modify format variables of math word problems. *Reading Research Quarterly*, 1981, *16* (2), 175–200.

COHEN, SANDRA B., ALBERTO, PAUL A., & TROUTMAN, ANN. Selecting and developing educational materials: An inquiry model. *Teaching Exceptional Children*, Fall 1979, *12*, 7–11.

COHN, MARVIN, & D'ALLESSANDRO, CYNTHIA. When is a decoding error not a decoding error? *The Reading Teacher*, December 1978, *32*, 341–344.

COHN, MARVIN, & STRICKLER, GEORGE. Reversal errors in strong, average, and weak letter namers. *Journal of Learning Disabilities*, October 1979, *12*, 533–537.

COLARUSSO, RONALD P., & GILL, SALLY. Selecting a test of visual perception. *Academic Therapy*, Winter 1975–76, *11*, 157–166.

COLBERT, PAT, *et al.* Learning disabilities as a symptom of depression in children. *Journal of Learning Disabilities*, June/July 1982, *15*, 333–336.

COLBURN, EVANGELINE. Advice for stimulating reading interests. *Elementary School Journal*, 1944, *44*, 539–541.

COLES, GERALD S. The learning-disabilities test battery: Empirical and social issues. *Harvard Educational Review*, August 1978, *48*, 313–340.

COLLINS, ALLAN, & HAVILAND, SUSAN E. Children's reading problems. Reading Education Report No. 8. Champaign, IL: Center for the Study of Reading, University of Illinois, June 1979.

COLLINS, ALLAN, & SMITH, EDWARD E. Teaching the process of reading comprehension. Technical Report No. 182. Champaign, IL: Center for the Study of Reading, University of Illinois, September 1982.

COLWELL, CLYDE, & HELFELDT, JOHN. The paragraph as a semantic unit: Theory and practice. *Reading World*, May 1983, *22*, 332–345.

COMPTON, CAROLYN. *A guide to 75 tests for special education*. Belmont, CA: Fearon, 1984.

CONAWAY, LARRY E. Setting standards in competency-based education: Some current practices and concerns. In M. Bunda & J. Sanders (Eds.), *Practices and problems in competency-based measurement*. Washington, DC: National Council of Measurement in Education, 1979. Pp. 72–88.

CONE, THOMAS E., & WILSON, LONNY R. Quantifying a severe discrepancy: A critical analysis. *Learning Disabilities Quarterly*, Fall 1981, *4*, 359–371.

CONLEY, MILLICENT. Increasing students' reading achievement via teacher inservice education. *The Reading Teacher*, April 1983, *36*, 804–808.

CONNERS, C. KEITH. *Food additives and hyperactive children*. New York: Plenum Press, 1980.

CONNOLLY, CHRISTOPHER. Social and emotional factors in learning disabilities. In H. R. Myklebust (Ed.), *Progress in learning disabilities*, Vol. II. New York: Grune & Stratton, 1971. Pp. 151–178.

COOK, WANDA D. *Adult literacy education in the United States*. Newark: DE: International Reading Association, 1977.

COOPER, J. LOUIS. The effect of adjustment of basal reading materials on reading achievement. Unpublished doctoral dissertation, Boston University, 1952.

COPELAND, WILLIS D. Teaching-learning behaviors and the demands of the classroom environment. *Elementary School Journal*, March 1980, *80*, 162–177.

COPPERMAN, PAUL. *The literacy hoax: The decline of reading, writing, and learning in the public schools and what we can do about it*. New York: William Morrow, 1978.

COPPERMAN, PAUL. The achievement decline of the 1970's. *Phi Delta Kappan*, June 1979, *60*, 736–739.

COPPLE, CAROL E. Effects of three variables on the performance of middle-class and lower-class children in discriminating similar letters in words. *Journal of Educational Research*, February 1975, *68*, 226–229.

CORBETT, EDWARD P. J. A literal view of literacy. In J. Raymond (Ed.), *Literacy as a human problem*. University, AL: University of Alabama Press, 1982. Pp. 137–153.

CORDEIRO, PATRICIA, GIACOBBE, MARY ELLEN, & CAZDEN, COURTNEY. Apostrophes, quotation marks, and periods: Learning punctuation in first grade. *Language Arts*, March 1983, *60*, 323–332.

CORDTS, ANNA D. And it's called phonics. *Elementary English*, 1955, *32*, 376–378.

CORMAN, CHERYL. Bibliotherapy—Insight for the learning handicapped. *Language Arts*, October 1975, *52*, 935–937.

CORNELIUS, PAULA L., & SEMMEL, MELVYN I. Effects of summer instruction on reading achievement of learning disabled students. *Journal of Learning Disabilities*, August/September 1982, *15*, 409–413.

CORNING, WILLIAM C., STEFFY, RICHARD A., & CHAPRIN, IAN C. EEG slow frequency and WISC-R correlates. *Journal of Abnormal Child Psychology*, December 1982, *10*, 511–530.

COTT, ALLAN. A reply. *Academic Therapy*, November 1977, *13*, 161–171.

COTTERELL, GILL. A case of severe learning disability. *Remedial Education*, February 1972, *7*, 5–9.

COURTNAGE, LEE. A survey of state policies on use of medication in schools. *Exceptional Children*, September 1982, *49*, 75–77.

COWAN, WILLIAM P. Remedial reading in secondary schools: Three-fourths of a century. In H. A. Robinson (Ed.), *Reading and writing instruction in the United States: Historical trends*. Newark, DE: International Reading Association, September 1977. Pp. 76–81.

COX, AYLETT R. *Structure and techniques*. Cambridge, MA: Educators Publishing Service, 1977.

COX, JUANITA, & WALLIS, BETH S. Books for the Cajun child—Lagniappe or a little something extra for multi-cultural teaching. *The Reading Teacher*, December 1982, *36*, 263–266.

COX, JUANITA, & WIEBE, JAMES H. Measuring reading vocabulary and concepts in mathematics in the primary grades. *The Reading Teacher*, January 1984, *37*, 402–410.

CRAIG, LINDA C. If it's too difficult for the kids to read—rewrite it. *Journal of Reading*, December 1977, *21*, 212–214.

CRANNEY, A. GARR, *et al.* Rate and Reading Dynamics reconsidered. *Journal of Reading*, March 1982, *25*, 526–533.

CRAWFORD, GAIL, & CONLEY, DICK. Meet you in reading lab! *Journal of Reading*, October 1971, *15*, 16–21.

CRAWLEY, SHARON J. Readabilities of the new basal programs. *The New England Reading Association Journal*, 1975, *10* (3), 35–38.

CRISCUOLO, NICHOLAS P. Book reports: Twelve creative alternatives. *The Reading Teacher*, May 1977, *30*, 893–895. (a)

CRISCUOLO, NICHOLAS P. Convincing the unconvinced to read: Twelve strategies. *Journal of Reading*, December 1977, *21*, 219–221. (b)

CRISCUOLO, NICHOLAS P. Successful motivation for children who can read but won't. *The New England Reading Association Journal*, 1978, *13* (1), 6–9.

CRISCUOLO, NICHOLAS P. Effective approaches for motivating children to read. *The Reading Teacher*, February 1979, *32*, 543–546.

CRISCUOLO, NICHOLAS P. *Look it up! 101 dictionary activities to develop word skills.* Belmont, CA: Fearon-Pitman, 1980.

CRISCUOLO, NICHOLAS P. Ten creative ways to build vocabulary skills. *Wisconsin State Reading Association Journal*, Fall 1981, *26*, 23–26.

CRISCUOLO, NICHOLAS P. Practical ways to motivate children to read and write: A baker's dozen. *New England Reading Association Journal*, Winter 1982, *17*, 25–26.

CRISCUOLO, NICHOLAS P. Different books for different children: A selected bibliography. *The Directive Teacher*, Winter/Spring 1983, *5*, 31.

CRISCUOLO, NICHOLAS P. A treasure trove for building a rich vocabulary. *The Reading Teacher*, January 1984, *37*, 444–446.

CRITCHLEY, MACDONALD. *The dyslexic child.* Springfield, IL: Charles C Thomas, 1970.

CRITCHLEY, MACDONALD. Dyslexia: An overview. In G. Pavlidis & T. Miles (Eds.), *Dyslexia research and its application to education.* New York: John Wiley & Sons, 1981. Pp. 1–11.

CROMER, WARD. The difference model: A new explanation for some reading difficulties. *Journal of Educational Psychology*, 1970, *61*, 471–483.

CRONBACH, LEE J. Test validation. In R. L. Thorndike (Ed.), *Educational measurement* (2nd ed.). Washington, DC: American Council on Education, 1971. Pp. 443–507.

CRONBACH, LEE J., & QUIRK, THOMAS J. Test validity. In *Encyclopedia of education* (Vol. 9). New York: Crowell-Collier, 1971. Pp. 165–175.

CRONBACH, LEE J., & SNOW, RICHARD E. *Aptitudes and instructional methods.* New York: Irvington, 1977.

CRONIN, B. A new technique for using Braille to teach reading to dyslexic children. *The New Outlook for the Blind*, 1972, *66*, 71–74.

CRONNELL, BRUCE. Cause and effect: An overview. *Reading World*, December 1981, *21*, 155–166.

CROWELL, DORIS C., AU, KATHRYN H., & BLAKE, KAREN M. Comprehension questions: Differences among standardized tests. *Journal of Reading*, January 1983, *26*, 314–319.

CRUICKSHANK, WILLIAM M. Myths and realities in learning disabilities. *Journal of Learning Disabilities*, January 1977, *10*, 51–64.

CRUICKSHANK, WILLIAM M. Learning disabilities: A neurophysiological dysfunction. *Journal of Learning Disabilities*, January 1983, *16*, 27–29.

CRUICKSHANK, WILLIAM M., *et al.* *A teaching method for brain-injured and hyperactive children.* Syracuse: Syracuse University Press, 1961.

CULLINAN, BERNICE E. (Ed.). *Black dialects and reading.* Urbana, IL: ERIC/RCS and National Council of Teachers of English, 1974.

CUNNINGHAM, PATRICIA. Transferring comprehension from listening to reading. *The Reading Teacher*, November 1975, *29*, 169–172.

CUNNINGHAM, PATRICIA M. Investigating a synthesized theory of mediated word identification,. *Reading Research Quarterly*, 1975–1976, *11* (2), 127–143.

CUNNINGHAM, PATRICIA M. Investigating the role of meaning in mediated word identification. In. P. D. Pearson & J. Hansen (Eds.), Reading: *Theory, research, and practice*. Clemson, SC: National Reading Conference, 1977. Pp. 168–171.

CUNNINGHAM, PATRICIA M. A comparison/contrast theory of mediated word identification. *The Reading Teacher*, April 1979, *32*, 774–778; Also in A. J. Harris, E. R. Sipay (Eds.), *Readings on reading instruction* (3rd ed.). New York: Longman, 1984. Pp. 202–207.

CUNNINGHAM, PATRICIA M. Applying a compare/contrast process to identifying polysyllabic words. *Journal of Reading Behavior*, Fall 1980, *12*, 213–223.

CUNNINGHAM, PATRICIA M. A teacher's guide to materials shopping. *The Reading Teacher*, November 1981, *35*, 180–184.

CUSHENBERY, DONALD C. The Joplin plan and cross grade groupings. In W. Z. Ramsey (Ed.), *Organizing for individual differences*. Newark, DE: International Reading Association, 1967. Pp. 33–46.

CZIKO, GARY A. Another response to Shanahan, Kamil, and Tobin: Further reasons to keep the cloze case open. *Reading Research Quarterly*, Spring 1983, *18*, 361–366.

DAHL, PATRICIA, & SAMUELS, S. JAY. Teaching children to read using hypothesis test strategies. *The Reading Teacher*, March 1977, *30*, 603–606.

DAHLBERG, CHARLES C, ROSWELL, FLORENCE G., & CHALL, JEANNE S. Psychotherapeutic principles as applied to remedial reading. *Elementary School Journal*, 1952, *52*, 211–217.

DALE, EDGAR. Vocabulary measurement: Techniques and major findings. *Elementary English*, 1965, *42*, 895–901, 948.

DALE, EDGAR, & CHALL, JEANNE S. A formula for predicting readability. *Educational Research Bulletin*, Ohio State University, 1948, *27*, 11–20; *28*, 37–54.

DALE, EDGAR, & O'ROURKE, JOSEPH. *Techniques for teaching vocabulary*. Menlo Park, CA: Benjamin Cummings, 1971.

DALE, EDGAR, & O'ROURKE, JOSEPH. *The living word vocabulary* (3rd ed.). Chicago: World Book-Childcraft International, 1981.

DALE, EDGAR, & O'ROURKE, JOSEPH. The need for a planned vocabulary program. In A. J. Harris & E. Sipay (Eds.), *Readings on reading instruction* (3rd ed.). New York: Longman, 1984. Pp. 226–230.

DALZELL, BONNIE. Exit Dick and Jane? *American Education*, July 1976, *12*, 9–13.

D'ANGELO, FRANK J. Luria on literacy: The cognitive consequences of reading and writing. In J. Raymond (Ed.), *Literacy as a human problem*. University, AL: University of Alabama Press, 1982. Pp. 154–169.

D'ANGELO, KAREN. Correction behavior: Implications for reading instruction. *The Reading Teacher*, January 1982, *35*, 395–398.

D'ANGELO, KAREN. Précis writing: Promoting vocabulary development and comprehension. *Journal of Reading*, March 1983, *26*, 534–539.

D'ANGELO, KAREN, & MAKLIOS, MARC. Insertion and omission miscues of good and poor readers. *The Reading Teacher*, April 1983, *36*, 778–782.

D'ANGELO, KAREN, & WILSON, ROBERT M. How helpful is insertion and omission miscue analysis? *The Reading Teacher*, February 1979, 519–520.

DANK, MARION. What effect do reading programs have on the oral reading behavior of children? *Reading Improvement*, Summer 1977, *14*, 66–69.

DANKS, JOSEPH H. Comprehension in listening and reading: Same or different? In F. Murray (Ed.), *Reading and understanding*. Newark, DE: International Reading Association, 1980. Pp. 1–39.

DANKS, JOSEPH H., & HILL, GREGORY O. An interactive analysis of oral reading. In A. Lesgold & C. Perfetti (Eds.), *Interactive processes in reading*. Hillsdale, NJ: LEA, 1981. Pp. 131–153.

DAS, JAGANNATH P., KIRBY, JOHN R., & JARMAN, RONALD F. Simultaneous and successive syntheses: An alternative model of cognitive abilities. *Psychological Bulletin*, January 1975, *82*, 87–103.

DAS, JAGANNATH P., KIRBY, JOHN R., & JARMAN, RONALD F. *Simultaneous and successive cognitive processes.* New York: Academic Press, 1979.

DAS, J. P., LEONG, C. G., & WILLIAMS, NOEL H. The relationships between learning disability and simultaneous-successive processing. *Journal of Learning Disabilities,* December 1978, *11,* 618–625.

DA SILVA, N. JORGE. A critical analysis of the proposed regulations to P.L. 94–142. *Academic Therapy,* January 1983, *18,* 375–379.

DAVEY, BETH. Think aloud—Modeling the cognitive processes of reading comprehension. *Journal of Reading,* October 1983, *27,* 44–47.

DAVIDSON, HELEN P. An experimental study of bright, average and dull children at the four-year mental level. *Genetic Psychology Monographs,* 1931, *9,* Nos. 3, 4.

DAVIDSON, JANE L. The group mapping activity for instruction in reading and thinking. *Journal of Reading,* October 1982, *26,* 52–56.

DAVIDSON, ROSCOE L. The effects of an interaction analysis system in the development of critical reading in elementary school children. Unpublished doctoral dissertation, University of Denver, 1967.

DAVIES, THOMAS R. Project Screen: A followup study of a pre-school screening battery. *Exceptional Child,* November 1980, *27,* 151–157.

DAVIES, WILLIAM C. Implicit speech—Some conclusions drawn from research. In R. C. Aukerman (Ed.), *Some persistent questions on beginning reading.* Newark, DE: International Reading Association, 1972. Pp. 171–177.

DAVIS, EVERETT E., & EKWALL, ELDON E. Mode of perception and frustration in reading. *Journal of Learning Disabilities,* September 1976, *9,* 448–454.

DAVIS, FREDERICK B. Research on comprehension in reading. *Reading Research Quarterly,* Summer 1968, *3,* 499–545.

DAVIS, FREDERICK B. *Psychometric research on comprehension in reading.* New Bruswick, NJ: Graduate School of Education, Rutgers University, 1971.

DAVIS, FREDERICK B. Psychometric research on comprehension in reading. *Reading Research Quarterly,* Summer 1972, *7,* 628–678.

DAVIS, JOANNE W. Teaching reading with paperbacks in an elementary school: Three models for classroom organization. *Elementary English,* December 1970, *47,* 1114–1120.

DAVIS, O. L., JR., & PERSONKE, CARL R., JR. Effects of administering the *Metropolitan Readiness Test* in English and Spanish to Spanish speaking school entrants. *Journal of Educational Measurement,* 1968, *5,* 231–234.

DAVIS, W. ALAN. & SHEPARD, LORRIE A. Specialists' uses of tests and clinical judgment in the diagnosis of learning disabilities. *Learning Disability Quarterly,* Spring 1983, *6,* 128–138.

DAVISON, ALICE. Readability—Appraising text difficulty. In R. Anderson *et al.* (Eds.), *Learning to read in American schools: Basal readers and content texts.* Hillsdale, NJ: LEA, 1984. Pp. 121–139.

DAVISON, ALICE, & KANTOR, ROBERT N. On the failure of readability formulas to define readable texts: A case study from adaptations. *Reading Research Quarterly,* 1982, *17* (2), 187–209.

DEARBORN, WALTER F. Structural factors which condition special disability in reading. *Proceedings of the American Association for Mental Deficiency,* 1933, *38,* 266–283.

DEATON, FRANK. A comparison of the effects of reinforcing accuracy and on task responses in a programmed remedial program with fourth-grade reading problem children. *Dissertation Abstracts International,* June 1975, *35* (12-B, Pt. 1), 6067–6068.

DECHANT, EMERALD V., & SMITH, HENRY P. *Psychology in teaching reading.* Englewood Cliffs, NJ: Prentice-Hall, 1977.

DECKER, SADIE N., & DEFRIES, J. C. Cognitive abilities in families with reading disabled children. *Journal of Learning Disabilities,* November 1980, *13,* 517–522.

DEFORD, DIANE E. Literacy: Reading, writing and other essentials. *Language Arts,* September 1981, *58,* 652–658.

DEFRIES, J. C., & BAKER, LAURA A. Parental contributions to longitudinal stability of cognitive measures in the Colorado Family Reading Study. *Child Development,* April 1983, *54,* 388–395.

DEFRIES, J. C., & DECKER, SADIE N. Genetic aspects of reading disability: A family study. In R. Malathesa & P. Aaron (Eds.), *Reading disorders: Varieties and treatment.* New York: Academic Press, 1982. Pp. 255–279.

DE HIRSCH, KATRINA, JANSKY, JEANETTE J., & LANGFORD, WILLIAM S. *Predicting reading failure: A preliminary study.* New York: Harper & Row, 1966.

DEIGHTON, LEE C. *Vocabulary development in the classroom.* New York: Teachers College Press, 1959.

DELACATO, CARL H. *Treatment and prevention of reading problems.* Springfield, IL: Charles C Thomas, 1959.

DELACATO, CARL H. *The diagnosis and treatment of speech and reading problems.* Springfield, IL: Charles C Thomas, 1963.

DELACATO, CARL H. *Neurological organization and reading.* Springfield, IL: Charles C Thomas, 1966.

DEN BUURMAN, RUDY, ROERSEMA, THEO, & GERRISSEN, JACK F. Eye movements and the perceptual span in reading. *Reading Research Quarterly,* 1981, *16* (2), 227–235.

DENBURG, SUSAN D. The interaction of picture and print in reading instruction (abstract). *Reading Research Quarterly,* 1976–1977, *12* (2), 176–189.

DENCKLA, MARTHA B. Clinical syndromes in learning disabilities: The case for "splitting" vs. "lumping." *Journal of Learning Disabilities,* August/September 1972, 5, 401–406.

DENCKLA, MARTHA B. Learning for language and language for learning. In U. Kirk (Ed.), *Neuropsychology of language, reading, and spelling.* New York: Academic Press, 1983. Pp. 33–43.

DENCKLA, MARTHA B., & RUDEL, RITA G. Rapid automatized naming (RAN): Dyslexia differentiated from other learning disabilities. *Neuropsychologia,* 1976, *14,* 471–479.

DENCKLA, MARTHA B., RUDEL, RITA G., & BROMAN, MELINDA. Tests that discriminate between dyslexic and other learning-disabled boys. *Brain & Language,* May 1981, *13,* 118–129.

DENK-GLASS, RITA, LABER, SUSAN S., & BREWER, KATHRYN. Prevalence of middle ear disease in preschool children, 1981. Mimeographed.

DENNIS, MAUREEN, LOVETT, MAUREEN, & WIEGEL-CRUMP, CAROLE ANN. Written language acquisition after left or right hemidecortification in infancy. *Brain & Language,* 1981, *12,* 54–91.

DENO, STANLEY L., & CHIANG, BERTRAM. An experimental analysis of the nature of reversal errors in children with severe learning disabilities. *Learning Disabilities Quarterly,* Summer 1979, *2,* 40–45.

DENO, STANLEY L., MIRKIN, PHYLLIS K., & CHIANG, BERTRAM. Identifying valid measures of reading. *Exceptional Children,* September 1982, *49,* 36–47.

DENO, STANLEY L., MIRKIN, PHYLLIS K., & WESSON, CAREN. How to write effective data-based IEPs. *Teaching Exceptional Children,* Winter 1984, *16,* 99–104.

DEPARTMENT OF EDUCATION AND SCIENCE. *A language for life (The Bullock Report).* London: Her Majesty's Stationery Office, 1975.

DE QUIROS, JULIO, & DELLA CELLA, M. La dislexia como sindrome: Estudio estadistico sobre la dislexia infantil en la Ciudad de Rosario—Santa Fe. *Acta Neuropsiquiatrica Argentina,* 1959, 5, 178–193.

DE QUIROS, JULIO B., & SCHRAGER, ORLANDO L. *Neuropsychological fundamentals in learning disabilities.* San Rafael, CA: Academic Therapy Publications, 1978.

DE STEFANO, JOHANNA S. Register: A concept to combat negative teachers' attitudes toward black English. In J. S. De Stefano (Ed.), *Language, society and education: A profile of black English.* Worthington, OH: Charles A. Jones, 1973. Pp. 189–195.

DE STEFANO, PHILIP, NOE, MICHAEL, & VALENCIA, SHEILA. Measurements of the effects of purpose and passage difficulty on reading flexibility. *Journal of Educational Research,* August 1981, *73,* 602–606.

DEVALL, YVONNA. Evaluating microcomputer software for reading instruction. *Journal of Reading,* March 1983, *26,* 553.

DICKERSON, DOLORES. A study of the use of games to reinforce sight vocabulary. *The Reading Teacher,* October 1982, *36,* 46–49.

DIEHL, DIGBY. Readership survey: Good, bad news. *Albany Times Union,* April 20, 1984, B-7.

DIETERICH, THOMAS, FREEMAN, CECILIA, & GRIFFIN, PEG. *Assessing comprehension in a school setting.* Arlington, VA: Center for Applied Linguistics, June 1978.

DIETRICH, DOROTHY M., & MATHEWS, VIRGINIA H. (Eds.). *Development of lifetime reading habits*. Newark, DE: International Reading Association, 1968.

DI LORENZO, LOUIS T., & SALTER, RUTH. Cooperative research in the nongraded primary. *Elementary School Journal*, 1965, *65*, 269–277.

DIONESIO, MARIE. "Write? Isn't this reading class?" *The Reading Teacher*, April 1983, *36*, 746–750.

Directory of education facilities for the learning disabled (9th ed.). Novato, CA: Academic Therapy Publications, 1985.

DISTAD, LOIS, & PARADIS, EDWARD. The effects of the temporal conjunctions *before* and *after* on reading comprehension by primary grade children. In J. Niles & L. A. Harris (Eds.), *Searches for meaning in reading/language processing and instruction*. Rochester, NY: National Reading Conference, 1983. Pp. 95–100.

DOBO, PAMELA J. Using literature to change attitudes toward the handicapped. *The Reading Teacher*, December 1982, *36*, 290–292.

DOCTOR, ESTELLE A. Considering reading cognitively: A review. *South African Journal of Psychology*, 1981, *11* (2), 55–66.

DOEHRING, DONALD G. *Patterns of impairment in specific reading disability: A neuropsychological investigation*. Bloomington, IN: Indiana University Press, 1968.

DOEHRING, DONALD G. *Acquisition of rapid reading responses*. Monographs of the Society for Research in Child Development, Vol. 41, Serial No. 165. Chicago, June 1976.

DOEHRING, DONALD G. The tangled web of behavioral research on developmental dyslexia. In A. L. Benton & D. Pearl (Eds.), *Dyslexia—an appraisal of current knowledge*. New York: Oxford University Press, 1978. Pp. 123–135.

DOEHRING, DONALD G., BACKMAN, JOAN, & WATERS, GLORIA. Theoretical models of reading disabilities, past, present, and future. *Topics in Learning & Learning Disorders*, April 1983, *3*, 84–94.

DOEHRING, DONALD G., & HOSHKO, IRENE M. Classification of reading problems by the Q-technique of factor analysis. *Cortex*, 1977, *13*, 281–294.

DOEHRING, DONALD G., HOSHKO, IRENE M., & BRYANS, B. N. Statistical classification of children with reading problems. *Journal of Clinical Neuropsychology*, 1979, *1* (1), 5–16.

DOEHRING, DONALD G., *et al. Reading disabilities: The interaction of reading, language, and neuropsychological deficits*. New York: Academic Press, 1981.

DOLAN, LAWRENCE. A follow-up evaluation of a transition class program for children with school and learning readiness problems. *Exceptional Child*, July 1982, *29*, 101–110.

DOLCH, EDWARD W. *A manual for remedial reading*. Champaign, IL: Garrard, 1939.

DOLCH, E. W. How to diagnose children's reading difficulties by informal classroom techniques. *The Reading Teacher*, January 1953, *6*, 10–14.

DOLCH, E. W., & BLOOMSTER, M. Phonic readiness. *Elementary School Journal*, 1937, *38*, 201–205.

DOLE, JANICE A., & JOHNSON, VIRGINIA P. Beyond the textbook: Science literature for young people. *Journal of Reading*, April 1981, *24*, 579–582.

DOLLENGER, ROBERTA, & WALKER, DAVID M. The effect of three methods of presentation and socioeconomic class on recognition performance in the presentation of low frequency words to kindergartners. *Journal of Reading Behavior*, Fall 1978, *10*, 303–305.

DORE-BOYCE, KATHLEEN, MISNER, MARILYN, & MCGUIRE, LORRAINE D. Comparing reading expectancy formulas. *The Reading Teacher*, October 1975, *29*, 8–14.

DORSEY, MARY E. *Reading games and activities*. Belmont, CA: Fearon-Pitman, 1972.

DOWDY, CAROL A., CRUMP, W. DONALD, & WELCH, MICHAEL W. Reading flexibility of learning disabled and normal students at three grade levels. *Learning Disabilities Quarterly*, Summer 1982, *5*, 253–263.

DOWNING, GERTRUDE, *et al. The preparation of teachers for schools in culturally deprived neighborhoods* (The Bridge Project). Cooperative Research Project No. 935. Flushing, NY: Queens College, 1965. Available through University Film Library Services.

DOWNING, JOHN. *Comparative reading: Cross-national studies of behavior and processes in reading and writing*. New York: Macmillan, 1973. (a)

DOWNING, JOHN. A summary of evidence related to the cognitive clarity theory of reading. In P. L. Nacke (Ed.), *Diversity in mature reading: Theory and research*. Boone, NC: National Reading Conference, 1973. Pp. 178–184. (b)

DOWNING, JOHN. Language arts in open schools. *Elementary English*, January 1975, *52*, 23–29.

DOWNING, JOHN. What is "comparative reading"? *Journal of Reading*, May 1978, *21*, 701–704.

DOWNING, JOHN. The psycholinguistic basis of cognitive clarity. In M. L. Kamil & A. J. Moe (Eds.), *Reading research: Studies and applications*. Clemson, SC: National Reading Conference, 1979. Pp. 279–283. (a).

DOWNING, JOHN. *Reading and reasoning*. New York. Springer-Verlag, 1979. (b)

DOWNING, JOHN. Learning to read with understanding. In C. McCullough (Ed.), *Inchworm, inchworm: Persistent problems in reading education*. Newark, DE: International Reading Association, 1980. Pp. 163–178.

DOWNING, JOHN. Research revisited: Jack Holmes' substrata-factor theory of reading. *Reading Psychology*, Spring 1981, *2*, 108–116.

DOWNING, JOHN. A source of cognitive confusion for beginning readers: Learning in a second language. *The Reading Teacher*, January 1984, *37*, 366–370.

DOWNING, JOHN, AYERS, DOUGLAS, & SCHAEFER, BRIAN. *Administrative Manual for the Linguistics Awareness in Reading Readiness Test* (LARR). Windsor, Great Britain: NFER-Nelson, 1983.

DOWNING, JOHN, & LEONG, CHE KAN. *Psychology of reading*. New York: Macmillan, 1982.

DOWNING, JOHN, MAY, RICHARD, & OLLILA, LLOYD. Sex differences and cultural expectations in reading. In E. Sheridan (Ed.), *Sex stereotypes and reading: Research and strategies*. Newark, DE: International Reading Association, 1982. Pp. 17–34.

DOWNING, JOHN, & THACKRAY, DEREK V. *Reading readiness*. London, England: University of London Press, 1971.

DRADER, DARIA. The role of verbal labeling in equivalence tasks as related to reading ability. *Journal of Learning Disabilities*, March 1975, *8*, 53–57.

DREYER, LOIS G. Readability and responsibility. *Journal of Reading*, January 1984, *28*, 334–338.

DREYER, SHARON S. *The bookfinder: A guide to children's literature about the needs and problems of youth*. Circle Pines, MN: American Guidance Service, 1977.

DRUM, PRISCILLA A. Vocabulary knowledge. In J. Niles & L. A. Harris (Eds.), *Searches for meaning in reading/language processing and instruction*. Rochester, NY: National Reading Conference, 1983. Pp. 163–171.

DUBOIS, DIANE, & STICE, CAROLE. Comprehension instruction: Let's recall it for repair. *Reading World*, December 1980, *20*, 173–184.

DUDLEY-MARLING, CURTIS, KAUFMAN, NANCY J., & TARVER, SARA G. WISC and WISC-R profiles of learning disabled children: A review. *Learning Disability Quarterly*, Summer 1981, *4*, 307–319.

DUFFELMEYER, FREDERICK A. A comparison of two noncomputational readability techniques. *The Reading Teacher*, October 1982, *36*, 4–7. (a)

DUFFELMEYER, FREDERICK A. Introducing words in context. *Wisconsin State Reading Association Journal*, Spring 1982, *26*, 4–6. (b)

DUFFY, FRANK H., *et al*. Dyslexia: Automated diagnosis by computerized classification of brain electrical activity. *Annals of Neurology*, May 1980, *7*, 421–428. (a)

DUFFY, FRANK H., *et al*. Regional differences in brain electrical activity by typographic mapping. *Annals of Neurology*, May 1980, *7*, 412–419. (b)

DUFFY, GERALD G. Maintaining a balance in objective-based reading instruction. *The Reading Teacher*, February 1978, *31*, 519–523.

DUFFY, GERALD G. Teacher effectiveness research: Implications for the reading profession. In M. Kamil & M. Boswick (Eds.), *Directions in reading: Research and instruction*. Washington, DC: National Reading Conference, 1981. Pp. 113–136.

DUFFY, GERALD G. Fighting off the alligators: What research in real classrooms has to say about reading instruction. *Journal of Reading Behavior*, 1982, *14* (4), 357–373.

DUFFY, GERALD G., & ROEHLER, LAURA R. An analysis of the instruction in reading instructional research. In J. Niles & L. A. Harris (Eds.), *New inquiries in reading research and instruction*. Rochester, NY: National Reading Conference, 1982. Pp. 14–23. (a)

DUFFY, GERALD G., & ROEHLER, LAURA R. The illusion of instruction. *Reading Research Quarterly*, 1982, *17* (3), 438–445. (b)

DUKE, DANIEL L. (Ed.). *Classroom management*. 78th Yearbook of the National Society for the Study of Education, Part II. Chicago: University of Chicago Press, 1979.

DUKER, SAM. *Individualized reading: An annotated bibliography.* Metuchen, NJ: Scarecrow Press, 1968.

DULIN, KEN L. Assessing reading interests of elementary and middle school students. In D. Monson & D. McClenathan (Eds.), *Developing active readers: Ideas for parents, teachers, and librarians.* Newark, DE: International Reading Association, 1979. Pp. 2–15. Also in A. J. Harris & E. Sipay (Eds.), *Readings on reading instruction* (3rd ed.). New York: Longman, 1984. Pp. 344–357.

DUNKELD, COHN G. M. The validity of the informal reading inventory for the designation of instructional levels: A study of the relationships between children's gains in reading achievement and the difficulty of instructional materials. Unpublished doctoral dissertation, University of Illinois, 1970.

DUNLAP, WILLIAM P., & MCKNIGHT, MARTHA B. Vocabulary translations for conceptualizing math word problems. *The Reading Teacher,* November 1978, *32,* 183–189.

DUNN, LLOYD M., POCHANART, PRAYOT, PFOST, PHILIP, & BRUININKS, ROBERT H. *The effectiveness of the Peabody Language Development Kits and the Initial Teaching Alphabet with disadvantaged children in the primary grades: A report after the third grade of the Cooperative Language Development Project.* IMRD Behavioral Science Monograph No. 9. Nashville: George Peabody College for Teachers, 1968.

DUNN, PAUL J. Orthomolecular therapy: Implications for learning disability. In G. Leisman (Ed.), *Basic visual processes and learning disability.* Springfield, IL: Charles C Thomas, 1976. Pp. 371–389.

DUNN, RITA. Teaching in a purple fog: What we don't know about learning style. *NASP Bulletin,* March 1981, *65,* 33–36.

DUNN, RITA, *et al.* Learning style: Research vs. opinion. *Phi Delta Kappan,* May 1981, *62,* 645–646.

DUNWANT, NOEL. *The relationship between learning disabilities and juvenile delinquency.* Williamsburg, VA: National Center for State Courts, 1982.

DUPUIS, MARY M. (Ed.). *Reading in the content areas.* Newark, DE: International Reading Association, 1984.

DUPUIS, MARY M., & SNYDER, SANDRA L. Develop concepts through vocabulary: A strategy for reading specialists to use with content teachers. *Journal of Reading,* January 1983, *26,* 297–305.

DURKIN, DOLORES. A six year study of children who learned to read in school at the age of four. *Reading Research Quarterly,* 1974–1975, *10* (1), 9–61.

DURKIN, DOLORES. *Strategies for identifying words.* Boston: Allyn & Bacon, 1976.

DURKIN, DOLORES. *Teaching them to read.* Boston: Allyn & Bacon, 1978.

DURKIN, DOLORES. What classrooom observations reveal about reading comprehension instruction. *Reading Research Quarterly,* 1978–1979, *14* (4), 481–533.

DURKIN, DOLORES. Reading comprehension instruction in five basal reader series. *Reading Research Quarterly,* 1981, *16* (4), 515–543. (a)

DURKIN, DOLORES. What is the value of the new interest in reading comprehension? *Language Arts,* January 1981, *58,* 23–43. (b) Also in A. J. Harris & E. Sipay (Eds.), *Readings on reading instruction* (3rd ed.). New York: Longman, 1984. Pp. 249–266.

DURKIN, DOLORES. A study of poor black children who are successful readers. Reading Education Report No. 33. Champaign, IL: Center for the Study of Reading, University of Illinois, April 1982.

DURKIN, DOLORES. Is there a match between what elementary teachers do and what basal reader manuals recommend? *The Reading Teacher,* April 1984, *37,* 734–744.

DURRELL, DONALD D. *Improvement of basic reading abilities.* New York: World Book, 1940.

DURRELL, DONALD D. *Improving reading instruction.* New York: Harcourt, Brace and World, 1956.

DURRELL, DONALD D. (Ed.). Adapting instruction to the learning needs of children in the intermediate grades. *Journal of Education,* December 1959, *42,* 1–78.

DURRELL, DONALD D. Letter-name value in reading and spelling. *Reading Research Quarterly,* 1980, *16* (1), 159–163.

DURRELL, DONALD D. Letter names controversy. *The Reading Teacher,* May 1984, *37,* 880.

DURRELL, DONALD D., & HAYES, MARY T. *Durrell Listening-Reading Series: Manual for listening and reading tests, primary level, Form OE.* New York: Psychological Corp., 1969.

DURRELL, DONALD D., & MURPHY, HELEN A. The auditory discrimination factor in reading readiness and reading disability. *Education*, 1953, *73*, 556–560.

DURRELL, DONALD D., & MURPHY, HELEN A. A prereading phonics inventory. *The Reading Teacher*, January 1978, *31*, 385–390.

DUTT, ANITA (Comp.). *Fifty creative ways to use paperbacks in the primary grades.* New York: Scholastic Book Services, 1980.

DUVAL, EILEEN V., JOHNSON, ROGER E., & LITCHER, JOHN. Learning stations and the reading class. In R. A. Earle (Ed.), *Classroom practice in reading.* Newark, DE: International Reading Association, 1977. Pp. 109–118.

DWORKIN, NANCY E. Changing teachers' negative expectations. *Academic Therapy*, May 1979, *14*, 517–531.

DWYER, CAROL ANN (Reviewer). *Woodcock reading mastery test.* In O. K. Buros (Ed.), *Eighth mental measurements yearbook*, Vol. II. Highland Park, NJ: Gryphon Press, 1978. Pp. 1303–1305.

DYKMAN, ROSCOE A., *et al.* Physiological manifestations of learning disability. *Journal of Learning Disabilities*, January 1983, *16*, 46–53.

DYKSTRA, ROBERT. Auditory discrimination abilities and beginning reading achievement. *Reading Research Quarterly*, Spring 1966, *1*, 5–34.

DYKSTRA, ROBERT. Summary of the second-grade phase of the cooperative research program in primary reading instruction. *Reading Research Quarterly*, Fall 1968, *4*, 49–70. (a)

DYKSTRA, ROBERT. The effectiveness of code- and meaning-emphasis beginning reading programs. *The Reading Teacher*, October 1968, *22*, 17–23. (b)

DYKSTRA, ROBERT. Phonics and beginning reading instruction. In C. C. Walcutt, J. Lamport, & G. McCracken, *Teaching reading: A phonic/linguistic approach to developmental reading.* New York: Macmillan, 1974. Pp. 373–397.

EAMES, THOMAS H. The effect of correction of refractive errors on the distant and near vision of school children. *Journal of Educational Research*, 1942, *36*, 272–279.

EAMES, THOMAS H. Comparison of eye conditions among 1000 reading failures, 500 ophthalmic patients, and 150 unselected children. *American Journal of Ophthalmology*, 1948, *31*, 713–717.

EAMES, THOMAS H. Some neurological and glandular bases of learning. *Journal of Education*, April 1960, *142*, 1–35.

EARLY, MARGARET. Reading in the secondary school. In J. E. Squire (Ed.), *The teaching of English.* 76th Yearbook of the National Society for the Study of Education, Part I. Chicago: University of Chicago Press, 1977. Pp. 189–196.

EARP, N. W. Procedures for teaching reading in mathematics. *Arithmetic Teacher*, 1970, *17*, 575–579.

EAST, ROBERT C. A study of the effectiveness of specific language disability techniques on reading ability of potentially retarded readers. *Bulletin of the Orton Society*, 1969, *19*, 95–99.

EBERSOLE, MARYLOU, KEPHART, NEWELL C., & EBERSOLE, JAMES B. *Steps to achievement for the slow learner.* Columbus, OH: Charles E. Merrill, 1968.

EBERWEIN, LOWELL. What do book choices indicate? *Journal of Reading*, December 1973, *17*, 186–191.

EBERWEIN, LOWELL. Does pronouncing unknown words really help? *Academic Therapy*, Fall 1975, *11*, 23–29.

ED 053 881 Model Programs: Reading. Bloom Township high school reading program, Chicago Heights, IL, 1971.

ED 053 882 Model programs: Reading. Summer junior high schools, New York, NY, 1971.

ED 053 883 Model programs: Reading. Programmed tutorial reading project, Indianapolis, IN, 1971.

ED 053 884 Model programs: Reading. Summer remedial and enrichment program, Thomasville, GA, 1971.

ED 053 885 Model programs: Reading. Elementary reading centers, Milwaukee, WI, 1971.

ED 053 886 Model programs: Reading. Intensive reading instructional teams, Hartford, CT, 1971.

ED 053 887 Model programs: Reading. Yuba County reading-learning center, Marysville, CA, 1971.

ED 053 888 Model programs: Reading. The Topeka reading clinic, centers and services, Topeka, KS, 1971.

ED 053 889 Model programs: Reading. School-within-a-school, Keokuk, IA, 1971.

ED 053 890 Model programs: Reading. Remedial reading program, Pojoaque, NM, 1971.

EDELSTEIN, RUTH R. Use of group processes in teaching retarded readers. *The Reading Teacher*, January 1970, *23*, 318–334.

EDFELDT, AKE W. *Silent speech and silent reading*. Chicago: University of Chicago Press, 1960.

EDWARDS, PETER. The effect of idioms on children's reading and understanding of prose. In B. S. Schulwitz (Ed.), *Teachers, tangibles, techniques: Comprehension of content in reading*. Newark, DE: International Reading Association, 1975. Pp. 37–46.

EEDS, MARYANN. What to do when they don't understand what they read—Research-based strategies for teaching reading comprehension. *The Reading Teacher*, February 1981, *34*, 565–571.

EFTA, MARTHA. Reading in silence: A chance to read. *Teaching Exceptional Children*, Fall 1978, *11*, 12–14. Also in A. J. Harris & E. Sipay (Eds.), *Readings on reading instruction* (3rd ed.). New York: Longman, 1984. Pp. 387–391.

EGELAND, BYRON. Effects of errorless training on teaching children to discriminate letters of the alphabet. *Journal of Applied Psychology*, August 1975, *60*, 533–536.

EHRI, LINNEA C. Word learning in beginning readers and prereaders: Effects of form class and defining contexts. *Journal of Educational Psychology*, December 1976, *68*, 832–842.

EHRI, LINNEA C. Beginning reading from a psycholinguistic perspective: Amalgamation of word identities. In F. B. Murray (Ed.), *The recognition of words*. Newark, DE: International Reading Association, 1978. Pp. 1–33.

EHRI, LINNEA C. Linguistic insight: Threshold of reading acquisition. In G. Waller & A. MacKinnon (Eds.). *Reading Research: Advances in theory and practice*, Vol. 1. New York: Academic Press, 1979. Pp. 63–114.

EHRI, LINNEA. The role of orthographic images in learning printed words. In J. Kavanagh & R. Venezky (Eds.), *Orthography, reading, and dyslexia*. Baltimore, MD: University Park Press, 1980. Pp. 155–170.

EHRI, LINNEA C. A critique of five studies related to letter-name knowledge and learning to read. In L. Gentile, M. Kamil, & J. Blanchard (Eds.), *Reading research revisited*. Columbus, OH: Charles E. Merrill, 1983. Pp. 143–153.

EHRI, LINNEA C., & ROBERTS, KATHLEEN T. Do beginners learn printed words better in context or in isolation? *Child Development*, September 1979, *50*, 675–685.

EHRI, LINNEA C., & WILCE, LEE S. Do beginners learn to read function words better in sentences or in lists? *Reading Research Quarterly*, 1980, *15* (4), 451–476.

EHRI, LINNEA C., & WILCE, LEE S. Recognition of spellings printed in lower and mixed case: Evidence for orthographic images. *Journal of Reading Behavior*, 1982, *14* (3), 219–230.

EHRLICH, SUSAN F. Children's word recognition in prose context. *Visible Language*, 1981, *15* (3), 219–244.

EISENBERG, LEON. Psychiatric aspects of language disability. In D. Duane & M. Rawson (Eds.), *Reading, perception, and language*. Baltimore: York Press, 1975. Pp. 215–229.

EKWALL, ELDON E. Measuring gains in remedial reading. *The Reading Teacher*, November 1972, *26*, 138–141.

ELDREDGE, ALICE R. An investigation to determine the relationships among self-concept, locus of control, and reading achievement (Abstracted). *Reading World*, October 1981, *21*, 59–64.

ELKONIN, D. B. USSR. In J. Downing (Ed.), *Comparative reading*. New York: Macmillan, 1973. Pp. 551–579.

ELLIOTT, PEGGY G., & STEINKELLNER, LESLEY L. Reading preferences of urban and suburban secondary school students: Topics and media. *Journal of Reading*, November 1979, *23*, 121–125.

ELLIOTT, STEPHEN N. Children's knowledge and uses of organizational patterns of prose in recalling what they read. *Journal of Reading Behavior*, Fall 1980, *12*, 203–212.

ELLIOTT, STEPHEN N., & PIERSAL, WAYNE C. Direct assessment of reading skills: An approach which links assessment to intervention. *School Psychology Review*, 1982, *11* (3), 267–280.

ELLIS, NICK. Visual and name coding in dyslexic children. *Psychological Research*, 1981, *43*, 201–218.

ELLSON, DOUGLAS G. Tutoring, In N. L. Gage (Ed.), *The psychology of teaching methods*. 75th Yearbook of the National Society for the Study of Education, Part I. Chicago: University of Chicago Press, 1976. Pp. 130–165.

ELLSON, DOUGLAS G., HARRIS, PHILIP, & BARBER, LARRY. A field test of programmed and directed tutoring. *Reading Research Quarterly*, Spring 1968, *3*, 306–368.

ELTERMAN, R. D., *et al.* Eye movements in dyslexic children. *Journal of Learning Disabilities*, January 1980, *13*, 11–16.

EMANS, ROBERT. When two vowels go walking and other such things. *The Reading Teacher*, December 1967, *21*, 262–269.

EMANS, ROBERT, & PATYK, GLORIA. Why do high school students read? *Journal of Reading*, February 1967, *10*, 300–304.

EMBREY, JAMES E. A study of the effects of mild hearing loss on educational achievement. Unpublished doctoral dissertation, University of Tulsa, 1971.

EMMER, EDMUND T., EVERTSON, CAROLYN M., & ANDERSON, LINDA M. Effective classroom management at the beginning of the school year. *Elementary School Journal*, May 1980, *80*, 219–231.

ENSTROM, E. A. A key to learning. *Academic Therapy*, Summer 1970, *5*, 295–297.

ENTIN, EILEEN B., & KLARE, GEORGE R. Factor analysis of three correlation matrices of readability variables. *Journal of Reading Behavior*, Fall 1978, *10*, 279–290. (a)

ENTIN, EILEEN B., & KLARE, GEORGE R. Some inter-relationships of readability, cloze and multiple-choice scores on a reading comprehension test. *Journal of Reading Behavior*, Winter 1978, *10*, 417–436. (b)

ERICKSON, LAWRENCE G. New Books? Yes. Better programs? Maybe. *The Reading Teacher*, January 1978, *31*, 378–380.

ERICKSON, MARILYN. The Z-score discrepancy method for identifying reading disabled children. *Journal of Learning Disabilities*, May 1975, 8, 308–312.

ERIKSON, ERIK H. *Childhood and society.* New York: Norton, 1950.

EVANS, JAMES R. Evoked potentials and learning disabilities. In L. Tarnopol & M. Tarnopol (Eds.)., *Brain function and reading disabilities.* Baltimore: University Park Press, 1977. Pp. 77–109.

EVANS, JAMES R. Neuropsychologically based remedial reading procedures: Some possibilities. In R. Malatesha & P. Aaron (Eds.), *Reading disorders: Varieties and treatments.* New York: Academic Press, 1982. Pp. 371–388.

EVANS, JAMES R., *et al.* Clinical neuropsychology in the schools: Some possibilities for assessment. *School Psychology International*, January–March 1982, *3*, 35–42.

EVELAND, LARRY W. Attitudes of elementary school principals and teachers toward individually prescribed instruction. Unpublished doctoral dissertation, University of Illinois, 1975.

EVERTSON, CAROLYN M., STANFORD, JULIE P., & EMMER, EDMUND T. Effects of class heterogenity in junior high school. *American Educational Research Journal*, Summer 1981, *18*, 219–232.

FADER, DANIEL N. *The new hooked on books.* New York: Berkley, 1977.

FARNSWORTH, KATHRYN. Storytelling in the classroom—not an impossible dream. *Language Arts*, February 1981, *58*, 162–167.

FARR, ROGER. *Reading: What can be measured?* Newark, DE: International Reading Association, 1969.

FARR, ROGER, & BLOMENBERG, PAULA. Contrary to popular opinion children today are exhibiting better reading skills than their predecessors. *Early Years*, May 1979, 9, 52–53, 68.

FARR, ROGER, & WOLF, ROBERT L. Evaluation and secondary reading programs. In A. Purves & O. Niles (Eds.), *Becoming readers in a complex society.* 83rd Yearbook of the National Society for the Study of Education, Part I. Chicago: University of Chicago Press, 1984. Pp. 271–292.

FAY, LEO. The status of reading achievement: Is there a halo around the past? In C. McCullough (Ed.), *Inchworm, inchworm: Persistent problems in reading education.* Newark, DE: International Reading Association, 1980. Pp. 13–21. Also in A. J. Harris & E. R. Sipay (Eds.), *Readings on reading instruction* (3rd ed.). New York: Longman, 1984. Pp. 20–25.

FAYNE, HARRIET R. A comparison of learning disabled adolescents with normal learners on an anaphoric pronominal reference task. *Journal of Learning Disabilities*, December 1981, *14*, 597–599.

FEELEY, JOAN T. Television and children's reading. *Elementary English*, January 1973, *50*, 141–150.

FEELEY, JOAN T. Interest patterns and media preferences of middle-grade children. *Reading World*, March 1974, *13*, 224–237.

FEELEY, JOAN T. Content interests and media preferences of middle-graders: Differences in a decade. *Reading World,* October 1982, 22, 11–16.

FEELEY, JOAN T. Help for the reading teacher: Dealing with the Limited English Proficient (LEP) child in the elementary classroom. *The Reading Teacher,* March 1983, 36, 650–655.

FEIN, RUTH L., & GINSBURG, ADRIENNE H. Realistic literature about the handicapped. *The Reading Teacher,* April 1978, 31, 802–805.

FEINGOLD, BENJAMIN F. Hyperkinesis and learning disabilities linked to the ingestion of artificial food colors and flavors. *Journal of Learning Disabilities,* November 1976, 9, 551–559.

FEINGOLD, BENJAMIN F. A critique of "Controversial medical treatment of learning disabilities." *Academic Therapy,* November 1977, 13, 173–183.

FEITELSON, DINA. Sequences and structure in a system with consistent sound-symbol correspondences. In J. E. Merritt (Ed.), *New horizons in reading.* Newark, DE: International Reading Association, 1976. Pp. 269–277.

FEITELSON, DINA (Ed.). *Mother tongue or second language? On the teaching of reading in multilingual societies.* Newark, DE: International Reading Association, 1979.

FENNIMORE, FLORA. Projective book reports. *Language Arts,* February 1977, 54, 176–179.

FERGUSON, JERRY. Teaching the reading of biology. In H. A. Robinson & E. L. Thomas (Eds.), *Fusing reading skills and content.* Newark, DE: International Reading Association, 1969. Pp. 114–119.

FERNALD, GRACE M. *Remedial techniques in basic school subjects.* New York: McGraw-Hill, 1943.

FERNALD, GRACE M., & KELLER, HELEN. The effect of kinesthetic factors in development of word recognition in the case of nonreaders. *Journal of Educational Research,* 1921, 4, 357–377.

FESHBACH, SEYMOUR, ADELMAN, HOWARD, & FULLER, WILLIAM W. Early identification of children with high risk of reading failure. *Journal of Learning Disabilities,* December 1974, 7, 639–644.

FILP, JOHANNA. Relationship among reading subskills: A hierarchical hypothesis. *Journal of Reading Behavior,* Fall 1975, 7, 229–239.

FINCHER, JACK. New machines may soon replace the doctor's black bag. *Smithsonian,* January 1984, 14, 64–71.

FINUCCI, JOAN M. Genetic considerations in dyslexia. In H. Myklebust (Ed.). *Progress in learning disabilities,* Vol. 4. New York: Grune & Stratton, 1978. Pp. 41–63.

FINUCCI, JOAN M., et al. The genetics of specific reading disability. *Annals of Human Genetics,* July 1976, 40, 1–23.

FINUCCI, JOAN M., et al. Empirical validation of reading and spelling quotients. *Developmental Medicine & Child Neurology,* December 1982, 24, 733–744.

FIRESTONE, PHILIP, POITRAS-WRIGHT, HELENE, & DOUGLAS, VIRGINIA. The effects of caffeine on hyperactive children. *Journal of Learning Disabilities,* March 1978, 10, 133–141.

FISCHER, F. WILLIAM, LIBERMAN, ISABELLE Y., & SCHANKWEILER, DONALD. Reading reversals and developmental dyslexia; A further study. *Cortex,* 1978, 14, 496–510.

FISHBEIN, HAROLD D. Braille-phonics: A new technique for aiding the reading disabled. *Journal of Learning Disabilities,* January 1979, 12, 60–64.

FISHER, CAROL J. 55 ways to respond to a book. *Instructor,* April 1979, 88, 94–96.

FISHER, CAROL J., & NATARELLA, MARGARET A. Of cabbages and kings! Or what kinds of poetry young children like. *Language Arts,* April 1979, 56, 380–385.

FISHER, CAROL J., & NATARELLA, MARGARET A. Young children's preferences in poetry: A national survey of first, second, and third graders. *Research in the Teaching of English,* December 1982, 16, 339–354.

FISHER, SHARON. Conceptual tempo and oral reading performance. Unpublished doctoral dissertation, State University of New York at Albany, 1977.

FISHER, THOMAS H. Implementing an instructional validity study of the Florida High School Graduation Test. *Educational Measurement: Issues and Practice,* Winter 1983, 2, 8–9.

FISK, JOHN L., & ROURKE, BYRON P. Identification of subtypes of learning-disabled children at three age levels: A neuro-psychological multivariate approach. *Journal of Clinical Neuropsychology,* 1979, 1 (4), 289–310.

FISKE, EDWARD B. General study replacing high school academics. *Albany Times Union,* April 26, 1983, 347, A-9.

FITE, JUNE H., & SCHWARTZ, LOUISE A. Screening culturally disadvantaged first-grade children for potential reading difficulties due to constitutional factors (Abstract). *American Journal of Orthopsychiatry*, 1965, *35*, 359–360.

FITZGERALD, GISELA G.. Reliability of the Fry sampling procedure. *Reading Research Quarterly*, 1980 *15* (4), 489–503.

FITZGERALD, GISELA G. How many samples give a good readability estimate? The Fry Graph. *Journal of Reading*, February 1981, *24*, 404–410.

FITZGERALD, JILL. Helping readers gain self-control over reading comprehension. *The Reading Teacher*, December 1983, *37*, 249–253.

FLANAGAN, JOHN C. Changes in school levels of achievement: Project TALENT ten and fifteen year retests. *Educational Researcher*, September 1976, *5*, 9–12.

FLAX, NATHAN. The contribution of visual problems to learning disability. *Journal of the American Optometric Association*, October 1970, *41*, 841–845.

FLEISHER, LISA, JENKINS, JOSEPH R., & PANY, DARLENE. Effects on poor reader's comprehension of training in rapid decoding. *Reading Research Quarterly*, 1979, *15* (1), 30–48.

FLEMING, JAMES T. Skimming: Neglected in research and teaching. *Journal of Reading*, December 1968, *12*, 211–214, 218.

FLESCH, RUDOLPH. *Why Johnny can't read.* New York: Harper & Row, 1955.

FLESCH, RUDOLPH. *Why Johnny still can't read: A new look at the scandal in our schools.* New York: Harper & Row, 1981.

FLETCHER, JACK M. Linguistic factors in reading acquisition. Evidence for developmental changes. In F. Pirozzolo & M. Wittrock (Eds.), *Neuropsychological and cognitive processes in reading.* New York: Academic Press, 1981. Pp. 261–294.

FLETCHER, JACK M., & SATZ, PAUL. Developmental changes in the neuropsychological correlates of reading achievement: A six-year longitudinal follow-up. *Journal of Clinical Neuropsychology*, 1980, *2* (1), 23–37.

FLETCHER, JACK M., SATZ, PAUL, & SCHOLES, ROBERT J. Developmental changes in the linguistic performance correlates of reading achievement. *Brain & Language*, May 1981, *13*, 78–90.

FLETCHER, JACK M., et al. Finger recognition skills and reading achievement: A developmental neuropsychological analysis. *Developmental Psychology*, January 1982, *18*, 124–132.

FLOOD, JAMES. Predictors of reading achievement: An integration of selected antecedents to reading. Unpublished doctoral dissertation, Stanford University, 1975. ED 116 123.

FOOD AND NUTRITION BOARD. *The relationship of nutrition to brain development and behavior.* National Academy of Sciences, National Research Council, Washington, DC, 1973.

FORESTER, LEONA M. Idiomagic! *Elementary English*, January 1974, *51*, 125–127.

FORGAN, HARRY W., & MANGRUM, CHARLES T. *Teaching content area reading skills* (2nd ed.). Columbus OH: Charles E. Merrill, 1981.

FOSTER, GLEN G., SCHMIDT, CARL R., & SABATINO, DAVID. Teacher expectations and the label "learning disabled." *Journal of Learning Disabilities*, February 1976, *9*, 111–114.

FOTHERINGHAM, JOHN B., & CREAL, DOROTHY. Family socioeconomic and educational-emotional characteristics as predictors of school achievement. *Journal of Educational Research*, July/August 1980, *73*, 311–314.

FOWLER, CAROL A. Some aspects of language perception by eye: The beginning reader. In O. Tzeng & H. Singer (Eds.), *Perception of print: Reading research in experimental psychology.* Hillsdale, NJ: LEA, 1981. Pp. 171–196.

FOWLER, GERALD L. Developing comprehension skills in primary students through use of story frames. *The Reading Teacher*, November 1982, *36*, 176–179.

FOWLER, JOSEPH W., & PETERSON, PENELOPE L. Increasing reading persistence and altering attributional style of learned helpless children. *Journal of Educational Psychology*, April 1981, *73*, 251–260.

FOX, BARBARA, & ROUTH, DONALD K. Phonemic analysis and synthesis as word attack skills. *Journal of Educational Psychology*, February 1976, *68*, 70–74.

FOX, BARBARA, & ROUTH, DONALD K. Phonemic analysis and severe reading disability in children. *Journal of Psycholinguistic Research*, 1980, *9*, 115–120.

FOX, BARBARA, & ROUTH, DONALD K. Reading disability, phonemic analysis, and dysphonetic spelling: A followup study. *Journal of Clinical Child Psychology*, Spring 1983, *12*, 28–32.

FRAGER, ALAN M. How good are content teachers' judgments of the reading abilities of secondary school students? *Journal of Reading*, February 1984, *27*, 402–406.

FRANK, JAN, & LEVINSON, HAROLD N. Dysmetric dyslexia and dyspraxia—Synopsis of a continuing research project. *Academic Therapy*, Winter 1975–1976, *11*, 133–143.

FRANK, JAN, & LEVINSON, HAROLD N. Compensatory mechanisms in cerebellar-vestibular dysfunction, dysmetric dyslexia, and dyspraxia. *Academic Therapy*, Fall 1976, *12*, 5–28.

FRANK, JAN, & LEVINSON, HAROLD N. Anti-motion sickness medications in dysmetric dyslexia and dyspraxia. *Academic Therapy*, Summer 1977, *12*, 411–424.

FRASHER, RAMONA S. Know your reluctant reader's interests. *Reading World*, October 1978, *18*, 67–71.

FRASHER, RAMONA S. A feminist look at literature for children: Ten years later. In E. Sheridan (Ed.), *Sex stereotypes and reading: Research and strategies*. Newark, DE: International Reading Association, 1982, Pp. 64–79.

FRAZIER, ALEXANDER. Developing a vocabulary of the senses. *Elementary English*, February 1970, *47*, 176–184.

FREASIER, AILEEN W. Teacher self-help IEP rating scale. *Academic Therapy*, March 1983, *18*, 487–493.

FREDERICKSEN, JOHN R. Sources of process interaction in reading. In A. Lesgold & C. Perfetti (Eds.), *Interactive processes in reading*. Hillsdale, NJ: LEA, 1981. Pp. 361–385.

FREDERICKSEN, JOHN R. A componential theory of reading skills and their interaction. Technical Report No. 227. Champaign, IL: Center for the Study of Reading, University of Illinois, January 1982. (a)

FREDERICKSEN, JOHN R. Sources of process interactions in reading. Technical Report No. 242. Champaign, IL: Center for the Study of Reading, University of Illinois, May 1982. (b)

FRENZEL, NORMAN J. Adjusting readability through rewriting. *Wisconsin State Reading Association Journal*, Spring 1982, *26*, 20–21, 24.

FREY, HERBERT. Improving the performance of poor readers through autogenic relaxation training. *The Reading Teacher*, May 1980, *33*, 928–932.

FRIED, ITZHAK, *et al.* Developmental dyslexia: Electrophysiological evidence of clinical subgroups. *Brain and Language*, January 1981, *12*, 14–22.

FRIEDMAN, GLENN, & REYNOLDS, ELIZABETH G. Enriching basal reader lessons with semantic webbing. *The Reading Teacher*, March 1980, *33*, 677–684.

FRITH, UTA. Unexpected spelling problems. In U. Frith (Ed.), *Cognitive processes in spelling*. New York: Academic Press, 1980. Pp. 495–515.

FRITH, UTA, & FRITH, CHRISTOPHER. Relationships between reading and spelling. In J. Kavanagh & R. Venesky (Eds.), *Orthography, reading, and dyslexia*. Baltimore: University Park Press, 1980. Pp. 287–295.

FROESE, VICTOR. Cloze readability versus the Dale–Chall formula. In B. S. Schulwitz (Ed.), *Teachers tangibles, techniques: Comprehension of content in reading*. Newark, DE: International Reading Association, 1975. Pp. 23–31.

FROESE, VICTOR. Functional reading levels: From graded word lists. *The Alberta Journal of Educational Research*, December 1976, *22*, 325–329.

FROESE, VICTOR. Judging global readability. *The Alberta Journal of Educational Research*, June 1981, *27*, 133–137.

FROST, BARRY P. The role of intelligence "C" in the selection of children for remedial reading. *The Alberta Journal of Educational Research*, 1963, *9*, 73–78.

FROSTIG, MARIANNE. Corrective reading in the classroom. *The Reading Teacher*, April 1965, *18*, 573–580.

FROSTIG, MARIANNE. Visual perception, integrative functions and academic learning. *Journal of Learning Disabilities*, January 1972, *5*, 1–15.

FROSTIG, MARIANNE, & MASLOW, PHYLLIS. Neuropsychological contributions to education. *Journal of Learning Disabilities*, October 1979, *12*, 538–552.

FRY, EDWARD. *Comparison of three methods of reading instruction (ITA, DMS, TO): Results at the end of third grade.* Final Report, Project No. 3050. New Brunswick: Rutgers, The State University, 1967.

FRY, EDWARD. A readability formula that saves time. *Journal of Reading*, April 1968, *11*, 513–516.

FRY, EDWARD. *Reading instruction for classroom and clinic.* New York: McGraw-Hill, 1972.

FRY, EDWARD. The readability principle. *Language Arts*, September 1975, *52*, 847–851.

FRY, EDWARD. Crossfire: No precision formulas. *The Reading Teacher*, April 1976, *29*, 686–687.

FRY, EDWARD. Fry's readability graph: Clarifications, validity, and extension to level 17. *Journal of Reading*, December 1977, *21*, 242–252.

FRY, EDWARD. Comments on the preceding Harris and Jacobson comparison of the Fry, Spache, and Harris-Jacobson readability formulas. *The Reading Teacher*, May 1980, *33*, 924–926. (a)

FRY, EDWARD. The new Instant Word List. *The Reading Teacher*, December 1980, *34*, 284–289. (b)

FRY, EDWARD. Graphical literacy. *Journal of Reading*, February 1981, *24*, 383–390. Also in A. J. Harris & E. Sipay (Eds.), *Readings on reading instruction* (3rd ed.). New York: Longman, 1984. Pp. 337–343.

FRY, EDWARD B., POLK, JACQUELINE K., & FOUNTOUKIDIS, DONA. *The reading teacher's book of lists.* Englewood Cliffs, NJ: Prentice-Hall, 1984.

FRY, EDWARD, WEBER, JANE, & DEPIERRO, JOSEPH. A partial validation of the kernel distance theory for readability. In P. D. Pearson & J. Hansen (Eds.), *Reading: disciplined inquiry in process and practice.* Clemson, SC: National Reading Conference, 1978. Pp. 121–124.

FRY, MAURINE A., & LAGOMARSINO, LINDA. Factors that influence reading: A developmental perspective. *School Psychology Review*, Summer 1982, *11*, 239–250.

FULLER, GERALD B., & FULLER, DIANE L. Reality therapy: Helping LD children make better choices. *Academic Therapy*, January 1982, *17*, 269–277.

FULLMER, ROBERT A. Maximal reading and auding rates. Unpublished doctoral dissertation, Harvard University, 1980.

FUNKHOUSER, G. R., & MACCOBY, N. Study on communicating science information to a lay audience, Phase II. Institute for Communication Research, Stanford University, September 1971.

FURNISS, DAVID W. Effects of stressing oral reading accuracy on comprehension. *Reading Psychology*, Fall 1980, *2*, 8–14.

FUSARO, JOSEPH. Eye-voice span and linguistic constraints in elementary school children. Unpublished doctoral dissertation, State University of New York at Albany, 1974.

FUSARO, JOSEPH A. Grapheme-phoneme and phoneme-grapheme correspondences. *Perceptual & Motor Skills*, 1978, *47*, 171–174.

FUSARO, JOSEPH A., & CONOVER, WILLIS M. Readability of two tabloid and two nontabloid papers. *Journalism Quarterly*, Spring 1983, *60*, 142–144.

GADDES, WILLIAM H. *Learning disabilities and brain function: A neuropsychological approach.* New York: Springer-Verlag, 1980.

GADOW, KENNETH D. School involvement in pharmacotherapy for behavior disorders. *Journal of Special Education*, Winter 1982, *16*, 385–399.

GALABURDA, ALBERT M. Developmental dyslexia: Current anatomical research. *Annals of Dyslexia*, 1983, *33*, 41–53.

GALABURDA, ALBERT M., & KEMPER, THOMAS L. Cytoarchitectonic abnormalities in developmental dyslexia. *Annals of Neurology*, August 1979, *6*, 94–100.

GALDA, S. LEE. Assessment: Responses to literature. In A. Berger & H. A. Robinson (Eds.), *Secondary school reading: What research reveals for classroom practice.* Urbana, IL: NCTE & ERIC/RCS, 1982. Pp. 111–125. (a)

GALDA, S. LEE. Playing about a story: Its impact on comprehension. *The Reading Teacher*, October 1982, *36*, 52–55. (b)

GAMBRELL, LINDA B. Think-time: Implications for reading instruction. *The Reading Teacher*, November 1980, *34*, 143–146.

GAMBRELL, LINDA B., & JARRELL, MARY. Summer reading: Description and evaluation of a program for children and parents. *Reading World*, October 1980, *20*, 1–9.

GAMBRELL, LINDA B., WILSON, ROBERT M., & GANITT, WALTER N. Classroom observations of task-attending behaviors of good and poor readers. *Journal of Educational Research*, July/August 1981, 74, 400–404.

GANS, ROMA. *Guiding children's reading through experiences*. New York: Teachers College Press, 1941; 2nd ed., 1979.

GARDINO, JOSEPH P. Twenty tips for better classroom management. *Academic Therapy*, May 1981, 16, 533–537.

GARDNER, KEITH. The initial teaching alphabet (i.t.a.) and remedial reading programme. *Slow Learning Child*, 1966, 13, 67–71.

GARMAN, DOROTHY. Language development and first-grade reading achievement. *Reading World*, October 1981, 21, 40–49.

GARNER, RUTH. Strategic behaviors in reading. *Topics in Learning and Learning Disabilities*, January 1983, 2, 12–19.

GARREN, RICHARD B. Hemispheric laterality differences among four levels of reading achievement. *Perceptual & Motor Skills*, 1980, 50, 119–123.

GARRETT, HENRY E. *Statistics in psychology and education* (5th ed.). New York: Longman, 1958.

GASKINS, IRENE W. Reading for learning: Going beyond basals in the elementary grades. *The Reading Teacher*, December 1981, 35, 323–328.

GATES, ARTHUR I. *The improvement of reading: A program of diagnostic and remedial methods*. New York: Macmillan, 1927; 2nd ed., 1935; 3rd ed., 1947.

GATES, ARTHUR I. The necessary mental age for beginning reading. *Elementary School Journal*, 1937, 27, 497–508.

GATES, ARTHUR I. The role of personality maladjustment in reading disability. *Journal of Genetic Psychology*, 1941, 59, 77–83.

GATES, ARTHUR I. Character and purposes of the yearbook. In N. B. Henry (Ed.), *Reading in the elementary school*. 48th Yearbook of the National Society for the Study of Education, Part II. Chicago: University of Chicago Press, 1949. Chapter I.

GATTEGNO, CALEB, & HINMAN, DOROTHY. Words in color. In J. Money (Ed.), *The disabled reader*. Baltimore: Johns Hopkins University Press, 1966. Pp. 175–192.

GAUS, PAULA J. The indispensable reading teacher. *The Reading Teacher*, December 1983, 37, 269–272.

GAZZANIGA, M. S., & SPERRY, R. W. Language after section of the cerebral commissures. *Brain*, 1967, 90, 131–248.

GEESLIN, DORINE H., & WILSON, RICHARD C. Effect of reading age on reading interests. *Elementary English*, May 1972, 49, 750–756.

GENNSEMER, IRA B., WALKER, C. CALVIN, & CADMAN, THOMAS E. Using the Peabody Picture Vocabulary Test with children having difficulty learning. *Journal of Learning Disabilities*, March 1976, 9, 179–181.

GENTILE, LANCE, & MCMILLAN, MERNA M. Humor and the reading program. *Journal of Reading*, January 1978, 21, 343–349. Also in A. J. Harris & E. Sipay (Eds.), *Readings on reading instruction* (3rd ed.). New York: Longman, 1984. Pp. 369–373.

GENTRY, J. RICHARD. An analysis of developmental spelling in GNYS AT WRK. *The Reading Teacher*, November 1982, 36, 192–200.

GEOFFRION, LEO D., & GEOFFRION, OLGA P. *Computers and reading instruction*. Reading, MA: Addison-Wesley, 1983.

GERRELL, HOLLY R., & MASON, GEORGE E. Computer-chunked and traditional text. *Reading World*, March 1983, 22, 241–246.

GESCHWIND, NORMAN. Disconnection syndromes in animals and man, Part I. *Brain*, 1965, 88, 237–294.

GESCHWIND, NORMAN. Biological associations of left-handedness. *Annals of Dyslexia* 1983, 33, 29–40.

GETTINGER, MARIBETH, & WHITE, MARY A. Which is the stronger correlate of school learning? Time to learn or measured intelligence: *Journal of Educational Psychology*, August 1979, 71, 405–412.

GEYER, JOHN J. Perceptual systems in reading: The prediction of a temporal eye-voice span. In H. K. Smith (Ed.), *Perception and reading*. Newark, DE: International Reading Association, 1968. Pp. 44–52.

GEYER, JOHN J. Comprehensive and partial models related to the reading process. *Reading Research Quarterly*, Summer 1972, 7, 541–587.

GIBSON, ELEANOR, & LEVIN, HARRY. *The psychology of reading*. Cambridge, MA: MIT Press, 1975.

GICKLING, EDWARD E., & ARMSTRONG, DAVID L. Levels of instructional difficulty as related to on-task behavior, task completion, and comprehension. *Journal of Learning Disabilities*, November 1978, 11, 559–566.

GILLESPIE, PATRICIA H., MILLER, TED L., & FIELDER, VIRGINIA D. Legislative definition of learning disabilities: Roadblocks to effective service. *Journal of Learning Disabilities*, December 1975, 8, 660–666.

GILLIAM, BETTYE, PEÑA, SYLVIA C., & MOUNTAIN, LEE. The Fry Graph applied to Spanish readability. *The Reading Teacher*, January 1980, 33, 426–430.

GILLIAM, JAMES E., & COLEMAN, MARGARET C. Who influences IEP committee decisions. *Exceptional Children*, May 1981, 47, 642–644.

GILLILAND, HAP. The new view of Native Americans in children's books. *The Reading Teacher*, May 1982, 35, 912–916.

GILLINGHAM, ANNA, & STILLMAN, BESSIE W. *Remedial training for children with specific difficulty in reading, spelling, and penmanship* (7th ed.). Cambridge, MA: Educators Publishing Service, 1966.

GIPE, JOAN P. Use of relevant context helps kids learn new word meanings. *The Reading Teacher*, January 1980, 33, 398–402.

GITTELMAN, RACHEL, & FEINGOLD, INGRID. Children with reading disorders: Efficacy of reading remediation. *Journal of Child Psychology & Psychiatry & Allied Disciplines*, April 1983, 24, 167–191.

GITTELMAN, RACHEL, KLEIN, DONALD F., & FEINGOLD, INGRID. Children with reading disorders II. Effects of methylphenidate in combination with reading remediation. *Journal of Child Psychology & Psychiatry & Allied Disciplines*, April 1983, 24, 193–212.

GLASS, GENE V., & ROBBINS, MELVYN P. A critique of experiments on the role of neurological organization in reading performance. *Reading Research Quarterly*, Fall 1967, 3, 5–52.

GLASS, GENE V., *et al. School class size: Research and policy*. Beverly Hills, CA: Sage Publications, 1982.

GLASS, GERALD G. *Teaching decoding as separate from reading*. Garden City, NY: Adelphi University Press, 1973.

GLASS, GERALD G., & BURTON, ELIZABETH H. How do they decode? Verbalizations and observed behaviors of successful decoders. *The Reading Teacher*, March 1973, 26, 645.

GLATTHORN, ALLAN A. Demystifying the teaching of writing. *Language Arts*, October 1982, 59, 722–725.

GLAZZARD, PEGGY. Kindergarten predictors of school achievement. *Journal of Learning Disabilities*, December 1979, 12, 689–694.

GLEITMAN, LILA R., & ROZIN, PAUL. Teaching reading by means of a syllabary. *Reading Research Quarterly*, Summer 1973, 8, 447–483.

GLUSHKO, ROBERT J. Principles for pronouncing print: The psychology of phonology. In A. Lesgold & C. Perfetti (Eds.), *Interactive processes in reading*. Hillsdale, NJ: LEA, 1981. Pp. 61–84.

GODFREY, JOHN J. *et al.* Performance of dyslexic children on speech perception tests. *Journal of Experimental Child Psychology*, December 1981, 32, 401–424.

GOINS, JEAN T. *Visual perceptual abilities and early reading progress*. Supplementary Educational Monograph No. 87. Chicago: University of Chicago Press, February 1958.

GOLD, JANET G. Writing composition activities to enhance reading comprehension, 1981. ED 205 903

GOLD, PATRICIA C. Cognitive mapping. *Academic Therapy*, January 1984, 19, 277–284.

GOLD, YVONNE. Helping students discover the origins of words. *The Reading Teacher*, December 1981, 35, 350–351.

GOLDBERG, HERMAN K., SHIFFMAN, GILBERT B., & BENDER, MICHAEL. *Dyslexia: Interdisciplinary approaches to reading disabilities*. New York: Grune & Stratton, 1983.

GOLDFIELD, BEVERLY, & SNOW, CATHERINE. Reading books with children: The mechanics of parental influences on children's reading achievement. In J. Flood (Ed.), *Promoting reading comprehension*. Newark, DE: International Reading Association, 1984. Pp. 204–215.

GOLDSMITH, JOSEPHINE S., NICOLICH, MARK J., & HAUPT, EDWARD J. A system for the analysis of word and context-based factors in reading. In J. Niles & L. A. Harris (Eds.), *New inquiries in reading research and instruction*. Rochester, NY: National Reading Conference, 1982. Pp. 185–190.

GOLINKOFF, ROBERTA M. A comparison of reading comprehension processes in good and poor comprehenders. *Reading Research Quarterly*, 1975–1976, *11* (4), 623–659.

GONZALES, PHILLIP C. How to begin language instruction for non-English-speaking students. *Language Arts*, February 1981, *58*, 175–180. (a)

GONZALES, PHILLIP C. Beginning English reading for ESL students. *The Reading Teacher*, November 1981, *35*, 154–162. (b) Also in A. J. Harris & E. Sipay (Eds.), *Readings on reading instruction* (3rd ed.). New York: Longman, 1984. Pp. 443–451.

GONZALES, PHILLIP C., & ELIJAH, DAVID V., JR. Rereading effect on error patterns and performance levels on the IRI. *The Reading Teacher*, April 1975, *26*, 647–652.

GONZALES, PHILLIP C., & ELIJAH, DAVID. Stability of error patterns on the informal reading inventory. *Reading Improvement*, Winter 1978, *15*, 279–288.

GOOD, THOMAS L. Teacher effectiveness in the elementary school: What we know about it now. *Journal of Teacher Education*, March/April 1979, *30*, 52–64.

GOOD, THOMAS L., & STIPEK, DEBORAH J. Individual differences in the classroom: A psychological perspective. In G. Fenstermacher & J. Goodlad (Eds.), *Individual differences and the common curriculum*. 82nd Yearbook of the National Society for the Study of Education, Part I. Chicago: University of Chicago Press, 1983. Pp. 9–43.

GOODLAD, JOHN L., & ANDERSON, ROBERT H. *The nongraded elementary school*. New York: Harcourt, Brace and World, 1959.

GOODMAN, KENNETH S. Reading: A psycholinguistic guessing game. *Journal of the Reading Specialist*, May 1967, *6*, 126–135. Also in A. J. Harris & E. Sipay (Eds.), *Readings on reading instruction* (3rd ed.). New York: Longman, 1984. Pp. 45–52.

GOODMAN, KENNETH S. Analyses of reading miscues: Applied psycholinguistics. *Reading Research Quarterly*, Fall 1969, *5*, 9–30.

GOODMAN, KENNETH S. Orthography in a theory of reading instruction. *Elementary English*, December 1972, *49*, 1254–1261.

GOODMAN, KENNETH S. Letters to the editor. *Reading Research Quarterly*, 1981, *16* (3), 477–478.

GOODMAN, KENNETH S. Revaluing readers and reading. *Topics in Learning and Learning Disorders*, January 1982, *1*, 87–93.

GOODMAN, KENNETH S. Unity in reading. In A. Purves & O. Niles (Eds.), *Becoming a reader in a complex society*. 83rd Yearbook of the National Society for the Study of Education, Part I. Chicago: University of Chicago Press, 1984. Pp. 79–114.

GOODMAN, KENNETH S., & BIRD, LOIS B. On the wording of texts: A study of intra-text word frequency. *Research in the Teaching of English*, May 1984, *18*, 119–145.

GOODMAN, KENNETH S., & GOLLASCH, FREDERICK V. Word omissions: Deliberate and non-deliberate. *Reading Research Quarterly*, 1980, *16* (1), 6–31.

GOODMAN, KENNETH S., & GOODMAN, YETTA M. Learning about psycholinguistic process by analyzing oral reading. *Harvard Educational Review*, August 1977, *47*, 317–333.

GOODMAN, KENNETH S., & GOODMAN, YETTA M. Learning to read is natural. In L. Resnick & P. Weaver (Eds.), *Theory and practice of early reading*, Vol. 1. Hillsdale, NJ: LEA, 1979. Pp. 137–154.

GOODMAN, KENNETH S., & GOODMAN, YETTA M. A whole-language comprehension-centered view of reading development. In L. Reed & S. Ward (Eds.), *Basic skills issues and choices: Approaches to basic skills instruction, 2*. St Louis: CEMREL, April 1982. Pp. 125–134.

GOODMAN, KENNETH, & GOODMAN, YETTA. Reading and writing relationships: Pragmatic function. *Language Arts*, May 1983, *60*, 590–599.

GOODMAN, YETTA M. Using children's reading miscues for new teaching strategies. *The Reading Teacher*, February 1970, *23*, 455–459. Also in A. J. Harris & E. Sipay (Eds.), *Readings on reading instruction* (3rd ed.). New York: Longman, 1984. Pp. 219–222.

GOODMAN, YETTA. Reading strategy lessons: Expanding reading effectiveness. In W. Page (Ed.), *Help for the reading teacher: New directions in research*. Urbana, IL: NCRE & ERIC/RCS, 1975. Pp. 34–41.

GOODMAN, YETTA M. Miscues, errors and reading comprehension. In J. E. Merritt (Ed.), *New horizons in reading*. Newark, DE: International Reading Association, 1976. Pp. 86–93.

GOODMAN, YETTA M. Beginning reading development: Strategies and principles. In R. Parker & F. A. Davis (Eds.), *Developing literacy: Young children's use of language*. Newark, DE: International Reading Association, 1983. Pp. 68–83.

GOODMAN, YETTA M., & BURKE, CAROLYN L. *Reading miscue inventory*. New York: Owen, 1972.

GOODMAN, YETTA, & BURKE, CAROLYN. *Reading strategies: Focus on comprehension*. New York: Holt, Rinehart and Winston, 1980.

GOODMAN, YETTA, & GREENE, JENNIFER. Grammar and reading in the classroom. In R. W. Shuy (Ed.), *Linguistic theory: What can it say about reading?* Newark, DE: International Reading Association, 1977. Pp. 18–30.

GORDON, BELITA. Teach them to read the questions. *Journal of Reading*, February 1983, *26*, 126–136.

GORDON, CHRISTIE J., & BRAUN, CARL. Using story schema as an aid to reading and writing. *The Reading Teacher*, November 1983, *37*, 116–121.

GORDON, EDMUND W. Implications for compensatory education drawn from reflections on the teaching and learning of reading. In L. Resnick & P. Weaver (Eds.), *Theory and practice of early reading*, Vol. 2. Hillsdale, NJ: LEA, 1979. Pp. 299–319.

GORDON, HAROLD W. The learning disabled are cognitively right. *Topics in Learning and Learning Disabilities*, April 1983, *3*, 29–39.

GORE, WILLIAM V., & VANCE, BOONEY. The micro meets the IEP. *Academic Therapy*, September 1983, *19*, 89–91.

GORRITI, CARLOS J. ROBLES, & MUÑIZ, ANA M. RODRIGUEZ. Learning problems in Argentina. In L. Tarnopol & M. Tarnopol (Eds.), *Reading disabilities: An international perspective*. Baltimore: University Park Press, 1976. Pp. 27–37.

GORTH, WILLIAM P., & PERKINS, MARCY R. Skill definitions in state competency testing programs. In L. Reed & S. Ward (Eds.), *Basic skills: Issues and choices, 2*. St. Louis: CEMREL 1982. Pp. 174–182.

GOUGH, PAULINE B. Introducing children to books via television. *The Reading Teacher*, January 1979, *32*, 458–461.

GOUGH, PHILIP B. One second of reading. In J. F. Kavanagh & I. G. Mattingly (Eds.), *Language by ear and eye*. Cambridge, MA: MIT Press, 1972. Pp. 331–358.

GOUGH, PHILIP B., ALFORD, JACK A., & HOLLEY-WILCOX, PAMELA. Words and context. In O. Tzeng & H. Singer (Eds.), *Perception of print: Reading research in experimental psychology*. Hillsdale, NJ: LEA, 1981. Pp. 85–102.

GOUGH, PHILIP B., & COSKY, MICHAEL J. One second of reading again. In N. Castellan *et al.* (Eds.), *Cognitive theory*, Vol. 2. Hillsdale, NJ: LEA, 1977. Pp. 271–288.

GRAESSER, ARTHUR C., HOFFMAN, NICHOLAS L., & CLARK, LESLIE F. Structural components of reading time. *Journal of Verbal Learning & Verbal Behavior*, April 1980, *19*, 135–151.

GRAHAM, KENNETH G., & ROBINSON, H. ALAN. *Study skills handbook: A guide for all teachers*. Newark, DE: International Reading Association, 1984.

GRANOWSKY, ALVIN, ROSE, ANGIE, & BARTON, NANCY. Parents as partners in education. Ginn Occasional Papers, No. 2. Columbus, OH: Ginn, 1981.

GRAVES, MICHAEL F. Selecting vocabulary to teach in the intermediate and secondary grades. In J. Flood (Ed.), *Promoting reading comprehension*. Newark, DE: International Reading Association, 1984. Pp. 245–260.

GRAVES, MICHAEL F., BOETTCHER, JUDITH A., & RYDER, RANDALL A. *Easy reading: Book series and periodicals for less able readers*. Newark, DE: International Reading Association, 1979.

GRAVES, MICHAEL F., BRUNETTI, GERALD J., & SLATER, WAYNE H. The reading vocabularies of primary grade children of varying geographic and social backgrounds. In J. Niles & L. A. Harris (Eds.), *New inquiries in reading: Research and instruction*. Rochester, NY: National Reading Conference, 1982. Pp. 99–104.

GRAVES, MICHAEL F., COOKE, CHERYL L., & LABERGE, MICHAEL. Effects of previewing difficult short stories on low ability junior high school students' comprehension, recall and attitudes. *Reading Research Quarterly*, Spring 1983, *18*, 262–276.

GRAVES, MICHAEL, & HAMMOND, HEIDI. A validated procedure for teaching prefixes and its effect on students's ability to assign meaning to novel words. In M. Kamil & A. Moe (Eds.), *Perspectives on reading research and instruction*. Washington, DC: National Reading Conference, 1980. Pp. 184–188.

GRAY, CLARENCE T. *Deficiencies in reading ability: Their diagnoses and remedies*. Boston: D. C. Heath, 1922.

GRAY, RICHARD A., *et al*. Is proficiency in oral language a predictor of academic success? *The Elementary School Journal*, May 1980, *80*, 261–268.

GRAY, WILLIAM S. *Remedial cases in reading: Their diagnosis and treatment*. Supplementary Educational Monographs, No. 22. Chicago: University of Chicago Press, 1922.

GRAY, WILLIAM S. A modern program of reading instruction for the grades and high school. In G. M. Whipple (Ed.), *Report of the national committee on reading*. 24th Yearbook of the National Society for the Study of Education, Part I. Bloomington, IL: Public School Publishing Co., 1925. Pp. 21–74.

GRAY, WILLIAM S. *On their own in reading*. Glenview, IL: Scott, Foresman, 1948.

GRAY, WILLIAM S. Reading. In C. W. Harris (Ed.), *Encyclopedia of educational research* (2nd ed.). New York: Macmillan, 1960. P. 1106.

GREANEY, VINCENT. Factors related to amount and type of leisure time reading. *Reading Research Quarterly*, 1980, *15* (3), 337–357.

GREEN, JUDITH, & BLOOME, DAVID. Ethnography and reading: Issues, approaches, criteria, and findings. In J. Niles & L. A. Harris (Eds.), *Searches for meaning in reading/language processing and instruction*. Rochester, NY: National Reading Conference, 1983. Pp. 6–30.

GREEN, JUDITH L., & HARKER, JUDITH O. Reading to children: A communicative process. In J. Langer & M. T. Burke-Smith (Eds.), *Reader meets author/bridging the gap: A psycholinguistic and sociolinguistic perspective*. Newark, DE: International Reading Association, 1982. Pp. 196–221.

GREEN, ORVILLE C., & PERLMAN, SUZANNE M. Endocrinology and disorders of learning. In H. R. Myklebust (Ed.), *Progress in learning disabilities*, Vol. II. New York: Grune & Stratton, 1971. Pp. 1–17.

GREEN, RICHARD R. Evaluation of materials designed to improve the balance in reading between comprehension and rate. Unpublished doctoral dissertation, Boston University, 1971.

GREENBAUM, JUDITH, VARAS, MARILYN, & MARKEL, GERALDINE. Using books about handicapped children. *The Reading Teacher*, January 1980, *33*, 416–419.

GREENBLATT, SAMUEL H. Localization of lesions in alexia. In A. Kertesz (Ed.), *Localization in neuropsychology*. New York: Academic Press, 1983. Pp. 323–356.

GREENE, ELLEN, & SCHOENFELD, MADALYNNE. *A multi-media approach to children's literature: A selective list of films, filmstrips, and records based on children's books* (2nd ed.). Chicago: American Library Association, 1977.

GREENE, JENNIFER C. Individual and teacher class effects in aptitude treatment studies. *American Educational Research*, Fall 1980, *17*, 291–302.

GREENEWALD, M. JANE, & PEDERSON, CAROLYN. Effects of sentence organization instruction in reading comprehension of poor readers. In J. Niles & L. A. Harris (Eds.), *Search for meaning in reading/language processing and instruction*. Rochester, NY: National Reading Conference, 1983. Pp. 101–103.

GREENLAW, M. JEAN. Reading interest research and children's choices. In N. Roser & M. Frith (Eds.), *Children's choices: Teaching with books children like*. Newark, DE: International Reading Association, 1983. Pp. 90–92.

GREENLAW, M. JEAN, & MOORE, DAVID W. What kinds of reading courses are taught in junior and senior high school? *Journal of Reading*, March 1982, *25*, 534–536.

GREENLINGER-HARLESS, CAROL S. Updated cross-referenced index to U.S. reading materials, grades K-8. *The Reading Teacher*, March 1984, *37*, 613–625. Errata are indicated in *The Reading Teacher*, May 1984, *37*, 871, 878–879.

GREER, JOHN G., & WETHERED, CHRIS E. Learned helplessness: A piece of the burnout puzzle. *Exceptional Children*, April 1984, *50*, 524–530.

GREER, MARGARET. Affective growth through reading. *The Reading Teacher*, January 1972, *25*, 336–341.

GRIESE, ARNOLD A. Focusing on students of different cultural backgrounds—the Eskimo and Indian pupil—special problems in reading comprehension. *Elementary English*, April 1971, *48*, 229–234.

GRIFFEN, GARY A. (Ed.). *Staff development*. 82nd Yearbook of the National Society for the Study of Education, Part II. Chicago, IL: University of Chicago Press, 1983.

GRIFFITHS, ANITA N. Self-concept in remedial work with dyslexic children. *Academic Therapy*, Winter 1970–1971, *6*, 125–133.

GRINNELL, PAULA C. Reading comprehension and picture usage: A study with first graders. In J. Niles & L. A. Harris (Eds.), *New inquiries in reading research and instruction*. Rochester, NY: National Reading Conference, 1982. Pp. 136–139.

GROFF, PATRICK. *The syllable: Its nature and pedagogical usefulness*. Portland, OR: Northwest Regional Educational Laboratory, April 1971.

GROFF, PATRICK. Research in brief: Shapes as cues in word recognition. *Visible Language*, Winter 1975, *9*, 67–71.

GROFF, PATRICK. Blending: Basic process or beside the point? *Reading World*, March 1976, *15*, 161–166. (a)

GROFF, PATRICK. Limitations of context cues for beginning readers. *Reading World*, December 1976, *16*, 97–103. (b)

GROFF, PATRICK J. Resolving the letter name controversy. *The Reading Teacher*, January 1984, *37*, 384–388.

GRONLUND, NORMAN E. *Stating behavioral objectives for classroom instruction*. New York: Macmillan, 1973.

GRONLUND, NORMAN E. *Preparing criterion-referenced tests for classroom instruction*. New York: Macmillan, 1978.

GROSS, ALICE D. The relationship between sex differences and reading ability in an Israeli kibbutz system. In D. Feitelson (Ed.), *Cross-cultural perspectives on reading and reading research*. Newark, DE: International Reading Association, 1978. Pp. 72–88.

GRUNDIN, HANS U., *et al*. Cloze procedure and comprehension: An exploratory study across three languages. In D. Feitelson (Ed.), *Cross-cultural perspectives on reading and reading* research. Newark, DE: International Reading Association, 1978. Pp. 48–61.

GUERRA, CATHY L., & PAYNE, DELORES B. Using popular books and magazines to interest children in general science. *Journal of Reading*, April 1981, *24*, 583–586.

GUILFORD, J. P. Cognitive styles: What are they? *Educational and Psychological Measurement*, Fall 1980, *40*, 715–735.

GUNN, V. PATRICIA, & ELKINS, JOHN. Clozing the reading gap. *Australian Journal of Reading*, August 1979, *2*, 144–151. Also in A. J. Harris & E. Sipay (Eds.), *Readings on reading instruction* (3rd ed.). New York: Longman 1984. Pp. 293–298.

GUNNING, ROBERT. Fog index of a passage. *Academic Therapy*, March 1979, *14*, 489–491.

GUNNISON, JUDY, KAUFMAN, NADEEN L., & KAUFMAN, ALAN S. Reading remediation based on sequential and simultaneous processing. *Academic Therapy*, January 1982, *17*, 297–307.

GURALNICK, MICHAEL J. Alphabet discrimination and distinctive features: Research review and educational implications. *Journal of Learning Disabilities*, August 1972, *5*, 427–434.

GUSZAK, FRANK J. Relations between teacher practice and knowledge of reading techniques in selected grade school classes. Madison: School of Education, University of Wisconsin, BR 5-8402, 1966. ED 010 191

GUSZAK, FRANK J. Teacher questioning and reading. *The Reading Teacher*, December 1967, *21*, 227–234.

GUTHRIE, JOHN T. Learnability versus readability of texts. *Journal of Educational Research*, February 1972, *65*, 273–280.

GUTHRIE, JOHN T. Models of reading and reading disability. *Journal of Educational Psychology*, August 1973, *65*, 9–18.

GUTHRIE, JOHN T. Time in reading programs. *The Reading Teacher*, January 1980, *33*, 500–502.

GUTHRIE, JOHN T. Acquisition of newspaper readership. *The Reading Teacher*, February 1981, *34*, 616–618. (a)

GUTHRIE, JOHN T. Invalidity of reading tests. *Journal of Reading*, December 1981, *25*, 300–302. (b)

GUTHRIE, JOHN T. Reading in New Zealand: Achievement and volume. *Reading Research Quarterly*, 1981, *17* (1), 6–27. (c)

GUTHRIE, JOHN T. Teaching methods. *The Reading Teacher*, January 1981, *34*, 492–494. (d)

GUTHRIE, JOHN T. Corporate education for the electronic culture. *Journal of Reading*, February 1982, *25*, 492–495.

GUTHRIE, JOHN T. Learning values form textbooks. *Journal of Reading*, March 1983, *26*, 574–576.

GUTHRIE, JOHN T. Lexical learning. *The Reading Teacher*, March 1984, *37*, 666–667.

GUTHRIE, JOHN T., MARTUZA, VICTOR, & SEIFORT, MARY. Impacts of instructional time in reading., In L. Resnick & P. Weaver (Eds.), *Theory and practice of early reading*, Vol. 3. Hillsdale, NJ: LEA, 1979. Pp. 153–178.

GUTHRIE, JOHN T., & SEIFORT, MARY. Profiles of reading activity in a community. *Journal of Reading*, March 1983, *26*, 498–508.

GUTHRIE, JOHN T., SEIFERT, MARY, & KLINE, LLOYD W. Clues from research on programs for poor readers. In S. J. Samuels (Ed.), *What research has to say about reading instruction*. Newark, DE: International Reading Association, 1978. Pp. 1–12.

GUTHRIE, JOHN T., *et al.* The maze technique to assess, monitor reading comprehension. *The Reading Teacher*, November 1974, *28*, 161–168.

GUZZETTI, BARBARA J., & MARZANO, ROBERT J. Correlates of effective reading instruction. *The Reading Teacher*, April 1984, *37*, 754–758.

HABER, LYN R., & HABER, RALPH N. Perceptual processes in reading: An analysis-by-synthesis model. In F. Pirozzolo & M. Wittrock (Eds.), *Neuropsychological and cognitive processes in reading*. New York: Academic Press, 1981. Pp. 167–200.

HABER, RALPH N., & HABER, LYN R. The shape of a word can specify its meaning. *Reading Research Quarterly*, 1981, *16* (3), 334–345. (a)

HABER, RALPH N., & HABER, LYN R. Visual components of the reading process. *Visible Language*, 1981, *15* (2), 147–182. (b)

HABER, LYN R., HABER, RALPH N., & FURLIN, KAREN R. Word length and word shape as sources of information in reading. *Reading Research Quarterly*, Winter 1983, *18*, 165–189.

HADDOCK, MARYANN. Effects of an auditory and auditory-visual method of blending instruction on the ability of prereaders to decode synthetic words. *Journal of Educational Psychology*, December 1976, *68*, 825–831.

HADDOCK, MARYANN. Teaching blending in beginning reading instruction is important. *The Reading Teacher*, March 1978, *31*, 654–657.

HAERTEL, EDWARD, & CALFEE, ROBERT. School achievement: Thinking about what to test. *Journal of Educational Measurement*, Summer 1983, *20*, 119–132.

HAGGARD, MARTHA R. The vocabulary self-collection strategy: An active approach to word learning. *Journal of Reading*, December 1982, *26*, 203–207.

HAINES, DEBORAH J., & TORGESEN, JOSEPH K. The effects of incentives on rehearsal and short-term memory in children with reading problems. *Learning Disability Quarterly*, Spring 1979, *2*, 48–55.

HAINES, L. P., & LEONG, C. K. Coding processes in skilled and less skilled readers. *Annals of Dyslexia*, 1983, *33*, 67–89.

HALE, GORDON A. Students' prediction of prose forgetting and the effects of study strategies. Research Report 88-46. Princeton, NJ: ETS, December 1982.

HALEY, BEVERLY. Once upon a time—they lived happily. *Language Arts*, November/December 1975, *52*, 1147–1153.

HALL, MARYANNE. *Teaching reading as a language experience*. Columbus, OH: Charles E. Merrill, 1970.

HALL, MARYANNE. *The language experience approach for teaching: A research perspective* (2nd ed.). Newark, DE: International Reading Association, 1978.

HALL, VERNON C., & TURNER, RALPH R. The validity of the "different language" explanation for poor scholastic performance by black students. *Review of Educational Research*, Winter 1974, *44*, 69–81.

HALL, WILLIAM S., & GUTHRIE, LARRY F. Situational differences in use of language. In J. Langer & M. Smith-Burke (Eds.), *Reader meets author/bridging the gap*. Newark, DE: International Reading Association, 1982. Pp. 132–146.

HALLAHAN, DANIEL P., & CRUICKSHANK, WILLIAM M. *Psychoeducational foundations of learning disabilities*. Englewood Cliffs, NJ: Prentice-Hall, 1973.

HALLAHAN, DANIEL P., MARSHALL, KATHLEEN J., & LLOYD, JOHN W. Self-recording during group instruction: Effects on attention to task. *Learning Disabilities Quarterly*, Fall 1981, *4*, 407–413.

HALLAHAN, DANIEL P., et al. A comparison of the effects of reinforcement and response cost on the selective attention of learning disabled children. *Journal of Learning Disabilities*, August/September 1978, *11*, 430–438.

HALLENBECK, PHYLLIS N. Remediating with comic strips. *Journal of Learning Disabilities*, January 1976, *9*, 11–15.

HALLGREN, BERTIL. Specific dyslexia. *Acta Psychiatrica Neurologica*, Supplement No. 65, 1950, 1–287.

HALPERN, HONEY. Contemporary realistic young adult fiction: An annotated bibliography. *Journal of Reading*, January 1978, *21*, 351–356.

HAMBLETON, RONALD K. On the use of cut-off scores with criterion-referenced tests in instructional settings. *Journal of Educational Measurement*, Winter 1978, *15*, 277–290.

HAMBLETON, RONALD K., & EIGNOR, DANIEL R. Guidelines for evaluating criterion-referenced tests and test manuals. *Journal of Educational Measurement*, Winter 1978, *15*, 321–327.

HAMBLETON, RONALD K., & EIGNOR, DANIEL R. Competency test development, validation, and standard setting. In R. Jaeger & C. Tittle (Eds.), *Minimum competency achievement testing: Motives, models, measures, and consequences*. Berkeley, CA: McCutchan, 1980. Pp. 367–396.

HAMBLETON, RONALD K., et al. Criterion-referenced testing and measurement: A review of technical issues and developments. *Review of Educational Research*, Winter 1978, *48*, 1–47.

HAMILTON, HARLAN. New heroes for old? In M. J. Weiss et al. (Eds.), *New perspectives in paperbacks*. York, PA: Strine, 1973. Pp. 43–50.

HAMILTON, HARLAN. TV tie-ins as a bridge to books. *Language Arts*, February 1976, *53*, 129–130.

HAMMILL, DONALD D., COLARUSSO, R. P., & WIEDERHOLT, J. LEE. Diagnostic value of the Frostig test: A factor analytic approach. *Journal of Special Education*, 1970, *4*, 279–282.

HAMMILL, DONALD, GOODMAN, LIBBY, & WIEDERHOLT, J. LEE. Visual-motor processes: Can we train them? *The Reading Teacher*, February 1974, *27*, 469–478.

HAMMILL, DONALD D., & LARSEN, STEPHEN C. The effectiveness of psycholinguistic training. *Exceptional Children*, September 1974, *41*, 5–14. (a).

HAMMILL, DONALD, & LARSEN, STEPHEN C. The relationship of selected auditory perceptual skills and reading ability. *Journal of Learning Disabilities*, August/September 1974, 7, 429–435. (b)

HAMMILL, DONALD D., & LARSEN, STEPHEN C. The effectiveness of psycholinguistic training: A reaffirmation of position. *Exceptional Children*, March 1978, *44*, 402–414.

HAMMILL, DONALD D., & MCNUTT, GAYE. *The correlates of reading: The consensus of thirty years of correlational research*. Austin, TX: Pro-Ed, 1981.

HANEY, WALTER, & MADAUS, GEORGE. Making sense of the competency testing movement. *Harvard Educational Review*, November 1978, *48*, 462–484.

HANLEY, JOHN, & SKLAR, BERNARD. Electroencephalographic correlates of developmental reading dyslexias: Computer analysis of recordings from normal and dyslexic children. In G. Leisman (Ed.), *Basic visual processes and learning disability*, Springfield, IL: Charles C Thomas, 1976. Pp. 217–243.

HANNA, GERALD S., DYCK, NORMA J., & HOLEN, MICHAEL C. Objective analysis of achievement—Aptitude discrepancies on LD classification. *Learning Disability Quarterly*, Fall 1979, *2*, 32–38.

HANNA, GERALD S., & SCHERICH, HENRY H. An empirical evaluation of three definitions of context dependence. *Journal of Reading Behavior*, Spring 1981, *13*, 75–80.

HANNA, PAUL R., & HANNA, JEAN S. Phoneme-grapheme correspondences as cues to spelling improvement. OE-32008. Washington, DC: U.S. Government Printing Office, 1966.

HANSEN, JANE. The effects of inference training and practice on young children's reading comprehension. *Reading Research Quarterly*, 1981, *16* (3), 391–417.

HANSEN, JANE, & HUBBARD, RUTH. Poor readers can draw inferences. *The Reading Teacher*, March 1984, *37*, 586–589.

HANSEN, JANE, & PEARSON, P. DAVID. An instructional study: Improving the inferential comprehension of good and poor fourth-grade readers. Technical Report No. 235. Champaign, IL: Center for the Study of Reading, University of Illinois, March 1982.

HANSFORD, B. C., & HATTIE, J. A. The relationship between self-concept and achievement/performance measures. *Review of Educational Research*, Spring 1982, *52*, 123–142.

HARBER, JEAN R. Achievement in black English. *The Reading Teacher*, April 1982, *35*, 848–849.

HARBER, JEAN R., & BEATTY, JANE N. (Comps.) *Reading and the black English speaking child: An annotated bibliography*. Newark, DE: International Reading Association, 1978.

HARDT, ULRICH H. Literature in the language arts program. In U. Hardt (Ed.), *Teaching reading with the other language arts*. Newark, DE: International Reading Association, 1983. Pp. 104–116.

HARE, VICTORIA C. Beginning reading theory and comprehension questions in teachers' manuals. *The Reading Teacher*, May 1982, *35*, 918–923. (a)

HARE, VICTORIA C. Preassessment of topical knowledge: A validation and an extension. *Journal of Reading Behavior*, 1982, *14* (1), 77–85. (b)

HARE, VICTORIA C. What's in a word? A review of young children's difficulties with the construct "word." *The Reading Teacher*, January 1983, *37*, 360–364.

HARE, VICTORIA C., & PULLIAM, CYNTHIA A. Teacher questioning: A verification and an extension. *Journal of Reading Behavior*, Spring 1980, *12*, 69–72.

HARDY, MADELINE, STENNETT, R. G., & SMYTHE, P. C. Auditory segmentation and auditory blending in relation to beginning reading. *Alberta Journal of Educational Research*, 1973, *17*, 144–158. (a)

HARDY, MADELINE, STENNETT, R. G., & SMYTHE, P. C. Word attack: How do they "figure them out"? *Elementary English*, January 1973, *50*, 99–102. (b)

HARGIS, CHARLES H., & GICKLING, EDWARD E. The function of imagery in word recognition development. *The Reading Teacher*, May 1978, *31*, 870–874.

HARKER, W. J. An evaluative summary of models of reading comprehension. *Journal of Reading Behavior*, Winter 1972–1973, *5*, 26–34.

HARNESCHFEGER, ANNEGRET, & WILEY, DAVID E. *Achievement test score decline: Do we need to worry?* St. Louis, MO: CEMREL, Inc., 1976. (a)

HARNESCHFEGER, ANNEGRET, & WILEY, DAVID E. Achievement test scores drop. So what? *Educational Researcher*, March 1976, *5*, 5–12. (b)

HARPER, ROBERT J., & KILARR, GARY. The law and reading instruction. *Language Arts*, November/December 1977, *54*, 913–919.

HARRIGAN, JOHN E. Initial reading instruction: Phonemes, syllables, or ideographs. *Journal of Learning Disabilities*, February 1976, *9*, 21–27.

HARRIS, ALBERT J. Egoistic learning. *American Journal of Orthopsychiatry*, 1954, *24*, 781–784. (a)

HARRIS, ALBERT J. Unsolved problems in reading, II. *Elementary English*, 1954, *31*, 416–418. (b)

HARRIS, ALBERT J. Lateral dominance, directional confusion, and reading disability. *Journal of Psychology*, 1957, *44*, 283–294.

HARRIS, ALBERT J. A critical reaction to *The Nature of Reading Disability. Journal of Developmental Reading*, 1960, *3*, 238–249.

HARRIS, ALBERT J. *How to increase reading ability* (4th ed.). New York: David McKay, 1961. (a)

HARRIS, ALBERT J. Perceptual difficulties in reading disability. In J. A. Figurel (Ed.), *Changing concepts in reading instruction*. Newark, DE: International Reading Association, 1961. Pp. 281–290. (b)

HARRIS, ALBERT J. Progressive education and reading instruction. *The Reading Teacher*, November 1964, *18*, 128–138.

HARRIS, ALBERT J. (Ed.). *Some administrative problems of reading clinics*. Newark, DE: International Reading Association, 1965.

HARRIS, ALBERT J. Diagnosis and remedial instruction in reading. In H. M. Robinson (Ed.), *Innovation and change in reading instruction.* 67th Yearbook of the National Society for the Study of Education, Part II. Chicago: University of Chicago Press, 1968. Chapter 5. (a)

HARRIS, ALBERT J. Five decades of remedial reading. In J. A. Figurel (Ed.), *Forging ahead in reading.* Newark, DE: International Reading Association, 1968. Pp. 25–34. (b)

HARRIS, ALBERT J. The effective teacher of reading. *The Reading Teacher*, December 1969, *23*, 195–204.

HARRIS, ALBERT J. *Casebook on reading disability.* New York: David McKay, 1970.

HARRIS, ALBERT J. A comparison of formulas for measuring degree of reading disability. In R. E. Liebert (Ed.), *Diagnostic viewpoints in reading.* Newark, DE: International Reading Association, 1971. Pp. 113–120. (a)

HARRIS, ALBERT J. Psychological and motivational problems. In D. K. Bracken & E. Malmquist (Eds.), *Improving reading ability around the world.* Newark, DE: International Reading Association, 1971. Pp. 97–103. (b)

HARRIS, ALBERT J. Some new developments in readability. In J. E. Merritt (Ed.), *New horizons in reading.* Newark, DE: International Reading Association, 1976. Pp. 331–340.

HARRIS, ALBERT J. The reading teacher as a diagnostician. In E. A. Earle (Ed.), *Classroom practice in reading.* Newark, DE: International Reading Association, 1977. Pp. 21–26. (a)

HARRIS, ALBERT J. Ten years of progress in remedial reading. *Journal of Reading*, October 1977, *21*, 29–35. (b)

HARRIS, ALBERT J. Practical suggestions for remedial teachers. *The Reading Teacher*, May 1978, *31*, 916–922.

HARRIS, ALBERT J. Discussion: Linguistic awareness and cognitive clarity in learning to read. In M. L. Kamil & A. J. Moe (Eds.), *Reading research: Studies and applications.* Clemson, SC: National Reading Conference, 1979. Pp. 295–296. (a)

HARRIS, ALBERT J. The effective teacher of reading, revisited. *The Reading Teacher*, November 1979, *33*, 135–140. (b)

HARRIS, ALBERT J. Lateral dominance and reading disability. *Journal of Learning Disabilities*, May 1979, *12*, 337–343. (c)

HARRIS, ALBERT J. Current issues in the diagnosis and treatment of reading disabilities. In C. M. McCullough (Ed.), *Inchworm, inchworm: Persistent problems in reading education.* Newark, DE: International Reading Association, 1980. Pp. 111–118. (a)

HARRIS, ALBERT J. An overview of reading disabilities and learning disabilities in the U.S. *The Reading Teacher*, January 1980, *33*, 420–425. (b)

HARRIS, ALBERT J. How many kinds of reading disability are there? *Journal of Learning Disabilities*, October 1982, *15*, 456–460.

HARRIS, ALBERT J., & JACOBSON, MILTON D. *Basic elementary reading vocabularies.* New York: Macmillan, 1972.

HARRIS, ALBERT J., & JACOBSON, MILTON D. Some comparisons between the Basic Elementary Reading Vocabularies and other word lists. *Reading Research Quarterly*, 1973–1974, *9* (1), 87–109.

HARRIS, ALBERT J., & JACOBSON, MILTON D. Predicting twelfth graders' comprehension scores. *Journal of Reading*, October 1976, *20*, 43–46.

HARRIS, ALBERT J., & JACOBSON, MILTON D. A framework for readability research: Moving beyond Herbert Spencer. *Journal of Reading*, February 1979, *22*, 390–398.

HARRIS, ALBERT J., & JACOBSON, MILTON D. A comparison of the Fry, Spache, and Harris-Jacobson readability formulas for primary grades. *The Reading Teacher*, May 1980, *33*, 920–923.

HARRIS, ALBERT J., & JACOBSON, MILTON D. *Basic reading vocabularies.* New York: Macmillan, 1982.

HARRIS, ALBERT J., & ROSWELL, FLORENCE G. Clinical diagnosis of reading disability. *Journal of Psychology*, 1953, *63*, 323–340.

HARRIS, ALBERT J., & SERWER, BLANCHE L. *Comparison of reading approaches in first-grade teaching with disadvantaged children (the CRAFT Project).* Final Report, Cooperative Research Project, No. 2677. New York: Division of Teacher Education, The City University of New York, 1966. (a) ED 010 037

HARRIS, ALBERT J., & SERWER, BLANCHE L. The CRAFT Project: Instructional time in reading research. *Reading Research Quarterly*, Fall 1966, *2*, 27–56. (b)

HARRIS, ALBERT J., & SIPAY, EDWARD R. *The Macmillan Reading Readiness Tests, RE: Manual for administering, scoring, and interpreting.* New York: Macmillan, 1970.

HARRIS, ALBERT J., & SIPAY, EDWARD R. *Readings on Reading Instruction* (2nd ed.). New York: David McKay, 1972.

HARRIS, ALBERT J., & SIPAY, EDWARD R. *How to teach reading: A competency-based program.* New York: Longman, 1979.

HARRIS, ALBERT J., & SIPAY, EDWARD R. *How to increase reading ability* (7th ed.). New York: Longman, 1980.

HARRIS, ALBERT J., et al. *A continuation of the CRAFT Project: Comparing reading approaches with disadvantaged urban negro children in primary grades.* Final Report, USOE Project No. 5-05-70-2-12-1. New York: Selected Academic Reading, 1968. ED 020 297

HARRIS, LARRY P. Attention and learning disorders of children: A review of theory and remediation. *Journal of Learning Disabilities,* February 1976, 9, 100–110.

HARRIS, MARY. Family forces for early school development of language fluency and beginning reading. In H. Sartain (Ed.), *Mobilizing family forces for worldwide reading success.* Newark, DE: International Reading Association, 1981. Pp. 55–73.

HARRIS, THEORDORE L. Reading flexibility: A neglected aspect of reading instruction. In J. Merritt (Ed.), *New horizons in reading.* Newark, DE: International Reading Association, 1976. Pp. 27–35.

HARRIS, THEODORE L., & HODGES, RICHARD E. (Eds.). *A dictionary of reading and related terms.* Newark, DE: International Reading Association, 1981.

HARRISON, COLIN. Assessing the readability of school texts. In E. Lunzer & K. Gardner (Eds.), *The effective use of reading.* London: Heinemann, 1979. Pp. 72–107.

HARSTE, JEROME C., & MIKULECKY, LARRY J. The context of literacy in our society. In A. Purves & O. Niles (Eds.), *Becoming readers in a complex society.* 83rd Yearbook of the National Society for the Study of Education, Part I. Chicago: University of Chicago Press, 1984. Pp. 47–78.

HARTLAGE, LAWRENCE C. Vision deficits and reading impairment. In G. Leisman (Ed.), *Basic visual processes and learning disability.* Springfield, IL: Charles C Thomas, 1976. Pp. 151–162.

HARTLAGE, LAWRENCE C., & TELZROW, CATHY F. Neuropsychological disorders in children: Effects of medication on learning and behavior modification. *Journal of Research and Development in Education,* Spring 1982, 15, 55–65.

HARZEM, P., LEE, I., & MILES, T. R. The effects of pictures on learning to read. *British Journal of Educational Psychology,* November 1976, 46, 318–322.

HASSILRIIS, PETER. IEPs and a whole-language model of language arts. *Topics in Learning & Learning Disabilities,* January 1982, 1, 17–21.

HATCH, EVELYN. Research on reading a second language. *Journal of Reading Behavior,* April 1974, 6, 53–61.

HAVIGHURST, ROBERT J. *Human development and education.* New York: Longman, 1953.

HAYES, DAVIS A., & TIERNEY, ROBERT J. Developing readers' knowledge through analogy. *Reading Research Quarterly,* 1982, 17 (2), 256–280.

HAYES, ROBERT B., & WUEST, RICHARD C. Factors affecting learning to read. Final Report, Project No. 6-1732. Harrisburg, PA: State Education Department, 1967.

HEALY, JANE M. The enigma of hyperlexia. *Reading Research Quarterly,* 1982, 27 (3), 319–338.

HEAP, JAMES L. Understanding classroom events: A critique of Durkin with an alternative. *Journal of Reading Behavior,* 1982, 14 (4), 392–411.

HEATHINGTON, BETTY S. What to do about reading motivation in the middle school. *Journal of Reading,* May 1979, 22, 709–713.

HEATHINGTON, BETTY S., & ALEXANDER, J. ESTILL. Do classroom teachers emphasize attitudes toward reading? *The Reading Teacher,* February 1984, 37, 484–488.

HEATHINGTON, BETTY S., & KOSKINEN, PATRICIA S. Interest inventory for adult beginning readers. *Journal of Reading,* December 1982, 26, 252–256.

HECKELMAN, R. G. Using the neurological impress remedial technique. *Academic Therapy Quarterly,* Summer 1966, 1, 235–239.

HECKELMAN, R. G. A Neurological Impress Method of remedial reading instruction. *Academic Therapy Quarterly,* Summer 1969, 4, 277–282.

HEITZMAN, ANDREW J. Effects of a token reinforcement system on the reading and arithmetic skills of migrant primary school pupils. *Journal of Educational Research*, July 1970, *63*, 455–458.

HELLRIEGEL, DIANE. *Fifty creative ways to use paperbacks in the middle grades.* New York: Scholastic Book Services, 1980.

HENDERSON, LESLIE. *Orthography and word recognition.* New York: Academic Press, 1982.

HENDERSON, LESLIE, & CHARD, JACKIE. The reader's implicit knowledge of orthographic structure. In U. Frith (Ed.), *Cognitive processes in spelling.* New York: Academic Press, 1980. Pp. 85–116.

HENDERSON, LINDA C., & SHANKER, JAMES L. The use of interpretive dramatics versus basal reader workbooks for developing comprehension skills. *Reading World*, March 1978, *17*, 239–243.

HENDERSON. RONALD W. Environmental predictors of academic performance of disadvantaged Mexican-American children. *Journal of Consulting and Clinical Psychology*, April 1972, *38*, 297.

HENDERSON, RONALD W. Social and emotional needs of culturally diverse children. *Exceptional Children*, May 1980, *46*, 598–605.

HENK, WILLIAM A. A response to Shanahan, Tobin, and Kamil: The case is not yet clozed. *Reading Research Quarterly*, 1982, *17* (4), 591–595.

HENK, WILLIAM A. Adapting the NIM to improve comprehension. *Academic Therapy*, September 1983, *19*, 97–101.

HENNINGS, DOROTHY G. A writing approach to reading comprehension—Schema theory in action. *Language Arts*, January 1982, *59*, 8–17.

HENRY, STEPHAN A., & WITTMAN, ROBERT D. Diagnostic implications of Bannatyne's recategorized WISC-R scores for identifying learning disabled children. *Journal of Learning Disabilities*, November 1981, *14*, 517–520.

HERBER, HAROLD L. *Teaching reading in content areas* (2nd ed.). Englewood Cliffs, NJ: Prentice-Hall, 1978.

HERBER, HAROLD L., & NELSON, JOAN. Questioning is not the answer. *Journal of Reading*, April 1975, *18*, 512–517. Also in A. J. Harris & E. Sipay (Eds.), *Readings on reading instruction* (3rd ed.). New York: Longman, 1984. Pp. 308–313.

HERBER, HAROLD L., & NELSON-HERBER, JOAN. Planning the reading program. In A. Purves & O. Niles (Eds.), *Becoming readers in a complex society.* 83rd Yearbook of the National Society for the Study of Education, Part I. Chicago: University of Chicago Press, 1984. Pp. 174–208.

HERMANN, KNUD. Specific reading disability. *Danish Medical Bulletin*, 1964, *11*, 34–40.

HERR, SELMA E. *Learning activities for reading* (3rd ed.). Dubuque, IA: William C. Brown, 1977.

HEWISON, JENNY., & TIZARD, J. Parental involvement and reading attainment. *British Journal of Educational Psychology*, 1980, *50*, 209–215.

HICKMAN, JANET. Children's responses to literature: What happens in the classroom. *Language Arts*, May 1980, *57*, 524–529. Also in A. J. Harris & E. Sipay (Eds.), *Readings on reading instruction* (3rd ed.). New York: Longman, 1984. Pp. 377–382.

HICKMAN, JANET. A new perspective on response to literature: Response in an elementary school setting. *Research in the Teaching of English*, December 1981, *15*, 343–354.

HICKMAN, JANET. Classrooms that help children like books. In N. Roser & M. Frith (Eds.), *Children's choices: Teaching with books children like.* Newark, DE: International Reading Association, 1983. Pp. 1–11.

HICKS, CAROLYN. The ITPA visual sequential memory task: An alternative interpretation and implications for good and poor readers. *British Journal of Educational Psychology*, February 1980, *50*, 16–25.

HICKS, CAROLYN, & SPURGEON, P. Two factor analytic studies of dyslexic subtypes. *British Journal of Educational Psychology*, 1982, *52*, 289–300.

HIEBERT, ELFRIEDA H. Developmental patterns and interrelationships of preschool children's print awareness. *Reading Research Quarterly*, 1981, *16* (2), 236–260.

HIEBERT, ELFRIEDA H. An examination of ability grouping in reading instruction. *Reading Research Quarterly*, Winter 1983, *18*, 231–255.

HIER, DANIEL B. Sex differences in hemispheric specialization: Hypothesis for the excess of dyslexia in boys. *Bulletin of the Orton Society*, 1979, *29*, 74–83.

HIER, DANIEL B., ATKINS, L., & PERLO, V. P. Learning disorders and sex chromosome aberrations. *Journal of Mental Deficiency Research*, March 1980, *24*, 17–26.

HIER, DANIEL, *et al.* Developmental dyslexia: Evidence for a subgroup with a reverse cerebral asymmetry. *Archives of Neurology*, February 1978, *35*, 90–92.

HILDYARD, ANGELA, & OLSON, DAVID P. On the structure and meaning of prose text. In W. Otto & S. White (Eds.), *Reading expository material*. New York: Academic Press, 1982. Pp. 155–184.

HILL, CAROL L., & HILL, KENNETH A. Achievement attributions of learning-disabled boys. *Psychological Reports*, December 1982, *51*, 979–982.

HILLERICH, ROBERT L. Word lists—Getting it all together. *The Reading Teacher*, January 1974, 27, 353–360.

HILLERICH, ROBERT L. Critical reading for slower learner to gifted (Part I). *Ohio Reading Teacher*, April 1980, *14*, 9–12. (a)

HILLERICH, ROBERT L. Critical reading for slower learner to gifted (Part II). *Ohio Reading Teacher*, July 1980, *14*, 4–7. (b)

HILLOCKS, GEORGE, JR., & LUDLOW, LARRY H. A taxonomy of skills in reading and interpretation of fiction. *American Educational Research Journal*, April 1984, *21*, 7–24.

HILLS, JOHN R. Interpreting grade-equivalent scores. *Educational Measurement: Issues and Practice*, Spring 1983, *2*, 15–21.

HINSHELWOOD, JAMES. *Letter, word, and mind-blindness.* London: H. K. Lewis, 1900.

HINSHELWOOD, JAMES. *Congenital word-blindness.* London: H. K. Lewis, 1917.

HIRSHOREN, ALFRED, HUNT, JACOB T., & DAVIS, CAROLINE. Classified ads as reading material for the educable retarded. *Exceptional Children*, September 1974, *41*, 45–47.

HIRST, LOIS T., & O'SUCH, TWILA. Using musical television commercials to teach reading. *Teaching Exceptional Children*, Winter 1979, *11*, 80–81.

HISCOCK, MERRILL. Do learning disabled children lack functional hemispheric lateralization? *Topics in Learning & Learning Disabilities*, April 1983, *3*, 14–28.

HISCOCK, MERRILL, & KINSBOURNE, MARCEL. Laterality and dyslexia: A critical review. *Annals of Dyslexia*, 1982, *32*, 177–228.

HITTLEMAN, DANIEL R. Seeking a psycholinguistic definition of readability. *The Reading Teacher*, May 1973, *26*, 783–789.

HITTLEMAN, DANIEL R. Readability, readability formulas and cloze: Selecting instructional materials. *Journal of Reading*, November 1978, *22*, 117–122.

HOAGLAND, JOAN. Bibliotherapy: Aiding children in personality development. *Elementary English*, March 1972, *49*, 390–394.

HOCKMAN, CAROL M. Black dialect reading tests in the urban elementary school. *The Reading Teacher*, March 1973, *26*, 581–583.

HODGES, CAROL A. Toward a broader definition of comprehension instruction. *Reading Research Quarterly*, 1981, *15* (2), 299–306.

HODGES, ELAINE J. A comparison of the functional reading levels of selected third grade students of varying reading abilities. Unpublished doctoral dissertation, University of Northern Colorado, 1972.

HODGES, RICHARD E. Language development: The elementary school years. In A. Marquardt (Ed.), *Linguistics in school programs*. 69th Yearbook of the National Society for the Study of Education, Part II. Chicago: University of Chicago Press, 1970. Pp. 215–228. Also in A. J. Harris & E. Sipay (Eds.), *Readings on reading instruction* (3rd ed.). New York: Longman, 1984. Pp. 59–65.

HODGES, RICHARD E. *Learning to spell.* Urbana, IL: ERIC/RCS and the National Council of Teachers of English, 1981.

HODGES, RICHARD E. Research update: On the development of spelling ability. *Language Arts*, March 1982, *59*, 284–290.

HOFFMAN, JAMES V. Developing flexibility through ReFlex Action. *The Reading Teacher*, December 1979, *34*, 323–329.

HOFFMAN, JAMES V., O'NEAL, SHARON, & BAKER, CHRISTOPHER. A comparison of inservice and preservice teachers verbal feedback to student miscues across two difficulty levels of text. In M. Kamil & M. Boswick (Eds.), *Directions in reading: Research and instruction*. Washington, DC: National Reading Conference, 1981. Pp. 150–156.

HOFFMAN, JAMES V., *et al.* Students' beliefs and attitudes about oral reading instruction. In J. Niles & L. A. Harris (Eds.), *New inquiries in reading research and instruction.* Rochester, NY: National Reading Conference, 1982. Pp. 140–145.

HOFFMAN, JAMES V., *et al.* Guided oral reading and miscue focused feedback in second-grade classrooms. *Reading Research Quarterly,* Spring 1984, *19,* 367–384.

HOFFMAN, M. S. Early indications of learning problems. *Academic Therapy,* Fall 1971, *7,* 23–25.

HOFLER, DONALD B. Word lines: An approach to vocabulary development. *The Reading Teacher,* November 1981, *35,* 216–218.

HOGABOAM, THOMAS W. Reading patterns in eye movement data. In K. Rayner (Ed.), *Eye movements in reading: Perceptual and language processes.* New York: Academic Press, 1983. Pp. 309–332.

HOLBROOK, HILARY T. Motivating reluctant readers: A gentle push. *Language Arts,* April 1982, *59,* 385–389.

HOLBROOK, HILARY T. Prereading in the content areas. *Journal of Reading,* January 1984, *27,* 368–370.

HOLDEN, MARJORIE H., & MACGINITIE, WALTER H. Children's conceptions of word boundaries in speech and print. *Journal of Educational Psychology,* December 1972, *63,* 551–557.

HOLDZKOM, DAVID, *et al.* How communication skill is developed. In D. Holdzkom *et al.* (Eds.), *Research within reach: Oral and written communication.* St. Louis. CEMREL, 1984. Pp. 21–47.

HOLLINGSWORTH, PAUL M. An experimental approach to the impress method of teaching reading. *The Reading Teacher,* March 1978, *31,* 624–626.

HOLMES, BETTY C. A confirmation strategy for improving poor readers' ability to answer inferential questions. *The Reading Teacher,* November 1983, *37,* 144–147. (a)

HOLMES, BETTY C. The effect of prior knowledge on the question answering of good and poor readers. *Journal of Reading Behavior,* 1983, *15* (4), 1–18. (b)

HOLMES, JACK A. *The substrata-factor theory of reading.* Berkeley, CA: California Book Co., 1953.

HOLMES, JACK A. The substrata-factor theory of reading: Some experimental evidence. In H. Singer & R. Ruddell (Eds.), *Theoretical models and processes of reading.* Newark, DE: International Reading Association, 1970. Pp. 187–197.

HOMAN, SUSAN P. LEA and basals unite! *The Reading Teacher,* March 1983, *36,* 693–694.

HONEL, MILTON F. The effectiveness of reading expectancy formulas for identifying underachievers. Unpublished doctoral dissertation, Northern Illinois University, 1973.

HOOD, JOYCE. Is miscue analysis practical for teachers? *The Reading Teacher,* December 1978, *32,* 260–266.

HOOD, JOYCE, & DUBERT, LEE ANN. Decoding as a component of reading comprehension among secondary students. *Journal of Reading Behavior,* 1983, *15* (4), 51–61.

HOOD, JOYCE, & KENDALL, JANET R. A qualitative analysis of oral reading errors of reflective and impulsive second graders: A followup study. *Journal of Reading Behavior,* Fall 1975, *7,* 269–281.

HOPKINS, CAROL J. Using every-pupil response techniques in reading instruction. *The Reading Teacher,* November 1979, *33,* 173–175.

HOPKINS, KENNETH D., & BRACHT, GLENN H. Ten-year stability of verbal and nonverbal IQ scores. *American Educational Research Journal,* Fall 1975, *12,* 469–477.

HOPKINS, LEE BENNETT. *The best of book bonanza.* New York: Holt, Rinehart and Winston, 1980.

HORMANN, ELIZABETH. Children's crisis literature. *Language Arts,* May 1977, *54,* 559–566.

HORN, ALICE. The uneven distribution of the effects of specific factors. *Southern California Education Monographs,* No. 12. Los Angeles: University of Southern California Press, 1941.

HORN, JANIS L. The reading teacher as an effective change agent. *The Reading Teacher,* January 1982, *35,* 408–411.

HORN, THOMAS D. (Ed.). *Reading for the disadvantaged: Problems of linguistically different learners.* New York: Harcourt Brace Jovanovich, 1970.

HORNE, MARCIA D. Criterion-referenced measurement in reading. Paper presented at the NCME Annual Meeting, San Francisco, 1979.

HORNE, MARCIA D. Attitudes and learning disabilities: A literature review for school psychologists. *Psychology in the Schools,* January 1982, *19,* 78–85.

HORNE, MARCIA D. *Attitudes toward handicapped students: Professional, peer, and parent reactions.* Hillsdale, NJ: LEA, 1985.

HORNE, MARCIA, POWERS, JAMES, & MAKABUB, PATRICIA. Reader and nonreader conception of the spoken word. *Contemporary Educational Psychology,* October 1983, *8,* 403–418.

HORNER, CATHERINE. *The single-parent family in children's books: An analysis and annotated bibliography with an appendix on audiovisual material.* Metuchen, NJ: Scarecrow, 1978.

HORNICK, ROBERT. Out-of-school television and schooling: Hypotheses and methods. *Review of Educational Research,* Summer 1981, *51,* 193–214.

HORODEZKY, BETTY. Comparative difficulty of beginning reading vacabulary: Set II. *The Alberta Journal of Educational Research,* December 1979, *25,* 259–263.

HORWITZ, ROBERT A. Psychological effects of the "open classroom." *Review of Educational Research,* Winter 1979, *49,* 71–86.

HOSKISSON, KENNETH. The many facets of assisted reading. *Elementary English,* March 1975, *52,* 312–315.

HOSKISSON, KENNETH. A response to "A critique of teaching reading as a whole-task venture." *The Reading Teacher,* March 1979, *32,* 653–659.

HUBA, MARY E. The relationship between linguistic awareness in prereaders and two types of experimental instruction. *Reading World,* May 1984, *23,* 347–363.

HUCK, CHARLOTTE S. Strategies for improving interest and appreciation in literature. In H. W. Painter (Ed.), *Reaching children and young people through literature.* Newark, DE: International Reading Association, 1971. Pp. 37–45.

HUEY, EDMUND B. *The psychology and pedagogy of reading.* New York: Macmillan, 1908. Reprinted by MIT Press, Cambridge, MA, 1968.

HUGGINS, A. W. F., & ADAMS, MARILYN J. Syntactic aspects of reading comprehension. In R. Spiro *et al.* (Eds.), *Theoretical issues in reading comprehension.* Hillsdale, NJ: LEA, 1980, Pp. 87–112.

HUGHES, JOHN R. Electroencephalography and learning disabilities. In H. R. Myklebust (Ed.), *Progress in learning disabilities,* Vol. II. New York: Grune & Stratton, 1971, pp. 18–55.

HUGHES, JOHN R. Electroencephalographic and neurophysiological studies in dyslexia. In A. L. Benton & D. Pearl (Eds.), *Dyslexia: An appraisal of current knowledge.* New York: Oxford University Press, 1978. Pp. 205–240.

HUGHES, JOHN R. The electroencephalogram and reading disorders. In R. Malatesha & P. Aaron (Eds.), *Reading disorders: Varieties and treatments.* New York: Academic Press, 1982. Pp. 233–253.

HULME, CHARLES. The effects of manual tracing on memory in normal and retarded readers: Some implications for multi-sensory teaching. *Psychological Research* (Developmental Dyslexia Issue), 1981, *43,* 179–191. (a)

HULME, CHARLES. *Reading retardation and multi-sensory teaching.* Boston: Routledge & Kegan Paul, 1981. (b)

HUNT, LYMAN C. Six steps to the individualized reading program (IRP). *Elementary English,* January 1971, *48,* 27–32. Also in A. J. Harris & E. Sipay (Eds.), *Readings on reading instruction* (3rd ed.). New York: Longman, 1984. Pp. 190–195.

HUNT, MORTON. Self-appointed censors: New threat to our schools. *Reader's Digest,* February 1982, *120,* 88–92.

HUUS, HELEN. The effects of reading on children and youth. In R. Karlin (Ed.), *Reading for all.* Newark, DE: International Reading Association, 1973. Pp. 132–141.

HUUS, HELEN. Approaches to the use of literature in the reading program. In B. Schulwitz (Ed.), *Teachers, tangibles, techniques: Comprehension of content in reading.* Newark, DE: International Reading Association, 1975. Pp. 140–149. Also in A. J. Harris & E. Sipay (Eds.), *Readings on reading instruction* (3rd ed.). New York: Longman, 1984. Pp. 363–368.

HUUS, HELEN. A new look at children's interests. In J. Shapiro (Ed.), *Using literature and poetry affectively.* Newark, DE: International Reading Association, 1979. Pp. 37–45.

HYMES, JAMES L., JR. *Before the child reads.* New York: Harper & Row, 1958.

HYND, GEORGE W., & OBRZUT, JOHN E. Reconceptualizing cerebral dominance: Implications for read-ing- and learning-disabled children. *Journal of Special Education*, Winter 1981, *15*, 447–457.

IGNOFFO, MATHEW F. The thread of thought: Analogies as a vocabulary building method. *Journal of Reading*, March 1980, *23*, 519–521.

ILG, FRANCIS L., & AMES, LOUISE B. *School readiness: Behavior tests used at the Gesell Institute.* New York: Harper & Row, 1964.

INDRISANO, ROSELMINA. An ecological approach to learning. *Topics in Learning & Learning Dis-abilities.* January 1982, *1*, 11–15.

INGRAM, T. T. S. The nature of dyslexia. *Bulletin of the Orton Society*, 1969, *19*, 18–50.

INGRAM, T. T. S., MASON, A. W. & BLACKBURN, I. A retrospective study of 82 children with reading disability. *Developmental Medicine & Child Neurology*, June 1970, *12*, 271–281.

INGRAM, T. T. S., & REID, JESSIE F. Developmental aphasia observed in a department of child psychiatry. *Archives of Diseases in Childhood*, 1956, *31*, 131.

INTERNATIONAL READING ASSOCIATION. Causes of reading disability. *The Reading Teacher*, December 1972, *26*, 341.

INTERNATIONAL READING ASSOCIATION. *Guidelines for the Professional Preparation of Reading Teach-ers.* Newark, DE: International Reading Association, May 1978.

INTERNATIONAL READING ASSOCIATION. A position on minimum competencies in reading. *The Reading Teacher*, October 1979, *33*, 54–55. (a)

INTERNATIONAL READING ASSOCIATION. *United States certification requirements* (2nd ed.). Newark, DE: International Reading Association, 1979. (b)

INTERNATIONAL READING ASSOCIATION. Checklist for evaluating adult basic education reading material. *Journal of Reading*, May 1981, *24*, 701–706.

INTERNATIONAL READING ASSOCIATION. Courts should not make reading policy. *Journal of Reading*, May 1982, *25*, 785. (a)

INTERNATIONAL READING ASSOCIATION. Misuse of grade equivalents. *The Reading Teacher*, January 1982, *35*, 464. (b)

INTERNATIONAL READING ASSOCIATION. *Adult illiteracy in the United States*, 1983. Pamphlet.

IRWIN, JUDITH W. Fifth grade readers' comprehension of explicit and implicit connective propositions. *Journal of Reading Behavior*, Fall 1979, *11*, 261–271.

IRWIN, JUDITH W. Implicit connectives and comprehension. *The Reading Teacher*, February 1980, *33*, 527–529.

IRWIN, JUDITH W., & DAVIS, CAROL A. Assessing readability: The checklist approach. *Journal of Reading*, November 1980, *24*, 124–130.

IRWIN, PI A., & MITCHELL, JUDY N. A procedure for assessing the richness of retellings. *Journal of Reading*, February 1983, *26*, 391–396.

ITO, H. RICHARD. Long-term effects of resource room programs on learning disabled children's reading. *Journal of Learning Disabilities*, June/July 1980, *13*, 322–326.

IWANICKI, EDWARD F. A new generation of standardized achievement test batteries: A profile of their major features. *Journal of Educational Measurement*, Summer 1980, *17*, 155–162.

JACKSON, GREGG B. The research evidence on the effects of grade retention. *Review of Educational Research*, Fall 1975, *45*, 613–635.

JACKSON, MERRILL S. Modes of adaptation to the first confrontation with English orthography in the visual modality. *Journal of Learning Disabilities*, January 1972, *5*, 25–30.

JACOBS, LELAND. Individualized reading is not a thing. In A. Miel (Ed.), *Individualizing reading practices.* New York: Teachers College, Columbia University, 1958. Pp. 1–17.

JACOBS, LELAND. Poetry books for poetry reading. *The Reading Teacher*, 1959, *13*, 45–48.

JAEGER, RICHARD M. Measurement consequences of selected standard-setting models. In M. Bunda & J. Sanders (Eds.), *Practices & problems in competency-based measurement.* Washington, DC: National Council on Measurement in Education, 1979. Pp. 48–58.

JAEGER, RICHARD M., & TITTLE, CAROL K. (Eds.). *Minimum competency achievement testing: Motives, models, measures, and consequences.* Berkeley, CA: McCutchan, 1980.

JANIAK, RICHARD. Listening/reading: An effective learning combination. *Academic Therapy*, Novem-ber 1983, *19*, 205–211.

JANICKE, EUGENE M. Massive oral decoding. *Academic Therapy*, November 1981, *17*, 157–161.

JANSEN, MOGENS, et al. Special education in Denmark. In L. Tarnopol & M. Tarnopol (Eds.), *Reading disabilities: An international perspective.* Baltimore: University Park Press, 1976. Pp. 155–174.

JANSKY, JEANETTE, & de HIRSCH, KATRINA. *Preventing reading failure: Prediction, diagnosis, intervention.* New York: Harper & Row, 1972.

JASON, MARTIN H., & DUBNOW, BEATRICE. The relationship between self-perceptions of reading abilities and reading achievement. In W. H. MacGinitie (Ed.), *Assessment problems in reading.* Newark, DE: International Reading Association, 1973. Pp. 96–100.

JEFFARES, DOLORES J., & COSENS, GRACE V. Effect of socio-economic status and auditory discrimination training on first-grade reading achievement and auditory discrimination. *Alberta Journal of Educational Research,* 1970, *16,* 165–178.

JENKINS, JOSEPH R., & DIXON, ROBERT. Vocabulary learning. *Contemporary Educational Psychology,* July 1983, 8, 237–260.

JENKINS, J. R., & LARSON, K. Evaluating error correction procedures for oral reading. Technical Report No. 55. Champaign, IL: Center for the Study of Reading, University of Illinois, June 1978.

JENKINS, JOSEPH R., & PANY, DARLENE. Curriculum biases in reading achievement tests. *Journal of Reading Behavior,* Winter 1978, *10,* 345–357.

JENKINS, JOSEPH R., & PANY, DARLENE. Instructional variables in reading comprehension. In J. Guthrie (Ed.), *Comprehension and teaching: Research reviews.* Newark, DE: International Reading Association, 1981. Pp. 163–202.

JENKINS, JOSEPH R., PANY, DARLENE, & SCHRECK, JANICE. Vocabulary and reading comprehension: Instructional effects. Technical Report No. 100. Champaign, IL: Center for the Study of Reading, University of Illinois, August 1978.

JENKINSON, EDWARD B. Forty targets of the textbook protesters. 1980. ED 199 716.

JENNINGS, FRANK G. What it means to be illiterate. *The New England Reading Association Journal,* 1975, *10* (3), 25–26.

JENSEN, JULIE M. (Ed.). *Composing and comprehending.* Urbana, IL: NCRE/CRCS, 1984.

JERROLDS, BOB W., CALLAWAY, BYRON, & GWALTNEY, WAYNE. A comparative study of three tests of intellectual potential; three tests of reading achievement, and the discrepancy scores between potential and achievement. *Journal of Educational Research,* December 1971, 65, 168–172.

JOBE, FRED W. *Screening vision in schools.* Newark, DE: International Reading Association, 1976.

JOHN, ROY E. Neurometric evaluation of brain dysfunction related to learning disorders. *Acta Neurological Scandinavia* (Supplement 89), 1981, *64,* 87–98.

JOHNS, JERRY L. What do inner city children prefer to read? *The Reading Teacher,* February 1973, *26,* 462–467.

JOHNS, JERRY L. Some comparisons between the Dolch Sight Vocabulary and the Word List for the 1970's. *Reading World,* March 1976, *15,* 144–150.

JOHNS, JERRY L. First graders' concepts about print. *Reading Research Quarterly,* 1980, *15* (4), 529–549. (a)

JOHNS, JERRY L. The growth of children's knowledge about spoken words. *Reading Psychology,* Spring 1980, *1,* 103–110. (b)

JOHNS, JERRY L. The development of the Revised Dolch List. *Illinois School Research and Development,* Spring 1981, *17,* 15–24.

JOHNS, JERRY L., & LUNN, MARY K. The Informal Reading Inventory: 1910–1980. *Reading World,* October 1983, *23,* 8–19.

JOHNS, JERRY L., & MCNAMARA, LAWRENCE P. The SQ3R study technique: A forgotten research target. *Journal of Reading,* May 1980, *23,* 705–708.

JOHNS, JERRY L., & WHEAT, THOMAS E. Newspaper readability: Two crucial factors. *Journal of Reading,* February 1984, *27,* 432–434.

JOHNSON, CAROLE S., & GREENBAUM, GLORIA R. Are boys disabled readers due to sex-role stereotyping? *Educational Leadership,* March 1980, *37,* 492–496.

JOHNSON, CAROLE S., & GREENBAUM, GLORIA R. Girls' and boys' reading interests: A review of the research. In E. Sheridan (Ed.), *Sex stereotypes and reading: Research and strategies.* Newark, DE: International Reading Association, 1982. Pp. 35–48.

JOHNSON, DALE D., & BARRETT, THOMAS C. Prose comprehension: A descriptive analysis of instructional practices. In C. Santa & B. Hayes (Eds.), *Children's prose comprehension: Research and practice*. Newark, DE: International Reading Association, 1980. Pp. 72–102.

JOHNSON, DALE D., MOE, ALDEN J., & BAUMANN, JAMES F. *The Ginn word book for teachers: A basic lexicon*. Columbus, OH: Ginn, 1983.

JOHNSON, DALE D., & PEARSON, P. DAVID. *Teaching reading vocabulary* (2nd ed.). New York: Holt, Rinehart and Winston, 1984.

JOHNSON, DORIS J. Process deficits in learning disabled children and implications for reading. In L. Resnick & P. Weaver (Eds.), *Theory and practice in early reading*, Vol. 2. Hillsdale, NJ: LEA, 1979, Pp. 207–227.

JOHNSON, DORIS J., & MYKLEBUST, HELMER R. *Learning disabilities: Educational principles and practices*. New York: Grune & Stratton, 1967.

JOHNSON, JEAN ANN. The etiology of hyperactivity. *Exceptional Children*, February 1981, *47*, 348–354.

JOHNSON, MAJORIE S. Tracing and kinesthetic techniques. In J. Money (Ed.), *The disabled reader*. Baltimore: Johns Hopkins Press, 1966. Pp. 147–160.

JOHNSON, MAVIS. Resources for teachers: 20 teacher tested ways to encourage reading. *Wisconsin State Reading Association Journal*, October 1980, *25*, 30–31.

JOHNSON, NEAL F. Integration processes in word recognition. In O. Tzeng & H. Singer (Eds.), *Perception of print: Reading research in experimental psychology*. Hillsdale, NJ: LEA, 1981. Pp. 29–63.

JOHNSON, RONALD J., JOHNSON, KAREN L., & KERFOOT, JAMES F. A massive decoding technique. *The Reading Teacher*, February 1972, *25*, 421–423.

JOHNSON, TERRY, MAYFIELD, MARGIE, & QUORM, KERRY. Organizing for instruction: Exploring different models of reading instruction. In L. Ollila (Ed.), *Handbook for administrators and teachers: Reading in the kindergarten*. Newark, DE: International Reading Association, 1980. Pp. 68–84.

JOHNSON, WILLIAM. Books for sale. *Elementary English*, February 1972, *49*, 233–234.

JOHNSTON, JAMES C. Understanding word perception: Clues from studying the word-superiority effect. In O. Tzeng & H. Singer (Eds.), *Perception of print: Reading research in experimental psychology*. Hillsdale, NJ: LEA, 1981. Pp. 65–84.

JOHNSTON, PETER. Implications of basic research for the assessment of reading comprehension. Technical Report No. 206. Champaign, IL: Center for the Study of Reading, University of Illinois, May 1981.

JOHNSTON, PETER. Prior knowledge and reading comprehension test bias. Technical Report No. 289. Champaign, IL: Center for the Study of Reading, University of Illinois, September 1983.

JOHNSTON, PETER, & AFFLERBACH, PETER. Measuring teacher and student change in a remedial reading class. In J. Niles & L. A. Harris (Eds.), *Searches for meaning in reading/language processing and instruction*. Rochester, NY: National Reading Conference, 1983. Pp. 304–312.

JOHNSTON, PETER, & BYRD, MARGIE. Basal readers and the improvement of reading comprehension ability. In J. Niles & L. A. Harris, (Eds.), *Searches for meaning in reading/language processing and instruction*. Rochester, NY: National Reading Conference, 1983. Pp. 140–147.

JOHNSTON, PETER, & PEARSON, P. DAVID. Assessment: Responses to exposition. In A. Berger & H. A. Robinson (Eds.), *Secondary school reading: What research reveals for classroom practice*. Urbana, IL: ERIC/RCS and NCRE, 1982. Pp. 127–141.

JOHNSTON, PETER, & WINOGRAD, PETER N. Passive failure in reading. Paper presented at the National Reading Conference Annual Meeting, Austin, TX, December 1983.

JOLLY, HAYDEN B., JR. Teaching basic function words. *The Reading Teacher*, November 1981, *35*, 136–140. Also In A. J. Harris & E. Sipay (Eds.), *Readings on reading instruction* (3rd ed.). New York: Longman, 1984. Pp. 215–219.

JONES, ASHBY, & STARK, LAWRENCE. Abnormal patterns of normal eye movements in specific dyslexia. In K. Rayner (Ed.), *Eye movements in reading: Perceptual and language processes*. New York: Academic Press, 1983. Pp. 481–498.

JONES, DON R. The dictionary: A look at "look it up." *Journal of Reading*, January 1980, *23*, 309–312.

JONES, JOHN P. A study of the relationship among intersensory transfer, intersensory perceptual shifting, modal preference and reading achievement at the third grade level. Unpublished doctoral dissertation, University of Georgia, 1970.

JONES, JOHN P. *Intersensory transfer, perceptual shifting, modal preference, and reading.* Newark, DE: International Reading Association, 1972.

JONGSMA, EUGENE A. *Cloze instruction research: A second look.* Newark, DE: International Reading Association and ERIC/RCS, 1980.

JORDAN, WILLIAM C. Prime-O-Tec: The new reading method. *Academic Therapy Quarterly*, Summer 1967, *2*, 248–250.

JORGENSON, GERALD W. An analysis of teacher judgments of reading levels. *American Educational Research Journal*, Winter 1975, *12*, 67–75.

JORGENSON, GERALD W. Relationship of classroom behavior to the accuracy of the match between material difficulty and student ability. *Journal of Educational Psychology*, February 1977, *69*, 24–32.

JORM, ANTHONY F. Effect of word imagery on reading performance as a function of reading ability. *Journal of Educational Psychology*, Feburary 1977, *69*, 46–54.

JORM, ANTHONY F. The cognitive and neurological basis of develop mental dyslexia. A theoretical framework and review. *Cognition*, March 1979, *7*, 19–33. (a)

JORM, ANTHONY F. The nature of the reading deficit in developmental dyslexia: A reply to Ellis. *Cognition*, December 1979, *7*, 421–433. (b)

JOSE, PAUL E., & BREWER, WILLIAM F. The development of story liking: Character identification, suspense and outcome resolution. Technical Report No. 219. Champaign, IL: Center for the Study of Reading, University of Illinois, October 1983.

JUDD, DOROTHY H. Avoid readability formula drudgery: Use your school's microcomputer. *The Reading Teacher*, October 1981, *35*, 7–8.

JUEL, CONNIE. The development and use of mediated word identification. *Reading Research Quarterly*, Spring 1983, *18*, 306–327.

JUEL, CONNIE, & HOLMES, BETTY. Oral and silent reading of sentences. *Reading Research Quarterly*, 1981, *16*, (4), 545–568.

JUEL, CONNIE, & ROPER-SCHNEIDER, DIANE. The influence of basal readers on first-grade reading. Paper presented at the American Educational Research Association Meeting, 1982.

JUOLA, JAMES F., *et al.* What do children learn when they learn to read? In L. Resnick & P. Weaver (Eds.), *Theory and practice in early reading*, Vol. 2. Hillsdale, NJ: LEA, 1979. Pp. 91–107.

KACHUCK, BEATRICE. Relative clauses may cause confusion for young readers. *The Reading Teacher*, January 1981, *34*, 372–377.

KAGAN, JEROME. Reflection-impulsivity and reading ability in primary grade children. *Child Development*, 1965, *36*, 609–628.

KAGAN, JEROME. Retrieval difficulty in reading disability. *Topics in Learning & Learning Disabilities*, April 1983, *3*, 75–83.

KAGAN, JEROME, & MOORE, MICHAEL J. Retrieval and evaluation of symbolic information in dyslexia. *Bulletin of the Orton Society*, 1981, *31*, 63–73.

KAMEENUI, EDWARD J., CARNINE, DOUGLAS W., & FRESCHI, ROGER. Effects of text construction and instructional procedures for teaching word meanings on comprehension and recall. *Reading Research Quarterly*, 1982, *17* (3), 367–388.

KAMIL, MICHAEL L. Research revisited: Early word recognition studies. *Reading Psychology*, Spring 1980, *1*, 133–136.

KAMMERLOHR, BARBARA, HENDERSON, ROBERT A., & ROCK, STEVE. Special education due process in Illinois. *Exceptional Children*, February 1983, *49*, 417–422.

KANN, ROBERT. The method of repeated readings: Expanding the neurological impress method for use with disabled readers. *Journal of Learning Disabilities*, February 1983, *16*, 90–92.

KAPELIS, LIA. Early identification of reading failure: A comparison of two screening tests and teacher forecasts. *Journal of Learning Disabilities*, December 1975, *8*, 638–641.

KAPPLEMAN, MURRAY M., KAPLAN, EUGENE, & GANTER, ROBERT L. A study of learning disorders among disadvantaged children. *Journal of Learning Disabilities*, May 1969, *2*, 262–268.

KARWEIT, NANCY L. Time-on-task: A research review. Report No. 332. Baltimore: Center for Social Organization of Schools, Johns Hopkins University, January 1983.

KARWEIT, NANCY, & SLAVIN, ROBERT E. Measurement and modeling choices in studies of time and learning. *American Educational Research Journal*, Summer 1981, *18*, 157–171.

KASDON, LAWRENCE M. Some problems in dealing with gain scores. *Reading World*, March 1977, *16*, 178–187.

KASS, CORRINE E. Identification of learning disability (dyssymbolia). *Journal of Learning Disabilities*, August/September 1977, *10*, 425–432.

KATZ, LEONARD, & FELDMAN, LAURIE B. Linguistic coding in word recognition: Comparisons between a deep and a shallow orthography. In A. Lesgold & C. Perfetti (Eds.), *Interactive processes in reading*. Hillsdale, NJ: LEA, 1981. Pp. 85–105.

KATZ, ROBERT B., SHANKWEILER, DONALD, & LIBERMAN, ISABELLE Y. Memory for item order and phonetic recording in the beginning reader. *Journal of Experimental Child Psychology*, December 1981, *32*, 474–484.

KAUFMAN, ALAN S. The WISC-R and learning disabilities assessment: State of the art. *Journal of Learning Disabilities*, November 1981, *14*, 520–526.

KAUFMAN, MAURICE. Measuring oral reading accuracy. *Reading World*, May 1976, *15*, 216–225.

KAVALE, KENNETH. Auditory-visual integration and its relationship to reading achievement: A meta-analysis. *Perceptual & Motor Skills*, December 1980, *51*, 947–955.

KAVALE, KENNETH. Functions of the Illinois Test of Psycholinguistic Abilities (ITPA): Are they trainable? *Exceptional Children*, April 1981, *47*, 496–510. (a)

KAVALE, KENNETH. The relationship between auditory perceptual skills and reading ability: A meta-analysis. *Journal of Learning Disabilities*, November 1981, *14*, 539–546. (b)

KAVALE, KENNETH. The efficacy of stimulant drug treatment for hyperactivity: A meta-analysis. *Journal of Learning Disabilities*, May 1982, *15*, 280–289. (a)

KAVALE, KENNETH. Meta-analysis of the relationship between visual perceptual skills and reading achievement. *Journal of Learning Disabilities*, January 1982, *15*, 42–51. (b)

KAVALE, KENNETH A., & LINDSEY, JIMMY D. Adult basic education: Has it worked? *Journal of Reading*, February 1977, *20*, 368–376.

KAVALE, KENNETH, & MATTSON, P. DENNIS. "One jumped off the balance beam": Meta-analysis of perceptual–motor training. *Journal of Learning Disabilities*, March 1983, *16*, 165–173.

KAWI, A. A., & PASAMANICK, B. Association factors of pregnancy with reading disorders of childhood. *Journal of the American Medical Association*, 1958, *166*, 1420–1423.

KAYE, STANLEY. Psychoanalytic perspectives on learning disability. *Journal of Contemporary Psychotherapy*, Spring/Summer 1982, *13*, 83–93.

KAZDIN, ALAN E., & BOOTZIN, RICHARD R. The token economy: An evaluative review. *Journal of Applied Behavioral Analysis*, Fall 1972, *5*, 343–372.

KEEFE, BARBARA, & SWINNEY, DAVID. On the relationship of hemispheric specialization and developmental dyslexia. *Cortex*, 1979, *15*, 471–481.

KEILITZ, INGO, ZAREMBA, BARBARA A., & BRODER, PAUL K. The link between learning disabilities and juvenile delinquency: Some issues and answers. *Learning Disabilities Quarterly*, Spring 1979, *2*, 2–11.

KELLAM, SHEPPARD G., & SCHIFF, SHELDON K. Effects of family life on children's adaptation to first grade. *American Journal of Orthopsychiatry*, March 1969, *39*, 276–278.

KELLER, PAUL F. G. Maryland Micro: A prototype readability formula for small computers. *The Reading Teacher*, April 1982, *35*, 778–782.

KENDALL, JANET R., MASON, JANA M., & HUNTER, WILLIAM. Which comprehension? Artifacts of the measurement of reading comprehension. *Journal of Educational Research*, March/April 1979, *73*, 233–235.

KENDER, JOSEPH P., & RUBENSTEIN, HERBERT. Recall versus reinspection in IRI comprehension tests. *The Reading Teacher*, April 1977, *30*, 776–779.

KEOGH, BARBARA K. The Bender Gestalt with children: Research implications. *Journal of Special Education*, 1961, *3*, 15–22.

KEOGH, BARBARA K. Hyperactivity and learning problems: Implications for teachers. *Academic Therapy*, Fall 1971, *7*, 47–50.

KEOGH, BARBARA K. Optometric vision training programs for children with learning disabilities: Review of issues and research. *Journal of Learning Disabilities*, April 1974, 7, 219–231.

KEOGH, BARBARA K., & DONLON, GENEVIEVE, M. Field dependence, impulsivity and learning disabilities. *Journal of Learning Disabilities*, June 1972, 5, 331–336.

KEOGH, BARBARA K., & GLOVER, ANNE T. The generality and durability of cognitive training effects. *Exceptional Children Quarterly*, May 1980, 1, 75–82.

KEOGH, BARBARA K., & MARGOLIS, JUDITH. Learn to labor and to wait: Attentional problems of children with learning disorders. *Journal of Learning Disabilities*, May 1976, 9, 276–286.

KEPHART, NEWELL C. *The slow learner in the classroom*. Columbus, OH: Charles E. Merrill, 1960.

KERSHNER, JOHN R. Laterality and learning disabilities: Cerebral dominance as a cognitive process. *Topics in Learning & Learning Disabilities*, April 1983, 3, 66–74.

KIBBY, MICHAEL W. The effects of certain instructional conditions and response modes on initial word learning. *Reading Research Quarterly*, 1979, 15 (1), 147–171. (a)

KIBBY, MICHAEL W. Passage readability affects the oral reading strategies of disabled readers. *The Reading Teacher*, January 1979, 32, 390–396. (b)

KIBBY, MICHAEL W. Intersentential processes in reading comprehension. *Journal of Reading Behavior*, 1980, 12, 299–312.

KIESLING, HENRY. Productivity of instructional time by mode of instruction for students at varying levels of reading skill. *Reading Research Quarterly*, 1977–1978, 13 (4), 544–582.

KIFER, EDWARD. The relationship between the home and school in influencing the learning of children. *Research in the Teaching of English*, Spring 1977, 11, 5–16.

KILTY, TED K. *The readability of commonly encountered materials*. Mimeographed. Western Michigan University, Kalamazoo, Michigan, 1976.

KIMMEL, SUSAN, & MACGINITIE, WALTER H. Identifying children who use a perseverative processing strategy. *Reading Research Quarterly*, Winter 1984, 19, 162–172.

KING, ETHEL M. Prereading programs: Direct versus incidental teaching. *The Reading Teacher*, February 1978, 31, 504–510.

KING, R. TOMMY. Learning from a PAL. *The Reading Teacher*, March 1982, 35, 682–685.

KINGORE, BERTHA W. Storytelling: A bridge from the university to the elementary school to the home. *Language Arts*, January 1982, 59, 28–32.

KINSBOURNE, MARCEL. Cerebral dominance, learning and cognition. In H. R. Myklebust (Ed.), *Progress in learning disabilities*, Vol. III. New York: Grune & Stratton, 1975. Pp. 201–218.

KINSBOURNE, MARCEL. Hemispheric specialization and the growth of human understanding. *American Psychologist*, April 1982, 37, 411–420.

KINSBOURNE, MARCEL. Models of learning disability. *Topics in Learning & Learning Disabilities*, April 1983, 3, 1–13.

KINSBOURNE, MARCEL, & CAPLAN, PAULA J. *Children's learning and attention problems*. Boston: Little, Brown, 1979.

KINSBOURNE, MARCEL, & HISCOCK, MERRILL. Cerebral lateralization and cognitive development. In J. S. Chall & A. F. Mirsky (Eds.), *Education and the brain*. 77th Yearbook of the National Society for the Study of Education, Part II. Chicago: University of Chicago Press, 1978. Pp. 169–222.

KINSBOURNE, MARCEL, & WARRINGTON, ELIZABETH K. Developmental factors in reading and writing backwardness. *British Journal of Psychiatry*, 1963, 54, 145–156.

KINSBOURNE, MARCEL, & WARRINGTON, ELIZABETH K. Developmental factors in reading and writing backwardness. In J. Money (Ed.), *The disabled reader*. Baltimore: Johns Hopkins Press, 1966. Pp. 59–71.

KIRBY, KIMBERLY, HOLBORN, STEPHEN W., & BUSHBY, HARRY T. Word game bingo: A behavioral treatment package for improving textual responding to sight words. *Journal of Applied Behavior Analysis*, Fall 1981, 14, 317–326.

KIRK, SAMUEL A., & KIRK, WINIFRED D. *Psycholinguistic learning disabilities: Diagnosis and remediation*. Urbana, IL: University of Illinois Press, 1971.

KIRK, SAMUEL A., & KIRK, WINIFRED. On defining learning disabilities. *Journal of Learning Disabilities*, January 1983, 16, 20–21.

KIRK, URSALA. Introduction: Toward our understanding of the neuropsychology of language, reading, and spelling. In U. Kirk (Ed.), *Neuropsychology of language, reading, and spelling.* New York: Academic Press, 1983. Pp. 3–31.

KIRSCH, DOROTHY. From athletes to zebras—young children want to read about them. *Elementary English,* January 1975, *52,* 73–78.

KIRSCH, DOROTHY I., PEHRSSON, ROBERT S. V., & ROBINSON, H. ALAN. Expressed reading interests of young children: An international study. In J. E. Merritt (Ed.), *New horizons in reading.* Newark, DE: International Reading Association, 1976. Pp. 302–317.

KIRSCH, IRWIN, & GUTHRIE, JOHN T. The concept and measurement of functional literacy. *Reading Research Quarterly,* 1977–1978, *13* (4), 485–507.

KLARE, GEORGE R. A table for rapid determination of Dale–Chall readability scores. *Educational Research Bulletin,* February 13, 1952, *31,* 43–47.

KLARE, GEORGE R. Assessing readability. *Reading Research Quarterly,* 1974–1975, *10* (1), 62–102.

KLARE, GEORGE R. A second look at the validity of readability formulas. *Journal of Reading Behavior,* Summer 1976, *8,* 129–152.

KLARE, GEORGE R. Readability. In P. D. Pearson (Ed.), *Handbook of reading research.* New York: Longman, 1984. Pp. 681–744.

KLASEN, EDITH. *The syndrome of specific dyslexia: With special consideration of its physiological, psychological, test psychological and social correlates.* Baltimore: University Park Press, 1972.

KLASEN, EDITH. Learning disabilities: The German perspective. In L. Tarnopol & M. Tarnopol (Eds.), *Reading disability: An international perspective.* Baltimore: University Park Press, 1976. Pp. 179–191.

KLAUER, KARL J. Intentional and incidental learning with instructional texts: A meta-analysis for 1970–1980. *American Educational Research Journal,* Summer 1984, *21,* 323–339.

KLAUSMEIER, HERBERT J., SORENSON, JUANITA S., & QUILLING, MARY. Instructional programming for the individual pupil in the multi-unit school. *Elementary School Journal,* November 1971, *72,* 88–101.

KLEIMAN, GLENN M. Comparing good and poor readers: A critique of the research. Technical Report No. 246. Champaign, IL: Center for the Study of Reading, University of Illinois, June 1982.

KLEIMAN, GLENN M., & HUMPHREY, MARY M. Phonological representations in visual word recognition: The adjunct access model. Technical Report No. 247. Champaign, IL: Center for the Study of Reading, University of Illinois, June 1982.

KLEIN, MARVIN. The development and use of sentence combining in the reading program. Paper presented at the International Reading Association Convention, St. Louis, May 1980. ED 186 845.

KLEINBERG, NORMAN M. Tachistoscopic vs. pseudo-tachistoscopic training and the Hawthorne effect in improving reading achievement. Unpublished doctoral dissertation, Columbia University, 1970.

KLESIUS, STEPHEN E. Perceptual motor development and reading—A closer look. In R. C. Aukerman (Ed.), *Some persistent questions on beginning reading.* Newark, DE: International Reading Association, 1972. Pp. 151–159.

KLIEGL, REINHOLD, OLSON, RICHARD K., & DAVIDSON, BRIAN J. On problems of confounding perceptual and language processes. In K. Rayner (Ed.), *Eye movements in reading: Perceptual and language processes.* New York: Academic Press, 1983. Pp. 333–343.

KLINE, CARL L., & KLINE, CAROLYN L. Follow-up study of 216 dyslexic children. *Bulletin of the Orton Society,* 1975, *25,* 127–144.

KLINK, HOWARD. Words and music. *Language Arts,* April 1976, *53,* 401–403.

KNOWLES, B. A. Behavior modification and special education. *Slow Learning Child,* November 1970, *17,* 170–177.

KOBASIGAWA, AKIRA, RANSOM, CHRISTINE, & HOLLAND, CORNELIUS. Children's knowledge about skimming. *Alberta Journal of Educational Research,* September 1980, *26,* 169–182.

KOENKE, KARL. The careful use of comic books. *The Reading Teacher,* February 1981, *34,* 592–595.

KOEPSEL, ERWIN O. A comparison of teaching reading to educationally handicapped children using Fernald's VAKT method, Blau's AKT method, existing methods. Unpublished doctoral dissertation, University of Colorado, 1974.

KOFFLER, STEPHEN L. A comparison of approaches for setting proficiency standards. *Journal of Educational Measurement,* Fall 1980, *17,* 167–178.

KOHLMORGEN, WILLIAM H. A study of the effects of Delacato's program of neurological organization on reading achievement. Unpublished doctoral dissertation, New York University, 1971.

KOLKER, BRENDA S., & TERWILLIGER, PAUL N. Sight vocabulary learning in first and second graders. *Reading World,* May 1981, *20,* 251–258.

KOPPELL, STEVEN. Testing the attentional deficit notion. *Journal of Learning Disabilities,* January 1979, *12,* 43–48.

KOPPITZ, ELIZABETH M. *The Bender–Gestalt Test for young children.* New York: Grune & Stratton, 1964.

KOSKINEN, PATRICIA S., & WILSON, ROBERT M. *Developing a successful tutoring program.* New York: Teachers College Press, 1982. (a)

KOSKINEN, PATRICIA S., & WILSON, ROBERT M. *A guide for student tutors.* New York: Teachers College Press, 1982. (b)

KOSKINEN, PATRICIA S., & WILSON, ROBERT M. *Tutoring: A guide for success.* New York: Teachers College Press, 1982. (c)

KRASNOW, ANITA. An Adlerian approach to the problem of school maladjustment. *Academic Therapy,* Winter 1971–1972, 7, 171–183.

KREESE, ELAINE C. Using reading as a thinking process to solve math story problems. *Journal of Reading,* April 1984, *27,* 598–601.

KREMIN, HELGARD. Alexia: Theory and research. In R. N. Malatesha & P. Aaron (Eds.), *Reading disorders: Varieties and treatments.* New York: Academic Press, 1982. Pp. 341–367.

KRESS, ROY A., & JOHNSON, MARJORIE S. Martin. In A. J. Harris (Ed.), *Casebook on reading disability.* New York: David McKay, 1970. Pp. 1–24.

KRETSCHMER, JOSEPH C. Computerizing and comparing the Rix readability index. *Journal of Reading,* March 1984, *27,* 490–499.

KRIPPNER, STANLEY. The use of hypnosis and the improvement of academic achievement. *Journal of Special Education,* Fall 1970, *4,* 451–460.

KRIPPNER, STANLEY. Hypnosis as verbal programming in educational therapy. *Academic Therapy,* Fall 1971, 7, 5–12.

KRONICK, DOREEN. *Three families.* San Rafael, CA: Academic Therapy Publications, 1976.

KUČERA, HENRY, & FRANCIS, W. NELSON. *Comparative analysis of present-day American English.* Providence, RI: Brown University Press, 1967.

KUO, W. F. A preliminary study of reading disabilities in the Republic of China. Collection of papers by National Taiwan Normal University, Graduate School of Education, 1978, *20,* 57–58. Cited by O. Tzeng & D. Hung. Reading in a nonalphabetic writing system: Some experimental studies. In J. Kavanagh & R. Venezky (Eds.), *Orthography, reading, and dyslexia.* Baltimore: University Park Press, 1980. Pp. 211–226.

KUYPERS, D. S., BECKER, W. C. & O'LEARY, K. D. How to make a token system fail. *Exceptional Children,* October 1968, *35,* 101–109.

KYÖSTIÖ, O. K. Is learning to read easy in a language in which the grapheme-phoneme correspondences are regular? In J. Kavanagh & R. Venezky (Eds.), *Orthography, reading, and dyslexia,* Baltimore: University Park Press, 1980. Pp. 35–49.

LABERGE, DAVID, & SAMUELS, S. JAY. Toward a theory of automatic information processing in reading. In H. Singer & R. B. Ruddell (Eds.), *Theoretical models and processes of reading* (2nd ed.). Newark, DE: International Reading Association, 1976. Pp. 548–579.

LABOV, WILLIAM. The logic of nonstandard English. In J. S. De Stefano (Ed.), *Language, society, and education: A profile of black English.* Worthington, OH: Charles A. Jones, 1973. Pp. 218–237.

LAFFEY, JAMES L. *Methods of reading instruction: An annotated bibliography.* Newark, DE: International Reading Association, 1971.

LAFFEY, JAMES L., & SHUY, ROGER (Eds.). *Language differences: Do they interfere?* Newark, DE: International Reading Association, 1973.

LAHADERNE, HENRIETTE M. Feminized schools—Unpromising myth to explain boys' reading problems. *The Reading Teacher,* May 1976, *29,* 776–786.

LAKE, MARY L. First aid for vocabularies. *Elementary English*, November 1967, *44*, 783–784. Also in A. J. Harris & E. Sipay (Eds.), *Readings on reading instruction* (2nd ed.). New York: Longman, 1972.

LAMB, POSE. Reading and television in the United States. In J. E. Merritt (Ed.), *New horizons in reading*. Newark, DE: International Reading Association, 1976. Pp. 370–382.

LAMME, LINDA L. Are reading habits and abilities related? *The Reading Teacher*, October 1976, *30*, 21–27. (a)

LAMME, LINDA L. Self-contained to departmentalized: How reading habits changed. *Elementary School Journal*, January 1976, *76*, 208–218. (b)

LANE, BRUCE A. The relationship of learning disabilities to juvenile delinquency: Current status. *Journal of Learning Disabilities*, October 1980, *13*, 425–434.

LANG, JANELL B. Self-concept and reading achievement—An annotated bibliography. *The Reading Teacher*, May 1976, *29*, 787–793.

LANGE, BOB. Promoting test-wiseness. *Journal of Reading*, May 1981, *24*, 740–743.

LANGE, BOB. Questioning techniques. *Language Arts*, February 1982, *59*, 180–185.

LANGE, JO-ANN T. Using S2RAT to improve reading skills in the content areas. *The Reading Teacher*, January 1983, *36*, 402–404.

LANGER, JUDITH A. Relation between levels of prior knowledge and the organization of recall. In M. Kamil & A. Moe (Eds.), *Perspectives in reading research and instruction*. Washington, DC: National Reading Conference, 1980. Pp. 28–33.

LANGER, JUDITH A. From theory to practice: A prereading plan. *Journal of Reading*, November 1981, *25*, 152–156.

LANGER, JUDITH A. Facilitating text processing: The elaboration of prior knowledge. In J. Langer & M. T. Burke-Smith (Eds.), *Reader meets author/bridging the gap: Psycholinguistic and sociolinguistic perspectives*. Newark, DE: International Reading Association, 1982. Pp. 149–162. (a)

LANGER, JUDITH A. Examining background knowledge and text comprehension. *Reading Research Quarterly*, Summer 1984, *19*, 468–481.

LANGER, JUDITH A., & NICOLICH, MARK. Prior knowledge and its relationship to comprehension. *Journal of Reading Behavior*, Winter 1981, *13*, 373–379.

LANGER, PHILIP, KALK, JOHN M., & SEARLS, DONALD T. Age of admission and trends in achievement: A comparison of blacks and caucasians. *American Educational Research Journal*, Spring 1984, *21*, 61–78.

LAOSA, LUIS M. Families as facilitator of children's intellectual development at three years of age: A causal analysis. Research report 81–45. Princeton, NJ: ETS, November 1981.

LAPP, DIANE (Ed.). *Making reading possible through effective classroom management*. Newark, DE: International Reading Association, 1980.

LARRICK, NANCY. *A parent's guide to children's reading* (4th ed.). New York: Doubleday, 1975.

LARRICK, NANCY. Classroom magazines: A critique of 45 top sellers. *Learning*, October 1978, *7*, 260–269.

LARRICK, NANCY. Random notes on recent research reflecting on children's reading. Paper presented at the International Reading Association Conference, Anaheim, CA, May 1983.

LARRIVEE, BARBARA. Modality preference as a model for differentiating beginning reading instruction: A review of the issues. *Learning Disability Quarterly*, Spring 1981, *4*, 180–188.

LARSEN, STEPHEN C., & EHLY, STEWART. Teacher-student interactions: A factor in handicapping conditions. *Academic Therapy*, January 1978, *13*, 267–273.

LARSEN, STEPHEN C., & HAMMILL, DONALD D. Relationships of selected visual perceptual abilities to school learning. *Journal of Special Education*, 1975, *9* (3), 282–291.

LARSEN, STEPHEN C., PARKER, RANDALL M., & HAMMILL, DONALD D. Effectiveness of psycholinguistic training: A reply to Kavale. *Exceptional Children*, September 1982, *49*, 60–66.

LASS, BONNIE. Trade books for black English speakers. *Language Arts*, April 1980, *57*, 413–419.

LASS, BONNIE. Do teachers individualize their responses to reading miscues? A study of feedback during oral reading. *Reading World*, March 1984, *23*, 242–254.

LASS, BONNIE, & BROMFIELD, MARCIA. Books about children with special needs: An annotated bibliography. *The Reading Teacher*, Feburary 1981, *34*, 530–533.

LASS-WOODFIN, MARY JO (Ed.). *Books on American Indians and Eskimos: A selected guide for children and young adults.* Chicago: American Library Association, 1978.

LASSEN, NIELS A., INGVAR, DAVID H., & SKINKØJ, ERIK. Brain function and blood flow. *Scientific American*, October 1978, *239*, 50–59.

LAUGHLIN, ROSEMARY M. Fun in the word factory: Exercises with the dictionary. *Language Arts*, March 1978, *55*, 319–321.

LAURITZEN, CAROL. A modification of repeated readings for group instruction. *The Reading Teacher*, January 1982, *35*, 456–458.

LAURITZEN, CAROL, & CHEVES, DEBORAH. Children's reading interests classified by age level. *The Reading Teacher*, April 1974, *27*, 694–700.

LAWRENCE, PAULA S., & SIMMONS, BARBARA M. Criteria for reading management systems. *The Reading Teacher*, December 1978, *32*, 332–336.

LAWSON, CORNELIA V. Children's reasons and motivations for the selection of favorite books. Unpublished doctoral dissertation, University of Kansas, 1972.

LAWSON, E. A. Note on the influence of different orders of approximations to the English language upon eye-voice span. *Quarterly Journal of Experimental Psychology*, 1961, *13*, 53–55.

LAYTON, JAMES R. A chart for computing the Dale–Chall Readability Formula above fourth grade level. *Journal of Reading*, December 1980, *24*, 239–244.

LAZAR, MAY. *Reading interests, activities, and opportunities of bright, average and dull children.* Contribution to Education No. 707. New York: Teachers College, Columbia University, 1937.

LECKY, P. *Self-consistency: A theory of personality.* New York: Island Press, 1951.

LEFTON, LESTER A., *et al.* Eye movement dynamics of good and poor readers: Then and now. *Journal of Reading Behavior*, Winter 1979, *11*, 319–328.

LEHR, FRAN. Bibliotherapy. *Journal of Reading*, October 1981, *25*, 76–79. (a)

LEHR, FRAN. Integrating reading and writing instruction. *The Reading Teacher*, May 1981, *34*, 958–961. (b). Also in A. J. Harris & E. Sipay (Eds.), *Readings on reading instruction* (3rd ed.). New York: Longman, 1984. Pp. 85–88.

LEHR, FRAN. Reading and the gifted secondary school student. *Journal of Reading*, February 1983, *26*, 456–458.

LEHR, FRAN. Peer teaching. *The Reading Teacher*, March 1984, *37*, 636–639.

LEIBERT, ROBERT E. A study of word errors by second, third, and fourth grade pupils reading the Dolch Word List. In J. Niles & L. A. Harris (Eds.), *New inquiries in reading research and instruction.* Rochester, NY: National Reading Conference, 1982. Pp. 166–169.

LEINHARDT, GAEA, & PALLAY, ALLAN. Restrictive educational settings: Exile or haven? *Review of Educational Research*, Winter 1982, *52*, 557–578.

LEINHARDT, GAEA, SEEWALD, ANDREA M., & ZIGMOND, NAOMI. Sex and race differences in learning disabilities classrooms. *Journal of Educational Psychology*, December 1982, *74*, 835–843.

LEINHARDT, GAEA, ZIGMOND, NAOMI, & COOLEY, WILLIAM W. Reading instruction and its effects. *American Educational Research Journal*, Fall 1981, *18*, 343–361.

LEMAY, MARJORIE. Are there radiological changes in the brains of individuals with dyslexia? *Bulletin of the Orton Society*, 1981, *31*, 135–141.

LEONG, CHE K. Laterality and reading proficiency in children. *Reading Research Quarterly*, 1980, *15* (2), 185–202.

LEONG, C. K., & HAINES, C. F. Beginning readers' awareness of words and sentences. *Journal of Reading Behavior*, Winter 1978, *10*, 393–407.

LESGOLD, ALAN M., & CURTIS, MARY E. Learning to read words efficiently. In A. Lesgold & C. Perfetti (Eds.), *Interactive processes in reading.* Hillsdale, NJ: LEA, 1981. Pp. 329–360.

LESGOLD, ALAN M., & PERFETTI, CHARLES A. Interactive processes in reading: Where do we stand? In A. Lesgold & C. Perfetti (Eds.), *Interactive processes in reading.* Hillsdale, NJ: LEA, 1981. Pp. 387–405.

LESLIE, LAUREN. The use of graphic and contextual information by average and below-average readers. *Journal of Reading Behavior*, Summer 1980, *12*, 139–149.

LESLIE, LAUREEN, & OSOL, PAT. Changes in oral reading strategies as a function of quantities of miscues. *Journal of Reading Behavior*, Winter 1978, *10*, 442–445.

LESLIE, LAUREEN, & SHANNON, ALBERT J. Recognition of orthographic structure during beginning reading. *Journal of Reading Behavior*, 1981, *13* (4), 313–324.

LESSLER, KEN, & BRIDGES, JUDITH S. The prediction of learning problems in a rural setting: Can we improve on readiness tests? *Journal of Learning Disabilities*, February 1973, 6, 90–94.

LEU, DONALD J. Differences between oral and written discourse and the acquisition of reading proficiency. *Journal of Reading Behavior*, 1982, *14* (2), 111–125. (a)

LEU, DONALD J. Oral reading error analysis: A critical review of research and application. *Reading Research Quarterly*, 1982, *17* (3), 420–437. (b)

LEVIN, HARRY, & ADDIS, ANN B. *The eye-voice span*. Cambridge, MA: MIT Press, 1979.

LEVIN, HARRY, & COHN, J. A. Effects of instruction on the eye-voice span. In H. Levin, E. J. Gibson, & J. J. Gibson (Eds.), *The analysis of reading skills: A program of basic and applied research*. Final Report, Project No. 5-1213, Cornell University, 1968. ED 034 663

LEVIN, HARRY, & KAPLAN, ELEANOR L. Grammatical structure and reading. In H. Levin & J. P. Williams (Eds.), *Basic studies on reading*. New York: Basic Books, 1970. Pp. 110–133.

LEVIN, HARRY, & TURNER, E. A. Sentence structure and the eye-voice span. Studies in oral reading IX, preliminary draft. Project No. B. R. 5-1213-9-OEC-6-10, September 1966. ED 011 957

LEVIN, HARRY, & WATSON J. The learning of variable grapheme-phoneme correspondence. In H. Levin et al., *A basic research program on reading*. Final Report, Cooperative Research Project No. 639, 1963.

LEVIN, JOEL R. The mnemonic '80's: Keywords in the classroom. *Educational Psychologist*, Summer 1981, *16*, 65–82. (a)

LEVIN, JOEL R. On functions of pictures in prose. In F. Pirozzolo & M. Wittrock (Eds.), *Neuropsychological and cognitive processes in reading*. New York: Academic Press, 1981. Pp. 203–228. (b)

LEVIN, JOEL R., et al. Frequency interference in children's recognition of sentence information. *American Educational Research Journal*, Winter 1978, *15*, 39–51.

LEVIN, JOEL R., et al. Mnemonic versus nonmnemonic vocabulary-learning strategies for children. *American Educational Research Journal*, Spring 1982, *19*, 121–136.

LEVINE, KENNETH. Functional literacy: Fond illusions and false economies. *Harvard Educational Review*, August 1982, *52*, 249–266.

LEVINE, MELVIN, & OBERKLAID, FRANK. Hyperactivity: Symptom complex or complex symptom? *American Journal of Diseases in Children*, April 1980, *134*, 409–414.

LEVINE, STEVEN G. USSR—A necessary component in teaching reading. *Journal of Reading*, February 1984, *27*, 394–400.

LEVINSON, HAROLD N. *A solution to the riddle dyslexia*. New York: Springer-Verlag, 1980.

LEVISON, BEATRICE. Raphael. In A. J. Harris (Ed.), *Casebook on reading disability*. New York: David McKay, 1970. Pp. 117–134.

LEWANDOWSKI, GLEN. A different look at some basic sight-word lists and their use. *Reading World*, May 1979, *18*, 333–341.

LEWIS, JENEVA. A comparison of kindergarten teachers' perceptions of children's preference in books with the children's actual preferences. Unpublished doctoral dissertation, East Texas State University, 1970.

LEWIS, RAMON, & TEALE, WILLIAM H. Another look at secondary school students' attitudes toward reading. *Journal of Reading Behavior*, Fall 1980, *12*, 187–201.

LEYS, MARGIE, et al. Does cloze measure intersentence comprehension? A modified replication of Shanahan, Kamil, and Tobin. In J. Niles & L. A. Harris (Eds.), *Searches for meaning in reading/ language processing and instruction*. Rochester, NY. National Reading Conference, 1983. Pp. 111–114.

LIBERMAN, ISABELLE Y. A language-oriented view of reading and its disabilities. In H. Myklebust (Ed.), *Progress in learning disabilities*, Vol. 5. New York: Grune & Stratton, 1983. Pp. 81–101.

LIBERMAN, ISABELLE Y. & SHANKWEILER, DONALD. Speech, the alphabet and teaching to read. In L. Resnick & P. Weaver (Eds.), *Theory and practice of early reading*, Vol. 2. Hillsdale, NJ: LEA, 1979. Pp. 109–132.

LIBERMAN, ISABELLE Y., *et al.* Letter confusion and reversals of sequence in the beginning reader: Implications for Orton's theory of developmental dyslexia. *Cortex*, June 1971, 7, 127–142.

LIBERMAN, ISABELLE Y., *et al.* Explicit syllable and phoneme segmentation in the young child. *Journal of Experimental Child Psychology*, October 1974, 18, 201–212.

LIBERMAN, ISABELLE Y., *et al.* Phonetic segmentation and recoding in the beginning reader. In A. S. Reber & D. L. Scarborough (Eds.), *Toward a psychology of reading*. Hillsdale, NJ: LEA 1977. Pp. 207–225.

LIBERMAN, ISABELLE, *et al.* Orthography and the beginning reader. In J. Kavanagh & R. Venezky (Eds.), *Orthography, reading, and dyslexia*. Baltimore: University Park Press, 1980. Pp. 137–153.

LICKTEIG, MARY JANE. A comparison of book selection preferences of innercity and suburban fourth and sixth graders. Unpublished doctoral dissertation, University of Oregon, 1972.

LIEBEN, BEATRICE. Attitudes, platitudes, and conferences in teacher-parent relations involving the child with a reading problem. *Elementary School Journal*, 1958, 57, 279–286. Reprinted in A. J. Harris & E. R. Sipay (Eds.), *Readings on reading instruction* (2nd ed.). New York: David McKay, 1972. Pp. 420–427.

LIEBERMAN, LAURENCE M. Territoriality—Who does what to whom? *Journal of Learning Disabilities*, March 1980, 13, 124–128.

LIGHT, RICHARD J., & PILLEMER, DAVID B. Numbers and narratives: Combining their strength in research reviews. *Harvard Educational Review*, February 1982, 52, 1–26.

LINCOLN, ROBERT D. The effect of single-grade and multi-grade primary school classrooms on reading achievement of children. *New England Reading Association Journal*, Spring 1982, 17, 19–24.

LINDAMOOD, CHARLES H., & LINDAMOOD, PATRICIA C. *Auditory discrimination in depth*. Boston: Teaching Resources Corp., 1969.

LINDSAY, G. A. The Infant Rating Scale. *British Journal of Educational Psychology*, 1980, 50, 97–104.

LINDSAY, G. A., & WEDELL, K. The early identification of educationally "at risk" children revisited. *Journal of Learning Disabilities*, April 1982, 15, 212–217.

LINDSEY, JAMES F., & RUNQUIST, ANNETTE D. Clinical supervision: A tool for the reading specialist. *Journal of Reading*, October 1983, 27, 48–50.

LINN, ROBERT L. Issues of reliability in measurement for competency-based programs. In M. Bunda & J. Sanders (Eds.), *Practices & problems in competency-based measurement*. Washington, DC: National Council on Measurement in Education, 1979. Pp. 90–107. (a)

LINN, ROBERT L. Issues of validity in measurement for competency-based programs. In M. Bunda & J. Sanders (Eds.), *Practices & problems in competency-based measurement*. Washington, DC: National Council on Measurement in Education, 1979. Pp. 108–123. (b)

LINN, ROBERT L. Testing and instruction: Links and distinctions. *Journal of Educational Measurements*, Summer 1983, 20, 179–189.

LINN, ROBERT L., & SLINDE, JEFFREY A. The determination of the significance of change between pre- and post-testing periods. *Review of Educational Research*, Winter 1977, 47, 121–150.

LINN, ROBERT L., *et al.* An investigation of item bias in a test of reading comprehension. Technical Report No. 163. Champaign, IL: Center for the Study of Reading, University of Illinois, March 1980.

LIPSON, ALICE M., & ALDEN, LEE. Mainstreaming: Unwanted side effects. *Academic Therapy*, January 1983, 18, 267–274.

LIPSON, MARJORIE Y. Some unexpected issues in prior knowledge and comprehension. *The Reading Teacher*, April 1984, 37, 760–764.

LIU, STELLA S. F. An investigation of oral reading miscues made by nonstandard dialect speaking black children (Abstract). *Reading Research Quarterly*, 1975–1976, 11 (2), 193–197.

LOHNES, PAUL R. Evaluating the schooling of intelligence. *Educational Researcher*, February 1973, 2, 6–11.

LOHNES, PAUL R., & GRAY, MARIAN M. Intelligence and the cooperative reading studies. *Reading Research Quarterly*, Spring 1972, 7, 466–476.

LOMAX, CAROL M. Interest in books and stories at nursery school. *Educational Research*, February 1977, 19, 100–112.

LONG, MARGO A. The interracial family in children's literature. *The Reading Teacher*, May 1978, *31*, 909–915.

LONG, RICHARD L., MCINTYRE, CURTIS W., & MURRAY, MICHAEL E. Visual selective attention in learning disabled and normal boys. *Bulletin of the Psychonomic Society*, January 1982, *19*, 15–18.

LONGO, JUDITH A. The Fry Graph: Validation of the college levels. *Journal of Reading*, December 1982, *26*, 229–234.

LORGE, IRVING. Predicting readability. *Teachers College Record*, March 1944, *45*, 404–419.

LOVETT, MAUREEN B. Reading skill and its development: Theoretical and empirical considerations. In G. MacKinnon & T. Waller (Eds.), *Reading research: Advances in theory and practice*, Vol. 3. New York: Academic Press, 1981. Pp. 1–37.

LOZANOV, GEORGI. The suggestological theory of communicating and instruction. *Suggestology & Suggestopedia*, 1975, *1*, 1–14.

LUCAS, PETER A., & MCCONKIE, GEORGE W. The definition of test items: A descriptive approach. *American Educational Research Journal*, Spring 1980, *17*, 133–140.

LUDLAM, WILLIAM M. Visual electrophysiology and reading/learning difficulties. *Journal of Learning Disabilities*, December 1981, *14*, 587–590.

LUFTIG, RICHARD L. Abstractive memory, the central-incidental hypothesis, and the use of structural importance in text: Control processes or structural features. *Reading Research Quarterly*, Fall 1983, *19*, 28–37.

LUITEN, JOHN, AMES, WILBUR, & ACHERSON, GARY A. A meta-analysis of the effects of advance organizers on learning and retention. *American Educational Research Journal*, Summer 1980, *17*, 211–218.

LUND, KATHRYN A., SCHNAPS, LAURA, & BIJOU, SIDNEY W. Let's take another look at record keeping. *Teaching Exceptional Children*, Spring 1983, *15*, 155–159.

LUNDAHL, FLEMMING. Split-half classes. In J. E. Merritt (Ed.), *New horizons in reading*. Newark, DE: International Reading Association, 1976. Pp. 428–433.

LUNSTRUM, JOHN P. Building motivation through the use of controversy. *Journal of Reading*, May 1981, *24*, 687–691.

LUNSTRUM, JOHN P., & TAYLOR, BOB L. *Teaching reading in the social studies*. Newark, DE: International Reading Association, 1978.

LUPICA, LENA. Skills for the future. In L. Reed & S. Ward (Eds.), *Basic skills: Issues and choices, 1*. St. Louis: CEMREL, April 1982. Pp. 117–123.

LURIA, A. R. *The working brain: An introduction to neuropsychology*. New York: Basic Books, 1973.

LYLE, J. G. Reading retardation and reversal tendency: A factorial study. *Child Development*, 1968, *40*, 833–843.

LYLE, J. G. Certain antecedent, perinatal and development variables and reading retardation in middle-class boys. *Child Development*, 1970, *41*, 481–491.

LYON, G. REID. Learning-disabled readers: Identification of subgroups. In H. Myklebust (Ed.), *Progress in Learning Disabilities*, Vol. 5. New York: Grune & Stratton, 1983. Pp. 103–133.

LYON, KATHLEEN. The effect on comprehension of increasing the single-word recoding speed of poor readers. Unpublished doctoral dissertation, State University of New York at Albany, 1984.

LYONS, KEVIN. Criterion referenced reading comprehension tests: New forms with old ghosts. *Journal of Reading*, January 1984, *27*, 293–298.

LYSAKOWSKI, RICHARD S., & WALBERG, HERBERT J. Instructional effects of cues, participation, and corrective feedback: A quantitative synthesis. *American Educational Research Journal*, Winter 1982, *19*, 559–578.

MACGINITIE, WALTER H. An introduction to some measurement problems in reading. In W. H. MacGinitie (Ed.), *Assessment problems in reading*. Newark, DE: International Reading Association, 1973. Pp. 1–7.

MACGINITIE, WALTER H. When should we begin to teach reading? *Language Arts*, November/December 1976, *53*, 878–882.

MACGINITIE, WALTER H. Children's understanding of linguistic units. In S. J. Samuels (Ed.), *What research has to say about reading instruction*. Newark, DE: International Reading Association, 1978. Pp. 43–56.

MACGINITIE, WALTER H., KIMMEL, SUSAN, & MARIA, KATHERINE. The role of cognitive strategies in certain reading comprehension disabilities. *The Forum*, Fall 1980, *6*, 10–13.

MACGINITIE, WALTER H., & TRETIAK, RICHARD. Sentence depth measures as predictors of reading difficulty. *Reading Research Quarterly*, Spring 1971, *6*, 364–376.

MACGINITIE, WALTER, et al. *Teacher's manual: Gates–MacGinitie Reading Tests* (2nd ed.). Boston: Houghton Mifflin, 1978.

MADDEN, NANCY A., & SLAVIN, ROBERT E. Mainstreaming students with mild handicaps: Academic and social outcomes. *Review of Educational Research*, Winter 1983, *53*, 519–569.

MADISON, JOANNE Y., CARROLL, BONNIE E., & DRUM, PRISCILLA A. The effects of directionality and proximity of context clues in the comprehension of unknown words. In J. Niles & L. A. Harris (Eds.), *New inquiries in reading: Research and instruction*. Rochester, NY: National Reading Conference, 1982. Pp. 105–109.

MAGER, ROBERT F. *Preparing instructional objectives* (2nd ed.). Belmont, CA: Fearon-Pitman, 1962.

MAGINNIS, GEORGE H. Measuring underachievement in reading. *The Reading Teacher*, May 1972, *25*, 750–753.

MAGINNIS, GEORGE H. Easier, faster, more reliable readability ratings. *Journal of Reading*, March 1982, *25*, 598–599.

MAKITA, KIYOSHI. The rarity of reading disability in Japanese children. *American Journal of Orthopsychiatry*, July 1968, *38*, 599–614.

MAKITA, KIYOSHI. Reading disability and the writing system. In J. E. Merritt (Ed.), *New horizons in reading*. Newark, DE: International Reading Association, 1976. Pp. 250–254.

MALATESHA, R. N., & DOUGAN, DEBORAH R. Clinical subtypes of developmental dyslexia: Resolution of an irresolute problem. In R. Malatesha & P. Aaron (Eds.), *Reading disorders: Varieties and treatment*. New York: Academic Press, 1982. Pp. 69–92.

MALMQUIST, EVE. *Factors related to reading disabilities in the first grade of the elementary school*. Stockholm: Almquist & Wiksell, 1958.

MALMQUIST, EVE. *Läs-och skrivsårigheter hos barn: Analys och behandlings metodik (Reading and writing disabilities in children: Diagnosis and remedial methods)*. Lund, Sweden: Gleerup, 1967.

MALMQUIST, EVE. Lässvårigheter på grundskolans lågstadium (Experimental studies on reading disabilities at the primary stage). Falkoping Sweden: Utbildningforlaget Liber. Research reports from the National School for Education Research No. 13, 1969.

MANGIERI, JOHN N., & CORBOY, MARGARET R. Recreational reading: Do we practice what is preached? *The Reading Teacher*, May 1981, *34*, 923–925.

MANGIERI, JOHN N., & HEIMBERGER, MARY J. Perceptions of the reading consultant's role. *Journal of Reading*, March 1980, *23*, 527–530.

MANLEY, MARY ANN, & SIMON, ALAN E. A reading celebration from K to 8. *The Reading Teacher*, February 1980, *33*, 552–554.

MANN, LESTER. Review of the Frostig Developmental Tests of Visual perception. In O. K. Buros (Ed.), *Seventh mental measurements yearbook*, Vol. 1. Highland Park, NJ: Gryphon Press, 1972. Pp. 1274–1276.

MANN, LESTER, et al. LD or not LD, that was the question: A retrospective analysis of Child Demonstration Centers' compliance with the Federal definition of learning disabilities. *Journal of Learning Disabilities*, January 1983, *16*, 14–17.

MANNA, ANTHONY L. Making language come alive through reading plays. *The Reading Teacher*, April 1984, *37*, 712–717.

MANNING, GARY L., & MANNING, MARYANN. What models of recreational reading make a difference? *Reading World*, May 1984, *23*, 375–380.

MANOLAKES, GEORGE. The effects of tachistoscopic training in an adult reading program. *Journal of Applied Psychology*, 1952, *36*, 410–412.

MANZO, ANTHONY. The ReQuest procedure. *Journal of Reading*, November 1969, *13*, 123–126, 163.

MARIA, KATHERINE, & MACGINITIE, WALTER H. Reading comprehension disabilities: Knowledge structures and non-accommodating text processing strategies. *Annals of Dyslexia*, 1982, *32*, 33–59.

MARR, MARY BETH, & GORMLEY, KATHLEEN. Children's recall of familiar and unfamiliar text. *Reading Research Quarterly*, Fall 1982, *18*, 80–104.

MARR, MARY BETH, & KAMIL, MICHAEL L. Single word decoding and comprehension: A constructive replication. *Journal of Reading Behavior*, 1981, *13*, 81–86.

MARR, MARY BETH, & LYON, KATHLEEN R. Passage independency and question characteristics: An analysis of three informal reading inventories. *Reading Psychology*, Spring 1981, *2*, 97–102.

MARSHALL, NANCY. Research: Readability and comprehensibility. *Journal of Reading*, March 1979, *22*, 542–544.

MARSHALL, NANCY. Using story grammar to assess reading comprehension. *The Reading Teacher*, March 1983, *36*, 616–620.

MARSHALL, NANCY. Discourse analysis as a guide for informal assessment of comprehension. In J. Flood (Ed.), *Promoting reading comprehension*. Newark, DE: International Reading Association, 1984. Pp. 79–96.

MARSTON, EMILY. Children's poetry preferences: A review. *Research in the Teaching of English*, Spring 1975, *9*, 107–110.

MARTIN, CHARLES E., CRAMOND, BONNIE, & SAFTER, TAMMY. Developing creativity through the reading program. *The Reading Teacher*, February 1982, *35*, 568–572.

MARTIN, HAROLD P. Vision and its role in reading disability and dyslexia. *Journal of School Health*, November 1971, *41*, 468–472.

MARTIN, L. S., & PAVAN, B. N. Current research on open space, nongrading, vertical grouping, and team teaching. *Phi Delta Kappan*, January 1976, *57*, 310–315.

MARTIN, SUE ANN. Techniques for the creative reading or telling of stories to children. *Elementary English*, May 1968, *45*, 611–618.

MARWIT, SAMUEL J., & NEUMANN, GAIL. Black and white children's comprehension of standard and nonstandard English passages. *Journal of Educational Psychology*, June 1974, *66*, 329–332.

MARZANO, ROBERT J., et al. The Graded Word List is not a shortcut to an IRI. *The Reading Teacher*, March 1978, *31*, 647–651.

MASLAND, RICHARD L. Neurological aspects of dyslexia. In G. Pavlidis & T. Miles (Eds.), *Dyslexia research and its application to education*. New York: John Wiley & Sons, 1981. Pp. 35–66.

MASON, GEORGE E. High interest–low vocabulary books: Their past and future. *Journal of Reading*, April 1981, *24*, 603–607.

MASON, GEORGE E., BLANCHARD, JAY S., & DANIEL, DANNY B. *Computer applications in reading* (2nd ed.). Newark, DE: International Reading Association, 1983.

MASON, GEORGE E., & MIZE, JOHN V. Twenty-two sets of methods and materials for stimulating teenage reading. *Journal of Reading*, May 1978, *21*, 735–741.

MASON, JANA M. Overgeneralization in learning to read. *Journal of Reading Behavior*, Summer 1976, *8*, 173–182.

MASON, JANA. Reading readiness: A definition and skills hierarchy from preschoolers' developing conceptions of print. Technical Report No. 59. Champaign, IL: Center for the Study of Reading, University of Illinois, September 1977.

MASON, JANA M. Prereading: A developmental perspective. Technical Report No. 198. Champaign, IL: Center for the Study of Reading, University of Illinois, February 1981.

MASON, JANA M. Acquisition of knowledge about reading: The preschool period. Technical Report No. 267. Champaign, IL: Center for the Study of Reading, University of Illinois, December 1982. (a)

MASON, JANA. A description of reading instruction: The tail is wagging the dog. Reading Education Report No. 35. Champaign, IL: Center for the Study of Reading, University of Illinois, August 1982. (b)

MASON, JANA M. An examination of reading instruction in third and fourth grades. *The Reading Teacher*, May 1983, *36*, 906–913.

MASON, JANA, ROEHLER, LAURA R., & DUFFY, GERALD G. A practioner's model of comprehension instruction. In G. Duffy et al. (Eds.), *Comprehension instruction: Perspectives and suggestions*. New York: Longman, 1984. Pp. 299–314.

MASON, JANA, et al. A schema-theoretic view of the reading process as a basis for comprehension instruction. In G. Duffy et al. (Eds.), *Comprehension instruction: Perspectives and suggestions*. New York: Longman, 1984. Pp. 26–38.

MATĚJČEK, ZDENĚK. Dyslexia in Czechoslovakian children. In L. Tarnopol & M. Tarnopol (Eds.), *Reading disabilities: An international perspective.* Baltimore: University Park Press, 1976. Pp. 131–154.

MATĚJČEK, ZDENĚK. Specific learning disabilities. *Bulletin of the Orton Society,* 1977, *27,* 7–25.

MATHEWS, MITFORD M. *Teaching to read: Historically considered.* Chicago: University of Chicago Press, 1966.

MATHEWSON, GROVER C. Teaching forms of negation in reading and reasoning. *The Reading Teacher,* January 1984, *37,* 354–358.

MATSUYAMA, UTAKO K. Can story grammar speak Japanese? *The Reading Teacher,* March 1983, *36,* 666–669.

MATTINGLY, IGNATIUS G. Reading, the linguistic process, and linguistic awareness. In J. F. Kavanaugh & I. G. Mattingly (Eds.), *Language by ear and by eye.* Cambridge, MA: MIT Press, 1972. Pp. 133–148.

MATTINGLY, IGNATIUS G. The psycholinguistic basis of linguistic awareness. In M. J. Kamil & A. J. Moe (Eds.), *Reading research: Studies and applications.* Clemson, SC: National Reading Conference, 1979. Pp. 274–278.

MATTIS, STEVEN. Dyslexia syndromes: A working hypothesis that works. In A. L. Benton & D. Pearl (Eds.), *Dyslexia: An appraisal of current knowledge.* New York: Oxford University Press, 1978. Pp. 43–58.

MATTIS, STEVEN. Dyslexia syndrome in children: Toward a development of syndrome-specific treatment programs. In F. Pirozollo & M. Wittrock (Eds.), *Neuropsychological and cognitive processes in reading.* New York: Academic Press, 1981. Pp. 93–107.

MATTIS, STEVEN, FRENCH, JOSEPH H., & RAPIN, ISABELLE. Dyslexia in children and young adults: Three independent neuropsychological syndromes. *Developmental Medicine and Child Neurology,* 1975, *17,* 150–163.

MATTLEMAN, MARCIENE. *101 activities for teaching reading.* Portland, ME: Walch, 1973.

MAVROGENES, NANCY A. Teaching implications of the schemata theory of comprehension. *Reading World,* May 1983, *22,* 295–305.

MAVROGENES, NANCY A., & GALEN, NANCY D. Cross-age tutoring: Why and how. *Journal of Reading,* January 1979, *22,* 344–353.

MAVROGENES, NANCY A., et al. Concise guide to standardized secondary and college reading tests. In W. J. Harker (Ed.), *Classroom strategies for secondary reading.* Newark, DE: International Reading Association, 1977. Pp. 8–18.

MAY, ANN B. All the angles of idiom instruction. *The Reading Teacher,* March 1979, *32,* 680–682.

MAY, JILL P. To think anew: Native American literature and children's attitudes. *The Reading Teacher,* April 1983, *36,* 790–794.

MAY, RICHARD B., & OLLILA, LLOYD O. Reading sex-role attitudes in preschoolers. *Reading Research Quarterly,* 1981, *16* (4), 583–595.

MAYER, RICHARD E. Can advance organizers influence meaningful learning? *Review of Educational Research,* Summer 1979, *49,* 371–383.

MAYRON, LEWIS W. Allergy, learning, and behavior problems. *Journal of Learning Disabilities,* January 1979, *12,* 32–42.

MAZURKIEWICZ, ALBERT J. The initial teaching alphabet. In J. Money (Ed.), *The disabled reader.* Baltimore: Johns Hopkins Press, 1966. Pp. 161–174.

MCAFEE, JACKSON K. Towards a theory of promotion: Does retaining students really work? Paper read at the annual meeting of the American Educational Research Association, Los Angeles, 1981. ED 204 871

MCANDREW, DONALD A. Underlining and notetaking: Some suggestions from research. *Journal of Reading,* November 1983, *27,* 103–108.

MCBRIDE, RALPH. Visual phrasing cues as an aid to comprehension of simple and complex sentences by learning disabled and normal pupils. *Journal of Research & Development in Education,* 1976, *9,* 109–110.

MCCABE, PATRICK P. The effect upon comprehension of mathematics material repatterned on the basis of oral language. *Reading World,* December 1981, *21,* 146–154.

MCCARTHY, J. M. Learning disabilities: Where have we been? Where are we going? *Learning disabilities: Selected conference papers.* Arlington, VA: Council for Exceptional Children, 1969. Pp. 33–39.

MCCARTHY, MARTHA M. Court cases with an impact on the teaching of reading. *Journal of Reading,* December 1979, *23,* 205–212.

MCCARTHY, MARTHA M. The Pennhurst and Rowley Decisions: Issues and implications. *Exceptional Children,* April 1983, *49,* 517–522.

MCCLAIN, LESLIE J. Study guides: Potential assets in content classrooms. *Journal of Reading,* January 1981, *24,* 321–325.

MCCLURE, ERICA, & STEFFENSON, MARGARET S. A study of the use of conjunctions across grades and ethnic groups. Technical Report No. 158. Champaign, IL: Center for the Study of Reading, University of Illinois, January 1980.

MCCONAUGHY, STEPHANIE H. Developmental changes in story comprehension and levels of questioning. *Language Arts,* September 1982, *59,* 580–589.

MCCONKIE, GEORGE W. Studying the reader's perceptual processes by computer. Reading Education Report No. 34. Champaign, IL: Center for the Study of Reading, University of Illinois, May 1982.

MCCONKIE, GEORGE W. Eye movements and perception during reading. In K. Rayner (Ed.), *Eye movements in reading: Perceptual and language processes.* New York: Academic Press, 1983. Pp. 65–96.

MCCONKIE, GEORGE W. The reader's perceptual process. In G. Duffy *et al.* (Eds.), *Comprehension instruction: Perspectives and suggestions.* New York: Longman, 1984. Pp. 10–25.

MCCONKIE, GEORGE W., WOLVERTON, GARY S., & ZOLA, DAVID. Instrumentation considerations in research involving eye-movement contingent stimulus control. Technical Report No. 305. Champaign, IL: Center for the Study of Reading, University of Illinois, January 1984.

MCCONKIE, GEORGE W., & ZOLA, DAVID. Eye movement control during reading: The effect of word units. Technical Report No. 310. Champaign, IL: Center for the Study of Reading, University of Illinois, March 1984.

MCCORMICK, CHRISTINE, & SAMUELS, S. JAY. Word recognition by second graders: The unit of perception and interrelationships among accuracy, latency, and comprehension. *Journal of Reading Behavior,* Summer 1979, *11,* 107–118.

MCCORMICK, SANDRA. Choosing books to read to preschool children. *Language Arts,* May 1977, *54,* 543–548. (a)

MCCORMICK, SANDRA. Should you read aloud to your children? *Language Arts,* February 1977, *54,* 139–143, 163. (b)

MCCORMICK, SANDRA, & COLLINS, BETTY M. A potpourri of game-making ideas for the reading teacher. *The Reading Teacher,* March 1981, *34,* 692–696.

MCCOY, LOIS E. Braille: A language for severe dyslexics. *Journal of Learning Disabilities,* May 1975, *8,* 288–292.

MCDERMOTT, R. P. Achieving school failure: An anthropological approach to illiteracy and social stratification. In H. Singer & R. B. Ruddell (Eds.), *Theoretical models and processes of reading* (2nd ed.). Newark, DE: International Reading Association, 1976. Pp. 389–428.

MCDERMOTT, R. P. The cultural context of learning to read. In S. F. Wanat (Ed.), *Issues in evaluating reading.* Arlington, VA: Center for Applied Linguistics, April 1977. Pp. 10–18.

MCDONALD, ARTHUR S. Television, books, and scholastic performance. In J. A. Figurel (Ed.), *Reading in a changing society.* Newark, DE: International Reading Association, 1959. Pp. 148–151.

MCDONALD, ARTHUR S. Research for the classroom: Rate and flexibility. *Journal of Reading,* January 1965, *8,* 187–191.

MCFEELEY, DONALD C. Syllabication usefulness in a basal and social studies vocabulary. *The Reading Teacher,* May 1974, *27,* 809–814.

MCFEELEY, DONALD C. Another look at the VCV controversy. *The Reading Teacher,* October 1981, *35,* 81.

MCGEE, DAVID W. Using the telephone directory as a learning tool. *Teaching Exceptional Children,* Fall 1979, *12,* 34–36.

MCGEE, LEA A. Good and poor readers: Ability to distinguish among and recall ideas on different levels of importance. In M. Kamil (Ed.), *Directions in reading: Research and instruction.* Washington, DC: National Reading Conference, 1981. Pp. 162–168.

MCGEE, LEA M. Awareness of text structure: Effects on children's recall of expository text. *Reading Research Quarterly,* 1982, *17* (4), 581–590. (a)

MCGEE, LEA M. The influence of metacognitive knowledge of expository text structure on discourse recall. In J. Niles & L. A. Harris (Eds.), *New inquiries in reading: Research and instruction.* Rochester, NY: National Reading Conference, 1982. Pp. 64–70. (b)

MCGINNIS, MAUREEN. *Reading resource guide.* Portland, ME: Walch, 1978.

MCGRADE, WILLIAM C. Probe questioning during reading lessons: Informational content and teacher evaluation of student responses. In J. Niles & L. A. Harris (Eds.), *Searches for meaning in reading/language processing and instruction.* Rochester, NY: National Reading Conference, 1983. Pp. 320–322.

MCGUIGNAN, F. J. The function of covert behavior ("silent speech") during silent reading. *International Journal of Psycholinguistics,* 1973, *2,* 39–47.

MCKENNA, MICHAEL. Portmanteau words in reading instruction. *Language Arts,* March 1978, *55,* 315–317.

MCKENNA, MICHAEL C., & ROBINSON, RICHARD D. *An introduction to the cloze procedure: An annotated bibliography.* Newark, DE: International Reading Association, 1980.

MCKENZIE, GARY R. Personalize your group teaching. *Instructor,* August/September 1975, *85,* 57–59. Also in A. J. Harris & E. Sipay (Eds.), *Readings on reading instruction* (3rd ed.). New York: Longman, 1984. Pp. 177–180.

MCKENZIE, GREGORY G., NEILSON, ALLAN R., & BRAUN, CARL. The effects of linguistic connectives and prior knowledge on comprehension of good and poor readers. In M. Kamil (Ed.), *Directions in reading: Research and instruction.* Washington, DC: National Reading Conference, 1981. Pp. 215–218.

MCKENZIE, JOANNA V. A survey of leisure time reading of adolescents. *Arizona English Bulletin,* April 1976, *18,* 13–22.

MCKEOWN, MARGARET G., *et al.* The effects of long-term vocabulary instruction on reading comprehension: A replication. *Journal of Reading Behavior,* 1983, *15* (1), 3–18.

MCKINNEY, JAMES D. Performance of handicapped students on the North Carolina Minimum Competency Test. *Educational Researcher,* April 1983, *49,* 547–550.

MCKNIGHT, JAN C. Using the manual alphabet in teaching reading to learning disabled children. *Journal of Learning Disabilities,* November 1979, *12,* 581–584.

MCLAUGHLIN, G. HARRY. SMOG grading—A new readability formula. *Journal of Reading,* May 1969, *12,* 639–646.

MCLAUGHLIN, JAMES A., & NETICK, ANNE. Defining learning disabilities: A new and cooperative direction. *Journal of Learning Disabilities,* January 1983, *16,* 21–23.

MCLEOD, JOHN. Reading expectancy from disabled readers. *Journal of Learning Disabilities,* February 1968, *1,* 97–104.

MCLEOD, JOHN. Educational underachievement: Toward a defensible psychometric definition. *Journal of Learning Disabilities,* May 1979, *12,* 322–330.

MCLEOD, JOHN. *Psychometric identification of children with learning disabilities* (2nd ed.). Saskatoon, Canada: Institute of Child Guidance and Development, University of Saskatchewan, 1981.

MCLEOD, JOHN. Learning disability is for educators. *Journal of Learning Disabilities,* January 1983, *16,* 23–24.

MCLOUGHLIN, WILLIAM P. *The non-graded school: A critical assessment.* Albany, NY: State Education Department, September 1967.

MCNAUGHTON, STUART. The influence of immediate teacher correction on self-corrections and proficient oral reading. *Journal of Reading Behavior,* Winter 1981, *13,* 367–371.

MCNEIL, JOHN D. *Auditory discrimination training in the development of word analysis skills.* Los Angeles: University of California at Los Angeles, 1967. ED 018 344

MCNEIL, JOHN D. False prerequisites in the teaching of reading. *Journal of Reading Behavior,* December 1974, *6,* 421–427.

MCNEIL, JOHN D. *Reading comprehension: New direction for classroom practice.* Glenview, IL: Scott, Foresman, 1984.

MCNEIL, JOHN, & DONANT, LISBETH. Summarization strategy for improving reading comprehension. In J. Niles & L. A. Harris (Eds.), *New inquiries in reading: Research and instruction.* Rochester, NY: National Reading Conference, 1982. Pp. 215–219.

MCNINCH, GEORGE. Determining the reading preferences of third, fourth, and fifth grade disadvantaged pupils. *Journal of Reading Behavior,* Spring 1970–1971, *3,* 32–38.

MCNINCH, GEORGE H., ARNOLD, ELIZABETH, & RICHMOND, MARK G. Recognition of perceived word units under different cuing conditions. *Educational Research Quarterly,* Summer 1981, *6,* 35–43.

MCPHAIL, IRVING P. Why teach test wiseness? *Journal of Reading,* October 1981, *25,* 32–38.

MCPHAIL, IRVING P. Toward an agenda for urban literacy: The study of schools where low-income black children read at grade level. *Reading World,* December 1982, *22,* 132–149.

MCWHIRTER, J. JEFFRIES. A parent education group in learning disabilities. *Journal of Learning Disabilities,* January 1976, *9,* 16–20.

MCWILLIAMS, LANA J. Riding and reading. *Journal of Reading,* January 1979, *22,* 337–339.

MEAGHER, JUDITH A. Affective development in reading. *New England Reading Association Journal,* 1981, *16* (2), 4–8.

MEARES, OLIVE. Figure/ground, brightness contrast, and reading disabilities. *Visible Language,* 1980, *14* (1), 13–29.

MEDLEY, DONALD M. *Teacher competence and teacher effectiveness: A review of process-product research.* Washington, DC: American Association of Colleges for Teacher Education, 1977.

MEDWAY, FREDERICK J., & LOWE, CHARLES A. Causal attribution for performance by cross-age tutors and tutees. *American Educational Research Journal,* Fall 1980, *17,* 377–387.

MEICHENBAUM, DONALD. *Cognitive-behavior modification: An integrative approach.* New York: Plenum Press, 1977.

MEICHENBAUM, DONALD. Cognitive behavior modification with exceptional children: A promise yet unfulfilled. *Exceptional Children Quarterly,* May 1980, *1,* 83–88.

MEICHENBAUM, DONALD, & ASARNOW, J. Cognitive-behavioral modification and meta-cognitive development: Implications for the classroom. In P. Kendall & S. Hollen (Eds.), *Cognitive behavioral interventions: Theory, research, and procedures.* New York: Academic Press, 1979.

MEINTS, DONALD W. The task system in an individualized reading class. *Journal of Reading,* January 1977, *20,* 301–304.

MEMORY, DAVID M. Record keeping for effective reading instruction. In D. Lapp (Ed.), *Making reading possible through effective classroom management.* Newark, DE: International Reading Association, 1980. Pp. 146–185.

MEMORY, DAVID M. Written questions as reading aids in the middle grades: A review of research. In J. Niles & L. A. Harris (Eds.), *New inquiries in reading: Research and instruction.* Rochester, NY: National Reading Conference, 1982. Pp. 71–76.

MEMORY, DAVID M. Constructing main idea questions: A test of a depth-of-processing perspective. In J. Niles & L. A. Harris (Eds.), *Searches for meaning in reading/language processing and instruction.* Rochester, NY: National Reading Conference, 1983. Pp. 66–70. (a).

MEMORY, DAVID M. Main idea prequestions as adjunct aids with good and low average middle grade readers. *Journal of Reading Behavior,* 1983, *15* (2), 37–48. (b)

MEMORY, DAVID M., & MOORE, DAVID W. Selecting sources in library research: An activity in skimming and critical reading. *Journal of Reading,* March 1981, *24,* 469–474.

MERLIN, SHIRLEY B., & ROGERS, SUE F. Direct teaching strategies. *The Reading Teacher,* December 1981, *35,* 292–297.

MERRY, R. The keyword method and children's vocabulary learning in the classroom. *British Journal of Educational Psychology,* 1980, *50,* 123–136.

MESSICK, SAMUEL. Cognitive styles in educational practice. Research Report 82–13. Princeton, NJ: ETS, June 1982.

MESSICK, SAMUEL. Assessment in context: Appraising student performance in relation to instructional quality. *Educational Researcher,* March 1984, *13,* 3–8.

METROPOLITAN SCHOOL STUDY COUNCIL. Five steps to reading success in science. In *Five steps to reading success in science, social studies, and mathematics.* New York: Teachers College,

Columbia University, 1960. Also in A. J. Harris & E. Sipay (Eds.), *Readings on reading instruction* (2nd ed). New York: Longman, 1972. Pp. 306–310.

MEWHORT, D. J. K., & CAMPBELL, A. J. Toward a model of skilled reading: An analysis of performance in tachistoscopic tasks. In G. MacKinnon & T. Waller (Eds.), *Reading research: Advances in theory and practice*, Vol. 3. New York: Academic Press, 1981. Pp. 39–118.

MEYER, BONNIE J. F. Organizational aspects of text: Effects on reading comprehension and applications for the classroom. In J. Flood (Ed.), *Promoting reading comprehension.* Newark, DE: International Reading Association, 1984. Pp. 113–138.

MEYER, BONNIE J. F., & RICE, G. ELIZABETH. The structure of text. In P. D. Pearson (Ed.), *Handbook of reading research.* New York: Longman, 1984. Pp. 319–351.

MEYER, LINDA A. The relative effects of word-analysis and word-supply correction procedures with poor readers during word-attack training. *Reading Research Quarterly,* 1982, *17* (4), 544–555.

MEYER, LINDA A. Long-term academic effects of Direct Instruction Follow Through: Technical Report No. 299. Champaign, IL: Center for the Study of Reading, University of Illinois, November 1983.

MEYER, LINDA A., GERSTEN, RUSSELL M., & GUTKIN, JOAN. Direct Instruction: A project follow-through success story. Technical Report No. 302. Champaign, IL: Center for the Study of Reading, University of Illinois, December 1983.

MEYER, SUSAN. What's the word on children's dictionaries? *Learning,* March 1980, *8,* 44–46.

MEZYNSKI, KAREN. Issues concerning the acquisition of knowledge: Effects of vocabulary training on reading comprehension. *Review of Educational Research,* Summer 1983, *53,* 253–279.

MICCINATI, JEANETTE. The Fernald technique: Modifications increase the probability of success. *Journal of Learning Disabilities,* March 1979, *12,* 139–142.

MICHIELUTTE, WILLIAM L. The use of group tutorial and group counseling methods in the investigation of causal relationships between self concept and reading achievement among underachieving sixth-grade boys. *Dissertation Abstracts International,* February 1977, *37* (8-B), 4156.

MICKLOS, JOHN, JR. Clouds and silver linings: A realistic look at reading achievement. *The Reading Teacher,* March 1982, *35,* 644–646. (a)

MICKLOS, JOHN, JR. A look at reading achievement in the United States: The latest data. *Journal of Reading,* May 1982, *25,* 760–762. (b)

MICKLOS, JOHN, JR. Is 1984 upon us? *Journal of Reading,* March 1983, *26,* 486–488.

MIER, MARGARET. Comprehension monitoring in the elementary classroom. *The Reading Teacher,* April 1984, *37,* 770–774.

MIKULECKY, LARRY. The International Reading Association's role in the politics of censorship, 1981. ED 205 934

MILES, J., FOREMAN, P. J., & ANDERSON, J. The long and short predictive efficiency of two tests of reading potential. *Slow Learning Child,* November 1973, *20,* 131–141.

MILES, W. R., & SEGEL, D. Clinical observation of eye movement in the rating of reading ability. *Journal of Educational Psychology,* 1929, *20,* 520–529.

MILLER, ARTHUR L. A study of reading tastes of children in grades four, five, and six in selected schools in the Lamar area school study council. *Dissertation Abstracts,* 1967, *27,* 2471A.

MILLER, EDITH F. Stimulate reading . . . with a dictionary. *Grade Teacher,* February 1962, *79,* 51–52, 106–07. Also in A. J. Harris & E. Sipay (Eds.), *Readings on reading instruction* (3rd ed.). New York: Longman, 1984. Pp. 242–245.

MILLER, ETTA. Relationships among modality preference, method of instruction, and reading achievement. Unpublished doctoral dissertation, State University of New York at Albany, 1974.

MILLER, GORDON W. Factors in school achievement and social class. *Journal of Educational Psychology,* 1970, *61,* 260–269.

MILLER, HARRY B., & HERING, STEVE. Teacher's ratings—Which reading group is number one? *The Reading Teacher,* January 1975, *28,* 389–391.

MILLER, MARGARET J. The primary child in the library. In L. Monson & D. McClenathan (Eds.), *Developing active readers: Ideas for parents, teachers and librarians.* Newark, DE: International Reading Association, 1979. Pp. 43–51.

MILLER, PHYLLIS A. Considering flexibility of reading rate for assessment and development of efficient reading behavior. In S. Jay Samuels (Ed.), *What research has to say about reading instruction.* Newark, DE: International Reading Association, 1978. Pp. 72–83.

MILLER, ROBERT. The Mexican approach to developing bilingual materials and teaching literacy to bilingual students. *The Reading Teacher,* April 1982, *35,* 800–804.

MILLER, WILMA H. The Joplin plan—Is it effective for intermediate-grade reading instruction? *Elementary English,* November 1971, *46,* 951–954.

MILLMAN, JASON, *et al.* Relation between perseverence and rate of learning: A test of Carroll's model of school learning. *American Educational Research Journal,* Fall 1983, *20,* 425–434.

MILLS, ROBERT E. An evaluation of techniques for teaching word recognition. *Elementary School Journal,* 1956, *56,* 221–225.

MIRSKY, ALLAN F. Attention: A neuropsychological perspective. In J. Chall & A. Mirsky (Eds.), *Education and the brain.* 77th Yearbook of the National Society for the Study of Education, Part II. Chicago: University of Chicago Press, 1978. Pp. 33–60.

MISHURA, S. P., & HURT, M., JR. The use of the Metropolitan Readiness Test with Mexican-American children. *California Journal of Educational Research,* 1970, *21,* 182–187.

MITCHELL, DON C. *The process of reading: A cognitive analysis of fluent reading and learning to read.* Somerset, NJ: John Wiley & Sons, 1982.

MITCHELL, JAMES V. (Ed.). *Tests in print, III.* Lincoln, NE: Buros Institute of Mental Measurements, University of Nebraska, 1983.

MITTERER, JOHN O. There are at least two kinds of poor readers: Whole-word poor readers and recoding poor readers. *Canadian Journal of Psychology,* September 1982, *36,* 445–461.

MOCKER, DONALD W. Cooperative learning process: Shared learning experience in teaching adults to read. In. L. Johnson (Ed.), *Reading and the adult learner.* Newark, DE: International Reading Association, 1980. Pp. 35–40.

MOE, ALDEN J., & HOPKINS, CAROL J. Jingles, jokes, limericks, poems, proverbs, puns, puzzles and riddles: Fast reading for reluctant readers. *Language Arts,* November/December 1978, *55,* 957–965, 1003.

MOE, ALDEN, HOPKINS, CAROL J., & RUSH, J. TIMOTHY. *The vocabulary of first-grade children.* Springfield, IL: Charles C Thomas, 1982.

MOLDENHAUER, DEBORAH L., & MILLER, WILMA H. Television and reading achievement. *Journal of Reading,* April 1980, *23,* 615–619.

MOLLER, BARBARA W. An instructional model for gifted advanced readers. *Journal of Reading,* January 1984, *27,* 324–327.

MONAGHAN, E. JENNIFER. A history of the syndrome of dyslexia with implications for its treatment. In C. McCullough (Ed.), *Inchworm, inchworm: Persistent problems in reading education.* Newark, DE: International Reading Association, 1980. Pp. 87–101.

MONEY, JOHN (Ed.). *Reading disability: Progress and research needs in dyslexia.* Baltimore: Johns Hopkins Press, 1962.

MONROE, MARION. *Children who cannot read.* Chicago: University of Chicago Press, 1932.

MONSON, DIANNE. Into a book and beyond: Responding to literature. In D. Monson & D. McClenathan (Eds.), *Developing active readers: Ideas for parents, teachers and librarians.* Newark, DE: International Reading Association, 1979. Pp. 58–64.

MONTARE, ALBERTO, ELMAN, ELAINE, & COHEN, JOANNE. Words and pictures: A test of Samuels' findings. *Journal of Reading Behavior,* Fall 1977, *9,* 269–285.

MONTEITH, MARY K. A whole word list catalog. *The Reading Teacher,* May 1976, *29,* 844–847.

MONTEITH, MARY K. Taped books and reading materials. *Journal of Reading,* March 1978, *21,* 554–557.

MONTEITH, MARY K. How well does the average American read? Some facts, figures, and opinions. *Journal of Reading,* February 1980, *23,* 460–464.

MONTEITH, MARY K. The magazine habit. *Language Arts,* November/December 1981, *58,* 965–969. (a)

MONTEITH, MARY K. The reading teacher vs. children of divorce. *The Reading Teacher,* October 1981, *35,* 100–103. (b)

MOORE, DAVID W., & READENCE, JOHN E. Processing main ideas through parallel lesson transfer. *Journal of Reading*, April 1980, *23*, 589–593.

MOORE, DAVID W., & READENCE, JOHN E. Approaches to content area reading instruction. *Journal of Reading*, February 1983, *26*, 397–402.

MOORE, DAVID W., READENCE, JOHN E., & RICKELMAN, ROBERT J. *Prereading activities for content area reading and learning.* Newark, DE: International Reading Association, 1982.

MOORE, DAVID W., READENCE, JOHN E., & RICKELMAN, ROBERT J. An historical explanation of content area reading instruction. *Reading Research Quarterly*, Summer 1983, *18*, 419–438.

MOORE, MICHAEL J., et al. Cognitive profiles in reading disability. *Genetic Psychology Monographs*, February 1982, *105* (1st half), 41–93.

MOORE, PHILLIP J. Children's thinking about reading. *Australian Journal of Reading*, March 1981, *4*, 23–32.

MORETZ, SARA, & DAVEY, BETH. Process and strategies in teaching decoding skills in middle and secondary schools. In L. E. Hafner (Ed.), *Improving reading in middle and secondary schools: Selected readings* (2nd ed.). New York: Macmillan, 1974. Pp. 76–101.

MORGAN, RAYMOND F., MEEKS, JANE W., & LAFFEY, JAMES L. Urban school reading programs. *New England Reading Association Journal*, Spring 1982, *17*, 42–46.

MORGAN, W. PRINGLE. A case of congenital word-blindness. *British Medical Journal*, 1896, *2*, 1543–1544.

MORRIS, DARRELL. Beginning reader's concept of word. In E. Henderson & J. Beers (Eds.), *Developmental and cognitive aspects of learning to spell: A reflection of word knowledge.* Newark, DE: International Reading Association, 1980. Pp. 97–111.

MORRIS, DARRELL. Concept of word and phoneme awareness in the beginning reader. *Research in the Teaching of English*, December 1983, *17*, 359–373.

MORRIS, GREGORY A. A comparison of fourth graders' oral and silent reading behavior in basal reader, science and social studies materials. Unpublished doctoral dissertation, University of Pittsburgh, 1970.

MORRIS, JOYCE M. *Standards and progress in reading.* London: National Foundation for Educational Research in England and Wales, 1966.

MORRISON, FREDERICK, & MANIS, FRANKLIN R. Cognitive processes and reading disability: A critique and proposal. In C. Brainerd & M. Pressley (Eds.), *Verbal processes in children: Progress in cognitive development research.* New York: Springer-Verlag, 1982. Pp. 59–93.

MORTON, J. The effects of context upon speed of reading, eye movement, and eye-voice span. *Quarterly Journal of Experimental Psychology*, 1964, *13*, 340–354.

MOSCOVITCH, MORRIS. Right-hemisphere language. *Topics in Language Disorders*, September 1981, *1*, 41–61.

MOSENTHAL, PETER. Psycholinguistic properties of aural and visual comprehension as determined by children's abilities to comprehend syllogisms. *Reading Research Quarterly*, 1976–1977, *12* (1), 55–92.

MOSS, JOY F. Growth in reading in an integrated day classroom. *Elementary School Journal*, March 1972, *72*, 304–320.

MUIA, JOSEPH A., & CONNORS, EUGENE T. Legal entanglement of reading clinic's diagnostic procedures. *Journal of Reading*, January 1978, *21*, 321–328.

MYERS, COLLIN A. Reviewing the literature on Fernald's technique of remedial reading. *The Reading Teacher*, March 1978, *31*, 614–619.

MYKLEBUST, HELMER R. Learning disabilities: Definition and overview. In H. R. Myklebust (Ed.), *Progress in learning disabilities*, Vol. I. New York: Grune & Stratton, 1968. Pp. 1–15.

MYKLEBUST, HELMER R. Toward a science of dyslexiology. In H. R. Myklebust (Ed.), *Progress in learning disabilities*, Vol. 4. New York: Grune & Stratton, 1978. Pp. 1–40.

MYKLEBUST, HELMER R. Toward a science of learning disabilities. *Journal of Learning Disabilities*, January 1983, *16*, 17–18.

NAGY, WILLIAM E., & ANDERSON, RICHARD C. The number of words in printed school English. Technical Report No. 253. Champaign, IL: Center for the Study of Reading, University of Illinois, July 1982.

NAGY, WILLIAM E., & ANDERSON, RICHARD C. How many words are there in printed school English? *Reading Research Quarterly*, Spring 1984, *19*, 304–330.

NAIDEN, NORMA. Ratio of boys to girls among disabled readers. *The Reading Teacher*, February 1976, *29*, 439–446.

NARANG, HARBANS L. Bibliotherapy: A review of the research. *Saskatchewan Journal of Educational Research and Development*, Spring 1977, *7*, 5–12.

NASH-WEBBER, BONNIE L. Inference as an approach to discourse anaphorad. Technical Report No. 77. Champaign, IL: Center for the Study of Reading, University of Illinois, January 1978.

NATIONAL ADVISORY COMMITTEE ON DYSLEXIA AND RELATED DISORDERS. *Reading disorders in the United States*. Washington, DC: Government Printing Office, 1969.

NATIONAL ASSESSMENT OF EDUCATIONAL PROGRESS. *Reading rate and comprehension, 1970–71 assessment*. Report 82-R-09. Denver, CO: Education Commission of the States, December 1972.

NATIONAL ASSESSMENT OF EDUCATIONAL PROGRESS. Achievement up among Title I students. *NAEP Newsletter*, Summer 1981, *14*, 5, 8. (a)

NATIONAL ASSESSMENT OF EDUCATIONAL PROGRESS. Reading, thinking, and writing. Results from the 1979–80 National Assessment of reading and literature. Report No. 11-L-35. Denver, CO: Education Commission of the States, July 1981. (b)

NAEP NEWSLETTER, Spring 1982, *15*, 3. (a)

NATIONAL ASSESSMENT OF EDUCATIONAL PROGRESS. *Reading comprehension of American youth: Do they understand what they read? Results from the 1979–80 National Assessment of reading and literature*. Report No. 11-R-02. Denver, CO: Education Commission of the States, July 1982. (b)

NATIONAL ASSESSMENT OF EDUCATIONAL PROGRESS. Linguistic background, achievement linked. *NAEP Newsletter*, Winter 1983, *16*, 3, 5. (a)

NATIONAL ASSESSMENT OF EDUCATIONAL PROGRESS. Low achievers improve reading skills, but top students lose ground in math, science. *NAEP Newsletter*, Winter 1983, *16*, 1–2. (b)

NATIONAL ASSESSMENT OF EDUCATIONAL PROGRESS. New objectives chart course for good writers to follow. *NAEP Newsletter*, Winter 1983, *16*, 4–5. (c)

NATIONAL CENTER FOR EDUCATION STATISTICS. *The condition of education, 1983 edition*. Washington, DC.: Superintendent of Documents, Government Printing Office, 1983. Stock No. 065–000–00183–7.

NATIONAL COMMISSION ON EXCELLENCE IN EDUCATION. *A nation at risk: The imperative for educational reform*. Washington, DC: Superintendent of Documents, Government Printing Office, 1983. Stock No. 065–000–00177–2. ED 226 006

NATIONAL INSTITUTE OF MENTAL HEALTH. *Television and behavior: Ten years of scientific progress and implications for the eighties*. DHMS Publication No. ADM 82–1195. Washington, DC: Government Printing Office, 1982.

NATIONAL JOINT COMMITTEE ON LEARNING DISABILITIES. Learning disabilities: Issues on definition. Baltimore, MD: Orton Dyslexia Society, January 30, 1981. Unpublished manuscript. Also appears in Jim Leigh, The NJCLD position papers (I–IV). *Learning Disabilities Quarterly*, Winter 1983, *6*, 4–54.

NATRIELLO, GARY, & DORNBUSH, STANFORD M. Bringing behavior back in: The effect of student characteristics and behavior on the classroom behavior of teachers. *American Educational Research Journal*, Spring 1983, *20*, 29–43.

NAYLOR, HILLARY. Reading disability and lateral asymmetry: An information processing analysis. *Psychological Bulletin*, May 1980, *87*, 531–545.

NEGIN, GARY A., & KRUGLER, DEE. Essential literacy skills for functioning in an urban community. *Journal of Reading*, November 1980, *24*, 109–115.

NEILSEN, ALLAN R. An investigation of the relationship of cohesion to linguistic marking, discourse structure, and content familiarity. In M. Kamil (Ed.), *Directions in reading: Research and instruction*. Washington, DC: National Reading Conference, 1981. Pp. 209–214.

NEILSEN, ALLAN R., RENNIE, BARBARA J., & CONNELL, ARLENE M. Allocation of instructional time to reading comprehension and study skills in intermediate grade social studies classrooms. In J. Niles & L. A. Harris (Eds.), *New inquiries in reading research and instruction*. Rochester, NY: National Reading Conference, 1982. Pp. 81–84.

NELSON, HAZEL E. Analyses of spelling errors in normal and dyslexic children. In U. Frith (Ed.), *Cognitive processes in spelling.* New York: Academic Press, 1980. Pp. 475–493.

NELSON, JOAN, & HERBER, HAROLD L. Organization and management of programs. In A. Berger & H. A. Robinson (Eds.), *Secondary school reading: What research reveals for classroom practice.* Urbana, IL: National Council for Research in English/ERIC, 1982. Pp. 143–157.

NELSON, ROSEMARY O., & WEIN, KENNETH S. The use of varying high-confusion versus low-confusion sequences to teach letter discrimination. *Journal of Reading Behavior,* Summer 1976, *8,* 161–171.

NEUMAN, SUSAN B. Teletext/videotex: The future of print media. *Journal of Reading,* January 1984, *27,* 340–344.

NEUMAN, SUSAN B., & PROWDA, PETER. Television viewing and reading achievement. *Journal of Reading,* April 1982, *25,* 666–670.

NEVI, CHARLES N. Cross-age tutoring: Why does it help the tutors? *The Reading Teacher,* May 1983, *36,* 892–898.

NEVILLE, DONALD. The relationship between reading skills and intelligence test scores. *The Reading Teacher,* January 1965, *18,* 257–262.

NEVILLE, DONALD, PFOST, P., & DOBBS, VIRGINIA. The relationship between test anxiety and silent reading gains. *American Educational Research Journal,* 1967, *4,* 45–50.

NEVINS, ROSEMARY V. The effect of training in letter names, letter sounds, and letter names and sounds on the acquisition of word recognition ability. Unpublished doctoral dissertation, State University of New York at Albany, 1972.

NEWCOMER, PHYLLIS L., & HAMMILL, DONALD D. ITPA and academic achievement: A survey. *The Reading Teacher,* May 1975, *28,* 731–741.

NEWCOMER, PHYLLIS L., & MAGEE, PATRICIA. The performance of learning (reading) disabled children on a test of spoken language. *The Reading Teacher,* May 1977, *30,* 896–900.

NEWHOUSE, ROBERT C., & LOKER, SUZANNE. Does bibliotherapy reduce fear among second-grade children? *Reading Psychology,* January–March 1984, *4,* 25–27.

NEWMAN, ANABEL P. Twenty lives revisited—A summary of a longitudinal study. *The Reading Teacher,* April 1982, *35,* 814–818.

NEWPORT, JOHN F. The Joplin Plan: The score. *The Reading Teacher,* November 1967, *21,* 158–162.

NEWTON, MARGARET. A neuropsychological investigation into dyslexia. In A. W. Franklin & S. Naidoo (Eds.), *Assessment and teaching of dyslexic children.* London: Invalid Children's Aid Association, 1970. Pp. 14–21.

New York Times. A therapy system for young scored. March 7, 1968.

NGUYEN, LIEM THANH, & HENKIN, ALAN B. A readability formula for Vietnamese. *Journal of Reading,* December 1982, *26,* 243–251.

NICHOLS, JAMES N. Foiling students who'd rather fake it than read it or how to get students to read and report on books. *Journal of Reading,* December 1978, *22,* 245–247.

NICHOLS, JAMES N. Using prediction to increase content area interest and understanding. *Journal of Reading,* December 1983, *27,* 325–328.

NICHOLSON, TOM. Why we need to talk to parents about reading. *The Reading Teacher,* October 1980, *34,* 19–21.

NICHOLSON, TONI, PEARSON, P. DAVID, & DYKSTRA, ROBERT. Effects of embedded anomalies and oral reading errors on children's understanding of stories. Technical Report No. 118. Champaign, IL: Center for the Study of Reading, University of Illinois, March 1979.

NICKERSON, RAYMOND S. Speech understanding and reading: Some differences and similarities. In O. Tzeng & H. Singer (Eds.), *Perception of print: Reading research in experimental psychology.* Hillsdale, NJ: LEA, 1981. Pp. 257–289.

NILSEN, ALEEN P., PETERSON, RALPH, & SEARFOSS, LYNDON W. The adult as critic vs. the child as reader. *Language Arts,* May 1980, *57,* 530–539.

NILSEN, DON L. F., & NILSEN, ALLEEN P. An exploration and defense of the humor in young adult literature. *Journal of Reading,* October 1982, *26,* 58–65.

NOLAND, RONALD G., & CRAFT, LYNDA H. Methods to motivate the reluctant readers. *Journal of Reading,* February 1976, *19,* 387–391.

NOONAN, NORMA. Parents as partners in reading development. *Australian Journal of Reading*, August 1978, *1*, 60–64. Also in A. J. Harris & E. Sipay (Eds.), *Readings on reading instruction* (3rd ed.). New York: Longman, 1984, Pp. 410–412.

NORVELL, GEORGE W. The challenge of periodicals in education. *Elementary English*, 1966, *43*, 402–408.

NORVELL, GEORGE W. Revolution in the English curriculum. *Elementary English*, May 1972, *49*, 760–767.

NORVELL, GEORGE W. *The reading interests of young people.* Ann Arbor: Michigan State University Press, 1973.

NOYCE, RUTH M., & CHRISTIE, JAMES F. Using literature to develop children's grasp of syntax. *The Reading Teacher*, December 1981, *35*, 298–304.

NURSS, JOANNE R. Assessment of readiness. In G. Waller & G. MacKinnon (Eds.), *Reading research: Advances in theory and practice*, Vol. 1. New York: Academic Press, 1979. Pp. 31–62. (a)

NURSS, JOANNE R. Learning to read in England: Some first-hand impressions. *Georgia Journal of Reading*, Fall 1979, *5*, 11–13. (b)

NURSS, JOANNE R., & TELEPAK, KATHLEEN. Planning for a prereading program. In L. Ollila (Ed.), *Handbook for administrators and teachers: Reading in the kindergarten*. Newark, DE: International Reading Association, 1980. Pp. 53–67.

ODLAND, NORINE. Planning a literature program for the elementary school. *Language Arts*, April 1979, *56*, 363–367.

O'DONNELL, HOLLY. The hyperactive child and drug treatment. *The Reading Teacher*, October 1982, *36*, 106–109.

O'DONNELL, HOLLY. The use of illustrations in textbooks. *The Reading Teacher*, January 1983, *36*, 462–464.

O'DONNELL, LINDA E. Intra-individual discrepancy in diagnosing specific learning disabilities. *Learning Disabilities Quarterly*, Winter 1980, *3*, 10–18.

OFMAN, WILLIAM, & SCHAEVITZ, MORTON. The kinesthetic method in remedial reading. *Journal of Experimental Education*, 1963, *31*, 319–320.

OJEMANN, GEORGE A. Interrelationships in the brain organization of language-related behavior: Evidence from electrical stimulation mapping. In U. Kirk (Ed.), *Neuropsychology of language, reading, and spelling*. New York: Academic Press, 1983, Pp. 129–192.

OLDRIDGE, O. A. Positive suggestion: It helps LD students learn. *Academic Therapy*, January 1982, *17*, 279–287.

OLIVER, LAWRENCE J., JR. Helping students overcome writer's block. *Journal of Reading*, November 1982, *26*, 162–168.

OLLILA, LLOYD O., & CHAMBERLIN, LARRY. The learning and retention of two classes of graphic words: High frequency nouns and non-noun words among kindergarten children. *The Journal of Educational Research*, May/June 1979, *72*, 288–293.

OLLILA, LLOYD, JOHNSON, TERRY, & DOWNING, JOHN. Adapting Russian methods of auditory discrimination training for English. *Elementary English*, November/December 1974, *51*, 1138–1141, 1145.

OLLILA, LLOYD O., & NURSS, JOANNE R. Beginning reading in North America. In L. Ollila (Ed.), *Beginning reading instruction in different countries*. Newark, DE: International Reading Association, 1981. Pp. 26–53.

OLSON, ARTHUR V. The questionable value of perceptual tests in diagnosing reading disabilities. *Journal of Research in Reading*, 1980, *3* (2), 129–139.

OLSON, MARY. A dash of story grammar and . . . Presto! A book report. *The Reading Teacher*, February 1984, *39*, 458–461.

OLSON, MARY W., & LONGION, BONNIE. Pattern guides: A workable alternative for content teachers. *Journal of Reading*, May 1982, *25*, 736–741.

OLSON, RICHARD K., KLIEGL, REINHOLD, & DAVIDSON, BRIAN J. Eye movements in reading disability. In K. Rayner (Ed.), *Eye movements in reading: Perceptual and language processes*. New York: Academic Press, 1983. Pp. 467–479.

O'MARA, DEBORAH A. The process of reading mathematics. *Journal of Reading*, October 1981, *25*, 22–30.

OMIZO, MICHAEL M., & MICHAEL, WILLIAM B. Biofeedback-induced relaxation training and impulsivity, attention to task, and locus of control among hyperactive boys. *Journal of Learning Disabilities,* August/September 1982, *15,* 414–416.

O'ROURKE, JOSEPH P. *Toward a science of vocabulary development.* The Hague: Mouton, 1974.

ORTIZ, ALBA A. Choosing the language of instruction for exceptional bilingual instruction. *Teaching Exceptional Children,* Spring 1984, *16,* 208–212.

ORTON, JUNE L. The Orton–Gillingham approach. In J. Money (Ed.), *The disabled reader.* Baltimore: Johns Hopkins Press, 1966. Pp. 119–146.

ORTON, JUNE L. *A guide to teaching phonetics.* Cambridge, MA: Educators Publishing Service, 1976.

ORTON, SAMUEL T. *Reading, writing, and speech problems in children.* New York: Norton, 1937.

ORTONY, ANDREW. Beyond literal similarity. Technical Report No. 105. Champaign, IL: Center for the Study of Reading, University of Illinois, October 1978.

ORTONY, ANDREW. Metaphor. In R. Spiro *et al.* (Eds.), *Theoretical issues in reading comprehension.* Hillsdale, NJ: LEA, 1980. Pp. 349–365. (a)

ORTONY, ANTHONY. Understanding metaphors. Technical Report No. 154. Champaign, IL: Center for the Study of Reading, University of Illinois, January 1980. (b)

ORTONY, ANTHONY. Understanding figurative language. In P. D. Pearson (Ed.), *Handbook of reading research.* New York: Longman, 1984. Pp. 453–470.

OSAKO, GARY N., & ANDERS, PATRICIA L. The effect of reading interest on comprehension of expository materials with controls for prior knowledge. In J. Niles & L. A. Harris (Eds.), *Searches for meaning in reading/language processes and instruction.* Rochester, NY: National Reading Conference, 1983. Pp. 56–60.

OSBURN, JEAN. The purposes, uses, and contents of workbooks and some guidelines for teachers and publishers. Reading Education Report No. 27. Champaign, IL: Center for the Study of Reading, University of Illinois, August 1981.

OSBURN, JEAN. The purposes, uses, and contents of workbooks and some guidelines for publishers. In R. Anderson *et al.* (Eds.), *Learning to read in American schools.* Hillsdale, NJ: LEA, 1984. Pp. 45–111. (a)

OSBURN, JEAN. Workbooks that accompany basal reading programs. In G. Duffy *et al.* (Eds.), *Comprehension instruction: Perspectives and suggestions.* New York: Longman, 1984. Pp. 163–186. (b)

O'SHEA, LAWRENCE J., & SINDELAR, PAUL T. The effects of segmenting written discourse on the reading comprehension of low- and high-performance readers. *Reading Research Quarterly,* Summer 1983, *18,* 458–465.

OSTERTAG, BRUCE, & RAMBEAU, JOHN. Reading success through rewriting for secondary LD students. *Academic Therapy,* September 1982, *18,* 27–32.

OTTO, WAYNE. The relationship of retroactive inhibition and school achievement: Theory, research, and implications. Occasional Paper No. 4. Madison, WI: Research and Development Center for Learning and Re-education, University of Wisconsin, 1966.

OTTO, WAYNE. Evaluating instruments for assessing needs and growth in reading. In W. H. MacGinitie (Ed.), *Assessment problems in reading.* Newark, DE: International Reading Association, 1973. Pp. 14–20.

OTTO, WAYNE, BARRETT, THOMAS C., & HARRIS, THEODORE L. Research in reading. *Journal of Experimental Education,* Fall 1968, *37,* 65–77.

OTTO, WAYNE, & STALLARD, CATHY. One hundred essential sight words. *Visible Language,* Summer 1976, *10,* 247–252.

OTTO, WAYNE, & WHITE, SANDRA. Editor's epilog: Look to the interaction. In W. Otto & S. White (Eds.), *Reading expository material.* New York: Academic Press, 1982. Pp. 279–290.

OTTO, WAYNE, WHITE, SANDRA, & CAMPERELL, KAY. Text comprehension research to classroom application: Developing an instructional technique. *Reading Psychology,* Summer 1980, *1,* 184–191.

OTTO, WAYNE, *et al.* A technique for improving the understanding of expository text: Gloss. Theoretical Paper No. 96. Madison, WI: Wisconsin Center for Education Research, University of Wisconsin, November 1981.

OWRID, H. L. Hearing impairment and verbal attainments in primary school children. *Educational Research,* June 1970, *12,* 209–214.

PAGE, WILLIAM D., & CARLSON, KENNETH L. The process of observing oral reading scores. *Reading Horizons,* Spring 1975, *15,* 147–150.

PALINSCAR, ANNEMARIE S. The quest for meaning from expository text: A teacher-guided journey. In G. Duffy *et al.* (Eds.), *Reading comprehension: Perspectives and suggestions.* New York: Longman, 1984. Pp. 251–264.

PALINSCAR, ANNEMARIE S., & BROWN, ANN L. Reciprocal teaching of comprehension-monitoring activites. Technical Report No. 269, Champaign, IL: Center for the Study of Reading, University of Illinois, January 1983.

PALMER, BARBARA C., & BRANNOCK, VIRGINA M. Specialized services. In A. Berger & H. A. Robinson (Eds.), *Secondary school reading: What research reveals for classroom practice.* Urbana, IL: NCRE/ERIC, 1982. Pp. 159–171.

PALMER, DOUGLAS J. An attributional perspective on labelling. *Exceptional Children,* February 1983, *49,* 423–429.

PALMER, WILLIAM S. What reading teachers can do before the censors come. *Journal of Reading,* January 1982, *25,* 310–314.

PANY, DARLENE, & JENKINS, JOSEPH R. Learning word meanings: A comparison of instructional procedures and effects on measures of reading comprehension with learning disabled students. Technical Report No. 25. Champaign, IL: Center for the Study of Reading, University of Illinois, March 1977.

PANY, DARLENE, JENKINS, JOSEPH R., & SCHRECK, JANICE. Vocabulary instruction: Effects on word knowledge and reading comprehension. *Learning Disabilities Quarterly,* 1982, *5,* 202–215.

PANY, DARLENE, MCCOY, KATHLEEN M., & PETERS, ELLEN E. Effects of corrective feedback on comprehension skills of remedial students. *Journal of Reading Behavior,* Summer 1981, *13,* 131–143.

PARADIS, EDWARD E. The appropriateness of visual discrimination exercises in reading readiness materials. *Journal of Educational Research,* 1974, *67,* 276–278.

PARISH, PEGGY. *Amelia Bedelia.* New York: Harper & Row, 1963; also a Scholastic paperback.

PARK, GEORGE E., & SCHNEIDER, KENNETH A. Thyroid function in relation to dyslexia (reading failures). *Journal of Reading Behavior,* Summer 1975, *7,* 197–199.

PARK, ROSEMARIE. A critical review of developments in adult literacy. In M. Kamil (Ed.), *Directions in reading: Research and instruction.* Washington, DC: National Reading Conference 1981. Pp. 279–289.

PARRISH, BERTA. Put a little romantic fiction into your reading program. *Journal of Reading,* April 1983, *26,* 610–615.

PASCARELLA, ERNEST T., & PFLAUM, SUSANNA W. The interaction of children's attribution and level of control over error correction in reading instruction. *Journal of Educational Psychology,* 1981, *73,* 533–540.

PASCARELLA, ERNEST T., PFLAUM, SUSANNA W., & PEARL, R. A. Interaction of internal attribution for effort and teacher response mode in reading instruction: A replication note. *American Educational Research Journal,* Summer 1983, *20,* 269–276.

PATBERG, JUDYTHE P., DEWITZ, PETER, & SAMUELS, S. JAY. The effect of context on the perceptual unit used in word recognition. *Journal of Reading Behavior,* Spring 1981, *13,* 33–48.

PATTEN, MAURINE D. Relationship between self-esteem, anxiety, and achievement in young learning disabled students. *Journal of Learning Disabilities,* January 1983, *16,* 43–45.

PATTERSON, KARALYN E. Neuropsychological approaches to the study of reading. *British Journal of Psychology,* May 1981, *72,* 151–174.

PAUK, WALTER. *How to study in college.* Boston: Houghton Mifflin, 1962.

PAUK, WALTER. Speed reading? *Journal of the Reading Specialist,* December 1964, *4,* 18–19.

PAUK, WALTER. A common system used in an uncommon way. *Reading World,* December 1982, *22,* 165–166.

PAUK, WALTER. The new SQ4R. *Reading World,* March 1984, *23,* 274–275.

PAULIN, MARY ANN. *Creative uses of children's literature.* Hamden, CT: Library Professional Publications, 1982.

PAVLIDIS, GEORGE T. Do eye movements hold the key to dyslexia? *Neuropsychologia*, 1981, *19* (1), 57–64. (a)

PAVLIDIS, GEORGE T. Sequencing, eye movements and the early objective diagnosis of dyslexia. In G. Pavlidis & T. Miles (Eds.), *Dyslexia research and its applications to education*. New York: John Wiley & Sons, 1981. Pp. 99–163. (b)

PAVLIDIS, GEORGE T. The "dyslexia syndrome" and its objective diagnosis by erratic eye movements. In K. Rayner (Ed.), *Eye movements in reading: Perceptual and language processing*. New York: Academic Press, 1983. Pp. 441–466.

PEARL, RUTH, BRYAN, TANIS, & DONAHUE, MAVIS. Learning disabled children's attibutions for success and failure. *Learning Disability Quarterly*, Winter 1980, *3*, 3–9.

PEARSON, GERALD H. A survey of learning difficulties in children. *Psychoanalytic Study of the Child*, 1952, *7*, 372–386.

PEARSON, P. DAVID. Asking questions about stories. Ginn Occasional Papers, No. 15. Columbus, OH: Ginn, 1982. Also in A. J. Harris & E. Sipay (Eds.), *Readings on reading instruction* (3rd ed.). New York: Longman, 1984. Pp. 274–283.

PEARSON, P. DAVID. A context for instructional research on reading comprehension. In J. Flood (Ed.), *Promoting reading comprehension*. Newark, DE: International Reading Association, 1984. Pp. 1–15. (a)

PEARSON, P. DAVID. Guided reading: A response to Isabel Beck. In R. Anderson, J. Osburn, & R. Tierney (Eds.), *Learning to read in American schools: Basal readers and content texts*. Hillsdale, NJ: LEA, 1984. Pp. 21–28. (b)

PEARSON, P. DAVID, & FIELDING, LINDA. Research update: Listening comprehension. *Language Arts*, September 1982, *59*, 617–629. Also in A. J. Harris & E. Sipay (Eds.), *Readings on reading instruction* (3rd ed.). New York: Longman, 1984. Pp. 74–85.

PEARSON, P. DAVID, & GALLAGHER, MARGARET C. The instruction of reading comprehension. Technical Report No. 297. Champaign, IL: Center for the Study of Reading, University of Illinois, October 1983. Also in *Contemporary Educational Psychology*, 1983, *8*, 317–345.

PEARSON, P. DAVID, & JOHNSON, DALE D. *Teaching reading comprehension*. New York: Holt, Rinehart and Winston, 1978.

PEARSON, P. DAVID, & KAMIL, MICHAEL L. Basic processes and instructional practices in teaching reading. Reading Education Report No. 7. Champaign, IL: Center for the Study of Reading, University of Illinois, December 1978.

PEARSON, P. DAVID, et al. The function of metaphor in children's recall of expository passages. *Journal of Reading Behavior*, 1981, *13* (3), 249–261.

PELLEGRINI, ANTHONY D., DESTEFANO, JOHANNA S., & THOMPSON, DEBORAH L. Saying what you mean: Using play to teach "literate language." *Language Arts*, March 1983, *60*, 380–384.

PELLEGRINI, ANTHONY D., & GALDA, LEE. The effects of thematic-fantasy play training in the development of children's story comprehension. *American Educational Research Journal*, Fall 1982, *19*, 443–452.

PELOSI, PETER L. The roots of reading diagnosis. In H. A. Robinson (Ed.), *Reading & writing instruction in the United States: Historical trends*. Newark, DE: International Reading Association, September 1977. Pp. 69–75.

PELOSI, PETER L. The disabled reader in years past. *Journal of Research and Development in Education*, Summer 1981, *14*, 1–10.

PELOSI, PETER L. A method for classifying remedial reading techniques. *Reading World*, December 1982, *22*, 119–128.

PENFIELD, W., & ROBERTS L. *Speech and brain mechanisms*. Princeton, NJ: Princeton University Press, 1959.

PENNINGTON, BRUCE F., & SMITH, SHELLEY D. Genetic influences on learning disabilities and speech and language disorders. *Child Development*, April 1983, *54*, 369–387.

PERFETTI, CHARLES A. Reading comprehension depends on language comprehension. Paper presented at the American Educational Research Association Convention, San Francisco, 1976. ED 120 688

PERFETTI, CHARLES A., FINGER, E., & HOGABOAM, T. W. Sources of vocalization latency differences between skilled and less skilled young readers. *Journal of Educational Psychology*, 1978, *70*, 730–739.

PERFETTI, CHARLES A., & LESGOLD, ALAN M. Discourse comprehension and sources of individual differences. Pittsburgh: Learning Research and Development Center, University of Pittsburgh, 1977. ED 145 400

PERFETTI, CHARLES A., & LESGOLD, ALAN M. Coding and comprehension in skilled reading and implications for reading instruction. In L. Resnick & P. Weaver (Eds.), *Theory and practice of early reading*, Vol. 1. Hillsdale, NJ: LEA, 1979. Pp. 57–84.

PERFETTI, CHARLES A., & ROTH, STEVEN. Some of the interactive processes in reading and their role in reading skill. In A. Lesgold & C. Perfetti (Eds.), *Interactive processes in reading*. Hillsdale, NJ: LEA, 1981. Pp. 269–297.

PERKINS, MARCY R. Minimum competency testing: What? Why? Why not? *Educational Measurement: Issues & Practices*, Winter 1982, *1*, 5–9, 26.

PERKINS, STANLEY A. Malnutrition and mental development. *Exceptional Children*, January 1977, *43*, 214–219.

PERTZ, DORIS L., & PUTNAM, LILLIAN R. An examination of the relationship between nutrition and learning. *The Reading Teacher*, March 1982, *35*, 702–706.

PERTZ, DORIS L., et al. What's in a name: Reading specialist? *Journal of Reading*, April 1979, *22*, 623–628.

PETERS, MICHAEL. Dyslexia: Why and when the visual-acoustic-kinesthetic-tactile remedial approach might work. *Perceptual & Motor Skills*, April 1981, *52*, 630.

PETERSON, JOE, & CARROLL, MARTHA. The cloze procedure as an indicator of the instructional level for disabled readers. In P. Nacke (Ed.), *Interaction: Research and practice for college-adult reading*. Clemson, SC: National Reading Conference, 1974. Pp. 153–157.

PETERSON, JOE, GREENLAW, M. JEAN, & TIERNEY, ROBERT J. Assessing instructional placement with the IRI: The effectiveness of comprehension questions. *Journal of Educational Research*, May/June 1978, *71*, 247–250.

PETERSON, J., PARADIS, E., & PETERS, N. Revalidation of the cloze procedure as a measure of the instructional level for high school students. In P. L. Nacke (Ed.), *Diversity in mature reading: Theory and research*. Boone, NC: National Reading Conference, 1973. Pp. 144–149.

PETERSON, PENELOPE L. Direct instruction reconsidered. In L. Reed & S. Ward (Eds.), *Basic skills issues and choices: Issues in basic skills planning and instruction*, Vol. 2. St. Louis: CEMREL, April 1982. Pp. 169–176.

PETRAUSKAS, RYMANTAS, & ROURKE, BYRON P. Identification of subgroups of retarded readers: A neuropsychological multivariate approach. *Journal of Clinical Neuropsychology*, 1979, *1* (1), 17–37.

PETRE, RICHARD M. Pupil response in open structured and close structured reading activities. In H. A. Klein (Ed.), *The quest for competency in teaching reading*. Newark, DE: International Reading Association, 1972. Pp. 192–197.

PETTY, WALTER T., HEROLD, CURTIS P., & STOLL, EARLINE. *The state of knowledge about the teaching of vocabulary*. Cooperative Research Project No. 3128. Urbana, IL: National Council of Teachers of English, 1968.

PFLAUM, SUSANNA W. The predictability of oral reading behaviors on comprehension in learning disabled and normal readers. *Journal of Reading Behavior*, Fall 1980, *12*, 231–236.

PFLAUM, SUSANNA W., & BRYAN, TANIS H. Oral reading behaviors in the learning disabled. *Journal of Educational Research*, May/June 1979, *73*, 252–258.

PFLAUM, SUSANNA W., & PASCARELLA, ERNEST T. Interactive effects of prior reading achievement and training in context on the reading of learning disabled children. *Reading Research Quarterly*, 1980, *16* (1), 138–158.

PFLAUM, SUSANNA W., & PASCARELLA, ERNEST T. Attribution retraining for learning disabled students: Some thoughts on the practical implications of the evidence. *Learning Disability Quarterly*, Fall 1982, *5*, 422–426.

PFLAUM, SUSANNA W., et al. Reading instruction: A quantitative analysis. *Educational Researcher*, July/August 1980, *9*, 12–18.

PHILIPS, SUSAN U. *The invisible culture: Communication in classroom and community on the Warm Springs Indian Reservation.* New York: Longman, 1983.

PHILLIPS, WILMA F. A study of dialect differences on comprehension of oral destructiveness given to intermediate grade children. *Dissertation Abstracts International,* July 1976, *37* (1-A), 126.

PHILPOTT, WILLIAM H. Professional opinion about dyslexia. *Journal of Orthomolecular Psychiatry,* 1977, *6* (1), 27–32.

PIAGET, JEAN. *The child's conception of the world.* Paterson, NJ: Littlefield, Adams, 1963.

PIAZZA, D. M. Cerebral lateralization in young children as measured by dichotic listening and finger tapping tests. *Neuropsychologia,* 1977, *15,* 417–425.

PIERONEK, FLORENCE T. Using basal guidebooks—The ideal integrated reading lesson plan. *The Reading Teacher,* November 1979, *33,* 167–172.

PIERONEK, FLORENCE T. Do basal readers reflect the interests of intermediate students? *The Reading Teacher,* January 1980, *33,* 408–412.

PIGGENS, W. R., & BARRON, RODERICK W. Why learning to read aloud more rapidly does not improve comprehension: Testing the coding sufficiency hypothesis. Paper presented at the American Educational Research Association, New York, March 1983.

PIHL, R., & PARKES, M. Hair element content in learning disabled children. *Science,* October 1977, *198,* 204–206.

PIKULSKI, JOHN J. The validity of three brief measures of intelligence for disabled readers. *Journal of Educational Research,* October 1973, *67,* 67–68, 80.

PIKULSKI, JOHN. A critical review: Informal reading inventories. *The Reading Teacher,* November 1974, *28,* 141–151.

PIKULSKI, JOHN J. Linguistics applied to reading instruction. *Language Arts,* April 1976, *53,* 373–377.

PIKULSKI, JOHN. Readiness for reading: A practical approach. *Language Arts,* February 1978, *55,* 192–197.

PIKULSKI, JOHN J., & KIRSCH, IRWIN S. Organization for instruction. In R. Calfee & P. Drum (Eds.), *Teaching reading in compensatory classes.* Newark, DE: International Reading Association, 1979. Pp. 72–86, 187–191.

PIKULSKI, JOHN J., & ROSS, ELLIOTT. Classroom teachers' perceptions of the role of the reading specialist. *Journal of Reading,* November 1979, *23,* 126–135.

PIKULSKI, JOHN J., & SHANAHAN, TIMOTHY. A comparison of various approaches to evaluating phonics. *The Reading Teacher,* March 1980, *33,* 692–702.

PIKULSKI, JOHN J., & SHANAHAN, TIMOTHY. Informal reading inventories: A critical analysis. In J. Pikulski & T. Shanahan (Eds.), *Approaches to the informal evaluation of reading.* Newark, DE: International Reading Association, 1982. Pp. 94–116.

PIKULSKI, JOHN J., & TOBIN, AILEEN W. The cloze procedure as an informal assessment technique. In J. Pikulski & T. Shanahan (Eds.), *Approaches to the informal evaluation of reading.* Newark, DE: International Reading Association, 1982. Pp. 42–62.

PILLAR, ARLENE. Individualizing book reviews. *Elementary English,* April 1975, *52,* 467–469.

PILLAR, ARLENE M. Literature and the language arts for middle grade students. In U. Hardt (Ed.), *Teaching reading with the other language arts.* Newark, DE: International Reading Association, 1983. Pp. 117–134.

PILON, A. BARBARA. Reading to learn about the nature of language. In J. Stewig & S. Sebesta (Eds.), *Using literature in the elementary classroom.* Urbana, IL: NCTE, 1978. Pp. 1–12. Also in A. J. Harris & E. Sipay (Eds.), *Readings on reading instruction* (3rd ed.). New York: Longman, 1984. Pp. 231–236.

PIROZZOLO, FRANCIS J. *The neuropsychology of developmental reading disorders.* New York: Praeger, 1979.

PIROZZOLO, FRANCIS J. Eye movements and reading disability. In K. Rayner (Ed.), *Eye movements in reading: Perceptual and language processes.* New York: Academic Press, 1983. Pp. 499–509.

PIROZZOLO, FRANCIS J., DUNN, KAY, & ZETUSKY, WALTER. Physiological approaches to subtypes of developmental reading disability. *Topics on Learning & Learning Disabilities,* April 1983, *3,* 40–47.

PIROZZOLO, FRANCIS J., & HANSCH, EDWARD C. The neurobiology of reading disorders. In R. Malatesha & P. Aaron (Eds.), *Reading disorders: Varieties and treatments.* New York: Academic Press, 1982. Pp. 215–231.

PIROZZOLO, FRANCIS J., & RAYNER, KEITH. Cerebral organization and reading disability. *Neuropsychologia,* 1979, *17* (5), 485–491.

PIROZZOLO, FRANCIS J., et al. Effects of cerebral dysfunction on neurolinguistic performance in children. *Journal of Consulting & Clinical Psychology,* December 1981, *49,* 791–806.

PLAS, JEANNE M. If not grade equivalent scores—then what? *Measurement in Education,* Spring 1977, *8,* 4–8.

PLATTS, MARY E. *Anchor: A handbook of vocabulary discovery techniques for the classroom teacher.* Stevensville, MI: Educational Services, 1970.

PLOGHOFT, MILTON, & SHELDON, WILLIAM D. Television viewing skills. In J. Cowen (Ed.), *Teaching reading through the arts.* Newark, DE: International Reading Association, 1983. Pp. 11–33.

PODSTAY, EDWARD J. Show me your underlines: A strategy to teach comprehension. *The Reading Teacher,* May 1984, *37,* 828–830.

POLLOWAY, EDWARD A., & POLLOWAY, CAROLYN H. Survival words for disabled readers. *Academic Therapy,* March 1981, *16,* 443–448.

POMERANTZ, HELEN. Subvocalization and reading. *The Reading Teacher,* April 1971, *24,* 665–667.

POPE, LILLIE. Reading instruction in modern China. *The Reading Teacher,* March 1982, *35,* 688–694.

POPHAM, W. JAMES. *Criterion-referenced measurement.* Englewood Cliffs, NJ: Prentice-Hall, 1978.

POPP, HELEN M. Current practices in the teaching of beginning reading. In J. B. Carroll & J. S. Chall (Eds.), *Toward a literate society.* New York: McGraw-Hill, 1975. Pp. 101–146.

POTTER, F. The use of the linguistic context: Do good and poor readers use different strategies? *British Journal of Educational Psychology,* 1982, *52,* 16–23.

POTTER, ROSEMARY L. The link between reading instruction and commercial television: Is there a bandwagon? *Journal of Reading,* February 1981, *24,* 377–383.

POVSIC, FRANCES F. Czechoslovakia: Children's fiction in English. *The Reading Teacher,* March 1980, *33,* 686–691. (a)

POVSIC, FRANCES F. Poland: Children's fiction in English. *The Reading Teacher,* April 1980, *33,* 806–815. (b)

POVSIC, FRANCES F. Yugoslavia: An annotated guide to children's fiction in English. *The Reading Teacher,* February 1980, *33,* 559–566. (c)

POVSIC, FRANCES F. Non-Russian tales from the Soviet Union. *The Reading Teacher,* November 1981, *35,* 196–202. (a)

POVSIC, FRANCES F. Russian folk and animal tales. *The Reading Teacher,* December 1981, *35,* 329–343. (b)

POVSIC, FRANCES F. Hungary—Children's fiction in English. *The Reading Teacher,* April 1982, *35,* 820–828. (a)

POVSIC, FRANCES F. The Ukraine—Children's stories in English. *The Reading Teacher,* March 1982, *35,* 316–322. (b)

POWELL, GLEN, & ZALUD, GARRETH. A SQ3R for secondary handicapped students. *Journal of Reading,* December 1982, *26,* 262–263.

POWELL, WILLIAM R. Acquisition of a reading repertoire. *Library Trends,* October 1973, *22,* 177–196.

POWERS, HUGH W. S., JR. Caffeine, behavior and the LD child. *Academic Therapy,* Fall 1975, *11,* 5–11.

PRAGER, BARTON B., & MANN, LESTER. Criterion-referenced measurement: The world of gray versus black and white. *Journal of Learning Disabilities,* February 1973, *6,* 72–84.

PRATT, MICHAEL W., KRANE, ANNE R., & KENDALL, JANET R. Triggering a schemata: The role of italics and intonation in the interpretation of ambiguous discourse. *American Educational Research Journal,* Fall 1981, *18,* 303–315.

PRESCOTT, GEORGE A. et al. *Teacher's manual for administering and interpreting the Metropolitan Achievement Tests, Intermediate Level.* New York: Psychological Corp., 1978.

PRESSLEY, MICHAEL. Imagery and children's learning: Putting the picture in developmental perspective. *Review of Educational Research,* Fall 1977, *47,* 585–622.

PRESSLEY, MICHAEL, LEVIN, JOEL, & MILLER, GLORIA E. How does the keyword method affect vocabulary comprehension and usage? *Reading Research Quarterly*, 1981, *16* (2), 213–226.

PRESSMAN, RAYMOND. The relationship of sensory-integration matching abilities and reading instructional approaches to word recognition ability. Unpublished doctoral dissertation, State University of New York at Albany, 1973.

PRESTON, RALPH C. Reading achievement of German boys and girls related to sex of teacher. *The Reading Teacher*, February 1979, *32*, 521–526.

PRITCHARD, ALLAN, & TAYLOR, JEAN. Suggestopedia for the disadvantaged reader. *Academic Therapy*, September 1978, *14*, 81–90.

PROUT, H. THOMPSON, & INGRAM, RICHARD E. Guidelines for the behavioral assessment of hyperactivity. *Journal of Learning Disabilities*, August/September 1982, *15*, 393–398.

PULLIAM, ROBERT. Child learning disabilities: Reported level of incidence as a function of defining criteria. Unpublished doctoral dissertation, Catholic University, 1975.

PUMFREY, P. D., & ELLIOTT, C. D. Play therapy, social adjustment and reading attainment. *Educational Research*, June 1970, *12*, 183–193.

PURVES, ALAN C. *Literature education in ten countries: An empirical study.* New York: John Wiley & Sons, 1973.

PURVES, ALAN C. The challenge to education to produce literate citizens. In A. Purves & O. Niles (Eds.), *Becoming readers in a complex society.* 83rd Yearbook of the National Society for the Study of Education, Part II. Chicago: University of Chicago Press, 1984. Pp. 1–15.

PURVES, ALAN C., & BEACH, RICHARD. *Literature and the reader: Research in response to literature, reading, interests, and the teaching of literature.* Urbana, IL: National Council of Teachers of English, 1972.

PURVES, ALAN C., et al. *Reading and literature: American achievement in international perspective.* Urbana, IL: National Council of Teachers of English, 1981.

PUTNAM, RUTH A. Cultivating a taste for non-fiction. *Elementary English Review*, 1941, *18*, 228–229.

PYRCZAK, FRED. Context-independence of items designed to measure the ability to derive the meanings of words from their context. *Educational and Psychological Measurement*, Winter 1976, *36*, 919–924.

PYRCZAK, FRED, & AXELROD, JEROME. Determining the passage-dependence of reading comprehension exercises: A call for replication. *Journal of Reading*, January 1976, *19*, 279–283.

RABINOVITCH, RALPH D. Dyslexia: Psychiatric considerations. In J. Money (Ed.), *Reading disability: Progress and research needs in dyslexia.* Baltimore: Johns Hopkins Press, 1962. Pp. 73–79.

RABINOVITCH, RALPH D. Reading problems in children: Definitions and classifications. In A. H. Keeney & V. T. Keeney (Eds.), *Dyslexia: Diagnosis and treatment of reading disorders.* St. Louis: C. V. Mosby, 1968. Pp. 1–10.

RADENBAUGH, MURIEL R. Using children's literature to teach mathematics. *The Reading Teacher*, May 1981, *34*, 902–906.

RAIM, JOAN. Influence of the teacher-pupil interaction on disabled readers. *The Reading Teacher*, April 1983, *36*, 810–813.

RAMSEY, WALLACE. The value and limitations of diagnostic reading tests for evaluation in the classroom. In T. C. Barrett (Ed.), *The evaluation of children's reading achievement.* Newark, DE: International Reading Association, 1967. Pp. 65–77.

RAND, MURIEL K. Story schema: Theory, research and practice. *The Reading Teacher*, January 1984, *37*, 377–382.

RANKIN, EARL F. How flexibly do we read? *Journal of Reading Behavior*, Summer 1970–71, *31*, 34–38.

RANKIN, EARL F. Grade level interpretation of cloze readability scores. In F. Greene (Ed.), *The right to participate.* Milwaukee, WI: National Reading Conference, 1971. Pp. 30–37.

RANKIN, EARL F. The cloze procedure revisited. In P. L. Nacke (Ed.), *Interaction: Research and practice for college-adult reading.* Clemson, SC: National Reading Conference, 1974. Pp. 1–8.

RANKIN, EARL F. Characteristics of the cloze procedure as a research tool in the study of language. In P. D. Pearson & J. Hansen (Eds.), *Reading: Disciplined inquiry in process and practice.* Clemson, SC: National Reading Conference, 1978. Pp. 148–153.

RANKIN, EARL F., & EBERWEIN, LOWELL. A critical evaluation of several methods for measuring gain in reading. In W. D. Miller & G. H. McNinch (Eds.), *Reflections and investigations on reading*. Clemson, SC: National Reading Conference, 1976. Pp. 181–189.

RANKIN, EARL F., & OVERHOLSER, BETSY M. Reaction of intermediate grade children to contextual clues. *Journal of Reading Behavior*, Summer 1969, *1*, 50–73.

RAPHAEL, TAFFY. Improving question-answering performance through instruction. Reading Education Report No. 32. Champaign, IL: Center for the Study of Reading, University of Illinois, March 1982. (a)

RAPHAEL, TAFFY. Question-answering strategies for children. *The Reading Teacher*, November 1982, *36*, 186–190. (b)

RAPHAEL, TAFFY E. Teaching learners about sources of information for answering comprehension questions. *Journal of Reading Behavior*, January 1984, *27*, 303–311.

RAPHAEL, TAFFY E., & GAVELEK, JAMES R. Question-related activities and their relationship to reading comprehension: Some instructional implications. In G. Duffy *et al.* (Eds.), *Comprehension instruction: Perspectives and suggestions*. New York: Longman, 1984. Pp. 234–250.

RASMUSSEN, T., & MILNER, B. Clinical and surgical studies of the cerebral speech areas in man. In K. J. Zulch, O. Creutzfeldt, & G. C. Galbraith (Eds.), *Otfred Foerster symposium on cerebral localization*. Heidelberg: Springer-Verlag, 1975. Pp. 238–257.

RAUCH, SIDNEY J. The administrator and the reading program—What to look for in a reading lesson. *Reading World*, March 1982, *21*, 264–265.

RAWSON, MARGARET B. *Developmental-language disability: Adult accomplishments of dyslexic boys.* Cambridge, MA: EPS, 1978.

RAYGOR, ALTON L. The Raygor readability estimate: A quick and easy way to determine difficulty. In P. D. Pearson & J. Hansen (Eds.), *Reading: Theory, research and practice*. Clemson, SC: National Reading Conference, 1977. Pp. 259–263.

RAYNER, KEITH. Eye movements and the perceptual span in reading. In F. Pirozzolo & M. Wittrock (Eds.), *Neuropsychological and cognitive processes in reading*. New York: Academic Press, 1981. Pp. 145–165.

RAYNER, KEITH. Eye movements, perceptual spans, and reading disability. *Annals of Dyslexia*, 1983, *33*, 163–173. (a)

RAYNER, KEITH. The perceptual span and eye movement control during reading. In K. Rayner (Ed.), *Eye movements in reading: Perceptual and language processes*. New York: Academic Press, 1983. Pp. 97–120. (b)

READ, CHARLES. Pre-school children's knowledge of English phonology. *Harvard Educational Review*, February 1971, *41*, 1–34.

READ, CHARLES. *Children's categorization of speech sounds in English*. Research Report No. 17. Urbana, IL: National Council of Teachers of English, 1975.

READ, MERRILL S. Malnutrition, hunger and behavior. In G. Leisman (Ed.), *Basic visual processes in learning disabilities*. Springfield, IL: Charles C Thomas, 1976. Pp. 58–72.

READENCE, JOHN E., BALDWIN, R. SCOTT, & RICKELMAN, ROBERT J. Instructional insights into metaphors and similies. *Journal of Reading*, November 1983, *27*, 109–112. (a)

READENCE, JOHN E., BALDWIN, R. SCOTT, & RICKELMAN, ROBERT J. Word knowledge and metaphorical interpretation. *Research in the Teaching of English*, December 1983, *17*, 349–358. (b)

READENCE, JOHN E., & MOORE, DAVID. Strategies for enhancing readiness and recall in content areas: The encoding specificity principle. *Reading Psychology*, Fall 1979, *1*, 47–54.

READENCE, JOHN E., & SEARFOSS, LYNDON W. Teaching strategies for vocabulary development. *English Journal*, October 1980, *69*, 43–46.

READING DEVELOPMENT CENTRE. *Games, games, games: Word recognition and listening activities* (4th ed.). Adelaide, South Australia: Education Department of South Australia, 1976. (a)

READING DEVELOPMENT CENTRE. *Resource book on the development of reading skills* (rev. ed.). Adelaide, South Australia: Education Department of South Australia, 1976. (b)

READING TEACHER STAFF. Who profits from self-learning kits? *The Reading Teacher*, January 1978, *31*, 391–392.

REDER, LYNNE M. The role of elaboration in the comprehension and retention of prose: A critical review. *Review of Educational Research*, Spring 1980, *50*, 5–33.

REED, JAMES C. The deficits of retarded readers—Fact or artifact? *The Reading Teacher*, January 1970, *23*, 347–352, 393.

REED, JAMES C., RABE, EDWARD F., & MANKINEN, MARGARET. Teaching reading to brain-injured children: A review. *Reading Research Quarterly*, Spring 1970, *5*, 379–401.

REED, LINDA, & WARD, SPENCER. Basic skills, issues and choices: An introduction. In L. Reed & S. Ward (Eds.), *Basic skills—Issues and choices: Approaches to basic skills instruction*, Vol. 1. St. Louis: CEMREL, April 1982. Pp. 1–24.

REICH, CAROL M., & REICH, PETER A. The construction of an orally based subject-word vocabulary list and its relationship to the vocabularies of beginning readers. *Journal of Educational Research*, 1979, *72* (4), 198–204.

REIMER, BECKY L. Recipes for language experience stories. *The Reading Teacher*, January 1983, *36*, 396–401.

RENTEL, VICTOR M. Concept formation and reading. *Reading World*, December 1971, *11*, 111–119.

RESNICK, DANIEL P., & RESNICK, LAUREN B. The nature of literacy: An historical exploration. *Harvard Educational Review*, August 1977, *47*, 370–385.

RESNICK, LAUREN B. Theories and prescriptions for early reading instruction. In L. Resnick & P. Weaver (Eds.), *Theory and practice in early reading*, Vol. 2. Hillsdale, NJ: LEA, 1979. Pp. 321–338. (a)

RESNICK, LAUREN B. Toward a usable psychology of reading instruction. In L. Resnick & P. Weaver (Eds.), *Theory and practice in early reading*, Vol. 3. Hillsdale, NJ: LEA, 1979. Pp. 355–372. (b)

RESNICK, LAUREN B., & BECK, ISABEL L. Designing instruction in reading: Interaction of theory and practice. In J. T. Guthrie (Ed.), *Aspects of reading acquisition*. Baltimore: Johns Hopkins University Press, 1976. Pp. 180–204.

REUTZEL, D. RAY. C^6: A reading mode for teaching arithmetic story solving. *The Reading Teacher*, October 1983, *37*, 28–34.

REYNOLDS, CECIL R. An examination for bias in a preschool test battery across race and sex. *Journal of Educational Measurement*, Summer 1980, *17*, 137–146.

REYNOLDS, CECIL R. The fallacy of "two years below grade level for age" as a diagnostic criterion for reading disorders. *Journal of School Psychology*, 1981, *19* (4), 350–358. (a)

REYNOLDS, CECIL R. Neuropsychological assessment and the habituation of learning: Considerations in the search for the aptitude X treatment interaction. *School Psychology Review*, Summer 1981, *10*, 343–349. (b)

REYNOLDS, CECIL R. Neuropsychological assessment in education: A caution. *Journal of Research and Development in Education*. Spring 1982, *15*, 76–79.

REYNOLDS, RALPH E., & ORTONY, ANDREW. Some issues in the measurement of children's comprehension of metaphorical language. Technical Report No. 172. Champaign, IL: Center for the Study of Reading, University of Illinois, May 1980.

REYNOLDS, RALPH E., *et al.* Cultural schemata and reading comprehension. *Reading Research Quarterly*, 1982, *17* (3), 353–366.

RIBOVICH, JERILYN K. Teachers plan ways for readers to get feedback. *Reading Improvement*, Summer 1978, *15*, 149–153.

RICHARDSON, ELLIS, DI BENEDETTO, BARBARA, & BRADLEY, C. MICHAEL. The relationship of sound blending to reading achievement. *Review of Educational Research*, Winter 1977, *47*, 319–334.

RICHARDSON, ELLIS, *et al.* Relationship of auditory and visual skills to reading retardation. *Journal of Learning Disabilities*, February 1980, *13*, 77–82.

RICHARDSON, SELMA K. *Magazines for children: A selection guide for librarians, teachers, and parents.* Chicago: American Library Association, 1983.

RICHEK, MARGARET ANN. Reading comprehension of anaphoric forms in varying linguistic contexts. *Reading Research Quarterly*, 1976–1977, *12* (2), 145–165.

RICHGELS, DONALD J., & HANSEN, RUTH. Gloss: Helping students apply both skills and strategies in reading content texts. *Journal of Reading*, January 1984, *27*, 312–317.

RICHGELS, DONALD J., & MATEJA, JOHN A. Gloss II: Integrating content and process for independence. *Journal of Reading*, February 1984, *27*, 424–431.

RICKARDS, JOHN P. Notetaking: Theory and research. *Improving Human Performance Quarterly*, Fall 1979, 8, 152–161. Also in A. J. Harris & E. Sipay (Eds.), *Readings on reading instruction* (3rd ed.). New York: Longman, 1984. Pp. 331–337.

RIEGEL, R. HUNT. Mainstreaming equals cooperative planning. *Academic Therapy*, January 1983, 18, 285–298.

RIGGS, CORINNE W. (Comp.), *Bibliotherapy: An annotated bibliography*. Newark, DE: International Reading Association, 1971.

RILEY, JOHN A., & LOWE, JAMES D., JR. A study of enhancing vs. reducing speech during reading. *Journal of Reading*, October 1981, 25, 7–13.

RINGLER, LENORE H., & WEBER, CAROL K. Comprehending narrative discourse: Implications for instruction. In J. Langer & M. T. Burke-Smith (Eds.), *Reader meets author/bridging the gap: Psycholinguistic and sociolinguistic perspectives*. Newark, DE: International Reading Association, 1982. Pp. 180–195.

RISPENS, J. Reading disorders as information-processing disorders. In R. Malatesha & P. Aaron (Eds.), *Reading disorders: Varieties and treatments*. New York: Academic Press, 1982. Pp. 177–197.

ROBBINS, LOUISE S. A way out of the book report dilemma. *Journal of Reading*, November 1981, 25, 165–166.

ROBBINS, MELVYN P. The Delacato interpretation of neurological organization. *Reading Research Quarterly*, Spring 1966, 1, 57–78.

ROBECK, CAROL P. An investigation of the relationship between concrete operational thought and reading achievement. *Reading World*, October 1981, 21, 2–13.

ROBECK, CAROL P. A study of cognitive style, knowledge of linguistic concepts, and reading achievement of first and third grade children. *Reading World*, December 1982, 22, 98–110.

ROBERGE, JAMES J., & FLEXER, BARBARA K. Cognitive style, operativity, and reading achievement. *American Educational Research Journal*, Spring 1984, 21, 227–236.

ROBERTS, CHRISTINE L. A new checklist for evaluating instructional materials in reading. *New England Reading Association Journal*, 1980, 15 (2), 25–34.

ROBERTS, R. W., & COLEMAN, J. An investigation of the role of visual and kinesthetic factors in reading failures. *Journal of Educational Research*, 1958, 57, 445–451.

ROBERTS, TESSA. Skills of analysis and synthesis in the early stages of reading. *British Journal of Educational Psychology*, February 1975, 45, 3–9.

ROBERTS, TESSA. Auditory blending in the early stages of reading. *Educational Research*, November 1979, 22, 49–53.

ROBERTS, TESSA. Strategies for helping the impulsive reader. *Reading*, July 1980, 14, 3–10.

ROBERTSON, JEAN E. Pupil understanding of connectives in reading. *Reading Research Quarterly*, Spring 1968, 3, 387–417.

ROBINSON, COLIN G. Cloze procedure: A review. *Educational Research*, February 1981, 23, 128–133.

ROBINSON, FRANCIS P. *Effective reading* (4th ed.). New York: Harper & Row, 1970.

ROBINSON, H. ALAN. A study of the techniques of word identification. *The Reading Teacher*, January 1963, 16, 238–241.

ROBINSON, H. ALAN. Reading instruction and research: An historical perspective. In H. A. Robinson (Ed.), *Reading and writing instruction in the United States: Historical trends*. Newark, DE: International Reading Association, 1977. Pp. 44–58.

ROBINSON, H. ALAN, & SCHATZBERG, KATHLEEN. The development of effective teaching. In A. Purves & O. Niles (Eds.), *Becoming readers in a complex society*. 83rd Yearbook of the National Society for the Study of Education, Part I. Chicago: University of Chicago Press, 1984. Pp. 233–270.

ROBINSON, HELEN M. *Why pupils fail in reading*. Chicago: University of Chicago Press, 1946.

ROBINSON, HELEN M. Perceptual training—Does it result in reading improvement? In R. C. Aukerman (Ed.), *Some persistent questions on beginning reading*. Newark, DE: International Reading Association, 1972. Pp. 135–150. (a)

ROBINSON, HELEN M. Visual and auditory modalities related to methods for beginning reading. *Reading Research Quarterly*, Fall 1972, 8, 7–39. (b)

ROBINSON, HELEN M., & SMITH, HELEN K. Reading clinic clients—Ten years after. *Elementary School Journal*, 1962, 63, 22–27.

ROBINSON, HELEN M., & WEINTRAUB, SAMUEL. Research related to children's interests and to developmental values of reading. *Library Trends,* October 1973, *22,* 81–108.

ROBINSON, RICHARD D., & PETTIT, NEILA T. The role of the reading teacher: Where do you fit in? *The Reading Teacher,* May 1978, *31,* 923–929.

ROBINSON, VIOLET, STRICKLAND, DOROTHY S., & CULLINAN, BERNICE. The child: Ready or not? In L. Ollila (Ed.), *The kindergarten child and reading.* Newark, DE: International Reading Association, 1977. Pp. 13–39.

ROCHE, ALEX F., LIPMAN, RONALD S., & OAERALL, WELLINGTON H. The effects of stimulant medication on the growth of hyperkinetic children. *Psychopharmacology Bulletin,* 1980, *16* (3), 13–18.

RODENBORN, LEO V. The importance of memory and integration factors to oral reading ability. *Journal of Reading Behavior,* Winter 1970–1971, *3,* 51–59.

ROE, BETTY D. Readability of elementary school textbooks. *Journal of the Reading Specialist,* May 1970, *9,* 163–167.

ROEDER, HAROLD H., & LEE, NANCY. Twenty-five teacher-tested ways to encourage voluntary reading. *The Reading Teacher,* October 1973, *27,* 48–50.

ROEHLER, LAURA R., & DUFFY, GERALD G. Matching direct instruction to reading outcomes. *Language Arts,* May 1982, *59,* 476–480.

ROEHLER, LAURA R., & DUFFY, GERALD G. Direct explanation of comprehension processes. In G. Duffy et al. (Eds.), *Comprehension instruction: Perspectives and suggestions.* New York: Longman, 1984. Pp. 265–280.

ROELKE, PATRICIA L. Reading comprehension as a function of three dimensions of word meaning. Unpublished doctoral dissertation, Indiana University, 1969.

ROGERS, CARL R. *Counseling and psychotherapy.* Boston: Houghton Mifflin, 1942.

ROGERS, JANETTE S. Reading practices in open education. *The Reading Teacher,* March 1976, *29,* 548–554.

ROGOSA, DAVID R., & WILLETT, JOHN B. Demonstrating the reliability of the difference score in the measurement of change. *Journal of Educational Measurement,* Winter 1983, *20,* 335–343.

ROHRLACK, C. R., BELL, B. J., & MCLAUGHLIN, T. F. The value of auditory blending skills for reading readiness programs. *Educational Research Quarterly,* Spring 1982, *7,* 41–47.

ROSE, CYNTHIA, ZIMET, SARA G., & BLOM, GASTON E. Content counts: Children have preferences in reading textbook stories. *Elementary English,* January 1972, *49,* 14–19.

ROSE, TERRY, KOORLAND, MARK A., & EPSTEIN, MICHAEL H. A review of applied behavioral analysis interventions with learning disabled children. *Education and Treatment of Children,* Winter 1982, *5,* 41–58.

ROSECKY, MARION. Are teachers selective when using basal guidebooks? *The Reading Teacher,* January 1978, *31,* 381–384.

ROSEN, CARL L. Visual deficiencies and reading. *Journal of Reading,* 1965, *9,* 57–61.

ROSENFELD, SYLVIA. Introducing behavior modification techniques to teachers. *Exceptional Children,* February 1979, *45,* 334–339.

ROSENSHINE, BARAK V. Review of *Teaching styles and pupil progress* by N. Bennett. *American Educational Research Journal,* 1978, *15,* 163–169. (a)

ROSENSHINE, BARAK V. Academic engaged time, content covered, and direct instruction. *Journal of Education,* August 1978, *160,* 38–66. (b)

ROSENSHINE, BARAK V., & BERLINER, DAVID C. Academic engaged time: Content covered and direct instruction. Paper presented at the Annual Meeting of the American Educational Research Association, April 1977.

ROSENTHAL, JOSEPH H., BODER, ELENA, & CALLAWAY, ENOCH. Typology of developmental dyslexia: Evidence for its construct validity. In R. Malatesha & P. Aaron (Eds.), *Reading disorders: Varieties and treatments.* New York: Academic Press, 1982. Pp. 93–120.

ROSENTHAL, ROBERT, & JACOBSON, LENORE. *Pygmalion in the classroom.* New York: Holt, Rinehart and Winston, 1968.

ROSER, NANCY, & FRITH, MARGARET (Eds.). *Children's choices: Teaching with books children like.* Newark, DE: International Reading Association, 1983.

ROSER, NANCY, & JUEL, CONNIE. Effects of vocabulary instruction on reading comprehension. In J. Niles & L. A. Harris (Eds.), *New Inquiries in reading: Research and instruction*. Rochester, NY: National Reading Conference, 1982. Pp. 110–118.

ROSNER, JEROME. Perceptual skills and achievement. *American Educational Research Journal*, Winter 1973, *10*, 59–67.

ROSNER, JEROME. *The perceptual skills curriculum. Program II—Auditory motor skills*. New York: Walker, 1976.

ROSS, ALAN O. *Psychological aspects of learning disabilities and reading disorders*. New York: McGraw-Hill, 1976.

ROSS, CAMPBELL. A comparative study of the responses made by grade 11 Vancouver students to Canadian and New Zealand poems. *Research in the Teaching of English*, December 1978, *12*, 297–306.

ROSS, ELINOR P. Checking the source: An essential component of critical reading. *Journal of Reading*, January 1981, *24*, 311–315.

ROSS, ELINOR P., & FLETCHER, RICHARD K. Reading preferences of children in the intermediate grades. *The Reading Instruction Journal*, Winter 1980, *23*, 45–49.

ROSS, PATRICIA A. Getting books into those empty hands. *The Reading Teacher*, January 1978, *31*, 397–399.

ROSSO, BARBARA R., & EMANS, ROBERT. Children's use of phonic generalizations. *The Reading Teacher*, March 1981, *34*, 653–658.

ROTH, KATHLEEN J., SMITH, EDWARD L., & ANDERSON, CHARLES W. Verbal patterns in teachers: Comprehension instruction in the content areas. In G. Duffy *et al.* (Eds.), *Comprehension instruction: Perspectives and suggestions*. New York: Longman, 1984. Pp. 281–293.

ROTH, STEVEN F., & PERFETTI, CHARLES A. A framework for reading, language comprehension and language disability. *Topics in Language Disorders*, December 1980, *1*, 15–27.

ROURKE, BYRON P. Reading retardation in children: Developmental lag or deficit? In R. M. Knights & D. J. Bakker (Eds.), *The neuropsychology of learning disorders: Theoretical approaches*. Baltimore: University Park Press, 1976. Pp. 125–137.

ROURKE, BYRON P., & FISK, JOHN L. Socio-emotional disturbances of learning disabled children: The role of central processing deficits. *Bulletin of the Orton Society*, 1981, *31*, 77–88.

ROURKE, BYRON P., & ORR, A. Prediction of the reading and spelling performances of normal and retarded readers: A four-year follow-up. *Journal of Abnormal Child Psychology*, 1977, *5*, 9–20.

ROWELL, E. H. Do elementary students read better orally or silently? *The Reading Teacher*, January 1976, *29*, 367–370.

ROWELL, RICHARD B. The effect of tachistoscopic and visual tracking training on the improvement of reading at the second grade level. *Dissertation Abstracts International*, December 1976, *37* (6-A), 3279.

ROYER, JAMES M., & CUNNINGHAM, DONALD J. On the theory and measurement of reading comprehension. *Contemporary Educational Psychology*, July 1981, *6*, 187–216.

ROZIN, PAUL, & GLEITMAN, LILA R. The structure and acquisition of reading II: The reading process and the acquisition of the alphabetic principle. In A. S. Reber & D. L. Scarborough (Eds.), *Toward a psychology of reading*. Hillsdale, NJ: LEA, 1977. Pp. 55–141.

RUBIN, ANDEE. Making stories, making sense. *Language Arts*, March 1980, *57*, 285–293, 298, 334. (a)

RUBIN, ANDEE. A theoretical taxonomy of the differences between oral and written language. In R. Spiro, B. Bruce, & W. Bower (Eds.), *Theoretical issues in reading comprehension*. Hillsdale, NJ: LEA, 1980. Pp. 411–438. (b)

RUBIN, ANDEE, & BRUCE, BERTRAM: QUILL: Reading and writing with a microcomputer. Reading Education Report No. 48. Champaign, IL: Center for the Study of Reading, University of Illinois, February 1984.

RUBIN, ROSALYN. Reading ability and assigned materials: Accommodations for the slow but not the accelerated. *Elementary School Journal*, March 1975, *75*, 374–377.

RUDDELL, ROBERT B. A longitudinal study of four programs of reading instruction varying in emphasis on regularity of grapheme-phoneme correspondences and language structure on reading achievement in grades two and three. Final Report Nos. 3099 and 78085. Berkeley: University of California, 1968.

RUDDELL, ROBERT B. (Ed.). *Accountability and reading instruction: Critical issues.* Urbana, IL: National Council of Teachers of English, 1973.

RUDDELL, ROBERT B. *Reading-language instruction: Innovative practices.* Englewood Cliffs, NJ: Prentice-Hall, 1974.

RUDDELL, ROBERT B. Developing comprehension abilities: Implications from research for an instructional framework. In S. J. Samuels (Ed.), *What research has to say about reading instruction.* Newark, DE: International Reading Association, 1978. Pp. 108–120.

RUDDELL, ROBERT B. Early prediction of reading success: Profiles of good and poor readers. In M. L. Kamil & A. J. Moe (Eds.), *Reading research: Studies and applications.* Clemson, SC: National Reading Conference, 1979. Pp. 150–158.

RUDDELL, ROBERT B. Improving classroom comprehension. In A. J. Harris & E. Sipay (Eds.), *Readings on reading instruction* (3rd ed.). New York: Longman, 1984. Pp. 283–286.

RUDE, ROBERT T. Objective-based reading systems: An evaluation. *The Reading Teacher,* November 1974, *28,* 169–175.

RUDE, ROBERT T. Microcomputers and the teaching of reading. *New England Reading Association Journal,* Spring 1982, *17,* 4–8.

RUDEL, RITA G. Learning disability: Diagnosis by exclusion and discrepancy. *Journal of the American Academy of Child Psychiatry,* 1980, *19,* 347–369.

RUDEL, R. G., & DENCKLA, MARTHA B. Relationship of IQ and reading scores to visual-spatial and visual-temporal matching tasks. *Journal of Learning Disabilities,* April 1976, *9,* 169–178.

RUDEL, RITA G., DENCKLA, MARTHA B., & BROMAN, MELINDA. The effect of varying stimulus context on word-finding ability: Dyslexia further differentiated from other learning disabilities. *Brain & Language,* May 1981, *13,* 130–144.

RUDISILL, MABEL. Children's preferences for color versus other qualities in illustrations. *Elementary School Journal,* 1952, *52,* 444–451.

RUDMAN, HERBERT C. The informational needs and reading interests of children in grades IV through VIII. *Elementary School Journal,* 1955, *55,* 502–512.

RUGG, MICHAEL D. Electrophysiological studies. In J. Beaumont (Ed.), *Divided visual field studies of cerebral organization.* New York: Academic Press, 1982. Pp. 129–146.

RUGGIERI, ELAINE, & PURNELL, RICHARD. A comparison of a standardized test and a graded word list test as indicators of reading level for remedial reading referrals. *The New England Reading Association Journal,* 1976, *11* (2), 24–27, 53–56.

RUMELHART, DAVID E. Toward an interactive model of reading. In S. Dormic (Ed.), *Attention and performance VI.* Hillsdale, NJ: LEA, 1977. Pp. 573–603.

RUMELHART, DAVID E. Understanding understanding. In J. Flood (Ed.), *Understanding reading comprehension.* Newark, DE: International Reading Association, 1984. Pp. 1–20.

RUMELHART, DAVID E., & MCCLELLAND, JAMES L. Interactive processing through spreading activation. In A. Lesgold & C. Perfetti (Eds.), *Interactive processes in reading.* Hillsdale, NJ: LEA, 1981. Pp. 37–60.

RUMELHART, DAVID E., & MCCLELLAND, JAMES L. An interactive activation model of context effects in letter perception: II. The contextual enhancement effect and some tests and extensions of the model. *Psychological Review,* January 1982, *89,* 60–94.

RUPLEY, WILLIAM H., & BLAIR, TIMOTHY R. Research revisited: Teacher effectiveness research in reading instruction: Early efforts to present focus. *Reading Psychology,* Fall 1980, *2,* 49–56.

RUSH, ROBERT J., & KLARE, GEORGE R. Re-opening the cloze blank issue. *Journal of Reading Behavior,* Summer 1978, *10,* 208–210.

RUSSELL, DAVID, KARP, ETTA E., & MUESER, ANNE MARIE. *Reading aids through the grades* (2nd ed.). New York: Teachers College Press, 1975.

RUSTED, JENNIFER, & COLTHEART, MAX. Facilitation of children's prose recall by the presence of pictures. *Memory & Cognition,* September 1979, *7,* 354–359.

RUTTER, MICHAEL. Syndromes attributed to "minimal brain dysfunction" in childhood. *American Journal of Psychiatry,* January 1982, *139,* 21–33.

RYAN, ELLEN B. Identifying and remediating failures in reading comprehension: Toward an instructional approach for poor comprehenders. In G. MacKinnon & T. Waller (Eds.), *Reading research: Advances in theory and practice,* Vol. 3. New York: Academic Press, 1981. Pp. 223–261.

RYAN, JOHN W. Linguistic factors in adult literacy. In J. Kavanagh & R. Venezky (Eds.), *Orthography, reading, and dyslexia.* Baltimore: University Park Press, 1980. Pp. 105–120.

RYCKMAN, DAVID B. Searching for a WISC-R profile for learning disabled children: An inappropriate task? *Journal of Learning Disabilities,* November 1981, *14,* 508–511.

RYDER, RANDALL J. Mapping techniques as study skills. *Wisconsin State Reading Association Journal,* Spring 1982, *26,* 7–10.

RYDER, RANDALL J., & GRAVES, MICHAEL F. Secondary students' internalization of letter-sound correspondences. *Journal of Educational Research,* 1980, *73,* 172–178.

SABATINO, DAVID A., & MILLER, TED L. The dilemma of diagnosis in learning disabilities: Problems and potential directions. *Psychology in the Schools,* 1980, *17* (1), 76–86.

SADOW, MARILYN W. The use of story grammar in the design of questions. *The Reading Teacher,* February 1982, *35,* 518–522.

SADOWSKI, MARK C. Ten years of uninterrupted sustained silent reading. *Reading Improvement,* Summer 1980, *17,* 153–156.

SADOWSKI, MARK. An exploratory study of the relationship between reported imagery and the comprehension and recall of a story. *Reading Research Quarterly,* Fall 1983, *19,* 110–123.

SAFFRAN, ELEANOR M., & MARIN, OSCAR S. M. Reading without phonology: Evidence from aphasia. *Quarterly Journal of Experimental Psychology,* 1977, *29,* 515–525.

SAGER, CAROL. *Secondary reading practices in New England: Results of a six-state survey.* New England Reading Association, 1980.

SAKAMOTO, TAKAHIKO. Writing systems in Japan. In J. E. Merritt (Ed.), *New horizons in reading.* Newark, DE: International Reading Association, 1976. Pp. 244–249.

SAKAMOTO, TAKAHIKO. Reading of hiragana. In J. Kavanagh & R. Venezky (Eds.), *Orthography, reading, and dyslexia.* Baltimore: University Park Press, 1980. Pp. 15–24.

SAKAMOTO, TAKAHIKO. Beginning reading in Japan. In L. Ollila (Ed.), *Beginning reading instruction in different countries.* Newark, DE: International Reading Association, 1981. Pp. 16–25.

SALEND, SPENCER J. Self-assessment: A model for involving students in the formulation of their IEPs. *Journal of School Psychology,* Spring 1983, *21,* 65–70.

SALEND, SPENCER J., & MOE, L. Modifying nonhandicapped students' attitudes toward their handicapped peers through children's literature. *Journal of Special Education,* 1983, *19,* 22–28.

SALTZ, ROSALYN. Children's interpretation of proverbs. *Language Arts,* May 1979, *56,* 508–514.

SAMPSON, MICHAEL R. A comparison of the complexity of children's dictation and instructional reading materials. In J. Niles & L. A. Harris (Eds.), *New inquiries in reading research and instruction.* Rochester, NY: National Reading Conference, 1982. Pp. 177–179.

SAMUELS, S. JAY. The method of repeated readings. *The Reading Teacher,* January 1979, *32,* 403–408.

SAMUELS, S. JAY. The effect of letter name knowledge on learning to read. *American Educational Research Journal,* Winter 1972, *9,* 65–74.

SAMUELS, S. JAY. Effect of distinctive feature training on paired associate learning. *Journal of Educational Psychology,* April 1973, *64,* 147–158. (a)

SAMUELS, S. JAY. Success and failure in learning to read: A critique of the research. *Reading Research Quarterly,* Winter 1973, *8,* 200–239. (b)

SAMUELS, S. JAY. Automatic decoding and reading comprehension. *Language Arts,* March 1976, *53,* 323–328. (a)

SAMUELS, S. JAY. Hierarchical subskills in the reading acquisition process. In J. T. Guthrie (Ed.), *Aspects of reading acquisition.* Baltimore: Johns Hopkins University Press, 1976. Pp. 141–161. (b)

SAMUELS, S. JAY. Can pictures distract students from the printed word: A rebuttal. *Journal of Reading Behavior,* Winter 1977, *9,* 361–364. (a)

SAMUELS, S. JAY. Introduction to theoretical models of reading. In W. Otto *et al.* (Eds.), *Reading problems: A multidisciplinary perspective.* Reading, MA: Addison-Wesley, 1977. Pp. 7–41. (b)

SAMUELS, S. JAY. The age-old controversy between holistic and subskill approaches to beginning reading instruction revisited. In C. McCullough (Ed.), *Inchworm, inchworm: Persistent problems in reading education*. Newark, DE: International Reading Association, 1980. Pp. 202–221.

SAMUELS, S. JAY. Some essentials of decoding. *Exceptional Education Quarterly*, May 1981, 2, 11–25.

SAMUELS, S. JAY. Diagnosing reading problems. *Topics in Learning and Learning Disabilities*, January 1983, 2, 1–11.

SAMUELS, S. JAY, & DAHL, PATRICIA R. Establishing appropriate purpose for reading and its effect on flexibility of reading rate. *Journal of Educational Psychology*, 1975, 67, 38–43.

SAMUELS, S. JAY, & EISENBERG, PETER. A framework for understanding the reading process. In F. Pirozzolo & M. Wittrock (Eds.), *Neuropsychological and cognitive processes in reading*. New York: Academic Press, 1981. Pp. 31–67.

SANACORE, JOSEPH. Guidelines for observing remedial reading lessons. *The Reading Teacher*, January 1981, 34, 394–399.

SANACORE, JOSEPH. Improving reading through prior knowledge and writing. *Journal of Reading*, May 1983, 26, 714–720.

SANACORE, JOSEPH. Metacognition and the improvement of reading: Some important links. *Journal of Reading*, May 1984, 27, 706–712.

SANDOVAL, JONATHAN. Hyperactive children: 12 ways to help them in the classroom. *Academic Therapy*, September 1982, 18, 107–113.

SANDOVAL, JONATHAN, & HUGHES, RENEE G. *Success in nonpromoted first grade children: Final report*. Davis, CA: University of California. Bethesda, MD: National Institute of Mental Health, 1981. ED 212 371

SARTAIN, HARRY W. The research base for individualized reading instruction. In J. A. Figurel (Ed.), *Reading and realism*. Newark, DE: International Reading Association, 1969. Pp. 523–530.

SARTAIN, HARRY W. Research summary: Family contributions to reading attainment. In H. Sartain (Ed.), *Mobilizing family forces for worldwide reading success*. Newark, DE: International Reading Association, 1981. Pp. 4–18.

SATZ, PAUL. Cerebral dominance and reading disability: An old problem revisited. In R. M. Knights & D. J. Bakker (Eds.), *The neuropsychology of learning disorders*. Baltimore: University Park Press, 1976. Pp. 273–294.

SATZ, PAUL, & FLETCHER, J. M. Early screening tests: Some uses and abuses. *Journal of Learning Disabilities*, January 1979, 12, 56–60.

SATZ, PAUL, & MORRIS, ROBIN. Learning disability subtypes: A review. In F. Pirozzolo & M. Wittrock (Eds.), *Neuropsychological and cognitive processes in reading*. New York: Academic Press, 1981. Pp. 109–141.

SATZ, PAUL, *et al.* Some developmental and predictive precursors of reading disabilities: A six-year follow-up. In A. Benton & D. Pearl (Eds.), *Dyslexia: An appraisal of current knowledge*. New York: Oxford University Press, 1978. Pp. 313–348.

SAUER, FREDA M. The determination of reading instructional level of disabled fourth grade readers utilizing cloze testing procedure. Unpublished doctoral dissertation, Oklahoma State University, 1969.

SAULS, CHARLES W. The relationship of selected factors to the recreational reading of sixth grade students. Unpublished doctoral dissertation, Louisiana State University and Agriculture and Mechanical College, 1971.

SCHACHTER, SUMNER W. Developing flexible reading rates. *Journal of Reading*, November 1978, 29, 149–152. Also in A. J. Harris & E. Sipay (Eds.), *Readings on reading instruction* (3rd ed.). New York: Longman, 1984. Pp. 402–404.

SCHADLER, MARGARET, & THISSEN, DAVID M. The development of automatic word recognition and reading skill. *Memory & Cognition*, March 1981, 9, 132–141.

SCHALE, FLORENCE C. Using special methods of learning, grades IX through XIV. In H. A. Robinson (Ed.), *Individual differences in reading*, Supplementary Educational Monograph No. 91. Chicago: University of Chicago Press, 1964. Pp. 41–44.

SCHALE, FLORENCE. Vertical methods of increasing rates of comprehension. *Journal of Reading*, April 1965, *8*, 296–300.

SCHALE, FLORENCE C. Exploring the potential of the monocularly blind for faster reading. *Academic Therapy*, Summer 1972, *7*, 401–410.

SCHALLBERT, DIANE L. The role of illustrations in reading comprehension. In R. Spiro *et al.* (Eds.), *Theoretical issues in reading comprehension*. Hillsdale, NJ: LEA, 1980. Pp. 503–524.

SCHALLERT, DIANE L., KLEIMAN, GLENN M., & RUBIN, ANN D. Analysis of differences between written and oral language. Technical Report No. 29. Champaign, IL: Center for the Study of Reading, University of Illinois, 1977.

SCHALLERT, DIANE L., & TIERNEY, ROBERT J. *Learning from expository test: The interaction of text structure with reader characteristics*. Champaign, IL: Center for the Study of Reading, University of Illinois, August 1982. Mimeographed report. NIE–G–79–0167.

SCHANK, ROGER C. *Reading and understanding: Teaching from the perspective of artificial intelligence*. Hillsdale, NJ: LEA, 1982.

SCHEERER-NEUMANN, GERHEID. The utilization of intraword structure in poor readers: Experimental evidence and a training program. *Psychological Research*, 1981, *43*, 155–178.

SCHEIRER, MARY ANN, & KRAUT, ROBERT E. Increasing educational achievement via self-concept change. *Review of Educational Research*, Winter 1979, *49*, 131–150.

SCHELL, LEO M. Teaching decoding to remedial readers. *The Reading Teacher*, May 1978, *31*, 877–882.

SCHELL, LEO M. (Ed.). *Diagnostic and criterion-referenced reading tests: Review and evaluation*. Newark, DE: International Reading Association, 1981.

SCHELL, LEO M. How accurate are oral reading tests? *Reading World*, December 1982, *22*, 91–97.

SCHELL, LEO M., & HANNA, GERALD S. Can informal reading inventories reveal strengths and weaknesses in comprehension subskills? *The Reading Teacher*, December 1981, *35*, 263–268.

SCHELL, VICKIE J. Learning partners: Reading and mathematics. *The Reading Teacher*, February 1982, *35*, 544–548.

SCHENK-DANZIGER, LOTTE. Probleme der legasthenie. *Schweizerische Zeitschrift fur Psychologie und Ihre Anwendungen*, 1960, *20*, 29–48.

SCHILKOWSKY, CARL, *et al.* Extending Schuyler's program. *Journal of Reading*, March 1983, *26*, 550–552.

SCHLIEF, MABEL, & WOOD, ROBERT W. A comparison of procedures to determine readability level of non-text materials. *Reading Improvement*, Fall 1974, *11*, 57–64.

SCHMITT, CLARA. Developmental alexia: Congenital word-blindness or inability to learn to read. *Elementary School Journal*, 1918, *18*, 680–700, 757–769.

SCHNAYER, SIDNEY W. Some relations between reading interest and reading comprehension. Unpublished doctoral dissertation, University of California at Berkeley, 1967.

SCHNEYER, J. WESLEY, & COWEN, SHEILA. *Comparison of a basal reader approach and linguistic approach in second and third grade reading instruction*. Final Report, Project 5–0601. Philadelphia: University of Pennsylvania, 1968.

SCHON, ISABEL. *A bicultural heritage: Themes for the exploration of Mexican and Mexican-American culture through books for children and adolescents*. Metuchen, NJ: Scarecrow Press, 1977.

SCHON, ISABEL. Recent notorious and noteworthy books about Mexico, Mexicans and Mexican-Americans. *Journal of Reading*, January 1981, *24*, 293–299.

SCHONHAUT, STEVEN, & SATZ, PAUL. Prognosis of the learning disabled child: A review of the followup studies. In M. Rutter (Ed.), *Behavioral syndromes of brain dysfunction in childhood*. New York: Guilford Press, 1983.

SCHORK, EDWARD J., & MILLER, STEPHEN C. Courts and public education: Possibilities and limits. In R. J. Harper & G. Killar (Eds.), *Reading and the law*. Newark, DE: International Reading Association, 1978. Pp. 1–9.

SCHRANK, FREDERICK A., ENGELS, DENNIS W., & SILKE, JAMES R. Using bibliotherapy in the elementary school: What does the research say? *Wisconsin State Reading Association Journal*, Winter 1983, *27*, 23–29.

SCHREIBER, PETER A. On the acquisition of fluency. *Journal of Reading Behavior*, Fall 1980, *12*, 177–186.

SCHUBERT, DELWYN G., & WALTON, HOWARD N. Visual screening—A new breakthrough. *The Reading Teacher*, November 1980, *34*, 175–177.

SCHULTE, EMERITA S. Independent reading interests of children in grades 4, 5, and 6. In J. A. Figurel (Ed.), *Reading and realism*. Newark, DE: International Reading Association, 1969. Pp. 728–732.

SCHULTHEIS, SISTER MIRIAM. *A guidebook for bibliotherapy*. Glenview, IL: Psychotechnics, 1972.

SCHULTZ, A. J. An investigation of the role of interest as a factor in reading comprehension. Unpublished master's thesis, Rutgers University 1975. ED 116 152

SCHUYLER, MICHAEL R. A readability formula program for use on microcomputers. *Journal of Reading*, March 1982, *25*, 560–591.

SCHWANTES, FREDERICK M. Effect of story context on children's ongoing word recognition. *Journal of Reading Behavior*, Winter 1981, *13*, 305–311.

SCHWORM, RONALD W. Hyperkinesis: Myth, mystery, and matter. *Journal of Special Education*, Summer 1982, *16*, 129–148.

SEARLEMAN, A. A review of right-hemisphere linguistic capabilities. *Psychological Bulletin*, 1977, *84*, 503–522.

SEAVER, JOANN T., & BOTEL, MORTON. A first-grade teacher teaches reading, writing, and oral communication across the curriculum. *The Reading Teacher*, March 1983, *36*, 656–664.

SEBESTA, SAM L. Choosing poetry. In N. Roser & M. Frith (Eds.), *Children's choices: Teaching with books children like*. Newark, DE: International Reading Association, 1983. Pp. 66–78.

SEIFERT, MARY (Comp.). *Graduate programs and faculty in reading* (3rd ed.). Newark, DE: International Reading Association, 1978.

SEITZ, VICTORIA. *Social class and ethnic group differences in learning to read*. Newark, DE: International Reading Association, 1977.

SELDEN, RAMSEY. On the validation of the original readability formulas. In A. Davison *et al.* (Eds.), *Text readability: Proceedings of the March 1980 Conference*. Technical Report No. 213. Champaign, IL: Center for the Study of Reading, University of Illinois, August 1981. Pp. 10–26.

SERAFICA, FELICISIMA C., & HARWAY, NORMAN I. Social relations and self-esteem of children with learning disabilities. *Journal of Clinical Child Psychology*, Fall 1979, 8, 227–233.

SHAFER, GARY F. An investigation of the relationship of selected components of readability and comprehension at the secondary school level. In P. D. Pearson & J. Hansen (Eds.), *Reading: Theory, research and practice*. Clemson, SC: National Reading Conference, 1977. Pp. 244–252.

SHANAHAN, TIMOTHY, & HOGAN, VIRGINIA. Parent reading style and children's print awareness. In J. Niles & L. A. Harris (Eds.), *Searches for meaning in reading/language processing and instruction*. Rochester, NY: National Reading Conference, 1983. Pp. 212–217.

SHANAHAN, TIMOTHY, & KAMIL, MICHAEL. The sensitivity of cloze to passage organization. In J. Niles & L. A. Harris (Eds.), *New inquiries in reading research and instruction*. Rochester, NY: National Reading Conference, 1982. Pp. 204–208.

SHANAHAN, TIMOTHY, & KAMIL, MICHAEL L. A further comparison of sensitivity of cloze and recall to passage organization. In J. Niles & L. A. Harris (Eds.), *Search for meaning in reading/language processing and instruction*. Rochester, NY: National Reading Conference, 1983. Pp. 123–128.

SHANAHAN, TIMOTHY, KAMIL, MICHAEL L., & TOBIN, AILEEN W. Cloze as a measure of intersentential comprehension. *Reading Research Quarterly*, 1982, *17* (2), 229–255.

SHANE, HAROLD G. The expanding role of oral reading in school and life activities. In H. M. Robinson (Ed.), *Oral aspects of reading*. Supplementary Educational Monographs, No. 82. Chicago: University of Chicago Press, 1955. Pp. 1–4.

SHANKER, JAMES L. *Guidelines for successful staff development*. Newark, DE: International Reading Association, 1982.

SHANKWEILER, DONALD, & LIBERMAN, ISABELLE Y. Misreading: A search for causes. In J. F. Kavanagh & I. G. Mattingly (Eds.), *Language by ear and by eye*. Cambridge, MA: MIT Press, 1972. Pp. 293–317.

SHANKWEILER, DONALD, LIBERMAN, ISABELLE Y., & MARK, LEONARD S. Phonetic coding in dyslexics and normal readers by Hall, Ewing, Tinzmann, and Wilson: A reply. *Bulletin of the Psychometric Society*, February 1982, *19*, 78–79.

SHANKWEILER, DONALD, *et al.* The speech code and learning to read. *Journal of Experimental Psychology: Human Learning & Memory*, November 1979, *5*, 531–545.

SHANNON, PATRICK. A retrospective look at teachers' reliance on commercial reading materials. *Language Arts*, November/December 1982, *59*, 844–853.

SHAPIRA, Y. A., JONES, M. H., & SHERMAN, S. P. Abnormal eye movements in hyperkinetic children with learning disabilities. *Neurpädiatrie*, February 1980, *11*, 36–44.

SHAPIRO, JON E. Developing an awareness of attitudes. In J. Shapiro (Ed.), *Using literature and poetry effectively.* Newark, DE: International Reading Association, 1979. Pp. 2–7.

SHAVELSON, RICHARD J., & BORKO, HILDA. Research on teachers' decisions in planning instruction. *Educational Horizons*, Summer 1979, *57*, 183–189.

SHAVELSON, RICHARD J., & STERN, PAULA. Research on teachers' pedogological thoughts, judgments, decisions, and behavior. *Review of Educational Research*, Winter 1981, *51*, 455–498.

SHAW, JULES H. Vision and seeing skills of preschool children. *The Reading Teacher*, October 1964, *18*, 33–36.

SHAYON, ROBERT L. *Television and our children.* New York: Longman, Green, 1951. P. 29.

SHEBILSKE, WAYNE L., & FISHER, DENNIS F. Eye movements and context effects during reading of extended discourse. In K. Rayner (Ed.), *Eye movements in reading: Perceptual and language processes.* New York: Academic Press, 1983. Pp. 153–179.

SHELDON, WILLIAM, *et al.* Comparison of thee methods of teaching reading in the second grade. 1967. OEC 6-10-076, CRP-3231, ED 023 524

SHEPARD, LORRIE. An evaluation of the regression discrepancy method for identifying children with learning disabilities. *Journal of Special Education*, Spring 1980, *14*, 79–91.

SHEPARD, LORRIE. The role of measurement in educational policy: Lessons from the identification of learning disabilities. *Educational Measurement: Issues & Practice*, Fall 1983, *2*, 4–8.

SHEPARD, LORRIE A., SMITH, MARY LEE, & VOJIR, CAROL P. Characteristics of pupils identified as learning disabled. *American Educational Research Journal*, Fall 1983, *20*, 309–331.

SHEPARD, LORRIE, *et al. Evaluation of the identification of perceptual-communicative disorders in Colorado: Executive summary.* Boulder, CO: Laboratory of Educational Research, University of Colorado, 1981. Mimeographed.

SHERER, PETER A. Those mystifying metaphors: Students can read them. *Journal of Reading*, April 1977, *20*, 559–566.

SHERIDAN, E. MARCIA. Literacy and language reform in the People's Republic of China. *The Reading Teacher*, April 1981, *34*, 804–808.

SHERIDAN, E. MARCIA. Early reading in Japan. *Reading World*, May 1982, *21*, 326–332.

SHERZER, JOEL. The ethnography of speaking. In R. W. Shuy (Ed.), *Linguistic theory: What can it say about reading?* Newark, DE: International Reading Association, 1977. Pp. 144–152.

SHIMADA, MUTSUO. Kana and Kanji processing in Japanese with special reference to functional hemisphere specialization. *Tohoku Psychologica Folia*, 1981, *40* (1–4), 24–34.

SHORES, HARLAN J., & HUSBANDS, KENNETH L. Are fast readers the best readers? *Elementary English*, 1950, *27*, 52–57.

SHOUP, BARBARA. Television: Friend, not foe of the teacher. *Journal of Reading*, April 1984, *27*, 629–631.

SHUCK, ANNETTE, ULSH, FLORENCE, & PLATT, JOHN S. Parents encouraging pupils (PEP): An innercity parent involvement reading project. *The Reading Teacher*, February 1983, *36*, 324–328.

SHUY, ROGER W. The mismatch of child language and school language: Implications for beginning reading instruction. In L. Resnick & P. Weaver (Eds.), *Theory and practice of early reading*, Vol. 1. Hillsdale, NJ: LEA, 1979. Pp. 187–207.

SHUY, ROGER W. Four misconceptions about clarity and simplicity. *Language Arts*, May 1981, *58*, 557–561. (a)

SHUY, ROGER W. A holististic view of language. *Research in the Teaching of English*, May 1981, *15*, 101–111. (b)

SHUY, ROGER W. What the teacher knows is more important than text or test. *Language Arts*, November/December 1981, *58*, 919–929. (c)

SHUY, ROGER W. What should the language strand in a reading program contain? *The Reading Teacher*, April 1982, *35*, 806–812.

SHWEDEL, ALLAN M. Must we use phonology to read? What Chinese can tell us. *Journal of Reading*, May 1983, *26*, 707–713.

SIEBEN, ROBERT L. Controversial medical treatments of learning disabilities. *Academic Therapy*, November 1977, *13*, 133–147.

SIEDOW, MARY D., & FOX, BARBARA J. Effect of training on good and poor readers' use of top-level structure. *Reading World*, May 1984, *23*, 340–346.

SIEGEL, MARY-ELLEN K. *Her way: A guide to biographies of women for young people.* Chicago: ALA, 1984.

SILBERBERG, NORMAN E., & SILBERBERG, MARGARET C. A note on reading tests and their roles in defining reading difficulties. *Journal of Learning Disabilities*, February 1977, *10*, 100–103.

SILVER, ARCHIE A., & HAGIN, ROSA A. *SEARCH: A scanning instrument for the identification of potential learning disability* (2nd ed.). New York: Walker, 1981.

SILVER, ARCHIE A., & HAGIN, ROSA A. A unifying concept for the neuropsychological organization of children with reading disabilities. *Journal of Developmental and Behavioral Pediatrics*, September 1982, *3*, 127–132.

SILVER, L. B. Acceptable and controversial approaches to treating the child with learning disabilities. *Pediatrics*, 1975, *55*, 406–415.

SILVERSTON, RANDALL, & DEICHMANN, JOHN W. Sense modality research and the acquisition of reading skills. *Review of Educational Research*, Winter 1975, *45*, 149–172.

SIMMONS, BEATRICE (Ed.). *Paperback books for children.* Chicago: American Library Association, 1972.

SIMONS, HERBERT D. Reading comprehension: The need for a new perspective. *Reading Research Quarterly*, Spring 1971, *6*, 338–363.

SIMONS, HERBERT D., & JOHNSON, KENNETH R. Black English syntax reading interference. *Research in the Teaching of English*, Winter 1974, *8*, 339–358.

SIMS, RUDINE. Miscue analysis: Emphasis on comprehension. In R. E. Shafer (Ed.), *Applied linguistics and reading.* Newark, DE: International Reading Association, 1979. Pp. 101–111.

SINDELAR, PAUL T., & MEISEL, C. JULIUS. Teacher-physician interaction in the treatment of children with behavioral disorders. *International Journal of Partial Hospitalization*, July 1982, *1*, 271–277.

SINGER, HARRY. The SEER technique: A non-computation procedure for quickly estimating readability level. *Journal of Reading Behavior*, Fall 1975, *7*, 255–267.

SINGER, HARRY. Theoretical models of reading. In H. Singer & R. B. Ruddell (Eds.), *Theoretical models and processes of reading* (2nd ed.). Newark, DE: International Reading Association, 1976. Pp. 634–654.

SINGER, HARRY. IQ is and is not related to reading. In S. Wanat (Ed.), *Issues in evaluating reading.* Arlington, VA: Center for Applied Linguistics, 1977. Pp. 43–55.

SINGER, HARRY (Reviewer). Reading miscue inventory. In O. K. Buros (Ed.), *Eighth mental measurements yearbook*, Vol. II. Highland Park, NJ: Gryphon Press, 1978. Pp. 1319–1322. (a)

SINGER, HARRY. Research in reading that should make a difference in classroom instruction. In S. J. Samuels (Ed.), *What research has to say about reading instruction.* Newark, DE: International Reading Association, 1978. Pp. 57–71. (b)

SINGER, HARRY. Active comprehension: From answering to asking questions. *The Reading Teacher*, May 1978, *31*, 901–908. (c). Also in C. McCullough (Ed.), *Inchworm, inchworm: Persistent problems in reading education.* Newark, DE: International Reading Association, 1980. Pp. 222–232. (a)

SINGER, HARRY. Sight word learning with and without pictures: A critique of Arlin, Scott, and Webster's research. *Reading Research Quarterly*, 1980, *15* (2), 290–298. (b)

SINGER, HARRY. Hypothesis on reading comprehension in search of classroom validation. In M. Kamil & M. Boswick (Eds.), *Directions in reading: Research and instruction.* Washington, DC: National Reading Conference, 1981. Pp. 1–20. (a)

SINGER, HARRY. Teaching the acquisition phase of reading development: An historical perspective. In O. Tzeng & H. Singer (Eds.), *Perception of print: Reading research in experimental psychology.* Hillsdale, NJ: LEA, 1981. Pp. 9–28. (b)

SINGER, HARRY, & DONLAN, DAN. *Reading and learning from text.* Boston: Little, Brown, 1980.

SINGER, HARRY, & DONLAN, DAN. Active comprehension: Problem-solving schema with question generation for comprehension of complex short stories. *Reading Research Quarterly*, 1982, *17* (2), 166–186.

SINGER, HARRY, & RUDDELL, ROBERT B. (Eds.), *Theoretical models and processes of reading* (2nd ed.). Newark, DE: International Reading Association, 1976.

SINGER, MARTIN H. Context use and reading disability. In M. Singer (Ed.), *Competent reader, disabled reader: Research and application*. Hillsdale, NJ: LEA, 1982. Pp. 55–68. (a)

SINGER, MARTIN H. Competent reading: A laboratory description. In M. Singer (Ed.), *Competent reader, disabled reader: Research and application*. Hillsdale NJ: LEA, 1982. Pp. 3–31. (b)

SINGER, MARTIN H. Insensitivity to ordered information and the failure to read. In M. Singer (Ed.), *Competent reader, disabled reader: Research and application*. Hillsdale, NJ: LEA, 1982. Pp. 69–80. (c)

SINGER, MARTIN H. Perceptual learning: Letter discrimination and orthographic knowledge. In M. Singer (Ed.), *Competent reader, disabled reader: Research and application*. Hillsdale, NJ: LEA, 1982. Pp. 151–158. (d)

SIPAY, EDWARD R. A comparison of standardized reading test scores and functional reading levels. *The Reading Teacher*, January 1964, *17*, 265–268.

SIPAY, EDWARD R. Interpreting the USOE cooperative reading studies. *The Reading Teacher*, October 1968, *22*, 10–16.

SIPAY, EDWARD R. Determining word identification difficulties. In B. Bateman (Ed.), *Learning disorders*, Vol. 4. Seattle: Special Child Publications, 1971. Pp. 215–247.

SIPAY, EDWARD R. Manual for the *Sipay Word Analysis Tests*. Cambridge, MA: EPS, 1973.

SIPERSTEIN, GARY N., BOPP, MICHAEL J., & BAK, JOHN J. Social status of learning disabled children. *Journal of Learning Disabilities*, February 1978, *11*, 98–102.

SITTIG, LINDA H. Involving parents and children in reading for fun. *The Reading Teacher*, November 1982, *36*, 166–168.

SLINGERLAND, BETH H. *A multi-sensory approach to language arts for specific language disability children: A guide for primary teachers*. Cambridge, MA: EPS, 1976.

SMARDO, FRANCES A. Using children's literature to clarify science concepts in early childhood programs. *The Reading Teacher*, December 1982, *36*, 267–273.

SMILANSKI, SARAH. Preventing accumulative learning deficits of disadvantaged children through reading instruction in kindergarten. Unpublished paper, University of Haifa, 1978.

SMILEY, SANDRA S., PASQUALE, FRANK L., & CHANDLER, CHRISTINE L. The pronunciation of familiar, unfamiliar, and synthetic words by good and poor adolescent readers. *Journal of Reading Behavior*, Fall 1976, 8, 289–297.

SMITH, DEBORAH D. The improvement of children's oral reading through the use of teacher modeling. *Journal of Learning Disabilities*, March 1979, *12*, 172–175.

SMITH, DON A., & WILBORN, BOBBIE L. Specific predictors of learning difficulties. *Academic Therapy*, Summer 1977, *12*, 471–477.

SMITH, DONALD E. P., & CARRIGAN, PATRICIA M. *The nature of reading disability*. New York: Harcourt Brace, 1959.

SMITH, E. A., & KINCAID, J. P. Derivation and validation of the Automated Readability Index for use with technical materials. *Human Factors*, 1970, *12*, 457–464.

SMITH, EDWARD E., & KLEIMAN, GLENN M. Word recognition: Theoretical issues and instructional hints. In L. Resnick & P. Weaver (Eds.), *Theory and practice in early reading*, Vol. 2. Hillsdale, NJ: LEA, 1979. Pp. 67–90.

SMITH, FRANK. *Understanding reading: A psycholinguistic analysis of reading and learning to read* (2nd ed.). New York: Holt, Rinehart and Winston, 1971, 1978.

SMITH, FRANK. *Comprehension and learning: A conceptual framework for teachers*. New York: Holt, Rinehart and Winston, 1975.

SMITH, FRANK. Learning to read by reading. *Language Arts*, March 1976, *53*, 297–299, 322.

SMITH, FRANK. Making sense of reading and of reading instruction. *Harvard Educational Review*, August 1977, *47*, 386–395.

SMITH, FRANK. *Reading without nonsense*. New York: Teachers College Press, 1978.

SMITH, FRANK. Conflicting approaches to reading research and instruction. In L. Resnick & P. Weaver (Eds.), *Theory and practice of early reading*, Vol. 2. Hillsdale, NJ: LEA, 1979. Pp. 31–42.

SMITH, FRANK. Reading like a writer. *Language Arts*, May 1983, *60*, 558–567.

SMITH, FRANK, & GOODMAN, KENNETH S. On the psycholinguistic method of teaching reading. *Elementary School Journal*, January 1971, *71*, 177–181.

SMITH, FREDERICK R., & FEATHERS, KAREN M. The role of reading in content classrooms: Assumptions vs. realities. *Journal of Reading*, December 1983, *27*, 262–267.

SMITH, JEFFREY K. Converging on correct answers: A peculiarity of multiple choice items. *Journal of Educational Measurement*, Fall 1982, *19*, 211–220.

SMITH, KENNETH. Intellectual and academic freedom: Issues and strategies for reading educators. *The Reading Teacher*, February 1982, *35*, 574–577.

SMITH, LAWRENCE L., *et al.* Using grade level vs. out-of-level reading tests with remedial students. *The Reading Teacher*, February 1983, *36*, 550–553.

SMITH, MARILYN, & BEAN, THOMAS W. Four strategies that develop children's story comprehension and writing. *The Reading Teacher*, December 1983, *37*, 295–301.

SMITH, MARY LEE, & GLASS, GENE V. Meta-analysis of research on class size and its relationship to attitudes and instruction. *American Educational Research Journal*, Winter 1980, *17*, 419–433.

SMITH, NILA B. *American reading instruction* (rev. ed.). Newark, DE: International Reading Association, 1965.

SMITH, NILA B. The quest for increased reading competency. In H. A. Klein (Ed.), *The quest for competency in teaching reading*. Newark, DE: International Reading Association, 1972. Pp. 45–56.

SMITH, PHILIP A., & MARK, RONALD W. Some cautions on the use of the Frostig test: A factor analytic study. *Journal of Learning Disabilities*, June/July 1972, *5*, 357–362.

SMITH, RICHARD J., & BARRETT, THOMAS C. *Teaching reading in the middle grades*. Reading, MA: Addison-Wesley, 1974.

SMITH, SHELLEY D., *et al.* Specific reading disability: Identification of an inherited form through linkage analysis. *Science*, March 18, 1983, *219*, 1345–1347.

SMITH, WILLIAM. Intermittent eye malfunctions and their effect on reading. *The Reading Teacher*, March 1984, *37*, 570–576.

SMITH, WILLIAM E., & BECK, MICHAEL D. Determining instructional reading level with the 1978 Metropolitan Achievement Tests. *The Reading Teacher*, December 1980, *34*, 313–319.

SMITH, WILLIAM L. Cloze procedure [Ebbinghaus completion method] as applied to reading. In O. K. Buros (Ed.), *Eighth mental measurements yearbook*, Vol. II. Highland Park, NJ: Gryphon Press, 1978. Pp. 1176–1178.

SMITH, WILLIAM L., & COMBS, WARREN E. The effects of overt and covert cues on written syntax. *Research in the Teaching of English*, February 1980, *14*, 19–38.

SNOWLING, MARGARET J. The development of grapheme-phoneme correspondence in normal and dyslexic readers. *Journal of Experimental Child Psychology*, April 1980, *29*, 294–305.

SNYDER, GERALDINE V. Learner verification of reading games. *The Reading Teacher*, March 1981, *34*, 686–691.

SOAR, R. S. Problems in analyzing process-product relationship in studies of teacher effectiveness. *Journal of Education*, August 1978, *160*, 96–116.

SOLAN, HAROLD A. A rationale for the optometric treatment and management of children with learning disabilities. *Journal of Learning Disabilities*, December 1981, *14*, 568–572.

SOLOMON, BERNARD. The television reading program. *Language Arts*, February 1976, *53*, 135–136.

SOMERS, ALBERT B., & WORTHINGTON, JANET E. *Response guides for teaching children's books*. Urbana, IL: National Council of Teachers of English, 1979.

SOMMERVILLE, MARY ANN. Dialect and reading: A review of alternative solutions. *Review of Educational Research*, Spring 1975, *45*, 247–262.

SOWDER-THREADGILL, JUDITH, *et al.* A case against telegraphing story problems for poor readers. *The Reading Teacher*, April 1984, *37*, 746–748.

SPACHE, EVELYN B. *Reading activities for child involvement* (2nd ed.). Boston: Allyn & Bacon, 1976.

SPACHE, GEORGE. A new readability formula for primary-grade reading materials. *Elementary School Journal*, March 1953, *53*, 410–413.

SPACHE, GEORGE D. Is this a breakthrough in reading? *The Reading Teacher*, 1962, *15*, 258–263.

SPACHE, GEORGE D. *Good reading for poor readers*. Champaign, IL: Garrard, 1974, 1978.

SPACHE, GEORGE D. *Good reading for the disadvantaged reader: Multi-ethnic resources*. Champaign, IL: Garrard, 1975.

SPANGLER, KATHERINE L. Reading interests vs. reading preferences: Using the research. *The Reading Teacher*, May 1983, *36*, 876–878.

SPEARRITT, DONALD. Identification of subskills and reading comprehension by maximum likelihood factor analysis. *Reading Research Quarterly*, Fall 1972, *8*, 92–111.

SPEARRITT, DONALD. *Measuring reading comprehension in the upper primary school*. Canberra, Australia: Government Publishing Service, 1977.

SPEARRITT, DONALD. Measuring reading comprehension in the upper primary school. *Australian Journal of Reading*, June 1980, *3*, 67–75.

SPERRY, R. W., GAZZANIGA, M. S., & BOGEN, J. H. Interhemispheric relationships: The neocortical commissures: Syndromes of hemisphere disconnection. In R. Vinken & G. Brown (Eds.), *Handbook of Clinical Neurology*, Vol. 4, New York: John Wiley & Sons, 1969. Pp. 273–290.

SPIEGEL, DIXIE LEE. Desirable teaching behaviors for effective instruction in reading. *The Reading Teacher*, December 1980, *34*, 324–330.

SPIEGEL, DIXIE LEE. *Reading for pleasure: Guidelines*. Newark, DE: International Reading Association & ERIC/RCS, 1981. (a)

SPIEGEL, DIXIE LEE. Six alternatives to the Directed Reading Activity. *The Reading Teacher*, May 1981, *34*, 914–920. (b). Also in A. J. Harris & E. Sipay (Eds.), *Readings on reading instruction* (3rd ed.). New York: Longman, 1984. Pp. 391–396.

SPIRO, RAND J. Etiology of reading comprehension style. Technical Report No. 124. Champaign, IL: Center for the Study of Reading, University of Illinois, 1979.

SPREEN, OTFRIED. Adult outcomes of reading disorders. In R. Malatesha & P. Aaron (Eds.), *Reading disorders: Varieties and treatments*. New York: Academic Press, 1982. Pp. 473–498.

SPRING, CARL, BLUNDEN, DALE, & GATHERAL, MARYANN. Effect on reading comprehension of training to automaticity in word reading. *Perceptual & Motor Skills*, December 1981, *53*, 779–786.

SPRING, CARL, & SANDOVAL, JONATHAN. Food additives and hyperkinesis: A critical evaluation of the evidence. *Journal of Learning Disabilities*, November 1976, *9*, 560–569.

SQUIRE, JAMES R. Instructional focus and the teaching of writing. Ginn Occasional Papers, No. 1. Columbus, OH: Ginn, November 1980.

STAHL, STEVEN. Differential word knowledge and reading comprehension. *Journal of Reading Behavior*, 1983, *15* (4), 33–50.

STAKE, JAYNE E., & KATZ, JONATHAN F. Teacher-pupil relationships in the elementary school classrooms: Teacher-gender and pupil-gender differences. *American Educational Research Journal*, Fall 1982, *19*, 465–471.

STALLARD, CATHY. Comparing objective-based reading programs. *Journal of Reading*, October 1977, *21*, 36–44.

STANCHFIELD, JO M., & FRAIM, SUSAN R. A follow-up study on the reading interests of boys. *Journal of Reading*, May 1979, *22*, 748–752.

STANLEY, JULIAN C. (Ed.). *Preschool programs for the disadvantaged*. Baltimore: Johns Hopkins University Press, 1972.

STANOVICH, KEITH E. Toward an interactive-compensatory model of individual differences in development of reading fluency. *Reading Research Quarterly*, 1980, *16* (1), 32–71.

STANOVICH, KEITH E. Individual differences in the cognitive processes of reading: I. Word decoding, *Journal of Learning Disabilities*, October 1982, *15*, 485–493. (a)

STANOVICH, KEITH E. Individual differences in the cognitive processes of reading: II. Text-level processing. *Journal of Learning Disabilities*, November 1982, *15*, 549–554. (b)

STANOVICH, KEITH E. Word recognition skill and reading ability. In M. Singer (Ed.), *Competent reader, disabled reader: Research and application*. Hillsdale, NJ: LEA, 1982. Pp. 81–102. (c)

STANOVICH, KEITH E., CUNNINGHAM, ANNE E., & FEEMAN, DOROTHY J. Intelligence, cognitive skills, and early reading progress. *Reading Research Quarterly*, Spring 1984, *19*, 278–303.

STANOVICH, KEITH E., CUNNINGHAM, ANNE E., & WEST, RICHARD F. A longitudinal study of the development of automatic recognition skills in first graders. *Journal of Reading Behavior*, Spring 1981, *13*, 57–74.

STAUFFER, RUSSELL G. A study of prefixes in the Thorndike list to establish a list of prefixes that should be taught in the elementary school. *Journal of Educational Research*, 1942, *35*, 453–458.

STAUFFER, RUSSELL G. (Ed.). *The first grade reading studies: Findings of individual investigations.* Newark, DE: International Reading Association, 1967.

STAUFFER, RUSSELL G. *Directing reading maturity as a cognitive process.* New York: Harper & Row, 1969.

STAUFFER, RUSSELL G. *The language-experience approach to the teaching of reading* (2nd ed.). New York: Harper & Row, 1980.

STAUFFER, RUSSELL G., & HAMMOND, W. DORSEY. The effectiveness of language arts and basic reader approaches to first-grade reading instruction—extended into third grade. *Reading Research Quarterly*, Summer 1969, *4*, 468–499.

STEIN, MIRIAM. Finger spelling: A kinesthetic aid in phonetic spelling. *Academic Therapy*, September 1982, *18*, 17–25.

STEIN, NANCY L., & TRABASSO, TOM. What's in a story: An approach to comprehension and instruction. Technical Report No. 200. Champaign, IL: Center for the Study of Reading, University of Illinois, April 1981.

STENSLAND, ANNA LEE. *Literature by and about the American Indian: An annotated bibliography* (2nd ed.). Urbana, IL: National Council of Teachers of English, 1979.

STERN, PAULA, & SHAVELSON, RICHARD J. Reading teachers' judgments, plans, and decision making. *The Reading Teacher*, December 1983, *37*, 280–286.

STERNBERG, LES, & TAYLOR, RONALD L. The insignificance of psycholinguistic training: A reply to Kavale. *Exceptional Children*, November 1982, *49*, 254–256.

STERNBERG, ROBERT J., & WAGNER, RICHARD K. Automation failure in learning disabilities. *Topics in Learning & Learning Disabilities*, July 1982, *2*, 1–11.

STETZ, F. P., & BECK, M. D. Attitudes toward standardized tests: Students, teachers, and measurement specialists. *Measurement in Education*, 1981, *12* (1), 1–11.

STEVENS, KATHLEEN. The effect of topic interest on the reading comprehension of higher ability students. *Journal of Educational Research*, July/August 1979, *73*, 365–368.

STEVENS, KATHLEEN C. Readability formulae and McCall–Crabbs Standard Test Lessons in Reading. *The Reading Teacher*, January 1980, *33*, 413–415.

STEVENS, KATHLEEN C. Chunking material as an aid to reading comprehension. *Journal of Reading*, November 1981, *25*, 126–129.

STEVENS, KATHLEEN C. Can we improve reading by teaching background information? *Journal of Reading*, January 1982, *25*, 326–329.

STEVENSON, HAROLD W. Orthography and reading disabilities. *Journal of Learning Disabilities*, May 1984, *17*, 296–301.

STEWART, ORAN, & GREEN, DAN S. Test-taking skills for standardized tests of reading. *The Reading Teacher*, March 1983, *36*, 634–638.

STEWIG, JOHN W., & SEBESTA, SAM L. (Eds.). *Using literature in the elementary classroom.* Urbana, IL: National Council of Teachers of English, 1978.

STICHT, THOMAS G. (Ed.). *Reading for working: A functional literacy anthology.* Alexandria, VA: Human Resources Research Organization, 1975.

STICHT, THOMAS G. Rate of comprehending by listening or reading. In J. Flood (Ed.), *Understanding reading comprehension.* Newark, DE: International Reading Association, 1984. Pp. 140–160.

STICHT, THOMAS G., & JAMES, JAMES H. Listening and reading. In P. D. Pearson (Ed.), *Handbook of reading research.* New York: Longman, 1984. Pp. 293–317.

STICHT, THOMAS G., et al. *Auding and reading: A developmental model.* Alexandria, VA: Human Resources Research Organization, 1974.

STIPEK, DEBORAH, & WEISZ, JOHN R. Perceived personal control and academic achievement. *Review of Educational Research*, Spring 1981, *51*, 101–137.

STONE, DAVID R. Speed of idea collecting. *Journal of Developmental Reading*, 1962, *5*, 149–156.

STONE, NORMAN M. Reversal errors in reading: Their diagnostic significance and implications for neuropsychological theories of reading disability. Unpublished doctoral dissertation, University of Iowa, 1976.

STONEHILL, ROBERT M., & ANDERSON, JUDITH I. An evaluation of ESEA Title I—Program operations and educational effects: A report to Congress. Washington, DC: U. S. Department of Education, March 1982. Mimeographed.

STOODT, BARBARA D. The relationship between understanding grammatical conjunctions and reading comprehension. *Elementary English*, April 1972, *49*, 502–505.

STOREY, DENISE C. Fifth graders meet elderly book characters. *Language Arts*, April 1979, *56*, 408–412.

STOREY, D. C. Reading in the content areas: Fictionalized biographies and diaries for social studies. *The Reading Teacher*, April 1982, *35*, 796–798.

STOTSKY, SANDRA L. Teaching prefixes in the elementary school. *Elementary School Journal*, March 1978, *78*, 278–283.

STOTSKY, SANDRA. The role of writing in developmental reading. *Journal of Reading*, January 1982, *25*, 330–340.

STOTSKY, SANDRA. Research on reading/writing relationships: A synthesis and suggested direction. *Language Arts*, May 1983, *60*, 627–642.

STOTT, DENIS H. *The hard-to-teach child: A diagnostic-remedial approach.* Baltimore: University Park Press, 1978.

STOTT, JON C. In search of the true hunter: Inuit folktales adapted for children. *Language Arts*, April 1983, *60*, 430–438.

STRANG, RUTH. *Reading diagnosis and remediation.* Newark, DE: International Reading Association, 1968.

STRANGE, MICHAEL. Instructional implications of a conceptual theory of reading comprehension. *The Reading Teacher*, January 1980, *33*, 391–397. Also in A. J. Harris & E. Sipay (Eds.), *Readings on reading instruction.* New York: Longman, 1984. Pp. 267–273.

STRAUSS, ALFRED, & LEHTINEN, LAURA E. *Psychopathology and education of the brain injured child.* New York: Grune & Stratton, 1947.

STRAW, STANLEY B., & SCHREINER, ROBERT. The effect of sentence manipulation on subsequent measures of reading and listening comprehension. *Reading Research Quarterly*, 1982, *17* (3), 339–352.

STRICKLAND, DOROTHY. The black experience in paperback (kindergarten through grade 6). In M. J. Weiss (Ed.), *New perspectives in paperbacks.* York, PA: Strine, 1973. Pp. 20–23. (a)

STRICKLAND, DOROTHY S. A program for linguistically different black children. *Research in the Teaching of English.* Spring 1973, *1*, 79–86. (b)

STRICKLAND, DOROTHY S. On reading. *Childhood Education*, November/December 1979, *56*, 67–74.

STRICKLER, DARRYL J. Planning the affective component. In R. A. Earle (Ed.), *Classroom practice in reading.* Newark, DE: International Reading Association, 1977. Pp. 3–9.

STRICKLER, EDWIN. Family interaction patterns in psychogenic learning disturbance. *Journal of Learning Disabilities*, March 1969, *2*, 147–154.

STURGE, CLAIRE. Reading retardation and anti-social behavior. *Journal of Child Psychology & Psychiatry & Allied Disciplines*, January 1982, *23*, 21–31.

SUCHER, FLOYD. Use of basal readers in individualized reading instruction. In J. A. Figurel (Ed.), *Reading and realism.* Newark, DE: International Reading Association, 1969. Pp. 136–143.

SUCHOFF, IRWIN B. Research in the relationship between reading and vision—What does it mean? *Journal of Learning Disabilities*, December 1981, *14*, 573–576.

SUHOR, CHARLES. The role of print as a medium in our society. In A. Purves & O. Niles (Eds.), *Becoming readers in a complex society.* 83rd Yearbook of the National Society for the Study of Education, Part I. Chicago: University of Chicago Press, 1984. Pp. 16–46.

SULZBY, ELIZABETH. Word concept development activities. In E. Henderson & J. Beers (Eds.), *Developmental and cognitive aspects of learning to spell: A reflection of word knowledge.* Newark, DE: International Reading Association, 1980. Pp. 127–137.

SUMMERS, EDWARD G. Instruments for assessing reading attitudes: A review of research and bibliography. *Journal of Reading Behavior*, September 1977, *9*, 137–165.

SUMMERS, EDWARD G., & LUKASEVICH, ANN. Reading preferences of intermediate-grade children in relation to sex, community, and maturation (grade level): A Canadian perspective. *Reading Research Quarterly*, Spring 1983, *18*, 347–360.

SUMMERS, JERRY A., & SHOBE, ROBERT E. Improving test-taking skills, 1983. ED 230 573

SWABY, BARBARA. Varying the ways you teach reading with basal stories. *The Reading Teacher*, March 1982, *35*, 676–680.

SWAIN, EMMA H. Using comic books to teach reading and language arts. *Journal of Reading*, December 1978, *22*, 253–258.

SWALM, J. E. A comparison of oral reading, silent reading, and listening comprehension. *Education*, 1972, *92*, 111–115.

SWAN, T. DESMOND. *Reading standards in Irish schools*. Walkinstown, Dublin, Ireland: Educational Company of Ireland, Ltd., 1978.

SWETT, SHIELA C. Math and LD: A new perspective. *Academic Therapy*, September 1978, *14*, 5–13.

SWISHER, LINDA, & ATEN, JAMES. Assessing comprehension of spoken language: A multifaceted task. *Topics in Language Disorders*, June 1981, *1*, 75–85.

SYVÄLAHTI, RAIJA. Reading-writing disabilities in Finland. In L. Tarnopol & M. Tarnopol (Eds.), *Reading disabilities: An international perspective*. Baltimore: University Park Press, 1976. Pp. 175–178.

TALLEL, PAULA. Auditory temporal perception, phonics, and reading disabilities in children. *Brain & Language*, March 1980, *9*, 182–198.

TANENHAUS, MICHAEL K., FLANAGAN, HELEN, & SEIDENBERG, MARK S. Orthographic and phonological activation in auditory and visual word recognition. Technical Report No. 178. Champaign, IL: Center for the Study of Reading, University of Illinois, August 1980.

TARNOPOL, LESTER, & TARNOPOL, MURIEL. Motor deficits that cause reading problems. *Journal of Learning Disabilities*, October 1979, *12*, 522–524.

TARVER, SARA D., & DAWSON, MARGARET M. Modality preference and the teaching of reading: A review. *Journal of Learning Disabilities*, January 1978, *11*, 17–29.

TARVER, SARA G., et al. The development of visual selective attention and verbal rehearsal in learning disabled boys. *Journal of Learning Disabilities*, October 1977, *10*, 491–500.

TAUBENHEIM, BARBARA, & CHRISTENSEN, JUDITH. Let's shoot "Cock Robin"! Alternatives to "round robin" reading. *Language Arts*, November/December, 1978, *55*, 975–977.

TAYLOR, BARBARA M. A summarizing strategy to improve middle grade students' reading and writing skills. *The Reading Teacher*, November 1982, *36*, 202–205.

TAYLOR, BARBARA M., & NOSBUSH, LINDA. Oral reading for meaning: A technique for improving word identification skills. *The Reading Teacher*, December 1983, *37*, 234–237.

TAYLOR, BARBARA M., & SAMUELS, S. JAY. Children's use of text structure in the recall of expository material. *American Educational Research Journal*, Winter 1983, *20*, 517–528.

TAYLOR, ERIC. Food additives, allergy and hyperkinesis. *Journal of Child Psychology & Psychiatry & Allied Disciplines*, October 1979, *20*, 357–363.

TAYLOR, H. GERRY, FLETCHER, JACK M., & SATZ, PAUL. Component processes in reading disabilities: Neuropsychological investigations of distinct reading subskill deficits. In R. Malatesha & P. Aaron (Eds.), *Reading disorders: Varieties and treatments*. New York: Academic Press, 1982. Pp. 121–147.

TAYLOR, H. GERRY, SATZ, PAUL, & FRIEL, JANETTE. Developmental dyslexia in relation to other childhood reading disorders: Significance and clinical utility. *Reading Research Quarterly*, 1979–1980, *15* (1), 84–101.

TAYLOR, INSUP. The Korean writing system. In P. Kolers *et al.* (Eds.), *Processing visible language*, Vol. 2. New York: Plenum Press, 1980. Pp. 67–82.

TAYLOR, INSUP. Writing systems and reading. In G. MacKinnon & T. Waller (Eds.), *Reading research: Advances in theory and practice*, Vol. 2. New York: Academic Press, 1981. Pp. 1–53.

TAYLOR, KARL K. Teaching summarization skills. *Journal of Reading*, February 1984, *27*, 389–393.

TAYLOR, MARION W., & SCHNEIDER, MARY A. What books are our children reading? *Chicago Schools Journal*, 1957, *38*, 155–160.

TAYLOR, MARSHA, & ORTONY, ANDREW. Figurative devices in black language: Some socio-psycholinguistic observations. Reading Education Report No. 20. Champaign, IL: Center for the Study of Reading, University of Illinois, May 1981.

TAYLOR, STANFORD E., *et al. EDL core vocabularies in reading, mathematics, science, and social studies.* New York: EDL/McGraw-Hill, 1979.

TAYLOR, W. L. Cloze procedures: A new tool for measuring readability. *Journalism Quarterly*, Fall 1953, *30*, 415–433.

TAYLOR-DELAIN, MARSHA, PEARSON, P. DAVID, & ANDERSON, RICHARD C. Reading comprehension and creativity in black language use: You stand to gain by playing the sounding game. Technical Report No. 295. Champaign, IL: Center for the Study of Reading, University of Illinois, October 1983.

TEALE, WILLIAM H. Assessing attitudes toward reading: Why and how. *Australian Journal of Reading*, June 1980, *3*, 86–94.

TEALE, WILLIAM H. Parents reading to their children: What we know and need to know. *Language Arts*, November/December 1981, *55*, 902–910.

TELFER, RICHARD J., & KANN, ROBERT S. Reading achievement, free reading, watching TV, and listening to music. *Journal of Reading*, March 1984, *27*, 536–539.

TEMPLETON, SHANE. Using the spelling/meaning connection to develop word knowledge in older students. *Journal of Reading*, October 1983, *27*, 8–14.

TERMAN, LEWIS M., & LIMA, MARGARET. *Children's reading.* New York: Appleton-Century-Crofts, 1937.

TERRY, ELLEN. *Children's poetry preference: A national survey of upper elementary grades.* Research Report No. 13. Urbana, IL: National Council of Teachers of English, 1974.

TERWILLIGER, PAUL N., & KOLKER, BRENDA S. The effects of learning confusable words on subsequent learning of high or low imagery words. *Reading World*, May 1982, *21*, 286–292.

TEST, DAVID W., & HEWARD, WILLIAM L. Teaching road signs and traffic laws to learning disabled students. *Learning Disability Quarterly*, Winter 1983, *6*, 80–83.

TEYLER, TIMOTHY J. *A primer of psychobiology: Brain and behavior.* San Francisco: W. H. Freeman, 1975.

TEYLER, TIMOTHY J. The brain sciences: An introduction. In J. Chall & S. Mirsky (Eds.), *Education and the brain.* 77th Yearbook of the National Society for the Study of Education, Part II. Chicago: University of Chicago Press, 1978. Pp. 1–32.

THARP, ROLAND. The effective instruction of comprehension: Results and description of the Kamehaameha Early Education Program. *Reading Research Quarterly*, 1982, *17* (4), 503–527.

THELEN, JUDY. Preparing students for content reading assignments. *Journal of Reading*, March 1982, *25*, 544–549.

THOM, E. Sensory integration and initial reading. Unpublished doctoral dissertation, University of Toronto, 1971.

THOMAS, ADELE. Learned helplessness and expectancy factors: Implications for research in learning disabilities. *Review of Educational Research*, Spring 1979, *49*, 208–221.

THOMAS, HUGH B. G. Genetic and psychodynamic aspects of developmental dyslexia—A cybernetic approach. *Journal of Learning Disabilities*, January 1973, *6*, 30–40.

THOMAS, KEITH J. Instructional application of the cloze technique. *Reading World*, October 1978, *18*, 1–12.

THOMPSON, J. S., *et al.* The role of computed axial tomography in the study of the child with minimal brain dysfunction. *Journal of Learning Disabilities*, June/July 1980, *13*, 334–337.

THOMPSON, LLOYD J. *Reading disability: Developmental dyslexia.* Springfield, IL: Charles C Thomas, 1966.

THOMPSON, RAY H., WHITE, KARL R., & MORGAN, DANIEL P. Teacher-student interaction patterns in classrooms with mainstreamed mildly handicapped students. *American Educational Research Journal*, Summer 1982, *19*, 220–236.

THOMPSON, RICHARD A. *Energizers for reading instruction.* West Nyack, NY: Parker, 1973.

THOMPSON, RICHARD A., & DZIUBEN, CHARLES D. Criterion-referenced reading tests in perspective. *The Reading Teacher*, December 1973, *27*, 292–294.

THOMPSON, RICHARD A., & MERRITT, KING, JR. Turn on to a reading center. *The Reading Teacher*, January 1975, *28*, 384–388.

THOMPSON, ROBERT J. The diagnostic utility of WISC-R measures with children referred to a developmental evaluation center. *Journal of Consulting and Clinical Psychology*, August 1980, *48*, 440–447.

THOMSON, MICHAEL E., & HARTLEY, GILL M. Self-concept in dyslexic children. *Academic Therapy*, September 1980, *16*, 19–36.

THONIS, ELEANOR W. *Literacy for America's Spanish-speaking children*. Newark, DE: International Reading Association, 1976.

THORNDIKE, EDWARD L. *The teacher's word book*. New York: Teachers College Press, Columbia University, 1921.

THORNDIKE, EDWARD L. The vocabulary of books for children in grades 3 to 8. *Teachers College Record*, 1936–1937, *38* (I), 196–205 (II), 316–323 (III), 416–429.

THORNDIKE, ROBERT L. *Children's reading interests*. New York: Teachers College Press, Columbia University, 1941.

THORNDIKE, ROBERT L. *The concepts of over- and underachievement*. New York: Teachers College Press, Columbia University, 1963.

THORNDIKE, ROBERT L. Reading as reasoning. *Reading Research Quarterly*, 1973–1974, 9 (2), 135–147.

THORNDIKE, ROBERT L. *Reading comprehension education in fifteen countries: An empirical study*. New York: John Wiley & Sons, 1973.

THORNLEY, GWENDELLA. Storytelling is fairy gold. *Elementary English*, January 1968, 45, 67–79.

TIERNEY, ROBERT J. Essential considerations for developing basic reading comprehension skills. *School Psychology Review*, 1982, 11 (3), 299–305.

TIERNEY, ROBERT J., & CUNNINGHAM, JAMES W. Research on teaching reading comprehension. In P. D. Pearson (Ed.), *Handbook of reading research*. New York: Longman, 1984. Pp. 609–655.

TIERNEY, ROBERT J., & MOSENTHAL, JAMES. Discourse comprehension and production: Analyzing text structure and cohesion. In J. Langer & M. T. Smith-Burke (Eds.), *Reader meets author/bridging the gap: Psycholinguistic and sociolinguistic perspectives*. Newark, DE: International Reading Association, 1982. Pp. 55–104.

TIERNEY, ROBERT J., MOSENTHAL, JAMES, & KANTOR, ROBERT N. Classroom applications of text analysis: Toward improving text selection and use. In J. Flood (Ed.), *Promoting reading comprehension*. Newark, DE: International Reading Association, 1984. Pp. 139–160.

TIERNEY, ROBERT J., & PEARSON, P. DAVID. Toward a composing model of reading. *Language Arts*, May 1983, *60*, 568–580.

TIERNEY, ROBERT J., & SCHALLERT, DIANE L. Learning from expository text: The interaction of text structures wtih reader characteristics. August 1982. Final Report ME-G-79-0167.

TIERNEY, ROBERT J., & SPIRO, RAND J. Some basic notions about reading comprehension: Implications for teachers. In J. Harste & R. Carey (Eds.), *New perspectives on comprehension*. Monographs in Teaching and Learning No. 3. Bloomington, IN: School of Education, Indiana University, October 1979. Pp. 132–137.

TIERNEY, ROBERT J., *et al.* Author's intentions and readers' interpretations. Technical Report No. 276. Champaign, IL: Center for the Study of Reading, University of Illinois, May 1983.

TIMKO, HENRY G. Configuration as a cue in the word recognition of beginning readers. *Journal of Experimental Education*, Winter 1970, *39*, 68–69.

TINKER, MILES A. Speed versus comprehension in reading as affected by level of difficulty. *Journal of Educational Psychology*, 1939, *30*, 81–94.

TINKER, MILES A. The study of eye movements in reading. *Psychological Bulletin*, 1946, *43*, 93–120.

TINKER, MILES A. Recent studies of eye movements in reading. *Psychological Bulletin*, 1958, *55*, 4.

TINKER, MILES A. *Bases for effective reading*. Minneapolis: University of Minnesota Press, 1965.

TIZARD, J., SCHOFIELD, W. W., & HEWISON, JENNY. Collaboration between teachers and parents in assisting children's reading. *British Journal of Educational Psychology*, February 1982, 52, 1–15.

TIZARD, J., *et al.* (Advisory Committee on Handicapped Children). *Children with specific reading difficulties*. London, England: HMSO, Secretary of State for Education and Science, February 8, 1972.

TORGESEN, JOSEPH. Performance of reading disabled children on serial memory tasks: Selective review of recent research. *Reading Research Quarterly*, 1978–1979, *14* (1), 57–87.

TORGESEN, JOSEPH K., & GREENSTEIN, JONATHAN J. Why do some learning disabled children have problems remembering? Does it make a difference? *Topics in Learning & Learning Disabilities*, July 1982, *2*, 54–67.

TORGESEN, JOSEPH K., & HOUCK, D. G. Processing deficiencies of learning disabled children who perform poorly on the digit span test. *Journal of Experimental Psychology*, 1980, 72, 141–160.

TORGESEN, JOSEPH K., MURPHY, HARRY A., & IVEY, CHARLES. The influence of an orientating task on the memory performance of children with learning problems. *Journal of Learning Disabilities*, June/July 1979, *12*, 396–401.

TORREY, JANE W. Black children's knowledge of standard English. *American Educational Research Journal*, Winter 1983, *20*, 627–643.

TOWNER, JOHN C., & EVANS, HOWARD M. The effect of three-dimensional stimuli versus two-dimensional stimuli on visual form discrimination. *Journal of Reading Behavior*, December 1974, *6*, 395–402.

TOWNSEND, MICHAEL A. Pupil achievement and adjustment under team and traditional classroom organizations: A review. *New Zealand Journal of Educational Studies*, November 1976, *11*, 113–123.

TRABASSO, THOMAS. On the making of inferences during reading and their assessment. In J. Guthrie (Ed.), *Comprehension and teaching: Research reviews*. Newark, DE: International Reading Association, 1981. Pp. 56–76.

TRAUB, NINA. Reading, spelling, handwriting: Traub Systematic Holistic Method. *Annals of Dyslexia*, 1982, *32*, 135–145.

TREIMAN, REBECCA, & BARON, JONATHAN. Segmental analysis ability: Development and relation to reading ability. In G. MacKinnon & T. Waller (Eds.), *Reading research: Advances in theory and practice*, Vol. 3. New York: Academic Press, 1981. Pp. 159–198.

TRELEASE, JIM. *The read-aloud handbook*. New York: Penguin, 1982.

TREVARTHEN, COLWYN. Development of the cerebral mechanism for language. In U. Kirk (Ed.), *Neuropsychology of language, reading, and spelling*. New York: Academic Press, 1983. Pp. 45–80.

TRESIZE, ROBERT L. Teaching reading to the gifted. *Language Arts*, November/December 1977, *54*, 920–924. Also in A. J. Harris & E. Sipay (Eds.), *Readings on reading instruction* (3rd ed.). New York: Longman, 1984. Pp. 452–455.

TROSKY, ODARKA S., & WOOD, CLIFFORD C. Using a writing model to teach reading. *Journal of Reading*, October 1982, *26*, 34–40.

TRUMBELL, ANN P., STRICKLAND, BONNIE, & HAMMER, SUSAN E. The Individualized Education Program—Part 1: Procedural guidelines. *Journal of Learning Disabilities*, January 1978, *11*, 40–46. (a)

TRUMBELL, ANN P., STRICKLAND, BONNIE, & HAMMER, SUSAN E. The Individualized Education Program—Part 2: Translating law into practice. *Journal of Learning Disabilities*. February 1978, *11*, 67–72. (b)

TRUSTY, KAY, & LINK, MARY. Reading teachers: Is aging in your book? *New England Reading Association Journal*, 1980, *15* (3), 6–12.

TUINMAN, J. JAAP. Determining the passage dependency of comprehension questions in 5 major tests. *Reading Research Quarterly*, 1973–1974, 9 (2), 206–223.

TUINMAN, J. JAAP (Reviewer). Woodcock Reading Mastery Test. In O. K. Buros (Ed.), *Eighth mental measurements yearbook*, Vol. II. Highland Park, NJ: Gryphon Press, 1978. Pp. 1306–1308.

TUINMAN, J. JAAP, ROWLS, MICHAEL, & FARR, ROGER. Reading achievement in the United States: Then and now. *Journal of Reading*, March 1976, *19*, 455–463.

TULMAN, CHESTER E. Bibliotherapy for adolescents: An annotated research review. *Journal of Reading*, May 1984, *27*, 713–719.

TURNER, SUSAN D. How to look at the testing components of basal reading series. *The Reading Teacher*, May 1984, *37*, 860–866.

TURNER, THOMAS N. Figurative language: Deceitful mirage or sparkling oasis for reading? *Language Arts*, October 1976, *53*, 758–761, 775. Also in A. J. Harris & E. Sipay (Eds.), *Readings on reading instruction* (3rd ed.). New York: Longman, 1984. Pp. 236–240.

TUTOLO, DANIEL J. The study guide—Types, purpose and value. *Journal of Reading*, March 1977, ew20, 503–507. Also in A. J. Harris & E. Sipay (Eds.), *Readings on reading instruction* (3rd ed.). New York: Longman, 1984. Pp. 313–317.

TUTOLO, DANIEL. Critical listening/reading of advertisements. *Language Arts*, September 1981, *58*, 679–683.

TWAY, EILEEN (Ed.). *Reading ladders for human relations* (6th ed.). Urbana, IL: NCTE, 1981.

TZAVARAS, A., KAPRINIS, G., & GATZOYAS, A. Literacy and hemispheric specialization for language: Digit dichotic listening for illiterates. *Neuropsychologia*, 1981, *19* (4), 565–570.

TZENG, OVID J. L., & HUNG, DAISY L. Linguistic determinism: A written language perspective. In O. Tzeng & H. Singer (Eds.), *Perception of print: Reading research in experimental psychology*. Hillsdale, NJ: LEA, 1981. Pp. 237–255.

TZENG, OVID J. L., & SINGER, HARRY. Failure of Steinberg and Yamada to demonstrate superiority of Kanji over Kana for initial reading instruction in Japan. *Reading Research Quarterly*, 1978–1979, *14* (4), 661–667.

UHL, WILLIS L. The use of the results of reading tests as bases for planning remedial work. *Elementary School Journal*, 1916, *17*, 266–275.

UNDERWOOD, N. RODERICK. The span of letter recognition of good and poor readers. Technical Report No. 251. Champaign, IL: Center for the Study of Reading, University of Illinois, July 1982.

VACCA, JO ANNE L. How to be an effective staff developer of teachers. *Journal of Reading*, January 1983, *26*, 293–296.

VACCA, JO ANNE L., & VACCA, RICHARD T. Learning stations: How to in the middle grades. *Journal of Reading*, April 1979, *19*, 563–567.

VACCA, RICHARD T. *Content area reading*. Boston: Little, Brown, 1981.

VAIL, PRISCILLA. 15 reading games you can adapt to any level. *Instructor*, October 1976, *86*, 60–62.

VALTIN, RENATE. Dyslexia: Deficit in reading or deficit in research? *Reading Research Quarterly*, 1978–1979, *14* (2), 201–221.

VALTIN, RENATE. Deficiencies in research on reading deficiencies. In J. Kavanagh & R. Venezky (Eds.), *Orthography, reading, and dyslexia*. Baltimore: University Park Press, 1980. Pp. 271–286.

VANCE, HUBERT B., WALLBROWN, FRED H., & BLAHA, JOHN. Determining WISC-R profiles for reading disabled children. *Journal of Learning Disabilities*, December 1978, *11*, 657–661.

VANDAMENT, WILLIAM E., & THALMAN, W. A. An investigation into the reading interests of children. *Journal of Educational Research*, 1956, *49*, 467–470.

VAN DEN HONERT, DOROTHY. A neuropsychological technique for training dyslexics. *Journal of Learning Disabilities*, January 1977, *10*, 21–27.

VAN DER VEUR, BARBARA W. Imagery ratings of 1,000 frequently used words. *Journal of Educational Psychology*, February 1975, *67*, 44–56.

VANDEVER, THOMAS, & NEVILLE, DONALD D. The effectiveness of tracing for good and poor readers. *Journal of Reading Behavior*, Spring 1972–1973, 5, 119–125.

VAN DE VOORT, LEWIS, SENF, GERALD M., & BENTON, ARTHUR L. Development of audiovisual integration in normal and retarded readers. *Child Development*, December 1972, *43*, 1260–1272.

VAUGHN, JOSEPH L., JR. The effect of interest on reading comprehension among ability groups and across grade levels. In G. H. McNinch & W. D. Miller (Eds.), *Reading: Convention and inquiry*. Clemson, SC: National Reading Conference, 1975. Pp. 172–176.

VAUGHN, JOSEPH L. Instructional strategies. In A. Berger & H. A. Robinson (Eds.), *Secondary school reading: What research reveals for classroom practice*. Urbana IL: NCTE & ERIC/RCS, 1982. Pp. 67–84.

VEALE, JAMES R., & FOREMAN, DALE I. Assessing cultural bias using foil response data: Cultural variation. *Journal of Educational Measurement*, Fall 1983, *20*, 249–258.

VEATCH, JEANNETTE, et al. *Key words to reading: The language experience approach begins* (2nd ed.). Columbus, OH: Charles E. Merrill, 1979.

VELLUTINO, FRANK R. Alternative conceptualizations of dyslexia: Evidence in support of a verbal deficit hypothesis. *Harvard Educational Review*, August 1977, *47*, 334–354.

VELLUTINO, FRANK R. *Dyslexia: Theory and research*. Cambridge, MA: MIT Press, 1979.

VELLUTINO, FRANK R. Theoretical issues in the study of word recognition: The unit of perception controversy reexamined. In S. Rosenberg (Ed.), *Handbook of applied psycholinguistics: Major thrusts of research and theory*. Hillsdale, NJ: LEA, 1982. Pp. 33–197.

VELLUTINO, FRANK R. Childhood dyslexia: A language disorder. In H. Myklebust (Ed.), *Progress in learning disabilities*, Vol. 5. New York: Grune & Stratton, 1983. Pp. 135–173.

VELLUTINO, FRANK R., & SCANLON, DONNA M. Verbal processing in poor and normal readers. In C. Brainerd & M. Pressley (Eds.), *Verbal processing in children: Progress in cognitive development research*. New York: Springer-Verlag, 1982. Pp. 189–264.

VELLUTINO, FRANK R., & SHUB, M. JEAN. Assessment of disorders in formal school language: Disorders in reading. *Topics in Language Disorders*, September 1982, *2*, 20–33.

VELLUTINO, FRANK R., *et al.* Developmental trends in the salience of meaning versus structural attributes of written words. *Psychological Research*, 1981, *43*, 131–153.

VENEZKY, RICHARD L. Nonstandard language and reading. *Elementary English*, March 1970, *47*, 334–345. (a)

VENEZKY, RICHARD L. *The structure of English orthography*. The Hague: Mouton, 1970. (b)

VENEZKY, RICHARD L. The curious role of letter names in reading instruction. *Visible Language*, Winter 1975, *9*, 7–23.

VENEZKY, RICHARD L. Harmony and cacophony from a theory-practice relationship. In L. Resnick & P. Weaver (Eds.), *Theory and practice of early reading*, Vol. 2. Hillsdale, NJ: LEA, 1979. Pp. 271–284. (a)

VENEZKY, RICHARD L. Orthographic regularities in English words. In P. Kolers *et al.* (Eds.), *Processing visible language*. New York: Plenum Press, 1979. Pp. 283–293. (b).

VENEZKY, RICHARD L. Overview: From Sumer to Leipzig to Bethesda. In J. Kavanagh & R. Venezky (Eds.), *Orthography, reading, and dyslexia*. Baltimore: University Park Press, 1980. Pp. 1–11.

VENEZKY, RICHARD L. Letter-sound regularity and orthographic structure. In M. Kamil & M. Boswick (Eds.), *Directions in reading: Research and instruction*. Washington, DC: National Reading Conference, 1981. Pp. 57–73.

VENEZKY, RICHARD, & JOHNSON, DALE D. Development of two letter-sound correspondences in grades one through three. *Journal of Educational Psychology*, 1973, *64*, 109–113.

VENEZKY, RICHARD L., & MASSARO, DOMINIC W. The role of orthographic regularity in word recognition. In L. Resnick & P. Weaver (Eds.), *Theory and practice in early reading*, Vol. 1. Hillsdale, NJ: LEA 1979, Pp. 85–107.

VERNON, MAGDALEN D. *Backwardness in reading: A study of its nature and origin*. Cambridge, England: Cambridge University Press, 1957, 1960.

VERNON, MAGDALEN D. *Reading and its difficulties: A psychological study*. Cambridge, England: Cambridge University Press, 1971.

VERNON, MAGDALEN D. Varieties of deficiency in the reading process. *Harvard Educational Review*, August 1977, *47*, 396–410.

VERNON, MCCAY, & COLEY, JOAN D. The sign language of the deaf and reading-language development. *The Reading Teacher*, December 1978, *32*, 297–301.

VERNON, MCCAY, COLEY, JOAN D., & DUBOIS, JAN H. Using sign language to remediate severe reading problems. *Journal of Learning Disabilities*, April 1980, *13*, 215–218.

VIK, GRETE HAGTVEDT. Reading disabilities in Norwegian elementary grades. In L. Tarnopol & M. Tarnopol (Eds.), *Reading disabilities: An international perspective*. Baltimore: University Park Press, 1976. Pp. 249–264.

VILSCEK, ELAINE C., & CLELAND, DONALD L. Two approaches to reading instruction. Final Report, Project No. 3195. Pittsburgh: University of Pittsburgh, 1968.

VINCENT, DENIS, *et al.* A review of reading tests: A critical review of reading tests and assessment procedures available for use in British schools. Berks, England: NFGR-Nelson, 1983.

VOSNIADOU, STELLA, & ORTONY, ANDREW. The influence of analogy in children's acquisition of new information from text: An exploratory study. In J. Niles & L. A. Harris (Eds.), *Searches for meaning in reading/language processing & instruction*. Rochester, NY: National Reading Conference, 1983. Pp. 71–79.

VOSNIADOU, STELLA, *et al*. Sources of difficulty in the young child's understanding of metaphorical language. Technical Report No. 290. Champaign, IL: Center for the Study of Reading, University of Illinois, October 1983.

VUGRENES, DAVID E. North American Indian myths and legends for classroom use. *Journal of Reading*, March 1981, *24*, 494–496.

VUKELICH, CAROL. Parent's role in the reading process: A review of practical suggestions and ways to communicate with parents. *The Reading Teacher*, February 1984, *37*, 472–477.

WADA, J., & RASMUSSEN, T. Intracarotid injection of sodium amytal for the lateralization of cerebral speech dominance: Experimental and clinical observation. *Journal of Neurosurgery*, 1960, *17*, 266–282.

WADE, SUZANNE E. A synthesis of the research for improving reading in the social studies. *Review of Educational Research*, Winter 1983, *53*, 461–497.

WAGNER, GUY, & HOSIER, MAX. *Strengthening reading skills with educational games*. Riverside, NJ: Teachers Publishing, 1970.

WAGNER, GUY, HOSIER, MAX, & CESINGER, JOAN. *Word power games*. Riverside, NJ: Teachers Publishing, 1972.

WAGNER, LILYA. The effects of TV on reading. *Journal of Reading*, December 1980, *34*, 201–206. Also in A. J. Harris & E. Sipay (Eds.), *Readings on reading instruction* (3rd ed.). New York: Longman, 1984. Pp. 358–362.

WAGONER, SHIRLEY A. Mexican-Americans in children's literature since 1970. *The Reading Teacher*, December 1982, *36*, 274–279.

WAGSCHAL, PETER H. Illiterates with doctorates: The future of education in an electronic age. *The Futurist*, 1978, *12*, 243–244.

WALBERG, HERBERT J., & TSAI, SHIOW-LING. Reading achievement and attitude productivity among 17-year-olds. *Journal of Reading Behavior*, 1983, *15* (3), 41–53.

WALKER, CHARLES M. High frequency word list for grades 3 through 9. *The Reading Teacher*, April 1979, *32*, 803–812.

WALKER, CLINTON B. *Standards for evaluating criterion-referenced tests*. CSE Report No. 103. Los Angeles, CA: Center for the Study of Evaluation, University of California, Los Angeles, January 1978.

WALKER, CLINTON B. *CSE criterion-referenced test handbook*. Los Angeles: Center for the Study of Evaluation, University of California, Los Angeles, 1979.

WALKER, LAURENCE. Newfoundland dialect interference in oral reading. *Journal of Reading Behavior*, Spring 1975, *7*, 61–78.

WALKER, L., & COLE, E. M. Familial patterns of expression of specifc reading disability in a population sample. Part I: Prevalence, distribution and persistence. *Bulletin of the Orton Society*, 1965, *15*, 12–24.

WALLBROWN, FRED H., BLAHA, JOHN, & VANCE, BOONEY. A reply to Miller's concerns about WISC-R profile analysis. *Journal of Learning Disabilities*, June/July 1980, *13*, 340–345.

WALLBROWN, FRED H., & COWGER, DORIS. Normative data for eight dimensions of reading attitude: III. Suburban parochial school students. *Psychology in the Schools*, January 1982, *19*, 45–48.

WALLBROWN, FRED H., & WISNESKI, PHILLIP D. Normative data for eight dimensions of reading attitude: II. Inner-city remedial readers. *Psychology in the Schools*, October 1981, *18*, 408–412.

WALLBROWN, FRED H., & WISNESKI, PHILLIP D. Test-retest reliability estimates for eight dimensions of reading attitude. *Psychology in the Schools*, July 1982, *19*, 305–309.

WALLER, MICHAEL, TRISMAN, DONALD A., & WILDER, GITA. A measure of student attitude toward reading and self as reader—A summary report. *Journal of Reading Behavior*, Summer 1977, *9*, 123–128.

WALLER, T. GARY. *Think first, read later: Piagetian prerequisites for reading*. Newark, DE: International Reading Association, 1977.

WANAT, STANLEY, & LEVIN, HARRY. Linguistic constraints in reader processing strategies. Paper delivered at the Eastern Psychological Association, 1970.

WANG, MARGARET C. The development of student self-management skills: Implication for effective use of instruction and learning time. *Educational Horizons*, Summer 1979, 57, 169–174.

WARD, BARBARA J. (Ed.). Elementary reading skills improve. *NAEP Newsletter*, Spring 1981, *14*, 1–3.

WARD, BARBARA J. (Ed.). Hispanic grade schoolers reading better. *NAEP Newsletter*, Summer 1982, *15*, 1–2.

WARDHAUGH, RONALD. Is the linguistic approach an improvement in reading instruction? In N. B. Smith (Ed.), *Current issues in reading*. Newark, DE: International Reading Association, 1969. Pp. 254–267.

WARNER, MICHAEL M. Learning disabled adolescents in the public schools: Are they different from other low achievers? *Exceptional Education Quarterly*, August 1980, *1*, 27–36.

WARTENBERG, HERBERT. The clip sheet. *The Reading Teacher*, January 1976, 29, 396–397, 398.

WARWICK, B. ELLEY. Cloze procedures (Ebbinghaus completion method) as applied to reading. In O. K. Buros (Ed.), *Eighth mental measurements yearbook*, Vol. II. Highland Park, NJ: Gryphon Press, 1978. Pp. 1174–1176.

WATSON, JERRY J. A positive image of the elderly in literature for children. *The Reading Teacher*, April 1981, *34*, 792–798.

WATTERS, ELISABETH. Reading in a family-grouped primary school. In H. K. Smith (Ed.), *Meeting individual needs in reading*. Newark, DE: International Reading Association, 1971. Pp. 29–35.

WAUGH, R. P., & HOVELL, K. W. Teaching modern syllabication. *The Reading Teacher*, October 1975, 29, 20–25.

WAY, JOYCE W. Achievement and self-concept in multiage classrooms. *Educational Research Quarterly*, Summer 1981, 6, 69–75.

WEAVER, PHYLLIS A. Improving reading comprehension: Effects of sentence organization instruction. *Reading Research Quarterly*, 1979, 15 (1), 129–146.

WEAVER, PHYLLIS A., & RESNICK, LAUREN B. *The theory and practice of early reading: An introduction.* In L. Resnick & P. Weaver (Eds.), *Theory and practice in early reading*, Vol. 1. Hillsdale, NJ: Erlbaum, 1979. Pp. 1–27.

WEBB, NOREEN M. Student interaction and learning in small groups. *Review of Educational Research*, Fall 1982, 52, 421–445.

WEBBER, ELIZABETH A. Organizing and scheduling the secondary reading program. *Journal of Reading*, April 1984, 27, 594–596.

WEBER, ROSE-MARIE. The study of oral reading errors: A review of the literature. *Reading Research Quarterly*, Fall 1968, 4, 96–119.

WEBER, ROSE-MARIE. Some reservations on the significance of dialect in the acquisition of reading. In J. A. Figurel (Ed.), *Reading goals for the disadvantaged*. Newark, DE: International Reading Association, 1970. Pp. 124–131.

WEBER, ROSE-MARIE. Review of *Findings of research on miscue analysis: Classroom implications*. *Journal of Reading Behavior*, Winter 1977, 9, 416–419.

WEBER, ROSEMARY. Bibliography. In H. Tanyzer & J. Karl (Eds.), *Reading, children's books, and our pluralistic society*. Newark, DE: International Reading Association, 1972. Pp. 81–89.

WEBSTER, RAYMOND E., & LAFAYETTE, ANN D. Distinguishing among three subgroups of handicapped students using Bannatyne's Recategorization. *Journal of Educational Research*, March/April 1979, 73, 237–240.

WECHSLER, DAVID. *The measurement of adult intelligence* (3rd ed.). Baltimore: Williams & Wilkens, 1944.

WEIGL, EGON. The written language is more than reading and writing. *The Reading Teacher*, March 1980, 33, 652–657.

WEINSCHENK, CURT, *et al.* Uber die Haufigkeit der kongenitalen legasthenie im zweiten Grund schuljahr: II. (On the frequency of dyslexia encountered in the second school year: II). *Psychologische Rundschau*, 1970, 21, 44–51.

WEINSTEIN, RHONA S. Reading group membership in first grade: Teacher behaviors and pupil experience over time. *Journal of Edcational Psychology*, February 1976, 68, 103–116.

WEINTRAUB, SAMUEL. Two significant trends in reading research. In H. A. Robinson (Ed.), *Reading & writing instruction in the United States*. Newark, DE: International Reading Association, 1977. Pp. 59–68.

WEINTRAUB, SAM, & COWAN, ROBERT J. *Vision/visual perception: An annotated bibliography*. Newark, DE: International Reading Association, 1982.

WENDELIN, KARLA H. Taking stock of children's preferences in humorous literature. *Reading Psychology*, Fall 1980, *2*, 34–42.

WENDER, PAUL H. Hypothesis for a possible biochemical basis for minimal brain dysfunction. In R. Knights & D. Bakker (Eds.), *The neuropsychology of learning disorders: Theoretical approaches*. Baltimore: University Park Press, 1976. Pp. 111–122.

WEPMAN, JOSEPH M. The interrelationship of hearing, speech, and reading. *The Reading Teacher*, March 1961, *14*, 245–247.

WERNER, DAVID B. Vision training: A review. Paper presented at The child with learning disabilities: Medical, psychological, and educational aspects (a symposium). Albany, NY: Albany Medical College, February 3, 1984.

WEST, RICHARD F. Efficient processing activities in reading. In F. Murray (Ed.), *Models of efficient reading*. Newark, DE: International Reading Association, 1979. Pp. 28–61.

WEST, RICHARD F., *et al*. The effect of sentence context on word recognition in second- and sixth-grade children. *Reading Research Quarterly*, Fall 1983, *19*, 6–15.

WESTCOTT, JANE. Native American children's literature. *New England Reading Association Journal*, Autumn 1982, *17*, 44–49.

WHALEY, JILL F. Readers' expectations for story structure. *Reading Research Quarterly*, 1981, *17* (1), 90–114. (a)

WHALEY, JILL F. Story grammars and reading instruction. *The Reading Teacher*, April 1981, *34*, 762–771. (b)

WHALEY, W. JILL. Closing the blending gap. *Reading World*, December 1975, *15*, 97–100.

WHALEY, W. JILL, & KIBBY, MICHAEL W. Word synthesis and beginning reading achievement. *Journal of Educational Research*, November/December 1979, *73*, 132–138.

WHEELER, LESTER R., & SMITH, EDWIN M. A practical readability formula for the classroom teacher in the primary grades. *Elementary English*, November 1954, *31*, 397–399.

WHIPPLE, GERTRUDE. Characteristics of a sound reading program. In N. B. Henry (Ed.), *Reading in the elementary school*. 48th Yearbook of the National Society for the Study of Education, Part II, 1949. Pp. 34–48.

WHIPPLE, GERTRUDE. Appraisal of the interest appeal of illustrations. *Elementary School Journal*, 1953, *53*, 262–269.

WHISLER, NANCY G. Pupil partners. *Language Arts*, April 1976, *53*, 387–389.

WHITE, C. STEPHEN. Learning style and reading instruction. *The Reading Teacher*, April 1983, *36*, 842–845.

WHITE, DAVID E. Language experience: Sources of information. *Language Arts*, November/December 1980, *57*, 888–889.

WHITE, MARY LOU. Long and funny poems: Children's favorites. *Ohio Reading Teacher*, April 1980, *14*, 17–20.

WHITE, VIRGINIA L., & SCHULTE, EMERITA S. (Comp.). *Books about children's books: An annotated bibliography*. Newark, DE: International Reading Association, 1979.

WHITE, WARREN J., *et al*. Are there learning disabilities after high school? *Exceptional Children*, November 1982, *49*, 273–274.

WICK, JOHN W. Reducing proportion of chance scores in inner-city standardized testing results: Impact on average scores. *American Educational Research Journal*, Fall 1983, *20*, 461–463.

WIDOMSKI, CHERYL L. Building foundations for reading comprehension. *Reading World*, May 1983, *22*, 306–313.

WIEDERHOLT, J. LEE, & HALE, GINGER. Indirect and direct treatment of reading disabilities. *Topics in Learning & Learning Disabilities*, January 1982, *1*, 79–85.

WIENER, MORTON, & CROMER, WARD. Reading and reading difficulty: A conceptual analysis. *Harvard Educational Review*, Fall 1967, *37*, 620–643.

WIENER, ROBERTA. A look at reading practices in the open classroom. *The Reading Teacher*, February 1974, *27*, 438–442.

WIGDOR, ALEXANDRA K. Ability testing: Uses, consequences, and controversies. *Educational Measurement*, Fall 1982, *1*, 6–8, 26.

WIGFIELD, ALLAN, & ASHER, STEVEN R. Social and motivational influences on reading. In P. D. Pearson (Ed.), *Handbook of reading research*. New York, Longman, 1984. Pp. 423–452.

WIIG, ELISABETH H., LAPOINTE, CONSTANCE, & SEMEL, ELEANOR M. Relationships among language processing and production of learning disabled adolescents. *Journal of Learning Disabilities*, May 1977, *10*, 292–299.

WIIG, ELISABETH H., SEMEL, ELEANOR M., & NYSTROM, LISA A. Comparison of rapid naming abilities in language-learning-disabled and academically achieving eight-year-olds. *Language, Speech & Hearing Services in Schools*, January 1982, *13*, 11–23.

WILDER, GITA. Five exemplary reading programs. In J. T. Guthrie (Ed.), *Cognition, curriculum and comprehension*. Newark, DE: International Reading Association, 1977. Pp. 257–278.

WILDMAN, DANIEL M., & KLING, MARTIN. Semantic, syntactic, and spatial anticipation in reading. *Reading Research Quarterly*, 1978–1979, *14* (2), 128–164.

WILGOSH, L., & PAITICH, D. Delinquency and learning disabilities: More evidence. *Journal of Learning Disabilities*, May 1982, *15*, 278–279.

WILKINSON, LOUISE C., & CALCULATOR, STEVE. Requests and responses in peer-directed reading groups. *American Educational Research Journal*, Spring 1982, *19*, 107–120.

WILLIAMS, FERN, & COLEMAN, MARGARET. A follow-up study of psycho-educational recommendations. *Journal of Learning Disabilities*, December 1982, *15*, 596–598.

WILLIAMS, JOANNA P. Learning to read: A review of theories and models. *Reading Research Quarterly*, Winter 1973, *8*, 121–146.

WILLIAMS, JOANNA. Training children to copy and to discriminate letterlike forms. *Journal of Educational Psychology*, December 1975, *67*, 790–795.

WILLIAMS, JOANNA. Building perceptual and cognitive strategies into a reading curriculum. In A. S. Reber & D. L. Scarborough (Eds.), *Toward a psychology of reading*. Hillsdale, NJ: LEA, 1977. Pp. 257–288.

WILLIAMS, JOANNA. Reading instruction today. *American Psychologist*, October 1979, *34*, 917–922.

WILLIAMS, JOANNA P., BLUMBERG, ELLEN L., & WILLIAMS, DAVID V. Cues used in visual word recognition. *Journal of Educational Psychology*, 1970, *61*, 310–315.

WILLIAMS, PATRICIA, *et al.* The impact of leisure time television on school learning: A research synthesis. *American Educational Research Journal*, Spring 1982, *19*, 19–50.

WILLIAMS, PETER. Reading and the law: The next step may be up to teachers. *Journal of Reading*, November 1981, *25*, 106–112.

WILLIAMS, ROBERT T. A table for the rapid determination of revised Dale–Chall readability scores. *The Reading Teacher*, November 1972, *26*, 158–165.

WILLIG, ANN C., *et al.* Sociocultural and educational correlates of success-failure attributions and evaluation anxiety in the school setting for Black, Hispanic, and Anglo children. *American Educational Research Journal*, Fall 1983, *20*, 385–410.

WILLIS, DONALD C. The effect of self-hypnosis on reading rate and comprehension. *American Journal of Clinical Hypnosis*, April 1972, *14*, 249–255.

WILLOWS, DALE M., BORWICK, DIANE, & HAYVREN, MAUREEN. The content of school readers. In G. MacKinnon & T. Waller (Eds.), *Reading research; Advances in theory and practice*, Vol. 2. New York: Academic Press, 1981. Pp. 97–175.

WILLOWS, DALE M., & RYAN, ELLEN B. Differential utilization of syntactic and semantic information by skilled and less skilled readers in the intermediate grades. *Journal of Educational Psychology*, October 1981, *73*, 607–615.

WILSON, MARILYN J. A review of recent research on the integration of reading and writing. *The Reading Teacher*, May 1981, *34*, 896–901.

WILSON, ROBERT M., & RIBOVICH, JERILYN K. Ability grouping? Stop and reconsider! *Reading World*, December 1973, *13*, 84–91.

WILSON, STEWART P., HARRIS, CHESTER, W., & HARRIS, MARGARET L. Effects of an auditory perceptual remediation program on reading performance. *Journal of Learning Disabilities*, December 1976, *9*, 670–678.

WILTON, SHIRLEY M. Juvenile science fiction involves reluctant readers. *Journal of Reading*, April 1981, *24*, 608–611.

WINKLEY, CAROL K. Building staff competence in identifying underachievers. In H. A. Robinson (Ed.), *The underachiever in reading*. Supplementary Educational Monograph No. 92. Chicago: University of Chicago Press, 1962. Pp. 155–162.

WINNIE, PHILIP H. Experiments relating teachers' use of higher cognitive questions to student achievement. *Review of Educational Research*, Winter 1979, *49*, 13–49.

WINOGRAD, PETER N. Strategic difficulties in summarizing texts. *Reading Research Quarterly*, Summer 1984, *19*, 404–425.

WIRT, JOHN. Implementing diagnostic-prescriptive reading innovations. *Teachers College Record*, February 1976, *77*, 352–365.

WISE, KATHLEEN. Activities for increasing hearing and speaking vocabularies. In A. J. Harris & E. Sipay (Eds.), *Readings on reading instruction* (2nd ed.). New York: Longman, 1972, Pp. 249–252.

WITELSON, SANDRA F. Developmental dyslexia: Two right hemispheres and none left. *Science*, January 1977, *195*, 309–311.

WITKIN, H. A., *et al.* Field-dependent and field-independent cognitive styles and their educational implications. *Review of Educational Research*, Winter 1977, *47*, 1–64.

WITMAN, CAROLYN C., & RILEY, JAMES D. Colored chalk and messy fingers: A kinesthetic-tactile approach to reading. *The Reading Teacher*, March 1978, *31*, 620–623.

WITTROCK, M. C. Education and the cognitive processes of the brain. In J. Chall & A. Mirsky (Eds.), *Education and the Brain*. 77th Yearbook of the National Society for the Study of Education, Part II. Chicago: University of Chicago Press, 1978. Pp. 61–102.

WITTROCK, M. C. Writing and the teaching of reading. *Language Arts*, May 1983, *60*, 600–606.

WITTY, PAUL A. Studies of the mass media—1949–1965. *Science Education*, 1966, *50*, 119–126.

WITTY, PAUL, & KOPEL, DAVID. Factors associated with the etiology of reading disability. *Journal of Educational Research*, February 1936, *29*, 440–450.

WITTY, PAUL A., & MELIS, LLOYD A. A 1964 study of TV: Comparisons and comments. *Elementary English*, February 1965, *42*, 134–141.

WITUCKE, VIRGINIA. The book talk: A technique for bringing together children and books. *Language Arts*, April 1979, *56*, 413–421.

WIXSON, KAREN L. Miscue analysis: A critical review. *Journal of Reading Behavior*, Summer 1979, *11*, 163–175.

WIXSON, KAREN L. Level of importance of post questions and children's learning from text. *American Educational Research Journal*, Summer 1984, *21*, 419–433.

WIXSON, KAREN, *et al.* An interview for assessing students' perceptions of classroom reading tasks. *The Reading Teacher*, January 1984, *37*, 346–352.

WOLF, ANNE E. Strategies for improving direction following in the content classroom. *Wisconsin State Reading Association Journal*, Summer 1982, *26*, 5–8.

WOLF, RONALD E. What is reading good for? Perspectives from senior citizens. In L. Johnson (Ed.), *Reading and the adult learner*. Newark, DE: International Reading Association, 1980. Pp. 13–15.

WOLF, WILLAVENE, KING, MARTHA L., & HUCK, CHARLOTTE S. Teaching critical reading to elementary school children. *Reading Research Quarterly*, Summer 1968, *3*, 435–498.

WOLFTHAL, MAURICE. Reading scores revisited. *Phi Delta Kappan*, May 1981, *62*, 662–663.

WONG, BERNICE. The effects of directive cues on the organization of memory and recall in good and poor readers. *Journal of Educational Research*, September/October 1978, *72*, 32–38.

WONG, BERNICE. The role of theory in learning disabilities research. Part 1. An analysis of problems. *Journal of Learning Disabilities*, November 1979, *12*, 585–595.

WONG, BERNICE. Understanding learning disabled students' reading problems: Contributions from cognitive psychology. *Topics in Learning & Learning Disabilities*, July 1982, *2*, 23–32.

WOOD, KAREN D., & MATEJA, JOHN A. Adapting secondary level strategies for use in elementary class-rooms. *The Reading Teacher*, February 1983, *36*, 492–496.

WOOD, KAREN D., & ROBINSON, NORA. Vocabulary, language and prediction: A prereading strategy. *The Reading Teacher*, January 1983, *36*, 392–395.

WOOD, MARGO. Invented spelling. *Language Arts*, October 1982, *59*, 707–717.

WOODWORTH, ROBERT S. *Psychology* (rev. ed.). New York: Holt, 1929. Pp. 103–104.

WORLEY, STINSON E. Developmental task situation in stories. *The Reading Teacher*, November 1967, *21*, 145–148.

WRIGHT, GARY. The comic book—a forgotten medium in the classroom. *The Reading Teacher*, November 1979, *33*, 158–161.

WRIGHT, LANCE, & MCKENZIE, CLANCY. "Talking" group therapy for learning-disabled children. *The Reading Teacher*, January 1970, *23*, 339–346, 385.

WYNE, MARVIN D. Time-on-task and classroom management. *The Directive Teacher*, Summer/Fall 1981, *3*, 10, 12.

YAMADORI, ATUSHI. Ideogram reading in alexia. *Brain*, June 1975, *98* Part II, 231–238.

YARBOROUGH, BETTY H. A study of the effectiveness of the Leavell language development service in improving the silent reading ability and other language skills of persons with mixed dominance. Unpublished doctoral dissertation, University of Virginia, 1964.

YENI-KOMSHIAN, GRACE H., ISENBERG, DAVID, & GOLDBERG, HERMAN. Cerebral dominance and reading disability: Left visual field deficit in poor readers. *Neuropsychologia*, January 1975, *13*, 83–94.

YNGVE, V. H. Computer programs for translation. *Scientific American*, 1962, *206*, 68–76.

YOAKAM, GERALD A. *Basal reading instruction.* New York: McGraw-Hill, 1955.

YOUNG, ANDREW W., & ELLIS, ANDREW W. Asymmetry of cerebral hemispheric function in normal and poor readers. *Psychological Bulletin*, 1981, *39* (1), 183–190.

YOUNG, LAURENCE R., & SHEENA, DAVID. Eye-movement measurement techniques. *American Psychologist*, March 1975, *30*, 315–330.

YSSELDYKE, JAMES E. Current practices in making psychoeducational decisions about learning disabled students. *Journal of Learning Disabilities*, April 1983, *16*, 226–233.

YSSELDYKE, JAMES E., & ALGOZZINE, BOB. Where to begin diagnosing reading problems. *Topics in Learning & Learning Disabilities*, January 1983, *2*, 60–69.

YSSELDYKE, JAMES E,, & MARSTON, DOUGLAS. A critical analysis of standardized reading tests. *School Psychology Review*, 1982, *11* (3), 257–266.

YULE, WILLIAM. Predicting reading ages on Neale's Analysis of Reading Ability. *British Journal of Educational Psychology*, June 1967, *37*, 252–255.

YULE, WILLIAM, & RUTTER, MICHAEL. Epidemiology and social implications of specific reading retardation. In R. M. Knights & D. J. Bakker (Eds.), *The neuropsychology of learning disorders: Theoretical approaches.* Baltimore: University Park Press, 1976. Pp. 25–39.

YULE, W., *et al.* Over- and under-achievement in reading: Distribution in the general population. *British Journal of Educational Psychology*, 1974, *44*, 1–12.

ZAESKE, ARNOLD. The validity of Predictive Index Tests in predicting reading failure at end of grade one. In W. K. Durr (Ed.), *Reading difficulties: Diagnosis, correction, and remediation.* Newark, DE: International Reading Association, 1970. Pp. 28–33.

ZANGWILL, O. L. Dyslexia in relation to cerebral dominance. In J. Money (Ed.), *Reading disability: Progress and research needs in dyslexia.* Baltimore: Johns Hopkins Press, 1962. Pp. 103–114.

ZELLER, LEROY. Prevent summer backsliding. *The Reading Teacher*, April 1980, *33*, 834–835.

ZIGMOND, NAOMI, VALLECORSA, ADA, & LEINHARDT, GAEA. Reading instruction for students with learning disabilities. *Topics in Language Disorders*, December 1980, *1*, 89–98.

ZOROTOVICH, BETTY. The bridge of hope: Hand centers that cause and cure dyslexia. *Academic Therapy*, March 1979, *14*, 469–477.

ZUCKERMAN, DIANA M., SINGER, DOROTHY G., & SINGER, JEROME L. Television viewing, children's reading, and related classroom behavior. *Journal of Communication*, Winter 1980, *30*, 166–174.

ZUCKERMAN, SAM. To own a book. *American Education*, November 1977, *13*, 13–16.

ZUTTELL, JERRY. Cognitive development, metalinguistic ability and invented spellings: Comparisons and correlations. In M. Kamil (Ed.), *Directions in reading: Research and instruction.* Washington, DC: National Reading Conference, 1981. Pp. 249–256.

Name Index

Subject Index